PUBLIC PAPERS OF THE PRESIDENTS
OF THE
UNITED STATES

PUBLIC PAPERS OF THE PRESIDENTS
OF THE
UNITED STATES

Barack Obama

2012

(IN TWO BOOKS)

BOOK I—JANUARY 1 TO JUNE 30, 2012

UNITED STATES GOVERNMENT PUBLISHING OFFICE
WASHINGTON : 2016

Published by the
Office of the Federal Register
National Archives and Records Administration

For sale by the Superintendent of Documents, U.S. Government Publishing Office
• Internet: bookstore.gpo.gov • Phone: (202) 512–1800 • Fax: (202) 512–1204
• Mail: Stop IDCC, Washington, DC 20401

Foreword

As 2012 began, our Nation looked forward with a renewed sense of hope. For the first time in 9 years, no Americans were fighting in Iraq. Consumer confidence was rising, and thanks to the grit and determination of the American people, we were pulling our way back from the worst recession since the Great Depression. But we still had much more to do. At stake was the basic bargain that built this country—the promise that hard work should pay off and responsibility should be rewarded.

Protecting that promise meant fighting for working families. With the payroll tax cut and unemployment insurance set to expire, I urged ordinary citizens to make their voices heard. They spoke up and persuaded the Congress to do the right thing, keeping taxes low for 160 million working Americans. A few months later, the Congress passed the JOBS Act, making it easier for aspiring entrepreneurs to turn a great idea into a job-creating small business. I was proud to sign that bipartisan bill into law.

I was ready to work with the Congress to keep strengthening the middle class, but I wouldn't allow partisanship and gridlock to stand in the way of progress. So I kept a promise I had made to the American people: where the Congress refused to act, I would. We found new ways to support American manufacturing and reward businesses that bring jobs to American shores. We cut red tape to speed the kinds of projects that keep us on the cutting edge, from laying broadband to repairing bridges. We launched an all-of-the-above energy strategy that taps into every available source, from domestic oil and natural gas to wind and solar. And we established a center to investigate trade abuses abroad and ensure our workers can compete on a level playing field.

Even as we worked to rebuild our economy, we continued to renew our leadership around the world. In Seoul, Cartagena, and Los Cabos, I joined leaders from every corner of the globe to strengthen our security and find new opportunities for economic cooperation. We led a coalition to confront the Iranian government with crippling sanctions, isolating it and slowing its nuclear program. I announced new guidance to keep our military the strongest in the world and to prepare for the challenges of the future. And I traveled to Afghanistan where I signed a Strategic Partnership Agreement that marked the beginning of the end of America's war in Afghanistan, because after a decade of war, it was time to do some nation-building here at home.

It was also time to renew the promises of equality and opportunity at the heart of our Nation's founding. This spring, I stated my personal belief that same-sex couples should be able to get married. I announced new steps to reform our broken immigration system and lift the shadow of deportation from young people who were brought to this country as children—Americans in every way but on paper. And as we continued to implement health care reform that will finally give millions of men and women a basic sense of security, the Supreme Court upheld the Affordable Care Act, affirming that this historic effort was not just moral, but constitutional.

During my State of the Union address, I asked our people to imagine the America that is within our reach. I described my vision of a country that leads the world in educating its students, attracts high-paying jobs, controls its own energy, and makes sure its economy is built to last. We still have a long way to go to claim that vision of the future. But America has taken important steps these past 6 months, and with hope and hard work, I know we can make it the rest of the way—together.

v

Preface

This book contains the papers and speeches of the President of the United States that were issued by the Office of the Press Secretary during the period January 1–June 30, 2012. The material has been compiled and published by the Office of the Federal Register, National Archives and Records Administration.

The material is presented in chronological order, and the dates shown in the headings are the dates of the documents or events. In instances when the release date differs from the date of the document itself, that fact is shown in the textnote. Every effort has been made to ensure accuracy: Remarks are checked against an audio recording, and signed documents are checked against the original. Textnotes and cross references have been provided by the editors for purposes of identification or clarity. Speeches were delivered in Washington, DC, unless otherwise indicated. The times noted are local times. All materials that are printed in full text in the book have been indexed in the subject and name indexes and listed in the document categories list.

The Public Papers of the Presidents series was begun in 1957 in response to a recommendation of the National Historical Publications Commission. An extensive compilation of messages and papers of the Presidents covering the period 1789 to 1897 was assembled by James D. Richardson and published under congressional authority between 1896 and 1899. Since then, various private compilations have been issued, but there was no uniform publication comparable to the Congressional Record or the United States Supreme Court Reports. Many Presidential papers could be found only in the form of mimeographed White House releases or as reported in the press. The Commission therefore recommended the establishment of an official series in which Presidential writings, addresses, and remarks of a public nature could be made available.

The Commission's recommendation was incorporated in regulations of the Administrative Committee of the Federal Register, issued under section 6 of the Federal Register Act (44 U.S.C. 1506), which may be found in title 1, part 10, of the Code of Federal Regulations.

A companion publication to the Public Papers series, the Weekly Compilation of Presidential Documents, was begun in 1965 to provide a broader range of Presidential materials on a more timely basis to meet the needs of the contemporary reader. Beginning with the administration of Jimmy Carter, the Public Papers series expanded its coverage to include additional material as printed in the Weekly Compilation. On January 20, 2009, the printed Weekly Compilation of Presidential Documents was superseded by the online Daily Compilation of Presidential Documents. The Daily Compilation provides a listing of the President's daily schedule and meetings, when announced, and other items of general interest issued by the Office of the Press Secretary. In 2012, the Government Printing Office and the Office of the Federal Register released a mobile web application (http://m.gpo.gov/dcpd) that catalogues the daily public activities of the President of the United States and enhances features of the online Daily Compilation with user-friendly search capability, allowing users to access Presidential content by date, category, subject, or location.

Also included in the printed edition are lists of the President's nominations submitted to the Senate, materials released by the Office of the Press Secretary that are not printed in full text in the book, and proclamations, Executive orders, and other Presidential documents released by the Office of the Press Secretary and published in the *Federal Register*. This information appears in the appendixes at the end of the book.

Volumes covering the administrations of Presidents Herbert Hoover, Harry S. Truman, Dwight D. Eisenhower, John F. Kennedy, Lyndon B. Johnson, Richard Nixon, Gerald R. Ford,

Jimmy Carter, Ronald Reagan, George H.W. Bush, William J. Clinton, and George W. Bush are also included in the Public Papers series.

The Public Papers of the Presidents publication program is under the direction of John Hyrum Martinez, Director of the Publications and Services Division, Office of the Federal Register. The series is produced by the Presidential and Legislative Publications Unit, Laurice A. Clark, Supervisor. The Chief Editor of this book was Joseph K. Vetter; the Manging Editor was Joshua H. Liberatore, assisted by Stacey A. Mulligan and Amelia E. Otovo.

The frontispiece and photographs used in the portfolio were supplied by the White House Photo Office. The typography and design of the book were developed by the Government Publishing Office under the direction of Davita E. Vance-Cooks, Director.

Oliver A. Potts
Director of the Federal Register

David S. Ferriero
Archivist of the United States

Contents

Cabinet

Vice President.. Joseph R. Biden, Jr.

Secretary of State... Hillary Rodham Clinton

Secretary of the Treasury............................ Timothy F. Geithner

Secretary of Defense................................... Leon E. Panetta

Attorney General... Eric H. Holder, Jr.

Secretary of the Interior .... Kenneth L. Salazar

Secretary of Agriculture.............................. Thomas J. Vilsack

Secretary of Commerce .... John E. Bryson
(resigned June 20)
Rebecca M. Blank, Acting
(designated June 20)

Secretary of Labor....................................... Hilda L. Solis

Secretary of Health and Human
Services.. Kathleen Sebelius

Secretary of Housing and Urban
Development.. Shaun L.S. Donovan

Secretary of Transportation .... Raymond H. LaHood

Secretary of Energy..................................... Steven Chu

Secretary of Education................................. Arne Duncan

Secretary of Veterans Affairs....................... Eric K. Shinseki

Secretary of Homeland Security................. Janet A. Napolitano

Chief of Staff .... William M. Daley
(resigned January 27)
Jacob J. "Jack" Lew
(appointed January 27)

Administrator of the Environmental
Protection Agency... Lisa P. Jackson

United States Trade Representative........... Ronald Kirk

Director of the Office of Management and
Budget .... Jacob J. "Jack" Lew
(resigned January 27)
Jeffrey D. Zients, Acting
(designated January 27)

Chair of the Council of Economic Advisers Alan B. Kreuger

United States Permanent Representative to
the United Nations...................................... Susan E. Rice

Administration of Barack Obama

2012

Remarks to Iowa Democratic Caucus Attendees and a Question-and-Answer Session
January 3, 2012

The President. Hello, Iowa! How are you guys? I miss you all. And I understand that it's actually warmer tonight than it was 4 years ago, which means, I'm sure, great turnout at the caucuses.

On the ride over here, I was reminiscing with David Plouffe. He was showing me, actually, an old advertisement from Iowa, in fact, the last advertisement we did in the Iowa campaign. And other than pointing out how much more gray I am and how much older I look now than I did then, we actually were just remembering the incredible energy and excitement and the spirit of common purpose that those Iowa caucuses represent. It was an example of how the campaign was not about one person, but it was about all of us coming together to try to deliver the kind of change that had been talked about a long time in Washington, but all too often hadn't been delivered on.

And it's because of you that I've had this extraordinary honor over the last 3 years of working to try to deliver on that change. And obviously, we didn't know at the time how severe the economic crisis was going to be. We didn't fully appreciate at the time the worldwide magnitude of the financial crisis. But we knew even then that the middle class had been taking it for a long time. Folks who had been trying to get into the middle class had found that the ladders that allowed for upward mobility had started to disintegrate for a lot of people.

And so we understood that what we were fighting for was an America where everybody had a fair shot, everybody did their fair share, that responsibility was rewarded and that the game wasn't fixed, that it wasn't rigged, and that if people did the right thing and worked hard, as so many families who in Iowa and throughout the country, that they were going to be able to live out their piece of the American Dream.

Now, we've still got a lot of work to do. But think about the change that was accomplished because of those caucuses 4 years ago. Because of those caucuses 4 years ago, we ended the war in Iraq, as promised; our troops are now coming home.

Because of the work that so many of you did even before the caucuses 4 years ago, health care is a reality for millions of Americans and seniors have seen the price of prescription drugs lowered and there are 2 million young Americans who are able to keep their insurance, even if they're not getting it through a job. And we're going to be able to say to every American out there who's got a preexisting condition or has gotten a raw deal from an insurance company that they're going to have some meaningful security, they're not going to be bankrupt if they get sick.

Because of you and the work that you did 4 years ago, there are millions of young people all across the country who are able to get more affordable student loans and Pell grants. They're able to afford college and apply themselves so that they can achieve a meaningful career that pays a good wage and provides good benefits. Because of you, we've been able to end the policy of "don't ask, don't tell" so that every American who wants to serve this country that they love had that opportunity, regardless of who they love.

So, across the board, whether it's doubling fuel efficiency standards on cars or making sure that we've got a more effective system to provide job training for people who've lost their jobs, across the board, you have made a difference. But we all know we've got a lot more work that we have to do.

Although we've passed health care reform, we've passed Wall Street reform, there are a lot of forces that want to push back against it and want to undo some of those changes. And we're battling millions of dollars of negative advertising and lobbyists and special interests who don't want to see the change that you worked so hard—to fully take root. And that's why this time out is going to be in some ways more important than the first time out. Mitch is right: Change is never easy. The problems that we've been dealing with over the last 3 years, they didn't happen overnight, and we're not going to fix them overnight. But we've been making steady progress, as long as we can sustain it. And that's what this is going to be all about.

So the only way we're going to be able to do that is if all of you maintain the same determination, the same energy, the same drive, the same hopefulness, the same optimism about this wonderful country of ours, as was on display 4 years ago. And I want you to know that because of you, because of all the memories I have of being in your living rooms or meeting you in a diner or seeing you over at a campaign office, I have never lost that same source of inspiration that drove me to embark on this journey in the first place. You guys inspire me every single day.

And I want us to remind each other that, as much work as there may be out there before us, there's nothing we can't accomplish when determined citizens come together to make a difference.

So thank you, everybody. I could not be prouder. And, Mitch, I think we've got a couple of—time for a couple questions.

Obama for America Battleground States Director Mitchell Stewart. Yes, we do, sir. And the first question comes out of Coralville. Coralville, can you hear us?

2012 Presidential Campaign

Q. Good evening, Mr. President. I'm Roseann, and I'm here, as you can see, at a full house in the beautiful Performing Arts Center in Coralville, Iowa. How are you tonight?

The President. I'm doing well. How are you?

Q. Well, Mr. President, I think we're having a little difficulty with audio, but I'm going to go ahead with my question.

Thinking about the caucuses 4 years ago, and as you reflected, you delivered your message of hope and change, but we didn't know in 2008 the extent of the problems we were facing, and certainly progress has been a challenge. So I'm wondering now, in 2012, if you still believe in hope and change for America. And I'm also wondering how your reelection campaign is going to help us better understand what we need to do, both as individual citizens and as a country, to achieve the fair society that you spoke about recently in Osawatomie, Kansas.

The President. Well, first of all, I want to make sure you can hear my answer. How's the sound coming through now?

[*At this point, the audience in Coralville applauded, indicating that they could hear the President.*]

Well, in some ways, I'm actually more optimistic now than I was when I first ran, because we've already seen change take place. And part of what 2012 is about is both reminding the American people of how far we've traveled and the concrete effects that some of our work has had in terms of making sure that people have health insurance or making sure that our troops are coming home or making sure that young people are able to go to college. But part of it is also framing this larger debate about what kind of country are we going to leave for our children and our grandchildren.

There is no problem that we face that we cannot solve. But in order to solve it, we've got to make sure that everybody gets a fair shot. And that means that we're investing in things like education, that we're investing in basic science and technology so we're making things again here in America and we're revitalizing manufacturing and we're not just buying from other countries, but we're selling to other countries and we're inventing things and encouraging entrepreneurship. It means that we're rebuilding our infrastructure, our roads and our bridges, but also our high-speed rail lines and high-speed Internet access in places like rural Iowa, making sure that everybody who wants to reach a worldwide market is able to do so because they've got the connection to do it.

It also means that those things are going to have to be paid for in a fair way. And obviously, a lot of the debate in Washington over the last several months and over the last year has revolved around how do we create a government that is lean and efficient and effective. And I'm proud of some of the tough decisions that we've been willing to make in terms of pruning back programs that don't work. But if we're going to make the investments that we need for our kids at the same time as we're controlling our deficit, then there's nothing wrong with saying to millionaires and billionaires that we're going to let your tax cuts expire. You can afford it. You've done very well in this society. And I know that—[*inaudible*]—in America, but they have to be asked. And the other party has a fundamentally different philosophy.

The same is true when it comes to the issue of fair play. We, through Wall Street reform, have rolled back policies that allowed credit card companies to jack up your interest rates without alerting you to it or other financial practices that disadvantage consumers.

And so we've said, you know what, we're going to have a consumer watchdog in place to look after you, to make sure that you're not being cheated on credit cards or mortgages. Because if you want to compete in a free market, then you should compete on the basis of price and service and quality, not on the basis of somebody not being able to understand what they're buying.

These basic principles are what's going to be at stake in order for us to succeed. And I think that they're principles that most Americans believe in, that everybody should act responsibly, everybody should do their part, and everybody should be able to travel as far as their work ethic and their dreams will carry them.

And right now all we're getting from the other side—you guys have been hearing it a lot more than I have. I know it's—you've been bombarded, I don't know how you watch TV in Iowa these days—with a different theory that says, we're going to cut taxes for the wealthiest among us and roll back regulations on things like clean air and health care reform and Wall Street reform, and that somehow, automatical-

ly, that assures that everybody is able to succeed. I don't believe that. And I don't think any of the people in that auditorium do either.

So it's going to be a big battle, though. I hope you guys are geared up. I'm excited.

Mr. Stewart. Great. Thank you very much, Coralville. Next, we have Cedar Rapids. Cedar Rapids, are you with us? Can you hear us, Cedar Rapids? Hello, Cedar Rapids. Can you hear us?

The President. Hold on one second.

Mr. Stewart. Yes, hold on one second.

The President. I can't hear you yet.

Mr. Stewart. We'll give it 5 more seconds. Folks in Cedar Rapids, can you hear us?

Q. Yes, we can. Yes.

Health Care Reform/2012 Presidential Campaign

Q. Good evening, Mr. President. This is Carol from Cedar Rapids, and I'm honored to be among your volunteers. On the cable talk shows, there is talk about your administration not accomplishing anything. However, I am a breast cancer survivor and was a social worker for 33 years before retiring and know firsthand what a great accomplishment the Affordable Care Act is, among your other achievements. How do you respond to people who say you have not done enough?

The President. I think the main message that we're going to have in 2012 is that we've done a lot, but we've got a lot more to do, and that's why we need another 4 years to get it all done. But you just mentioned the Affordable Care Act. We know that somebody who's had an illness like cancer, who's a survivor, has trouble getting insurance. Because of the Affordable Care Act, insurance companies are not going to be able to ban people with preexisting conditions. That makes a direct impact on your life and your family's life.

We know that there are 2 million young people who have insurance because of the Affordable Care Act who didn't have it before. We know that seniors have seen discounts in their prescription drugs. They're saving billions of dollars all across the country. We know that preventive care, like mammograms, are now available through your insurance, and they can't arbitrarily deny you coverage right when you need care.

So that's just on health care. And it's making an impact on people's lives day to day. But here's the thing. Frankly, not that many people watch cable TV. What they do is they listen to their friends, their neighbors, their coworkers. And that's why what you guys are doing today at the caucus and what you will be doing every day from now until November makes such a difference. Because nobody is a better messenger for the kind of change we're talking about than you. You can tell a story about the difference these policies make in your life in a way that any politician in Washington, including me, can't do.

And one of the things that we learned 4 years ago was that when people at grassroots level are getting involved and they're getting engaged and they're feeling empowered and they're joining hands with each other, that's a powerful force. It can't be stopped. But unfor-tunately, over the—[*inaudible*]—it's not as focused and concentrated as an election campaign. And so the forces of big money and special interests and lobbyists, they all come to the fore, and the pundits and the cable TV dominates the political conversation.

Well, you know what, fortunately in 2012 we've got a chance to respond. And I will put my money on you. I find you a lot more persuasive than anybody on cable TV, and that's why I know we're going to win.

Thank you.

Mr. Stewart. Great. Thank you very much, sir. We appreciate your time. We appreciate Cedar Rapids. We're going to let you get back to the remainder of your caucuses.

NOTE: The President spoke at 8:10 p.m. via videoconference from the Capital Hilton hotel in Washington, DC, to caucus attendees. A portion of these remarks could not be verified because the audio was incomplete.

Remarks in Cleveland, Ohio
January 4, 2012

The President. Well, I just want to thank the Easons and Ms. Kirkpatrick for welcoming us. As some of you may be aware, just in terms of background, the Easons, who have been married for 42 years now—Mr. Eason is a former marine and so served our country in the Korean war—were living in their home, were taken advantage by a mortgage broker, and as a consequence, ended up being $80,000 in debt. The repairs that had originally been promised to be made for a few thousands dollars were never completed, and they almost lost their home.

And thanks to Ms. Kirkpatrick's organization and some timely intervention, they were able to stay in their home and prevent foreclosure. But it's a good example of the kinds of trickery and abuse in the nonbank financial sector that we're going to have to do something about. And we're so glad that we've got somebody like Rich Cordray who's willing to take this on and make sure that families like the Easons, who've done the right thing, who've been responsible, who've served their country, that they're not taken advantage of and they're able to live in security and dignity in their golden years.

So thank you so much for letting us be in your home, Mr. Eason and Mrs. Eason. Thank you.

William Eason. It's an honor you being here.

The President. Well, we appreciate your service all the way around.

Now, he's not mentioning he also used to be a boxer, so if you guys break anything in here, you could be in trouble. [*Laughter*]

Thanks, guys.

NOTE: The President spoke at 12:25 p.m. at the residence of William and Endia Eason. In his remarks, he referred to Richard A. Cordray, Director-designate, Consumer Financial Protection Bureau; and Deonna Kirkpatrick, communications director, Empowering and Strengthening Ohio's People. Audio was not available for verification of the content of these remarks.

Remarks at Shaker Heights High School in Shaker Heights, Ohio
January 4, 2012

The President. Hello, Ohio! Ah, it is good to be back in Ohio. It is good to be back in Shaker Heights, home of the Red Raiders.

Audience member. Mr. President, I love you!

The President. I love you back. And I'm glad to be back. I'm glad to be here.

I want to thank your mayor, Earl Leiken, for hosting us today; your superintendent, Mark Freeman; the principal here, Mike Griffith. Well, and I know—I'm pretty sure we've got a couple of Congresspeople here, but I don't see them. Where are they? The—okay, we got Marcia Fudge. Marcy Kaptur is here. Dennis Kucinich, Betty Sutton in the house. Outstanding Members of Congress, doing the right thing every day, so we thank them all for being here.

Now, I understand the folks here at this school have a pretty good basketball team—boys and girls. Unfortunately, I have no eligibility left. [*Laughter*] So I can't play with you.

I want to wish everybody a happy New Year; 2012 is going to be a good year. It's going to be a good year. And one of my New Year's resolutions is to make sure that I get out of Washington and spend time with folks like you. Because folks here in Ohio and all across the country, I want you to know you're the reason why I ran for this office in the first place. You remind me what we are still fighting for. You inspire me.

Audience member. [*Inaudible*]

The President. Okay. You do? [*Laughter*]

No, you remind me that this country is all about folks who work hard and where responsibility pays off, an America where anybody who puts in the effort and plays by the rules can get ahead.

That's the America you deserve. That's the America we're working to build. That's why I told Congress before the new year they couldn't leave for vacation until we made sure 160 million working Americans wouldn't get hit with a tax hike on January 1.

Now, this wasn't easy. It should have been easy, but it wasn't. But in the end, we got members of both parties to come together and make sure that you could keep more money in your paychecks each month. And you're keeping that extra $40 in every paycheck because we made sure that we didn't stunt the recovery. We made sure that families got the break that they need. And that means more security for your families. It also means a boost for our economy at a time when we've got to do everything we can to keep it growing. Because more money spent by more Americans means more businesses hiring more workers.

And so when I—when Congress returns, I'm going to urge them to extend this tax cut all the way through 2012, with no drama, no delay. Do the right thing. It is a no-brainer. Let's get it done. Let's pass these tax cuts.

Now, we still have more to do. So today we're taking another important step, one that will bring us closer to the economy that we need, an economy where everybody plays by the same rules.

And to help us do that, I'm joined by somebody you might recognize, Richard Cordray. Son of Ohio; a good, good man. Today I'm appointing Richard as America's consumer watchdog. And that means he is going to be in charge of one thing: looking out for the best interests of American consumers, looking out for you.

His job will be to protect families like yours from the abuses of the financial industry. His job will be to make sure that you've got all the information you need to make important financial decisions. Right away, he'll start working to make sure millions of Americans are treated fairly by mortgage brokers and payday lenders and debt collectors. In fact, just this week, his agency is opening up a simple 1–800 number that you can call to make sure you're getting a fair deal on your mortgage and hold banks and brokers accountable if you're not.

Now, I nominated Richard for this job last summer, so you may be wondering why am I

5

appointing him today. It would be a good question. [*Laughter*] For almost half a year, Republicans in the Senate have blocked Richard's confirmation.

They refused to even give Richard an up-or-down vote. Now, this is not because Richard is not qualified. There's no question that Richard is the right person for the job. He's got the support of Democrats and Republicans around the country. A majority of attorney generals—Richard's a former attorney general—a majority of attorney generals from both parties across the country have called for Richard to be confirmed. Your local Members of Congress who are here today, they support him. He has the support of a majority in the Senate. Everyone agrees Richard is more than qualified.

So what's the problem, you might ask. The only reason Republicans in the Senate have blocked Richard is because they don't agree with the law that set up a consumer watchdog in the first place. They want to weaken the law. They want to water it down. And by the way, a lot of folks in the financial industry have poured millions of dollars to try to water it down.

That makes no sense. Does anybody think that the reason that we got in such a financial mess—the worst financial crisis since the Great Depression, the worst economic crisis in a generation—that the reason was because of too much oversight of the financial industry?

Audience members. No!

The President. Of course not. We shouldn't be weakening oversight. We shouldn't be weakening accountability. We should be strengthening it, especially when it comes to looking out for families like yours.

The financial firms have armies of lobbyists in Washington looking out for their interests. You need somebody looking out for your interests and fighting for you, and that's Richard Cordray.

Now, I have to say, Richard's a really nice guy. [*Laughter*] You know, you look at him and you think, this guy is not somebody who's going around picking fights. And yet this fight on behalf of consumers is something that Richard

has been waging here in Ohio for the better part of two decades, so—[*applause*].

As your attorney general, he helped recover billions of dollars in things like pension funds on behalf of retirees. He protected consumers from dishonest lending practices. Before that, Richard was the State treasurer, where he earned a reputation for working with folks from across the spectrum—Democrats, Republicans, bankers, consumer advocates—had a great reputation across the board, doing the right thing.

And, Cleveland, you've seen the difference that Richard can make for consumers, and I have too. And that's why I want Richard to keep standing up for you, not just here in Ohio, but for consumers all across the country.

Now, every day that Richard waited to be confirmed—and we were pretty patient. I mean, we kept on saying to Mitch McConnell and the other folks, let's go ahead and confirm him. Why isn't he being called up? Let's go. Every day that we waited was another day when millions of Americans were left unprotected. Because without a director in place, the consumer watchdog agency that we've set up doesn't have all the tools it needs to protect consumers against dishonest mortgage brokers or payday lenders and debt collectors who are taking advantage of consumers. And that's inexcusable. It's wrong. And I refuse to take no for an answer.

So I've said before that I want to look for every possible opportunity to work with Congress to move this country forward and create jobs. I'm going to look for every opportunity to try to bridge the partisan divide and get things done, because that's what the American people need right now. And that means putting construction workers back on the jobs repairing our roads and our bridges. That means keeping our teachers in the classrooms. That means keeping our cops and firefighters doing what they do, protecting us every day. That means helping small businesses get ahead. That means serving our veterans as well as they've served us, like this young man right in the front. We are grateful for him, for his service.

These are ideas that have support from Democrats; they have support from Republicans around the country, Independents around the country. I want to work with Congress to get them done.

But when Congress refuses to act, and as a result, hurts our economy and puts our people at risk, then I have an obligation as President to do what I can without them. I've got an obligation to act on behalf of the American people. And I'm not going to stand by while a minority in the Senate puts party ideology ahead of the people that we were elected to serve. Not with so much at stake, not at this make-or-break moment for middle class Americans. We're not going to let that happen.

For way too long, we've had a financial system that was stacked against ordinary Americans. Banks on Wall Street played by different rules than businesses on Main Street. They played by different rules than a lot of community banks who were doing the right thing across the country: hidden fees, fine print that led consumers to make financial decisions that they didn't always understand.

Richard and I, before we came here, had an opportunity to visit with a wonderful elderly couple, the Easons. And Mr. Eason is a former marine, served in the Korean war. Mrs. Eason makes a really good sweet potato pie. She gave me one. I'm going to eat it later, after. [*Laughter*] I didn't want to eat it before because I didn't want to get sleepy having a big piece of pie right before. [*Laughter*]

But their story was the story of a lot of folks in this region, where a mortgage broker came to them, said that they could do some home repair for a few thousand dollars, and they ended up getting scammed. The loans got flipped. They ended up owing $80,000, almost losing their home, and the repairs were never made.

Those kinds of practices, that's not who we are. We cannot allow people to be taken advantage of. And it's not just because it's bad for those individuals. All that risky behavior led— helped to contribute to the economic crisis that we're all still digging ourselves out of. All those subprime loans, all those foreclosures, all the problems in the housing market, that's all

contributing to an economy that's not moving as fast as we want it.

And that's why, last year, we put in place new rules, new rules of the road to make sure that a few bad apples in the financial sector can't break the law, they can't cheat consumers, they can't put our entire economy in danger. And many of these provisions are already starting to make a difference. For the first time in history, we put in place a consumer watchdog, someone whose only job is to look out for the interests of everyday Americans.

And we are so fortunate to have somebody like Richard who's willing to do it, despite great sacrifice to his family. He's the right man for the job.

So if you're a student—I see some young people out here—his job will be to protect you from dishonest lending practices and to make sure that you've got the information you need on student loans. He's already started up an initiative called Know Before You Owe. [*Laughter*] That's a good slogan: Know Before You Owe. You don't want to owe and then know. [*Laughter*]

If you're a veteran, he'll help make sure that you aren't taken advantage of when you're coming home from serving your country. And it turns out that military families are some of the folks who are most vulnerable to some of these financial abuses.

If you're a senior, Richard's going to help make sure you don't lose your home or your retirement because somebody saw you as an easier target. And that's what happened to the Easons. Endia, who I think is here—Mrs. Eason, are you here? You're somewhere here. There's—Mrs. Eason's down there. Ninety-one years old. And as I mentioned, Mrs. Eason's husband William is a former marine, also a former boxer. So don't mess with him. [*Laughter*]

And I just want to repeat, 10 years ago they were approached by a broker who offered them a loan to make needed repairs on their home, made everything sound easy. Easons agreed. Broker ended up disappearing. They get left with $80,000 in debt, almost lose their home. They didn't lose it because of the

7

intervention of some terrific non-for-profits that Richard, when he was treasurer here in Ohio, helped to support. Now—[*applause*].

Audience member. [*Inaudible*].

The President. East Side, that's right.

Now, the Easons are good people. They're what America is all about. They worked hard. They served their country. They saved their money. They didn't live high on the hog. It's a modest house. They earned the right to retire with dignity and with respect, and they shouldn't have to worry about being tricked by somebody who's out to make a quick buck. And they need somebody who is going to stand up for them, and millions of Americans need somebody who is going to look out for their interests. And that person is Richard Cordray.

And we know what would happen if Republicans in Congress were allowed to keep holding Richard's nomination hostage. More of our loved ones would be tricked into making bad financial decisions. More dishonest lenders could take advantage of some of the most vulnerable families. And the vast majority of financial firms who do the right thing would be undercut by those who don't.

See, most people in the financial services industry do the right thing, but they're at a disadvantage if nobody is enforcing the rules. We can't let that happen. Now is not the time to play politics while people's livelihoods are at stake. Now's the time to do everything we can to protect consumers, prevent financial crises like the one that we've been through from ever happening again. That starts with letting Richard do his job.

So I know—let me just close by saying this. I know that you're hearing a lot of promises from a lot of politicians lately. Today you're only going to hear one from me. As long as I have the privilege of serving as your President, I promise to do everything I can every day, every minute, every second, to make sure this is a country where hard work and responsibility mean something and everybody can get ahead. Not just those at the very top, not just those who know how to work the system, but everybody.

That's what America's always been about. That's what America is going to be about today and tomorrow and 10 years from now and 20 years from now. And with the help of people like Richard Cordray, that's the country that we will always be.

Thank you. God bless you. God bless the United States of America.

NOTE: The President spoke at 1:26 p.m. in the North Gymnasium. In his remarks, he referred to Richard A. Cordray, Director-designate, Consumer Financial Protection Bureau.

Remarks at the Pentagon in Arlington, Virginia
January 5, 2012

Good morning, everybody. The United States of America is the greatest force for freedom and security that the world has ever known. And in no small measure, that's because we've built the best trained, best led, best equipped military in history, and as Commander in Chief, I'm going to keep it that way.

Indeed, all of us on this stage—every single one of us—have a profound responsibility to every soldier, sailor, airman, marine, and coastguardsman who puts their life on the line for America. We owe them a strategy with well-defined goals, to only send them into harm's way when it's absolutely necessary, to give them the equipment and the support that they need to get the job done, and to care for them and their families when they come home. That is our solemn obligation.

And over the past 3 years, that's what we've done. We've continued to make historic investments in our military: our troops and their capabilities, our military families, and our veterans. And thanks to their extraordinary service, we've ended our war in Iraq. We've decimated Al Qaida's leadership. We've delivered justice to Usama bin Laden, and we've put that terrorist network on the path to defeat. We've made important progress in Afghanistan, and we've begun to transition so Afghans can assume more responsibility for their own security. We joined allies and partners to protect the Libyan people as they ended the regime of Muammar Qadhafi.

Now we're turning the page on a decade of war. Three years ago, we had some 180,000 troops in Iraq and Afghanistan. Today, we've cut that number in half. And as the transition in Afghanistan continues, more of our troops will continue to come home. More broadly, around the globe we've strengthened alliances, forged new partnerships, and served as a force for universal rights and human dignity.

In short, we've succeeded in defending our Nation, taking the fight to our enemies, reducing the number of Americans in harm's way, and we've restored America's global leadership. That makes us safer, and it makes us stronger. And that's an achievement that every American, especially those Americans who are proud to wear the uniform of the United States Armed Forces, should take great pride in.

This success has brought our Nation once more to a moment of transition. Even as our troops continue fight—to fight in Afghanistan, the tide of war is receding. Even as our forces prevail in today's missions, we have the opportunity and the responsibility to look ahead to the force that we are going to need in the future.

At the same time, we have to renew our economic strength here at home, which is the foundation of our strength around the world. And that includes putting our fiscal house in order. To that end, the Budget Control Act passed by Congress last year, with the support of Republicans and Democrats alike, mandates reductions in Federal spending, including defense spending. I've insisted that we do that responsibly. The security of our Nation and the lives of our men and women in uniform depend on it.

And that's why I called for this comprehensive defense review to clarify our strategic interests in a fast-changing world and to guide our defense priorities and spending over the coming decade, because the size and the structure of our military and defense budgets have to be driven by a strategy, not the other way around. Moreover, we have to remember the

lessons of history. We can't afford to repeat the mistakes that have been made in the past, after World War II, after Vietnam, when our military was left ill prepared for the future. As Commander in Chief, I will not let that happen again. Not on my watch.

We need a start—we need a smart, strategic set of priorities. The new guidance that the Defense Department is releasing today does just that. I want to thank Secretary Panetta and General Dempsey for their extraordinary leadership during this process. I want to thank the service secretaries and chiefs, the combatant commanders, and so many defense leaders—military and civilian, Active, Guard, and Reserve—for their contributions. Many of us met repeatedly, asking tough questions, challenging our own assumptions, and making hard choices. And we've come together today around an approach that will keep our Nation safe and our military the finest that the world has ever known.

This review also benefits from the contributions of leaders from across my national security team, from the Departments of State, Homeland Security, and Veterans Affairs, as well as the intelligence community. And this is critical, because meeting the challenges of our time cannot be the work of our military alone or the United States alone. It requires all elements of our national power, working together in concert with our allies and our partners.

So I'm going to let Leon and Marty go into the details. But I just want to say that this effort reflects the guidance that I personally gave throughout this process. Yes, the tide of war is receding. But the question that this strategy answers is what kind of military will we need long after the wars of the last decade are over. And today, we're fortunate to be moving forward from a position of strength.

As I made clear in Australia, we will be strengthening our presence in the Asia-Pacific, and budget reductions will not come at the expense of that critical region. We're going to continue investing in our critical partnerships and alliances, including NATO, which has demonstrated time and again—most recently in Libya—that it's a force multiplier. We will stay vigilant, especially in the Middle East.

As we look beyond the wars in Iraq and Afghanistan and the end of long-term nation-building with large military footprints, we'll be able to ensure our security with smaller conventional ground forces. We'll continue to get rid of outdated cold war–era systems so that we can invest in the capabilities that we need for the future, including intelligence, surveillance and reconnaissance, counterterrorism, countering weapons of mass destruction, and the ability to operate in environments where adversaries try to deny us access.

So yes, our military will be leaner, but the world must know the United States is going to maintain our military superiority with Armed Forces that are agile, flexible, and ready for the full range of contingencies and threats.

We're also going to keep faith with those who serve by making sure our troops have the equipment and capabilities they need to succeed and by prioritizing efforts that focus on wounded warriors, mental health, and the well-being of our military families. And as our newest veterans rejoin civilian life, we'll keep working to give our veterans the care, the benefit—the benefits, and job opportunities that they deserve and that they have earned.

Finally, although today is about our defense strategy, I want to close with a word about the defense budget that will flow from this strategy. The details will be announced in the coming weeks. Some will no doubt say that the spending reductions are too big; others will say that they're too small. It will be easy to take issue with a particular change in a particular program. But I'd encourage all of us to remember what President Eisenhower once said, that "each proposal must be weighed in the light of a broader consideration: the need to maintain balance in and among national programs." After a decade of war, and as we rebuild the source of our strength at home and abroad, it's time to restore that balance.

I think it's important for all Americans to remember, over the past 10 years, since 9/11, our defense budget grew at an extraordinary pace. Over the next 10 years, the growth in the defense budget will slow, but the fact of the matter is this: It will still grow, because we have global responsibilities that demand our leadership. In fact, the defense budget will still be larger than it was toward the end of the Bush administration. And I firmly believe, and I think the American people understand, that we can keep our military strong and our Nation secure with a defense budget that continues to be larger than roughly the next 10 countries combined.

So again, I want to thank Secretary Panetta, Chairman Dempsey, all the defense leaders who are on this stage, and some who are absent, for their leadership and their partnership throughout this process. Our men and women in uniform give their very best to America every single day, and in return they deserve the very best from America. And I thank all of you for the commitment to the goal that we all share: keeping America strong and secure in the 21st century and keeping our Armed Forces the very best in the world.

And with that, I will turn this discussion over to Leon and to Marty, who can explain more and take your questions.

So thank you very much. I understand this is the first time a President's done this. It's a pretty nice room. [*Laughter*]

Thank you, guys.

NOTE: The President spoke at 11 a.m. in the Pentagon Briefing Room.

Remarks at the Consumer Financial Protection Bureau
January 6, 2012

Thank you. Well, it is wonderful to see all of you. I thought I would just drop by to help your new Director move in. [*Laughter*] He's been a little busy. So I thought maybe some boxes, a little plant. [*Laughter*]

I also just wanted to say hello to all of you who have just been doing extraordinary work in standing up what I think is going to be one of the most important agencies for people that there is. And I know that all of you have devoted enormous amounts of time and energy, and many of you are here making significant sacrifices with your families to make sure that this agency gets up and running really well. And so I just wanted to say thank you to all of you.

Let me begin by saying a few words about the latest economic news. This morning we learned that American businesses added another 212,000 jobs last month. All together, more private sector jobs were created in 2011 than any year since 2005. And there are a lot of people that are still hurting out there. After losing more than 8 million jobs in the recession, obviously, we have a lot more work to do. But it is important for the American people to recognize that we've now added 3.2 million new private sector jobs over the last 22 months, nearly 2 million new jobs last year alone. So, after shedding jobs for more than a decade, our manufacturing sector is also adding jobs 2 years in a row now. So we're making progress. We're moving in the right direction.

And one of the reasons for this is the tax cut for working Americans that we put in place last year. And when Congress returns, they should extend the middle class tax cut for all of this year to make sure that we keep this recovery going. It's the right thing to do. There should not be delay. There should not be a lot of drama. We should get it done.

And the American people, I think, rightly understand that there are still a lot of struggles that people are going through out there. A lot of families are still having a tough time. A lot of small businesses are still having a tough time. But we're starting to rebound. We're moving in the right direction. We have made real progress. Now is not the time to stop. So I would urge Congress to make sure that they stay on top of their jobs, to make sure that everybody else is able to enjoy, hopefully, an even more robust recovery in 2012.

So the economy is moving in the right direction. We're creating jobs on a consistent basis.

We're not going to let up, not until everybody who wants to find a good job can find one. But we have a responsibility to do even more than just try to recover from this devastating recession and financial crisis. We have a responsibility to make sure that the economy that we're rebuilding is one where middle class families feel like they can get ahead again. A lot of the problems that we're dealing with are problems that existed even before the recession, even before the financial crisis. For a decade or more, middle class families felt like they were treading water, that they were losing ground.

And what we want to do is make sure not just that we're getting back to the status quo, we want to make sure that we're dealing with those underlining problems. Getting to a point where middle class families feel like they can get ahead again, where hard work pays off again, where everybody gets a fair shot and everybody does their fair share and everybody is playing by the same set of rules.

And that's where all of you come in. Every one of you here has a critical role to play in making sure that everybody plays by the same rules. To make sure that the big banks on Wall Street play by the same rules as community banks on Main Street. To make sure that the rules of the road are enforced and that a few bad actors in the financial sector can't break the law, can't cheat working families, can't threaten our entire economy all over again.

That's your mission: to make sure that the American people have somebody in their corner, that American consumers have somebody who's got their back. And you finally got a great Director who is tailormade to lead this agency in Richard Cordray.

You've also got an extraordinary team that is lined up behind me here, who did a great job in getting this agency up and running and are going to continue to show extraordinary leadership in all the various issues that you're going to be addressing. And I also want to give a special shout-out to the woman who dreamt up this agency and spent so much time turning it into a reality, our friend Elizabeth Warren.

Just to be a little more specific, millions of working Americans use financial products like

11

credit cards and student loans and mortgages. And that's a good thing. These products have a tremendous potential to make people's lives better—to buy products, to earn an education, to afford a home, to raise a family. And we all use them. But when they're sold in an irresponsible fashion they can also make life brutally hard on people. They can turn the dreams of a family into a nightmare. Things like hidden fees and traps on credit cards and student loans cost working American billions of dollars. Things like subprime loans and skyrocketing interest that you can't escape can not only bring families to their knees, but the entire economy to its knees.

And Richard just mentioned the example of this elderly couple that we met when we were in Ohio yesterday. These are folks—the gentleman was a marine who served in Korea. They had been married for 42 years. He had worked all his life; they had poured their savings into this home.

Because of a code violation—obviously, they're on a fixed income, they don't have a lot of money—they thought, well, maybe we can get a loan to make some modest repairs. And what initially was promised as an $8,000 line of credit to make these repairs, ended up being an $80,000 debt with no repairs that threatened them going into foreclosure.

And those kinds of stories are replicated all across the country. And it not only hurts those individuals, it hurts the entire economy. That shouldn't happen, not in America. And that's why we're here. We're here to put an end to stories like these.

And already, your work is making a difference. The "Know Before You Owe" campaign you've been working on for months is doing three big things. It's making home loan applications more transparent so that families will know what they owe on their mortgages. It's making it easier for students to compare financial aid packages and know what they owe each month when they graduate. I could have used that. [*Laughter*] It's making—in fact, I've got a law school classmate here who, she probably went through the same thing I did. [*Laughter*] It's making credit card agreements shorter and

simpler, so that credit card holders will know what they owe and what they're getting into. And I know that folks all across America have been sending in their stories to help shape these new initiatives.

This is not something where it's just a Washington top-down process. You are gathering the experiences of individual families, seeing how they got hurt, how they might have gotten cheated. And that's helping to define how you enforce these rules. And that's vitally important.

And now that Richard is your Director, you can finally exercise the full power that this agency has been given to protect consumers under the law. Now that he's here, irresponsible debt collectors and payday lenders and independent mortgage servicers and loan providers, they're all bound by the same rules as everybody else. No longer are consumers left alone to face the risk of unfair or deceptive or abusive practices, not anymore.

So we can make sure that folks don't lose their homes or their life savings just because somebody saw them as an easy target. We can make sure that students don't start out in life saddled with debt that they can never pay back just because of a lousy deal. We can safeguard families and seniors and veterans from toxic financial products. We can help give everybody the clear and transparent information that they need to make informed financial decisions and have companies compete for their business in an open and honest way.

That's Richard's commitment. That's my commitment. That's the commitment of everybody standing on this stage. And that's your commitment. That's why this agency is so important.

So I want to thank all of you for choosing to serve your country in these challenging times. Your mission is extraordinarily important. It's vital to the strength of our economy. It's really important to the security of working families. And I know that it might be personal for some of you. You may know a friend or a family member whose life was turned upside down because of some of these unsavory practices that this agency is designed to root out, and maybe you were then determined to prevent that from happening to somebody else. Now you can. And we're not going to let those folks down all across the country.

When I meet Americans all across the country or I read letters that I get every night, they really don't ask for much. They're not looking for a handout; they're not looking for special treatment. They just want a fair shake; they just want a fair deal. And we have a chance to give it to them.

So let's do everything that we can to make sure that middle class families can regain some of the security that they've lost over the last de-cade. Let's help to protect what they've worked so hard for and give them the chance to hand it down to their kids. I know you guys are ready to go to work. I am too. I couldn't be prouder of you.

So congratulations.

NOTE: The President spoke at 12:02 p.m. In his remarks, he referred to Elizabeth H. Warren, former Assistant to the President and Special Adviser to the Secretary of the Treasury on the Consumer Financial Protection Bureau; and Cleveland, OH, residents William and Endia Eason.

Statement on the Observance of the Coptic Orthodox Christmas
January 6, 2012

Michelle and I wish Coptic Orthodox Christians in the United States and around the world a blessed and joyous Christmas. On this special day, we give thanks for the extraordinary contributions that Coptic Christians have made to the United States. I want to reaffirm the commitment of the United States to work for the protection of Christian and other religious minorities around the world. As events in Egypt and elsewhere have illustrated, and as history repeatedly reminds us, freedom of religion, the protection of people of all faiths, and the ability to worship as you choose are critical to a peaceful, inclusive, and thriving society. In this Christmas season, we join our Coptic brothers and sisters around the globe in prayers for peace.

The President's Weekly Address
January 7, 2012

Happy New Year, everybody.

This week, I traveled to Cleveland, Ohio, to talk with folks about the biggest challenge we face as a country: rebuilding our economy so that, once again, hard work pays off, responsibility is rewarded, and anyone, regardless of who they are or where they come from, can make it if they try. That's the economy America deserves. That's the economy I'm fighting every day to build.

Now, to get there, the most important thing we need to do is to get more Americans back to work. And over the past 3 years, we've made steady progress. We just learned that our economy added 212,000 private sector jobs in December. After losing more than 8 million jobs in the recession, we've added more than 3 mil-lion private sector jobs over the past 22 months. And we're starting 2012 with manufacturing on the rise and the American auto industry on the mend.

We're heading in the right direction, and we're not going to let up. On Wednesday, the White House will host a forum called Insourcing American Jobs. We'll hear from business leaders who are bringing jobs back home and see how we can help other businesses follow their lead.

Because this is a make-or-break moment for the middle class and all those working to get there. We've got to keep at it. We've got to keep creating jobs. And we've got to keep rebuilding our economy so that everyone gets a fair shot, everyone does their fair share, and everyone plays by the same rules. We can't go back to the days when the financial system was stacking the deck against ordinary Americans. To me, that's not an option, not after all we've been through.

That's why I appointed Richard Cordray as our Nation's new consumer watchdog this week. Richard's job is simple: to look out for you. Every day, his sole mission is to protect consumers from potential abuses by the financial industry and to make sure that you've got all the transparent information you need to make the important financial decisions in your lives.

I nominated Richard for this job last summer. And yet Republicans in the Senate kept blocking his confirmation, not because they objected to him, but because they wanted to weaken his agency. That made no sense. Every day we waited was a day you and consumers all across the country were at greater financial risk.

So this year, I'm going to keep doing whatever it takes to move this economy forward and to make sure that middle class families regain the security they've lost over the past decade. That's my New Year's resolution to all of you.

Thanks, and have a great weekend.

NOTE: The address was recorded at approximately 4:40 p.m. on January 6 in the East Room at the White House for broadcast on January 7. In the address, the President referred to Richard A. Cordray, Director, Consumer Financial Protection Bureau. The transcript was made available by the Office of the Press Secretary on January 6, but was embargoed for release until 6 a.m. on January 7.

Remarks Honoring the 2011 National Basketball Association Champion Dallas Mavericks
January 9, 2012

The President. Hello, everybody! Everybody, please have a seat, have a seat. Welcome to the White House, and congratulations to the world champion Dallas Mavericks. Obviously, we got some Texas people here.

This was the Mavericks' first title, so I want to start by recognizing everybody who stuck with the team through good times and through bad, from Don Carter, the original owner, to the arena staff, to all the fans back home.

We've got some Members of Congress who've waited a long time for this—[laughter]—as well as my Trade Representative, Ron Kirk, who happens to be a former mayor of Dallas.

Of course, none of this would be possible if it hadn't been for the shy and retiring owner—[laughter]—of the Dallas Mavericks, Mark Cuban. So not only did Mark help put together an outstanding group of players and coaches, he was also responsible for making this event happen today. And so we are thrilled to have you guys here.

It turns out that because of the lockout, Dallas wasn't scheduled to play in Washington this season. That did not sit well with Mark. [*Laughter*] He knew this team had worked hard. He wanted them to get all the perks of a world championship, including a visit to the White House. It is tough to say no to Mark Cuban. And so they made a separate trip, and here we are.

And I'm glad it worked out, because this is a special group. Last season, they called themselves the Bad News Bears because from the very beginning nobody gave them much of a chance. People said that Jason Kidd was too old. And I will say that this is the first time I've been with some world champions who are my contemporaries. [*Laughter*] They said J.J. Barea was too small, that Dirk Nowitzki was too slow. They did say that, Dirk, I'm sorry. [*Laughter*] That's what they said. They said you had a great jump shot, but—[*laughter*]. They said DeShawn Stevenson was too crazy. [*Laughter*] They said "The JET" was terrific, but they weren't sure whether that tattoo was such a good idea. [*Laughter*]

But these players got it done because they know how good teams win, not just by jumping higher or running faster, but by finding the open man, working together, staying mentally tough, being supportive of each other, playing smarter.

And that's how the Mavericks took down some of the league's best teams, including the Miami Heat, who got a little bit of attention last year. This was especially sweet for Dirk and Jason who were around the first time that the Mavericks and the Heat met in the finals and lost 5 years ago.

In fact, the Mavericks played—before the Mavericks played a single game last season, when Jason got his tattoo, he said, "When you do something as crazy as I did, you've got to back it up." And he did, by the way, score 27 points to help win the deciding game six.

Dirk joined the Mavericks 13 years ago as a skinny kid from Germany with what he describes as a goofy haircut. [*Laughter*] Last year he became the second European player ever to be named Finals MVP. And it wasn't easy. He bent a finger so badly in game two that he had to shoot left-handed. In game four, he played through a 101-degree fever. But every time, he came through when it counted. And I think it's fair to say that we have very rarely seen a better playoff run than Dirk Nowitzki had last year. It was remarkable.

So, clearly, Dirk is a tough guy. Although the most painful thing may have been his rendition of "We Are the Champions"—[*laughter*]—during the victory celebration. That was—[*laughter*]—did you—you said you worked on that? [*Laughter*] Seriously? Okay.

Now, none of these players would have gotten so far without the rest of the folks on this stage. Obviously, Jason Kidd now has the second most assists and third most steals in NBA history. It wouldn't have worked without an outstanding coach. And Coach Rick Carlisle has now won a player as—or won a title as a player, with Larry Bird in the eighties, has a title as a coach, and then he just informed me

that he had also won—what was it? The Pantoons? What were they called?

Head Coach Richard P. Carlisle. The Patroons, the Albany Patroons.

The President. The Albany Patroons. Many of you did not know that Rick Carlisle had also won one of those. [*Laughter*]

Mr. Carlisle. It's minor league.

The President. It's a minor league team. [*Laughter*]

So these players and coaches will always share a bond that comes with being the best. And it's a bond they share with the Dallas community, where they do everything from setting up scholarships to helping military families get back on their feet. Today, in fact, they met with some wounded warriors here at the White House. I want to really thank them for taking the time to do that. That means so much to people.

So this team really does have a heart that's the size of Texas. This was a remarkable run, a great victory, a great vindication for all the effort Mark Cuban put into building this team, and for long-time players like Dirk Nowitzki and long-suffering fans like all of you. [*Laughter*]

And so I just want to give a heartfelt congratulations to all of you. I told them that it's too bad that next year it will be the Chicago Bulls here—[*laughter*]—but they said I shouldn't be so confident. So congratulations, everybody. Give it up for the Dallas Mavericks.

Dirk, you got something for me?

Forward Dirk Nowitzki. Yes.

[*At this point, the President was presented with a team jersey.*]

The President. That's it. That's what I'm talking about.

Mr. Nowitzki. That's it. I heard you're a big, big fan of Michael Jordan.

The President. Thank you so—well, you know, I was actually—I was 23 before Jordan.

Mr. Nowitzki. Oh, you were?

The President. I was. [*Laughter*] So he got the number from me, I think. [*Laughter*]

Mr. Nowitzki. He stole it.

The President. He stole it.

Mr. Nowitzki. Yes. I got you.

The President. That's what happened. That's beautiful.

NOTE: The President spoke at 12:09 p.m. in the East Room at the White House. In his remarks, he referred to Donald J. Carter, former owner, Mark Cuban, current owner, Richard P. Carlisle, head coach, and Jason Kidd, Jose J. Barea, Jason E. "The JET" Terry, and DeShawn Stevenson, guards, Dallas Mavericks; and former NBA players Larry J. Bird and Michael Jordan.

Remarks on the Resignation of White House Chief of Staff William M. Daley and the Appointment of Jacob J. "Jack" Lew as White House Chief of Staff
January 9, 2012

Hello, everybody. Hope you all had a good weekend.

Last week, my Chief of Staff, Bill Daley, informed me that after spending time reflecting with his family over the holidays, he decided it was time to leave Washington and return to our beloved hometown of Chicago.

Obviously, this was not easy news to hear. And I didn't accept Bill's decision right away. In fact, I asked him to take a couple of days to make sure that he was sure about this. But in the end, the pull of the hometown we both love—a city that's been synonymous with the Daley family for generations—was too great. Bill told me that he wanted to spend more time with his family, especially his grandchildren, and he felt it was the right decision.

One of the things that made it easier was the extraordinary work that he has done for me during what has been an extraordinary year. Bill has been an outstanding Chief of Staff during one of the busiest and most consequential years of my administration.

We were thinking back, just a year ago this weekend, before he was even named for the job, Bill was in the Situation Room getting updates on the shooting in Tucson. On his very first day, Bill took part in a meeting where we discussed Usama bin Laden's compound in Abbottabad. This was all before he even had time to unpack his office.

Over the last year, he's been intimately involved in every decision surrounding the end of the war in Iraq and our support of the people of Libya as they fought for their freedom. He was instrumental in developing the "American Jobs Act" and making sure taxes didn't go up on middle class families. He helped us reach an agreement to reduce the deficit by over $2 trillion. And he played a central role in passing historic trade agreements with South Korea, Colombia, and Panama. Given his past record of service as Secretary of Commerce, he was invaluable in all these negotiations.

So no one in my administration has had to make more important decisions more quickly than Bill. And that's why I think this decision was difficult for me. Naturally, when Bill told me his plans to go back to Chicago, I asked him who I thought could fill his shoes. He told me that there was one clear choice, and I believe he's right. So today I'm pleased to announce that Jack Lew has agreed to serve as my next Chief of Staff.

Let me begin, first of all, by thanking Ruth for allowing Jack to serve in what I know is one of the most difficult jobs in Washington. But Jack has had one of the other most difficult jobs in Washington. For more than a year, Jack has served as the Director of the Office of Management and Budget. As anyone who's been following the news lately can tell you, this is not an easy job.

During his first tour at OMB under President Clinton, Jack was the only Budget Director in history to preside over budget surpluses for 3 consecutive years. And over the last year, he has helped strengthen our economy and streamline the Government at a time when we need to do everything we can to keep our recovery going.

Jack's economic advice has been invaluable, and he has my complete trust, both because of his mastery of the numbers, but because of the values behind those numbers. Ever since he began his career in public as a top aide to Speaker Tip O'Neill, Jack has fought for an America where hard work and responsibility pay off, a place where everybody gets a fair shot, everybody does their fair share, and everybody plays by the same rules. And that belief is reflected in every decision that Jack makes.

Jack also has my confidence on matters outside the borders. Before he served at OMB for me, Jack spent 2 years running the extremely complex and challenging budget and operations process for Secretary Clinton at the State Department, where his portfolio also included managing the civilian operations in Iraq and Afghanistan. And over the last year, he has weighed in on many of the major foreign policy decisions that we've made.

So there is no question that I'm going to deeply miss having Bill by my side here at the White House. But as he will soon find out, Chicago is only a phone call away, and I'm going to be using that phone number quite a bit. I plan to continue to seek Bill's advice and counsel on a whole range of issues in the months and years to come. And here in Washington, I have every confidence that Jack will make sure that we don't miss a beat and continue to do everything we can to strengthen our economy and the middle class and keep the American people safe.

So I want to thank, once again, Bill for his extraordinary service, but also his extraordinary friendship and loyalty to me. It's meant a lot. And I want to congratulate Jack on his new role. I know he is going to do an outstanding job, so thank you.

Thank you, everybody.

NOTE: The President spoke at 3:02 p.m. in the State Dining Room at the White House. In his remarks, he referred to Ruth Lew, wife of White House Chief of Staff Lew.

Remarks at an Obama Victory Fund 2012 Fundraiser
January 9, 2012

The President. Thank you. Happy New Year, everybody. It looks like Gaspard got you all fired up.

A few acknowledgements that I want to make: First of all, the OFA Virginia State director, Lise Clavel, is here, and we just want to thank our directors in the State because they do such hard work every day. Give them a big round of applause. The chair of our event this evening, Spencer Overton, thank you. One of my favorite singers, but more importantly, one of Michelle's favorite singers, Sara Bareilles—thank you for doing—and her band. We are grateful to them.

And I am grateful to you.

Audience member. We love you!

The President. I love you back. I do.

But I'm here not just to say I love you. [*Laughter*] I'm here because I need your help. And more importantly, I'm here because the country needs your help. There were a lot of reasons that many of you got involved in our campaign, worked your hearts out back in 2008. And it wasn't because you thought it was going to be easy. It wasn't because you thought it was a sure thing. You decided to support a candidate named Barack Hussein Obama. You didn't need a poll to know that that might be an uphill struggle. [*Laughter*]

But what evolved during the course of that campaign, I think people more and more became aware of the fact that the campaign wasn't about me. It was about us. It was about our shared vision of America. It was about a vision of America that wasn't narrow, it wasn't cramped. It wasn't an idea that in America everybody goes out and fends for themselves and plays by their own rules and an America that's built on "what's in it for me." It was a vision of a big, bold, ambitious, compassionate, just America, where everybody who works hard has a chance to get ahead, not just those at the very top, but everybody. And it was a vision that said we're greater together than we are on our own. It was a vision that says everybody deserves a fair shot and everybody needs to do their fair share and everybody has to play by the same set of rules, and that when that happens, we all advance together.

That's the vision that we shared. That's the change we believed in. You helped me believe in that change. It wasn't just me, it was you. And we knew it wasn't going to be easy. We knew the change we wanted wasn't going to come quickly.

I was just talking to a group, they were reminiscing about the 2008 campaign. I said, you guys are engaging in some selective memory here. [*Laughter*] First of all, 2008 wasn't easy at all. There were all kinds of setbacks and all kinds of miscues, and there were times where I screwed up. But just over 3 years later, because of what you did in 2008, because you had faith, because you had confidence in the possibilities of this country, we've begun to see what change looks like.

Think about it. Think about what's happened over the last 3 years.

Change is the first bill I signed into law, a bill that says an equal day's work should mean an equal day's pay, because our daughters should have the same opportunities as our sons.

Change is the decision we made to rescue an auto industry that was on the brink of collapse, even when some politicians said we should let them all go bankrupt. And 1 million jobs were saved, and the local businesses were picking up again. And now we've got the Big Three making money and rehiring workers, and fuel-efficient cars are rolling off the assembly line stamped with three proud words: Made in America. That's what change is.

Change is the decision we made to stop waiting for Congress to do something about our oil addiction and go ahead and finally raise fuel efficiency standards on cars. And now, by the next decade, we are going to be driving cars that get 55 miles to a gallon. And that is going to help our environment. That will help

our economy. That's going to help consumers. That's because of you. That's what change is.

Change is the fight we won to stop handing $60 billion of subsidies to banks to manage the student loan program and go ahead and give it directly to students, and as a consequence, millions of young people have greater access to college than ever before.

Change is the health care reform that we passed, after a century of trying, that will ensure that in America nobody goes bankrupt because they get sick. Already, 2.5 million young people have health insurance today because that law let them stay on their parent's plan. Seniors are already seeing discounts on their prescription drugs, preventive care available to everybody, folks with preexisting conditions in a position to finally get insurance instead of being left out in the cold. That's what change is, because of you. That's what we were fighting for: millions of Americans who can no longer be denied or dropped by their insurance companies when they need it most. That's what change is.

Change is the fact that for the first time in our history, you don't have to hide who you love in order to serve the country you love. Because "don't ask, don't tell" is history. It is over.

And change is keeping one of the first promises I made in 2008: ending the war in Iraq and bringing our troops home. The war is over, and our troops are home. And instead, we refocused our efforts on the terrorists who actually attacked us on 9/11. And thanks to our brave men and women in uniform, Al Qaida is weaker than it's ever been and Usama bin Laden will never again walk the face of this Earth. That's what change is.

And now, a lot of these changes weren't easy. A lot of these changes weren't easy, and some of them were risky. They all came in the face of tough opposition, powerful lobbyists, special interests spending millions to keep things the way they were. And it's no secret I haven't always taken the politically popular course, certainly not with the crowd in Washington. But this progress has been possible nevertheless because of you, because you guys didn't stop believing. You stood up. You made your voices heard. You were out there knocking on doors. You made phone calls. You kept up the fight for change long after the election was over.

And that should make you proud, but it should also make you hopeful. It shouldn't make you satisfied. It shouldn't make us complacent. We have so much more work to do. And everything we fought for during the last election is at stake in this election. The very core of what this country stands for is on the line, the basic promise that no matter what you look like, no matter where you come from, this is a place where you could make it if you try. The notion that we're all in this together, that we look out for one another, that's at stake in this election. Don't take my word for it. Watch some of these debates that have been going on up in New Hampshire.

The crisis that struck in the months before I took office put more Americans out of work than any time since the Great Depression. But it was the culmination of a decade where the middle class had been losing ground. More good jobs and manufacturing left our shores. More of our prosperity was built on risky financial deals and homes that we couldn't afford. And we racked up greater debt, and incomes fell, and wages flatlined. And the cost of everything from college to groceries went through the roof.

Now, these problems didn't happen overnight. And the truth is they're not going to be solved overnight. It is going to take us a few more years to meet all the challenges that have been decades in the making. And the American people understand that. What the American people don't understand are leaders who refuse to take action. They're sick and tired of watching people who are supposed to represent them put party ahead of country and the next election ahead of the next generation. That's what they don't understand. That's what they don't understand.

You know, President Kennedy used to say after he took office what surprised him most about Washington was that things were just as bad as he had been saying they were. [*Laughter*] And I understand what he meant. [*Laughter*] When you've got the top Republican in the Senate saying his party's number-one priority is not to create jobs, not to fix the economy, but to beat me, that gives you a sense of the mentality here. Things aren't on the level. That's how you end up with Republicans in Congress voting against all kinds of proposals that they supported in the past. Tax cuts for workers and small businesses, rebuilding roads and bridges, putting cops and teachers back to work used to be bipartisan ideas.

Now, I've said I will continue to look for every opportunity during the course of this year to work with Congress to move this country forward and create jobs.

Audience member. We can't wait!

The President. But we can't wait. [*Laughter*] When Congress—whenever this Congress refuses to act, in a way that hurts our economy and puts our people at risk, I've got an obligation as President to do what we can without them. I've got an obligation to work on behalf of you and the American people. I'm not going to let Members of Congress put party ideology ahead of the people that they were elected to serve, not when there's this much at stake.

This is a make-or-break moment for this country, for the middle class in this country and folks who want to get into the middle class. So, for example, that's why last week I appointed Richard Cordray as America's consumer watchdog. Now, this is a man whose sole job is to look out for the best interests of American consumers, to protect families from the kinds of unfair or deceptive, abusive financial practices that helped to bring the economy to its knees. That shouldn't be controversial. Why would somebody be against that? [*Laughter*]

And yet, for almost half a year, Republicans in the Senate blocked his appointment. They wouldn't even vote on it, not because they said he wasn't qualified, because they couldn't say that. Former attorney general—you had Democrats and Republicans across the country, including his home State of Ohio, saying he was qualified. They just wanted to weaken Wall Street reforms. They thought, well, this might be too tough on these financial firms.

Now, does anybody here think that the reason we got into this financial mess was because we had too much oversight?

Audience members. No!

The President. Too much accountability?

Audience members. No!

The President. We shouldn't be weakening these rules, we should be strengthening these rules. When it comes to American workers and American families, we should be looking to protect them more, not less. And that's what we've been doing, and that's what we're going to keep on doing.

That's also why I fought so hard last month to make sure that Congress didn't go home without preventing a tax increase on 160 million working Americans. And I'm glad. I'm glad Republicans finally came around and agreed to extend the payroll tax cut for working families into this year. But they've got to now extend it for the entire year. A lot of Republicans, they've sworn an oath: I will never raise taxes on anybody as long as I live. [*Laughter*] Well, don't make an exception for ordinary folks. It can't just apply to the wealthiest. Now is the time to prove you'll fight at least as hard for middle class folks and folks trying to get into the middle class as you do for the wealthiest Americans.

So we've got a clear choice this year. People are hurting out there. They're going through a tough time. Everybody understands that the economy is not where it needs to be. It's growing. We've had 22 consecutive months of job growth in the private sector. But everybody understands we still got more work to do. Of course, it's got to move faster. Of course, the economy still has a long way to go. Everybody understands that.

The question is what are we going to do about it. The debate we're going to have in this election is about where do we go from here. Because the Republicans in Congress and the candidates who are running for President, they've got a very specific idea of where they want to take this country. They say they want to reduce the deficit, but they're going to do it by gutting our investments in education and

research and technology and infrastructure, our roads and our bridges and our airports.

Look, I've already signed a trillion dollars' worth of spending cuts, but it's time to reduce the deficit by asking the wealthiest people in our society to pay their fair share. There's nothing wrong with that. People like me can afford it.

Republicans in Congress and on the campaign trail, they want to make Medicare a form of private insurance that seniors have to shop for with a voucher, but the voucher might not cover all the costs. I think we can lower the cost of Medicare with reforms that still guarantee the dignified retirement of seniors, because they've earned it.

Republicans in Congress and these candidates, they think that the best way for America to compete for new jobs and businesses is to follow other countries in a race to the bottom. They figure, well, China pays low wages, we should pay low wages. Let's roll back the minimum wage. Let's prevent folks from organizing for collective bargaining in this country. Since other countries allow corporations to pollute as much as they want, why not get rid of the protections that ensure our air is clean and our water is clean.

I don't think we should have any more regulation than the health and the safety of the American people require. I've already made reforms that will save businesses billions of dollars. We are creating a smart Government. We've issued fewer regulations than the Bush administration.

But I don't believe a race to the bottom is one that we should be trying to win. We should be trying to win the race to the top. We should be competing to make sure that we've got the best schools in the world and our workers have the best training and skills in the world and we've got a college education within reach of everybody who wants to go. That's the race we should be trying to win.

We should be in a race to give our businesses the best roads and airports and railroads and best Internet access. We should be in a race to support the best scientists and researchers who are trying to make the next breakthrough in clean energy and medicine. And those should happen right here in the United States of America. That's the race we should be trying to win.

We should be in a race to make sure that the next generation of manufacturing—the new products, the new services—that they're not created in Asia, they're not created in Europe, they're created here. They're created in America, in Detroit and Pittsburgh and Cleveland, Baltimore, Virginia. I want—I don't want us to just be known for buying stuff from other places. I want us to be known for building stuff and selling stuff all around the world—Made in America. That's what I want us to win.

This competition for new jobs and new businesses and middle class security, that's a race we can win. But we can't win it if we just go back to the same things that got us into this mess in the first place. The same old tune: Hand out more tax cuts to folks who don't need them, and let companies play by their own rules, and hope that everything eventually trickles down to the rest of us. [*Laughter*]

That doesn't work. It's never worked. We tried it. It didn't work in the Great Depression. It's not what led to the incredible postwar boom of the fifties and sixties. It didn't work when we tried it between 2000 and 2008. It won't work now.

We can't go back to this brand of you're-on-your-own economics. We are not a country that was built on the idea of survival of the fittest. We were built on the idea that we survive as a nation. We thrive when we work together, all of us. Every race, every creed.

We believe we've got a stake in each other's success, that if we attract outstanding teachers into a profession, give her the pay she deserves, the support she deserves, she's going to teach the next Steve Jobs. And we'll all end up benefiting. If we provide a faster Internet out into some rural community, that owner is going to be selling goods around the world, and he's going to be able to hire more workers. And that's going to be good for all of us.

If we build that new bridge and it saves the shipping company some time and money,

workers and customers all over the country will do better. That's our idea.

And that idea has never been Democratic or Republican; that's an American idea. It was a Republican President, Abraham Lincoln, launched the transcontinental railroad, the National Academy of Sciences, the first land-grant colleges. It was a Republican, Teddy Roosevelt, who called for a progressive income tax. Republican Dwight Eisenhower built the Interstate Highway System. There were Republicans who voted with FDR to give millions of returning heroes, including my grandfather, a chance to go to college under the GI bill. This is an American idea.

And you know what, here's the good news. Here's the good news. That same common purpose, that still exists today. Maybe it doesn't exist here in Washington and maybe not on the Presidential debate stage up in New Hampshire. [*Laughter*] But out in America, it's there. It's there when you talk to folks on Main Streets, in barbershops, in town halls. Our political parties may be divided, but most Americans, they still understand that we are greater together. No matter where we come from, we rise or fall as one Nation and one people. And that's what's at stake right now. That's what this election is about.

I know this has been a tough 3 years. I know that the change we fought for in 2008, we have had to grind it out to make it happen. And after all that's been going on in Washington, all the nonsense that takes place here sometimes, it's tempting to believe, well, maybe it's not possible to do everything we wanted. But I want to remind everybody what I said in the last campaign: Real change, big change, is hard. It's always been hard. It takes more than a single term. It may take more than a single President. It takes you, ordinary citizens committed to fighting and pushing, inching this country forward bit by bit so we get closer to our highest ideals.

That's how this country was built. That's how we freed ourselves from an empire. That's how the greatest generation was able to overcome more than a decade of war and depression and end up building the largest middle

21

class in history. That's how young people beat back the billy clubs and the dogs and the fire hoses to make sure that race was no longer a barrier to what you can become in this country.

Change is hard, but it's possible. I've seen it. I've lived it. And if you want to end the cynicism and the game-playing and the point-scoring here in Washington, then this is the election to send a message that you refuse to back down, you will not give up. You intend to keep hoping. You intend to keep fighting for the change that we talked about, the change that we believe in.

I said in 2008—I warned you all, I said—I said I'm not a perfect man; I said I won't be a perfect President. But I promised you—I promised you this. I made a commitment to you, and I've kept this commitment. I will always tell you what I think. I always will tell you where I stand. And I wake up every single day thinking about you and fighting for you and trying to figure out how can we make sure that everybody has access to the American Dream.

And if you stick with us, if you keep pushing, if we just keep on going through the setbacks, through the tough times, if you keep reaching for a vision of America that I know you still hold in your hearts, then change will continue to come. And this election may be harder than the last one, but I promise you we will finish what we started in 2008. We're going to keep on. We will press forward. We will remind the world once more why the United States of America is the greatest nation on Earth.

Let's get to work. Thank you. God bless you. God bless the United States of America.

NOTE: The President spoke at 8:16 p.m. at the Capital Hilton hotel. In his remarks, he referred to Patrick H. Gaspard, executive director, Democratic National Committee; Lise Clavel, Virginia State director, Obama for America; and Richard A. Cordray, Director, Consumer Financial Protection Bureau.

Remarks at the Environmental Protection Agency
January 10, 2012

Thank you, EPA! Thank you, everybody. Thank you so much. It is wonderful to see you. It is great to see you. Thank you, thank you.

Now, everybody can have a seat. I know Lisa is making you guys all stand up. [*Laughter*] But you can all relax.

It is wonderful to be here with all of you. Thank you so much for all the great work you do. I want to first acknowledge your outstanding Administrator, Lisa Jackson. She has done an extraordinary job leading this agency. But here's what I want all of you to know: Not only is she good on policy, not only is she tough and able to present the EPA's mission so effectively to the public, but she also has your back. She is an advocate on behalf of all the people who work so hard here at the EPA. And so you should know that your boss loves you, even if she doesn't always show it—I don't know. [*Laughter*]

The main reason I'm here is simple: I just want to say thank you. I want to say thank you to each and every one of you, because the EPA touches on the lives of every single American every single day. You help make sure that the air we breathe, the water we drink, the foods we eat are safe. You protect the environment not just for our children, but their children. And you keep us moving towards energy independence.

And it is a vital mission. Over the past 3 years, because of your hard work, we've made historic progress on all these fronts. Just a few weeks ago, thanks to the hard work of so many of you, Lisa and I were able to announce new commonsense standards to better protect the air we breathe from mercury and other harmful air pollution. And that was a big deal. And part of the reason it was a big deal was because, for over 20 years, special interest groups had successfully delayed implementing these standards when it came to our Nation's power plants. And what we said was: Enough; it's time to get this done.

And because we acted, we're going to prevent thousands of premature deaths, thousands of heart attacks and cases of childhood asthma. There are families that are going to be directly impacted in a positive way because of the work that you do. Because you kept fighting—and some of you have been fighting this fight for a long time, long before I was here, and long before Lisa was here. And so your tenacity and stick-to-it-ness is making a difference.

Because of you, across the board, we're cutting down on acid rain and air pollution. We're making our drinking water cleaner and safer. We're creating healthier communities. But that's not all. Safeguarding our environment is also about strengthening our economy. I do not buy the notion that we have to make a choice between having clean air and clean water and growing this economy in a robust way. I think that is a false debate.

Think about it. We established new fuel economy standards, a historic accomplishment that is going to slash oil consumption by about 12 billion barrels, dramatically reduces pollution that contributes to climate change, and saves consumers thousands of dollars at the pump, which they can then go spend on something else.

As part of the Recovery Act, you cleaned up contaminated sites across the country, which helped to rid neighborhoods of environmental blight while putting Americans back to work.

We don't have to choose between dirty air and dirty water or a growing economy. We can make sure that we are doing right by our environment and, in fact, putting people back to work all across America. That's part of our mission.

When we put in place new commonsense rules to reduce air pollution, we create new jobs building and installing all sorts of pollution-control technology. When we put in place new emissions standards for our vehicles, we make sure that the cars of tomorrow are going to be built right here in the United States of America, that we're going to win that race. When we clean up our Nation's waterways, we generate more tourists for our local communities. So what's good for the environment can also be good for our economy.

Now, that doesn't mean that there aren't going to be some tensions. That doesn't mean that there aren't going to be legitimate debates that take place. That doesn't mean that it's not important for every single one of us to think about how can we make sure that we are achieving our goals in the smartest way possible, in the most efficient ways possible, in the least bureaucratic ways possible, in the clearest ways possible. That's also part of our mission.

There's not a Federal agency that can't get better and be smarter in accomplishing our mission, and we have an obligation every single day to think about how can we do our business a little bit better. How can we make sure the taxpayers are getting every dime's worth that they're paying in order to achieve these important common goals that we have?

But I believe we can do it, and you've shown me that we can do it over these last 3 years. So I could not be prouder of the work that you all do every single day as Federal employees. I know the hours can be long. I know that sometimes spending time getting these policies right means less time at home than you'd like, and you're missing birthday parties, or you're missing a soccer game, and the spouse is not happy with you. I know a little bit about that sometimes. [*Laughter*] I know these jobs are demanding.

But I also know what compelled you to enter public service in the first place, and that's the idea that you could make a difference, that you could leave behind a planet that is a little cleaner, a little safer than the one we inherited.

And I have to tell you that part of why I get excited when I see some of the work that you're doing is because our next generation is so much more attuned to these issues than I was when I was growing up. I can tell you when I sit down and I talk to my kids, probably the area where they have the most sophisticated understanding of policy is when it comes to the environment. They understand that the decisions we make now are going to have an impact on their lives for many years to come. And their instincts are right. So your mission is vital.

23

And just think of what this agency has been able to do over the last four decades. There's so many things we now take for granted. When I hear folks grumbling about environmental policy, you almost want to do a "Back to the Future"—[*laughter*]—kind of reminder of folks of what happens when we didn't have a strong EPA. The year before President Nixon created the EPA, the Cuyahoga River was so dirty from industrial pollution and oil slicks that it literally caught on fire. In my hometown, the Chicago River could—you probably could not find anything alive in there—[*laughter*]—four decades ago. Now it's thriving, to the benefit of the city. Today, because of your work, 92 percent of Americans have access to clean water that meets our national health standards.

Before the EPA was created, our cars were spewing harmful lead pollution into the air, with all sorts of impacts, especially on children. Today, because of your work, air pollution is down by more than half and lead pollution is down more than 90 percent from a generation ago.

So, all of you, and all of those who served before you, have made a difference. Our environment is safer because of you. Our country is stronger because of you. Our future is brighter because of you. And I want you to know that you've got a President who is grateful for your work and will stand with you every inch of the way as you carry out your mission to make sure that we've got a cleaner world.

So thank you. God bless you. God bless the United States of America. Thank you.

NOTE: The President spoke at 2:51 p.m. in the Andrew W. Mellon Auditorium.

Remarks at a White House Forum on Insourcing American Jobs
January 11, 2012

Thank you, everybody. Please, please have a seat. Thank you. Well, welcome to the White House, everybody. And, Tim, thank you for that introduction.

I could not have enjoyed more the meeting that I had this morning, because what these companies represent is a source of optimism and enormous potential for the future of America. What they have in common is that they're part of a hopeful trend: They are bringing jobs back to America.

You've heard of outsourcing. Well, these companies are insourcing. These companies are choosing to invest in the one country with the most productive workers, the best universities, and the most creative and innovative entrepreneurs in the world, and that is the United States of America. [*Applause*] That's worth applauding.

That's exactly the kind of commitment to country that we need, especially right now, when we're in a make-or-break moment for the middle class and those aspiring to get in the middle class here in the United States.

All across this country, I meet folks who grew up with a faith that in America hard work paid off and responsibility was rewarded and anybody could make it if they tried, no matter where you came from, no matter what you looked like, no matter how you started out. Those are the values that my grandparents and my mother taught me. Those are the values that built the best products and the strongest economy and the largest middle class that the world has ever known.

I think we understand that over the last few decades, that bargain has eroded for too many Americans. The economy has changed rapidly. And for many, that change has been painful. Factories where people thought they would retire packed up and went overseas, where labor costs were cheaper.

At the same time, we live in a global economy, and as other countries grow and develop middle classes of their own, of course global companies are going to pursue those markets and employ workers and make investments all over the world.

But right now we're at a unique moment, a inflection point, a period where we've got the opportunity for those jobs to come back. And the business leaders in this room, they're ahead of the curve, they recognize it. I'll give you just a few examples. After shedding jobs for more than a decade, American manufacturers have now added jobs for 2 years in a row. That's good news. But when a lot of folks are still looking for work, now is the time for us to step on the gas.

So that's why I pushed Congress to extend the payroll tax cut this year, so that 160 million working Americans weren't hit with a tax hike. Now is the time to extend that middle class tax hike for—tax cut for all of this year. It's the right thing to do, and we need to get that done.

But we're going to have to do more. And that's why, in the next few weeks, we're also going to put forward new tax proposals that reward companies that choose to bring jobs home and invest in America. And we're going to eliminate tax breaks for companies that are moving jobs overseas.

Because there is an opportunity to be had right here and right now. There are workers ready to work right now. That's why I set a goal of doubling our exports of goods and services by 2014, and it's a goal, by the way, that we're on track to meet. In fact, we're a little ahead of schedule in meeting that goal.

That's why, with the help of our outstanding USTR, I was able to sign trade agreements with Korea and Colombia and Panama so our businesses can sell more goods to those markets. That's why I've fought for investments in schools and community colleges, so that our workers remain the best you'll find anywhere, and investments in our transportation and communication networks, so that your businesses have more opportunities to take root and grow.

I don't want America to be a nation that's primarily known for financial speculation and racking up debt buying stuff from other nations. I want us to be known for making and selling products all over the world stamped with three proud words: Made in America. And we can make that happen.

I don't want the next generation of manufacturing jobs taking root in countries like China or Germany. I want them taking root in places like Michigan and Ohio and Virginia and North Carolina. And that's a race that America can win. That's the race businesses like these will help us win.

These are CEOs who take pride in hiring people here in America, not just because it's increasingly the right thing to do for their bottom line, but also because it's the right thing to do for their workers and for our communities and for our country. And they're leading by example. I'm proud of that, as an American. But as President, I also want to make sure they get some credit for it.

Just 3 years ago, for example, we almost lost the American auto industry. Today, the Big Three automakers are turning a profit and manufacturing the next generation of fuel-efficient cars that the rest of the world wants to buy. Ford Motor Company—that's represented by workers and management on this stage—has committed to investing $16 billion in the United States by 2015—$16 billion. And that includes bringing back about 2,000 jobs and shifting production from countries like Japan, Mexico, and China to States like Michigan and Ohio and Missouri.

Master Lock, iconic company. When Master Lock looked at their numbers, they saw that union workers in America could do the same job at competitive costs as nonunion workers in China. In fact, Master Lock is now exporting their products from the United States to China and Europe. And today, for the first time in 15 years, Master Lock's Milwaukee complex is running at full capacity.

But you don't have be a big manufacturer to insource jobs. Bruce Cochrane's family had manufactured furniture in North Carolina for five generations. But in 1966—1996, rather, as jobs began shifting to Asia, the family sold their business, and Bruce spent time in China and Vietnam as a consultant for American furniture makers who had shifted their production. While he was there, though, he noticed something he didn't expect: Their customers actually wanted to buy things made in America. So he came home and started a new company, Lincolnton Furniture, which operates out of the old family factories that had been shut down. He's even rehired many of the former workers from his family business.

You also don't have to be a manufacturer to insource jobs. You just heard Tim, CEO of a health care IT company in New Jersey called GalaxE.Solutions. They've already hired 150 workers with their Outsource to Detroit program, and they plan on hiring up to 500. And Tim was quoted as saying, "There are some really talented people in Detroit, and we're putting them back to work."

Whether you're a small business that are—some of which are represented here—or a large manufacturing corporation or a technology company, whether you're a historic brand or a brandnew startup, insourcing jobs is a smart strategy right now. We live in a global economy with opportunities for global investment. But we heard from several experts this morning and business leaders that we're at this point in time where factors like incredibly rising American productivity and increasingly competitive costs mean the economic case to invest in America and bring jobs back home is strong, and it's getting stronger.

Labor costs are going up in places like China. We have become much more productive. We continue to be the largest market in the world. And so we have this outstanding opportunity if everybody is partnering and getting together. That's the economic case.

I believe there's also a moral case. Andy Grove, the former CEO of Intel, said it well. He said: "Those of us in business have two obligations. One that's undebatable is that we have a fiduciary responsibility to the shareholders who put us in our place." But he also said, "There's another obligation that I feel personally, given that everything I've achieved in my career and a lot of what Intel has achieved in its career were made possible by a climate of democracy, an economic climate and investment climate provided by our domicile—the United States."

All these folks onstage, they are businesspeople first, and they're looking at the bottom line. But they also feel good about the fact that they're restoring hope and creating jobs here in the United States. And that's part of the responsibility that comes with being a leader in America, a responsibility not just to the shareholders or the stakeholders, but to the country that made all this incredible wealth and opportunity possible. That's a responsibility that we all have to live up to, whether we're in the private sector or the public sector, whether we're in Washington or we're on Wall Street. Because the more Americans who succeed, the more America succeeds.

So my message to business leaders today is simple: Ask yourselves what you can do to bring jobs back to the country that made our success possible. And I'm going to do everything in my power to help you do it. We're going to have to seize this moment. American workers are the most productive and competitive in the world right now. When you factor in all the costs, we have a outstanding market, we have the most innovative entrepreneurs, the best research universities. And part of what our session this morning was all about was just helping people to take a look at what this moment is and where we're going to be 5 years from now. Because when people take a second look, it turns out that the potential for job growth and American manufacturing and the service industry is incredible.

I said in a speech a while back, this moment is perfectly suited for our advantages. It's perfectly suited for who we are. The global marketplace is becoming more innovative, more creative, more transparent, faster, more adaptable. That's who we are. That's our strength. We've got to take advantage of it.

And if we've got leadership of the sort that we're seeing on this stage, I'm absolutely confident that not only can it make a difference for our middle class and folks who are working their way into the middle class, it also gives us an incredible opportunity to assure the future for our children and our grandchildren. And that's my central goal and focus as President. That should be our central goal as a country: how we rebuild an economy where hard work pays off, responsibility is rewarded, a nation where those values continue for generations to come.

So thanks to all the people on this stage for being such a great example. For all the press who are here, I hope you get a chance to hear their stories, because it's exciting, and it gives you a sense of why I'm incredibly optimistic about our prospects.

Thank you very much, everybody.

NOTE: The President spoke at 12:51 p.m. in the East Room at the White House. In his remarks, he referred to Timothy M. Bryan, chief executive officer and chairman, GalaxE.Solutions.

Remarks at an Obama Victory Fund 2012 Fundraiser in Chicago, Illinois
January 11, 2012

The President. Hello, Chicago! Thank you! Thank you so much.

Audience member. Hello!

The President. Hello! Oh, it's good to be home. It is good to be home. No place like it.

It is great to see so many old friends. I don't mean in years, although you guys are getting older, some of you. I'll be honest with you, I wouldn't mind popping over to the United Center. I think the Bulls are playing tonight. They are off to a fine start. You might have heard the Dallas Mavericks came to the White House on Monday to celebrate their championship, and I told them, enjoy it, because the Bulls will be here next year. That's what I said.

I want to thank Jessica——

Audience member. [*Inaudible*]

The President. [*Laughter*] I want to thank Jessica for sharing her extraordinary story. And Jessica is so representative of all the folks who did so much 4 years ago and are doing so much now. So give her a big round of applause. We are appreciative of her.

I want to thank Janelle Monae for her wonderful performance. Her whole crew is here. We had them at the state dinner, and the Korean President and his whole family, they were moving around and—[*laughter*]. You remember that? Oh, they loved it. So music is the universal language, and Janelle and her team are incredibly talented.

I want to thank my dear friend. He and I went to law school together; he decided to make something of his life. [*Laughter*] You see him on TV all the time. Hill Harper is in the house. Thank you, Hill.

One of the finest public servants and one of the finest Senators in the land, Dick Durbin is here. Thank you, Dick. Two of the finest Members of Congress in the land, and great friends, Danny Davis and Jan Schakowsky, and we've got Cook County Board President Toni Preckwinkle, who is here as well.

Now, I also want to say a special word about a friend of ours, a man who's done extraordinary work for me and performed extraordinary service for our country over the past year, and that is Bill Daley, who—[*applause*]. Now, first of all, Bill and I, we got off the plane, and we said, is it really 45 degrees in January? [*Laughter*] So we were a little confused, thought we had landed in the wrong place. [*Laughter*] But when Bill first told me it was time for him to return to our hometown, I asked him to take a couple days to reconsider. But it is tough to resist the greatest city in the world. And as much as I will miss him in the White House, he's going to be an extraordinary asset to our campaign. He's going to be helping us win in 2012. So I just want to publicly say how much I appreciate him.

Now, I also want to say how much I appreciate you.

Audience member. We love you!

The President. I love you.

Audience members. We love you!

The President. I love you too.

Audience member. I love you!

The President. I love you back, man. [*Laughter*] You know, I'm here not just because I need your help, but I'm also here because the country needs your help. There was a reason why so many people like Jessica worked your hearts out in our 2008 campaign. And it wasn't because you thought it was going to be easy. When you support a guy named Barack Hussein Obama—[*laughter*]—for President of the United States, you've got to assume that the odds may not be in your favor. [*Laughter*] You didn't need a poll to know that it wasn't a sure thing.

But what you understood was that the campaign was not about me. It was about our common vision for America. It wasn't a cramped, narrow vision of an America where everybody is left to fend for themselves and the most powerful are able to play by their own rules. It was a vision of a big and compassionate and ambitious and bold America where everybody has a chance to get ahead: everybody, not just those who are advantaged. A vision that says we're greater together than we are on our own. A vision where everybody gets a fair shot and everybody does their fair share and there's a sense of fair play, that the rules apply to everybody.

That's the vision we shared. That's the change we believed in. And we knew it wouldn't come easy, and we knew it wouldn't come quickly. But I'm here to tell you that 3 years later, because of what you did in 2008, we've begun to see what change looks like.

Change—we've begun to see—and sometimes, because things are moving so fast and the media moves from thing to thing to thing, we don't take time to step back and ask ourselves what happened because of the work you did in 2008.

Change is the first bill I signed into law, a law that says an equal day's work should mean an equal day's pay, because our daughters should be treated the same and have the same opportunities as our sons. That's what change is.

Change is the decision we made—that was unpopular at the time—to go in and help the auto industry retool, prevent its collapse, even when you had a lot of folks who said we should just let Detroit go bankrupt. And as a consequence, we saved 1 million jobs, and local businesses are picking up again, and fuel-efficient cars are rolling off the assembly line stamped with three proud words—Made in America— and the automakers are back, and folks are working. That's because of you.

Change is the decision we made to stop waiting for Congress to do something about our oil addiction and go ahead and raise fuel efficiency standards on cars. And by the next decade, we'll be driving cars that get 55 miles to a gallon. That's what change is. Save us billions of barrels of oil and save consumers billions of dollars from their pocketbooks, and it means that we'll have a better chance of making sure that we leave the planet a little bit cleaner and a little bit better off for our kids.

And change is the fight we had, and the fight we won, to stop handing out $60 billion in taxpayer subsidies to banks that issue student loans and give that money directly to students so that millions of more young people are able to get the kind of education that they need in this 21st-century economy. That's what change is.

And as Jessica pointed out, change is finally, after a century of talking about it, passing health care reform that ensures that in the United States of America nobody goes bankrupt because they get sick. And 2.5 million young people already have health insurance because they can stay on their parent's plan. And nobody is denied coverage or dropped by their insurance company when they need it most. That's what change is.

Change is the fact that for the first time in our history, you don't have to hide who you love in order to serve the country you love. That's what change is. "Don't ask, don't tell" is over.

And change is keeping one of the first promises I made back in 2008, and that is ending the war in Iraq and bringing our troops home so we can focus our attention on rebuilding America.

Focus our attention on rebuilding America, but also focusing our efforts on the terrorists who actually attacked us on 9/11. And thanks to the brave men and women in uniform, Al Qaida is weaker than it has ever been and Usama bin Laden will never walk this Earth again.

Now, these changes weren't easy. Some were risky. Almost all of them came in the face of fierce opposition, powerful lobbyists, special interests who spent millions trying to maintain the status quo. And not all the steps we took were politically popular at the time, certainly not politically popular with the crowd in Washington.

But you know, what kept me going is you. See, I remembered all the work you put in. I remembered your hopes and your dreams. And I knew that on every one of these fights, you guys were out there making your voices heard, knocking on doors, making phone calls, keeping up the fight for change long after the election was over.

And that should make you proud. It should make you hopeful. It shouldn't make you complacent. It shouldn't make you satisfied, because everything that we fought for is now at stake in this election. The very core of what this country stands for is on the line, the basic promise that no matter who you are, where you come from, this is a place where you can make it if you try. That's at stake in this election.

The crisis that struck in the months before I took office put more Americans out of work than at any time since the Great Depression. But it was also a culmination of a decade of neglect, a decade where the middle class fell further behind and more jobs in manufacturing left our shores. And suddenly, our prosperity was built on risky financial deals and homes that we couldn't afford. And we racked up greater debt. Even as incomes fell, wages flatlined, the cost of everything from college and health care kept on going through the roof.

And those problems built up over a decade, in some cases more. They didn't happen overnight. We knew we couldn't solve them overnight. It's going to take more than a few years to meet the challenges that have been decades in the making. And the American people understand that.

What they don't understand are leaders who refuse to take action. What they're sick and tired of is watching people who are supposed to represent them put their party ahead of the country, put the next election ahead of the next generation. That's what they don't understand.

President Kennedy used to say that after he took office, what surprised him most about Washington was it was just as bad as he had said it was. [*Laughter*]

I can relate to that. [*Laughter*] When you've got the top Republican saying his number-one priority isn't creating more jobs, isn't solving the health care problems, isn't making sure that we're competitive in the 21st century, but is to beat me, then you know things aren't on the level. That's how you end up with Republicans in Congress voting against all kinds of proposals that they—even proposals they supported in the past: tax cuts for workers, tax cuts for small businesses, rebuilding roads, bridges, putting cops and teachers back to work. Suddenly, they're opposed.

They'll fight with their last breath to protect tax cuts for the most fortunate of Americans, but they'll play political games with tax cuts for the middle class. I guess they thought it was a smart political strategy, but it's sure not a strategy to create jobs. It's not a strategy to strengthen the middle class or help people who are trying to get into the middle class to get there. It's not a strategy to help America succeed.

So we've got a clear choice this year. The question is not whether people are still hurting, the economy is still recovering. Of course, folks are still hurting. We've got a long way to go. The question is what are we going to do about it, where are we going to go, what direction does this country move towards.

The Republicans in Congress, the Presidential candidates who are running, they've got a very specific idea about where they want to take this country. I mean, they've said it. They said they want to reduce the deficit by gutting our investments in education and gutting our investments in research and technology, letting our infrastructure further deteriorate.

Now, my attitude is, I've already signed a trillion dollars' worth of spending cuts; I proposed even more. It's time, when we're talking about reducing the deficit, to also ask people like me to pay our fair share in taxes. We can do that. We can have a system in which folks who have been incredibly blessed by this Nation do a little bit more so that the next generation is able to get on the ladder of success.

The Republicans in Congress and on the campaign trail, they want to make Medicare a form of private insurance, where seniors have to shop with a voucher, and it may not cover all their costs. I think we can lower the cost of Medicare, but still guarantee the dignified retirement that our seniors have earned. They've earned it. They've earned it.

When I hear some of them talk about, oh, this is just an entitlement. These folks earned it. They worked hard. They paid into it.

This crowd, they think the best way for America to compete for new jobs and businesses is to follow other countries in a race to the bottom. They figure, well, since China pays really low wages, let's roll back the minimum wage here and bust unions; since some of these other countries allow corporations to pollute as much as they want, let's get rid of protections that help make sure our air is clean and our water is safe.

Audience member. Go EPA!

The President. Yes. You know—now, I don't think we should have any more regulations than what are necessary for our health and safety. And we've made reforms that will make sure that businesses save billions of dollars. We want government that is smart and efficient and lean. And by the way, we've issued fewer regulations than the Bush administration. They've been better regulations. [*Laughter*]

But I don't believe in a race to the bottom. I think we should be in a race to the top. We should be competing to make sure we've got the best schools. We should be competing to make sure we've got the most highly trained workers. We should make sure that a college education is within reach for everybody.

We should be in a race to make sure our businesses have the best access to the fastest Internet, the fastest railroads, the best airports. I want a race where we got—we continue to have the best scientists and researchers, making the next breakthroughs in medicine and clean energy. I want to make sure that happens right here in America. That's the race we can win.

We should be in a race to make sure the next generation of manufacturing takes root not in Asia, not in Europe, but right here in Chicago, in Detroit, in Pittsburgh, in Cleveland, in Charlotte, in Nashville.

I don't want this Nation to be known for what we buy, what we consume. I want us to be known for building and selling products all around the world.

And you know it's possible. I had a meeting this morning with CEOs from—some of them very big companies like Intel, some of them small manufacturers. They're starting to bring jobs back to the United States. They've started to figure out that, yes, some of these countries may have lower wages, but when you factor in all the costs and quality and the productivity of American workers, that it actually makes sense to build plants here. And they're moving plants back from China and plants back from Mexico, because they know that businesses who succeed here will succeed anywhere.

But what they also said was we can only come here if we know that we've got the best workers. And that means the education system has to work. We can't come here if we don't think that the Internet and our roads and our transportation infrastructure is the best in the world.

The competition for new jobs, for businesses, for middle class security, that's a race I know we can win. But America is not going to win if we give in to those who think that we can only respond to our challenges with the same tired old tune, just hand out more tax cuts to folks who don't need them and weren't even asking for them, let companies do whatever they want, hope that prosperity somehow trickles down on everybody else's head.

It doesn't work. It didn't work when it was tried in the decade before the Great Depression. It's not what led to the incredible postwar boom in the fifties and the sixties. It didn't work when we tried it under the previous President, and it's not going to work now.

We cannot go back to this brand of you're-on-your-own economics. We believe that everybody has a stake in each other and that if we attract an outstanding teacher to the profession by giving her the pay and training and support that she needs, she'll go out and educate the next Steve Jobs. And suddenly, a whole new industry will blossom.

And we believe that if you provide rural—faster Internet to some little town out in rural America, that store owner now suddenly has a whole world marketplace. And if we build a new bridge that saves a shipping company time and money, then workers and customers all over the country are going to do better. And if we invest in basic science and research, that the next new thing will be invented.

And so instead of listening to Janelle on the iPod—who knows what the next thing is, but it will be because we have invested in the innovation that makes us the greatest nation on Earth.

Now, this has never been a Democratic idea or a Republican idea. This isn't a partisan idea. It was a Republican President from Illinois named Abraham Lincoln who launched the transcontinental railroad and the National Academy of Sciences and the first land-grant colleges. Teddy Roosevelt called for a progressive income tax; he was a Republican. Dwight Eisenhower built the Interstate Highway System, invested in boosting our science and math and engineering education here in this country. It was with the help of Republicans that FDR helped millions of people—returning heroes, including my grandfather—get a chance to go college on the GI bill. This should not be a partisan idea.

And that same spirit of common purpose, it still exists today. It may not exist in Washington. But out in America, when you talk to people on main streets and in town halls, they'll tell you, we still believe in those values. Our political parties may be divided, but most Americans, they understand, no, we're in this together. We rise and fall together as one Nation, as one people.

That's what's at stake right now. That's what this election is about. So, Chicago, yes, it has been 3 tough years. There are times where the changes we want didn't come as fast as we

wanted. And after all the noise in Washington, I know it's tempting to believe sometimes that, gosh, maybe change isn't possible.

But remember what we said during the last campaign: Yes, we can.

We said real change and big change isn't easy. I warned you it was going to take time. I said it was going to take more than a year, maybe more than one term. Some of it's going to take more than one President. It takes ordinary citizens who keep fighting, keep pushing, keep inching this country closer and closer and closer to our ideals.

That's how the greatest generation overcame a decade of depression and ended up building the largest middle class in the history of the world. That's how young people beat back billy clubs and fire hoses and ensured that their kids could grow up in a country where you can be anything, including the President of the United States.

Change is hard, but it is possible. I've seen it. You've seen it. We have lived it. And if you want to end the cynicism and stop the game playing that passes for politics these days and you want to send a message about what is possible, then you can't back down. Not now.

We won't give up. Not now.

You've got to send a message. We are going to keep pushing and fighting for the change that we believe in.

I've said before, I am not a perfect man. I'm not a perfect President. But I've promised you this, and I've kept this promise: I will always tell you what I believe, I will always tell you where I stand. I will wake up every single day thinking about how I can make this country better, and I will spend every ounce of energy that I have fighting for you.

So, if you've still got that energy, if you're still fired up, if you are not weary, if you're ready to put on your walking shoes and get to work and knock on some doors and make some phone calls and talk to your friends and talk to your neighbors and push through all the obstacles and keep reaching for that vision that you hold in your hearts, I promise you change will come.

If you're willing to work even harder in this election than you did in that last election, I promise you change will come. If you stick with me, we're going to finish what we started in 2008. We will remind this country and we will remind the world just why we are the greatest nation on Earth.

God bless you, Chicago. I love you. God bless the United States of America. Thank you.

NOTE: The President spoke at 5:49 p.m. at the UIC Forum at the University of Illinois at Chicago. In his remarks, he referred to Glen Ellyn, IL, resident Jessica Hierbaum, who introduced the President; President Lee Myung-bak of South Korea; actor Hill Harper; and Senate Minority Leader A. Mitchell McConnell.

Remarks at an Obama Victory Fund 2012 Fundraiser in Chicago
January 11, 2012

Hello, everybody! Oh, it is good to be home. And it is—you are right, Stuart, I see so many familiar faces. But first of all, obviously, I've got to thank the Taylor family for their wonderful hospitality. To all the folks who helped make this evening possible, I appreciate you. I just see all my neighbors. Is somebody mowing the grass in front of my house? [*Laughter*] I'm going to go over there and check. [*Laughter*] Because I don't want you guys talking about me. "He's a good President, but nobody's mowing the lawn." [*Laughter*] "Bringing down property values." [*Laughter*]

A couple of people I want to acknowledge who are here. Oops, that's the wrong one. [*Laughter*] Hold on a second, because these folks—there we go. First of all, somebody who has been a great friend of mine, one of the finest public servants in the land, our senior Senator Dick Durbin is in the house. Dick is around here somewhere. Somebody who I knew before she got into politics as an extraordinary advocate for youth, continues to do great work—Heather Steans is here.

We've got Alderman Willie Cochran is here. Where's Alderman? He's over there. Hey, Willie. And then I've got another alderman who used to work for me—[*laughter*]—and in my first State senate campaign was basically my only staff person. [*Laughter*] And now he is a big shot, but I will always remember the fact that he was there back when nobody could pronounce my name—Will Burns is in the house. Where's Will? There he is. Will Burns. It's good to see you.

And then all of you are here. [*Laughter*] And I'm looking around, I see folks who first hired me for—as a summer associate. Between

Eden and Tom, they can take—and John—they can take responsibility for me meeting Michelle. If it had not been for them, it would not have happened.

I've got Allison and folks who stole me from Sidley, so you can blame them if—[*laughter*]—but I've got folks here who watched our kids grow up, who we played basketball together, we worked out together, we saw each other at various functions and events. And friends who, if it weren't for you, could have never gone on this extraordinary journey that I've gone on.

And it's interesting, Michelle and I, we're always reflecting on the nature of the work at the White House and—whoops. That's okay. You all right? Hope that didn't break. And we could not be more privileged to be able to serve the American people and couldn't be more grateful for the opportunity they've given us. And every day is just this remarkable adventure. But I will tell you, we're not shy about saying the one thing we miss is, we don't get to see our friends as much. And as I look around this room, it's a reminder that you guys do have our backs, have continued to have our backs, and we're grateful for you and couldn't be more appreciative of everything that you've done.

Now, I mentioned at a previous event, a friend of mine and a friend of some of yours, Ab Mikva, once said that having a friend who's a politician is like permanently having a child in college. [*Laughter*] And basically every few months a tuition check comes, and you keep on thinking, haven't they graduated yet? [*Laughter*] Golly. I'm still working—[*laughter*]—I want to remodel the kitchen and basement.

Here's the good news, is we're about to graduate. This is—this will be the last campaign. [*Laughter*] And you know, when you think about what's at stake, I hope you end up feeling that there hasn't been a more important investment to make than the one that needs to be made this year, not just in terms of money, but in terms of time and energy and effort and enthusiasm.

Back in 2008, when we first got started, I think we all had a shared vision, a common vision, of a country that came together to try to solve problems that had been put off for decades, whether it was fixing a health care system that was broken, making sure that our education system was functioning for this extraordinarily competitive 21st century, making sure that our foreign policy reflected the best of our values, dealing with energy in a way that was smart and intelligent and not only improved our economy, but also helped our environment and made sure that we could leave a planet for the next generation, an America that was inclusive and made sure that everybody had a chance to succeed.

And that vision that we had, there were specific policies attached to it, but what it really came down to was this belief in an America where everybody gets a fair shot, everybody does their fair share, everybody is playing by the same set of rules, that all of us are invested in hard work and responsibility and we're all in it together. That we don't have a country in which some people are consigned to poverty because of circumstances, that if they're willing to work hard, they can do it, and we all have a responsibility to make that happen.

That's what 2008 was about, and that's what the excitement was about, and that was the essence of the "hope, change" message, was this belief that in America, it's just different from other countries in the sense that it's diverse and everybody has a stake.

And we didn't know at the time that we were going to go through the worst economic crisis since the Great Depression. We didn't know that we were going to go through this extraordinary financial crisis. And so a lot of the last 3 years had been just dealing with emergencies.

And they've been dealt with. And sometimes it wasn't popular. Sometimes it was risky. But we've now had an auto industry that has come surging back. We have seen private sector job growth for 22 months in a row. We are seeing the return of manufacturing to America for 2 years in a row now, some of the strongest manufacturing growth in a decade.

And so there's reason to believe that we're now getting past the worst of what was a very difficult situation.

But what was important to me over these last 3 years was that we also didn't lose sight of the things that had gotten me into this race in the first place, that we still worked on some of those long-term challenges.

And so we fought for health care. Because unless we could honestly say that nobody in this country is going bankrupt because they get sick, unless we could say that if you're working hard and you're carrying out your responsibilities, you shouldn't have to worry about whether an insurance company drops you or whether as a young person getting started off in life, that you're going to have some assurance that you've got health care coverage, that we're not living up to that vision that got us—that got me into this race. And so we got it done.

The first bill I signed, a bill that said that we're going to have equal pay for equal work because I want my daughters treated the same way as my sons. We got that done.

Making sure that college was accessible. We made sure that we took $60 billion that were going through banks as a pass-through for student loan programs, and we said, let's use that $60 billion and expand Pell grants and make student loans more accessible so that millions of young people have opportunity all across the country.

And if we're going to deal seriously with energy, we've got to get started now, even though we still have an economic crisis, especially because we've got an economic crisis. So we doubled fuel efficiency standards on cars and on trucks. And we made sure that we didn't have any more regulations than were necessary to keep our air clean and our water clean, but we were going to enforce those laws to make sure

33

that we're leaving a planet behind for our kids and grandkids that is at least as clean as the one that we inherited.

And we said that we're going to have to end this war in Iraq, and we did. And we said that there are certain values that we're not going to back off of, like making sure that if you want to serve this country that you love, you don't have to answer for who you love. And we ended "don't ask, don't tell."

And so there were just—there were a series of things that met a lot of resistance, lot of the lobbyists opposed, that at times caused controversy. But 3 years into it, we can honestly say that the vision that motivated me to run, the vision that motivated you to work so hard, that we've been true to that vision.

Now, we still have a lot more work to do. We've got a lot more unfinished business. I was mentioning at a previous event I was at—I had a forum this morning with CEOs, some from very large companies like Intel, some from medium-sized companies, some from very small companies. The common theme was they were all bringing jobs back from China and Mexico. They decided to relocate back in the United States.

Now they were making this not out of a charitable decision. [*Laughter*] They were making this decision because American workers continue to be the most productive in the world and their productivity has shot up even in the midst of this recession, that our research and our innovation remains unparalleled around the world. And they started figuring out, you know what, it might actually be cheaper for us and more productive for us to create jobs here in the United States.

The interesting thing, though, was—is that when you asked them what more can we do to encourage this trend, every one of them said we still have to have a better education system; we need to make an investment in that. Every one of them said we've got to make sure we've got the best infrastructure in the world, and we've been falling behind. Every one of them said that we've got to have a smart energy policy.

Every one of them said that we've got to maintain our primacy in research and science and technology. And that was gratifying, because I said, well, that's my agenda. [*Laughter*] That's what I've been fighting for. And that's what this year's debate is going to be about. It's going to be about not only consolidating the extraordinary achievements that we've been able to get done thanks to you over the last 3 years, making sure that health care reform is implemented and financial regulatory reform is implemented and we don't have a rollback of our environmental protections. Those are all important things.

But what we're also going to be debating is are we going to pursue a vision that says our only way to compete in this world is to slash spending on education and slash spending on research and development and not upgrade our infrastructure and take away worker protections and just kind of see how we do in a race to the bottom. Or are we going to pursue a vision that says we're going to continue to have the best scientists and universities, but we're also going to get down into K through 12 and community colleges and we're going to train our young people, and we're going to invest in human capital, and we're going to have the best infrastructure. And there's no conflict between environment and economics because we're going to continue to make sure that we're at the cutting edge on advanced vehicles and electric cars.

That vision of a future that is inclusive and forward looking, that's what we're fighting for. Now, we've still got a difficult economy, and that's why this is still going to be a close race. I've got to tell you that if we weren't coming out of this extraordinary recession, I think the American people would make their decision very quickly.

But we've gone through 3 tough years. And the other side has been able to just sit on the sidelines and say no to everything, not cooperate, and then simply try to point the finger and say that somehow this should have been fixed. And I understand that. That's politics. That's how Washington generally works. And so this is going to be a tough battle, and I'm going to need all of you just as much now, more now, than I needed you in 2008.

But the main message I've got is that if you guys are willing to invest the same kind of blood, sweat, and tears as we invested in 2008, I'm confident we're going to win. And the reason I'm confident is that common vision of ours is one that's shared all across the country. I rose to national prominence by a speech that said there is no red—there are no red States and no blue States; it was the United States of America. Now, sometimes people say, ah, well, you learned, didn't you? [*Laughter*] You go to Washington, and you'll find out.

But that's Washington. That's not America. And when I travel around the country—I don't care whether I'm going to a tiny town or a big city, I don't care whether I'm talking to Black people or White people or Latinos or Native Americans or Asian Americans. Wherever I go, I still hear and see on display that core decency and common sense and confidence in the future and belief in community that I was talking about way back when. Making that real, translating that into policy, getting it through Con-gress, signing these things into laws, that's tough. It's not easy.

But the animating spirit? That's still there. And I am just as determined as I ever was—more determined with all that I've seen over the last several years—more determined than ever to make sure that we've got a Government that is reflective of those values. That's what we're fighting for.

And if you guys stand with me, if you guys have my back as you guys have had my back for all these years, I guarantee you that we are going to win this election. We will deliver for the American people. And I won't be back here in that house for another 5 years. [*Laughter*]

All right? Thank you very much, everybody. God bless you. Thank you.

NOTE: The President spoke at 9 p.m. at the residence of Stuart and Evonne Taylor. In his remarks, he referred to State Sen. Heather Steans of Illinois; and former White House Counsel Abner J. Mikva. Audio was not available for verification of the content of these remarks.

Remarks at an Obama Victory Fund 2012 Fundraiser in Chicago
January 11, 2012

It is wonderful to be back home! It is great to see so many friends that I haven't seen in too long, and some folks who visited me in my new residence. But let me begin by just thanking Fred for opening up this extraordinary home to us. And thank everybody else who helped put this together. I particularly want to thank Sonia and Eric for all that they did—[*applause*].

I want to acknowledge some outstanding public servants who are here—my former seat mate in Springfield, the attorney general of Illinois—[*applause*]. My former teacher of the ways of the Senate and one of the finest public servants that we know, Dick Durbin. The outstanding Governor of Illinois, Pat Quinn, is in the house. And finally, we have sort of a carpetbagger here. [*Laughter*] I just love her, so whenever I have an excuse to see her I'm hap-py, and she is a fellow Midwesterner, the Senator from Missouri, Claire McCaskill.

So I'm going to make my opening remarks very, very brief because—Fred and I were talking, particularly a crowd like this that knows me—I want to spend as much time as possible answering questions.

I was talking about a meeting I had this morning with companies from all across the country, some of them very large corporations, Intel and Siemens, some medium-sized companies, and some very small companies. The common theme was that they were all insourcing. They were bringing jobs back to America. Many of them had located plants in China, located plants in Mexico, and because of the extraordinary growth in productivity in the United States over the last several years, because wages are going up pretty rapidly in places like China, because of energy costs and transportation costs and a whole range of other factors, we're getting to this point where when you account for everything, that America is fully competitive in manufacturing and more than competitive in services with any other country in the world. Those are a good news story.

But I asked them, what is it that's going to make the biggest difference in accelerating this trend so you start seeing more and more companies decide, let's move back into the United States, let's move our plants back? And some of them mentioned education. They said the single most important reason for us to move back here is because they're more highly skilled workers here, and as long as we're investing in K through 12 and our community colleges and have enough engineers and scientists, then that's going to be a reason for us to locate here.

And a number of them said the fact that we've got the most innovative research taking place in the United States, that's what's going to make a difference. And another one said, well, logistically—I think this was maybe Otis Elevators—he said it's kind of hard to move elevators around—[laughter]—and so making sure we've got the best infrastructure in the world is going to be what is the determining factor in whether or not we locate a plant here in the United States.

And as I listened to each one of these companies, I was reminded that everything we've done over the last 3 years—but more importantly, everything we have to do over the next 5 years—has to be designed to making sure that this economy is once again one that is built on a solid foundation, one that is not done with bubbles, one that is not based on simply shuffling paper, but one that's based on making things and selling things and one in which everybody—business, workers, communities—all feel invested in each other.

And that's what we've been trying to do over the last 3 years as we've dug ourselves out of the worst recession since the Great Depression. That's why it's been so important for us to invest in education like never before, and that's why it's been so important for us to make sure,

with the help of folks like Claire and Dick, that we continue to invest in research. That's why we pushed so hard to make sure that we're rebuilding not just our roads and our bridges, but also high-speed rail lines and a faster Internet all across the country.

And I make this point because as important as 2008 was, I actually think 2012 is more important, because what we're seeing developing, what we're seeing over the last 2 years—but I think what we're going to see this year in a pretty decisive way is a decision about contrasting visions about where the country should go.

You've got one theory that says if we slash our education, our research, and our infrastructure budgets and weaken our social safety net and make sure that unions aren't out there operating and we essentially eliminate EPA— and I'm not exaggerating, there are candidates and Members of Congress who've called for that—that somehow we're going to be able to win this competition in the 21st century. And that's one vision, and it is being starkly stated.

And I have a different vision. Most of the people in this room have a fundamentally different vision about how this country was formed. Our vision is based on the notion that everybody deserves a fair shot, everybody has to do their fair share, and everybody has got to play by the same set of rules, and America succeeds best when we're all in it together, we're all rising together. And that big, inclusive, generous, bold, ambitious vision of America is what's at stake, is what we're fighting for.

But I guess in these initial remarks, what I just want to say is that many of you got involved in my campaign back in 2008, many of you got involved in my Senate campaign back in 2004, some of you got involved in my State senate campaign back in—[laughter]—I don't remember when that was. [Laughter] I think that the reason we were successful was not because I was a flawless candidate or I ran a flawless campaign, but it was because together we were able to give voice to this shared vision of what America should be. And I want you to know that I have kept faith with that vision all these years, and that's not wavered.

And whether it's making a decision about getting all of our troops out of Iraq or it was making a decision about ending "don't ask, don't tell" or it was making a decision about expanding Pell grants so more people have access to college or it's trying to present a balanced approach to deficit reduction, what animates me continues to be the same vision that you guys helped me realize way back when.

This will be my last campaign. A friend of many of us, Ab Mikva, used to say that being friends with a politician is like permanently having a child in college. [*Laughter*] Every year there's another tuition check. [*Laughter*] But I'm finally graduating. [*Laughter*] And I'm confident that as difficult as these last 3 years have been, as challenging as they've been—not so much for me, but for Americans all across the country who lost their jobs or have seen their home values decline or been worrying about their retirement and their 401(k)s—I absolutely believe that the American people still have confidence and faith in this country and there's a core decency and strength and resilience to be tapped and that most of the time the better angels of our nature win out. I think that's what's going to happen this time as well. But we're going to have to work hard to get it done.

NOTE: The President spoke at 7:30 p.m. at the residence of Fred Eychaner. In his remarks, he referred to State Attorney General Lisa Madigan of Illinois; and former White House Counsel Abner J. Mikva. The transcript was released by the Office of the Press Secretary on January 12. Audio was not available for verification of the content of these remarks.

Letter to Congressional Leaders Certifying the Public Debt Limit Increase
January 12, 2012

Dear Mr. Speaker: (Dear Mr. President:)

Pursuant to section 3101A(a)(2)(A) of title 31, United States Code, I hereby certify that the debt subject to limit is within $100,000,000,000 of the limit in 31 U.S.C. 3101(b) and that further borrowing is required to meet existing commitments.

Sincerely,

BARACK OBAMA

NOTE: Identical letters were sent to John A. Boehner, Speaker of the House of Representatives, and Joseph R. Biden, Jr., President of the Senate.

Remarks on Government Reform
January 13, 2012

Good morning, everybody. Please have a seat.

Welcome to the White House. I see all sorts of small-businesspeople here, and I am thrilled to have you here. As small-business owners, you know as well as anybody that if we're going to rebuild an economy that lasts—an economy that creates good, middle class jobs—then we're all going to have to up our game.

The other day, I met with business leaders who are doing their part by insourcing, by bringing jobs back to the United States. And I told them that if you are willing to keep asking yourselves what you can do to bring jobs back, then I'll make sure that you've got a Government that helps you succeed.

And that's why we're here today. I ran for office pledging to make our Government leaner and smarter and more consumer friendly. And from the moment I got here, I saw up close what many of you know to be true: The Government we have is not the Government that we need.

We live in a 21st-century economy, but we've still got a Government organized for the 20th century. Our economy has fundamentally changed, as has the world, but our Government, our agencies, have not. The needs of our citizens have fundamentally changed, but their Government has not. Instead, it's often grown more complicated and sometimes more confusing.

Give you a few examples. There are five different entities dealing with housing. There are more than a dozen agencies dealing with food safety. My favorite example, which I mentioned in last year's State of the Union Address: As it turns out, the Interior Department is in charge of salmon in freshwater, but the Commerce Department handles them in saltwater. [*Laughter*] If you're wondering what the genesis of this was, apparently it had something to do with President Nixon being unhappy with his Interior Secretary for criticizing him about the Vietnam War, and so he decided not to put NOAA in what would have been a more sensible place.

No business or nonprofit leader would allow this kind of duplication or unnecessary complexity in their operations. You wouldn't do it when you're thinking about your businesses. So why is it okay for our Government? It's not. It has to change.

Now, what we've tried to do over the first three years of my administration is to do a whole range of steps administratively to start making processes, procedures, agencies more consumer friendly. But we need to do more, and we need authority to do more.

So today I'm calling on Congress to reinstate the authority that past Presidents have had to streamline and reform the executive branch. This is the same sort of authority that every business owner has to make sure that his or her company keeps pace with the times. And let me be clear: I will only use this authority for reforms that result in more efficiency, better service, and a leaner Government.

Now, a little bit of history here. Congress first granted this authority to Presidents in the midst of the Great Depression so that they could swiftly reorganize the executive branch to respond to the changing needs of the American people and the immediate challenges of the Depression. For the next 52 years, Presi-

dents were able to streamline or consolidate the executive branch by submitting a proposal to Congress that was guaranteed a simple up or down vote.

In 1984, while Ronald Reagan was President, Congress stopped granting that authority. And when this process was left to follow the usual congressional pace and procedures, not surprisingly, it bogged down. So congressional committees fought to protect their turf and lobbyists fought to keep things the way they were because they were the only ones who could navigate the confusion. And because it's always easier to add than to subtract in Washington, inertia prevented any real reform from happening. Layers kept getting added on and added on and added on. The Department of Homeland Security was created to consolidate intelligence and security agencies, but Congress didn't consolidate on its side. So now the Department of Homeland Security reports to over 100 different congressional panels. That's a lot of paperwork. That's a lot of reports to prepare. That's not adding value. It's not making us safer to file a whole bunch of reports all the time.

It has been a generation since a President had the authority to propose streamlining the Government in a way that allowed for real change to take place. Imagine all the things that have happened since 1984. Nineteen-eighty-four didn't have—we didn't have the Internet, just to take one example. A generation of Americans has come of age. Landlines have turned to smartphones. The cold war has given way to globalization. So much has happened, and yet the Government we have today is largely the Government we had back then. And we deserve better.

Go talk to the skilled professionals in Government who are serving their country—and by the way, you won't meet harder working folks than some of the folks in these Federal agencies—devote countless hours to trying to make sure that they're serving the American people. But they will tell you their efforts are constantly undermined by an outdated bureaucratic maze. And of course, if you go talk to ordinary Americans, including some of the small-business leaders here today, they'll tell you that to deal with Government on a regular basis is not always the highlight of their day. [*Laughter*]

Over the past 3 years, as I said, we've tried to take some steps to fix the problem, to bring our Government into this century and, in doing so, to root out waste. So, just to take some examples: We made sure that Government sends checks to the right people in the right amount, which should be obvious, but we've been able to prevent $20 billion in waste over the last 2 years, just by making sure that checks are sent properly and we're reducing error.

We cut Government contracting for the first time in more than a decade. We cut a whole range of overlapping programs. We have tried to yank the Federal Government into the 21st century when it comes to technology and making everything we do a little more Web friendly. And by the way, that also helps in terms of accountability and transparency, because the public can get on whitehouse.gov or the various other websites and they can see what's happening and track where money goes.

So we've done a lot, but we've got to do more. We need to think bigger. So today I'm outlining changes we could make if Congress gives the green light to allow us to modernize and streamline. These changes would help small-business owners like you. It would also help medium and large businesses. And as a consequence, they would help create more jobs, sell more products overseas, grow our economy faster, improve our quality of life.

Right now there are six departments and agencies focused primarily on business and trade in the Federal Government—six. Commerce Department, Small Business Administration, the U.S. Trade Representative's Office—in this case, six is not better than one. Sometimes more is better; this is not one of those cases, because it produces redundancy and inefficiency. With the authority that I'm requesting today, we could consolidate them all into one department, with one website, one phone number, one mission: helping American businesses succeed. That's a big idea.

Now, we've put a lot of thought into this. Over the past year, we spoke with folks across the Government and across the country. And most importantly, we spoke with businesses, including hundreds of small businesses, to hear what works and what doesn't when you deal with the Government; what's frustrating, what's actually value added. And frankly, in those conversations, we found some unsatisfied customers. A lot of times what we heard was, "You know what, the individual who I'm working with was really helpful to me, but the process itself is too confusing." Most of the complaints weren't about an unresponsive Federal worker, they were about a system that was too much of a maze.

So take a look at this slide. I don't usually use props in my speeches—[*laughter*]—but I thought this was useful. This is the system that small-business owners face. This is what they have to deal with if they want even the most basic answers to the most basic questions like how to export to a new country or whether they qualify for a loan. And by the way, this is actually simplified because there are some color codes. [*Laughter*] The business owners don't get the blue and the purple—and it's all just—there's a whole host of websites, all kinds of toll-free numbers, all sorts of customer service centers, but each are offering different assistance. It's a mess. This should be easy for small-business owners. They want to concentrate on making products, creating services, selling to customers. We're supposed to make it easier for them. And we can. There are some tools that we can put in place that every day are helping small-business owners all across the country, but we're wasting too much time getting that help out. And if Congress would reinstate the authority that previous Presidents have had, we would be able to fix this.

We'd have one department where entrepreneurs can go from the day they come up with an idea and need a patent to the day they start building a product and need financing for a warehouse to the day they're ready to export and need help breaking into new markets overseas. One website, easy to use, clear. One department where all our trade agencies would work together to ensure businesses and workers can better export by better enforcing our trade agreements. One department dedicated to helping our businesses sell their products to the 95 percent of global consumers who live beyond our shores. So, with this authority, we could help businesses grow, save businesses time, save taxpayer dollars.

And this is just one example of what we could do. The contrast between this and this sums up what we could do on the business side, but these kinds of inefficiencies exist across Government. And there's a real opportunity right now for us to fundamentally rethink, reform, and remake our Government so that it can meet the demands of our time, so that it's worthy of the American people, and so that it works.

This should not be a partisan issue. Congress needs to reinstate this authority that has in the past been given to Democratic and Republican presidents for decades. In the meantime, as long as folks are looking for work and small businesses are looking for customers, I'm going to keep doing everything I can with my current authority to help.

So, to take one example, as of today, I am elevating the Small Business Administration to a Cabinet-level agency. Karen Mills, who's here today and who's been doing an outstanding job leading that agency, is going to make sure that small-business owners have their own seat at the table in our Cabinet meetings.

In the coming weeks, we're also going to unveil a new website: Business USA. And this site will be a one-stop shop for small businesses and exporters, and it will consolidate information that right now is spread across all these various sites so that it's all in one place, and it's easy to search.

So, with or without Congress, I'm going to keep at it. But it would be a lot easier if Congress helped. [*Laughter*] This is an area that should receive bipartisan support, because making our Government more responsive and strategic and leaner, it shouldn't be a partisan issue.

We can do this better. We can provide taxpayers better value. So much of the argument out there all the time is up in 40,000 feet, these abstract arguments about who's conservative or who's liberal. Most Americans, and certainly most small-business owners, you guys are just trying to figure out, how do we make things work? How do we apply common sense? And that's what this is about.

So I'm going to keep fighting every day to rebuild this economy so that hard work pays off, responsibility is rewarded, and we've got a government that is helping to create the foundation for the incredible energy and entrepreneurship that all of you represent. And I'm going to keep fighting to make sure that middle class families regain the security that they've lost over the last decade. I've said before, this—I believe this is a make-or-break moment for families who are trying to get in the middle class, folks who are trying to maintain their security, folks who are trying to start businesses. There's enormous potential out there. The trend lines in our global economy are moving in our direction, towards innovation and openness and transparency.

But we've got to take advantage of it. And you need a strong ally in an effective, lean Government. That's what this authority can do.

Thank you very much, everybody. Thank you.

NOTE: The President spoke at 11:25 a.m. in the East Room at the White House.

Statement on the Release of Political Prisoners in Burma
January 13, 2012

President Thein Sein's decision to release hundreds of prisoners of conscience is a substantial step forward for democratic reform.

Two months ago, I spoke with Aung San Suu Kyi and President Thein Sein about how America's engagement can help empower democratic reform and improve relations between our countries. Shortly afterwards, Hillary Clinton became the first Secretary of State to travel to Burma in over half a century. In her meetings in Nay Pyi Taw and Rangoon, she discussed with President Thein Sein and other leaders the steps that would advance a new beginning between our countries. A key part of that discussion was the need to unconditionally release prisoners of conscience and allow them to participate fully in public and political life.

Since that visit, there have been a number of positive developments, including the announcement of elections to be held on April 1 and the decision to allow Aung San Suu Kyi and her party to participate. There has also been an important ceasefire agreement reached with the Karen National Union, which the United States welcomes. Today I applaud President Thein Seins's decision to release hundreds of prisoners of conscience, which is a crucial step in Burma's democratic transformation and national reconciliation process. I'm pleased that Aung San Suu Kyi has welcomed this step as she continues to pursue a dialogue with the Government. I urge the Government to ensure that these and all other former political prisoners are allowed to participate fully and freely in the political process, particularly the upcoming by-elections, and to free all remaining prisoners of conscience.

In Indonesia, I spoke about the flickers of progress that were emerging in Burma. Today that light burns a bit brighter as prisoners are reunited with their families and people can see a democratic path forward. Much more remains to be done to meet the aspirations of the Burmese people, but the United States is committed to continuing our engagement with the Government in Nay Pyi Taw. I have directed Secretary Clinton and my administration to take additional steps to build confidence with the Government and people of Burma so that we seize this historic and hopeful opportunity. We will continue to support universal rights and engage the Government as it takes the additional steps necessary to advance freedom for prisoners of conscience, democratic governance, and national reconciliation.

NOTE: The statement referred to Aung San Suu Kyi, leader of the National League for Democracy in Burma.

Letter to Congressional Leaders on Review of Title III of the Cuban Liberty and Democratic Solidarity (LIBERTAD) Act of 1996
January 13, 2012

Dear _____:

Consistent with section 306(c)(2) of the Cuban Liberty and Democratic Solidarity (LIBERTAD) Act of 1996 (Public Law 104–114) (the "Act"), I hereby determine and report to the Congress that suspension, for 6 months beyond February 1, 2012, of the right to bring an action under title III of the Act is necessary to the national interests of the United States and will expedite a transition to democracy in Cuba.

Sincerely,

BARACK OBAMA

NOTE: Identical letters were sent to Daniel K. Inouye, chairman, and W. Thad Cochran, vice chairman, Senate Committee on Appropriations; John F. Kerry, chairman, and Richard G. Lugar, ranking member, Senate Committee on Foreign Relations; Harold D. Rogers, chairman, and Norman D. Dicks, ranking member, House Committee on Appropriations; and Ileana Ros-Lehtinen, chairman, and Howard L. Berman, ranking member, House Committee on Foreign Affairs.

The President's Weekly Address
January 14, 2012

Hi there. As you can see, I brought a few things with me for this week's video: a padlock, a pair of boots, a candle, and a pair of socks.

We are not having a yard sale, and these products may not appear to have much in common. But they're united by three proud words: Made in America. They're manufactured by American workers, in American factories, and shipped to customers here and around the world.

The companies that make these products are part of a hopeful trend: They're bringing jobs back from overseas. You've heard of outsourcing; well, this is insourcing. And in this make-or-break moment for the middle class and those working to get into the middle class, that's exactly the kind of commitment to country that we need.

This week, I invited executives from businesses that are insourcing jobs to a forum here at the White House. These are CEOs who take pride in hiring people here in America, not just because it's increasingly the right thing to do for their bottom line, but also because it's the right thing to do for their workers and for our communities and for our country.

I told those CEOs what I'll tell any business leader: Ask yourself what you can do to bring more jobs back to the country that made your success possible, and I'll make sure that you've got a Government that does everything in its power to help you succeed.

That's why, in the next few weeks, I'll put forward new tax proposals that reward companies that choose to do the right thing by bringing jobs home and investing in America, and we'll eliminate tax breaks for companies that move jobs overseas.

It's also why, on Friday, I called on Congress to help me make Government work better for you. Right now we have a 21st-century economy, but we've still got a Government organized for the 20th century. Over the years, the needs of Americans have changed, but our Govern-

ment has not. In fact, it's gotten even more complex, and that has to change.

That's why I asked Congress to reinstate the authority that past Presidents have had to streamline and reform the executive branch. This is the same sort of authority that every business owner has to make sure that his or her company keeps pace with the times. It's the same authority that Presidents had for over 50 years, until Ronald Reagan. And let me be clear: I will only use this authority for reforms that result in more efficiency, better service, and a leaner Government.

These changes will make it easier for small-business owners to get the loans and support they need to sell their products around the world. For example, instead of forcing small-business owners to navigate the six departments and agencies in the Federal Government that focus on business and trade, we'll have one department, one place where entrepreneurs can go from the day they come up with an idea and need a patent, to the day they start building a warehouse, to the day they're ready to ship their products overseas.

And in the meantime, we're creating a new website, BusinessUSA, that will serve as a one-stop shop with information for businesses small and large that want to start selling their stuff around the world.

This means that more small-business owners will see their hard work pay off. More companies will be able to hire new workers. And we'll be able to rebuild an economy that's not known for paper profits or financial speculation, but for making and selling products like these, products made in America.

Thank you, and have a great weekend.

NOTE: The address was recorded at approximately 4:40 p.m. on January 13 in the Map Room at the White House for broadcast on January 14. The transcript was made available by the Office of the Press Secretary on January 13, but was embargoed for release until 6 a.m. on January 14.

Statement on Elections in Taiwan
January 14, 2012

We congratulate Ma Ying-jeou on his re-election and the people of Taiwan on the successful conduct of their Presidential and legislative elections.

Through the hard work of its people and its remarkable economic and political development over the past decades, Taiwan has proven to be one of the great success stories in Asia. In this year's elections, Taiwan has again demonstrated the strength and vitality of its democratic system. We are confident Taiwan will build on its many accomplishments, and we will continue to work together to advance our many common interests, including expanding trade and investment ties.

Cross-Strait peace, stability, and improved relations in an environment free from intimi-dation are of profound importance to the United States. We hope the impressive efforts that both sides have undertaken in recent years to build cross-Strait ties continue. Such ties and stability in cross-Strait relations have also benefited U.S.-Taiwan relations.

The relationship between the people of the United States and the people of Taiwan is based on common interests and a shared commitment to freedom and democracy. As we have done for more than 30 years, we will maintain our close unofficial ties with the people on Taiwan through the American Institute in Taiwan and according to our "one China" policy based on the three joint communiques with the People's Republic of China and the Taiwan Relations Act.

Remarks at a Service Event at Browne Education Campus
January 16, 2012

The President. Well, good morning, everybody!

Audience members. Good morning!

The President. Oh, this looks like an outstanding group. I can already tell. I'm not going to make a long speech because we're here to do some work. But mainly what I want to do is just to say thank you to all of you for participating. I know there are a lot of organizations that are represented here today. We are so glad to be at this outstanding school where we're going to be doing a whole bunch of stuff to make it—make the facilities even better than they already are.

But this is the third year now that Michelle and Malia and usually Sasha is here—she couldn't make it today—that we provide or engage in some sort of service on Dr. King's birthday. And there's no better way to celebrate Dr. King than to do something on behalf of others.

I know there's been a lot of controversy lately about the quote on the memorial, and they're changing it and making some modifi-cations, but if you look at that speech talking about Dr. King as a drum major, what he really said was that all of us can be a drum major for service, all of us can be a drum major for justice. There's nobody who can't serve, nobody who can't help somebody else. And whether you're 7 or 6 or whether you're 76, then you can find opportunities to make an enormous difference in your community. And at a time when the country has been going through some difficult economic times, for us to be able to come together as a community, people from all different walks of life, and make sure that we're giving back, that's ultimately what makes us the strongest, most extraordinary country on Earth, is because we pull together when times are good, but also when times are hard. And you guys all represent that.

So, on behalf of our family, we want to say thank you. I'm sure Dr. King, were he here, he'd want to say thank you. And I look forward to spending some time next to you guys. Hopefully, I have some good instructors here so that

43

I don't mess anything up. So, if you're putting a paintbrush in my hands, make sure that I've got some very clear lines, and I'll try to stay within them.

All right? Thank you, everybody. God bless you. Thank you.

NOTE: The President spoke at 9:57 a.m.

Remarks During a Meeting With the President's Council on Jobs and Competitiveness
January 17, 2012

The President. Please have a seat, everybody. For those of you who I have not seen since before the break, happy New Year.

I am extraordinarily grateful for all the work that you have done. I want to start off by thanking Jeff for his continued outstanding leadership of this Jobs Council. I think that the plan is for me to maybe just open up with a few remarks and then we've got a whole bunch of presentations, so I don't want to take too much time.

General Electric Co. Chairman and Chief Executive Officer Jeffrey R. Immelt. Great.

The President. Is that all right with you, Mr. Chairman?

Mr. Immelt. That's great.

The President. One of the things that's been striking about this Jobs Council is how focused and how hard-working everybody has been around this table. This has not been a show council, this has been a work council. And because of the extraordinary commitments that each and every one of you have made, we have generated, I think, as good a set of proposals as we have seen coming out of the private sector to help to guide and steer our economic agenda and our approach to jobs and growth over the next couple of years.

In each of the earlier meetings, we discussed the key role that we all play in accelerating growth and improving America's competitiveness and that the economic recovery has to be driven by the private sector. We have moved aggressively to implement your recommendations. As I think you've heard, of your 35 executive action recommendations, we've taken action on 33 of them; we've completed the implementation of 16 of them. And I'll highlight a couple of examples.

Building on some of the Job Council's National Investment Initiative recommendations, last week the Vice President and I hosted a forum on the increasing trend of insourcing, companies choosing to invest in the United States. And Intel and DuPont participated, along with several dozen other companies. We discussed tangible ways that we can encourage domestic investment, and I announced a number of new initiatives and new tax proposals to provide further incentives for companies to increase investment in the United States, including expanding on SelectUSA, one of the recommendations in your last report. And we actually had a company there that had benefited from the services of SelectUSA, and it confirmed the power and capacity of one-stop shops and a coordinated approach from the Federal Government for somebody who is interested in investment here in the United States.

I've personally emphasized to the White House team and to the Cabinet the importance of aggressively implementing the recommendations of this Job Council. I have been tracking implementation of your recommendations, and we've seen substantial progress across the board.

Let me highlight a couple other areas where your ideas and focus have had significant impact. First, on permitting: This is something that I know that Matt and others really emphasized. As we all agreed, we needed to make a big investment in this country in infrastructure to assure our competitiveness. We also agreed that we can't be bogged down by redtape and bureaucracy if we're actually going to get every bang for the buck. Building on administration efforts to streamline permitting, I issued an

Executive order to expedite review of job-creating infrastructure projects and to track their progress on a new public dashboard. All 14 projects are on track. Most importantly, we're using these projects to learn lessons that we can scale across a whole range of projects throughout the Federal Government moving forward. And I want you to know that as a result of your input, we're going to establish a permitting project manager effort, overseen by OMB, to establish performance metrics, track progress against goals, and adapt best practices across agencies. So, see? Mark can cross this off—check this off his list. [*Laughter*] I know he was coming here, and he was going to make sure that happened; it's happening.

A second example: On regulatory review—and we're going to have an opportunity for Jeff and Cass to expand on what we've been doing in this area—but I tasked Federal agencies to cut inefficient or excessively burdensome regulations and issued an Executive order to independent agencies to look back at their regulations for inefficiencies and excessive burdens. Currently, we're estimating savings of $10 billion over 10 years by implementing just a fraction of the reforms that have already been proposed and identified. Cass is going to provide you with a fuller update in a moment, but the preliminary results are exciting. And this includes, by the way, the independent agencies. So, for example, the FCC, prompted by our request, but also due to some excellent work by Julius Genachowski, they've already eliminated a hundred and ninety rules—a hundred and ninety. And that gives you some sense of the scale of the work that can be done as a consequence of some of your recommendations.

I announced last Friday that I'm going to ask Congress to give me authority to reorganize the Government to make it work better for the American people, while eliminating duplication and waste and inefficiencies. Much of this was embodied in some of the recommendations that you had in particular areas.

My legislative proposal would create a consolidation authority that would for the first time require that any reorganization proposal reduce the size of Government and cut costs.

So this is not just a matter of moving boxes around. The question is, can you actually achieve better integration, better streamlining, better efficiency, and ultimately better consumer service and better payoff for taxpayers.

The first proposal we identified was to consolidate the six agencies focusing primarily on business and trade into a new department with a single mission: to spur job creation and expand the U.S. economy. And this new department would consolidate the core business and trade functions of six agencies. It would be focused solely on helping entrepreneurs and businesses of all size to grow and to compete and to hire, while also cutting costs and provide better customer service.

So I make these points just to say that not only have you guys exceeded all expectations in providing specific, thoughtful recommendations. Hopefully, we've at least met your expectations in followthrough and implementation; what we haven't seen is a bunch of white papers sitting on a shelf somewhere collecting dust. We have tried to take very seriously everything that you proposed and to try to integrate it into not only legislative proposals, but also the executive proposals out there.

So I read your first-year report. I was pleased to see that there's consistency and shared urgency about America playing to win. Education, innovation, streamlining regulations, energy, manufacturing, all these are critical issues, and they're all interwoven, and they impact each other.

I recognize a lot of these issues are difficult. They've proven challenging for decades. The good news is on each of these fronts we've made progress this year. I feel confident in being able to say that every one of the agencies in this Government has been focused on how do they improve, get smarter, get better, get faster, become more focused on delivering good value to the end user. And I believe that we've made genuine progress on all these fronts. We would not have made this progress without this Jobs Council. And I think it will pay off in terms of solidifying this recovery and allowing us to move forward in a way where it actually translates into jobs, which has obviously been our principal and primary focus: making sure that we're creating a fair shot for every American who wants to work hard and get out there and succeed in this economy.

So with that, Jeff, I just want to say thank you for your being able to provide such outstanding leadership for this effort. And with that, I'm looking forward to hearing——

Mr. Immelt. Great.

The President. ——all the good work that's already been done.

Mr. Immelt. Thanks, Mr. President.

[*At this point, the meeting continued, and no transcript was provided. The meeting concluded as follows.*]

The President. Well, I just, again, want to thank all of you for the seriousness and effort that you've put into this Jobs Council. We're going to continue to gather recommendations from you and are going to continue to try to implement them as quickly as we can.

Those where we think there's an issue, we'll get back to you, and there will be an iterative process where we'll be in discussions in terms of how we can achieve some of the goals that have been set.

I want you to know that obviously this year is an election year, and so getting Congress focused on some of these issues may be difficult. But we have been struck by the degree of capacity we have administratively to at least chip away at some of these problems. Oftentimes, it's hard to get the kind of comprehensive solutions that you want without legislative involvement. But those small, incremental steps, they add up, and we're going to continue to make sure that we push that as hard as possible.

I did notice that we didn't have time to talk about manufacturing, although Jeff, I know that you and Rich Trumka and others have spent a good deal of time on it. In some ways that's all right because essentially that whole insourcing conversation was really a manufacturing conversation. And I was incredibly impressed with the potential at least for us to start getting manufacturing back in the United

States in selective industries, understanding that if you've got products that involve high volume, lots of labor, unskilled labor, that it's going to be difficult to move those back.

On the other hand, where you have skilled labor, our competitive advantages are accelerating. And we're going to really be pushing hard on that front along with issues like basic research, et cetera, partly because my understanding—and John and others, I think you guys helped—Steve Jobs and others—helped educate me on the fact that if all our manufacturing facilities move offshore that it's actually hard over time to keep our R&D here because so much of this ends up being a matter of seeing how something works in an applied fashion and tinkering with it and going back at it.

Mr. Immelt. We've set a goal here, Mr. President, to try to get back four points of global market share and value added in manufacturing. We think we can do that. People like Paul and I that travel the world, I think we see the U.S. more competitive today than we have in the last 20 or 25 years, so that's—I think that's another great initiative here.

The President. It's a good news story. It merges directly with our export initiative and the great work that people like Fred and Ron and others are doing. So we're going to keep on pushing that. You'll see that is a significant focus in our State of the Union as well.

So thank you, everybody. Great work. Appreciate it.

Mr. Immelt. Thanks, Mr. President.

NOTE: The President spoke at 11:13 a.m. in the State Dining Room at the White House. In his remarks, he referred to Matthew Rose, chairman and chief executive officer, BNSF Railway, and Mark T. Gallogly, founder and managing partner, Centerbridge Partners, L.P., in their capacity as members of the President's Council on Jobs and Competitiveness; Cass R. Sunstein, Office of Information and Regulatory Affairs Administrator, Office of Management and Budget; Richard L. Trumka, president, AFL–CIO; John Doerr, partner, Kleiner Perkins Caufield & Byers; Fred P.

Hochberg, Chairman, Export-Import Bank; and U.S. Trade Representative Ronald Kirk.

Mr. Immelt referred to Paul S. Otellini, president and chief executive officer, Intel Corp.

Remarks Following a Meeting With King Abdullah II of Jordan
January 17, 2012

President Obama. Good afternoon, everybody. It is a great pleasure for me to once again welcome His Majesty King Abdullah of Jordan, as well as his delegation.

We have very few countries around the world that are better friends and better partners than the Jordanians. The fact that they are in such a difficult neighborhood makes the relationship between our two countries that much more important.

And so I want to publicly express my appreciation for His Majesty's leadership not only in forging a strong bilateral relationship, but also all the multilateral efforts that he is engaged in to encourage peace and prosperity during what has been an extraordinary time.

The last time we met, the face of the region was very different. Since that time, you've seen new governments emerging in Egypt, in Libya, transitions taking place and a new government in Tunisia, transitions taking place in Yemen, and now obviously great volatility in Syria. Throughout this period we consult closely with the Jordanians, and we value the advice and the thoughtful leadership that His Majesty provides.

We spent a great deal of time discussing a number of key subjects. We talked about the importance of us continuing to consult closely together to encourage the Palestinians and the Israelis to come back to the table and negotiate in a serious fashion a peaceful way forward. And the Jordanians have taken great leadership on this issue, and we very much appreciate their direction on this issue.

We discussed, as well, the extraordinary efforts that have been made by His Majesty, as well as the Prime Minister, in guiding political reform inside of Jordan. I think His Majesty has been ahead of the curve in trying to respond to the legitimate concerns and aspirations, both politically and economically, of the Jordanian population. And so we have said that

we want to be as helpful as we can in encouraging this ongoing reform process that's taking place.

We also talked about a number of regional issues, including Iraq and Iran, but uppermost on our minds right now is the issue of Syria. His Majesty was the first Arab leader to publicly call on President Asad to step down in the face of the terrible brutality we've been seeing inside of Syria. I want to thank him for his willingness to stand up. As a consequence, Jordan has been part of an overall Arab League effort to encourage this sort of peaceful transition inside of Syria that is needed.

Unfortunately, we're continuing to see unacceptable levels of violence inside that country, and so we will continue to consult very closely with Jordan to create the kind of international pressure and environment that encourages the current Syrian regime to step aside so that a more democratic process of transition can take place inside of Syria.

Finally, Jordan, just like the rest of the world, has been grappling with a very difficult economic environment, and we are proud to have been able to provide some timely assistance in areas like food security this week. I think wheat from the United States will be arriving that will help to make sure that there's bread in Jordan.

But there's more work to do. And so through a wide range of bilateral efforts, including the Millennium Challenge grant and other mechanisms, what we're trying to do is encourage entrepreneurship, market-based reforms, small business and medium-sized businesses developing and prospering inside of Jordan. And we pledge to continue to work in strong partnership with His Majesty to make sure that all the people of Jordan have the kind of opportunity that they deserve.

So, generally speaking, our bilateral relationship could not be stronger. And I want to thank, once again, His Majesty for being not only a leader in the region, but also being a great friend of the United States.

Thank you.

King Abdullah II. Mr. President, thank you very much. It's obviously a great honor for me and my delegation to be back here in Washington. We so much appreciate the historical support that we always get from our friends in the United States to Jordan's challenges. And again, our personal friendship, which is very, very strong, has allowed us to look at the challenges that the Israelis and Palestinians face, as you just mentioned.

Although this is still in the very early stages, we have to keep our fingers crossed and hope that we can bring the Israelis and Palestinians out of the impasse that we're facing. We're in coordination on a regular basis with the President, as well as with his administration.

We're very, very grateful to the economic support that you're showing Jordan in this very difficult time. As we move into political reform, obviously the economy and the situation that challenges the livelihood of Jordanians is very, very important as we move forward. But we are very, very optimistic. We had the opportunity to talk about the full impact with the President this afternoon.

So again, sir, wonderful to be back. We will be in close consultation with you on all these issues. And thank you for your kind words and your wonderful support to our country.

President Obama. Good. Thank you very much, everybody.

NOTE: The President spoke at 3:07 p.m. in the Oval Office at the White House. In his remarks, he referred to Prime Minister Awn Shawkat al-Khasawnah of Jordan.

Remarks Honoring the 2011 World Series Champion St. Louis Cardinals
January 17, 2012

The President. Thank you. It is wonderful to be here. It is wonderful to be joined by my wife. It is her birthday today. When we first married, it was a little controversial that she was 20 years younger than me, but—[*laughter*]—now it seems to have worked out okay. [*Laughter*]

The First Lady. I'm 48. [*Laughter*]

The President. And I want to join her in congratulating the world champion St. Louis Cardinals. I won't lie, I'm a little disappointed I had to leave my White Sox jacket in the closet for another year. [*Laughter*] But this is a special team, both because of what they do for our military and their families, but also what they did on the field last season. And I know we've got Mayor Slay from St. Louis and some Members of Congress who agree with me. I see the delegation here; they're beaming. [*Laughter*] They are quite pleased.

Now, when we talk about baseball, we're talking about a sport, obviously, with a long history. Over 200,000 games have been played since Major League Baseball began. Seventeen

thousand players have gone through the league. So this is a sport that has seen it all.

But every once in a while, something happens that we have never seen before, something unique. And that's why it is my pleasure to stand here with the greatest comeback team in the history of baseball.

Last August, with just 31 games to play in the regular season, the Cardinals were 10½ games out of the playoff race. At one point, they had a less than 4-percent mathematical chance of making the playoffs. In Las Vegas, they were 500-to-1 longshots to win the World Series. And when Chris Carpenter pulled the team together for a meeting, his message was simple: Let's not embarrass ourselves. [*Laughter*] But through skills and guts and, I think the team would agree, just a little bit of luck—just a touch—this team made the playoffs. And even though they trailed in each of the series that followed, they somehow had the spirit and the determination and the resolve to survive.

Of course, the most memorable moment was game six of the World Series. I've got to say, that has to be one of the best baseball games of all time—unbelievable game. I will tell you guys, I had a bunch of early morning stuff the next day, and you kept me up. [*Laughter*] It was painful waking up the next morning, but what an incredible game. Five times, the Cardinals found themselves trailing; twice, they were down to the last strike. Then Mr. Freese here hits the first walk-off homer of his entire career to send it into game seven. Then the Cardinals put the Rangers away for good.

This team essentially played 2 months of elimination games, both to get into the playoffs, and then to win it all. But in Tony La Russa's words, "Sometimes, you can't be afraid to make a mistake. Sometimes, you just roll the dice and you let it go." That's what the former teammate of these folks, Albert Pujols, did when he joined Babe Ruth and Reggie Jackson as the only player to hit three home runs in a World Series game. That's what the outstanding ace, Chris Carpenter, did when he pitched the lights out against the Phillies and then came back to put the nail in the coffin against the Rangers. That's what David Freese did in game six—not bad for a kid who grew up dreaming of playing for the Cardinals. And even though he can't be here today, that's what Tony La Russa did, winning his third title and then stepping down with the third most wins of any manager in history.

I will point out that he began as a White Sox, so—[*laughter*].

The First Lady. Let it go, honey. [*Laughter*]

The President. Everyone on this team follows the Cardinals way: They play all 27 outs, they never quit, they carry on the legacy of so many great Cardinals that have come before them.

Last year, I was honored to present Stan "The Man" Musial with one of the highest honors a President can bestow, the Medal of Freedom. And you could see Stan coming from about a mile away, because he was wearing that bright red blazer. There's no question he will always be a Cardinal at heart. And now this team is part of that long line of heroes.

So I want to congratulate not only the players, the owners, all the managers, and team officials, but also the fans, for a historic year. And

I also want to thank them for visiting Walter Reed this morning, spending some time with our wounded warriors over there. That's what this organization's all about; it represents baseball at its best. And I wish them all the best this season.

Congratulations. Fantastic. Come on up.

St. Louis Cardinals President William O. DeWitt III. We've got a gift for you.

The President. Yes, tell me what I got here. Tell me what I got.

St. Louis Cardinals Chairman and Chief Executive Officer William O. DeWitt, Jr. Thank you for those warm remarks and nice hospitality here. We've got a couple of gifts for you and Mrs. Obama.

The President. There you go.

William O. DeWitt, Jr. A World Series jersey with your name on the back, number 44.

The President. That's nice right there. [*Laughter*] There we go.

William O. DeWitt III. One for each.

William O. DeWitt, Jr. One for each. That one's yours.

The President. Yes.

William O. DeWitt, Jr. You can have that.

The President. Okay.

William O. DeWitt, Jr. And a World Series bat, for your——

The President. I'm a little bit worried about giving my wife a bat, though, if I—[*laughter*]—if I mess up.

The First Lady. I'll take my bat. [*Laughter*]

The President. [*Inaudible*]

William O. DeWitt, Jr. It's great to be here. Thank you.

The President. Thank you so much.

NOTE: The President spoke at 3:33 p.m. in the East Room at the White House. In his remarks, he referred to Mayor Francis G. Slay of St. Louis, MO; Christopher J. Carpenter, pitcher, David R. Freese, third baseman, J. Alberto Pujols, first baseman, and Stanley F. Musial, former outfielder, St. Louis Cardinals; and Reginald M. Jackson, former right fielder, New York Yankees. The transcript released by the Office of the Press Secretary included the introductory remarks of the First Lady.

Statement on the Keystone XL Pipeline
January 18, 2012

Earlier today I received the Secretary of State's recommendation on the pending application for the construction of the Keystone XL Pipeline. As the State Department made clear last month, the rushed and arbitrary deadline insisted on by congressional Republicans prevented a full assessment of the pipeline's impact, especially the health and safety of the American people, as well as our environment. As a result, the Secretary of State has recommended that the application be denied. And after reviewing the State Department's report, I agree.

This announcement is not a judgment on the merits of the pipeline, but the arbitrary nature of a deadline that prevented the State Department from gathering the information necessary to approve the project and protect the American people. I'm disappointed that Republicans in Congress forced this decision, but it does not change my administration's commitment to American-made energy that creates jobs and reduces our dependence on oil. Under my administration, domestic oil and natural gas production is up, while imports of foreign oil are down. In the months ahead, we will continue to look for new ways to partner with the oil and gas industry to increase our energy security—including the potential development of an oil pipeline from Cushing, Oklahoma, to the Gulf of Mexico—even as we set higher efficiency standards for cars and trucks and invest in alternatives like biofuels and natural gas. And we will do so in a way that benefits American workers and businesses without risking the health and safety of the American people and the environment.

NOTE: The related memorandum is listed in Appendix D at the end of this volume.

Remarks at Walt Disney World Resort in Lake Buena Vista, Florida
January 19, 2012

The President. Hello, everybody! I am glad to be at Disney World, the Magic Kingdom. This is outstanding.

Well, let me begin by thanking Ruben for that extraordinary introduction. And he was too bashful; maybe he's not supposed to do this. I will do it. His restaurant is called Zaza [Yaya's]°—new Cuban diners. So everybody check it out. And I told him, he was—on the way out, he was wondering, I don't know, I don't do this a lot. He's a natural. [*Laughter*] We're going to have to run him for something. [*Laughter*]

But thank you so much for taking the time. It is great to be here. It is rare that I get to do something that Sasha and Malia envy me for. [*Laughter*] That doesn't happen very often. Maybe for once they'll actually ask me at dinner how my day went. [*Laughter*]

And I confess, I am excited to see Mickey. It's always nice to meet a world leader who has bigger ears than me. [*Laughter*]

I want to acknowledge the presence of one of Florida's outstanding mayors, the mayor of Orlando, Buddy Dyer is in the house. We've got two outstanding members of my Cabinet, Interior Secretary Ken Salazar and Commerce Secretary John Bryson. Because they're focused on what brings us here today, and that's creating jobs and boosting tourism.

You just heard what a huge difference tourism makes for small businesses like Ruben's. Every year, tens of millions of tourists all over the world come to visit America. Makes sense. You got the greatest country on Earth, people want to come. As folks in Orlando know, that's good for our economy. It means people are renting cars and they're staying in hotels and

---

° White House correction.

they're eating at restaurants and they're checking out the sights. It means people are doing business here in the United States. In 2010, nearly 60 million international visitors helped the tourism industry generate over $134 billion. Tourism is the number-one service that we export—number one. And that means jobs.

More money spent by more tourists means more businesses can hire more workers. This is a pretty simple formula. And that's why we're all here today, to tell the world that America is open for business. We want to welcome you and to take concrete steps to boost America's tourism industry so that we can keep growing our economy and creating more jobs here in Florida and all across the country.

Now, here's the good news: We've got the best product to sell. I mean, look at where we are. We've got the most entertaining destinations in the world. This is the land of extraordinary natural wonders, from the Rocky Mountains to the Grand Canyon, from Yellowstone to Yosemite.

This is the land where we do big things, and so have incredible landmarks, like the Golden Gate Bridge and the Empire State Building, the Hoover Dam, the Gateway Arch. This is the land of iconic cities and all their sights, from Independence Hall in Philadelphia to Faneuil Hall in Boston, from the Space Needle in Seattle to the skyline of my hometown in Chicago. It's a nice skyline, for those of you who have never been there. [*Laughter*] All right, a couple of Chicagoans back there. [*Laughter*]

But I'm here today because I want more tourists here tomorrow. I want America to be the top tourist destination in the world—[*applause*]—the top tourist destination in the world. And this is something that we've been focused on for some time.

Two years ago, I signed a bill into law called the Travel Promotion Act. It had broad support of both Democrats and Republicans. And as you know, that doesn't always happen. [*Laughter*] And it set up a new nonprofit organization called Brand USA. Its job is to pitch America as a travel destination for the rest of the world to come to visit.

You guys see advertising for other countries, other destinations, here in the United States, right? Well, we've got to do the same thing so that when people are thinking about where they want to travel, where they want to spend their vacation, we want them to come here. And so that's already in place, but we've got to do more.

So today I directed my administration to send me a new national tourism strategy focused on creating jobs. And some of America's most successful business leaders—some who are here today—have signed up to help. We're going to see how we can make it easier for foreign tourists to find basic information about visiting America. And we're going to see how we can attract more tourists to our national parks. We want people visiting not just Epcot Center, but the Everglades too. The more folks who visit America, the more Americans we get back to work. It's that simple.

Now, just as we do a better job of marketing our tourist destinations, we've also got to make it easier for tourists to make the visit. There's a good reason why it's not easy for anybody to get a visa to come to America. Obviously, our national security is a top priority. We will always protect our borders and our shores and our tourist destinations from people who want to do us harm. And unfortunately, such people exist, and that's not going to change.

But we also want to get more international tourists coming to America. And there's no reason why we can't do both. We can make sure that we're doing a good job keeping America secure while at the same time maintaining the openness that's always been the hallmark of America and making sure that we're welcoming travelers from all around the world.

So one step we're taking is the expansion of something called the Global Entry Program. It's a program that protects our borders and makes life easier for frequent travelers to and from the United States. Now, getting into the program requires an extensive background check. But once you're in, once you've proven yourself to be a solid individual who is coming here for business or recreation purposes, instead of going through long lines at immigration, we can scan your passport, your fingerprints, and you're on your way.

So it's a great example of how we're using new technology to maintain national security and boost tourism at the same time. And we're now going to make it available to almost all international travelers coming to the United States. If they're willing to submit themselves to the background checks necessary, we can make sure that we're facilitating their easy travel into the United States.

There are some additional steps, though, that we can take. Right now there are 36 countries around the world whose citizens can visit America without getting a tourist visa. After they go online they get precleared by Homeland Security, and there's only one thing they have to do and that's book a flight. And that's been a great boost for tourism. Over 60 percent of our visitors don't require a visa, and in most cases, that's because of this program.

Today I'm directing my administration to see if we can add more countries to it. We want more folks to have an easier time coming to the United States.

And let's also realize that in the years ahead, more and more tourists are going to come from countries not currently in this program, countries with rapidly growing economies, huge populations, and emerging middle classes, countries like China and India, and especially important here in Florida, Brazil, a huge population that loves to come to Florida. But we make it too hard for them. More and more of their people can now afford to visit America who couldn't come before, and in fact, over the next 4 years, the tourists traveling from those countries we expect to more than double.

But we want them coming right here. We want them spending money here, in Orlando, in Florida, in the United States of America, which will boost our businesses and our economy.

So today I'm directing the State Department to accelerate our ability to process visas by 40 percent in China and in Brazil this year.

We're not talking about 5 years from now or 10 years from now—this year.

We've already made incredible progress in this area. We've better staffed our Embassies and our consulates. We've streamlined services with better technology. Waiting times for a visa are down. But applications keep on going up; they are skyrocketing. People want to come here. And China and Brazil are the two countries which have some of the biggest backlogs. And these are two of the countries with some of the fastest growing middle classes that want to visit and have disposable income, money that they want to spend at our parks and our monuments and at businesses like Ruben's.

So that's what this is all about: telling the world that America is open for business, making it as safe and as simple as possible to visit, helping our businesses all across the country grow and create jobs, helping those businesses compete and win.

Ultimately, that's how we're going to rebuild an economy where hard work pays off, where responsibility is rewarded, and where anybody can make it if they try. That's what America is all about. That's part of the reason why people want to come here, because they know our history. They know what the American Dream has been all about. And a place like Disneyland represents that quintessentially American spirit. This image is something that's recognized all around the world, and this weather is something that people appreciate all around the world, including the northern parts of this country. [*Laughter*]

So we want everybody to come. All who are watching, Disney World and Florida are open for business, but we want people all around the world to know the same. And we are going to do everything we can to make sure that we're continuing to boost tourism for decades to come.

Thank you very much, everybody. God bless you. God bless the United States of America.

NOTE: The President spoke at 12:40 p.m. In his remarks, he referred to Ruben Perez, owner, Yaya's Cuban Cafe and Bakery.

Remarks at an Obama Victory Fund 2012 Fundraiser in New York City
January 19, 2012

Thank you, everybody. Please have a seat. It is wonderful to be back in New York, and it is wonderful to be among so many wonderful friends. As I look around the room, I've got people who've supported me when nobody could pronounce my name—[*laughter*]—and I was running for the United States Senate. In fact, I've got a couple people here who supported me when I was running for the State senate—my Chicago contingent here. [*Laughter*]

I want to thank all the organizers who helped pull this together. I also want to give a special shout-out to one of the finest mayors that this city has ever had, Ed Koch, who's here. We are grateful to him.

We're going to spend most of our time in a conversation. I don't want to give a long speech, partly because I have three more events tonight. [*Laughter*] But the main reason is I want to save most of the time for a conversation and a dialogue between us.

But let me just, first of all, say that we're obviously living in historic times. When I first came into office, we were going through the worst financial crisis since the Great Depression, and so understandably, a lot of my time and most of the country's attention was consumed by how do we get America back on its feet.

But we were also in the midst of two wars. We were also coming out of a period in which America's leadership around the world had declined. And what we've been able to do, I think, over the last 3 years is to not only avert a Great Depression, not only save an auto industry, not only get the economy moving in the right direction—although we've still got a long way to go—but we were also able to end a war that had distracted us from our most ardent enemies, we were able to decimate Al Qaida, we were able to beef up what we were doing in Afghanistan in a way that now allows us to take a transition and start bringing our troops home there and turn over the security needs of the Afghan people to Afghan security forces.

But what we were also able to do, I think, is to restore a sense of America as the sole, indispensable power, a country that, whether it's responding to an earthquake or a tsunami, or it's dealing with a dictator that is about to ruthlessly butcher his people, we aren't out there alone. We're able to mobilize around a set of values and a set of principles and ensure that the international rules of the road are followed.

And it's because of that extraordinary work that my Secretary of State, Hillary Clinton, has been able to do, that our entire national security team has been able to execute, that America is stronger now than it was 3 years ago. But what's also true is the world is going through the kinds of changes that we haven't seen in a generation. And obviously, nowhere is that more true than in the Middle East.

Now, I'm sure we're going to have a chance to take some questions on these issues, but I want to just make a couple of key points.

Since I've been in office, we have unequivocally said that Israel's security is non-negotiable, and that we will do everything that's necessary to make sure that Israel is able to thrive and prosper as a secure Jewish state. Part of that has been to make sure that we've got the strongest military cooperation that we've ever had between our two nations. That's not my opinion, by the way, that's the Israeli Government's opinion.

Part of it is by making sure that as the Arab Spring swept through the region, that we are pushing hard on countries like Egypt to make sure that they continue to abide by the peace treaties that have served both countries well.

Part of it is mobilizing an unprecedented campaign of sanctions and pressure on Iran and stating unequivocally that we're not going to tolerate a nuclear weapon in the hands of this Iranian regime. And we've been able to organize folks like China and Russia that previously would have never gone along with something like this. And it's been so effective that even the Iranians have had to acknowledge that their economy is in a shambles.

When I came into office, Iran was united and the world was divided. And now what we have is a united international community that is saying to Iran, you've got to change your ways.

Now, this doesn't mean that we're where we need to be. The Arab Spring can still go in a whole multitude of directions, and this is going to be a very delicate time for us to make sure that the legitimate aspirations of ordinary people for democracy and economic opportunity doesn't get channeled by demagogues in ways that are dangerous for America's security interests or Israel's security interests.

We still have situations like Syria where people are being slaughtered. And obviously, that has huge ramifications for the region. Iran still has not made the right choice in terms of taking a path that would allow it to rejoin the community of nations and set aside its nuclear ambitions. And obviously, we still have not made the kind of progress that I would have liked to have seen when it comes to peace between Israel and the Palestinians, a peace, by the way, that I believe is not just good for the Palestinians, but is profoundly in the strategic interest of Israel.

So we've still got a lot of work to do. And my main message tonight is going to be, I'm going to need you in order for us to finish that work. We're not going to be able to succeed in fully transitioning from a time in which the United States was isolated and at war and disregarded around the world, to one in which we have restored a sense of balance and vision and purpose to world affairs, unless we can continue on the effective path that we're on.

And obviously, the American people are still keenly interested in making sure that the economy is working. And that's going to dominate the debate. And although I believe that we've got a great story to tell on that front, although I can tick off statistics about how we've had 22 straight months of private sector job growth and that we're starting to see companies actually bringing jobs back to the United States because of our renewed competitive posture, and I can talk about the investments that we're making in basic research and science to make sure that we maintain our innovative edge, and

I can talk about all the things we've done in Government to make it more efficient and leaner so that it can more effectively serve the American people, despite all those stories that we've got to tell, unemployment is still too high and a lot of people are still hurting and the housing market is still weak and State and local governments are still trying to figure out how to balance their books.

So, in that environment, this is still going to be a tough race, regardless of who they nominate. And the most important thing that we can do on the foreign policy front is make sure that we've got an America in which everybody has got a fair shot, everybody is doing their fair share, everybody is playing by the same rules, and we once again create a sense of opportunity and optimism here in the United States. Because when that happens, then America looks outward and it realizes the critical role that it plays in world affairs. And when folks are struggling, we turn inward, and sometimes we don't realize how important it is for us to be involved in some of these critical issues.

This is a group obviously that spends a lot of time thinking both about domestic issues and international issues. And my main message to you is I intend to win, but I'm going to need your help doing it.

And over the next 10 months, when we are having as clear a contrast between the parties and as profound a debate as we've seen in a very long time about the direction that America needs to take, I hope you know that the values you cherish, what you stand for, what you believe in, are the things I cherish and I believe in and I'm willing to fight for.

And if you have that confidence in me—because I certainly have that confidence in you—then I'm absolutely positive that not only will we win the election but, more importantly, we're going to be able to continue this path that we started in 2008.

Thank you very much, everybody. Thank you.

NOTE: The President spoke at 5:18 p.m. in the main reception area of Daniel restaurant. Audio was not available for verification of the content of these remarks.

Statement on Representative Maurice D. Hinchey's Decision Not To Seek Reelection
January 19, 2012

As a native New Yorker, Maurice Hinchey has served the people of the Empire State for over 35 years. Prior to his time in office, Maurice proudly served his country as a member of the United States Navy. He then went on to serve as a member in the State Assembly for 18 years, followed by 10 consecutive terms as a U.S. Representative for the 22d congressional district of New York. Throughout his career Maurice has been a champion for the middle class, leading the charge for renewable energy and Wall Street reform and working tirelessly to get Americans back to work. Michelle and I join the people of New York in thanking Congressman Hinchey for his service.

Letter to Congressional Leaders on Continuation of the National Emergency With Respect to Terrorists Who Threaten To Disrupt the Middle East Peace Process
January 19, 2012

Dear Mr. Speaker: (Dear Mr. President:)

Section 202(d) of the National Emergencies Act (50 U.S.C. 1622(d)) provides for the automatic termination of a national emergency unless, within 90 days prior to the anniversary date of its declaration, the President publishes in the *Federal Register* and transmits to the Congress a notice stating that the emergency is to continue in effect beyond the anniversary date. In accordance with this provision, I have sent to the *Federal Register* for publication the enclosed notice stating that the national emergency declared with respect to foreign terrorists who threaten to disrupt the Middle East peace process is to continue in effect beyond January 23, 2012.

The crisis with respect to grave acts of violence committed by foreign terrorists who threaten to disrupt the Middle East peace process that led to the declaration of a national emergency on January 23, 1995, has not been resolved. Terrorist groups continue to engage in activities that have the purpose or effect of threatening the Middle East peace process and that are hostile to United States interests in the region. Such actions constitute an unusual and extraordinary threat to the national security, foreign policy, and economy of the United States. For these reasons, I have determined that it is necessary to continue the national emergency with respect to foreign terrorists who threaten to disrupt the Middle East peace process and to maintain in force the economic sanctions against them to respond to this threat.

Sincerely,

BARACK OBAMA

NOTE: Identical letters were sent to John A. Boehner, Speaker of the House of Representatives, and Joseph R. Biden, Jr., President of the Senate. The notice is listed in Appendix D at the end of this volume.

Remarks at an Obama Victory Fund 2012 Fundraiser in New York City
January 19, 2012

The President. Hello! Everybody, please have a seat. Have a seat. Thank you. You're going to make me blush. [*Laughter*] Well, it is wonderful to be back in New York, and it is wonderful to be with all of you.

I understand that you already had a chance to talk with the outstanding junior Senator from New York, and Kirsten is doing a wonderful job, so all of you guys should be very proud. I'm sure that a number of you supported her in previous campaigns and will continue to do so.

As I look around the room, I see some old friends—not in years, but—some of you in years—[*laughter*]—but who have known me for a very long time, people who supported me in my first U.S. Senate race. Andy supported me in my first State senate race.

Audience member. Bobby Rush.

The President. That's exactly right.

I'm going to speak very briefly at the top because I want to spend most of my time in conversation. We're obviously living through a historic time. We just went through the worst financial crisis in our history since the Great Depression—worst financial crisis. We have an Arab Spring that is transforming an entire region of the world. The structure of the global economy, the changes in technology all are happening at a breathless pace.

And I think that—when I think back to the last 3 years, I could not be prouder of what we've been able to do in averting a depression, saving an auto industry. We've now seen 22 consecutive months of job growth in the private sector. We're starting to see manufacturing come back to the United States.

On the international stage, we've been able to manage the end of one war and the beginning of a transition of another. We have been on the right side of democracy. We've strengthened our alliances, restored respect for the United States around the world.

On issues of equity and the values that we care most deeply about, we've made enormous advances: ending "don't ask, don't tell," making sure that equal pay for equal work is—[*applause*]—appointing two really smart women to the Supreme Court.

But we have so much more work to do. We've got so many things that remain to tackle. We have an economy that, although now is getting close to where we were before the financial crisis struck, continues to struggle with these long-term trends that had been going on

for decades, where middle class families felt less and less secure, where the education system wasn't equipping our kids to compete in a global economy, where we had an absence of an energy policy, a health care system that was bleeding companies and the Federal Treasury dry and not providing any care for millions of people.

And so part of our task is to tell a story about everything that we've gotten done over the last 3 years so that people have confidence that change is possible. It's not easy, it's messy. There are times where it's frustrating, sometimes we experience setbacks, but change occurs, meaningful change that concretely helps people's lives. But even as we tell that story, we've also got to tell a story about where this country needs to go.

I've never felt more confident about the capacity of America to meet the moment and assure a solid future for our kids and our grandkids. But it's going to require more work, and it's going to require us making good choices. And this year is going to be as stark a choice as we have seen—a starker choice than we saw in 2008.

I mean, think about it. In 2008, I was running against a Republican nominee who agreed that we should ban torture, agreed that we should close Guantanamo, believed in climate change, had worked on immigration reform. And so as profound as the differences were between myself and John McCain, there was some sense of convergence when it came to some very important issues.

If you've been listening to the Republican debates, they have moved. [*Laughter*] I've stayed here. [*Laughter*] They've gone in a different direction.

Now, that's going to make for a hugely important, hugely consequential election, partly because we need to win this election to consolidate all the gains that we've made over the last 3 years and make sure that financial reform is actually implemented effectively and not watered down, and somebody like a Richard Cordray as the head of the Consumer Financial Protection Bureau is able to prevent people from being subjected to predatory lending, partly because health care reform still has to be implemented.

We already have 2.5 million young people who have insurance because of that bill and millions of seniors who are saving money on prescription drugs because of that bill. But there are a whole bunch of folks with preexisting conditions who are still going to need help and a whole bunch of working families who still don't have health insurance, and they're going to need those exchanges that we're setting up put in place so that they can get affordable health care.

But it's not just a matter of implementing many of the things we've already done. It's a matter of meeting the requirements to get to where we need to go. We're going to have to solve this fiscal crisis that we're in, in a way that's balanced and fair, and in which everybody does their fair share.

We're going to have to make sure that we are investing in community colleges and early childhood education so that everybody genuinely has a fair shot. We're going to have to rebuild America. In a city like New York, we've got tens, hundreds of billions of dollars of infrastructure work where we could put construction workers, right now, who are sitting at home, back to work, making ourselves more productive to meet the challenges of a 21st-century economy.

We're going to have to make sure that the budgets for the NIH and NSF and all our basic research in science is maintained so that we continue to be the leading innovators in the world.

We're going to have to make sure that all the work we've done over the last 3 years to restore America's standing in the world, that that's preserved, and that people everywhere continue to see America as the one indispensable nation in assuring that there's an international order that thinks about everybody and not just thinks in terms of raw power.

So this is a big deal, this race. And I am very confident about our prospects. As tough as the economic environment is, as many headwinds as we're experiencing, I believe we're going to win. But that belief is premised on my confidence in you, that you guys are going to step up, that you are going to show the same kind of resolve and determination and enthusiasm that you showed in 2008.

If you do, then I think we'll win the argument, because I think we have a better vision for the future. And I continue to have this profound confidence and faith in the American people and that a vision of a America that gives everybody opportunity and is inclusive and considers our values important to project around the world and in our own Government—I think that's what they want to—that's how they think about America as well.

So I hope all you guys are ready to go——

Audience member. Fired up.

The President. I hope you're fired up. [*Laughter*] And I don't—I'm glad you guys wrote checks, but I don't just want your money. I'm going to want your ideas and your time and your energy and your effort. And if you give me that, I promise you I will be working harder this time than I did in 2008. All right?

Thank you very much, everybody.

NOTE: The President spoke at 6:15 p.m. in the Bellcour reception area of Daniel restaurant. Audio was not available for verification of the content of these remarks.

Remarks at an Obama Victory Fund 2012 Fundraiser in New York City
January 19, 2012

The President. I am so thrilled to be here, not only because of the extraordinary hospitality of Spike and Tonya and Jackson and Satchel, but also because I see a lot of good friends around the room. And so I just want to thank you in advance for everything that you've done in the past and everything that I know you're committed to doing this year.

Tonya, I saw "Bamboozled" a while back. [*Laughter*]

Filmmaker Spike Lee. Sleep and eat!

Tonya L. Lee. Sometimes, you got to wonder. [*Laughter*]

The President. Some of you may not remember that film, which is okay. [*Laughter*] On the other hand, I prefer to tell the story, which I told when you guys hosted us in Martha's Vineyard, about a little-known fact—I'm not sure this has been reported by the press—that on my first official date with Michelle, I took Michelle to see "Do the Right Thing," first official date.

Mr. Lee. You remember what I said?

The President. Yes.

Mr. Lee. I said, good thing you didn't choose "Driving Miss Daisy." [*Laughter*]

The President. That's true. Spike wasn't maybe quite as famous, as the movie had just come out, and I was showing my sophistication in selecting this independent filmmaker, and she was impressed. And I think——

Mr. Lee. Glad to help you. [*Laughter*]

The President. I'm just saying, I think you helped me out that day. [*Laughter*] So it worked out, which is why I've always had a soft spot for Spike Lee in my heart. What I've also always enjoyed is Spike serving as a foil for my Chicago Bulls—[*laughter*]—year after year after year after year. [*Laughter*]

But these guys, it's true, they have been great friends ever since I started this incredible journey in politics on the national scene. And to see their incredibly accomplished and good-looking children and to see how well Tonya has done with her writing, it's just wonderful.

So thank you so much for hosting this——

Mr. Lee. Thank you.

The President. ——spectacular event.

I'm going to be very brief so that we have some time for questions and conversation. We're obviously at a historic moment in this country's history. We're coming off of the worst financial crisis since the Great Depression, an economic contraction of the likes that we haven't seen in our lifetime. Around the world there are transformations taking place in the Middle East, in Eastern Europe, and Asia that are extraordinarily challenging.

But this is also a moment of great promise. And what we've tried to do over the last 3 years is to not only solve a crisis, not only make sure that we didn't tip into a Great Depression and started getting economic growth going again and jobs growing again—we've now had 22 straight months of private sector job growth and the economy is on the mend, although not where it needs to be; not only have we been able to end a war in Iraq and start managing a transition in Afghanistan; not only have we passed historic health care legislation that's already having an impact on 2.5 million young people who have health insurance as we speak because of that law, and been able to end practices like "don't ask, don't tell," that were so fundamentally contrary to who we are as a country, but what we've also tried to do is begin to lay the foundation to deal with problems that have been building up for decades.

An education system that is still not where it needs to be to make sure that our young people can compete in the 21st century, making sure that we have a Tax Code that is fair and equitable so that hard-working Americans don't feel like other folks are playing by a different set of rules, making sure that our financial system is stable and conducive to economic growth, as opposed to just speculation and arbitrage.

And so what we've also tried to do is to take a long view about where America needs to be in order for us to succeed in this 21st century, not for us—everybody in this room is going to be doing fine—but for children and grandchildren and future generations who are going to be able to proudly say that America continues to be the land of opportunity, and it continues to be the one indispensable nation around the world that people look to for leadership and clarity of values.

I couldn't be prouder of the track record we've established over the last 3 years. But we've got a lot more work to do. And the only way we're going to accomplish it is to win this election. We could not have a sharper contrast this year than is going to be presented. And if some of you want to wander off to watch the debate—[*laughter*].

Audience member. No, thank you!

The President. If you need some motivation—[*laughter*]—feel free. Because the country actually is not as divided as Washington is. I think people still are looking for commonsense solutions. I think people believe that we can have economic growth and make sure that the ladders of upward mobility are still there for everybody. I think people believe that we can be tough on those who would try to do us harm, but still abide by due process and our values.

I think people believe that it's possible for us to grow and to build, but still conserve our incredible natural resources and make sure we're passing on a planet that is livable for the next generation.

I think people believe that there's no contradiction between excellence and diversity and that making sure that everybody, regardless of race or gender or sexual orientation, is able to live out their dreams if they're willing to work hard and be responsible, that that's what America is all about. I think most people believe that. But it's those values of hard work and responsibility, everybody getting a fair share—everybody getting a fair shake and everybody doing their fair share and everybody playing by the same set of rules, that's what's at stake in this election.

And I'm absolutely confident we're going to win this thing. But the reason I'm confident is because of the people in this room. The reason I'm confident is because of the folks I meet out on the campaign trail. The reason I'm confident is I have extraordinary faith in the American people. And if we're working hard, if we've got as much passion and energy and focus as we did in 2008, we're going to win, because our vision of the country, I think, is more consistent with who we are and our history.

But we can't take it for granted. There are going to be a lot of headwinds. The economy is still in tough shape for a lot of people. And I am, as the most visible elected official in the land, rightly held more responsible than anybody else for things I control and for things I don't control. And that means that we're going to have to go out there and actively make the case.

So part of my message to all of you is, as wonderful as it is to be in this elegant setting with these elegant people, we're also going to have to hit the streets. And we're also going to have to persuade friends and family and coworkers and knock on doors and make phone calls and raise money.

And not all of it is going to be glamorous and not all of it is going to be elegant and not all of it is going to be fun. But things that are worthwhile are always hard. And change is hard, but you should take confidence from the last 3 years that change is possible.

And I promise you that one commitment I will make to you tonight is that I will work even harder this year than I did in 2008, and I'm even more passionate about this election. I'm more determined than I was in 2008 that we're going to win in 2012.

So thank you very much, everybody. Thank you.

NOTE: The President spoke at 8:04 p.m. at the residence of Spike and Tonya L. Lee. In his remarks, he referred to Jackson and Satchel Lee, children of Mr. and Mrs. Lee. Audio was not available for verification of the content of these remarks.

Remarks at an Obama Victory Fund 2012 Fundraiser in New York City
January 19, 2012

The President. Hello, New York! Hello, New York! Hello, Harlem! Oh, it is good to be here tonight!

Audience members. Four more years! Four more years! Four more years!

The President. All right.

Audience members. Four more years! Four more years! Four more years!

The President. Thank you. Thank you so much.

I want to begin by just thanking Ny for the incredible introduction and being such a great mom. And we're so proud of her. Thank you. I want to thank our emcee, Lin-Manuel Miranda. We appreciate you.

I want to thank the incredible performers this evening; one of my favorites, India Arie in the house. There she is. I love India.

And then, to know that Reverend Al Green was here——

[At this point, the President sang as follows.]

The President. "I"—*[applause]*—"so in love with you." *[Applause]*

You—those guys didn't think I would do it. I told you I was going to do it. *[Laughter]* The Sandman did not come out. I—now, don't worry, Rev, I cannot sing like you. But I did—I just wanted to show my appreciation. *[Laughter]*

I also want to acknowledge a couple of outstanding Members of Congress with us here today: Congressman Charlie Rangel and Congressman Jerry Nadler are in the house.

All right, you guys, have a seat. I've got something to say.

Audience member. Thank you, Mr. President.

The President. Thank you. No, thank you. Because I am here tonight not just because I need your help, I'm here because your country needs your help.

There was a reason why so many of you got involved in the campaign in 2008, worked your hearts out. And it wasn't because you thought it was going to be easy. When you decide to support somebody named Barack Hussein Obama for President, you're not doing it because you think it's a cakewalk. *[Laughter]*

You did it because you understood the campaign wasn't about me. It was about a vision that we shared for America. A vision that wasn't narrow and cramped. It wasn't an idea that in America you just look out for yourself and the most powerful among us can just play by their own rules. It was a vision that was big and compassionate and bold, and it said, in America, if you work hard, you've got a chance. You've got a chance to get ahead. Doesn't matter where you were born. It doesn't matter what you look like. It doesn't matter what your name is. If you're willing to work hard, if

you've got some talent, some idea, if you're motivated, you can make it.

And it was a vision that said we're greater together than we are on our own, that when everybody gets a fair shot and everybody does their fair share and everybody's playing by the same set of rules, then we all do better. We all do better.

That's the vision we shared. That was the change we believed in. And we knew it wasn't going to come easy. We knew it wouldn't come quickly. We knew there would be resistance. We knew there would be setbacks. But because of what you did in 2008, we've started to see concrete examples of that change.

Think about it. Change is the first bill I signed into law that enshrines a very simple proposition: You get an equal day's pay for an equal's day work, because we want our daughters treated just as well as our sons. That's what change is.

Change is the decision we made to rescue the auto industry from collapse, even when there were folks saying no and wanted to let Detroit go bankrupt. And now, 1 million jobs were saved and local businesses have picked up again and GM is once again the largest auto company in the world. And we are seeing cars rolling off those assembly lines stamped with three proud words: Made in America.

Change is the decision we made to stop waiting for Congress to do something about our oil addiction and finally raised our fuel efficiency standards on our cars so that by the next decade, every car is going to be getting 55 miles per gallon. That will save you money. That will save our environment. It's good for our national security. That's what change is. We got that done.

Change was the fight that we had to stop sending $60 billion in unnecessary subsidies to the banks in the student loan program, take that $60 billion out, give it directly to the students so that millions of young people all across America are able to afford a college education. That's change.

Change is the health care reform bill that we passed after a century of trying that says, if you get sick in America, you will not go bankrupt.

And we've already got 2½ million young people with health insurance who didn't have it and seniors getting help on their prescription drugs. And Americans won't be denied coverage because of preexisting conditions or insurance companies dropping them right when they need the care most. That's what change is.

Change is the fact that for the first time in our history, you don't have to hide who you love in order to serve this country that you love. "Don't ask, don't tell" is over. We don't believe in discrimination in this country. That's part of who we are. That's what change is.

And change is keeping one of the first promises I made in 2008. We ended the war in Iraq, and we brought our troops home. And in the meantime, we refocused our efforts on the terrorists who actually attacked us on 9/11. And thanks to the extraordinary men and women in our—in uniform and our intelligence agencies, Al Qaida is weaker than it's ever been and Usama bin Laden will never walk this Earth again. That's what change is.

Now, you guys have been paying attention. None of this has been easy. Some of it was risky. We were opposed by lobbyists and special interests. Millions of dollars were spent trying to maintain the status quo. And a lot of the things we did weren't always popular at the time, certainly not with the crowd in Washington.

But part of the reason we were able to get it done is because of you, because I knew that all across America your voices were still being heard. You guys were still knocking on doors. You were making phone calls. You were rooting for us, because you understood that as hard as this was, it was consistent with the vision that we campaigned so hard to bring about.

You kept up the fight long after the election was over. And that should make you proud. And it should make you hopeful. It shouldn't make you complacent, it shouldn't make you satisfied, because everything we did over the last 3 years is now at stake in this election. The very core of what this country stands for, that idea that no matter who you are, you can make it, that idea that we're all in it together, the idea that if there's a child somewhere who's

not getting a good education, that affects me, the idea that if there's a senior somewhere losing her home, that affects me, that idea is at stake in this election.

The crisis that struck in the months before I took office put more Americans out of work than any time since the Great Depression. We've got a chart that shows in the months right before I took office, 4 million jobs lost; the months right after I took office, another 4 million, before our economic policies had a chance to take effect.

We've been growing ever since. We've been adding jobs ever since. But this was a profound crisis. But it was also a culmination of a decade where middle class families fell further and further behind and more and more good jobs, manufacturing jobs, left our shores. And suddenly, our prosperity was built on risky financial deals or homes we couldn't afford or everybody running up their credit cards. And we racked up greater and greater debt, and incomes fell, and wages flatlined, and the cost of everything from college to health care to food went through the roof.

These problems didn't happen overnight; we weren't going to solve them overnight. It's going to take more than a few years to meet the challenges that have been decades in the making. The American people understand that. What they don't understand is leaders who refuse to take action. They're sick and tired of watching people who are supposed to represent them put party ahead of country or the next election before the next generation.

President Kennedy had a—once said, after he took office, he said, the thing that surprised him most about Washington was that it was as bad as he had been saying it was. [*Laughter*] I can relate to that. [*Laughter*] You've got the top Republican in the Senate who said his top priority was beating me. [*Laughter*] That's his top priority.

My top priority is putting Americans back to work. My top priority is making sure our kids are getting a good education. My top priority is making sure that everybody has affordable, accessible health care.

His top priority is beating me. That shows you things aren't in—on the level. That's how you end up with the Republicans in Congress voting against proposals that they used to support.

You saw them in December all tied up in knots because we were proposing tax cuts for workers and small businesses, and they always said they were the party of tax cuts. Suddenly—[*laughter*]—didn't know what to do. Proposals to rebuild roads and bridges, that didn't used to be a Democratic issue. It used to be we understood building America was good for America—putting cops and teachers back to work, back in the classroom, back on the streets. They will fight with everything they have to protect tax cuts for me, for the wealthiest Americans, and then suddenly, they get confused when it comes to tax cuts for the middle class.

Now, maybe they thought this was smart political strategy. Maybe they thought it would advance Mitch McConnell's agenda to beat me. But it's not a strategy to create jobs. It's not a strategy to strengthen our middle class. It's not a strategy to help America succeed.

So we've got a choice this year. It's—we have not seen a choice this stark in years. I mean, even in 2008, the Republican nominee wasn't a climate change denier. [*Laughter*] He was in favor of immigration reform. He was opposed to torture. [*Laughter*]

The contrast this year could not be sharper. So the question is not whether people are still hurting; people are still hurting profoundly. A lot of folks out there still out of work looking for work. The question is, what do we do about it? The debate that we need to have in this election is about where do we go from here.

The Republicans in Congress, the candidates running for President, they've got a very specific idea about where they want to take this country. They want to reduce—[*laughter*]—they want to reduce the deficit by gutting our investments in education, by gutting our investments in research and technology, by letting our roads and our bridges and our airports deteriorate.

I've already signed a trillion dollars' worth of spending cuts, proposed even more. And I think it's time for us to reduce the deficit by asking those of us who are most fortunate to pay their fair share—to pay their fair share.

And by the way, let me just say this, because I've been hearing a lot of these Republicans talking about, oh, that's class warfare, and he just wants to redistribute and doesn't believe in work, and he's trying to create an entitlement society, and this and that and the other. Let me be absolutely clear: I should pay more taxes and folks in my income bracket should pay more taxes and certainly folks who are making billions of dollars should pay more taxes not because I want to take their money and just give it to somebody else. It's because we've got basic investments and basic functions that have to be carried out in this 21st century if we're going to be able to compete.

We're going to have to train our young people so that they can get the high-skilled jobs of the future. We're going to have to make sure that we've got the best broadband lines and the best infrastructure to move products and services. We're going to have to make sure that we have the basic science and technology research that allows us to stay on the cutting edge of innovation, because other countries are making these investments and they're catching up.

And if we are going to do all that without leaving a mountain of debt for our kids, while still maintaining the strongest military on Earth, while still making sure that Social Security and Medicare are there for future generations, that our seniors are protected, then all of us have to do our part.

That is—should not be a Democratic idea or a Republican idea. That should be an American idea. It's about responsibility. It's about taking responsibility for the country. And when all of us take responsibility, we all do better. That's the idea.

The Republicans in Congress and on the campaign trail, these guys running for President—[*laughter*]—want to—why do you laugh? They're running for President. [*Laughter*] They are. And they want to take Medicare and make it a form of private insurance, of—so that seniors shop around with a voucher, even if it doesn't cover the costs of their medicine or their care.

Now, I think that we can lower the cost—we have to lower the cost of Medicare with reforms that still guarantee a dignified retirement for seniors, because they've earned it. These folks act like this is an entitlement that was unearned. Folks paid into this system. They worked hard to have some sense of security. Our reforms should reflect that.

They think the best way for America to compete for new jobs and businesses is to follow other countries in a race to the bottom. So they say, well, look, if—China lets you pay low wages, so they want to roll back our minimum wage or our right to collectively bargain. They say, well, if companies can pollute in some of these other countries, so they want to get rid of protections that ensure we have clean air and clean water.

Look, we should not have any more regulation than is required for the health and safety of the American people. Nobody likes redtape. Nobody likes bureaucracy. That's why I actually—I've reformed Government so that we initiated fewer regulations than the previous administration, with a lot more benefit, much lower costs relative to the benefits, looking to streamline Government. We're saving businesses billions of dollars in reduced paperwork. So we are not interested in regulation for regulation's sake. But I do not believe in this notion that we should have a race to the bottom. That shouldn't be what we're competing for.

We should be competing to win that race to the top. We should be competing to make our schools the best in the world. We should be competing to make sure that our workers have the best skills and the best training so they get the best pay. We should be making sure that college is within reach of everybody.

We should be in a race to give our businesses the best roads and airports. We should be in a race to support the scientists and the researchers that create the next clean energy breakthrough or the medicine that might cure pernicious diseases. We should be in a race to make sure that the next generation of manufacturing doesn't take root in Asia or in Germany, but takes root in Detroit and in Pittsburgh and in Cleveland and in New York. I don't want this to be a nation that just buys and consumes and borrows. I want us to be known for building and selling all over the world.

And that's a race—this competition for middle class security, for advanced technology, for having the best workers in the world—this is a race I know we can win. But America is not going to win if we do the same things, if we respond to our economic challenges with the same old, tired "cut taxes for wealthy people, let companies do whatever they want even if it's harming other folks, and somehow prosperity is going to trickle down to everybody else."

Look, we tried that. [*Laughter*] I don't know if you remember, but we tried that. It never worked. It didn't work when it was tried in the decade before the Great Depression. It's not what led to the incredible boom in the fifties and the sixties that created the greatest middle class on Earth. It did not work back in 2001 and 2 and 3 and 4 and 5 and 6—[*laughter*]—where we had the slowest job growth of any decade.

We can't go back to this brand of you're-on-your-own economics. I believe we've got a stake in everybody's success. If we can attract outstanding teachers by giving her the pay and the support and the training she deserves, she is going to educate the next Steve Jobs. And not only will we have whatever the next iPad is, but we'll also all see the economy grow.

If we provide faster Internet service to some rural business somewhere and now suddenly they have access to the entire global market, or some business right here in Harlem that's selling something that previously they could only sell in a few blocks and now they can sell it anywhere, that means suddenly they can start hiring more workers. They've got customers now all over the world. Countries will do better—our whole country will do better.

This is not a Democratic idea or a Republican idea. Abraham Lincoln, first Republican President, he understood this, launched the transcontinental railroad, the National Academy of Scientists—or of Sciences, the first land-grant college, all while dealing with a Civil War—a Republican.

Teddy Roosevelt called for a progressive income tax, because he understood that you can't pretend you're for equality of opportunity when you have huge inequality and you're not creating ladders for success for people—a Republican.

Dwight Eisenhower built the Interstate Highway System, invested in math and science education so we could compete in the race to space—Republican.

There were Republicans in Congress that supported FDR giving millions of returning heroes, including my grandfather, the chance to go college on the GI bill. That idea is as old as this country.

And you know, that idea, it's still there. That sense of common purpose, it's still there. We tapped into it in 2008, and it's still out there all across the country. I see it everywhere I go. It may not be in Washington, it may not be in Congress, but it's out there. You talk to folks on Main Streets, town halls, VFW halls, barbershops, they understand this. Our politics may be divided, but people understand we're all in this together. They understand that no matter who we are, we rise or fall as one Nation and as one people.

And that's what's at stake right now. That's what this election is about.

Now, I know these have been 3 tough years. I know that some of the change folks wanted hasn't come as fast as people hoped for. I know that after all the stuff that has gone on in Washington, it's tempting sometimes to just say, you know what, it's not possible, the system's broken, we give up. That's tempting. But remember what I used to say in the last campaign. I said this—I repeated it over and over again: Real change, big change, it's hard. It takes time. It takes more than a single term. It takes more than a single President.

What it takes is ordinary citizens like you who just keep on fighting, keep pushing, keep inching the country closer and closer and closer to our ideals. That's how the greatest gener-

ation defeated fascism and yanked us out of a great depression and built the largest middle class in history. That's how young people from every background were able to suffer billy clubs and firehoses to ensure that our children grew up in a country where your race is no barrier to what you can become.

I mean, change is hard, but we know it's possible. We've seen it. I've lived it. I've lived it. I've seen it.

And so, as we go into this election year, I want everybody to understand, yes, my hair is grayer, yes, we've got some dings and some dents, and yes, this financial crisis has been a wakeup call. But you know what, there is no other country that doesn't envy our position. They understand that this country is still that last, best hope. And they are counting—the world is counting and our fellow citizens are counting on us not giving up, not giving in to despair.

If you want to end the cynicism and the game-playing and the point-scoring and the sound bites that pass for politics these days, then you've got to send a message this year, starting right now, that you refuse to back down, that you will not give up, that you intend to keep hoping and keep pushing and keep fighting just as hard as you did 4 years ago. You are going to keep believing in change.

And if you are willing to do that, if you are going to work just as hard, if you're able to generate that same passion and commitment, then I'll be there next to you. Because I've often said—I said in 2008, I'm not a perfect man. I'm not a perfect President. But I promise you that I've kept that promise I made to you in 2008: I would always tell you what I thought, I would always tell you where I stood, and I would wake up every single day fighting as hard as I can for you.

I am just as determined now as I was then. And if you are willing to stand alongside me, we will knock those obstacles out of the way. We will reach for that vision of America that we believe in in our hearts, and change will come. If you will work harder than you did last time, change will come.

If you keep on believing, we'll finish what we started in 2008. Change will come. If you fight with me and press on with me, I promise you change will come. And we will remind everybody just why it is that the United States of America is the greatest nation on Earth.

Thank you. God bless you. God bless the United States of America.

NOTE: The President spoke at 9:56 p.m. at the Apollo Theater. In his remarks, he referred to Ny Whittaker, organizer, Obama for America; composer, lyricist, and actor Lin-Manuel Miranda; and Sen. John S. McCain III, in his capacity as the 2008 Republican Presidential nominee.

The President's Weekly Address
January 21, 2012

Hello, everybody. On Thursday, I went down to Florida to visit Disney World, and to Sasha and Malia's great disappointment, I was not there to hang out with Mickey or ride Space Mountain. Instead, I was there to talk about steps we're taking to boost tourism and create jobs.

Tourism is the number-one service we export. Every year, tens of millions of tourists come from all over the world to visit America. They stay in our hotels, eat at our restaurants, and see all the sights America has to offer.

That's good for local businesses. That's good for local economies. And the more folks who visit America, the more Americans we get back to work. It's that simple.

We can't wait to seize this opportunity. As I've said before, I will continue to work with Congress, States, and leaders in the private sector to find ways to move this country forward. But where they can't act or won't act, I will. Because we want the world to know that America is open for business. And that's why I announced steps we're taking to promote America and make it easier for tourists to come and visit.

Frequent travelers who pass an extensive background check will be able to scan their passports and fingerprints and skip long lines at immigration at more airports. We're going to expand the number of countries where visitors can get precleared by Homeland Security so they don't need a tourist visa. And we're going to speed up visa processing for countries with growing middle classes that can afford to visit America, countries like China and Brazil.

We want more visitors coming here. We want them spending money here. It's good for our economy, and it will help provide the boost more businesses need to grow and hire. And we can't wait to make it happen.

Too often over the last few months, we've seen Congress drag its feet and refuse to take steps we know will help strengthen our economy. That's why this is the latest in a series of actions I've taken on my own to help our economy keep growing, creating jobs, and restoring security for middle class families.

In September, we decided to stop waiting for Congress to fix No Child Left Behind and give States the flexibility they need to help our kids meet higher standards. We made sure that small businesses that have contracts with the Federal Government can get paid faster so they can start hiring more people. We made it easier for veterans to get jobs and put their skills to work. We took steps to help families whose home values have fallen refinance their mortgages and save up to thousands of dollars a year. We sped up the loan process for companies that want to rebuild our roads and bridges, putting construction workers back on the job. And I appointed Richard Cordray to be America's consumer watchdog and protect working Americans from the worst abuses of the financial industry.

These are all good steps. Now we need to do more.

On Tuesday evening, I'll deliver my State of the Union Address, where I'll lay out my blueprint for actions we need to take together—not just me, or Congress, but every American—to rebuild an economy where hard work and responsibility are rewarded, an economy that's built to last. I hope you'll tune in.

In the meantime, I'm going to keep doing everything I can to make this country not only the best place to visit and do business, but the best place to live and work and build a better life.

Thanks for watching, have a great weekend, and I'll see you on Tuesday.

NOTE: The address was recorded at approximately 1:55 p.m. on January 20 in the East Room at the White House for broadcast on January 21. In the address, the President referred to Richard A. Cordray, Director, Consumer Financial Protection Bureau. The transcript was made available by the Office of the Press Secretary on January 20, but was embargoed for release until 6 a.m. on January 21.

Statement on the 39th Anniversary of the Supreme Court Decision in *Roe* v. *Wade*
January 22, 2012

As we mark the 39th anniversary of *Roe* v. *Wade*, we must remember that this Supreme Court decision not only protects a woman's health and reproductive freedom, but also affirms a broader principle: that Government should not intrude on private family matters. I remain committed to protecting a woman's right to choose and this fundamental constitutional right. While this is a sensitive and often divisive issue, no matter what our views, we must stay united in our determination to prevent unintended pregnancies, support pregnant woman and mothers, reduce the need for abortion, encourage healthy relationships, and promote adoption. And as we remember this historic anniversary, we must also continue our efforts to ensure that our daughters have the same rights, freedoms, and opportunities as our sons to fulfill their dreams.

Statement on the Resignation of Representative Gabrielle D. Giffords
January 22, 2012

Gabby Giffords embodies the very best of what public service should be. She's universally admired for qualities that transcend party or ideology: a dedication to fairness, a willingness to listen to different ideas, and a tireless commitment to the work of perfecting our Union. That's why the people of Arizona chose Gabby: to speak and fight and stand up for them. That's what brought her to a supermarket in Tucson last year: so she could carry their hopes and concerns to Washington. And we know it is with the best interests of her constituents in mind that Gabby has made the tough decision to step down from Congress.

Over the last year, Gabby and her husband Mark have taught us the true meaning of hope in the face of despair, determination in the face of incredible odds, and now, even after she's come so far, Gabby shows us what it means to be selfless as well.

Gabby's cheerful presence will be missed in Washington. But she will remain an inspiration to all whose lives she touched—myself included. And I'm confident that we haven't seen the last of this extraordinary American.

NOTE: The statement referred to Mark E. Kelly, husband of Rep. Giffords.

Remarks Honoring the 2011 Stanley Cup Champion Boston Bruins
January 23, 2012

Hello, everybody! Thank you so much. Thank you. Everybody, please have a seat.

Well, I am happy to welcome the Stanley Cup champion Boston Bruins to the White House. I know you are all wicked happy to be here. [*Laughter*]

I know there are some Members of Congress, members of my Cabinet who are joining us today who are also pretty excited to see you. I understand we got Mayor Menino here. Where is he? There he is right in front of me. Great to see you.

The Bruins, the Sox, the Celtics, now the Patriots. [*Laughter*] Enough already, Boston. [*Laughter*] What's going on, huh?

Last year, this team endured a long season and even longer playoffs. They are the first team in NHL history to win three full seven-game series. They had some pretty long playoff beards to show it—to show for it. And I appreciate them looking a little more clean cut as they come here today. [*Laughter*]

These Bruins finally brought the Stanley Cup back to Causeway Street for the first time since 1972, when Bobby Orr was leading the team. And obviously, that was before most of the guys on this stage were born. [*Laughter*]

Now, Bobby Orr is obviously a hockey legend. He took the ice without a helmet, and kids, don't try that at home. He attacked every puck, and he lived by the motto, "Forget about style; worry about results."

Well, that's what this year's offense delivered: big-time results.

Brad Marchand went into the season playing on the fourth line, but "The Little Ball of Hate" shrugged off the rookie jitters and— [*laughter*]—what's up with that nickname, man?—[*laughter*]—scored five goals in the last five games of the finals series.

After two series-winning goals to lead the Bruins to the championships, Nathan Horton went down hard in game three of the finals. But that didn't stop him from doing everything he could to help his team win. He even brought some Boston water all the way to Van-

couver and poured it in the ice before decisive game seven. So Beantown delivered.

And there is no better image of the Bruins dominance than the tallest player in NHL history—I'll let you guess which one that is— [*laughter*]—Zdeno Chara, hoisting the cup above the ice in Vancouver, which is, I'm sure, the highest that the Stanley Cup had ever been. [*Laughter*]

This Stanley Cup was won by defense as much as by offense. Tim Thomas posted two shutouts in the Stanley Cup's finals, set an all-time record for saves in the postseason. He also earned the honor of being only the second American ever to be recognized as the Stanley Cup's Playoffs MVP.

And together, these players proved that teamwork is everything. It can overcome injuries, it can overcome long odds. The wise old man of the team, Mark Recchi, summed up the season by saying, "We played together, we drank together"—how much did you drink?— [*laughter*]—"we lost together, and we never wavered."

I know that loyalty is important in Boston, which is why the Boston Bruins Foundation has raised and donated more than $7 million in charitable contributions for organizations all across New England.

I want to thank them for bringing their spirit of service to Washington. They led a hockey clinic at the Boys and Girls Club—or they're going to do that later this afternoon.

These Bruins understand that winning the Stanley Cup is more than just men on ice. It's about the people that stand behind them. And that's why, since the last buzzer sounded in June, the Bruins have been taking their Cup all over the world to share it with their fans.

Zdeno invited his mailman to check it out, wheeled it around town in a baby carriage. [*Laughter*] Coach Julien's daughter ate her morning Cheerios out of it. [*Laughter*] That's pretty cool. The Cup has traveled from the back of a duck boat in the streets of Boston to the greens of Pebble Beach and from a sauna in Finland to a Slovakian castle. Dennis Seidenberg even brought it to his son's [daughters']° christening.

Under the leadership of owner Jeremy Jacobs and Coach Julien, this team has shown a commitment to the game and to each other that is a testament to them, but obviously also a testament to fans who cheer for the black and gold all around the world. They know that being a champion doesn't end when you hang up your skates at the end of practice or at the end of the season. And the new banner that hangs from the rafters of the Garden commemorates the place that they have earned in history.

And I know that the season is heating up again, so I don't want to be too long. I just want to make sure that I wish everybody good luck on the ice tomorrow night and during the rest of the season as well.

Congratulations, gentlemen. Great job. All right.

NOTE: The President spoke at 1:45 p.m. in the East Room at the White House. In his remarks, he referred to Mayor Thomas M. Menino of Boston, MA; Robert G. Orr, former defenseman, Brad Marchand, left wing, Nathan Horton, right wing, Zdeno Chara, defenseman, Tim Thomas, goaltender, Mark Recchi, former right wing, Claude Julien, head coach, and Dennis Seidenberg, defenseman, Boston Bruins; Katryna C. Julien, daughter of Mr. Julien; and Story and Noah Grace Seidenberg, daughters of Mr. Seidenberg.

Statement on the European Union's Sanctions Against Iran
January 23, 2012

I applaud today's actions by our partners in the European Union to impose additional sanctions on Iran in response to the regime's continuing failure to fulfill its international obligations regarding its nuclear program. These sanctions demonstrate once more the unity of the international community in addressing the serious threat presented by Iran's nuclear program. The United States will continue to impose new sanctions to increase the pressure on Iran. On December 31, I signed into law a new set of sanctions targeting Iran's Central Bank and its oil revenues. Today the Treasury Department announced new sanctions on Bank Tejerat for its facilitation of proliferation, and we will continue to increase the pressure unless Iran acts to change course and comply with its international obligations.

Address Before a Joint Session of the Congress on the State of the Union
January 24, 2012

Mr. Speaker, Mr. Vice President, Members of Congress, distinguished guests, and fellow Americans: Last month, I went to Andrews Air Force Base and welcomed home some of our last troops to serve in Iraq. Together, we offered a final, proud salute to the colors under which more than a million of our fellow citizens fought and several thousand gave their lives.

We gather tonight knowing that this generation of heroes has made the United States safer and more respected around the world. For the first time in 9 years, there are no Americans fighting in Iraq. For the first time in two decades, Usama bin Laden is not a threat to this country. Most of Al Qaida's top lieutenants have been defeated. The Taliban's momentum has been broken, and some troops in Afghanistan have begun to come home.

These achievements are a testament to the courage, selflessness, and teamwork of America's Armed Forces. At a time when too many of our institutions have let us down, they exceed all expectations. They're not consumed with

---

° White House correction.

personal ambition. They don't obsess over their differences. They focus on the mission at hand. They work together.

Imagine what we could accomplish if we followed their example. Think about the America within our reach: a country that leads the world in educating its people; an America that attracts a new generation of high-tech manufacturing and high-paying jobs; a future where we're in control of our own energy and our security and prosperity aren't so tied to unstable parts of the world; an economy built to last, where hard work pays off and responsibility is rewarded.

We can do this. I know we can, because we've done it before. At the end of World War II, when another generation of heroes returned home from combat, they built the strongest economy and middle class the world has ever known. My grandfather, a veteran of Patton's army, got the chance to go to college on the GI bill. My grandmother, who worked on a bomber assembly line, was part of a workforce that turned out the best products on Earth.

The two of them shared the optimism of a nation that had triumphed over a depression and fascism. They understood they were part of something larger, that they were contributing to a story of success that every American had a chance to share, the basic American promise that if you worked hard, you could do well enough to raise a family, own a home, send your kids to college, and put a little away for retirement.

The defining issue of our time is how to keep that promise alive. No challenge is more urgent. No debate is more important. We can either settle for a country where a shrinking number of people do really well while a growing number of Americans barely get by, or we can restore an economy where everyone gets a fair shot and everyone does their fair share and everyone plays by the same set of rules. What's at stake aren't Democratic values or Republican values, but American values. And we have to reclaim them.

Let's remember how we got here. Long before the recession, jobs and manufacturing began leaving our shores. Technology made businesses more efficient, but also made some jobs obsolete. Folks at the top saw their incomes rise like never before, but most hard-working Americans struggled with costs that were growing, paychecks that weren't, and personal debt that kept piling up.

In 2008, the house of cards collapsed. We learned that mortgages had been sold to people who couldn't afford or understand them. Banks had made huge bets and bonuses with other people's money. Regulators had looked the other way or didn't have the authority to stop the bad behavior.

It was wrong, it was irresponsible, and it plunged our economy into a crisis that put millions out of work, saddled us with more debt, and left innocent, hard-working Americans holding the bag. In the 6 months before I took office, we lost nearly 4 million jobs. And we lost another 4 million before our policies were in full effect.

Those are the facts. But so are these: In the last 22 months, businesses have created more than 3 million jobs. Last year, they created the most jobs since 2005. American manufacturers are hiring again, creating jobs for the first time since the late 1990s. Together, we've agreed to cut the deficit by more than $2 trillion. And we've put in place new rules to hold Wall Street accountable so a crisis like this never happens again.

The state of our Union is getting stronger. And we've come too far to turn back now. As long as I'm President, I will work with anyone in this Chamber to build on this momentum. But I intend to fight obstruction with action, and I will oppose any effort to return to the very same policies that brought on this economic crisis in the first place.

No, we will not go back to an economy weakened by outsourcing, bad debt, and phony financial profits. Tonight I want to speak about how we move forward and lay out a blueprint for an economy that's built to last, an economy built on American manufacturing, American energy, skills for American workers, and a renewal of American values.

Now, this blueprint begins with American manufacturing.

On the day I took office, our auto industry was on the verge of collapse. Some even said we should let it die. With a million jobs at stake, I refused to let that happen. In exchange for help, we demanded responsibility. We got workers and automakers to settle their differences. We got the industry to retool and restructure. Today, General Motors is back on top as the world's number-one automaker. Chrysler has grown faster in the U.S. than any major car company. Ford is investing billions in U.S. plants and factories. And together, the entire industry added nearly 160,000 jobs.

We bet on American workers. We bet on American ingenuity. And tonight, the American auto industry is back.

What's happening in Detroit can happen in other industries. It can happen in Cleveland and Pittsburgh and Raleigh. We can't bring every job back that's left our shore. But right now it's getting more expensive to do business in places like China. Meanwhile, America is more productive. A few weeks ago, the CEO of Master Lock told me that it now makes business sense for him to bring jobs back home. Today, for the first time in 15 years, Master Lock's unionized plant in Milwaukee is running at full capacity.

So we have a huge opportunity at this moment to bring manufacturing back. But we have to seize it. Tonight my message to business leaders is simple: Ask yourselves what you can do to bring jobs back to your country, and your country will do everything we can to help you succeed.

We should start with our Tax Code. Right now companies get tax breaks for moving jobs and profits overseas. Meanwhile, companies that choose to stay in America get hit with one of the highest tax rates in the world. It makes no sense, and everyone knows it. So let's change it.

First, if you're a business that wants to outsource jobs, you shouldn't get a tax deduction for doing it. That money should be used to cover moving expenses for companies like Master Lock that decide to bring jobs home.

Second, no American company should be able to avoid paying its fair share of taxes by moving jobs and profits overseas. From now on, every multinational company should have to pay a basic minimum tax. And every penny should go towards lowering taxes for companies that choose to stay here and hire here in America.

Third, if you're an American manufacturer, you should get a bigger tax cut. If you're a high-tech manufacturer, we should double the tax deduction you get for making your products here. And if you want to relocate in a community that was hit hard when a factory left town, you should get help financing a new plant, equipment, or training for new workers.

So my message is simple: It is time to stop rewarding businesses that ship jobs overseas and start rewarding companies that create jobs right here in America. Send me these tax reforms, and I will sign them right away.

We're also making it easier for American businesses to sell products all over the world. Two years ago, I set a goal of doubling U.S. exports over 5 years. With the bipartisan trade agreements we signed into law, we're on track to meet that goal ahead of schedule. And soon there will be millions of new customers for American goods in Panama, Colombia, and South Korea. Soon there will be new cars on the streets of Seoul imported from Detroit and Toledo and Chicago.

I will go anywhere in the world to open new markets for American products. And I will not stand by when our competitors don't play by the rules. We've brought trade cases against China at nearly twice the rate as the last administration, and it's made a difference. Over a thousand Americans are working today because we stopped a surge in Chinese tires. But we need to do more. It's not right when another country lets our movies, music, and software be pirated. It's not fair when foreign manufacturers have a leg up on ours only because they're heavily subsidized.

Tonight I'm announcing the creation of a trade enforcement unit that will be charged with investigating unfair trading practices in countries like China. There will be more inspections to prevent counterfeit or unsafe goods from crossing our borders. And this Congress should make sure that no foreign company has an advantage over American manufacturing when it comes to accessing financing or new markets like Russia. Our workers are the most productive on Earth, and if the playing field is level, I promise you, America will always win.

I also hear from many business leaders who want to hire in the United States, but can't find workers with the right skills. Growing industries in science and technology have twice as many openings as we have workers who can do the job. Think about that: openings at a time when millions of Americans are looking for work. It's inexcusable, and we know how to fix it.

Jackie Bray is a single mom from North Carolina who was laid off from her job as a mechanic. Then, Siemens opened a gas turbine factory in Charlotte and formed a partnership with Central Piedmont Community College. The company helped the college design courses in laser and robotics training. It paid Jackie's tuition, then hired her to help operate their plant.

I want every American looking for work to have the same opportunity as Jackie did. Join me in a national commitment to train 2 million Americans with skills that will lead directly to a job. My administration has already lined up more companies that want to help. Model partnerships between businesses like Siemens and community colleges in places like Charlotte and Orlando and Louisville are up and running. Now you need to give more community colleges the resources they need to become community career centers, places that teach people skills that businesses are looking for right now, from data management to high-tech manufacturing.

And I want to cut through the maze of confusing training programs so that from now on, people like Jackie have one program, one website, and one place to go for all the information and help that they need. It is time to turn our unemployment system into a reemployment system that puts people to work.

These reforms will help people get jobs that are open today. But to prepare for the jobs of tomorrow, our commitment to skills and education has to start earlier.

For less than 1 percent of what our Nation spends on education each year, we've convinced nearly every State in the country to raise their standards for teaching and learning, the first time that's happened in a generation. But challenges remain, and we know how to solve them.

At a time when other countries are doubling down on education, tight budgets have forced States to lay off thousands of teachers. We know a good teacher can increase the lifetime income of a classroom by over $250,000. A great teacher can offer an escape from poverty to the child who dreams beyond his circumstance. Every person in this Chamber can point to a teacher who changed the trajectory of their lives. Most teachers work tirelessly, with modest pay, sometimes digging into their own pocket for school supplies, just to make a difference.

Teachers matter. So, instead of bashing them or defending the status quo, let's offer schools a deal. Give them the resources to keep good teachers on the job and reward the best ones. And in return, grant schools flexibility to teach with creativity and passion, to stop teaching to the test, and to replace teachers who just aren't helping kids learn. That's a bargain worth making.

We also know that when students don't walk away from their education, more of them walk the stage to get their diploma. When students are not allowed to drop out, they do better. So tonight I am proposing that every State—every State—requires that all students stay in high school until they graduate or turn 18.

When kids do graduate, the most daunting challenge can be the cost of college. At a time when Americans owe more in tuition debt than credit card debt, this Congress needs to stop the interest rates on student loans from doubling in July.

Extend the tuition tax credit we started that saves millions of middle class families thousands of dollars, and give more young people the chance to earn their way through college by doubling the number of work-study jobs in the next 5 years.

Of course, it's not enough for us to increase student aid. We can't just keep subsidizing skyrocketing tuition; we'll run out of money. States also need to do their part by making higher education a higher priority in their budgets. And colleges and universities have to do their part by working to keep costs down.

Recently, I spoke with a group of college presidents who have done just that. Some schools redesign courses to help students finish more quickly. Some use better technology. The point is, it's possible. So let me put colleges and universities on notice: If you can't stop tuition from going up, the funding you get from taxpayers will go down. Higher education can't be a luxury. It is an economic imperative that every family in America should be able to afford.

Let's also remember that hundreds of thousands of talented, hard-working students in this country face another challenge: the fact that they aren't yet American citizens. Many were brought here as small children, are American through and through, yet they live every day with the threat of deportation. Others came more recently, to study business and science and engineering, but as soon as they get their degree, we send them home to invent new products and create new jobs somewhere else. That doesn't make sense.

I believe as strongly as ever that we should take on illegal immigration. That's why my administration has put more boots on the border than ever before. That's why there are fewer illegal crossings than when I took office. The opponents of action are out of excuses. We should be working on comprehensive immigration reform right now.

But if election-year politics keeps Congress from acting on a comprehensive plan, let's at least agree to stop expelling responsible young people who want to staff our labs, start new businesses, defend this country. Send me a law that gives them the chance to earn their citizenship. I will sign it right away.

You see, an economy built to last is one where we encourage the talent and ingenuity of every person in this country. That means women should earn equal pay for equal work. It means we should support everyone who's willing to work and every risk taker and entrepreneur who aspires to become the next Steve Jobs.

After all, innovation is what America has always been about. Most new jobs are created in startups and small businesses. So let's pass an agenda that helps them succeed. Tear down regulations that prevent aspiring entrepreneurs from getting the financing to grow. Expand tax relief to small businesses that are raising wages and creating good jobs. Both parties agree on these ideas. So put them in a bill and get it on my desk this year.

Innovation also demands basic research. Today, the discoveries taking place in our federally financed labs and universities could lead to new treatments that kill cancer cells but leave healthy ones untouched, new lightweight vests for cops and soldiers that can stop any bullet. Don't gut these investments in our budget. Don't let other countries win the race for the future. Support the same kind of research and innovation that led to the computer chip and the Internet, to new American jobs and new American industries.

And nowhere is the promise of innovation greater than in American-made energy. Over the last 3 years, we've opened millions of new acres for oil and gas exploration, and tonight I'm directing my administration to open more than 75 percent of our potential offshore oil and gas resources. Right now—right now—American oil production is the highest that it's been in 8 years. That's right, 8 years. Not only that, last year, we relied less on foreign oil than in any of the past 16 years.

But with only 2 percent of the world's oil reserves, oil isn't enough. This country needs an all-out, all-of-the-above strategy that develops every available source of American energy, a strategy that's cleaner, cheaper, and full of new jobs.

We have a supply of natural gas that can last America nearly 100 years. And my administration will take every possible action to safely develop this energy. Experts believe this will support more than 600,000 jobs by the end of the decade. And I'm requiring all companies that drill for gas on public lands to disclose the chemicals they use. Because America will develop this resource without putting the health and safety of our citizens at risk.

The development of natural gas will create jobs and power trucks and factories that are cleaner and cheaper, proving that we don't have to choose between our environment and our economy. And by the way, it was public research dollars, over the course of 30 years, that helped develop the technologies to extract all this natural gas out of shale rock, reminding us that Government support is critical in helping businesses get new energy ideas off the ground.

Now, what's true for natural gas is just as true for clean energy. In 3 years, our partnership with the private sector has already positioned America to be the world's leading manufacturer of high-tech batteries. Because of Federal investments, renewable energy use has nearly doubled, and thousands of Americans have jobs because of it.

When Bryan Ritterby was laid off from his job making furniture, he said he worried that at 55 no one would give him a second chance. But he found work at Energetx, a wind turbine manufacturer in Michigan. Before the recession, the factory only made luxury yachts. Today, it's hiring workers like Bryan, who said, "I'm proud to be working in the industry of the future."

Our experience with shale gas, our experience with natural gas, shows us that the payoffs on these public investments don't always come right away. Some technologies don't pan out, some companies fail. But I will not walk away from the promise of clean energy. I will not walk away from workers like Bryan. I will not cede the wind or solar or battery industry to China or Germany because we refuse to make the same commitment here.

We've subsidized oil companies for a century. That's long enough. It's time to end the taxpayer giveaways to an industry that rarely has

been more profitable and double down on a clean energy industry that never has been more promising. Pass clean energy tax credits. Create these jobs.

We can also spur energy innovation with new incentives. The differences in this Chamber may be too deep right now to pass a comprehensive plan to fight climate change. But there's no reason why Congress shouldn't at least set a clean energy standard that creates a market for innovation. So far, you haven't acted. Well, tonight I will. I'm directing my administration to allow the development of clean energy on enough public land to power 3 million homes. And I'm proud to announce that the Department of Defense, working with us, the world's largest consumer of energy, will make one of the largest commitments to clean energy in history, with the Navy purchasing enough capacity to power a quarter of a million homes a year.

Of course, the easiest way to save money is to waste less energy. So here's a proposal: Help manufacturers eliminate energy waste in their factories and give businesses incentives to upgrade their buildings. Their energy bills will be a hundred billion dollars lower over the next decade, and America will have less pollution, more manufacturing, more jobs for construction workers who need them. Send me a bill that creates these jobs.

Building this new energy future should be just one part of a broader agenda to repair America's infrastructure. So much of America needs to be rebuilt. We've got crumbling roads and bridges, a power grid that wastes too much energy, an incomplete high-speed broadband network that prevents a small-business owner in rural America from selling her products all over the world.

During the Great Depression, America built the Hoover Dam and the Golden Gate Bridge. After World War II, we connected our States with a system of highways. Democratic and Republican administrations invested in great projects that benefited everybody, from the workers who built them to the businesses that still use them today.

In the next few weeks, I will sign an Executive order clearing away the redtape that slows down too many construction projects. But you need to fund these projects. Take the money we're no longer spending at war, use half of it to pay down our debt, and use the rest to do some nation-building right here at home.

There's never been a better time to build, especially since the construction industry was one of the hardest hit when the housing bubble burst. Of course, construction workers weren't the only ones who were hurt. So were millions of innocent Americans who've seen their home values decline. And while Government can't fix the problem on its own, responsible homeowners shouldn't have to sit and wait for the housing market to hit bottom to get some relief.

And that's why I'm sending this Congress a plan that gives every responsible homeowner the chance to save about $3,000 a year on their mortgage by refinancing at historically low rates. No more redtape. No more runaround from the banks. A small fee on the largest financial institutions will ensure that it won't add to the deficit and will give those banks that were rescued by taxpayers a chance to repay a deficit of trust.

Let's never forget: Millions of Americans who work hard and play by the rules every day deserve a Government and a financial system that do the same. It's time to apply the same rules from top to bottom. No bailouts, no handouts, and no copouts. An America built to last insists on responsibility from everybody.

We've all paid the price for lenders who sold mortgages to people who couldn't afford them and buyers who knew they couldn't afford them. That's why we need smart regulations to prevent irresponsible behavior. Rules to prevent financial fraud or toxic dumping or faulty medical devices, these don't destroy the free market. They make the free market work better.

There's no question that some regulations are outdated, unnecessary, or too costly. In fact, I've approved fewer regulations in the first 3 years of my Presidency than my Republican predecessor did in his. I've ordered every Federal agency to eliminate rules that don't make sense. We've already announced over 500 reforms, and just a fraction of them will save business and citizens more than $10 billion over the next 5 years. We got rid of one rule from 40 years ago that could have forced some dairy farmers to spend $10,000 a year proving that they could contain a spill, because milk was somehow classified as an oil. With a rule like that, I guess it was worth crying over spilled milk. [*Laughter*]

Now, I'm confident a farmer can contain a milk spill without a Federal agency looking over his shoulder. Absolutely. But I will not back down from making sure an oil company can contain the kind of oil spill we saw in the Gulf 2 years ago. I will not back down from protecting our kids from mercury poisoning or making sure that our food is safe and our water is clean. I will not go back to the days when health insurance companies had unchecked power to cancel your policy, deny your coverage, or charge women differently than men.

And I will not go back to the days when Wall Street was allowed to play by its own set of rules. The new rules we passed restore what should be any financial system's core purpose: getting funding to entrepreneurs with the best ideas and getting loans to responsible families who want to buy a home or start a business or send their kids to college.

So, if you are a big bank or financial institution, you're no longer allowed to make risky bets with your customers' deposits. You're required to write out a "living will" that details exactly how you'll pay the bills if you fail, because the rest of us are not bailing you out ever again. And if you're a mortgage lender or a payday lender or a credit card company, the days of signing people up for products they can't afford with confusing forms and deceptive practices, those days are over. Today, American consumers finally have a watchdog in Richard Cordray, with one job: to look out for them.

We'll also establish a financial crimes unit of highly trained investigators to crack down on large-scale fraud and protect people's investments. Some financial firms violate major antifraud laws because there's no real penalty for being a repeat offender. That's bad for consumers, and it's bad for the vast majority of bankers and financial service professionals who do the right thing. So pass legislation that makes the penalties for fraud count.

And tonight I'm asking my Attorney General to create a special unit of Federal prosecutors and leading State attorney general to expand our investigations into the abusive lending and packaging of risky mortgages that led to the housing crisis. This new unit will hold accountable those who broke the law, speed assistance to homeowners, and help turn the page on an era of recklessness that hurt so many Americans.

Now, a return to the American values of fair play and shared responsibility will help protect our people and our economy. But it should also guide us as we look to pay down our debt and invest in our future.

Right now our most immediate priority is stopping a tax hike on 160 million working Americans while the recovery is still fragile. People cannot afford losing $40 out of each paycheck this year. There are plenty of ways to get this done. So let's agree right here, right now. No side issues. No drama. Pass the payroll tax cut without delay. Let's get it done.

When it comes to the deficit, we've already agreed to more than $2 trillion in cuts and savings. But we need to do more, and that means making choices. Right now we're poised to spend nearly $1 trillion more on what was supposed to be a temporary tax break for the wealthiest 2 percent of Americans. Right now, because of loopholes and shelters in the Tax Code, a quarter of all millionaires pay lower tax rates than millions of middle class households. Right now Warren Buffett pays a lower tax rate than his secretary.

Do we want to keep these tax cuts for the wealthiest Americans? Or do we want to keep our investments in everything else, like education and medical research, a strong military and care for our veterans? Because if we're serious about paying down our debt, we can't do both.

The American people know what the right choice is. So do I. As I told the Speaker this summer, I'm prepared to make more reforms

that rein in the long-term costs of Medicare and Medicaid and strengthen Social Security, so long as those programs remain a guarantee of security for seniors. But in return, we need to change our Tax Code so that people like me, and an awful lot of Members of Congress, pay our fair share of taxes.

Tax reform should follow the Buffett rule. If you make more than a million dollars a year, you should not pay less than 30 percent in taxes. And my Republican friend Tom Coburn is right: Washington should stop subsidizing millionaires. In fact, if you're earning a million dollars a year, you shouldn't get special tax subsidies or deductions. On the other hand, if you make under $250,000 a year, like 98 percent of American families, your taxes shouldn't go up. You're the ones struggling with rising costs and stagnant wages. You're the ones who need relief.

Now, you can call this class warfare all you want. But asking a billionaire to pay at least as much as his secretary in taxes? Most Americans would call that common sense.

We don't begrudge financial success in this country. We admire it. When Americans talk about folks like me paying my fair share of taxes, it's not because they envy the rich. It's because they understand that when I get a tax break I don't need and the country can't afford, it either adds to the deficit or somebody else has to make up the difference, like a senior on a fixed income or a student trying to get through school or a family trying to make ends meet. That's not right. Americans know that's not right. They know that this generation's success is only possible because past generations felt a responsibility to each other and to the future of their country, and they know our way of life will only endure if we feel that same sense of shared responsibility. That's how we'll reduce our deficit. That's an America built to last.

Now, I recognize that people watching tonight have differing views about taxes and debt, energy and health care. But no matter what party they belong to, I bet most Americans are thinking the same thing right about now: Nothing will get done in Washington this year or next year or maybe even the year after that, because Washington is broken.

Can you blame them for feeling a little cynical?

The greatest blow to our confidence in our economy last year didn't come from events beyond our control. It came from a debate in Washington over whether the United States would pay its bills or not. Who benefited from that fiasco?

I've talked tonight about the deficit of trust between Main Street and Wall Street. But the divide between this city and the rest of the country is at least as bad, and it seems to get worse every year.

Now, some of this has to do with the corrosive influence of money in politics. So together, let's take some steps to fix that. Send me a bill that bans insider trading by Members of Congress. I will sign it tomorrow. Let's limit any elected official from owning stocks in industries they impact. Let's make sure people who bundle campaign contributions for Congress can't lobby Congress and vice versa, an idea that has bipartisan support, at least outside of Washington.

Some of what's broken has to do with the way Congress does its business these days. A simple majority is no longer enough to get anything—even routine business—passed through the Senate. Neither party has been blameless in these tactics. Now both parties should put an end to it. For starters, I ask the Senate to pass a simple rule that all judicial and public service nominations receive a simple up-or-down vote within 90 days.

The executive branch also needs to change. Too often, it's inefficient, outdated, and remote. That's why I've asked this Congress to grant me the authority to consolidate the Federal bureaucracy so that our Government is leaner, quicker, and more responsive to the needs of the American people.

Finally, none of this can happen unless we also lower the temperature in this town. We need to end the notion that the two parties must be locked in a perpetual campaign of mutual destruction, that politics is about clinging to rigid ideologies instead of building consensus around commonsense ideas.

I'm a Democrat, but I believe what Republican Abraham Lincoln believed: that Government should do for people only what they cannot do better by themselves and no more. That's why my education reform offers more competition and more control for schools and States. That's why we're getting rid of regulations that don't work. That's why our health care law relies on a reformed private market, not a Government program.

On the other hand, even my Republican friends who complain the most about Government spending have supported federally financed roads and clean energy projects and Federal offices for the folks back home.

The point is, we should all want a smarter, more effective Government. And while we may not be able to bridge our biggest philosophical differences this year, we can make real progress. With or without this Congress, I will keep taking actions that help the economy grow. But I can do a whole lot more with your help. Because when we act together, there's nothing the United States of America can't achieve.

That's the lesson we've learned from our actions abroad over the last few years. Ending the Iraq war has allowed us to strike decisive blows against our enemies. From Pakistan to Yemen, the Al Qaida operatives who remain are scrambling, knowing that they can't escape the reach of the United States of America.

From this position of strength, we've begun to wind down the war in Afghanistan. Ten thousand of our troops have come home. Twenty-three thousand more will leave by the end of this summer. This transition to Afghan lead will continue, and we will build an enduring partnership with Afghanistan so that it is never again a source of attacks against America.

As the tide of war recedes, a wave of change has washed across the Middle East and North Africa, from Tunis to Cairo, from Sana'a to Tripoli. A year ago, Qadhafi was one of the world's longest serving dictators, a murderer with American blood on his hands. Today, he is gone. And in Syria, I have no doubt that the Asad regime will soon discover that the forces of change cannot be reversed and that human dignity cannot be denied.

How this incredible transformation will end remains uncertain. But we have a huge stake in the outcome. And while it's ultimately up to the people of the region to decide their fate, we will advocate for those values that have served our own country so well. We will stand against violence and intimidation. We will stand for the rights and dignity of all human beings: men and women; Christians, Muslims, and Jews. We will support policies that lead to strong and stable democracies and open markets, because tyranny is no match for liberty.

And we will safeguard America's own security against those who threaten our citizens, our friends, and our interests. Look at Iran. Through the power of our diplomacy, a world that was once divided about how to deal with Iran's nuclear program now stands as one. The regime is more isolated than ever before. Its leaders are faced with crippling sanctions, and as long as they shirk their responsibilities, this pressure will not relent.

Let there be no doubt: America is determined to prevent Iran from getting a nuclear weapon, and I will take no options off the table to achieve that goal. But a peaceful resolution of this issue is still possible, and far better. And if Iran changes course and meets its obligations, it can rejoin the community of nations.

The renewal of American leadership can be felt across the globe. Our oldest alliances in Europe and Asia are stronger than ever. Our ties to the Americas are deeper. Our ironclad commitment—and I mean ironclad—to Israel's security has meant the closest military cooperation between our two countries in history.

We've made it clear that America is a Pacific power, and a new beginning in Burma has lit a new hope. From the coalitions we've built to secure nuclear materials to the missions we've led against hunger and disease, from the blows we've dealt to our enemies to the enduring power of our moral example, America is back.

Anyone who tells you otherwise, anyone who tells you that America is in decline or that our influence has waned, doesn't know what they're talking about. That's not the message we get from leaders around the world who are eager to work with us. That's not how people feel from Tokyo to Berlin, from Cape Town to Rio, where opinions of America are higher than they've been in years. Yes, the world is changing. No, we can't control every event. But America remains the one indispensable nation in world affairs, and as long as I'm President, I intend to keep it that way.

That's why, working with our military leaders, I've proposed a new defense strategy that ensures we maintain the finest military in the world, while saving nearly half a trillion dollars in our budget. To stay one step ahead of our adversaries, I've already sent this Congress legislation that will secure our country from the growing dangers of cyber threats.

Above all, our freedom endures because of the men and women in uniform who defend it. As they come home, we must serve them as well as they've served us. That includes giving them the care and the benefits they have earned, which is why we've increased annual VA spending every year I've been President. And it means enlisting our veterans in the work of rebuilding our Nation.

With the bipartisan support of this Congress, we're providing new tax credits to companies that hire vets. Michelle and Jill Biden have worked with American businesses to secure a pledge of 135,000 jobs for veterans and their families. And tonight I'm proposing a veterans jobs corps that will help our communities hire veterans as cops and firefighters, so that America is as strong as those who defend her.

Which brings me back to where I began. Those of us who've been sent here to serve can learn a thing or two from the service of our troops. When you put on that uniform, it doesn't matter if you're Black or White, Asian, Latino, Native American; conservative, liberal; rich, poor; gay, straight. When you're marching into battle, you look out for the person next to you or the mission fails. When you're in the thick of the fight, you rise or fall as one unit, serving one Nation, leaving no one behind.

You know, one of my proudest possessions is the flag that the SEAL team took with them on the mission to get bin Laden. On it are each of their names. Some may be Democrats, some may be Republicans, but that doesn't matter. Just like it didn't matter that day in the Situation Room, when I sat next to Bob Gates, a man who was George Bush's Defense Secretary, and Hillary Clinton, a woman who ran against me for President.

All that mattered that day was the mission. No one thought about politics. No one thought about themselves. One of the young men involved in the raid later told me that he didn't deserve credit for the mission. It only succeeded, he said, because every single member of that unit did their job: the pilot who landed the helicopter that spun out of control, the translator who kept others from entering the compound, the troops who separated the women and children from the fight, the SEALs who charged up the stairs. More than that, the mission only succeeded because every member of that unit trusted each other. Because you can't charge up those stairs into darkness and danger unless you know that there's somebody behind you, watching your back.

So it is with America. Each time I look at that flag, I'm reminded that our destiny is stitched together like those 50 stars and those 13 stripes. No one built this country on their own. This Nation is great because we built it together. This Nation is great because we worked as a team. This Nation is great because we get each other's backs. And if we hold fast to that truth, in this moment of trial, there is no challenge too great, no mission too hard. As long as we are joined in common purpose, as long as we maintain our common resolve, our journey moves forward, and our future is hopeful, and the state of our Union will always be strong.

Thank you, God bless you, and God bless the United States of America.

NOTE: The President spoke at 9:10 p.m. in the House Chamber of the U.S. Capitol. In his remarks, he referred to John Heppner, president and chief executive officer, Master Lock Co.; former President George W. Bush; Richard A. Cordray, Director, Consumer Financial Protection Bureau; Warren E. Buffett, chief executive officer and chairman, and Debbie Bosanek, assistant, Berkshire Hathaway Inc.; President Bashar al-Asad of Syria; and Jill T. Biden, wife of Vice President Joe Biden.

Remarks at Conveyor Engineering and Manufacturing in Cedar Rapids, Iowa
January 25, 2012

Thank you! Hello, Iowa! Hello, Cedar Rapids! All right. Thank you. Thank you, everybody. Please have a seat.

It is great to be back in Iowa, although it is a little colder here—[*laughter*]—than it was in Washington. I want to thank Jeff for the introduction. It's good to see your Governor, Governor Branstad, and Mayor Corbett, outstanding members of the congressional delegation, all kinds of good friends. In fact, this whole row here, if I start introducing them, it will make my speech twice as long, but I love these guys. And it is wonderful to be back here in Iowa.

I know there's been a lot of excitement here over the past couple of months. It kind of made me nostalgic. [*Laughter*] I used to have a

lot of fun here in Iowa. I remember a great backyard barbecue out in Marion way back in 2007. Good burgers. I did not have as much gray hair back then. [*Laughter*]

But when I think about all the days I spent in Iowa, so much of my Presidency, so much about what I care about, so much what I think about every day, has to do with the conversations that I had with you. People's backyards, VFW halls—those conversations I carry with me.

All across this State, in all 99 counties—and I was in, I think, just about every county—we talked about how for years the middle class was having a tougher time. Hard work had stopped paying off for too many people. Good jobs and manufacturing were leaving our shores.

Folks at the very, very top saw their incomes rise like never before, but most Americans, most folks in Iowa, were just trying to stay afloat. And that was before the financial crisis hit in 2008.

The crisis stuck—struck right at the end of a long campaign, but we didn't even understand at that point how bad that crisis was going to be. And millions of our neighbors were put out of work.

But we did know then what we know today: That when we come together as a country, there's no reason why we can't restore that basic American promise, that if you work hard, you can do well.

America is not about handouts. America is about earning everything you've got. But if you're willing to put in the work, the idea is that you should be able to raise a family and own a home, not go bankrupt because you got sick, because you've got some health insurance that helps you deal with those difficult times; that you can send your kids to college; that you can put some money away for retirement. That's all most people want.

Folks don't have unrealistic ambitions. They do believe that if they work hard, they should be able to achieve that small measure of an American Dream. That's what this country is about. That's what you deserve. That's what we talked about during the campaign.

Now today, 3 years after the worst economic storm in three generations, we are making progress. Our businesses have created more than 3 million jobs over the last 22 months. If you look at a job chart, if you look at a chart of what's happened in terms of jobs in America, we lost 4 million jobs before I took office, another 4 million in the few months right after I took office, before our economic policies had a chance to take effect, and we've been growing and increasing jobs ever since—3 million over the last 22 months. Last year, we created the most jobs since 2005. And today, American manufacturers like this one are hiring again, creating jobs for the first time since the 1990s. And that's good news.

Our economy is getting stronger. We've got a lot of work to do, but it's getting stronger. And we've come way too far to turn back now. After everything that's happened, there are people in Washington who seem to have collective amnesia. They seem to have forgotten how we got into this mess. They want to go back to the very same policies that got us into it, the same policies that have stacked the deck against middle class Americans for years.

And their philosophy, what there is of it, seems to be pretty simple: We're better off when everybody is left to fend for themselves and everybody can play by their own rules. And I'm here to say they're wrong. We're not going to go back to an economy weakened by outsourcing and bad debt and phony financial profits. That's not how America was built. We're not going to go back to that.

So last night in the State of the Union, I laid out my vision for how we move forward. I laid out a blueprint for an economy that is built to last.

It's an economy built on American manufacturing with more good jobs and more products made right here in the United States of America. It's an economy built on American energy, fueled by homegrown and alternative energy sources that make us more secure and less dependent on foreign oil. And by the way, there's a connection between those two things. This company right here, some of its key customers are folks who are active in alternative energy. There are jobs to be had—and Iowa knows all about it—when we are pursuing aggressively clean energy and alternative energy.

It's an economy built on the skills of American workers, getting people the education and the training they need so they're prepared for the jobs of today and they're ready to compete for the jobs of tomorrow.

And most importantly, it's an economy that's built on a renewal of American values, heartland values, values that Iowa knows something about: hard work, responsibility, and the same set of rules for everybody, from Main Street to Wall Street.

That has to be our future. That's how we restore that basic American promise. And it starts with manufacturing.

Look what happened in our auto industry. On the day I took office, it was on the verge of collapse. And some even said we should let it die. I've got the clips in case—[*laughter*]—because I remember. They were beating the heck out of me. "Why are you doing this? Why are you intervening?"

But we stood to lose a million jobs, not just in the auto industry, but all the suppliers, all the related businesses. So I refused to let that happen.

In exchange for help—see, keep in mind that the administration before us, they had been writing some checks to the auto industry with asking nothing in return. It was just a bailout, straightforward. We said we're going to do it differently.

In exchange for help, we also demanded responsibility from the auto industry. We got the industry to retool and to restructure. We got workers and management to get together, figure out how to make yourselves more efficient.

And over the past 2 years, that entire industry has added nearly 160,000 jobs. GM is number one in the world again. Ford is investing billions in new plants. Chrysler is growing faster. So today, the American auto industry is back.

And I want what's happening in Detroit to happen in other industries. I want it to happen in Cleveland and Pittsburgh and Raleigh. And I want it to happen right here in Cedar Rapids, Iowa.

Now, it's already happening at places like Conveyor. These folks make some big stuff. I just got a tour, a quick tour from Graig and Jeff, met some of the workers here, and they told me the story of how Conveyor started. Like so many other wonderful American companies, it started in a garage—couldn't make that up. Today, they employ 65 people, from engineers and welders to assembly-line workers and salespeople. They specialize in making augers, those giant screws, and they're used to mix and move everything from cement to choc-

olate. They don't use the same ones for—[*laughter*]—just in case you were wondering.

So Conveyor has doubled in size twice over the last 16 years, and over the next several years, they're hoping to double again.

See, right now we have a huge opportunity to help companies like this hire more workers, because what's—here's what's happening globally. Obviously, the economy had shifted all around the world. And we were getting more competition from other countries like China that were catching up and had very low wage rates. We had technology that was displacing a lot of workers. But here's what's going on: It's getting more expensive to do business in China now. Their wages are going up. Transportation costs to ship a big auger over here, it starts becoming cost prohibitive.

Meanwhile, America is getting more productive. We've become more efficient. We are as competitive as we've ever been. So, for a lot of companies, it's starting to make a lot more sense to bring jobs back home.

But we've got to seize that opportunity. We've got to help these companies succeed. And it starts with changing our Tax Code. [*Applause*] It starts with changing our Tax Code.

Now, right now companies get all kinds of tax breaks when they move jobs and profits overseas. Think about that. A company that chooses to stay in America gets hit with one of the highest tax rates in the world. That's wrong. It doesn't make sense. We've got to stop rewarding businesses that ship jobs overseas. Reward companies like Conveyor that are doing business right here in the United States of America.

Now, before the other side gets all excited, let me be clear: If you're a company that wants to outsource jobs or do business around the world, that's your right. It's a free market. But you shouldn't get a tax break for it. Companies that are bringing jobs back from overseas should get tax breaks. High-tech manufacturers should get tax breaks. Manufacturers like Conveyor that stamp products with three proud words: Made in America. Those are the folks who should be rewarded through our Tax Code.

Jeff and Graig told me that if we passed tax reforms like these, they'd be able to buy more equipment for their facility. So let's do it. Today my administration is laying out several concrete actions we could take right now to discourage outsourcing and encourage investing in America. You need to tell Congress to send me this tax reform plan. I will sign it right away.

We need to make it easier for American businesses to do business here in America, and we also need to make it easier for American businesses to sell our products other places in the world. I don't want to export our jobs; I want to export our goods and our services.

So, 2 years ago, I set a goal of doubling U.S. exports within 5 years. And by the way, Iowa, you should be interested that obviously a big chunk of those exports are also agricultural, which is doing wonders for this State's economy. The agricultural sector is doing very well. But I also want us to export manufacturing.

And we're on track to meet our goal of doubling exports. Actually we're ahead of schedule. Exports has been one of the strengths of this recovery. And soon, thanks to new trade agreements I've signed, not only are we going to be sending more soy beans into South Korea, but we're also going to start seeing new cars on the streets of Seoul, South Korea, imported from Detroit and Toledo and Chicago.

I don't mind Kias being sold here. I just want to make sure that they're also buying some Chevys and some Fords. So we're going to keep boosting American manufacturing. We're going to keep training workers with the skills they need to find these jobs. We're going to keep creating new jobs in American energy, including alternative energy that's been a source of strength for a lot of rural communities in Iowa. And an economy built to last also means making sure that there's a sense of fair play and shared responsibility.

Now, most immediately—I was talking about taxes on business—the most immediate thing we need to do with our Tax Code is make sure that we stop a tax hike on 160 million working Americans at the end of next month. People can't afford losing $40 out of each pay-

check. Not right now. Your voices convinced Congress to extend this middle class tax cut before. You remember there was a little resistance there at the end of last year? But you guys sent a message: Renew that payroll tax cut, strengthen the economy. But they only extended it for 2 months. We now have to extend it for the entire year. So I need your help to make sure they do it again. Tell Congress to pass this tax cut without drama, without delay, no soap operas. Just get it done.

In the longer run, if we're going to invest in our future, we've also got to get our fiscal house in order. You hear a lot of talk about deficits and debt. And those are legitimate concerns, although the most important thing we can do to actually reduce the debt is to grow the economy. So we can't abandon our investments in things like manufacturing and education investment, because if we're growing faster, the debt and deficits start coming down, the numbers get easier to manage. You can't just cut your way out of it. It's just like a family. If you are struggling to get out of debt, but you decide, well, I'll just—I won't repair the roof or the boiler, and I'll stop sending my kid to college, that's not the way you're going to solve your long-term problems.

Now, we're going to have to make some tough choices though. And right now we are scheduled to spend nearly $1 trillion more on what was intended to be a temporary tax cut for the wealthiest 2 percent of Americans. A quarter of all millionaires pay lower tax rates than millions of middle class households. Warren Buffett pays a lower tax rate than his secretary. Warren Buffett's secretary was at the State of the Union last night, just to confirm—[*laughter*]—that fact.

Now, does that make any sense to you? Do we want to keep these tax cuts for folks like me who don't need them? I'm doing okay. [*Laughter*] I really am. And look, nobody likes paying taxes. I understand that. So, if we didn't need it, if the country was in a surplus like it was back in 2000, I'd understand us saying, well, let's try to let millionaires keep every last dime. I get that. But that's not the situation we're in. And so we've got to make choices.

Do we want to keep investing in everything that's important to our long-term growth: education, medical research, our military, caring for our veterans, all of which are expensive? Or do we keep these tax cuts for folks who don't need them and weren't even asking for them? Because we can't do both. I want to be very clear about this. We cannot do both. You've got to choose.

So I believe we should follow what we call the Buffett rule: If you make more than a million dollars a year—I don't mean that you've got a million dollars' worth of assets. I don't mean a family that's been saving all their lives and doing well, but—and is comfortable, and finally they've got a little nest egg. If you make more than a million dollars a year, you should pay a tax rate of at least 30 percent. If, on the other hand, you make less than $250,000 a year, which includes 98 percent of you, your taxes shouldn't go up.

And by the way, if we do that and we make some smart cuts in other areas, we can get this deficit and debt under control and still be making the investments we need to grow the economy.

A lot of—I hear folks running around calling this class warfare. This is not class warfare. Let me tell you something, asking a billionaire to pay at least as much as his secretary, that's just common sense. That's common sense. I mean, we're talking about going back to tax rates that we had under Bill Clinton, when, by the way, the economy grew faster and jobs increased much faster. And in the meantime, Warren Buffett will do fine. [*Laughter*] I will do fine. We don't need tax breaks; you do. You're the ones who've seen your wages stall, the cost of everything from groceries to college tuition going up. So I want to give you a break. I don't need a break.

Look, we don't begrudge success in America. This family business right here, I want them to thrive. I want these guys to keep growing and growing and growing and hire and hire. When we talk—when Americans talk about folks like me paying my fair share in taxes, it's not because Americans envy the rich. Most of them want to get rich. Most of them

will work hard to try to do well financially. It's because if I get a tax break I don't need and the country can't afford, then either it's going to add to our deficit, and that's what happened between 2000 and 2008, basically. All these tax cuts just added to the deficit because they weren't paid for, so it takes money out of the Treasury.

Or alternatively, if we're going to close that deficit, somebody else is going to have to pick up the tab. It might be a senior who now suddenly has to pay more for their Medicare. It's got to be a student who's suddenly having to pay more for their student loan. It might be a family that's just trying to get by, and suddenly, their tax rates go up. That's not right. That's not who we are.

One of the biggest disagreements I have with some folks in Washington is the nature of America's success. Each of us is only here because somebody somewhere felt a responsibility to each other and felt a responsibility to our country's future. And that starts within our own families. It starts with us making sure our kids are responsible and we're instilling in them the values of hard work and doing your homework and treating other people with respect. But then it expands from there to our neighborhoods and our communities. And we recognize that if everybody is getting a fair shot, everybody has a chance to do better.

That's what built this country. Now it's our turn to be responsible. Now it's our turn to leave an America that's built to last. And I think we can do it. I'm confident we can do it. I believe it because of what I see in places like Cedar Rapids, what I hear when I meet the folks who are gathered here today.

I mean, think about what you've accomplished coming back from those floods. Now, that wasn't a matter of just each person being on their own. It was a matter of everybody pulling together to rebuild a city and make it stronger than it was before. That's how we work. And that FEMA assistance wasn't—it didn't come out of nowhere. It came around because, as a country, as a United States of America, we decide, you know what, when any part of the country gets in trouble, we're going to step in and help out. That's what we do.

This country only exists because generations of Americans worked together and looked out for each other and believed that we're stronger when we rise together. And those values are not Democratic values or Republican values. Those are American values. Those are the values we have to return to.

So we're going to keep on moving on American energy. We're going to keep on moving on American manufacturing. We are going to push hard to make sure that American workers have the skills they need to compete. And we're going to make sure that everything we do abides by those core American values that are so important.

And I know that if we work together and in common purpose, we can build an economy that gives everybody a fair shot. We can meet this challenge. And we'll remind everybody just why it is the United States of America is the greatest nation on Earth.

Thank you, everybody. God bless you. God bless America.

NOTE: The President spoke at 11:47 a.m. In his remarks, he referred to Jeff Baxter, operations supervisor, and Graig Cone, president, Conveyor Engineering & Manufacturing; Mayor Ron Corbett of Cedar Rapids, IA; and Warren E. Buffett, chief executive officer and chairman, and Debbie Bosanek, assistant, Berkshire Hathaway Inc.

Remarks at the Intel Corporation Ocotillo Campus in Chandler, Arizona
January 25, 2012

The President. Hello, Arizona! Thank you. Well, thank you, everybody. It is good to be in Arizona. The weather is good. You can't have better weather than this. Can't do it.

I want to thank Preston for that wonderful introduction. I want to acknowledge a few folks we have with us this afternoon. Mayor Tibshraeny is here. Give him a big round of applause. Mayor Stanton is here. All the tribal leaders who are here today.

Audience member. Clap your hands for Barack, *mi hermano!* [*Laughter*]

The President. Mi hermano. Mucho gusto. [*Laughter*]

Let me say how happy I was to see one particular Arizonan last night: Gabby Giffords. I was able to give her a big hug and just tell her we could not be happy—more happy to see her. I mean, she just looked gorgeous last night. And she's been an inspiration. Her husband Mark has been just a great friend and a great public servant and a hero to so many of us. And Michelle and I are going to be thinking of her as she continues her recovery here in Arizona. And she loves this State, and she loves all of you. So it was wonderful to see her.

Audience member. Gabby! Gabby!

Now last year, I had the chance to tour one of Intel's plants in Oregon. And basically, the engineers explained what happens inside these factories, and I pretended that I understood—[*laughter*]—what they were talking about. No, it's true. We were on this tour, and we were looking through these microscopes, and you'd look at some little spots in the microscope, and you'd say, "Well, what's that?" And they'd say, "Well, that's atoms." [*Laughter*] "Really?" And it was so remarkable that my Trip Director, who was with me, he said, "This stuff's like magic." [*Laughter*] "How do they do this?"

And while I was there, Intel's CEO, Paul Otellini, someone whose advice I rely on as a member of my Jobs Council, announced—he announced that Intel would be building a new factory here in Arizona. A factory which will turn out some of the fastest and most powerful computer chips on Earth. A factory so big, I'm told that right there is the world's largest land-based crane—can pull up to, what is it, 4,000 tons? Is that right, Preston?

Ocotillo Campus Construction Program Manager Preston McDaniel. Yes, sir.

The President. Four thousand. So not only that, but Paul informs me that the microscopes that they're going to have here will be twice as good as the ones they had—[*laughter*]—up in Oregon. So I decided I had to check this out for myself, because, honestly, first of all, who wants to miss out a chance to see the crane? [*Laughter*] That thing is huge.

But there's a more important reason that I'm here. I'm here because the factory that's being built behind me is an example of an America that is within our reach, an America that attracts the next generation of good manufacturing jobs, an America where we build stuff and make stuff and sell stuff all over the world.

We can do that. But we've got to come together. We've got to come together and restore the basic American promise that if you work hard, you can do well enough to raise a family and own a home, send your kids to college, put a little away for retirement, maybe come down to Arizona, where the weather is like this all the time. [*Laughter*] It never gets above 70 degrees, does it? [*Laughter*] Look, that's what people are looking for. They don't expect anybody to give them anything, but they want to be able to earn and deserve security, the ability to take care of their families, dignity in their retirement. That's what Americans are looking for. That's what they deserve.

Now, we're still recovering from one of the worst economic crises in three generations. We lost nearly 4 million jobs in the 6 months before I took office, another 4 million before our policies had a chance to take full effect. But here's the good news: Over the last 22 months, our businesses have created more than 3 million jobs. Last year, they created the most jobs since 2005. Today, American manufacturers are hiring again and creating jobs for the first time since the 1990s.

So our economy is getting stronger, and we've come too far to turn back now. After all that's happened, there are folks in Washington who want to do that, who want to turn back. It's like they're suffering from a case of collective amnesia. [*Laughter*] They want to go back to the very same policies that got us into this mess, same policies that have stacked the deck against middle class Americans for too many years. A philosophy that says we're better off if

everybody is just fending for themselves and everybody can play by their own rules.

I'm here to say they're wrong. I don't accept the notion that there's nothing we can do to accept—to meet our Nation's greatest challenges. There are all kinds of steps we can take. We can't go back to an economy that's weakened by outsourcing and bad debt and phony financial profits.

And last night at the State of the Union, I laid out a vision of how we move forward, laid out a blueprint for an economy built to last. It's an economy built on American manufacturing, with more good jobs and more products made in America. It's an economy built on American energy fueled by homegrown and alternative energy sources that make us more secure and less dependent on foreign oil. It's an economy built on the skills of American workers, getting people the education and the training they need so they're prepared for the jobs of today and ready to compete for the jobs of tomorrow.

And most importantly, it's an economy that's built on a renewal of American values: hard work, responsibility, the same set of rules for everybody, from Wall Street to Main Street. That has to be our future. That's how we restore the basic American promise. And it starts with manufacturing, both old industries, but also new industries, like Intel.

Look at what's happened in the auto industry. On the day I took office, it was on the verge of collapse. Some people said we should let it die. But we had a million jobs at stake, and I refused to let that happen. And so we said to the auto companies, in exchange for help, we're going to demand responsibility. We've got to make sure that the industry retools and restructures. And that's what they did. And over the past 2 years, the entire industry has added nearly 160,000 jobs. GM is number one in the world again. Ford is investing in new plants. Chrysler's on the mend. The American auto industry is back.

Now, what's happening in Detroit can happen in other industries. I want it to happen all across Arizona. This project—thanks to the leadership of Paul and the incredible engineering prowess of Intel. This project's going to employ thousands of construction workers who will put in more than 10 million hours on the job. When this factory is finished, Intel will employ around a thousand men and women, making the computer chips that power everything from your smart phone to your laptop to your car.

As an American, I'm proud of companies like Intel, who create jobs here. We all are. So let's help them grow and hire even faster. We have a huge opportunity to create more high-tech manufacturing jobs in the United States and bring some of these jobs back from overseas. But we're going to have to seize the moment. That starts with changing our tax system.

Right now companies get all kinds of tax breaks when they move jobs and profits overseas. But when a company chooses to stay in America, it gets hit with one of the highest tax rates in the world. That doesn't make sense. We've been talking about changing it for years. Republicans and Democrats have said that doesn't make sense. Well, let's get it done. Let's stop rewarding businesses that ship jobs overseas. Let's reward companies like Intel that are investing and creating jobs right here in the United States of America.

Now look, we live in a global economy. If a company wants to do business overseas, of course it's their right. But we shouldn't subsidize it. What we should do are subsidize and help and give tax breaks to companies that are investing here, that bring jobs back from overseas, high-tech manufacturers like Intel.

Today my administration is laying out several concrete actions we could take right now that would discourage companies from outsourcing jobs, encourage them to invest in the United States. Congress needs to send me this tax reform. I want to sign it right away, because I want to put more people to work right here in the United States.

Now, while we're at it, we need to make it easier for American businesses to sell our products all over the world. Two years ago, I set a goal of doubling U.S. exports within 5 years, which will create good, new manufacturing jobs. And we are on track to meet that goal. And soon, thanks to the new trade agreements

that I've signed, there are going to be new cars on the streets of other countries that are imported from Detroit and Toledo and Chicago.

And we need to invest in education. We want tomorrow's workers—we want Arizona's workers—to have the skills they need for the jobs like the ones that will be opening up here. And I have to tell you, I've been to these plants at Intel—young people, you'd better have done some math before you get in here. [*Laughter*] There—you know, you can't just kind of wander in and you didn't do some math in school. [*Laughter*]

And I want to thank Intel for leading the way, because they're investing in startups, they're supporting science and math education, they're helping to train new engineers. Paul is chairing a project that we initiated through the Jobs Council. We're looking to get thousands more engineers all across America. And for the young people who are out there who are thinking about a profession, think about engineering. We can use more engineers all across America.

We're also going to need to look at clean energy and innovation in the energy field. We have—as I said last night, oil production is higher than it's been in 8 years. We're actually importing less oil as a percentage than any time in the last 16 years. So we're opening up the oil and the gas industry here in the United States. But they don't need subsidies. We need to stop subsidizing oil companies and use that money to invest in clean energies like wind and solar and high-tech batteries. Those are industries that are already creating new jobs and making us even less dependent on foreign oil.

And an economy built to last also means we've got to renew American values: fair play, shared responsibility.

When it comes to tax policy, my first priority right now is to stop a tax hike on 160 million working Americans at the end of next month. People can't afford losing $40 out of each paycheck. Not right now. Your voices convinced Congress to extend this middle class tax cut before. I need your help again. Let Congress know: Pass this tax cut without drama, without delay. Get it done. It's good for the economy.

But in the longer run, we're going to have to both invest in our future—invest in education so we're producing more engineers, invest in clean energy, invest in our infrastructure—and we have to do all this at the same time as we've got to get our fiscal house in order. And that means we've got to make choices.

Right now we're supposed to spend nearly a trillion dollars more on what was intended to be a temporary tax cut for the wealthiest 2 percent of Americans. A quarter of all millionaires pay lower tax rates than millions of middle class households. Warren Buffett pays a lower tax rate than his secretary. I know because his secretary was at the State of the Union yesterday. [*Laughter*] Now, that just doesn't make any sense.

Because we've got to make choices: We could keep those tax breaks for folks like me, or we could keep investing in everything that's going to make this country strong: education and basic research and our military and caring for our veterans.

So I've said, let's follow the Buffett rule, named after Warren: If you make more than a million dollars a year, you should pay a tax rate of at least 30 percent. On the other hand, if you make less than $250,000 a year, which is 98 percent of you, your taxes shouldn't go up. And I just want to make clear, the reason I proposed this is not because we begrudge financial success in this country. We strive for it. We encourage it. I want everybody here to be rich. Go out there, work, create new businesses. Fulfill your dreams. But I think asking a billionaire to pay at least as much as his secretary in taxes is just common sense, especially when we're trying to figure out how to reduce our deficit.

And I promise you, look, Warren Buffett will do fine. [*Laughter*] I will do fine. We don't need more tax breaks. The middle class needs help. They're the ones who've seen wages stall. They're the ones who've seen the cost of everything from groceries to college tuition go up. You're the ones who need a break.

Again, we don't begrudge success in America. We encourage it. We aspire to it. When we talk about everybody paying their fair share,

it's not because anybody envies the rich. Earlier today Bill Gates said that he agrees that Americans who can afford it should pay their fair share. I promise you, Bill Gates doesn't envy rich people. [*Laughter*] He feels pretty comfortable that he's doing okay. It just has to do with basic math. We're going to have to reduce our deficit, and if I get tax breaks that I don't need and the country can't afford, if a Bill Gates or a Warren Buffett get tax breaks that they don't need and can't afford, then one of two things is going to happen. Either it adds to our deficit, or it's going to take away from somebody else, whether it's a senior or a student or a family who's trying to get by. And that's not right. That's not who we are.

Each of us is only here because somebody somewhere felt a responsibility to the country and people felt a responsibility to each other, because we understood that we're all in this together.

Intel's former CEO, the legendary Andy Grove, he put—he said it best. He said, look, I feel an obligation to my shareholders. I run a business; they've invested; I've got to make sure they get a good return. That's how the free market works, that's how it's supposed to work, that's what produces the extraordinary wealth of this country. But he also said—and I'm quoting here—"There is another obligation I feel personally, given that—given everything I've achieved in my career—and a lot of what Intel has achieved—were made possible by a climate of democracy, an economic climate and investment climate provided by the United States."

So his argument was, his first obligation to his shareholders, but he also has an obligation to this country that provided extraordinary opportunity. And that's something that all of us feel, or something that we should all feel.

I think Andy Grove was right. This Nation is great because we built it together, because we overcame challenges together. I believe we can do it again. I believe it because we've done it in the past. I believe it because I see it in places like Chandler. I believe it when I talk to folks like you. I know this country exists only because generations of Americans have worked hard, have fulfilled their responsibilities, have cared for their families, but they've also cared for their communities, and they've also looked out for each other. They've lived out the idea that we're in this together.

These values are not Democratic values or Republican values, they're American values. We've got to return to those values. It's our turn to be responsible. It's our turn to leave an America that's built to last.

So we're going to keep moving on American manufacturing. We are going to keep moving on American energy. We are going to keep making sure that American workers get the skills they need. We are going to invest in American innovation and basic science and research. We are going to make sure that we are training those engineers that we need. We are going to make sure that we return to the values of fair play and responsibility.

And I know that if we work together with common purpose, we can build an economy that gives everybody a fair shot. We can meet this challenge, and we'll remind the world once again just why the United States of America is the greatest nation on Earth.

Thank you very much, Arizona. God bless you. God bless America.

NOTE: The President spoke at 4:31 p.m. In his remarks, he referred to Mayor Jay Tibshraeny of Chandler, AZ; Mayor Gregory J. Stanton of Phoenix, AZ; Rep. Gabrielle D. Giffords and her husband Mark E. Kelly; White House Trip Director Marvin Nicholson; Warren E. Buffett, chief executive officer and chairman, and Debbie Bosanek, assistant, Berkshire Hathaway Inc.; and William H. Gates III, chairman, Microsoft Corp.

Statement on the Rescue of Jessica Buchanan
January 25, 2012

On Monday, I authorized an operation to rescue Jessica Buchanan, an American citizen who was kidnapped and held against her will for 3 months in Somalia. Thanks to the extraordinary courage and capabilities of our Special Operations Forces, yesterday Jessica Buchanan was rescued and she is on her way home. As Commander in Chief, I could not be prouder of the troops who carried out this mission and the dedicated professionals who supported their efforts.

Jessica Buchanan was selflessly serving her fellow human beings when she was taken hostage by criminals and pirates who showed no regard for her health and well-being. Last night I spoke with Jessica Buchanan's father and told him that all Americans have Jessica in our thoughts and prayers and give thanks that she will soon be reunited with her family. The United States will not tolerate the abduction of our people and will spare no effort to secure the safety of our citizens and to bring their captors to justice. This is yet another message to the world that the United States of America will stand strongly against any threats to our people.

NOTE: The statement referred to John Buchanan, father of Ms. Buchanan.

Remarks at UPS Las Vegas South in Las Vegas, Nevada
January 26, 2012

The President. Hello, Nevada! It is great to be back in Las Vegas.

Audience member. I love you!

The President. I love you back. [*Laughter*] Although I always say, when we stay here for the night, I've got to watch my staff to make sure that they get on the plane when we leave. [*Laughter*] Sometimes, they conveniently miss the flight. [*Laughter*]

But everybody please have a seat, have a seat. It is great to see you. Joe, thanks for the introduction. Scott, thank you and the folks at

UPS for hosting us today. I want to thank all of the elected officials and the tribal leaders who took the time to join us.

Before I get into the core of my remarks, I just want to mention something that I said to Scott and I said to Joe, and that is that UPS, I think, deserves just extraordinary credit for being the best in its space, one of the best businesses we have in the United States. But the reason is because it's got such outstanding workers, and the relationship between its workforce and management, cooperating, constantly figuring out how to make things better—it is just an outstanding organization. And so you guys all need to be congratulated for everything that you do.

Now, I'm here to talk a little more about what I talked about at the State of the Union on Tuesday night. And what I want to focus on is how we're going to restore the basic promise of America, something that folks at UPS understand, which is, if you work hard, if you do the right thing, you should be able to do well enough to raise a family and own a home and send your kids to college and put a little away for retirement. That's the American Dream. That's what most people are looking for.

They don't expect a handout. They don't expect anything to come easy. They do expect, if they're willing to work hard to try to get ahead, if they're doing the right thing, then they can have a sense of security and dignity and help make sure that their family is moving forward. That's what Americans are looking for. That's what Americans deserve.

And today, 3 years after the worst economic storm in three generations, our economy is growing again. Our businesses have created more than 3 million jobs. Last year, businesses created the most jobs since 2005. American manufacturers are hiring again and creating jobs for the first time since the 1990s.

Now, we've got more work to do. But what we can't do is go back to the very same policies that got us into a mess in the first place. We can't go backwards. We have to move forward. I said on Tuesday, and I will repeat today, we will not—we cannot—go back to an economy weakened by outsourcing and bad debt and phony financial profits. So, on Tuesday, at the State of the Union, I laid out my vision for how we move forward. I laid out a blueprint for an economy that's built to last, that has a firm foundation, where we're making stuff and selling stuff and moving it around and UPS drivers are dropping things off everywhere.

That's the economy we want, an economy built on American manufacturing with more good jobs and more products made here in the United States of America; an economy built on American energy, fueled by homegrown and alternative sources that make us more secure and less dependent on foreign oil; an economy built on the skills of American workers, getting people the education and the training they need to prepare for the jobs of today, but also to compete for the jobs of tomorrow.

And most importantly, I talked about an economy that's built on a renewal of American values: hard work, responsibility, and the same set of rules for everybody, from Wall Street to Main Street. That has to be our future. That's how we restore that basic American promise.

Now, part of my blueprint, and what I want to focus on a little bit today, is for an economy built to last with American energy. That's why we're here. For decades, Americans have been talking about how do we decrease our dependence on foreign oil. Well, my administration has actually begun to do something about it.

Over the last 3 years, we negotiated the toughest new efficiency standards for cars and trucks in history. We've opened millions of new acres for oil and gas exploration. Right now American oil production is the highest that it's been in 8 years—8 years. Last year, we relied less on foreign oil than in any of last the 16 years. That hasn't gotten a lot of attention, but that's important. We're moving in the right direction when it comes to oil and gas production.

And today I'm announcing that my administration will soon open up around 38 million acres in the Gulf of Mexico for additional exploration and development, which could result in a lot more production of domestic energy.

But as I said on Tuesday, and as the folks here at UPS understand, even with all this oil production, we only have about 2 percent of the world's oil reserves. So we've got to have an all-out, all-in, all-of-the-above strategy that develops every source of American energy, a strategy that is cleaner and cheaper and full of new jobs.

Now, a great place to start is with natural gas. Some of you may not have been following this, but because of new technologies, because we can now access natural gas that we couldn't access before in a economic way, we've got a supply of natural gas under our feet that can last America nearly a hundred years—nearly a hundred years. Now, when I say under our feet, I don't know that there's actually gas right here, but—[*laughter*]—I mean in all the United States.

And developing it could power our cars and our homes and our factories in a cleaner and cheaper way. The experts believe it could support more than 600,000 jobs by the end of the decade. We, it turns out, are the Saudi Arabia of natural gas. We've got a lot of it. We've got a lot of it.

Now, removing that natural gas obviously has to be done carefully. And I know that there are families that are worried about the impact this could have on our environment and on the health of our communities. And I share that concern. So that's why I'm requiring, for the first time ever, that all companies drilling for gas on public lands disclose the chemicals they use. We want to make sure that this is done properly and safely. America will develop this resource without putting the health and safety of our citizens at risk.

But we've got to keep at it. We've got to take advantage of this incredible natural resource. And think about what could happen if we do. Think about an America where more cars and trucks are running on domestic natural gas than on foreign oil. Think about an America where our companies are leading the world in developing natural gas technology and creating a generation of new energy jobs, where our natural gas resources are helping make our manufacturers more competitive for decades. We can do this. And by the way, natural gas burns cleaner than oil does, so it's also potentially good for our environment as we make this shift.

So, last April, we issued a challenge to shipping companies like UPS. We said, if you upgrade your fleets to run on less oil or no oil at all, we're going to help you succeed. We want to help you with that experiment. So we started out with five companies that accepted the challenge. And of course, UPS was one of the first. That's how they roll. [*Laughter*]

So, less than a year later, we've got 14 companies on board, and together, they represent 1 million vehicles on the road. That's a lot of trucks.

We should do more though. And that's why we're here today. First, let's get more of these natural gas vehicles on the road. Let's get more of them on the road. The Federal fleet of cars is leading by example. Turns out the Federal Government has a lot of cars. [*Laughter*] We buy a lot of cars. So we've got to help not only the Federal Government, but also local governments upgrade their fleet. If more of these brown trucks are going green, more city buses should too. There's no reason why buses can't go in the same direction.

Second, let's offer new tax incentives to help companies buy more clean trucks like these.

Third, let's make sure all these new trucks that are running on natural gas have places to refuel. That's one of the biggest impediments, is the technology. We know how to make these trucks, but if they don't have a place to pull in and fill up, they got problems.

So we're going to keep working with the private sector to develop up to five natural gas corridors along our highways. These are highways that have natural gas fueling stations between cities, just like the one that folks at UPS, South Coast Air, and Clean Energy Fuels are opening today between Los Angeles and Salt Lake City. That's a great start. So now one of these trucks can go from Long Beach all the way to Salt Lake City. And they're going to be able to refuel along the way.

And finally, to keep America on the cutting edge of clean energy technology, I want my Energy Secretary, Steven Chu, to launch a new competition that encourages our country's brightest scientists and engineers and entrepreneurs to discover new breakthroughs for natural gas vehicles.

So we're going to keep moving on American energy. We're going to keep boosting American manufacturing. We're going to keep training our workers for these new jobs. But an economy that's built to last also means a renewal of the values that made us who we are: hard work, fair play, and shared responsibility.

Now, right now that means, first of all, stopping a tax hike on 160 million working Americans at the end of next month. People cannot afford right now losing $40 out of each paycheck. Your voices convinced Congress to extend this middle class tax cut before. I need your help to make sure they do it again. No drama, no delay. Let's just get this done for the American people and for our economy as a whole.

But we've got a longer run issue—Scott and I were talking about this before we came out—and that is, how do we get America's fiscal house in order? And we're going to have to make some choices. The reason that we've got these debts and deficit is because we're not making hard choices. Right now we're supposed to spend nearly $1 trillion more on what was intended to be a temporary tax cut for the wealthiest 2 percent of Americans—supposed to be temporary, back in 2001. [*Laughter*] That's a long time ago. [*Laughter*] A quarter of all millionaires pay lower tax rates than millions of middle class households. Warren Buffett pays a lower tax rate than his secretary. I know because she was at the State of the Union. [*Laughter*] She told me.

Now, that's not fair. That doesn't make sense. And the reason it's important for us to recognize that is, if we're going to reduce our deficit, then we've got to have a balanced approach that has spending cuts. And we've already agreed to $2 trillion worth of spending cuts. We got to get rid of programs that don't work. We've got to make Government more efficient. I have asked Congress for authority to consolidate some of these agencies to make them run better. We're going to have to be

much more effective when it comes to Government spending. We all acknowledge that, and we're making progress on that front.

But that alone doesn't do it. So, if we want to actually deal with the deficit, we've got to look at the other side of the ledger. Do we want to keep these tax cuts for the wealthiest Americans? Or do we want to keep investing in everything else, like education, like clean energy, like a strong military, like caring for our veterans who are coming home from Iraq and Afghanistan? We can't do both. We can't do both.

So what I've said is let's follow the Buffett rule: If you make more than a million dollars a year, you should pay a tax rate of at least 30 percent, which, by the way, is lower than you would have been paying under Ronald Reagan. Nobody's talking about anything crazy here. On the other hand, if you make less than $250,000 a year, which 98 percent of all Americans do, then your taxes shouldn't go up. That's a—I think that's a fair approach.

And a lot of folks have been running around saying, well, that's class warfare. Asking a billionaire to pay at least as much as his secretary in taxes, that's just common sense. [*Laughter*] And I promise you, if we make this change, Warren Buffett will be doing fine. [*Laughter*] I will be doing fine. Scott will be doing fine. We don't need more tax breaks. You're the ones who have seen your wages and your incomes stall while the cost of everything from groceries to college to health care have been going up. You're the ones who deserve a break.

And I want to make one last point: We do not begrudge success in America. We aspire to it. We want everybody to succeed. We want everybody to be rich. We want everybody to be working hard, making their way, creating new products, creating new services, creating jobs. That's the American way. We don't shy away from financial success. We don't apologize for it.

But what we do say is when this Nation has done so much for us, shouldn't we be thinking about the country as a whole? When Americans talk about folks like me paying their fair share of taxes, it's not because they envy the rich. Just yesterday Bill Gates said he agrees with me that most—that Americans who can afford it should pay their fair share. I promise you, Bill Gates does not envy the rich. [*Laughter*] He doesn't envy wealthy people.

This has nothing to do with envy. It has everything to do with math. It's what I talked about earlier. We've got to make choices. Americans understand, if I get a tax break I don't need and a tax break the country can't afford, then one of two things are going to happen. Either it's going to add to our deficit, right? Or somebody else is going to have to make up the difference.

A senior suddenly is going to have to start paying more for their Medicare, or a student is going to have to pay more for their student loan, or a family that's trying to get by, they're going to have to do with less. And that's not right. That's not who we are. Each of us is only here because somebody somewhere felt a responsibility to each other and to our country and helped to create all this incredible opportunity that we call the United States of America.

Now, it's our turn to be responsible. And it's our turn to leave an America that is built to last for the next generation. That's our job, and we can do it. We can do it. We can do it. And I know we can do it because I've seen in States like Nevada and with people like you that I meet all across this country, you understand the history of this country, generations of Americans working together, looking out for each other, living by the idea that we rise or fall

together. Those are the values we have to return to.

I mentioned praise for our military at the State of the Union and the incredible work that they do. And the reason our military is so good, the reason why they're so admired is because they—it's not like everybody in the military agrees on everything. You got Democrats in the military. You got Republicans in the military. You've got folks who are conservative or liberal, different races, different religions, different backgrounds, but they figure out how to focus on the mission. They figure out how to do their job.

And that sense of common purpose is what we're going to need to build an economy that lasts. And if we work together in common purpose, we can build that economy and we can meet the challenges of our times. And we'll remind the entire world once again just why it is that the United States is the greatest country on Earth.

Thank you, everybody. God bless you, and God bless the United States of America.

NOTE: The President spoke at 10:11 a.m. In his remarks, he referred Joseph Mueller, employee, and D. Scott Davis, chairman and chief executive officer, UPS; Warren E. Buffett, chief executive officer and chairman, and Debbie Bosanek, assistant, Berkshire Hathaway Inc.; and William H. Gates III, chairman, Microsoft Corp.

Remarks at Buckley Air Force Base, Colorado
January 26, 2012

The President. Hello, everybody! Hello, Team Buckley! It is great to be here. Everybody, please have a seat, have a seat.

Al, thank you for that introduction and for your years of service. I brought a few folks with me here today: the Secretary of the Air Force, Michael Donley; the Secretary of the Navy, Ray Mabus, is here; our Assistant Secretary of Defense for Energy Planning, Sharon Burke, is in the house. They are all doing great work with Secretary Panetta to keep our military the

strongest in the world and to make our military more energy efficient.

I want to thank our host, Colonel Dant, for welcoming us here today. Lieutenant Governor Joe Garcia is here as well. Give him a round of applause. And the mayor of the great city of Denver, Michael Hancock, is here as well. You'll notice they have the same hairdo. [*Laughter*]

And of course, we've got some outstanding men and women in uniform from Buckley Air

Force Base. And that includes the 460th Space Wing. To all of you, on behalf of a grateful nation, I want to thank you for your extraordinary service.

During a decade of war, these folks, so many of you, exhibited the very best of America: courage, selflessness, teamwork. As I said this past Tuesday, you've exceeded all expectations, because you focus on your mission. You work together. You get the job done.

And so on Tuesday, I talked about the job we've got to get done as a nation—all of us—the job of restoring the American promise, the idea that if you work hard, if you fulfill your responsibilities, then you can do well enough to raise a family and own a home, send your kids to college, put a little away for retirement, live out that American Dream.

That's what most people are reaching for. They don't expect a handout. They don't expect anything to come easy. But they do expect, if they're applying themselves, if they're working hard, if they're able to overcome setbacks and obstacles and they can cooperate with the folks they're working with, if they're doing the right thing, then they should be able to achieve some security and some dignity in their lives. Something very basic—it's a basic promise that we've got to restore.

So, at the State of the Union, I tried to lay out my vision for how we would do that. I laid out a blueprint for an economy that's built to last. It's an economy built on American manufacturing, more good jobs and products made here in the United States that we're selling all around the world.

It's an economy built on American energy, fueled on homegrown and alternative energy sources that make us more secure and less dependent on foreign oil, which obviously is not just good for our prosperity, but also for our security. We all know that. It's an economy built on the skills of American workers, getting people the education and the training that they need so that they're prepared for the jobs of today and ready to compete for the jobs of tomorrow.

And most importantly, it's an economy that's built on a renewal of American values: hard work, responsibility, and the sense that the same rules apply to everybody, from Wall Street to Main Street.

That's also part of what makes our military so strong. Doesn't matter if you're a general, you're a private. There are some rules you got to follow. That has to be our future. That's how we restore that basic American promise.

Now, today we've been focusing on American energy. For all our lives, America has been talking about decreasing our dependence on foreign oil. I've been hearing it—I'm older than most of you guys—[*laughter*]—I've been hearing it all my life. Well, my administration has actually tried to do something about it.

Over the last 3 years, we negotiated the toughest new efficiency standards for cars and trucks in history. That will save us and consumers billions of gallons of gas and a lot of money. We've opened millions of new acres for oil and gas exploration here in the United States. Right now American oil production is the highest it's been in 8 years—8 years.

Last year, we relied less on foreign oil than any time in the past 16 years. Hasn't gotten a lot of attention, but it's important. We're moving in the right direction when it comes to oil and gas production.

But we've got to do more, because even if we tapped every drop of domestic oil, we've only got 2 percent of the world's oil reserves. We've got to have an all-out, all-of-the-above strategy, develop every available source of American energy, and it's got to be a strategy that is cleaner and cheaper and will create all kinds of new jobs.

So this morning I was in Nevada talking about how natural gas is a enormous energy source for the United States. We are the Saudi Arabia of oil—or Saudi Arabia of natural gas. We've just got to develop it, and if we do effectively, then we're going to create jobs, and it's going to power trucks that are cleaner and cheaper and factories that are cleaner and cheaper.

The same promise is true for clean energy. Because of Federal investments, renewable energy use—sources like wind and solar—has nearly doubled. Thousands of Americans have jobs because of those efforts.

So, as I said on Tuesday, I'm not going to walk away from the promise of clean energy. We're not going to cede the wind industry or the solar industry or the battery industry to China or Germany because we're too timid to make that same commitment here in the United States. We subsidized oil for a very long time, long enough. It's time to stop giving taxpayer giveaways to an industry that's never been more profitable. We've got to double down on a clean energy industry that's never been more promising. And Congress is going to need to act.

They need to pass clean energy tax credits. They need to set a clean energy standard so that we create a market for innovation. These are the industries of the future, and they're the jobs of the future.

So this is common sense. But we're not going to wait for Congress. We're also going to do some things administratively. It's why I'm directing my administration to allow the development of clean energy on enough public lands to power 3 million homes. And the reason we're at Buckley is because the military is doing its part. The military is doing its part, as usual—as usual. Now, it's important for the military to do its part because we're the largest—our military is the largest energy consumer in the world. So we can set a good example and help create an additional market for clean energy. The Navy is going to purchase enough clean energy capacity to power a quarter of a million homes a year. And it won't cost taxpayers a dime.

What does it mean? It means that the world's largest consumer of energy, the Department of Defense, is making one of the largest commitments to clean energy in history. That will grow this market, it will strengthen our energy security.

And I promise you, the Department of Defense is not just embracing clean energy because it feels good. [*Laughter*] We got some tough-minded folks. Our number-one priority is always the security of this Nation. But what our military understands is that if we're smart

on energy, that saves DOD budgets that allow them to do a whole bunch of other things.

Leading on this issue is the right thing to do. Yes, it's the right thing to do to prevent climate change. Yes, it's the right thing to do in terms of reducing pollution. But it's also important for our national security.

Ray Mabus has said: "We wouldn't allow some of the places that we buy fossil fuels from to build our ships or to build our aircrafts, to build our ground equipment. We wouldn't do that. And yet we give them say on whether those ships sail or whether those aircrafts fly or whether those vehicles run, because we buy fuel from them." Why would we do that if we don't have to? The less we depend on foreign oil, the more secure we become as a nation.

That's why in December, the Navy made the single largest purchase of biofuel in Government history. This summer, that fuel will power ships and subs during the world's largest naval exercise. By the way, 2 years ago, I got a chance to see a Navy F–18 Green Hornet that flies on biofuel. It was a pretty impressive sight. They wouldn't let me fly it. [*Laughter*] But it was impressive to see.

The rest of the military, including here at Buckley, is doing its part as well. In 2010, you started installing thousands of solar panels here on the base. That same year, the Air Force flew an A–10 Thunderbolt entirely on alternative fuels, a first for the military. Overall, the Air Force is on track to save $500 million in fuel costs over the next 5 years because you guys have changed the way you operate. Think about that: half a billion dollars. [*Applause*] Yes, that's worth clapping.

Reducing our dependence on oil is going to strengthen our national security. It will make our environment cleaner for our kids. It will make energy cheaper for our businesses and for our families. And doubling down on a clean energy industry will create lots of jobs in the process.

So we're going to keep moving on American energy. We're going to stay focused on boosting American manufacturing. We're going to keep training our workers so that they are equipped for the high-skill jobs of tomorrow, including in the clean energy space. And we're going to restore those American values of fair play and responsibility that made us who we are.

We've got to follow the lead of the members of our military who are here today. You rise or fall as one unit, serving one Nation. You have each other's backs. That's the same spirit that you'll find in communities all over America. Each of us is here only because somebody was looking out for us. Not just our parents, but we had neighbors and communities and churches and synagogues, people who were coaching Little League. And we had a country that was investing in community colleges and universities and research and caring for our vets. Everybody was taking responsibility for each other and for our country, as well as for ourselves.

Somebody had our back. Otherwise, we wouldn't have been successful. Certainly, I wouldn't have been. This country exists because generations of Americans worked together and looked out for each other. Out of many, we came together as one. These are the values we have to return to. That's how we're going to create an economy that is built to last. That's how we're going to make sure that we have the best energy policy in the world. That's how we're going to put people back to work. That's how we're going to continue to make sure we have the finest military in the history of the world.

If we work together in common purpose, nobody can stop us. We will rebuild this economy. We will meet these challenges. We'll remind everybody why the United States is the greatest country on Earth.

Thank you, everybody. God bless you. God bless America.

NOTE: The President spoke at 3:34 p.m. In his remarks, he referred to Maj. Alberto Mezarina, USAF (Ret.), energy manager, and Col. Daniel A. Dant, USAF, commander, 460th Space Wing, Buckley Air Force Base.

Statement on North Carolina Governor Beverly E. Perdue's Decision Not To Seek Reelection
January 26, 2012

As the first woman to serve as North Carolina's Lieutenant Governor and Governor, Bev Perdue has never been afraid to break barriers. For over 25 years, she has fought for the people of the Tar Heel State, working to transform the State's public schools, improve the health care system, protect and attract jobs for members of the military and their families, and create the jobs of the future. Michelle and I want to congratulate Governor Perdue on her historic tenure, and we wish Bev and her family well in the future.

Statement on Representative R. Bradley Miller's Decision Not To Seek Reelection
January 26, 2012

Brad Miller has served the people of North Carolina for two decades. In the House of Representatives, Brad helped lead the fight to protect families from abuses by the financial industry and is a key reason why today we finally have a strong watchdog in place looking out for American consumers. Michelle and I thank Brad for his service and wish him the very best in the future.

Letter to Congressional Leaders Reporting on the Rescue of Jessica Buchanan
January 26, 2012

Dear Mr. Speaker: (Dear Mr. President:)

At my direction, on January 24, 2012, U.S. Special Operations Forces conducted an operation in Somalia to rescue Ms. Jessica Buchanan, a U.S. citizen. The operation was successfully completed. Ms. Buchanan was kidnapped in Galcayo, Somalia on October 25, 2011, by a group linked to Somali pirates and financiers. Also rescued in the course of the operation was a Danish national, Poul Hagen Thisted, who was kidnapped with Ms. Buchanan. The operation was undertaken by a small number of joint combat-equipped U.S. forces, after we received reliable intelligence indicating Ms. Buchanan's location in Somalia along with that of Mr. Thisted. These forces left Somalia on January 25, 2012.

I directed this action consistent with my responsibility to protect U.S. citizens both at home and abroad, and in furtherance of U.S. national security interests, pursuant to my constitutional authority to conduct U.S. foreign relations and as Commander in Chief and Chief Executive.

I am providing this report as part of my efforts to keep the Congress fully informed, consistent with the War Powers Resolution (Public Law 93–148). I appreciate the support of the Congress in this action.

Sincerely,

BARACK OBAMA

NOTE: Identical letters were sent to John A. Boehner, Speaker of the House of Representatives, and Daniel K. Inouye, President pro tempore of the Senate.

Remarks at the University of Michigan in Ann Arbor, Michigan
January 27, 2012

The President. Hello, Michigan! Oh, it is good to be back in Ann Arbor.

Thank you, Christina, for that wonderful introduction. I also want to thank your president, Mary Sue Coleman. The mayor of Ann Arbor, John Hieftje, is here. My outstanding Secretary of Education, Arne Duncan, is in the house. We have some outstanding Members of Congress who are here as well, who are representing you each and every day. Give them a round of applause, come on.

Audience member. I love you, President Obama!

The President. I love you back.

So in terms of—boy, we've got all kinds of Members of Congress here, so the—[*laughter*].

Oh, where's Denard? Denard Robinson is in the house. I hear you're coming back, man. That is a good deal for Michigan.

Audience member. Denard Robinson in 2012! [*Laughter*]

The President. Oh, oh, come on. They're trying to draft you for President. [*Laughter*] He's got to graduate before he runs for President. [*Laughter*] There's an age limit. [*Laughter*]

Well, it is wonderful to be here. I want to thank all of you for coming out this morning. I know for folks in college, this is still really early. I remember those days. It is good home— good to be in the home of the Sugar Bowl champion Wolverines. And with Denard Robinson coming back, this will be a team to be reckoned with. I understand your basketball team is pretty good this year too. All right. Go Blue! It's always good to start with a easy applause line. [*Laughter*]

Look, the reason I'm here today—in addition to meeting Denard Robinson—[*laughter*]—is to talk with all of you about what most of you do here every day, and that is to think about how you can gain the skills and the training you need to succeed in this 21st-century economy. And this is going to be one of the most important issues that not just you face, but this entire country faces. How can we make sure that everybody is getting the kind of education they need to personally succeed, but also to build up this Nation, because in this economy, there is no greater predictor of individual success than a good education.

Today, the unemployment rate for Americans with a college degree or more is about half the national average. Their incomes are twice as high as those who don't have a high school diploma. College is the single most important investment you can make in your future, and I'm proud that all of you are making that investment.

And the degree you earn from Michigan will be the best tool you have to achieve that basic American promise, the idea that if you work hard, if you are applying yourself, if you are doing the right thing, you can do it well enough to raise a family and own a home and send your own kids to college, put away a little for retirement, create products or services, be part of something that is adding value to this country and maybe changing the world. That's what you're striving for. That's what the American Dream is all about.

And how we keep that promise alive is the defining issue of our time. I don't want to be in a country where we only are looking at success for a small group of people. We want a country where everybody has a chance—[*applause*]— where everybody has a chance. We don't want to become a country where a shrinking number of Americans do really well while a growing number barely get by. That's not the future we want. Not the future I want for you, it's not the future I want for my daughters. I want this to be a big, bold, generous country where everybody gets a fair shot, everybody is doing their fair share, everybody is playing by the same set of rules. That's the America I know. That's the America I want to keep. That's the future within our reach.

Now, in the State of the Union on Tuesday, I laid out a blueprint that gets us there. Blueprint—it's blue—[*laughter*]—that's no coincidence; I planned it that way, Michigan—

[*laughter*]—a blueprint for an economy that's built to last.

It's an economy built on new American manufacturing, because Michigan is all about making stuff. If there's anybody in America who can teach us how to bring back manufacturing, it is the great State of Michigan.

On the day I took office, with the help of folks like Debbie Stabenow, your Senator, and Carl Levin and John Conyers—the American auto industry was on the verge of collapse. And some politicians were willing to let it just die. We said no. We believe in the workers of this State. I believe in American ingenuity. We placed our bets on the American auto industry, and today, the American auto industry is back. Jobs are coming back, 160,000 jobs.

And to bring back even more jobs, I want this Congress to stop rewarding companies that are shipping jobs and profits overseas, start rewarding companies who are hiring here and investing here and creating good jobs here in Michigan and here in the United States of America.

So our first step is rebuilding American manufacturing. And by the way, not all the jobs that have gone overseas are going to come back. We have to be realistic. And technology means that a larger and larger portion of you will work in the service sector as engineers and computer scientists. [*Applause*] There you go. We got the engineering school—there you go—and entrepreneurs. So there's going to be a lot of activity in the service sector. But part of my argument, part of the argument of Michigan's congressional delegation is that when manufacturing does well, then the entire economy does well.

The service sector does well if manufacturing is doing well, so we've got to make sure that America isn't just buying stuff, but we're also selling stuff, all around the world, products stamped with those three proud words: Made in America.

An economy built to last is also one where we control our energy needs. We don't let foreign countries control our energy supplies. Right now America is producing more of our own oil than we were 8 years ago. That's good news. As a percentage, we're actually importing less than any time in the last 16 years.

But—I think young people especially understand this—no matter how much oil we produce, we've only got 2 percent of the world's oil reserves. And that means we've got to focus on clean, renewable energy. We've got to have a strategy that, yes, is producing our own oil and natural gas. But we've also got to develop wind and solar and biofuels. And that is good for our economy. It creates jobs. But it's also good for our environment. It's also—makes sure that this planet is sustainable. That's part of the future that you deserve. We've subsidized oil companies for a century. That's long enough. Congress needs to stop giving taxpayer dollars to an oil industry that's never been more profitable and double down on a clean energy future that's never been more promising.

I don't want to cede the wind or the solar or the battery industry to China or Germany because we were too timid, we didn't have the imagination to make the same commitment here. And I want those jobs created here in the United States of America. And I also want us to think about energy efficiency, making sure—we've already doubled fuel efficiency standards on cars. Part of Detroit coming back is creating more fuel-efficient cars here in Michigan, and more fuel-efficient trucks. And we've got to revamp our buildings to make them more fuel efficient. And we—if we are focused on this, we can control our energy future. That's part of creating an America that's built to last.

And we've got to have an economy in which every American has access to a world-class higher education, the kind you are getting right here at the University of Michigan. My grandfather got the chance to go to college because this country decided that every returning veteran of World War II should be able to afford it. My mother was able to raise two kids by herself because she was able to get grants and work her way through school. I am only standing here today because scholarships and student loans gave me a shot at a decent education. Michelle and I can still remember how long it took us to pay back our student loans. [*Laughter*]

Audience member. Tell the First Lady we wish her happy birthday!

The President. I will tell Michelle you said happy birthday.

But I just want all of you to understand, your President and your First Lady were in your shoes not that long ago. [*Laughter*] We didn't come from wealthy families. The only reason that we were able to achieve what we were able to achieve was because we got a great education. That's the only reason. And we could not have done that unless we lived in a country that made a commitment to opening up opportunity to all people.

The point is, this country has always made a commitment to put a good education within the reach of all who are willing to work for it, and that's part of what helped to create this economic miracle and build the largest middle class in history.

And this precedes even college. I mean, we were—we helped to begin the movement in industrialized countries to create public schools, public high schools, understanding that as people are moving from an agricultural sector to an industrial sector, they were going to need training. Now we've moved to an Information Age, a digitalized age, a global economy. We've got to make that same commitment today.

Now, we still have, by far, the best network of colleges and universities in the world. Nobody else comes close. [*Applause*] Nobody else comes close. But the challenge is, it's getting tougher and tougher to afford it. Since most of you were born, tuition and fees have more than doubled. That forces students like you to take out more loans and rack up more debt. In 2010, graduates who took out loans left college owing an average of $24,000. That's an average. Are you waving because you owe $24,000 or—[*laughter*].

Student loan debt has now surpassed credit card debt for the first time ever. Think about that. That's inexcusable. In the coming decade, 60 percent of new jobs will require more than a high school diploma. Higher education is not a luxury. It's an economic imperative that every family in America should be able to afford.

97

And when I say higher education, I don't just mean 4-year colleges and universities, I also mean our community colleges and providing lifelong learning for workers who may need to retrain for jobs when the economy shifts. All those things cost money, and it's harder and harder to afford. So we've got to do something to help families be able to afford—and students to be able to afford—this higher education. We've all got a responsibility here.

Thanks to the hard work of Secretary Duncan, my administration is increasing Federal student aid so more students can afford college. And one of the things I'm proudest of, with the help of all these Members of Congress, we won a tough fight to stop handing out tens of billions of dollars in taxpayer subsidies to banks that issue student loans and shift that money to where it should go, directly to the students and to the families who need it.

Tens of billions of dollars that were going to subsidies for banks are now going to students in the form of more grants and lower rates on loans. We've capped student loan payments so that nearly 1.6 million students, including a bunch of you, are only going to have to pay 10 percent of your monthly income towards your loans once you graduate—10 percent of your monthly income.

So that's what we've been doing. Now Congress has to do more. Congress needs to do more. They need to stop the interest rates on student loans from doubling this July. That's what's scheduled to happen if Congress doesn't act. That would not be good for you. [*Laughter*] So you should let your Members of Congress know: Don't do that. Don't do it. [*Applause*] Don't do it.

They need to extend the tuition tax credit that we've put in place that's saving some of you and millions of folks all across the country thousands of dollars. And Congress needs to give more young people the chance to earn their way through college by doubling the number of work-study jobs in the next 5 years.

So the administration has a job to do. Congress has a job to do. But it's not just enough to increase student aid, and you can imagine why. Look, we can't just keep on subsidizing sky-rocketing tuition. If tuition is going up faster than inflation, faster than even health care is going up, no matter how much we subsidize it, sooner or later, we're going to run out of money. And that means that others have to do their part. Colleges and universities need to do their part to keep costs down as well.

Recently, I spoke with a group of college presidents who've done just that. Here at Michigan, you've done a lot to find savings in your budget. We know this is possible. So, from now on, I'm telling Congress we should steer Federal campus-based aid to those colleges that keep tuition affordable, provide good value, serve their students well. We are putting colleges on notice. You can't keep—you can't assume that you'll just jack up tuition every single year. If you can't stop tuition from going up, then the funding you get from taxpayers each year will go down. We should push colleges to do better. We should hold them accountable if they don't.

Now, States also have to do their part. I was talking to your president—and this is true all across the country—States have to do their part by making higher education a higher priority in their budgets. Last year, over 40 States cut their higher education spending—40 States cut their higher education budget. And we know that these State budget cuts have been the largest factor in tuition increases at public colleges over the past decade.

So we're challenging States: Take responsibility as well on this issue. What we're doing is, today we're going to launch a Race to the Top for college affordability. We're telling the States, if you can find new ways to bring down the cost of college and make it easier for more students to graduate, we'll help you do it. We will give you additional Federal support if you are doing a good job of making sure that all of you aren't loaded up with debt when you graduate from college.

And finally, today I'm also calling for a new report card for colleges. Parents like getting report cards. I know you guys may not always look forward to it. [*Laughter*] But we parents, we like to know what you're doing. From now on, parents and students deserve to know how a college is doing, how affordable is it, how well are its students doing. We want you to know how well a car stacks up before you buy it. You should know how well a college stacks up.

We call this—one of the things that we're doing at the Consumer Finance Protection board that I just set up with Richard Cordray is to make sure that young people understand the financing of colleges. He calls it "Know Before You Owe"—[*laughter*]—"Know Before You Owe." So we want to push more information out so consumers can make good choices, so you as consumers of higher education understand what it is that you're getting.

The bottom line is that an economy built to last demands we keep doing everything we can to bring down the cost of college. That goes along with strengthening American manufacturing. It means we keep on investing in American energy. It means we double down on the clean energy that's creating jobs across this State and guaranteeing your generation a better future.

And you know what else it means? It means that we renew the American values of fair play and shared responsibility—[*applause*]—shared responsibility.

I talked about this at the State of the Union. We've got to make sure that as we're paying for the investments of the future that everybody is doing their part, that we're looking out for middle class families and not just those at the top. Right—the first thing that means is making sure taxes don't go up on 160 million working Americans at the end of next month. People can't afford to lose $40 out of every paycheck. Not right now. Students who are working certainly can't afford it.

Your voices encouraged and ultimately convinced Congress to extend the payroll tax cut for 2 months. Now we've got to extend it for the whole year. I need your help to get it done again. Tell them to pass this tax cut, without drama, without delay. Get it done. It's good for the economy.

Audience member. Four more years! Yes, we can!

The President. Okay. [*Laughter*]

Now, in the longer run, we're also going to have to reduce our deficit. We've got to invest in our future, and we've got to reduce our deficit. And to do both, we've got to make some choices. Let me give you some examples.

Right now we're scheduled to spend nearly one trillion more dollars on what was intended to be a temporary tax cut for the wealthiest 2 percent of Americans.

Audience member. That's not fair.

The President. That's not fair. A quarter of all millionaires pay lower tax rates than millions of middle class households.

Audience member. Boo!

The President. Not fair. Warren Buffett pays a lower tax rate than his secretary. I know because she was at the State of the Union. She told me. [*Laughter*] Is that fair?

Audience members. No!

The President. Does it make sense to you?

Audience members. No!

The President. Do we want to keep these tax cuts for folks like me who don't need them? Or do we want to invest in the things that will help us in the long term, like student loans and grants and a strong military and care for our veterans and basic research?

Those are the choices we've got to make. We can't do everything. We can't reduce our deficit and make the investments we need at the same time and keep tax breaks for folks who don't need them and weren't even asking for them. Well, some of them were asking for them. I wasn't asking for them. [*Laughter*] We've got to choose.

When it comes to paying our fair share, I believe we should follow the Buffett rule: If you make more than $1 million a year—and I hope a lot of you do after you graduate—[*applause*]—then you should pay a tax rate of at least 30 percent. On the other hand, if you decide to go into a less lucrative profession, if you decide to become a teacher—and we need teachers—if you decide to go into public service, if you decide to go into a helping profession, if you make less than $250,000 a year, which 98 percent of Americans do, then your taxes shouldn't go up.

This is part of the idea of shared responsibility. I know a lot of folks have been running around calling this class warfare. I think asking a billionaire to pay at least as much as his secretary in taxes is just common sense. Yesterday Bill Gates said he doesn't think people like him are paying enough in taxes. I promise you, Warren Buffett is doing fine, Bill Gates is doing fine, I'm doing fine.

Audience member. Koch brothers.

The President. They're definitely doing fine. [*Laughter*]

We don't need more tax breaks. There are a lot of families out there who are struggling, who have seen their wages stall, and the cost of everything from a college education to groceries and food have gone up. You're the ones who need that. You're the ones who need help. And we can't do both.

There have been some who have been saying, well, the only reason you're saying that is because you're trying to stir people up, make them envious of the rich. People don't envy the rich. When people talk about me paying my fair share of taxes or Bill Gates or Warren Buffett paying their fair share, the reason that they're talking about it is because they understand that when I get a tax break that I don't need, that the country can't afford, then one of two things are going to happen. Either the deficit will go up, and ultimately, you guys are going to have to pay for it. Or alternatively, somebody else is going to foot the bill, some senior who suddenly has to pay more for their Medicare, or some veteran who's not getting the help that they need readjusting after they have defended this country, or some student who's suddenly having to pay higher interest rates on their student loans.

We do not begrudge wealth in this country. I want everybody here to do well. We aspire to financial success. But we also understand that we're not successful just by ourselves. We're successful because somebody started the University of Michigan. We're successful because somebody made an investment in all the Federal research labs that created the Internet. We're successful because we have an outstanding military; that costs money. We're successful because somebody built roads and bridges and laid broadband lines. And these things didn't just happen on their own.

And if we all understand that we've got to pay for this stuff, it makes sense for those of us who've done best to do our fair share. And to try to pass off that bill onto somebody else, that's not right. That's not who we are. That's not what my grandparents' generation worked hard to pass down. That's not what your grandparents and your great-grandparents worked hard to pass down. We've got a different idea of America, a more generous America.

Everybody here is only here because somebody somewhere down the road decided we're going to think not just about ourselves, but about the future. We've got responsibilities, yes, to ourselves, but also to each other. And now it's our turn to be responsible. Now it's our turn to leave an America that's built to last. And I know we can do it. We've done it before, and I know we can do it again because of you.

When I meet young people all across this country, with energy and drive and vision, despite the fact that you've come of age during a difficult, tumultuous time in this world, it gives me hope. You inspire me. You're here at Michigan because you believe in your future. You're working hard. You're putting in long hours, hopefully, some at the library. [*Laughter*] Some of you are balancing a job at the same time. You know that doing big things isn't always easy, but you're not giving up.

You've got the whole world before you. And you embody that sense of possibility that is quintessentially American. We do not shrink from challenges. We stand up to them. And we don't leave people behind. We make sure everybody comes along with us on this journey that we're on.

That's the spirit right now that we need, Michigan. Here in America, we don't give up. We look out for each other. We make sure everybody has a chance to get ahead. And if we work in common purpose, with common resolve, we can build an economy that gives everybody a fair shot. And we will remind the world just why it is that the United States of America is the greatest nation on Earth.

Thank you, everybody. God bless you. God bless the United States of America. Thank you.

NOTE: The President spoke at 10 a.m. in the Al Glick Field House. In his remarks, he referred to Christina Beckman, sophomore, University of Michigan; Denard Robinson, quarterback, University of Michigan football team; Richard A. Cordray, Director, Consumer Financial Protection Bureau; Warren E. Buffett, chief executive officer and chairman, and Debbie Bosanek, assistant, Berkshire Hathaway Inc.; William H. Gates III, chairman, Microsoft Corp.; and Charles G. Koch, chief executive officer and chairman of the board, and David H. Koch, executive vice president, Koch Industries, Inc. He also referred to his sister Maya Soetoro-Ng.

Remarks at the House Democratic Issues Conference in Cambridge, Maryland
January 27, 2012

The President. Thank you. All right, everybody, have a seat. Now, let me begin by saying I was told that on a CD that I've just received—[*laughter*]—that all of you participated in a rendition of Al Green. [*Laughter*] What I did not realize was that you also had a reverend who can preach as good as Al Green in John Larson. So I kept on looking for the collection plate getting passed. [*Laughter*] But, John, thank you for that rousing introduction.

To the leader of this august body and soon to be, once again, Speaker of the House, Nancy Pelosi; to the rest of the leadership team— Steny Hoyer, Jim Clyburn, Xavier Becerra— and the best possible chair we could have for the DNC, Debbie Wasserman Schultz, we've got an all-star team assembled and ready to get to work.

I know that you guys have been here quite a bit. You already had to suffer through a relatively long speech from me this week, so I'm not going to speak too long. What I wanted to do, first of all, was just say thank you.

So many of you have served this country, your districts, for years, through good times and through bad times. And let's face it, public service doesn't always get the credit that it deserves. But knowing each and every one of you personally, understanding the sacrifices that you and your family members—some who are here today—make each and every day, understanding how much your heart bleeds when you see constituents are going through a tough time and how much you want to make sure

that Government serves as a force for good in their lives, I just want to say thank you for everything that you do.

You guys are putting it all on the line because you believe in an America in which everybody gets a fair shot and everybody does their fair share and everybody plays by the same set of rules. That's what you have been about, that's what this caucus is about, and that's the vision that we're fighting for, this year and in years to come.

Now, as I said at the State of the Union, the critical debate in this country right now, the defining question that faces all of us, is whether we are going to restore that sense of an American promise, where if you work hard, if you're carrying out your responsibilities, if you're looking out for your family, if you're participating in your community, if you're doing what you're supposed to be doing, you have the chance to get a job that allows you to support your family, you won't be bankrupt when you get sick, you can send your children to college, you can retire with some dignity and some respect, you can expect that the next generation—your children and grandchildren— will do better than you did. That American promise, that central driving force in what has created the greatest country, the largest economy, and the broadest middle class on Earth, that promise has been eroding for too many people. And all of you know it.

And this is not a new trend. This is something that's been going on for years now.

Wages and incomes stagnant at the same time that costs keep going up and up and up, outsourcing and jobs moving elsewhere, young people wondering, even if they invest in a college degree, are they going to be able to find a job that supports an ever-increasing load of debt, and all of that was before the economic crisis hit in 2008, 2009 that put millions of people out of work.

Now, here's the good news. The good news is that we are moving in the right direction. Thanks to your efforts, thanks to some tough votes that all of you took, thanks to the leadership that Nancy Pelosi and the rest of the leadership team showed, we righted the ship. We did not tip into a Great Depression. The auto industry was saved. Credit started flowing to small businesses again. And over the last 22 months, we have seen 3 million jobs created, the most jobs last year since 2005, more jobs in manufacturing than we've seen since the nineties. A lot of that has to do with tough decisions that you took.

I just came from Michigan. And there are very few States that have been harder hit by these long-term trends than Michigan. But you can feel this sense of renewed purpose and renewed hope in that State. They understand that had we not acted, a million jobs might have been lost. They understand that had we not acted, the Big Three automakers—but then, all the suppliers, the entire ecosystem of the economy in that State—would have been decimated. And now, they're thinking, GM is number one again and Chrysler is on the move again and Ford is investing in plants and equipment again. And you get a sense of movement, a restoration of hope and possibility.

But people understand that the job is not done, not even close to being done yet. And they understand that if we're going to finish the job, then we've got to, first of all, make sure that American manufacturing is strong. And that means that we're out there creating a Tax Code that doesn't provide tax breaks for companies that are shipping jobs overseas. We are focusing on companies that are investing right here in the United States, because we believe that when you make it in America everybody benefits, everybody does well.

They understand that we need American energy. And part of my goal on Tuesday was to dispel this notion that somehow we haven't been on top of developing American energy—oil and gas production up higher than they've been in 8 years, percentage of imports lower than in the last 16. We've been developing and opening up millions of acres to develop.

But what we've also said is oil is not enough. We've got to think about the future, not just look backwards at the past. We've got to invest in solar and wind and biofuels. We've already doubled our fuel efficiency standards on cars and trucks. We've got to make sure that we build on these successes, which are good for our economy and create jobs and, by the way, are also good for our environment. And that's important to the American people as well.

I know the other side doesn't always believe in this agenda. They think that the only subsidy that's worth providing is subsidies to oil companies. Well, as I said, we've been subsidizing oil companies for close to a century now. Rarely have they been more profitable. Let's take some of that money, let's take some of those tax breaks, and make sure that we're investing in a clean energy future that's just as promising.

Skills for American workers, making sure that every young person in this country has the skills to succeed—I told the story at the State of the Union, but I want to make sure everybody hears this, because we're going to have to work hard on this. Companies are starting to say it makes economic sense for us to move back here into the United States. Wages in places like China are going up faster than productivity. American workers have never been more productive. Energy costs increasingly are competitive here in the United States, partly because of all of the development that's taking place around natural gas. Transportation costs are higher from other places.

When you look at the whole package, a lot of companies are saying, we want to be here, close to our market. But one of the biggest impediments is we've got to be able to find the skilled workers that are going to be managing million-dollar pieces of equipment.

They don't all have to go to 4-year colleges and universities, although we need more engineers and we need more scientists and we've got to make sure that college is affordable and accessible. But we also need skilled workers who are going to community colleges or middle-aged workers who are allowed to retrain, have a commitment to work, have that work ethic, but want to make sure that technology is not passing them by—and so focusing on our community colleges and making sure that they're matched up with businesses that are hiring right now and making sure that they help to design the programs that are going to put them, put people in place to get those jobs right away.

Making college more affordable, which I just spoke about at Michigan—we've got an average of $24,000 worth of debt for every young person that's graduating right now. They're starting off in a hole that most of us didn't have to start off with, and it's brutal. And there are ways we can solve it. This caucus helped to make sure that we increased Pell grants, and we increased student aid, but now—there's some concrete things we've got to do right now, like making sure that the interest rates don't double on student loans this year in July. We're going to require Congress to act.

We're going to also put pressure on States to make sure they're prioritizing higher education. We're going to make sure that colleges and universities are held accountable and that they do what they need to do to hold down costs, but most of all, we've got to restore a commitment to the American values of hard work and responsibility and shared responsibility.

Over the last 3 days, I've traveled around the country amplifying what we said on Tuesday. One of the points I make—and everybody understands this—I say, if we're going to make the investments we need, if we're going to invest in basic science and research that leads to inventions like the Internet that create entire industries, entire platforms for long-term economic growth, if we're going to invest in the skills of our workers, if we're going to make

sure we've got the best infrastructure in the world, if we're going to pay for this incredible military that just saved this young woman out of Somalia, if we're going to take care of the veterans once they're finished serving so that we serve them as well as they serve us, all those things cost money. We've got to pay for it.

And if we're serious about paying for it, then yes, we've got to cut out programs that don't work. This caucus has gone ahead and been willing to make some of the toughest cuts we've ever made—$2 trillion—over $2 trillion in deficit reduction. But we've also said, at a certain point, you know what, everybody has got to participate in this.

And when we've got a trillion—more than a trillion dollars' worth of tax breaks that were supposed to be temporary for the top 2 percent slated to continue, we've got a Tax Code full of loopholes for folks who don't need them and weren't even asking for them, we've got to ask ourselves, what's more important to us? Is it more important for me to get a tax break, or is it more important for that senior to know that they've got Medicare and Social Security that's stable? Is it more important for me to get a tax break, or is it better for that young person to get a break on their college education? Is it more important for me to get a tax break, or is it more important that we care for our veterans?

This is—one of the biggest things I'm going to be pushing back against this year is this notion that somehow this is class warfare, that we're trying to stir up envy. Nobody envies rich people. [*Laughter*] Everybody wants to be rich. [*Laughter*] Everybody aspires to be rich, and everybody understands you got to work hard if you're going to be financially successful. That's the American way. The question is, are we creating opportunity for everybody, which requires some investments? And the question is, how do we pay for that? Because when you give me a tax break that I don't need and the country can't afford, two things happen: Either the deficit increases, or alternatively, somebody else has to pay the tab—that senior or that student or that family who's struggling to make ends meet.

So we're going to push hard for the Buffett rule. We're going to push hard to make sure that millionaires, somebody making over a million dollars a year isn't getting tax breaks and subsidies that they don't need. Not out of envy, but out of a sense of fairness and a sense of mutual responsibility and a sense of commitment to this country's future.

That's what we're fighting for. And the American people understand that.

The same way that they understand we're going to have to keep in place smart regulations that assure that a health care company can't drop you right when you get sick or charge women differently than men. These other folks want to roll back financial regulatory reform. After all that we've been through, you want to water down and weaken rules that make sure that big banks and financial institutions have to play by the same rules as everybody else? That makes no sense.

The American people understand that. You understand that. That's what you've been fighting for.

So, obviously, we're in an election season, and when the other side decides who it is that they want to be their standard bearer, then we're going to have a robust debate about whose vision is more promising when it comes to moving this country forward. And it's going to be a tough election, because a lot of people are still hurting out there and a lot of people have lost faith, generally, about the capacity of Washington to get anything done.

The main thing I want to urge all of you is that even as we are out there making our case, even as we push hard to persuade not just the American people, but hopefully, some folks on the other side about the brightness of our future if we work together, I think it's important during the course of this year not to forget that there's still work that we can do right now.

We can extend the payroll tax cut right now without drama and without delay. We can work together right now to help startups and entrepreneurs get easier financing and use R&D more effectively. There are things we can do right now.

And so even as we engage in a robust debate with the other side, I want us all to remember that there are folks out there that are still counting on us. There are people out there who are still hurting, and wherever we have an opportunity, wherever there is the possibility that the other side is putting some politics aside for just a nanosecond in order to get something done for the American people, we've got to be right there ready to meet them. We've got to be right there ready to meet them.

On the other hand, where they obstruct, where they're unwilling to act, where they're more interested in party than they are in country, more interested in the next election than the next generation, then we've got to call them out on it. We've got to call them out on it. We've got to push them. We can't wait. We can't be held back.

At the State of the Union, obviously, I talked about our military. I had a chance to see some folks out at Buckley in Colorado as well.

Audience member. Yay, Colorado!

The President. There you go. [*Laughter*] Obviously, the work that our military has done this last decade has filled us with awe. I think, as you saw during the State of the Union, everybody stands up when you mention the military and appropriately so. That's something that should not be partisan. But the point that I tried to make on Tuesday, and I hope we all keep in mind, is there's a reason we admire them, and it's not just because they do their job so well. It's not just because of their incredible capacity and training and skill. It's also because of an ethic that says, you know what, we're all in this together. I can only succeed if the guy next to me and the gal next to me are successful as well. I can only succeed if somebody has got my back.

We do not succeed on our own. We all have to pull our weight. We all have to do our work. America is not about handouts or bailouts or copouts. We all have to focus on what our responsibilities are. We have to do our jobs, but we also understand that we are always more successful when we do it together.

Black, White, Hispanic, Asian, Latino, Native American, gay, straight—it doesn't matter. What matters is that we have this sense of common purpose and common resolve. That's what is going to help ensure that this recovery continues. That's what is going to make sure that this country's future is bright. That is at the core, I believe, not only of what it means to be a Democrat, but I also think that's at the core of what it means to be an American.

I believe in you guys. You guys have had my back through some very tough times. I'm going to have your back, as well. And together, we're going to move this country forward.

God bless you. God bless the United States of America. And thank you, Democratic caucus, for all the great work that you do. Let's go out there and change the country. Thank you.

NOTE: The President spoke at 1:36 p.m. at the Hyatt Regency Chesapeake Bay Golf Resort, Spa & Marina. In his remarks, he referred to musician Al Green; Rep. John B. Larson; Jessica Buchanan, an aid worker held hostage in Somalia and rescued by U.S. Armed Forces on January 25; and Warren E. Buffett, chief executive officer and chairman, Berkshire Hathaway Inc.

Remarks at an Obama Victory Fund 2012 Fundraiser
January 27, 2012

Thank you, everybody. Please, please have a seat. It is wonderful to see all of you here this afternoon. Some old friends and some new friends.

As you know, I'm not here tonight just as President, but also as an adopted member of the Crow Nation. If my adoptive parents were here, I know what they'd say: Kids just grow up so fast. [*Laughter*]

When I made that visit to Montana, I said that my job wasn't just to win an election. It was to make sure that Washington started to focus on you. And I took that commitment seriously.

My commitment is deeper than our unique nation-to-nation relationship. It's a commitment to making sure that we get that relationship right. Native Americans have to be full partners in our economy. Your children and your grandchildren have to have an equal shot at the American Dream.

And that's why for 3 years in a row now, we've brought tribal leaders to Washington to develop an agenda that reflects your hopes and your aspirations and the needs of your tribes. I've appointed Native Americans to senior positions in my administration and in my White House. And many of you have had a chance to work with Kim Teehee, who does an extraordinary job coordinating our Native American affairs in the White House. And we've worked

together to tackle some of the most difficult challenges facing Native American families.

And we should be proud of what we've done so far, but it should also sharpen our resolve to do even more. As long as Native Americans face unemployment rates that are far higher than the national average, we've got more work to do. And I wake up every day focused on how do we restore America's promise for all our people, including our first Americans.

So, in my State of the Union Address this week, I laid out my blueprint for an economy that's built to last, an economy built on American manufacturing and American energy, skills for American workers, and a return to American values of fair play and responsibility. And that's what we're fighting for.

And I want you guys to be full partners in that fight because I believe that one day we're going to be able to look back on these years and say that this was a turning point in nation-to-nation relations; that this was a turning point when the nations all across the country recognized that they were full partners, treated with dignity and respect and consultation; that this wasn't just a side note on a White House agenda, but this was part and parcel of our broader agenda to make sure that everybody has opportunity.

And it's also a moment when we build a strong middle class in Indian Country. It's not

105

simply a ward, but is able to marshal the resources to create its own agenda and its own destiny and its own economic development and its own businesses. That's what we're looking for.

We want new businesses and new opportunities to take root on the reservation. We want to stop repeating the mistakes of the past and begin building a better future, one that honors old traditions and also welcomes every single Native American into the American Dream.

We've done some great work together. Whether it's making sure that Indian Health was permanently extended and that we were putting additional resources to make sure that we're picking up the health of Native Americans all across the country, whether it's an Executive order that specifies our focus on education with all of your tribes, whether it's making sure that we are working hard to allow the expansion of land in trust on behalf of nations to go further, we've made some significant progress. But we've got a lot more to do.

And I'm going to need all of you to continue to consult with us, to continue to work with us, continue to partner with us. I guarantee you that the work we've done over these first 3 years is not the end, it's just the beginning.

And if you stick with me, I promise you guys I'm going to be sticking with you. All right, God bless you. Thank you. Thank you.

[*At this point, the President answered questions from members of the audience, and no transcript was provided.*]

NOTE: The President spoke at 4:44 p.m. at the Mandarin Oriental hotel. In his remarks, he referred to Kimberly Teehee, Senior Policy Adviser for Native America Affairs, White House Domestic Policy Council. He also referred to the Indian Health Care Improvement Act; and Executive order 13592.

Statement on International Holocaust Remembrance Day
January 27, 2012

This International Holocaust Remembrance Day, Michelle and I join people in the United States, in Israel, and across the globe as we remember the 6 million Jews and millions of others who were murdered at the hands of the Nazis.

We commit ourselves to keeping their memories alive not only in our thoughts, but through our actions. As we remember all those who perished in camps from Auschwitz to Treblinka, Dachau to Sobibor, we pledge to speak truth to those who deny the Holocaust.

As we celebrate the strength and resilience of survivors, we pledge to stand strong against all those who would commit atrocities, against the resurgence of anti-Semitism, and against hatred in all its forms.

As we draw inspiration from the righteous gentiles who risked their lives to save friends, neighbors, and even strangers, we pledge to continue the hard work of repairing the world.

Together with the State of Israel and all our friends around the world, we dedicate ourselves to giving meaning to those powerful words: "Never forget. Never again."

Statement on the Resignation of Aneesh P. Chopra as United States Chief Technology Officer
January 27, 2012

As the Federal Government's first Chief Technology Officer, Aneesh Chopra did groundbreaking work to bring our Government into the 21st century. Aneesh found countless ways to engage the American people using technology, from electronic health records for veterans to expanding access to broadband for rural communities to modernizing Government records. His legacy of leadership and innovation will benefit Americans for years to come, and I thank him for his outstanding service.

The President's Weekly Address
January 28, 2012

On Tuesday, in my State of the Union Address, I laid out a blueprint for an economy built to last, an economy built on American manufacturing, American energy, skills for American workers, and a renewal of American values.

This week, I took that blueprint across the country, and what I saw was people who work hard and believe in each other. They believe in the America that's within our reach. But they're not sure that the right thing will get done in Washington this year or next year or the year after that. And frankly, when you look at some of the things that go on in this town, who could blame them for being a little cynical?

Just 2 days ago, a Senator promised to obstruct every single American I appoint to a judgeship or a public service position unless I fire the consumer watchdog I put in place to protect the American people from financial schemes or malpractice.

For the most part, it's not that this Senator thinks these nominees are unqualified. In fact, all of the judicial nominees being blocked have bipartisan support. And almost 90 percent have unanimous support from the Judiciary Committee.

Instead, one of the Senator's aides told reporters that the Senator plans to, and I'm quoting here, "Delay and slow the process in order to get the President's attention."

Well, this isn't about me. We weren't sent here to wage perpetual political campaigns against each other. We were sent here to serve the American people. And they deserve better than gridlock and games. One Senator gumming up the whole works for the entire country is certainly not what our Founding Fathers envisioned.

The truth is, neither party has been blameless in tactics like these. But it's time for both parties to put an end to them. I'm asking Congress, both Democrats and Republicans, to stop this kind of behavior by passing a rule that allows all judicial and public service nominations a simple up-or-down vote within 90 days.

We should also stem the corrosive influence of money in politics. The House and Senate should send me a bill that bans insider trading by Members of Congress, and I will sign it immediately. They should limit any elected official from owning stocks in industries they impact. And they should make sure people who bundle campaign contributions for Congress can't lobby Congress, and vice versa.

During my address on Tuesday night, I spoke about the incredible example set by the men and women of our Armed Forces. At a time when too many of our institutions have let us down, they exceed all expectations. They're not consumed with personal ambition. They don't obsess over their differences. They focus on the mission at hand. They work together.

If you agree with me that leaders in Washington should follow their example, then make your voice heard. Tell your Member of Congress that it's time to end the gridlock and start tackling the issues that really matter: an economy built on American manufacturing, American energy, American skills and education, and a return to American values—an economy built to last.

Thanks. God bless you, and have a great weekend.

NOTE: The address was recorded at approximately 6 p.m. on January 27 in the East Room at the White House for broadcast on January 28. In the address, the President referred to Sen. Michael S. Lee; and Richard A. Cordray, Director, Consumer Financial Protection Bureau. The transcript was made available by the Office of the Press Secretary on January 27, but was embargoed for release until 6 a.m. on January 28.

Remarks Following a Meeting With President Mikheil Saakashvili of Georgia
January 30, 2012

President Obama. Well, I want to welcome President Saakashvili and his delegation here. And it's a wonderful occasion to have him here as we'll be celebrating this year 20 years of independence for Georgia and the eighth anniversary of the Rose Revolution.

I think Georgia should be extraordinarily proud of the progress that it has made in building a sovereign and democratic country. And one of the first things that I did was express my appreciation for the institution-building that's been taking place in Russia—in Georgia, the importance of making sure that minorities are respected, the importance of a police—and a system of rule of law that is being observed, the kinds of institution-building that is going to make an enormous difference in the future of not just this generation of Georgians, but future generations of Georgians.

And so I want to express my appreciation for the work that's been done in the past, but also anticipating fair and free elections here, the formal transfer of power that will be taking place in Georgia, which I think will solidify many of these reforms that have already taken place.

We discussed how we can continue to strengthen the strong bilateral relationship between our two countries. Part of this is economic. Obviously, Georgia has made strides in creating a effective free market system, and more progress needs to be made. The United States wants to help in that progress.

And so one of the most important things that we're doing in addition to things like the MCC and OPIC loans is also what we've agreed to is a high-level dialogue between our two countries about how we can continue to strengthen trade relations between our two countries, including the possibility of a free trade agreement. Obviously, there's a lot of work to be done and there are going to be a lot of options that are going to be explored. The key point though is we think it's a win-win for the United States and for Georgia as we continue to find opportunities for businesses to invest in Georgia, for us to be able to sell Georgia our goods and services, and Georgia to be able to sell theirs as well.

On defense and security, I expressed my gratitude to the President for the extraordinary contributions that have been made by the Georgian military in Afghanistan. They have been one of the most dedicated contributors outside of NATO to the ISAF effort, and in fact have taken on some significant casualties as a consequence of those efforts.

We have talked about how we will continue to strengthen our defense cooperation, and there are a wide range of areas where we are working together. And I reaffirmed to the President and assured him that the United States will continue to support Georgia's aspirations to ultimately become a member of NATO.

Finally, I wanted to say to the President that we appreciate the model of democracy and transparency that they've been setting not just for their own country, but also for the region as a whole. And we think that with continued progress over the next several years that a lot of countries will say to themselves that if Georgia can perform these transformations, then we can as well. They've been a responsible player on the world scene and in multilateral fora.

And so under the President's leadership, I think that they've made enormous strides. And we will continue to look for opportunities to strengthen what is already a very strong bilateral relationship.

So welcome, Mr. President. Thank you so much for being here.

President Saakashvili. Thank you so much. Thank you.

Well, Mr. President, I'm incredibly honored to be back in the Oval Office. And I can tell you we are incredibly grateful as a nation for continued support and strong basically cooperation that we'll be getting from your administration and from the United States of America at every level. And for my country's independence, for its future, for the future of our democracy, for the future of our region, that has been absolutely decisive and key in all different directions.

Obviously, there's a very good understanding at a number of levels. We are grateful for your support for our NATO aspirations. We are very grateful for elevating our defense cooperation further and talking about Georgia's self-defense capabilities and developing it, because that's also, of course, an important message back to my nation.

It's very important that you mentioned, obviously, the prospect of a free trade agreement with Georgia, because that's going to attract lots of additional activity to my country and basically helping our nation-building process.

Thank you again for complimenting us on our reforms. Obviously, the reform process is never over, but these reforms would not have happened without strong commitment and support and advice from your administration and from the United States and your people on the ground. We deeply appreciate all this.

Obviously, next—this year we have parliamentary elections which will mark also bringing in another political system, constitution system, with more parliamentary government. And as you rightly mentioned, there is—well, there will be—next year a new President will be elected in Georgia. And that's also important because that's also—will move our democracy forward and will generally get much more to a diversified and pluralistic political scene.

And obviously, I will continue to cooperate with you in all these directions that these gains get solidified, irreversible. And nothing can take Georgia away from this track of progress. Nothing can bring us back to a less democratic, corrupt, retrograde political system or political actors.

And obviously, this was very, very—from my point of view, I'll be—again, my personal gratitude. I'll be leaving this office very happy because we basically got what we wanted to get. Thanks so much.

President Obama. Thank you.

President Saakashvili. Thank you.

NOTE: The President spoke at 2:59 p.m. in the Oval Office at the White House.

Remarks Prior to a Cabinet Meeting and an Exchange With Reporters
January 31, 2012

The President. Hello, everybody. This is our first Cabinet meeting after my State of the Union Address, and it gives me an opportunity to share my ideas and initiatives with my Cabinet, but also to get some feedback from them.

One of the top priorities that I mentioned during the State of the Union was the need for us to small—promote small business. And I'm very pleased that we've got Karen Mills here, who has participated in our meetings before, but is now an official member of the Cabinet. It is a symbol of how important it is for us to spur entrepreneurship, to help startups, to move aggressively so that we can assure more companies that create the most jobs in our economy are getting a leg up from the various programs that we have in our Government.

I mentioned at the State of the Union that there have been discussions, bipartisan discussions between Republicans and Democrats, about a whole set of measures that can accelerate financing to startup companies, can provide tax breaks to startups and small businesses that are interested in either hiring more workers or increasing their wages, that looks at innovative ways for them to raise capital. And my expectation and hope is, is that they will get a bill together quickly, that they will pass it and get it on my desk. I will sign it right away, and I would like to see that bill signed this year.

In addition, we've got all the Cabinet agencies who are here represented; they are putting forward their own initiatives to enhance the ability of entrepreneurs to get up and running. So, for example, the Department of Homeland Security, my understanding is we're going to be talking about how we can improve the visa process for those who are interested in investing in the United States and starting businesses here in the United States.

109

I know that the Department of Commerce, Energy, and Education, as well as the SBA, are all launching complementary initiatives to support entrepreneurship as well. And so what we want to do is to make sure that every single agency, even as they're tending to their energy initiatives or providing homeland security or transportation or defense, that we're also thinking about how are we advancing the cause of giving small businesses and entrepreneurs opportunities to start creating the next Google or the next Apple or the next innovative company that's going to create jobs and improve our economy.

It's that kind of all-hands-on-deck approach that is really going to make a difference. And we're looking forward to hearing additional ideas from our Business Council and from those who are involved in startups that can help to promote these—this agenda.

So thank you all for participating. I'm looking forward to hearing your ideas, and I will see you guys later.

Housing Market

Q. Will we get details on your housing plan tomorrow?

The President. I will talk to you then about it. I wouldn't want to use up all my good stuff now. [*Laughter*]

Q. Thank you, sir.

NOTE: The President spoke at 10:48 a.m. in the Cabinet Room at the White House. A portion of these remarks could not be verified because the audio was incomplete.

Remarks at the Washington Auto Show
January 31, 2012

Let me just say, when you look at all these cars, it is testimony to the outstanding work that's been done by workers: American workers, American designers. The U.S. auto industry is back. The fact that GM is back, number one, I think shows the kind of turnaround that's possible when it comes to American manufacturing.

And it's good to remember that—the fact that there were some folks who were willing to let this industry die. Because of folks coming together, we are now back in a place where we can compete with any car company in the world. And these are not only selling here in the United States, they also serve as a platform for us to sell product all around the world.

So I'm just very proud of what we're seeing here. That Camaro with the American eagle and the American flag, that helps tell the story.

So thank you very much.

NOTE: The President spoke at 2:50 p.m. at the Walter E. Washington Convention Center.

Remarks at an Obama Victory Fund 2012 Fundraiser
January 31, 2012

Thank you so much, Rob, for the introduction. And it's wonderful to see all of you. I'm going to be very brief at the top because I want to spend most of this time in a dialogue.

As Rob said, I see a lot of friends here, people who supported me since way back when, before people could say my name. And as I look around the room, folks from all across the country, I am mindful of the fact that not only have you done so much to help me be in a position where I can make a difference in America, but separate and apart from my election, so many of you have supported good causes that are making a difference day in and day out. And so I just want to say thank you for that.

As Rob said, the last 3 years, we've obviously gone through historic times, a set of historic challenges: the worst economic crisis and financial crisis since the Great Depression, two wars, a transformation of our geopolitics. And I couldn't be prouder of the track record that we've been able to put together over the last 3 years, not only in preventing us from sliding into a Great Depression, not only shifting from a situation where we were losing 800,000 jobs per month to 22 consecutive months of job growth, the highest manufacturing job growth since the nineties, the largest job growth, period, last year since 2005, passing historic health care legislation that we're in the process now of implementing, tough Wall Street reform legislation that is going to make sure that we don't see the same kind of reckless behavior that got us into this mess in the first place, along with a set of laws that are going to make sure that the values we care so deeply about are the law of the land, things like ending "don't ask, don't tell" or making sure that people are actually getting equal pay for equal work, one of the strongest environmental records of any President in the modern era.

So, across the board, I couldn't be prouder of what we've accomplished. On the other hand, what I'm also mindful of is how much remains to be done.

What led me to run in 2008 was a sense that there had been a fundamental shift in the social compact, a fundamental shift in the American promise, the notion that if you worked hard, if you met your responsibilities, that you could get ahead, support a family, send your kid to college, avoid being bankrupted by an illness, retire with dignity and respect. That basic bargain felt like it was slipping away from far too many Americans.

And so in addition to dealing with crises, our goal since before I came into office was how do we restore that sense that any American, no matter where they're from, no matter what they look like, that they've got a shot to succeed; how do we restore an America where everybody gets a fair shot, everybody is doing their fair share, and we're all playing by the same set of rules.

This past Tuesday, I tried to lay out that vision, that blueprint for how we move forward, involving resuscitating American manufactur-

ing—the same way we've done with the auto industry, we can do that across the board. American energy—how do we, yes, make sure that American oil production and natural gas are properly produced, but how do we also make sure that we're still investing in clean energy and looking 10, 20, 30 years down the road and making sure that we're at the forefront of the kind of clean energy economy that I think everybody is going to have to adjust to?

How do we make sure that we've got a tax system that reflects everybody doing their fair share? Because if we're going to bring down our deficits and make investments in our infrastructure and our basic research, then we're going to have to do it in a balanced way?

And how do we make sure that we've got a set of regulations in place that aren't designed to squelch entrepreneurial activity and the free market, but are designed to make sure that our consumers are protected and that our air is clean and our water is clean and that we don't see another crisis like we saw in the housing market.

And those are going to be huge fights. And that's why I think this year is going to be extraordinarily exciting. In some way, the spirit of this year's race will be different because in 2008, obviously everybody was full of hope and possibility, and we had not yet gone through a crisis. And it's worn on people, and it's been tough for folks. Now I think what we're really struggling for is the kind of America that most of the people here believe in and I believe that most Americans believe in.

But we're going to have to fight for it, because the other party has a fundamentally different vision about where to take this country. Their basic argument is, is that if we strip out regulations, if we disregard environmental concerns, if we take away protections for consumers, if we lower taxes even further for the kind of folks who are in this room, that somehow growth and the American Dream will be restored. And I fundamentally disagree with that vision. I think it's the wrong vision for America.

But given the difficulties that Americans have gone through over the last 3 years, this is going to be a tough fight, and we're all going to have to be focused on making sure that every single day the American people understand not only where we want to take the country, but also so that we're willing to fight for them; that this is not an abstract ideological argument, but this is a practical, concrete argument about whether or not they're going to be able to find a good job that pays a living wage, whether they're going to have health care that protects their families, whether or not, as consumers, they're going to be protected from being taken advantage of. They've got to feel that we are actively advocating on their behalf.

The last point I'd make is, is that—and I made this point at the State of the Union—as I travel around the world, and obviously, we've been extraordinarily active, not only ending the war in Iraq, but managing a responsible transition in Afghanistan, helping to usher in an Arab Spring that is still uncertain in terms of its outcome, what's striking to me is the degree to which for all of the challenges we've gone through over the last 3 years, the world still looks to us for leadership. They're still looking to America because for all our power, they also understand we are invested in a set of international rules and international norms and a set of universal values that, historically, superpowers have not paid a lot of attention to.

And so when we went to Asia, for example, what was striking was, yes, people understand that China is on the rise and economically their fates are going to be tied not only to us, but also to a rapidly growing China, but when it comes to putting together an architecture out there that assures that small countries are protected, that everybody is abiding by the same sets of rules, that their natural resources are properly developed and not exploited, they're still looking to us.

And so part of the message I wanted to send last week at the State of the Union was, we've been through tougher times before, we've been through bigger challenges before, and we've always come out stronger, more united, and have remained a beacon of hope around the world because—I think it was Churchill who said that the Americans always end up doing the right thing after they've tried every other alternative. [*Laughter*] And that's true. We muddle our way through because of messy democracy, and it's in our nature to be contentious and have these big arguments, but ultimately, we choose the right path. And that's what the world is counting on right now as well.

I think we're going to get there, but—in fact, I know we're going to get there—but I'm going to need all of your help to get there as well.

So thanks for the support in the past, and I'm looking forward to you guys being in the foxhole with me this year. Thank you very much.

NOTE: The President spoke at 7:05 p.m. at the St. Regis Hotel.

Remarks at an Obama Victory Fund 2012 Fundraiser in Chevy Chase, Maryland
January 31, 2012

The President. First of all, I just want to thank Stewart and Sandra for setting up this extraordinary event. It is true that this is now the third time I've been here. It's been said by a friend of mine, Abner Mikva, former Member of Congress, that being friends with a politician is like perpetually having a student in college. [*Laughter*] But this is the last campaign. I'm about to graduate. [*Laughter*] So those tuition checks will slowly diminish.

There was also suggestion that we might sing a duet together. And I have to tell you, though, you try to limit these appearances so that you leave them hungry for more. [*Laughter*] So we may not hear me singing for quite some time.

I'm going to be very brief on the front end because I want to spend most of my time in a conversation with you guys and make sure that we have time for questions.

There he is. [*Laughter*] She stole your thunder, man.

Audience member. I decided to show up. [*Laughter*]

The President. But look, we've gone through 3 of the toughest years that we've seen in our lifetimes. And a lot of folks are still hurting out there. But as I said at the State of the Union last week, we're beginning to see progress. We averted a great depression. The auto industry has come back, and GM is number one again. I just went to the auto show today to see some of the terrific cars that Detroit is churning out.

We've had 3 million jobs created over the last 22 months, and we had the highest job growth last year since 2005, the highest manufacturing job growth since the 1990s. There is a sense that although there's still a lot of uncertainties out there—Europe, the price of oil—that America is slowly repairing from this extraordinary economic and financial crisis.

And during the last 3 years, even as we singularly focused on making sure that we were able to right the ship, we were also able to accomplish a lot of goals that we had set for ourselves in 2008, whether it was passing health care reform so that already 2.5 million young people have insurance that wouldn't have it otherwise and senior citizens are seeing discounts on their prescription drugs, and we're now setting up exchanges all across the country so that never again would somebody with a preexisting condition finds themselves barred from being able to get health insurance.

We were able to end "don't ask, don't tell" so that it doesn't matter who you love, you can serve the country that you love. We were able to take billions of dollars that were going to banks as middlemen for students' loans, and now it's being channeled directly to students so that millions of young people across the country find college a little bit more affordable.

We have made progress on a whole variety of fronts domestically. And obviously, internationally we kept one of the first promises I made as President of the United States, and that was to end the war in Iraq in a responsible way. And we're now in the process of transitioning in Afghanistan.

But having said all that, we have so much more work to do, because what compelled me to run in the first place back in 2008 was a larger challenge. It had to do with what had happened to the American promise, the idea if you work hard, then you can find a job that supports a family and you can send your kids to college and you can retire with dignity and respect. That basic compact that said no matter who you are, no matter where you came from, you could make it if you try, that had been slipping away from too many people for too long.

And that was a set of challenges that were decades in the making. We never expected to solve those overnight, but what we understand is that the defining issue of our time is how we restore the basic promise of the American Dream.

And last week at the State of the Union, I laid out a blueprint for how we get there that involves rebuilding American manufacturing and replicating the success we've had in the auto industry across the board. It means revitalizing how we train our young people for the jobs of the 21st century, creating skills for American workers, not just through 4-year colleges, but also through 2-year colleges.

It means having an American energy policy that doesn't just look to the past, but also looks to the future: clean energy, solar, wind, biodiesel, and electric cars.

And it means the restoration of American values where we're certain that everybody is playing by the same set of rules, whether it comes to Wall Street and how they treat their customers, whether it comes to dealing with polluters and making sure that we still have clean air and clean water, but also when it comes to our Tax Code and ensuring that those investments we have to make in basic research and science and infrastructure—all the things that help make us an economic superpower—that we're able to pay for those without adding to the deficit. And that means that we have a tax system that's more equitable and we're

113

stripping out the loopholes and the special deals that have been carved out for so long.

That's our challenge. That's what we're fighting for. And the other side has a fundamentally different idea about how to move this country forward. It's a vision that got us into this mess in the first place, and we can't go back to it. And frankly, the American people are not buying this notion that what will cure our ills is more tax cuts for the wealthiest of Americans and a rolling back of regulations designed to protect American consumers and our children from pollution. People don't believe that that somehow is a recipe for success over the long term.

The challenge we have is people have gone through 3 years of really tough times. And so they don't experience the economy in some abstract way; they're experiencing it in terms of not being able to find a job or their house being underwater or their kids having to come back even after they've gotten a college education and tens of thousands of dollars in debt and still not being able to find a job. And given the difficulties that a lot of folks are still going through, it's not surprising that they're feeling doubtful. Even if we're moving in the right direction, their sense is, gosh, we sure hope—we sure wish that it went faster.

So this is going to be a tough race because of that economic reality, not because of the ideas of the other side. And our job over the next year is to make sure that, number one, we

make the case about what we've done, because we have an extraordinary record, a story to tell that resonates with the American people when they have the facts; and number two, to lift up the prospects, the possibility, of an America where once again people who are responsible and are doing the right thing are able to get ahead.

And I think we can accomplish those things, but I'm going to need your help. This is not going to be easy. This is going to be tough. And since 2008, as I often say, my hair is now grayer, and I've got a few more dings. [*Laughter*] Sometimes, I look at pictures of the campaign and I say, gosh, I was really young. [*Laughter*]

But you know, my determination, my passion for making sure that everybody has a chance in this country, the same sense of determination that I had in 2008, it's stronger now than it was then. I am absolutely convinced that we're on the right track and we just got to fight for it.

I'm going to need you to help, but if you do, then we're going to have 5 more years to be able to get everything done that needs to get done so that this country reflects the values that we all care so deeply about.

Thanks.

NOTE: The President spoke at 8:43 p.m. at the residence of Stewart Bainum, Jr., and Sandra Bainum. Audio was not available for verification of the content of these remarks.

Remarks at the James Lee Community Center in Falls Church, Virginia
February 1, 2012

Thank you so much. Everybody, please have a seat. Have a seat. It is great to be back in Falls Church. Thank you for having me.

Last week, in my State of the Union, I laid out my blueprint for an economy that's built to last. And I want to assure you I am not going to go over the whole thing again this morning. [*Laughter*] That was a long speech. I'm not going to repeat the whole thing. But I do want to talk about some of the issues that I discussed last week, because the blueprint we put forward was one that focuses on restoring what

have always been this country's greatest strengths: American manufacturing, American energy, skills and education for American workers so that we can compete with anybody around the world in this 21st-century economy, and most importantly, the American values of fairness and responsibility—fairness and responsibility.

Now, we know what happens, because we've just seen it—what happened when we stray from those values. We saw what happened over the past decade when we strayed from those values, especially when it comes to the massive housing bubble that burst and hurt so many people. Millions of families who did the right and the responsible thing, folks who shopped for a home that they could afford, secured a mortgage, made their payments each month, they were hurt badly by the irresponsible actions of other people who weren't playing by the same rules, weren't taking the same care, weren't acting as responsibly: by lenders who sold loans to people who they knew couldn't afford the mortgages and buyers who bought homes they knew they couldn't afford and banks that packaged those mortgages up and traded them to reap phantom profits, knowing that they were building a house of cards.

It was wrong. It was wrong. It triggered the worst economic crisis of our lifetimes. And it has been the single biggest drag on our recovery from a terrible recession. Crushing debt has kept millions of consumers from spending. A lack of building demand has kept hundreds of thousands of construction workers idle. Everybody involved in the home-building business—folks who make windows, folks who make carpets—they've all been impacted. The challenge is massive in size and in scope because we've got a multitrillion-dollar housing industry. And economists can tell you how it's affected all sorts of statistics, from GDP to consumer confidence.

But what's at stake is more than just statistics. It's personal. I've been saying that this is a make-or-break moment for the middle class. And this housing crisis struck right at the heart of what it means to be middle class in America: our homes, the place where we invest our nest egg, place where we raise our family, the place where we plant roots in a community, the place where we build memories.

It's personal. It affects so much of how people feel about their lives, about their communities, about the country, about the economy. We need to do everything in our power to repair the damage and make responsible families whole again—everything we can.

Now, the truth is, it's going to take more time than any of us would like for the housing market to fully recover from this crisis. This was a big bubble, and when it burst, it had a big effect. Home prices started a pretty steady decline about 5 years ago. And Government certainly can't fix the entire problem on its own. But it is wrong for anybody to suggest that the only option for struggling, responsible homeowners is to sit and wait for the housing market to hit bottom. I refuse to accept that, and so do the American people.

There are more than 10 million homeowners across the country right now who, because of an unprecedented decline in home prices that is no fault of their own, owe more on their mortgage than their homes are worth. It means your mortgage, your house is underwater.

Here in Falls Church, home values have fallen by about a quarter from their peak. In places like Las Vegas, more than half of all homeowners are underwater—more than half. So it's going to take a while for those prices to rise again. But there are actions we can take right now to provide some relief to folks who've been responsible, have done the right thing, and are making their payments on time.

Already, thanks to the outstanding work, in part, of my Secretary of Housing and Urban Development, Shaun Donovan, who's here today—yes, there he is, the good-looking guy in the front here—[*laughter*]—the housing plan we launched a couple years ago has helped nearly 1 million responsible homeowners refinance their mortgages, and they're saving an average of $300 on their payments each month—$300, which is great.

But I'll be honest, the programs that we put forward haven't worked at the scale that we hoped. Not as many people have taken advantage of it as we wanted. Mortgage rates are as low as they've been in half a century, and when that happens, usually homeowners flock to refinance their mortgages. So a lot of people take advantage of it and save a lot of money. But this time too many families haven't been able to take advantage of the low rates, because falling prices lock them out of the market. They were underwater; made it more difficult for them to refinance.

Then, you've got all the fees involved in refinancing. And a lot of people just said, you know what, even though I'd like to be, obviously, cutting down my monthly payment, the banks just aren't being real encouraging.

So, last year, we took aggressive action that allowed more families to participate. And today we're doing even more. This is the main reason I'm here today.

As I indicated at the State of the Union last week, I am sending Congress a plan that will give every responsible homeowner in America the chance to save about $3,000 a year on their mortgage by refinancing at historically low rates. No more redtape. No more runaround from the banks. And a small fee on the largest financial institutions will make sure it doesn't add to our deficit.

Now, I want to be clear: This plan, like the other actions we've taken, will not help the neighbors down the street who bought a house they couldn't afford and then walked away and left a foreclosed home behind. It's not designed for those who've acted irresponsibly, but it can help those who've acted responsibly. It's not going to help those who bought multiple homes just to speculate and flip the house and make a quick buck, but it can help those who've acted responsibly.

What this plan will do is help millions of responsible homeowners who make their payments on time but find themselves trapped under falling home values or wrapped up in redtape.

If you're ineligible for refinancing just because you're underwater on your mortgage, through no fault of your own, this plan changes that. You'll be able to refinance at a lower rate. You'll be able to save hundreds of dollars a month that you can put back in your pocket. Or you can choose those savings to rebuild equity in your homes, which will help most underwater homeowners come back up for air more quickly.

Now, to move this part of my plan, we're going to need Congress to act. We're going to need Congress to act. I hear some—[*laughter*]—murmuring in the audience here. We need them to act. But we're not just going to wait for Congress. We're going to keep building a firewall to prevent the same kinds of abuses that led this crisis—that led to this crisis in the first place. So there are things we can do administratively that are also going to help responsible homeowners.

Already, we've set up a special Task Force I asked my Attorney General to establish to investigate the kind of activity banks took when they packaged and sold risky mortgages. And that Task Force is ramping up its work as we speak. We're going to keep at it and hold people who broke the law accountable and help restore confidence in the market. We're going to speed assistance to homeowners. And we're going to turn the page on an era of recklessness that hurt so many hard-working Americans.

Today I'm also proposing a homeowner's bill of rights, one straightforward set of commonsense rules of the road that every family knows they can count on when they're shopping for a mortgage. No more hidden fees or conflicts of interest, no more getting the runaround when you call about your loan, no more fine print that you use to get families to take a deal that is not as good as the one they should have gotten, new safeguards against inappropriate foreclosures, new options to avoid foreclosure if you've fallen on hardship or a run of bad luck, and a new, simple, clear form for buying—for new buyers of a home.

Now, think about it. This is the most important purchase a family makes. But how many of you have had to deal with overly complicated mortgage forms and hidden clauses and complex terms? I remember when Michelle and I bought our first condo. And we're both lawyers. [*Laughter*] And we're looking through the forms and kind of holding it up—[*laughter*]—reading it again—"What does this phrase mean?" And that's for two trained lawyers. The forms, the confusion, the potential for abuse is too great just because the forms were too complicated.

So this is what a mortgage form should look like.

[*At this point, the President held up a mortgage disclosure form.*]

This is it. Now that our new consumer watchdog agency is finally running at full steam, now that Richard Cordray is in as the Director of the Consumer Finance Protection Bureau, they're moving forward on important protections like this new, shorter mortgage form: simple, not complicated; informative, not confusing; terms are clear, fees are transparent.

This is, by the way, is what some of the folks in Congress are trying to roll back and prevent from happening.

I guess they like complicated things that confuse consumers and allow them to be cheated. I prefer actions that are taken to make things simpler and easier to understand for consumers so that they can get the best deal possible, especially on the biggest single investment that most people will ever make.

Americans making a downpayment on their dreams shouldn't be terrified by pages and pages of fine print. They should be confident they're making the right decision for their future.

Now, there's more that we're announcing today. We're working to turn more foreclosed homes into rental housing, because as we know and a lot of families know, that empty house or for sale sign down the block can bring down the price of homes across the neighborhood. We're working to make sure people don't lose their homes just because they lose their jobs. These are steps that can make a concrete difference in people's lives right now.

As I said earlier, no program or policy will solve all the problems in a multitrillion-dollar housing market. The heights of the housing bubble reached before it burst, those were unsustainable, and it's going to take time to fully recover. That requires everybody to do their part.

As much as our economic challenges were born of eroding home values and portfolio values, they were also born of an erosion of some old-fashioned American values. An economy that's built to last, that's on a firm foundation, so that middle class families have a sense of security and those who want to get in the middle class can make it if they're working hard, that demands responsibility from everyone.

Government must take responsibility for rules that are fair and fairly enforced. Banks and lenders must be held accountable for ending the practices that helped cause this crisis in the first place. And all of us have to take responsibility for our own actions or lack of action.

So I urge Congress to act. Pass this plan. Help more families keep their homes. Help more neighborhoods remain vibrant. Help keep more dreams defended and alive. And I promise you that I'll keep doing everything I can to make the future brighter for this community, for this Commonwealth, for this country.

Thank you, everybody. God bless you. God bless the United States of America. Thank you.

NOTE: The President spoke at 11:05 a.m.

Remarks at the National Prayer Breakfast
February 2, 2012

Thank you. Please, please, everybody have a seat. Well, good morning, everybody. It is good to be with so many friends united in prayer. And I begin by giving all praise and honor to God for bringing us together here today.

I want to thank our cochairs, Mark and Jeff; to my dear friend, the guy who always has my back, Vice President Biden; all the Members of Congress—[*applause*]—Joe deserves a hand— all the Members of Congress and my Cabinet

who are here today; all the distinguished guests who've traveled a long way to be part of this. I'm not going to be as funny as Eric—[*laughter*]—but I'm grateful that he shared his message with us. Michelle and I feel truly blessed to be here.

This is my third year coming to this prayer breakfast as President. As Jeff mentioned, before that, I came as Senator. I have to say, it's easier coming as President. [*Laughter*] I don't have to get here quite as early. But it's always been an opportunity that I've cherished. And it's a chance to step back for a moment, for us to come together as brothers and sisters and seek God's face together. At a time when it's easy to lose ourselves in the rush and clamor of our own lives or get caught up in the noise and rancor that too often passes as politics today, these moments of prayer slow us down. They humble us. They remind us that no matter how much responsibility we have, how fancy our titles, how much power we think we hold, we are imperfect vessels. We can all benefit from turning to our Creator, listening to Him, avoiding phony religiosity, and listening to Him.

This is especially important right now, when we're facing some big challenges as a nation. Our economy is making progress as we recover from the worst crisis in three generations, but far too many families are still struggling to find work or make the mortgage, pay for college or, in some cases, even buy food. Our men and women in uniform have made us safer and more secure, and we were eternally grateful to them, but war and suffering and hardship still remain in too many corners of the globe. And a lot of those men and women who we celebrate on Veterans Day and Memorial Day come back and find that, when it comes to finding a job or getting the kind of care that they need, we're not always there the way we need to be.

It's absolutely true that meeting these challenges requires sound decisionmaking, requires smart policies. We know that part of living in a pluralistic society means that our personal religious beliefs alone can't dictate our response to every challenge we face.

But in my moments of prayer, I'm reminded that faith and values play an enormous role in motivating us to solve some of our most urgent problems, in keeping us going when we suffer setbacks, and opening our minds and our hearts to the needs of others.

We can't leave our values at the door. If we leave our values at the door, we abandon much of the moral glue that has held our Nation together for centuries and allowed us to become somewhat more perfect a Union. Frederick Douglass, Abraham Lincoln, Jane Addams,

Martin Luther King, Jr., Dorothy Day, Abraham Heschel, the majority of great reformers in American history did their work not just because it was sound policy or they had done good analysis or understood how to exercise good politics, but because their faith and their values dictated it and called for bold action, sometimes in the face of indifference, sometimes in the face of resistance.

This is no different today for millions of Americans, and it's certainly not for me.

I wake up each morning, and I say a brief prayer, and I spend a little time in Scripture and devotion. And from time to time, friends of mine, some of who are here today, friends like Joel Hunter or T.D. Jakes, will come by the Oval Office or they'll call on the phone or they'll send me a e-mail, and we'll pray together, and they'll pray for me and my family and for our country.

But I don't stop there. I'd be remiss if I stopped there, if my values were limited to personal moments of prayer or private conversations with pastors or friends. So instead, I must try—imperfectly, but I must try—to make sure those values motivate me as one leader of this great Nation.

And so when I talk about our financial institutions playing by the same rules as folks on Main Street, when I talk about making sure insurance companies aren't discriminating against those who are already sick or making sure that unscrupulous lenders aren't taking advantage of the most vulnerable among us, I do so because I genuinely believe it will make the economy stronger for everybody. But I also do it because I know that far too many neighbors in our country have been hurt and treated unfairly over the last few years, and I believe in God's command to "love thy neighbor as thyself." I know that a version of that Golden Rule is found in every major religion and every set of beliefs, from Hinduism to Islam to Judaism to the writings of Plato.

And when I talk about shared responsibility, it's because I genuinely believe that in a time when many folks are struggling, at a time when we have enormous deficits, it's hard for me to ask seniors on a fixed income or young people with student loans or middle class families who can barely pay the bills to shoulder the burden alone. And I think to myself, if I'm willing to give something up as somebody who's been extraordinarily blessed and give up some of the tax breaks that I enjoy, I actually think that's going to make economic sense.

But for me as a Christian, it also coincides with Jesus' teaching that "for unto whom much is given, much shall be required." It mirrors the Islamic belief that those who've been blessed have an obligation to use those blessings to help others or the Jewish doctrine of moderation and consideration for others.

When I talk about giving every American a fair shot at opportunity, it's because I believe that when a young person can afford a college education or someone who's been unemployed suddenly has a chance to retrain for a job and regain that sense of dignity and pride and contributing to the community as well as supporting their families, that helps us all prosper.

It means maybe that research lab on the cusp of a lifesaving discovery or the company looking for skilled workers is going to do a little bit better, and we'll all do better as a consequence. It makes economic sense. But part of that belief comes from my faith in the idea that I am my brother's keeper and I am my sister's keeper, that as a country, we rise and fall together. I'm not an island. I'm not alone in my success. I succeed because others succeed with me.

And when I decide to stand up for foreign aid or prevent atrocities in places like Uganda or take on issues like human trafficking, it's not just about strengthening alliances or promoting democratic values or projecting American leadership around the world, although it does all those things and it will make us safer and more secure. It's also about the Biblical call to care for the least of these, for the poor, for those at the margins of our society; to answer the responsibility we're given in Proverbs to "speak up for those who cannot speak for themselves, for the rights of all who are destitute." And for others, it may reflect the Jewish belief that the highest form of charity is to do our part to help others stand on their own.

Treating others as you want to be treated, requiring much from those who have been given so much, living by the principle that we are our brother's keeper, caring for the poor and those in need, these values are old. They can be found in many denominations and many faiths, among many believers and among many nonbelievers. And they're values that have always made this country great when we live up to them, when we don't just give lip service to them, when we don't just talk about them 1 day a year. And they're the ones that have defined my own faith journey.

And today, with as many challenges as we face, these are the values I believe we're going to have to return to in the hopes that God will buttress our efforts.

Now, we can earnestly seek to see these values lived out in our politics and our policies, and we can earnestly disagree on the best way to achieve these values. In the words of C.S. Lewis, "Christianity is not, and does not profess to have a detailed political program. It is meant for all men at all times, and the particular program which suited one place or time would not suit another."

Our goal should not be to declare our policies as Biblical. It is God who is infallible, not us. Michelle reminds me of this often. [*Laughter*] So instead, it is our hope that people of good will can pursue their values and common ground—and the common good as best they know how, with respect for each other. And I have to say that sometimes we talk about respect, but we don't act with respect towards each other during the course of these debates.

But each and every day, for many in this room, the Biblical injunctions are not just words, they are also deeds. Every single day, in different ways, so many of you are living out your faith in service to others.

Just last month, it was inspiring to see thousands of young Christians filling the Georgia Dome at the Passion Conference to worship the God who set the captives free and work to end modern slavery. Since we've expanded and strengthened the White House faith-based initiative, we've partnered with Catholic Charities to help Americans who are struggling with poverty, worked with organizations like World Vision and American Jewish World Service and Islamic Relief to bring hope to those suffering around the world.

Colleges across the country have answered our Interfaith Campus Challenge, and students are joined together across religious lines in service to others. From promoting responsible fatherhood to strengthening adoption, from helping people find jobs to serving our veterans, we're linking arms with faith-based groups all across the country.

I think we all understand that these values cannot truly find voice in our politics and our policies unless they find a place in our hearts. The Bible teaches us to "be doers of the word and not merely hearers." We're required to have a living, breathing, active faith in our own lives. And each of us is called on to give something of ourselves for the betterment of others and to live the truth of our faith not just with words, but with deeds.

So, even as we join the great debates of our age—how we best put people back to work, how we ensure opportunity for every child, the role of Government in protecting this extraordinary planet that God has made for us, how we lessen the occasions of war—even as we debate these great issues, we must be reminded of the difference that we can make each day in our small interactions, in our personal lives.

As a loving husband or a supportive parent or a good neighbor or a helpful colleague, in each of these roles, we help bring His kingdom to Earth. And as important as government policy may be in shaping our world, we are reminded that it's the cumulative acts of kindness and courage and charity and love, it's the respect we show each other and the generosity that we share with each other that in our everyday lives will somehow sustain us during these challenging times. John tells us that, "If anyone has material possessions and sees his brother in need but has no pity on him, how can the love of God be in him? Dear children, let us not love with words or tongue but with actions and in truth."

Mark read a letter from Billy Graham, and it took me back to one of the great honors of my life, which was visiting Reverend Graham at his mountaintop retreat in North Carolina when I was on vacation with my family at a hotel not far away.

And I can still remember winding up the path up a mountain to his home. Ninety-one years old at the time, facing various health challenges, he welcomed me as he would welcome a family member or a close friend. This man who had prayed great prayers that inspired a nation, this man who seemed larger than life, greeted me and was as kind and as gentle as could be.

And we had a wonderful conversation. Before I left, Reverend Graham started praying for me, as he had prayed for so many Presidents before me. And when he finished praying, I felt the urge to pray for him. I didn't really know what to say. What do you pray for when it comes to the man who has prayed for so many? But like that verse in Romans, the Holy Spirit interceded when I didn't know quite what to say.

And so I prayed—briefly, but I prayed from the heart. I don't have the intellectual capacity or the lung capacity of some of my great preacher friends here to pray for a long time, but I—[*laughter*]—I prayed. And we ended with an embrace and a warm goodbye.

And I thought about that moment all the way down the mountain, and I've thought about it in the many days since. Because I thought about my own spiritual journey: growing up in a household that wasn't particularly religious, going through my own period of doubt and confusion, finding Christ when I wasn't even looking for him so many years ago, possessing so many shortcomings that have been overcome by the simple grace of God. And the fact that I would ever be on top of a mountain, saying a prayer for Billy Graham, a man whose faith had changed the world and that had sustained him through triumphs and tragedies and movements and milestones, that simple fact humbled me to my core.

I have fallen on my knees with great regularity since that moment, asking God for guidance not just in my personal life and my Christian walk, but in the life of this Nation and in the values that hold us together and keep us strong. I know that He will guide us. He always has, and He always will. And I pray his richest blessings on each of you in the days ahead.

Thank you very much.

NOTE: The President spoke at 9:10 a.m. at the Washington Hilton hotel. In his remarks, he referred to Sens. Mark L. Pryor and Jefferson B. Sessions III, cochairs, and Eric Metaxas, keynote speaker, National Prayer Breakfast; Joel C. Hunter, senior pastor, Northland Church in Longwood, FL; Thomas D. Jakes, senior pastor, The Potter's House in Dallas, TX; and William F. Graham, chairman of the board, Billy Graham Evangelistic Association.

Statement on Senate Passage of Legislation To Ban Insider Trading by Members of Congress
February 2, 2012

In my State of the Union Address, I laid out a blueprint for an economy built to last, where everyone gets a fair shot, everyone does their fair share, and everyone plays by the same set of rules, especially those of us who have been sent here to serve the American people.

Last week, I called on Congress to pass a bill that makes clear that Members of Congress may not engage in insider trading. No one should be able to trade stocks based on nonpublic information gleaned on Capitol Hill. So I'm pleased the Senate took bipartisan action to pass the "STOCK Act." I urge the House of Representatives to pass this bill, and I will sign it right away.

And while this is an important step to rebuild the trust between Washington and the American people, there is much more work to be done, like prohibiting elected officials from owning stocks in industries they impact and prohibiting people who bundle campaign contributions for Congress from lobbying Congress, an idea that has bipartisan support outside of Washington. These are straightforward proposals that will help eliminate the corrosive influence of money in politics.

NOTE: The statement referred to H.R. 1148.

Remarks at Fire Station 5 in Arlington, Virginia
February 3, 2012

The President. Thank you so much. Everybody, please have a seat. Well, good morning, everybody.

Audience members. Good morning!

The President. Jacob, thank you for that introduction. More importantly, thank you for your extraordinary service to our country.

I want to acknowledge two outstanding members of my Cabinet who are here today. Secretary of Veterans Affairs Ric Shinseki is in the house, also one of our finest—[*applause*]—himself one of our finest veterans and obviously an extraordinary leader when he was in our Army. And I also want to acknowledge Interior Secretary Ken Salazar, who's in the house.

And we're joined by another president, the International Association of Fire Fighters president, Harold Schaitberger, is here.

Now, this is a fire station that holds some special significance for our country. On September 11, the firefighters of this house were among the first to respond to the attack on the Pentagon. You guys answered this Nation's call during its hour of need. And in the years that followed, as Americans went to war, some of you answered that call as well.

Today's 9/11 generation of veterans has already earned a special place in our history. Our veterans and all the brave men and women who serve our country are the reason why America's military is the greatest in the history of the world. In the face of great odds and grave danger, they get the job done. They work as a team. They personify the very best that America has to offer.

That's true on the battlefront. But we're here today because it's also true on the homefront. After a decade of war, our Nation needs to do some building right here in the United States of America.

Now, this morning we received more good news about our economy. In January, American businesses added another 257,000 jobs. The unemployment rate came down because more people found work. And all together, we've added 3.7 million new jobs over the last 23 months.

Now, these numbers will go up and down in the coming months, and there's still far too many Americans who need a job or need a job that pays better than the one they have now. But the economy is growing stronger. The recovery is speeding up. And we've got to do everything in our power to keep it going.

We can't go back to the policies that led to the recession. And we can't let Washington stand in the way of our recovery. We want Washington to be helping with the recovery, not making it tougher.

The most important thing Congress needs to do right now is to stop taxes from going up on 160 million Americans at the end of this month. They've got to renew the payroll tax cut that they extended only for a couple of months. They need to pass an extension of the payroll tax cut and unemployment insurance and do it without drama, without delay, without linking it to some ideological side issues. They just need to get it done. It shouldn't be that complicated. Now is not the time for self-inflicted wounds to our economy. Now is the time for action.

So I want to send a clear message to Congress: Do not slow down the recovery that we're on. Don't muck it up. Keep it moving in the right direction.

Beyond preventing a tax hike, we need to do a lot more to create an economy that's built to last. To restore American manufacturing, we need to stop giving tax breaks to companies that ship jobs overseas. Give those tax breaks to companies that are investing in plants and equipment and hiring workers right here in the United States of America. That makes a lot of sense.

To reduce our dependency on foreign oil, we need to stop subsidizing oil companies that are already making record profits and double down on clean energy that creates jobs and creates opportunities in new industries, but also improves our security because we're not as dependent on foreign oil.

To make sure our businesses don't have to move overseas to find skilled workers, we've got to invest in education and make sure college is affordable for every hard-working American.

And—this is the reason we're here today— we need to make sure that as our troops return from battle, they can find a job when they get home. That's what I want to talk about today.

The war in Iraq is over. The war in Afghanistan is moving to a new phase; we're transitioning to Afghan lead. Over the past decade, nearly 3 million servicemembers have transitioned back to civilian life, and more are joining them every day.

And when these men and women come home, they bring unparalleled skills and experience. Folks like Jacob, they've saved lives in some of the toughest conditions imaginable. They've managed convoys and moved tons of equipment over dangerous terrain. They've tracked millions of dollars of military assets. They've handled pieces of equipment that are worth tens of millions of dollars. They do incredible work. Nobody is more skilled, more precise, more diligent, more disciplined.

Our veterans are some of the most highly trained, highly educated, highly skilled workers that we've got. These are Americans that every business should be competing to attract. These are the Americans we want to keep serving here at home as we rebuild this country. So we're going to do everything we can to make sure that when our troops come home, they come home to new jobs and new opportunities and new ways to serve their country.

Now, this has been a top priority of mine since I came into office. Already, we've helped 600,000 veterans and their family members go back to school on the post-9/11 GI bill. We've hired over 120,000 veterans to serve in the Federal Government. We've made it easier for veterans to access all sorts of employment services. We've set up online tools to connect veterans with job openings that match their skills.

Michelle and Jill Biden have worked with the private sector, with businesses, to secure a pledge of 135,000 jobs for veterans and their families. And with the support of Democrats and Republicans, we've put in place two new tax credits for companies that hire veterans. So these are all important steps. We've made progress. But we've got to do more. There's more we can do.

In my State of the Union Address, I proposed a new initiative called the Veterans Jobs Corps to put veterans back to work protecting and rebuilding America. And today we're laying out the details of this proposal.

First, we want to help communities hire more veterans as cops and firefighters. You guys have seen what a great job Jacob is doing. Well, there are a whole bunch of folks like that who could be doing that same outstanding work all across the country. But it's not that easy these days to get a job at a firehouse.

Over the past few years, tight budgets have forced a lot of States, a lot of local communities to lay off a lot of first-responders. Now, my administration, when I first came into office, one of the first things we did was, through the Recovery Act, make sure that States and local governments helped—or got the help that they needed to prevent some of these layoffs. And thousands of jobs were saved all across the country.

Harold and I were talking as we came over here. Thousands of firefighter jobs were saved because of the actions we took. But budgets are still tight, and that's a problem we need to fix. Jobs that protect our families and our communities shouldn't be the first on the chopping block. They should be one of our highest priorities as a nation.

Over the past 3 years, my administration has made it possible for States to keep thousands of first-responders on the job. But today we're announcing that communities who make it a priority to recruit veterans will be among the first in line when it comes to getting help from the Federal Government. And I know that's one of the things, Chief, that you've been doing here in Arlington. So we want to prioritize veterans, and we want to help States and local communities hire veterans to firehouses and police stations all across the country.

The second thing we want to do is to connect up to 20,000 veterans with jobs that involve rebuilding local communities or national parks. That's why Ken Salazar is here as the Interior Secretary. He needs some help. And our veterans are highly qualified to help him. They've already risked their lives defending America. They should have the opportunity to rebuild America. We've got roads and bridges in and around our national parks in need of repair. Let's fix them.

Of course, Congress needs to fund these projects. Congress should take the money that we're no longer spending on war, use half of it to pay down our debt, and use the rest to do some nation-building here at home, to improve the quality of life right here in the United States of America and put our veterans to work.

So let's get more cops on the beat. Let's gets more rangers in the parks. Let's get more firefighters on call. And in the process, we're going to put more veterans back to work. It's good for our communities, it's good for our economy, and it's good for our country.

And for veterans who want to do something else—maybe put their leadership skills to use starting a small business—we're going to start offering entrepreneurial training to our veterans. We want servicemembers prepared for battle and for professional success when they come home. So we should do all that we can to support our troops and our veterans in helping them start a business, in helping them get a foothold in a fire station like this one and start moving up the ranks, doing outstanding work the way Jacob's been doing.

But we also need to follow their lead. We want to help them, but we should also learn from them. We should remember from our veterans that no matter what the circumstances, those men and women in uniform—a lot like the firefighters in this fire station—work together, act as a team, finish the job. That's what we've got to do when it comes to our Nation's recovery.

Now, these are challenging times for America, but we've faced challenging times before. On the grounds here you've got a stone from the Pentagon and a beam from the World Trade Center. And that reminds us of our resolve as a people. They remind us that when we come together as one people and as one community and one Nation, then we prevail. That's who we are.

This is a nation that exists because generations of Americans worked together to build it. This is a nation where, out of many, we come together as one. Those are the values that every veteran understands. Those are values that this fire station understands. We've got to make sure that we return to those values. And if we do, then I guarantee you we'll remind everybody around the world just why it is the United States is the greatest country on Earth.

Thank you very much, everybody. God bless you. God bless America.

NOTE: The President spoke at 11:30 a.m. In his remarks, he referred to Lt. Jacob Johnson and Chief James H. Schwartz of the Arlington County Fire Department; and Jill T. Biden, wife of Vice President Joe Biden.

Message to the Congress on Continuation of the National Emergency With Respect to the Situation in or in Relation to Cote d'Ivoire
February 3, 2012

To the Congress of the United States:

Section 202(d) of the National Emergencies Act (50 U.S.C. 1622(d)) provides for the automatic termination of a national emergency, unless, within 90 days prior to the anniversary date of its declaration, the President publishes in the *Federal Register* and transmits to the Congress a notice stating that the emergency is to continue in effect beyond the anniversary date. In accordance with this provision, I have sent to the *Federal Register* for publication the enclosed notice stating that the national emergency declared in Executive Order 13396 of February 7, 2006, with respect to the situation in or in relation to Cote d'Ivoire is to continue in effect beyond February 7, 2012.

The situation in or in relation to Cote d'Ivoire, which has been addressed by the United Nations Security Council in Resolution 1572 of November 15, 2004, and subsequent resolutions, has resulted in the massacre of large numbers of civilians, widespread human rights abuses, significant political violence and unrest, and fatal attacks against international peacekeeping forces. Since the inauguration of President Alassane Ouattara in May 2011, the Government of Cote d'Ivoire and its people have made significant advances in the promotion of democratic, social, and economic development. Although considerable progress has been made, the situation in or in relation to Cote d'Ivoire continues to pose an unusual and extraordinary threat to the national security and foreign policy of the United States. For these reasons, I have determined that it is necessary to continue the national emergency and related measures under Executive Order 13396 of February 7, 2006, Blocking Property of Certain Persons Contributing to the Conflict in Cote d'Ivoire.

BARACK OBAMA

The White House,
February 3, 2012.

NOTE: The notice is listed in Appendix D at the end of this volume.

The President's Weekly Address
February 4, 2012

Over the last couple of weeks, I've been traveling around the country and talking with folks about my blueprint for an economy built to last. It's a blueprint that focuses on restoring the things we've always done best, our strengths: American manufacturing, American energy, the skills and education of American workers, and most importantly, American values like fairness and responsibility.

We know what happened when we strayed from those values over the past decade, especially when it comes to our housing market. Lenders sold loans to families who couldn't afford them. Banks packaged those mortgages up and traded them for phony profits. It drove up prices and created an unsustainable bubble that burst and left millions of families who did everything right in a world of hurt.

It was wrong. The housing crisis has been the single biggest drag on our recovery from the recession. It has kept millions of families in debt and unable to spend, and it has left hundreds of thousands of construction workers out of a job.

But there's something even more important at stake. I've been saying this is a make-or-break moment for the middle class. And the housing crisis struck right at the heart of what it means to be middle class in this country: owning a home, raising our kids, building our dreams.

Right now there are more than 10 million homeowners in this country who, because of a decline in home prices that is no fault of their own, owe more on their mortgages than their homes are worth. It is wrong for anyone to suggest that the only option for struggling, responsible homeowners is to sit and wait for the housing market to hit bottom. I don't accept that. None of us should.

That's why we launched a plan a couple years ago that's helped nearly 1 million responsible homeowners refinance their mortgages and save an average of $300 on their payments each month. I'll be the first to admit it didn't help as many folks as we'd hoped. But that doesn't mean we shouldn't keep trying.

That's why I'm sending Congress a plan that will give every responsible homeowner the chance to save about $3,000 a year on their mortgages by refinancing at historically low rates. No more redtape. No more endless forms. And a small fee on the largest financial institutions will make sure it doesn't add a dime to the deficit.

I want to be clear: This plan will not help folks who bought a house they couldn't afford and then walked away from it. It won't help folks who bought multiple houses just to turn around and sell them in speculation.

What this plan will do is help millions of responsible homeowners who make their payments every month, but who, until now, couldn't refinance because their home values kept dropping or they got wrapped up in too much redtape.

Here's the catch. In order to lower mortgage payments for millions of Americans, we need Congress to act. They're the ones who have to pass this plan. And as anyone who has followed the news in the last 6 months can tell you, getting Congress to do anything these days is not an easy job.

That's why I'm going to keep up the pressure on Congress to do the right thing. But I also need your help. I need your voice. I need everyone who agrees with this plan to get on the phone, send an e-mail, tweet, pay a visit, and remind your representatives in Washington who they work for. Tell them to pass this plan. Tell them to help more families keep their homes and more neighborhoods stay vibrant and whole.

The truth is, it will take time for our housing market to recover. It will take time for our economy to fully bounce back. But there are steps we can take right now to move this country forward. That's what I promise to do as your President, and I hope Members of Congress will join me.

Thanks, and have a great weekend.

NOTE: The address was recorded at approximately 5:10 p.m. on February 3 in the Library at the White House for broadcast on February 4. The transcript was made available by the Office of the Press Secretary on February 3, but was embargoed for release until 6 a.m. on February 4.

Statement on the Situation in Syria
February 4, 2012

Thirty years after his father massacred tens of thousands of innocent Syrian men, women, and children in Hama, Bashar al-Asad has demonstrated a similar disdain for human life and dignity. Yesterday the Syrian Government murdered hundreds of Syrian citizens, including women and children, in Homs through shelling and other indiscriminate violence, and Syrian forces continue to prevent hundreds of injured civilians from seeking medical help. These brutal killings take place at a time when so many Syrians are also marking a deeply meaningful day for their faith. I strongly condemn the Syrian Government's unspeakable assault against the people of Homs, and I offer my deepest sympathy to those who have lost loved ones. Asad must halt his campaign of killing and crimes against his own people now. He must step aside and allow a democratic transition to proceed immediately.

The Syrian people demonstrated in large numbers across Syria yesterday to participate in peaceful protests commemorating the 30th anniversary of the Hama massacre. They labeled the protests, "We are Sorry, Hama—Forgive Us." We owe it to the victims of Hama and Homs to learn one lesson: that cruelty must be confronted for the sake of justice and human dignity. Every government has the responsibility to protect its citizens, and any government that brutalizes and massacres its people does not deserve to govern. The Syrian regime's policy of maintaining power by terrorizing its people only indicates its inherent weakness and inevitable collapse. Asad has no right to lead Syria and has lost all legitimacy with his people and the international community.

The international community must work to protect the Syrian people from this abhorrent brutality. Earlier this week, our Arab partners called on U.N. Security Council members to take action to support a political solution to the crisis in Syria and stop Asad's "killing machine." The Council now has an opportunity to stand against the Asad regime's relentless brutality and to demonstrate that it is a credible advocate for the universal rights that are written into the U.N. Charter.

We must work with the Syrian people toward building a brighter future for Syria. A Syria without Asad could be a Syria in which all Syrians are subject to the rule of law and where minorities are able to exercise their legitimate rights and uphold their identities and traditions while acting as fully enfranchised citizens in a unified republic. The United States and our international partners support the Syrian people in achieving their aspirations and will continue to assist the Syrian people toward that goal. We will help because we stand for principles that include universal rights for all people and just political and economic reform. The suffering citizens of Syria must know: We are with you, and the Asad regime must come to an end.

Message to the Congress on Blocking Property of the Government of Iran and Iranian Financial Institutions
February 5, 2012

To the Congress of the United States:

Pursuant to the International Emergency Economic Powers Act (50 U.S.C. 1701 *et seq.*) (IEEPA), I hereby report that I have issued an Executive Order (the "order") that takes additional steps with respect to the national emergency declared in Executive Order 12957 of March 15, 1995.

In Executive Order 12957, the President found that the actions and policies of the Government of Iran threaten the national security, foreign policy, and economy of the United States. To deal with that threat, the President in Executive Order 12957 declared a national emergency and imposed prohibitions on certain transactions with respect to the development of Iranian petroleum resources. To further respond to that threat, Executive Order 12959 of May 6, 1995, imposed comprehensive trade and financial sanctions on Iran. Executive Order 13059 of August 19, 1997, consolidated and clarified the previous orders. To take additional steps with respect to the national emergency declared in Executive Order 12957 and to implement section 105(a) of the Comprehensive Iran Sanctions, Accountability, and Divestment Act of 2010 (Public Law 111–195) (22 U.S.C. 8501 *et seq.*) (CISADA), I issued Executive Order 13553 on September 28, 2010, to impose sanctions on officials of the Government of Iran and other persons acting on behalf of the Government of Iran determined to be responsible for or complicit in certain serious human rights abuses. To take further additional steps with respect to the threat posed by Iran and to provide implementing authority for a number of the sanctions set forth in the Iran Sanctions Act of 1996 (Public Law 104–172) (50 U.S.C. 1701 note) (ISA), as amended by CISADA, I issued Executive Order 13574 on May 23, 2011, to authorize the Secretary of the Treasury to implement certain sanctions imposed by the Secretary of State pursuant to ISA, as amended by CISADA. Finally, to take additional steps with respect to the threat posed by Iran, I issued Executive Order 13590 on November 20, 2011, to authorize the Secretary of State to impose sanctions on persons providing certain goods, services, technology, information, or support that contribute either to Iran's development of petroleum resources or to Iran's production of petrochemicals, and to authorize the Secretary of

the Treasury to implement some of those sanctions.

I have determined that additional sanctions are warranted, particularly in light of the deceptive practices of the Central Bank of Iran and other Iranian banks to conceal transactions of sanctioned parties, the deficiencies in Iran's anti-money laundering regime and the weaknesses in its implementation, and the continuing and unacceptable risk posed to the international financial system by Iran's activities.

The order also implements section 1245(c) of the National Defense Authorization Act for Fiscal Year 2012 (Public Law 112–81) (NDAA) by blocking the property and interests in property of Iranian financial institutions pursuant to IEEPA.

The order blocks the property and interests in property of the following:

- The Government of Iran, including the Central Bank of Iran;

- Any Iranian financial institution, including the Central Bank of Iran; and

- Persons determined by the Secretary of the Treasury, in consultation with the Secretary of State, to be owned or controlled by, or to have acted or purported to act for or on behalf of, directly or indirectly, any person whose property and interests in property are blocked pursuant to the order.

The prohibitions of the order do not apply to property and interests in property of the Government of Iran that were blocked pursuant to Executive Order 12170 of November 14, 1979, and thereafter made subject to the transfer directives set forth in Executive Order 12281 of January 19, 1981, and implementing regulations thereunder. In addition, nothing in the order prohibits transactions for the conduct of the official business of the Federal Government by employees, grantees, or contractors thereof.

I have delegated to the Secretary of the Treasury the authority, in consultation with the Secretary of State, to take such actions, including the promulgation of rules and regulations, and to employ all powers granted to the President by IEEPA as may be necessary to carry out the blocking-related purposes of the order. All agencies of the United States Government are directed to take all appropriate measures within their authority to carry out the provisions of the order.

I have also delegated certain functions and authorities conferred by section 1245 of the NDAA to the Secretary of the Treasury and the Secretary of State in consultation with other appropriate agencies as specified in the order.

I am enclosing a copy of the Executive Order I have issued.

BARACK OBAMA

The White House,
February 5, 2012.

NOTE: This message was released by the Office of the Press Secretary on February 6. The Executive order is listed in Appendix D at the end of this volume.

Remarks at the White House Science Fair
February 7, 2012

Thank you, everybody. Everybody, have a seat. Well, welcome to the White House Science Fair. It is—I just spent some time checking out some of the projects that were brought here today, and I've got to say, this is fun. It's not every day that you have robots running all over your house. [*Laughter*] I am trying to figure out how you got through the metal detectors. I also shot a marshmallow through a air gun, which was very exciting. [*Laughter*]

Science is what got several of our guests where they are today, so I just want to make a couple of introductions. We've got a real-life astronaut and the head of NASA, Charles Bolden, in the house. We have the Administrator of the EPA; Lisa Jackson is here. The Director of the National Science Foundation, Subra Suresh, is here. My science—there's Subra, over here. My science adviser, John Holdren, is in the house. We've got a couple of people who've dedicated themselves to making science cool for young people. We've got Neil deGrasse Tyson and Bill Nye the Science Guy.

Now, it is fitting that this year's fair is happening just 2 days after the Super Bowl. I want to congratulate the New York Giants and all their fans. I just talked to Coach Coughlin; I'm looking forward to having the Giants here at the White House so we can celebrate their achievements. But what I've also said—I've said this many times—is if we are recognizing athletic achievement, then we should also be recognizing academic achievement and science achievement. If we invite the team that wins the Super Bowl to the White House, then we need to invite some science fair winners to the White House as well.

Now I'm going to talk about how great all of you are in a second. But before I do, I want to give the parents a big round of applause, because they work hard to help you succeed, and I know this is their day. They're really proud of you. As a parent, I know that seeing your kids do extraordinary things is—brings the greatest happiness that a parent can have. So congratulations to all the parents of all these incredible young people.

But parents aren't the only ones who helped you get this far. Every one of you can think of a teacher, or maybe a couple of teachers, without whom you would not be here. So I want you to promise that the next time you see those teachers, that you give them a big thank you, not just for yourselves, but also from me. Because teachers matter, they deserve our support, and I want to make sure that we are constantly lifting up how important teachers are to making sure that not only you succeed, but this country succeeds. So give teachers a big round of applause.

Now, as I was walking around the Science Fair, I was thinking back to when I was your age. And basically, you guys put me to shame. [*Laughter*] What impresses me so much is not just how smart you are, but it's the fact that you recognize you've got a responsibility to use your talents in service of something bigger than yourselves.

Some of you, that means developing new products that will change the way we live. So Hayley Hoverter—where's Hayley? There she is, right over here—invented a new type of sugar packet that dissolves in hot water. It's flavorless, it's colorless, and potentially could save up to 2 million pounds of trash each year—and that's just at Starbucks. [*Laughter*] So Master-Card has already awarded her $10,000 to help turn her idea into a business.

Some of you are here because you saw a problem in your community and you're trying to do something to solve it. Benjamin Hylak—where's Benjamin? There's Benjamin right here—was worried that folks at his grandmother's senior center were getting lonely. So he built a robot with a monitor and a video camera, so it's like a moving Skype. And it moves around the center, and it allows seniors to talk to their kids and their grandkids, even when they can't visit in person. So inventions like Benjamin's could make life better for millions of families.

For some of you, the journey you took to get here is just as inspiring as the work that you brought with you today. There's a rocketry team from Presidio, Texas. Where's my team here? Where are you? Stand up, guys. Stand up. This is part of the fourth-poorest school district in the State of Texas. And I was told that teachers cooked food to sell after church, supporters drove 200 miles to pick up doughnuts for bake sales, they even raffled off a goat—[*laughter*]—is that right? Just so they could raise enough money for the rocketry team to compete. And the majority of the kids at the school are ESL, English as a second language. And the presentation they made could not make you prouder. So way to go.

There's a group of young engineers from Paul Robeson-Malcolm X Academy. And nobody needs to tell them the kinds of challenges that Detroit still faces. Where's my team from Detroit? In the house—there they are. Stand up. They believe in their city, and they're coming up with new ideas to keep Detroit's comeback going.

And there's Samantha Garvey—where's Samantha? Just saw Samantha. There she is. Stand up, Samantha. Samantha spent years studying mussel populations in the Long Island Sound. And when she learned that she was a semifinalist for the Intel Science Talent Search—when she found this out—her family was living in a homeless shelter, so think about what she's overcome. She wants to, by the way, work maybe for NOAA or EPA. So this is Dr. Lubchenco; she's the head of NOAA. [*Laughter*] Lisa Jackson, right there, head of EPA. [*Laughter*] You might just want to hook up with them before you leave. [*Laughter*]

The young people I met today, the young people behind me, you guys inspire me. It's young people like you that make me so confident that America's best days are still to come. When you work and study and excel at what you're doing in math and science, when you compete in something like this, you're not just trying to win a prize today. You're getting America in shape to win the future. You're making sure we have the best, smartest, most skilled workers in the world, so that the jobs and industries of tomorrow take root right here. You're making sure we'll always be home to the most creative entrepreneurs, the most advanced science labs and universities. You're making sure America will win the race to the future.

So, as an American, I'm proud of you. As your President, I think we need to make sure your success stories are happening all across the country.

And that's why when I took office, I called for an all-hands-on-deck approach to science, math, technology, and engineering. Let's train more teachers. Let's get more kids studying these subjects. Let's make sure these fields get the respect and attention that they deserve.

But it's not just a Government effort. I'm happy to say that the private sector has answered that call as well. They understand how important it is to their future. So today, led by the Carnegie Corporation, a group of businesses and foundations is announcing a $22 million fund to help train 100,000 new science and math teachers. A coalition of more than 100 CEOs is expanding innovative math and science programs to 130 sites across the country. And other companies are partnering from—everybody from will.i.am to Dean Kamen, to make sure we celebrate young scientists and inventors and engineers, not just at the White House, but in every city and every town all across America.

And many of these leaders are here today, and I want to thank them for doing their part. We're going to do everything we can to partner to help you succeed in your projects. And I'm proud to announce that the budget I unveil next week will include programs to help prepare new math and science teachers and to meet an ambitious goal, which is 1 million more American graduates in science, technology, engineering, and math over the next 10 years. That is a goal we can achieve. That's a goal we can achieve.

Now, in a lot of ways, today is a celebration of the new. But the belief that we belong on the cutting edge of innovation, that's an idea as old as America itself. I mean, we're a nation of tinkerers and dreamers and believers in a better tomorrow. You think about our Founding Fathers, they were all out there doing experiments. And folks like Benjamin Franklin and Thomas Jefferson, they were constantly curious about the world around them and trying to figure out how can we help shape that environment so that people's lives are better.

It's in our DNA. We know that innovation has helped each generation pass down that basic American promise, which is no matter who you are, no matter where you come from, you can make it if you try. So there's nothing more important than keeping that promise alive for the next generation. There's no priority I have that's higher than President—as President than this.

And I can't think of a better way to spend a morning than with the young people who are here doing their part and creating some unbelievable stuff in the process. So I'm proud of you. I want you to keep up your good work.

I'm going to make a special plea to the press, not just the folks who are here, but also your editors: Give this some attention. I mean, this is the kind of stuff, what these young people are doing, that's going to make a bigger difference in the life of our country over the long term than just about anything. And it doesn't belong just on the back pages of a newspaper. We've got to lift this up. We've got to emphasize how important this is and recognize these incredible young people who are doing things that I couldn't even imagine thinking about at fifth grade or eighth grade or in high school.

And so pay attention to this. This is important. This is what's going to make a difference in this country over the long haul. This is what inspires me and gets me up every day. This is what we should be focusing on in our public debates.

And as for all the folks who are here, don't let your robots wander off anywhere. [*Laughter*] All right?

Thank you, everybody. Appreciate it. Congratulations.

NOTE: The President spoke at 11:53 a.m. in the East Room at the White House. In his remarks, he referred to Neil deGrasse Tyson, director, Hayden Planetarium; William S. Nye, television personality and executive director of the Planetary Society; Tom Coughlin, head coach, National Football League's New York Giants; Science Fair student participants Janet Nieto, Gwynelle Condino, and Ana Karen of Presidio, TX, and Lucas C. Beal, Jayla M. Dogan, and Ashley C. Thomas of Detroit, MI; musician William J. "will.i.am" Adams, Jr.; and Dean Kamen, founder and president, DEKA Research and Development Corporation.

Remarks on the National Foreclosure Abuse Settlement
February 9, 2012

All right, good afternoon, everybody. Before I start, I just want to introduce the folks on stage here, because the extraordinary work that they did is the reason that a lot of families are going to be helped all across the country. First of all, our Attorney General Eric Holder; Secretary of Housing and Urban Development Shaun Donovan; Associate Attorney General, and former classmate of mine, Tom Perrelli; we've got Attorney General George Jepsen from Connecticut; Roy Cooper, attorney general from North Carolina; Lisa Madigan from my home State of Illinois, and former seatmate of mine when we were in the State legislature together; Dustin McDaniel from Arkansas; Gregory Zoeller from Indiana; and Tom Miller from Iowa. And I also want to acknowledge Bob Ryan, who worked with Shaun Donovan extensively on this issue, as well as Tim Massad of Treasury. And I'm going to acknowledge also Gene Sperling, who doesn't always get the credit he deserves for doing outstanding work.

The housing bubble that burst nearly 6 years ago triggered, as we all know, the worst economic crisis of our lifetimes. It cost millions of innocent Americans their jobs and their homes, and it remains one of the biggest drags on our economy.

Last fall, my administration unveiled a series of steps to help responsible homeowners refinance their mortgages to take advantage of historically low rates. And last week, I urged Congress to pass a plan that would help millions more Americans refinance and stay in their homes. And I indicated that the American people need Congress to act on this piece of legislation.

But in the meantime, we can't wait to get things done and to provide relief to America's homeowners. We need to keep doing everything we can to help homeowners and our economy. And today, with the help of Democratic and Republican attorney generals from nearly every State in the country, we are about to take a major step on our own.

We have reached a landmark settlement with the Nation's largest banks that will speed relief to the hardest hit homeowners, end some of the most abusive practices of the mortgage industry, and begin to turn the page on an era of recklessness that has left so much damage in its wake.

By now, it's well known that millions of Americans who did the right thing and the responsible thing—shopped for a house, secured a mortgage that they could afford, made their payments on time—were nevertheless hurt badly by the irresponsible actions of others: by lenders who sold loans to people who couldn't afford them, by buyers who knew they couldn't afford them, by speculators who were looking to make a quick buck, by banks that took risky mortgages, packaged them up, and traded them off for large profits.

It was wrong, and it cost more than 4 million families their homes to foreclosure. Even worse, many companies that handled these foreclosures didn't give people a fighting chance to hold onto their homes. In many cases, they didn't even verify that these foreclosures were actually legitimate. Some of the people they hired to process foreclosures used fake signatures to—on fake documents to speed up the foreclosure process. Some of them didn't read what they were signing at all.

We've got to think about that. You work and you save your entire life to buy a home. That's where you raise your family. That's where your kids' memories are formed. That's your stake, your claim on the American Dream. And the person signing the document couldn't take enough time to even make sure that the foreclosure was legitimate.

These practices were plainly irresponsible. And we refused to let them go unanswered. So, about a year ago, our Federal law enforcement agencies teamed up with State attorneys general to get to the bottom of these abuses. The settlement we've reached today, thanks to the work of some of the folks who are on this stage—this is the largest joint Federal-State settlement in our Nation's history—is the result of that extraordinary cooperation.

Under the terms of this settlement, America's biggest banks—banks that were rescued by taxpayer dollars—will be required to right these wrongs. That means more than just paying a fee. These banks will put billions of dollars towards relief for families across the Nation. They'll provide refinancing for borrowers that are stuck in high interest rate mortgages. They'll reduce loans for families who owe more on their homes than they're worth. And they will deliver some measure of justice for families that have already been victims of abusive practices.

All told, this isn't just good for these families; it's good for their neighborhoods, it's good for their communities, and it's good for our economy. This settlement also protects our ability to further investigate the practices that caused this mess. And this is important. The mortgage fraud Task Force I announced in my State of the Union Address retains its full authority to aggressively investigate the packaging and selling of risky mortgages that led to this crisis. This investigation is already well underway. And working closely with State attorneys general, we're going to keep at it until we hold those who broke the law fully accountable.

Now, I want to be clear. No compensation, no amount of money, no measure of justice is enough to make it right for a family who's had their piece of the American Dream wrongly taken from them. And no action, no matter how meaningful, is going to, by itself, entirely heal the housing market. But this settlement is a start. And we're going to make sure that the banks live up to their end of the bargain. If they don't, we've set up an independent inspector, a monitor, that has the power to make sure they pay exactly what they agreed to pay, plus a penalty if they fail to act in accordance with this agreement. So this will be a big help.

Of course, even with this settlement, there's still millions of responsible homeowners who are out there doing their best. And they need us to do more to help them get back on their feet. We've still got to stoke the fires of our economic recovery. So now is not the time to pull back.

To build on this settlement, Congress still needs to send me the bill I've proposed that gives every responsible homeowner in America the chance to refinance their mortgage and save about $3,000 a year. It would help millions of homeowners who make their payments on time save hundreds of dollars a month, and it can broaden the impact building off this settlement.

That's money that can be put back into the homes of those folks who are saving money on the refinancing, helping to build their equity back up. They may decide to spend that money on local businesses. Either way, it's good for families, and it's good for our economy. But it's only going to happen if Congress musters the will to act. And I ask every American to raise your voice and demand that they do.

Because there really is no excuse for inaction. There's no excuse for doing nothing to help more families avoid foreclosure. That's not who we are. We are Americans, and we look out for one another; we get each other's backs. That's not a Democratic issue, that's not a Republican issue. That's who we are as Americans.

And the bipartisan nature of this settlement and the outstanding work that these State attorneys general did is a testament to what happens when everybody is pulling in the same direction. And that's what today's settlement's all about: standing up for the American people, holding those who broke the law accountable, restoring confidence in our housing market and our financial sector, getting things moving. And we're going to keep on at it until everyone shares in America's comeback.

So, ladies and gentlemen, thank you for your outstanding efforts. We are very, very proud of you. And we look forward to seeing this settlement lead to some small measure of relief to a lot of families out there that need help. And that's going to strengthen the American economy overall.

So thank you very much.

NOTE: The President spoke at 12:28 p.m. in Room 430 of the Dwight D. Eisenhower Executive Office Building. In his remarks, he referred to Attorney General Lisa Madigan of Illinois; Attorney General Dustin McDaniel of Arkansas; Attorney General Gregory F. Zoeller of Indiana; Attorney General Thomas J. Miller of Iowa; Robert C. Ryan, Acting Assistant Secretary for Housing/Federal Housing Commissioner, Department of Housing and Urban Development; Timothy G. Massad, Assistant Secretary for Financial Stability, Department of the Treasury; and National Economic Council Director Eugene B. Sperling.

Remarks on the No Child Left Behind Act
February 9, 2012

Please have a seat, have a seat. Thank you so much. Well, hello, everybody, and welcome to the White House.

I want to start by thanking all the chief State school officers who have made the trip from all over the country. Why don't you all stand up just so we can see you all, right here. It's a great group, right here. Thank you. And I want to recognize someone who is doing a pretty good job right here in Washington, DC, and that is my Secretary of Education, Arne Duncan. Love Arne.

We've also got some outstanding Members of Congress who are here who have always been on the frontlines when it comes to education reform. But above all, I want to thank all the teachers who are here today. Where are the teachers? Come on, stand up, teachers. There you go. We got some teachers here.

Earlier this week, we hosted our second White House Science Fair. Some of you may have seen this on TV. I got a chance to shoot a marshmallow out of an air cannon, which I don't usually get to do. [*Laughter*] But I met these incredibly talented young people, kids who are working on everything from portable housing for disaster victims to technology that can detect smuggled uranium before it became a threat; this young man had built a prototype. And I asked him how he came up with this idea, and he said, "I've always just been really interested in nuclear materials, and I collect samples." [*Laughter*] And I asked him, "How does your mom feel about this?" [*Laughter*] He said she wasn't that happy about it.

But just unbelievable young people; it was extraordinary. And before they left, I gave them some homework. I told them go find a teacher who helped them make it here and say thank you, because every single one of us can point to a teacher who in some way changed the course of our lives. I certainly can; I know Arne can. And the impact is often much bigger than we realize.

One study found that a single good teacher can increase the lifetime earnings of a classroom by $250,000—single teacher. A great teacher can help a young person escape poverty, allow them to dream beyond their circumstances.

So teachers matter. And in an economy where employers are looking for the most skilled, educated workers, few people are going to have a bigger impact on that than the men and women who are in our classrooms. And that ultimately is why we're here today. It's about our classrooms and our children and what's happening to them and how they can perform.

In September, after waiting far too long for Congress to act, I announced that my administration would take steps to reform No Child Left Behind on our own. This was one of the first and the biggest We Can't Wait announcements that we've made, because our kids and our schools can't be held back by inaction.

I want to point out, by the way, the Members of Congress who are here, they're ready to act, but we haven't been able to get the entire House and Senate to move on this.

I said back then the goals of No Child Left Behind were the right ones. Standards and accountability, those are the right goals. Closing the achievement gap, that's a good goal. That's the right goal. We've got to stay focused on those goals. But we've got to do it in a way that

133

doesn't force teachers to teach to the test or encourage schools to lower their standards to avoid being labeled as failures. That doesn't help anybody. It certainly doesn't help our children in the classroom.

So we determined we need a different approach. And I've always believed that each of us has a role to play when it comes to our children's education. As parents, we've got a responsibility to make sure homework gets done, but also to instill a love of learning from the very start. As a nation, we've got a responsibility to give our students the resources they need, from the highest quality schools to the latest textbooks to science labs that actually work.

In return, we should demand better performance. We should demand reform. And that was the idea behind Race to the Top. For less than 1 percent of what our Nation spends on education each year, we've gotten almost every State in the Nation to raise their standards for teaching and learning. And that's the first time that's happened in a generation.

So, when it comes to fixing what's wrong with No Child Left Behind, we've offered every state the same deal. We've said, if you're willing to set higher, more honest standards than the ones that were set by No Child Left Behind, then we're going to give you the flexibility to meet those standards. We want high standards, and we'll give you flexibility in return. We combine greater freedom with greater accountability. Because what might work in Minnesota may not work in Kentucky, but every student should have the same opportunity to reach their potential.

So, over the last 5 months, 39 States have told us that they were interested. Some have already applied. And today I am pleased to announce that we are giving 10 States—the first 10 States the green light to continue making the reforms that are best for them.

Each of these States has set higher benchmarks for student achievement. They've come up with ways to evaluate and support teachers fairly, based on more than just a set of test scores. And along with promoting best practices for all of our children, they're also going to be focusing on low-income students and Eng-

lish language learners and students with disabilities, not just to make sure that those children don't fall through the cracks, but to make sure they have every opportunity to go as far as their talents will take them.

So Massachusetts, for example, has set a goal to cut the number of underperforming students in half over the next 6 years. I like that goal.

Colorado has launched a website that will allow teachers and parents to see exactly how much progress students are making and how different schools are measuring up. So nothing creates more accountability than when parents are out there taking a look and seeing what's going on.

New Jersey is developing an early warning system to reduce the number of dropouts. Tennessee is creating a statewide school district to aggressively tackle its lowest performing schools. And Florida has set a goal to have their test scores rank among the top 5 States in the country, and the top 10 countries in the world. I like that ambition.

This is good news for our kids; it's good news for our country. And I'm confident that we're going to see even more States come forward in the months ahead. Because if we're serious about helping our children reach their full potential, the best ideas aren't going to just come from here in Washington. They're going to come from cities and towns from all across America. They're going to come from teachers and principals and parents. They're going to come from you who have a sense of what works and what doesn't.

And our job is to harness those ideas, to lift up best practices, to hold States and schools accountable for making them work. That's how we're going to make sure that every child in America has the skills and the education they need to compete for the jobs of the future and to be great citizens. And that's how we're going to build an economy that lasts.

So to all the educators who are in the room, thank you for what you do every day. We are very proud of your efforts. We know it's not easy. We're proud of you. And working together, I am absolutely confident that year after year we're going to see steady improvement.

I told the superintendents that I met backstage before I came out here, this is not a 1-year project. This isn't a 2-year project. This is going to take some time. But we can get it done with the kind of determination and the kind of commitment that so many of you have shown.

So I'm proud of you. I'm proud of Arne Duncan. Let's make this happen.

Thank you very much, everybody.

NOTE: The President spoke at 1:57 p.m. in the East Room at the White House. In his remarks, he referred to White House Science Fair student participant Taylor Wilson.

Remarks Following a Meeting With Prime Minister Mario Monti of Italy
February 9, 2012

President Obama. Well, hello, everybody. *Benvenuto.* I want to welcome Prime Minister Monti to the White House for his first visit. I had the opportunity to congratulate him after he took on the extraordinary responsibilities that he has accepted.

I want to begin by saying that it's nice to be able to return the hospitality of the Italian people. Every time I've been to Rome, L'Aquila, the warmth that has been extended not just to me, but to my family has been extraordinary. And obviously, we have a deep and special connection with the Italian people. The Italian American community here in the United States has had as much of an impact as any group within our country.

I personally cannot claim Italian ancestry, although my name ends in a vowel—[*laughter*]—so sometimes, I try to pretend.

The Prime Minister came in at a very difficult time in Italian politics and the Italian economy. And I just want to say how much we appreciate the strong start that he has embarked on and the very effective measures that he is promoting inside of Italy. You've already seen because of his stewardship and his experience and his knowledge of economics, that not only has he boosted confidence within Italy about a reform agenda, but he's also been able to generate confidence throughout Europe and in the marketplace that Italy has a plan that takes seriously its fiscal responsibilities, but also emphasizes the need for structural reforms that can promote growth.

And so one of the topics of our conversation obviously was my continuing to encourage the fine work that has already been done by the Prime Minister and to express our interest in doing whatever we can do to help stabilize the situation in the euro zone, including something that we both agree on, which is the need for a stronger European firewall that will allow for a more stable path for repayment of debt, but also the promotion of a growth strategy within Europe, which is obviously important not only to Europe, but the entire world economy and to our economy back here in the United States of America.

In addition to all the burdens that he has economically, Prime Minister Monti also is the leader of one of our most important friends and allies when it comes to security issues. So I emphasized to him how much we appreciate the sacrifices and outstanding work that are made by Italian forces in Afghanistan, and we reaffirmed our commitment to the Lisbon schedule in which we transition to full Afghan lead by the end of 2014.

I emphasized the fact that we could not have been successful in our Libya campaign without the extraordinary contributions of our Italian partners, and we both expressed our interest in working with the transitional government there to create a stable pathway towards democracy and economic prosperity.

We discussed the extraordinary efforts that Italian forces have taken in Kosovo to continue to maintain the peace there and to deal with ongoing tensions. And we discussed a wide range of diplomatic concerns, including the situation in Syria, where we both have a great interest in ending the outrageous bloodshed that we've seen and seeing a transition from the

135

current Government that has been assaulting its people.

We also discussed how we can continue to encourage a peaceful and effective transition elsewhere in the Middle East. And we discussed the situation in Iran, and I thanked Italy for its participation in a strong sanctions regime. We also both said that we would work as hard as we can to find a diplomatic resolution to that very difficult situation.

So overall, I think that the relationship between Italy and the United States has never been stronger. I personally have great confidence in the Prime Minister's leadership and his ability to navigate Italy through this difficult time and to stabilize the economic situation there and then put it on a footing so that it can grow and prosper over the long term.

And I know given the extraordinary talents and gifts of the Italian people that, with these structural reforms, there's no reason why the future for Italy will—should not be extraordinarily bright.

So, Mr. Prime Minister, welcome. We thank you very much for your friendship, and we wish you the very best in the months to come.

Thank you so much, thank you.

Prime Minister Monti. Mr. President, thank you so much for having me today at the White House. It is a great privilege and an honor to have the first meeting with you after our telephone conversation and to hear directly from you your vision about world affairs, and in particular, the economic cooperation and the common challenges that the U.S. and the European Union and, within it, Italy, have to tackle.

The meeting with the President has been ranging through a number of topics, as the President himself just mentioned. We of course devoted particular attention to the efforts going on in Italy. And I do wish to warmly thank the President for his generous and supportive words, which in itself are an encouragement for my Government to persist along these lines.

And I'm glad to say the lines towards budgetary consolidation and structure reforms, however painful they may be in the short term,

seem to be widely understood by the Italian public opinion. And I think this is a good basis for also the future of the country and for whatever will be there after the time-limited duration of the current government.

With President Obama, we went through the interactions that exist in Europe between the efforts by any particular member state and the overall governance of the European Union. I found in him a deep interest and, can I also say, thorough knowledge of these intricate mechanisms of us, the Europeans.

And we agreed on the strategy in order for Europe to consolidate its budgetary position, to cope with the financial tensions, and in particular, you heard the President mention the importance of adequate firewalls and also the imperative of growth, a growth which can only come, particularly in Europe, from structural transformations giving more role to productivity, enhanced efficiency.

And I think the U.S. is a very good case in point, providing examples on the benefits of well-functioning markets. And of course, the U.S. is the living example of what a single market can provide in terms of growth. And this explains why, in Europe, Italy is so insisting, finding more and more audience among the other member states on the fact that Europe's programs for growth should rely heavily on an enhanced effort for the single market.

I will not go through the various points concerning the strategic agenda, the area of security that the U.S. and Italy share. I confirmed the firm willingness of Italy to play its role within this alliance, which is a strategic alliance, but which is, first of all, an alliance of values, common values that we defend. And I promised to President Obama the renewed intention of Italy to provide not only the necessary resources and women and men for these tasks, but also the knowledge and expertise that Italy may have, as regards particularly some countries in the Mediterranean and Middle Eastern region, due to geographic and historical links.

So we are, Mr. President, and I personally am very encouraged by this thorough exchange of views. It was difficult to identify points where there isn't agreement. But it was easy to identify points—first and foremost, economic growth—where we have common views, but we need to step up joint actions in order for our wishes to become a reality.

And finally, if I may conclude with a sentence in Italian, Mr. President.

[*At this point, Prime Minister Monti spoke in Italian, and no translation was provided. He then continued in English as follows.*]

Prime Minister Monti. Thank you so much, Mr. President.

President Obama. Thank you so much. And I apologize; I forgot my translation during my long speech. But rather than try to repeat it now, if anybody needs a translation, we've got the translator right here.

So thank you very much, Mr. Prime Minister.

Prime Minister Monti. Thank you, Mr. President.

NOTE: The President spoke at 3:30 p.m. in the Oval Office at the White House.

Remarks at an Obama Victory Fund 2012 Fundraiser
February 9, 2012

Thank you. Thank you, Laura, for the wonderful introduction, the best introduction that a Cubs fan has ever given me. [*Laughter*] The rivalry is fierce in Chicago, but I'll make an exception here.

And I want to thank Karen and Nan for opening up their incredible home. To all of you, and to everybody who helped put this together, thank you so much. I am very grateful.

I'm going to be very brief at the top, because I want to—usually, in these things, I like to spend most of my time in a conversation. I do want to acknowledge that I have as good a Cabinet as I think any President in modern history has had. And one of the stars of that Cabinet is sitting right here, Kathleen Sebelius.

All of America has gone through an incredibly difficult, wrenching time these last 3 years. And it doesn't matter whether you are Black or White, whether you are northern or southern, rich or poor, gay or straight; I think all of us have been deeply concerned over these last 3 years to making sure that our economy recovers, that we're putting people back to work, that we stabilize the financial system. The amount of hardship and challenge that ordinary families have gone through over the last 3 years has been incredible. And there are still a lot of folks hurting out there.

The good news is that we're moving in the right direction. And when I came into office,

we were losing 750,000 jobs a month, and this past month we gained 250,000. That's a million-job swing. And for the last 23 months, we've now created 3.7 million jobs. And that's more than any time since 2000—or, yes, since 2005—the number of jobs that we created last year, and more manufacturing jobs than any time since the 1990s.

So we're making progress on that front now, but we've still got a long way to go. Today we announced a housing settlement, brought about by our Attorney General and States attorneys all across the country. And as a consequence, we're going to see billions of dollars in loan modifications and help to folks who are seeing their homes underwater. And that's going to have a huge impact.

In my State of the Union, we talked about the need for American manufacturing—companies coming back, insourcing, and recognizing how incredibly productive American workers are—and our need to continue to double down on investments in clean energy and making sure that our kids are getting trained so that they are competing with any workers in the world and are also effectively equipped to be great citizens and to understand the world around them.

And we talked about the fact that we've got to have the same set of values of fair play and responsibility for everybody, whether it's Wall

137

Street or Main Street. It means that we have a Consumer Finance Protection Board that is enforcing rules that make sure that nobody is getting abused by predatory lending or credit card scams. It means that we have regulations in place that protect our air and our water.

And it also means that we ensure that everybody in our society has a fair shot, is treated fairly. That's at the heart of the American Dream. For all the other stuff going on, one thing every American understands is you should be treated fairly, you should be judged on the merits. If you work hard, if you do a good job, if you're responsible in your community, if you're looking after you family, if you're caring for other people, then that's how you should be judged. Not by what you look like, not by how you worship, not by where you come from, not by who you love.

And so the work that we've done with respect to the LGBT community I think is just profoundly American and is at the heart of who we are. And that's why I could not be prouder of the track record that we've done, starting with the very beginning when we started to change, through Executive order, some of the Federal policies. Kathleen—the work that she did making sure that hospital visitation was applied equally to same-sex couples, just like with anybody else's loved ones. The changes we made at the State Department. The changes we made in terms of our own personnel policies, but also some very high-profile work like "don't ask, don't tell."

And what's been striking over the course of these last 3 years is, because we've rooted this work in this concept of fairness, and we haven't gone out of our way to grab credit for it, we haven't gone out of our way to call other folks names if they didn't always agree with us on stuff, but we just kept plodding along, because of that, in some ways what's been remarkable is how readily the public recognizes this is the right thing to do.

Think about—just take "don't ask, don't tell" as an example. The perception was somehow that this would be this huge, ugly issue. But because we did it methodically, because we brought the Pentagon in, because we got some very heroic support from people like Bob Gates and Mike Mullen, and they thought through institutionally how to do it effectively—since it happened, nothing's happened. [*Laughter*] Nothing's happened.

We still have the best military by far on Earth. There hasn't been any notion of erosion and unit cohesion. It turns out that people just want to know, are you a good soldier, are you a good sailor, are you a good airman, are you a good marine, good coastguardsman? That's what they're concerned about. Do you do your job? Do you do your job well?

It was striking—when I was in Hawaii, there is a Marine base close to where we stay. Probably the nicest piece of real estate I think the Marines have. [*Laughter*] It is very nice. And they have this great gym, and you go in there, you work out, and you always feel really inadequate because they're really in good shape, all these people. [*Laughter*] They're lifting 100-pound dumbbells and all this stuff. At least three times that I was at that gym, people came up, very quietly, to say, you know what, thank you for ending "don't ask, don't tell."

Now, here's the thing. I didn't even know whether they were gay or lesbian. I didn't ask, because that wasn't the point. The point was these were outstanding marines who appreciated the fact that everybody was going to be treated fairly.

We're going to have more work to do on this issue, as is true on a lot of other issues. There's still areas where fairness is not the rule. And we're going to have to keep on pushing in the same way: persistently, politely, listening to folks who don't always agree with us, but sticking to our guns in terms of what our values are all about. What American values are all about.

And that's going to be true on the issues that are of importance to the LGBT community specifically, but it's also going to be true on a host of other issues where we're just going to have to make persistent steady progress. Whether it is having an energy policy that works for America, whether it is having an immigration policy that is rational so that we are actually both a nation of laws and a nation of immigrants, whether it's making sure that as we get our fiscal house in order we do it in a balanced way where everybody is doing their fair share to help close this deficit. It's not just being done on the backs of people who don't have enough political clout on Capitol Hill, but it's broadly applied and everybody is doing their fair share.

On all these issues, my view is that if we go back to first principles and we ask ourselves, what does it mean for us as Americans to live in a society where everybody has a fair shot, everybody is doing their fair share, we're playing by a fair set of rules, everybody is engaging in fair play, then we're going to keep on making progress.

And that's where I think the American people are at. It doesn't mean this is going to be smooth. It doesn't mean that there aren't going to be bumps in the road. It's not always good politics; sometimes, it's not. But over the long term, the trajectory of who we are as a nation, I believe that's our national character. We trend towards fairness and treating people well. And as long as we keep that in mind, I think we should be optimistic not just about the next election, but about the future of this country.

Thank you.

NOTE: The President spoke at 7:09 p.m. at the residence of Karen Dixon and Nan Schaffer. In his remarks, he referred to Laura Ricketts, co-owner, Major League Baseball's Chicago Cubs; former Secretary of Defense Robert M. Gates; and Adm. Michael G. Mullen, USN (Ret.), former Chairman, Joint Chiefs of Staff.

Remarks on Preventive Health Care Insurance Coverage and an Exchange With Reporters
February 10, 2012

Q. Here we go.
The President. Here we go.
Q. Here he is.
The President. Here I am.
Q. "Hello, everybody." You like that?
The President. That was pretty good.
Q. I've been working on that.
The President. Hello, everybody. [*Laughter*]
Q. "Hello, everybody." [*Laughter*]
The President. I was actually going to say good morning, but it—I guess it's afternoon by now.

As part of the health care reform law that I signed last year, all insurance plans are required to cover preventive care at no cost. That means free checkups, free mammograms, immunizations, and other basic services. We fought for this because it saves lives and it saves money for families, for businesses, for Government, for everybody. And that's because it's a lot cheaper to prevent an illness than to treat one.

We also accepted a recommendation from the experts at the Institute of Medicine that when it comes to women, preventive care should include coverage of contraceptive services such as birth control. In addition to family planning, doctors often prescribe contraception as a way to reduce the risks of ovarian and other cancers and treat a variety of different ailments. And we know that the overall cost of health care is lower when women have access to contraceptive services.

Nearly 99 percent of all women have relied on contraception at some point in their lives— 99 percent. And yet more than half of all women between the ages of 18 and 34 have struggled to afford it. So, for all these reasons, we decided to follow the judgment of the Nation's leading medical experts and make sure that free preventive care includes access to free contraceptive care.

Whether you're a teacher or a small-businesswoman or a nurse or a janitor, no woman's health should depend on who she is or where she works or how much money she makes. Every woman should be in control of the decisions that affect her own health—period. This basic principle is already the law in 28 States across the country.

Now, as we move to implement this rule, however, we've been mindful that there's another principle at stake here, and that's the principle of religious liberty, an inalienable right that is enshrined in our Constitution. As a citizen and as a Christian, I cherish this right.

In fact, my first job in Chicago was working with Catholic parishes in poor neighborhoods, and my salary was funded by a grant from an arm of the Catholic Church. And I saw that local churches often did more good for a community than a government program ever could, so I know how important the work that faith-based organizations do and how much impact they can have in their communities.

I also know that some religious institutions, particularly those affiliated with the Catholic Church, have a religious objection to directly providing insurance that covers contraceptive services for their employees. And that's why we originally exempted all churches from this requirement, an exemption, by the way, that eight States didn't already have.

And that's why, from the very beginning of this process, I spoke directly to various Catholic officials, and I promised that before finalizing the rule as it applied to them, we would spend the next year working with institutions like Catholic hospitals and Catholic universities to find an equitable solution that protects religious liberty and ensures that every woman has access to the care that she needs.

Now, after the many genuine concerns that have been raised over the last few weeks, as well as, frankly, the more cynical desire on the part of some to make this into a political football, it became clear that spending months hammering out a solution was not going to be an option, that we needed to move this faster. So, last week, I directed the Department of Health and Human Services to speed up the process that had already been envisioned. We weren't going to spend a year doing this, we're going to spend a week or two doing this.

Today we've reached a decision on how to move forward. Under the rule, women will still have access to free preventive care that includes contraceptive services, no matter where they work. So that core principle remains. But if a woman's employer is a charity or a hospital that has a religious objection to providing contraceptive services as part of their health plan, the insurance company—not the hospital, not the charity—will be required to reach out and offer the woman contraceptive care free of charge, without copays and without hassles.

The result will be that religious organizations won't have to pay for these services, and no religious institution will have to provide these services directly. Let me repeat: These employers will not have to pay for or provide contraceptive services. But women who work at these institutions will have access to free contraceptive services just like other women, and they'll no longer have to pay hundreds of dollars a year that could go towards paying the rent or buying groceries.

Now, I've been confident from the start that we could work out a sensible approach here, just as I promised. I understand some folks in Washington may want to treat this as another political wedge issue, but it shouldn't be. I certainly never saw it that way. This is an issue where people of good will on both sides of the debate have been sorting through some very complicated questions to find a solution that works for everyone. With today's announcement, we've done that. Religious liberty will be protected, and a law that requires free preventive care will not discriminate against women.

Now, we live in a pluralistic society where we're not going to agree on every single issue or share every belief. That doesn't mean that we have to choose between individual liberty and basic fairness for all Americans. We are unique among nations for having been founded upon both these principles, and our obligation as citizens is to carry them forward. I have complete faith that we can do that.

Thank you very much, everybody.

NOTE: The President spoke at 12:15 p.m. in the James S. Brady Press Briefing Room at the White House.

Statement on Signing the Ultralight Aircraft Smuggling Prevention Act of 2012
February 10, 2012

This bill gives our Nation's law enforcement expanded authority to combat illicit drug trafficking on our northern and southern borders, and being able to sign it next to my friend Gabby Giffords gives me enormous pride. She has spent her career fighting for the safety of the people of Arizona and the fact that it passed unanimously shows just how much Gabby is respected by her colleagues in Congress in both parties. Her dedication to fairness and to this country has been an inspiration to so many, including myself. I wished Gabby well in her recovery and told her that I expect to see more of her in the months and years to come. I'm confident that while this legislation may have been her last act as a Congresswoman, it will not be her last act of public service.

NOTE: The statement referred to former Rep. Gabrielle D. Giffords. H.R. 3801, approved February 10, was assigned Public Law No. 112–93.

The President's Weekly Address
February 11, 2012

Hello, everybody. In recent weeks, we've seen signs that our economy is growing stronger and creating jobs at a faster clip. While numbers and figures will go up and down in the coming months, what cannot waver is our resolve to do everything in our power to keep stoking the fires of the recovery.

And the last thing we should do is let Washington stand in the way. You see, at the end of the month, taxes are set to go up on 160 million working Americans. If you're one of them, then you know better than anyone that the last thing you need right now is a tax hike. But if Congress refuses to act, middle class taxes will go up. It's that simple.

Now, if this sounds familiar, it's because we've been here before. Back in December, Congress faced this exact same predicament. Ultimately, thanks to your voices, they did the right thing, but only after a great deal of bickering and political posturing that put the strength of our economy and the security of middle class families at risk. We can't go through that again.

Congress needs to stop this middle class tax hike from happening—period. No drama, no delay, and no ideological side issues that have nothing to do with this tax cut. Now is not the time for self-inflicted wounds to our recovery.

Now is the time for commonsense action, and this tax cut is common sense. If you're a family making about $50,000 a year, this tax cut amounts to about $1,000 a year. That's about $40 in every paycheck. I know there are some folks in this town who think $40 isn't a lot of money. But to a student or a senior who's trying to stretch the budget a little bit further, to a parent who's filling up the tank and looking at rising gas prices—to them, $40 can make all the difference in the world.

And so can your voice. I hope you'll pick up the phone, send a tweet, write an e-mail, and tell your Representative that they should get this done before it's too late. Tell them not to play politics again by linking this debate to unrelated issues. Tell them not to manufacture another needless standoff or crisis. Tell them not to stand in the way of the recovery. Tell them to just do their job. That's what our middle class needs. That's what our country needs.

In the wake of the worst economic crisis of our lifetimes, we're getting things going again. And we're going to keep at it until everyone shares in America's comeback.

Thanks, and have a great weekend.

NOTE: The address was recorded at approximately 4:50 p.m. on February 10 in the

East Room at the White House for broadcast on February 11. The transcript was made available by the Office of the Press Secretary on February 10, but was embargoed for release until 6 a.m. on February 11.

Remarks at the Northern Virginia Community College Annandale Campus in Annandale, Virginia
February 13, 2012

The President. Thank you very much. Thank you, Virginia! Thank you, NOVA! Thank you so much. Thank you very much. Everybody who has a chair please have a seat. I know not everybody has a chair.

Audience member. Love you!

The President. I love you back. [*Laughter*] Great to be here.

First of all, I want to thank Mike for the wonderful introduction. Please give Mike a big round of applause.

It is great to be back here at NOVA. I've been here so many times I'm about three credits short of graduation. [*Laughter*] But there are a couple of reasons that I keep on coming back. First of all, I think that Dr. Templin and the whole administration here is doing a great job, so I want to give them a big round of applause. The other reason is because Jill Biden keeps talking up how great you are. And just as I do what Michelle tells me to do, I also do what Jill Biden tells me to do. [*Laughter*]

In addition, by the way, I just want to acknowledge that we also have our Secretary of Labor here, Hilda Solis, who's doing an outstanding job.

But the main reason I keep on coming back is I think this institution is an example of what's best about America. Some of you may have your eye on a 4-year college. Some of you may be trying to learn new skills that could lead to a new job, like Mike, or a job that pays more, gives you more opportunity. But all of you are here because you believe in yourselves, you believe in your ability, you believe in the future of this country. And that's something that inspires me, and you guys should take great pride in.

Now the truth is, the skills and training you get here will be the best tools you have to achieve the American promise, the promise that if you work hard, you can do well enough to raise a family, own a home, send your kids to college, and put a little away for retirement.

And the defining issue of our time is how to keep this promise alive today, for everybody. Because we've got a choice. We can settle for a country where a few people do really, really well and everybody else struggles to get by. Or we can restore an economy where everybody gets a fair shot, everybody does their fair share, everybody plays by the same set of rules, from Washington to Wall Street to Main Street. That's the America we believe in.

Now, we're still recovering from one of the worst economic crises in three generations. We've got a long way to go before everybody who wants a good job can find one, before middle class Americans regain that sense of security that's been slipping away for too long, long before the recession hit.

But over the last 23 months, we've added 3.7 million new jobs. American manufacturers are creating jobs for the first time since the 1990s. The economy is growing stronger. The recovery is speeding up. And the last thing we can afford to do right now is to go back to the very policies that got us into this mess in the first place. We can't afford it. The last thing we need is for Washington to stand in the way of America's comeback.

Now, what does that mean concretely? For starters, Congress needs to stop taxes from going up on 160 million Americans by the end of this month. And if they don't act, that's exactly what will happen. Congress needs to pass an extension of the payroll tax cut and unemployment insurance without drama and without delay and without linking it to some other ideological side issues.

We've been through this before, remember? We've seen this movie. We don't need to see it again. The time for self-inflicted wounds to our economy has to be over. Now is the time for action. Now is the time for all of us to move forward.

But preventing a tax hike on the middle class, that's only the beginning, that's just starters. In the State of the Union, I outlined a blueprint for an economy that is built to last, an economy built on new manufacturing and new sources of energy and new skills and education for the American people.

Today we're releasing the details of that blueprint in the form of next year's budget. And don't worry, I will not read it to you. [*Laughter*] It's long and a lot of numbers. But the main idea in the budget is this: At a time when our economy is growing and creating jobs at a faster clip, we've got to do everything in our power to keep this recovery on track.

Part of our job is to bring down our deficit. And if Congress adopts this budget, then along with the cuts that we've already made, we'll be able to reduce our deficit by $4 trillion by the year 2022—$4 trillion. I'm proposing some difficult cuts that frankly I wouldn't normally make if they weren't absolutely necessary. But they are. And the truth is we're going to have to make some tough choices in order to put this country back on a more sustainable fiscal path.

By reducing our deficit in the long term, what that allows us to do is to invest in the things that will help grow our economy right now. We can't cut back on those things that are important for us to grow. We can't just cut our way into growth. We can cut back on the things that we don't need, but we also have to make sure that everyone is paying their fair share for the things that we do need.

We need to restore American manufacturing by ending tax breaks for companies that ship jobs overseas, giving them to companies that are creating jobs right here in the United States of America. That's something that everybody should agree on.

We need to reduce our dependence on foreign oil by ending the subsidies for oil companies and doubling down on clean energy that generates jobs and strengthens our security.

And to make sure our businesses don't have to move overseas to find skilled workers, we've got to invest in places like NOVA and make sure higher education is affordable for every hard-working American.

That's what I want to focus on today, what we need to do in terms of higher education and community colleges in particular. Employers today are looking for the most skilled, educated workers. I don't want them to find them in India or China. I want businesses to find those workers right here in the United States. The skills and training that employers are looking for begins with the men and women who educate our children.

All of us can point to a teacher who's made a difference in our lives, and I know I can. So I want this Congress to give our schools the resources to keep good teachers on the job and reward the best teachers. And in return, they also need to give schools the flexibility to stop just teaching to the test and replace teachers who aren't helping kids learn. That's something that we can do.

So making sure we've got the most skilled workers starts early. It starts with K through 12—it starts before K through 12, making sure every child is prepared. And when an American of any age wants to pursue any kind of higher education, whether it's that high school grad who's just trying to get that first couple years of college education or somebody like Mike who's in the process of retraining, whether it's 2 years or 4 years or more, we've got to make sure that education is affordable and available to everybody who wants to go.

Now, this Congress needs to stop the interest rates on student loans from doubling this July. That's pretty important. That's in our budget. We're saying to Congress, now is not the time to make school more expensive for young people. And they can act right now to make that change.

They also need to take the tuition tax credit that my administration put in the budget over these last few years—a tax credit that saves families thousands of dollars on tuition—and we need to make that permanent. It shouldn't be temporary, it should be permanent.

So, between the increases we've provided in Pell grants, these tax credits, keeping interest rates low, all that's going to help. And millions of students across the country have benefited from that. But students and taxpayers can't just keep on subsidizing skyrocketing tuition; we're going to run out of money. So that's why I've asked States and colleges to do their part to keep costs down.

We're putting colleges and universities on notice: You can't just keep on raising tuition and expect us to keep on coming up with more and more money. Because tuition inflation has actually gone up even faster than health care. That's hard to do. [*Laughter*]

So what we're saying to States, colleges, and universities: If you can't stop tuition from going up, then funding you get from taxpayers will go down because higher education cannot be a luxury. It is an economic imperative that every family in America should be able to afford. That's part of the American promise in the 21st century.

So that's what we need to do to get more Americans ready for the jobs of the future. But what about the jobs that are open today? I talked about this at the State of the Union. There are millions of jobs open right now, and there are millions of people who are unemployed. And the question is, how do we match up those workers to those jobs? What about the companies that are looking to hire right now?

I hear from business leaders all the time who want to hire in the United States, but at the moment, they cannot always find workers with the right skills. Growing industries in science and technology have twice as many openings as we have workers who can do those jobs. Think about that. At a time when millions of Americans are looking for work, we shouldn't have any job openings out there. They should all be getting filled up.

Here in America, we've got the best workers and some of the fastest growing companies in the world. There's no reason we can't connect the two. And places like NOVA are proving that we know how to do it. This institution proves we know how to do it.

So let's say you are a single parent or a returning veteran or somebody who just wants a shot at a better paying job. You're a hard worker, you're a fast learner, you're motivated. You know there are companies looking to hire. You just need to figure out how to acquire some of the specific skills, the specialized skills that the companies need, and you need to figure that out as quickly as possible, hopefully without taking on tons of debt. Everybody in America should be able to get those skills at a community college like NOVA. And companies looking to hire should be able to count on these schools to provide them with a steady stream of workers qualified to fill those specific jobs.

That's why Mike was sharing his story. As Mike mentioned, he worked in the mortgage and real estate industry for 10 years, but when business declined after 9/11, he decided to start over. So he began selling building materials. Then the bottom fell out of the housing market, so Mike had to start all over again. He's got a knack for computers. So he figured he'd try a career in cybersecurity, where there is a lot of hiring—that is going to be a growth industry.

Luckily for Mike, NOVA is home to a program called CyberWatch. So he signed up; even though he's driving a limo on the side, he's still got to pay the bills. So he's working while going to school. But in December, Mike earned two certificates and, by the way, finished with a 4.0. So we're proud of that. Now he's working towards his associate's degree. And when he graduates, Mike will have access to a network of over 40 companies and Government agencies to help him find a job.

So we need more stories like Mike's. That's why my administration is helping community colleges redesign training programs, so students can learn the skills that are most in demand in industries like health care sciences and advanced manufacturing. And that's why we're making a national commitment to train 2 million Americans with skills they need to get a job right now or start their own business right now.

We've lined up more companies that want to help. We've already got model partnerships between major businesses like Siemens and community colleges in places like Charlotte and Orlando and Louisville. They're already up and running. We know how they work. And that's why I've asked Dr. Biden, Secretary Solis to take a bus tour through several States, including Ohio and Kentucky and North Carolina, to highlight businesses and community colleges that are working together to train workers for careers that are in demand right now. We've got to make these examples a model for the entire Nation.

And we also need to give more community colleges the resources they need to become community career centers, places where folks can learn the skills that local business are looking for right now, from data management to high-tech manufacturing. This should be an engine of job growth all across the country, these community colleges, and that's why we've got to support them. That's why it's such a big priority.

So an economy built to last demands that we keep doing everything we can to help students learn the skills that businesses are looking for. It means we have to keep strengthening American manufacturing. It means we've got to keep investing in American energy. We've got to double down on the clean energy that's creating jobs. But it also means we've got to renew the American values of fair play and shared responsibility.

The budget that we're releasing today is a reflection of shared responsibility. It says that if we're serious about investing in our future and investing in community colleges and investing in new energy technology and investing in basic research, well, we've got to pay for it. And that means we've got to make some choices.

Right now we're scheduled to spend nearly $1 trillion more on what was intended to be a temporary tax cut for the wealthiest 2 percent of Americans. We've already spent about that much. Now we're scheduled to spend another trillion. Keep in mind, a quarter of all millionaires pay lower tax rates than millions of middle class households. You've heard me say it:

Warren Buffett pays a lower tax rate than his secretary. That's not fair. It doesn't make sense at a time when we've got to pull together to get the country moving.

I don't need a tax break. We don't need to be providing additional tax cuts for folks who are doing really, really, really well. Do we want to keep these tax cuts for the wealthiest Americans? Or do we want to keep investing in everything else: education, clean energy, a strong military, care for our veterans? We can't do both. We can't afford it.

Some people go around, they say, well, the President is engaging in class warfare. That's not class warfare. That's common sense. That's common sense. Asking a billionaire to pay at least as much as his secretary when it comes to his tax rate—that's just common sense. Because Warren Buffet is doing fine, I'm doing fine. We don't need the tax breaks. You need them. You're the ones who see your wages stall. You're the one whose costs of everything from college to groceries has gone up. You're the ones who deserve a break.

And we don't begrudge success in America; we aspire to it. Everybody here—I want everybody here to go out there and do great. I want you to make loads of money if you can. That's wonderful. And we expect people to earn it, study hard, work hard for it. So we don't envy the wealthy. But we do expect everybody to do their fair share, so that everybody has opportunity, not just some.

And given where our deficit is, it's just a matter of math that folks like me are going to have to do a little bit more. Because Americans understand if I get a tax break I don't need and the country can't afford, then one of two things is going to happen: Either that means we have to add to our deficit, or it means you've got to pay for it. It means a senior has got to pay for it, in terms of suddenly their Medicare benefits are costing more. It means a student suddenly sees their interest rates go up higher at a time when they can't afford it. It means a family that's struggling to get by is having to do more because I'm doing less.

That's not right. It's not who we are. Each of us is here only because somebody, somewhere, felt a responsibility to each other and to our country's future. That's why they made investments in places like NOVA.

Here in America, the story has never been about what we can do just by ourselves; it's about what we can do together. It's about believing in our future and the future of our country. You believe in that future. That's why you're working hard. That's why you're putting in the long hours. That's why Mike is doing what he's doing. Some of you are balancing a job at the same time as you're going to school. You're scrimping and scratching to make sure that you can pay tuition here. You know that doing big things isn't easy, but you haven't given up.

That's the spirit we've got to have right now. We don't give up in this country. We look out for each other. We pull together. We work hard. We reach for new opportunities. We pull each other up. That's who we are. And if we work together in common purpose, we will build an economy that lasts and remind people around the world why America is the greatest country on Earth.

Thank you very much, everybody. God bless you. God bless the United States of America.

NOTE: The President spoke at 11:12 a.m. In his remarks, he referred to Mike Phillips, student, and Robert G. Templin, Jr., president, Northern Virginia Community College; Jill T. Biden, wife of Vice President Joe Biden; and Warren E. Buffett, chief executive officer and chairman, Berkshire Hathaway Inc.

Remarks on Presenting the 2011 National Medal of Arts and National Humanities Medal
February 13, 2012

The President. Thank you, everybody. Please, please have a seat. Thank you. Thank you so much for joining us in this celebration of the arts and the humanities. Two outstanding public servants and ambassadors for the arts are here: Rocco Landesman—where's Rocco? There he is, right here—Chairman of the National Endowment of the Arts. And Jim Leach—where's Jim? Good to see you, Jim— the Chairman of the National Endowment for the Humanities.

We also have two good friends and Cochairs of the President's Committee on the Arts and the Humanities who are here: Margo Lions and George Stevens. And I also want to acknowledge one of our honorees who unfortunately could not make it. Ever the artist, Andre Watts had a concert to give in Salt Lake City. [*Laughter*] So give him a big round of applause in his absence.

Michelle and I love this event. This is something we look forward to every single year because it's a moment when America has a chance to pay tribute to extraordinary men and women who have excelled in the arts and the humanities and who, along the way, have left an indelible mark on American culture. That's all the honorees we see here today. We honor your talents, we honor your careers, and your remarkable contributions to this country that we love.

Throughout our history, America has advanced not only because of the will of our citizens, not only because of the vision of our leaders or the might of our military. America has also advanced because of paintings and poems, stories and songs, the dramas and the dances that provide us comfort and instilled in us confidence, inspired in us a sense of mutual understanding and a calling to always strive for a more perfect Union.

Emily Dickinson wrote, "I dwell in possibility." I dwell in possibility. And so does the American spirit. That's who we are as a people. And that's who our honorees are. Each of you have traveled a unique path to get here, and your fields represent the full spectrum of the arts and humanities. With us are actors and poets, authors, singers, philosophers, sculptors, curators, musicians, and historians. We even have an economist, which we don't always get on stage, but—[*laughter*]—what connects every one of you is that you dwell in possibilities. You create new possibilities for all of us.

And that's a special trait. And it assigns you a special task. Because in moments of calm, as in moments of crisis, in times of triumph as in times of tragedy, you help guide our growth as a people. The true power of the arts and the humanities is that you speak to everyone. There is not one of us here who hasn't had their beliefs challenged by a writer's eloquence or their knowledge deepened by a historian's insights or their sagging spirits lifted by a singer's voice. Those are some of the most endearing and memorable moments in our lives.

Equal to the impact you have on each of us every day as individuals is the impact you have on us as a society. And we are told we're divided as a people, and then suddenly, the arts have this power to bring us together and speak to our common condition.

Recently, I've been reminded of Walt Whitman's famous poem "I Hear America Singing." And it's a poem that with simple eloquence spotlights our diversity and our spirit of rugged individualism, the messy, energized, dynamic sense of what it is to be an American. And Whitman lifts up the voices of mechanics and carpenters, masons and boatmen, shoemakers, woodcutters, the mother and the young wife at work, "each singing what belongs to him or her and to none else."

And it's true that we all have songs in our souls that are only ours. We all have a unique part in the story of America. But that story is bigger than any one of us. And it endures because we are all heirs to a fundamental truth: that out of many are one, this incredible multitude.

I hear America singing today. I hear America singing through the artists and the writers that we honor this afternoon, the men and women who are following in the footsteps of Whitman and Hemingway, Souza and Armstrong, and Eakins and Rockwell. But I also hear America singing through the artists and writers who will be sitting here a few decades from now with another President, the students

in Denver who recently wrote a play about teenage homelessness or the kids in Grand Rapids who designed a mural to bring joy to a struggling community. They're singing what Whitman called "strong melodious songs."

And somewhere in America, the next great writer is wrestling with the first draft of an English paper. [*Laughter*] Somewhere the next great actor is mustering up the courage to try out for that school play. Somewhere the next great artist is doodling on their homework. Somewhere the next great thinker is asking their teacher, "Why not?" They're out there right now, dwelling in possibility.

So, as we honor the icons of today, we also have to champion the icons of tomorrow. They need our support; we need them to succeed. We need them to succeed as much as we need engineers and scientists. We also need artists and scholars. We need them to take the mantle from you, to do their part to disrupt our views and to challenge our presumptions and most of all to stir in us a need to be our better selves.

The arts and the humanities do not just reflect America, they shape America. And as long as I am President, I look forward to making sure they are a priority for this country, so—[*applause*].

It is now my distinct privilege to present these medals to the award winners who we have here today. And as the citations are read, I'm sure you've gotten extensive instructions from our Military Aides, so—[*laughter*].

[*At this point, Maj. Gary Marlowe, USAF, Air Force Aide to the President, read the citations, and the President presented the medals.*]

The President. Will you please stand and give a big hand to our award winners today.

Well, we are just blessed to have this incredible array of talent and inspiration with us here today. We are so glad we had the opportunity to make this small gesture of appreciation and thanks to all that you have contributed to us.

Each and every day you continue to inform who we are as a people, and we could not be prouder of everything that you've done, and we know you've got a lot more to do, so keep at it.

In the meantime, for everybody who is gathered here today, we have a wonderful reception. So please enjoy. The food is usually pretty good around here. [*Laughter*] The music is even better. I think the Marine Band will probably be out there playing a few tunes. And again, we are very thankful to all the honorees here today for everything that you've done for our country. Congratulations.

NOTE: The President spoke at 1:52 p.m. in the East Room at the White House. In his remarks, he referred to Amartya Sen, professor of economics and philosophy, Harvard University.

Remarks on Payroll Tax Cut and Unemployment Insurance Legislation
February 14, 2012

Thank you. Everybody, please have a seat. Well, good morning. And let me start with a quick public service announcement for all the gentlemen out there: Today is Valentine's Day. [*Laughter*] Do not forget. I speak from experience here. [*Laughter*] It is important that you remember this. And go big, that's my advice. [*Laughter*]

Lately, I've been saying that this is a make-or-break moment for the middle class in America and for folks who want to be in the middle class. We face a choice. We can settle for a country where a few people do really, really well and everybody else struggles just to get by. Or we can restore an economy where everybody gets a fair shot, and everybody is doing their fair share, and everybody is playing by the same set of rules. And that second option is, I strongly believe, the kind of America that we want for our kids and our grandkids. That's who we are. That's the America that we believe in. That's what we have to roll up our sleeves and get back to doing, is creating an America where everybody is doing their fair share, everybody gets a fair shot, everybody is engaging in fair play.

We're still fighting our way back from the worst economic crisis in our lifetimes, and we've still got a lot of work to do and a long way to go. It's going to take time to recover all the jobs that were lost when the recession was at its depths. But the fight is beginning to turn our way.

Over the past 2 years, our businesses have added over 3.7 million new jobs. Our manufacturers are hiring more new workers to make more new things here in America than at any time since the 1990s. So our economy is growing stronger. And the last thing we need, the last thing we can afford to do, is to go back to the same policies that got us in this mess in the first place. The last thing we need is for Washington to stand in the way of America's comeback.

First and foremost, that means Washington shouldn't hike taxes on working Americans right now. That's the wrong thing to do. But that's exactly what's going to happen at the end of this month, in a couple of weeks, if Congress doesn't do something about it. The payroll tax cut we put in place last year will expire. The typical American family will shell out nearly a thousand dollars more in taxes this year. You'll lose about $40 out of every paycheck if Congress does not act.

And that can't happen. Not now. And it doesn't have to. Congress needs to extend that tax cut, along with vital insurance lifelines for folks who've lost their jobs during this recession, and they need to do it now, without drama and without delay. No ideological sideshows to gum up the works. No self-inflicted wounds. Just pass this middle class tax cut. Pass the extension of unemployment insurance. Do it before it's too late. And I will sign it right away.

Now, the good news is over the last couple of days, we've seen some hopeful signs in Congress that they realize that they've got to get this done, and you're starting to hear voices talk about how can we go ahead and make this happen in a timely way on behalf of the American people. That is good news. But as you guys know, you can't take anything for granted here in Washington until my signature is actually on it.

So we've got to keep on making sure that the American people's voices keep breaking through until this is absolutely, finally, completely done. Until you see me sign this thing, you've got to keep on speaking up. Until you see that photograph of me signing it at my desk—[*laughter*]—make sure it's verified, certified. If it's not on the White House website, it hasn't happened. And I'm going to need to make sure that your voices are heard.

Last December, when we had this same fight, your voices made all the difference. We asked folks to tell what it was like—what it would be like if they lost $40 out of every one of their paychecks, because we wanted to make sure that people understood this is not just an abstract argument. This is concrete. This makes a difference in the lives of folks all across the country in very important ways.

Tens of thousands of working Americans flooded us with their stories, and some of them are here with me today. And their feedback has been pretty unanimous. Allowing this tax cut to expire would make people's lives harder right now. It would make their choices more difficult. It would be $40 less for groceries to feed your kids. It would be $40 less for the medications you depend on, $40 less to cover bills and the rent, $40 less to take care of an elder parent or to donate to a church or a charity. And when gas prices are on the rise again—because as the economy strengthens, global demand for oil increases—and if we start seeing significant increases in gas prices, losing that $40 could not come at a worse time.

One local entrepreneur named Thierry—where's Thierry? He's right here. He told us that $40 would cover the gas that gets him to his day job or, alternatively, the Internet service that his small business depends on. So he'd have to start making a choice: Do I fill up my gas tank to get to my work, or do I give up my entrepreneurial dream? "Forty dollars," he wrote, "means a heck of a lot." Means a heck of a lot.

And that's what this debate is all about. This is what's at stake for millions of Americans. This is why it matters to people; it mat-

ters a heck of a lot. And I'm asking the American people to keep their stories coming. Tell us what $40 means to you. If you tweet it, use the hashtag #40dollars. [*Laughter*] Call, tweet, write your Congressmen, write your Senators. Tell them, do not let up until this thing gets done. Don't let taxes go up on 160 million working Americans. Don't let millions of Americans who are out there looking for work right now—and the economy is starting to improve, but they don't have a job yet—don't leave them without a lifeline in terms of cutting off their unemployment insurance.

When a plane is finally lifting off the ground, you don't ease up on the throttle. You keep the throttle on full. You keep going. And our plane is up there, but we're not at cruising altitude yet. [*Laughter*]

After all, extending this tax cut and the unemployment insurance is the least of what we should be doing for working Americans. It's just a start. We need to rebuild an economy where middle class folks can focus on more than just getting by and folks who want to get in the middle class have those ladders to get into the middle class. We've got to rebuild an economy where the middle class thrives and more Americans have a chance to earn their way into it: an economy built to last.

Yesterday I released a blueprint for how we get there. It's a blueprint for an economy built on new American manufacturing and new American energy sources and new skills and education for American workers and a new focus on the values that are the bedrock of this country, values like fairness and responsibility for all and from all. We're going to be better off if we start building that economy right now.

And we can do it because we've done it before. We have a common challenge; it's time for us to meet it with a common purpose and to show a sense of seriousness that's equal to the task.

So, on behalf of all the hard-working Americans who are standing behind me, I want to thank you for helping to tell your story and tell the story of why this is so important. And I just want everybody, all across the country, to keep the pressure so that we get this done. It is going to make our economy stronger, and it's going to put us in a position where we can start really rebuilding on behalf of not just this generation, but future generations.

Thank you very much, everybody. God bless you. God bless America.

NOTE: The President spoke at 10:55 a.m. in the South Court Auditorium of the Dwight D. Eisenhower Executive Office Building.

Remarks Prior to a Meeting With Vice President Xi Jinping of China
February 14, 2012

President Obama. I want to welcome Vice President Xi to the Oval Office and welcome him to the United States. This is obviously a great opportunity for us to build on the U.S.-China relationship, but also an opportunity to return the extraordinary hospitality that Vice President Xi showed Vice President Biden during his recent visit to China.

As I indicated during my recent visit to APEC and the East Asia Summit, the United States is a Pacific nation. And we are very interested and very focused on continuing to strengthen our relationships, to enhance our trade and our commerce, and make sure that we are a strong and effective partner with the Asia-Pacific region. And obviously, in order to do that, it is absolutely vital that we have a strong relationship with China.

Over the last 3 years I've had a great opportunity to develop a strong working relationship with President Hu. And we have continually tried to move forward on the basis of recognizing that a cooperative relationship based on mutual interest and mutual respect is not only in the interests of the United States and China, but is also in the interest of the region and in the interest of the United States, in the interest of the world.

On the basis of that understanding, we have established very extensive strategic and economic dialogues between our two countries. We have been able to pursue a significant consultation on opportunities for both countries to improve their economic relationship and their strategic relationship and also manage areas of tension in a way that is constructive.

That includes working together in the G–20 to manage the world economic crisis that had such an impact not only on both our countries, but on the entire world. And because of U.S.-China cooperation, I think that we were able to help stabilize the situation at a very difficult time. It also includes the work that we've been able to do together in dealing with regional hotspot issues, like the Korean Peninsula and issues like Iran, that obviously have an impact on everybody.

Throughout this process, I have always emphasized that we welcome China's peaceful rise, that we believe that a strong and prosperous China is one that can help to bring stability and prosperity to the region and to the world. And we expect to be able to continue on the cooperative track that we've tried to establish over the last 3 years.

We have tried to emphasize that because of China's extraordinarily—extraordinary development over the last two decades, that with expanding power and prosperity also comes increased responsibilities. And so we want to work with China to make sure that everybody is working by the same rules of the road when it comes to the world economic system and that includes ensuring that there is a balanced trade flow between not only the United States and China, but around world.

It also means that on critical issues like human rights, we will continue to emphasize what we believe is the importance of recognizing the aspirations and rights of all people. And we expect that China will continue to take a growing role in world affairs. And we believe that it is critically important that the United States and China develop a strong working relationship to help to bring stability, order, and security that ultimately provides a better life for both the people of the United States and the people of China.

So, Mr. Vice President, I hope you have a wonderful visit while you're here. I'm sure the American people welcome you. I'm glad that you're going to get an opportunity to get out of Washington. I know you'll be visiting Iowa, where you visited many years ago when you were a governor. And I understand you're also going to be going to Los Angeles and maybe even taking in a Lakers game. So I hope you enjoy that very much.

But I want to extend my deepest welcome to you and look forward to a future of improved dialogue and increased cooperation in the years to come.

Vice President Xi. Honorable President Obama, it's my great pleasure to meet you again. First of all, I'd like to convey the sincere greetings from President Hu Jintao, the National People's Congress Chairman Wu Bangguo, and Premier Wen Jiabao.

I am paying an official visit to the United States at the kind invitation of Vice President Biden. And we have received the warm and extraordinary hospitality from our hosts. So here, I want to thank you for your personal attention and what you did to help prepare and ensure a successful visit for myself.

The main purpose of my visit is to implement the important agreement you had reached with President Hu Jintao and to do some work to move forward the China-U.S. relationship along in the right direction, set by

you and President Hu—that is for our two countries to work together to build a cooperative partnership based on mutual respect and mutual interests. And I hope to engage with a broad cross-section of American society during my current visit, so as to deepen mutual understanding, expand consensus, strengthen cooperation, and deepen the friendship between the Chinese and American people.

Yesterday evening, soon after my arrival in Washington, DC, I met with a very distinguished group of veteran U.S. political leaders. I sought their advice on the future development of our relationship, and their wise and practical suggestions have provided me with much food for thought.

Just now I've had a set of large and small talks with Vice President Biden. He and I had an extensive, candid, and indepth exchange of views on the bilateral relationship and international and regional issues of shared interest. Building on our discussions last August in Beijing and Chengdu, the Vice President and I reached some new consensus.

I look forward to my indepth discussion with you, President Obama, in our meeting today.

President Obama. Thank you, everybody.

NOTE: The President spoke at 11:29 a.m. in the Oval Office at the White House. Vice President Xi spoke in Chinese, and his remarks were translated by an interpreter.

Remarks at Master Lock Company in Milwaukee, Wisconsin
February 15, 2012

The President. Hello, Milwaukee! It is good to be back in the great State of Wisconsin. This is the closest I've been to home in a while. I was thinking about getting on the 90/94 and just driving down to my house. [*Laughter*]

Thank you, DiAndre, for that outstanding introduction and for sharing your story. I can tell, though, DiAndre is a little shy. He doesn't necessarily like to get out in front of people. [*Laughter*]

Before I begin, I want to thank some additional special guests who are here. Milwaukee Mayor Tom Barrett is in the house. Your Con-

gresswoman, Gwen Moore, is here. You heard from your local UAW representative, John Drew, and I got a great tour from the president of UAW Local 469, Mike Bink. And finally, I want to thank Master Lock CEO John Heppner for inviting us here today.

It is wonderful to be at Master Lock. I have to say, though, it brought back some memories. I was thinking about my gym locker in high school. [*Laughter*] And you know, if you go into the boys' locker room in high school, sometimes it's a little powerful, the odor in there. [*Laughter*] So I was thinking about the fact that we weren't washing our stuff enough. [*Laughter*] And then I was thinking about, as I got older and I kept on using Master Locks, I became an even better customer because I couldn't always remember my combination. [*Laughter*] So I'd end up having to have the lock sawed off and buy a new one. So I was giving you guys a lot of business.

And now, as I was looking at some of the really industrial-size locks, I was thinking about the fact that I am a father of two girls who are soon going to be in high school, and that it might come in handy to have these super locks. [*Laughter*] For now, I'm just counting on the fact that when they go to school there are men with guns with them. [*Laughter*]

But I'm actually here today because this company has been making the most of a huge opportunity that exists right now to bring jobs and manufacturing back to the United States of America.

I talked about this during the State of the Union. Over the last few decades, revolutions in technology have made a lot of businesses more efficient and more productive. And that's a great thing. It means you generally have a better choice of products, you get better prices. But as some of you know, technology has also made a lot of jobs obsolete. And it's allowed companies to set up shop and hire workers almost anywhere in the world where there's an Internet connection; you can produce things that previously you could only produce here in the United States.

So the result has been a pretty painful process for a lot of families and for a lot of communities, especially here in the Midwest. Too many factories where people thought they'd retire suddenly left town. Too many jobs that provided a decent living got shipped overseas. And now the hard truth is, a lot of those jobs are not going to come back. In a global economy, some companies are always going to find it more profitable to pick up and do business in some other part of the world. That's just a fact.

But that doesn't mean we have to just sit by and settle for a lesser future. That doesn't mean there's nothing we can do to create new jobs and restore middle class security here in America. There is always something we can do.

For starters, I'm glad to see that Congress seems to be on the way of making progress on extending the payroll tax cut so taxes don't go up on all of you and 160 million working Americans. This tax cut means that the typical American family will see an extra $40 in every paycheck this year. And that's going to help speed up this recovery. It will make a real difference in the lives of millions of people. And as soon as Congress sends me that extension of tax cuts and unemployment insurance to my desk, I will sign it right away. We're going to get that signed.

Audience member. Love you, Mr. President!

The President. I love you back. [*Laughter*]

But that's only a start. There's a lot more we can do—a lot more we have to do—to help create jobs and bring back manufacturing and middle class security to Milwaukee and Wisconsin and the United States of America.

Look, what—and we've got examples of success. When I took office—a lot of UAW workers here, you guys remember this—when I took office, the American auto industry was on the verge of collapse. And there were some folks who said we should let it die. With a million jobs at stake, I refused to let that happen. I refused to let that happen.

We said, in exchange for help, we're going to demand responsibility. We got workers and automakers to settle their differences. We got the industry to restructure and retool, come up with better designs. Today, the American auto industry is back. And General Motors is once again the number-one automaker in the world. Chrysler has grown faster in the U.S. than any major car company. Ford is investing billions in U.S. plants and equipment and factories. And all together, over the past 2 years, the entire industry has added nearly 160,000 jobs—well-paying jobs.

What's happening in Detroit can happen in other industries. What happens in Cleveland and Pittsburgh and Raleigh and Milwaukee, that's what we've got to be shooting for, is to create opportunities for hard-working Americans to get in there and start making stuff again and sending it all over the world, products stamped with three proud words: Made in America. That's our goal.

And that's what's happening right here at Master Lock, because of you. Over the last few years, it's become more expensive to do business in countries like China. Meanwhile, American workers, we've become even more productive. So, when John Heppner was at the White House in January, he told me how it makes more business sense for Master Lock to bring jobs back home here to Milwaukee. And today, for the first time in 15 years, this plant is running at full capacity. And that's an example of what happens when unions and employers work together to create good jobs. Today, you're selling products directly to customers in China stamped with those words: Made in America.

And the good news is this is starting to happen around the country. For the first time since 1990, American manufacturers are creating new jobs. That's good for the companies, but it's also good up and down the supply chain, because if you're making this stuff here, that means that there are producers and suppliers in and around the area who have a better chance of selling stuff here. It means the restaurant close by suddenly has more customers. Everybody benefits when manufacturing is going strong.

So you all have heard enough about outsourcing. More and more companies like Master Lock are now insourcing, deciding that if the cost of doing business here isn't too much different than the cost of doing business in places like China, then why wouldn't you rather do it right here in the United States of America? Why not? Why not put some Americans to work?

Companies would rather bet on the country with the best colleges and universities to train workers with new skills and produce cutting-edge research. They'd rather place their bet on the Nation with the greatest array of talent and ingenuity, the country with the greatest capacity for innovation that the world has ever known.

During the State of the Union, I issued a challenge to America's business leaders, folks like John. I said, ask yourself what you can do to bring jobs back to your country, and your country will do everything we can to help you succeed. And since then, a number of companies—large and small, domestic, but also even some foreign companies—have said they now plan to open new facilities and create new jobs right here in America, which is still the largest market on Earth.

These include Wisconsin companies like Diamond Precision, which is a machine manufacturer that's going to be adding dozens of jobs here in Milwaukee, a company that's growing because its customers are choosing to buy American-made products instead of supplies from China. There's a company called Collaborative Consulting, an information technology company that wants to open a new call center here in Wausau. And across the Nation, there are well-known companies like Caterpillar that are planning to bring jobs back home.

So, last month, we decided to hold a summit—that's where John was at—a summit at the White House so we could hear from companies like these who've decided to insource jobs. We wanted to learn how can we accelerate this trend. And this last fall, for the first time, we'll be bringing companies from around the world together with Governors and mayors and other leaders to discuss the benefits of investing and creating more jobs here in the United States.

So our job as a nation is to do everything we can to make the decision to insource more attractive for more companies. That's our top priority. That's our top priority. We've got to seize this moment of opportunity. We can't let it slip away. We've got an opportunity to create new American jobs and American manufacturing, put that back where it needs to be.

Now, one place to start is with our Tax Code. I talked about this a little bit at the State of the Union. Right now companies get tax breaks for moving jobs and profits overseas.

Audience members. Boo!

The President. They're taking deductions for the expenses of moving out of the United

States. Meanwhile, companies that are doing the right thing and choosing to stay here, they get hit with one of the highest tax rates in the world. That doesn't make sense. Everybody knows it doesn't make sense. Politicians of both parties have been talking about changing it for years. So my message to Congress is: Don't wait. Get it done. Do it now. Let's get it done.

As Congress thinks about tax reform principles, there are some basic things they can do. First, if you're a business that wants to outsource jobs, you have that right, but you shouldn't get a tax deduction for doing it. That money should be used to cover moving expenses for companies like Master Lock that decide to bring jobs home. Give them the tax break.

Second of all, no American company should be able to avoid paying its fair share of taxes by moving jobs and profits overseas. So we've said, from now on, every multinational company should have to pay a basic minimum tax. And every penny should go towards lowering taxes for companies that choose to stay and hire here in the United States of America. Give them a bigger tax break.

Third, if you're an American manufacturer, you should get a bigger tax cut. If you're a high-tech manufacturer, creating new products, new services, we should double the tax deduction you get for making products here in America. If you want to relocate in a community like this one that's been hard hit when factories left town, you should get help financing a new plant, financing new equipment, training new workers.

It is time to stop rewarding companies that ship jobs overseas and start rewarding companies that are creating jobs right here in the United States of America. And this Congress should send me these tax reforms right now. I will sign them right away.

Audience member. Right now!

The President. Right now.

Audience members. Right now! Right now! Right now!

The President. Right now. Right now. [*Laughter*]

Now, another thing we're doing to support American jobs is to make it easier for business-es like Master Lock to sell their products all over the world. Everybody knows Master Lock makes the best lock. So, 2 years ago, I set a goal of doubling U.S. exports over 5 years. With the bipartisan trade agreements I signed into law, we're on track to meeting that goal ahead of schedule. Pretty soon, there are going to be millions of new customers for American goods in places like Panama and Colombia and South Korea. I want new cars on the streets of Seoul, South Korea, imported from Detroit and Toledo and Milwaukee.

There's nothing wrong with them being able to sell cars here. I just want to be able to sell cars there.

Audience member. Even playing field, Mr. President——

The President. Even playing field is what we want.

Audience member. Yeah!

The President. I'm going anywhere in the world to open up new markets for American products. And I'm not going to stand by when our competitors don't play by the same rules. It's not fair when foreign manufacturers have a leg up on ours just because they're getting heavy subsidies from their government.

So I directed my administration to create a trade enforcement unit, and it's only got one job: investigating unfair trade practices in countries like China, making sure we've got an even playing field. Because when we've got an even playing field, I promise you, nobody is going to outcompete America. We've got the most productive workers on Earth. We've got the most creative entrepreneurs on Earth. Give us a level playing field, we will not lose.

Now part of creating that level playing field is also making sure that American workers have the skills that today's jobs require. And DiAndre talked about how he's—even though he's working, he's still going back to school. I know that Master Lock's decision to create even more jobs here in Milwaukee in part is going to depend—and this is part—something that John raised when we were at our meeting—it's going to depend on finding enough workers with the right training.

I had a chance to meet one of your coworkers, Eric—where's—is Eric here? There he is right there. So Eric and I were talking—been a diemaker for a long time. He's older than he looks—[*laughter*]—although we were comparing the gray in his beard to the gray on my head. [*Laughter*] But he was pointing out that he's actually been able to help make the machinery that he works on more efficient, which is making the company able to do more because it's not lying idle when certain orders aren't coming in. But that's an accumulation of experience that he's had over a couple of decades.

Now, not everybody is going to have all that experience, but the question is, can we make sure if they're—if they haven't already been working in this job, can they get that kind of training even before they're hired here at Master Lock so that they can provide that same value-added across the board? That's what's going to separate the companies that succeed from the companies that don't, is how skilled and talented the workers are and whether management is listening to the workers. Because that's important. Part of what allowed Eric to be successful was somebody—his supervisor said, hey, this guy has got pretty good ideas.

So that's why it's so important for the companies investing in training programs and partnering with nearby community colleges to help design courses and curriculum, so that when workers show up they're already ready to hit the ground running. That's why I've asked Congress to join me in a national commitment to train 2 million American workers with skills that will lead directly to a job. We need to give more community colleges the resources they need to become community career centers, places that teach people the skills that businesses like Master Lock are looking for right now.

Audience members. Right now!

The President. Right now.

There are jobs from data management to high-tech manufacturing that right now are open. And we've got a lot of folks out of work, but we've got to match up the folks who are out of work with the jobs. And sometimes the businesses may not be able to afford to train that person on the job, so let's have the community college help get the training.

At a time when so many Americans are out of work, there should not be any job openings, because every single job opening that comes up, somebody should be able to say, I want that job and I'm prepared and skilled to get it.

We're still recovering from one of the worst economic crises in three generations. And I'm not going to lie to you guys. You know it. We've still got a long way to go before everyone who wants a good job can find it. I'm sure that if we traveled all around here, there are a lot of folks who want work and can't find it. And when you're out of work, that wears on you. It's not just the income. It has to do with your sense of place and your sense of dignity and your ability to support your family and the pride that you take in making a good product. That's part of what America has always been about, is what our work means to us, the values we put behind our work. We don't just do it for a paycheck.

And so this has been hard on folks. It's been hard on our country. And it's going to take some time before middle class Americans regain the sense of security that's been slipping away way before this recession hit. A lot of these factories were moving out before this recession hit. There was a lot of outsourcing going on over the last 20 years. So we've got a long way to go.

But here's what I want everybody to remember. Over the last 23 months, businesses have added nearly 3.7 million new jobs. Manufacturing is coming back. Companies are starting to bring jobs back. The economy is getting stronger. The recovery is speeding up. We're moving in the right direction. And now we have to do everything in our power to keep our foot on the gas. And the last thing we can afford to do is go back to the same policies that got us into this mess.

Milwaukee, we are not going back to an economy that's weakened by outsourcing and bad debt and phony financial profits. We need an economy that is built to last, that is built on American manufacturing and American know-how and American-made energy and skills for

American workers and the renewal of American values of hard work and fair play and shared responsibility. That's what we're about. That's what we're about.

And let me say this. These are not Democratic values or Republican values. These are American values. They have seen us through the most difficult challenges, through war and depressions and civil strife. But we've always come out on the other side stronger than we were before. We don't give up. This country does not give up.

And we make sure that everybody is brought along. We don't leave people behind. We look out for one another. We reach out to one another. We are going for new opportunities, but we pull each other up. That's who we are.

If we work together with common purpose, if we pull together with common effort, I've got no doubt we will rebuild this economy so it lasts. We're going to create more success stories like Master Lock, and we will remind the world just why it is the United States is the greatest nation on Earth.

Thank you, everybody. God bless you. God bless America.

NOTE: The President spoke at 12:50 p.m. In his remarks, he referred to Master Lock Co. employees DiAndre Jackson and Eric Hammerer; and John R. Drew, servicing representative, UAW Region 4.

Remarks at an Obama Victory Fund 2012 Fundraiser in Los Angeles, California
February 15, 2012

Hello, L.A.! Oh, it is good to be in L.A., although you guys are not used to this kind of weather, are you? You're all cold. This is balmy, people. I'm trying to let you know. [*Laughter*]

A few folks I just want to acknowledge. First of all, to Colleen and Brad and the entire Bell family, thank you for making this incredible night possible. We're so grateful to them. What about the Foo Fighters? Love the Foo Fighters. They were tired of winning so many awards, so they said, let's do something else tonight. [*Laughter*] We are so grateful to them. Jack Black, one of my favorites; Rashida Jones—we love Rashida; the mayor of Los Angeles, Antonio Villaraigosa, who was announced tonight as the permanent chair of the 2012 Democratic National Convention. And our host and cochair in Charlotte, North Carolina, Mayor Anthony Foxx of Charlotte is here. So we are grateful to him.

Now, some of you are back for a return engagement because you were around in 2008. A few of you guys in the front row, you were only 1 year old so you may not remember this. [*Laughter*] But sometimes I have occasion to think back to the 2008 campaign, and I think about that magical night in Grant Park—when it was actually 60 degrees in November, which does not happen in Chicago very often—and I remind people of what I said that night. I said change is never easy. Change doesn't happen overnight. Change is hard, especially when you're dealing with challenges that have been building up over decades. But if everyone maintains their determination, their sense of purpose, the bonds that we have with each other as Americans, then there's no challenge we can't overcome.

Now it's hard to remember that, because those were such heady days, those last few days of the campaign. Some of you had gotten involved in the campaign very early, before anybody could pronounce my name. [*Laughter*] Right here. And obviously, you didn't do it because it was a sure thing because, let's face it, the odds of Barack Obama—Barack Hussein Obama—becoming President were not high. [*Laughter*]

The reason you got involved, and the reason you were a constant source of inspiration to me, was because you recognized that the America that you grew up in, your idea of America wasn't matching up to what was happening all across the country; that the idea that if you work hard, if you are responsible, if you're looking after your family, if you're doing your very best, that somehow you can live out that American Dream and get ahead and support your family and have health care that protects your family if something goes wrong and you're able to retire with dignity and respect and watch your kids exceed your greatest dreams by going to college and doing great things; that too many folks felt that that dream had been betrayed. And this was before this extraordinary financial crisis that we ended up having in 2007 and 2008.

People were already feeling that there was a mismatch between our idea of what America should be and what was happening around the country. That's what you were fighting for. That's what this campaign was about. It was not about me. It was about you and the commitments you make to each other, to your families and your children, your grandchildren, your neighbors and your coworkers and your friends and your fellow citizens.

And because of the incredible work that you did, we began to transform the country. We knew it was going to be a long journey. We didn't know maybe how steep it was going to be. We didn't realize in 2008 the nature of the crisis, how profound it was going to be. Four million jobs lost before I even took office; 4 million jobs lost in the 6 months after I took office before any of our economic policies had a chance to take effect. The worst economic crisis since the Great Depression, all across the country, people struggling to find a job, seeing their home values deteriorate. We did not fully comprehend at that point how deep this crisis would be.

But because of you, because of your commitment, because of your determination and your vision, we began to see change happening all across the country. And when you think about change that we can believe in, as hard as these last 3 years have been, don't underestimate the changes we've made.

The month I took office, we were losing 750,000 jobs every month; last month we created 250,000 jobs. We've now created 3.7 million jobs all across the country over the last 23 months. We've seen more manufacturing jobs created than any time since the 1990s. An auto industry is saved, and GM is the number-one automaker in the world again.

So, slowly, steadily, as difficult as it's been, we've started to see the economy rebound and recover. We've started to see people who were starting to lose hope see once again the possibilities in their lives.

But that's not all that we did. You know, I was talking to a young person who told me that they had been diagnosed with cancer—they had written me a letter, actually. And fortunately, the diagnosis was one where the prospects are good. But she told me that she wouldn't even have gone to a doctor had it not been for the fact that we passed something that had eluded Presidents for a century, the idea that everybody in America deserves health care. Nobody should be left out. And because of those changes, already 2.6 million young people have health care that they wouldn't otherwise have. And because she had health care, including preventive care, she was able to get a checkup and this cancer was diagnosed early and her prospects are good.

And she said, "This wouldn't have happened had it not been for what you did." And what I have to tell you today is that's something you did. There are people whose lives have been saved because of the work that you did in 2008.

I was at a Marine base in Hawaii—my hometown. And we were working out. And you don't want to really work out with marines because they're all in really good shape and they make you feel bad about yourself. [*Laughter*] But during the course of the 10 days that I was there, at least three times a marine would come up and say: "Mr. President, thank you for passing laws rescinding 'don't ask, don't tell,' because I am proud to serve my country, and I didn't think it was ever going to happen. And to see that happen makes all the difference in my life."

And you know what I told them? I said, don't thank me, thank all the people who worked in 2008 to make this campaign a reality. That's what you did, because of your commitment.

The first bill I signed into law, the Lilly Ledbetter Act, that says a very simple principle: There's got to be equal pay for equal work, and I don't want my daughters being treated [differently]° than anybody else's sons when it comes to how they're treated on the job. That happened because of you. That's what change means.

Making sure that young people all across America have a little bit of a better shot going to college. We took $60 billion that was going to banks, subsidizing banks through the student loan program, and we said let's give that money directly to students. And there are millions more students now who are able to go to college and accrue less debt because of you, because of what you did.

And then I was down in North Carolina and talking to some troops, the last troops to come home from Iraq, a war that I said we would end, and it is now over. And seeing them greet their families and hug their loved ones, I thought back to the campaign and all the volunteers who had knocked on doors and made phone calls. That was what you did. That's what you did.

So the point is, is that as tough as things are, the changes we've made are remarkable, and they're making a difference in the lives of people every single day. And that should be a source of satisfaction, but it can't be a source of complacency, because we're not done. We've got so much more work to do.

All the challenges that existed before the crisis are still there. We've still got a middle class that's struggling. We still have a make-or-break moment for folks who are in the middle class or trying to get in the middle class, who want to live out that American Dream.

And that's why at the most recent State of the Union I laid out a vision for where we need to go, and it means that we're once again making things in America, not just buying things in America, but we are building cars and creating new products and new services, and we're selling them all over the world.

It means American manufacturing resurging. It means American sources of energy—and not just the old energy, but the new energy—solar energy and wind energy and biodiesel that can not only free ourselves from dependence on foreign oil, but also help save a planet.

We've got more work to do making sure that every single one of our young people have the skills that they need to compete in the 21st century. We still have schools where half the kids are dropping out. And despite the amazing changes that we've been able to make and the reforms we've been able to push, we got to follow through, we've got to finish up.

And we've got to make sure that health care gets implemented, because there are folks who want to roll it back. And we've got to make sure that the Wall Street reform process that we put into place to make sure that never again do we have those kinds of bailouts and the kind of recklessness that almost brought this economy to its knees, we've got to make sure that those who are trying to roll it back do not succeed at rolling it back.

We've got more work to do so that America once again is a place where everybody has a fair shot, everybody does their fair share, and everybody is playing by the same set of rules. That's our vision.

And the other side has a fundamentally different vision of America. Their view is that everybody is on their own. If you don't have health care, tough luck, you're on your own. If you were born into poverty, pull yourself up by your bootstraps, you're on your own. They've got a different vision that basically says, let's go back to the old policies where a few do really well and everybody else struggles just to get by. And they're explicit about it. This is not me putting spin on the ball. [*Laughter*] They've been very clear about what their agenda is.

And so we're going to have to push back. We're going to have to preserve the changes we've made, and we've got to keep on driving. We've got to make sure that our schools are number one. We've got to make sure that col-

---

° White House correction.

lege is affordable. We've got to make sure health care is implemented. We've got to have immigration reform, because we are a nation of laws and we are a nation of immigrants.

On the foreign policy front, we've got to make sure that now that we've ended the war in Iraq responsibly, we've got to make sure that we're transitioning in Afghanistan responsibly and start bringing our troops home there.

One of the proudest things of my 3 years in office is helping to restore a sense of respect for America around the world, a belief that we are not just defined by the size of our military, despite the incredible feats of our military and the incredible sacrifices of our men and women in uniform, but we're also defined by our values and our respect for rule of law and our willingness to help countries in need. We've got to preserve that, and we've got to build on that.

So we've got enormous work to do. And the main message I've got for you tonight is it's not going to be easier this time, it's going to be harder this time. We're not going to have to just have as much energy as we did last time, we've got to have more energy than we did last time. It's not going to be enough for us to just sit back and say, look at all the great things we've done, because people out there are hurting and they need us to do more.

So I'm going to need you. You are going to have to carry this thing the same way that you did in 2008. And part of what's going to make it more difficult—I'll be honest with you—is look, I'm older now. I'm gray. [*Laughter*] I've been a little dinged up. It's not quite as cool to be on the Obama bandwagon. Back in 2008, it was the new thing. [*Laughter*] Everybody had their poster, and you'd be talking to your coworkers: "Oh, have you heard about Obama? Yes! Oh, no, you haven't? Let me tell you about him." [*Laughter*] Now, everybody can pronounce my name. They don't always say it nicely, but—[*laughter*].

But that determination, the values that got us this far, are undiminished. I believe even more in the possibility of change now than I did when I first got into office, not only because we've made those changes, but also be-cause as President, I have a chance to travel all across the country and meet people of every walk of life: Black, White, Latino, Asian, gay, straight, rich, poor, north, south, east, west. And what's remarkable to me is, as hard as these last 3 years have been, that core decency, that sense that we can overcome whatever challenges are ahead of us, that we are still a nation full of possibility, that we still have the best workers on Earth, and we have the best universities on Earth, and we've got the best entrepreneurs on Earth and we've got a democracy that, as flawed and as frustrating as it can be sometimes, still gives everybody a chance to make their voices heard, and we work things out. As bitter and tough as they seem sometimes, we work it out, and we end up on the other side stronger and more unified than we were before. That's what gives me confidence. That's what inspires me. You inspire me.

And so if you are ready for one more round, if you are ready for one more fight, if, despite all the naysayers and all the cynicism and all the tough times we've been through, you're staying—still saying to yourself, "Yes, we can," you're still saying to yourself, "There's change out there I can believe in," and if you're willing not just to talk the talk, but walk the walk and knock on doors and make phone calls and send out e-mails and tweet and do whatever it is that you do to mobilize your neighborhoods and your friends and your coworkers and your family. And if we get folks out to vote, I promise you there is nothing that can stop the United States of America. And we will remind them just why it is that this is the greatest nation on Earth.

Thank you, everybody. God bless you. God bless America.

NOTE: The President spoke at 6:31 p.m. at the residence of Bradley P. and Colleen B. Bell. In his remarks, he referred to actors Thomas J. "Jack" Black and Rashida L. Jones. The transcript was released by the Office of the Press Secretary on February 16. Audio was not available for verification of the content of these remarks.

Remarks at an Obama Victory Fund 2012 Fundraiser in Los Angeles
February 15, 2012

Hello, everybody. It is great to see you. Obviously, I want to, first of all, thank the Bell family, Colleen and Brad, for opening up this spectacular venue and for being such incredible friends. And thanks your kids, too, for putting up with all of us. [*Laughter*]

I want to just make—in addition to the host committee, I want to make two other acknowledgements. First of all, your outstanding mayor, Antonio Villaraigosa, is in the house. And the mayor who is going to be responsible for making sure that we have a great convention in Charlotte, North Carolina, Anthony Foxx is here as well.

So I'm going to be very brief at the top because I want to spend most of this time in conversation and answering your questions, getting your comments and advice.

We've gone through 3 pretty tough years in this country. And as I was just telling the crowd outside, I think when I think back to 2008, nobody here got involved in that campaign because you thought it was going to be easy. The odds were not in favor of Barack Hussein Obama ending up as President of the United States. [*Laughter*] The reason you got involved was because we shared a vision of what this country should be.

We believed in a country where everybody gets a fair shot. It doesn't matter who you are, what you look like, where you come from, if you're willing to put in the sweat and hard work, you're able to achieve. And we believed in a country where everybody does their fair share. It's not just some people who are required to be good citizens, not just some who are required to the common good, but everybody has to pull their weight. Whether it comes to service, whether it comes to taxes, whether it comes to participation, whether it comes to caring for those who are vulnerable, all of us are called.

The third idea was a country in which everybody follows the same set of rules, a country based on fair play. We don't have one set of rules for Wall Street and a different set of rules for Main Street. We don't have one set of rules for kids who are born into wealthy neighborhoods and another set of rules for kids that are born into poor neighborhoods, that we expect everybody is showing responsibility and everybody is acting in accordance with some of our deepest held values.

And that's what the campaign was about. There were issues, specific things we wanted to accomplish. We wanted to end the war in Iraq; we ended the war in Iraq. We wanted to reinstate rule of law as we're fighting terrorism and stop torture, and we did that. We wanted to make sure that we reversed this economic chaos coming out of the recession where we were losing 750,000 jobs a month, and we're now gaining 250,000 jobs a month and have created 3.7 million jobs over the last 23 months.

We said that in this country nobody should go bankrupt because they get sick. This country is too wealthy for us to allow something like that to happen. And despite all the frustrations and barriers and setbacks that we experienced, we got it done. And right now 2.5 million kids have insurance right now that didn't have it before—2.5 million.

I get letters from young people who say, you know what, I got diagnosed with a treatable cancer—wouldn't have had a chance if it hadn't been for the fact that this health care bill passed, and I was on my parent's health care plan, and I was able to go in and get a checkup. That's happening right now.

We said that it shouldn't matter who you love if you want to serve the country you love. And we ended "don't ask, don't tell." And I was telling the folks outside about the fact that when I was out in Kaneohe Marine Base, working out with marines—which is a bad idea because they're in better shape than you are—[*laughter*]—on three separate occasions, the marines came up and said, thank you for ending "don't ask, don't tell." And you know what, I didn't even ask them, did it apply to you, because it didn't matter. The point was they understood that the integrity of our Armed Forces would be enhanced, not debilitated, when we got rid of that law.

And so there were a bunch of specific objectives and specific issues that we wanted: making sure that the kids got health care; making sure that we expanded student loans for young people so that the circumstances they were born into wouldn't be a barrier to their ability to achieve; being able to project an America around the world that is based not just on our might, but also on our values.

There were specific things that we did in each of those categories. But the bigger mission in 2008 was everybody getting a fair shot, everybody doing their fair share, everybody playing by the same set of rules. And that's still what this election is about. It's still what this battle is about in this country.

The other side has a very different vision about where they want to take this country. And they've got fervor and sincerity, a vision that says, you know what, it's okay if just a few people do very well and those who are left behind, it's probably their fault. And if we just go back to a philosophy that says we slash taxes for those of us who've been most fortunate—the folks in this room—that somehow that's going to be good for everybody else. If we get rid of regulations that keep our air clean and our water clean, that somehow business will be unleashed. That if we roll back reforms that were designed to make sure that the kind of recklessness that got us in this mess in the first place, that those same institutions have a free hand, that somehow we're going to better off.

That's their working theory. And it's wrong. And it's not who we are.

And so we've got to fight for what we believe in as much now as we fought for it in 2012. And it's not going to be easy because there are a lot of folks out there who are still hurting. And there are a lot of people out there who, understandably, after just slogging for 3 years and after maybe in some cases slogging for a decade or two decades and seeing their standard of living deteriorating and seeing their home underwater and seeing their families struggling and folks losing jobs. It's under-

standable that some of them may feel discouraged and feel cynical, and say, you know what, nothing changes.

But part of our job is to say, as tough as it is, as incremental as it sometimes seems, things have changed. And they can change more if we fight for it, if we're determined, if we have confidence in each other, if we decide to unite instead of divide.

And I think the American people, beneath all the pain and hurt and frustration that they feel, they still want to believe that that change is possible and there's still that hope there. They're optimistic, fundamentally, about this country. They love it so deeply.

And our job over the next year is to make sure that they can channel that fundamental optimism and decency and courage and come together to create the kind of country that we want for our kids and our grandkids.

I mentioned outside I am much grayer now than I was when I started this thing. [*Laughter*] And Mario Cuomo once said that campaigning is poetry and governance is prose. And we've been slogging through prose for the last 3 years and sometimes that gets people discouraged. Because people, they like the poetry. That's what's inspiring. The prose is frustrating because it involves compromises and it involves half-loaves and it involves getting some progress, but not as much as you want. And so people get frustrated.

And I guarantee you, there are all kinds of friends of yours who, when you talk to them: "Well, Guantanamo is not closed yet, or the war in Afghanistan is still raging. Or why isn't it that the housing crisis hasn't been completely fixed and climate change is still going on?" And I understand that. I feel the same way sometimes.

Every morning I wake up and I say, are we doing everything we can to get everything that needs to be done done right now? But one of the things that's happened over the last 3 years is a recognition that nothing beats persistence. Inspiration is wonderful, nice speeches are wonderful, pretty posters—that's great. [*Laughter*] But what's required at the end of the day to create the kind of country we want is stick-to-it-ness. It's determination. It's saying we don't quit.

And we'll be tacking and zigging and zagging, and sometimes it will feel like there's no wind behind us and we're just sitting there and it's frustrating. But that north star is still out there. And if you are determined, then you'll get there.

And this country has always gotten there. We have always been able to tack towards that north star. And we're not going to stop now. That's what this election is about. That's why you're here. And I couldn't be more excited about the prospect.

All right. Thank you very much, everybody. Thank you. Thank you.

NOTE: The President spoke at 8:07 p.m. at the residence of Bradley P. and Colleen B. Bell. In his remarks, he referred to Bradley C., Caroline C., Charlotte C., and Oliver P. Bell, children of Mr. and Mrs. Bell; and former Gov. Mario M. Cuomo of New York. The transcript was released by the Office of the Press Secretary on February 16. Audio was not available for verification of the content of these remarks.

Remarks at an Obama Victory Fund 2012 Fundraiser in Corona del Mar, California
February 16, 2012

Thank you, Orange County! Thank you. Thank you. Everybody, please have a seat. It is great to be here on such a spectacular day. This is what California weather is supposed to look like. I have to say, yesterday, up in L.A., I could see my breath when I was speaking. [*Laughter*] I was a little concerned. But today you guys are living up to your billing.

I want to thank everybody who's here, but obviously I want to, first of all, thank Janet for the wonderful introduction, but also being such a powerhouse in terms of helping making this thing happen. Janet Keller, thank you. As well as Bernie—thank you so much for letting Janet spend all this time on this. [*Laughter*]

I want to thank Jeff and Nancy and their entire family for opening up their spectacular home to us. Thank you so much. Thanks for your hospitality. To Wylie and Bette and so many other who've helped to pull this together, you guys have been with me through thick and thin, so thank you so much. We love you guys.

And a couple of wonderful elected officials—one, your own Representative, Loretta Sanchez, is in the house. But we also have an import here. He is going to be hosting us at the Democratic National Convention. He's the mayor of Charlotte. Anthony Foxx is here—Charlotte, North Carolina.

Now, usually in these things what I like to do is be brief at the top and then I have some time to answer questions and take comments and suggestions, and so it ends up being a little more informal.

But picking up on something that Janet said, we've obviously gone through 3 of the toughest years that America has seen in our lifetime: the worst economic crisis since the Great Depression; the worst financial crisis since the 1930s; 4 million people losing their jobs in the 6 months before I took office, 4 million more in the 6 months after I was sworn in, but before our economic policies had a chance to take effect; an auto industry on the brink of collapse; layoffs all across the country; State and local governments struggling; at the same as we faced enormous global challenges from two wars to a global economy that was shrinking.

And as we look back over these last 3 years, I think we can all say that we're not yet where we need to be, we haven't solved every challenge, but what we've been able to accomplish—in part because of you, in part because of your support and your voices—has been remarkable.

The month I took office we were losing 750,000 a month. Last month we created 250,000. That's a million-job swing. And that's representative of the progress that the economy has made. We now have more manufacturing jobs being created than any time since the 1990s. And although unemployment is still too high, over the last 23 months we've created 3.7 million jobs and people are starting to get a sense that the economy is on the rebound.

Even as that has been our singular focus, we recognize that there are a whole bunch of issues and a whole bunch of challenges that faced us even before this recession hit. That's what led me to get in this race in the first place, the sense that folks who were working hard were treading water, that we were becoming a country where just a few did well and so many others were struggling to get by. Problems like health care that had been escalating for decades, a lack of an energy policy that had put us in a vulnerable position every time there was turmoil in the Middle East, issues that had been lingering, but we kept on kicking down the road because we didn't have enough political will and political courage to do something about it.

So, even as we were grappling with this enormous economic crisis, we did not forget those challenges that led us to start that campaign in 2008 in the first place.

And so yes, we pushed and pushed and pushed, until we finally were able to pass legislation that ensures that every American is going to be able to get health care in the country and nobody is going to go bankrupt when they get sick. And already we've got 2.6 million young people who have coverage who did not have it before because of this law, seniors all across the country benefiting from lower prescription drug plan, and the promise not only of making sure health care is affordable and preventive care and mammograms and other things are available and people aren't being dropped from their health insurance when they get sick because they now have the Patient's Bill of Rights, but it also promises to actually, over time, lower health care costs, which will help reduce our deficits and help businesses and families well into the future.

We kept on focusing on energy, even though we were grappling with this economic crisis, and have doubled the production of clean energy in this country from wind and solar and biodiesel. And even as we have said that we're going to have to continue to develop American energy and traditional energy sources like oil and gas, we've also said we're not going to compromise on making sure that there are strong environmental controls in place, because we want our kids having clean air and clean water. We want them growing up in the kind of country that protects and preserves its natural resources and conserves our land and this incredible bounty that God has given us.

Even as we were focusing on the economy, we said, we want an America where everybody is treated fairly. So first bill I passed—equal pay for equal work. I want my daughters to be treated just like somebody else's sons when it comes to a job.

And we said, given the incredible sacrifices that our military makes, we don't want your capacity to serve the country you love to be dependent on who you love. And we ended "don't ask, don't tell," because that's part of fairness. That's part of who we are as Americans.

Whether it was doubling fuel efficiency standards on cars—probably the most significant environmental action that's been taken in two or three decades—to making sure that student loans were more accessible to folks who are going to college, to trying to revamp our job training system so that our workers are getting the best skills in the world and can compete in this 21st century, even as we were dealing with the immediate crisis, the immediate emergency, we've tried to keep our eye on our long-term goal, which is restoring an America where everybody gets a fair shot, everybody does their fair share, and everybody is playing by the same set of rules, an America where everybody feels a sense of responsibility not only to themselves, but also to the larger community and the larger country.

163

And we've done all this obviously with some fairly vocal opposition. [*Laughter*] And we've done this even as the weight of the economic crisis made it more difficult. We did this at a time when changes around the world were taking place more quickly than we've ever seen before. And so even as I was managing two wars, we also had to deal with an Arab Spring in which suddenly millions of people, especially young people, said, we want a different way of life.

And there have been setbacks. There have been times where progress was not as fast as we wanted. And there's so much more work that remains to be done. We still have a broken immigration system that has to be reformed so that we are a nation of laws and a nation of immigrants. We still have more work to do on energy, because the fact of the matter is that, for example, if America simply matched the energy efficiency of a country like Japan, we would lower our overall energy utilization by 20 or 25 percent. Nothing could be more important in terms of our economy and the long-term health of this planet. That's more work to do.

We are going to have to make sure that we close this deficit and reduce our debt in a responsible and balanced way, which means that we get rid of programs that don't work and we evaluate carefully our spending to make sure we're getting a good bang for the buck. And we say to those who can afford to do a little bit more, like me, that you've got to be part of the solution in terms of lowering this deficit. It can't be just done on the backs of seniors or students in the forms of higher loans or more expensive Medicare.

So we've still got a lot of work to do. And that's hopefully why all of you are here today. I always joke that back in 2008, if you got behind my campaign it wasn't because you thought it was a sure thing. [*Laughter*] Electing Barack Hussein Obama was not the—[*laughter*]—easy route to take. So you got involved because you had a sense of possibility, a sense of how this country could be brought together and start moving in a new direction.

We've begun that process, but the journey is not complete. And although I'm a little grayer now than I was, a little dinged up—[*laughter*]—and some of the newness and excitement that possessed us in 2008 naturally will have dissipated. That sense of urgency and determination and the values that are at stake are no less today than they were back in 2008. If anything, it's more urgent and we have to be more determined and more energized and work even harder. And if we do, we're going to have 4½ more years to change America.

Thank you. Thank you, everybody.

NOTE: The President spoke at 9:52 a.m. at the residence of Jeff and Nancy Stack. In his remarks, he referred to Janet Keller, National Finance Committee member, Democratic National Committee, and her husband Bernard E. Schneider; and fundraiser cohosts Wylie A. and Bette Aitken. Audio was not available for verification of the content of these remarks.

Statement on Congressional Action on Payroll Tax Cut and Unemployment Insurance Legislation
February 16, 2012

Leaders of both parties have done the right thing for our families and for our economy by reaching an agreement that will prevent a tax hike on 160 million working Americans. I urge Congress to pass this agreement so that the payroll tax cut we put in place last year will not expire at the end of this month. The typical American family will still see an extra $40 in every paycheck, keeping nearly $1,000 of their hard-earned money this year. And millions of Americans who are out pounding the pavement looking for new work to support their families will still be able to depend on the vital lifeline of unemployment insurance.

I thank the many Americans who lent their voices to this debate in recent months. You made all the difference. This is real money that will make a real difference in people's lives. It includes important reforms that I proposed in the "American Jobs Act" to help discourage businesses from laying off workers and to connect workers with jobs. It includes a critical element in the plan I outlined in the State of the Union to outinnovate the rest of the world by unleashing mobile broadband, investing in innovation, and building a nationwide public safety network. It will mean a stronger economy and hundreds of thousands of new jobs. And as soon as Congress sends this bipartisan agreement to my desk, I will sign it into law right away. But this must be only the start of what we do together this year. There's much more the American people need and expect from us: to help our businesses keep creating jobs, to help restore security for middle class families, and to leave an economy that's built to last.

Remarks at an Obama Victory Fund 2012 Fundraiser in San Francisco, California
February 16, 2012

The President. Thank you. Oh, I've got a little blues track going on here. I like that. Please, everybody have a seat. Instead of ruffles and flourishes, we might have to get this crew every time I come on stage. It sounded smooth. [*Laughter*]

I want to—first of all, obviously, I want to thank Robert and Nicola and all the kids for letting us crash their house. They have been extraordinary friends and supporters for so long, and for them to help to organize this is something that means so much to me. So I want to thank them.

In addition, I want to thank Reverend Al Green for taking the time to be here. I took a chance at the Apollo—[*laughter*]—and I'm not going to take a chance again.

Audience members. Aww!

The President. No. No, I'm sorry. Now, what is possible is after reelection—[*laughter*]—I might go on tour with the good Reverend, be his opening act. But I don't want to lose any further votes because of my singing voice. But we are greatly honored to have you here. Thank you so much.

To Booker T. Jones, Les Claypool, Charlie Musselwhite, thank you so much, gentlemen, for being here. We are all big fans. We are all huge fans of your music, and it is a great honor to have you guys here. As Robert and Nicole know, the arts are part of what brings us together, what binds us together as a people. And one of the things—we're actually having a blues night next week, which is going to be part of our effort at the White House to lift up the importance of the arts in our lives and make sure that our kids understand the power of expression.

And then finally, I just want to acknowledge—those of you who are going to come down to North Carolina for our outstanding convention, we've got the person who will be our host. The mayor of Charlotte, North Carolina, Anthony Foxx is here.

As I look around the room, I've got some new friends, and I've got some folks who have supported me since I had just been elected to the U.S. Senate and who I've known for quite some time. All of you have been doing good work, separate and apart from my campaign, for a lot of years, making this community better, making sure that folks who are vulnerable got the help they need, making sure that our kids have a chance to excel in this globalized world, helping to promote understanding. And so we've got a lot of do-gooders in this room, and I'm grateful for everything that you guys do day in, day out.

I am not going to speak long at the top, because usually in a setting like this, what I love to do is take questions and bounce things around. But I just want to reflect a little bit on where we've been over the last 3 years.

We've gone through the toughest economy, the worst financial crisis, worst economic crisis, since the Great Depression, since our lifetimes—in our lifetimes. And things are still tough. There are a lot of people here in California and all across the country who are still struggling each and every day. Their homes may be underwater. They may be out of work. If they've got work, they're struggling to pay the bills. And what was true before 2008 is still true for too many today, which is the sense that their concept of the American Dream, what it means to be an American, feels like it's slipping away from them, that idea that if you work hard, if you're responsible, if you're looking out for your family and a good citizen, that you can make it, you can afford to buy a house and send your kids to school and retire with some dignity and respect, that sense was slipping away from too many people far before this economic crisis. And this economic crisis made it that much tougher.

Having said that, 3 years from when I took office, America is moving on the right track. We are stronger than we were. The month that I took office, we were losing 750,000 jobs; last month we gained 250,000. That's a turnaround of a million jobs in this country. We've seen 3.7 million jobs created over the last 23 months, the strongest job growth in a long time—since 2005—and the strongest manufacturing job growth since the 1990s.

An economy that was in danger of tipping into a great depression is starting to heal and rebuild itself. And our challenge right now is not just to settle for getting back to where we were in 2008. Our challenge is how do we address all those accumulated problems that helped to lead to the crisis and how do we restore a sense for folks in the middle class and those aspiring to the middle class or beyond that they've got a fair shot and everybody is doing their fair share and fair play reigns across the country and our core values as Americans are being respected and honored. That's what's at stake.

And so, even as we were dealing with the economic crisis, we tried not, over the last 3 years, to take our eye off the larger purpose of rebuilding an economy that has a firmer foundation. And that meant making sure, for example, that people in this country don't go bank-

rupt when they get sick. And as tough as it was for us to be able to pass universal health care that had alluded previous Presidents—and 2.6 million young people already have health insurance now because of that law that didn't have it before, and millions of seniors across the country are seeing the cost of prescription drugs going down for them—and us setting the stage so that in my second term we will have fully implemented this law and 30 million people will have coverage that didn't have it before and prevention is covered and insurance companies can't drop people because of the fine print right when they need it the most. That's part of building an economy that's built to last.

We wanted to make sure that at a time when education has never been more important, that we made sure that we started digging in and figuring out how do we guarantee every child has a decent education. And that meant taking on our friends and not just our enemies and saying, yes, we're going to put more money into the system, but we're also going to insist on reform, and we're going to do a better job training our teachers and giving them the support that they need, but also demanding some accountability, and instead of just teaching to the test, making sure that we have a way of measuring outcomes so that our young people can compete in math and science, but also the arts and the humanities.

And 40 States now across the country have made significant education reforms because of our efforts—unprecedented effort at school reform over the last several years. It doesn't get a lot of notice.

And then we realized, you know, it's not enough for them just to get through high school these days; they're going to have to go college. But the barriers of college costs, tuition costs have been so great we decided let's stop sending $60 billion in subsidies to the banks and let's channel that money directly into student loans and increase Pell grants so that now you've got millions of students who are less burdened by debt and have greater opportunity not just to go to 4-year colleges, but also to go to 2-year colleges, or in some cases, adults who have the capacity now to go and get retrained so that they can get back into the workforce with the new skills that they need.

And we decided that if we're going to have economy built to last that we've got to finally take on energy. But it's not enough for us to just drill our way out of the problem. We recognize that we're not going to immediately transition off of fossil fuels and we've got to increase American energy production. But it can't just be oil and natural gas. We also have to make sure that we're investing in the energies of the future.

And so we've doubled clean energy because of the investments that we've made, created entire industries here in the United States in things like advanced battery manufacturing. Because we understand that we can't keep on going every spring—we basically, like clockwork, say to ourselves, well, gas prices are going up and the economy is now going to be held hostage. Not to mention our concern about the planet that we're going to be leaving our kids and our grandkids.

And we decided, although the global economy shifted and because manufacturing has become more efficient, we are going to have to recognize that a bigger and bigger portion of the economy will be service based, we still want America to have the best manufacturing capacity in the world, which is part of the reason why at a time when it was unpopular not just with the Republicans, but also Democrats to save the auto industry, we decided to go in there and restructure and force workers and management to work together. And GM, which was on the verge of liquidation, is now once again the number-one automaker in the world, with the highest profits that they have ever seen.

And part of our commitment to that economy of the future was making sure that we restored science to its rightful place. And so we increased our investments in NIH and NSF and made sure that stem cell research could proceed, and insisted that we place the highest priority on technology and innovation—in Government, through our research—because nobody understands better than this region of

the country and how important that is to our economic future.

And then finally, we had to make sure that fair play meant something. And so the first bill I signed said, equal pay for equal work, because I want my daughters to have the same opportunities that anybody's sons have when they go out into the job market.

And we determined that your capacity to fight for the country you love shouldn't be contingent on who you love, and we ended "don't ask, don't tell." Because there was something quintessentially American about treating everybody equally and judging them on the merits.

And there were great predictions that this was going to be impossible to do, but we did it. And you know what, I was in Marine Base Kaneohe in Hawaii during vacation, and while I was working out at the Marine base, which is a bad idea because they're all in much better shape than you are—[*laughter*]—on three different occasions people came up and said, thank you for doing that. And I don't know whether they were directly impacted or they just had a fellow marine that was impacted, but they understand this makes us stronger. It doesn't make us weaker.

And then, as Robert mentioned, we recognize that our strength at home has to be matched with strength abroad. But that strength is not just defined by our military might. It's also defined by our values and our diplomacy and our respect for rule of law, which is why we ended torture and why we kept our commitment to responsibly end that war in Iraq.

That didn't make us weaker. It gave us the capacity to refocus our attention on those who had attacked us on 9/11. And there is a direct line between the strategic decisions we made there and our ability to begin dismantling Al Qaida and to restore a sense of respect for America all around the world that has huge dividends over the long term, so that when I took a trip to Asia, rather than feeling neglected or feeling America was no longer relevant, people were hungry for American leadership. People recognized that we remain the one indispensable nation, not just because we're big and powerful, but also because we have this idea that there are certain universal principles and universal rights and international norms that have to be observed and that we are perhaps the only superpower in history that obviously is looking out for our own self-interest, but also thinks about what's good for everybody. And that is part of our power.

So we've been busy these last 3 years. And for all the difficulties and all the challenges and all the political twists and turns that this journey has taken, I'm here to report to you that all that work you did back in 2008, it's paid off. And you should feel pride and confidence in the fact that change remains possible if you're persistent, if you're focused.

But I'm also here to report that you shouldn't feel complacent, because we've got a lot more to do. We've got to fully implement health care reform. We've got to fully implement financial reform. We've got to make sure that our Consumer Financial Protection Bureau that is protecting consumers for the first time isn't rolled back. We've still got to get immigration reform done, because we are a nation of immigrants and we're a nation of laws, and those two things don't contradict each other. We have to have an even more robust energy policy if we're going to create the kind of jobs in this new energy sector that are needed and we're going to deal with climate change in a serious way.

We've still got to follow through on the education reforms that we're doing, and that's going to require enormous effort. And we're going to have to figure out how to pay for all this stuff. And part of fair play and everybody doing their fair share is making sure that we have an economy in which we're getting rid of programs that don't work and we're making Government more efficient. But it also means people like those of us in this room that have been unbelievably blessed can do a little bit more to

make sure that kid around the corner has a chance like we did and to make sure that that senior is protected, make sure that student can get a loan that doesn't leave them broke after they graduate and to make sure that senior is able to live with dignity and respect after they retire.

All these things can be accomplished, but we're going to have to feel as determined, we're going to have to be as focused as we were in 2008. And that's not going to be easy because, first of all, I'm older and I'm grayer. [*Laughter*] So it's not as new, it's not as trendy to be part of the Obama campaign, although some of you still have your posters, I'm sure. [*Laughter*] And part of it is, we've gone through 3 tough years, and so people want to hope, but they've been worn down by a lot of hardship.

But as I travel around the country, I have to tell you, there's a core decency to the American people. There is a resilience to the American people. There is, under all the cynicism, a basic optimism to the American people. That's what we tapped into in 2008, and it's still there. It's still there.

And if we pull together and if we work just as hard, I guarantee you that 5 years from now we're going to be able to look back and say, you know what, that change we believed in we delivered.

Thank you very much, everybody. Thank you.

NOTE: The President spoke at 7:26 p.m. at the residence of Robert M. Anderson and Nicola Miner. In his remarks, he referred to Dashiell, Lucinda, Frances, Callum, and Stephen, children of Mr. Anderson and Ms. Miner; and musician Al Green. The transcript was released by the Office of the Press Secretary on February 17. Audio was not available for verification of the content of these remarks.

Remarks at an Obama Victory Fund 2012 Fundraiser in San Francisco
February 16, 2012

The President. Hello, San Francisco! Thank you! Thank you! Thank you so much. Thank you, everybody. First of all, everybody, please give a huge round of applause to Patty for sharing her story. Thank you, Patty. We appreciate it.

I want to thank Chris Cornell for his wonderful performance. Give Chris a big round of applause. And I want to thank Vernon Davis for being here. If you want to come and play for the Bears, you are welcome to do it. Vernon had a great playoff. I mean, he had a great playoff. Unbelievable.

You guys can take a seat. Just relax. I'm going to be here a while. I'm going to be here awhile. I am going to be here awhile.

So, San Francisco, I am here—I am——

Audience member. [*Inaudible*]

The President. You look great. Got the Statue of Liberty right here. [*Laughter*] That is outstanding.

Audience member. We love you!

The President. I love you back.

Now, I'm here not just because I need your help, San Francisco. I am here because this country needs your help. A lot of you worked very, very hard, worked your hearts out, in 2008. And it wasn't because you thought electing Barack Hussein Obama was a sure thing. [*Laughter*] That wasn't guaranteed. You didn't need a poll to tell you that might be difficult. [*Laughter*] The campaign was not about me; it was about you, and the vision that we share for America.

A vision that doesn't say we leave everything to the free market by itself, and everybody is left to fend for themselves and play by their own rules. It's a vision that says, yes, we believe in the free market and we believe in entrepreneurship and individualism. But we also believe that anybody who works hard should have the chance to get ahead, not just a few. A vision that says we're greater together than we are on our own and that everybody should get a fair shot and everybody should do their fair share and everybody should play by the same set of rules. And when we do that, then the entire country does better.

The market does better. Business does better. Workers do better. Our children do better. The future is brighter. That's the vision we shared. That's the change we believed in. And we knew it wasn't going to be easy. I told you it wasn't going to be easy. [*Laughter*] I did. We knew it wasn't going to come quickly. But think about the journey we've traveled over the last 3 years. Because of what you did in 2008, because of your effort, we're starting to see what change looks like.

Change is the first bill I signed into law, the Lilly Ledbetter Act, that says women deserve an equal day's pay for an equal day's work. That's what change is.

Change is the decision we made to rescue the American auto industry from collapse, even when it wasn't popular and some people said we should let Detroit go bankrupt. With 1 million jobs on the line, I wasn't going to let that happen. And today, GM is back on top as the world's number-one automaker. It just reported the highest profits in the 100-year history of that company. With more than 200,000 new jobs created in the last 2½ years, the American auto industry is back. That's change.

Change is the decision we made to stop waiting for Congress to do something about our oil addiction and go ahead and raise our fuel efficiency standards for the first time in decades. And by the next decade, we'll be driving American-made cars that get almost 55 miles to a gallon. That's what change is.

Change is the fight that we won to stop handing out over $60 billion in taxpayer subsidies to banks that issue student loans. We said, let's give that money directly to the students, and that way we can increase the number of students that are getting loans and the amount of loans that they're getting, so that millions of young people have opportunities they didn't have before.

And yes, change is the health care reform bill that we passed after a century of trying, a reform that has already allowed 2.6 million young people to stay on their parent's insurance. A reform that will ensure that in the United States of America, nobody is going to go broke just because they get sick. And Americans will no longer be denied or dropped by their insurance companies just when they need care the most. That's what change is.

Change is the fact that for the first time in our history, you don't have to hide who you love to serve the country you love. That's what change is. "Don't ask, don't tell" is over. That's change.

For the first time in 9 years, there are no Americans fighting in Iraq. That has changed. We refocused our efforts on the terrorists who actually attacked us on 9/11. And thanks to the brave men and women in uniform, Al Qaida is weaker than it has ever been and bin Laden isn't around anymore. That's what change is.

Now none of this change has been easy, and we still got a lot more work to do. There are still too many Americans out there that are looking for work. There are still too many families who can barely pay the bills, still see their homes underwater. We're still recovering from the worst economic situation in our lifetimes.

But as tough as this economy is and has been, think about what's changed the day I took office. That month we were losing 750,000 jobs. Over the past 2 years, businesses have added about 3.7 million new jobs. Our manufacturers are creating jobs for the first time since the 1990s. Our economy is getting stronger. The recovery is accelerating. America is coming back. And the last thing we can afford to do is go back to the same policies that got us back—got us into this mess in the first place.

That's what is at stake in this election. And that's what the other candidates want to do, take us back——

Audience member. I love you, Obama!

The President. I told you I loved you already. [*Laughter*]

These other folks, they make no secret about where they want to go. They want to go back to the days when Wall Street played by its own rules.

[*At this point, there was a disruption in the audience.*]

Audience members. Boo!

The President. We're okay. No, this is what San Francisco is always about. There's always something going on in San Francisco. Folks are not shy about sharing their ideas in San Francisco. Yes, it's fun. [*Laughter*]

But here's what's at stake in this election. Look, the other folks—these folks who are running for President—[*laughter*]—that's what they're doing—[*laughter*]—they want to go back to the days when insurance companies could deny coverage or jack up premiums without any reason. They want to spend trillions of dollars more on tax breaks for folks like me who don't need it and aren't asking for it, even if it means adding to the deficit or gutting things like education or clean energy or basic research or Medicare. Their philosophy is simple: We are better off when everybody fends for themselves and everybody plays by their own set of rules.

And I'm here to tell them they are wrong. They are wrong. Because in the United States of America, we are greater together than we are on our own. We're better off when we keep that basic American promise that if you work hard, you can do well—you can raise a family, you can own a home, send your kids to college, put a little away for retirement—and that that promise is open to everybody. If you're born into tough circumstances, we're going to give you ladders to climb up into that middle class. And if you're in that middle class, then we're going to make sure that you've got the tools to, even in a changing world, have some security and some stability in your life.

That's what we're fighting for. That's the choice in this election. This is not just another political debate. This is the defining issue of our time, a make-or-break moment for middle class Americans and all those who are trying to get into it. And we can go back to an economy that's based on outsourcing and bad debt or phony financial profits, or we can fight for an economy that is built to last, an economy built on American manufacturing and American-made energy and skills and education for American workers and the values that have made America great: hard work and fair play and shared responsibility. That is what we're fighting for. That's what's at stake in this election.

I want to make sure the next generation of manufacturing isn't taking root just in Asia or Europe. I want it taking root in factories in Detroit and Pittsburgh and Cleveland and California. I don't want this Nation to be known just for buying and consuming stuff. I want to be known for building and selling products all over the world. And I want to stop rewarding businesses that are shipping jobs overseas. I want to reward companies that are investing here in the United States and creating jobs all throughout this country.

I want to make our schools the envy of the world, and that starts with the men and women who are in front of the classroom. A good teacher—we've got some teachers here? I want to say thank you to you. A good teacher can increase the lifetime income of a classroom by over $250,000. A great teacher can offer a path, an escape for a child who is born into really tough circumstances.

I don't want to hear folks in Washington bashing teachers, but I also don't want them just defending the status quo because too many kids aren't making it. So I want us to pull together and give schools the resources they need to keep good teachers on the job and reward the best ones. And in return, let's grant schools the flexibility to teach with creativity and with passion and not just teach to the test, but also to say to teachers who aren't doing the job, you know what, you got to improve or we're going to find somebody else.

And when kids do graduate, you heard from Patty, the cost of college just keeps on going up and up and up. At a time when more Americans owe more in tuition debt than credit card debt, this Congress has to take some immediate steps. We got to stop interest rates on student loans from doubling in July, which it's scheduled to do. This Congress needs to keep in place the tuition tax credits we've already put into place.

But colleges and universities, they've got to do their part. And I said this at the State of the Union: If you can't stop tuition from going up, the funding that you get from taxpayers needs to go down, because we've got to incentivize colleges and universities to do the right thing. Higher education can't be a luxury. It is an economic imperative that every family in America should be able to afford. That's what we're going to work for.

I want an economy that supports our scientists and our researchers who are trying to make sure the next breakthrough in clean energy happens right here in the United States of America. We have subsidized oil companies long enough. It's time to end nearly 100 years of taxpayer subsidies to an oil industry that's never been more profitable and double down on a clean energy that's never been more promising: solar and wind and biofuels and electric vehicles. We can make progress and create jobs and get ahead of the curve, not be behind it.

We need to give our businesses the best access to newer roads and airports and faster railroads, Internet access. I was telling somebody the other day, I'm a chauvinist; I want America to have the best stuff. [*Laughter*] I want us to have the best airports and the best roads. I want us to have the fastest broadband lines. And we can do that. It's time to take the money we are no longer spending in Iraq, use half of that to pay down our debt and use the rest to do some nation-building right here at home.

And we've got to make sure we have a tax system that reflects everybody doing their fair share. I've talked about the Buffett rule: If you make more than a million dollars a year, you shouldn't pay a lower tax rate than your secretary. That's a pretty simple concept to understand. Now, if, like 98 percent of American families, you make less than $250,000 a year, your taxes shouldn't go up.

This is not class warfare. It has nothing to do with envy. It's simple math. If somebody like me is getting a tax break that I don't need, then two things can happen. Either the deficit goes up further, our debt increases, or alternatively, we are balancing our budget on the backs of

171

seniors who are paying more for Medicare, or students who are paying more for their student loans, or a veteran who really needs help, or a family trying to get by. Why would I ask them to sacrifice and I do nothing when this country has blessed me like no other country could ever do? That's not right. That's not who we are.

We're only here because somebody, somewhere felt a responsibility to each other and to our country's future. Our story has never been about what we do alone. It's about what we can do together. That's why we won't win the competition for new jobs and new businesses and middle class security, we will not be as competitive as we need to be in this 21st-century economy, the market will not work as well if we just respond to these same economic challenges with the same old you're-on-your-own economics.

It just doesn't work. In fact, it's never worked. It didn't work in the decade before the Great Depression. It didn't work when we tried it during the last decade. Why do we think it would work now? It's not as if we didn't try it. We tried it. It didn't work. And middle class families lost more and more ground. And those folks trying to get in the middle class saw those ladders to success erode. We saw it.

That's part of what our campaign in 2008 was about. That's what we're trying to reverse. And we've begun to make progress, but we've got a lot more work to do. We got to build an economy that lasts because we've all got a stake in each other's success.

Look, think about it this way: If we attract an outstanding teacher to their—to the teaching profession by giving her the pay she deserves and the support that she needs, and that teacher goes on and educates the next Steve Jobs, we all benefit; America is stronger. That was a good investment. We get a good return. If we provide faster Internet service to some rural part of America that doesn't have it right now and suddenly there's a store owner there who is able to connect with the global economy and start selling their stuff around the world, that benefits us. It makes our country stronger. If we build a new bridge that saves a shipping company time

and money, workers and customers all over the country end up doing better.

This is not a Democratic idea or a Republican idea. It was a Republican President, Abraham Lincoln, the first Republican President, who launched the transcontinental railroad, the National Academy of Sciences, the first land-grant colleges in the midst of a Civil War. Republican Teddy Roosevelt called for a progressive income tax, carved out land to conserve for future generations. It was a Republican, Dwight Eisenhower, who built the Interstate Highway System. And with the help of Republicans in Congress, FDR was able to give millions of returning heroes, including my grandfather, the chance to go to college on the GI bill.

This is an American idea, and sometimes the other side seems to have lost its way. It doesn't seem to remember these are American ideas. That sense of common purpose and that spirit of common purpose still exists today. In Washington, sometimes the political rhetoric, it's all about us and them. And the notion is if it wasn't for them, everyone would be okay. And then, the circle of who is us gets smaller. [*Laughter*] But you know, that's Washington. In America, that spirit is still there. It's there when you talk to people on main streets and town halls, if you go to VFW halls. It's there when you talk to our members of the Armed Forces. It's there in places of worship.

Our politics may be divided, but if you watched cable TV you'd think we're all tearing at each other's throats. But most Americans, they still understand we are greater together, that no matter who we are, no matter where we come from—Black, White, Hispanic, Asian, Native American, gay, straight, rich or poor—we rise or fall as one Nation and one people. That's what people understand. That's the politics that we built in 2008. That's what's at stake right now. That's what this election is all about.

I know these last 3 years have been tough. I know the change that we fought for in 2008 has come in fits and starts and sometimes it hasn't come as fast as folks wanted. We've had setbacks. I've made mistakes. After all that's happened in Washington, I know it's tempting sometimes to believe that maybe what we imagined isn't possible. But remember what we used to say during the campaign, that real change, big change is hard and it takes time. And it takes more than a single term. And it takes more than a single President. What it requires is ordinary citizens who come together with a shared vision and who are committed and persistent and just stay at it and keep fighting and keep pushing and inching this country closer and closer and closer to our highest ideals.

And I said in 2008, I'm not a perfect man and I will not be a perfect President. But I promised you then that I would always tell you what I thought, I would always tell you where I stood, and I would wake up every single day fighting for you as hard as I know how. And I have kept that promise.

And so if you're willing to stand with me and keep pushing and keep fighting and keep believing and, yes, keep hoping, then change will come. If you're willing to work even harder than you were in 2008, then we're going to finish what we started. Stand with me, walk with me, organize with me, hope with me, and we will remind the world just why it is that America is the greatest nation on Earth.

God bless you, and God bless this country of ours.

NOTE: The President spoke at 9:10 p.m. at the Nob Hill Masonic Auditorium. In his remarks, he referred to Vernon Davis, tight end, National Football League's San Francisco 49ers; and Warren E. Buffett, chief executive officer and chairman, Berkshire Hathaway Inc. The transcript was released by the Office of the Press Secretary on February 17.

Remarks at the Boeing Company Production Facility in Everett, Washington
February 17, 2012

The President. Hello, Everett! It is great to be in Washington—not Washington, DC, in Washington State. And it is great to be here at Boeing.

I want to begin by first of all thanking Kathleen for that wonderful introduction. We were up there talking a little bit, and she's a pretty good representative of Boeing workers. Kathleen told me, "I have a motto: Every day, nobody will outwork me." And that's a pretty good motto for Boeing, but it's also a pretty good motto for America. So give Kathleen a big round of applause.

I've been told we're standing in the biggest building in the world, so big you could fit Disneyland inside. Your heating bills must be crazy. [*Laughter*]

I want to thank Jim McNerney and Jim Albaugh for hosting us here today. Give them a big round of applause. Your Machinists leadership, Tom Buffenbarger, Rich Michalski, Tom Wroblewski and SPEEA President Tom McCarty are here. One of the finest Governors in the country, Chris Gregoire, is in the house.

And I want to thank the mayor of Everett, Ray Stephanson, for having us here today.

Now, I want to thank all of you for also giving me a pretty smooth ride. [*Laughter*] As some of you may know, Air Force One was built right here in Everett, 25 years ago. In fact, I met—one of my guys that I met during the tour worked on the plane. So I told him he did a pretty good job. [*Laughter*] It's flying smooth. I get to see your handiwork in action every single day. But as wonderful as it is to fly Air Force One—and it is wonderful—it's hard not to be amazed by the Dreamliner. I notice this one is going to United, one of our outstanding carriers. And I have to mention that just because I'm from Chicago, so I've got to—[*laughter*]—give a few extra props there.

But this is the first commercial airplane to be made with 50 percent composite materials. It's lighter, it's faster, it's more fuel efficient than any airplane in its class. And it looks cool. [*Laughter*] The Dreamliner is the plane of the future. And by building it here, Boeing is taking advantage of a huge opportunity that exists

173

right now to bring more jobs and manufacturing back to the United States of America.

We know that the last few decades haven't been easy for manufacturing. New technology has made businesses more efficient and more productive, and that's a good thing. That's what raises our standards of living. It means we can get better products for less. But that also means that companies need fewer workers to make the same amount of product as they used to. And technology makes it easier for companies to set up shop and hire workers anywhere where there's an internet connection. And so the result has been this transition process that's been incredibly painful for a lot of families and a lot of communities. A lot of communities that used to rely on a lot of factory jobs, they saw those shrink. They saw those get shipped off overseas. Too many factories, where people thought they'd retire, left home. Too many jobs that provided a steady, stable life, a middle class life for people, got shipped overseas.

And look, the hard truth is, a lot of those jobs aren't going to come back because of these increased efficiencies. And in a global economy, some companies are always going to find it more profitable to pick up and do business in other parts of the world. That's just the nature of a global economy. But that does not mean that we've got to just sit there and settle for a lesser future. I don't accept that idea. You don't accept that idea. America is a place where we can always do something to create new jobs and new opportunities and new manufacturing and new security for the middle class, and that's why I'm here today. That's our job. That's what we're going to do together.

Now, just today we actually took an important short-term step to strengthen our economy. Just before we got here, Congress did the right thing and voted to make sure that taxes would not go up on middle class families at the end of this month. Congress also agreed to extend unemployment insurance for millions of Americans—maybe some of your family members—who are still out there looking for a job. So I'm going to sign this bill right away when I get back home.

You guys may remember, this middle class tax cut is something I proposed in my jobs bill back in September. And because you kept the pressure on Congress, because you reminded people what it means to have 40 bucks taken out of your paycheck every week, it got done. This is a big deal. And I want to thank Members of Congress for listening to the voices of the American people. It is amazing what happens when Congress focuses on doing the right thing instead of just playing politics. This was a good example, and Congress should take pride in it.

But the payroll tax cut is just a start. If we want middle class families to get ahead, we've got to deal with a set of economic challenges that existed even before this recession hit.

And we've got a choice right now: We can either settle for a country where a few people do really well and everybody else is struggling, or we can restore an economy where everybody gets a fair shot and everybody does their fair share and everybody plays by the same set of rules, from Washington to Wall Street to Main Street. Everybody is doing their part.

We're still recovering from one of the worst economic crises in three generations, the worst in our lifetimes, for most of us. And we've still got a long way to go to make sure everybody who can—everybody who wants a job can find one and every family can regain that sense of security that was slipping away even before this recession hit.

But the tide is turning. The tide is beginning to turn our way. Over the last 23 months, businesses have created 3.7 million new jobs and American manufacturers are hiring for the first time since 1990 and the American auto industry is back and our economy is getting stronger. And that's why we can look towards a promising future. And Boeing is an example of that. But to keep it going, the last thing we can afford to do is to go back to the very same policies that got us into this mess in the first place. We can't go backwards, we got to go forwards. We can't go back to an economy that was weakened by outsourcing and bad debt and phony financial profits.

I want us to make stuff. I want us to sell stuff. So in the State of the Union, I outlined a blueprint for an economy that's built to last, that has a strong foundation, an economy based on American manufacturing and American know-how, American-made energy, skills for American workers, and the values that made America great, the values that Kathleen talked about: hard work and fair play and shared responsibility. That's what America is about.

And that blueprint starts with American manufacturing. It starts with companies like this one. A lot of people say, well, there are going to be fewer manufacturing jobs than there were in the past. I already said we're more efficient now. What used to take a thousand people to make, you might only need a hundred now. We understand that. We understand that there are going to be more service jobs. That's important. We want to make sure that we're promoting service industries as well. But manufacturing has a special place in America. When we make stuff and we're selling stuff, that creates jobs beyond just this plant. It raises standards of living for everybody.

And here at Boeing, business is booming—booming. Last year, orders for commercial aircraft rose by more than 50 percent. And to meet that demand, Boeing hired 13,000 workers all across America, including 5,000 right here in Everett. Now the biggest challenge is how to turn out planes fast enough. Jay, that's a high-class problem to have.

So this company is a great example of what American manufacturing can do, in a way that nobody else in the world can do it. And the impact of your success, as I said, goes beyond the walls of this plant. Every Dreamliner that rolls off the assembly line here in Everett supports thousands of jobs in different industries all across the country. Parts of the fuselage are manufactured in South Carolina and Kansas. Wing edges, they come from Oklahoma. Engines assembled in Ohio. The tail fin comes from right down the road in Frederickson. And the people in every one of these communities, some of whom—who are here today, they are benefiting from the work that you do.

All those workers, they spend money at the local store. They go to restaurants. So the service economy does better because you're doing well. And what's happening here in Everett can happen in other industries. It can happen not just here, but it can happen in Cleveland, in Pittsburgh, in Raleigh. We can't bring every job back. Anybody who says we can, they're not telling you the truth. But right now it's getting more expensive to do business in places like China. Meanwhile, American workers have never been more productive. And companies like Boeing are finding out that even when we can't make things faster or cheaper than China, we can make them better. Our quality can be higher. And that's what America is about. That's how we're going to compete.

Now, during the State of the Union, I issued a challenge to America's business leaders. I said, ask yourselves what you can do to bring and create jobs here in this country, and your country will do everything we can to help you succeed. And I'm encouraged. We're actually seeing a number of companies—large and small, domestic, but even some foreign companies—recognizing, you know what, we're going to open new facilities and create new jobs here in America.

This is a good place to work. This is a good place to be. And our job as a nation is to make it easier for more of these companies to do the right thing.

That starts with our Tax Code. Right now companies get tax breaks for moving jobs and profits overseas. Meanwhile, companies that choose to stay in America get hit with one of the highest tax rates in the world. That doesn't make any sense. So my message to Congress is, what are we waiting for? Let's get this done right now. Let's make some changes to the Tax Code.

And let's follow some simple principles. First, if you're a business that wants to outsource jobs, that's your choice, but you shouldn't get a tax deduction for doing it. That money should be used to cover moving expenses for companies that are deciding to bring jobs back home. That's who should be getting tax breaks.

Second, no American company should be able to avoid paying its fair share of taxes by moving jobs and profits overseas. My attitude is every multinational company should have to pay a basic minimum tax. You should not have an advantage by building a plant over there, over somebody who's investing here and hiring American workers. And every penny of that minimum tax should go towards lowering taxes for companies like Boeing that choose to stay and hire here in the United States of America.

Number three, if you're an American manufacturer, you should get a bigger tax cut. And if you're a high-tech manufacturer, we should double the tax deductions you get for making your products here.

And finally, if you want to relocate in a community that's been hard hit by factories leaving town, then you should get help financing that new plant or financing that equipment or training for new workers.

Everett, it is time to stop rewarding companies that ship jobs overseas. Reward companies that are creating jobs right here in the United States of America. Congress should send me these tax reforms. I'll sign them right away.

Now, another thing we're doing to support American jobs is making it easier for businesses like Boeing to sell their products all over the world. Two years ago, I set a goal of doubling U.S. exports in 5 years. We're on track to meet that goal. We're actually ahead of schedule. So, last November, when I was in Indonesia, Boeing announced a deal with the help of the Export-Import Bank to sell more than 200 planes to one of the fastest growing airlines in the world. Boeing is one of the largest exporters in America; this was one of the biggest deals Boeing had ever done. Over the years, it will help support thousands of American jobs, including jobs here in Everett. So I tease Jay every time I see him. I said, I deserve a gold watch because I'm selling your stuff all the time. [*Laughter*]

I will go anywhere in the world to open up new markets for American products. And by the way, I will not stand by when our competitors don't play by the rules. That's why I directed my administration to create a trade enforcement unit that just has one job: investigating unfair trade practices in countries like China or places like Europe.

That's why it's so important for Congress to reauthorize the Export-Import Bank. This bank is led by Fred Hochberg, who is right here. He's out there working with Jay all the time, selling on behalf of Boeing. And the Export-Import Bank helps companies like this one sell its products. It also helps thousands of small businesses.

And today the bank will be launching a new program to help small businesses get the financing they need to sell more products overseas. I'm also instructing the bank to give American companies a fair shot by matching the unfair export financing that their competitors receive from other countries.

American workers—you guys, folks like Kathleen—you're the most productive on Earth. You can compete with anybody. You will outwork anybody, as long as the level—as long as the playing field is level. You can compete with any worker, anywhere, any time, in China, in Europe, it does not matter. If we have a level playing field, America will always win because we've got the best workers.

It's also because we've always believed in the power of innovation. Innovation requires basic research. Look at this plane. This plane was first designed virtually using the same technology that was developed by NASA. Government research helped to create this plane. We got—I was in there fooling around with those windows, where you press them and they dim on their own. [*Laughter*] I kept on pressing the button, and—dimmed and got light—one touch with a finger. And the display is in the cockpit. They're projected on the windshield so pilots don't have to look down at their instruments; they can maintain their line of sight, even as they're getting all these readings.

Now, some of the work—the most advanced work—was done by engineers down in Huntsville, Alabama, who used to work on the International Space Station. Their expertise, a lot of those ideas, came out of Government research. We've got to support this kind of cutting-edge research. We need to maintain our innovative edge so that jobs and industries take root right here in the United States, not someplace else.

So, Everett, if we want to build an economy that lasts, that is strong, that has a strong foundation, that helps families get into the middle class and stay in the middle class, we've got to do everything we can to strengthen American manufacturing. We've got to make sure we're making it easier for companies like Boeing to create jobs here at home and sell our products abroad. We've got to keep on investing in American-made energy, and we've got to keep training American workers. And above all, we've got to renew the values that have always made this country great: hard work, fair play, shared responsibility.

These are not Democratic values or Republican values. These are American values. They've seen us through some tough challenges, but we've always emerged stronger than before because of these values. And we're going to come out stronger than before this time as well. And I know it because of the people who are here.

In December of 2009, the first Dreamliner took off on its maiden flight right here in Everett. Some of you were probably out there seeing it. It was a cold and windy day. That didn't stop 13,000 employees all from coming out and seeing what they had built, seeing the product of all their hard work suddenly filling the skies.

And one of these people was Sharon O'Hara. Is Sharon here? Where is Sharon? There's Sharon right there. Sharon works as an executive office administrator for the leaders of the Dreamliner team. Now, executive assistant means, basically, you're doing all the work. [*Laughter*] Now, some of you may know that Sharon has been undergoing some treatment for cancer recently, so she's got her own battle. But her doctors recently told her she's healthy enough to come back to work. That's worth applauding. Sharon, there are a lot of people who are happy to see you back at work.

And I was hearing about this, and as Sharon tells the story about watching the first plane lift gently off the runway, just the way it was designed to do, she thought about everything that had gone into making this day possible, all the challenges, all the setbacks, the thousands of hours of brainpower and manpower—and womanpower. And what Sharon says is—this is a quote—"I had goosebumps and tears. We said we would do it, and we did." That's a pretty good motto. You said you would do it, and you did.

That's what we do as Americans. That's the spirit we need right now. In this country, we don't give up, even when times are tough. We look out for one another. We reach for new opportunities. We pull each other up. We stay focused on the horizon. That's who we are. That's who we've always been. And if we work together right now, with common purpose and common effort, I have no doubt we will build an economy that lasts, and we will remind the world just why it is that the United States of America is the greatest country on Earth. We said it, we will do it.

God bless you. God bless the United States. Thank you.

NOTE: The President spoke at 11:47 a.m. In his remarks, he referred to Kathleen Hughbanks, mechanic, Boeing Co. production facility, Everett, WA; W. James McNerney, Jr., chief executive officer, and James F. Albaugh, executive vice president, Boeing Co.; and R. Thomas Buffenbarger, international president, Richard P. Michalski, general vice president, and Tom Wroblewski, district president, International Association of Machinists.

Remarks at an Obama Victory Fund 2012 Fundraiser in Medina, Washington
February 17, 2012

The President. That was a one-time affair. The fewer the shows, the higher the admission. [*Laughter*]

But first of all, I just want to thank Jeff and Susan for opening up their extraordinary home. We're thrilled to be here. It is wonderful to be back in the Pacific Northwest. I was reminding some folks who may not know, I've got Seattle roots. My mother went to Puget Sound High School.

Audience members. Mercer Island.

The President. They lived in Puget Sound and went to Mercer Island High School. Some of you did not know this. But that's why I love this place, every time I come up.

So many of you have been extraordinary friends in the past. More importantly, so many of you have done such important philanthropic work and charitable work that in some ways you guys just feel like a bunch of old friends, and I don't want to spend too much time giving a long speech at the front end. I want to spend more of our time in discussion. But maybe what I can do is give you a sense of where I think the country is right and give you a sense of where we need to go over the next 5 years.

We've obviously gone through the toughest 3 years in my lifetime, the toughest 3 years economically since the Great Depression. The month I was sworn in, we were losing 750,000 jobs a month. We had lost 4 million jobs in the 6 months before I was sworn into office. We would lose another 4 million in the 6 months after I was sworn in, before our economic policies had a chance to take effect. The housing market was decimated. People lost jobs. They saw their homes underwater, in some cases hundreds of thousands of dollars, where they would never probably recover all the equity in their homes.

And so there has obviously been a lot of pain and a lot of hardship for a lot of families for a long time, and that's not over. There are people in this region of the country, like communities all across America, that are still hurting, folks who are still looking for work, still struggling to get by, still having a tough time paying the bills.

At the same time, though, what we're starting to see is the incredible resilience of the American people and the American economy. So, this month, we saw 250,000 jobs created. I'm sure some of it had to do with Microsoft. [*Laughter*] That's a million-job swing. We've now had 23 consecutive months of job growth, about 3.7 million jobs being created, the highest manufacturing job growth since the 1990s. And you get a sense as you talk to small businesses, large businesses, people across the country, there is a sense that we may have gotten through the heaviest storms.

But what is also true is that when I ran for office in 2008, my goal wasn't simply to get us back to where we were. We had decades of challenges that had been accumulating that nobody attended to. And what I determined was, in addition to righting the ship, in addition to making sure we didn't tip into a great depression, that we stayed focused on those things that are going to ensure that this country is competitive, but that it is also a country where no matter what you look like, no matter where you come from, you can still make it if you try, that that central American promise that's based on everybody getting a fair shot, everybody doing their fair share, and all of us playing by the same set of rules—that we had to rebuild that foundation for an economy that was built to last.

And so, even as we were working to stem a crisis, we were still focused on some long-term issues. Health care: The fact that we spent 17 percent of our GDP on health care—every other advanced industrial country spends 11 percent on average and gets better outcomes—was unsustainable. And so as difficult as it was, we pushed through reforms that not only are going to give 30 million people without health insurance health insurance, that not only are currently providing 2.6 million young people health insurance because they can stay on their parents' plans, but that promises actually to start bending the cost curve because we've changed delivery systems and we changed incentives within this incredibly complicated piece of our economy in a way that will save businesses and families and ultimately both Federal and State governments a whole lot of money and make us better equipped to meet the challenges of the 21st century.

Education: We said that we keep on issuing reports and talking about how important it is, and every President is the education President, but we don't seem to make real progress, partly because there was an ideological division between Democrats and Republicans—Republicans saying the public schools don't work and teachers unions are the problem and let's tear them down, and Democrats saying the only problem is not enough money, but we don't want to initiate real changes.

And what we were able to do was to break through that logjam. Through programs like Race to the Top, we now have a situation where we're putting more money into education, but we're also asking for accountability. We're saying more resources and more reform, that we are going to respect, in fact elevate, teachers, because the single most important criteria for whether our kids succeed is that person standing in front of the classroom. And we're going to give them more flexibility, make sure they don't teach to the test, so that they can teach with creativity and passion, but we're also going to insist on greater accountability and high standards, because that's the only way we're going to succeed.

And then we said it's not going to be enough if they just graduate from high school. So, even though we got 40 States to initiate K–12 reform, we said we've got to do more with community colleges and higher education. And the biggest barrier, in addition to performance in K–12, is financial. And so we took $60 billion that was being funneled to banks to manage to student loans programs, and we said, you know what, let's cut out the middleman and take that $60 billion, and now millions of kids all across the country are able to afford college that they couldn't afford before.

And we said, let's stop—let's not stop there. We need more scientists and mathematicians and engineers. This group knows a little something about that. And so working not only in the public sector, but the private sector, we've initiated a whole range of programs to start elevating and lifting up the importance of STEM education and redesigning how it's taught, so that my daughters are starting to get interested in math and science early. We're not waiting until it's too late.

Well, we still had to do something about energy. And although we were not able to get, at this stage, the kind of climate legislation that, I think, is ultimately going to be necessary, we were able, without a lot of fanfare, to initiate the most significant environmental legislation

probably since the Clean Air Act by doubling fuel efficiency standards on cars and trucks and heavy trucks, which is not only good for our environment, but good for our economy.

And what we've also started to say is, is that we've got to have an even bolder program to get the low-hanging fruit when it comes to our energy challenges, and that's making everything more energy efficient. If we had the energy efficiency that exists in Japan right now, we would lower our energy consumption by 20 percent. It's remarkable. It's doable. It doesn't require new technologies.

Ultimately, Bill Gates is right. What we need to actually solve the problem is a massive technological breakthrough. But for us to spend the next 10, 20 years focused on what we know we can do right now, even as we're investing in the basic research, is critical.

And then we said, on the international front, if we're going to adapt to a changing world, we're going to have to wind down one war that probably should not have been fought in the first place. We've got to transition another war so that Afghans start taking more responsibility, and we have to stay focused on the folks who actually did us harm. And as difficult as that's been over the last three years, we were able to effectuate the plan and the promise that I made back in 2008.

Across the board, we have made tough decisions, whether it's saving the auto industry or making sure that we have a health care system that actually works for our economy. And there have been times, let's face it, during the last 3 years, where some of you have said, hmm, I'm not sure it's working out. But what we've always been convinced of, what I've always been convinced of, is that if we sustain this effort, even in the face of huge political obstacles, that eventually not only would the economy come back, but eventually, our politics would align with common sense and our traditions of hard work and mutual responsibility, the basic idea that, yes, we're rugged individualists and we're entrepreneurs and we focus on what we can accomplish on our own and we don't ask for handouts or expect anybody to do anything for us, but we're also part of something bigger, part of neighborhoods and communities and a United States of America, and that if we keep that in mind, then there's nothing we can't accomplish.

Now, this election is not going to be as sexy as 2008. [*Laughter*] You know, my hair is grayer. I've got little dings and bruises—although you're right, I can still sing. [*Laughter*] It's not going to be as new as it was in 2008. But I have to tell you, the stakes are so much higher, in some ways.

I think in 2008, everybody recognized, there was unanimity that change had to happen. And frankly, I think that I had a very capable Democratic opponent who also could have won. In this situation, we've got fundamentally different visions about the direction where our country is going, fundamentally different visions between us and the [other]° party's. Never has it been as probably as stark, in my lifetime, as it is now. Because on every single issue, you've got a party that says they are not willing to balance our budget, even if you've got a 10-to-1 deal, spending cuts to tax increases.

We've got a party that denies climate change even exists rather than debates how do we best address it. We've got a party that, when it comes to foreign policy, seems to only talk about military adventures and never seems to talk about how can we create a diplomatic climate that allows the world to organize itself to ensure mutual security and prosperity.

Across the board, I have not seen in my lifetime as stark a choice as we've got in 2012. And that means we're going to have to work harder this time than we did last time. If you agree with Mr. Gates here, who's spoken so eloquently about the fact that we've got to have a balanced approach to how we reduce our deficits, well, this is for all the marbles right here. Because the Bush tax cuts are going to expire at the end of this year, and whoever is the President is going to shape what our tax policy is and how we reduce our deficits and how we maintain fiscal stability for the next 20, 30 years.

And unless you think that it makes sense for us to cut basic research by 35 percent and edu-

cation support from the Federal Government by 35 percent and add about $6,000 of additional costs on every senior, whether they can afford it or not, for Medicare and Medicaid, then this election is going to require a lot of work.

I'm optimistic that the American people want common sense. I'm optimistic that the American people want balance. I'm optimistic the American people don't want to just think about the next election, they want us to think about the next generation. But we're going to have to fight for that. And I have to tell you that it is true I look a little older, but in some ways my determination is even greater now than it was in 2008.

One of the great things about occupying this job is that every single day, you're wrestling with these enormous, sometimes seemingly insoluble problems, right? Nothing hits my desk if it was easy to solve because then somebody else would have solved it. [*Laughter*] But in addition to just being fascinating, what's also amazing about this job is you're able to see sort of the spectrum of American life.

There's not an inch of this country that I haven't seen. There's not a group of people I haven't talked to. And that's an enormous source of inspiration and optimism. We've got really good people, and we have to make sure that we've got a Government that is reflective of their core decency. That's what we're fighting for, that's what this is all about. And the fact that you're joining me here today is just one more reason why I feel encouraged. So let me stop there.

Thank you.

NOTE: The President spoke at 2:41 p.m. at the residence of Jeffrey H. and Susan Brotman. In his remarks, he referred to William H. Gates III, chairman, Microsoft Corp.; and Secretary of State Hillary Rodham Clinton, in her capacity as a 2008 Democratic Presidential candidate. Audio was not available for verification of the content of these remarks.

° White House correction.

Remarks at an Obama Victory Fund 2012 Fundraiser in Bellevue, Washington
February 17, 2012

Hello, Bellevue! Hello, Seattle! It is good to be here back in the Pacific Northwest. Everybody can have a seat. I'm going to be talking for a while. [*Laughter*]

Let me start by just saying thank you to Peter for sharing his story. I love bookstores, so it was fun hearing how he's coming back. And we are very grateful to him and small-business owners all across the country who, every day, are getting up and doing what's required to make payroll and support a lot of families out there.

We also have somebody who's doing an outstanding job in public service. Your outstanding Governor, Chris Gregoire, is in the house. And your Lieutenant Governor, Brad Owens, is here. Or he was here. There he is over there. Good to see you, Brad.

I am here as well. I'm here because not only do I need your help, but I'm here because your country needs your help. There are so many reasons why a lot of you worked hard, worked your hearts out, in the 2008 campaign. It was not because my election was preordained. Electing Barack Hussein Obama was not, like, the odds-on favorite thing to happen. [*Laughter*] You didn't need a poll to know that could be tricky. [*Laughter*]

You joined it because the campaign wasn't simply about me. It was because of a shared vision that we had about the kind of country we want for not just ourselves, but our kids and our grandkids, a vision that doesn't assume a few people doing really well at the top and then everybody else struggling to get by. It was a vision that was inclusive and bold and generous, and it says here in America everybody who works hard has a chance to get ahead, no matter where you come from, no matter what you look like. It's a vision that says we're greater together than we are on our own and that when everybody gets a fair shot and everybody is doing their fair share and everybody is playing by the same set of rules, that's when America progresses.

That's the vision that we shared. That's the change we believed in. We knew it wasn't going to be easy. We knew it wasn't going to come quickly. But think about what's happened over these last 3 years. With all the opposition that we've had, with all the challenges we face, think about what's happened because of what you did in 2008. Think about what change looks like.

The first bill I signed into law, a law that says women deserve an equal day's pay for an equal day's work, so our daughters are treated the same as our sons, that's what change is.

Our decision to rescue the American auto industry from collapse, even when there were a bunch of politicians saying we should let Detroit go bankrupt, and now, because we didn't let a million jobs go, today GM is back on top as the world's number-one automaker, just reported the highest profits in its 100-year history, and with more than 200,000 new jobs created in the last 2½ years, the American auto industry is back. That's what change is. That's what you did.

Change is the decision we made to stop waiting for Congress to do something about our oil addiction and finally raise our fuel efficiency standards. And now, by the next decade, we'll be driving American-made cars that get almost 55 miles to the gallon, and trucks for the first time are covered. That's what change is: doubling fuel efficiency standards on cars. That's because of you—because of you.

Change is the fight we had to stop handing over $60 billion to banks in the student loan program and say let's cut out the middleman, let's give that money directly to students. And as a consequence, we've got millions of young people who are benefiting from less debt and greater college affordability. That happened because of you.

Because of you, we were able to put middle class tax cuts in the back pockets of working Americans every single year I've been in office. And today Congress did the right thing and extended the payroll tax cut for working

Americans through the rest of the year. That's about a thousand dollars for the typical American family. And that's part of what lifted the economy when it was on the verge of a great depression. That's what change is.

And yes, change is the health care reform bill we passed after a century of trying. That's a reform that will finally ensure that in the United States of America, nobody goes broke because they get sick. And already, 2.5 million young people have health insurance today because the law allows them to stay on their parent's plan. And because of this law, Americans no longer can be denied or dropped by their insurance companies when they need care the most. That's what change is.

Change is the fact that, for the first time in our history, it doesn't matter who you love, you can still serve the country you love, because "don't ask, don't tell" is finally over.

And change is keeping another promise. For the first time in 9 years, there are no Americans fighting in Iraq. And we've refocused our efforts on the terrorists who actually attacked us on 9/11. And thanks to the brave men and women in uniform, Al Qaida is weaker than it has ever been and Usama bin Laden is no longer a threat to the United States of America. That's what change is.

Now, none of this change was easy. And we've got so much more work we have to do. There are so many Americans out there that are still looking for work and so many families that are still struggling to pay the bills or make their mortgage payment, and we're still recovering from the worst economic crisis in our lifetimes. But over the past 2 years, businesses have added about 3.7 million jobs. Our manufacturers are creating the most jobs since the 1990s. Our economy is getting stronger.

The recovery is accelerating. America is coming back, which means the last thing we can do is go back to the same failed policies, the very same policies that got us into this mess in the first place. And that's what's at stake in this election. That's exactly what the other candidates want to do. They don't make any secret about it. They want to go back to the days when Wall Street played by its own rules. They want to go back to the days when insurance companies could deny you coverage or jack up premiums without reason. They want to go back to spend trillions of dollars more on tax breaks for folks like me, for the wealthiest Americans, even if it means adding to the deficit or gutting things like education or clean energy or making Medicare more expensive for seniors.

The philosophy is simple: We are better off when everybody else is left to fend for themselves and the most powerful can write their own rules. And they're wrong. That's not how America was built. In the United States of America, we're greater together than we are on our own. And we are going to keep that basic promise that if you work hard, you can raise a family and send your kids to college and put a little away for retirement. That's what we're going to be fighting for. That's the choice in this election.

This isn't just another political debate. This is the defining issue of our time, a make-or-break moment for middle class Americans and those who want to get into the middle class. We could go back to an economy that's built on outsourcing and debt and phony financial profits. That's an option. But we got a better option: We can fight for an economy that's built to last, an economy that's based on American manufacturing and American-made energy and American innovation and skills and education for American workers and the values that have always made this country great: hard work and fair play and shared responsibility. That's what we're fighting for. That's what this election's about. That's why you're here tonight.

We need to make sure that the next generation of manufacturing, companies like Boeing, take root not in Asia, not in Europe, but in factories of Detroit, Pittsburgh, and Cleveland, here in Washington State. I don't want this Nation to just be known for buying and consuming. I want us to be known for building and selling products all around the world. And part of that means we've got to stop rewarding companies that ship jobs overseas and start rewarding companies that create jobs right here in the United States.

We've got to change our Tax Code to incentivize investment here. It means we have to make our schools the envy of the world, which starts, by the way, with the man or woman in front of the classroom. A good teacher can increase the lifetime earnings of a classroom by over $250,000. A great teacher offers a path for a child to go where their dreams might carry them even if they're born into poverty, even if they've got tough circumstances.

So I don't want to hear folks in Washington bashing teachers; I don't want to hear them defending the status quo. I want us to give schools the resources they need to hire good teachers and keep good teachers and reward the best teachers. And in return, I want to give schools the flexibility to teach with creativity and passion and still maintain accountability. Stop teaching to the test, but still make sure that teachers are meeting high standards and replace those who aren't helping our kids learn. That's what we're fighting for. That's a vision of America of shared responsibility.

And when kids do graduate, I want them to be able to afford to go to college. Americans now owe more tuition debt than credit card debt, which means, for starters, this Congress needs to stop the interest rates on student loans from doubling in July, which is what's scheduled to happen. But that's just the start. Colleges and universities have to do their part.

I said in the State of the Union, we want to give incentives to colleges and universities, and we will help them contain their costs, and State legislatures are going to have to do the same thing. Because my attitude is if colleges and universities that are supposed to be serving students are pricing themselves so that students can't go, then fundings from taxpayers should go down. Higher education can't be a luxury. It's an economic imperative that every family in America should be able to afford. And if we are persistent and creative about it, we can make that happen.

An economy built to last is one where we support science and scientists and researchers that are making the next breakthroughs in clean energy right here in the United States of America. We are a nation of inventors and tin-

kerers. We come up with new ideas, and we try things that the world hasn't seen before. And that has to be an area where we are thinking not just about now, but we're thinking about tomorrow and the next generation. And nowhere is that truer than when it comes to energy.

We've subsidized oil companies for nearly a hundred years. It's time to end a hundred years of taxpayer giveaways to an industry that's rarely been more profitable so we can double down on the clean energy industry that has never been more promising, in solar power and wind power and biofuels. That's good for our economy, it's good for our national security, and it is good for the planet. And that is part of what's at stake in this election.

I want us to rebuild in America. I'm a chauvinist; I want America to have the best stuff. I don't want to go to China and see their airports better than ours. I don't want to go to Europe and see that they've got faster high-speed rail than we do. I want to give our businesses and our people the best access to newer roads and airports and the fastest railways and the best Internet access. We should—and I've proposed this—let's take the money that we are no longer spending in Iraq, use half of that to pay down our debt, use the rest of it to do some nation-building here at home. Let's put people to work here at home rebuilding this Nation.

Now, even if we do that, we're still going to have to bring down our deficit and our debt. And that comes to the issue of everybody doing their fair share. We need a tax system that reflects our best values, everybody carrying their weight. I believe we should follow the Buffett rule: If you make more than $1 million a year, you shouldn't pay a lower tax rate than your secretary. If, like 98 percent of Americans, you make $250,000 a year or less, your taxes don't need to go up right now—period.

This has nothing to do with class warfare. It has nothing to do with envy. It has everything to do with math. [*Laughter*] If somebody likes—if somebody like me gets a tax break that I don't need, wasn't asking for, at a time when we're trying to get our fiscal house in order, then one of two things happens. Either that adds to our deficit, or alternatively, we've got to take something else away from somebody else. Maybe a student suddenly has to pay higher interest on their student loans or a senior has got to pay more for their Medicare or a homeless veteran doesn't get the support that they need or a family doesn't have the opportunity to get the kind of job training they need to adapt in this changing economy.

Those are the choices. And the notion that we would ask sacrifice from folks who are already struggling in order to protect folks who have never been better—never been better off—that's not who we are.

Every one of us, we're here because somebody else, somewhere, was looking out for us and looking out for the country, taking responsibility for the future, made an investment in us. I don't care how successful you are, you didn't do it just on your own. And here in America, our story has never been about what we do just on our own; it's about what we do together.

Yes, we are rugged individualists, and we expect everybody to carry their weight and work hard and take responsibility for yourself and your family. But we also recognize that for all of us to succeed, we have to have an investment in each other's success. We won't win the competition for new jobs and new businesses and middle class security if we just respond to the same economic challenges with the same, old, you're-on-your-own economics. It doesn't work. We've tried it. It didn't work in the Depression, it didn't work in the last decade, it won't work now.

So, if we're going to build an economy that's built to last, we've got to have a stake in each other's success and we've got to think about the future. And think about it, this is something everybody here understands instinctually. If we attract an outstanding teacher to the profession by giving teachers the pay they deserve and the training and professional development they deserve, and that teacher goes on to educate the next Bill Gates, we all benefit. If we provide faster Internet to a rural part of Washington, and suddenly that storeowner can sell his or her goods around the world, that

makes everybody better off here in the State of Washington and in the United States. If we build a new bridge that saves a shipping company time or money, workers and customers everywhere are going to be better off. We'll be more competitive.

This idea is not a Democratic idea or a Republican idea. It's an American idea. The first Republican President, Abraham Lincoln, he launched the transcontinental railroad, the National Academy of Science, the first land-grant colleges in the middle of a Civil War, because he understood that for us to succeed, we've got to invest in the future. A Republican, Teddy Roosevelt, called for a progressive income tax. Dwight Eisenhower built the Interstate Highway System. It was with the help of Republicans in Congress that FDR gave millions of returning heroes, including my grandfather, a chance to go to college on the GI bill.

That spirit of common purpose, that's still at the heart of the American experience. It still exists today. Maybe not in Washington, but as I travel around the country, I know it's there. You hear it. You see it. It's there when you talk to folks on Main Street or in town halls. It's certainly there when you talk to members of our Armed Forces, when you talk to somebody who's out there coaching Little League or in their place of worship, volunteering and helping people that are less fortunate.

Our politics sometimes seems just so divided, almost irrational. And obviously, that gets a lot of attention because conflict sells newspapers, attracts viewers. But most Americans understand that for all our differences, what binds us together is more important. No matter who we are—Black, White, Latino, Asian, Native American, gay, straight, rich, poor, disabled or not—we rise and fall as one Nation and as one people. And that's what this election's about.

It's been a tough 3 years, and the change we fought for in 2008 didn't always come fast and didn't always come easy. And after all that's happened in Washington and all the noise and sound and fury, I know it's tempting sometimes to believe, well, maybe the vision we had is beyond our grasp. But I remind all of you, those of you who were involved in 2008, or even those of you who were just casual observers at the time, I said big change, real change is hard. It takes time. It takes more than a single term. And it may take more than a single President. It takes ordinary citizens who are committed to fighting and pushing and inching this country, day by day, week by week, month by month, year by year, towards our highest ideals.

And I told you then, I may not be a perfect man and I will never be a perfect President, but I pledged that I would always tell you what I thought and where I stood, and I would wake up every single day fighting for you as hard as I know how. And I have kept that promise. I have kept that promise. That promise I've kept.

And if you're willing to push with me through all the obstacles and keep reaching for that vision of a better America, then change will come.

Thank you very much, everybody. God bless you. God bless America.

NOTE: The President spoke at 4:34 p.m. at the Westin Bellevue hotel. In his remarks, he referred to Peter Aaron, owner, Elliott Bay Book Co., who introduced the President; Warren E. Buffett, chief executive officer and chairman, Berkshire Hathaway Inc.; and William H. Gates III, chairman, Microsoft Corp.

The President's Weekly Address
February 18, 2012

Hello, everybody. I'm speaking to you this week from the Boeing Plant in Everett, Washington. Boeing has been in this community for half a century, but it's what they're doing here today that has folks really excited, because at this plant they're building the plane of the future, the Dreamliner. It's an impressive sight. And to be honest, part of why I came was to see it up close. But I also came because this is a great example of how we can bring jobs and manufacturing back to America.

You see, the last few decades haven't been easy for manufacturing in this country. New technology has made businesses more efficient and productive, and that's good, but it's also made a lot of jobs obsolete. The result has been painful for a lot of families and a lot of communities. Factories where people thought they'd retire have left town. Jobs that provided a decent living have been shipped overseas. And the hard truth is that a lot of those jobs aren't coming back.

But that doesn't mean we have to settle for a lesser future. I don't accept that idea. In America, there's always something we can do to create new jobs and new manufacturing and new security for the middle class. In America, we don't give up, we get up.

Right now that's exactly what we're doing. Over the past 23 months, businesses have created 3.7 million new jobs. And manufacturers are hiring for the first time since the 1990s. It's now getting more expensive to do business in places like China. Meanwhile, America is more productive than ever. And companies like Boeing are realizing that even when we can't make things cheaper than China, we can make things better. That's how we're going to compete globally.

For Boeing, business right now is booming. Last year, orders for commercial aircraft rose by more than 50 percent. To meet that rising demand, they've put thousands of folks to work all over the country. And we want to see more of this. We need to make it as easy as we can for our companies to create more jobs in America, not overseas. And that starts with our Tax Code.

No company should get a tax break for outsourcing jobs. Instead, tax breaks should go to manufacturers who set up shop here at home. Bigger tax breaks should go to high-tech manufacturers who create the jobs of the future. And if you relocate your company in a struggling community, you should get help financing that new plant, that new equipment, or for training for new workers. It's time to stop rewarding businesses that ship jobs overseas and start rewarding businesses that create jobs here in America. And Congress should send me that kind of tax reform right away.

Another thing we're doing is to make it easier for companies like Boeing to sell their products all over the world, because more exports mean more jobs. Two years ago, I set a goal of doubling U.S. exports over 5 years. And we're on track to meet that goal, ahead of schedule.

We have a big opportunity right now to build not only an economy that will help us succeed today, but an economy that will help our kids and their kids succeed tomorrow. We know what we need to do. We need to strengthen American manufacturing. We need to invest in American-made energy and new skills for American workers. And above all, we need to renew the values that have always made this country great: hard work, fair play, shared responsibility.

We can do this. Ask the folks in Everett. Right here, a few years ago, the first Dreamliner took off on its maiden trip. Thousands of employees came to watch. One was an executive office administrator named Sharon O'Hara. And as Sharon saw that first plane take flight—a result of so much hard work—she got goose bumps. In her words, she said, "We said we would do it, and we did." That's the story of America. We said we would do it, and we did. That's the can-do spirit that makes us who we are. We've seen challenging times before. But we always emerge from them stronger. And that's what we're going to do again today.

Thanks, and have a great weekend.

NOTE: The address was recorded at approximately 12:30 p.m. on February 17 at the Boeing Co. production facility in Everett, WA, for broadcast on February 18. The transcript was made available by the Office of the Press Secretary on February 17, but was embargoed for release until 6 a.m. on February 18.

Remarks on Payroll Tax Cut and Unemployment Insurance Legislation
February 21, 2012

Hello! Good to see everybody. Please, have a seat. Have a seat. Good morning. I want to thank all of you for coming.

I want to thank my outstanding Vice President, Joe Biden, who is here today, and members of my administration for joining us. But most of all, I want to thank the men and women who are standing with me today, as well as all the Americans who made their voices heard during the debate about extending the payroll tax cut and unemployment insurance.

We are here because of you. This got done because of you. Because you called, you e-mailed, you tweeted your Representatives, and you demanded action. You made it clear that you wanted to see some common sense in Washington. And because you did, no working American is going to see their taxes go up this year. That's good news. Because of what you did, millions of Americans who are out there still looking for work are going to continue to get help with unemployment insurance. That's

because of you. I called on—[*applause*]—that's worth applauding as well.

You'll remember, I called on Congress to pass this middle class tax cut back in September as part of my broader jobs plan. And for the typical American family, it is a big deal. It means $40 extra in their paycheck. And that $40 helps to pay the rent, the groceries, the rising cost of gas, which is on a lot of people's minds right now. LaRonda Hill—right here—told us how $40 covers the water bill for a month. So this tax cut makes a difference for a lot of families. You can get back over here, Joe. [*Laughter*] And more people spending more money means more businesses will be able to hire more workers and the entire economy gets another boost just as the recovery is starting to gain some steam.

So Congress did the right thing here. They listened to the voices of the American people. Each side made a few compromises. We passed some important reforms to help turn unemployment insurance into reemployment insurance so that more people get training and the skills they need to get back in a job. We passed an initiative that will create jobs by expanding wireless broadband and ensuring that first-responders have access to the latest life-saving technologies. And we've got some first-responders here. We're very grateful for the work that they do.

So, in the end, everyone acted in the interests of the middle class and people who are striving to get into the middle class through hard work. And that's how it should be. That's what Americans expect, and that's what Americans deserve.

Now my message to Congress is: Don't stop here. Keep going. Keep taking the action that people are calling for to keep this economy growing. This may be an election year, but the American people have no patience for gridlock and just a reflexive partisanship and just paying attention to poll numbers and the next election instead of the next generation and what we can do to strengthen opportunity for all Americans. Americans don't have the luxury to put off tough decisions, and neither should we. There's a lot more we can do—and there's plenty of time to do it—if we want to build an economy where every American has a chance to find a good job that pays well and supports a family.

For example, Congress needs to pass my plan to help responsible homeowners save about $3,000 a year by refinancing their homes, their mortgages, at historically low rates. We're doing what we can administratively to provide some Americans that opportunity. I want all Americans to have that opportunity, and we need Congress to act to do it.

Congress needs to step up and support America's small businesses and especially companies that want to export. It's time we stop rewarding businesses that send jobs overseas, start rewarding companies right here that want to create jobs in the United States and sell to other countries as opposed to exporting jobs to other countries. That's what we need to do. Congress can act on that.

Congress needs to make the Buffett rule a reality. This is common sense. If you make more than a million dollars a year—make more than a million dollars a year—you should pay a tax rate of at least 30 percent. And if you do that, that means that if you make less than $250,000 a year, like 98 percent of Americans do, you shouldn't see your taxes go up. And we won't be adding to the deficit.

These are things we can do today. It shouldn't be that difficult. Now, whenever Congress refuses to act, Joe and I, we're going to act. In the months to come, wherever we have an opportunity, we're going to take steps on our own to keep this economy moving. Because we've got a choice right now. We can either settle for a country where a few people are doing very well and everybody else is having to just struggle to get by, or we can build an economy where everybody gets a fair shot and everybody is doing their fair share and everybody is taking responsibility and everybody is playing by the same set of rules. And that's the economy that I want.

We still have some struggles out there. We're coming out of the worst economic crisis in our lifetimes. We've got a long way to go before every single person who's looking for a job can find a job. But where we stand now looks a lot different than where we stood a few years ago. Over the last 23 months, businesses have created 3.7 million new jobs. Manufacturers are hiring for the first time since the 1990s. The auto industry is back on top. Our recovery is gaining steam. Our economy is getting stronger. So we're headed in the right direction. And the last thing we should do is turn around and go back to the policies that weren't working in the first place.

That's why it's so important for us to stay focused and Congress to continue to do the things that the American people want to see done in order to improve the economy. We've got to build an economy that is built on American manufacturing and American-made energy and is improving the skills and capacity of American workers. We've got to make sure that when we think about energy, that we're fueling America by homegrown and alternative energy sources that make us more secure and less dependent on foreign oil. When we think about skills for American workers, we got to make sure that everybody has the opportunity not only for 4-year colleges, but also 2-year colleges, the community colleges that Dr. Jill Biden is doing such a great job promoting all across the country.

We've put forward plans on each of these areas that can make a huge difference. But most of all, we've got to have a return to some homespun American values: hard work, fair play, shared responsibility. That's who we are as a people.

And the reason I'm so confident in our future is because the folks who are standing with me today, some of the folks who are in the audience, because of all the families and workers and small-business owners and students and seniors that I've met over the last few weeks and that I've met during the course of my political career. When times are tough, Americans don't give up. They push ahead. They do

whatever it takes to make their lives better, their communities, better and their countries better.

And with or without Congress, every day I'm going to be continuing to fight with them. I do hope Congress joins me. Instead of spending the coming months in a lot of phony political debates, focusing on the next election, I hope that we spend some time focusing on middle class Americans and those who are struggling to get into the middle class. We've got a lot more work to do. Let's do it.

Thank you very much, everybody. Thanks for the great job you did. Appreciate you, proud of you. Thank you.

NOTE: The President spoke at 11:41 a.m. in the South Court Auditorium of the Dwight D. Eisenhower Executive Office Building. In his remarks, he referred to Warren E. Buffett, chief executive officer and chairman, Berkshire Hathaway Inc.; and Jill T. Biden, wife of Vice President Biden.

Remarks at PBS's "In Performance at the White House: Red, White, and Blues"
February 21, 2012

Thank you. Everybody, please have a seat. That sounded pretty good. [*Laughter*] I might try that instead of ruffles and flourishes. [*Laughter*]

Well, first of all, I want to wish everybody a happy Mardi Gras. I hear Trombone Shorty brought some beads up from New Orleans. And I see that we've got some members of our Cabinet here. We've got some Members of Congress. And we have elected officials from all across the country.

One of the things about being President—I've talked about this before—is that some nights when you want to go out and just take a walk, clear your head, or jump into a car just to take a drive, you can't do it. Secret Service won't let you. And that's frustrating. But then there are other nights where B.B. King and Mick Jagger come over to your house to play for a concert. So I guess things even out a little bit. [*Laughter*]

In 1941, the folklorist Alan Lomax traveled throughout the Deep South, recording local musicians on behalf of the Library of Congress. In Stovall, Mississippi, he met McKinley Morganfield, a guitar player who went by the nickname Muddy Waters. And Lomax sent Muddy two pressings from their sessions together, along with a check for $20.

Later in his life, Muddy recalled what happened next. He said: "I carried that record up to the corner, and I put it on the jukebox. Just played it and played it and said, I can do it." I can do it. In many ways, that right there is the story of the blues.

This is music with humble beginnings, roots in slavery and segregation, a society that rarely treated Black Americans with the dignity and respect that they deserved. The blues bore witness to these hard times. And like so many of the men and women who sang them, the blues refused to be limited by the circumstances of their birth.

The music migrated north, from Mississippi Delta to Memphis to my hometown in Chicago. It helped lay the foundation for rock and roll and R&B and hip-hop. It inspired artists and audiences around the world. And as tonight's performers will demonstrate, the blues continue to draw a crowd. Because this music speaks to something universal. No one goes through life without both joy and pain, triumph and sorrow. The blues gets all of that, sometimes with just one lyric or one note.

And as we celebrate Black History Month, the blues reminds us that we've been through tougher times before. That's why I'm proud to have these artists here, and not just as a fan, but also as the President. Because their music teaches us that when we find ourselves at a crossroads, we don't shy away from our problems. We own them. We face up to them. We deal with them. We sing about them. We turn them into art. And even as we confront the challenges of today, we imagine a brighter tomorrow, saying, I can do it, just like Muddy Waters did all those years ago.

With that in mind, please join me in welcoming these extraordinary artists to the White House. And now, it is my pleasure to bring out our first performer to the stage, the King of the Blues, Mr. B.B. King.

NOTE: The President spoke at 7:22 p.m. in the East Room at the White House. In his remarks, he referred to musician Troy "Trombone Shorty" Andrews.

Remarks at a Groundbreaking Ceremony for the National Museum of African American History and Culture
February 22, 2012

Thank you so much. Please, have a seat. Thank you very much. Well, good morning, everybody.

I want to thank France for that introduction and for her leadership at the Smithsonian. I want to thank everybody who helped to make this day happen. I want to thank Laura Bush; Secretary Salazar; Sam Brownback; my hero, Congressman John Lewis; Wayne Clough; and everybody who's worked so hard to make this possible.

I am so proud of Lonnie Bunch, who came here from Chicago, I want to point out. [*Laughter*] I remember having a conversation with him about this job when he was planning to embark on this extraordinary journey. And we could not be prouder of the work that he has done to help make this day possible.

I promise to do my part by being brief.

As others have mentioned, this day has been a long time coming. The idea for a museum dedicated to African Americans was first put forward by Black veterans of the Civil War. And years later, the call was picked up by members of the civil rights generation, by men and women who knew how to fight for what was right and strive for what is just. This is their day. This is your day. It's an honor to be here to see the fruit of your labor.

It's also fitting that this museum has found a home on the National Mall. As has been mentioned, it was on this ground long ago that lives were once traded, where hundreds of thousands once marched for jobs and for freedom. It was here that the pillars of our democracy were built, often by Black hands. And it is on this spot, alongside the monuments to those who gave birth to this Nation and those who worked so hard to perfect it, that generations will remember the sometimes difficult, often inspirational, but always central role that African Americans have played in the life of our country.

This museum will celebrate that history. Because just as the memories of our earliest days have been confined to dusty letters and faded pictures, the time will come when few people remember drinking from a colored water fountain or boarding a segregated bus or hearing in person Dr. King's voice boom down from the Lincoln Memorial. That's why what we build here won't just be an achievement for our time, it will be a monument for all time. It will do more than simply keep those memories alive.

Just like the Air and Space Museum challenges us to set our sights higher, or the Natural History Museum encourages us to look closer, or the Holocaust Museum calls us to fight persecution wherever we find it, this museum should inspire us as well. It should stand as proof that the most important things in life rarely come quickly or easily. It should remind us that although we have yet to reach the mountaintop, we cannot stop climbing.

And that's why, in moments like this, I think about Malia and Sasha. I think about my daughters, and I think about your children, the millions of visitors who will stand where we stand long after we're gone. And I think about what I want them to experience. I think about what I want them to take away.

When our children look at Harriet Tubman's shawl or Nat Turner's Bible or the plane flown by Tuskegee Airmen, I don't want them to be seen as figures somehow larger than life. I want them to see how ordinary Americans could do extraordinary things, how men and women just like them had the courage and determination to right a wrong, to make it right.

I want my daughters to see the shackles that bound slaves on their voyage across the ocean and the shards of glass that flew from the 16th Street Baptist church and understand that injustice and evil exist in the world. But I also want them to hear Louis Armstrong's horn and learn about the Negro League and read the poems of Phyllis Wheatley. And I want them to appreciate this museum not just as a record of tragedy, but as a celebration of life.

When future generations hear these songs of pain and progress and struggle and sacrifice, I hope they will not think of them as somehow separate from the larger American story. I want them to see it as central, an important part of our shared story, a call to see ourselves in one another, a call to remember that each of us is made in God's image. That's the history we will preserve within these walls, the history of a people who, in the words of Dr. King, "injected new meaning and dignity into the veins of civilization."

May we remember their stories. May we live up to their example. Thank you, God bless you, and God bless the United States of America.

NOTE: The President spoke at 11:21 a.m. on the National Mall. In his remarks, he referred to France A. Cordova, Chair, Smithsonian Institution Board of Regents; former First Lady Laura Bush; and Lonnie G. Bunch, Director, National Museum of African American History and Culture.

Statement on the Observance of Ash Wednesday
February 22, 2012

Today Michelle and I honor Ash Wednesday with Christians around the country and across the world. This is at once a solemn and joyous occasion, an opportunity to remember both the depths of sacrifice and the height of redemption. We join millions in entering the Lenten season with truly thankful hearts, mindful of our faith and our obligations to one another.

Statement on Tax Code Reform
February 22, 2012

In my State of the Union, I laid out a blueprint for an economy that's built to last, where everyone gets a fair shot, everyone pays their fair share, and everyone plays by the same set of rules. That includes a Tax Code that rewards companies who invest and create jobs in the United States of America.

Our current corporate tax system is outdated, unfair, and inefficient. It provides tax breaks for moving jobs and profits overseas and hits companies that choose to stay in America with one of the highest tax rates in the world. It is unnecessarily complicated and forces America's small businesses to spend countless hours and dollars filing their taxes. It's not right, and it needs to change.

That's why my administration released a framework for reform that simplifies the Tax Code, eliminates dozens of tax loopholes and subsidies, and promotes job creation right here at home. It's a framework that lowers the corporate tax rate and broadens the tax base in order to increase competitiveness for companies across the Nation. It cuts tax rates even further for manufacturers that are creating new products and manufacturing goods here in America. Finally, because no company should be able to avoid paying its fair share of taxes by moving jobs and profits overseas, this framework includes a basic minimum tax for every multinational company. This reform is fully paid for, and it won't add a dime to the deficit.

As I said in the State of the Union, it is time to stop rewarding businesses that ship jobs overseas and start rewarding companies that create jobs right here in America.

Remarks During a Tour of the Industrial Assessment Center at the University of Miami in Coral Gables, Florida
February 23, 2012

This is for background because you guys just came in. What this facility does is teach these outstanding young engineers how to do energy assessments for manufacturers—industrial buildings across the board. And so far they have—how many?—200 assessments, saving these companies up to 25 percent in their energy usage. And that's going to end up saving them millions of dollars.

So it's a great example of how people are being trained right now to make our businesses more energy efficient all across the country.

All right.

NOTE: The President spoke at 1:55 p.m. in the McArthur Engineering Building. Audio was not available for verification of the content of these remarks.

Remarks at the University of Miami in Coral Gables
February 23, 2012

The President. Hello, Miami! The U! It is good to see all of you here today.

I want to thank Erica for that outstanding introduction. She said her parents were tweeting. [*Laughter*] We're so proud of you, Erica.

I also want to thank your president, this country's former Secretary of Health and Human Services, Donna Shalala. Senator Bill Nelson is here. Give him a big round of applause—former astronaut—that's too cool. [*Laughter*] And my outstanding friend, Congresswoman Debbie Wasserman Schultz, is in the house.

It is good to be back in sunny Florida. I must say I don't know how you guys go to class. [*Laughter*] I'm assuming you do go to class. [*Laughter*] Too—it's just too nice outside. But in another life, I would be staying for the Knicks-Heat game tonight, then go up to Orlando for a NBA All-Star Weekend. But these days, I've got a few other things on my plate. [*Laughter*] Just a few.

I just got a fascinating demonstration of the work that some of you are doing at the College of Engineering. And let me say at the outset, we need more engineers. So I could not be prouder of those of you who are studying engineering.

It was fascinating stuff. I understood about 10 percent of what they told me. [*Laughter*] But it was very impressive. [*Laughter*] And the work couldn't be more important, because what they were doing was figuring out how our buildings, our manufacturers, our businesses can waste less energy. And that's one of the fastest, easiest ways to reduce our dependence on oil and save a lot of money in the process and make our economy stronger.

So some cutting-edge stuff is being done right here at the U. Now, that's what I'm here to talk about today. In the State of the Union, I laid out three areas where we need to focus if we want to build an economy that lasts and is good for the next generation, all of you. We need new American manufacturing. We've got to have new skills and education for America's workers, and we need new sources of American-made energy.

Now, right now we are experiencing just another painful reminder of why developing new energy is so critical to our future. Just like last year, gas prices are climbing across the country. This time, it's happening even earlier. And when gas prices go up, it hurts everybody: everybody who owns a car, everybody who owns a business. It means you've got to stretch a paycheck even further. It means you've got to find even more room in a budget that was already really tight. And some folks have no choice but to drive a long way to work, and high gas prices are like a tax straight out of your paycheck.

I got a letter last night; I get these letters, 10 letters every night that I read out of the 40,000 that are sent to me. And at least two of them said, I'm not sure I'm going to be able to keep my job if gas prices keep on going up so high, because it's just hard to manage the budget and fill up the tank. A lot of folks are going through tough times as a consequence.

Now, some politicians, they see this as a political opportunity. I know you're shocked by that. [*Laughter*] Last week, the lead story in one newspaper said, "Gasoline prices are on the rise, and Republicans are licking their chops." [*Laughter*] That's a quote. That was the lead. "Licking their chops." Only in politics do people root for bad news, do they greet bad news so enthusiastically. You pay more; they're licking their chops.

You can bet that since it's an election year, they're already dusting off their three-point plan for $2 gas. And I'll save you the suspense. Step one is to drill, and step two is to drill. And

then step three is to keep drilling. [*Laughter*] We heard the same line in 2007 when I was running for President. We hear the same thing every year. We've heard the same thing for 30 years.

Well, the American people aren't stupid. They know that's not a plan, especially since we're already drilling. That's a bumper sticker. It's not a strategy to solve our energy challenge. That's a strategy to get politicians through an election.

You know there are no quick fixes to this problem. You know we can't just drill our way to lower gas prices. If we're going to take control of our energy future and can start avoiding these annual gas price spikes that happen every year—when the economy starts getting better, world demand starts increasing, turmoil in the Middle East or some other parts of the world—if we're going to avoid being at the mercy of these world events, we've got to have a sustained, all-of-the-above strategy that develops every available source of American energy. Yes, oil and gas, but also wind and solar and nuclear and biofuels and more.

We need to keep developing the technology that allows us to use less oil in our cars and trucks, less energy for our buildings and our plants and our factories. That's the strategy we're pursuing, and that's the only real solution to this challenge.

Now, it starts with the need for safe, responsible oil production here in America. We're not going to transition out of oil anytime soon. And that's why under my administration, America is producing more oil today than at any time in the last 8 years. That's why we have a record number of oil rigs operating right now, more working oil and gas rigs than the rest of the world combined.

Over the last 3 years, my administration has approved dozens of new pipelines, including from Canada. And we've opened millions of acres for oil and gas exploration. All told we plan to make available more than 75 percent of our potential offshore oil and gas resources from Alaska to the Gulf of Mexico.

Last week, we announced the next steps towards further energy exploration in the Arctic.

Earlier this week, we joined Mexico in an agreement that will make more than 1.5 million acres in the Gulf available for exploration and production, which contains an estimated 172 million barrels of oil and 304 billion cubic feet of natural gas.

So we're focused on production. That's not the issue. And we'll keep on producing more homegrown energy. But here's the thing: It's not enough. The amount of oil that we drill at home doesn't set the price of gas by itself. The oil market is global; oil is bought and sold in a world market. And just like last year, the single biggest thing that's causing the price of oil to spike right now is instability in the Middle East, this time around Iran. When uncertainty increases, speculative trading on Wall Street increases, and that drives prices up even more.

So those are the biggest short-term factors at work here.

Over the long term, the biggest reason oil prices will probably keep going up is growing demand in countries like China and India and Brazil. I want you to all think about this. In 5 years, the number of cars on the road in China more than tripled—just in the last 5 years. Nearly 10 million cars were added in China in 2010 alone—10 million cars in 1 year in one country. Think about how much oil that requires. And as folks in China and India and Brazil, they aspire to buy a car just like Americans do, those numbers are only going to get bigger.

So what does this mean for us? It means that anybody who tells you that we can drill our way out of this problem doesn't know what they're talking about or just isn't telling you the truth.

And young people especially understand this, because I think—it's interesting, when I talk to Malia and Sasha—you guys are so much more aware than I was of conserving our natural resources and thinking about the planet. The United States consumes more than a fifth of the world's oil—more than 20 percent of the world's oil—just us. We only have 2 percent of the world's oil reserves. We consume 20; we've got 2.

And that means we can't just rely on fossil fuels from the last century. We can't just allow ourselves to be held hostage to the ups and downs of the world oil market. We've got to keep developing new sources of energy. We've got to develop new technology that helps us use less energy and use energy smarter. We've got to rely on American know-how and young engineers right here at the "U" who are focused on energy. That is our future. And that's exactly the path that my administration has been trying to take these past 3 years.

And we're making progress. That's the good news. In 2010, our dependence on foreign oil was under 50 percent for the first time in over a decade. We were less reliant on foreign oil than we had been. In 2011, the United States relied less on foreign oil than in any of the last 16 years. That's the good news. And because of the investments we've made, the use of clean, renewable energy in this country has nearly doubled, and thousands of American jobs have been created as a consequence.

We're taking every possible action to develop, safely, a near hundred-year supply of natural gas in this country; something that experts believe will support more than 600,000 jobs by the end of the decade. We supported the first new nuclear power plant in three decades. Our cooperation with the private sector has positioned this country to be the world's leading manufacturer of high-tech batteries that will power the next generation of American cars, that use less oil, maybe don't use any oil at all.

And after three decades of inaction, we put in place the toughest fuel economy standards in history for our cars and pickup trucks and the first standards ever for heavy-duty trucks. And because we did this, our cars will average nearly 55 miles per gallon by the middle of the next decade. That's nearly double what they get today.

Now, I remember what it was like being a student. You guys probably have one of those old beaters. Who knows what kind of mileage you guys get. [*Laughter*] I can tell you some stories about the cars I had. I bought one for $500. But by the middle of the next decade, you guys are going to be buying some new cars—hopefully, sooner than that. And that means you'll be able to fill up your car every 2 weeks instead of every week, something that, over time, will save the typical family more than $8,000 at the pump.

And it means this country will reduce our oil consumption by more than 2 million barrels a day. That's not only good for your pocketbook, that's good for the environment.

All right, but here's the thing: We've got to do more. We've got to act even faster. We have to keep investing in the development of every available source of American-made energy. And this is a question of where our priorities are. This is a choice that we face.

Now, first of all, while there are no silver bullets short term when it comes to gas prices, and anybody who says otherwise isn't telling the truth. I have directed my administration to look for every single area where we can make an impact and help consumers in the months ahead, from permitting to delivery bottlenecks to what's going on in the oil markets. We're going to look at every single aspect of gas prices, because we know the burden that it's putting on consumers. And we will keep taking as many steps as we can in the coming weeks.

That's short term. But over the long term, an all-of-the-above energy strategy requires us having the right priorities. We've got to have the right incentives in place. I'll give you an example. Right now 4 billion of your tax dollars subsidize the oil industry every year—$4 billion. They don't need a subsidy. They're making near-record profits. These are the same oil companies that have been making record profits off the money you spend at the pump for several years now. How do they deserve another $4 billion from taxpayers and subsidies?

It's outrageous. It's inexcusable. And every politician who's been fighting to keep those subsidies in place should explain to the American people why the oil industry needs more of their money, especially at a time like this.

I said this at the State of the Union: A century of subsidies to the oil companies is long enough. It's time to end taxpayer giveaways to an industry that has never been more profitable, double down on clean energy industries that have never been more promising. That's what we need to do. This Congress needs to

renew the clean energy tax credits that will lead to more jobs and less dependence on foreign oil.

The potential of a sustained, all-of-the-above energy strategy is all around us. Here in Miami—2008, Miami became the first major American city to power its city hall entirely with solar and renewable energy. Right here in Miami. The modernization of your power grid so that it wastes less energy is one of the largest projects of its kind in the country. On a typical day, the wind turbine at the Miami-Dade Museum can meet about 10 percent of the energy needs in a South Florida home, and the largest wind producer in the country is over at Juno Beach. Right here at this university, your work is helping manufacturers save millions of dollars in energy bills by making their facilities more energy efficient.

So a lot of work is already being done right here, just in this area. And the role of the Federal Government isn't to supplant this work, take over this work, direct this research. It is to support these discoveries. Our job is to help outstanding work that's being done in universities, in labs, and to help businesses get new energy ideas off the ground, because it was public dollars, public research dollars, that over the years helped develop the technologies that companies are right now using to extract all this natural gas out of shale rock.

The payoff on these public investments, they don't always come right away, and some technologies don't pan out, and some companies will fail. But as long as I'm President, I will not walk away from the promise of clean energy. Your future is too important. I will not cede, I will not give up. I will not cede the wind or the solar or the battery industry to China or Germany because some politicians in Washington have refused to make the same commitment here in America.

With or without this Congress, I will continue to do whatever I can to develop every source of American energy so our future isn't controlled by events on the other side of the world.

Today we're taking a step that will make it easier for companies to save money by investing in energy solutions that have been proven here in the University of Miami: new lighting systems, advanced heating and cooling systems that can lower a company's energy bills and make them more competitive.

We're launching a program that will bring together the Nation's best scientists and engineers and entrepreneurs to figure out how more cars can be powered by natural gas, a fuel that's cleaner and cheaper and more abundant than oil. We've got more of that. We don't have to import it. We may be exporting it soon.

We're making new investments in the development of gasoline and diesel and jet fuel that's actually made from a plant-like substance, algae. You've got a bunch of algae out here, right? [*Laughter*] If we can figure out how to make energy out of that, we'll be doing all right.

Believe it or not, we could replace up to 17 percent of the oil we import for transportation with this fuel that we can grow right here in the United States. And that means greater energy security. That means lower costs. It means more jobs. It means a stronger economy.

Now, none of the steps that I've talked about today is going to be a silver bullet. It's not going to bring down gas prices tomorrow. Remember, if anybody says they got a plan for that, what?

Audience members. They're lying.

The President. I'm just saying. We're not going to, overnight, solve the problem of world oil markets. There is no silver bullet. There never has been.

And part of the problem is, is when politicians pretend that there is, then we put off making the tough choices to develop new energy sources and become more energy efficient. We got to stop doing that. We don't have the luxury of pretending. We got to look at the facts, look at the science, figure out what we need to do.

We may not have a silver bullet, but we do have in this country limitless sources of energy, a boundless supply of ingenuity, huge imagination, amazing young people like you—all of which can put—all of which we can put to work to develop this new energy source.

Now, it's the easiest thing in the world to make phony election-year promises about lower gas prices. What's harder is to make a serious, sustained commitment to tackle a problem. And it won't be solved in 1 year, it won't be solved in one term, it may not be completely solved in one decade. But that's the kind of commitment we need right now. That's what this moment requires.

So I need all of you to keep at it. I need you guys to work hard. I need you guys to dream big. I need those of you who are a lot smarter than me to figure out how we're going to be able to tap into new energy sources. We've got to summon the spirit of optimism and that willingness to tackle tough problems that led previous generations to meet the challenges of their times: to power a nation from coast to coast, to send a man to the Moon, to connect an entire world with our own science and our own imagination.

That's what America is capable of. That's what this country is about. And that history teaches us that whatever our challenges—all of them—whatever, whatever we face, we always have the power to solve them.

This is going to be one of the major challenges for your generation. Solving it is going to take time; it's going to take effort. It's going to require our brightest scientists, our most creative companies. But it's going to also require all of us as citizens—Democrats, Republicans, everybody in between—all of us are going to have to do our part.

If we do, the solution is within our reach. And I know we can do it. We have done it before. And when we do, we will remind the world once again just why it is that the United States of America is the greatest country on Earth.

Thank you, everybody. God bless you. God bless America.

NOTE: The President spoke at 2:26 p.m. In his remarks, he referred to Erica C. Hord, student, University of Miami.

Remarks at an Obama Victory Fund 2012 Fundraiser in Coral Gables
February 23, 2012

Hello, hello! Hello, Miami! It is good to see all of you. Thank you so much. Everybody, please have a seat. Thank you.

First of all, I just want you to know that I am resentful I'm not going to the game tonight. [*Laughter*] I am mad about that. It's not right. It's not fair. [*Laughter*] The—but I wish you guys all the best.

I want to, first of all, acknowledge a couple of people who are in the audience. First of all, you just heard from somebody who I don't know where she gets her energy from—[*laughter*]—but is just doing a remarkable job as our DNC chair—Debbie Wasserman Schultz. Give her a big round of applause. Your senior Senator, who I expect to—you will send back to Washington, Bill Nelson is in the house. And my great friend and Florida finance chair, Kirk Wagar is here.

And of course, all of you are here. And this is a good-looking crowd. [*Laughter*]

Audience member. [*Inaudible*]

The President. You, especially. [*Laughter*] You're all raising your hand—"Yes, that's me." [*Laughter*]

Miami, I am here today not just because I need your help, although I do. But I'm here because your country needs your help. There was a reason that so many of you got involved in the campaign back in 2008, and it wasn't because Barack Obama was a sure thing in the campaign. When you're named Barack Hussein Obama, the odds are not in your favor—[*laughter*]—in any election campaign. The reason you got involved was not because of me.

The reason you got involved was because we had a shared vision about what America could be, what America should be. We had an idea of a shared vision of an America in which everybody who works hard, everybody who has a vision of where they want to take their life, they can succeed. Doesn't matter where you come from, doesn't matter what you look like, doesn't matter what your name is. That idea that if you worked hard and took responsibility, that you could buy a home and send your kids

to college and retire with dignity and respect, put a little bit away, that core American Dream felt like it was slipping away for too many people all across the country.

And we shared a vision in which we started making good decisions about energy and health care and education. And instead of trying to divide the country, we tried to bring it together—and that we could assure that America for the next generation and generations to come. That's why you got involved, because of that shared vision we had for America.

Now, 3 years later, I'm a little grayer—[*laughter*]—I'm a little dinged up here and there. But the message I have for you is that because of you, that change that you believed in has begun to happen. As tough as these last 3 years have been, think about everything that we've accomplished together.

Because of you, we averted a great depression. When I took office, 750,000 jobs were being lost every month. Last month, we gained 250,000 jobs. We are moving the economy in the right direction. That's because of you.

Because of you, there are millions of people around the country who didn't have health care and either already have health care or will soon have health care and will never again have to think about going bankrupt just because they get sick. That happened because of you.

Because of you, we were able to take $60 billion that was going to subsidize banks in the student loan program, and we said, why aren't we sending that money directly to students? And as a consequence, we now have millions of young people all across the country who are getting higher Pell grants or are eligible for Pell grants for the first time or are seeing their student loan interest rates lower have access to college and the keys to the American Dream. That happened because of you. That's what change is.

Change is the decision to rescue the American auto industry from collapse. You remember there were a lot of people who didn't believe in that. Even when some politicians said we should just let Detroit go bankrupt, we stepped up. And as a consequence, probably a million jobs were saved and the American auto industry has come roaring back and GM is now once again the number-one automaker in the world. That happened because of you.

Change is the decision we made to start doing something about our oil addiction, not waiting for Congress. And so in a historic step, even without legislation, we doubled fuel efficiency standards on cars, applied them to light trucks, heavy trucks for the first time. It will save consumers billions of dollars. It will help our environment. It puts us at the forefront of the electric car industry, at the forefront of the clean energy industry. That all happened because of you.

Because of you, people across the country are going to still be able to serve the country they love, regardless of who they love. "Don't ask, don't tell" is history. That happened because of you.

Change is keeping another promise that I made back in 2008. For the first time in 9 years, there are no Americans fighting in Iraq. We have refocused our efforts on those who carried out 9/11. Al Qaida is being dismantled, and Usama bin Laden will never again walk the face of the Earth. And that happened because of you.

So a lot's happened in 3 years. And none of this has been easy. None of this was automatic. Oftentimes we faced enormous opposition. And obviously, we're still recovering from the worst recession that we've had in our lifetimes. So we've got so much more work to do. But as I said, the good news is we're moving in the right direction.

Over the last 2 years, the private sector has created about 3.7 million new jobs—3.7 million new jobs. Our manufacturers are creating jobs for the first time since the 1990s. Our economy is getting stronger. The recovery is accelerating. America is coming back, which means the last thing we can afford to do is to go back to the same policies that got us into this mess in the first place. That's what we can't afford.

Now, that's what the other candidates want to do. Now, I don't know if you guys have been watching the Republican primary debates, in case you need an incentive. [*Laughter*] They make no secret about what they want to do. They want to go back to the days when Wall Street played by its own rules. They want to go back to the days when insurance companies could deny you coverage or jack up your premiums without reason. They want to spend trillions more on tax breaks for the wealthiest individuals, for people like me, who don't need it, weren't even asking for it, even if it means adding to the deficit, even if it means gutting our investments in education or clean energy or making it harder for seniors on Medicare. Their philosophy is simple: We are better off when everybody is left to fend for themselves, everybody makes their own rules, a few do very well at the top, and everybody else is struggling to get by. That's their core vision for America.

We've got a different vision. We see America as a bigger, bolder place. I'm here to tell them they are wrong about America. Because in America, we understand, yes, we're rugged individuals, yes, we don't expect a handout, we are going to do everything we can to make it and fulfill our dreams, but we also understand we are greater together than we are on our own. We're better off when we keep that basic American promise that if you work hard, you can do well, you can succeed, that you can own that home and send that—send your kids to college and put away something for retirement.

And that's the choice in this election. This is not just a political debate. This goes to who we are as a people, because we are in a make-or-break moment for the middle class and people who are trying to get in the middle class. And we can go back to an economy that is built on outsourcing and bad debt and phony financial profits; or we can build an economy that lasts, an economy that's built on American manufacturing, skills and education for American workers, and American-made energy, and most importantly, the values that have always made America great: hard work, fair play, shared responsibility.

We've got to make sure that the next generation of manufacturing ideas take place right here in the United States of America. Not in factories in Europe or China, but in Detroit and Pittsburgh and Cleveland. I don't want this Nation to be known just for buying and consuming things. I want us to be selling our products and making our products, inventing products, all around the world. That's who we are. It's time for us to stop rewarding businesses that ship jobs overseas. We need to reward companies that are investing and hiring right here in the United States of America.

We need to make our schools the envy of the world. And that starts with the man or woman at the front of the classroom. A study recently showed a good teacher can increase the lifetime income of a classroom by $250,000. A great teacher can help a child escape poor circumstances and achieve their dreams.

So I don't want to hear folks in Washington bash teachers. I don't want them defending the status quo. I want to give schools the resources they need to keep good teachers on the job. Reward the best ones, give schools flexibility to teach with creativity, stop teaching to the test.

Audience member. That's right.

The President. Replace teachers who aren't helping our kids. We can do those things. [*Applause*] We've got some teachers in the house. [*Applause*]

When kids graduate, I want them to be able to afford to go to college. If they've been working hard, if they've gotten the grades to go to college, I don't want them to cut their dreams short because they don't think they can afford it.

Right now Americans owe more in tuition debt than they do in credit card debt. And that means Congress is going to have to stop the interest rates on student loans from going up. They're scheduled to go up in July right now. Colleges and universities are going to have to do their part. I've said to them—and I've met with university and college presidents—we're going to keep on helping students afford to go to college. You've got to do your job in terms of keeping tuition down, because taxpayers can't fund this stuff forever. Higher education can't be a luxury; it's an economic necessity, an economic imperative for every family in America. And they should be able to afford it.

An America built to last is one where we're supporting scientists and researchers trying to find the next breakthrough in clean energy, making sure that happens right here in the United States. You know, we've subsidized oil companies for a century. It's time to end a hundred years of subsidies for an industry that's rarely been more profitable and make sure that we're doubling down on clean energy that's never been more promising: solar power and wind power, biofuels that can break our addiction to foreign oil, create jobs here in America. It's good for our national security, it's good for our economy, it's good for your pocketbook.

We need to build our infrastructure. I'm a chauvinist; I want America to have the best stuff. I want us to have the best airports and the best roads and the best ports right here in Miami that can create more jobs.

So what I've said is, let's take the money we're no longer spending on war, let's use half of it to reduce the deficit, let's spend the other half to do some nation-building right here at home. Let's put folks to work.

And we've got to make sure that everybody is doing their fair share. Everybody needs a fair shot, everybody has got to play by the same set of rules, everybody has got to do their fair share.

And when it comes to paying for our Government and making sure the investments are there so that future generations can succeed, everybody has got to do their part. Which is why I put forward the Buffett rule: If you make more than a million dollars a year, you should not pay a lower tax rate than your secretary. That's common sense. We've said if you make $250,000 a year or less, you don't need your taxes going up right now. But folks like me, we can afford to do a little bit more.

That's not class warfare. That's not envy. It has to do with simple math. If somebody like me gets a tax break that the country can't afford, then one of two things happen: Either the deficit goes up, which is irresponsible, or we're taking it out of somebody else: that student who is now suddenly having to pay a higher student loan rate or that senior who's having to pay more for Medicare or that veteran who's not getting the help they need after having served our country.

That's not right. That's not who we are. Everybody in this room, we are here, successful, because somebody down the road was not just thinking about themselves, they were taking responsibility for the country as a whole. They we're thinking about their future. The American story has never been about what we just do by ourselves, it's about what we do together. We're not going to win the race for new jobs and new businesses and middle class security if we're responding to today's challenges with the same old, tired, worn-out, you're-on-your-own economics that hasn't worked.

What these other guys are peddling has not worked. It didn't work in the decade before the Great Depression. It did not work in the decade before I became President. It will not work now.

And this is not just a matter of economics. Look, we all have a stake in everybody's success. If we attract an outstanding teacher by giving her the pay that she deserves and giving her the training that she needs and she goes on to teach the next Steve Jobs, we all benefit. If we provide faster Internet service so that some storeowner in rural America suddenly can sell their products all around the world, or if we build a new bridge that saves a shipping company time and money, workers, consumers, all of us benefit. We all do better.

This has never been a Democratic or Republican idea. This is an American idea. It was the first Republican President, Abraham Lincoln, who launched a transcontinental railroad, the National Academy of Sciences, the first land-grant colleges, all in the middle of the Civil War. Think about that. I'm sure there were some folks at the time who were saying: "Why are we doing all that? I don't want to pay for that." But that laid the groundwork for a national economy.

A Republican, Teddy Roosevelt, called for a progressive income tax. Dwight Eisenhower built the Interstate Highway System. Republicans supported FDR when he gave millions of returning heroes, including my grandfather, the chance to go to college on the GI bill.

Everybody here has a similar story. I mean, think about Florida, think about Miami; it's a microcosm of the country, people from all over the world coming here, seeking opportunity. And the reason people came here, people—the reason people continue to come to America, is because there is a recognition that in America we will create the platform for people to succeed if they work hard. That's what is at stake in this election.

And I have to tell you that that sense of common purpose that binds us together regardless of our backgrounds, that still exists today. It may not exist in Washington, but out in the country it's there. You talk to folks on Main Streets, town hall meetings, you go to a VFW hall, you go to a coffee shop—it's there. You talk to the incredible members of our Armed Forces, the men and women in uniform—it's there. You go to places of worship, that sense of a bond to something larger—it's there.

So our politics may be divided—and obviously, the media loves to portray conflict—but most Americans, they understand that we're in this together, that no matter who we are, where we come from, whether you are Black or White or Latino or Asian or Native American, gay, straight, disabled or not, that we rise or fall as one Nation, as one people. And that's what's at stake right now. That's what we are fighting for. That's what we've been fighting for, for the last 3 years.

And so the main message I have to all of you is, as tough as these last 3 years have been, that that vision you had that led you to get involved, you're not alone in that vision.

I know the change we fought for in 2008 sometimes hasn't come as fast as we want it. There have been setbacks. There have been controversies. And with everything that's happened in Washington, sometimes, it's tempting to believe that, well, maybe that change we hoped for isn't completely possible. But remember what I said during the last campaign. People don't remember. People have a revisionist history. They remember the time from Grant Park until the inauguration. They don't remember how hard it was to get to Grant Park. [*Laughter*]

But I told you then, I said real change, big change is hard and it's going to take time. It takes more than a single term. It takes more than a single President. Most of all, what it requires is individual citizens like you who are committed to keeping up the fight, to pushing and struggling and nudging the country so that it slowly inches closer and closer and closer to our highest ideals.

The other thing I told you in 2008 was I'm not a perfect man. If you hadn't talked to Michelle, you—[*laughter*]—in the interest of full disclosure, I told you I'm not perfect, and I won't be a perfect President. But you know what I promised? I said I'd always tell you what I thought, I'd always tell you where I stood,

and I'd wake up every single day fighting as hard as I can for you. I've kept that promise. I've kept that promise.

So, if you're willing to keep pushing with me, if you're willing to keep struggling with me, if you're continuing to reach out for that vision of America that we all share, I promise you change will come. If you are willing to get just as involved and engaged and motivated in 2012 as you were in 2008, I promise you we're going to finish what we started. If you stick with me, if you press with me, we will remind the world once again just why it is that America is the greatest country on Earth.

Thank you, everybody. God bless you. Thank you. God bless America.

NOTE: The President spoke at 4:03 p.m. at the Biltmore Hotel. In his remarks, he referred to Warren E. Buffett, chief executive officer and chairman, Berkshire Hathaway Inc.

Remarks at an Obama Victory Fund 2012 Fundraiser in Pinecrest, Florida
February 23, 2012

Thank you. Well, good afternoon, everybody. What a spectacular setting and a beautiful evening. I want to thank Chris and Irene and the whole Korge family. You guys have been great friends for a really long time. So please give them a big round of applause.

You have one of the finest Senators in the country, Bill Nelson. I expect you to send him back to Washington. Plus, he's an astronaut. I always say this. [*Laughter*] You know, there are a lot of folks who are Senators; there aren't that many astronauts. So we are so proud of him. And what can I say about Debbie Wasserman Schultz? She is tireless, she is smart, and she is just fearless. And so we could not have a better person to help lead the party.

And to so many of you who have been supportive for so long, all the people that Chris mentioned, but a lot of folks who are here who have worked tirelessly not only on behalf of my campaign, but on behalf of good causes here in Florida and around the country, I am grateful to all of you.

I just noticed, by the way, we've got one other person that needs to be acknowledged because some of you will be spending some time with him in September, and that is the mayor of Charlotte, North Carolina, our host for the Democratic National Convention, Anthony Foxx is in the house.

Now, in settings like this, where I'm among friends, I try to not speak long at the top because I want to spend most of my time in a conversation with you, in answering questions and getting ideas and comments from you. And part of the reason I don't have to speak long at the top is because Chris stole a bunch of my lines. [*Laughter*]

Think about where we were in 2008. And sometimes people forget. The stock market was in a freefall. We were losing 750,000 jobs a month. The bottom had fallen off of the housing market. The entire financial system was locked up. Blue-chip companies couldn't borrow money. And people weren't certain whether we were going to spiral into a Great Depression.

Three years later, instead of losing 750,000 jobs a month, we created 250,000 last month. Over the last 2 years, we've created 3.7 million jobs in the private sector. And we've actually seen manufacturing job growth for the first time since the 1990s. So the economy is moving in the right direction. We've got some headwinds: Europe is still weak; gas prices are a huge burden on families. But overall, considering where we were and where we could have been, I think most Americans recognize that things have stabilized and we're moving in a better direction.

The challenge we have is we don't want to just get back to where we were, because part of what led me to run in the first place was the recognition that for too many families, the middle class idea, the American Dream was slipping away. Wages were stagnant. A few of us were doing very well, including most of us who are here today. But there were a whole bunch of folks who were having trouble just hanging on to their home, hanging on to the idea of sending their kids to college. And those who wanted to get in the middle class, who wanted to follow the same path that so many of our families, our parents, our grandparents followed—working hard, playing by the rules, dreaming big dreams—those ladders were being taken away from too many people.

So what we've done, even as we focused on the economy, was also to say, what are those ingredients that are going to make sure that America has an economy that's built to last over the long term? And that means resuscitating, reviving American manufacturing, which is why I am so proud of what's happened in the auto industry, because it's an example of what can happen in manufacturing across the board. We had some folks who said let's let that die. Instead, GM is back to number one, seeing the greatest profits that it's seen in its history, hired back tens of thousands of workers. And that's true across the U.S. auto industry.

We said that we've got to start developing American energy. We've doubled clean energy since I've been President. And even as we've increased production of oil, we've recognized we've got to transition so that our kids and our grandkids are able to enjoy not only economic growth and not be dependent on what's happening in the Middle East or someplace else, but also we're able to protect the planet.

We said that we've got to focus on American skills and education. And we now have 40 States that have initiated reforms because of what we did. And college is more accessible to more young people—millions of young people—because of policies that we put forward.

And at the same time, we said we've got to make sure that America is fair, that everybody gets a fair shot, which means that you don't have to worry about who you love to serve the country that you love, and we ended "don't ask, don't tell." It means that the first bill I signed into law said equal pay for equal work. I want my daughters paid the same as your sons when they get a job.

And it means that we have a tax system that encourages economic growth, that helps to bring down our deficit, that pays for the investments that we need and says folks like me can afford to do a little bit more, that it doesn't make sense to give me tax breaks I don't need if it means making some senior citizen pay more for her Medicare or making a student pay more for their student load or a veteran maybe doesn't get the kind of help that they need coming home and they've got posttraumatic stress disorder.

Internationally, I promised to end one war; it's ended. We're transitioning to end another one. We've restored respect for the United States around the world. And don't take my word for it. If any of you do international business, they will tell you that the attitude about America is fundamentally different now than it was when we first took office. And that makes us safer. And we've been able to do that without lessening the pressure—in fact, increasing the pressure—on those who carried out 9/11 and threatened to do us the most harm, which is why Al Qaida is on the ropes and bin Laden is no more.

So we've got a good story to tell about the last 3 years, but I'm not done yet. I need 5 more years. We need 5 more years to reform an immigration system that doesn't work and make sure that we are a nation of laws and a nation of immigrants. We need 5 more years because we still have to implement energy policies that work for everybody. And that means continuing to push on clean energy and energy efficiency.

I was over at the University of Miami, where these amazing engineering students are helping businesses right now save millions of dollars just by making their physical plants and equipment more energy efficient.

That's more work to do. We've got to follow through and implement health care reform legislation so that 30 million people have health insurance who wouldn't otherwise have it and to make sure that 2.5 million young people who already have health care because of that health care bill—because they can stay on their parents' health insurance—that they don't lose it.

We're going to have to make sure that we effectively implement Wall Street reform. I want our financial sector to be the most vibrant in the world, but I also want it to not engage in the kind of recklessness that may lead to another big bailout. We can't afford it.

And we're going to have to continue to invest in our infrastructure: the Port of Miami, all across the country, roads, bridges, airports, school buildings, science labs.

There's so much more that we've got to do, and I'm only going to be able to do it because of you. You are going to have to send back Bill Nelson. You're going to have to elect Mr. Murphy. We're going to need strong partners in Congress, but—well, Debbie is probably—I don't know, what are you, 30 in the polls? [*Laughter*]

But the most important thing I'm going to need is all of you sustaining that same sense of hope and vision for the future that led you to get involved in that campaign back in 2008. And if you do that, we can't lose. Because the American people, they have deep in their core, deep in their gut, a belief that we are all in this together, that we look out for one another, that our country is at its best when everybody, regardless of what you look like, where you come from, what your last name is, what your sexual orientation is, regardless of who you are, you deserve a fair shot in life.

That's what America is about. That's what we're fighting for. That's what this election is going to be about. And that's why I'm grateful for your help.

Thanks, everybody. And thank you to the staff back there for all the great help. I appreciate you.

NOTE: The President spoke at 5:35 p.m. at the residence of Christopher G. and Irene Korge. In his remarks, he referred to Rep. Deborah Wasserman Schultz, chair, Democratic National Committee; and Democratic congressional candidate Patrick E. Murphy. Audio was not available for verification of the content of these remarks.

Letter to Congressional Leaders on Continuation of the National Emergency With Respect to Cuba and of the Emergency Authority Relating to the Regulation of the Anchorage and Movement of Vessels
February 23, 2012

Dear Mr. Speaker: (Dear Mr. President:)

Section 202(d) of the National Emergencies Act (50 U.S.C. 1622(d)) provides for the automatic termination of a national emergency unless, within 90 days prior to the anniversary date of its declaration, the President publishes in the *Federal Register* and transmits to the Congress a notice stating that the emergency is to continue in effect beyond the anniversary date. In accordance with this provision, I have sent the enclosed notice to the *Federal Register* for publication, stating that the national emergency declared with respect to the Government of Cuba's destruction of two unarmed U.S.-registered civilian aircraft in international airspace north of Cuba on February 24, 1996, as amended and expanded on February 26, 2004, is to continue in effect beyond March 1, 2012.

Sincerely,

BARACK OBAMA

NOTE: Identical letters were sent to John A. Boehner, Speaker of the House of Representatives, and Joseph R. Biden, Jr., President of the Senate. The notice is listed in Appendix D at the end of this volume.

Letter to Congressional Leaders on Continuation of the National Emergency With Respect to Libya
February 23, 2012

Dear Mr. Speaker: (Dear Mr. President:)

Section 202(d) of the National Emergencies Act (50 U.S.C. 1622(d)) provides for the automatic termination of a national emergency unless, within 90 days prior to the anniversary date of its declaration, the President publishes in the *Federal Register* and transmits to the Congress a notice stating that the emergency is to continue in effect beyond the anniversary date. In accordance with this provision, I have sent to the *Federal Register* for publication the enclosed notice stating that the national emergency declared in Executive Order 13566 of February 25, 2011, is to continue in effect beyond February 25, 2012.

Colonel Muammar Qadhafi, his government, and close associates took extreme measures against the people of Libya, including by using weapons of war, mercenaries, and wanton violence against unarmed civilians. In addition, there was a serious risk that Libyan state assets would be misappropriated by Qadhafi, members of his government, members of his family, or his close associates if those assets were not protected. The foregoing circumstances, the prolonged attacks, and the increased numbers of Libyans seeking refuge in other countries caused a deterioration in the security of Libya, posed a serious risk to its stability, and led me to declare a national emergency to deal with this threat to the national security and foreign policy of the United States.

We are in the process of winding down the sanctions in response to the many positive developments in Libya, including the fall of Qadhafi and his government. We are working closely with the new Libyan government and with the international community to effectively and appropriately ease restrictions on sanctioned entities, including by taking actions consistent with the U.N. Security Council's decision to lift sanctions against the Central Bank of Libya and two other entities on December 16, 2011. However, the situation in Libya continues to pose an unusual and extraordinary threat to the national security and foreign policy of the United States and we need to protect against this threat and the diversion of assets or other abuse by certain members of Qadhafi's family and other former regime officials. Therefore, I have determined that it is necessary to continue the national emergency with respect to Libya.

Sincerely,

BARACK OBAMA

NOTE: Identical letters were sent to John A. Boehner, Speaker of the House of Representatives, and Joseph R. Biden, Jr., President of the Senate. The notice is listed in Appendix D at the end of this volume.

Remarks at an Obama Victory Fund 2012 Fundraiser in Orlando, Florida
February 23, 2012

Thank you, everybody. Everybody, please have a seat. Have a seat. First of all, I just want to thank Vince and the whole family for setting up this unbelievable event. This is a nice gym. [*Laughter*] So Vince said that he left the other side open in case I wanted to get in a dunk contest with him. But I told him I didn't bring my sneakers, so not tonight. [*Laughter*]

But Vince has been so generous, along with his mom and the whole family, for the last couple of years. And it's a huge treat for me because I'm such a fan of his ever since he was playing for the Tar Heels. I know Reggie Love is not here, so I can praise the Tar Heels. [*Laughter*] But always conducting himself with such dignity and class and now doing such great work with the Mavericks. I know that Mark Cuban is pretty happy about having Vince around.

I see a lot of other friends in the room. Alonzo and Tracy have been there for me every time I've come to Florida. I could not be more grateful for that. Magic and Cookie, wherever I go in California, they're there for us. Chris is helping out on our Fitness Council and allowed me to cross over on him when we played during my birthday. [*Laughter*] He insists that he could have stolen the ball at any time. [*Laughter*] But I'm going to still claim it.

In addition, I want to make sure that I acknowledge, first of all, the mayor of Orlando, Buddy Dyer is here. An outstanding Senator for Florida, but also just a great Senator for the country, Bill Nelson is here. And I always have to remind people Bill was an astronaut before he was a Senator. So being a Senator is cool. Being an astronaut is cooler. [*Laughter*] And his lovely wife Grace, it's wonderful to see you.

And the chair of the Democratic National Committee, Debbie Wasserman Schultz is here. So we love Debbie.

I also understand that Commissioner Stern is here. And I just want to say that—thank you so much for settling the lockout. [*Laughter*] Because I don't know what I would be doing with myself if I didn't at least have some basketball games around. And obviously, we're looking forward to the All-Star Game. The game down in Miami is tight, by the way. I just—I was checking on the score as I was flying up.

We've gone through 3 of the toughest years this country has gone through in my lifetime. And there are a lot of people who are still hurting all across the country, a lot of people here in Florida, a lot of people everywhere. There are still folks whose homes are underwater because the housing market collapsed. There are people who are still struggling because they can't find a job. There are folks who are just barely able to make ends meet. And obviously, those of us who are here, we've been incredibly blessed. But one of the great things about America and one of the great things about those who are in professional sports is we've all got cousins, uncles, family members who are still struggling and are a reminder that we have a lot more work to do.

The good news is that the country has begun to move in the right direction. So, when I took office, we were losing 750,000 jobs a month; last month, we gained 250,000. We stabilized the financial system. We've now created 3.7 million jobs over the last 2 years. Businesses are starting to invest again. Consumer confidence is up. People are buying tickets to the games. And there's a general sense that we may have weathered the worst of the storm.

That's the good news. The challenge, though, is when I ran in 2008, it wasn't just to tread water, it wasn't just to avert a great depression and then get back to where we were in 2007 and 2008, because people were already struggling then. There were too many communities where if a child was born in poverty, they didn't have any ladders to get out, where middle class families were struggling to get by, even though now you had both mom and dad working and they still didn't have enough in their paychecks to be able to make ends meet.

A few people were doing very well. And what used to be the core of America's middle class felt like it was falling behind. And so as a consequence, even as we've made sure to do everything we can to dig ourselves out of this incredible hole that I inherited, even as we have strengthened the economy and focused like a laser on how do we put people back to work, we've also tried to say, how do we rebuild America in a way where everybody has got a fair shot, everybody is doing their fair share, everybody is playing by the same set of rules, everybody who is willing to take responsibility and work hard, they can get ahead? And that's been our challenge.

And so in addition to the stuff that we've done to make sure that folks are getting back to work, we've also said nobody should go bankrupt because they get sick in this country, and we were able to pass a health care bill that is already providing 2.5 million young people insurance who didn't have it before and, by the time it's fully implemented, will give 30 million people health insurance, the kind of security that we take for granted where if our child gets sick or a family member falls ill, that they know that they're going to be able to get well without having to lose their home.

That's why we focused on education, and we've said that not only do we want to improve K through 12 so that every child is getting the basics—math and science and English—but we want everybody to be able to go to college. And we took $60 billion that was going to—that was being channeled to the banks as subsidies through the student loan program, and we said let's take that money and give it directly to students so that we could expand Pell grants and we could make sure that every—young people who want to go to college can afford to do so. Because right now, actually, student loan debt is higher than credit card debt in this country. And it's a huge burden on the next generation, and we have to start relieving it.

We said, we've got to have an energy policy that makes sense and that includes developing oil and gas resources in this country, but it also means focusing on clean energy. And here in Florida, we've seen enormous progress on things like solar and wind and biodiesel. But we've got to do more: making sure that our

cars are more energy efficient, making sure that we're not prey to, every year right around this time, oil spiking because something is going on in the Middle East, and our whole economy is suddenly vulnerable.

And we focused on making sure that our tax system is fair. What I've said consistently is, look, I don't like paying taxes any more than anybody else does, and I'm the President. Now, here's the thing about being President, you pay every dime. You don't take advantage of any loopholes—[*laughter*]—because everybody sees your income tax returns. So I'm probably in the top bracket in every category.

But what I've said is Michelle and I have been so blessed, we can afford to do a little bit more to make sure that the next generation is able to come back up, is able to achieve their dreams the same way Michelle and I did. Because we think about our stories. I was raised by a single mom. Michelle was raised by a blue-collar worker and a secretary. My mother-in-law, even though she lives with us now, she's kept her home back in Chicago. It's now her house, but when they were growing up it was actually my mother-in-law's sister's house and Michelle's family lived on the top floor, the second floor of this bungalow. It couldn't have been more than 600 square feet where four people grew up.

And yet she was able to go to a quality public school, go to Princeton, go to Harvard Law School, because somebody made an investment in her. Somebody said, you know what, we want to make sure everybody has opportunity. And that's the same way I was able to get ahead, is because somebody made an investment in me.

And so what I've said is, as President, we welcome success. We want somebody like a Vince Carter to be able to build a house like this. But we want to make sure that that next generation is able to do just as well, because they're young people, just as—they might not have the same vertical as Vince—[*laughter*]. But they've got the same talents in something else, maybe in science, maybe in the arts, maybe in engineering, maybe they could be a doctor or a lawyer. And I don't want to pull up the ladder behind me. And I don't think anybody here does either.

And that's what's at stake in this election. What's at stake in this election is whether we as a country are going to continue to look out for one another and be able to say that it doesn't matter what you look like, where you come from, what your name is, that if you're willing to work hard, you can get ahead.

And that is an experience that is true for everybody in this room at some level. Somewhere in your past you had an immigrant mother or grandmother or great-grandmother or great-grandfather who came to this country with not much and was able to create a life for themselves. And in the debate that's going to be unfolding over the next several months, you seem to see a philosophy on the other side that says, basically, you know what, it's fine if a few of us do well and everybody else is struggling.

And that's not how America got built. That's not what makes America strong. The reason we were the envy of the world is because we had this massive middle class and you could get rich here in America, but there was also the possibility of everybody getting ahead.

I love looking at Magic's story, for example. His dad, when you talk about basketball, you learned your work ethic from your dad, right, working every day driving a truck, right? Well, you know what, that was a life of dignity and respect. You weren't a celebrity. You might not make millions of dollars, but you could raise a family and have a home and pass on to your son those same values.

And that's what we're fighting for here. That's the struggle. It has to do with our values and who we are as Americans. So the good

news is, as I travel around the country, most Americans agree with me.

One of the things about being President is when things are going tough everybody looks to you and says, why haven't you fixed it yet? And that's okay. That's what you sign up for. As Michelle always reminds me, you volunteered for this. [*Laughter*]

But no matter where I go around the country, whether it's in a big city or a rural community—north, south, east, west—I meet the most incredible people, and they still have confidence and optimism in America's possibilities. They get frustrated with Washington, but they still believe in what we can accomplish as a country when we work together.

And that's what we're going to continue to strive for over the next several months. And that's what we're going to continue to strive for over the next 5 years with your help.

So thank you very much, everybody, for being here. I appreciate it.

NOTE: The President spoke at 9 p.m. at the residence of Vince Carter, guard-forward, National Basketball Association's Dallas Mavericks. In his remarks, he referred to Michelle Carter-Scott, mother of Mr. Carter; Reginald L. Love, former Personal Aide to the President; Mark Cuban, owner, Dallas Mavericks; Alonzo Mourning, center, NBA's Miami Heat, and his wife Tracy; former NBA player Earvin "Magic" Johnson, Jr., his wife Earlitha "Cookie" Johnson, and his father Earvin Johnson, Sr.; Chris Paul, point guard, NBA's Los Angeles Clippers; and David J. Stern, commissioner, National Basketball Association. He also referred to his mother-in-law Marian Robinson. Audio was not available for verification of the content of these remarks.

Remarks Following a Meeting With Prime Minister Helle Thorning-Schmidt of Denmark
February 24, 2012

President Obama. Well, I want to welcome Prime Minister Thorning-Schmidt to the White House and to the Oval Office. This is the first time that we've had a chance to meet,

but obviously, we've been very impressed with the first 5 months of her Prime Ministership. I shared with her how much Michelle and I appreciated the extraordinary hospitality that was shown to Michelle and I when I visited Copenhagen in the past. And I also wanted to just say how much we appreciate the great alliance and partnership that we have with the Danish people on a whole range of international issues.

Obviously, most recently, the operations in Libya could not have been as effective had it not been for the precision and the excellence of the Danish armed forces and their pilots. But that's fairly typical of the way that Danes have punched above their weight in international affairs.

In Afghanistan, I thanked the Prime Minister for the extraordinary contributions of Danish troops in the Helmand area. They operate without caveat, have taken significant casualties, for which obviously all of us extend our condolences to the families that have been affected. But because of the outstanding work that's been done by Danish soldiers in Afghanistan, we're seeing great progress in the areas where they operate.

We had a chance to talk about the economy. We—as we were exchanging notes, it turns out that, like folks here in the United States, everybody in Denmark wants to talk about the economy all the time and jobs and growth. And we agreed that there has been some progress in resolving the sovereign debt issues, that there's been some progress with respect to the agreements between the EU and the IMF and Greece, the new Government in Italy, new Governments in Spain and Portugal are all making some significant progress, but that there's a lot more work to do. And we will be consulting closely with Denmark.

And we exchanged ideas on how we can ensure not only economic stability in Europe, but also growth in Europe, because if Europe is growing, then that benefits the U.S. economy as well. And we've emphasized, are there additional ways that we can encourage trade and reduce economic frictions between the two sides of the transatlantic relationship.

In preparation for our meeting in Chicago, at NATO, in my hometown, we talked about the transition that was already agreed to in Lisbon, when it comes to putting Afghans in the lead in security over the next several years.

And we are going to be consulting closely with not only Denmark, but our other allies in making sure that that is a smooth transition and one that is sustainable, where we continue to help the Afghan Government to support its own sovereignty and to effectively control its borders.

We also discussed the extraordinary counterterrorism cooperation that's taking place between our two countries. And I thanked the Prime Minister for the excellent work that her intelligence team has done. We are in constant communication on a whole host of issues. The Danes are very much one of the leaders when it comes to counterterrorism and are obviously familiar with the significant threats that are posed by terrorism. So we appreciated that very much.

And we had a chance to talk about a wide range of international issues, including the situation in Syria. And I have to say that all of us who've been seeing the terrible pictures coming out of Syria and Homs recently recognize it is absolutely imperative for the international community to rally and send a clear message to President Asad that it is time for a transition, it is time for that regime to move on, and it is time to stop the killing of Syrian citizens by their own Government.

And I'm encouraged by the international unity that we are developing, the meeting that took place in Tunisia that Secretary Clinton had attended. And we are going to continue to keep the pressure up and look for every tool available to prevent the slaughter of innocents in Syria. And this is an area where I think the Prime Minister and I deeply agree. It's important that we not be bystanders during these extraordinary events.

At the same time, there are other threats in the region, including the situation in Iran. And I thanked the Prime Minister and the Danish Government for their leadership role in applying the toughest sanctions we've ever seen coming out of the EU. Difficult sanctions to apply, but we both agreed that we're making progress and they are working in sending a message to Iran that it needs to take a different path if it wants to rejoin the international community and that there is a expectation on the part of the world that they abide by their international obligations when it comes to their nuclear program.

So the final thing we talked about was the fact that we both have two daughters. [*Laughter*] They're roughly the same ages. We traded notes. The Prime Minister's daughters are slightly older than Malia and Sasha. She assures me that they continue to behave themselves, even well into their teenage years. So I'm encouraged by that report. [*Laughter*]

Prime Minister Thorning-Schmidt. Very good.

President Obama. And I thank you very much. I hope that you have a wonderful stay while you're here, and we look forward to working with you again in the near future.

Prime Minister Thorning-Schmidt. Thank you, Mr. President. And thank you so much for your kind words. I mean, the Danish people have a very strong sense of closeness to the United States. We always have had that sense. We have close economic, political ties with each other. But not only that, we exchange— we have exchanged tourism, students, ideas, culture. But perhaps most important of all, we have—we share common values. And I think in a turbulent time, this is very, very important.

So, basically, the friendship and the alliance between our two countries is in a very good shape right now. And I thank you for that.

As you said, we discussed the economic situation. Denmark holds the Presidency of the EU right now, and we talk about the debt situation most of the time in Europe. I conveyed the message to the President that I am convinced that we will see our self through this crisis. We have now put some very important measures in place. We have fiscal consultation, we have reforms, and we have a focus on growth and jobs right now.

In doing that, in this endeavor, I think a closer transatlantic relationship would be important. We are dependent on each other, and we should have closer trade with each other, and I think that would be part of creating a sustainable growth in our countries.

As you were saying, Mr. President, we also have close ties in terms of security. It is clear— it has been for a long time—that Danish soldiers are serving alongside American soldiers in Afghanistan, and I used the opportunity today to thank you and the American people for the great effort you have put in Afghanistan. It is greatly appreciated worldwide. And I know that the Danish people really appreciate the global leadership that you and your people have taken also in that context.

I look forward, of course, to coming back to the States, to your hometown, Chicago, to participate in the NATO summit. What we will be discussing there is Afghanistan, of course. One of the major issues there is to transition to the next phase in Afghanistan, and where—what we want to see is the Afghans taking responsibility for their own security. And we are, in Europe, with the—under Danish leadership, trying to gather donors in this—in securing that the Afghans are capable of taking over their own security.

We have some great examples of our alliance. We have worked together, again, in Libya, where we made sure that we—that Libya came out on a path of democracy. And I think, again, the Americans showed leadership in that context.

Another area that we discussed, as you've said, was Syria, which is quite the opposite situation. It is horrendous what we see in Syria right now. But I think it is also very, very true that we have worked together in that area. We must continue that endeavor, and just today we have seen that, under the leadership of the League of Arab States, there has been a step forward in trying to put pressure on Syria, which is very, very important. The same, of course, goes for Iran.

Another area in security where we work together is in terms of piracy, and I used the opportunity of thanking sincerely the President for the courageous operation that led to the freeing of two aid workers that worked for the Danish Refugee Council. They are now safe because of the Americans. Thank you for that.

So, basically, our security—our cooperation in terms of security are very great indeed.

I will finish here just by saying that I think our meeting here today has confirmed the friendship and the alliance between our two countries. We—there's a lot we can do that—you're always welcome to come to Denmark—and I think it is very, very important that we have these kind of meetings to renew the friendship, and this is what we've done today.

Thank you.

President Obama. Okay. Thank you very much, everybody.

NOTE: The President spoke at 3:41 p.m. in the Oval Office at the White House. In his remarks, he referred to Johanna and Camilla Kinnock, daughters of Prime Minister Thorning-Schmidt. Prime Minister Thorning-Schmidt referred to Jessica Buchanan of the United States, and Poul Hagen Thisted of Denmark, who were rescued in a Navy SEAL operation on January 24, after being held hostage by Somali pirates in Galcayo, Somalia, since October 25, 2011.

The President's Weekly Address
February 25, 2012

Hi, everybody. In the State of the Union, I laid out three areas we need to focus on if we're going to build an economy that lasts: new American manufacturing, new skills and education for American workers, and new sources of American-made energy.

These days, we're getting another painful reminder why developing new energy is so important to our future. Just like they did last year, gas prices are starting to climb. Only this time, it's happening earlier. And that hurts everyone: everybody who owns a car, everybody who owns a business. It means you have to stretch your paycheck even further. Some folks have no choice but to drive a long way to work, and high gas prices are like a tax straight out of their paychecks.

Now, some politicians always see this as a political opportunity. And since it's an election year, they're already dusting off their same three-point plan for $2 gas. I'll save you the suspense: Step one, according to them, is drill; step two is drill; and step three is to keep drilling. We hear the same thing every year. We've heard the same thing for 30 years.

Well the American people aren't stupid. You know that's not a plan, especially since we're already drilling. It's a bumper sticker. It's not a strategy to solve our energy challenge. It's a strategy to get politicians through an election.

You know there are no quick fixes to this problem, and you know we can't just drill our way to lower gas prices. If we're going to take control of our energy future and avoid these gas price spikes down the line, then we need a sustained all-of-the-above strategy that develops every available source of American energy: oil, gas, wind, solar, nuclear, biofuels, and more. We need to keep developing the technology that allows us to use less oil in our cars and trucks, in our buildings and plants. That's the strategy we're pursuing, and that's the only real solution to this challenge.

Now, we absolutely need safe, responsible oil production here in America. And that's why under my administration, America is producing more oil today than at any time in the last 8 years. In 2010, our dependence on foreign oil was under 50 percent for the first time in more than a decade. And while there are no short-term silver bullets when it comes to gas prices, I've directed my administration to look for every single area where we can make an impact and help consumers in the months ahead, from permitting, to delivery bottlenecks, to what's going on in the oil markets.

But over the long term, an all-of-the-above energy strategy means we have to do more. It means we have to make some choices.

Here's one example: Right now 4 billion of your tax dollars subsidize the oil industry every year. Four billion dollars, imagine that. Maybe some of you are listening to this in your car right now, pulling into a gas station to fill up; and as you watch those numbers rise, know that oil company profits have never been higher. Yet, somehow, Congress is still giving those same companies another $4 billion of your money. It's outrageous, and it has to stop.

A century of subsidies to the oil companies is long enough. It's time to end taxpayer giveaways to an industry that's never been more profitable and use that money to reduce our deficit and double down on a clean energy industry that's never been more promising. Because of the investments we've already made, the use of wind and solar energy in this country has nearly doubled and thousands of Americans have jobs because of it. And because we put in place the toughest fuel economy standards in history, our cars will average nearly 55 miles per gallon by the middle of the next decade, something that, over time, will save the typical family more than $8,000 at the pump. Now Congress needs to keep that momentum going by renewing the clean energy tax credits that will lead to more jobs and less dependence on foreign oil.

Look, we know there's no silver bullet that will bring down gas prices or reduce our dependence on foreign oil overnight. But what we can do is get our priorities straight and make a sustained, serious effort to tackle this problem. That's the commitment we need right now. And with your help, it's a commitment we can make. Thanks.

NOTE: The address was recorded at approximately 5:15 p.m. on February 24 in the Blue Room at the White House for broadcast on February 25. The transcript was made available by the Office of the Press Secretary on February 24, but was embargoed for release until 6 a.m. on February 25.

Statement on the Presidential Election in Yemen
February 25, 2012

Just over 1 year ago, thousands of men and women gathered in city squares across Yemen to demand a government that was responsive to their democratic aspirations. The determination and sacrifice of the Yemeni people in the struggle for their universal rights has been inspiring and has brought about unprecedented political change in Yemen. This week, millions of Yemenis voted for a new President and the beginning of a promising new chapter in Yemen's history.

Today I called Yemeni President Abd Rabuh Mansur Hadi to congratulate him and the Yemeni people as they mark this historic and peaceful transfer of power that honors all the brave Yemenis who have set their country on a path for a more stable, secure, and democratic future. I told President Hadi that the United States will stand with the people of Yemen as they continue their efforts to forge a brighter future for their country. I also offered my condolences for the lives lost at the Presidential compound in Mukalla, Hadramawt.

The Yemeni people have achieved a new beginning for their country, but much work lies ahead. Going forward, as part of their political agreement, Yemenis must convene an inclusive national dialogue, reform their Constitution, reorganize the military and security services, and hold Presidential and Parliamentary elections by 2014. This is an ambitious agenda, but with the determination they have shown over the past year, Yemenis have proven they are up to the task. Under President Hadi's leadership, Yemen has the potential to serve as a model for how peaceful transitions can occur when people resist violence and unite under a common cause. The United States will remain a steadfast partner to Yemen and its people as they transition to a democracy worthy of their struggle.

Remarks at the National Governors Association Dinner
February 26, 2012

Good evening, everybody. Welcome to the White House. [*Laughter*] Did I hear an "aloha" back there? Yes. [*Laughter*] All right, Neil. [*Laughter*]

Let me begin by acknowledging your outstanding chair, Dave Heineman, who's doing an outstanding job in the great State of Nebraska, as well as your vice chair, Jack Markell, of the great State of Delaware, for their hard work.

I have heard that you've had some very productive meetings this weekend. I'm looking forward to having you back tomorrow. We'll be able to discuss a wide range of policy.

But tonight it's about having some fun. We've got the help of the great Dianne Reeves, who is going to be here, and we'll be hearing from later on. So I'm going to be brief because, although some may disagree, she has a better voice than I do. [*Laughter*]

I've always said that Governors have one of the best, but also one of the toughest, jobs around. On the one hand, you guys are in charge, which means that folks know where you live and they know how to find you if something doesn't work. [*Laughter*] They expect you to deliver when times are tough. But you're also in a position to make real and lasting change every single day. You're where rubber hits the road. And as a consequence, you can see your streets safer, your schools doing better by our children, our businesses growing faster, and our communities growing stronger because of the work that you do each and every day.

In recent months, I've had the privilege of seeing firsthand some of the outstanding work that you're doing in your respective States. I've seen the kinds of businesses that are growing in States like Iowa and Washington. I've seen States like Florida who are really doing great work increasing tourism and developing renewable energies. I often get a chance to go to Virginia and Maryland and States in the vicinity, where community colleges are doing a wonderful job retraining our people for the jobs of the future.

So, every time I get a sense of what's happening in your States, I'm reminded that the progress is possible. And I want you to know that you've got a partner here in the White House. We're not going to agree on every single issue, every single day. But the thing about Governors is that by nature, and if not by nature, then by virtue of the position, you end up having to be pragmatic, because you have to figure out what works. And that's why I'm confident that we're going to be able to find more and more common ground going forward.

So I want everybody to have a great time tonight. By the way, you all look fabulous. [*Laughter*] You clean up very well. This house has actually seen its share of good times. The story goes that after the Inauguration, Andrew Jackson opened the White House to the public and was nearly crushed by the crowd. As things started getting out of hand, the staff decided to pass barrels of ice cream and whiskey out the window—[*laughter*]—to get people out on the lawn, so they wouldn't cause damage and break the chandeliers and the furniture.

So I just want you to know, in case things get rowdy, we also have barrels standing by. [*Laughter*]

But now I'd like to propose a toast to all the Governors for your outstanding work, but especially to all the spouses who put up with us. Cheers. Thank you so much.

Cheers, everybody. All right. I hope you guys have a wonderful time. Let's serve it up. [*Laughter*]

NOTE: The President spoke at 7:18 p.m. in the State Dining Room at the White House. In his remarks, he referred to Gov. Neil Abercrombie of Hawaii; and musician Dianne Reeves. The transcript released by the Office of the Press Secretary also included the remarks of Gov. David E. Heineman of Nebraska.

Remarks to the National Governors Association
February 27, 2012

The President. Thank you, everybody. Thank you so much. Please, everybody, have a seat. Have a seat.

Thank you, Joe, for the outstanding work you're doing on behalf of the American people every day. I want to thank all the members of my Cabinet and administration who are here today. I want to thank Dave Heineman and Jack Markell for the outstanding leadership that they've shown as they've chaired and cochaired the NGA.

I'm glad to see that everybody has recovered from the wild time we had last night. [*Laughter*] It was wonderful to have all of you here.

And I always look forward to this event because Governors are at the frontline of America's recovery. You see up close what's working, what's not working, and where we can take it. And the thing that connects all of us—and no matter what part of the country we're from and certainly no matter what party we belong to— is that we know what it means to govern, what it means to make tough choices during tough times, and hopefully, to forge some common ground. We've all felt the weight of big decisions and the impact that those decisions have on the people that we represent.

I first addressed this group 3 years ago, and it was the moment, as Joe mentioned, when the economy was in a freefall. Some of you were just coming into office at that time as well. Hundreds of thousands of Americans were losing their jobs or their homes every month. Businesses were closing their doors at a heartbreaking pace. Our entire auto industry was on the verge of collapse, and all told, the prospects of us going into a full-blown depression were very real.

Today, there's no doubt that enormous challenges remain. But the fact of the matter is that over the last 2 years American businesses have created 3.7 million new jobs. Manufacturers are hiring for the first time since the 1990s. The auto industry is back. Our recovery is gaining speed, and the economy is getting strong.

And we've got to do everything we can to make sure that we sustain this progress.

That means we've got to strengthen American manufacturing so that more and more good jobs and products are made here in America. It means that we've got to develop new sources of American energy so that we're less dependent on foreign oil and yearly spikes in gas prices. And it means that we've got to make sure that every American is equipped with the skills, with the education that they need to compete for the jobs of tomorrow as well as the jobs of today. And that's what I want to talk to these Governors a little bit about.

No issue will have a bigger impact on the future performance of our economy than education. In the long run it's going to depend—determine whether or not businesses stay here. It will determine whether businesses are created here, whether businesses are hiring here. And it will determine whether there's going to be an abundance of good middle class jobs in America.

Today, the unemployment rate for Americans with at least a college degree is about half the national average. Their incomes are about twice as high as those who only have a high school diploma. So this is what we should be focused on as a nation. This is what we should be talking about and debating. The countries who outeducate us today will outcompete us tomorrow. That's a simple fact. And if we want America to continue to be number one and stay number one, we've got some work to do.

Now, in the last 3 years, the good news is, we've made some important progress, working together. We've broken through the traditional stalemate between left and right by launching a national competition to improve our schools. And I think Arne has done an outstanding job of saying we've got to get past the old dogmas—whether it's the dogmas on the liberal side or the conservative side—and figure out what works. We've invested, but we've invested in reform. And for less than 1 percent of what our Nation spends on education each year, almost all of you have agreed to raise standards for teaching and learning. And that's the first time that's happened in a generation.

We've also worked with all of you—Democrats and Republicans—to try to fix No Child Left Behind. We said that if you're willing to set higher, more honest standards, then we will give you more flexibility to meet those standards. Earlier this month, I announced the first 11 States to get a waiver from No Child Left Behind, and I hope that we are going to be adding more States soon.

I believe education is an issue that is best addressed at the State level. And Governors are in the best position to have the biggest impact. I realize that everybody is dealing with limited resources. Trust me, I know something about trying to deal with tight budgets. We've all faced some stark choices over the past several years. But that is no excuse to lose sight of what matters most. And the fact is that too many States are making cuts to education that I believe are simply too big.

Nothing more clearly signals what you value as a State than the decisions you make about where to invest. Budgets are about choices. So today I'm calling on all of you: Invest more in education. Invest more in our children and in our future. That does not mean you've got to invest in things that aren't working. That doesn't mean that it doesn't make sense to break some china and move aggressively on reform. But the fact of the matter is, we don't have to choose between resources and reform; we need resources and reform.

Now, there are two areas in education that demand our immediate focus. First, we've just got to get more teachers into our classrooms. Over the past 4 years, school districts across America have lost over 250,000 educators—250,000 teachers, educators have been lost. Think about that. A quarter-million educators, responsible for millions of our students, all laid off when America has never needed them more.

Other countries are doubling down on education and their investment in teachers, and we should too. And each of us is here only because

at some point in our lives a teacher changed our life trajectory. The impact is often much bigger than even we realize. One study found that a good teacher can increase the lifetime income of a classroom by over $250,000: one teacher, one classroom. And a great teacher offers potentially an escape for a child who is dreaming beyond his circumstances. The point is, teachers matter, and all of us have to recognize that, and we've got to put our money behind that.

Now, we want to help you every place that we can. At the Federal level, we've already provided billions of dollars in funding to help keep hundreds of thousands of teachers in the classroom. And a cornerstone of the jobs plan that I put forward in September—a chunk of which has gotten done, but a chunk of which remains undone—was to provide even more funding, so that you could prevent further layoffs and rehire teachers that had lost their jobs. And I'd like to thank those of you in this room who voiced support for that effort.

Congress still is in a position to do the right thing. They can keep more teachers in the classroom, but you've got to keep the pressure up on them to get this done.

The second area where we have to bring greater focus is higher education. The jobs of the future are increasingly going to those with more than a high school degree. And I have to make a point here. When I speak about higher education, we're not just talking about a 4-year degree. We're talking about somebody going to a community college and getting trained for that manufacturing job that now is requiring somebody walking through the door, handling a million-dollar piece of equipment. And they can't go in there unless they've got some basic training beyond what they received in high school.

We all want Americans getting those jobs of the future. So we're going to have to make sure that they're getting the education that they need. It starts, by the way, with just what kinds of expectation and ground rules we're setting for kids in high school. Right now 21 States require students to stay in high school until they graduate or turn 18—21 States. That means 29 don't. I believe that's the right thing to do, for us to make sure to send a message to our young people: You graduate from high school at a minimum. And I urge others to follow suit of those 21 States.

Now, for students that are ready for college, we've got to make sure that college is affordable. Today, graduates who take out loans leave college owing an average of $25,000. That's a staggering amount for young people. Americans now owe more in student loan debt than they do in credit card debt. There's so many Americans out there with so much to offer who are saddled with debt before they even start out in life. And the very idea of owing that much money puts college out of reach for far too many families.

So this is a major problem that must be fixed. I addressed it at the State of the Union. We have a role to play here. My grandfather got a chance to go to college because Americans and Congress decided that every returning veteran from World War II should be able to afford it. My mother was able to raise two kids by herself while still going to college and getting an advanced degree because she was able to get grants and work-study while she was in school. Michelle and I are only here today because of scholarships and student loans that gave us a good shot at a great education. And it wasn't easy to pay off these loans, but it sure wasn't as hard as it is for a lot of kids today.

So my administration has tried to do our part by making sure that the student loans program puts students before banks, by increasing aid like the Pell grants for millions of students and their families and by allowing students to cap their monthly loan payments at 10 percent of their income, which means that their repayment schedule is manageable.

Congress still needs to do its part by, first of all, keeping student interest rates low. Right now they are scheduled to double at the end of July if Congress does not act. And that would be a real tragedy for an awful lot of families around the country. They also need to extend the tuition tax credit for the middle class, protect Pell grants, and expand work-study programs.

But it's not enough to just focus on student aid. We can't just keep on, at the Federal level, subsidizing skyrocketing tuition. If tuition is going up faster than inflation—faster, actually, than health care costs—then no matter how much we subsidize it, sooner or later we are going to run out of money. So everybody else is going to have to do their part as well. This is not just a matter of the Federal Government coming up with more and more money.

That means colleges and universities are going to have to help to make their tuition more affordable. And I've put them on notice: If they are not taking some concrete steps to prevent tuition from going up, then Federal funding from taxpayers is going to go down. We've got to incentivize better practices in terms of keeping costs under control. And all of you have a role to play by making higher education a higher priority in your budgets.

Over two-thirds of students attend public colleges and universities where, traditionally, tuition has been affordable because of State investments. And that's something that every State takes pride in. That's the crown jewel, in fact, of our economic system—is, by far, we've got the best network of colleges, universities, and community colleges in the world.

But more than 40 States have cut funding for higher education over the past year. And this is just the peak of what has been a long-term trend in reduced State support for higher education. And State budget cuts have been among the largest factor in tuition hikes at public colleges over the past decade.

So my administration can do more, Congress can do more, colleges have to do more. But unless all of you also do more, this problem will not get solved. It can be done, though.

Jack O'Malley—where's Jack—not—Martin. Where's Martin? Sorry. I was——

Gov. Martin J. O'Malley of Maryland. I thought my son was right here. [*Laughter*]

The President. Right, right, right.

Martin in Maryland is doing some outstanding work on this front. He worked with the legislature to keep tuition down by controlling costs and cutting spending on college campuses, and you're seeing a real impact, from the flagship University of Maryland all the way down. And a lot of you are starting to experiment with this as well.

We can't allow higher education to be a luxury in this country. It's an economic imperative that every family in America has to be able to afford. And frankly, I don't think any of this should be a partisan issue. All of us should be about giving every American who wants a chance to succeed that chance.

So let me wrap up by saying a few weeks ago I held, right here in this room and in the adjoining room, one of my favorite events and that is the White House Science Fair. We invited students from a lot of your States, and they showcased projects that covered the full range of scientific discovery.

We had a group of kids from Texas, young Latino women, who came from the poorest section of Texas and yet were winning rocket competitions. And they were so good because they could only afford one rocket, so they couldn't test them, and they had to get it just right. [*Laughter*] And their parents ran bake sales just so they could travel to these events.

You had a young woman who was from Long Island, had been studying mussels and wanted to be an oceanographer, and won the Intel Science Award while she was homeless. Her family had lost their home, and she was living out of a car and out of her family's—on her family's couch and yet still was able to stay focused and achieve what was just remarkable.

There was a kid—the kid who actually got the most attention was a young man named Joey Hudy of Arizona. That's because Joey let me fire off a extreme marshmallow cannon. [*Laughter*] We did it right here in this room. We shot it from here. We pumped it up—it almost hit that light. [*Laughter*] I thought it was

a lot of fun. [*Laughter*] And while the cannon was impressive, Joey left a bigger impression because he had already printed out his own business cards: He was 14 years old. And he was handing them out to everybody, including me. [*Laughter*] He's on a short list for a Cabinet post. [*Laughter*]

Under his name on each card was a simple motto: "Don't be bored; do something." Don't be bored; do something. Don't be bored; make something.

All across this country there are kids like Joey who are dreaming big and are doing things and making things. And we want them to reach those heights. They're willing to work hard. They are willing to dig deep to achieve. And we've got a responsibility to give them a fair shot. If we do, then I'm absolutely convinced that our future is going to be as bright as all of us want.

So this is going to be something that I want to collaborate with all of you on. If you've got ideas about how we can make our education system work better, I want to hear them today, and Arne Duncan is going to want to hear them for the rest of the time that he's Education Secretary and the rest of the time I'm President.

All right? Thank you very much, everybody.

NOTE: The President spoke at 11:30 a.m. in the State Dining Room at the White House. In his remarks, he referred to Vice President Joe Biden, who introduced the President; Gov. David E. Heineman of Nebraska, chair, and Gov. Jack A. Markell of Delaware, cochair, National Governors Association; and White House Science Fair participants Janet Nieto, Gwynelle Condino, and Ana Karen of Presidio, TX, and Samantha Garvey of Bay Shore, NY. He also referred to his sister Maya Soetoro-Ng.

Remarks to the United Auto Workers Convention
February 28, 2012

The President. How's it going, UAW? It is good to be with some autoworkers today! All right. Everybody have a seat, get comfortable. Go ahead and get comfortable. I'm going to talk for a little bit.

First of all, I want to say thank you to one of the finest leaders that we have in labor, Bob King. Give it up for Bob. I want to thank the International Executive Board and all of you for having me here today. It is a great honor. I brought along somebody who is proving to be one of the finest Secretaries of Transportation in our history, Ray LaHood is in the house. Give Ray a big round of applause.

It is always an honor to spend time with folks who represent the working men and women of America. It's unions like yours that fought for jobs and opportunity for generations of American workers. It's unions like yours that helped build the arsenal of democracy that defeated fascism and won World War II. It's unions like yours that forged the American middle class, that great engine of prosperity, the greatest that the world has ever known.

So you guys helped to write the American story. And today, you're busy writing a proud new chapter. You are reminding us that no matter how tough times get, Americans are tougher. No matter how many punches we take, we don't give up. We get up. We fight back. We move forward. We come out on the other side stronger than before. That's what you've shown us. You're showing us what's possible in America. So I'm here to tell you one thing today: You make me proud. You make me proud.

Take a minute and think about what you and the workers and the families that you represent have fought through. A few years ago, nearly one in five autoworkers were handed a pink slip—one in five. Four hundred thousand jobs across this industry vanished the year before I took office. And then as the financial crisis hit with its full force, America faced a hard and once unimaginable reality, that two of the Big Three automakers, GM and Chrysler, were on the brink of liquidation.

The heartbeat of American manufacturing was flatlining, and we had to make a choice. With the economy in complete freefall, there were no private investors or companies out there willing to take a chance on the auto industry. Nobody was lining up to give you guys loans. Anyone in the financial sector can tell you that.

So we could have kept giving billions of dollars of taxpayer dollars to automakers without demanding the real changes or accountability in return that were needed. That was one op-

tion. But that wouldn't have solved anything in the long term. Sooner or later we would have run out of money. We could have just kicked the problem down the road. The other option was to do absolutely nothing and let these companies fail. And you will recall, there were some politicians who said we should do that. Some even said we should "let Detroit go bankrupt."

You remember that? You know. [*Laughter*] Think about what that choice would have meant for this country, if we had turned our backs on you, if America had thrown in the towel, if GM and Chrysler had gone under. The suppliers, the distributors that get their business from these companies, they would have died off. Then even Ford could have gone down as well. Production shut down, factories shuttered, once-proud companies chopped up and sold off for scraps, and all of you—the men and women who built these companies with your own hands—would have been hung out to dry.

More than 1 million Americans across the country would have lost their jobs in the middle of the worst economic crisis since the Great Depression. In communities across the Midwest, it would have been another Great Depression. And then, think about all the people who depend on you. Not just your families, but the schoolteachers, the small-business owners, the server in the diner who knows your order, the bartender who's waiting for you to get off. [*Laughter*] That's right. Their livelihoods were at stake as well.

And you know what was else at stake? How many of you who've worked the assembly line had a father or a grandfather or a mother who worked on that same line? How many of you have sons and daughters who said, "You know, Mom, Dad, I'd like to work at the plant too?"

These jobs are worth more than just a paycheck. They're a source of pride. They're a ticket to a middle class life that make it possible for you to own a home and raise kids and maybe send them, yes, to college. Give you a chance to retire with some dignity and some respect. These companies are worth more than just the cars they build. They're a symbol of

American innovation and know-how. They're the source of our manufacturing might. If that's not worth fighting for, what's worth fighting for?

So no, we were not going to take a knee and do nothing. We were not going to give up on your jobs and your families and your communities. So, in exchange for help, we demanded responsibility. We said to the auto industry, you're going to have to truly change, not just pretend like you're changing. And thanks to outstanding leadership like Bob King, we were able to get labor and management to settle their differences.

We got the industry to retool and restructure, and everybody involved made sacrifices. Everybody had some skin in the game. And it wasn't popular. And it wasn't what I ran for President to do. I—that wasn't originally what I thought I was going to be doing as President. [*Laughter*] But you know what, I did run to make the tough calls and do the right things, no matter what the politics were.

And I want you to know: You know why I knew this rescue would succeed?

Audience member. How did you do it? [*Laughter*]

The President. You want to know? It wasn't because of anything the Government did. It wasn't just because of anything management did. It was because I believed in you. I placed my bet on the American worker. And I'll make that bet any day of the week.

And now, 3 years later, that bet is paying off. Not just paying off for you, it's paying off for America. Three years later, the American auto industry is back. GM is back on top as the number-one automaker in the world, highest profits in its 100-year history. Chrysler is growing faster in America than any other car company. Ford is investing billions in American plants, American factories, plans to bring thousands of jobs back to America.

All told, the entire industry has added more than 200,000 new jobs over the past 2½ years—200,000 new jobs. And here's the best part: You're not just building cars again, you're building better cars.

After three decades of inaction, we're gradually putting in place the toughest fuel economy standards in history for our cars and pickups. That means the cars you build will average nearly 55 miles per gallon by the middle of next decade, almost double what they get today. That means folks, every time they fill up, they're going to be saving money. They'll have to fill up every 2 weeks instead of every week. That saves the typical family more than $8,000 at the pump over time. That means we'll cut our oil consumption by more than 2 million barrels a day. That means we have to import less oil while we're selling more cars all around the world.

Thanks to the bipartisan trade agreement I signed into law, with you in mind, working with you, there will soon be new cars in the streets of South Korea imported from Detroit and from Toledo and from Chicago.

And today—I talked about this at the State of the Union, we are doing it today—I am creating a trade enforcement unit that will bring the full resources of the Federal Government to bear on investigations, and we're going to counter any unfair trading practices around the world, including by countries like China. America has the best workers in the world. When the playing field is level, nobody will beat us. And we're going to make sure that playing field is level.

Because America always wins when the playing field is level. And because everyone came together and worked together, the most high-tech, fuel-efficient, good-looking cars in the world are once again designed and engineered and forged and built not in Europe, not in Asia, right here in the United States of America.

I've seen it myself. I've seen it myself. I've seen it at Chrysler's Jefferson North Plant in Detroit, where a new shift of more than 1,000 workers came on 2 years ago, another 1,000 slated to come on next year. I've seen it in my hometown at Ford's Chicago Assembly, where workers are building a new Explorer and selling it to dozens of countries around the world.

Audience member. I'm buying one too!

The President. There you go. [*Laughter*]

I've seen it at GM's Lordstown plant in Ohio, where workers got their jobs back to build the Chevy Cobalt, and at GM's Hamtramck plant in Detroit, where I got to get inside a brandnew Chevy Volt fresh off the line, even though Secret Service wouldn't let me drive it. But I liked sitting in it. It was nice. I'll bet it drives real good. [*Laughter*] And 5 years from now, when I'm not President anymore, I'll buy one and drive it myself. [*Applause*] Yes, that's right.

Audience members. Four more years! Four more years! Four more years!

The President. Look, I know our bet was a good one because I had seen it pay off firsthand. But here's the thing. You don't have to take my word for it. Ask the Chrysler workers near Kokomo who were brought on to make sure the newest high-tech transmissions and fuel-efficient engines are made in America. Or ask the GM workers in Spring Hill, Tennessee, whose jobs were saved from being sent abroad. Ask the Ford workers in Kansas City coming on to make the F–150, America's best selling truck, a more fuel-efficient truck. And you ask all the suppliers who are expanding and hiring, and the communities that rely on them, if America's investment in you was a good bet. They'll tell you the right answer.

And who knows, maybe the naysayers would finally come around and say that standing by America's workers was the right thing to do. Because, I've got to admit, it's been funny to watch some of these folks completely try to rewrite history now that you're back on your feet. The same folks who said, if we went forward with our plan to rescue Detroit, "you can kiss the American automotive industry goodbye," now they're saying, we were right all along. [*Laughter*]

Or you've got folks saying, well, the real problem is—what we really disagreed with was the workers, they all made out like bandits, that saving the auto industry was just about paying back the unions. Really? I mean, even by the standards of this town, that's a load of you know what. [*Laughter*]

About 700,000 retirees had to make sacrifices on their health care benefits that they had earned. A lot of you saw hours reduced or pay or wages scaled back. You gave up some of your rights as workers. Promises were made to you over the years that you gave up for the sake and survival of this industry, its workers, their families. You want to talk about sacrifice? You made sacrifices. This wasn't an easy thing to do.

Let me tell you, I keep on hearing these same folks talk about values all the time. You want to talk about values? Hard work, that's a value. Looking out for one another, that's a value. The idea that we're all in it together and I'm my brother's keeper and sister's keeper, that's a value.

They're out there talking about you like you're some special interest that needs to be beaten down. Since when are hard-working men and women who are putting in a hard day's work every day, since when are they special interests? Since when is the idea that we look out for one another a bad thing?

I remember my old friend Ted Kennedy. He used to say, what is it about working men and women they find so offensive? [*Laughter*] This notion that we should have let the auto industry die, that we should pursue antiworker policies in the hopes that unions like yours will buckle and unravel, that's part of that same old you-are-on-your-own philosophy that says we should just leave everybody to fend for themselves, let the most powerful do whatever they please.

They think the best way to boost the economy is to roll back the reforms we put into place to prevent another crisis, to let Wall Street write the rules again. They think the best way to help families afford health care is to roll back the reforms we passed that's already lowering costs for millions of Americans. They want to go back to the days when insurance companies could deny your coverage or jack up your rates whenever and however they pleased. They think we should keep cutting taxes for those at the very top, for people like me, even though we don't need it, just so they can keep paying lower tax rates than their secretaries.

Well, let me tell you something. Not to put too fine a point on it, they're wrong. [*Laughter*] They are wrong. That's the philosophy that got us into this mess. We can't afford to go back to it. Not now.

We've got a lot of work to do. We've got a long way to go before everybody who wants a good job can get a good job. We've got a long way to go before middle class Americans fully regain that sense of security that's been slipping away since long before this recession hit. But, you know what, we've got something to show. All of you show what's possible when we pull together.

Over the last 2 years, our businesses have added about 3.7 million new jobs. Manufacturing is coming back for the first time since the 1990s. Companies are bringing jobs back from overseas. The economy is getting stronger. The recovery is speeding up. Now is the time to keep our foot on the gas, not put on the brakes. And I'm not going to settle for a country where just a few do really well and everybody else is struggling to get by.

We're fighting for an economy where everybody gets a fair shot, where everybody does their fair share, where everybody plays by the same set of rules. We're not going to go back to an economy that's all about outsourcing and bad debt and phony profits. We're fighting for an economy that's built to last, that's built on things like education and energy and manufacturing. Making things, not just buying things, making things that the rest of the worlds want to buy. And restoring the values that made this country great: hard work and fair play, the chance to make it if you really try, the responsibility to reach back and help somebody else make it too, not just you. That's who we are. That's what we believe in.

I was telling you I visited Chrysler's Jefferson North Plant in Detroit about a year and a half ago. Now, the day I visited, some of the employees had won the lottery. Not kidding. They had won the lottery. Now you might think that after that, they'd all be kicking back and retiring. [*Laughter*] And no one would fault them for that. Building cars is tough work.

But that's not what they did. The guy who bought——

Audience member. What did they do?

The President. Funny you ask. [*Laughter*] The guy who bought the winning ticket, he was a proud UAW member who worked on the line. So he used some of his winnings to buy his wife the car that he builds because he's really proud of his work. Then he bought brand new American flags for his hometown, because he's proud of his country. And he and the other winners are still clocking in at that plant today, because they're proud of the part they and their coworkers play in America's comeback.

See, that's what America is about. America is not just looking out for yourself. It's not just about greed. It's not just about trying to climb to the very top and keep everybody else down. When our assembly lines grind to a halt, we work together and we get them going again. When somebody else falters, we try to give them a hand up, because we know we're all in it together.

I got my start standing with working folks who'd lost their jobs, folks who had lost their hope, because the steel plants had closed down. I didn't like the idea that they didn't have anybody fighting for them. The same reason I got into this business is the same reason I'm here today. I'm driven by that same belief that everybody—everybody—should deserve a chance.

So I promise you this: As long as you've got an ounce of fight left in you, I'll have a ton of fight left in me. We're going to keep on fighting to make our economy stronger, to put our friends and neighbors back to work faster, to give our children even more opportunity, to make sure that the United States of America remains the greatest nation on Earth.

Thank you, UAW. I love you. God bless you. God bless the work you do. God bless the United States of America.

NOTE: The President spoke at 11:30 a.m. at the Washington Marriott Wardman Park hotel. In his remarks, he referred to Robert T. King, president, United Auto Workers; and Curtice, OH, resident William Shanteau, a worker at the Chrysler Jefferson North Assembly Plant in Detroit, MI, who purchased a winning Powerball lottery ticket in June 2010, and his wife Lisa.

Statement on Senator Olympia J. Snowe's Decision Not To Seek Reelection
February 28, 2012

For nearly four decades, Olympia Snowe has served the people of the great State of Maine. Elected to the statehouse in 1973, Olympia went on to be the first woman in American history to serve in both houses of a State legislature and both Houses of Congress. From her unwavering support for our troops, to her efforts to reform Wall Street, to fighting for Maine's small businesses, Senator Snowe's career demonstrates how much can be accomplished when leaders from both parties come together to do the right thing for the American people. Michelle and I join Mainers in thanking Senator Snowe for her service, and we wish her and her family all the best in the future.

Directive on Procedures Implementing Section 1022 of the National Defense Authorization Act for Fiscal Year 2012
February 28, 2012

Presidential Policy Directive/PPD–14

Subject: Procedures Implementing Section 1022 of the National Defense Authorization Act for Fiscal Year (FY) 2012

The executive branch must utilize all elements of national power—including military, intelligence, law enforcement, diplomatic, and economic tools—to effectively confront the threat posed by al-Qa'ida and its associated forces, and must retain the flexibility to determine how to apply those tools to the unique facts and circumstances we face in confronting this diverse and evolving threat.

Under the Authorization for Use of Military Force of September 18, 2001 (Public Law 107–40)(2001 AUMF), the executive branch has the authority to detain in military custody individuals who planned, authorized, committed, or aided the terrorist attacks that occurred on September 11, 2001, and persons who harbored those responsible for the September 11 attacks, as well as individuals who are part of or substantially supported Taliban or al-Qa'ida forces or associated forces that are engaged in hostilities against the United States or its coalition partners. Section 1021 of the National Defense Authorization Act for FY 2012 (Public Law 112–81)(NDAA) affirms that authority.

A rigid, inflexible requirement to place suspected terrorists into military custody would undermine the national security interests of the United States, compromising our ability to collect intelligence and to incapacitate dangerous individuals. This Directive specifies policies and procedures designed to ensure that section 1022 of the NDAA is implemented in a manner that is consistent with the national security and foreign policy interests of the United States. Specifically, this Directive sets forth the procedures required by section 1022 of the NDAA for determining when the military custody requirement of section 1022 applies to non-citizens detained by the United States, when and how any such determination will be implemented, and when and how to waive the requirements of section 1022(a)(1) when it is in the national security interests of the United States. This Directive also issues several national security waivers.

I. SCOPE OF PROCEDURES AND STANDARD FOR COVERED PERSON DETERMINATIONS

A. *Scope of Procedures.* Subject to sections I(B) through I(F), the procedures set out in sections II through V of this Directive apply only when (1) an individual is arrested or otherwise taken into custody by the Federal Bureau of Investigation (FBI) or another Federal law enforcement agency on or after the date of this Directive; and (2) officials of the agency detaining the individual have probable cause to believe that the individual is a "Covered Person" under section 1022 of the NDAA.

B. *Covered Persons.* For purposes of this Directive, the phrase "Covered Person" applies only to a person who is not a citizen of the United States and:

    1. whose detention is authorized under the 2001 AUMF, as informed by the laws of war, and affirmed in section 1021 of the NDAA; and

    2. (a) who is a member of, or part of, al-Qa'ida or an associated force that acts in coordination with or pursuant to the direction of al-Qa'ida; and (b) who participated in the course of planning or carrying out an attack or attempted attack against the United States or its coalition partners.

C. *Attack or Attempted Attack.*

    1. An "attack" means the completion of an act of violence or the use of force that involves serious risk to human life.

    2. An "attempted attack" means an overt act or acts beyond a substantial step when (a) performed with specific intent to commit an attack; and (b) no further step or act by the individual would be necessary to complete the attack.

D. *Application to Individuals Captured or Detained by, or in the Custody of, the Department of Defense.* Any time an individual is captured or detained by, or otherwise taken into the custody of, the Department of Defense,
the requirement under section 1022(a)(1) of the NDAA will have been satisfied, regardless of whether there has been a final determination as to whether the individual is a Covered Person, and regardless of the authorities under which the individual is captured, detained, or otherwise taken into custody. Therefore, individuals captured or detained by, or otherwise taken into the custody of, the Department of Defense shall not be subject to the procedures outlined in sections II through IV of this Directive. Any subsequent law of war disposition of the individual effectuated by the Department of Defense consistent with section 1021(c) and 1022(a)(3) of the NDAA satisfies all requirements of section 1022 of the NDAA, subject to the conditions on transfer in section 1028 for any individual detained at Guantanamo.

E. *No Effect on Individuals Held by State or Local Authorities.* The requirement in section 1022(a) of the NDAA does not apply to individuals arrested by, or otherwise taken into the custody of, State or local law enforcement agencies, and the procedures and requirements set out in this Directive shall not apply while individuals are held in the custody of State or local law enforcement agencies.

F. *No Effect on Individuals Held by Foreign Governments.* The requirement in section 1022(a) of the NDAA does not apply to individuals who are arrested by, or otherwise taken into the custody of, a foreign government, and the procedures and requirements set out in this Directive shall not apply to individuals held in the custody of foreign governments, including but not limited to circumstances where intelligence, law enforcement, or other officials of the United States are granted access to an individual who remains in the custody of a foreign government.

II. WAIVERS TO PROTECT NATIONAL SECURITY INTERESTS

A. *Statutory Authority under NDAA.* Section 1022(a)(4) of the NDAA authorizes the President to waive application of the military custody requirement under section 1022(a)(1) where doing so is "in the national security interests of the United States." Such waivers ("National Security Waivers") apply to the requirements of section 1022 of the NDAA.

B. *Protection of U.S. National Security Interests.* In accordance with section 1022(a)(4) of the NDAA, and consistent with section 1022(c)(2), which provides the executive branch with broad discretion to design implementing procedures to ensure that the requirements of section 1022 do not interfere with various authorities necessary to disrupt or respond to terrorism threats, and to ensure that counterterrorism professionals have clear guidance and appropriate tools at their disposal to accomplish their mission effectively, I hereby waive the requirements of section 1022(a)(1), regardless of whether an individual has yet been determined to be a Covered Person, and certify that it is in the national security interests of the United States to do so, when:

1. placing a foreign country's nationals or residents in U.S. military custody will impede counterterrorism cooperation, including but not limited to sharing intelligence or providing other cooperation or assistance to the United States in investigations or prosecutions of suspected terrorists;
2. a foreign government indicates that it will not extradite or consent to the transfer of individuals to the United States if such individuals may be placed in military custody;
3. an individual is a lawful permanent resident of the United States who is arrested inside the United States or is arrested by a Federal agency on the basis of conduct taking place in the United States, to the extent the individual is subject to the requirement of section 1022(a)(1);
4. an individual has been arrested by a Federal agency in the United States on charges other than terrorism offenses (unless such individual is subsequently charged with one or more terrorism offenses and held in Federal custody in connection with those offenses);

5. an individual has been arrested by State or local law enforcement, pursuant to State or local authority, and is transferred to Federal custody;
6. transferring an individual to U.S. military custody could interfere with efforts to secure an individual's cooperation or confession; or
7. transferring an individual to U.S. military custody could interfere with efforts to conduct joint trials with co-defendants who are ineligible for U.S. military custody or as to whom a determination has already been made to proceed with a prosecution in a Federal or State court.

C. *Authority to Issue Additional Categorical National Security Waivers.* The Attorney General, in consultation with other senior national security officials, shall have authority to waive the requirements of section 1022(a)(1) of the NDAA in the national security interests of the United States for categories of conduct or categories of individuals consistent with section 1022(a)(4).

D. *Authority to Issue Individual National Security Waivers.* The Attorney General, in consultation with other senior national security officials, shall have the authority to waive the requirements of section 1022(a)(1) of the NDAA in the national security interests of the United States on an individual, case-by-case basis, consistent with section 1022(a)(4). A decision to issue such a waiver shall take into account factors such as: the legal and evidentiary strength of any criminal charges that may be brought against the individual; the likely punishment if convicted; the impact on intelligence collection of maintaining the individual in law enforcement custody; the legal and investigative risks posed by a transfer to U.S. military custody; the effect any transfer to U.S. military custody would likely have on cooperation by the individual in custody; the effect any transfer to U.S. military custody would likely have on cooperation by foreign governments in a particular investigation or related investigations; the risk associated with litigation concerning the legal authority to detain the individual pursuant to the 2001 AUMF, as informed by the laws of war; and the need to preserve a long-term disposition of the individual that adequately mitigates the threat the individual poses and protects the national security interests of the United States. A waiver is also appropriate if the Attorney General determines, in consultation with other senior national security officials, that a prosecution of the individual in Federal, State, or a foreign court will best protect the national security interests of the United States. The Attorney General may delegate this authority to any appropriate subordinate officials of the Department of Justice who hold positions for which Senate confirmation is required.

E. *Timing and Effect of National Security Waiver Determination.* The Attorney General shall have the authority to issue a National Security Waiver at any time, including before a determination is made that an individual is a Covered Person. If the Attorney General issues a National Security Waiver or determines that an existing National Security Waiver applies, no determination whether an individual is a Covered Person is required.

III. LAW ENFORCEMENT ARRESTS OF INDIVIDUALS BELIEVED TO BE COVERED PERSONS

A. *Notice to Attorney General of Arrests of Proposed Covered Persons.* As soon as is practicable after the FBI or another Federal law enforcement agency arrests or otherwise takes into custody a person it has probable cause to believe is a Covered Person under section I(B) of this Directive, the arresting agency shall notify the Attorney General that it has arrested or taken into custody such a person. The arresting agency may also submit to the Attorney General its views as to whether a National Security Waiver applies or would be appropriate.

B. *Screening.* For each individual in custody about whom the Attorney General has been notified in accordance with paragraph (A), a screening shall commence as soon as practicable after sufficient information is available, in the estimation of the Attorney General, to establish that probable cause exists to believe

that the individual is a Covered Person and that the individual is not currently subject to a National Security Waiver. In the event the Attorney General determines that there is not probable cause to believe that the individual is a Covered Person or determines that the individual is subject to an existing National Security Waiver, no further action shall be required under section 1022 or this Directive.

C. *Process for Making Covered Person Determinations.*

1. Where the Attorney General determines that there is sufficient information to establish probable cause to believe that the individual is a Covered Person and that the individual is not subject to an existing National Security Waiver, the Attorney General, in coordination with other senior national security officials, shall be responsible for determining whether the individual is a Covered Person for purposes of section 1022(a) of the NDAA. In consultation with other senior national security officials, the Attorney General is authorized to issue further implementing guidelines as necessary to ensure that Covered Person determinations are made efficiently, accommodate the operational concerns of all relevant departments and agencies of the Federal Government, and are consistent with the NDAA and the requirements in section III(C) of this Directive.

2. The Attorney General, in coordination with other senior national security officials, shall, to the extent reasonably practicable, review information in the possession of the United States Government relevant to determining whether the individual is a Covered Person under section I(B) of this Directive, as well as whether the individual is subject to a National Security Waiver under section II(B) or II(C) or whether a separate National Security Waiver should be issued under section II(D). Such information shall include available information from the

Department of Homeland Security and other agencies as to the citizenship and/or immigration status of the individual. All relevant departments and agencies shall assist the Attorney General in collecting the information required for determining whether an individual is a Covered Person or is or should be subject to a National Security Waiver.

3. On the basis of the information reviewed, the Attorney General, in coordination with other senior national security officials, shall determine whether there is clear and convincing evidence that the individual is a Covered Person under section 1022 of the NDAA.

a. No further action shall be required under section 1022(a)(1) of the NDAA or the procedures set out in this Directive if the Attorney General, in coordination with other senior national security officials,

i. determines that there is not clear and convincing evidence that such individual is a Covered Person;

ii. determines that such individual is subject to a categorical National Security Waiver specified in section II(B) or issued pursuant to section II(C) of this Directive; or

iii. issues an individual National Security Waiver under section II(D) of this Directive.

D. *Final Determinations.* If the Attorney General, with the concurrence of the Secretary of State, the Secretary of Defense, Chairman of the Joint Chiefs of Staff, the Secretary of Homeland Security, and the Director of National Intelligence, concludes that there is clear and convincing evidence that such individual is a Covered Person, that the individual is not subject to an existing National Security Waiver, and that a National Security Waiver with respect to that individual should not be issued, then the Attorney General shall make a final determination that the individual is a Covered Person and provide notice of that final determination to other senior national security officials.

E. *Effect of National Security Waiver.* As provided in section II(E) of this Directive, nothing in this Directive precludes the Attorney General, in consultation with other senior national security officials, from issuing a National Security Waiver at any time. Once such a waiver is issued, the Covered Person determination process for an individual covered by that waiver shall cease, and no further action shall be required under section 1022 or this Directive.

F. *Effect of Covered Person Determination.* A determination that an individual is a Covered Person not subject to a National Security Waiver shall be without prejudice to that individual's appropriate disposition under the law of war in accordance with sections 1021(c) and 1022(a)(3) of the NDAA, the national security and foreign policy interests of the United States, and the interests of justice.

IV. IMPLEMENTATION OF COVERED PERSON DETERMINATIONS

The FBI or any other Federal law enforcement agency that has taken a Covered Person into custody shall, in consultation with the Attorney General and the Secretary of Defense, ensure that any transfer to U.S. military custody occasioned by a Covered Person determination does not result in the interruption of any ongoing interrogation, the compromise of any national security investigation, or the interruption of any ongoing surveillance or intelligence gathering with regard to persons not already in the custody or control of the United States. In no event may a Covered Person arrested in the United States or taken into the custody of the United States by the FBI (or any other Federal law enforcement agency) be transferred to military custody unless and until the Director of the FBI or his designee has determined such a transfer will not interrupt any ongoing interrogation, compromise any national security investigation, or interrupt any ongoing surveillance or intelligence gathering with regard to persons not already in the custody or control of the United States, consistent with section

1022(c)(2)(B) of the NDAA. For these purposes, and to ensure that vital intelligence is not lost, an "interrogation" is not limited to a single interview session and extends until the interrogating agency or agencies determine that all necessary intelligence gathering efforts have been exhausted.

V. NO ABRIDGMENT OF DOMESTIC LAW ENFORCEMENT

The agency with custody of the proposed Covered Person shall continue to operate in accordance with the agency's standard authorities and practices and consistent with applicable law, unless and until (1) the Attorney General, in coordination with other senior national security officials, makes a final determination that the individual is a Covered Person not subject to a National Security Waiver; (2) the Attorney General provides notice of that determination to other senior national security officials, including the head of the department or agency with custody of the proposed Covered Person; and (3) the Attorney General and the Secretary of Defense, in consultation with other senior national security officials, determine that the individual can safely and securely be transferred to the custody or control of the United States Armed Forces, consistent with applicable laws, including the law of armed conflict, and all applicable Department of Defense policies and procedures. After a Covered Person determination is made and implemented, the Department of Justice and the FBI shall retain lead responsibility for coordinating the investigation, including interrogation, while the Covered Person is held in military custody pending disposition under the law of war.

Nothing in the NDAA nor in this Directive alters the existing law enforcement and national security authorities of the Department of Justice, the FBI, or other Federal law enforcement agencies. In particular, nothing in this Directive shall be construed to affect the existing law enforcement and national security authorities of the FBI or any other law enforcement agency with regard to a Covered Person (or proposed Covered Person), regardless of whether such person is held in U.S. military custody. The FBI continues to have lead responsibility for investigations of terrorist acts or terrorist threats by individuals or groups within the United States, as well as for related intelligence collection activities within the United States.

VI. DISPOSITION DETERMINATIONS

In the event that an individual is determined to be a Covered Person not subject to a National Security Waiver, relevant departments and agencies shall determine the individual's disposition under the law of war.

VII. GENERAL PROVISIONS

This Directive shall be implemented consistent with the Constitution and other applicable law including: the Convention Against Torture; Common Article 3 of the Geneva Conventions; the Detainee Treatment Act of 2005; and other laws and Executive Orders relating to the transfer, treatment, and interrogation of individuals detained in an armed conflict.

Any determination that there is not clear and convincing evidence that an individual is a Covered Person shall be without prejudice to the question of whether the individual may be subject to detention under the 2001 AUMF, as informed by the laws of war, and affirmed by section 1021 of the NDAA. Nothing in this Directive is intended to affect or alter the jurisdiction of Federal courts to determine the legality of detention or the substantive or procedural standards that apply to such determinations.

The procedures set out in this Directive are not designed to resolve legal issues with respect to the detention by the United States of any Covered Person or individual proposed to be a Covered Person. If, at any time, material information calls into question the legality of an individual's detention, the matter shall be referred to the Attorney General for appropriate action, consistent with this Directive.

For purposes of this Directive, the phrase "senior national security officials" includes the Secretary of State, Secretary of Defense, Attorney General, Secretary of Homeland Security, Chairman of the Joint Chiefs of Staff,

Director of National Intelligence, Director of the FBI, and Director of the Central Intelligence Agency, as well as any other official I designate. Such officials may delegate their responsibilities under this Directive to appropriate subordinate officials.

This Directive is not intended to, and does not, create any right or benefit, substantive or procedural, enforceable at law or in equity by any party against the United States, its departments, agencies, or entities, its officers, employees, or agents, or any other person.

NOTE: The related memorandum is listed in Appendix D at the end of this volume.

Message to the Congress on the Directive on Procedures Implementing Section 1022 of the National Defense Authorization Act for Fiscal Year 2012
February 28, 2012

To the Congress on the United States:

Attached is the text of a Presidential Policy Directive establishing procedures to implement section 1022 of the National Defense Authorization Act for Fiscal Year 2012 (Public Law 112–81) (the "Act"), which I hereby submit to the Congress, as required under section 1022(c)(1) of the Act. The Directive also includes a written certification that it is in the na-

tional security interests of the United States to waive the requirements of section 1022(a)(1) of the Act with respect to certain categories of individuals, which I hereby submit to the Congress in accordance with section 1022(a)(4) of the Act.

BARACK OBAMA

The White House,
February 28, 2012.

Remarks at a Dinner Honoring Veterans of United States Military Operations in Iraq
February 29, 2012

Thank you so much, everyone. Please, please. Please, everyone, have a seat.

Thank you, Joe Biden, for not only outstanding remarks, but the extraordinary leadership you showed in helping to guide our policies.

To Secretary Panetta, General Dempsey, to all the commanders who are here and did so much under such extraordinary circumstances to arrive at an outcome in which the Iraqi people have an opportunity to chart their own destiny, thank you for the great work that you've done.

I do have to say, despite Deanie's advice, I thought Dempsey was going to burst into song. [*Laughter*] You have not lived until you hear him belt out an Irish ballad. His voice is better than mine. I think you're never a prophet in your own land, Marty, so your wives are there to cut you down a peg. [*Laughter*]

Distinguished guests, ladies and gentlemen: This house has stood for more than two centuries, through war and peace, through hardship and through prosperity. These rooms have hosted Presidents and Prime Ministers and kings and queens. But in the history of this house, there's never been a night quite like this. Because this evening, we welcome not the statesmen who decide great questions of war and peace, but citizens, men and women from every corner of our country, from every rank of our military, every branch of our service, who answer the call, who go to war, who defend the peace.

And in a culture that celebrates fame and fortune, yours are not necessarily household names. They're something more: the patriots who serve in our name. And after nearly 9 years of war in Iraq, tonight is an opportunity for us to express our gratitude and to say once more: Welcome home.

This is not the first time that we've paid tribute to those who served courageously in Iraq. This will not be the last. And history reminds us of our obligations as a nation at moments like this. This year will mark the 50th anniversary of the Vietnam war, a time when our veterans didn't always receive the respect and the thanks that they so richly deserved, and that's a mistake that we must never repeat.

The good news is, already, we've seen Americans come together—in small towns and big cities all across the country—to honor your service in Iraq. And tonight, on behalf of Michelle and myself, on behalf of over 300 Americans— 300 million Americans, we want to express those simple words that we can never say enough, and that's thank you.

In your heart, each of you carries your own story: the pride of a job well done, the pain of losing a friend, a comrade. Ernie Pyle, who celebrated our GIs in World War II, said that your world can never be known to the rest of us. Tonight what we can do is convey what you've meant to the rest of us, because through the dust and the din and the fog of war, the glory of your service always shone through. In your noble example, we see the virtues and the values that sustain America, that keep this country great.

You taught us about duty. Blessed to live in the land of the free, you could have opted for an easier path, but you know that freedom is not free. And so you volunteered, and you stepped forward, and you raised your hand, and you took an oath to protect and defend, to serve a cause greater than yourself, knowing, in a time of war, you could be sent into harm's way.

You taught us about resolve. Invasion turned to insurgency and then sectarian strife. But you persevered, tour after tour, year after year. Indeed, we're mindful that even as we gather here, Iraq veterans continue to risk their lives in Afghanistan, and our prayers are with them all tonight.

In one of our Nation's longest wars, you wrote one of the most extraordinary chapters in American military history. Now the Iraqi people have a chance to forge their own destiny, and every one of you who served there can take pride in knowing you gave the Iraqis this opportunity, that you succeeded in your mission.

You taught us about devotion to country and to comrades, but most of all, to family. Because I know that some of the hardest days of war were the moments you missed back home: the birthdays, the anniversaries, when your little girl or boy took their first wobbly steps. And behind every one of you was a parent, a spouse, a son or a daughter, trying to stay strong and praying for the day that you'd come home safe. And that's why Michelle and Dr. Biden have made it their mission to make sure America takes care of your families, because they inspire us as much as you do. And they deserve that honor as much as you do.

That's why I'd ask all the spouses and the partners and families to stand up and accept our gratitude for your remarkable service, especially because you look so good tonight.

You taught us about sacrifice, a love of country so deep, so profound, you were willing to give your lives for it. And tonight we pay solemn tribute to all who did. We remember the first, on that first day of war: Major Jay Thomas Aubin, Captain Ryan Anthony Beaupre, Corporal Brian Matthew Kennedy, Staff Sergeant Kendall Damon Waters-Bey. And we remember the last, Specialist David Emanuel Hickman, November 14, 2011.

Separated by nearly 9 years, they are bound for all time, among the nearly 4,500 American patriots who gave all that they had to give. To their families, including the Gold Star families here tonight, know that we will never forget their sacrifice and that your loved ones live on in the soul of our Nation, now and forever.

You taught us about strength, the kind that comes from within, the kind that we see in our wounded warriors. For you, coming home was the start of another battle: the battle to recover, to stand, to walk, to serve again. And in your resilience we see the essence of America, because we do not give up. No matter the hardship, we push on. And just as the wounds of war can last a lifetime, so does America's commitment to you and all who serve to give you the care you earned and the opportunities you need as you begin the next proud chapter in your lives.

And finally, all of you taught us a lesson about the character of our country. As you look across this room tonight, you look at our military, we draw strength from every part of our American family: every color, every creed, every background, every belief. And every day, you succeed together, as one American team.

As your Commander in Chief, I could not be more proud of you. As an American, as a husband and father of two daughters, I could not be more grateful for your example of the kind of country we can be, of what we can achieve when we stick together.

So I'll leave you with a picture that captures this spirit. It's from that day in December, when the last convoy rolled out, five American soldiers standing beside their vehicle, marked with the words, "Last vehicle out of Iraq." They're young, men and women, shoulder to shoulder, proud, heads held high, finally going home. And they were asked what it was like to be, literally, the last troops out of Iraq. And one of them gave a simple reply: "We completed the mission." We completed the mission. We did our jobs.

So I propose a toast: To the country we love, to the men and women who defend her, and to that faith—that fundamental American faith—that says no mission is too hard, no challenge is too great, through tests and through trials, we don't simply endure, we emerge stronger than before, knowing that America's greatest days are still to come, and they are great because of you.

Cheers.

[At this point, the President offered a toast.]

God bless you and your families, and may God continue to bless those in uniform and the United States of America.

Thank you very much, everybody. May dinner be served.

NOTE: The President spoke at 8:07 p.m. in the East Room at the White House. In his remarks, he referred to Deanie Dempsey, wife of Gen. Martin E. Dempsey, USA, Chairman, Joint Chiefs of Staff; and Jill T. Biden, wife of Vice President Joe Biden. The transcript released by the Office of the Press Secretary also included the remarks of Gen. Dempsey, Secretary of Defense Leon E. Panetta, and Vice President Biden. The transcript was released by the Office of the Press Secretary on March 1.

Remarks at Nashua Community College in Nashua, New Hampshire
March 1, 2012

The President. Hello, Nashua! It is good to be back in New Hampshire!

Thank you, Mike, for that wonderful introduction and for your service to our country. I want to thank the president of Nashua Community College, Lucille Jordan, for hosting us here today. Give Lucille a big round of applause. We've got Professor Paul [Karl]° Wunderlich, who gave me a great tour. Where's Paul? Where is he? He's got a beard; you can see him. [*Laughter*] There he is. And I want to thank your mayor, Donnalee Lozeau, for join-

ing us here today. Where's Donnalee? Right over there—there. Right in there. It is— [*laughter*].

Audience member. We love you!

The President. I love you back. It is good to be back in New Hampshire.

Audience member. [*Inaudible*]—9–1–1! 9–1–1!

The President. Oh——

Audience member. Somebody's down!

The President. Okay, we'll be all right. They probably were just standing too long. Just give

---

° White House correction.

them a little space. Do—where's our EMS folks? They'll be okay. Just give them a little space. This happens sometimes. You guys been here a while after the magging?

Audience members. Yes.

The President. Well, no, you have to eat ahead of time. [*Laughter*] Keep your blood sugar high. We got somebody over there? Jordan, right in the middle. There we go. Here's our guy. Make a little room, everybody. All right, let's make sure everybody is okay.

[*At this point, the President paused in his remarks momentarily.*]

You all right? All good? Okay. I think you're going to be all right. Okay. So remember, eat before you come to a Presidential event. [*Laughter*]

Now, I am from Chicago, so you know a little snow was not going to keep me away, which is why I can relate to New Hampshirites, because this is just, like, a dusting. [*Laughter*] It's like, what's the big deal? There's no big deal. When Air Force One landed, there were, like, 50 people waiting to shake my hand. They got icicles on their eyebrows. [*Laughter*] I—hey, great weather. [*Laughter*] So I want to thank all of you for making the trek out here. I really appreciate it.

I just had a chance to look at some of the cutting-edge work that's being done here at the auto shop. Earlier this week, I gave a speech to American autoworkers where I said that one reason this country has an auto industry today is because we're not just building cars again, we're building better cars, cars that— [*applause*]—we're building cars that use less oil, cars that go further on a gallon of gas. And in part, that's because of what's happening in places like this community college. It's because of so many of you.

I don't need to tell you why fuel efficiency is so important, especially right now. Most of you filled up your gas tanks in the last week or two, am I right?

It hasn't been a happy experience. You've seen the prices go up almost every day, and you've already felt the pinch, whether you own a car or maybe you own a small business that uses energy. Some of you have no choice but to drive a long way to work. And higher gas prices are like a tax straight out of your paycheck. And in the winter, the rising price of oil is also making it more expensive to heat your homes.

Now, I know this is hard to believe, but some politicians are seeing higher gas prices as a political opportunity. You're shocked, I know. [*Laughter*] But it's true—right in the middle of an election year. Who would have thought? [*Laughter*] So, recently, the lead in one news story said, and I'm quoting here, "Gasoline prices are on the rise, and Republicans are licking their chops." Licking their chops. Now let me tell you, only in politics do people respond to bad news with such enthusiasm. [*Laughter*] That doesn't happen anywhere else.

And so as a consequence, you can anticipate we're going to be hearing a lot about how people have these magic three-point plans to make sure that you're only paying 2-dollar-a-gallon gas. Just like we heard about it in the last election, just like we've heard about it for the last 30 years. And you know what the essence of their plan is going to be, which is: Step one, drill; step two, drill; step three, keep drilling. And by the way, we'll drill in your backyard. We'll—wherever it is, we're just going to put up more rigs.

Now, if there's one thing I know about New Hampshire, it's that your political bull detector is pretty keen. It's pretty sharp. You know that we can't just drill our way to lower gas prices. There are no quick fixes or silver bullets. If somebody's—tells you there are, they're not telling you the truth.

If we're going to take control of our energy future, which we have to do, if we're going to avoid high gas prices every single year, with a lot of politicians talking every single year, but nothing happening, if we're going to avoid that, then we've got to have an all-of-the-above strategy that develops every single source of American energy. Not just oil and gas, but also wind and solar and biofuels. We've got to keep developing the technology that allows us to use less oil in our cars and trucks, less oil in our buildings and our factories. And that's the strategy we've been pursuing for the last 3 years, and it's the only real solution to this challenge.

Now, here's the good news. We're making progress. And you can see it in this chart. There's a chart behind me right here. We're using visual aids today. [*Laughter*] The bar on the left shows that 6 years ago, 60 percent of the oil we used was imported. Since I took office, America's dependence on foreign oil has gone down every single year—every single year. In fact, in 2010, it was under 50 percent for the first time in 13 years—for the first time.

And we gave one of these handy charts to everybody who came today, so you can impress your family and friends—[*laughter*]—with your knowledge. It makes a great conversation piece at parties. [*Laughter*]

Now, one of the reasons our oil—our dependence on foreign oil is down is because of policies put in place by our administration, but also the—our predecessor's administration. And whoever succeeds me is going to have to keep it up. This is not going to be solved by one party. It's not going to be solved by one administration. It's not going to be solved by slogans. It's not going to be solved by phony rhetoric. It's going to be solved by a sustained, all-of-the-above energy strategy.

And no matter what you hear from some folks in an election year, the key part of this strategy over the last 3 years has been to increase safe, responsible oil production here at home while also pursuing clean energy for the future. We don't have to choose between one or the other, we got to do both.

So, when it comes to oil production, under my administration, America is producing more oil today than at any time in the last 8 years. That is a fact. That's a fact. Under my administrations, we have a near-record number of oil rigs operating right now, more working oil and gas rigs than the rest of the world combined. Think about that. That's a fact.

We've opened up millions of new acres for oil and gas exploration where appropriate and where it is done safely, and we've approved more than 400 drilling permits since we put in place new safety standards to make sure that we don't have the same kind of spill that we had down in the Gulf a couple of years ago.

And we've approved dozens of new pipelines to move oil around, including from Canada. Just this week, we announced that we'll do whatever we can to help speed the construction of a pipeline in Oklahoma that will relieve a bottleneck for oil that needs to get to the Gulf. And that's going to help create jobs and encourage production.

So we're focused on American oil production. We are doing all that we can in a safe, responsible way to make sure that American oil production and gas production is high. But here's the thing. The amount of oil that we drill at home doesn't set the price of gas on its own. And the reason is, is because oil is bought and soiled—bought and sold on the world energy market. And just like last year, the biggest thing that's causing the price of oil to rise right now is instability in the Middle East. This time it's Iran. But a lot of folks are nervous about what might happen there, and so they're anticipating there might be a big disruption in terms of flow. And when uncertainty increases, speculation on Wall Street can drive up prices even more. Those are the short-term factors at work here.

So when you start hearing a bunch of folks saying somehow that there's some simple solution, you can turn a nozzle and suddenly we're going to be getting a lot more oil, that's just not how it works. Over the long term, the biggest reason oil prices will rise is because of growing demand in countries like China and India and Brazil.

Just think about this. In 5 years, the number of cars on the road in China more than tripled. Over the last 5 years, the number of cars tripled. Nearly 10 million cars were added in China alone in 2010; 10 million cars just in one country in 1 year. So that's using up a lot of oil, and those numbers are only going to get bigger over time. As places like China and India get wealthier, they're going to want to buy cars like we do, and they're going to want to fill them up like we do, and that's going to drive up demand.

So what does this mean for us? What does this mean for America? It means that anybody who tells you that we can just drill our way out of this problem does not know what they're talking about or they're not telling you the truth, one or the other.

Here's another way to think about it. The United States consumes more than 20 percent of the world's oil, but we only have 2 percent of the world's oil reserves. Twenty percent we use; we only produce 2 percent. And no matter what we do, it's not going to get much above 3 percent. So we're still going to have this huge shortfall. That's why if we really want energy security and energy independence, we've got to start looking at how we use less oil and use other energy sources that we can renew and that we can control so we are not subject to the whims of what's happening in other countries.

We have to keep developing new technology that helps us use less energy. We've got to keep relying on American know-how and ingenuity that comes from places like this one, Nashua Community College. That's our future. And that, that's exactly the path that we've been taking these last 3 years. Because of the investments we've made, the use of clean, renewable energy in this country has nearly doubled, and thousands of Americans have jobs because of it.

We're taking every possible action to develop a near-hundred-year supply of natural gas, which releases fewer carbons. Now that's something that experts believe will support more than 600,000 jobs by the end of the decade. Our cooperation with the private sector has positioned this country to be the world's leading manufacturer of high-tech batteries that will power the next generation of American cars.

And after three decades of doing nothing, we put in place fuel economy standards that will make sure our cars average nearly 55 miles per gallon by the middle of the next decade. That's nearly double what we have today. And that, by the way, applies not just to cars, it applies to light trucks, and now it's going to apply to heavy trucks as well.

So that means that every time you fill up, you can think to yourself, you know what, I won't have to fill up again for 2 weeks instead of 1 week. Yes, that's worth applauding. [*Applause*] Because what that means is that will save the typical family more than $8,000 at the pump. And it means that this country will reduce our oil consumption by more than 2 million barrels a day, which means we can continue to see a decline in how much imported oil we need. And that's good for our national security, that's good for our economy, and it's good for our environment.

So that's the strategy we've got to pursue. But we've got to do more, and we've got to do more even faster. We've got to keep investing in developing every available type of American-made energy. And this means that we've got to set some priorities. We've got to make some choices.

First, while there are no short-term silver bullets when it comes to gas prices, I've directed my administration to look for every single area where we can make an impact and help consumers, from helping to relieve bottlenecks in the places like the one we've got in Oklahoma to making sure speculators aren't taking advantage of what's going on in the oil markets. And we're just going to keep on announcing steps in the coming weeks; every time we find something that can provide a little bit of relief right now, we're going to do it.

But over the long term, an all-of-the-above strategy requires the right incentives. And here's one of the best examples. Right now 4 billion of your tax dollars—4 billion—subsidizes the oil industry every year. Hmm.

Audience members. Boo!

The President. Four billion dollars. Now, these companies are making record profits right now, tens of billions of dollars a year. Every time you go to the gas tank or fill up your gas tank, they're making money—every time. Now, does anyone really think that Congress should give them another $4 billion this year?

Audience members. No!

The President. Of course not. It's outrageous. It's inexcusable. And I am asking Congress: Eliminate this oil industry giveaway right away. I want them to vote on this in the next few weeks. Let's put every single Member of Congress on record: You can stand with the oil companies, or you can stand up for the American people. You can keep subsidizing a fossil fuel that's been getting taxpayer dollars for a century, or you can place your bets on a clean energy future.

So I'm asking everybody here today, anybody who is watching at home, let your Member of Congress know where you stand. Will you do that?

Audience members. Yes!

The President. Because I know, I know where I stand, New Hampshire. I know where I stand on this. We want to have successful oil companies that are able to get the oil that we have in our country, but we also understand that our future requires us to make investments in clean, renewable energies. And that has to start now. We can't wait. We can't wait until gas has skyrocketed more and people are desperate. We need to start making those investments now.

And most of you guys agree. That's why you're putting your time—that's why folks here at this community college are learning about building cars and repairing cars that use less oil, cars that are powered with alternative fuels, like natural gas. That's why the city of Nashua is purchasing a new fleet of trash trucks that run on natural gas. They're going to go cleaner, they're going to last longer, they're going to be cheaper to fill up.

I saw one of them. It was a good-looking truck. And it put a smile on the mayor's face, because she knows she's saving money. She's saving taxpayer money. Good job, Mayor.

So that's part of what that $4 billion that's going to the oil companies right now, that's where it could be going, to help cities like this one convert their fleets to fuel-efficient cars and trucks, to help private sector companies— big companies like UPS or Federal Express— convert their fleets. That can save us money. In fact, since we announced the National Clean Fleets Partnership last year, the companies interested in transitioning their fleets have tri-

pled. And that's part of why this chart is going down.

And I'm proud to say that the Federal Government is leading by example. One thing the Federal Government has a lot of is cars. I don't know if you guys are aware of this, but— [*laughter*]—we have a lot of cars. And I've directed every department, every agency—every single one—to make sure that by 2015, a hundred percent of the vehicles that the Federal Government buys are fuel-efficient cars and trucks. Let's save us money.

So this is our future. This is the ultimate solution to our energy challenge. It's not going to be a smooth, easy ride. Some of the clean energy technologies that are discovered, they won't pan out. Some companies will fail. There's going to be experiments and research that take time. But as long as I'm President, I will not walk away from the promise of clean energy, because our future depends on it. I'm not going to cede the wind or the solar or the battery industry to China or Germany because some politicians in Washington refused to make the same commitment here in the United States of America.

With or without this Congress, I'm going to continue to do whatever I can to develop every source of American energy, to make sure that 3 years from now our dependence on foreign oil is even lower, to make sure that our future is not controlled by events on the other side of the world.

We may not have a silver bullet to bring down gas prices tomorrow or reduce our dependence on foreign oil overnight. But what we do have in this country are limitless sources of energy and a boundless supply of ingenuity and imagination and talent that we can put to work to develop the energy of the future. We've got you. We've got you.

The easiest thing in the world is to make phony election-year promises about lowering gas prices. But what's harder is to make a serious, sustained commitment to tackle a problem that we've been talking about for 30 years and has not been tackled, has not been solved. It's not going to be solved in 1 year or one term, maybe not completely even in one decade. But that's the kind of commitment that we need. That's what this moment requires.

And so when I see all the young people who are here today—or the young at heart—[*laughter*]—we need you guys to keep at it. This is your future at stake. We need you to work hard. We need you to dream big. We need you to summon the same spirit of unbridled optimism, that bold willingness to tackle tough problems that led previous generations to meet the challenges of their time, to power a nation from coast to coast, to touch the Moon, to connect an entire world with our own science and imagination. That's what America is capable of doing.

And it's that history that teaches us that all of our challenges—all of them—are within our power, within our grasp to solve. This one is no different. This one's no different. It will require our brightest scientists, our most creative companies, but it's also going to require all of us—Democrats, Republicans, everybody in between—to do our part. That's what this moment requires.

And I know we can do it. And when we do, we'll remind the world once again just why it is that the United States of America is the greatest nation on Earth.

Thank you, everybody. God bless you. God bless the United States of America.

NOTE: The President spoke at 1:28 p.m. In his remarks, he referred to Mike Kapel, student, Nashua Community College.

Remarks at an Obama Victory Fund 2012 Fundraiser in New York City
March 1, 2012

Thank you. Wow, you are making me blush. [*Laughter*]

It is just wonderful to be here. And I want to thank Victor and Sarah for opening up their extraordinary home. Although, I will say they have some pictures of me before I had gray hair—[*laughter*]—which is a little troubling. They should have put the photo down. [*Laughter*] But it's a testimony to how long the two of them have been friends and supporters. And those of you who know them know the passion and the extraordinary energy that they bring to issues of social justice and democratic politics.

I'm grateful for all you being here. I'm going to keep my remarks at the top relatively brief so that we can have more of an exchange of ideas and I can answer questions and you guys can give me good advice.

But I'll tell you, obviously, we've gone through 3 of the toughest years that America has gone through in our lifetimes. And when I think back to those early months—at a time when we were losing 800,000 jobs a month and the banking sector had completely locked up and the auto industry was on the verge of liquidation here in the United States and globally no one was sure whether the center would hold—the thing that gave me confidence was the incredible resilience and energy and hopefulness that I had seen during my travels as a Presidential candidate. And so as scary as those moments were, I had confidence that America could bounce back.

Now, we're not all the way back. There is still a lot of hardship out there. There are a lot of folks who still are looking for a job, or if they're employed, are still just barely getting by. There are millions of Americans who have seen their homes decline in value and they're underwater, and they're wondering whether they're going to be able to retire as they had planned or send their kid to college.

We still have an enormous amount of work to do. But the good news is that here in the United States, the trend lines are good. Last month, we saw 250,000 jobs created. We've created 3.7 million jobs over the last 2 years. We've seen the highest growth in manufacturing jobs since the 1990s. Unemployment is still high, but it's been moving in the right direction.

And across the country, what you're seeing are businesses small and large saying to themselves, you know what, investing in America makes sense, because for all of our challenges, there's still no country that other folks would

233

rather be because they understand that there is something about this place, that there's a set of values that are core to who we are, that are woven into our DNA, that allow you to make it if you try.

Now the challenge is that for a lot of folks, that essential American Dream that brought a lot of our forebears here to the United States has been slipping away. And so even as we've tried to right the ship of the economy, even as we saved the auto industry, even as we stayed focused on putting people back to work, we were also looking at what are the fundamentals that ensure that everybody is going to get a fair shot, everybody is going to do their fair share, everybody is going to play by the same set of rules.

And that's why, over the last 3 years, we've focused on making sure that you don't go bankrupt if you get sick and that 30 million people will have health insurance that didn't have it before and insurance companies can't deny you coverage at a time when you need it most.

It's the reason we've put such an emphasis on education, not just through reform of the K–12 system, so every kid, no matter what their circumstances, can move ahead, but also, that once they graduate from high school, they can actually afford to go to college. And we've made a bigger commitment at the Federal level to education than any administration in recent history. And our basic argument has been, not only are we going to put more money in, but we're also going to reform the system and raise standards and infuse school districts with the kind of creativity and passion that's required to make sure that kids can learn.

It's the reason why, on the environmental front, we've doubled fuel efficiency standards on cars so that we know that a decade from now your average vehicle will get 55 miles a gallon, which is part of the reason why we're starting to see our dependence on foreign oil decline; and having an energy policy that is not just drill, drill, drill, but is also investing in clean energy and advanced battery technologies and making sure that we're using energy more efficiently. That's going to be one of the

foundations for making sure that we can succeed over the long term.

So, in addition to just saving the economy, what we've been trying to do is make sure that we provide a better foundation for long-term economic growth. And we're poised to make that happen.

Of course, over the last 3 years, I haven't just been able to worry about what happened here in this country, we've also had to do a little bit of worrying about what happened around the world. The first promise I made as a Presidential candidate was that I would end the war in Iraq. Last night, I had the great honor of hosting a representative sample of the incredible young men and women, and some not so young men and women, in uniform who helped allow us to stabilize Iraq. And that war is now over.

We're in the process of transitioning in Afghanistan so that, increasingly, Afghans can take a lead for their own security and we can start bringing our troops home. And we've been able to do all this while focusing attention on those who actually perpetrated 9/11. And Al Qaida is weaker than it's ever been, and bin Laden is no more. Which goes to show that there's no contradiction between having a smart foreign policy, a foreign policy that is consistent with our values, but also being tough and looking out for America's national security.

Now, just as there's a lot more work to do here in the United States, there's a lot more work that we have to do internationally. What's happening in the Middle East and North Africa right now is as profound, as transformative, as what happened when the Berlin Wall fell, and the jury is still out in terms of the direction that it will go. And my administration's commitment has been to say that we will continue to affirm our values, the things we believe in, that we will, where we can, defend people from brutality of their own governments, that we will stand up for human rights, we will stand up for free speech, we will stand up for women's rights. We will oppose torture. We will oppose the kind of oppressiveness that unfortunately had been too common in too many countries in that region.

And one of our long-term goals in that region is to make sure that the sacrosanct commitment that we make to Israel's security is not only a matter of providing them the military capabilities they need, not only providing the sort of qualitative military edge that they need in a very tough neighborhood, but also that we are a partner with them to try to bring about a peace in the region that can be lasting. And that is a challenge.

What we're seeing around that region is, is it used to be easier just to deal with one person who was an autocrat when it came to knowing who you could strike a deal with. Part of what happens as a consequence of these regimes dissolving is that we're going to have to take into account the politics and the attitudes of people in this region. And that's going to be challenging because there have been years of venom and anti-Semitism and anti-Israeli rhetoric that had been floating around for a long time.

At the same time, one of the things that I'm absolutely convinced of is that for Israel's long-term security, it is going to be necessary for us—even as we draw sharp lines in terms of Israel's security—to also continue to reach out to people of good will on the other side and try to shape the kind of lasting, two-state solution that will allow Israel not only to preserve its security, but also to preserve its essence as a democratic, Jewish state.

And so as I look out over the next several years, America has probably had—never had a clearer choice about where we go next, because the other side has a very different vision across the board about who we are and what's important. On the domestic front, their basic vision is if a very few people at the top are doing well and everybody else is struggling to get by, that's okay. On the foreign policy side, their view is, is that as long as we are flexing our muscles militarily, the need for engagement and diplomacy is a sign of weakness rather than strength.

And so this election has huge consequences. And what I've been saying to folks as I travel around the country—a lot of supporters back in 2008—it was so much fun and so fresh to support this young guy who nobody could pronounce his name and there were those posters there and—there's a little bit of revisionist history. People remember that campaign as being flawless and so much fun. I don't remember it that way. [*Laughter*] I remember us screwing up all the time.

And so I acknowledge, yes, I've got a little more gray hair now. And the last 3 years, despite, I think, the extraordinary work that my team has done, that we've got some dings and some nicks and some cuts from the battles we've had to fight. But I am as determined as I ever was, and I believe as deeply as I ever have, about the core decency of the American people and the importance of a Government that reflects those values.

And that's what we're going to be fighting for over the next year. And I'm going to need your help. So I hope you're ready, and I hope you will be just as determined, just as fired up, just as ready to go as you were in 2008.

Thank you very much, everybody. Thank you.

NOTE: The President spoke at 5 p.m. at the residence of Victor and Sarah Kovner. Audio was not available for verification of the content of these remarks.

Remarks at an Obama Victory Fund 2012 Fundraiser in New York City
March 1, 2012

[*The President's remarks were joined in progress.*]

——first of all, your outstanding Congresswoman of this district, Carolyn Maloney, is here, and we want to give her a big round of applause. And my understanding is we also have the chairman of our convention effort in Charlotte, North Carolina, Jim Rogers. Where's Jim? Where is he? Jim Rogers, right here. Thank you, Jim. Here—is working hard to make sure that is a good event, and we're going to make sure that North Carolina is blue again.

So I'm not going to be long at the top. I'm just going to make a few brief remarks, and then what I want to do is save as much time as possible for us to have a conversation and to take questions.

Four years ago, we were losing 800,000 jobs a month; last month, we gained 250,000 jobs. Three years ago, the banking system had frozen up completely; today, credit is flowing again. Three years ago, the auto industry was on the verge of liquidation; today, GM not only is the number-one automaker in the world again, but also saw the highest profits in its entire history. Over the last 2 years, we've created 3.7 million jobs in the private sector. Manufacturing is the strongest it's been since the 1990s.

None of this argues that we're out of the woods. Many of you are in business, and you know better than I do that there are a lot of folks out there who are still having a tough time. There are a lot of small businesses that still have trouble getting credit. The unemployment rate remains too high. We still have enormous challenges to make sure that we are the most competitive, most productive economy in the world in the 21st century. But the trend lines are good. The economy is stronger, we are more productive, and we are poised to be able to take advantage of a moment where all the things that we're good at—innovation, dynamism, entrepreneurship—all those things are going to be at a greater premium than ever before.

And the question then becomes, do we continue down the path that allows us to compete and create good jobs with good wages and ensures that the essence of the American Dream, which is everybody gets a fair shot, no matter where you come from, no matter what you look like; if you work hard and you've got a good idea, you're able to succeed; that everybody does their fair share so that, in addition to this incredible individualism and enterprise that we rightly are proud of, we also are looking out for one another; and everybody is playing by the

same set of rules, that the notion of fair play exists in all sectors of our economy—the question is, is that going to be the vision that guides us over the next 10, 20, 50 years? Or are we going to pursue a vision that says it's okay for a few of us to do really well while the rest of America is struggling?

And this election is going to give us a starker choice than we have had in my lifetime. Now, if you agree with me that it's good for all of us to ensure everybody has a fair shot, everybody is doing their fair share, and fair play reigns, then that has to translate into some concrete policy. It means that we continue to make investments in education and we follow the path that we've been following over the last 3 years, which is, yes, we put more money into education, but we also demand more reform.

It means we continue to make investments in American-made energy. But that doesn't just include oil production and gas production, as much as we're promoting that. It also includes us preparing for the future by investing in clean energy.

It means we're investing in science and technology, recognizing that that's how we got here, was we invented more stuff and operationalized it and commercialized it better than anybody else in the world. And the Federal Government historically has had a role in that.

It means we rebuild our infrastructure so that we can compete and move goods and services around the world better than anybody else can.

And it means that even as we are getting our fiscal house in order, that we're doing so in a way that doesn't just put the burden on the senior citizen on Medicare or the student who is trying to finance their way through college, but those of us that have been incredibly blessed by this society, that we're doing our part as well.

Now, the proposals that I've put forward in terms of balancing our budget, making our Government more efficient, but making sure that it's still creating ladders of opportunity, making sure that we're still investing in those things that help us succeed economically, that made us an engine of economic growth and created this incredible middle class that we have—all those things that we've done are ideas that traditionally received Democratic and Republican support.

It's only in this environment that we've seen the other party suddenly say that that's socialism, that that somehow is un-American. That somehow the critical role that Government has played as a partner with the marketplace to create opportunity for everybody, that somehow there's something wrong with that. I reject that vision, and I think the American people do too.

Now, they've gone 3 tough years, and so this is going to be a close election. Nobody is under any illusion that this isn't going to be a tight race for us. But as I travel around the country and I talk to folks, including people who don't support me, when you break down the individual items that are being debated right now—how do we balance this budget, what our tax policy should be, should we be investing in education, should we make sure that science and basic research continue to be paramount in our economy, do we have an obligation to make sure that our seniors can retire with dignity and respect—we win that argument every time.

And when it comes to foreign policy, I'm actually finding it very interesting. The other side traditionally seems to feel that Democrats are somehow weak on defense, and they've had a little trouble making that argument this year. Because I think that what we've shown is there's no contradiction between being tough and strong and protecting the American people, but also abiding by those values that make

America great and believing in diplomacy and believing in engagement and believing that it's not a sign of weakness when we try to resolve issues peacefully, even as we're prepared, when we need to for our own security, to act militarily.

So let me just close by saying this. So many people in this room were active in 2008. So many of you have had to defend me from your coworkers over the last 3 years. [*Laughter*] And it's true that over the last 3 years I'm a little grayer than I was. Being an Obama supporter is not as trendy as it was. [*Laughter*] Those old "Hope" posters that we had, they're a little dog eared. [*Laughter*] But I am more determined and more confident than I have ever been that if we keep at it, that America is poised to be stronger, more unified, more competitive, bolder, more generous than we ever have been before.

And you will see me working harder and making those arguments as passionately as anything that I did in 2008. And if you guys are with me, then I'm pretty confident not only are we going to win, but more importantly, America is going to be in good stead for years to come.

Thank you very much, everybody. Thank you.

NOTE: The President spoke at 6:04 p.m. at the ABC Kitchen. In his remarks, he referred to James E. Rogers, chairman, president, and chief executive officer, Duke Energy. Audio was not available for verification of the content of these remarks.

Remarks at an Obama Victory Fund 2012 Fundraiser in New York City
March 1, 2012

The President. Hello, New York! Oh, it is good to be back in New York City.

We've got some folks here that I want to acknowledge. First of all, the event cochairs: Deepak Chopra, thank you; Paulette Cole, thank you; Reshma Saujani, thank you; Russell Simmons, thank you.

Got a couple of elected officials who are here: Congresswoman Carolyn Maloney is

here, and Public Advocate Bill de Blasio is here. I want to thank all the talent who participated: Ben Folds; Ingrid Michaelson; the Roots are always in the house; and Aziz Ansari.

Now, this is big because Malia is a big "Parks and Recreation" fan. So having Aziz here is, like, the only thing she thinks is worth me doing. [*Laughter*] I want to thank him for what he said earlier. I know he's backstage, but I just want to remind him, I've got more Twitter followers than you, man. [*Laughter*] I just want to keep him humble and hungry. [*Laughter*] We all need somebody who does that; fortunately, I have Michelle. [*Laughter*]

Now, this is a incredible tapestry of what New York is all about. But I also want to thank all the Asian American and Pacific Islanders who helped get this program off the ground. It is a incredible reminder of my roots back in Hawaii and the incredible visit that we made to India just over a year ago. Although it was a little discouraging because the day after our first visit, I opened up the papers, there were two headlines: "President Obama Visits India," and then there was, "Michelle Obama Rocks India." [*Laughter*] So this is kind of my life, keeps me humble.

I am here today not just because I need your help, although I do, but I'm here because your country needs your help. There was a reason why so many of you worked your hearts out in 2008. And I see some friends out here who were active in that campaign. And you got involved not because you thought it was going to be easy. I mean, think about it. You supported a candidate named Barack Hussein Obama— [*laughter*]—for President of the United States. You did not need a poll to know that was not going to be a sure thing. [*Laughter*]

And besides, you didn't join the campaign because of me. It was not about one person. It was because of a shared vision that we had for America. It was because of your commitments to each other. It's not a vision of America where everybody is left to fend for themselves. It's a vision of America where everybody works together and everybody who works hard has a chance to get ahead, not just those at the very top.

That's the vision we share. That's the change we believed in, that no matter who you are, no matter where you come from, no matter what you look like, no matter what your name is, that in this country you can make it if you try. That was the change we believed in.

And we knew it wasn't going to come easy. We knew it wouldn't come quickly. But I want you to think about what we have done in just 3 years because of what you did in 2008. Think about it. Think about what change looks like. Change is the first bill I signed into law, a pretty simple law. It says women deserve an equal day's pay for an equal day's work, because we want—[*applause*]—because I want my daughters to have the same opportunity as someone's sons. That happened because of you.

Change is the decision we made to rescue the American auto industry from collapse, even when there were some politicians who were saying, let's let Detroit go bankrupt. And with 1 million jobs on the line, we weren't going to let that happen. And today, GM is back on top as the world's number-one automaker, just reported the highest profits in 100 years. With 200,000 new jobs created in the last 2½ years, the American auto industry is back. That happened because of you.

Change is the decision we made to stop just waiting for Congress to do something about our addiction to oil and finally raise our fuel efficiency standards. And by the next decade, we will be driving American-made cars that get almost 55 miles to the gallon. And that will save the typical family $8,000 at the pump and reduce our dependence on foreign oil and start actually giving us some independence from these gas prices that have been going up. That's what change is. That's what you did.

Change is the fight we won to stop handing $60 billion in taxpayer subsidies to banks to process student loans and give that money directly to students and families who need it so that millions of young people around the country are able to afford college just a little bit better.

Change is health care reform that we passed after a century of trying, a reform that ensures that in the United States of America, nobody will go bankrupt just because they get sick. And already, 2.5 million young people have health insurance today because this law let them stay on their parent's plan. And every American can no longer be denied or dropped by their insurance company when they need care the most. That happened because of you, because of what you were willing to fight for back in 2008.

Change is the fact that for the first time in history, you don't have to hide who you love to serve the country you love, because we got rid of "don't ask, don't tell." And change is keeping another promise I made in 2008: For the first time in 9 years there are no Americans fighting in Iraq. We put that war to an end, and we refocused our efforts on the terrorists who actually attacked us on 9/11. And thanks to the incredible men and women in uniform, Al Qaida is weaker than it has ever been and Usama bin Laden will never again walk the face of this Earth.

We've restored respect for America around the world, made clear that America will abide by those core values that made us a great country. We ended torture. We promoted human rights. We made it clear that America is a Pacific power. We demonstrated that if countries like Burma travel down the road of democratic reform, they will find a new relationship with the United States. And we are leading again by the power of our moral example. That's what change is.

Audience member. No more war!

The President. None of this—nobody has announced a war, young lady. But we appreciate your sentiment. You're jumping the gun a little bit there.

None of this change has been easy. And we've got a lot more work to do. There are still too many Americans out there looking for work. There are too many families out there who are having a tough time paying their bills or making their mortgage or their house is underwater. They're still recovering from the worst economic storm in our lifetimes, in generations.

But over the last 2 years, businesses have added about 3.7 million new jobs. Our manufacturing sector is creating jobs again for the very first time since the 1990s. Our economy is getting stronger. The recovery is accelerating. America is coming back.

And the last thing we can afford to do right now is to go back to the very same policies that got us into this mess in the first place. But you know, that is exactly what the other folks for

this office—who are running for this office want to do.

I don't know if you've been paying attention—[*laughter*]—but they make no secret about their agenda. They want to go back to the days when Wall Street played by its own rules. They want to go back to the days when insurance companies could deny coverage or jack up your premiums without a reason. They want to spend a trillion dollars more on tax breaks for the wealthiest individuals, even if it means adding to our deficit or gutting education or gutting our investment in clean energy or making it tougher for seniors who are on Medicare. And their philosophy is simple: We are better off when everybody is left to fend for themselves, the most powerful can play by their own rules.

We're at a crossroads here. We've got as stark a choice as we've seen in a very long time. And their vision of America is fundamentally wrong, because in the United States of America we are greater together than we are on our own. We're better off—[*applause*]—we are better off when we keep to that basic American promise that if you work hard, you can do well enough to raise a family and own a home, send your kids to college and let them dream bigger than you ever imagined. Maybe you can retire with some dignity and respect and put a little bit away after a lifetime of labor. If you have a good idea to start a business, you can go out there and start one. If you want to serve, then there's a place for you teaching, helping kids who are having a tough time. That's the choice in this election.

This is not just another political debate. What's at stake is the defining issue of our time, because middle class Americans, but also those striving to get in the middle class, those of us who know we would not be here had it not been for the opportunities given our parents and our grandparents and our great-grandparents, some of us immigrants, some of us who are here because of that basic American promise. That's what we're fighting for. They are in a make-or-break moment.

We can go back to an economy that's built on outsourcing and phony debt and phony financial profits, or we can fight for an economy that works for everybody, an economy that's built to last, that's built on American manufacturing and American energy and education and skills for our workers and the values that made us great: hard work and fair play and shared responsibility. That's the vision of America that I believe in. That's the vision of America you believe in. That's what's at stake in this election.

I want an America where we are still attracting the best and the brightest from around the world. I want an America where the next generation of manufacturing is taking root here in the factories of Detroit and Pittsburgh and Cleveland. I don't want this Nation to just be known for how much we buy and consume. I want us to be inventing products and building products and selling products all around the world.

And we've got to have a Tax Code that incentivizes people to invest here, not just rewarding companies that are sending jobs overseas. We want capital and talent here, creating here in America.

We need to make our schools the envy of the world. And that starts with the man or woman at the front of the classroom. Because a good teacher—a recent study showed a good teacher can increase the lifetime earnings of just one class by over $250,000. So I don't want to hear folks in Washington bashing teachers; I don't want them defending the status quo. Let's give schools the resources they need to keep good teachers on the job and reward the best teachers. Let's grant schools flexibility to teach with creativity and passion and stop teaching to the test, even as—and demanding accountability and replacing teachers who aren't helping kids learn, but making sure that teachers who love to teach, that they're supported.

And when kids graduate, the most daunting challenge is, how do they afford college. Right now we've got more tuition debt than credit card debt in America. Now there's some immediate things we need to do. Congress needs to stop the interest rates on student loans from doubling in July. That's coming up. Colleges and universities have to do their part to be more affordable. If they can't stop tuition from going up, the funding they get from taxpayers should go down. Because higher education can't be a luxury, it's an economic imperative that every American family should be able to afford.

We've got to invest in our people. That's what will determine who can compete in the 21st century. And other countries are—they understand this. They're catching up. They're making the investments. Why aren't we? Why are we seeing teachers laid off all across the country? Why are we seeing it harder for young people to get a college education? Our priorities have gotten a little skewed.

An economy built to last is one where we're supporting scientists and researchers trying to make sure that the next breakthrough in clean energy happens right here in the United States of America. We've subsidized oil companies for over a hundred years. It's time to end those taxpayer giveaways to an oil industry that's rarely been more profitable, and let's double that on clean energy that has never been more promising: solar, wind, and biofuels.

We need to rebuild America. I'm a chauvinist when it comes to—I want America to have the best stuff. I want us to have the best roads and the best airports and the fastest railroads and Internet access. It's time to take the money that we're no longer spending at war, use half of it to pay down the debt, use the other half for some nation-building here at home. Let's put people back to work rebuilding America.

And in order to create this economy built to last, we've got to make sure that we've got a tax system that reflects everybody doing their fair share. That's why I've said we should follow the Buffett rule: If you make more than a million dollars a year, you should not pay a lower tax rate than your secretary. Now, if you make less than $250,000 a year, which is 98 percent of Americans, your taxes shouldn't go up. You're already challenged right now.

When I lay this out, I try to remind folks this is not class warfare. This isn't about envy. This is about basic math. Because if somebody like me gets a tax break I don't need and that the country cannot afford, then one of two things has to happen. Either that's going to add to the deficit; it's a tax cut that's not paid for, and we've just gone through a decade of that. Or alternatively, we're going to reduce the deficit on the backs of folks who can't afford it: the student who has to pay more for their student loans or the senior who suddenly has to pay more for their Medicare or a family that's trying to get by. That's not fair. It's not right. It's not who we are.

You hear a lot about values during election season. Politicians love to talk about values. And I think back, when I hear some of this talk, about the values my mother, my grandparents taught me when I was growing up. Hard work, that's a value. Looking out for one another, compassion, that's a value. The idea that we're all in this together and that we're—that we trust and care for one another, that I am my brother's keeper, I am my sister's keeper, that's a value.

Each of us is here because somewhere, somebody took responsibility not just for themselves, but also for the future, for their family, for their community, for their Nation. The American story has never been about what we do alone. It's what we do together. And we won't win the race for new jobs and businesses and security for middle class families with this same old "you're on your own" economics that the other side is peddling. It doesn't work.

It never worked. It didn't work when we tried it back in the decade before the Great Depression. It didn't work when we tried it in the last decade. And it won't work now. It will not work.

And what everybody here understands instinctively is if we attract an outstanding teacher to the profession by giving her the pay that she deserves, and that teacher goes on to educate the next Steve Jobs, we all benefit. If we provide faster Internet to rural America so a storeowner could suddenly sell his goods around the world or the next Russell Simmons, entrepreneur, can start promoting some unbelievable music, even though you don't have a lot of capital, that benefits all of us.

If we build a new bridge that saves shipping companies time and money or make airports work a little bit better so everybody saves a couple hours when you have to fly somewhere, we all do better: businesses, workers, customers—America.

And this has never been a Democratic or a Republican idea. The first Republican President, Abraham Lincoln, launched the transcontinental railroad, the National Academy of Sciences, the first land-grant colleges in the middle of a Civil War, because he understood those investments will pay dividends for decades to come. Teddy Roosevelt, Republican, called for a progressive income tax because he understood that we don't want a system in which barriers are created for the majority of people to be able to succeed.

Dwight Eisenhower, Republican, built the Interstate Highway System, stitching us together as one Nation. Republicans in Congress supported FDR when he gave millions of returning heroes, including my grandfather, a chance to go to college on the GI bill.

This is not a left-right idea. This is an American idea. And that same sense of common purpose, it still exists. Not always in Washington, but out in America, it's there. You go to a Main Street, you go to a town hall, you go to a VFW hall, you go to a diner, you go to a small business, you talk to the members of our Armed Forces, you go to a synagogue or a mosque or a church, a temple; our politics may be divided, but Americans, they know we have a stake in each other. They know no matter who you are, where you come from, we rise or fall as one Nation, as one people. And that's what's at stake right now. That's what this election is about.

So let me say this, New York, I know it's been a tough few years for America. We've taken some shots. The change we fought for in 2008 hasn't always happened as fast as we would have liked. After all that's happened in Washington, sometimes you look and you just see the mess—[*laughter*]—and it's tempting, I think, to sometimes say, you know what, maybe change isn't possible. Maybe that spirit that we had, maybe we were naive.

I know it's tempting to believe that. But remember what I always used to say during the last campaign, including that night at Grant Park. I said, real change, big change, is always hard. It's always hard. The civil rights movement was hard. Winning the vote for women was hard. Making sure that workers had some basic protections was hard. Around the world, Gandhi, Nelson Mandela, what they did was hard. It takes time. It takes more than a single term. It takes more than a single President. It takes more than a single individual. What it takes is ordinary citizens who keep believing, who are committed to fighting and pushing and inching this country closer and closer to our highest ideals.

And I said in 2008 that I am not a perfect man and I will not be a perfect President. But I promised you—[*laughter*]—I promised you back then that I would always tell you what I believed, I would always tell you where I stood, and that I would wake up every single day thinking about you and fight for you as hard as

I could and do everything possible to make sure that this country that has given me and Michelle and our kids so much, that that country is there for everybody. And you know what, I have kept that promise.

So, if you're willing to work with me and push through the obstacles and push through the setbacks and get back up when we get knocked down, and if you're willing to hold that vision that we have for America in your hearts, then I promise you change will come. And if you're willing to work as hard as you did in the last election in this election, then we will finish what we started and remind the world just why it is that America is the greatest nation on Earth.

God bless you, everybody. God bless the United States of America. Thank you.

NOTE: The President spoke at 8:45 p.m. at ABC Carpet & Home. In his remarks, he referred to former President Nelson R. Mandela of South Africa.

Remarks at an Obama Victory Fund 2012 Fundraiser in New York City
March 1, 2012

The President. Hello, New York? Hello, New York!

So let me start off by thanking Michael and James. They could not be better friends. And for them to open up their home to us just means so much.

It is a special treat for me because, as some of you know, Michael has been redesigning the White House. [*Laughter*] And he has some strong opinions. [*Laughter*] And sometimes doesn't always agree with my taste. And so it is good to come to his house and critique it. [*Laughter*] I don't know about this whole thing right here. [*Laughter*] Actually, he has done a remarkable job, despite me. So I'm grateful to him.

I see a lot of friends here, people who've supported me for a long time, and I just want to begin by saying thank you. I also want to announce because John Legend is here, I will not sing tonight. [*Laughter*]

Musician John Legend. Don't steal my job. [*Laughter*]

The President. Three years ago—a little over 3 years ago now, when I took office, America was in a place that I think some of us don't fully appreciate. We had lost 800,000 jobs the month I was sworn in. The banking system was locked up. There was worldwide panic. The stock market was about half what it is right now. And when I reflect back over the last 3 years, all the battles, all the challenges, what is remarkably encouraging is just how resilient America has proven to be.

That instead of losing 800,000 jobs, last month we gained 250,000. Over the last 2 years, we've created over 3.5 million jobs just in the private sector. Manufacturing is stronger than it's been since the 1990s. We've now had 10 consecutive quarters of growth. Slowly, businesses are recovering. Slowly, families are recovering. And the auto industry is back. GM is once again the number-one automaker in the world.

The trend lines are moving in the right direction. But there are still a lot of folks out there who are hurting: a lot of people who are still looking for jobs, lot of people whose homes are still underwater, a lot of small businesses that shuttered and haven't reopened.

And so when I think about why I ran in 2008, it wasn't simply to rescue the country from a great depression, because at that—at the time I announced, didn't know we were going into a great depression. It wasn't to save an auto industry. It wasn't to just get back to the status quo. The reason I ran was because there were challenges that had been building up for decades that were preventing America from being the America we dream about and we believe in. An America where everybody gets a fair shot and everybody does their fair share and everybody is playing by the same set of rules, an America where everybody, no matter what you look like, no matter where you come from, no matter what you believe, no matter who you love, you've got a chance to make it in this country.

And that's why I ran. And so as much satisfaction as I take from what we've accomplished over the last 3 years, we've got so much more to do.

It's part of the reason why, even as we restored the economy, even as we focused on making sure that we didn't spill into a depression, we also focused on the things that were going to matter in fulfilling that original vision: making sure that people don't go bankrupt when they get sick, making sure that we're investing in education so that young people can afford to go to college and that young people have the skills to go to college, making sure that we get rid of things like "don't ask, don't tell" that prevent people who love this country from serving this country just because of who they love or having to hide who they are. Making sure that we end things like torture and that we project an image around the world that is based on our values and what we care about and rejecting this notion that somehow we

have to choose between our security and our values.

Making sure that, in a country like America, that we are investing in not just now, but the future, and we're rebuilding our roads and our bridges, and we're investing in science and basic research. That we're thinking about how to not only reduce gas prices here and now, but also, how are we transitioning to a new economy that's not dependent on foreign oil and doubling fuel efficiency standards on cars and investing in clean energy and creating whole new industries in advanced battery manufacturing so that the cars of the future can get 100 or 200 miles a gallon or maybe at some point not have to use any oil.

So what we've tried to do is deal with immediate crises, but also make sure that we're keeping our eye on that long-term vision that got me into this campaign in 2008 and got many of you to support that campaign in 2008.

Now, the good news is, we've made incredible progress. The bad news is, is that we haven't had much cooperation from the other side. And I won't make this too sharply political. If you're wondering what I'm talking about, I recommend you watch the recent debates. We're thinking about just running those as advertisements—[*laughter*]—little snippets, without commentary. We'll just sort of—here you go, this is what they said a while back. [*Laughter*]

But I think what you're seeing now in the Republican primary underscores what's at stake in this election. There is a fundamental choice here about who we are. Do we have a vision of America that is big and bold and generous and inclusive and is built on hope? Or do we prefer a vision for America that is narrow and cramped and says there's an "us" and a "they" and is satisfied if a few people are doing very, very well at the very top and everybody else is struggling?

And that's going to apply to every issue that comes up, everything that we've done in the past, but also things that are not yet finished. For example, I believe that we've got to reform our immigration system, because it's not right if we've got 10 million people in this country who are living in the shadows, working for us, looking after our children in some cases, whose kids are U.S. citizens, playing with our kids, and somehow we can't figure out a way to give them some pathway to be a full part of this community or somehow we're afraid of attracting a talent from around the world. I mean, this is a nation of immigrants. When did we lose that sense that we welcome the "huddled masses"? Because it enriches us, it makes us who we are.

On deficits and debt, unlike Greece, even unlike England, our deficits and debts actually are entirely manageable if we make some sensible decisions. And the question is, are we going to cut education by 30 percent or Medicare by 30 percent or basically eliminate NIH funding or NSF funding or other basic research because the people in this room, we can't just pay just a little bit more in taxes? Or are we going to solve that problem in a balanced way where everybody is doing their part?

And so yes, we're reforming programs like Medicare and Medicaid, but we're also saying to ourselves we can step up and do a little bit more because we figure we're going to do better and our kids are going to do better if our neighbors have a shot as well. That's what built America.

On energy, right now, obviously, this happens every year—gas prices come up and somebody starts yelling, "Drill, drill, drill." And they want to drill in the South Lawn, and they want to drill in—[*laughter*]—have a drill every—have a rig every 2 miles along the California coast. And the fact of the matter is we've actually—oil production has been—is higher now than it's been in 8 years, and our dependence on foreign oil is lower than it's been in 16. We've got more rigs and more drilling in this country than all other countries combined.

And we welcome that. It's good that we develop the resources that we have. But the notion that with 2 percent of the world's reserves consuming 20 percent of the world's oil, that you don't hear just a smidgen of an idea from the other side about how we might want to enhance energy efficiency, how we might want to develop new sources of energy, how we might

want to restore our buildings so they're energy efficient or create more energy-efficient cars— not even a mention of it. In fact, somehow that's weak. It's un-American.

On every one of these issues, we've got a really sharp, stark choice. And the fact is they're wrong. They're wrong about what's going to ensure we've got the kind of future we want.

So the bottom line is that, as exciting and fun as 2008 was, at least in retrospect—[*laughter*]—I know I was younger then. I didn't have gray hair. It was cooler, it was trendier. There was posters and—[*laughter*]—you know. What's at stake this time is even more profound than what was at stake in 2008.

In 2008, I was running against a general election candidate who believed in banning torture, believed in doing something about climate change, somebody who, frankly, could never get a nomination in the Republican Party this time out, would be considered too liberal, right?

So the stakes are higher this time. And the question then is going to be, given that I'm a little older and it's not as trendy, are we able to summon the same kind of energy and the same kind of determination that's required to finish what we started?

And I'm just here to report that I'm ready. I've got the energy, I've got the determination. I've never been more convinced about what is possible in this country if we stick with it. There are times when people say, how did you get such a fine woman as Michelle to marry you? [*Laughter*] And my main response is, "Persistence." I stick to it if I believe in something. And I fight for it. And I believe in the America that the people in this room believe in, and it's worth fighting for. So I hope you'll join me.

Thanks, everybody.

NOTE: The President spoke at 9:49 p.m. at the residence of Michael S. Smith and James Costos. In his remarks, he referred to Sen. John S. McCain III, in his capacity as the 2008 Republican Presidential nominee. Audio was not available for verification of the content of these remarks.

Remarks at the Department of the Interior
March 2, 2012

Thank you so much. Thank you. Everybody, have a seat. Have a seat. Well, it is good to have all of you in here. Welcome to Washington.

I want to thank Ken Salazar for the introduction. Did everybody know that it's his birthday today? All right, has he milked that enough? [*Laughter*] I just want to make sure everybody wished him a happy birthday. Turning 40 is tough. [*Laughter*]

We've also got our outstanding Secretary of Agriculture, Tom Vilsack, in the house. Our wonderful EPA Administrator, Lisa Jackson, is with us. And I want to thank all of you for being a part of this conference.

Now, I have to say that this is a pretty diverse group here today. We've got hunters and fishermen, we've got farmers and ranchers, we've got conservationists, we've got small-business owners, we've got local government leaders, we've got tribal leaders. And some of you may have just wandered in, I don't know. [*Laughter*] But you're all here for the same reason: Each of you has a deep appreciation for the incredible natural resources, the incredible bounty that we've been blessed with as a nation. And you're working hard every day to make sure those resources are around for my daughters and your children and, hopefully, their children to enjoy.

Doing that takes creativity. The great Aldo Leopold once said that conservation is "a positive exercise of skill and insight, not merely a negative exercise of abstinence and caution." It's not just about doing nothing. It's about doing something affirmative to make sure that we are passing on this incredible blessing that we have. And you also know that effective conservation is about more than just protecting our environment. It's about strengthening our economy. When we put in place new common-sense rules to reduce air pollution, like we did in December, it was to prevent our kids from breathing in dangerous chemicals. That's something we should all be able to agree on. But it will also create new jobs building and installing all sorts of pollution control technolo-

gy. And since it will prevent thousands of heart attacks and cases of childhood asthma, it will also take some strain off our health care system.

When we make a commitment to restore a million acres of grasslands and wetlands and wildlife habitat, like the Department of Agriculture and Interior did today, we're not just preserving our land and water for the next generation. We're also making more land available for hunting and fishing. And we're bolstering our—an outdoor economy that supports more than 9 million jobs and brings in more than a trillion dollars a year.

And when we make it easier to visit this country, like we've done recently accelerating the process for foreign travelers to get visas, we're not just boosting tourism in big cities and places like Disney World. We're helping more people discover our parks and our mountains and our beaches. And more visitors means more people renting cars and staying in hotels and eating at our restaurants and buying our equipment.

So the work you're doing today is important if we're going to grow our economy and put more people back to work. But conservation is also important when it comes to another issue that I've been talking about lately, and that's developing new sources of American-made energy.

Obviously, gas prices are on a lot of folks' minds right now. And we're getting another painful reminder of why developing new energy is so important for our future. Of course, because it's an election year, everybody is trotting out their three-point plans for $2 gas. And you know what that involves, is you drill, and then you drill, and then you drill some more. We've heard this for 30 years.

The American people know better. They understand we can't just drill our way out of high gas prices. We're doing everything we can to boost U.S. production. But if we're going to take control of our energy future and avoid these gas price spikes in the future, then we've got to have a sustained all-of-the-above strategy that develops every available source of American energy: yes, oil and gas, but also wind and solar and biofuels and more.

And we're making progress on this front. In 2010, our dependence on foreign oil was under 50 percent for the first time in 13 years. Because of the investments we've made, the use of clean, renewable energy in this country has nearly doubled. And in my State of the Union Address, I announced that we're allowing the development of clean energy on enough public land to power 3 million homes—3 million homes. That protects our environment, and it helps families and businesses save money.

But while it's important to use public lands to develop things like wind and solar energy and reduce our dependence on foreign oil, we've also got to focus on protecting our planet. Now, that's why Teddy Roosevelt made sure that as we build this country and harvest its bounty, we also protect its beauty. That's part of our national character. And historically, it's been bipartisan.

That's why, even as our country grew by leaps and bounds, we made sure to set aside places like the Grand Canyon for our children and our grandchildren. It's why my administration has stood up to protect its waters. That's why President Kennedy directed a portion of the revenues from oil and gas production to help communities build trails and ball fields, and why my administration has fought to protect the Land and Water Conservation Fund.

That's why the hunters and anglers in this country have always been willing to pay a few extra bucks for a fishing license or a duck stamp that helps protect streams and habitats, because they want to make sure that their grandkids can enjoy these same pastimes. That's why my administration is expanding access to public lands so that more Americans can cast a rod or teach their children how to hunt.

We have to keep investing in the technology and manufacturing that helps us lead the world. But we've also got to protect the places that help define who we are, that help shape our character and our soul as a nation, places

that help attract visitors and create jobs, but that also give something to our kids that is irreplaceable.

And all of us have a role to play. One of the first bills I signed after taking office was the public lands bill that protected more than a thousand miles of rivers and established new national parks and trails. And 2 years ago, thanks to some great work by my Cabinet, and Ken Salazar especially, I kicked off the America's Great Outdoors Initiative to support conservation projects happening in all 50 States, including Fort Monroe in Virginia, which just became America's 396th national park.

Right now we're restoring the River of Grass in the Everglades, providing clean water to millions of residents, creating thousands of jobs, construction jobs, in southern Florida. We need to keep moving forward on projects like these. And I know we've got ranchers and farmers and landowners here today who represent places like the Crown of the Continent in Montana, the Dakota Grasslands, and everywhere in between. We need to keep working to protect these incredible landscapes that all of you know so well.

The bottom line is this: There will always be people in this country who say we've got to choose between clean air and clean water and a growing economy, between doing right by our environment and putting people back to work. And I'm here to tell you that is a false choice. [*Applause*] That is a false choice. With smart, sustainable policies, we can grow our economy today and protect our environment for ourselves and our children.

We know it's possible. And we know it because of what's been happening in communities like yours, where compromise isn't a dirty word, where folks can recognize a good idea no matter where it comes from.

A while back, I heard a story about the Rogue River in Oregon. And every year, the Rogue is filled with salmon swimming upstream to spawn. But because factories were allowed to—allowing warm water to run back into the river, the temperature was becoming too high for the salmon to survive. So to fix the problem, the town could have required the company to buy expensive cooling equipment, but that would have hurt the local economy. Instead, they decided to pay farmers and ranchers to plant trees along the banks of the river, and that helped to cool the water at a fraction of the cost. So it worked for business, it worked for farmers, it worked for salmon.

And those are the kinds of ideas that we need in this country. Ideas that preserve our environment, protect our bottom line, and connect more Americans to the great outdoors.

And this is personally important to me. Some of you know that I grew up in Hawaii mostly, and we got some pretty nice outdoors in Hawaii. [*Laughter*] And you spend a lot of time outdoors, and you learn very early on to appreciate this incredible splendor. But I remember when I was 11, I had never been to the mainland, and my grandmother and my mother and my sister, who at the time was 2, decided we were going to take a big summer trip. And we traveled across the country. And mostly we took Greyhound buses. My grandmother was getting—she had some eye problems, and so she couldn't see that well, so she was a little nervous about driving long distances. Sometimes we took the train. And we went to the usual spots, Disneyland and—yeah, I was 11, right? So—[*laughter*].

But I still remember traveling up to Yellowstone and coming over a hill and suddenly just hundreds of deer and seeing bison for the first time and seeing Old Faithful. And I remember that trip giving me a sense of just how immense and how grand this country was and how diverse it was. And watching folks digging for clams in Puget Sound and watching ranchers and seeing our first Americans guide me through a canyon in Arizona, and it gave you a sense of just what it is that makes America special.

And so when I went back to Yellowstone with Ken and my daughters—that was the first time they had been—and I'm standing there. I'm thinking not only about them and the first time they're seeing this, but I'm also remembering back to when my grandmother and my mother had shown me this amazing country so many years before.

And that is part of what we have to fight for. That's what's critical, is making sure that we're always there to bequeath that gift to the next generation. And if you'll work with me, I promise I'll do everything I can to help protect our economy, but also protect this amazing planet that we love and this great country that we've been blessed with.

Thank you very much, everybody. God bless you. God bless America.

NOTE: The President spoke at 5:32 p.m. In his remarks, he referred to his sister Maya Soetoro-Ng.

Statement on Representative Norman D. Dicks's Decision Not To Seek Re-election
March 2, 2012

I want to thank Norm Dicks for more than 30 years of service on behalf of the people of Washington State. Norm has spent his career working to protect our national security, championing the men and women of our Armed Forces, and fighting for the many natural resources of Washington State and the Pacific Northwest. Norm's dedication to our Nation's intelligence personnel and his leadership on the Appropriations Committee will be missed in Congress, and Michelle and I wish him and family well in the future.

Message to the Congress on Continuation of the National Emergency With Respect to the Situation in Zimbabwe
March 2, 2012

To the Congress of the United States:

Section 202(d) of the National Emergencies Act (50 U.S.C. 1622(d)) provides for the automatic termination of a national emergency unless, within 90 days prior to the anniversary date of its declaration, the President publishes in the *Federal Register* and transmits to the Congress a notice stating that the emergency is to continue in effect beyond the anniversary date. In accordance with this provision, I have sent to the *Federal Register* for publication the enclosed notice stating that the national emergency with respect to the actions and policies of certain members of the Government of Zimbabwe and other persons to undermine Zimbabwe's democratic processes or institutions is to continue in effect beyond March 6, 2012.

The crisis constituted by the actions and policies of certain members of the Government of Zimbabwe and other persons to undermine Zimbabwe's democratic processes or institutions has not been resolved. These actions and policies continue to pose an unusual and extraordinary threat to the foreign policy of the United States. For these reasons, I have determined that it is necessary to continue this national emergency and to maintain in force the sanctions to respond to this threat.

The United States welcomes the opportunity to modify the targeted sanctions regime when blocked persons demonstrate a clear commitment to respect the rule of law, democracy, and human rights. The United States has committed to continue its review of the targeted sanctions list for Zimbabwe to ensure it remains current and addresses the concerns for which it was created. We hope that events on the ground will allow us to take additional action to recognize progress in Zimbabwe in the future. The goal of a peaceful, democratic Zimbabwe remains foremost in our consideration of any action.

BARACK OBAMA

The White House,
March 2, 2012.

NOTE: The notice is listed in Appendix D at the end of this volume.

The President's Weekly Address
March 3, 2012

Hello, everybody. Earlier this week, I spent some time with the hard-working men and women of the American auto industry, who are busy writing a new chapter in America's story.

Just a few years ago, their industry was shedding hundreds of thousands of jobs. Two of the Big Three—GM and Chrysler—were on the brink of failure. If we had let this great American industry collapse, if we had let Detroit go bankrupt, more than 1 million Americans would have lost their jobs in the middle of the worst recession since the Great Depression.

I refused to let that happen. These jobs are worth more than just a paycheck. They're a source of pride and a ticket to the middle class. These companies are worth more than just the cars they build. They're a symbol of American innovation and a source of our manufacturing might.

So, in exchange for help, we demanded responsibility. We got the companies to retool and restructure. Everyone sacrificed. And 3 years later, the American auto industry is back.

Today, GM is the number-one automaker in the world. Chrysler is growing faster in America than any other car company. Ford is investing billions in American plants and factories and plans to bring thousands of jobs back home. All told, the entire industry has added more than 200,000 new jobs over the past 2½ years.

And they're not just building cars again, they're building better cars. Thanks to new fuel efficiency standards we put in place, they're building cars that will average nearly 55 miles per gallon by the middle of the next decade. That's almost double what they get today. That means folks will be able to fill up every 2 weeks instead of every week, saving the typical family more than $8,000 at the pump over time. That's a big deal, especially as families are yet again feeling the pinch from rising gas prices.

So what's happening in Detroit will make a difference. But it won't solve everything. There's no silver bullet for avoiding spikes in gas prices every year. There's no shortcut to taking control of our energy future. We have to pursue an all-of-the-above strategy that helps develop every source of American energy. And we have to do it now.

The good news is, we've been making progress. Here, take a look at this chart. Six years ago, 60 percent of the oil we used was imported. Since I took office, America's dependence on foreign oil has decreased every single year. In fact, in 2010, for the first time in 13 years, less than half the petroleum we consumed was imported. Part of that's because we're producing more oil here at home than at any time in the last 8 years.

But we can't just drill our way out of this problem. While we consume 20 percent of the world's oil, we only have 2 percent of the world's oil reserves. We've got to develop new technologies that will help us use new forms of energy. That's been a priority of mine as President. And because of the investments we've made, our use of clean, renewable energy has nearly doubled, and thousands of Americans have jobs because of it.

Now we need to keep at it. And to do that, we need to make the right choices.

Here's one choice we can make right now. Every year, 4 billion of your tax dollars goes to subsidizing the oil industry. These are the same companies making record profits: tens of billions of dollars a year. I don't think oil companies need more corporate welfare. Congress should end this taxpayer giveaway. If you agree with me, I'm asking you to e-mail, call, or tweet your Representative. Tell them to stop fighting for oil companies, and tell them to start fighting for working families. Tell them to fight for the clean energy future that's within our reach. Because the sooner we all get started, the sooner we'll get there together.

Thanks, and have a great weekend.

NOTE: The address was recorded at approximately 4:30 p.m. on March 2 in the State Dining Room at the White House for broadcast on March 3. The transcript was made available by the Office of the Press Secretary on March 2, but was embargoed for release until 6 a.m. on March 3.

Remarks at the American Israel Public Affairs Committee Policy Conference
March 4, 2012

Thank you. Everyone, please have a seat. Well, good morning, everyone.

Rosy, thank you for your kind words. I have never seen Rosy on the basketball court. I'll bet it would be a treat. [*Laughter*] Rosy, you've been a dear friend of mine for a long time and a tireless advocate for the unbreakable bonds between Israel and the United States. And as you complete your term as President, I salute your leadership and your commitment.

I want to thank the board of directors. As always, I'm glad to see my longtime friends in the Chicago delegation. I also want to thank the Member of Congress who are here with us today and who will be speaking to you over the next few days. You've worked hard to maintain the partnership between the United States and Israel. And I especially want to thank my close friend and leader of the Democratic National Committee, Debbie Wasserman Schultz.

I'm glad that my outstanding young Ambassador to Israel, Dan Shapiro, is in the house. I understand that Dan is perfecting his Hebrew on his new assignment, and I appreciate his constant outreach to the Israeli people. And I'm also pleased that we're joined by so many Israeli officials, including Ambassador Michael Oren. And tomorrow I'm very much looking forward to welcoming Prime Minister Netanyahu and his delegation back to the White House.

Every time I come to AIPAC, I'm especially impressed to see so many young people here. You don't yet get the front seats, I understand. [*Laughter*] You have to earn that. But students from all over the country who are making their voices heard and engaging deeply in our democratic debate, you carry with you an extraordinary legacy of more than six decades of friendship between the United States and Israel. And you have the opportunity and the responsibility to make your own mark on the world. And for inspiration, you can look to the man who preceded me on this stage, who's being honored at this conference, my friend President Shimon Peres.

Shimon was born a world away from here, in a shtetl in what was then Poland, a few years after the end of the First World War. But his heart was always in Israel, the historic homeland of the Jewish people. And when he was just a boy, he made his journey across land and sea toward home.

In his life, he has fought for Israel's independence and he has fought for peace and security. As a member of the Haganah and a member of the Knesset, as a Minister of Defense and Foreign Affairs, as a Prime Minister and as President, Shimon helped build the nation that thrives today: the Jewish State of Israel. But beyond these extraordinary achievements, he has also been a powerful moral voice that reminds us that right makes might, not the other way around.

Shimon once described the story of the Jewish people by saying it proved that "slings, arrows, and gas chambers can annihilate man, but cannot destroy human values, dignity, and freedom." And he has lived those values. He

has taught us to ask more of ourselves and to empathize more with our fellow human beings. I am grateful for his life's work and his moral example. And I'm proud to announce that later this spring, I will invite Shimon Peres to the White House to present him with America's highest civilian honor, the Presidential Medal of Freedom.

In many ways, this award is a symbol of the broader ties that bind our nations. The United States and Israel share interests, but we also share those human values that Shimon spoke about: a commitment to human dignity, a belief that freedom is a right that is given to all of God's children, an experience that shows us that democracy is the one and only form of government that can truly respond to the aspirations of citizens.

America's Founding Fathers understood this truth, just as Israel's founding generation did. President Truman put it well, describing his decision to formally recognize Israel only minutes after it declared independence. He said: "I had faith in Israel before it was established. I believe it has a glorious future before it—as not just another sovereign nation, but as an embodiment of the great ideals of our civilization."

For over six decades, the American people have kept that faith. Yes, we are bound to Israel because of the interests that we share in security for our communities, prosperity for our people, the new frontiers of science that can light the world. But ultimately is—it is our common ideals that provide the true foundation for our relationship. That is why America's commitment to Israel has endured under Democratic and Republican Presidents and congressional leaders of both parties. In the United States, our support for Israel is bipartisan, and that is how it should stay.

AIPAC's work continually nurtures this bond. And because of AIPAC's effectiveness in carrying out its mission, you can expect that over the next several days, you will hear many fine words from elected officials describing their commitment to the U.S.-Israel relationship. But as you examine my commitment, you don't just have to count on my words. You can look at my deeds. Because over the last 3 years, as President of the United States, I have kept my commitments to the State of Israel. At every crucial juncture, at every fork in the road, we have been there for Israel—every single time.

Four years ago, I stood before you and said that "Israel's security is sacrosanct. It is nonnegotiable." That belief has guided my actions as President. The fact is, my administration's commitment to Israel's security has been unprecedented. Our military and intelligence cooperation has never been closer. Our joint exercises and training have never been more robust. Despite a tough budget environment, our security assistance has increased every single year. We are investing in new capabilities. We're providing Israel with more advanced technology, the types of products and systems that only go to our closest friends and allies. And make no mistake: We will do what it takes to preserve Israel's qualitative military edge, because Israel must always have the ability to defend itself, by itself, against any threat.

This isn't just about numbers on a balance sheet. As a Senator, I spoke to Israeli troops on the Lebanese border. I visited with families who've known the terror of rocket fire in Sderot. And that's why, as President, I have provided critical funding to deploy the Iron Dome system that has intercepted rockets that might have hit homes and hospitals and schools in that town and in others. Now our assistance is expanding Israel's defensive capabilities so that more Israelis can live free from the fear of rockets and ballistic missiles. Because no family, no citizen, should live in fear.

And just as we've been there with our security assistance, we've been there through our diplomacy. When the Goldstone report unfairly singled out Israel for criticism, we challenged it. When Israel was isolated in the aftermath of the flotilla incident, we supported them. When the Durban conference was commemorated, we boycotted it, and we will always reject the notion that Zionism is racism.

When one-sided resolutions are brought up at the Human Rights Council, we oppose them. When Israeli diplomats feared for their lives in Cairo, we intervened to save them. When there are efforts to boycott or divest from Israel, we will stand against them. And whenever an effort is made to delegitimize the State of Israel, my administration has opposed them. So there should not be a shred of doubt by now: When the chips are down, I have Israel's back.

Which is why, if during this political season—[*laughter*]—you hear some questions regarding my administration's support for Israel, remember that it's not backed up by the facts. And remember that the U.S.-Israel relationship is simply too important to be distorted by partisan politics. America's national security is too important. Israel's security is too important.

Of course, there are those who question not my security and diplomatic commitments, but rather my administration's ongoing pursuit of peace between Israelis and Palestinians. So let me say this: I make no apologies for pursuing peace. Israel's own leaders understand the necessity of peace. Prime Minister Netanyahu, Defense Minister Barak, President Peres, each of them have called for two states, a secure Israel that lives side by side with an independent Palestinian state. I believe that peace is profoundly in Israel's security interest.

The reality that Israel faces—from shifting demographics to emerging technologies to an extremely difficult international environment—demands a resolution of this issue. And I believe that peace with the Palestinians is consistent with Israel's founding values, because of our shared belief in self-determination and because Israel's place as a Jewish and democratic state must be protected.

Of course, peace is hard to achieve. There's a reason why it's remained elusive for six decades. The upheaval and uncertainty in Israel's neighborhood makes it that much harder, from the horrific violence raging in Syria to the transition in Egypt. And the division within the Palestinian leadership makes it harder still, most notably, with Hamas's continued rejection of Israel's very right to exist.

But as hard as it may be, we should not and cannot give in to cynicism or despair. The changes taking place in the region make peace more important, not less. And I've made it clear that there will be no lasting peace unless Israel's security concerns are met. That's why we continue to press Arab leaders to reach out to Israel, and we'll continue to support the peace treaty with Egypt. That's why, just as we encourage Israel to be resolute in the pursuit of peace, we have continued to insist that any Palestinian partner must recognize Israel's right to exist and reject violence and adhere to existing agreements. And that is why my administration has consistently rejected any efforts to shortcut negotiations or impose an agreement on the parties.

As Rosy noted, last year, I stood before you and pledged that "the United States will stand up against efforts to single Israel out at the United Nations." As you know, that pledge has been kept. Last September, I stood before the United Nations General Assembly and reaffirmed that any lasting peace must acknowledge the fundamental legitimacy of Israel and its security concerns. I said that America's commitment to Israel's security is unshakeable, our friendship with Israel is enduring, and that Israel must be recognized. No American President has made such a clear statement about our support for Israel at the United Nations at such a difficult time. People usually give those speeches before audiences like this one, not before the General Assembly.

And I must say, there was not a lot of applause. [*Laughter*] But it was the right thing to do. And as a result, today there is no doubt anywhere in the world that the United States will insist upon Israel's security and legitimacy. That will be true as we continue our efforts to pursue—in the pursuit of peace. And that will be true when it comes to the issue that is such a focus for all of us today: Iran's nuclear program, a threat that has the potential to bring together the worst rhetoric about Israel's destruction with the world's most dangerous weapons.

Let's begin with a basic truth that you all understand: No Israeli Government can tolerate a nuclear weapon in the hands of a regime that denies the Holocaust, threatens to wipe Israel off the map, and sponsors terrorist groups committed to Israel's destruction. And so I understand the profound historical obligation that weighs on the shoulders of Bibi Netanyahu and Ehud Barak and all of Israel's leaders. A nuclear-armed Iran is completely counter to Israel's security interests. But it is also counter to the national security interests of the United States.

Indeed, the entire world has an interest in preventing Iran from acquiring a nuclear weapon. A nuclear-armed Iran would thoroughly undermine the nonproliferation regime that we've done so much to build. There are risks that an Iranian nuclear weapon could fall into the hands of a terrorist organization. It is almost certain that others in the region would feel compelled to get their own nuclear weapon, triggering an arms race in one of the world's most volatile regions. It would embolden a regime that has brutalized its own people, and it would embolden Iran's proxies, who have carried out terrorist attacks from the Levant to southwest Asia.

And that is why, 4 years ago, I made a commitment to the American people and said that we would use all elements of American power to pressure Iran and prevent it from acquiring a nuclear weapon. And that is what we have done.

When I took office, the efforts to apply pressure on Iran were in tatters. Iran had gone from zero centrifuges spinning to thousands, without facing broad pushback from the world. In the region, Iran was ascendant, increasingly popular and extending its reach. In other words, the Iranian leadership was united and on the move, and the international community was divided about how to go forward.

And so from my very first months in office, we put forward a very clear choice to the Iranian regime: a path that would allow them to rejoin the community of nations if they meet their international obligations or a path that leads to an escalating series of consequences if they don't. In fact, our policy of engagement—quickly rebuffed by the Iranian regime—allowed us to rally the international community as never before, to expose Iran's intransigence, and to apply pressure that goes far beyond anything that the United States could do on our own.

Because of our efforts, Iran is under greater pressure than ever before. Some of you will recall, people predicted that Russia and China wouldn't join us to move towards pressure. They did. And in 2010, the U.N. Security Council overwhelmingly supported a comprehensive sanctions effort. Few thought that sanctions could have an immediate bite on the Iranian regime. They have, slowing the Iranian nuclear program and virtually grinding the Iranian economy to a halt in 2011. Many questioned whether we could hold our coalition together as we moved against Iran's Central Bank and oil exports. But our friends in Europe and Asia and elsewhere are joining us. And in 2012, the Iranian Government faces the prospect of even more crippling sanctions.

That is where we are today because of our work. Iran is isolated, its leadership divided and under pressure. And by the way, the Arab Spring has only increased these trends, as the hypocrisy of the Iranian regime is exposed and its ally, the Asad regime, is crumbling.

Of course, so long as Iran fails to meet its obligations, this problem remains unresolved. The effective implementation of our policy is not enough. We must accomplish our objective. And in that effort, I firmly believe that an opportunity still remains for diplomacy, backed by pressure, to succeed.

The United States and Israel both assess that Iran does not yet have a nuclear weapon, and we are exceedingly vigilant in monitoring their program. Now the international community has a responsibility to use the time and space that exists. Sanctions are continuing to increase, and this July, thanks to our diplomatic coordination, a European ban on Iranian oil imports will take hold. Faced with these increasingly dire consequences, Iran's leaders still have the opportunity to make the right decision. They can choose a path that brings them back into the community of nations, or they can continue down a dead end.

And given their history, there are, of course, no guarantees that the Iranian regime will make the right choice. But both Israel and the United States have an interest in seeing this challenge resolved diplomatically. After all, the only way to truly solve this problem is for the Iranian Government to make a decision to forsake nuclear weapons. That's what history tells us.

Moreover, as President and Commander in Chief, I have a deeply held preference for peace over war. I have sent men and women into harm's way. I've seen the consequences of those decisions in the eyes of those I meet who've come back gravely wounded and the absence of those who don't make it home. Long after I leave this office, I will remember those moments as the most searing of my Presidency. And for this reason, as part of my solemn obligation to the American people, I will only use force when the time and circumstances demand it. And I know that Israeli leaders also know all too well the costs and consequences of war, even as they recognize their obligation to defend their country.

So we all prefer to resolve this issue diplomatically. Having said that, Iran's leaders should have no doubt about the resolve of the United States, just as they should not doubt Israel's sovereign right to make its own decisions about what is required to meet its security needs.

I have said that when it comes to preventing Iran from obtaining a nuclear weapon, I will take no options off the table, and I mean what I say. That includes all elements of American power: a political effort aimed at isolating Iran, a diplomatic effort to sustain our coalition and ensure that the Iranian program is monitored, an economic effort that imposes crippling sanctions, and yes, a military effort to be prepared for any contingency.

Iran's leaders should understand that I do not have a policy of containment; I have a policy to prevent Iran from obtaining a nuclear weapon. And as I have made clear time and again during the course of my Presidency, I will not hesitate to use force when it is necessary to defend the United States and its interests.

Moving forward, I would ask that we all remember the weightiness of these issues, the stakes involved for Israel, for America, and for the world. Already, there is too much loose talk of war. Over the last few weeks, such talk has only benefited the Iranian Government by driving up the price of oil, which they depend on to fund their nuclear program. For the sake of Israel's security, America's security, and the peace and security of the world, now is not the time for bluster. Now's the time to let our increased pressure sink in and to sustain the broad international coalition we have built. Now's the time to heed the timeless advice from Teddy Roosevelt: Speak softly; carry a big stick. And as we do, rest assured that the Iranian Government will know our resolve and that our coordination will—with Israel will continue.

Now, these are challenging times. But we've been through challenging times before, and the United States and Israel have come through them together. Because of our cooperation, citizens in both our countries have benefited from the bonds that bring us together. I'm proud to be one of those people. In the past, I've shared in this forum just why those bonds are so personal for me: the stories of a great-uncle who helped liberate Buchenwald, to my memories of returning there with Elie Wiesel; from sharing books with President Peres to sharing Seders with my young staff in a tradition that started on the campaign trail and continues in the White House; from the countless friends I know in this room to the concept of *tikkun olam* that has enriched and guided my life.

As Harry Truman understood, Israel's story is one of hope. We may not agree on every single issue; no two nations do, and our democracies contain a vibrant diversity of views. But we agree on the big things, the things that matter. And together, we are working to build a better world, one where our people can live free from fear, one where peace is founded upon justice, one where our children can know a future that is more hopeful than the present.

There is no shortage of speeches on the friendship between the United States and Israel. But I'm also mindful of the proverb, "A man is judged by his deeds, not his words." So, if you want to know where my heart lies, look no further than what I have done to stand up for Israel, to secure both of our countries, and to see that the rough waters of our time lead to a peaceful and prosperous shore.

Thank you very much, everybody. God bless you. God bless the people of Israel. God bless the United States of America.

NOTE: The President spoke at 11:10 a.m. at the Walter E. Washington Convention Center. In his remarks, he referred to Lee "Rosy" Rosenberg, president, American Israel Public Affairs Committee; Richard J. Goldstone, head, United Nations Fact-Finding Mission on the Gaza Conflict; President Bashar al-Asad of Syria; and Elie Wiesel, Nobel Prize winner, author, and Holocaust survivor. He also referred to his great-uncle Charles Payne.

Statement on the 47th Anniversary of the 1965 Voting Rights March From Selma to Montgomery, Alabama
March 4, 2012

Today we mark the 47th anniversary of "Bloody Sunday," the march from Selma to Montgomery, Alabama, where hundreds of courageous men and women risked their lives in the name of equality. Those brave marchers knew the danger that awaited them on the other side of the Edmund Pettus Bridge, but they pressed on, stepping into history as they challenged the Nation's conscience. Today we remember their courage in the face of danger and the spirit of perseverance that helped lead to iconic legislation like the Civil Rights Act and the Voting Rights Act. We also recommit ourselves to their struggle and to the idea that we should always seek a more perfect Union.

Remarks Prior to a Meeting With Prime Minister Benjamin Netanyahu of Israel
March 5, 2012

President Obama. Well, I want to welcome Prime Minister Netanyahu and the entire Israeli delegation back to the White House, back to the Oval Office.

This visit obviously comes at a critical time. We are seeing incredible changes that are taking place in the Middle East and in North Africa. We have seen the terrible bloodshed that's going on in Syria, the democratic transition that's taking place in Egypt. And in the midst of this, we have an island of democracy and one of our greatest allies in Israel.

As I've said repeatedly, the bond between our two countries is unbreakable. My personal commitment—a commitment that is consistent with the history of other occupants of this Oval Office—our commitment to the security of Israel is rock solid. And as I've said to the Prime Minister in every single one of our meetings, the United States will always have Israel's back when it comes to Israel's security. This is a bond that is based not only on our mutual security interests and economic interests, but is also based on common values and the incredible people-to-people contacts that we have between our two countries.

During the course of this meeting, we'll talk about the regional issues that are taking place, and I look forward to the Prime Minister sharing with me his ideas about how we can increase the prospects of peace and security in the region. We will discuss the issues that continue to be a focus of not only our foreign policy, but also the Prime Minister's: how we can, potentially, bring about a calmer set of discussions between the Israelis and the Palestinians and arrive at a peaceful resolution to that long-standing conflict. It is a very difficult thing to do in light of the context right now, but I know that the Prime Minister remains committed to trying to achieve that.

And obviously, a large topic of conversation will be Iran, which I devoted a lot of time to in my speech to AIPAC yesterday and I know that the Prime Minister has been focused on for a long period of time. Let me just reiterate a couple of points on that.

Number one, we all know that it's unacceptable from Israel's perspective to have a country with a nuclear weapon that has called for the destruction of Israel. But as I emphasized yesterday, it is profoundly in the United States' interest as well to prevent Iran from obtaining a nuclear weapon. We do not want to see a nuclear arms race in one of the most volatile regions in the world. We do not want the possibility of a nuclear weapon falling into the hands of terrorists. And we do not want a regime that has been a state sponsor of terrorism being able to feel that it can act even more aggressively or with impunity as a consequence of its nuclear power.

That's why we have worked so diligently to set up the most crippling sanctions ever with respect to Iran. We do believe that there is still a window that allows for a diplomatic resolution to this issue, but ultimately, the Iranians' regime has to make a decision to move in that direction, a decision that they have not made thus far.

And as I emphasized, even as we will continue on the diplomatic front, we will continue to tighten pressure when it comes to sanctions, I reserve all options, and my policy here is not going to be one of containment. My policy is prevention of Iran obtaining nuclear weapons. And as I indicated yesterday in my speech, when I say all options are at the table, I mean it.

Having said that, I know that both the Prime Minister and I prefer to resolve this diplomatically. We understand the costs of any military action. And I want to assure both the American people and the Israeli people that we are in constant and close consultation. I think the levels of coordination and consultation between our militaries and our intelligence not just on this issue, but on a broad range of issues, has been unprecedented. And I intend to make sure that that continues during what will be a series of difficult months, I suspect, in 2012.

So, Prime Minister, we welcome you, and we appreciate very much the friendship of the Israeli people. You can count on that friendship always being reciprocated from the United States.

Prime Minister Netanyahu. Thank you.

President Obama. Thank you.

Prime Minister Netanyahu. Mr. President, thank you for those kind words. And thank you too for that strong speech yesterday. And I want to thank you also for the warm hospitality that you've shown me and my delegation.

The alliance between our two countries is deeply appreciated by me and by everyone in Israel. And I think that, as you said, when Americans look around the Middle East today, they see one reliable, stable, faithful ally of the United States, and that's the democracy of Israel.

Americans know that Israel and the United States share common values, that we defend common interests, that we face common enemies. Iran's leaders know that too. For them, you're the "Great Satan," we're the "Little Satan." For them, we are you, and you're us. And you know something, Mr. President, at least on this last point, I think they're right. We are you, and you are us. We're together. So, if there's one thing that stands out clearly in the Middle East today, it's that Israel and America stand together.

I think that above and beyond that are two principles, longstanding principles of American policy that you reiterated yesterday in your speech: that Israel must have the ability always to defend itself, by itself, against any threat and that when it comes to Israel's security, Israel has the right, the sovereign right to make its own decisions. I believe that's why you appreciate, Mr. President, that Israel must reserve the right to defend itself.

And after all, that's the very purpose of the Jewish state: to restore to the Jewish people control over our destiny. And that's why my supreme responsibility as Prime Minister of Israel is to ensure that Israel remains the master of its fate.

So I thank you very much, Mr. President, for your friendship, and I look forward to our discussions. Thank you, Mr. President.

President Obama. Thank you very much.

NOTE: The President spoke at 10:53 a.m. in the Oval Office at the White House.

The President's News Conference
March 6, 2012

The President. Good afternoon, everybody. Now, I understand there are some political contests going on tonight, but I thought I'd start the day off by taking a few questions, which I'm sure will not be political in nature. [*Laughter*] But before I do, I want to make a few announcements about some steps we're taking to help responsible homeowners who've been struggling through this housing crisis.

Now, we've clearly seen some positive economic news over the last few months. Businesses have created about 3.7 million new jobs over the last 2 years. Manufacturers are hiring for the first time since the 1990s. The auto industry is back and hiring more than 200,000 people over the last few years. Confidence is up, and the economy is getting stronger.

But there are still millions of Americans who can't find a job. There are millions more who are having a tough time making the rent or the mortgage, paying for gas or groceries. So our job in Washington isn't to sit back and do nothing. And it's certainly not to stand in the way of the recovery. Right now we've got to do everything we can to speed it up.

Now, Congress did the right thing when they passed part of my jobs plan and prevented a tax hike on 160 million working Americans this year. And that was a good first step. But it's not enough. They can't just stop there and wait for the next election to come around. There are a few things they can do right now that could make a real difference in people's lives.

This Congress should, once and for all, end tax breaks for companies that are shipping jobs overseas and use that money to reward companies that are creating jobs here in the United States. I've put forward a proposal that does just that, and there's no reason why Congress can't come together and start acting on it.

This Congress could hold a vote on the Buffett rule so that we don't have billionaires paying a lower tax rate than their secretaries. That's just common sense. The vast majority of Americans believe it's common sense. And if we're serious about paying down our deficit, it's a—as good a place to start as any.

And finally, this Congress should pass my proposal to give every responsible homeowner a chance to save an average of $3,000 a year by refinancing their mortgage at historically low rates, no redtape, no runaround from the banks. If you've been on time on your payments, if you've done the right thing, if you've acted responsibly, you should have a chance to save that money on your home, perhaps to build up your equity or just to have more money in your pocket that you can spend on businesses in your community. That would make a huge difference for millions of American families.

Now, if Congress refuses to act, I've said that I'll continue to do everything in my power to act without them. Last fall, we announced an initiative that allows millions of responsible homeowners to refinance at low interest rates. Today we're taking it a step further. We are cutting by more than half the refinancing fees that families pay for loans ensured by the Federal Housing Administration. That's going to save the typical family in that situation an extra $1,000 a year, on top of the savings that they'd also receive from refinancing. That would make refinancing even more attractive to more families. It's like another tax cut that will put more money in people's pockets. We're going to do this on our own. We don't need congressional authorization to do it.

We're also taking a series of steps to help homeowners who have served our country. It is unconscionable that members of our Armed Forces and their families have been some of those who have been most susceptible to losing their homes due to the actions of unscrupulous

banks and mortgage lenders. Over the last few years that happened, a lot.

So, as part of the landmark settlement we reached with some of the Nation's largest banks a few weeks ago, here's what we're going to do: If you are a member of the Armed Forces whose home was wrongfully foreclosed, you will be substantially compensated for what the bank did to you and your family. If you are a member of the Armed Forces with a high interest rate who was wrongfully denied the chance to lower it while you were in active service, which banks are required to do by law, the banks will refund you the money you would have saved along with a significant penalty.

The settlement will make sure that you aren't forced into foreclosure just because you have a permanent change in station, but can't sell your home because you owe more than it's worth. Some of the money will also go into a fund that guarantees loans on favorable terms to our veterans, and there will be more foreclosure protections for every man and woman who is currently serving this country in harm's way.

As I've said before, no amount of money is going to be enough to make it right for a family who has had their piece of the American Dream wrongfully taken away from them, and no action, no matter how meaningful, will entirely heal our housing market on its own. This is not something the Government by itself can solve. But I'm not one of those people who believe that we should just sit by and wait for the housing market to hit bottom. There are real things that we can do right now that would make a substantial difference in the lives of innocent, responsible homeowners. That's true in housing, and that's true in any number of different areas when it comes to ensuring that this recovery touches as many lives as possible. That's going to be my top priority as long as I hold this office, and I will do everything I can to make that progress.

So with that, I'm going to take some questions, and I will start with Mike Viqueira [NBC News].

Iran/Situation in the Middle East

Q. Yes, sir. On the Middle East and as it relates to American politics, a little less than a year ago Muammar Qadhafi gave a speech, and he said he was going to send his forces to Benghazi, he was going to rout opponents from their bedrooms, and he was going to shoot them. You frequently cited that speech as a justification for NATO, the no-fly zone, and military action against Libya. In Syria, Bashar al-Asad is killing people. There's a massacre underway. And your critics here in the United States, including, most notably, John McCain, said you should start air strikes now.

And on Iran, Mitt Romney, on Sunday, went so far as to say that if you are reelected, Iran will get a bomb and the world will change. How do you respond to those criticisms?

The President. All right, Mike, you've asked a couple of questions there, so let me—let's start with the Iran situation since that's been the topic in the news for the last few days.

When I came into office, Iran was unified, on the move, had made substantial progress on its nuclear program, and the world was divided in terms of how to deal with it. What we've been able to do over the last 3 years is mobilize unprecedented, crippling sanctions on Iran. Iran is feeling the bite of these sanctions in a substantial way. The world is unified; Iran is politically isolated.

And what I have said is, is that we will not countenance Iran getting a nuclear weapon. My policy is not containment; my policy is to prevent them from getting a nuclear weapon, because if they get a nuclear weapon, that could trigger an arms race in the region, it would undermine our nonproliferation goals, it could potentially fall into the hands of terrorists. And we've been in close consultation with all our allies, including Israel, in moving this strategy forward.

At this stage, it is my belief that we have a window of opportunity where this can still be resolved diplomatically. That's not just my view. That's the view of our top intelligence officials; It's the view of top Israeli intelligence officials. And as a consequence, we are going

to continue to apply the pressure even as we provide a door for the Iranian regime to walk through where they could rejoin the community of nations by giving assurances to the international community that they're meeting their obligations and they are not pursuing a nuclear weapon.

That's my track record. Now, what's said on the campaign trail, those folks don't have a lot of responsibilities. They're not Commander in Chief. And when I see the casualness with which some of these folks talk about war, I'm reminded of the costs involved in war. I'm reminded that the decision that I have to make in terms of sending our young men and women into battle and the impacts that has on their lives, the impact it has on our national security, the impact it has on our economy.

This is not a game, and there's nothing casual about it. And when I see some of these folks who have a lot of bluster and a lot of big talk, but when you actually ask them specifically what they would do, it turns out they repeat the things that we've been doing over the last 3 years, it indicates to me that that's more about politics than actually trying to solve a difficult problem.

Now, the one thing that we have not done is we haven't launched a war. If some of these folks think that it's time to launch a war, they should say so. And they should explain to the American people exactly why they would do that and what the consequences would be. Everything else is just talk.

Syria/Libya

Q. That goes to Syria as well?

The President. With respect to Syria, what's happening in Syria is heartbreaking and outrageous, and what you've seen is the international community mobilize against the Asad regime. And it's not a question of when Asad leaves or if Asad leaves, it's a question of when. He has lost the legitimacy of his people. And the actions that he's now taking against his own people is inexcusable, and the world community has said so in a more or less unified voice.

On the other hand, for us to take military action unilaterally, as some have suggested, or to think that somehow there is some simple solution, I think is a mistake. What happened in Libya was we mobilized the international community, had a U.N. Security Council mandate, had the full cooperation of the region, Arab States, and we knew that we could execute very effectively in a relatively short period of time. This is a much more complicated situation.

So what we've done is to work with key Arab States, key international partners—Hillary Clinton was in Tunisia—to come together and to mobilize and plan how do we support the opposition, how do we provide humanitarian assistance, how do we continue the political isolation, how do we continue the economic isolation. And we are going to continue to work on this project with other countries. And it is my belief that ultimately this dictator will fall, as dictators in the past have fallen.

But the notion that the way to solve every one of these problems is to deploy our military, that hasn't been true in the past, and it won't be true now. We've got to think through what we do through the lens of what's going to be effective, but also what's critical for U.S. security interests.

Jake Tapper [ABC News].

Situation in the Middle East/Iran/Israel

Q. Thank you, Mr. President. What kind of assurances did you give Prime Minister Netanyahu about the role that the U.S. would play if diplomacy and economic sanctions fail to work to convince Iranian—Iran's leaders to change their behavior, and Israel goes ahead and prepares to strike a nuclear facility? What kind of assurances did you tell him? And shouldn't we—I recognize the difference between debate and bluster—but shouldn't we be having in this country a vigorous debate about what could happen in the case of a Middle East war in a way that, sadly, we did not do before going into Iraq?

The President. Well, I think there's no doubt that those who are suggesting or proposing or beating the drums of war should explain clearly to the American people what they think the costs and benefits would be.

I'm not one of those people, because what I've said is, is that we have a window through which we can resolve this issue peacefully. We have put forward an international framework that is applying unprecedented pressure. The Iranians just stated that they are willing to return to the negotiating table. And we've got the opportunity, even as we maintain that pressure, to see how it plays out.

I'm not going to go into the details of my conversation with Prime Minister Netanyahu. But what I said publicly doesn't differ greatly from what I said privately. Israel is a sovereign nation that has to make its own decisions about how best to preserve its security. And as I said over the last several days, I am deeply mindful of the historical precedents that weigh on any Prime Minister of Israel when they think about the potential threats to Israel and the Jewish homeland.

What I've also said is that because sanctions are starting to have significant effect inside of Iran—and that's not just my assessment, that's, I think, a uniform assessment—because the sanctions are going to be even tougher in the coming months, because they're now starting to affect their oil industry, their central bank, and because we're now seeing noises about them returning to the negotiating table, that it is deeply in everybody's interests, the United States, Israel, and the world's, to see if this can be resolved in a peaceful fashion.

And so this notion that somehow we have a choice to make in the next week or 2 weeks, or month or 2 months, is not borne out by the facts. And the argument that we've made to the Israelis is that we have made an unprecedented commitment to their security. There is an unbreakable bond between our two countries, but one of the functions of friends is to make sure that we provide honest and unvarnished advice in terms of what is the best approach to achieve a common goal, particularly one in which we have a stake. This is not just an issue of Israeli interest, this is an issue of U.S. interests. It's also not just an issue of consequences for Israel if action is taken prematurely. There are consequences to the United States as well.

And so I do think that any time we consider military action, that the American people understand there's going to be a price to pay. Sometimes, it's necessary. But we don't do it casually.

When I visit Walter Reed, when I sign letters to families that haven't—whose loved ones have not come home, I am reminded that there is a cost. Sometimes, we bear that cost. But we think it through. We don't play politics with it. When we have in the past—when we haven't thought it through and it gets wrapped up in politics—we make mistakes. And typically, it's not the folks who are popping off who pay the price. It's these incredible men and women in uniform and their families who pay the price.

And as a consequence, I think it's very important for us to take a careful, thoughtful, sober approach to what is a real problem. And that's what we've been doing over the last 3 years. That's what I intend to keep doing.

Q. Sir, I'm sorry, if I could just quickly follow up, you didn't——

The President. Jake——

Q. You might not be beating the drums of war, but you did very publicly say, we've got Israel's back. What does that mean?

The President. What it means is, is that historically, we have always cooperated with Israel with respect to the defense of Israel, just like we do with a whole range of other allies—just like we do with Great Britain, just like we do with Japan. And that broad statement, I think, is confirmed when you look at what we've done over the last 3 years on things like Iron Dome that prevents missiles from raining down on their small towns along border regions of Israel, that potentially land on schools or children or families. And we're going to continue that unprecedented security commitment.

It was not a military doctrine that we were laying out for any particular military action. It was a restatement of our consistent position that the security of Israel is something I deeply care about and that the deeds of my administration over the last 3 years confirms how deeply we care about it. That's a commitment we've made.

Jackie [Jackie Calmes, New York Times]. Where's Jackie? There you are.

Iran/Israel

Q. With the news this morning that the U.S. and its allies are returning to the table, are taking up Iran's offer to talk again, more than a year after those talks broke up in frustration, is this Israel's—Iran's last chance to negotiate an end to this nuclear question?

And you said 3 years ago—nearly 3 years ago, in a similar one-on-one meeting with Prime Minister Netanyahu, that the time for talk—by the end of that year, 2009, you would be considering whether Iran was negotiating in good faith. And you said at that time that "we're not going to have talks forever." So here we are nearly 3 years later. Is this it? And did you think you would be here 3 years after those first talks?

The President. You know, there is no doubt that over the last 3 years, when Iran has engaged in negotiations, there has been hemming and hawing and stalling and avoiding the issues in ways that the international community has concluded were not serious. And my expectations, given the consequences of inaction for them, the severe sanctions that are now being applied, the huge toll it's taking on their economy, the degree of isolation that they're feeling right now, which is unprecedented, they understand that the world community means business.

To resolve this issue will require Iran to come to the table and discuss in a clear and forthright way how to prove to the international community that the intentions of their nuclear program are peaceful. They know how to do that. This is not a mystery. And so it's going to be very important to make sure that on an issue like this—there are complexities; it obviously has to be methodical. I don't expect a breakthrough in a first meeting, but I think we will have a pretty good sense fairly quickly as to how serious they are about resolving the issue.

And there are steps that they can take that would send a signal to the international community and that are verifiable, that would allow them to be in compliance with international norms, in compliance with international mandates, abiding by the nonproliferation treaty, and provide the world an assurance that they're not pursuing a nuclear weapon. They know how to do it, and the question is going to be whether in these discussions they show themselves moving clearly in that direction.

Ed Henry [FOX News].

Price of Gasoline/Alternative and Renewable Energy Sources and Technologies/Israel

Q. Thank you, Mr. President. I wanted to follow up on Israel and Iran, because you have said repeatedly you have Israel's back. And so I wonder why, 3 years in office, you have not visited Israel as President. And related to Iran and Israel, you have expressed concern about this loose talk of war, as you call it, driving up gas prices further. Your critics will say on Capitol Hill that you want gas prices to go higher because you have said before, that will wean the American people off fossil fuels, onto renewable fuels. How do you respond to that?

The President. Ed, just from a political perspective, do you think the President of the United States going into reelection wants gas prices to go up higher? [*Laughter*] Is that—is there anybody here who thinks that makes a lot of sense?

Look, here's the bottom line with respect to gas prices. I want gas prices lower because they hurt families. Because I meet folks every day who have to drive a long way to get to work, and them filling up this gas tank gets more and more painful, and it's a tax out of their pocketbooks, out of their paychecks, and a lot of folks are already operating on the margins right now.

And it's not good for the overall economy, because when gas prices go up, consumer spending oftentimes pulls back. And we're in the midst right now of a recovery that is starting to build up steam, and we don't want to reverse it.

What I have also said about gas prices is that there is no silver bullet and the only way we're going to solve this problem over the medium and long term is with an all-of-the-above strategy that says we're going to increase produc-

tion, which has happened; we are going to make sure that we are conserving energy—that's why we doubled fuel efficiency standards on cars, which will save consumers about $1.7 trillion and take about 12 billion barrels of oil offline, which will help to reduce prices; and we're going develop clean energy technologies that allow us to continue to use less oil.

And we've made progress. I mean, the good news is, 2010, first time in a decade that our oil imports were actually below 50 percent, and they have kept on going down. And we're going to keep on looking at every strategy we can to, yes, reduce the amount of oil that we use, while maintaining our living standards and maintaining our productivity and maintaining our economic growth, and we're going to do everything we can to make sure that consumers aren't hurt by it.

Now, there are some short-term steps that we're looking at with respect to—for example, there are certain potential bottlenecks in refineries around the country that we've been concerned about. We're concerned about what's happening in terms of production around the world. It's not just what's happening in the Gulf. You've had, for example, in Sudan, some oil that's been taken offline that's helping to restrict supply.

So we're going to look at a whole range of measures, including, by the way, making sure that my Attorney General is paying attention to potential speculation in the oil markets. We—I've asked him to reconstitute a Task Force that's examining that.

But we go through this every year. We've gone through this for 30 years. And if we are going to be competitive, successful, and make sure families are protected over the long term, then we've got to make sure that we've got a set of options that reduce our overall dependence on oil.

And with respect to Israel, I am not the first President who has been unable, because of a whole range of issues, not to visit Israel as President in their first term. I visited Israel twice as Senator, once right before I became President. The measure of my commitment to Israel is not measured by a single visit. The measure of my commitment to Israel is seen in the actions that I've taken as President of the United States. And it is indisputable that I've had Israel's back over the last 3 years.

Aamer Madhani [USA Today].

Radio Talk Show Host Rush Limbaugh/Civility in Political Discourse

Q. Thank you, Mr. President. Do you believe Rush Limbaugh's apology to the Georgetown law student was sufficient and heartfelt? Do you agree with the decision of the growing number of sponsors that have decided to drop his show or stop supporting his show? And has there been a double standard on this issue? Liberal commentators have made similarly provocative or distasteful statements, and there hasn't been such an outrage.

The President. I'm not going to comment on what sponsors decide to do. I'm not going to comment on either the economics or the politics of it. I don't know what's in Rush Limbaugh's heart, so I'm not going to comment on the sincerity of his apology. What I can comment on is the fact that all decent folks can agree that the remarks that were made don't have any place in the public discourse.

And the reason I called Ms. Fluke is because I thought about Malia and Sasha, and one of the things I want them to do as they get older is to engage in issues they care about, even ones I may not agree with them on. I want them to be able to speak their mind in a civil and thoughtful way. And I don't want them attacked or called horrible names because they're being good citizens. And I wanted Sandra to know that I thought her parents should be proud of her, and that we want to send a message to all our young people that being part of a democracy involves argument and disagreements and debate, and we want you to be engaged, and there's a way to do it that doesn't involve you being demeaned and insulted, particularly when you're a private citizen.

All right.

Q. [*Inaudible*]

The President. Jessica Yellin [CNN].

Q. Mr. President——

[*At this point, a different reporter asked a question.*]

Q. Bill Maher apologized for what he said about—[*inaudible*].

The President. Jessica.

Q. Thank you——

Q. ——should apologize for what they said about that?

Women Voters

Q. Thank you, Mr. President.

The President. Thank you.

Q. Top Democrats have said that Republicans on a similar issue are engaged in a war on women. Some top Republicans say it's more like Democrats are engaged in a war for the women's vote. As you talk about loose talk of war in another arena and women are—this could raise concerns among women, do you agree with the chair of your Democratic National Committee that there is a war on women?

The President. Here is what I think. Women are going to make up their own mind in this election about who is advancing the issues that they care most deeply about. And one of the things I've learned being married to Michelle is I don't need to tell her what it is that she thinks is important.

And there are millions of strong women around the country who are going to make their own determination about a whole range of issues. It's not going to be narrowly focused just on contraception. It's not going to be driven by one statement by one radio announcer. It is going to be driven by their view of what's most likely to make sure they can help support their families, make their mortgage payments; who's got a plan to ensure that middle class families are secure over the long term; what's most likely to result in their kids being able to get the education they need to compete.

And I believe that Democrats have a better story to tell to women about how we're going to solidify the middle class and grow this economy, make sure everybody got—has a fair shot, everybody's doing their fair share, and we got a fair set of rules of the road that everybody has to follow.

So I'm not somebody who believes that women are going to be single-issue voters. They never have been. And—but I do think that we've got a strong story to tell when it comes to women.

Civility in Political Discourse

Q. Would you prefer this language be changed?

The President. Jessica, as you know, if I start being in the business of arbitrating——

Q. You talk about civility.

The President. ——the—right, and what I do is I practice it. And so I'm going to try to lead by example in this situation, as opposed to commenting on every single comment that's made by either politicians or pundits. I would be very busy. I would not have time to do my job. That's your job, to comment on what's said by politicians and pundits.

All right. Lori Montenegro [Telemundo].

Immigration Reform

Q. Mr. President, thank you.

The President. There you go.

Q. Mr. President, polls are showing that Latino voters seem to be favoring your reelection over a Republican alternative. Yet some of them are still disappointed, others upset, about a promise that you've made on immigration reform that has yet to come to pass. If you are reelected, what would be your strategy, what would you do different to get immigration reform passed through the Congress, especially if both Houses continue as they are right now, which is split?

The President. Well, first of all, just substantively, every American should want immigration reform. We've got a system that's broken. We've got a system in which you have millions of families here in this country who are living in the shadows, worried about deportation. You've got American workers that are being undercut because those undocumented workers can be hired and the minimum wage laws may not be observed, overtime laws may not be observed.

You've got incredibly talented people who want to start businesses in this country or to work in this country, and we should want those folks here in the United States. But right now the legal immigration system is so tangled up that it becomes very difficult for them to put down roots here.

So we can be a nation of laws and a nation of immigrants. And it is not just a Hispanic issue. This is an issue for everybody. This is an American issue that we need to fix.

Now, when I came into office I said, I am going to push to get this done. We didn't get it done. And the reason we haven't gotten it done is because what used to be a bipartisan agreement that we should fix this ended up becoming a partisan issue.

I give a lot of credit to my predecessor, George Bush, and his political advisers, who said this should not be just something the Democrats support; the Republican Party is invested in this as well. That was good advice then; it would be good advice now.

And my hope is, is that after this election, the Latino community will have sent a strong message that they want a bipartisan effort to pass comprehensive immigration reform that involves making sure we've got tough border security, and this administration has done more for border security than just about anybody; that we are making sure that companies aren't able to take advantage of undocumented workers; that we've got strong laws in place; and that we've got a path so that all those folks whose kids often are U.S. citizens, who are working with us, living with us and in our communities, and not breaking the law and trying to do their best to raise their families, that they've got a chance to be a fuller part of our community.

So what do I think will change?

Q. What would you do differently?

The President. What I will do—look, we're going to be putting forward, as we have done before, a framework, a proposal, legislation that can move it—move the ball forward and actually get this thing done.

But ultimately, I can't vote for Republicans. They're going to have to come to the conclusion that this is good for the country and that this is something that they themselves think is important. And depending on how Congress turns out, we'll see how many Republican votes we need to get it done.

Norah O'Donnell [CBS News]. How are you?

2012 Presidential Election

Q. Thank you, Mr. President. Today is Super Tuesday, so I wonder if you might weigh in on some of your potential Republican opponents. Mitt Romney has criticized you on Iran and said, "Hope is not a foreign policy." He also said that you are "America's most feckless President since Carter." What would you like to say to Mr. Romney?

The President. Good luck tonight. [*Laughter*]

Q. No, really.

The President. Really. [*Laughter*]

Lynn [Lynn Sweet, Chicago Sun-Times], since you've been hollering and you're from my hometown, make it a good one.

Group of Eight Summit/NATO Summit

Q. My question is about the switch of the G–8 summit from Chicago to Camp David. A reason given from the White House is that now you wanted a more intimate summit. People of Chicago would like to know, what do you know now that you did not know when you booked hometown Chicago for the G–8 that led to the switch? And what role did security threats possibly play in the decision?

The President. Well, keep in mind, Lynn, we're still going to be showing up with a whole bunch of world leaders. We've got this NATO summit. Typically, what's happened is, is that we try to attach the G–8 summit to the NATO summit so that the leaders in the G–8 summit don't have to travel twice to whatever location. So, last year, in France, we combined a G–8 with a NATO summit. We'll do so again.

I have to say, this was an idea that was brought to me after the initial organizing of the NATO summit. Somebody pointed out that I hadn't had any of my counterparts, who I've

worked with now for 3 years, up to Camp David. G–8 tends to be a more informal setting in which we talk about a wide range of issues in a pretty intimate way. And the thinking was that people would enjoy being in a more casual backdrop. I think the weather should be good that time of year. It will give me a chance to spend time with Mr. Putin, the new Russian President. And from there, we will then fly to Chicago.

I always have confidence in Chicago being able to handle security issues. Whether it's Taste of Chicago or Lollapalooza—[*laughter*]—or Bulls championships, we know how to deal with a crowd. And I'm sure that your new mayor will be quite attentive to detail in making sure that everything goes off well.

All right? Okay. Go ahead, last one.

Q. Thank you.

The President. Last question.

U.S. Military Operations in Afghanistan/NATO Summit

Q. Thank you. Mr. President, just to continue on that, when the NATO leaders gather in Chicago in May, do you expect that they'll be able to agree on a transition strategy? And are you concerned at all that the Koran burning and the episodes that have followed since then threaten your ability to negotiate with partners?

The President. Well, keep in mind that the transition policy was in place and established at Lisbon, and we've been following that strategy that calls for us turning over increasing responsibility to Afghans and a full transition so that our combat role is over by the end of 2014. And our coalition partners have agreed to it. They are sticking with it. That continues to be the plan.

What we are now going to be doing over the next—at this NATO meeting and planning for the next 2 years is to make sure that that transition is not a cliff, but that there are benchmarks and steps that are taken along the way, in the same way that we reduced our role in Iraq, so that it is gradual, Afghan capacity is built, the partnering with Afghan security forces is effective, that we are putting in place the kinds of support structures that are needed in order for the overall strategy to be effective.

Now, yes, the situation with the Koran burning concerns me. I think that it is an indication of the challenges in that environment, and it's an indication that now is the time for us to transition.

Obviously, the violence directed at our people is unacceptable. And President Karzai acknowledged that. But what is also true is President Karzai, I think, is eager for more responsibility on the Afghan side. We're going to be able to find a mechanism whereby Afghans understand their sovereignty is being respected and that they're going to be taking a greater and greater role in their own security. That, I think, is in the interest of Afghans. It's also in our interests. And I'm confident we can execute, but it's not going to be a smooth path. There are going to be bumps along the road just as there were in Iraq.

Afghanistan-U.S. Relations

Q. Well, are these bumps along the road, or are you seeing a deterioration in the relationship, based on the Koran burning itself, the violence that has followed, that inhibits your ability to work out things like how to hand off the detention center?

The President. No, I—none of this stuff is easy, and it never has been. And obviously, the most recent riots or protests against the Koran burning were tragic, but remember, this happened a while back when a pastor in Florida threatened to burn a Koran. In Iraq, as we were making this transition, there were constant crises that would pop up and tragic events that would take place and there would be occasional setbacks.

But what I've tried to do is to set a course, make sure that up and down the chain of command everybody knows what our broader strategy is. And one of the incredible things about

our military is that when they know what our objective is, what our goal is, regardless of the obstacles that they meet along the way, they get the job done.

And I think that President Karzai understands that we are interested in a strategic partnership with the Afghan people and the Afghan Government. We are not interested in staying there any longer than is necessary to assure that Al Qaida is not operating there and that there is sufficient stability that it doesn't end up being a free-for-all after ISAF has left.

And so we share interests here. It will require negotiations, and there will be time where things don't look as smooth as I'd like. That's kind of the deal internationally on a whole range of these issues.

All right? Thank you guys.

Oh, let—can I just make one other comment? I want to publicly express condolences to the family of Donald Payne, Congressman from New Jersey, a wonderful man, did great work, both domestically and internationally. He was a friend of mine. And so my heart goes out to his family and to his colleagues.

All right.

NOTE: The President's news conference began at 1:15 p.m. in the James S. Brady Press Briefing Room at the White House. In his remarks, the President referred to Georgetown University law student Sandra K. Fluke, who testified before the House Democratic Steering and Policy Committee on student health insurance coverage of contraceptive services; Prime Minister Vladimir Vladimirovich Putin of Russia, in his capacity as President-elect of Russia; Mayor Rahm I. Emanuel of Chicago; and Terry Jones, pastor, Dove World Outreach Center in Gainesville, FL. Reporters referred to William Maher, Jr., host, HBO's "Real Time With Bill Maher" program; and Rep. Deborah Wasserman Shultz, chair, Democratic National Committee.

Statement on the Death of Representative Donald M. Payne
March 6, 2012

Michelle and I were saddened to hear about the passing of Congressman Donald Payne, chairman of the Congressional Black Caucus Foundation and former chairman of the Congressional Black Caucus. By any standard, Don lived a full and meaningful life. After serving as the first African American president of the national council of YMCAs and then several years in local government, Don went on to become the first African American Congressman to represent the State of New Jersey. In Washington, he made it his mission to fight for working families, increase the minimum wage, ensure worker safety, guarantee affordable health care, and improve the educational system. He was a leader in U.S.-Africa policy, making enormous contributions towards helping restore democracy and human rights across the continent. Don will be missed, and our thoughts and prayers go out to his family and friends during this difficult time.

Remarks to the Business Roundtable
March 6, 2012

Thank you very much, everybody. It is good to see all of you. Jim, thank you for the introduction. It is a privilege to be with the men and women of the Business Roundtable. Over the past 3 years, we've worked together on a number of issues, and we've found common ground on an awful lot of them.

Some of you have dedicated your time and energy and expertise to serving on my Jobs Council or my Export Council. Others have hosted me or Cabinet members at your companies, at your plants, at your distribution centers. And this engagement has been incredibly productive for us. It's helped to shape our collective work and to get this economy growing again. So I just wanted to say thank you for that.

Tonight I want to keep that engagement going, so I'm going to keep my remarks at the top relatively brief. I'm looking forward to hearing about your new "Taking Action for America" report. And I'm going to, hopefully, spend as much time listening as I do talking.

But the last time I addressed this group was just over 2 years ago, when we were still working to clear away the wreckage from what turned out to be the worst economic crisis that we've seen since the Great Depression. And obviously, we've got a long way to go. We've still got millions of people who are out of work.

We still have a lot of folks whose homes are underwater. There are enormous economic challenges that lie ahead, and we're going to have to think strategically and systematically about how we restore a sense of middle class security for Americans who are doing the right thing, working hard, looking to support their families.

The good news is, over the last 2 years, businesses like yours have created over 3.7 million new jobs. The American auto industry has come back. Companies are bringing jobs back to America. Manufacturers are adding new jobs for the first time since the 1990s.

And I've seen it firsthand in many of your companies. Most recently, I went to the Boeing plant out in Washington State. And Jim informed me that last year, orders for commercial aircraft rose by more than 50 percent, and they had to hire 13,000 workers all across America just to keep up. And I have to say that given the number of planes that I've been selling around the world, I expect a golden watch upon my retirement. [*Laughter*]

So the economy is getting stronger, and the recovery is speeding up. And the question now is, how do we make sure that it keeps going?

I've been talking a lot recently about how we can do that: how we can help companies like yours hire more workers, bring more jobs back to America; how we can leave an economy that's not just restored to precrisis levels, but positions ourselves to be competitive in this 21st-century economy over the long term, an economy built to last.

I think we have to focus on our core strengths: American manufacturing, American energy, American innovation, the best skills and education for American workers.

Right now, on the manufacturing front, I think we've got a huge opportunity. What's happened in the auto industry can happen in other areas, and we've got to make sure that we understand even though manufacturing will not be the same percentage of our economy as it once was, it still remains this incredible multiplier for services and consumers and prosperity all across America. That's why I want to thank Andrew Liveris. Where's Andrew? There he is. Andrew is helping us to do some terrific work as part of our Advanced Manufacturing Partnership. And obviously, part of our job as the Federal Government is to make sure that the R&D, the basic research is continuing to be done, and figuring out how we commercialize that, create products here in America, and sell them all around the world is going to be absolutely critical.

Thanks to new bipartisan trade agreements that I've signed with Panama, Colombia, and, most significantly, South Korea, we're on track to meet our goal of doubling American exports over the next 5 years. And I know the BRT was very helpful in making sure that that happened.

I think I've shown that I will go anywhere in the world to open new markets for American goods. That's why we worked so hard to secure Russia's invitation into the WTO. That's why I have asked Congress to repeal Jackson-Vanik, to make sure that all your companies and American companies all across the country can take advantage of it. And that's something that we're going to need some help on.

This is about creating a level, rules-based playing field in the growing Russian market. Because when it comes to competing for the jobs and the industries of tomorrow, no foreign company should have an advantage over American companies. When the playing field is lev-

el, American companies will win, American workers will win, and this country will win.

And one of the most important things Congress can do right now for companies like yours, to sell your ideas and your products and your services around the world, is to reauthorize the Export-Import Bank at the appropriate funding level. This is something that we're going to be focused on in the coming weeks and months.

During the financial crisis, trade finance dried up all around the world, and the Ex-Im Bank lived up to its mission. It stepped up to fill the void at record levels, and at no cost to taxpayers. In fact, since 2005, Ex-Im has returned billions back to the U.S. Treasury. So this is a smart thing to do for American businesses and American jobs.

It is an indispensable resource for our exporters, especially since many of your competitors are getting aggressive financing from their governments. So I'm asking your help in making sure Congress does the right thing on this front.

I've also shown that I won't stand by when our competitors don't play by the rules. A lot of you are expanding into growth markets, in emerging markets in Asia-Pacific region. But many of you, at least privately, have indicated to me that it gets harder and harder to do business there in terms of protecting your intellectual property, competing against indigenous innovation laws. And so what we are doing is setting up a trade enforcement unit to aggressively investigate and counter unfair trade practices all around the world, including countries like China.

And if you're a CEO that's willing to bring jobs back to America, we want to do everything we can to help you succeed. That means working together to reform our tax system so that we are rewarding companies that are investing here in the United States, making sure that we are able to cut our tax rate here, but also broaden the base. That is going to be a difficult task. Anybody who has been involved in tax discussions in any legislature, but especially Congress, knows that it's like pulling teeth. But it is the right thing to do for us to become more competitive.

We're also going to have to make significant investments in American energy. I am very proud of the fact that American energy output is reaching record levels. We are seeing the highest oil production in the last 8 years. At the same time, because so many of your companies have become more efficient, we're actually seeing a reduction in imports—in fact, below 50 percent for the first time back in 2010, the first time in a decade.

But we've got more work to do, and it's going to require an all-of-the-above strategy. Obviously, folks are getting killed right now with gas prices. And that has an impact on all of your companies, because consumers are more price sensitive when it comes to filling up their gas tank than just about anything else. That means, yes, we've got to produce more oil and more natural gas, and we are game for that. It also means, though, we've got to invest in the energy sources of the future.

We've got to invest in clean energy. We've got to invest in efficiency. We've got to make sure that the advanced batteries for electric cars, for example, are manufactured here in the United States.

And then, the final thing we're going to have to do is make sure that we have the skills and the training for our workers that are unmatched around the world. There has been a lot of talk about education reform; we've actually implemented education reform. And we've been able to get more than 40 States to raise standards, to start looking at best practices to figure out how we can train teachers more effectively, make sure that teachers who aren't doing a good job are getting the kind of training they need or they're not in the classroom, but also rewarding those folks who are stepping up to the plate and making sure our kids are prepared.

It also means matching up companies with our community colleges to train people for the jobs that actually exist. And I know that companies like Siemens and UPS are doing a great job on this front. We want to continue to push that forward.

Two last points: One is, I will not give up on the need for us to rebuild America's infrastructure. When you think about your own businesses, if you know that you've got to make some capital investments and interest rates are

historically low and it is a buyer's market, you act, understanding that you've got to project 5 years out, 10 years out, 20 years out. Well, that's the situation our country faces. I make no apologies for being chauvinistic when it comes to wanting to have the best airports, the best roads, the fastest broadband lines, the best wireless connections here in the United States of America. And now is the time for us to do it, and we're going to need BRT's help.

That will be good for business. It will allow you to move goods and services more quickly around the world. It will put people back to work. It will be a boost for our economy. And it will increase our productivity and efficiency over the long term.

And the final thing I just want to make mention of is the issue of how we pay for all these things. There obviously, over the last couple of years, has been an enormous debate about deficits and debt, and I'm sure we'll have a chance to talk about that more during the Q&A.

The fact of the matter is that we have already made significant cuts when it comes to discretionary spending. We are pruning this Government to make sure the programs that don't work we eliminate, so that we can invest in the programs that are necessary for our growth. We're going to have to make some continued reforms when it comes to, particularly, our health care system, because it is still too expensive and we've got an aging population that we're going to have to take care of.

But we're also going to have to deal with revenue. And that's something that I think that the American people instinctually understand, that if we do this in a balanced way, we can solve our problems. This is not a situation that is analogous to Greece. We don't have to cut by 25 percent and raise taxes by 25 percent. That's not the situation we find ourselves in. These are relatively modest adjustments that can stabilize our economy, give you the kind of business confidence you need to invest, and make sure that America wins for the future.

I'm prepared to be a partner in that process. But we're going to have to have everybody pulling together. The business community is going to have an important voice in how that moves forward.

So with that, I want to thank you again, and I look forward to the questions and the comments.

NOTE: The President spoke at 7:06 p.m. at the Newseum. In his remarks, he referred to W. James McNerney, chairman, Business Roundtable; and Andrew N. Liveris, chairman and chief executive officer, Dow Chemical Co.

Remarks at Daimler Trucks North America Manufacturing Plant in Mount Holly, North Carolina
March 7, 2012

The President. Hello, North Carolina! Hello, Mount Holly! Thank you, Juan, for that introduction. I did not know he was a preacher. [*Laughter*] He must be at least a deacon. [*Laughter*] I was—"Well"—[*laughter*]. He was starting to get the spirit up here. I'm going to take Juan on the road to introduce me everywhere. [*Laughter*] Can I hear an "amen"?

Audience members. Amen!

The President. Amen.

I want to thank Mark Hernandez, Ricky McDowell, and Martin Daum for hosting us and being such great tour guides. Thank you so much, everybody. Give them a big round of applause.

We've got a few outstanding North Carolinians in the house. You've got your Governor, Bev Perdue is here. Your mayors, Bryan Hough and Anthony Foxx, are here. Two outstanding Congressmen, Mel Watt and Heath Shuler, are here. Thank you all for being here.

It is good to be in North Carolina. Anthony Foxx pointed out that I decided to wear a tie that could be a Tar Heel, but it's got a little Duke color in there too. I didn't want to get in trouble with anybody, so I was hedging my bets. [*Laughter*]

I always tell people I am one of the best advertisers for North Carolina. I love this State. Love this State. Everybody here is so nice, so welcoming. Even the folks who don't vote for me, they're nice to me. They usually wave five fingers. [*Laughter*] So it's just a great pleasure.

And I just had a chance to see some of the folks who are doing the work here today. I couldn't be more impressed. Some people have been here—like Juan—32 years, 25 years. Some folks had been here for 4 months or 6

months, had just gotten hired. But everybody had such pride in their work.

And the Freighterline trucks that you're making here at this plant run on natural gas, and that makes them quieter, it makes them better for the environment, it makes them cheaper to fill up than they would be with diesel. I hear you sold your 1,000th natural gas truck last November, the first company to reach that milestone. And it was made right here in Mount Holly. And last year, this plant added more than 1,000 workers, hiring back a lot of folks who were laid off during the recession. That is something to be proud of.

Now, here at Daimler, you're not just building trucks. You're building better trucks. You're building trucks that use less oil. And you know that's especially important right now because most of you have probably filled up your gas tank a time or two in the last week, and you've seen how quickly the price of gas is going up. A lot of you may have to drive a distance to work. Higher gas prices are like a tax straight out of your paycheck.

And for companies that operate a whole fleet of trucks, the higher costs can make a big difference in terms of the profitability of the company.

Now, here's the thing, though. This is not the first time we've seen gas prices spike. It's been happening for years. Every year about this time, gas starts spiking up, and everybody starts wondering, how high is it going to go? And every year, politicians start talking when gas prices go up. They get out on the campaign trail, and you and I both know there are no quick fixes to this problem, but listening to them, you'd think there were.

As a country that has 2 percent of the world's oil reserves, but uses 20 percent of the world's oil—I'm going to repeat that—we've got 2 percent of the world oil reserves; we use 20 percent. What that means is, as much as we're doing to increase oil production, we're not going to be able to just drill our way out of the problem of high gas prices. Anybody who tells you otherwise either doesn't know what they're talking about or they aren't telling you the truth.

Here is the truth: If we are going to control our energy future, then we've got to have an all-of-the-above strategy. We've got to develop every source of American energy, not just oil and gas, but wind power and solar power, nuclear power, biofuels. We need to invest in the technology that will help us use less oil in our cars and our trucks, in our buildings, in our factories. That's the only solution to the challenge. Because as we start using less, that lowers the demand, prices come down. It's pretty straightforward. That's the only solution to this challenge.

And that's the strategy that we've now been pursuing for the last 3 years. And I'm proud to say we've made progress. Since I took office, America's dependence on foreign oil has gone down every single year. In fact, in 2010, it went under 50 percent for the first time in 13 years.

Now, you wouldn't know it from listening to some of these folks out here—[*laughter*]—some of these folks—[*laughter*]—but a key part of our energy strategy has been to increase safe, responsible oil production here at home. Under my administration, America is producing more oil today than any time in the last 8 years. Under my administration, we've quadrupled the number of operating oil rigs to a record high. We've got more oil rigs operating now than we've ever seen. We've opened up millions of new acres for oil and gas exploration. We've approved more than 400 drilling permits that follow new safety standards after we had that mess down in the Gulf.

We're approving dozens of new pipelines. We just announced that we'll do whatever we can to speed up construction of a pipeline in Oklahoma that's going to relieve a bottleneck

and get more oil to the Gulf, to the refineries down there, and that's going to help create jobs, encourage more production.

So these are the facts on oil production. If somebody tells you we're not producing enough oil, they just don't know the facts.

But how much oil we produce here at home—because we only have 2 percent and we use 20—that's not going to set the price of gas worldwide or here in the United States. Oil is bought and sold on the world market. And the biggest thing that's causing the price of oil to rise right now is instability in the Middle East. You guys have been hearing about what's happening with Iran; there are other oil producers that are having problems. And so people have gotten uncertain. And when uncertainty increases, then sometimes you see speculation on Wall Street that drives up gas prices even more.

But here's the thing: Over the long term, the biggest reason oil prices will go up is there's just growing demand in countries like China and India and Brazil. There are a lot of people there. In 2010 alone, China added nearly 10 million cars on its roads. Think about that—2010, 10 million new cars. People in China, folks in India, folks in Brazil, they're going to want cars too, as their standard of living goes up, and that means more demand for oil, and that's going to kick up the price of oil worldwide. Those numbers are only going to get bigger over time.

So what does that mean for us? It means we can't just keep on relying on the old ways of doing business. We can't just rely on fossil fuels from the last century. We've got to continually develop new sources of energy.

And that's why we've made investments that have nearly doubled the use of clean, renewable energies in this country. And thousands of Americans have jobs because of it. It also means we've got to develop the resources that we have that are untapped, like natural gas. We're developing a near hundred-year supply of natural gas, and that's something that we expect could support more than 600,000 jobs by the end of the decade.

And that's why we've worked with the private sector to develop a high-tech car battery that costs half as much as other batteries and can go up to 300 miles on a single charge. Think about that. That will save you some money at the pump. And that is why we are helping companies like this one right here and plants like this one right here to make more cars and trucks that use less oil.

When I ran for office, I went to Detroit and I gave a speech to automakers where I promised that I was going to raise fuel standards on our cars, so that they'd go further on a gallon of gas. I said we should do the same thing on trucks. I have to tell you, when I said it, I didn't get a lot of applause in the room, because there was a time when automakers were resisting higher fuel standards because change isn't easy. But you know what, after three decades of not doing anything, we got together with the oil companies, we got together with the unions, we got together with folks who usually do not see eye to eye, and we negotiated new fuel economy standards that are going to make sure our cars average nearly 55 miles per gallon by the middle of the next decade. That's nearly double what they get today—nearly double.

Now, because of these new standards for cars and trucks, they're going to—all going to be able to go further and use less fuel every year. And that means pretty soon you'll be able to fill up your car every 2 weeks instead of every week, and over time that saves you, a typical family, about $8,000 a year.

Audience member. We like that.

The President. You like that, don't you?

Audience members. Yes!

The President. Eight thousand dollars, that's no joke. We can reduce our oil consumption by more than 12 billion barrels. And thanks to the SuperTruck program that we've started with companies like this one, trucks will be able to save more than $15,000 in fuel costs every year. Think about that, 15,000.

It looks like somebody might have fainted up here. Have we got some of the EMS—somebody. Don't worry about—folks do this all the time in my meetings. [*Laughter*] You've always got to eat before you stand for a long

time. That's a little tip. But they'll be okay. Just make sure that—give them a little room. All right, everybody, all right? Okay.

So these trucks can save $15,000 every year. I want people to think about what that means for businesses, what it means for consumers. It is real progress. And it's happening because of American workers and American know-how. It's happening because of you. It's happening because of you.

We're also making it easier for big companies—some of your customers, like UPS and FedEx—to make the shift to fuel-efficient cars and trucks. We call it the National Clean Fleets Partnership. And since we announced it last year, the number of companies that are taking part in it has tripled. And that means more customers for your trucks. We're creating more customers for your trucks.

And I am proud to say that the Federal Government is leading by example. One thing the Federal Government has a lot of is cars and trucks. We got a lot of cars and we got a lot of trucks. And so what I did was I directed every department, every agency in the Federal Government, to make sure that by 2015, 100 percent of the vehicles we buy run on alternative fuels—100 percent.

So we're one of the biggest customers in the world for cars and trucks, and we want to set that bar high. We want to set a standard that says by 2015, 100 percent of cars, alternative fuels.

So we're making progress, Mount Holly. But at the end of the day, it doesn't matter how much natural gas or flex-fuel or electric vehicles you have if there's no place to charge them up or fill them up. So that's why I'm announcing today a program that will put our communities on the cutting edge of what clean energy can do.

To cities and towns all across the country, what we're going to say is, if you make a commitment to buy more advanced vehicles for your community, whether they run on electricity or biofuels or natural gas, we'll help you cut through the redtape and build fueling stations nearby. And we'll offer tax breaks to families that buy these cars, companies that buy

271

alternative fuel trucks like the ones that are made right here at Mount Holly. So we're going to give communities across the country more of an incentive to make the shift to more energy-efficient cars.

In fact, when I was up in New Hampshire, in Nashua, they had already converted all their dump trucks—they were in a process because of this program—they were converting it to natural gas–driven trucks.

This is something that we did in education. We called it Race to the Top. We said, we'll put in more money, but we want you to reform. We're going to give you an incentive to do things in a different way. And if we do the same thing with clean energy, we can save consumers money and we can make sure the economy is more secure. So we've got to keep investing in American-made energy, and we've got to keep investing in the vehicles that run on it. That's where our future is.

And in order to continue this progress, we're going to have to make a choice. We've got to decide where our priorities are as a country. And that's up to all of you. And I'll give you an example. Right now 4 billion of your tax dollars goes straight to the oil industry every year, $4 billion in subsidies that other companies don't get. Now keep in mind, these are some of the same companies that are making record profits every time you fill up your gas tank. We're giving them extra billions of dollars on top of near-record profits that they're already making. Anybody think that's a good idea?

Audience members. No!

The President. Me neither. [*Laughter*] It doesn't make any sense. The American people have subsidized the oil industry long enough. They don't need the subsidies. It's time to end that taxpayer giveaway to an industry that's never been more profitable, invest in clean energy that's never been more promising.

So I called on Congress, eliminate these subsidies right away. There's no excuse to wait any longer. And we should put every Member of Congress on record: They can stand up for the oil companies, or they can stand up for the

American people and this new energy future. We can place our bets on the fuel of the past, or we can place our bets on American know-how and American ingenuity and American workers like the ones here at Daimler. That's the choice we face. That's what's at stake right now.

So, in between shifts, get on the phone or e-mail or send a letter or tweet—[*laughter*]—your Member of Congress, ask them where they stand on this, because it will make a difference. And you'll know where I stand on this. Let's make sure our voices are heard. The next time you hear some politician trotting out some three-point plan for $2 gas—[*laughter*]—you let them know, we know better.

Tell them we're tired of hearing phony election-year promises that never come about. What we need is a serious, sustained, all-of-the-above strategy for American-made energy, American-made efficiency, American innovation, American fuel-efficient trucks, American fuel-efficient cars. We may not get there in one term. It's going to take us a while to wean ourselves off of the old and grab the new. But we're going to meet this challenge because we are Americans. Our destiny is not written for us; it is written by us. We decide what that next chapter is going to be.

And I'm confident, working with folks like you, the outstanding working people of Mount Holly, of this plant, of North Carolina, of States all across the country, we can pull together and remind everybody around the world just why it is that the United States of America is the greatest nation on Earth.

Thank you very much, everybody. God bless you. God bless the United States of America.

NOTE: The President spoke at 12:50 p.m. In his remarks, he referred to Juan Smith, Mark Hernandez, and Ricky McDowell, employees, and Martin Daum, president and chief executive officer, Daimler Trucks North America; Mayor Bryan Hough of Mount Holly, NC; and Mayor Anthony R. Foxx of Charlotte, NC.

Remarks Following a Meeting With President John Evans Atta Mills of Ghana
March 8, 2012

President Obama. Well, it is a great pleasure to welcome President Mills and his delegation from Ghana. This gives me the opportunity to return the extraordinary hospitality that they showed not only me, but also Michelle and Sasha and Malia, and when we had the opportunity to visit last year.

There are sometimes—there's sometimes a tendency to focus on the challenges that exist in Africa and rightfully so. But I think it's important for us to also focus on the good news that's coming out of Africa, and I think Ghana continues to be a good-news story.

This is a country that has established a strong tradition of democracy, and President Mills and I were comparing notes—we're both up for reelection—but what we agreed to is the fact that regardless of who wins and who loses, our countries' commitment to making sure that the people have a voice and determine who it is that represents them in their government is what gives both our countries such strength.

And Ghana has proven, I think, to be a model for Africa in terms of its democratic practices. And I very much appreciate the efforts that President Mills has taken not only to ensure fair and free elections, but also to root out corruption, increase transparency, make sure that government is working for the people of Ghana and not just for the few. So we're very appreciative of those efforts.

In addition, Ghana has become a wonderful success story economically on the continent. In part because of the initiatives of President Mills, you've seen high growth rates over the last several years. Food productivity and food security is up. There's been strong foreign investment. That trade and investment benefits folks back home here in the United States as well.

In fact, the President's Government recently is collaborating with a number of American businesses to build infrastructure inside of Ghana, which will create thousands of jobs here in the United States. And the trade that we engage in creates jobs for tens of thousands of people back in Ghana. So that's a good-news story.

And what we've also been able to do is collaborate with the Ghanaian Government through the Millennium Challenge Corporation—they are a grant recipient—and it has helped to improve a wide range of infrastructure and institutions inside of Ghana. Our Feed the Future program—we've been able to help increase productivity there. And the Partnership for Growth—that is also another mechanism where we're collaborating, for example, on power generation and credit to small businesses and medium-size businesses inside of Ghana.

Ghana's also been a leader, a responsible actor on the international stage, working in the region to help stabilize and reduce conflict there. They've been a strong partner with us in the United Nations on a whole range of international issues. And as important, President Mills has consistently spoken out on behalf of human rights and making sure that everyone is treated fairly and not discriminated against inside of his country.

So I am very proud of the friendship and the partnership between Ghana and the United States. I am confident that it will continue well into the future, beyond the tenures of these two Presidents. And I'm looking forward to having an opportunity to visit Ghana once again sometime in the future.

But in the meantime, Mr. President, welcome to the United States, welcome to your delegation, and we wish you all the best.

President Mills. Thank you, Mr. President, for this very warm reception. My delegation and I are really honored to be here today. First, to say a big thank you to you, Mr. President, for the honor done us by singling us out for your first visit to Africa on assumption of office. It's really inspired us.

And I'm also here to also thank you for the help that we have been enjoying and for the high level of cooperation and collaboration that exists between our two countries. We share the

273

same values of democracy. We have come to accept that democracy is the only way.

And democracy goes with development. And if you come to Africa, our people are yearning for only one thing: improvement in their daily lives. And there can be no development without peace, which means that we should do the things which will ensure that there is peace and that there's no room for conflict.

The United States has been a model, and I'm happy that we are cooperating with one another on all kinds of fronts and they are yielding results. And I was telling Mr. President that when one of the roads was commissioned, and it was built with money provided by the MCC under our first compact; you should have seen the joy on the faces of the Ghanaians because there had been a radical transformation in their lives. I mean, that is what governance is all about: to see people happy because they now have what they did not have.

So I've assured the President that we have elections this year, but we are going to ensure that there is peace before, during, after the elections, because when there is no peace, it's not the leaders who will suffer, it's the ordinary people who have elected us into office.

So we have a big challenge, and we know that some of our friends in Africa are looking up to us, and we dare not fail them. I have no doubt at all that we have embarked on a useful journey, and we'll get to the very end. I've told him that both of us are facing elections, but our ships will be able to sail safely to their final destination, I want to assure you.

So thanks a lot for the wonderful reception. We'll go back with happy memories. And of course, this will also reassure our people that the kind of cooperation, which started with Osagyefo Dr. Kwame Nkrumah, our first President, is growing from strength to strength.

President Obama. Thank you, Mr. President.

President Mills. Thank you, Mr. President.

President Obama. Thank you, everybody.

NOTE: The President spoke at 3:55 p.m. in the Oval Office at the White House.

Statement on International Women's Day
March 8, 2012

On International Women's Day, the United States celebrates the many achievements and milestones in the ongoing struggle for gender equality around the world and reaffirms our commitment to accelerating progress. We are committed to a future in which our daughters and sons have equal opportunities to thrive, because when women succeed, communities and countries succeed. With this promise in mind, we are launching new initiatives on women's political participation and economic empowerment, combating violence against women, promoting women's roles and perspectives in conflict prevention and peacebuilding, and supporting the work of U.N. Women and other key partners.

Experience shows that true democracy cannot be built without the full and equal partici-

pation of half our population. Women's economic empowerment is essential for economic recovery and growth worldwide. Successful transitions in the Middle East and North Africa will depend on women's ability to shape their countries' futures. From Egypt to Yemen and beyond, over the last year, we have seen women lead local and national efforts to protest corruption, demand accountability, and establish new institutions.

The United States also recognizes the need to elevate the perspectives of particularly marginalized women worldwide, including refugees and displaced persons, ethnic and religious minorities, and women with disabilities. On this day, and every day, we stand with the women and men who bravely champion dignity, freedom, and opportunity for all.

Remarks at the Rolls-Royce Crosspointe Plant in Petersburg, Virginia
March 9, 2012

The President. Hello, Virginia! Thank you so much. Thank you, everybody. Wow, what a unbelievable crowd. Everybody, please have a seat, if you have one. [*Laughter*]

Well, thank you, James, for that rousing introduction and letting me hang out a little bit with your workers. We've got a few other folks I want to acknowledge: The Governor of the great Commonwealth of Virginia, Bob McDonnell, is here. Outstanding Congressman Bobby Scott is in the house. We've got your mayor, Brian Moore. And I want to very much say thank you to our outstanding Secretary of Commerce, Secretary Bryson, who was here, and he is doing great work trying to create jobs and investment and opportunity all across the country.

It is great to be back in Petersburg. Last time I was here was during the campaign. I had my bus pull over so I could get a cheeseburger—[*laughter*]—at Longstreet's Deli. You guys have eaten there. [*Laughter*] Some of you may think this violates Michelle's "Let's Move!" program—[*laughter*]—but she gives me a pass when it comes to a good burger—[*laughter*]—and fries.

Now, back then, in 2008, we were talking about how working Americans were already having a tough go of it. Folks were working harder and longer for less. It was getting tougher to afford health care or to send your kids to college. The economy was already shedding jobs, and in less than a decade, nearly one in three manufacturing jobs had vanished. Then the bottom fell out of the economy, and things got that much tougher. We were losing seven to eight hundred thousand jobs a month. The economy was hemorrhaging.

And 3½ years later, we're still recovering from the worst economic crisis in our lifetimes. And we've got a lot of work to do before everybody who wants a good job can find one, before middle class folks regain that sense of security that had been slipping away even before the recession hit and before towns like Petersburg get fully back on their feet.

But here's the good news: Over the past 2 years, our businesses have added nearly 4 million new jobs. We just found out that last month in February we added 233,000 private-sector jobs. More companies are bringing jobs back and investing in America. And manufacturing is adding jobs for the first time since the 1990s. We just had another good month last month in terms of adding manufacturing jobs. And this facility is part of the evidence of what's going on all across the country. This company is about to hire more than 200 new workers, 140 of them right here in Petersburg, Virginia.

So the economy is getting stronger. And when I come to places like this, and I see the work that's being done, it gives me confidence there are better days ahead. I know it because I would bet on American workers and American know-how any day of the week.

The key now—our job now is to keep this economic engine churning. We can't go back to the same policies that got us into this mess. We can't go back to an economy that was weakened by outsourcing and bad debt and phony financial profits. We've got to have an economy that's built to last. And that starts with American manufacturing. It starts with you.

For generations of Americans, manufacturing has been the ticket into the middle class. Every day, millions clocked in at foundries and on assembly lines, making things. And the stuff we made—steel and cars and jet engines—that was the stuff that made America what it is. It was understood around the world.

The work was hard, but the jobs were good. They paid enough to own a home and raise kids and send them to college, gave you enough to retire on with dignity and respect. They were jobs that told us something more important than how much we were worth; they told us what we were worth. They told us that we were building more than just products. They told us we were building communities and neighborhoods, we were building a country. It gave people pride about what America was about.

And that's why one of the first decisions I made as President was to stand by manufacturing, to stand by the American auto industry when it was on the brink of collapse. The heartbeat of American manufacturing was at stake, and so were more than a million jobs. And today, the American auto industry is coming back, and GM is number one in the world again, and Ford is investing billions in American plants and factories. And together, over the past 2½ years, the entire auto industry has added more than 200,000 jobs.

And here's the thing. They're not just building cars again, they're building better cars. For the first time in three decades, we raised fuel standards in this country so that by the middle of the next decade the cars that are built in America will average nearly 55 miles to the gallon. That will save the typical family about $8,000 at the pump over time. That's real savings. That's real money.

And it shows that depending on foreign oil doesn't have to be our future. It shows that when we harness our own ingenuity, our technology, then we can control our future. See, America thrives when we build things better than the rest of the world. I want us to make stuff here and sell it over there. I don't want stuff made over there and selling it over here. And that's exactly what you're doing here at the largest Rolls-Royce facility in the world. That's what you're doing by building the key components of newer, faster, more fuel-efficient jet engines.

I just took a tour, and I learned a bit about how a jet engine comes together. Don't quiz me on it. [*Laughter*] I'm a little fuzzy on some of the details. [*Laughter*] I did press some buttons back there. [*Laughter*]

But a few weeks ago, I actually got to see the finished product. I went to Boeing, in Washington State, and I checked out a new Dreamliner. I even got to sit in the cockpit, which was pretty sweet. I didn't press any buttons there, though—[*laughter*]—because if it had started going, it would have been a problem.

So this plane, the Dreamliner, is going to keep America at the cutting edge of aerospace technology. American workers are manufacturing various components for it in Ohio and Oklahoma and South Carolina and Kansas and right here in Petersburg. In fact, the demand for their planes was so high last year that Boeing had to hire 13,000 workers all across America just to keep up. And Boeing is gaining more and more share all the time.

So think about that. Rolls-Royce is choosing to invest in America. You're creating jobs here, manufacturing components for jet engines, for planes that we're going to send all around the world. And that's the kind of business cycle we want to see. Not buying stuff that's made someplace else and racking up debt, but by inventing things and building things and selling them all around the world stamped with three proud words: Made in America. Made in America.

Think about how important this is. I mean, imagine if the plane of the future was being built someplace else. Imagine if we had given up on the auto industry. Imagine if we had settled for a lesser future.

But we didn't. We're Americans. We are inventors. We are builders. We're Thomas Edison, and we're the Wright Brothers, and we are Steven Jobs. That's who we are. That's what we do. We invent stuff, we build it. And pretty soon, the entire world adapts it. That's who we are. And as long as I'm President, we're going to keep on doing it. We're going to make sure the next generation of life-changing products are invented and manufactured here in the United States of America.

So that's why we launched an all-hands-on-deck effort. We brought together the brightest academic minds, the boldest business leaders, the most dedicated public servants from our science and our technology agencies all with one big goal: a renaissance in American manufacturing. We called it the Advanced Manufacturing Partnership. The Advanced Manufacturing Partnership. And today, we're building on it.

I'm laying out my plans for a new national network of manufacturing innovation, and these are going to be institutes of manufacturing excellence where some of our most advanced engineering schools and our most innovative manufacturers collaborate on new ideas, new technology, new methods, new processes.

And if this sounds familiar, that's because what you're about to do right here at Crosspointe. Later this summer, the Commonwealth Center for Advanced Manufacturing will open its doors. And it's a partnership between manufacturers, including this one, UVA, Virginia Tech, Virginia State University—*[applause]*—VSU is a little overrepresented here, obviously—*[laughter]*—the Commonwealth, and the Federal Government. So think of this as a place where companies can share access to cutting-edge capabilities. At the same time, students and workers are picking up new skills, they're training on state-of-the-art equipment, they're solving some of the most important challenges facing our manufacturers.

You just got all this brain power and skill and experience coming together in this hub, and that makes the whole greater than the sum of its parts. It allows everybody to learn from each other and figure out how we're going to do things even better. It's going to help get that next great idea from a paper or a computer to the lab, to the factory, to the global marketplace. And that's especially important for the one in three Americans in manufacturing who work for a small business that doesn't always have access to resources like these.

Obviously, big companies—the Boeings, the Intels, the Rolls-Royces—they've got the resources, the capital, to be able to create these platforms. But some of the small to medium-sized businesses, it's a little bit harder. So this gives them access and allows them to take part in this new renaissance of American inventiveness. And we've got to build these institutes all across the country—all across the country. I don't want it just here at Crosspointe, I want it everywhere.

To do that, we need Congress to act. Hmm. We—*[laughter]*—it's true. *[Laughter]* But that doesn't mean we have to hold our breath. We're not going to wait; we're going to go ahead on our own. Later this year, we're going

to choose the winner of a competition for a pilot institute for manufacturing innovation, help them get started. With that pilot in place, we'll keep on pushing Congress to do the right thing because this is the kind of approach that can succeed, but we've got to have this all across the country. I want everybody thinking about how are we making the best products, how are we harnessing the new ideas and making sure they're located here in the United States.

And sparking this network of innovation across the country, it will create jobs and it will keep America in the manufacturing game. Of course, there's more we can do to seize this moment of opportunity to create new jobs and manufacturing here in America.

We've got to do everything we can to encourage more companies to make the decision to invest in America and bring jobs back from overseas. And we're starting to see companies do that. They're starting to realize this is the place with the best workers, the best ideas, the best universities. This is the place to be. We've got to give them a little more encouragement.

Right now companies get tax breaks for moving jobs and profits overseas. Companies that choose to invest in America, they get hit with one of the highest tax rates in the world. Does that make any sense?

Audience members. No!

The President. It makes no sense. Everybody knows it. So it's time to stop rewarding businesses that ship jobs overseas; reward companies that create good jobs right here in the United States of America. That's how our Tax Code can work. That's how our Tax Code should work.

At the same time, we've got to do everything we can to make sure our kids get an education that gives them every chance to succeed. I've been told that last year's valedictorian at Petersburg High, whose name is Kenneisha Edmonds, she had a pretty good statement. She said her cap and gown was "the best gown that anybody can hang in their closet." *[Laughter]* I like that. So let's make sure students like Kenneisha have teachers who bring out the best in them. Let's make sure if they want to go to college, their families can afford them to go to college.

And let's make sure all our workers have the skills that companies like this one are looking for, because we've got to have folks engaged in lifelong learning. The days when you started out at 20 at one company and you just kept on doing the same thing for 40 years, that's not going to happen anymore.

So even if—as I was meeting some of the folks here, they had been in the industry, they'd been machinists, they'd been in manufacturing for years. But they're constantly upgrading their skills and retraining. And some of them had been laid off and had gone back to school before they came to this company. And so we've got to make sure those opportunities for people midcareer and onward, that they can constantly go back to a community college and retool so that they can make sure they're qualified for the jobs of tomorrow.

At a time when so many Americans are looking for work, no job opening should go unfilled just because people didn't have an opportunity to get the training they needed. And that's why I've asked Congress, join me in a national commitment to train 2 million Americans with the skills that will lead directly to a job, right now.

We need to create more partnerships like the one this plant has with John Tyler Community College. We should give more community colleges the resources they need. I want them to be community career centers, places that teach people skills that companies are looking for right now, from data management to the kind of high-tech manufacturing that's being done at this facility.

So, day by day, we're restoring this economy from crisis. But we can't stop there. We've got to make this economy ready for tomorrow. Day by day, we're creating new jobs, but we can't

stop there, not until everybody who's out there pounding the pavement, sending out their résumés has a chance to land one of those jobs.

Every day we're producing more oil and gas than we have in years, but we can't stop there. I want our businesses to lead the world in clean energy too. We've got the best colleges and universities in the world, but we can't stop there. I want to make sure more of our students can afford to go to those colleges and universities. Everybody knows we've got the best workers on Earth, but we can't stop there. We've got to make sure the middle class doesn't just survive these times, we want them to thrive. We want them to dream big dreams and to feel confident about the future.

I did not run for this office just to get back to where we were. I ran for this office to get us to where we need to be. And I promise you we will get there. Some of these challenges may take a year, some may take one term, some may take a decade, but we're going to get there. Because when we work together, we know what we're capable of. We've got the tools, we've got the know-how, we've got the toughness to overcome any obstacle. And when we come together and combine our creativity and our optimism and our willingness to work hard, and if we're harnessing our brainpower and our manpower and our horsepower, I promise you we will thrive again. We will get to where we need to go. And we will leave behind an economy that is built to last. We will make this another American century.

Thank you. God bless you. God bless the United States of America.

NOTE: The President spoke at 12:57 p.m. In his remarks, he referred to James M. Guyette, president and chief executive officer, Rolls-Royce North America Inc.

Statement on the First Anniversary of the March 11 Earthquake, Tsunami, and Nuclear Disaster in Japan
March 9, 2012

As we mark 1 year since the catastrophic earthquake, tsunami, and nuclear disasters in Japan, Michelle and I join all Americans in honoring the memory of the 19,000 victims lost or missing. We continue to be inspired by the Japanese people, who faced unimaginable loss with extraordinary fortitude. Their resilience and determination to rebuild stronger than before is an example for us all.

Since the first moments of the disaster, the United States mobilized to help our friends in Japan. At the peak of Operation Tomodachi—our single, largest bilateral military operation with Japan ever—the Department of Defense had 24,000 personnel, 190 aircraft, and 24 Navy ships supporting humanitarian assistance and disaster relief efforts. One year later, we remain committed to assist the people of Japan to rebuild. This effort, led by the Japanese Government, has benefited from the compassion of the American people, who in difficult economic times have given generously to help. Today, U.S. experts continue to support Japan's ongoing efforts to deal with the challenges associated with Fukushima, and the TOMODACHI public-private partnership is investing in the next generation to strengthen

cultural and economic ties. We are grateful for the contributions of Americans, civilian and military, who have joined with people from around the world to support Japan's recovery.

No one can forget the tragic images of disaster in the immediate aftermath of the earthquake and tsunami or the heartbreak of friends who lost homes, belongings, and most importantly, loved ones. Even as it works to rebuild its devastated northeastern region, Japan has never wavered from its steadfast commitment to help other countries around the world. So, on this day when our thoughts and prayers are with the Japanese people in remembrance of the hardship faced 1 year ago, let us also celebrate the recovery underway in Japan and pay tribute to Japan's unflagging dedication to bettering the lives of others throughout the world. The friendship and alliance between our two nations is unshakeable and, going forward, the people of Japan will continue to have an enduring partner in the United States.

Remarks at an Obama Victory Fund 2012 Fundraiser in Houston, Texas
March 9, 2012

The President. Hello, Texas! Oh, it is good to be back in Houston. The weather wasn't quite cooperating. [*Laughter*] But we got here. And so did you.

We've got some wonderful folks here, but first of all, can everybody please give Debra Jones a big round of applause for the wonderful introduction.

We have in the house your outstanding mayor, Annise Parker. We've got Congressman Gene Green. We've got Congressman Al Green. He's the one who taught me how to sing. [*Laughter*] We've got Congresswoman Sheila Jackson Lee. And we have all of you.

It is good to be in this facility. As a White Sox fan, I have a fond memories——

Audience members. Boo!

The President. ——of this facility. [*Laughter*] I want to thank Jim Crane for helping to make it available. And I want to thank all of you for being part of this thing here today.

Audience member. I love you!

The President. I love you back.

So I'm here today not just because I need your help. I'm here because the country needs your help. Now, there was a reason why so many of you worked your hearts out back in 2008. It wasn't because you thought it was going to be easy. After all, you decided to support a candidate named Barack Obama. You knew that wasn't going to be a sure thing. [*Laughter*]

You didn't join the campaign just because of me. You joined it because of your commitment to each other. You joined it because you had a common vision for America. Not a vision where everybody is left to fend for themselves; it was a vision where everyone who works hard has a chance to get ahead, not just those at the very top, but everybody.

That's the vision that we shared. That's the change that we believed in. And we knew it wouldn't come easy. We knew it wouldn't come quickly. We knew problems had been building up for decades. But I tell you what, in just 3 years, because of what you did, we've begun to see what change looks like.

Change is the first bill I signed into law that says women deserve an equal day's pay for an equal day's work. Our daughters should be treated just the same and have the same opportunities as our sons.

Change is the decision that we made that Debra alluded to, to rescue the American auto industry, save it from collapse, even when some politicians were saying let's let Detroit go bankrupt. With 1 million jobs on the line, I wasn't going to let that happen. And today, GM is back as the number-one automaker in the world, reporting the highest profits in its history. And with 200,000 new jobs created in the last 2½ years, the American auto industry is back. That's what change is. That happened because of you.

Change is the decision that we made to stop waiting for Congress to do something about our oil addiction and finally raise our fuel efficiency standards. And by the next decade, we will be driving American-made cars that are getting 55 miles a gallon, and that saves American families about $8,000 at the pump. That's what change is. That happened because of you.

Change is the fight we won to stop handing over $60 billion in taxpayer subsidies to banks in the student loan program, give that money directly to students. And as a consequence, millions of young people all across the country are getting help that they didn't have before. That happened because of your change.

Audience members. TSU loves you!

The President. We've got TSU in the house. Change is the fact that for the first time in history, you don't have to hide who you love in order to serve the country you love. "Don't ask, don't tell" is over.

And yes, change is health care reform that we passed after a century of trying. This is reform that makes sure that nobody in this country goes bankrupt just because they get sick. And already 2½ million young people have health insurance today that did not have it before because this law lets them stay on their parent's plan. Because of this law, preventive care is now covered. And yes, that includes preventive care for women: checkups, mammograms, birth control.

We fought for this because the top doctors, the medical experts in the country said this kind of preventive care saves women's lives. We fought for it because we know it saves money. It's a lot cheaper to prevent an illness than to treat one. So, when you see politicians who are trying to take us back to the days when this care was more expensive and harder to get for women—and I know you're seeing some of that here in Texas—you just remember, we can't let them get away with it. We fought for this change. We're going to protect this change. It's the right thing to do.

And change is keeping another promise I made in 2008. For the first time in 9 years, we do not have any Americans who are fighting in Iraq. We refocused our efforts on the terrorists who actually attacked us on 9/11. And thanks to our brave men and women in uniform—and there are a lot, a lot of servicemembers and a lot of veterans here in the great State of Texas—Al Qaida is weaker than it's ever been and Usama bin Laden will never again walk the face of this Earth.

None of this has been easy. We've got a lot more work to do. There's still too many Americans out there looking for work, still too many families struggling to pay the bills or make the mortgage. We're still recovering from the worst economic crisis of our generation or many generations. But over the past 2 years, businesses have added almost 4 million new jobs. Our manufacturers are creating jobs for the first time since the 1990s. Our economy steadily has been getting stronger. The recovery is accelerating. America is coming back. And the last thing we can afford to do is go back to the same policies that got us into this mess in the first place.

Of course, that's exactly what the other folks running for this office want us to do. They think you all have amnesia. [*Laughter*] They think you've forgotten how we got into this mess. They want to go back to the days when Wall Street played by its own rules. They want to go back to the days when insurance companies could deny you coverage or jack up your premiums without any reason. They want to go back to spending trillions of dollars more on tax breaks for the wealthiest individuals—folks like me—even if it means adding to the deficit or gutting education or gutting investments in clean energy or gutting Medicare. They're philosophy is simple: We're better off when everybody is left to fend for themselves.

Let me tell you something: They are wrong. In the United States of America, we're always greater together than we are on our own. We're better off when we keep that basic American promise where if you work hard, you can do well enough to raise a family or own a home, start your own business, send your kids to college, put a little away for retirement, maybe someday own the Astros. That's the choice we face in this election.

Look, we want everybody to succeed. We want everybody to do well—not just a few, but everybody to have that chance. That's what America's about. No matter where you come from, no matter what you look like, if you are willing to work hard, if you are willing to roll up your sleeves, you can make it. That's the American way.

And this is not just another political debate; this is the defining issue of our times. This is a make-or-break moment for middle class families and everybody who's trying to get into the middle class. I mean, we can go back to an economy that's built on outsourcing and bad debt and phony financial profits, or we can fight for an economy that's built to last.

And that's what we've been talking about for the last 3 years: an economy built on American manufacturing and American energy and the skills that American workers need, the education that our kids deserve, and the values that always made this country great: hard work and fair play and shared responsibility, everybody, from top to bottom, everybody pitching in.

And you know what? That's actually what everybody wants to do. When you hear some of these political debates—poor people, they want to work hard, they want to find a job. Wealthy people, they believe in this country, they want to give back. But we've gotten into

this pattern where our politics divides us and pushes us apart.

We need to make sure that the next generation of manufacturing takes root not in Asia, not in Europe, but right here, in Detroit and Pittsburgh and Cleveland and Houston. We don't want to be a nation—nobody should want us to be a nation known for just buying and consuming things. We want to build things, make things, invent things, sell things all around the world, which is why we need to stop giving tax breaks to businesses that ship jobs overseas. Let's reward companies that are creating jobs right here in the United States of America.

We've got to make our schools the envy of the world, and that starts with the men and women in front of the classroom. You know, an interesting statistic: A great teacher can increase the lifetime incomes of a classroom by over $250,000—just one teacher. So I don't want folks bashing teachers. I don't want folks defending the status quo. I want us to give the schools the resources they need to recruit and keep good teachers on the job, to reward the best ones.

Let's grant schools the flexibility to teach with creativity and passion, stop teaching to the test, replace teachers—train our teachers, and those who aren't helping our kids learn, we're going to have to replace.

And when kids do graduate, the most daunting challenge is affording the cost of college. Right now Americans owe more in tuition debt than credit card debt. So this Congress—and I know these Members of Congress agree with me here—we've got to stop the interest rates on student loans from doubling in July. And colleges and universities have to do their part. If they can't stop tuition from going up, then there should be some penalties, because taxpayers are willing to help young people, but ultimately, colleges and universities have got to do their part too. Higher education can't be a luxury; it's an economic imperative that every family in America should be able to afford.

An economy that's built to last is one that supports our scientists and our researchers that are trying to make the next breakthrough, invent the next product, discover the next source of clean energy right here in the United States of America.

You know, the—Houston—this is an oil town. And that's good. We need oil. And we've got a high production of oil right now. When you hear folks saying, oh, Obama's not supporting oil production—we've got the highest production we've had in 8 years. We're opening up millions of acres to new production, got more rigs than the entire world combined right here in the United States.

But we don't need to subsidize oil companies when they're doing this well. So what I've said is, rather than continue a hundred years of taxpayer subsidies to an industry that's very, very profitable, let's double down on our investments in clean energy that's never been more promising. That will create jobs in Texas—solar power and wind power, biofuels. We want an all-of-the-above strategy. Yes, oil. Yes, gas. Yes, solar. Yes, wind.

Audience member. Yes, we can.

The President. Yes, we can. We can do it.

We've got to rebuild our infrastructure. I—you know, I'm biased; I want America to have the best stuff. I want us to have the best roads, the best airports, the fastest railroads, the quickest Internet access. So I've said, let's take the money that we're no longer spending in Iraq, let's use half of it to pay down our debt. Let's use the rest to do some nation-building right here in Houston, right here in Texas, right here in the United States of America.

And let's make sure our tax system has everybody doing their fair share. I've called for something called the Buffett rule: If you make more than a million dollars a year, you should not pay a lower tax rate than your secretary. And you know what, most folks who've done well, they agree. They understand. They understand that folks making $250,000 a year or less—98 percent of American families—can't see their taxes going up.

Audience member. That's right.

The President. You agree with that. [*Laughter*] But folks like me, we can afford to do a little bit more if it means protecting our kids and making sure that we're investing in the future.

This isn't class warfare. This isn't about envy. This is just basic math. Because if somebody like me gets a tax break that I don't need, that I wasn't asking for, and that the country can't afford, then one of two things happens: Either it adds to our deficit, or it's going to take something away from somebody else. From a student, suddenly their college tuition gets more expensive; or a senior citizen who suddenly is paying higher on their prescription drugs; or a veteran who desperately needs help to recover from sacrificing on our behalf.

That's not right.

Audience member. It ain't right!

The President. Not only is it not right, it ain't right. [*Laughter*] That's not who we are as Americans.

You hear a lot of politicians during election years, they talk about values. Well, look, I agree, we should be talking about what are our values as Americans. Hard work, that's a value. Looking out for one another, that's a value. The idea that we're all in this together, as Debra said, that I am my brother's keeper, I am my sister's keeper, that's a value.

Everybody here, whatever success we have, it's because someone, somewhere, took responsibility not only for themselves, but also for their kids, for their neighborhood, for their church, for their community, for our country's future. Our American story has never been just about what we can do on our own. It's about what we can do together. We're not going to be able to compete around the world, win the race for new jobs and businesses and creating—recreating middle class security with the same old you-are-on-your-own economics. It doesn't work. It didn't work when it was tried right before the Great Depression. It didn't work when we tried it in the last decade. Why would we think it would work now? That's another example of amnesia some of these folks have. [*Laughter*]

We tried what they're peddling; it did not work. You understand that. Look, let me give you just some examples. You know that if we attract an outstanding teacher to the profession by giving her the pay and respect and support that she deserves, and that teacher then goes on and educates the next Steve Jobs, we all benefit. If we provide faster Internet to some rural town in Texas, so suddenly that storeowner in that little town can start selling his goods all around the country and all around the world, we benefit. The economy benefits, America benefits. If we build a new bridge that saves a shipping company time and money, workers, customers, that business, everybody, we all do better.

This isn't a Democratic idea or a Republican idea. It was a Republican President, Abraham Lincoln, who launched the transcontinental railroad, the National Academy of Sciences, and the first land-grant colleges in the middle of a civil war. It was a Republican, Teddy Roosevelt, who called for a progressive income tax. Dwight Eisenhower built the Interstate Highway System. Republicans helped FDR pass the law that gave millions of returning heroes, including my grandfather, the chance to go to college on the GI bill.

This should not be a partisan idea. And you know what, that same spirit of common purpose that lies at the heart of America, it's still there. It might not be there in Washington, but out in America, it's there. It's there where you talk to people in Main Streets or town halls or VFW halls. It's there when you talk to the members of our Armed Forces. If you go into a church or a synagogue or a mosque, you'll find out people are supporting each other and believe in the notion of everyone pulling together.

Our politics may be divided, but most Americans understand that we're in this together. No matter who we are or what we look like, where we come from, what our names are, we rise and fall as one Nation and as one people. And that's what's at stake right now. That's what this election is all about.

I know it's been a tough few years. I know the change that we fought for hasn't always come as fast we'd like. And after all that's happened in Washington, sometimes it may be tempting to start feeling cynical again and think maybe change isn't possible. But I want you to remember what we used to say during the last campaign. We didn't promise easy. I— you never heard me say change was easy. Real change—big change—is hard. It takes time. It takes more than a single year, a single term. It will take more than a single President.

What it really requires is ordinary citizens, all across the country, committed to fighting and pushing and inching this country, step by step, closer to our common ideals, our highest ideals.

You know what else I said in 2008? I said I'm not a perfect man. I didn't promise I'd be a perfect President. But what I promised you was that I would always tell you what I thought, I'd always tell you where I stood, and I would wake up every single day fighting as hard as I could, fighting as hard as I know how, for you. And I've kept that promise. I have kept that promise, Texas.

So, if you're willing to keep working with me and marching with me and standing with me, pushing through the obstacles to reach for that vision that you hold in your hearts, change will come. If you're willing to work as hard in this election as you did in last election, change will come. We'll finish what we started in 2008.

God bless you. God bless the United States of America. Thank you.

NOTE: The President spoke at 6:58 p.m. at Minute Maid Park. In his remarks, he referred to Houston, TX, resident Debra Jones; and James R. Crane, owner, Major League Baseball's Houston Astros.

Remarks at an Obama Victory Fund 2012 Fundraiser in Houston
March 9, 2012

Well, it is wonderful to see all of you here today. I just want to, first of all, obviously thank Tony and Dina. They have been great friends for a very long time. In fact, the first time I met

Tony, I was still in law school, and Tony was an alum, and he came back to law school, and he was a big cheese and important and—but he was willing to shake my hand and—

[*laughter*]—couldn't really pronounce my name—[*laughter*]. But he was very nice to me, and I will never forget that. And we've been great friends ever since. So I'm so grateful to him.

I want to acknowledge somebody who has also been a good friend for a long time and did a lot of work for this, Rodney Ellis—outstanding State senator. State Representative Garnet Coleman is in the house.

And so many of you—as we were looking around the room, folks here—there are folks who—first Houston event, second Houston event—[*laughter*]. I mean, I've just got—they're dispersed throughout the crowd. But we just have a lot of good friends here.

And I also want to acknowledge, by the way, Mayor White is here, and the—just want to thank him for the great work that he has done.

I want to spend most of my time just interacting and answering questions. So I'm going to keep my remarks at the top relatively brief.

We've obviously gone through 3 of the toughest years that any of us can recall: worst financial crisis, worst economic crisis in our lifetimes. And yet, 3 years later, we can look then and look now and say to ourselves that we have made progress. When I took office, we were losing 800,000 jobs a month. We found out last month that we created another 233,000 jobs, which gets us close to 4 million jobs created over the last 2 years, the strongest manufacturing growth since the 1990s.

We're obviously still in the midst of a lot of struggles for a lot of people, but the trend lines are good. And the reason is because so many of you believed in the same vision that I believe in: an America where if you work hard, if you take responsibility, if you're willing to apply yourself, you can make it if you try here, no matter what you look like, no matter where you come from, no matter what your name. And that was the premise of our campaign back in 2008. Part of what I think allowed us to be successful against some very long odds was, at its core, our campaign reaffirmed our basic faith and confidence and optimism in America.

And it's that optimism that has carried me through these difficult 3 years, because every-where I go I meet people who, despite hardship, despite losing a job, despite a plant closing in town, people are resilient, and they come back, and they're not willing to quit or say no. And that's what's really carried me through. And because of that enormous decency at the core of the American people, I'm confident that we're going to be able to keep moving over the next year, the next 5 years, the next 10 years, the next 20 years.

But our ability to bounce back and then thrive is also going to depend on some choices that we make right now. And as important as 2008 was, I think this election is even more important. Because very rarely are you going to see such a stark choice about how one party sees the country and where we need to go and how the other party sees the country and where we need to go.

I strongly believe that we're going to have to invest in American manufacturing. I was at a plant today in Virginia where they make the jet engines for Boeing. And we're starting to set up pilot programs around the country where we're connecting universities with manufacturers, community colleges with businesses, bringing scientists and engineers together, to make sure that we're innovating and making things and building things right here in America. I don't want a country where we're just consuming. I want a country where we're building and we're selling stuff.

And that requires the private sector taking the lead, but it also requires investments in research and science and education, making sure we've got the engineers that are needed for us to compete. And that's something that historically has been an important role of Government. But we've got a party that somehow believes that those investments are unimportant, despite the fact that's what made us into an economic superpower.

I believe that we've got to make sure that our K–12 education system works. And that's not just a function of money, it's a function of reform. And we've initiated bolder reforms on education than at any time in the last 20, 30 years. Forty-six States have revamped their education system so that we're holding schools more accountable, we're asking them to make sure that they're thinking about students first, but we're also giving them the resources to train their teachers and succeed and to teach more creatively, not just teach to the test. That involves us making an investment. That involves us being involved.

Same thing when our kids get to college. There's actually more tuition debt now than there is credit card debt. And one of the things we're very proud of over the last 3 years is we revamped our student loan programs to free up $60 billion to make college more accessible to young people all across the country.

The other—you don't hear much in the debates of the other party right now about education. In fact, I don't think it's been mentioned. And yet nothing is going to be more significant in whether or not we can compete in the 21st century. There's a stark choice there.

When it comes to energy—Texas is an energy State. And over the last several weeks, I've had to remind people we actually have higher production now in oil than at any time in the last 8 years. We are starting to tap into the natural gas resources of this country that could provide energy for 100 years. But we only have 3 percent of the world's oil reserves, which means that we're going to have to focus on efficiency. And when we double fuel efficiency standards on cars, that's not bad for the oil industry, but it does make sure that American businesses and American families are going to be able to keep on going even as demand goes up in China and India and Brazil and other places.

And we've got to invest in clean energy, solar and wind and biodiesel. It's not an either-or, it's a all-of-the-above strategy in order for us to free ourselves from dependence of the—on foreign oil and the winds of what happens in the Middle East. That's a choice.

We've got a choice that we're going to have to make about the deficit and how we solve that problem and bring down our debt. And the fact of the matter is, is that we've already made more discretionary cuts than had been proposed by the Bowles-Simpson commission. We have cut programs that aren't working to make sure that we're funding those that do.

We're revamping and reforming Government so it's more efficient. I'm prepared to make some significant reforms on entitlements to ensure that they're there for future generations.

But even after we've done all that, it's not going to work unless those of us in this room also agree that we've got to make sure that we're doing our fair share. Because the tax rate right now is the lowest it's been in 50 years, and we disproportionately benefit from that. So the idea of shared responsibility, which has been rejected by the other side, you know what, I think that's central to who we are. And if we're going to get a handle on this thing, it's just basic math. We can't just do one side of the equation, we've got to deal with both sides of the equation, both revenues and spending.

So, whether it's health care, whether it's the role of women, whether it's how serious we're going to take immigration reform and making sure we're a nation of laws and a nation of immigrants, whether it's foreign policy and whether we have—whether we continue the course that we've set over the last 3 years, which says, we're going to go after those who would do us harm, but we also understand that our security doesn't just depend on our military, it depends on the respect we're held in the world and how we reach out diplomatically and whether we're helping other countries feed themselves and prosper—on each of these issues there is a stark choice.

And here's the good news: I am absolutely confident that our vision about where America needs to go is shared by the American people. Not 100 percent—this is a big, diverse, complicated country, and the democratic debate is always messy. But when you travel to town halls or VFW halls or churches or synagogues, or wherever you go around the country, what you'll find is a common belief that everybody should get a fair shot, everybody should do their fair share, everybody should play by the same set of rules, and that we're stronger together than we are when we're apart. And those basic principles, I think, are consistent with what we fought for in 2008. And they are the foundation for my campaign in 2012.

And so if you're with me in pursuing that vision, we've gotten a lot of stuff done over these last 3½ years, but I'd say I've got about 5 more years to finish the job.

So all right. Thank you, everybody.

NOTE: The President spoke at 8:52 p.m. at the residence of Anthony R. Chase and Dina Also-wayel. In his remarks, he referred to former Mayor William H. White of Houston, TX; and Erskine B. Bowles and Alan K. Simpson, Co-chairs, National Commission on Fiscal Responsibility and Reform. The transcript was released by the Office of the Press Secretary on March 10. Audio was not available for verification of the content of these remarks.

The President's Weekly Address
March 10, 2012

Hi, everybody. I'm speaking to you this week from a factory in Petersburg, Virginia, where they're bringing on more than a hundred new workers to build parts for the next generation of jet engines.

It's a story that's happening more frequently across our country. Our businesses just added 233,000 jobs last month, for a total of nearly 4 million new jobs over the last 2 years. More companies are choosing to bring jobs back and invest in America. Manufacturing is adding jobs for the first time since the 1990s, and we're building more things to sell to the rest of the world, stamped with three proud words: Made in America.

And it's not just that we're building stuff. We're building better stuff. The engine parts manufactured here in Petersburg will go into the next-generation planes that are lighter, faster, and more fuel efficient.

That last part is important. Because whether you're paying for a plane ticket or filling up your gas tank, technology that helps us get more miles to the gallon is one of the easiest ways to save money and reduce our dependence on foreign oil.

The recent spike in gas prices has been another painful reminder of why we have to invest in this technology. As usual, politicians have been rolling out their three-point plans for $2 gas: drill, drill, and drill some more. Well, my response is: We have been drilling. Under my administration, oil production in America is at an 8-year high. We've quadrupled the number of operating oil rigs and opened up millions of acres for drilling.

But you and I both know that with only 2 percent of the world's oil reserves, we can't just drill our way to lower gas prices, not when we consume 20 percent of the world's oil. We need an all-of-the-above strategy that relies less on foreign oil and more on American-made energy: solar, wind, natural gas, biofuels, and more.

That's the strategy we're pursuing. It's why I went to a plant in North Carolina earlier this week, where they're making trucks that run on natural gas and hybrid trucks that go further on a single tank.

And it's why I've been focused on fuel-efficient cars since I took office. Over the last few years, the annual number of miles driven by Americans has stayed roughly the same, but the total amount of gas we use has been going down. In other words, we're getting more bang for our buck.

If we accelerate that trend, we can help drivers save a significant amount of money. That's why, after 30 years of inaction, we finally put in place new standards that will make sure our cars average nearly 55 miles per gallon by the middle of the next decade, nearly double what they get today. This wasn't easy: We had to bring together auto companies and unions and folks who don't ordinarily see eye to eye. But it was worth it.

Because these cars aren't some pie-in-the-sky solution that's years away. They're being built right now, by American workers, in factories right here in the U.S.A. Every year, our cars and trucks will be able to go further and use less fuel, and pretty soon, you'll be able to fill up every 2 weeks instead of every week, something that, over time, will save the typical family more than $8,000 at the pump. We'll reduce our oil consumption by more than 12 billion barrels. That is a future worth investing in.

So we have a choice. Right now some folks in Washington would rather spend another $4 billion on subsidies to oil companies each year. Well, you know what? We've been handing out these kinds of taxpayer giveaways for nearly a century. And outside of Congress, does anyone really think that's still a good idea? I want this Congress to stop the giveaways to an oil industry that's never been more profitable and invest it in a clean energy industry that's never been more promising. We should be investing in the technology that's building the cars and trucks and jets that will prevent us from dealing with these high gas prices year after year after year.

Ending this cycle of rising gas prices won't be easy, and it won't happen overnight. But that's why you sent us to Washington: to solve tough problems like this one. So I'm going to keep doing everything I can to help you save money on gas, both right now and in the future. I hope politicians from both sides of the aisle join me. Let's put aside the bumper-sticker slogans and remember why we're here and get things done for the American people.

Thank you, God bless you, and have a great weekend.

NOTE: The address was recorded at approximately 1:45 p.m. on March 9 at the Rolls-Royce Crosspointe plant in Petersburg, VA, for broadcast on March 10. The transcript was made available by the Office of the Press Secretary on March 9, but was embargoed for release until 6 a.m. on March 10.

Statement on the Resignation of Representative Jay R. Inslee
March 10, 2012

Through the course of more than 20 years working on behalf of Washington State, including more than a decade in Congress, Jay Inslee has never forgotten where he came from. A son of the Pacific Northwest, Jay has been a champion of our natural resources while pushing for new sources of clean energy. Jay has supported new frontiers in technology and worked to increase fairness in our Nation's health care system. While Jay's voice in Congress will be missed, I know he will continue his dedicated service to the people of Washington State. Michelle and I wish him and his family well in the future.

Statement on Civilian Deaths in Afghanistan
March 11, 2012

I am deeply saddened by the reported killing and wounding of Afghan civilians. I offer my condolences to the families and loved ones of those who lost their lives and to the people of Afghanistan, who have endured too much violence and suffering. This incident is tragic and shocking and does not represent the exceptional character of our military and the respect that the United States has for the people of Afghanistan. I fully support Secretary Panetta's and General Allen's commitment to get the facts as quickly as possible and to hold accountable anyone responsible.

NOTE: The statement referred to Gen. John R. Allen, USMC, commander, NATO International Security Assistance Force, Afghanistan.

Statement on "The Blueprint for a Secure Energy Future: Progress Report"
March 12, 2012

The progress report I received today from members of my administration underscores the headway our Nation has made towards reducing our reliance on foreign oil, while also expanding American made energy. As the report highlights, we have made progress, with imports of foreign oil decreasing by a million barrels a day in the last year alone. Our focus on increased domestic oil and gas production, currently at an 8-year high, combined with the historic fuel economy standards we put in place, means that we will continue to reduce our Nation's vulnerability to the ups and downs of the global oil market. We've also made progress in the expansion of clean energy, with renewable energy from sources like wind and solar on track to double, along with the construction of our first advanced biofuel refineries. And yet, despite the gains we've made, today's high gas prices are a painful reminder that there's much more work to do free ourselves from our dependence on foreign oil and take control of our energy future. And that's exactly what our administration is committed to doing in the months ahead.

Remarks on Trade Policy
March 13, 2012

Good morning, everybody. Before I make an announcement about our efforts to stand up for U.S. businesses and U.S. workers, I'd like to say a few words about the situation in Afghanistan.

Civilian Deaths in Afghanistan

Over the weekend, as many of you know, there was a tragic incident in which a number of Afghan civilians were killed. What I've made to President Karzai when I spoke to him is that the United States takes this as seriously as if it was our own citizens and our own children who were murdered. We're heartbroken over the loss of innocent life. The killing of innocent civilians is outrageous, and it's unacceptable. It's not who we are as a country, and it does not represent our military.

And for that reason, I've directed the Pentagon to make sure that we spare no effort in conducting a full investigation. I can assure the American people and the Afghan people that we will follow the facts wherever they lead us, and we will make sure that anybody who was involved is held fully accountable with the full force of the law.

Yesterday I met with General Allen and Ambassador Crocker, who were here in Washington, and I've extraordinary confidence in them and in the many Americans who are serving in Afghanistan and who have made extraordinary sacrifices to be there. Today I'll be meeting with Prime Minister Cameron, who is part of our broad coalition serving in Afghanistan, and we'll have an opportunity to consult about the way forward as we prepare for the NATO summit in Chicago later this spring.

So make no mistake, we have a strategy that will allow us to responsibly wind down this war. We're steadily transitioning to the Afghans who are moving into the lead, and that's going to allow us to bring our troops home. Already we're scheduled to remove 23,000 troops by the end of this summer, followed by—following the 10,000 that we withdrew last year. And meanwhile, we will continue the work of devastating Al Qaida's leadership and denying them a safe haven.

There's no question that we face a difficult challenge in Afghanistan, but I am confident that we can continue the work of meeting our objectives, protecting our country, and responsibly bringing this war to a close.

Free and Fair Trade

Now, one of the things that I talked about during the State of the Union Address was making America more competitive in the global economy. The good news is that we have the best workers and the best businesses in the world. They turn out the best products. And when the playing field is level, they'll always be able to compete and succeed against every other country on Earth.

But the key is to make sure that the playing field is level. And frankly, sometimes it's not. I will always try to work our differences through with other countries. We prefer dialogue. That's especially true when it comes to key trading partners like China. We've got a constructive economic relationship with China, and whenever possible, we are committed to working with them to addressing our concerns. But when it is necessary, I will take action if our workers and our businesses are being subjected to unfair practices.

Since I took office, we've brought trade cases against China at nearly twice the rate as the last administration, and these actions are making a difference. For example, we halted an unfair surge in Chinese tires, which has helped put over 1,000 American workers back on the job. But we haven't stopped there.

Two weeks ago, I created a trade enforcement unit to aggressively investigate any unfair trade practices taking place anywhere in the world. And as they ramp up their efforts, our competitors should be on notice: You will not get away with skirting the rules. When we can, we will rally support from our allies. And when it makes sense to act on our own, we will.

I just signed a bill to help American companies that are facing unfair foreign competition. These companies employ tens of thousands of Americans in nearly 40 States. Because of subsidies from foreign governments, some of their foreign competitors are selling products at an artificially low price. That needs to stop.

This morning we're taking an additional step forward. We're bringing a new trade case against China, and we're being joined by Japan and some of our European allies. This case involves something called rare earth materials, which are used by American manufacturers to make high-tech products like advanced batteries that power everything from hybrid cars to cell phones.

We want our companies building those products right here in America. But to do that, American manufacturers need to have access to rare earth materials, which China supplies. Now, if China would simply let the market work on its own, we'd have no objections. But their policies currently are preventing that from happening. And they go against the very rules that China agreed to follow.

Being able to manufacture advanced batteries and hybrid cars in America is too important for us to stand by and do nothing. We've got to take control of our energy future, and we can't let that energy industry take root in some other country because they were allowed to break the rules. So our administration will bring this case against China today, and we will keep working every single day to give American workers and American businesses a fair shot in the global economy.

We're going to make sure that this isn't a country that's just known for what we consume. America needs to get back to doing what it's always done best—a country that builds and sells products all over the world that are stamped with the proud words "Made in America." That's how we create good, middle class jobs at home, and that's how we're going to create an economy that's built to last.

Thank you very much, everybody.

NOTE: The President spoke at 11:35 a.m. in the Rose Garden at the White House. In his remarks, he referred to Gen. John R. Allen, USMC, commander, NATO International Security Assistance Force, Afghanistan; U.S. Ambassador to Afghanistan Ryan C. Crocker; and Prime Minister David Cameron of the United Kingdom.

Letter to Congressional Leaders on Continuation of the National Emergency With Respect to Iran
March 13, 2012

Dear Mr. Speaker: (Dear Mr. President:)

Section 202(d) of the National Emergencies Act (50 U.S.C. 1622(d)) provides for the automatic termination of a national emergency unless, within 90 days prior to the anniversary date of its declaration, the President publishes in the *Federal Register* and transmits to the Congress a notice stating that the emergency is to continue in effect beyond the anniversary date. In accordance with this provision, I have sent the enclosed notice to the *Federal Register* for publication stating that the national emergency with respect to Iran that was declared on March 15, 1995, is to continue in effect beyond March 15, 2012.

The crisis between the United States and Iran resulting from the actions and policies of the Government of Iran has not been resolved.

The actions and policies of the Government of Iran are contrary to the interests of the United States in the region and continue to pose an unusual and extraordinary threat to the national security, foreign policy, and economy of the United States. For these reasons, I have determined that it is necessary to continue the national emergency declared with respect to Iran and maintain in force comprehensive sanctions against Iran to respond to this threat.

Sincerely,

BARACK OBAMA

NOTE: Identical letters were sent to John A. Boehner, Speaker of the House of Representatives, and Joseph R. Biden, Jr., President of the Senate. The notice is listed in Appendix D at the end of this volume.

Remarks at a Welcoming Ceremony for Prime Minister David Cameron of the United Kingdom
March 14, 2012

President Obama. Good morning, everyone.

The storied relationship between the United States and the United Kingdom is steeped in tradition. And last night, as President, I shared with the Prime Minister a uniquely American tradition of bracketology—*[laughter]*—March Madness. He's learned to appreciate one of our great national pastimes. His team has told me he has decided to install a hoop at 10 Downing Street. *[Laughter]*

Today we carry on another tradition, an official visit for one of our closest friends and our dearest allies. Prime Minister Cameron, Mrs. Cameron, members of the British delegation, on behalf of the American people, it is my great honor to welcome you to the United States.

David, Samantha, on behalf of Michelle and myself, we welcome you to the White House. And, Samantha, just let me say that we are de-

lighted that you've made America your first official foreign trip.

It's now been 200 years since the British came here, to the White House, under somewhat different circumstances. *[Laughter]* They made quite an impression. *[Laughter]* They really lit up the place. *[Laughter]* But we moved on. *[Laughter]* And today, like so many Presidents and Prime Ministers before us, we meet to reaffirm one of the greatest alliances the world has ever known.

This visit is also an opportunity to reciprocate the extraordinary and gracious hospitality shown to us by Her Majesty Queen Elizabeth, by David and Samantha, and by the British people during our visit to London last year. And we are proud that this visit comes as Her Majesty begins her Diamond Jubilee, celebrating 60 extraordinary years on the British throne.

It is remarkable to consider: Down the decades, we've seen nations rise and fall; wars fought and peace defended; a city divided, a wall come down; countries imprisoned behind an Iron Curtain, then liberated. We've seen the demise of a cold war and the rise of new threats, the transition from an industrial revolution to an Information Age where new technologies empower our citizens and our adversaries like never before. Our world has been transformed over and over, and it will be again. Yet, through the grand sweep of history, through all its twists and turns, there is one constant: the rock-solid alliance between the United States and the United Kingdom.

And the reason is simple. We stand together, and we work together, and we bleed together, and we build together, in good times and in bad, because when we do, our nations are more secure, our people are more prosperous, and the world is a safer and better and more just place. Our alliance is essential—it is indispensable—to the security and prosperity that we seek not only for our own citizens, but for people around the world.

And that is why, as President, I've made strengthening this alliance and our alliances around the world one of my highest foreign policy priorities. And because we have, I can stand here today and say with pride and with confidence—and I believe with David's agreement—that the relationship between the United States and the United Kingdom is the strongest that it has ever been.

And so in the sunlight of this beautiful morning, with children from both nations in attendance, we reaffirm the enduring values in which our alliance is forever rooted. We believe that every person, if they're willing to work hard, if they play by the rules, deserve a fair shot, deserve a chance to succeed. So, in these tough economic times, we stand united in our determination to create the jobs that put our people back to work, in expanding trade that is both free and fair, and in fighting for a global economy where every nation plays by the same rules.

We believe that our citizens should be able to live free from fear. So, like generations before us, we stand united in the defense of our countries and against those who would terrorize our people or endanger the globe with the world's most dangerous weapons.

We believe in the universal rights of all people, so we stand united in our support for those who seek to choose their leaders and forge their future, including the brave citizens of the Middle East and North Africa, who deserve the same God-given rights and freedoms as people everywhere.

And we believe in the inherent dignity of every human being. So we will stand united in advancing the developments that lift people and nations out of poverty: the new crops that feed a village, the care that saves a mother in childbirth, the vaccine that allows a child to live a long and healthy life.

This is what we believe. This is who we are. This is what we do together, what we achieve together every single day. And this is the alliance that we renew today, guided by the interests we share, grounded in the values that we cherish not just for our time, but for all time.

And finally, I would just note that while this is not the first official visit of my Presidency, it is one of the few where I have not had to pause for translation. [*Laughter*] We Americans and Brits speak the same language, most of the time. [*Laughter*] So let me just say, David, we are chuffed to bits that you are here—[*laughter*]—and I'm looking forward to a great natter. I'm confident that together we're going to keep the relationship between our two great nations absolutely top notch. [*Laughter*]

David, Samantha, the warmest of welcomes from Michelle and myself, but more importantly, from the American people. We are honored to have you here.

Prime Minister Cameron. President Obama, First Lady, Mr. Vice President, members of both Cabinets, guests of honor, ladies and gentlemen: Thank you for such an incredibly warm welcome. Am I—I have to say, Barack, with that spectacular command of our shared language—[*laughter*]—with all these Union flags and with so many friends at home, you are really making me feel very at home here in Washington.

So I am a little embarrassed, as I stand here, to think that 200 years ago—[*laughter*]—my ancestors tried to burn this place down. [*Laughter*] Now, looking around me, I can see you've got the place a little better defended today. [*Laughter*] You're clearly not taking any risks with the Brits this time. [*Laughter*]

And thank you also for the lessons last night. I will leave America with some new words—alley-oops—[*laughter*]—brackets, fast breaks, and who knows, maybe that hoop will be installed in Downing Street after all. It was a great evening. Thank you very much indeed.

Now, of course, since that unfortunate episode 200 years ago, generations of British and American service men and women have fought together. Our grandparents fought in the same campaign. My grandfather, wounded a few days after D-day, the greatest ever British and American operation in history. And yours, Barack, serving under General Patton as the Allies swept through France. Whether it is defeating the Nazis, standing up to the Soviets, defending the Korean Peninsula, or hunting down Al Qaida in Afghanistan, there can be no more tangible illustration of our two nations defending our values and advancing our interests than the mutual sacrifice made by our service men and women. And let us once again pay tribute to their valor, their courage, their professionalism, and their dedication here in Washington today.

From the Balkans to Baghdad, across the world and across the decades, we have been proud to serve with you. When the chips are down, Britain and America know that we can always count on each other because we are allies not just prepared to say the right thing, but to do the right thing and to do it in the right way: promoting our values, standing up for our ideals.

The partnership between our countries, between our peoples, is the most powerful partnership for progress that the world has ever seen. That is why whenever an American President and a British Prime Minister get together, there is a serious and important agenda to work through. And today is no different. Afghanistan, Iran, the Arab Spring, the need for

trade, for growth, for jobs in the world economy, the biggest issues in the world, that is our agenda today.

But what makes our relationship so vigorous and so lasting is that it draws its strength from roots far deeper and broader than government or the military. It is a meeting of kindred spirits. When the world's brightest minds want to generate the innovations that will make tomorrow more free and more fair, they look to our great universities, like Harvard and Stanford, Cambridge and Oxford.

When the most audacious and entrepreneurial philanthropists, like the Gates Foundation, want not just to give out to charity, but to eliminate polio and other avoidable diseases so that no child in our world should die unnecessarily, they find partners across the Atlantic in the British aid agencies, like Save the Children, Oxfam, and Christian Aid.

And when a great innovator like Sir Tim Berners-Lee wanted a partner to make the World Wide Web a reality, he turned to America. Why? Because he knew that it was in America that he would find that same spirit of creativity, innovation, and risk-taking that defines our unique approach to enterprise and to business.

He's not alone. In 2010, transatlantic partnerships produced eight of the nine Nobel Prizes in science. Foreign direct investment between Britain and America is the largest in the world and now stands at $900 billion. This creates and sustains around a million jobs each side of the Atlantic. And it provides a strong foundation for bilateral trade worth nearly $200 billion a year. In fact, American investment in the U.K. is eight times larger than China, and U.K. investment in America is nearly a hundred and forty times that of China.

So yes, the world is changing at a faster rate than ever before, and the ways we will influence events are changing with it. But one thing remains unchanged: the ceaseless back-and-forth between our two nations through ideas, friendship, business, and shared endeavor. And that's why I believe that we can be sure that in 50 years' time, an American President and a British Prime Minister will stand on this very spot, just as we do now; they will stand here, as we do, for freedom and for enterprise; our two countries, the united states of liberty and enterprise.

That is why I'm so pleased to be here today to celebrate an essential relationship that, as you say, has never been stronger, and to work with you to make sure we deliver that, and to make our countries closer and closer still.

Thank you.

NOTE: The President spoke at 9:33 a.m. on the South Lawn at the White House, where Prime Minister Cameron was accorded a formal welcome with full military honors. In his remarks, Prime Minister Cameron referred to Timothy J. Berners-Lee, director, World Wide Web Consortium (W3C).

The President's News Conference With Prime Minister David Cameron of the United Kingdom
March 14, 2012

President Obama. Good afternoon, everyone. Please have a seat. Again, it is a great honor to welcome my friend and partner, Prime Minister David Cameron, back to the White House for this official visit.

I know there's been a lot of focus on last night's game. Some have asked how it came about. So I want to set the record straight. During my visit to London last year, David arranged for us to play some local students—table tennis. As they would say in Britain, we got thrashed. So, when it came to sports on this visit, I thought it would be better if we just watched. That said, I'm still trying to get David to fill out his bracket.

We've just finished up a very good discussion, and it was a reminder of why I value David's leadership and partnership so much. He appreciates how the alliance between our countries is a foundation not only for the security and prosperity of our two nations, but for international peace and security as well. David shares my belief that in a time of rapid change, the leadership of the United States and the United Kingdom is more important than ever. And we share the view that the future we seek is only possible if the rights and responsibilities of nations and people are upheld. And that's a cause that we advanced today.

At a time when too many of our people are still out of work, we agree that we've got to stay focused on creating the growth and jobs that put our people back to work, even as both our countries make difficult choices to put our fis-

cal houses in order. Between us, we have the largest investment relationship in the world, and we've instructed our teams to continue to explore ways to increase transatlantic trade and investment. And I very much appreciate David's perspective on the fiscal situation in the euro zone, where both our countries—our economies, our businesses, our banks—are deeply connected.

We moved on to discuss Afghanistan, where we are the two largest contributors of forces to the international mission and where our forces continue to make extraordinary sacrifices. The tragic events of recent days are a reminder that this continues to be a very difficult mission. And obviously, we both have lost a number of extraordinary young men and women in theater. What's undeniable, though, and what we can never forget, is that our forces are making very real progress: dismantling Al Qaida, breaking the Taliban's momentum, and training Afghan forces so that they can take the lead and our troops can come home.

That transition is already underway, and about half of all Afghans currently live in areas where Afghan security forces are taking responsibility. Today the Prime Minister and I reaffirmed the transition plan that we agreed to with our coalition partners in Lisbon. Specifically, at the upcoming NATO summit in my hometown of Chicago, we'll determine the next phase of transition. This includes shifting to a support role next year, in 2013, in advance of Afghans taking full responsibility for security in 2014. We're going to complete this mission, and we're going to do it responsibly. And NATO will maintain an enduring commitment so that Afghanistan never again becomes a haven for Al Qaida to attack our countries.

We also discussed the continuing threat posed by Iran's failure to meet its international obligations. On this we are fully united. We are determined to prevent Iran from acquiring a nuclear weapon. We believe there is still time and space to pursue a diplomatic solution, and we're going to keep coordinating closely with our P–5-plus-1 partners. At the same time, we're going to keep up the pressure, with the strongest U.S. sanctions to date and the European Union preparing to impose an embargo on Iranian oil. Tehran must understand that it cannot escape or evade the choice before it: Meet your international obligations, or face the consequences.

We reaffirmed our commitment to support the democratic transitions underway in the Middle East and North Africa. British forces played a critical role in the mission to protect the Libyan people, and I want to commend David personally for the leadership role he's—plays in mobilizing international support for the transition in Libya.

We also discussed the horrific violence that the Asad regime continues to inflict on the people of Syria. Right now we're focused on getting humanitarian aid to those in need. We agreed to keep increasing the pressure on the regime: mobilizing the international community, tightening sanctions, cutting the regime's revenues, isolating it politically, diplomatically, and economically.

Just as the regime and security forces continue to suffer defections, the opposition is growing stronger. I'll say it again: Asad will leave power. It's not a question of if, but when. And to prepare for that day, we'll continue to support plans for a transition to support the legitimate aspirations of the Syrian people.

More broadly, we recommitted ourselves and our leadership to the goal of global development. Along with our international partners, we've saved countless lives from the famine in the Horn of Africa. David, you've done an out-standing job in bringing the international community to support progress in Somalia, including lifesaving aid. At the same time, we're renewing our commitment to improve maternal health and preventable deaths of children and supporting the Global Fund for AIDS, TB and Malaria so that we can realize our goal, and that's the beginning of the end of AIDS. And let me say that it's a tribute to David's leadership that the U.K. will be playing a leading role in the global partnership to strengthen the open government upon which human rights and development depend.

Finally, I'm very pleased that we're bringing our two militaries, the backbone of our alliance, even closer. As I told David, I can announce that next month, we intend to start implementing our long-awaited defense trade treaty with the U.K. This will put advanced technologies in the hands of our troops, and it will mean more jobs for workers in both our countries. And we're moving ahead with our joint initiative to care for our men and women in uniform.

For decades, our troops have stood together on the battlefield. Now we're working together for them when they come home, with new partnerships to help our wounded warriors recover, assist our veterans' transition back to civilian life, and to support our remarkable military families.

So, David, thank you, as always, for being such an outstanding ally, partner, and friend. As I said this morning, because of our efforts, our alliance is as strong as it has ever been. And Michelle and I are very much looking forward to hosting you and Samantha at tonight's state dinner. I look forward as well to welcoming you to Camp David and my hometown of Chicago in May to carry on the work upon which both our nations and the world depend.

So, David, welcome, and thank you.

Prime Minister Cameron. Well, thank you very much for that, Barack. And thank you for last night's sporting event. I thought there was a link between that and the table tennis. I remember it well. And because I know America doesn't like being on the losing side, I'm trying to make up to you with the gift of a tennis—a table tennis table, which I hope will be there in the White House——

President Obama. We should practice this afternoon.

Prime Minister Cameron. I think—well, I certainly need the practice. And one of these days I'll get my own back by getting you to a cricket match—[*laughter*]—and explaining the rules to you and some of the terminology that you'll have to try and get straight, as I tried last night. But thank you.

We've had excellent discussions today, and it was great that our teams had time to join those talks as well. And, Barack, thank you, because there are some countries whose alliance is a matter of convenience, but ours is a matter of conviction. Two states, as I said this morning, united for freedom and enterprise, working together, day in, day out, to defend those values and advance our shared interests.

That has been the fundamental business of this visit, and we've just made important progress on four vital areas: Afghanistan, Syria, Iran, and economic growth. And I want to take each in turn.

First, Afghanistan. Recent days have reminded us just how difficult our mission is and how high the cost of this war has been for Britain, for America, and for Afghans themselves. Britain has fought alongside America every day since the start. We have 9,500 men and women still serving there. More than 400 have given their lives. And today, again, we commemorate each and every one of them.

But we will not give up on this mission because Afghanistan must never again be a safe haven for Al Qaida to launch attacks against us. We won't build a perfect Afghanistan, although let's be clear, we are making some tangible progress, with more markets open, more health centers working, more children going to school, more people able to achieve a basic standard of living and security. But we can help ensure that Afghanistan is capable of delivering its own security without the need for large numbers of foreign troops.

We are now in the final phases of our military mission. That means completing the training of the Afghan forces so that they can take over the tasks of maintaining security themselves. That transition to Afghan control, as agreed at Lisbon, is now well underway. And next year, as the President said, in 2013, this includes shifting to a support role as Afghans take the lead. This is in advance of Afghan forces taking full responsibility for security in 2014. And as we've always said, we won't be in a combat role after 2014. At the same time, we will also back President Karzai in working towards an Afghan-led political settlement.

Second, a year on from the United Nations Security Council resolution on Libya, we agreed we must maintain our support for the people of the Arab world as they seek a better future. And let me just say, in response to what you said, Mr. President—Barack—about Libya, that I'm very proud of the action that Britain and France and others took, but let us be absolutely clear. None of that would have been possible without the overwhelming support and overwhelming force that the United States provided in the early stages of that campaign—exactly what you promised you would do—that actually made that intervention possible and has given that chance—that country a chance of prosperity and stability and some measure of democracy.

Most urgently now in Syria, we are working to get humanitarian aid to those who need it. And Britain is today pledging an additional £2 million in food and medical care. At the same time, we must properly document the evidence so that those guilty of crimes can be held to account, no matter how long it takes.

Above all, we must do everything we can to achieve a political transition that will stop the killing. So we must maintain the strongest pressure on all those who are resisting change at all costs. We'll give our support to Kofi Annan as he makes the case for the transition. And we are ready to work with Russia and China for the same goal, including through a new United Nations Security Council resolution.

But we should be clear. What we want is the quickest way to stop the killing. That is through transition rather than revolution or civil war. But if Asad continues, then civil war or revolution is the inevitable consequence. So we will work with anyone who is ready to build a stable, inclusive, and democratic Syria for all Syrians.

Third, we've discussed Iran's nuclear program. The President's tough, reasonable approach has united the world behind unprecedented sanctions pressure on Iran. And Britain has played a leading role in helping to deliver an EU-wide oil embargo. Alongside the financial sanctions being led by America, this embargo is dramatically increasing the pressure on the regime.

Now, we are serious about the talks that are set to resume, but the regime has to meet its international obligations. If it refuses to do so, then Britain and America, along with our international partners, will continue to increase the political and economic pressure to achieve a peaceful outcome to this crisis. The President and I have said nothing is off the table. That is essential for the safety of the region and the wider world.

Fourth, growth. Both Britain and America are dealing with massive debts and deficits. Of course, the measures we take in our domestic economies reflect different national circumstances, but we share the same goals: delivering significant deficit reduction over the medium term and stimulating growth.

One of the keys to growth is trade. The EU and the U.S. together account for more than half of all global trade. Foreign direct investment between Britain and America is the largest in the world. It creates and sustains around a million jobs each side of the Atlantic, and it provides a strong foundation for bilateral trade worth nearly $200 billion a year. So deepening trade and investment between us is crucial and can really help to stimulate growth. Barack and I have agreed to prioritize work ahead of the G–8 on liberalizing transatlantic trade and investment flows.

So we've had some very important discussions this morning, and I'm looking forward to continuing our talks at the G–8 and at NATO summits, and to visiting you, Barack, at Camp David and in your hometown of Chicago. Who knows what sport we will be able to go and see there?

As Barack has said, the relationship between Britain and America is the strongest that it has ever been. And I believe that's because we're working together as closely as at any point in our history. And together, I'm confident that we can help secure the future of our nations and the world for generations to come.

Thank you.

President Obama. Thank you, David.

So we've got questions from each respective press corps. We're going to start with Ari Shapiro of NPR.

U.S. Military Operations in Afghanistan/Global Economic Stabilization

Q. Thank you, Mr. President. Given the extraordinarily difficult circumstances in Afghanistan from the last few weeks, I wonder what makes you confident that 2 years from now, when the last troops leave, it will be better than it is today. And I wonder if you could also talk about the pace of withdrawal, whether you see something more gradual or speedier.

And, Mr. Prime Minister, you and the President take very different approaches to economic growth. Whereas you emphasize more austerity measures, the President focuses more on stimulative measures. And I wonder whether you could explain why you believe that your approach is likely to create more jobs than President Obama's approach.

Thank you.

President Obama. Well, first of all, on Afghanistan, I think both David and I understand how difficult this mission is because we've met with families whose sons or daughters or husbands or wives made the ultimate sacrifice. We visit our wounded warriors, and we understand the sacrifices that they've made there.

But as I indicated, we have made progress. We're seeing an Afghan National Security Force that is getting stronger and more robust and more capable of operating on its own. And our goal, set in Lisbon, is to make sure that over the next 2 years, that Afghan security force continues to improve, enhance its capabilities, and so will be prepared to provide for that country's security when we leave.

We also think it's important that there is a political aspect to this, that all the various factions and ethnic groups inside of Afghanistan recognize that it's time to end 30 years of war. And President Karzai has committed to a political reconciliation process. We are doing what we can to help facilitate that. Ultimately, it's going to be up to the Afghans to work together to try to arrive at a path to peace. And we can't be naive about the difficulties that are going to be involved in getting there.

But if we maintain a steady, responsible transition process, which is what we've designed, then I am confident that we can put Afghans in a position where they can deal with their own security. And we're also underscoring, through what we anticipate to be a strategic partnership that's been signed before we get to Chicago, that the United States, along with many other countries, will sustain a relationship with Afghanistan. We will not have combat troops there, but we will be working with them both to ensure their security, but also to ensure that their economy continues to improve.

There are going to be multiple challenges along the way. In terms of pace, I don't anticipate, at this stage, that we're going to be making any sudden, additional changes to the plan that we currently have. We have already taken out 10,000 of our troops. We're slated to draw down an additional 23,000 by this summer. There will be a robust coalition presence inside of Afghanistan during this fighting season to make sure that the Taliban understand that they're not going to be able to regain momentum.

After the fighting season, in conjunction with all our allies, we will continue to look at how do we effectuate this transition in a way that doesn't result in a steep cliff at the end of 2014, but rather is a gradual pace that accommodates the developing capacities of the Afghan National Security Forces.

Although you asked it to David, I want to make sure that I just comment quickly on the economic issues, because this is a question that David and I have been getting for the last 2 years. We always give the same answer, but I figure it's worth repeating. The United States

and Great Britain are two different economies in two different positions. Their banking sector was much larger than ours. Their capacity to sustain debt was different than ours. The—and so as a consequence, each of us are going to be taking different strategies at—and employing different timing.

But our objectives are common, which is we want to make sure that we have a—we have governments that are lean, that are effective, that are efficient, that are providing opportunity to our people, that are properly paid for so that we're not leaving it to the next generation. And we want to make sure that ultimately our citizens in both our countries are able to pursue their dreams and opportunities by getting a good education and being able to start a small business, being able to find a job that supports their families and allows them to retire with dignity and respect.

And so this notion that somehow two different countries are going to have identical economic programs doesn't take into account profound differences in position. But the objectives, the goals, the values I think are the same. And I'm confident that because of the resilience of our people and our businesses and our workers, our systems of higher education, that we are both countries that are incredibly well positioned to succeed in this knowledge-based economy of the 21st century.

Prime Minister Cameron. I very much agree with that. I mean, there are differences because we're not a reserve currency, so we have to take a different path. But I think it would be wrong to think that Britain is just taking measures to reduce its deficit. We're also taking a series of measures to help promote growth.

Just before coming here, we took a series of steps to try and unblock and get moving our housing market. We're—we've cut corporation tax in our country to show that it's a great destination for investment. We're investing in apprenticeships. So a series of steps are being taken.

But there are differences, as Barack has said, between the states of the two economy and the circumstances we face. But we're both trying to head in the same direction of growth and low deficits. And actually, if you look at the U.S. plans for reducing the deficit over coming years, in many ways they are actually steeper than what we're going to be doing in the U.K.

So different starting points, different measures on occasions, but the same destination, and a very good shared understanding as we try to get there.

I think I've got Joey Jones from Sky News.

U.S. Military Operations in Afghanistan

Q. [*Inaudible*]—and Mr. President, can I ask you both whether you have any information about an apparent car bombing at Camp Bastion this afternoon? And on the general Afghan question, why do you think it is that people feel that you talk a good game but they don't buy it? Why do you think it is that the British and American people look at a situation that they think is frankly a mess—they see terrible sacrifice, they see two men who are unable to impose their wills—and they just are not persuaded by your arguments?

Prime Minister Cameron. Well, first of all, on the—what has happened at Camp Bastion, it is very early, details still coming through. Obviously, we'll want to examine and investigate exactly what has happened before making clear anything about it.

But the security of our people, of our troops, security of both our nations' forces is absolutely the priority. And if there are things that need to be done in the coming hours and days to keep them safer, be in no doubt we will do them.

On the broader issue of Afghanistan, what I—I would make this point: If you compare where we are today with where we've been 2, 3 years ago, the situation is considerably improved. I think the U.S. surge and the additional U.K. troops we put in, particularly into Helmand Province, had a transformative effect. The level of insurgent attacks are right down. The level of security is right up. The capital of Helmand Province, Lashkar Gah, is now fully transitioned over to Afghan lead control. The markets are open. You're able to do and take part in economic activity in that town,

which simply wasn't possible when I first visited it several years ago.

So look, it's still a very difficult situation. There are many challenges we have to overcome. But what's happening in Afghanistan today is quite different to the situation we had 3, 4, 5 years ago.

Do I think we can get to a situation by the end of 2014 where we have a larger Afghan National Army, a larger Afghan police force, both of which are pretty much on track, and that with the Afghan Government, they're capable of taking care of their own security in a way that doesn't require large numbers of foreign troops and that country isn't a threat in the way that it was in the past in terms of a base for terrorism? Yes, I think we can achieve that.

Now, it's been very hard work. The sacrifices have been very great. But we have to keep reminding ourselves and everybody why we are there, what we are doing. You have to go back and remember that the vast majority of terrorist plots that were affecting people in the U.K., people in the U.S., came out of that country and that region. That's why we went in there; that's why we're there today.

It's not some selfish, long-term strategic interest. It's simply that we want Afghanistan to be able to look after its own security with its own security forces so we are safe at home. That's the key. That's the message we need to keep explaining to people. But I think what we're trying to do by the end of 2014 is achievable and doable.

President Obama. I concur with everything David said. The only thing I would add: You asked, why is it that poll numbers indicate people are interested in ending the war in Afghanistan? It's because we've been there for 10 years, and people get weary, and they know friends and neighbors who have lost loved ones as a consequence of war. No one wants war. Anybody who answers a poll question about war saying enthusiastically, we want war, probably hasn't been involved in a war.

But as David said, I think the vast majority of the American people and British understand why we went there. There is a reason why Al

Qaida is on its heels and has been decimated. There is a reason why Usama bin Laden and his lieutenants are not in a position to be able to execute plots against the United States or Great Britain. There is a reason why it is increasingly difficult for those who are interested in carrying out transnational operations directed against our interests, our friends, our allies, to be able to do that—is because the space has shrunk and their capacity to operate is greatly diminished.

Now, as David indicated, do—this is a hard slog, this is hard work. When I came into office, there had been drift in the Afghanistan strategy, in part because we had spent a lot of time focusing on Iraq instead. Over the last 3 years, we have refocused attention on getting Afghanistan right. Would my preference had been that we started some of that earlier? Absolutely. But that's not the cards that were dealt. We're now in a position where, given our starting point, we're making progress. And I believe that we're going to be able to make our—achieve our objectives in 2014.

Alister Bull [Reuters].

Iran/Syria

Q. Thank you, Mr. President, Mr. Prime Minister. Mr. President, switching to Iran——

President Obama. Can I just point out that somehow Alister gets to ask a question on behalf of the U.S. press corps—[*laughter*]—but he sounds like——

Q. It's the special relationship. [*Laughter*]

President Obama. Did—were you upset about that, Chuck [Chuck Todd, NBC News]? [*Laughter*]

Q. It's the special relationship.

The President. Yes, what's going on with that, Jay? Come on, man. [*Laughter*]

Q. So——

White House Press Secretary James F. "Jay" Carney. It's a special relationship.

The President. It's a special relationship.

Q. It is a special relationship. So—on Iran, do you believe that the six-power talks represent a last chance for the country to diffuse concerns over its nuclear program and avert military action?

And, Prime Minister, on Syria, how are you approaching the Russians to get them on board for a fresh Security Council resolution? And do you believe President Bashar al-Asad ought to be tried as a war crime—a war criminal?

Thank you.

President Obama. As David said, we have applied the toughest sanctions ever on Iran, and we've mobilized the international community with greater unity than we've ever seen. Those sanctions are going to begin to bite even harder this summer. And we're seeing significant effects on the Iranian economy.

So they understand the seriousness with which we take this issue. They understand that there are consequences to them continuing to flout the international community. And I have sent a message very directly to them publicly that they need to seize this opportunity of negotiations with the P–5-plus-1 to avert even worse consequences for Iran in the future.

Do I have a guarantee that Iran will walk through this door that we're offering them? No. In the past there has been a tendency for Iran in these negotiations with the P–5-plus-1's to delay, to stall, to do a lot of talking but not actually move the ball forward.

I think they should understand that because the international community has applied so many sanctions, because we have employed so many of the options that are available to us to persuade Iran to take a different course, that the window for solving this issue diplomatically is shrinking.

And as I said in a speech just a couple of weeks ago, I am determined not simply to contain Iran that is in possession of a nuclear weapon; I am determined to prevent Iran from getting a nuclear weapon, in part for the reasons that David mentioned. It would trigger a nuclear arms race in the most dangerous part of the world. It would raise nonproliferation issues that would have—carry significant risks to our national security interests. It would embolden terrorists in the region who might believe that they could act with more impunity if they were operating under the protection of Iran.

And so this is not an issue that is simply in one country's interests or two countries' interests. This is an issue that is important to the entire international community. We will do everything we can to resolve this diplomatically, but ultimately, we've got to have somebody on the other side of the table who's taking this seriously. And I hope that the Iranian regime understands that, that this is their best bet for resolving this in a way that allows Iran to rejoin the community of nations and to prosper and feel secure themselves.

Prime Minister Cameron. Thank you. On Syria, when you see what is happening in Homs and elsewhere, I think we need to appeal to people's humanity to stop this slaughter, to get aid and assistance to those into—who've been affected, and to ratchet up the pressure on this dreadful regime.

But in the case of Russia, I think we should also appeal to their own interest. It's not in their interest to have this bloodied, broken, brutal regime butchering people nightly on the television screens. The irony is that people in Syria often felt that the Russians were their friends, and many in the West they were more suspicious of. Now they can see people in the West wanting to help them, raising their issues, calling for the world to act on their problems. And we need to make sure that Russia joins with that.

So it's going to take a lot of hard work. It's going to take a lot of patient diplomacy. But I think it's actually in Russia's interest that we deal with this problem, that we achieve transition, and that we get peace and stability in Syria. And that's the appeal that we should make.

On the issue of holding people responsible, I do. They're not a signatory to the ICC, but what is being done in Homs—and I've spoken personally to one of the photographers who was stuck in Homs, when he got out to the U.K.—what he witnessed, what he saw is simply appalling and shouldn't be allowed to stand in our world.

And that's why Britain and others have sent monitors to the Turkish border and elsewhere to make sure we document these crimes, we write down what has been done so that no matter how long it takes, people should always remember that international law has got a long reach and a long memory, and the people who are leading Syria at the moment and committing these crimes need to know that.

Tom Bradby from ITN.

Syria

Q. Mr. President, it's great you've agreed to learn about cricket. I noticed the Prime Minister neglected to tell you that a test match usually takes 5 days. [*Laughter*] So it's going to be a long trip. [*Laughter*]

On the serious subject of Syria, you say you want Asad to go. You wanted Qadhafi to go, and he didn't for a long, long time. So could you just answer specifically, have you discussed today the possibility of a no-fly zone? Have you discussed how you might implement it? Have you discussed how you would degrade the Syrian defenses? Have you discussed time scales on any of those issues?

Prime Minister Cameron. What I'd say, Tom, is that our teams work incredibly closely together on this issue, and the focus right now is, as I said, on trying to achieve transition, not trying to foment revolution. We think that the fastest way to end the killing, which is what we all want to see, is for Asad to go. So the way we should try to help bring that about is through diplomatic pressure, sanctions pressure, political pressure, the pressure that Kofi Annan can bring to bear. That is where our focus is.

Of course, our teams, all the time, as I put it, kick the tires, push the system, ask the difficult questions: What are the other options, what are the other things that we could do? And it's right that we do that. But they're not without their difficulties and complications, as everybody knows. So the focus is transition and all the things that we can to do bring that pressure to bear. And that has been the focus of our discussions.

President Obama. I'd echo everything that David said. Our military plans for everything. That's part of what they do. But I was very clear during the Libya situation that this was unique. We had a clear international mandate; there was unity around the world on that. We were able to execute a plan in a relatively short timeframe that resulted in a good outcome.

But each country is different. As David just mentioned with respect to Syria, it is a extremely complicated situation. The best thing that we can do right now is to make sure that the international community continues to unify around the fact that what the Syrian regime is doing is unacceptable. It is contrary to every international norm that we believe in.

And for us to provide strong support to Kofi Annan, to continue to talk to the Russians, the Chinese, and others about why it is that they need to stand up on behalf of people who are being shelled mercilessly, and to describe to them why it is in their interest to join us in a unified international coalition, that's the most important work that we can do right now.

There may be some immediate steps that we've discussed just to make sure that humanitarian aid is being provided in a robust way and to make sure that a opposition unifies along principles that ultimately would provide a clear platform for the Syrian people to be able to transition to a better form of government.

But when we see what's happening on television, our natural instinct is to act. One of the things that I think both of us have learned in every one of these crises—including in Libya—is that it's very important for us to make sure that we have thought through all of our actions before we take those steps. And that's not just important for us, it's also important for the Syrian people. Because ultimately, the way the international community mobilizes itself, the signals we send, the degree to which we can facilitate a more peaceful transition or a soft landing, rather than a hard landing that results in civil war and, potentially, even more deaths—the people who are going to ultimately be most affected by those decisions are the people in Syria itself. All right?

Thank you very much, everybody. Enjoy the day. See some of you tonight.

NOTE: The President's news conference began at 12:27 p.m. in the Rose Garden at the White House. In his remarks, the President referred to former Secretary-General Kofi A. Annan of the United Nations, in his capacity as Joint U.N.-Arab League Special Envoy for Syria. Prime Minister Cameron referred to Sunday Times photographer Paul Conroy, who was wounded in an attack by Government forces in Homs, Syria, on February 22, and later rescued by Syrian anti-Government activists.

Remarks at a State Dinner Honoring Prime Minister David Cameron of the United Kingdom
March 14, 2012

President Obama. Good evening, everyone. Please have a seat. Welcome to the White House. I was just telling the Prime Minister that, so far, the evening has been successful because I have not stepped on Michelle's train—[*laughter*]—my main goal this evening. Michelle and I could not be more honored that you could join us as we host our great friends the Prime Minister of the United Kingdom, David Cameron, and his remarkable wife Samantha. You can give them a round of applause. Why not?

As I said this morning, this visit also gives us an opportunity to return the gracious hospitality that Her Majesty Queen Elizabeth as well as David and Samantha and all the British people showed us during our visit to London last year. And I know Michelle looks forward to returning, because, as she announced yesterday, she will be leading the U.S. delegation to the opening ceremonies of the Summer Olympics in London. I am jealous. [*Laughter*]

Now, I'm so grateful for all the time that David and I have had together. But as we've learned, you can never tell how things will get reported as a consequence of our interactions. When we met 2 years ago, we exchanged beers from our hometowns. One newsstory said: "David Cameron and Barack Obama cemented their special relationship by hitting the bottle." [*Laughter*]

When we had a barbecue at Downing Street for some of our servicemembers, David and I rolled up our sleeves, threw away the aprons, decided to flip the burgers ourselves. One reporter called it a "brave and foolish move." [*Laughter*] Another expressed amazement at our "surprising competence." [*Laughter*] Michelle and Samantha often remark the same way. [*Laughter*]

And finally, when David and I got beat pretty badly in table tennis by some local London kids, one newspaper asked the head coach of the British Olympic women's team to critique our performance. Obama, the coach said, "talked a lot." [*Laughter*] David "overhits the ball." [*Laughter*] Both of them—I'm quoting here—"looked a little confused." [*Laughter*]

But in moments like that and in all of our interactions, including today, I've learned something about David. In good times and in bad, he's just the kind of partner that you want at your side. I trust him. He says what he does, and he does what he says. And I've seen his character. And I've seen his commitment to human dignity during Libya. I've seen his resolve, his determination to get the job done, whether it's righting our economies or succeeding in Afghanistan.

And I will say something else, David: All of us have seen how you, as a parent, along with Samantha, have shown a measure of strength that few of us will ever know. Tonight I thank you for bringing that same strength and solidarity to our partnership, even if you do overhit the ball. [*Laughter*]

We are by no means the first President and Prime Minister to celebrate the deep and abiding bonds between our people. There has been no shortage of words uttered about our special relationship. And as—and I was humbled to offer my own last year when I had the opportunity to address Parliament in Westminster Hall.

So, rather than words, I'd like to leave you tonight with two simple images. They're from different times and places, decades apart. But they're moments, I think, that reveal the spirit of our alliance and the character of our countries.

The first is from the Blitz, when, month after month, the British people braved the onslaught from the sky. And one of those most enduring images from those days is of the London skyline, covered in smoke, with one thing shining through: the dome of St. Paul's Cathedral, tall and proud and strong. The other image we know from our own lives, from that awful September day, that unforgettable picture of the Manhattan skyline, covered in smoke and dust, with one thing shining through: our Statue of Liberty, tall and proud and strong.

In those two moments, I think you see all you need to know about who we are and what brings us together tonight. In war and in peace, in times of plenty and times of hardship, we stand tall and proud and strong together. And as free peoples committed to the dignity of all human beings, we will never apologize for our way of life, nor waver in its defense.

It's why David's grandfather fought alongside us Yanks after D-day, why my grandfather marched across Europe in Patton's army. It's why tonight, at dusty bases in Afghanistan, both American and British soldiers are getting ready to go on patrol, like generations before them, shoulder to shoulder. It's why our diplomats and development workers are side by side, standing with the activists who dare to demand their rights, save a child from drought or famine.

It's why leaders of our two countries can embrace the same shared heritage and the promise of our alliance, even if we come from different political traditions, even if the Prime Minister is younger than nearly 200 years of his predecessors, even if the President looks a little different than his predecessors. And, David, it's why tonight our young children, and children across our countries, can sleep well, knowing that we're doing everything in our power to build a future that is worthy of their dreams.

So, in closing, let me just say that I intended to make history tonight. I thought that I could be the first American President to make it through an entire visit of our British friends without quoting Winston Churchill. [*Laughter*] But then I saw this great quote, and I thought, "Come on, this is Churchill!" [*Laughter*] So I couldn't resist.

It was December 1941, and the attack on Pearl Harbor had finally thrust America into war, alongside our British friends. And these were the words Sir Winston spoke to his new American partners: "I will say that he must indeed have a blind soul who cannot see that some great purpose and design is being worked out here below, of which we have the honor to be the faithful servants."

And so I'd like to propose a toast: To Her Majesty the Queen, on her Diamond Jubilee, to our dear friends David and Samantha, and to the great purpose and design of our alliance. May we remain, now and always, its faithful servants. Cheers, everyone.

[*At this point, President Obama offered a toast.*]

David.

Prime Minister Cameron. President Obama, First Lady, ladies and gentlemen: It is a tremendous honor to be here this evening. And I want to thank you for putting on such a great dinner and for making our visit so special over the last 2 days. And thank you also for those strong and beautiful words that you've just spoken.

Now, Michelle, I'm sure that, like Sam, you often wonder what happens when your husband goes for a night out with the guys. [*Laughter*] So maybe I should come clean about last night. [*Laughter*] We went to basketball, and we had a real man-to-man chat. Barack tried to confuse me by talking about bracketology—[*laughter*]—but I got my own back by running him gently through the rules of cricket. [*Laughter*]

The truth is, we have to have a guys' night out because so often we find we are completely overshadowed by our beautiful wives.

As I rolled into bed last night, I said, "Samantha, do you want to hear about what I got up to on this great guys' night out?" And she— she's not too impressed by these things. She said: "Well, everything you did was on television. You were surrounded by the Presidential

bodyguard, so presumably, you didn't get up to anything." [*Laughter*]

Now, both Barack and I have said a lot today about the importance of the relationship between our two countries and our peoples. Like my predecessors, I'm proud of our essential relationship and of Britain's strong national bond with the United States of America. I feel it in my bones.

Now, there is, of course, a great history of close relationships between U.S. Presidents and British Prime Ministers. Importantly, these have been regardless of the political parties they happen to represent. Her Majesty the Queen is a great authority on the matter. She has seen—and she likes to tell me this—no fewer than 12 British Prime Ministers and 11 American Presidents during her time on the throne. And I'm sure everyone here would want to pay tribute to her incredible service and selfless duty in this, her special Diamond Jubilee year.

Now, Her Majesty's first Prime Minister was, of course, Winston Churchill, a regular guest here at the White House. I'm not going to quote from Churchill, I'm going to quote about Churchill, because it seems his visits were not always the easiest experience for his American hosts.

As Roosevelt's secretary wrote after one visit: "Churchill is a trying guest. He drinks like a fish. He smokes like a chimney. He has irregular routines, works nights, sleeps days, and turns the clocks upside down." And for those of you who wonder why the British Prime Minister now stays at Blair House rather than the White House—[*laughter*]—I simply observe this. We all know the story of Winston Churchill famously found naked in his bath by President Roosevelt. This happened while he stayed at the White House in December 1941, and the Federal Government bought Blair House in 1942. [*Laughter*]

Now, for every genuine Presidential-Prime Ministerial friendship, there have been some—I think we could call them—total disconnects. Edward Heath and Richard Nixon took personal awkwardness with each other to new and excruciating levels. [*Laughter*] And yet, despite this, Richard Nixon arranged for someone to pay for the swimming pool at the Prime Minister's country residence of Chequers. Incidentally, this swimming pool now has a serious and possibly terminal leak. [*Laughter*] So I hope you won't find it amiss as I say here in the White House, for the first time in 40 years, these words: It is time to call in the plumbers. [*Laughter*]

Now, turning to Obama-Cameron, as fellow parents, Barack and Michelle have both been personally very kind to Sam and me. And as fellow leaders, we've struck up, I believe, a really good partnership. It is frank and honest. We talk through issues very rationally. We don't need to remind each other of the basic threats that we face; we know them. But there are three things about Barack that really stand out for me: strength, moral authority, and wisdom.

Strength, because Barack has been strong when required to defend his national interests. Under President Obama's leadership, America got bin Laden. And together with British and coalition forces, America has fundamentally weakened Al Qaida. The President says what he will do, and he sticks to it. I'll never forget that phone call on Libya, when he told me exactly what role America would play in Libya, and he delivered his side of the bargain to the letter. We delivered our side of the bargain too. And let us all agree that the world is better off without bin Laden, but the world is better off without Qaddafi too.

Moral authority, because Barack understands that the means matter every bit as much as the ends. Yes, America must do the right thing, but to provide moral leadership, America must do it in the right way too. The first President I studied at school was Theodore Roosevelt. He talked of speaking softly and carrying a big stick. That is Barack's approach. And in following it, he has pressed the reset button on the moral authority of the entire free world.

Wisdom, because Barack has not rushed into picking fights, but has stewarded America's resources of hard and soft power. He's taken time to make considered decisions, drawing down troops from Iraq and surging in Afghani-

stan. He's found a new voice for America with the Arab people. And at home, he's recognized that in America, as in Britain, the future depends on making the best of every citizen. Both our nations have historically been held back by inequality. But now there's a determined effort in both our countries—most notably through education reform—to ensure that opportunity is truly available for all.

Half a century ago, the amazing courage of Rosa Parks, the visionary leadership of Martin Luther King, and the inspirational actions of the civil rights movement led politicians to write equality into the law and make real the promise of America for all her citizens. But in the fight for justice and the struggle for freedom, there is no end, because there is so much more to do to ensure that every human being can fulfill their potential.

That is why our generation faces a new civil rights struggle, to seek the prize of a future that is open to every child as never before. Barack has made this one of the goals of his Presidency, a goal he's pursuing with enormous courage. And it is fitting that a man whose own personal journey defines the promise and potential of this unique nation should be working to fulfill the hopes of his country in this way.

Barack, it is an honor to call you an ally, a partner, and a friend. You don't get to choose the circumstances you have to deal with as a President or a Prime Minister. And you don't get to choose the leaders that you have to work with. But all I can say is that it is a pleasure to work with someone with moral strength, with clear reason, and with fundamental decency in this task of renewing our great national alliance for today and for the generations to follow.

And with that, I propose a toast: To the President, to the First Lady, and to the people of the United States of America. Cheers.

NOTE: The President spoke at 9:01 p.m. on the South Grounds at the White House. In his remarks, he referred to Alan Cooke, head coach, United Kingdom's women's Olympic table tennis team.

Remarks at Prince George's Community College in Largo, Maryland
March 15, 2012

The President. Thank you. Well, I am so—what a wonderful reception. That is so nice. Thank you. You're all just cheering because I know Michelle. [*Laughter*] Well, the—it is wonderful to be here. Folks who have a seat, feel free to take a seat.

I want to thank Roy for that introduction. He talks pretty smooth, right? That whole—[*laughter*]. It's great to be back in Maryland. It's great to be here at Prince George's Community College.

Audience member. We love you!

The President. I love you back. Now, but before I start, I want to thank your other president, Dr. Charlene Dukes. Your Governor, Martin O'Malley, is in the house. Lieutenant Governor Brown is here. We've got one of the finest Members of the United States Senate that you could hope to have in Ben Cardin. Congresswoman Donna Edwards is here. And County Executive Rushern Baker is here. And I want to thank all of you for coming out here today.

Now, I just finished learning about some of the work that you're doing here at this community college to make sure that homes are using less energy and helping folks save money on their heating and their air-conditioning bills. And I was very impressed. I'm even more impressed because I know this program is giving a lot of people a chance to make a decent living, everyone from veterans to folks with disabilities to folks who've just been down on their luck, but want to work. So I want you to know how proud I am of this program, of this institution, of all of you.

The skills that you gain here at this community college will be the surest path to success in this economy. Because if there's one thing that we're thinking about a lot these days, is, first of all, how do we make sure that American workers have the skills and education they need to be able to succeed in this competitive global economy? And community colleges all across the country and all across Maryland are doing an outstanding job providing young people that

first opportunity after high school, but also helping older workers retrain for the jobs of the future, because the economy is constantly adapting.

So community colleges are big. Community colleges are critical to our long-term success. What's also critical to our long-term success is the question of energy: How do we use less energy? How do we produce more energy right here in the United States of America?

And I know this is an especially important topic for everybody right now because you guys have to fill up at the gas station. And it's rough. Gas prices and the world oil markets right now are putting a lot of pressure on families right now. And one of the things that it is important to remember is for a lot of folks, just doing what you have to do to get your kids to school, to get to the job, to do grocery shopping, you don't have an option. You've got to be able to fill up that gas tank. And when prices spike on the world market, it's like a tax; it's like somebody is going into your pocket.

We passed the payroll tax at the beginning of this year to make sure that everybody had an extra $40 in their paycheck, on average, in part because we anticipated that gas prices might be going up like they did last year, given tight world oil supplies.

But that doesn't make it easier for a lot of families out there that are just struggling to get by. This is tough. Now the question is, how do we meet this challenge? Because right now we're starting to see a lot of politicians—talking a lot, but not doing much. And we've seen this movie before. Gas prices went up around this time last year. Gas prices shot up in the spring and summer of 2008; I remember, I was running for President at the time. This has been going on for years now.

And every time prices start to go up, especially in an election year, politicians dust off their three-point plans for $2 gas. [*Laughter*] I guess this year they decided, we're going to make it $2.50. [*Laughter*] I don't know where—you know, why not $2.40? Why not

$2.10? [*Laughter*] But they tell the same story. They head down to the gas station; they make sure a few cameras are following them, and then they start acting like we've got a magic wand and we will give you cheap gas forever if you just elect us. [*Laughter*] Every time—been the same script for 30 years. It's like a bad rerun. [*Laughter*]

Now, here's the thing: Because we've seen it all before, we know better; you know better. There is no such thing as a quick fix when it comes to high gas prices. There's no silver bullet. Anybody who tells you otherwise isn't really looking for a solution; they're trying to ride the political wave of the moment.

Usually, the most common thing, when you actually ask them, all right, how is it that you're going to get back to 2-dollar-a-gallon gas, how are you going to do it, specifically, what is your plan—then typically what you'll hear from them is, well, if we just drilled more for oil, then gas prices would immediately come down and all our problems would go away. That's usually the response.

Now, Maryland, there are two problems with that answer. First of all, we are drilling. Under my administration, America is producing more oil today than at any time in the last 8 years—any time. That's a fact. [*Applause*] That's a fact. We've quadrupled the number of operating oil rigs to a record high. I want everybody to listen to that: We have more oil rigs operating now than ever. That's a fact. We've approved dozens of new pipelines to move oil across the country. We announced our support for a new one in Oklahoma that will help get more oil down to refineries on the Gulf Coast.

Over the last 3 years, my administration has opened millions of acres of land in 23 different States for oil and gas exploration. Offshore, I've directed my administration to open up more than 75 percent of our potential oil resources. That includes an area in the Gulf of Mexico we opened up a few months ago that could produce more than 400 million barrels of oil.

So do not tell me that we're not drilling. We're drilling all over this country. I mean, I guess there are a few spots where we're not drilling. We're not drilling in the National Mall. [*Laughter*] We're not drilling at your house. [*Laughter*] Right? I mean, I guess we could try to have, like, 200 oil rigs in the middle of the Chesapeake Bay.

Audience members. No!

The President. Well, that's the question. We are drilling at a record pace, but we're doing so in a way that protects the health and safety and the natural resources of the American people.

All right, so that's point number one. If you start hearing this "drill, baby, drill; drill, drill, drill"—if you start hearing that again, just remember you've got the facts. We're doing that. Tell me something new. That's problem number one.

Here's the second problem with what some of these politicians are talking about. There's a problem with a strategy that only relies on drilling, and that is, America uses more than 20 percent of the world's oil. If we drilled every square inch of this country—so we went to your house, and we went to the National Mall, and we put up those rigs everywhere—we'd still have only 2 percent of the world's known oil reserves. Let's say we miss something; maybe it's 3 percent instead of 2. We're using 20; we have 2.

Now, you don't need to be getting an excellent education at Prince George's Community College to know that we've got a math problem here. Right? [*Laughter*] I help out Sasha occasionally with her math homework, and I know that if you've got 2 and you've got 20, there's a gap. [*Laughter*] There's a gap, right? Do we have anybody who's good at math here? Am I right? Okay.

So, if we don't develop other sources of energy, if we don't develop the technology to use less energy to make our economy more energy efficient, then we will always be dependent on foreign countries for our energy needs.

And that means every time there's instability in the Middle East, which is the main thing that's driving oil prices up right now—it's the same thing that was driving oil prices up last year—every time that happens, every time that there's unrest, any time that there's concern about a conflict, suddenly, oil futures shoot up, you're going to feel it at the pump. It will happen every single time.

We will not fully be in control of our energy future if our strategy is only to drill for the 2 percent, but we still have to buy the 20 percent. And there's another wrinkle to this. Other countries use oil too. We're not the only ones. So you've got rapidly growing nations like China and India, and they're all starting to buy cars. They're getting wealthier. They want cars too. And that means the price of gas will rise.

Just to give you an example: In 2010, China alone added 10 million new cars. That's just in 1 year. And there are about a billion Chinese. So they've got a lot more people who are going to want cars in the future, which means they are going to want to get some of that oil, and that will drive prices up. So we can't just drill our way out of the problem. We are drilling, but it's not going to solve our problem.

That's not the future I want for the United States of America. We can't allow ourselves to be held hostage to events on the other side of the globe. That's not who we are. America controls its own destiny. We're not dependent on somebody else.

So we can't have an energy strategy for the last century that traps us in the past. We need an energy strategy for the future, an all-of-the-above strategy for the 21st century that develops every source of American-made energy. Yes, develop as much oil and gas as we can, but also develop wind power and solar power and biofuels. Make our buildings more fuel efficient. Make our homes more fuel efficient. Make our cars and trucks more fuel efficient so they get more miles for the gallon. That's where I want to take this country.

And here's—the best part of it is thousands of Americans have jobs right now because we've doubled the use of clean energy in this country since I came into office. And I want to keep on making those investments. I don't want to see wind turbines and solar panels and high-tech batteries made in other countries by other workers. I want to make them here. I want to make them here in Maryland. I want to make them here in the United States of America, with American workers. That's what I want.

So, when I came into office, we said, all right, how are we going to start moving America in that direction? It's not a thing you get done in 1 year, but how do we start moving in that direction? So, after 30 years of not doing anything, we raised fuel economy standards on cars and trucks so that by the middle of the next decade, our cars will average nearly 55 miles per gallon. That's double what we get today, 55 miles per gallon—55 miles a gallon.

So the young people here who were driving those beaters that—[*laughter*]—getting 5 miles per gallon—[*laughter*]. We're going to get you to 55. And that will save the average family more than $8,000 over the life of a car—$8,000. That will help pay some bills. That means you'll be able to fill up every 2 weeks instead of every week. And those are the cars we need to keep building here in the United States.

Audience member. Yes, we can!

The President. Yes, we can do that.

All right, so now, to fuel these cars and trucks, obviously, if they're using less gas, that's great. That saves us; we're using less oil. But we also want to invest in clean advanced biofuels that can replace some of the oil that we're currently using. That's important.

Already, we're using these biofuels to power everything from city buses to UPS trucks to Navy ships. I want to see more of these fuels in American cars—homegrown fuels—because that means we're buying less oil from foreign countries and we're creating jobs here in the United States, including big parts of rural America, big parts of rural Maryland, where the economy oftentimes is struggling, you have a real opportunity to create entire new industries and put people to work. And it's happening all across the country.

So all of these steps have put us on a path of greater energy independence. Here's a statistic I want everybody to remember next time you're talking to somebody who doesn't know what they're talking about. [*Laughter*] Since I took office, America's dependence on foreign oil has gone down every single year. All right? In 2010, our oil dependence, the amount that we're bringing in, the percentage we're bringing in, was under 50 percent for the first time in 13 years. We've got to do better than that, and we can do better than that.

Audience member. Yes, we can!

The President. Yes, we can. But in order to do better than that, we've got to tell the folks who are stuck in the past that our future depends on this all-of-the-above energy strategy. That's our job. That it can't just be—it can't just be—drilling for more oil. We're drilling for more oil, but that can't be all the solution; that's just part of the solution.

Now, the—here's the sad thing. Lately, we've heard a lot of professional politicians, a lot of the folks who are running for a certain office—[*laughter*]—who shall go unnamed—they've been talking down new sources of energy. They dismiss wind power. They dismiss solar power. They make jokes about biofuels. They were against raising fuel standards. I guess they like gas guzzlers. They think that's good for our future. We're trying to move towards the future; they want to be stuck in the past.

And we've heard this kind of thinking before. Let me tell you something. If some of these folks were around when Columbus set sail—[*laughter*]—they must have been founding members of the Flat Earth Society. [*Laughter*] They would not have believed that the world was round. We've heard these folks in the past. They probably would have agreed with one of the pioneers of the radio who said: "Television won't last. It's a flash in the pan." [*Laughter*] One of Henry Ford's advisers was quoted as saying, "The horse is here to stay, but the automobile is only a fad." [*Laughter*]

There have always been folks like that. There always have been folks who are the naysayers and don't believe in the future and don't believe in trying to do things differently. One of my predecessors, Rutherford B. Hayes, reportedly said about the telephone, "It's a great invention, but who would ever want to use one?" [*Laughter*] That's why he's not on Mount Rushmore—[*laughter*]—because he's looking backwards. He's not looking forwards. He's explaining why we can't do something, instead of why we can do something.

The point is, there will always be cynics and naysayers who just want to keep on doing things the same way that we've always done them. They want to double down on the same ideas that got us into some of the mess that we've been in. But that's not who we are as Americans. See, America has always succeeded because we refuse to stand still. We put faith in the future. We are inventors. We are builders. We are makers of things. We are Thomas Edison. We are the Wright Brothers. We are Bill Gates. We are Steve Jobs. That's who we are.

That's who we need to be right now. [*Applause*] That's who we need to be right now. I don't understand when I hear folks who are in elected office or aspiring to elected office, who ignore the facts and seem to just want to get a cute bumper-sticker line, instead of actually trying to solve our problems.

What I just said about energy, by the way, is not disputed by any energy expert. Everybody agrees with this. So why is it that somebody who wants to help lead the country would be ignoring the facts?

If you want an example of what I'm talking about, consider an important issue that's before Congress right now.

I think somebody may have fainted. All right. Remember next time, if you're going to stand for a long time, you got to eat. [*Laughter*] I'm—no, no, it's true. You got to get something to eat. You got to get some juice. I'm just saying. It's true. They'll be okay; just make sure to give them space.

The question—there's a question before Congress I want everybody to know about. The question is whether or not we should keep giving $4 billion in taxpayer subsidies to the oil industry.

The oil industry has been subsidized by you, the taxpayer, for about a hundred years—100 years. One hundred years, a century. So some of the same folks who are complaining about biofuels getting subsidies or wind or solar energy getting subsidies or electric cars and advanced batteries getting subsidies to help get them off the ground, these same folks, when you say, why are we still giving subsidies to the oil industry, "Well, no, we need those."

Oil companies are making more money right now than they've ever made. On top of the money they're getting from you at the gas station every time you fill up, they want some of your tax dollars as well.

That doesn't make any sense. Does it make sense?

Audience members. No!

The President. It's inexcusable. It is time for this oil industry giveaway to end. So, in the next few weeks, I expect Congress to vote on ending these subsidies. And when they do, they'll put every single Member of Congress on record. I guess you can stand up for the oil companies who really don't need much help, or they can stand up for the American people, because we can take that $4 billion, we could be investing it in clean energy in a good energy future, in fuel efficiency. We could actually be trying to solve a vital problem.

They can bet—they can place their bets on the energy of the past, or they can place their bets on America's future: on American workers, American ingenuity, American technology, American science, American-made energy, American efficiency, American productivity. We can bet on America and our own capacity to solve this problem. That's the choice we face. That's what's at stake right now.

Maryland, we know what direction we have to go in. And every American out there, as frustrated as they are about gas prices right now, when you actually ask people, they'll tell you, yes, we've got to find new sources of energy. We got to find new ways of doing things. People understand that. We just got to get Washington to understand it. We got to get politicians to understand it.

We've got to invest in a serious, sustained, all-of-the-above energy strategy that develops every resource available for the 21st century. We've got to choose between the past and the future. And that's a choice we shouldn't be afraid to make because we've always bet on the future, and we're good at it. America is good at the future. We are good at being ahead of the curve. We're good at being on the cutting edge.

Ending these subsidies won't bring down gas prices tomorrow. Even if we drilled every inch of America, that won't bring gas prices down tomorrow. But if we're tired of watching gas prices spike every single year, and being caught in this position, where what happens in the Middle East ends up taking money out of your pocket, if we want to stabilize energy prices for the long term and the medium term, if we want America to grow, we're going to have look past what we've been doing and put ourselves on the path to a real, sustainable energy future.

That's the future you deserve. So I need all of you to make your voices heard. Get on the phone, write an e-mail, send a letter, let your Member of Congress know where you stand. Tell them to do the right thing. Tell them we can win this fight. Tell them we're going to combine our creativity and our optimism, our brainpower, our manpower, our womanpower. Tell them: Yes, we can. Tell them we are going to build an economy that lasts. Tell them we're going to make this the American century just like the last century.

Thank you, Prince George's County. Thank you, Prince George's Community College. Thank you, Maryland. Let's get to work. God bless you. God bless America.

NOTE: The President spoke at 11:05 a.m. In his remarks, he referred to W. Roy Dunbar, chairman, Sustainable Star Renewable Energy & Construction; Rushern L. Baker III, county executive, Prince George's County, MD; and William H. Gates III, chairman, Microsoft Corp.

Statement on a Meeting of the Interagency Task Force To Monitor and Combat Trafficking in Persons
March 15, 2012

Nearly 150 years ago, in issuing the Emancipation Proclamation, President Abraham Lincoln reaffirmed the commitment of the United States to the enduring cause of freedom. Then as now, we remain steadfast in our resolve to see that all men, women, and children have the opportunity to realize this greatest of gifts. Yet millions around the world, including here in the United States, toil under the boot of modern slavery. Mothers and fathers are forced to work in fields and factories against their will or in service to debts that can never be repaid. Sons and daughters are sold for sex, abducted as child soldiers, or coerced into involuntary labor. In dark corners of our world and hidden in plain sight in our own communities, human beings are exploited for financial gain and subjected to unspeakable cruelty.

Slavery remains the affront to human dignity and stain on our collective conscience that it has always been. That is why members of my Cabinet and senior advisers gathered at the White House today, at a meeting chaired by Secretary of State Hillary Clinton, to lay out their plans for meeting this challenge. The United States is committed to eradicating trafficking in persons, and we will draw on tools ranging from law enforcement and victim service provision to public awareness building and diplomatic pressure. Because we know that Government efforts are not enough, we are also increasing our partnerships with a broad coalition of local communities, faith-based and nongovernmental organizations, schools, and businesses.

To bring all these elements together and to be sure we are maximizing our efforts, today I am directing my Cabinet to find ways to strengthen our current work and to expand on partnerships with civil society and the private sector so that we can bring more resources to bear in fighting this horrific injustice. In the coming weeks, the White House will build on this gathering on behalf of human dignity. I am confident that we will one day end the scourge of modern slavery because I believe in those committed to this issue: young people, people of faith and station, Americans who refuse to accept this injustice and will not rest until it is vanquished. Today I reaffirm that the United States stands with them and that together we will realize the promise of the Emancipation Proclamation and our country's ideal of freedom.

Letter to Congressional Leaders Regarding the Comprehensive Interagency Strategy for Public Diplomacy and Strategic Communication
March 15, 2012

Dear _____:

Pursuant to section 1055 of the Duncan Hunter National Defense Authorization Act for Fiscal Year 2009, I am providing an update on my Administration's comprehensive interagency strategy for public diplomacy and strategic communication, which was submitted to the Congress in March 2010.

Sincerely,

BARACK OBAMA

NOTE: Identical letters were sent to Daniel K. Inouye, chairman, and W. Thad Cochran, vice chairman, Senate Committee on Appropriations; Carl M. Levin, chairman, and John S. McCain III, ranking member, Senate Committee on Armed Services; John F. Kerry, chairman, and Richard G. Lugar, ranking member, Senate Committee on Foreign Relations; Harold D. Rogers, chairman, and Norman D. Dicks, ranking member, House Committee on Appropriations; Howard P. "Buck" McKeon, chairman, and Adam Smith, ranking member,

House Committee on Armed Services; and Ileana Ros-Lehtinen, chairman, and Howard L.

Berman, ranking member, House Committee on Foreign Affairs.

Remarks at an Obama Victory Fund 2012 Fundraiser in Chicago, Illinois
March 16, 2012

Hello, Chicago! Thank you! Thank you so much. It is good to be home! Good to be home. Thank you very much. Thank you. Everybody, please have a seat. Thank you so much.

I have never seen the city look prettier, I have to say. And every time I come back, I am just overwhelmed with not only the beauty of this city, but I was explaining to folks as we were flying over—Dick Durbin flew in with me—what makes this place so special is not just that this is where my daughters were born, not just where I really started my political career, but I've got so many good friends, so many relationships. And as I look out across the room, seeing so many folks who put up with me—[*laughter*]—before I was President and helped me get there, it is just extraordinary.

So I miss you guys. I wish I could stay the weekend—[*laughter*]—especially this weekend, because we all know there is no better place to be on St. Patrick's Day than in Chicago.

Let me say just thank you to, first of all, one of the finest attorney generals in the country. She proved it again in helping us to get this settlement on the housing issue—Lisa Madigan is doing outstanding work. The senior Senator of the great State of Illinois and one of my dearest friends, Dick Durbin is in the house. The Governor of the great State of Illinois, Pat Quinn; you've got a new mayor here—[*laughter*]—I don't know how he's doing, but he seems to have a little bit of energy—Mr. Rahm Emanuel.

We got Representatives Bobby Rush and Jan Schakowsky in the house. County Board President and my former Alderwoman, Toni Preckwinkle. The trees were always trimmed. [*Laughter*] Snow was shoveled when Toni was in charge. And I want to thank Axelrod and Penny and Daley for the preprogram.

Now, you might have noticed that we have some guests in Illinois this week. Apparently, things haven't quite wrapped up on the other side. [*Laughter*] So there is actually some interest in the primary that we have here on Tuesday.

And my message to all the candidates is, "Welcome to the Land of Lincoln"—[*laughter*]—because I'm thinking maybe some Lincoln will rub off on them while they are here. [*Laughter*]

Now, we remember Lincoln as the leader who saved our Union, but this is a President who, in the midst of the Civil War, launched the transcontinental railroad, understanding that in order for America to grow, we had to stitch ourselves together, to be connected, coast to coast.

He set up the first land-grant colleges in the midst of war, because this largely self-taught man understood that education could give people the chance to real their—realize their potential, and if we were able to give that kid on a farm the opportunity to learn, that that would be good for all of us, not just for that kid; created the National Academy of Sciences to promote the discovery and innovation that would lead to new jobs and entire new industries.

Lincoln, the first Republican President, knew that if we as a nation, through our Federal Government, didn't act to facilitate these things, then they likely wouldn't happen, and as a result, we'd all be worse off. He understood that we are a people that take great pride in our self-reliance and our independence but that we are also one Nation and one people and that we rise or fall together.

So I hope that while my counterparts on the other side enjoy the outstanding hospitality of the people of Illinois and spend some money here to promote our economy—[*laughter*]—I hope they also take a little bit of time to reflect on this great man, the first Republican President.

Of course, you may not feel confident that will happen. You may be watching some of this

311

avalanche of attack ads and think this is not appealing to the better angels of our nature, but hope springs eternal. [*Laughter*]

And that vision of Lincoln's—a vision of a big, bold, generous, dynamic, active, inclusive America—that's a vision that has driven this country for more than 200 years. That's the vision that helped create Chicago. That's why we don't make little plans here. And that's not a Democratic vision or a Republican vision. That is a quintessentially American vision.

And that's the vision that drove our campaign in 2008 and that so many of you worked your hearts out to see realized. It wasn't because you were willing to settle for an America where people are left to fend for themselves and everybody is playing by their own rules. What you believed in was an America where everyone who works hard has a chance to get ahead—everybody. It doesn't matter what you look like, where you come from, what your name is. Everybody has a chance.

That's the vision we shared. That's the change we believed in. That's why you got involved. You didn't get involved because the odds were that a guy named Barack Hussein Obama was going to be President. [*Laughter*]

And we knew it wasn't going to be easy or that it would come quickly. We knew it was going to be hard. But as you just saw in that video, just think about what happened over the last 3 years because of what you did in 2008. Because of your efforts, your commitment not to me, but to the country and to each other, we started to see what change looks like.

So change is the first bill I signed into law, a law that says women deserve an equal day's pay for an equal day's work, because our daughters should have the same opportunities as our sons.

Change is the decision we made to rescue the American auto industry from collapse, even when some were saying, let's let Detroit go bankrupt. We had a million jobs on the line, the entire economy of the Midwest and the country at stake. So I wasn't about to let that happen. And because of your efforts, it didn't happen.

Today, GM is back on top as the world's number-one automaker, just reported the highest profits in 100 years. The factory here in Chicago is going gangbusters. With more than 200,000 new jobs created in the last 2½ years, the auto industry in America is back. That's change. That happened because of you.

Change is the decision we decided—we made to stop waiting for Congress to do something about our oil addiction and finally raise fuel efficiency standards on our cars and on our trucks, so that by the next decade we will be driving American-made cars that get 55 miles to the gallon, which will save the typical family $8,000 at the pump over time and do some good for the environment in the bargain. That's what change is.

Change is us no longer handing out $60 billion in taxpayer subsidies to banks who are managing student loans, and instead, giving that money directly to students who need it and families who want to see a better life for the next generation, so that millions of kids all across the country have benefited.

And change is the fact that in the first—for the first time in our history, you don't have to hide who you love in order to serve the country you love, because "don't ask, don't tell" is over.

Change is health care reform that we passed after a century of trying, which means nobody will go bankrupt in this country just because they get sick. We got 2½ million young people who already have health insurance today because they can stay on their parent's plan, millions of seniors who are already seeing benefits in terms of more preventive care, lower drug prices.

And not only is preventive care now covered, it also means that families with children with preexisting conditions aren't going to have to worry that somehow their child is going to be left on their own or that they're going to have to mortgage their business or lose their home because of that illness. That's what change is.

Change is fulfilling the first promise I made in this campaign, that we would end the war in Iraq. We do not have troops in Iraq anymore because of the extraordinary work of our men and women in uniform.

We've made sure that Wall Street is playing by the rules, stabilizing our economy. All this happened because of your efforts.

Now, the question is, what happens next? None of this has been easy. We've got a lot more work to do. There are still too many Americans out there who are struggling, whose homes are underwater, who are still looking for work. There are too many families right here in Chicago who can barely pay the bills, who are trying to figure out how they can scrap enough money together to let their kids go to college.

But, over the past 2 years, we've created close to 4 million new jobs. We've got the biggest growth in manufacturing since the 1990s. The economy is stronger. Our exports are on track to double. Businesses feel more confident. And so we've got an opportunity to build on all the work that we've done over the last 3 years, and the question is, are we going to be able to stay on track and move in the right direction?

Because the other side, they've got an entirely different idea. Their basic theory is that we go back to doing things the same way we were doing them before the crisis hit, promoting the same policies that got us into this mess in the first place. And it's my belief that the last thing we can afford to do is go back to the same policies that got us into this mess. That's the last thing we can afford to do. But that's what they're talking about.

Look, they're not making any secret of it. You can watch these ads on TV. They want to go back to the days when Wall Street played by its own rules. They want to go back to the days when insurance companies could deny coverage or jack up premiums without reason. They want to spend trillions of dollars more on tax breaks for the veriest wealthiest individuals, even if it means adding to the deficit or gutting things like energy or education or Medicare. We got a simple philosophy: We are better off when everybody's left on their own. Everybody writes their own rules.

They are wrong. In the United States of America, we have always been greater together than we are on our own. We are better off when we keep to that basic American promise that you can—that if you work hard, you can do well enough to raise a family and own a home, send a kid to college, put a little away for retirement. We're better off when the laws are applied fairly to everybody, not just some. And that's the choice in this election.

This is not just another political debate. This is the defining issue of our time, because we are in a make-or-break moment, not only for the middle class in this country, but everybody who is fighting to get into the middle class. We can go back to an economy built on outsourcing and bad debt and phony financial profits, or we can fight for an economy that's built to last, an economy built on American manufacturing and American energy and skills and education for American workers and the values that made this country great and made this city great and made this State great: hard work and fair play and shared responsibility.

That's what's at stake. And so over the coming months we're going to have a great debate about whose vision will deliver for the American people. I think we need to make sure that the next generation of manufacturing takes root not in Asia, not in Europe, but in the factories of Detroit and Pittsburgh and Cleveland and Chicago. That's what I believe.

I don't want this Nation to be known just for buying and consuming things. I want us to be known for building and selling products all around the world. Which is why I've said let's stop rewarding businesses that ship jobs overseas. Let's start rewarding companies that are creating jobs right here in the United States of America.

I think most Americans agree with us. We should be making our schools the envy of the world. And by the way, there is a Chicago export named Arne Duncan, who is doing unbelievable work at a national level. And he understands, as I understand, that we—it starts with the man or woman at the front of the classroom.

A good teacher can increase the lifetime earnings of a classroom by over $250,000. So I don't want to hear Washington either defend the status quo or spend all their time bashing teachers. What Arne and I have been talking about is giving schools the resources they need to hire good teachers and keep good teachers and train good teachers and reward the best ones and provide schools the flexibility to teach with creativity and passion and stop teaching to the test and replacing teachers who aren't helping our kids. That's what we expect: reform, resources, accountability. That's what I believe.

When kids do graduate, the biggest challenge they're facing right now is how to afford a college education. We've got more tuition debt now than credit card debt, which means this Congress has to pay attention, because in July, student interest—interest rates on student loans are scheduled to double if we don't do anything about it. We've got to focus on how are we making sure our kids can get good value, that they're making informed choices, and that they're getting some help.

And colleges and universities have to do their part. I've said to university presidents and college presidents, we want to work with you and help with you—help you. But we're not going to just keep on funding tuition rates that are skyrocketing. Higher education cannot be a luxury. It's an economic imperative that every family in America should be able to afford.

An economy that's built to last is one where we support scientists and researchers trying to make sure the next breakthrough in clean energy and biotechnology happens right here in the United States of America. We've restored science to its rightful place. On things like stem cell research, we said, let's follow the science, but we also have to make investments in science. We have to make investments in basic research. Lincoln understood that; you understand it.

Nowhere is that truer, by the way, in the—than in the area of energy. We've been subsidizing oil companies for a hundred years. Now's the time to stop subsidizing an oil industry that's rarely been more profitable, double down on a clean energy industry that's never been more promising: solar and wind and biofuels, homegrown, American energy. That's

what we believe. The other side has a different view.

We believe we need to give our businesses the best access to newer roads and airports, faster railroads and internet access. I'm biased; maybe it's because I'm a Chicagoan. I believe in having the best stuff. I don't—I'm a chauvinist in this way. I don't want to go to China and see a better airport in China than O'Hare. I don't want to ride on a road in Germany and see a better road than Lake Shore Drive.

It is time for us to take the money we we are no longer spending at war and use half of that to pay down our debt and use the rest to do some nation-building here at home. Let's put people back to work.

And we need to make sure that we've got a tax system that reflects everybody doing their fair share. I was with Warren Buffett a couple of days ago, and he's quite pleased that I named a rule after him—[*laughter*]—the Buffett rule, which is common sense. It says, if you make more than a million dollars a year, you shouldn't pay a lower tax rate than your secretary. I—this is not—look, if you make $250,000 a year or less, which is 98 percent of Americans, your taxes shouldn't go up. You're—a lot of folks in that category are struggling.

But for folks like me, we can do a little bit more. I know. You know it. This isn't class warfare. This isn't envy. It's basic math. Because if somebody like me and some of you are getting tax breaks we don't need, weren't even asking for, and the country can't afford, then either it's going to add to the deficits—which the other side claims is their top priority—or we've got to take something from somebody else.

That student who's trying to go to college, suddenly their interest rate goes higher. That senior who's trying to afford their prescription drugs, their costs go up. That veteran who desperately needs help right now, they get short-changed. That family that's trying to get by, they're forgotten. That's not right. That's not who we are.

You hear a lot of politicians talk about values in election years. And I'm sure some of the ads have been talking about that here in Illinois. Let me tell you about values. Hard work is a value. Looking out for one another, that's a value. The idea we're all in this together, that I'm my brother's keeper and sister's keeper, that's a value. Caring for our own, that's a value. Making sure that seniors can retire with dignity and respect, that's a value. Making sure our veterans are cared for—and that costs money—that's a value.

You understand that. One of the great things about this town is we come from everywhere. You look—I guess you can't look in a phonebook anymore; they don't have phonebooks these days. [*Laughter*] But when you think about Chicago, part of what you think about is all the last names, right? The Emanuels, the Obamas, the Sanchezes, the Polaskis—we all come from someplace else. And the only reason that we can be in this magnificent ballroom is because somebody, somewhere, took responsibility. They took responsibility for their families, first and foremost: generations of immigrants making sure that they were leaving something behind for the next generation; our grandparents, our great-grandparents striking out, sometimes falling down, picking themselves back up.

But also, they took responsibility for our country's future. They understood the American story is never about just what we can do by ourselves. It's about what we can do together. And we will not win the race for new jobs and new businesses and middle class security with the same old you-are-on-your-own economics, because it hasn't worked in the past. It won't work now.

It didn't work in the decade before the Great Depression. It did not work when we tried it in the last decade. It's not like we haven't tried it. It does not work. And we've got a stake in each other's success. And we all understand that. If we attract an outstanding teacher to the profession, giving her the pay she deserves, the support she deserves, and she educates the next Steve Jobs, we all benefit.

We get faster Internet to rural Illinois, rural America, so that some store owner or entrepreneur there can suddenly have access to a worldwide marketplace, that's good for the entire economy. We build a new bridge that saves

a shipping company time and money—workers, consumers, we all do better.

This is not a Democratic or Republican idea. Lincoln understood it. It was a Republican President, Teddy Roosevelt, who called for a progressive income tax; Republican Dwight Eisenhower that built the Interstate Highway System. It was with the help of Republicans in Congress that FDR was able to give millions of returning heroes, including my grandfather, the chance to go to college on the GI bill.

And here's the thing: That same spirit of common purpose, that desperate desire to pull the country together and focus on what needs to get done in a serious way, that spirit still exists today, maybe not in Washington, but exists here in Chicago. It exists out there in America. You go to Main Streets, you go to town halls, you go to VFW halls, you go to a church or a synagogue, it's there when you talk to members of our Armed Forces, when you talk to folks at a Little League game or at their places of worship.

Our politics may be divided. But most Americans understand we are greater together and that no matter who we are or where we come from, we rise or fall as one Nation and one people. And that's what's at stake. That's what's at stake in this election. That's what we're fighting for. As much as 2008 was exciting, and as much as all of us, I think, saw that night at Grant Park as the culmination of something, it was actually just the beginning of what we're fighting for. That's what 2012 is about.

And I know it's been a tough few years, and I know there are times where people have said, change just isn't coming fast enough. And I know that when you see what's going on in Washington sometimes it's tempting to believe that what we believed in, in 2008, was an illusion; maybe it's just not possible. It's easy to slip back into cynicism.

But remember what we said in the last campaign, that real change, big change would be hard. It takes time. It may take more than a single term. It may take more than a single President. What it really takes is ordinary citizens who are committed to continuing to fight and to push and to keep inching this country closer to its ideals, its highest ideals.

And I said in 2008, I am not a perfect man and I will never be a perfect President. But I made a commitment then that I would always tell you what I believed, I would always tell you where I stood, and I would wake up every single day fighting as hard as I know how for you. And I've kept that promise to the American people.

So I'm a little grayer now. [*Laughter*] It's not as trendy to be involved in the Obama campaign as it was back then. [*Laughter*] Some of you have rolled up those "Hope" posters, and they're in a closet somewhere. [*Laughter*] But I am more determined and more confident that what drove us in 2008 is the right thing for America, than I've ever been before.

And if you're willing to keep pushing through the obstacles and reach for that vision of America that we all believe in, I promise you change will continue to come. And if you work as hard as you did then now, I promise you we will finish what we started in 2008, and we will remind the world just why it is that America is the greatest nation on Earth.

Thank you, everybody. God bless you. God bless the United States of America.

NOTE: The President spoke at 12:13 p.m. at the Palmer House Hilton hotel. In his remarks, he referred to former White House Senior Adviser David M. Axelrod; Penny S. Pritzker, chairman and founder, Pritzker Realty Group; former White House Chief of Staff William M. Daley; Secretary of Education Arne Duncan; and Warren E. Buffett, chief executive officer and chairman, Berkshire Hathaway Inc.

Statement on Representative Gary L. Ackerman's Decision Not To Seek Re-election
March 16, 2012

For over 30 years, Gary Ackerman has represented the people of Queens and Long Island, first as a New York State senator and then as a Member of Congress. Gary's bipartisan efforts helped our Nation confront significant challenges at home and abroad. He was a leader in the fight to pass Wall Street reform and helped strengthen the bonds between the United States and our allies, particularly Israel. Always a champion of his fellow New Yorkers,

Gary was also successful in enacting a bill to create the "Heroes" postage stamp, which benefited the families of rescue workers killed or permanently disabled while responding to the 9/11 attacks. Gary's unique enthusiasm will be greatly missed in the halls of Congress, but I am confident he will continue to serve the people of New York for years to come. Michelle and I wish him and his family well in the future.

Letter to Congressional Leaders Regarding High-Performance Computer Export Controls
March 16, 2012

Dear _____:

In accordance with the provisions of section 1211(d) of the National Defense Authorization Act for Fiscal Year 1998 (Public Law 105–85), I hereby notify you of my decision to establish a new level for the notification procedure for digital computers set forth in section 1211(a) of Public Law 105–85. The new level will be 3.0 Weighted TeraFLOPS. The attached report provides the rationale supporting this decision and fulfills the requirements of Public Law 105–85, sections 1211(d) and (e).

I have made this change based on the recommendation of the Departments of State, Defense, Commerce, and Energy.

Sincerely,

BARACK OBAMA

NOTE: Identical letters were sent to Carl M. Levin, chairman, Senate Committee on Armed Services; Timothy P. Johnson, chairman, Senate Banking, Housing, and Urban Affairs Committee; Howard P. "Buck" McKeon, chairman, House Committee on Armed Services; and Ileana Ros-Lehtinen, chairman, House Committee on Foreign Affairs.

Remarks at an Obama Victory Fund 2012 Fundraiser in Atlanta, Georgia
March 16, 2012

The President. Hello, Atlanta! Hello, Georgia! Oh, it is good to be in Atlanta, Georgia. Thank you. Thank you.

Audience member. I love you!

The President. I love you back. I do. [*Laughter*]

So let me first of all acknowledge a few people who are here. The outstanding young mayor of Atlanta, Georgia, Kasim Reed is in the house. One of the finest men I know, somebody upon whose shoulders I stand, the great Congressman John Lewis is in the house; other outstanding members of the congressional delegation here in Georgia: Sanford Bishop, David Scott, Hank Johnson.

Somebody who—I was just reminiscing. When I first started to run for office, a lot of people weren't sure whether a guy named Barack Obama could win. And so we went down to the Selma commemoration—Edmund Pettus Bridge—and we're in church. And a lot of folks at that point are still wondering whether this is a good idea, that this young guy is running for President. And this man gets up onstage, and he explains how people call him a little crazy, but "there is good crazy, and there's bad crazy." He tells me now that he came up with the idea when his doctor explained to him there was good cholesterol and bad cholesterol. [*Laughter*] But he decided that supporting Barack Obama was a "good kind of crazy," he said. We have been dear friends ever since. The Reverend Dr. Joseph Lowery is in the house.

And finally, let me just say about—something about the man who introduced us, Tyler Perry, hosting us all at his incredible facility.

He and I were talking, and there's something about America where somebody from my background can do what I'm doing and somebody from Tyler's background can do what he's doing. And as tough as things get sometimes and as frustrated and cynical people can get about politics, when you look at a Tyler Perry and all that he's achieved and the humility and graciousness with which he's achieved it, you can't help but be proud of him and to be proud of our country. So give it up for Mr. Tyler Perry.

Now, I'm here today not only because I need your help. I'm here because the country needs your help. There was a lot of reasons why so many of you decided to get involved and then just work your hearts out in the campaign in 2008. It was not because you thought it would be easy. The odds of me becoming President were long. You didn't need a poll to know it was going to be tough. You didn't join the campaign because of me. You joined it because of your commitment to each other and the vision that we share about America.

It wasn't a vision where just a few people do well and everybody else is on their own and the most powerful are able to make their own rules. It wasn't a cramped vision or a selfish vision of America. It wasn't a limited vision about our future. It was a vision of America where everybody who works hard has a chance to get ahead, not just those who are born into it, but a Tyler Perry or a Barack Obama or a child in Georgia or a child in a barrio in Texas or a poor child in some rural community in the Midwest. It didn't matter. They would have a chance if they were willing to work hard.

That's the vision we shared. That's the change we believed in. We knew it wouldn't come easy. We knew it wouldn't come quickly. But we believed. And, in just 3 years, because of what you did in 2008, we've begun to see what change looks like.

Change is the first bill I signed into law—a law that says women deserve an equal day's pay for an equal day's work—because I don't want my daughters treated any differently than your sons. I want them to have the same opportunities. That's what change is.

Change is the decision we made to rescue the American auto industry at a time when it was on the verge of collapse and some folks were saying let Detroit go bankrupt. We had 1 million jobs on the line, and I wasn't going to let them go. Today, GM is back on top, the number-one automaker in the world, just reported the highest profits in a hundred-year history. With more than 200,000 new jobs added, the United States auto industry is back. That's what change is. That's what you did.

Change is the decision we made to stop waiting for Congress to do something about energy. We've been listening to politicians for three decades, four decades, saying they were going to do something about energy. We went ahead and did it: raised fuel efficiency standards on cars. By the next decade, we'll be driving American-made cars getting 55 miles a gallon. That will save the average family $8,000 at the pump. That's what change is. And it happened because of you.

Change is us deciding, you know what, why are we giving $60 billion to the banks to manage the student loan program; let's give it directly to the students, so that millions of more young people are either getting higher Pell grants or finally eligible, being able to invest in things like early education and community colleges and HBCUs.

Change is attacking the cycle of poverty not by just pouring money into a broken system, but by building on what works. Promise Neighborhoods—the idea of pulling all our resources together to make sure that everybody has a chance, rebuilding our public services, public housing, making sure that our education system is working, making sure that we've got partnerships with local leaders like Kasim Reed. All across the country, rebuilding cities, one block, one neighborhood at a time. That's what change is.

Change is, yes, health care reform. You want to call it Obamacare, that's okay, because I do care. That's why we passed it. [*Applause*] That is why we passed it, because I care about folks who were going bankrupt because they were getting sick. And I care about children who have preexisting conditions and their families couldn't get them any kind of insurance. And so now we've got reforms that will ensure that in this great country of ours you won't have to mortgage your house just because you get sick.

Right now 2.5 million young people already have health insurance who didn't have it before because of this law. It let them stay on their parents' policies. Insurance companies can't just deny you coverage or drop your coverage at a time when you need it most. Seniors are seeing more help when it comes to their prescription drugs and preventive care. That's what change is.

Change is the fact that for the first time in history, you don't have to hide who you love in order to serve the country you love. We ended "don't ask, don't tell."

Change is keeping the promise I made in 2008: For the first time in 9 years, there are no Americans fighting in Iraq. We decided to refocus on the folks who actually attacked us on 9/11. And thanks to the brave men and women in uniform, Al Qaida is weaker than it's ever been and Osama bin Laden is not walking this face—the face of this Earth.

None of this has been easy. And we still have a lot of work to do, because there are a lot of folks who are still hurting out there, a lot of folks still pounding the pavement looking for work, a lot of people whose homes—values have dropped, a lot of people who are still struggling to make the rent. There are still too many families who can barely pay their bills, too many young people still living in poverty.

I was reading a statistic the other day: Fewer than half of African Americans believe we'll reach the dream Dr. King left for us. So we've still got so much work to do.

And I know when we look at what is, it can be heartbreaking and frustrating. But I ran for President—and you joined this cause—because we don't settle just for what is, we strive for what might be. We want to help more Americans reach that dream. I ran for President to give every child a chance, whether he's born in Atlanta or comes from a rural town in the Delta. I ran for President not just to get us back to where we were, but to take us forward to where we need to be.

And I'm telling you, Atlanta, we are going to get there. Step by step, we are going to get there. Already over the past 2 years, our businesses have added almost 4 million new jobs. Manufacturers are creating jobs for the first time since the 1990s. The recovery is accelerating. Our economy is getting stronger. We're moving on the right track. What we can't do is go back to the same policies that got us into this mess in the first place.

Of course, that's exactly what the other folks want to do, the folks who are running for President. And they make no secret about it. They want to roll back the laws that we put in place so that now Wall Street can play by its own rules again. They want to go back to the day when insurance companies could deny you coverage or jack up your premiums any time they wanted without reason. They want to spend trillions more on tax breaks for the very wealthiest of individuals, even if it means adding to the deficit, even if it means gutting things like education or our investment in clean energy or making sure Medicare is stable.

Their philosophy is simple: Everybody is just left to fend for themselves, if those in power could make their own rules, and somehow it's all going to trickle down to you. And they're wrong. They're wrong. They were wrong when they tried it, and they're wrong now.

In the United States of America, we are always greater together than we are on our own. We're always better off when we keep that basic American promise that if you work hard, you can do well enough to raise a family and own a home and send your kids to college and put a little away for retirement. And that's the choice in this election.

We've got different visions being presented. This is not just another political debate, this is the defining issue of our time. What are we going to do to make sure that middle class families are secure and that we continue to build ladders for people who are trying to get into the middle class? We don't need an economy that's built on outsourcing and bad debt and phony financial profits. We need an economy that's built to last, an economy that's built on American manufacturing, American energy, and giving skills to American workers, and holding up those values that we cherish: hard work, fair play, shared responsibility.

When we think about the next generation of manufacturing, I don't want it taking root in Asia, I want it taking root in Atlanta. I don't want this Nation just to be known for buying and consuming things from other countries. I want to build and sell to other countries products made in the United States of America. I want to stop rewarding businesses that are shipping jobs overseas. I want to reward companies, like this one, that are creating jobs right here in the United States of America.

I want to make sure that our schools are the envy of the world. And that means investing in the men and women who stand in front of the classroom. A good teacher increases the income of a classroom by over $2,500. A great teacher can help a child move beyond their immediate circumstances and reach out for their dreams. I don't want Washington to defend the status quo, but I don't want them to be just bashing teachers. I want to give schools the resources they need to keep good teachers on the job and reward the best teachers and grant schools flexibility to teach with creativity and passion, stop teaching to the test, replace teachers that aren't helping kids learn. I want us to create in this country the kind of passion and reverence for education that's not just, by the way, a job of government, but a job of each of us: as parents, as community leaders.

And when kids do graduate, I want them to be able to afford to go to college. We've got more tuition debt than credit card debt today.

And by the way, right now interest rates are scheduled to go up on student loans in July if Congress does not act, so you guys need to get on Congress about that.

And I've said to colleges and universities, you've got to stop tuition from just going up and up and up and up. Higher education cannot be a luxury; it is an economic imperative that every family should be able to afford.

I want an economy that's supporting the scientists and researchers that will make sure we discover the next breakthrough in biotechnology, in clean energy. We have subsidized oil companies for 100 years, given them $4 billion worth of tax breaks when they are making near-record profits. It is time to stop giving tax giveaways to an industry that's never been more profitable and start investing in clean energy that can create jobs here in the United States in solar power and wind power and biofuels.

We need to give our businesses the best infrastructure in the world: newer roads and airports and faster railroads and Internet access. You take half the money that we've been spending on the wars in Iraq, as we phase down the war in Afghanistan—let's pay down—use half of it to pay down our debt. Let's use the other half to do some nation-building here at home. Let's put people to work rebuilding schools, rebuilding our bridges, rebuilding our ports.

And to pay for this, we've got to have a tax system that is fair. I was with Warren Buffett a couple days ago. He says, "Thanks for naming a rule after me." [*Laughter*] We—it's a very simple principle, the Buffett rule. It says if you make more than a million dollars a year, you should not pay a lower tax rate than your secretary. We've said if you make less than $250,000 a year, which is 98 percent of Americans, your taxes shouldn't go up. But folks like me, we can afford to do a little more. Tyler can afford to do a little more. Tyler? [*Laughter*] He knows he—[*laughter*]—he knows that.

When we say that, this is not class warfare, this is not envy. This is just basic math. Because if Tyler or I or others get tax breaks we don't need, weren't asking for, that the country can't afford, then one of two things are going to happen. Either the deficit goes up—all these other folks they say they want to do something about the deficit; every single one of their plans actually increases the deficit. Or alternatively, they've got to make up for it by taking it away from somebody who really needs it: the student who suddenly sees their interest on their loans going up, the senior who suddenly has to pay more for Medicare, the veteran who's not getting help after having protected us, the family that's trying to get by. It's not right. It's not who we are.

I hear a lot of politicians talk about values during election year. You know what, I'm happy to have a values debate. I'm happy to have a debate about values. I think about the values my mother and my grandparents taught me. Hard work, that's a value. Looking out for one another, that's a value. I am my brother's keeper, I am my sister's keeper, that is a value. Each of us is only here because somebody somewhere was looking out for us. It started in the family, but it wasn't just the immediate family. There was somebody in church. There was somebody in the neighborhood. There was the coach of the Little League. There was somebody who made an investment in our country's future.

Our story has never been about what we can do alone. It's what we do together. We don't win the race for new jobs and middle class security and new businesses with the same old you-are-on-your-own economics. I am telling you, it does not work. It did not work in the decade before the Great Depression. It did not work in the decade before I took office. It won't work now.

This is about who we are as a country, the opportunities we've always, always passed on to future generations. When I think about Michelle and me and where we come from—[*applause*]—I know you all love Michelle, I know. [*Applause*] I know. I love her too. [*Laughter*] But I think about—sometimes we'll be in the White House, and we think about my mother-in-law who lives upstairs and was a secretary. Michelle's dad had multiple sclerosis and still went to work every day, blue-collar job; my mom raising me, a single mom. I think about what they did for us and the sacrifices they made.

And so then I think, well, the sacrifices that I have to make, given all the blessings that I've received, they can't just extend to Malia and Sasha. I've got to be thinking about somebody else's kids. I've got to be making sure that somebody else gets a student loan who's maybe a single mom going back to school just like my mom, who was able to get a student loan so— to get an education. I'm thinking, we've got to make sure that jobs are out there for folks who are willing to work and overcoming barriers. And I'm willing to make some sacrifices for that. And that makes my life better. Right?

And most of you understand that. You understand if you invest in a teacher and then she teaches somebody who is the next Steve Jobs or invents some cure for a major disease, that makes us all better. If we invest in Internet services for rural Georgians, there is a little store out there that, suddenly, business starts booming because they now have a worldwide market through the Internet, and that creates economic opportunity for everybody.

That idea is not a Democratic idea, it is not a Republican idea. That is an American idea. Abraham Lincoln understood it. The first Republican President during a war invested in the transcontinental railroad, the National Academy of Sciences, land-grant colleges.

Dwight Eisenhower, Republican, built the Interstate Highway System. Teddy Roosevelt, Republican, called for a progressive income tax. This is not just a Democratic idea. This is an American idea, that we invest in our future and that we are stronger together than we are on our own.

And you know, sometimes, that spirit may seem to have vanished in Washington. Sometimes it may seem like our politics is just a bad reality show—[*laughter*]—people arguing and fussing and trying to score points and—[*laughter*]. But you know, out in the country, when I go to town halls, when I go to a VFW hall, that spirit it still there.

People still understand, this country that gave us so much, we want to pass that on to the next generation. They understand that it's not just about us, it's about what we can do for each other. It's not just about the next election, it's about the next generation. You talk to our men and women in uniform, they understand it. You talk to folks in our places of worship, they recognize it. And all of you recognize it. And that's what we tapped into in 2008: that spirit, that spirit.

So let me just say this: I'm a little grayer now. [*Laughter*] I'm a little—got some bumps and bruises. I know that over the last 3 years there have been times where we've suffered setbacks and change hasn't come as fast as we would have liked. And people still got the old "Hope" posters; it's, like, fading a little bit. [*Laughter*] And I know that there are times where you might start feeling cynical about what's possible.

But I just want to remind you of what I said back in 2008. I said change is hard. I said this may not happen in 1 year, it may not happen in one term, it may not happen with one President. But if we stick with it, if we're determined, if we understand the rightness of our cause, if we continue to think not in terms of just what's good for me, but what's good for us, we will get there.

And I also told you—I told you I'm not a perfect man, and I won't be a perfect President. But I said I'd always tell you what I thought, I would always tell you where I stood, and I would wake up every single day thinking about you and working as hard as I know how to make your lives a little bit better.

And I have kept that promise. I have kept that promise these last 3 years. And so if you're willing to get back to organizing, if you're willing to get on the phone and e-mail and tweet and knock on doors and do what needs to be done, if you feel the same passion and same energy and same determination as I do—and I feel it more now than I have ever felt it in my life—then I promise you we will finish what we started. Two thousand and eight was a beginning. We're still on that journey. We've got 5 more years of work before us.

I promise you change will come. The change you believe in will come. And we will remind the world once again just why it is the United States of America is the greatest country on Earth.

God bless you. God bless the United States of America.

NOTE: The President spoke at 8:05 p.m. at the Tyler Perry Studios. In his remarks, he referred to actor and comedian Tyler Perry; Warren E. Buffett, chief executive officer and chairman, Berkshire Hathaway Inc.; and his mother-in-law Marian Robinson.

Remarks at an Obama Victory Fund 2012 Fundraiser in Atlanta
March 16, 2012

The President. So, usually, I have better accommodations for our events. [*Laughter*] But we decided to slum it here today. Everybody, have a seat. Everybody, have a seat.

It is wonderful to see all of you. I've got a bunch of good friends here. It is a nice, intimate setting, which means that I'm going to have time to have a conversation instead of giving a long speech. And since I've been giving long speeches all day, I'm—and most of you have heard it before—I'm glad that it's going to be more of a dialogue.

First of all, I just want to thank Tyler for this event. I was saying to him, when we were over at his studio, there is something about America, with all the struggles we've been going through and all the changes that have taken place in our history, for him to come from where he is and be who he is, for me to come from where I am and have this extraordinary privilege. It says something special about this place. And for Tyler to continue to be so humble and thoughtful and generous is just a—is a testimony to him and his family. And so we are just so grateful to him and just feel blessed to see his success. So thank you so much, Tyler. Appreciate it.

We've got a couple of elected officials who are doing outstanding work. First of all, your own mayor, who is blowing up, as they say. [*Laughter*] He is a star, and people all across the country are starting to get a sense of how astute he is and how effective he is in leading this city; Mr. Kasim Reed is in the house.

Our host when we get to Charlotte, North Carolina, Mayor Anthony Foxx is here.

And then there is my good friend Oprah, who very early on, when I was still running, just decided that she would support this guy with a name that nobody could pronounce. And just like books and skin cream—[*laughter*]—when Oprah decides she likes you, then other people like you too. [*Laughter*] And she has continued to be just—not just a friend, but somebody who Michelle and I seek out in thinking about not just the day-to-day issues of the day but trying to keep our focus on the big picture. And what she's done for so many people, not just in America, but around the world, is extraordinary. So I just want to say thank you to Oprah.

We've had a good day. I was back home in Chicago, came down to Atlanta. It's warm every place. It gets you a little nervous about what's happening to global temperatures, but when it's 75 degrees in Chicago in the beginning of March, you start thinking——

Audience member. Something is wrong.

The President. Yes. On the other hand, really have enjoyed the nice weather. [*Laughter*]

And we're starting to gear up, starting to get into—back into that campaign mode. And it makes you reflect on the journey we've traveled so far over the last 3 years. As some of you may have seen, we released a video yesterday. If you haven't seen it, it's worth catching. Because what it reminds us of is where we were, because you can't understand where we are unless you have a good sense of where we've been.

And this time—around this time 4 years ago—or 3 years ago, we were losing 800,000 jobs a month. The banking system had completely locked up. The auto industry was on the verge of collapse. The world economy was hemorrhaging. And 3 years later, we've now created close to 4 million jobs. The banking system is healthy again. Credit is flowing.

Small businesses are starting to get back on their feet. Manufacturing is as strong as it's been in a couple of decades in terms of job growth. We still have enormous challenges, but we've made extraordinary progress.

Now, what I always remind people of is, I ran for President not just to get back to where we were before the crisis; I ran because the status quo precrisis wasn't good enough. But it was for too many people a betrayal of the American Dream, the idea that if you work hard, you can make it, regardless of what you look like, where you come from, what your name is, that as a consequence of hard work you could support a family, buy a home, send your kids to college, retire with dignity and respect. That core American Dream had been fraying for too many people.

And so even as these last 3 years we have been dealing with crises and getting the auto industry back on its feet and making sure the banking system was sounder and dealing with two wars and going after Al Qaida and trying to clean up after these extraordinary challenges, I've still tried to stay focused on the fact that the promises we made in the campaign had to do with building an economy that sustained itself and that was built on a solid foundation, not phony financial profits or debt, but was built on something more sound and more lasting and that we would reopen opportunity for everybody and give people more security as they pursue their dreams.

And that's what we've done. The health care bill will give 30 million people health care for the first time. But it also means that everybody who already has health care, the insurance companies can't drop you just because you get sick or you've got a preexisting condition or—young people, 2½ million people right now have health care that didn't have it before because they can stay on their parent's plan.

The changes we're making in education, 46 States have initiated reforms across the country that are reemphasizing training teachers, and not just teaching to the test, but allowing creativity and passion in the classroom, holding folks accountable, saying we're going to get rid of teachers who aren't doing a good job, but al-

so rewarding teachers who are doing a great job and lifting them up.

Across the country, we are seeing a renaissance of advanced manufacturing, so we're not just a country that's known for buying stuff and consuming stuff, but we're starting to build and sell and export things that are made in America.

We want to rebuild our infrastructure, and we began to do that through the Recovery Act, so that once again we've got the best airports and the best roads and the best bridges and the best Internet service, accessing rural communities and inner cities so that everybody can tap into this new 21st-century economy.

We've tried to make sure that fairness is not just something we give lip service to, but that we actually deliver on. And so whether it's reinvigorating the Justice Department's Office of Civil Rights or ending "don't ask, don't tell," we've tried to make sure that we mean what we say when we say that this is a country where everybody is equal before the law.

Internationally, we've restored respect for America. We've ended one war. We're transitioning out of another one. We went after the people who actually attacked us on 9/11, and Al Qaida is weaker than it's been in years. And Usama bin Laden is not around.

We strengthened our alliances, the respect for the United States, the restoration of our moral standing by banning torture and upholding rule of law. That makes all kinds of differences for people as they travel overseas and they try to do business overseas.

So here's the thing though: This is not a 3-year project; this is an 8-year project. So I need you one more time. And we're confident we can get there, but we're going to need your help. So I've said this—I was saying this at the speech that I gave at Tyler's studio: I know I'm a little grayer now—[*laughter*]—and it's not as trendy to be an Obama supporter, because it's not as fresh. Those posters are kind of rolled up in some closet somewhere. [*Laughter*] But my determination—my determination is unwavering. My passion to bring about change is undiminished. The need is still great. The American people are still relying on us.

And so I hope that you are game to work just as hard, if not harder, in the coming months to make sure we finish what we began. I'll be counting on you, and more importantly, the American people are counting on you.

All right. Thank you very much.

The President's Weekly Address
March 17, 2012

Hi, everybody. As I know you've noticed over the past few weeks, the price at your local pump has been going up and up. And because it's an election year, so has the temperature of our political rhetoric.

What matters most to me right now is the impact that rising prices have on you. When you've got to spend more on gas, you've got less to spend on everything else. It makes things harder. So I wanted to take a minute this weekend to explain what steps my administration is taking when it comes to energy—most importantly, producing more of it while using less of it.

The truth is, the price of gas depends on a lot of factors that are often beyond our control. Unrest in the Middle East can tighten global oil supply. Growing nations like China or India adding cars to the road increases demand. But one thing we should control is fraud and manipulation that can cause prices to spike even further.

For years, traders at financial firms were able to game the energy markets, distort the price of oil, and make big profits for themselves at your expense. And they were able to do all that because of major gaps and loopholes in our regulations. When I took office, we did something about it.

The Wall Street reforms I signed into law are helping bring energy markets out of the shadows and under real oversight. They're strengthening our ability to go after fraud and to prevent traders from manipulating the market. So it's not just wrong, but dangerous that some in Congress want to roll back those protections and return to the days when companies like Enron could avoid regulation and reap enormous profits, no matter who it hurt.

NOTE: The President spoke at 9:14 p.m. at the residence of Tyler Perry. In his remarks, he referred to talk show host Oprah Winfrey. Audio was not available for verification of the content of these remarks.

What's more, at a time when big oil companies are making more money than ever before, we're still giving them 4 billion of your tax dollars in subsidies every year. Your Member of Congress should be fighting for you. Not for big financial firms. Not for big oil companies.

In the next few weeks, I expect Congress to vote on ending these subsidies. And when they do, we're going to put every single Member of Congress on record: They can either stand up for the oil companies, or they can stand up for the American people. They can either place their bets on a fossil fuel from the last century, or they can place their bets on America's future. So make your voice heard. Send your Representative an e-mail, give them a call, tell them to stand with you.

And tell them to be honest with you. It's easy to promise a quick fix when it comes to gas prices. There just isn't one. Anyone who tells you otherwise—any career politician who promises some three-point plan for $2 dollar gas—they're not looking for a solution. They're just looking for your vote.

If we're truly going to make sure we're not at the mercy of spikes in gas prices every year, the answer isn't just going to be to drill more, because we're already drilling more. Under my administration, we're producing more oil here at home than at any time in the last 8 years. That's a fact. We've quadrupled the number of operating oil rigs to a record high. That's a fact. And we've opened millions of acres of land and offshore to develop more of our domestic resources.

Those are the facts. But we can't just rely on drilling. Not when we use more than 20 percent of the world's oil, but still only have 2 percent of the world's known oil reserves. If we don't develop other sources of energy and the technology to use less energy, we'll continue to be dependent on foreign countries for our energy needs. That's why we're pursuing an all-of-the-above strategy. As we develop more oil and gas, we're also developing wind and solar power, biofuels, and next-generation vehicles, and thousands of Americans have jobs right now because of it. We need to keep making those investments, because I don't want to see those jobs go to other countries. I want to create even more of them right here in America.

And after three decades of inaction, we raised fuel economy standards so that by the middle of the next decade, our cars will average nearly 55 miles per gallon. That's nearly double what they get today. That means you only have to fill up every 2 weeks instead of every week. And that will save the typical family more than $8,000 over the life of the car, just by using less gas.

Combined, these steps have helped put us on a path to greater energy independence. Since I took office, America's dependence on foreign oil has gone down every single year. In 2010, for the first time in 13 years, less than half the oil we used came from foreign countries.

But we can do even better, and we will. What we can't do is keep depending on other countries for our energy needs. In America, we control our own destiny. And that's the choice we face: the past or the future. America is what it is today because we've always placed our bets on the future. Thanks, and have a great weekend.

NOTE: The address was recorded at approximately 6 p.m. on March 15 in the Cross Hall foyer at the White House for broadcast on March 17. The transcript was made available by the Office of the Press Secretary on March 16, but was embargoed for release until 6 a.m. on March 17.

Statement on the Death of Pope Shenouda III
March 17, 2012

Michelle and I are saddened to learn of the passing of Coptic Christian Pope Shenouda III, a beloved leader of Egypt's Coptic Christians and an advocate for tolerance and religious dialogue. We stand alongside Coptic Christians and Egyptians as they honor his contributions in support of peace and cooperation.

We will remember Pope Shenouda III as a man of deep faith, a leader of a great faith, and an advocate for unity and reconciliation. His commitment to Egypt's national unity is also a testament to what can be accomplished when people of all religions and creeds work together. On behalf of the American people, we extend our thoughts and prayers to Coptic Christians, Egyptians, and all those who mourn Pope Shenouda III today.

Statement on Transportation Infrastructure Improvement Legislation
March 19, 2012

Last week, the Senate passed a bipartisan transportation bill that will keep construction workers on the job and keep our economy growing. Now the House of Representatives needs to take bipartisan action so I can sign this into law.

An economy built to last depends on a world-class infrastructure system that allows us to transport our people and goods as quickly and effectively as possible. That's

why we need to continue to make investments that will create jobs by rebuilding and modernizing our roads, bridges, and railways. And that's why my administration will continue to fight for the long-term investments needed to ensure that America continues to compete and succeed in a global economy.

NOTE: The statement referred to S. 1813.

Statement on the Death of King George Tupou V of Tonga
March 19, 2012

With the passing yesterday of King George Tupou V of Tonga, the United States has lost a friend and the people of Tonga have lost a visionary leader. Upon ascending to the throne, King George championed a process of peaceful democratization that led to the first majority elected Parliament of Tonga taking office in 2010. As I said when I met with the King at the U.S. Coast Guard Academy graduation last spring, Tonga is one of the United States closest partners among the Pacific Island States, and we are grateful for its role in Afghanistan, where Tonga makes an active contribution to the international coalition. On behalf of all Americans, I extend my deepest condolences to the Queen Mother Halaevalu Mata'aho, the royal family, and the people of Tonga on the passing of King George Tupou V.

Videotaped Remarks on the Observance of Nowruz
March 20, 2012

Today Michelle and I extend our best wishes to all those who are celebrating Nowruz around the world. In communities and homes from America to Southwest Asia, families and friends are coming together to celebrate the hope that comes with renewal.

To the people of Iran, this holiday comes at a time of continued tension between our two countries. But as people gather with their families, do good deeds, and welcome a new season, we're also reminded of the common humanity that we share.

There is no reason for the United States and Iran to be divided from one another. Here in the United States, Iranian Americans prosper and contribute greatly to our culture. This year, an Iranian production, "A Separation," won America's highest honor for a foreign film. Our navies have confronted the danger of piracy, with U.S. sailors even rescuing Iranian citizens who had been taken hostage. And from Facebook to Twitter, from cell phones to the Internet, our people use the same tools to talk to one another and to enrich our lives.

Yet, increasingly, the Iranian people are denied the basic freedom to access the information that they want. Instead, the Iranian Government jams satellite signals to shut down television and radio broadcasts. It censors the Internet to control what the Iranian people can see and say. The regime monitors computers and cell phones for the sole purpose of protect-ing its own power. And in recent weeks, the Internet restrictions have become so severe that Iranians can't communicate freely with their loved ones within Iran or beyond its borders. Technologies that should empower citizens are being used to repress them.

Because of the actions of the Iranian regime, an electronic curtain has fallen around Iran, a barrier that stops the free flow of information and ideas into the country and denies the rest of the world the benefit of interacting with the Iranian people, who have so much to offer.

I want the Iranian people to know that America seeks a dialogue to hear your views and understand your aspirations. That's why we set up a virtual Embassy so you can see for yourselves what the United States is saying and doing. We're using Farsi on Facebook, Twitter, and Google+. And even as we've imposed sanctions on the Iranian Government, today my administration is issuing new guidelines to make it easier for American businesses to provide software and services into Iran that will make it easier for the Iranian people to use the Internet.

The United States will continue to draw attention to the electronic curtain that is cutting the Iranian people off from the world. And we hope that others will join us in advancing a basic freedom for the Iranian people: the freedom to connect with one another and with their fellow human beings.

Over the last year, we have learned once more that suppressing ideas never succeeds in making them go away. The Iranian people are the heirs to a great and ancient civilization. Like people everywhere, they have the universal right to think and speak for themselves. The Iranian Government has a responsibility to respect these rights, just as it has a responsibility to meet its obligations with regard to its nuclear program. Let me say again that if the Iranian Government pursues a responsible path, it will be welcome once more among the community of nations and the Iranian people will have greater opportunities to prosper.

So, in this season of new beginnings, the people of Iran should know that the United States of America seeks a future of deeper connections between our people, a time when the electronic curtain that divides us is lifted and your voices are heard, a season in which mistrust and fear are overcome by mutual understanding and our common hopes as human beings.

Thank you, and *Eid-eh Shoma Mobarak*.

NOTE: The President's remarks were recorded at approximately 12:05 p.m. on March 19 in the Blue Room at the White House. The transcript was released by the Office of the Press Secretary on March 20. The Office of the Press Secretary also released Persian and Arabic language transcripts of these remarks.

Remarks Following a Meeting With Prime Minister Enda Kenny of Ireland
March 20, 2012

President Obama. Well, it is my great pleasure to welcome once again Taoiseach, Mr. Kenny, who has done, I think, extraordinary work during a very difficult time. Over the last several years, we've been able to strike up a friendship. And you'll notice that even though technically it is not St. Patrick's Day, we like to prolong the party around here. Technically, most of the Americans who celebrate St. Patrick's Day aren't Irish anyway—[*laughter*]—so we shouldn't go on technicalities.

I want to thank the Taoiseach, his lovely wife, and all of the people of Ireland for the extraordinary hospitality they showed Michelle and I when we had the chance to travel there recently. It was a magical day. It was too short, so I provided assurances that we will be returning. But the warmth and the good will that was expressed towards us I think was really representative of the deep bonds that exist between the United States and Ireland, bonds that are almost unique among two countries around the world. And the impact obviously that Ireland and Irish American—that Irish culture has had on the United States is almost unparalleled.

We have had a terrific discussion about a wide range of issues. Obviously, for both of our countries, one of the biggest priorities is getting the economy moving in the right direction and putting our people back to work. And the Taoiseach described to me the steps that they've taken to try to stabilize the banking system there, to get control of their budget, and to be in a position to grow in the future.

And it is important that both the people of Ireland and the American people understand the extraordinary benefits of trade, commerce, and investment between our two countries. We are obviously an extraordinary contributor to investment in Ireland, and that's something of great importance to the people of Ireland. Conversely, Irish businesses invest and employ huge numbers of Americans as well.

And so we are continuing to identify and describe additional areas where we can strengthen those strong economic bonds. And I expressed to the Taoiseach my confidence in not only his government's ability to get Ireland moving again, but also we consulted on the broader issue of how Europe can begin to grow again, which obviously has an impact on our economy.

I also had an opportunity to thank him for the continued exemplary efforts by the men and women in uniform in Ireland who contribute to peacekeeping and humanitarian efforts all around the world, from Kosovo to Lebanon. As I've said before, Ireland punches above its weight internationally and has a long history rooted in its own experience of making sure that not only is peace a priority, but also that the human needs of—on issues like hunger are addressed. And even in the midst of a relatively austere time, Ireland has continued to step up internationally, and we greatly appreciate that.

I'm pleased to see that progress continues to be made with respect to the agreement in Northern Ireland, and we discussed how the United States wants to continue to be supportive on that issue as well.

So once again, Taoiseach, welcome. We are always pleased to see you here. And the expressions of affection that I experienced when I was in Ireland I'm sure you are experiencing in return while you are here, because the American people have just an extraordinary affinity and fondness for the Irish people. And we are looking forward to you having a very productive visit, and we look forward to going over to Capitol Hill well—where even when it's not St. Patrick's Day, everybody claims to have a little bit of Irish roots.

Prime Minister Kenny. [*Inaudible*]—pleasure.

President Obama. Thank you.

Prime Minister Kenny. Could I say, first of all, I want to thank the President and the First Lady for the accommodation last evening. It's always good to have a place to stay in Washington. And it's a signal honor to be allowed to stay in Blair House, but also to come here to the Oval Office and have this conversation this morning.

I'd just like to say that I've given the President a rundown on the decisions taken by my government in the last 12 months to stabilize our public finances and to put our own house in order, but also to play a part, clearly, in the European Union, which is so important in a global sense. And from that point of view, I gave the President a rundown on the changes in the structure of banks, the decisions taken by government in relation to public sector numbers, the forcing down of costs and therefore the increase in competitiveness, and to report to him signs of confidence returning to the Irish economy. But we still have a very long

way to go. Otherwise, we've made a good, solid start but clearly there are challenges ahead.

I also reported to the President that the conversation around the table of Europe in the last 10 months has shifted from one of being just austerity to being one of good budgetary discipline, but also where clearly the agenda for growth and jobs will now be central to every European Council meeting.

I gave the President an outline of my views in respect of the fiscal compact treaty and how I will expect the Irish people, in their pragmatism and understanding of what the future holds, to vote strongly in favor of the treaty and that this represents a real insurance policy both for the country and for the next generation of children, but also not to allow any future government to run riot with the people's money as has happened in the past.

We discussed the question of the development of the European economies and how other countries are making efforts aligned with our own to have that as a central issue for the time ahead. We also discussed the trading links between the U.S. and Ireland. I pointed out to the President my interaction with the American Chamber of Commerce and the chief executives of multinationals in Ireland. We discussed the question of the possibility of semesters, either way, for young people involved in innovation and research and education, which is so important in the context of what multinational companies are actually looking for.

As well as that, we discussed the issue of Syria, and I gave the President a rundown on the last discussions at the European Council meeting. We also discussed the question of Iran and what the U.S. has said very clearly about this and the short time window that there is in that regard.

We referred to the possibility of an opportunity to travel again to Ireland, and the President has confirmed that in due course. Obviously, he's got a little matter to attend to here in America between this and then. But I just wanted to say to you that it's a reestablishment, if you like, and a redefining of the absolutely unique relationship that there is between Ireland and the United States.

I pointed out to President Obama since my visit here to Chicago, his home city, the extraordinary outpouring of enthusiasm and exuberance in the streets of Chicago on Saturday and my visit to Notre Dame in South Bend and the opportunities that we had in New York to meet with Irish American business, with American investment business, the Ireland investment day in the stock exchange.

And here in Washington for the past 2 days has been simply outstanding. And it confirms my belief that the reputation of our country has been restored internationally and that the unique relationship that we've always had with the United States for so many reasons is exceptionally strong. And I told the President of the great work being done by Ambassador Rooney, but also that Ireland respects America for what it does, both in our own context, but also to keep the world a safer place for the hundreds

of millions of people who look for real leadership in this regard.

I thank President Obama and his Government and his First Lady for all they do for so many people around the world. And as I say, it's a privilege to be here in the Oval Office to represent our country and have this opportunity on St. Patrick's week. [*Laughter*]

Thank you.

President Obama. Thank you very much. Thank you.

Thank you, everybody.

NOTE: The President spoke at 11:09 a.m. in the Oval Office at the White House. In his remarks, he referred to Fionnuala Kenny, wife of Prime Minister Kenny. Prime Minister Kenny referred to U.S. Ambassador to Ireland Daniel M. Rooney.

Remarks at the Friends of Ireland Luncheon
March 20, 2012

Thank you. Please. Well, thank you, John. Thank you, everybody. I know we are all glad to welcome Taoiseach Kenny and his lovely wife back to Washington. Technically, you may be aware, it is not St. Patrick's Day. [*Laughter*] Of course, technically, most Americans who celebrate St. Patrick's Day are not Irish. So it's a wash. [*Laughter*]

I want to thank our top Irishman in the White House, Joe Biden, who is here, and Speaker Boehner for being such a gracious host. I want to welcome Ambassador Collins and Mrs. Collins, distinguished Members of the House and the Senate, leaders from Ireland, Northern Ireland, and Britain. Thank you all for coming.

I always think about how every Taoiseach must leave this luncheon marveling at how cheerful and bipartisan Washington is. It's remarkable. And that's something worth aspiring to, even during an election year.

As John mentioned, this wonderful tradition began with Speaker Tip O'Neill and Ronald Reagan. And when I was getting ready this morning, I came across some advice that Tip

gave to anybody who was making a St. Patrick's Day speech. As the story goes, Tip was once asked to deliver a speech to the Friendly Sons of St. Patrick in Pennsylvania. He figured the Irishmen would arrive early, perhaps have a few drinks, relax a little bit, and by the time he stood up to speak, they would applaud anything he said as long as he kept it short.

Then, as Tip was getting dressed, one of the—his aides ran up to him, out of breath, and said he had just found out that no drinking was allowed before dinner, only afterwards. And Tip panicked a little bit. He realized he had to prepare. So he grabbed a few pages from "Famous Irishmen of America," underlined some passages, acted like he had planned it all along. The speech went extraordinarily well, and afterwards, he was complimented on his thoroughness and studiousness in preparing for the speech.

So Tip's lesson was: Always know your audience, and don't count on drinks getting you through the evening. [*Laughter*]

But Tip also taught us something else. He taught us that even in the midst of partisanship and passion, true friendship can exist in this town. Tip and President Reagan famously had fierce battles and genuine disagreements. But after the work ended, the two men did their best to put partisanship aside. According to Tip, President Reagan used to begin calls with, "Hello, Tip, is it after 6 o'clock?" [*Laughter*] To which the Speaker would reply, "Absolutely, Mr. President." And then they could enjoy each other's company.

For his part, the President said he always knew Tip was behind him, even if it was just at the State of the Union—[*laughter*]—whispering to the Vice President after every policy proposal, "Forget it." [*Laughter*] "No way." "Fat chance." [*Laughter*] I can relate. [*Laughter*]

So it is no surprise that the two proud Irishmen came together to start this luncheon, with the Speaker promising to cook some Boston corned beef and the President offering to "polish up some new Irish jokes." Later, our friend Ted Kennedy and others persuaded Taoiseach to join them. And today, the only argument we have is over who has more green in their family tree.

For once, I have some bragging rights here. Last spring, the Taoiseach and Mrs. Kenny hosted Michelle and I for a wonderful visit to Ireland. And one of the highlights was a trip to the small village of Moneygall, where my great-great-great-grandfather on my mother's side lived before he set sail for America. I met my eighth cousin Henry, who has my ears, I might point out. [*Laughter*] We had a pint of Guinness at the local pub. And I got a chance to see firsthand the kind of hospitality that the big-hearted people of Ireland have always been known for.

So today is about celebrating those people, as well as the tens of millions of Americans who trace their heritage across the ocean to the Emerald Isle. Never has a nation so small had such an enormous impact on another. Never has anyone taught us more about the value of faith and friendship, about the capacity of the human spirit, about the simple truth that it's harder to disagree when we recognize ourselves in each other, which is easier to do when we're all wearing green.

So to Taoiseach Kenny, I want to thank you and Fionnuala for joining us here today. And I want to thank the people of Ireland for their friendship, now and always. Cheers.

NOTE: The President spoke at 12:58 p.m. in the Rayburn Room at the U.S. Capitol. In his remarks, he referred to Prime Minister Enda Kenny of Ireland and his wife Fionnuala; and Ireland's Ambassador to the U.S. Michael Collins and his wife Marie. He also referred to his cousin Henry Healy of Moneygall, Ireland. Audio was not available for verification of the content of these remarks.

Remarks at a St. Patrick's Day Reception
March 20, 2012

President Obama. Hello, everybody!

Audience members. Hello!

President Obama. Well, welcome to the White House. This does not sound like a shy crowd. [*Laughter*]

As you may have noticed, today is not, in fact, St. Patrick's Day. [*Laughter*] We just wanted to prove that America considers Ireland a dear and steadfast friend every day of the year. Some of you may have noticed, we even brought the cherry blossoms out early for our Irish and Northern Irish visitors. And we will be sure to plant these beautiful shamrocks right away.

I want to welcome back my good friend Taoiseach Kenny; his extraordinary wife Fionnuala. This has been our third working visit in just over a year, and each one has been better than the last.

I've had the pleasure to welcome back First Minister Peter Robinson; Deputy First Minister Martin McGuinness of Northern Ireland as well.

And, everyone, please welcome my new friends from Moneygall. My long-lost cousin

Henry; his mother Mary is here as well. And my favorite pub keeper, Ollie Hayes, is here with his beautiful wife. He was interested in hiring Michelle—[*laughter*]—when she was pouring a pint. I said, she's too busy, maybe at the end of our second term.

In return, I did take them out for a pint at the Dubliner here in Washington, DC, on Saturday. That's right, I saw some of you there. [*Laughter*] I won't—I didn't take pictures. And I've asked them to please say hello to everybody back home for me.

Now, while there are too many Irish Americans to acknowledge by name here tonight, I do want to thank Martin O'Malley and his band for rocking the White House for the evening. It's said that the curse of the Irish, as the Governor must know, is not that they don't know the words to a song—it's that they know them all. [*Laughter*]

As you may know, I finally got to spend a day in Ireland with Michelle last May. I visited my ancestral village of Moneygall, saw my great-great-great-grandfather's house. I had the distinct honor of addressing the Irish people from College Green in Dublin. And when it comes to their famous reputation for hospitality and good cheer, the Irish outdid themselves. Michelle and I received absolutely the warmest of welcomes, and I've been trying to return the favor as best I can.

There really was something magical about the whole day, and I know that I'm not the only person who feels that way when they visit Ireland. Even my most famously Irish American predecessor was surprised about how deeply Ireland affected him when he visited in his third year as President. "It is strange," President Kennedy said on his last day in Ireland, "that so many years and so many generations pass, and still some of us who come on this trip could feel ourselves among neighbors, even though we are separated by generations, by time, and by thousands of miles."

I know most of you can relate to that. I think anyone who's had a chance to visit can relate. And that's why Jackie Kennedy later visited Ireland with her children and gave one of President Kennedy's dog tags to his cousins in

Dunganstown. And that's why I felt so at home when I visited Moneygall.

When my great-great-great-grandfather arrived in New York City after a voyage that began there, the St. Patrick's Society in Brooklyn had just held its first annual banquet. And a toast was made to family back home enduring what were impossibly difficult years: "Through gloomy shadows hang over thee now, as darkness is densest, even just before day, so thy gloom, truest Erin, may soon pass away."

Because for all the remarkable things the Irish have done in the course of human history—keeping alive the flame of knowledge in dark ages, outlasting a great hunger, forging a peace that once seemed impossible—the green strands they have woven into America's heart, from their tiniest villages through our greatest cities, is something truly unique on the world stage. And these strands of affection will never fray, nor will they come undone.

While those times and the troubles of later generations were far graver than anything we could fathom today, many of our people are still fighting to get back on solid ground after several challenging years. But we choose to rise to these times for the same reason we rose to those tougher times: Because we are all proud peoples who share more than sprawling family trees. We are peoples who share an unshakeable faith, an unbending commitment to our fellow man, and a resilient and audacious hope. And that's why I say of Ireland tonight what I said in Dublin last May: This little country that inspires the biggest things, its best days are still ahead.

So I propose a toast to the Taoiseach and the people of Ireland. Do I have any—where's my drink? [*Laughter*] Here it is, here it is. All right, here we go. It's only water but—obviously, somebody didn't prepare. [*Laughter*]

To quote your first President, Douglas Hyde: "A word is more lasting than the riches of the world." And tonight, grateful for our shared past and hopeful for our common future, I give my word to you, Mr. Prime Minister, and to the people of Ireland: As long as I am President, you will have a strong friend, a steadfast ally, and a faithful partner in the United States of America.

Ladies and gentlemen, Taoiseach Kenny. Cheers!

[At this point, Prime Minister Enda Kenny of Ireland made brief remarks, during which he presented President Obama with a certificate of Irish heritage and a bowl of shamrocks.]

President Obama. Well, thank you. First of all, this will have a special place of honor alongside my birth certificate. [*Laughter*] Absolutely. Absolutely. The shamrocks have brought good luck to our garden over the past few years. And I am extraordinarily grateful to you, Taoiseach and Fionnuala, for just being such wonderful hosts to us when we were there. But I think that you get a sense from this crowd that you have a second home on the other side of the Atlantic and that good cheer and warmth is fully reciprocated.

So happy St. Patrick's week, everybody. God bless you. May God bless both our countries. Have a wonderful time while you're here. Don't break anything.

NOTE: The President spoke at 7:04 p.m. in the East Room at the White House. In his remarks, he referred to his cousin Henry Healy of Moneygall, Ireland, and his mother Mary Healy; Ollie Hayes, owner, Ollie Hayes Bar in Moneygall, Ireland, and his wife Majella; and Gov. Martin J. O'Malley of Maryland. The transcript released by the Office of the Press Secretary also included the remarks of Vice President Joe Biden, who introduced the President, and Prime Minister Kenny.

Remarks at the Copper Mountain Solar 1 Facility in Boulder City, Nevada
March 21, 2012

The President. Hello, everybody. Good afternoon. Everybody, please have a seat. Have a seat. It is wonderful to be here. Thank you so much. It is great to be in Boulder City.

A couple people I want to thank for their outstanding work. First of all, our Interior Secretary, Ken Salazar, is in the house. He's the guy in the nice-looking hat. Not only does it look good, but it protects his head, because the hair has gotten a little thin up there. [*Laughter*]

Audience member. One is a good-looking guy.

The President. He is a good-looking guy.

Audience member. One of them. One of them.

The President. One of them. [*Laughter*] There— that's right. There's the other guy. [*Laughter*]

I also want to thank your mayor—a big supporter of solar energy—and that's Roger Tobler, for being here. Where's Roger? Here he is right there. I just met his beautiful daughter. It's great to see you.

I want to thank Jeffrey Martin, CEO of Sempra, and John and Kevin, who helped just give me this tour.

And Boulder City is the first stop on a tour where I'll be talking about what we're calling an all-of-the-above energy strategy—all of the above—a strategy that relies on producing more oil and gas here in America, but also more biofuels, more fuel-efficient cars, more wind power, and as you can see, a whole lot more solar power.

This is the largest solar plant of its kind anywhere in the country. That's worth applauding. Every year, you produce enough clean energy to power around 17,000 homes. And that's just the beginning. Things are going so well that another plant is already under construction down the road that will eventually power another 45,000 homes. And a third plant is in development that will be one day able to power around 66,000 homes.

Now, this is an area that was hit hard by the recession, and that's true of the whole State. You guys have been through a lot. But you haven't given up. You looked around at this flat, beautiful land and all this sun—I just—I asked the question, how many days of sun do you get a year—320; that's pretty good—and decided that Boulder City was the perfect place to generate solar power.

In fact, as I was talking to the folks from Sempra, they were explaining that this location is almost optimal for solar power generation, not only because it's flat. Transmission lines were already here, the sun is traveling, and there's no haze, and it's absolutely clear. And so this is an extraordinary opportunity for the community. And when a business showed up with plans to build a new solar plant, hundreds of local workers got jobs because of it. Thousands of families are now powering their homes with a cleaner, renewable source of energy.

And this is not just happening here in Boulder City, it's happening in cities and towns all across America. According to experts, we've now got more than 5,600 solar companies nationwide, and many of them are small businesses. There are solar companies in every single State in the Union. And today, we're producing enough solar energy to power 730,000 American homes. And because of the investments we've made as a nation, the use of renewable energies has actually doubled.

So this is an industry on the rise. It's a source of energy that's becoming cheaper; we all know it's cleaner. And more and more businesses are starting to take notice. They're starting to look around for more places like Boulder City to set up shop.

And when I took office I said, why not give these businesses some access to public lands that aren't otherwise being utilized? At the time, there wasn't a single solar project in place on public lands, not one. Today, thanks to some great work by Ken Salazar, we've got 16 solar projects approved. And when they're complete, we'll be generating enough energy to power 2 million homes. And that's progress.

We're also enforcing our trade laws to make sure countries like China aren't giving their solar companies an unfair advantage over ours. And that's important because countries all around the world—China, Germany, you name it—they understand the potential. They understand the fact that as countries all around the world become more interested in power generation—their population is expanding, their income level is going up, they use more electricity—and we're going to have to make

sure that we're the guys who are selling them the technology and the know-how to make sure that they're getting the power that they need.

In fact, just yesterday our administration determined China wasn't playing fair when it came to solar power. And so we took the first step towards leveling the playing field, because my attitude is, when the playing field is level, then American workers and American businesses are always going to win. And that's why we've got to make sure that our laws are properly enforced.

Now, you'd think, given this extraordinary site, given the fact that this is creating jobs, generating power, helping to keep our environment clean, making us more competitive globally, you'd think that everybody would be supportive of solar power. That's what you'd think. And yet, if some politicians had their way, there won't be any more public investment in solar energy. There won't be as many new jobs and new businesses.

Some of these folks want to dismiss the promise of solar power and wind power and fuel-efficient cars. In fact, they make jokes about it. One Member of Congress who shall remain unnamed called these jobs "phony"—called them phony jobs. I mean, think about that mindset, that attitude that says because something is new, it must not be real. If these guys were around when Columbus set sail, they'd be charter members of the Flat Earth Society. [*Laughter*] It's—we were just talking about this: that a lack of imagination, a belief that you can't do something in a new way. That's not how we operate here in America. That's not who we are. That's not what we're about.

These politicians need to come to Boulder City and see what I'm seeing. They should talk to the people who are involved in this industry, who have benefited from the jobs, who benefit from ancillary businesses that are related to what's going on right here.

Now, all of you know that when it comes to new technologies, the payoffs aren't always going to come right away. Sometimes you need a jumpstart to make it happen. That's been true of every innovation that we've ever had. And we know that some discoveries won't pan out.

There's the VCR and the Beta and the—all that stuff. [*Laughter*]

And each successive generation recognizes that some technologies are going to work, some won't; some companies will fail, some companies will succeed. Not every auto company succeeded in the early days of the auto industry. Not every airplane manufacturer succeeded in the early days of the aviation. But we understood as Americans that if we keep on this track, and we're at the cutting edge, then that ultimately will make our economy stronger, and it will make the United States stronger. It will create jobs. It will create businesses. It will create opportunities for middle class Americans and folks who want to get into the middle class. That's who we are. That's what we're about.

So I want everybody here to know that as long as I'm President, we will not walk away from the promise of clean energy. We're not going to walk away from places like Boulder City. I'm not going to give up on the new to cede our position to China or Germany or all the other competitors out there who are making massive investments in clean energy technology. I refuse to see us stand by and not make the same commitment. That's not what we do in America. It's not who we are as a country.

One of the main reasons I ran for this office is I didn't think that our leaders were doing enough to tackle the big challenges, the hard challenges, to seize the big opportunities. And energy is one of the best examples. We have been talking about changing our energy policies for 30 years. When I was the age of these guys right here, when I was 10, 11, right, in the seventies, and my grandparents were complaining about long gas lines, we were talking about how we were going to do things differently. Thirty, forty years, and we keep on doing the same stuff. We keep on punting. We keep on putting it off. For decades, Washington kept kicking the can down the road.

I don't want to do that anymore. I want to make sure when these guys are grown up that they're seeing solar panels all across the country. They're seeing American-made energy and

American-made power. They're benefiting from a cleaner environment. They're seeing jobs and opportunity. That's what I want to see.

So, as long as I'm President, we're going to develop every available source of energy. That is a promise that I'm making to you.

And yes, that means we make investments in stuff that is new, and we stop subsidizing stuff that's old. The current members of the Flat Earth Society in Congress—[*laughter*]—they would rather see us continue to provide $4 billion in tax subsidies, tax giveaways, to the oil companies, $4 billion to an industry that is making record profits. Every time you fill up the pump, they're making money. They are doing just fine. They're not having any problems.

And yet, on top of what we're paying at the pump, we're also going to give them $4 billion in subsidies that could be going into making sure there were investments in clean energy for the future? That doesn't make any sense. Does that make any sense?

Audience members. No!

The President. All right, I just wanted to make sure. Because I didn't think it was a wise use of your tax dollars. [*Laughter*]

We have subsidized oil companies for a century. We want to encourage production of oil and gas and make sure that wherever we've got American resources, we are tapping into them. But they don't need an additional incentive when gas is $3.75 a gallon, when oil is $120 a barrel, $125 a barrel. They don't need additional incentives. They are doing fine.

Audience member. [*Inaudible*]—our retirement!

The President. Yes. A century of subsidies to oil companies is long enough. It's time to end the taxpayer giveaways to an industry that's rarely been more profitable and double down on investments in an energy industry that has never been more promising. That's what we need to do.

So Congress needs to pass more tax credits for projects like this one, needs to provide certainty when it comes to these tax credits. We need to go out there and do what a lot of States are doing right now, which is saying, let's get a certain percentage of our energy from clean energy sources. Because when we do that, that gives a company like this one certainty that they're going to have customers, and they can invest more and build more.

We need to keep Americans on the job. We need to keep these homes powered by clean energy. We need to support the businesses that are doing it.

And again, I just want everybody to be clear, because sometimes, when you listen to the news and you listen to some of these other politicians, they seem a little bit confused about what I'm saying. We are going to continue producing oil and gas at a record pace. That's got to be part of what we do. We need energy to grow. That's why we're producing more oil right now, here in America, than at any time in the last 8 years—any time in the last 8 years. We're opening up more land for oil exploration. We've got more oil rigs operating. There are more pipelines out there that are being approved. I'll be visiting one of those rigs and one of those pipelines this week.

But an energy strategy that focuses only on drilling and not on an energy strategy that will free ourselves from our dependence on foreign oil, that's a losing strategy. And that's not a strategy I'm going to pursue. America uses 20 percent of the world's oil, and we've got 2 percent of the world's oil reserves. Think about—I wasn't a math major, but I just want—[*laughter*]—if you're using 20, you've only got 2, that means you got to bring in the rest from someplace else. Why wouldn't we want to start finding alternatives that make us less reliant, less dependent on what's going on in the Middle East?

So we've got to develop new energy technologies, new energy sources. It's the only way

forward. And here in Boulder City, you know that better than anybody. You know the promise that lies ahead because this city has always been about the future. Eight decades ago, in the midst of the Great Depression, the people of Boulder City were busy working on another energy project you may have heard of. Like today, it was a little bit ahead of its time. It was a little bit bigger than this solar plant; it was a little louder too. It was called the Hoover Dam. And at the time, it was the largest dam in the world. Even today, it stands as a testimony to American ingenuity, American imagination, the power of the American spirit, a testimony to the notion we can do anything.

That was true back then; it is true today. You know the choice we need to make when it comes to energy. We've got to invest in a sustained, all-of-the-above strategy that develops every available source of energy. We've got to stay ahead of the curve. We've got to make sure that we're taking some risks. We've got to make sure that we're making the investments that are necessary. We've got to support extraordinary entrepreneurs that are on the cutting edge. That's who we are. That's what we do. And if we keep on doing it, nothing's going to stop us.

Thank you very much, everybody. God bless you. God bless the United States of America. Thank you.

NOTE: The President spoke at 1:10 p.m. In his remarks, he referred to Alyssa Tobler, daughter of Mayor Roger L. Tobler of Boulder City, NV; Jeffrey W. Martin, president and chief executive officer, John A. Sowers, vice president of operations, and Kevin Gillespie, director of operations, Sempra U.S. Gas and Power, LLC; and Rep. John C. Fleming.

Remarks in Maljamar, New Mexico
March 21, 2012

Hello, New Mexico! Thank you so much for being here! Everybody, have a seat. I know it's a little windy out here, but you guys are used to it. It is wonderful to be back in New Mexico.

I want to acknowledge a couple of folks who are here. Well, first, mainly I want to thank Concho Resources and the Southwest New Mexico ConocoPhillips team for helping to set this up. Thank you. Good job, everybody.

It was a wonderful trip over here. We took the helicopter. We had landed in Roswell. I announced to people when I landed that I had come in peace. [*Laughter*] Let me tell you, there are more 9- and 10-year-old boys around the country—when I meet them, they ask me, "Have you been to Roswell, and is it true what they say?" [*Laughter*] And I tell them, "If I told you, I'd have to kill you." So—and their eyes get all big. [*Laughter*] So we're going to keep our secrets here.

I'm here to talk about what we're calling an all-of-the-above energy strategy: a strategy that relies on producing more oil and gas here in America, but also producing more biofuels in America, more fuel-efficient cars in America, more wind power in America, and more solar power in America. I believe this all-of-the-above approach is the only way we can continue to reduce our dependence on foreign oil and ultimately put an end to some of these gas spikes that we're going through right now and that obviously hurt a lot of families all across the country.

Now, you wouldn't know it from listening to some of these folks who are running for office—I won't mention their names, you know who they are—but producing more oil here in our own country has been and will continue to be a key part of my energy strategy. Under my administration, America is producing more oil today than at any time in the last 8 years. That's a fact. That is a fact. We've approved dozens of new oil and gas pipelines, and we've announced our support for more, including one that I'm going to be visiting tomorrow in Oklahoma.

And we've quadrupled the number of operating oil rigs to a record high. More than 70 of those rigs are right here in this area. And I had a chance to see them all, I think, as I was flying over here. [*Laughter*] In fact, business is so good that today the biggest problem is finding enough qualified truck drivers to move all the oil that's coming out of these wells down to the refinery. Too much oil, that's a good problem to have.

Now, this is public land, it's been leased to the oil companies by the Federal Government.

And over the last 3 years, I've directed my administration to open up millions of acres, just like this, for oil and gas exploration in 23 different States. Let me repeat that: millions of acres in 23 different States. That's just onshore. Offshore, I've directed my administration to open up more than 75 percent of our potential oil resources. And that includes an area in the Gulf of Mexico that we opened up a few months ago that could produce more than 400 million barrels of oil—about 38 million acres in the Gulf.

And I want to thank my Secretary of the Interior, Ken Salazar, who is here, because he helped make it happen. Where did Ken go? He's right over here.

Now, I make this point so that if you hear anybody on TV saying that somehow we're against drilling for oil, then you'll know that they either don't know what they're talking about, or they're not telling you the truth. We're drilling all over the place. That's one of the reasons we've been able to reduce our dependence on foreign oil every year since I took office. In 2010, it was under 50 percent for the first time in 13 years. And you have my word that we will keep drilling everywhere we can, and we'll do it while protecting the health and safety of the American people. That's a commitment that I'm making.

Now, there's no contradiction to say that we're going to keep on producing American oil and American gas and also saying drilling can't be the only part of our energy strategy. A recent independent analysis showed that over the last 36 years, there has been no connection between the amount of oil that we drill in this country and the price of gasoline. There's no connection. And the reason is that we've got a worldwide oil market. And so even if we produce more, the fact of the matter is we use 20 percent of the world's oil. And even if we drilled every square inch of this country, we'd still only have 2 or 3 or 4 percent of the world's known oil reserves.

So what ends up happening is, the price is impacted not just by us, but by everybody, in the amount of oil that's used worldwide. And that means if we don't develop new sources of energy along with oil and gas, and if we don't develop technologies to use less energy for the same amount of output, we're always going to depend on other countries for our energy needs.

If we do nothing, every time there's instability in the Middle East, we will feel it at the pump even if we're drilling nonstop here in New Mexico and all across the country. If we only drill for our 2 percent of the world's oil reserves, the price of gas will continue to rise. Part of the reason is because China and India, they're growing. China added 10 million cars in 2010—10 million cars just in this one country. And they're just going to keep on going, which means they're going to use more and more oil. That's not a future I want for America.

In this country we control our own destiny. We control our own resources. We control our own economy. We chart our own course. I don't want to be subject to the whim of somebody, somewhere else. And that's why we need an all-of-the-above energy strategy.

So we're going to develop every possible source of American-made energy. Oil and gas, wind power, solar power, biofuels, fuel-efficient cars and trucks that get more miles to the gallon, that's our future. And the good news is we're already seeing progress.

I just came from Boulder City, Nevada, which is home to the Nation's largest solar plant, a plant that was built by hundreds of American workers and that's now powering tens of thousands of homes. I've been visiting universities and factories where American workers are building cars that get more miles per gallon, because after 30 years of not doing anything, we put in place some of the toughest fuel economy standards in our history. And now, by the middle of the next decade, our cars will average nearly 55 miles per gallon, which is going to save the average family about $8,000 during the life of that car. I know you can use $8,000.

Audience member. [*Inaudible*]

The President. Absolutely—[*laughter*]—I don't know anybody who can't.

We've got to continue down this path. And that means we've got to make some important choices for our future. The oil companies that are drilling here in New Mexico and all over the country are making record profits. And like I said, as long as we drill safely and responsibly, I'm committed to making sure that we open more acres to gas and oil exploration. I want American oil companies to do well. I have said, though, it doesn't make sense for us be providing a $4 billion subsidy when oil and gas are doing plenty well on their own. Oil companies are making record profits and that's good. But we don't need to subsidize them. Four billion dollars is a lot of money, and we've been subsidizing them for a hundred years.

So my attitude is, let's make sure that we use that money in smarter ways to develop a whole range of new energy sources, since the oil industry is mature and has already taken off. Instead of investing tax dollars in profitable companies, let's invest in our future. Let's tell Congress to get their act together, let's allocate these subsidies in a smart kind of way.

Because if we're going to end our dependence on foreign oil and bring gas prices down once and for all, we've got to develop every single source of American energy. We've got to develop new technologies that help use less energy in our cars, our homes, our buildings, our businesses. That's where we need to go. That's what's at stake right now. And with your help, we're going to build that future.

So we're going to keep on seeing this incredible part of America's legacy, this incredible natural resource that we have, but we're also going to use our ingenuity and our brainpower to develop new sources of energy. That's going to be the key to our future. That's how we're going to build an economy that lasts. And I'm going to need your help, New Mexico, to make it happen.

Thank you very much, everybody. Appreciate you. God bless you. God bless New Mexico and the United States of America. Thank you.

NOTE: The President spoke at 6:16 p.m. at a well site on Federal land outside of Maljamar, NM.

Remarks at the TransCanada Pipe Storage Yard in Stillwater, Oklahoma
March 22, 2012

The President. Hello, Oklahoma! Well, it's good to be here. Everybody, have a seat. Have a seat.

Audience member. I love you, Mr. President!

The President. I love you back. It's wonderful to see you.

It is good to be back in Oklahoma. I haven't been back here since the campaign, and everybody looks like they're doing just fine. [*Laughter*] Thank you so much for your hospitality. It is wonderful to be here.

Yesterday I visited Nevada and New Mexico to talk about what we're calling an all-of-the-above energy strategy. It's a strategy that will keep us on track to further reduce our dependence on foreign oil, put more people back to work, and ultimately help to curb the spike in gas prices that we're seeing year after year after year.

So today I've come to Cushing, an oil town, because producing more oil and gas here at home has been and will continue to be a critical part of an all-of-the-above energy strategy.

Now, under my administration, America is producing more oil today than at any time in the last 8 years. Over the—[*applause*]—that's important to know. Over the last 3 years, I've directed my administration to open up millions of acres for gas and oil exploration across 23 different States. We're opening up more than 75 percent of our potential oil resources offshore. We've quadrupled the number of operating rigs to a record high. We've added enough new oil and gas pipeline to encircle the Earth and then some.

So we are drilling all over the place right now. That's not the challenge. That's not the problem. In fact, the problem in a place like Cushing is that we're actually producing so much oil and gas in places like North Dakota and Colorado that we don't have enough pipeline capacity to transport all of it to where it needs to go, both to refineries, and then eventually all across the country and around the world. There's a bottleneck right here because we can't get enough of the oil to our refineries fast enough. And if we could, then we would be able to increase our oil supplies at a time when they're needed as much as possible.

Now, right now a company called TransCanada has applied to build a new pipeline to speed more oil from Cushing to state-of-the-art refineries down on the Gulf Coast. And today I'm directing my administration to cut through the redtape, break through the bureaucratic hurdles, and make this project a priority, to go ahead and get it done.

Now, you wouldn't know all this from listening to the television set. [*Laughter*] This whole issue of the Keystone pipeline has generated obviously a lot of controversy and a lot of politics. And that's because the original route from Canada into the United States was planned through an area in Nebraska that supplies some drinking water for nearly 2 million Americans and irrigation for a good portion of America's croplands. And Nebraskans of all political stripes, including the Republican Governor there, raised some concerns about the safety and wisdom of that route.

So to be extra careful that the construction of the pipeline in an area like that wouldn't put the health and the safety of the American people at risk, our experts said that we needed a certain amount of time to review the project. Unfortunately, Congress decided they wanted their own timeline. Not the company, not the experts, but Members of Congress, who decided this might be a fun political issue, decided to try to intervene and make it impossible for us to make an informed decision.

So what we've said to the company is, we're happy to review future permits. And today we're making this new pipeline from Cushing to the Gulf a priority. So the southern leg of it we're making a priority, and we're going to go ahead and get that done. The northern portion of it we're going to have to review properly to make sure that the health and safety of the American people are protected. That's common sense.

But the fact is that my administration has approved dozens of new oil and gas pipelines over the last 3 years, including one from Canada. And as long as I'm President, we're going to keep on encouraging oil development and infrastructure, and we're going to do it in a way that protects the health and safety of the American people. We don't have to choose between one or the other. We can do both.

So I just—if you guys are talking to your friends, your neighbors, your coworkers, your aunts, or your uncles and they're wondering what's going on in terms of oil production, you just tell them anybody who suggests that somehow we're suppressing domestic oil production isn't paying attention. They are not paying attention.

What you also need to tell them is anybody who says that just drilling more gas and more oil by itself will bring down gas prices tomorrow or the next day or even next year, they're also not paying attention. They're not playing it straight. Because we are drilling more, we are producing more. But the fact is, producing more oil at home isn't enough by itself to bring gas prices down.

And the reason is we've got an oil market that is global, that is worldwide. And I've been saying for the last few weeks, and I want everybody to understand this, we use 20 percent of the world's oil; we only produce 2 percent of the world's oil. Even if we opened up every inch of the country, if I put a oil rig on the South Lawn—[*laughter*]—if we had one right next to the Washington Monument, even if we drilled every little bit of this great country of ours, we'd still have to buy the rest of our needs from someplace else if we keep on using the same amount of energy, the same amount of oil.

The price of oil will still be set by the global market. And that means every time there's tensions that rise in the Middle East, which is what's happening right now, so will the price of gas. The main reason the gas prices are high right now is because people are worried about what's happening with Iran. It doesn't have to do with domestic oil production. It has to do with the oil markets looking and saying, you

know what, if something happens, there could be trouble, and so we're going to price oil higher just in case.

Now, that's not the future that we want. We don't want to be vulnerable to something that's happening on the other side of the world somehow affecting our economy or hurting a lot of folks who have to drive to get to work. That's not the future I want for America. That's not the future I want for our kids. I want us to control our own energy destiny. I want us to determine our own course.

So yes, we're going to keep on drilling. Yes, we're going to keep on emphasizing production. Yes, we're going to make sure that we can get oil to where it's needed. But what we're also going to be doing as part of an all-above—all-of-the-above strategy is looking at how we can continually improve the utilization of renewable energy sources, new clean energy sources, and how do we become more efficient in our use of energy.

That means producing more biofuels, which can be great for our farmers and great for rural economies. It means more fuel-efficient cars. It means more solar power. It means more wind power, which, by the way, nearly tripled here in Oklahoma over the past 3 years, in part because of some of our policies.

We want every source of American-made energy. I don't want the energy jobs of tomorrow going to other countries. I want them here in the United States of America. And that's what an all-of-the-above energy strategy is all about. That's how we break our dependence on foreign oil.

Now, the good news is we're already seeing progress. Yesterday I went, in Nevada, to the largest solar plant of its kind anywhere in the country. Hundreds of workers built it. It's powering thousands of homes, and they're expanding to tens of thousands of homes more as they put more capacity online.

After 30 years of not doing anything, we've finally increased fuel efficiency standards on cars and trucks, and Americans are now designing and building cars that will go nearly twice as far on the same gallon of gas by the middle of the next decade. And that's going to save the average family $8,000 over the life of a car. And it's going to save a lot of companies a lot of money, because they're hurt by rising fuel costs as well.

All of these steps have helped put America on the path to greater energy independence. Since I took office, our dependence on foreign oil has gone down every single year. Last year, we imported 1 million fewer barrels per day than the year before. Think about that. America, at a time when we're growing, is actually importing less oil from overseas because we're using it smarter and more efficiently. America is now importing less than half the oil we use for the first time in more than a decade.

So the key is to keep it going, Oklahoma. We've got to make sure that we don't go backwards, that we keep going forwards. If we're going to end our dependence on foreign oil, if we're going to bring gas prices down once and for all, as opposed to just playing politics with it every single year, then what we're going to have to do is to develop every single source of energy that we've got, every new technology that can help us become more efficient.

We've got to use our innovation. We've got to use our brain power. We've got to use our creativity. We've got to have a vision for the future, not just constantly looking backwards at the past. That's where we need to go. That's the future we can build.

And that's what America has always been about, is building the future. We've always been at the cutting edge. We're always ahead of the curve. Whether it's Thomas Edison or the Wright Brothers or Steve Jobs, we're always thinking about what's the next thing. And that's how we have to think about energy. And if we do, not only are we going to see jobs and growth and success here in Cushing, Oklahoma, we're going to see it all across the country.

All right? Thank you very much, everybody. God bless you. God bless the United States of America.

NOTE: The President spoke at 10:22 a.m. In his remarks, he referred to Gov. David E. Heineman of Nebraska. The related Executive order and memorandum are listed in Appendix D at the end of this volume.

Remarks at Ohio State University in Columbus, Ohio
March 22, 2012

The President. Hello, Buckeyes! Oh, yes. Well, it is good to be back at the Ohio State University. I want to thank you——

Audience member. I love you!

The President. I love you back. I am thrilled to be here. I want to thank a couple of people. First of all, the outstanding mayor of Columbus, Michael Coleman, is here. I want to thank OSU Provost Joe Alutto.

And I just got this extraordinary tour from Giorgio Rizzoni, who's the director of the Center for Automotive Research. So give him a big round of applause.

Now, let's face it, a Presidential visit isn't even close to being the biggest thing this weekend on campus. [*Laughter*] And despite what Vijay said, I did have the Buckeyes heading to the Final Four. I'm just saying. I think Sullinger is going to have a big game tonight. And I promise you I didn't do it because I knew I was

coming here, because I am coldblooded when it comes to filling out my brackets. [*Laughter*] So I genuinely think you guys are looking good.

And by the way, I just read somewhere that 1 in every 4 teams in the Sweet 16 is from Ohio. You've got Ohio State, Ohio University, Xavier—Xavier is in the—Cincinnati.

Audience members. Boo!

The President. I'm not going to get in the middle of this. [*Laughter*] I do want to just say no State has ever done this before. So it's a testimony to Ohio basketball.

And I want to thank Vijay for the outstanding introduction, very much appreciate that.

Now, this is our last stop on a trip where we've been talking about an all-of-the-above energy strategy for America, a strategy where we produce more oil, produce more gas, but also produce more American biofuels and more fuel-efficient cars, more solar power, more wind power, more power from the oceans, more clean and renewable energy—[*applause*]—more clean and renewable energy.

You know what I'm talking about here, because this school is a national leader in developing new sources of energy and advanced vehicles that use a lot less energy.

I just had a chance to take a tour of the Center for Automotive Research. Now, I admit the best part of it was seeing the Buckeye Bullet, which has gone over 300 miles an hour and is now shooting for 400 miles an hour. And I asked the guys who were helping to design this whether mom was going to let them actually test-drive this thing, and the answer was no. [*Laughter*] Only professional drivers are permitted.

But for anybody who's not familiar with this, the Buckeye Bullet is the fastest electric car in the world—the fastest in the world. I don't know who's going to need to go that fast. [*Laughter*] But it is a testament to the ingenuity here at Ohio State and what is essential to American leadership when it comes to energy: our brain power.

I will say, though, when Malia gets her license in a few years, she will not be allowed to go 300 miles per—an hour. [*Laughter*]

Now, one of the reasons that I've been talking so much about fuel-efficient cars and new sources of energy is obviously because we're seeing another spike in gas prices right now. And that's tough on folks. I remember when I was a student, filling up was always tough. And gas prices are putting pressure not just on students, but on a lot of families all across Ohio, all across the country. Whether you're trying to get to school, go to work, go grocery shopping, dropping off your kids, you've got to be able to fill up that gas tank. Right now, for most people, you don't have a choice.

So, when prices spike, that tax hike feels like a—or that gas spike feels like a tax hike coming right out of your pocket. That's part of the reason that we passed a payroll tax cut at the beginning of this year so that the average American would get an extra $40 in every paycheck to help offset the price of gas. So that's going to offer some relief.

But the bigger question is how do we make sure that these spikes in gas prices don't keep on happening, because we've seen this movie before. This happens just about every year. This happened this time last year. Gas prices were even higher in the spring and summer of 2008. It has been going on for years, for decades.

And every time prices start to go up, especially during an election year, politicians, they start dusting off their three-point plan for $2 gas. [*Laughter*] Although this year, they decided it was going to be $2.50. [*Laughter*] This year they decided it was going to be $2.50. Now, I don't know where they pick that number, $2.50. Because it could have been $2.40, I guess. They could have said $2.10. They could have said 50 cents a gallon. But they all make the same promise. They head down to the gas station, and they make sure a few cameras are following them, and then they tell you how we're going to have cheap gas forever if you just vote for them. And it has been the same script for 30 years, the same thing. It has been like a bad rerun.

And when you ask them, what specifically is your——

[*At this point, there was a disruption in the audience.*]

Sir, I'm here to speak to these folks. You can hold your own rally. You're being rude. Sir, we're trying to talk to these people. Show—I'll be happy to read your book; if you want to give me your book, I'll be happy to read it. But don't interrupt my conversation with these folks, all right? Show me some courtesy. All right? Show me some courtesy. I'll be happy to take your book. But don't interrupt everybody else. All right? Okay.

Now, where was I? [*Laughter*] Go ahead and get that book from him, guys. He wants to give me a book. Please feel free to grab it. You're touting this book; make sure that you've given it to us.

All right, now that we've gotten that settled. [*Laughter*] Now, the question is, why is it that every year we hear the same story about how we're going to have $2 gas or $1.50 gas or whatever price they come up with, if we would just drill for more oil? That's the solution that you always here. Prices will immediately come down, and all our problems will go away, like magic.

There are two problems with that. First of all, we have been drilling. We're drilling right now. Under my administration, America is producing more oil today than at any time in the last 8 years—at any time. That's a fact. Over the last 3 years, we've opened millions of acres of land in 23 different States for oil and gas exploration. That's a fact. Offshore, I've directed my administration to open up more than 75 percent of potential oil resources. We've quadrupled the number of operating oil rigs to a record high.

I just visited New Mexico. Their big problem is they don't have enough truck drivers to transport all the oil that they are producing. We've added enough oil and gas pipeline to circle the entire Earth and then some. I just visited one of those new pipelines in Oklahoma, and today I directed my administration to make sure that we cut the redtape in terms of reducing some of these bottlenecks.

So the problem is not that we're not drilling or that we're not producing more oil. We are producing more oil than any time in the last 8 years. That's not the problem. There are probably a few spots where we're not drilling, it's true. I'm not drilling in the South Lawn. [*Laughter*] We're not drilling next to the Washington Monument. We're not drilling in Ohio Stadium.

So there are some spots out there that we are not drilling. But we're doing so in a way that protects the health and safety of the American people and protects America's incredible bounty that God gave us, our resources.

So that's point number one. But the second issue, which, because we got a lot of young people, you guys understand, is that a strategy that relies only on drilling defies the fact that America uses 20 percent of the world's oil, but we only have 2 percent of the world's known oil reserves. So we use 20 percent; we have 2 percent. Who's a math major here? [*Laughter*]

All right. If I'm not mistaken, that leaves us about 18-percent short. [*Laughter*]

We can't simply drill our way out of the problem. Even if we drilled every square inch of this country right now, we're going to be relying on other countries for oil. Does anybody here think that's a good strategy?

Audience members. No!

The President. Of course it isn't. We shouldn't have to pay more at the pump every time there's instability in the Middle East, which is the main reason gas prices are going up right now. We should not be held hostage to events on the other side of the world. This is America. We control our own destiny. We forge our own future. And I will not accept an energy strategy that traps us in the past. We're not going to do it.

So, as long as I'm President, America is going to be pursuing an all-of-the-above energy strategy. Yes, we'll develop as much oil and gas as we can, in a safe way, but we're also going to develop wind power and solar power and advanced biofuels. We can build the next-generation nuclear reactors that are smaller and safer and cleaner and cheaper, but we've got to also look at renewable energy as the key to our future. And we've got to build cars and trucks that get more miles to the gallon. We've got to build homes and businesses that waste less energy and put consumers in control of their energy bills.

And we'll do it by harnessing the same type of American ingenuity and imagination that's on display right here at Ohio State—right here at Ohio State.

So already, we've made progress. After decades of inaction, we raised fuel economy standards, so that by the middle of the next decade, our cars will average nearly 55 miles per gallon, almost double what we get today. That means you'll be able to fill up your car every 2 weeks instead of every week. You like that?

That will save the average family about $8,000 at the pump over the life of a car, which is real money. To use even less oil, we're going to have to keep investing in clean, renewable, homegrown biofuels. And already, we're using these biofuels to power everything from city buses to UPS trucks, even to Navy ships. And the more we rely on these homegrown fuels, the less oil we buy from other countries and the more jobs we create right here in America.

We also need to keep investing in clean energy like wind power and solar power. I just visited the biggest American solar plant of its kind in Boulder City, Nevada. It's powering thousands of homes. It put hundreds of local people at work. There are thousands of companies like that all across America. And today, thousands of Americans have jobs because of public investments that have nearly doubled the use of clean energy in this country.

And as long as I'm President, we are going to keep on making those investments. I am not going to cede the wind and solar and advanced battery industries to countries like China and Germany that are making those investments. I want those technologies developed and manufactured here in Ohio, here in the Midwest, here in America, by American workers. That's the future we want.

So all these steps, all these steps have put us on a path of greater energy independence. Here's a statistic I want everybody to remember: Since I took office, America's dependence on foreign oil has gone down every single year. In 2010, our oil dependence was under 50 percent for the first time in 13 years. Even as the economy was growing, we've made progress in reducing the amount of oil that we have to import because we're being smarter, we're doing things better.

But now we've got a choice. We can keep moving in that direction, we can keep developing new energy and new technology that uses less oil, or we can listen to these folks who actually believe that the only thing we can do is drill our way out of this problem. In fact, they make fun of clean energy. They call the jobs produced by them "phony" jobs. They make jokes about them at their rallies.

Lately, we've heard a lot of politicians, a lot of folks who are running for a certain office— [*laughter*]—they shall go unnamed—[*laughter*]—they dismiss wind power. They dismiss solar power. They make jokes about biofuels. I guess they like gas guzzlers because they're

against raising fuel standards. Imagine if these guys had been around when Columbus set sail. They'd be charter members of the Flat Earth Society. [*Laughter*] They don't ask what we can do; they explain what we can't do and why we can't do it.

And the point is there will always be cynics and naysayers who just want to keep on doing the same things the same way that we've always done them.

Audience member. Then we wouldn't have a Black President, but we do!

The President. Well, that's true.

They want to double down on the same ideas that got us exactly into this mess that we've been in and we've been digging our way out of. That's not who we are as Americans.

We've always succeeded because we refused to stand still. We put faith in the future. We are inventors. We are builders. We're makers of things. We're Thomas Edison and the Wright Brothers and Steve Jobs. By the way, the Wright Brothers were from Ohio. Just want to point that out. But that's who we are. That's who we need to be right now. We can't be afraid of the future.

The flat Earth crowd, they've got a different view. They would rather give $4 billion in taxpayer subsidies to oil companies this year than to invest in clean energy. Four billion dollars to an industry that's making record profits because of what you're paying at the gas station. Does anybody think that they need help, that they don't have enough incentive to drill for oil? Does anybody think that's a wise use of your tax dollars?

Audience members. No!

We have been subsidizing oil companies for a century. That's long enough. It is time to stop a taxpayer giveaway to an industry that's rarely been more profitable and start making investments in a clean energy industry that has never been more promising.

And when Congress votes on this, you guys should put some pressure on to tell them, do the right thing. Bet on our future, not on our past. Put them on record: They can either stand with the oil industry, or they can stand with the American people. They can place their bets on the energy of the past or place their bets on America's future, on American workers, American technology, American ingenuity, American-made energy.

Audience member. Our children.

The President. Our children. The—that's the choice we face. That's what's at stake right now.

And, Ohio, we know the direction that we've got to go in. Ending these oil subsidies won't bring gas prices down tomorrow. Even if we drilled every inch of America, that won't bring gas prices down tomorrow. But if we're tired of watching gas prices spike every single year, if we're tired of being caught in this position, knowing that China and India are growing—China had 10 million cars purchased in 2010 alone. You've got a billion people—2 billion people out there, who are interested in buying cars, which means that unless we develop alternatives, oil prices are going to keep on going up.

I don't want folks in the Middle East taking your money out of your pocket because we did not develop the kind of strategies that will sustain our future and our independence.

So I need all of you guys to make your voices heard. Get on the phone, write an e-mail, send a tweet, let your Members of Congress know where you stand. Tell them to do the right thing. Tell them that we can win this fight. Tell them: Yes, we can. We can build an economy that lasts. We can make this another American century. We can remind the entire world just why it is the United States of America is the greatest nation on Earth.

Thank you. God bless you. God bless the United States of America.

NOTE: The President spoke at 4:27 p.m. In his remarks, he referred to Mayor Michael B. Coleman of Columbus, OH; Joseph A. Alutto, provost, and Vijay Gadepally, student, Ohio State University; and Jared Sullinger, forward, Ohio State University men's basketball team.

Statement on Congressional Passage of Legislation To Prevent Members of Congress From Engaging in Insider Trading
March 22, 2012

In my State of the Union Address, I laid out a blueprint for an economy where everyone gets a fair shot, everyone does their fair share, and everyone plays by the same set of rules, including those who have been elected to serve the American people.

Today I'm pleased Congress took bipartisan action to pass the "STOCK Act." After I sign this bill into law, Members of Congress will not be able to trade stocks based on nonpublic information they gleaned on Capitol Hill. It's a good first step. And in the months ahead, Congress should do even more to help fight the destructive influence of money in politics and rebuild the trust between Washington and the American people.

NOTE: The statement referred to S. 2038.

Statement on the Death of John A. Payton
March 22, 2012

Michelle and I were saddened to hear about the passing of our dear friend John Payton. As president and director-counsel of the NAACP Legal Defense and Education Fund, John led the organization's involvement in five Supreme Court cases. A true champion of equality, he helped protect civil rights in the classroom and at the ballot box. The legal community has lost a legend, and while we mourn John's passing, we will never forget his courage and fierce opposition to discrimination in all its forms.

Our thoughts and prayers go out to John's family, the many students he taught, and those who love him.

Remarks on the Nomination of Jim Yong Kim To Be President of the World Bank and an Exchange With Reporters
March 23, 2012

The President. Good morning, everybody.

In February, Bob Zoellick, the current President of the World Bank, announced that he would be stepping down at the end of his term in June. Bob's been a strong and effective leader at the bank for the last 5 years, and when he told me about his plans, I immediately began to search for someone to fill his shoes.

Now, despite its name, the World Bank is more than just a bank. It's one of the most powerful tools we have to reduce poverty and raise standards of living in some of the poorest countries on the planet, and in a world that is growing smaller and more connected every day, that's a critical mission, not just for those who are struggling, but for all of us.

When we reduce hunger in the world or help a farmer recover from a flood or a drought, it strengthens the entire world economy. When we put an end to a preventable disease, all of us are safer because of it. When an entrepreneur can start a new business, it creates jobs in their country, but also opens up new markets for our country. And ultimately, when a nation goes from poverty to prosperity, it makes the world stronger and more secure for everybody.

That's why the World Bank is so important. And that's why the leader of the World Bank should have a deep understanding of both the role that development plays in the world and the importance of creating conditions where assistance is no longer needed.

I believe that nobody is more qualified to carry out that mission than Dr. Jim Kim. It's time for a development professional to lead the world's largest development agency. And that's why today, after a careful and thorough search, I am nominating Dr. Jim Kim to be the next President of the World Bank.

Jim has spent more than two decades working to improve conditions in developing countries around the world. As a physician and an anthropologist, he cofounded Partners in Health and led a World Health Organization campaign to treat 3 million patients with HIV/AIDS. I have made HIV/AIDS and the fight against that dreaded disease and the promotion of public health a cornerstone of my development agenda, building on some of the outstanding work that was done by President Bush.

We pursue these efforts around the globe because it's the right thing to do, and also because healthy populations enable growth and prosperity. And I'm pleased that Jim brings this particular experience with him to his new job.

Jim was also the chair of the Department of Global Health and Social Medicine at Harvard Medical School. He's earned a MacArthur "Genius" Fellowship. And for the last 3 years he has served as the president of Dartmouth College.

I should also mention that after immigrating to this country from Korea at age 5, Jim went on to become the president of his high school class, the quarterback of the football team, the point guard of the basketball team. I just found out he is a 5 handicap in golf. I'm a little resentful about that last item. [*Laughter*] But he does it all.

Jim has truly global experience. He's worked from Asia to Africa to the Americas, from capitals to small villages. His personal story exemplifies the great diversity of our country and the fact that anyone can make it as far as he has as long as they're willing to work hard and look out for others. And his experience makes him ideally suited to forge partnerships all around the world.

So I could not be more pleased to nominate Jim for this job, and I think I can speak for Secretary Clinton and Secretary Geithner, when I say that we are looking forward to working with him.

And I also want to take a minute to thank Bob Zoellick once again for all his hard work. Over the last 5 years, Bob has made the bank more transparent. He has helped shore up progress made in places like Afghanistan. He's raised billions of dollars to help some of the world's poorest communities.

Jim is the right person to carry on that legacy, and I know his unique set of skills and years of experience will serve him well. So I'm grateful to him for his willingness to serve. I do not think that the World Bank could have a better leader. So thank you.

President-designate Kim. Mr. President, thank you.

The President. Thank you.

President-designate Kim. Thank you, sir.

The President. You're going to do great. Thank you. All right?

Death of Trayvon Martin

Q. Mr. President, may I ask you about this current case in Florida, very controversial, allegations of lingering racism within our society—the so-called do not—I'm sorry—"Stand Your Ground" law and the justice in that? Can you comment on the Trayvon Martin case, sir?

The President. Well, I'm the head of the executive branch, and the Attorney General reports to me, so I've got to be careful about my statements to make sure that we're not impairing any investigation that's taking place right now.

But obviously, this is a tragedy. I can only imagine what these parents are going through. And when I think about this boy, I think about my own kids. And I think every parent in America should be able to understand why it is absolutely imperative that we investigate every aspect of this and that everybody pulls together—Federal, State, and local—to figure out exactly how this tragedy happened.

So I'm glad that not only is the Justice Department looking into it, I understand now that the Governor of the State of Florida has formed a Task Force to investigate what's taking place. I think all of us have to do some soul searching to figure out how does something like this happen. And that means that we examine the laws and the context for what happened, as well as the specifics of the incident.

But my main message is to the parents of Trayvon Martin. If I had a son, he'd look like Trayvon. And I think they are right to expect that all of us as Americans are going to take this with the seriousness it deserves and that we're going to get to the bottom of exactly what happened.

Thank you.

NOTE: The President spoke at 10:09 a.m. in the Rose Garden at the White House. In his remarks, he referred to former President George W. Bush; Gov. Richard L. Scott of Florida; Trayvon Martin, who was allegedly killed by neighborhood watch volunteer George Zimmerman in Sanford, FL, on February 26; and Tracy Martin and Sybrina Fulton, parents of Trayvon Martin.

The President's Weekly Address
March 24, 2012

Hello, everybody. This week, I traveled across the country to talk about my all-of-the-above energy strategy for America, a strategy where we produce more oil and gas here at home, but also more biofuels and fuel-efficient cars, more solar power and wind power and other sources of clean, renewable energy.

Now, you wouldn't know it by listening to some of the folks running for office out there today, but producing more oil at home has been, and will continue to be, a key part of my energy strategy. Under my administration, we're producing more oil than at any other time in the last 8 years. We've quadrupled the number of operating oil rigs to a record high. And we've added enough oil and gas pipeline to circle the entire Earth and then some. Those are the facts.

But as I've been saying all week, even though America uses around 20 percent of the world's oil, we only have around 2 percent of the world's known oil reserves. So, even if we drilled everywhere, we'd still be relying on other countries for oil.

That's why we're pursuing an all-of-the-above strategy. We're producing more biofuels, more fuel-efficient cars, more solar power, more wind power. This week, I was in Boulder City, Nevada, where they've got the largest solar plant of its kind anywhere in the country—that's the future. I was at Ohio State University, where they've developed the fastest electric car in the world—that's the future. I don't want to cede these clean energy industries to China or Germany or some other country. I want to see solar panels and wind turbines and fuel-efficient cars manufactured right here, in America, by American workers.

Now, getting these clean energy industries to locate here requires us to maintain a national commitment to new research and development, but it also requires us to build world-class transportation and communications networks, so that any company can move goods and sell products all around the world as quickly and efficiently as possible. So much of America needs to be rebuilt right now. We've got crumbling roads and bridges, a power grid that wastes too much energy, an incomplete high-speed broadband network. And we've got thousands of unemployed construction workers who've been looking for a job ever since the housing market collapsed.

But once again, we're waiting on Congress. You see, in a matter of days, funding will stop for all sorts of transportation projects. Construction sites will go idle, workers will have to go home, and our economy will take a hit.

This Congress cannot let that happen, not at a time when we should be doing everything in our power—Democrats and Republicans—to keep this recovery moving forward. The Senate did their part. They passed a bipartisan transportation bill. It had the support of 52 Democrats and 22 Republicans. Now it's up to the House to follow suit: to put aside partisan posturing, end the gridlock, and do what's right for the American people.

This is common sense. Right now, all across this country, we've got contractors and construction workers who've never been more eager to get back on the job. A long-term transportation bill would put them to work. And those are good jobs. We just released a report that shows nearly 90 percent of the construction, manufacturing, and trade jobs created through investments in transportation projects are middle class jobs. Those are exactly the jobs we need right now, and it will make the economy stronger for everybody.

We've done this before. During the Great Depression, America built the Hoover Dam and the Golden Gate Bridge. After World War II, we connected our States with a system of highways. Democratic and Republican administrations invested in great projects that benefited everybody, from the workers who actually built them to the businesses that still use them today.

So tell Congress that if we invest in new technology and new energy, in new roads and bridges and construction projects, we can keep growing our economy, put our people back to work, and remind the world why the United States is the greatest nation on Earth.

Thanks, and have a great weekend.

NOTE: The address was recorded at approximately 4:40 p.m. on March 23 in the State Dining Room at the White House for broadcast on March 24. In the address, the President referred to S. 1813. The transcript was made available by the Office of the Press Secretary on March 23, but was embargoed for release until 6 a.m. on March 24.

Remarks to United States Military Personnel at Camp Bonifas, South Korea
March 25, 2012

It's good to see you. Thank you.

Well, listen, I'm not going to give a long speech, because I just want to make sure that I get a chance to shake everybody's hands. I just want to point out that I was just presented this spiffy jacket. And so whoever arranged to make sure that it fit—I'm sure it wasn't the General—I appreciate it. [*Laughter*]

But as I told General Thurman and your commander here, you guys are the—at freedom's frontier. When you think about the transformation that has taken place in South Korea during my lifetime, it is directly attributed to this long line of soldiers, sailors, airmen, marines, coastguardsmen who were willing to create the space and the opportunity for freedom and prosperity. And the contrast between South Korea and North Korea could not be clearer, could not be starker, both in terms of freedom, but also in terms of prosperity.

And the reason that the South is doing so well is obviously attributable to the incredible resilience of their people and their incredible talents and hard work, but it also has to do with you guys. And so my main message is the same obviously to every base that I go to all across—all around the world, which is, I could not be prouder of what you're doing. Everybody back home could not be prouder of what you guys do each and every day: the dedication, the professionalism that you show. But there's something about this spot in particular, where there's such a clear line and there's such an obvious impact that you have for the good each and every day that should make all of you proud.

And I'll just share with you real briefly, last time I was here, I was having lunch with the President of South Korea, President Lee. And he talked about how he was a small child when the Korean war was taking place and its aftermath, and the brutal poverty, the fact that they had nothing. And he went on to be a auto executive and ultimately the President of his country and watch it grow. And he specifically said to me—and this was a private moment, he didn't say this in front of the press, so you knew he meant it—he said, the only reason that was able to happen—and I still think back to all those American soldiers and the sacrifices that they made.

That's the legacy you're carrying on here. So we're grateful to you. We're proud of you. And I hope that all your family back home knows how proud your Commander in Chief is of you.

And the only other thing I'll say is, for those of you guys who missed the ball games—[*laughter*]—Florida got beat by Louisville, and Ohio State just beat Syracuse. So I don't know how your brackets are doing. [*Laughter*]

But anyway, thank you, God bless you, and let me just shake some hands and take some pictures. All right.

NOTE: The President spoke at 11:26 a.m. In his remarks, he referred to Gen. James D. Thurman, USA, commander, United Nations Command, Combined Forces Command, U.S. Forces Korea; and Col. Patrick McKenzie, USAF, commander, 51st Fighter Wing.

Remarks Following a Meeting With Prime Minister Recep Tayyip Erdogan of Turkey in Seoul, South Korea
March 25, 2012

President Obama. I just want to say how much I appreciate the opportunity to once again meet with my friend and colleague, Prime Minister Erdogan. I think it's fair to say that over the last several years, the relationship between Turkey and the United States has continued to grow across every dimension. And I find Prime Minister Erdogan to be an outstanding partner and an outstanding friend on a wide range of issues.

We devoted a lot of this meeting to the issue of Syria, where the United States and Turkey have worked with a broad-based coalition: an international coalition of countries in the region, as well as around the world, who deeply object to the killings that have been taking place in Syria and are absolutely committed to trying to help those innocent civilians who are being killed by the Asad regime. And we are very much in agreement that there should be a process whereby a transition to a representative and legitimate government in Syria takes place.

So I expressed my thanks for Turkey hosting the next Friends of Syria meeting. And we worked on a common agenda, in terms of how we can support both humanitarian efforts, political efforts—the efforts of Kofi Annan—to bring about much-needed change inside of Syria. And not only Prime Minister Erdogan, but his entire team has shown outstanding leadership on this critical issue.

We also had the opportunity to discuss the issue of Iran and its nuclear program. I emphasized to the Prime Minister once again that I believe there is a window of time to resolve this question diplomatically, but that window is closing. And it's absolutely critical for us to be able to move forward in an effective way, in a serious way, in concert based on negotiations through the P–5-plus-1 and other channels, to ensure that Iran abides by its international obligations, which also then confers upon it the right to engage in peaceful nuclear power. And I very much appreciate the Prime Minister's insights, obviously, as a neighbor of Iran and as someone who is interested in seeing this issue resolved in a peaceful fashion.

Beyond those two specific issues, we had a wide-ranging conversation about our continued support of counterterrorism efforts, including the efforts that are taking place in Turkey with respect to the PKK. And we are very supportive of making sure that the kinds of terrorist attacks that we've seen in the past are not occurring. I congratulated the Prime Minister on the efforts that he's made within Turkey to protect religious minorities. I was pleased to hear of his decision to reopen the Halki Seminary.

We discussed our joint NATO efforts, and I look forward to welcoming him to my hometown of Chicago to discuss the transition process in Afghanistan, to provide support for an effort within Afghanistan so that they can provide for their own security and a stable Government that's representative of its people and providing them with opportunity and prosperity.

And we discussed some of the important humanitarian efforts that are being made jointly in places like Somalia.

So the bottom line is that we have found ourselves in frequent agreement upon a wide range of issues. Our discussions are frank and honest, and I very much appreciate our collaboration. And I also appreciate the advice he gives me, because he has two daughters that are a little older than mine; they've turned out very well, so I'm always interested in his perspective on raising girls.

Prime Minister Erdogan. My dear friend, Barack, thank you very much for a very fruitful meeting today. The first topic that we discussed was Syria. We extensively evaluated the situation in Syria. Of course, for a country like Turkey, which has a border of 910 kilometers with Syria, the events that are taking place in Syria is very close to us, and we feel it in our hearts, and we're very sorry to see some of the developments.

Our country has become a center of migration; we have more than 17,000 people who have had to come over from the Syrian side to Turkey as a result of the events in Syria. And we also see significant number of people who are killed, and there seems to be continuous action in terms of bombing and burning cities and settlement areas by headquarters and the need to do more of this.

And of course, as human beings, people with conscience, we cannot remain a spectator to these developments, which are things that we have to be doing something about within the framework of international law. And I'm also very pleased to see that our views in general very much overlap on this subject.

We've also had an opportunity to talk about, with respect to Syria again, developments in the region: Iran, Russia, and China, in that context.

On my return from South Korea, I will be visiting Iran, specifically on the issue of Syria. And I was hoping that we would have a chance to discuss that aspect as well, which we did today.

And there are also developments in Iraq, which was—which were important, which we wanted to discuss, and those have also been discussed in our meeting. We discussed about developments in Iraq to see how we can create greater impetus towards greater peace in Iraq. And I'm hoping that all efforts will in the end help contribute to greater peace in Iraq.

We're also very pleased to see the United States standing with us in our fight against the separatist terrorist organization. Our fight against the separatist terrorist organization will continue, but we also have to continue to have discussions with the political extensions of this organization.

We also had a chance to evaluate the situation with respect to Cyprus. Our hope is that we can achieve the desired future for Cyprus sooner.

A very, very important point has been that from the moment Barack became President, we upgraded the status of our relations from a strategic partnership to a model partnership, which he also placed a lot of importance on.

And as a result of the steps we have taken within the context of this model partnership, our trade in 2011 reached $20 billion.

A second meeting, after the first one that was held in Washington, will be held in Turkey in June this year to talk about those relations, which, in turn, in my opinion, will also lead to a significant increase once again for our relations.

And I also told you about my—[*inaudible*].

Thank you.

NOTE: The President spoke at 4:49 p.m. at the Grand Hyatt Seoul hotel. In his remarks, he referred to President Bashar al-Asad of Syria; former Secretary-General Kofi A. Annan of the United Nations, in his capacity as Joint U.N.-Arab League Special Envoy for Syria; and Esra and Sumeyye Erdogan, daughters of Prime Minister Erdogan. He also referred to the Kurdistan Workers' Party (PKK). Prime Minister Erdogan spoke in Turkish, and his remarks were translated by an interpreter.

The President's News Conference With President Lee Myung-bak of South Korea in Seoul
March 25, 2012

President Lee. I apologize for running a little late, ladies and gentlemen.

Mr. President, distinguished members of the press, it's good to see my good friend again. The last time we met was 4 months ago. Welcome to Korea, Mr. President.

And I wish to thank you, Mr. President, for taking time to visit the DMZ early this morning, soon after your arrival in Seoul. Mr. President, I'm sure it was a chance to witness firsthand the reality of division that has been a part of Korea for such a long time. And I gather you had a good time meeting with the members of the armed forces from both Korea and the United States. And thank you for the encouragement that you gave these men and women in uniform.

Today, ladies and gentlemen, we had a very useful and constructive discussion on a wide array of issues, from North Korea's nuclear and missile development and including other security issues, and also how to promote bilateral

trade between our two countries, and of course, other topics of mutual interest.

And we talked about the security situation in the region and the situation on the Korean Peninsula and agreed to continue working closely together in implementing our North Korea policy. Both countries agreed that North Korea's announcement to test-fire its long-range missile is a violation of U.N. Security Council resolutions, not to mention the latest agreement between the U.S. and North Korea. Therefore, President Obama and I both agreed that North Korea must immediately repeal its decision and abide by its international obligations.

President Obama and I agreed that we will continue to enhance and strengthen our combined defense capabilities and, at the same time, firmly respond to any threats or provocations from the North. If North Korea gives up its pursuit of nuclear weapons and missile development and instead chooses a path towards peace and cooperation, our two countries will work together, along with the international community, to help improve the lives of the people in North Korea and provide necessary assistance that will help North Korea open up a new era.

And we reaffirmed the value and importance of our enduring alliance and discussed a future vision of our partnership. Following the adoption of the future vision of the alliance, which was adopted in June 2009, our alliance is evolving into a truly global partnership where we are working shoulder to shoulder to resolve global challenges.

Furthermore, we reviewed the progress being made in our alliance, such as the transfer of OPCON two-plus-two security consultations, and agree that we will strengthen our deterrence capabilities through enhanced policy coordination and strive towards a future-oriented alliance.

Ladies and gentlemen, we will also work together so that the KORUS FTA that came into effect last March 15 will fulfill its goal. That is creating jobs for our workers, expand trade and investments, and overall improve the lives of our peoples. And accordingly, in order to ensure the faithful implementation of the KORUS FTA, we will establish a ministerial-level joint committee, as previously agreed, and check upon the progress.

President Obama and I also exchanged views on the state of the global economy and shared our concern regarding the uncertainties that still remain. In particular, we share the concern that rising oil prices is an obstacle to speedy recovery of the global economy and agree that international cooperation needed to be further strengthened to bring about stability in the world oil market.

And of course, we also talked about regional issues—issues in the Middle East, Afghanistan, and other issues, including Iran—and how we can strengthen international cooperation to bring about a resolution to these issues.

I welcome President Obama once again on his visit. The Nuclear Security Summit was President Obama's initiative, born out of his vision to leave behind a safer, more prosperous world for the future generation. And we will continue to strive together to achieve a world without nuclear weapons. I thank him and his team for all the help in ensuring a successful Nuclear Security Summit meeting.

Thank you.

President Obama. Well, good evening, everyone. Thank you to my good friend and partner, President Lee, for your very kind words. And thank you, to the people of Korea, for your gracious welcome. This is my third visit to the Republic of Korea as President. It is wonderful to be back. And once again, I'm grateful for the hospitality.

This visit reflects the extraordinary friendship between our two people. My wife and I were proud to help strengthen those ties when we had the honor of hosting President Lee and First Lady Kim for a state visit at the White House last fall. And during that visit I learned a Korean word that I believe captures the deep affection between our people: *jeong*. And I feel that spirit again today.

My visits to Korea reflect the leadership role that South Korea is playing in this region and around the world: a global Korea. I was last here for the G–20, which was a success under President Lee's leadership. Now we're back, along with more than 50 world leaders, for the second Nuclear Security Summit.

In fact, just today we saw another important step forward. We learned that Ukraine completed the removal of highly enriched uranium from its territory. This fulfills a commitment Ukraine made at our last Nuclear Security Summit in Washington, and I believe it's a preview of the kind of progress we're going to see over the next 2 days in confronting one of the most urgent challenges of global security: securing the world's nuclear weapons and preventing nuclear terrorism.

My visit to Korea also reflects the enduring strength of our alliance. My last visit to Seoul came as we marked both the 60th anniversary of the Korean war and Veterans Day. And today I traveled, as President Lee mentioned, to the DMZ to thank our men and women in uniform, American and Korean, who serve shoulder to shoulder. They're the reason that we can stand here free today and prosperous here today. And we salute them all.

My visit to Korea reflects the fact that the United States is leading again in the Asia-Pacific, a region that will affect American security and prosperity in the 21st century like no other. As I declared in Australia last year, the United States as a Pacific nation will play a larger and long-term role in shaping this region and its future. And the cornerstone of our efforts is our strong alliances, including our alliance with the Republic of Korea.

This is the context for our meeting today. And as President Lee indicated, we had a very good discussion on a wide range of issues. We reviewed our ongoing efforts to modernize our security alliance. We agreed to have our foreign and defense ministers meet in June to discuss concrete measures we can take to continue strengthening that alliance. We're on track for South Korea to assume operational control for the alliance in 2015.

I reaffirmed, as I said in Australia, that reductions in U.S. defense spending will not come at the expense of the Asia-Pacific, and that includes South Korea. America's Armed Forces are going to stay ready for the full range of contingencies and threats. And the alliance between the United States and the Republic of Korea remains unshakable.

We reviewed our great progress in bringing our economies even closer. During my last visit to Seoul, we pledged to get our landmark trade agreement done. On President Lee's visit to Washington, it passed our Congress. On this visit, we can say that our trade agreement is now in force. We got it done. This is a win for both of our countries: more jobs and opportunities for our workers and businesses on both sides of the Pacific. That includes supporting some 70,000 American jobs and keeping us on track to meet my goal of doubling American exports.

We discussed regional security, and that obviously includes the issue of North Korea. Last month, North Korea agreed to a series of steps, including a moratorium on long-range missile launches. This month, North Korea announced its intention to conduct a missile launch. As President Lee mentioned, this would constitute a direct violation of Pyongyang's own commitments and its international obligations. Moreover, it would only deepen North Korea's isolation, damage further its relations with its neighbors, and seriously undermine the prospect of future negotiations.

I'll have more to say in my speech tomorrow about our commitment to security and peace on the Korean Peninsula and the choice Pyongyang must make. Today I'll simply say that North Korea will achieve nothing by threats or by provocations. North Korea knows its obligations, and it must take irreversible steps to meet those obligations. On this, the United States and the Republic of Korea are absolutely united.

Since South Korea is one of our key global partners, we discussed a range of challenges to international security. I again want to thank South Korea for its important contributions to reconstruction in Afghanistan, and I updated the President on our preparations for the NATO summit in Chicago, where we will chart the next phase of the transition to Afghan lead.

And I also thanked the President of South Korea's strong support of sanctions on Iran because its failure to meet its international obligations. I know this decision does not come without costs, both to the Republic of Korea, as well as our own country, but the prospects of an Iran with nuclear weapons would be a threat to the world, and this is one more example of South Korea stepping up and playing a leadership role on the world stage.

Finally, we're deepening the ties between our people. We agreed to expand educational exchanges, which will give more Korean students the opportunity to study in the United States, which benefits both of our countries.

So once again, President Lee, I thank you for your hospitality, for your leadership. Our alliance is strong. Our commitment to the security and prosperity of our people is unwavering. And I'm confident that under South Korea's leadership, the Nuclear Security Summit is going to be a great success.

President Lee. Thank you.

We will now take questions from the press. [*Inaudible*]—from Korean Broadcasting Service.

North Korean Long-Range Missile Test/South Korean Defense Capabilities

Q. A question going out to President Lee. As predicted, you just explained that you and President Obama discussed the issue of North Korea's impending rocket launch. But despite the international community's warnings, how will you respond if North Korea goes ahead and test-fires its long-range missile? What will Korea do? What kind of sanctions are you planning to impose on North Korea? And could you explain the status of the negotiations regarding extending the missile range of South Korea?

You—in a recent press interview you spoke about the fact that discussions are proceeding between the U.S. and Korea regarding extending the missile range of South Korea. Can you explain or—the status of the negotiations?

President Lee. Thank you—[*inaudible*]. You asked about North Korea's impending launch of its long-range missile, and let me just reiterate once again, ladies and gentlemen: If North Korea goes ahead with its plan to test-launch its long-range missile, this is a clear violation of U.N. Security Council Resolution 1874. North Korea, if it goes ahead with its plan, will be going straight against its pledges that it made with the international community.

The international community is urging the North Koreans to repeal its announcement to test-fire its long-range missile. Now, your question was, what—how are we going to respond? I just want to answer that question by saying that if North Korea goes ahead with it, North Korea must be the sole country to bear the entire responsibility. As President Obama just mentioned, if it goes ahead with its plan, it will only deepen its isolation and all the consequences North Korea will have to face.

And from the perspective of the people of North Korea, they will understand that its leader is spending hundreds of millions of dollars just to launch a long-range missile. And watching their leader do so, they're not going

to feel proud that their country was able to launch a long-range missile, but rather, they will get—truly understand the nature of their leaders and understand why they have to go through such hardships today.

So, domestically, I'm sure the North Korean leaders are hoping to achieve some sort of—an objective by test-launching its long-range missile. But they must clearly understand that if they go ahead with the plan, that they will put themselves in a very difficult position. I urge the North Koreans to come out as a responsible member of the international community, and that is the surest way to ensure a better life for the people of North Korea.

In this regard, there is no difference of opinions between the U.S. and South Korea. We'll remain very calm and rational, and we will be wise in dealing with the North Koreans if in fact they do go ahead with their announcement.

You asked about extending the missile range of South Korea. We did not discuss that issue. Of course, working-level officials have been discussing this issue. But you have to look at this from a more holistic framework in that extending the missile range is part of increasing and enhancing our defense capabilities vis-a-vis North Korea.

President Obama. Ben Feller [Associated Press].

North Korea

Q. Good evening. President Obama, President Lee, thank you for the question. I'd like to follow up on the North Korean threat on two fronts. The first is to follow up on the question my colleague had. Could you be more specific, from your perspective, what the consequences would be that you would bring to bear on North Korea should there be a rocket launch, in terms of the overall relationship, but also specifics, such as food aid and negotiations?

And also, I'm wondering, sir, if you could give us some insights about whether you've developed an impression of North Korea's new leader, and whether you've been able to yet take a measure of the man.

And to President Lee, good to see you again. I wanted to ask you about the Nuclear Security Summit. Can you explain how it would have any true and lasting credibility when the two major antagonists of North Korea and Iran are on the sidelines?

President Obama. Well, first of all, with respect to the consequences should there be a launch by the North Koreans, as President Lee indicated, North Korea is already under an extraordinary battery of sanctions. They are the most isolated country in the world. They are cut off from basic commerce and exchanges beyond their borders that every other country—almost every other country—takes for granted.

Their people are extraordinarily impoverished. The contrast between living standards in the North and living standards in the South could not be greater and couldn't be a greater testimony to the benefits of living in a free society.

And so the real consequence, should they go forward with a launch, is they will have missed an opportunity, because what we presented to them, and what we've consistently presented to them, is an opportunity for them to take a different path than the one they've been taking, which is resulting in not simply hardship for their people, but a state that is decades behind their counterparts in the region in terms of development, in terms of economic strength, in terms of influence in world affairs.

And so immediate, concrete, tangible effects: We had offered them the possibility, as part of a series of confidence-building measures to move forward with a nutritional aid package, for example. We've indicated to them very directly—because this was part of discussions that had taken place among negotiators—that it would be difficult to move forward with that package if they show themselves unable to make commitments that they've made even a month earlier. Because part of the challenge for any nutrition aid package, for example, is that you makes sure it actually gets to the people who need it, and it doesn't go to serve elites in that country or their military. That requires monitors. It's very difficult to have monitors at a period of tension and friction. And it is diffi-

cult to provide aid if you don't think that it's going to get to the people who actually need it. So that's just one example of the kinds of consequence that will take place.

I'll also note that every time North Korea has violated international resolution—the Security Council resolution, it's resulted in further isolation, tightening of sanctions, stronger enforcement, greater support on part of the international community for stronger enforcement. I suspect that will happen this time as well.

So they need to understand that bad behavior will not be rewarded. There'd been a pattern, I think, for decades, in which North Korea thought that if they acted provocatively then somehow they would be bribed into ceasing and desisting acting provocatively. And President Lee and I have agreed from the start of our relationship that we're going to break that pattern. And I suspect that it will ultimately end up having the impact intended, but in the meantime, it's the people of North Korea that are most likely to suffer.

I do want to comment on the issue you raised with respect to the Nuclear Security Summit. Understand that the concept of the Nuclear Security Summit that we set up was not directed at the specific issue of Iran or North Korea, but was directed at one leg of a multilegged stool when it comes to our nuclear security. Specifically, if you've got a lot of loose nuclear material, if countries, either historically because of old nuclear programs or currently in terms of how they operate their nuclear energy facilities, are leaving a bunch of material out there that could potentially fall in the hands of terrorists, that poses an extraordinary threat to the United States, to South Korea, and to countries all around the world.

And so our goal with this Nuclear Security Summit has always been to be very specific, concrete, around a set of issues that if we act with some deliberateness, can actually enhance everybody's security and should not be controversial. And it's a testament, I think, to that well-defined agenda that 2 years later we're seeing all these deliverables take place that are taking a whole bunch of nuclear material out of vulnerable positions that could fall into the wrong hands.

It doesn't solve every problem; it doesn't address every issue that I raised in my Prague speech 3½ years ago. We still have issues of how can we reduce nuclear weapons among those countries that currently have nuclear weapons, consistent with the long-term obligations of the NPT.

We still have outliers like Iran and North Korea that are potentially pursuing nuclear weapons and that pose a significant danger and are engaging in potential nonproliferation activities. But that doesn't diminish in any way the concrete work that's gotten done here. That is significantly reducing the risk that an Al Qaida or a terrorist organization could get a dirty bomb and explode it in Seoul or New York City. And that's always been the objective of the Nuclear Security Summit, and I think that because of the fine leadership that's been shown by President Lee and his delegation, we're going to see a whole bunch of concrete stuff get done over the next 2 days.

North Korean Leadership/Nuclear Security Summit

Q. Kim Jong Un?

President Obama. Oh. I think it's hard to have an impression of Kim Jong Un, in part because the situation in North Korea still appears unsettled. It's not clear exactly who's calling the shots and what their long-term objectives are. But regardless of the North Korean leadership, what is clear is that they have not yet made that strategic pivot where they say to themselves, what we're doing isn't working. It's leading our country and our people down a dead end.

And, Ben, you were there at the DMZ, and it's like you're in a time warp. It's like you're looking across 50 years into a country that has missed 40 years or 50 years of progress. And if a country can't feed its people effectively, if it can't make anything of any use to anybody, if it has no exports other than weapons, and even those aren't ones that in any way would be considered state of the art, if it can't deliver on any indicators of

well-being for its people, then you'd think you'd want to try something different.

I don't get a sense that they've made that decision yet. But my suspicion is, is that, at some point, that's what the North Korean people are going to be looking for. And they do have that opportunity. And when they make that decision, I know I speak for President Lee, no one will welcome it more than we do, because it is in our interests to see every country provide opportunity and prosperity for its people. But there are certain things that just don't work, and what they're doing doesn't work.

President Lee. Regarding the Nuclear Security Summit, President Obama just explained what kind of objectives that we want to achieve by holding this second Nuclear Security Summit. So I just want to add to what President Obama said and say that during the Seoul summit, which begins tomorrow, first of all, we're going to review the kind of progress that we made back in Washington, DC, and then what we're going to do is we're going to make more pledges to reduce and eliminate nuclear materials. We are going to set up more concrete benchmarks, and as a result of the Seoul summit, we will be able to reduce and eliminate about 20,000 nuclear weapons. We still have about 100,000 nuclear weapons left. This is a tremendous amount of nuclear weapons, but I have hope that as we continue to engage in— with this problem that we will be able to achieve and attain our goal of a world without nuclear weapons.

And another important point that President Obama also mentioned is that 50-plus leaders gathered here in Seoul are going to be discussing how we can prevent nuclear materials and weapons from falling into the wrong hands. We are going to discuss how we can share intelligence and information so that we can prevent individuals and organizations from acquiring nuclear weapons.

You can just only imagine the kind of work that will go into coming up with an agreement between 50-plus states, but nonetheless, we share a common vision and a commitment. And I'm confident that following the meeting in Washington, DC, the meeting that will start tomorrow will contribute to enhancing our safety and security.

Mr. Choi from—[*inaudible*]—from Chosun Daily.

North Korea/South Korean Defense Capabilities

Q. A question going out to President Obama. Mr. President, you just visited the DMZ, the Panmunjom, this morning, and today the North Koreans are commemorating the 100th anniversary of the birth of Kim Il Sung, and so they were having this big parade in North Korea, also celebrating the new leadership of Kim Jung Un. If you can share with us your thoughts in visiting the DMZ and what you think about the leaders in North Korea.

And second question has to do with extending the missile range of South Korea. The South Korean Government's position is that since North Korea has a capability of more than 3,000 kilometers in its missile range, that is one reason why you hope to extend the missile range of—here in South Korea. What are your thoughts on this? And what are some of the preconditions in order to resume the six-party talks?

The last question was also going out to both President Obama and President Lee.

President Lee. You just asked three questions. [*Laughter*]

President Obama. It's hard to remember them. [*Laughter*] Well, the first question I think I basically answered: my impressions with respect to the DMZ and the North Korean leadership.

With respect to the issue of extending missile ranges, I think President Lee got it exactly right. We have this incredibly powerful alliance that is multidimensional and involves a whole range of coordination, training activities, making sure that there's interoperability with respect to various weapon systems and our defensive capabilities. And so all these issues are being discussed as we move forward to implementing the 2015 plan.

And so there are no specific preconditions around—or specific obstacles around the missile range issue. Rather, it's a broader question

of what are the needs in order for us to fulfill our enduring goals around the alliance. And a lot of that is technical. A lot of it takes place not at the Presidential level, but rather at the military level. And we will continue to instruct our teams that they work closely together to ensure what is the ultimate outcome, which is not any particular weapon system or any particular missile range, but rather, can we protect our people, can we make sure that the objectives of the alliance are achieved.

With respect to the six-party talks, look, we've been very clear about this again and again. It's not that complicated. If the North Koreans are serious about entering into six-party talks, they have to show that they are operating in good faith. At minimum, that requires them suspending activities that right now clearly are contrary to previous obligations that they've made and international law. And when they do that, then we'll be able to sit down and resolve, hopefully, some of these longer term issues.

In the absence of that, it's hard to figure out how these discussions would be productive. And frankly, President Lee and I both have a lot of things to do, and so we try not to have our team sit around tables talking in circles without actually getting anything done. And my hope is, is that at some point the North Koreans make the decision that it is in their interests to try to figure out how to feed their people and improve their economy rather than have big parades where they show off weapons.

Mark Landler [New York Times]. You can use them both, Mark. [*Laughter*]

China-North Korea Relations/North Korean Leadership

Q. Exactly. Thank you both. A question first for President Obama. Mr. President, in the past you've been, particularly when frustrated with China on the issue of North Korea, not shy about telling President Hu that the U.S. will do what's necessary to protect its national security interest. As you're meeting President Hu tomorrow, I wonder what message will you give him regarding North Korea. Are you satisfied with the pressure that China has brought to bear on North Korea? Is there more they could be doing? And is it realistic to think that if they pushed hard enough they might persuade the North Koreans not to go ahead with the satellite launch?

And a question for President Lee. As long as my colleague asked President Obama for his views on Kim Jong Un, I'd like to ask you your views. You live here. You've paid attention to North Korea for longer than our President has, I daresay. And I just wonder whether you think he is, as the President suggested, still in a very tenuous situation, or whether you see him as really establishing quite some control.

President Obama. Well, first of all, I look forward to my meeting with President Hu tomorrow. Obviously, the issue of North Korea will be one among a number of topics that we discuss.

My communications with the Chinese have been very consistent on this issue. It is my firm belief that it is in none of our interests to see either tension and instability on the Peninsula, and it's not in anybody's interest to see a nuclearized Peninsula. The Chinese say they agree with that. The question then is, given that they have more influence and closer diplomatic relations with North Korea than any other country on Earth, what are they doing to help guide or encourage North Korea to take a more constructive approach? And that certainly will be a topic of conversation.

Now, I am sympathetic to the fact that they share a border with North Korea; they are deeply concerned about potential instability in that country and what ramifications it might have on China. And it is important to recognize that they have a broad range of equities when it comes to how they operate with North Korea, given that they're neighbors. But what I've said to them consistently is rewarding bad behavior, turning a blind eye to deliberate provocations, trying to paper over these not just provocative words, but extraordinarily provocative acts that violate international norms, that that's not obviously working.

So, in the same way that North Korea needs to do something new if it actually wants to do right by its people, my suggestion to China is, is that how they communicate their concerns to North Korea should probably reflect the fact that the approach they've taken over the last several decades hasn't led to a fundamental shift in North Korea's behavior.

And the irony of course is, is that during the last 20 years, China has leapt into the 21st century, in part by abandoning some of the practices that North Korea still clings to. You couldn't ask for a better model of the difference, at least on the economic front, that different policies have made.

And again, I believe China is very sincere that it does not want to see North Korea with a nuclear weapon. But it is going to have to act on that interest in a sustained way. And if it does, I think together, between the South Koreans, the Japanese, the Russians, the Chinese, and ourselves, I think we can have a real impact.

President Lee. With regards to your question about Kim Jong Un and my impression on him, it's a difficult question. I think it's safe to say that it's rather premature for anyone to make any initial assessment or analysis of Kim Jong Un or have an accurate impression on Kim Jong Un. And I think it's safe to say that the majority of North Korean people themselves are probably having a difficult time trying to assess their own leader because it hasn't been very long since he assumed the leadership role.

So I don't think any leader around the world is going to give you a definitive impression or an answer to your question. But having said that, I initially did have a bit of an expectation that he will take a different path. But his recent announcement was a source of disappointment. Nonetheless, I will wait and see and give you a more definitive answer of my impression on Kim Jong Un, and I think that will be more accurate.

And new leader in North Korea will have to understand that he cannot survive alone in this world. In this day and age, no country or people—or leader, for that matter—cannot stand alone. It's imperative that all leaders and countries work together as a responsible member of the international community. And this is the surest way to ensure a better life for the people of that country. And if they do so, of course, including the Republic of Korea and the United States and many other members of the international community, will help the North Koreans realize a better life for their people.

Thank you very much

President Obama. Thank you very much.

NOTE: The President's news conference began at 6:44 p.m. at the Blue House. In his remarks, the President referred to Kim Yoon-ok, wife of President Lee; and Supreme Commander Kim Jong Un of North Korea. President Lee and some reporters spoke in Korean, and their remarks were translated by an interpreter.

Remarks at Hankuk University of Foreign Studies in Seoul
March 26, 2012

Thank you. Please, thank you very much.

To President Park, faculty, staff, and students, thank you so much for this very warm welcome. It is a great honor to be here at Hankuk University of Foreign Studies. I want to thank Dr. Park for, a few moments ago, making me an honorary alumni of the university.

Now, I know that this school has one of the world's finest foreign language programs, which means that your English is much better than my Korean. [*Laughter*] All I can say is *kamsa hamnida.*

Now, this is my third visit to the Republic of Korea as President. I've now been to Seoul more times than any other capital, except for Washington, DC, of course. This reflects the extraordinary bonds between our two countries and our commitment to each other. I'm pleased that we're joined by so many leaders here today, Koreans and Americans, who help keep us free and strong and prosperous every day. That includes our first Korean American Ambassador to the Republic of Korea, Ambassador Sung Kim.

I've seen the deep connections between our peoples in my own life among friends and colleagues. I've seen it in so many patriotic Korean Americans, including a man born in the city of Seoul, who came to America and has dedicated his life to lifting up the poor and sick of the world. And last week I was proud to nominate him to lead the World Bank, Dr. Jim Yong Kim.

I've also seen the bonds in our men and women in uniform, like the American and Korean troops I visited yesterday along the DMZ, freedom's frontier. And we salute their service and are very grateful for them. We honor all those who have given their lives in our defense, including the 46 brave souls who perished aboard the *Cheonan* 2 years ago today. And in their memory, we reaffirm the enduring promise at the core of our alliance: We stand together, and the commitment of the United States to the defense and the security of the Republic of Korea will never waver.

Most of all, I see the strength of our alliance in all of you. For decades, this school has produced leaders—public servants, diplomats, businesspeople—who've helped propel the modern miracle that is Korea, transforming it, from crushing poverty to one of the world's most dynamic economies, from authoritarianism to a thriving democracy, from a country focused inward to a leader for security and prosperity not only in this region, but also around the world: a truly global Korea.

So to all the students here today, this is the Korea your generation will inherit. And I believe there's no limits to what our two nations can achieve together. For like your parents and grandparents before you, you know that the future is what we make of it. And you know that in our digital age, we can connect and innovate across borders like never before: with your smart phones and Twitter and Me2Day and Kakao Talk. [*Laughter*] It's no wonder so many people around the world have caught the Korean wave, *Hallyu.*

Or consider this: In advance of my visit, our Embassy invited Koreans to send us your questions using social media. Some of you may have sent questions. And they called it "Ask President Obama." Now, one of you—maybe it was you, maybe it was somebody else; this is true—asked this question: "Have you posted, yourself, a supportive opinion on a website under a disguised name, pretending you are one of the supporters of President Obama?" [*Laughter*] I hadn't thought of this. [*Laughter*] But the truth is I have not done this. Maybe my daughters have. [*Laughter*] But I haven't done that myself.

So our shared future—and the unprecedented opportunity to meet shared challenges together—is what brings me to Seoul. Over the next 2 days, under President Lee's leadership, we'll move ahead with the urgent work of preventing nuclear terrorism by securing the world's nuclear materials. Now, this is an important part of the broader, comprehensive agenda that I want to talk with you about today: our vision of a world without nuclear weapons.

Three years ago, I traveled to Prague, and I declared America's commitment to stopping the spread of nuclear weapons and to seeking a world without them. I said I knew that this goal would not be reached quickly, perhaps not in my lifetime, but I knew we had to begin, with concrete steps. And in your generation, I see the spirit we need in this endeavor, an optimism that beats in the hearts of so many young people around the world. It's that refusal to accept the world as it is, the imagination to see the world as it ought to be, and the courage to turn that vision into reality. So today, with you, I want to take stock of our journey and chart our next steps.

Here in Seoul, more than 50 nations will mark our progress toward the goal we set at the summit I hosted 2 years ago in Washington: securing the world's vulnerable nuclear materials in 4 years so that they never fall into the hands of terrorists. And since then, nations, including the United States, have boosted security at nuclear facilities.

South Korea, Japan, Pakistan, and others are building new centers to improve nuclear security and training. Nations like Kazakhstan have moved nuclear materials to more secure locations. Mexico, and just yesterday Ukraine, have joined the ranks of nations that have removed all the highly enriched uranium from their territory. All told, thousands of pounds of nuclear material have been removed from vulnerable sites around the world. This was deadly material that is now secure and can now never be used against a city like Seoul.

We're also using every tool at our disposal to break up black markets in nuclear material. Countries like Georgia and Moldova have seized highly enriched uranium from smugglers. And countries like Jordan are building their own countersmuggling teams, and we're tying them together in a global network of intelligence and law enforcement. Nearly 20 nations have now ratified the treaties and international partnerships that are at the center of our efforts. And I should add that with the death of Usama bin Laden and the major blows that we've struck against Al Qaida, a terrorist organization that has actively sought nuclear weapons is now on the path to defeat.

So, in short, the international community has made it harder than ever for terrorists to acquire nuclear weapons, and that has made us all safer. We're building an international architecture that can ensure nuclear safety. But we're under no illusions. We know that nuclear material, enough for many weapons, is still being stored without adequate protection. And we know that terrorists and criminal gangs are still trying to get their hands on it as well as radioactive material for a dirty bomb. We know that just the smallest amount of plutonium—about the size of an apple—could kill hundreds of thousands and spark a global crisis. The danger of nuclear terrorism remains one of the greatest threats to global security.

And that's why here in Seoul, we need to keep at it. And I believe we will. We're expecting dozens of nations to announce over the next several days that they've fulfilled the promises they made 2 years ago. And we're now expecting more commitments—tangible, concrete action—to secure nuclear materials and, in some cases, remove them completely. This is the serious, sustained global effort that we need, and it's an example of more nations bearing the responsibility and the costs of meeting global challenges. This is how the international community should work in the 21st century. And Korea is one of the key leaders in this process.

The United States will continue to do our part: securing our own material and helping others protect theirs. We're moving forward with Russia to eliminate enough plutonium for about 17,000 nuclear weapons and turn it instead into electricity. I can announce today a new agreement by the United States and several European partners toward sustaining the supply of medical isotopes that are used to treat cancer and heart disease without the use of highly enriched uranium. And we will work with industry and hospitals and research centers in the United States and around the world to recover thousands of unneeded radiological materials so that they can never do us harm.

Now, American leadership has been essential to progress in a second area: taking concrete steps towards a world without nuclear weapons. As a party to the Nuclear Nonproliferation Treaty, this is our obligation, and it's one that I take very seriously. But I believe the United States has a unique responsibility to act; indeed, we have a moral obligation. I say this as President of the only nation ever to use nuclear weapons. I say it as a Commander in Chief who knows that our nuclear codes are never far from my side. Most of all, I say it as a father who wants my two young daughters to grow up in a world where everything they know and love can't be instantly wiped out.

Over the past 3 years, we've made important progress. With Russia, we're now reducing our arsenal under the New START Treaty, the most comprehensive arms control agreement in nearly 20 years. And when we're done, we will have cut American and Russian deployed nuclear warheads to their lowest levels since the 1950s.

As President, I changed our nuclear posture to reduce the number and role of nuclear weapons in our national security strategy. I made it clear that the United States will not develop new nuclear warheads. And we will not pursue new military missions for nuclear weapons. We've narrowed the range of contingencies under which we would ever use or threaten to use nuclear weapons. At the same

time, I've made it clear that so long as nuclear weapons exist, we'll work with our Congress to maintain a safe, secure, and effective arsenal that guarantees the defense not only of the United States, but also our allies, including South Korea and Japan.

My administration's nuclear posture recognizes that the massive nuclear arsenal we inherited from the cold war is poorly suited to today's threats, including nuclear terrorism. So, last summer, I directed my national security team to conduct a comprehensive study of our nuclear forces. That study is still underway. But even as we have more work to do, we can already say with confidence that we have more nuclear weapons than we need. Even after New START, the United States will still have more than 1,500 deployed nuclear weapons and some 5,000 warheads.

I firmly believe that we can ensure the security of the United States and our allies, maintain a strong deterrent against any threat, and still pursue further reductions in our nuclear arsenal.

Going forward, we'll continue to seek discussions with Russia on a step we have never taken before, reducing not only our strategic nuclear warheads, but also tactical weapons and warheads in reserve. I look forward to discussing this agenda with President Putin when we will meet in May. Missile defense will be on the agenda, but I believe this should be an area of cooperation, not tension. And I'm confident that, working together, we can continue to make progress and reduce our nuclear stockpiles. Of course, we'll consult closely with our allies every step of the way, because the security and defense of our allies, both in Europe and Asia, is not negotiable.

Here in Asia, we've urged China, with its growing nuclear arsenal, to join us in a dialogue on nuclear issues. That offer remains open. And more broadly, my administration will continue to pursue ratification of the Comprehensive Test Ban Treaty. And after years of delay, it's time to find a path forward on a new treaty that verifiably ends the production of fissile materials for nuclear weapons, ends it once and for all.

By working to meet our responsibilities as a nuclear power, we've made progress in a third area: strengthening the global regime that prevents the spread of nuclear weapons. When I came into office, the cornerstone of the world's effort, which is the Nuclear Non-Proliferation Treaty, was fraying. Iran had started spinning thousands of centrifuges. North Korea conducted another nuclear test. And the international community was largely divided on how to respond.

Over the past 3 years, we have begun to reverse that dynamic. Working with others, we've enhanced the global partnership that prevent proliferation. The International Atomic Energy Agency is now conducting the strongest inspections ever. And we've upheld the basic bargain of the NPT: Countries with nuclear weapons, like the United States and Russia, will move towards disarmament; countries without nuclear weapons will not acquire them; and all countries can have access to peaceful nuclear energy.

Because of these efforts, the international community is more united and nations that attempt to flout their obligations are more isolated. Of course, that includes North Korea.

Here in Korea, I want to speak directly to the leaders in Pyongyang. The United States has no hostile intent toward your country. We are committed to peace. And we are prepared to take steps to improve relations, which is why we have offered nutritional aid to North Korean mothers and children.

But by now it should be clear: Your provocations and pursuit of nuclear weapons have not achieved the security you seek; they have undermined it. Instead of the dignity you desire, you're more isolated. Instead of earning the respect of the world, you've been met with strong sanctions and condemnation. You can continue down the road you are on, but we know where that leads. It leads to more of the same: more broken dreams, more isolation, ever more distance between the people of North Korea and the dignity and the opportunity that they deserve.

And know this: There will be no rewards for provocations. Those days are over. To the leaders of Pyongyang, I say, this is the choice before you. This is the decision that you must make. Today we say, Pyongyang, have the courage to pursue peace and give a better life to the people of North Korea.

This same principle applies with respect to Iran. Under the NPT, Iran has the right to peaceful nuclear energy. In fact, time and again, the international community, including the United States, has offered to help Iran develop nuclear energy peacefully. But time and again, Iran has refused, instead taking the path of denial, deceit, and deception. And that is why Iran also stands alone as the only member of the NPT unable to convince the international community that its nuclear program is for peaceful purposes—the only member. That's why the world has imposed unprecedented sanctions, slowing Iran's nuclear program.

The international community is now poised to enter talks with Iran's leaders. Once again, there is the possibility of a diplomatic resolution that gives Iran access to peaceful nuclear energy while addressing the concerns of the international community. Today I'll meet with the leaders of Russia and China as we work to achieve a resolution in which Iran fulfills its obligations.

There is time to solve this diplomatically. It is always my preference to solve these issues diplomatically. But time is short. Iran's leaders must understand they too face a choice. Iran must act with the seriousness and sense of urgency that this moment demands. Iran must meet its obligations.

For the global response to Iran and North Korea's intransigence, a new international norm is emerging: Treaties are binding, rules will be enforced, and violations will have consequences. We refuse to consign ourselves to a future where more and more regimes possess the world's most deadly weapons.

And this brings me to the final area where we've made progress: a renewed commitment to harnessing the power of the atom, not for war, but for peaceful purposes. After the tragedy at Fukushima, it was right and appropriate that nations moved to improve the safety and security of nuclear facilities. We're doing so in the United States. It's taking place all across the world.

As we do, let's never forget the astonishing benefits that nuclear technology has brought to our lives. Nuclear technology helps make our food safe. It prevents disease in the developing world. It's the high-tech medicine that treats cancer and finds new cures. And of course, it's the energy—the clean energy—that helps cut the carbon pollution that contributes to climate change. Here in South Korea, as you know, as a leader in nuclear energy, you've shown the progress and prosperity that can be achieved when nations embrace peaceful nuclear energy and reject the development of nuclear arms.

And with rising oil prices and a warming climate, nuclear energy will only become more important. That's why, in the United States, we've restarted our nuclear industry as part of a comprehensive strategy to develop every energy source. We supported the first new nuclear power plant in three decades. We're investing in innovative technologies so we can build the next generation of safe, clean nuclear power plants. And we're training the next generation of scientists and engineers who are going to unlock new technologies to carry us forward.

One of the great challenges they'll face and that your generation will face is the fuel cycle itself in producing nuclear energy. We all know the problem: The very process that gives us nuclear energy can also put nations and terrorists within the reach of nuclear weapons. We simply can't go on accumulating huge amounts of the very material, like separated plutonium, that we're trying to keep away from terrorists.

And that's why we're creating new fuel banks to help countries realize the energy they seek without increasing the nuclear dangers that we fear. That's why I've called for a new framework for civil nuclear cooperation. We need an international commitment to unlocking the fuel cycle of the future. In the United States we're investing in the research and development of new fuel cycles so that dangerous materials can't be stolen or diverted. And today I urge nations to join us in seeking a future

where we harness the awesome power of the atom to build and not to destroy.

In this sense, we see how the efforts I've described today reinforce each other. When we enhance nuclear security, we're in a stronger position to harness safe, clean nuclear energy. When we develop new, safer approaches to nuclear energy, we reduce the risk of nuclear terrorism and proliferation. When nations, including my own, fulfill our responsibilities, it strengthens our ability to ensure that other nations fulfill their responsibilities. And step by step, we come closer to the security and peace of a world without nuclear weapons.

I know that there are those who deride our vision. There are those who say ours is an impossible goal that will be forever out of reach. But to anyone who doubts the great progress that is possible, I tell them, come to Korea. Come to this country, which rose from the ashes of war—[*applause*]—a country that rose from the ashes of war, turning rubble into gleaming cities. Stand where I stood yesterday, along a border that is the world's clearest contrast between a country committed to progress, a country committed to its people, and a country that leaves its own citizens to starve.

Come to this great university, where a new generation is taking its place in the world, helping to create opportunities that your parents and grandparents could only imagine. Come and see some of the courageous individuals who join us today: men and women, young and old, born in the North, but who left all they knew behind and risked their lives to find freedom and opportunity here in the South. In your life stories we see the truth: Koreans are one people. And if just given the chance, if given their freedom, Koreans in the North are capable of great progress as well.

Looking out across the DMZ yesterday, but also looking into your eyes today, I'm reminded of another country's experience that speaks to the change that is possible in our world. After a terrible war, a proud people was divided. Across a fortified border, armies massed, ready for war. For decades, it was hard to imagine a different future. But the forces of history and hopes of man could not be denied. And today, the people of Germany are whole again, united, and free.

No two places follow the same path, but this much is true: The currents of history cannot be held back forever. The deep longing for freedom and dignity will not go away. So too on this divided peninsula, the day all Koreans yearn for will not come easily or without great sacrifice. But make no mistake, it will come. And when it does, change will unfold that once seemed impossible. And checkpoints will open, and watchtowers will stand empty, and families long separated will finally be reunited. And the Korean people, at long last, will be whole and free.

Like our vision of a world without nuclear weapons, our vision of a Korea that stands as one may not be reached quickly. But from this day until then, and all the days that follow, we take comfort in knowing that the security we seek, the peace we want, is closer at hand because of the great alliance between the United States and the Republic of Korea and because we stand for the dignity and freedom of all Koreans. And no matter the test, no matter the trial, we stand together. We work together. We go together. *Katchi kapshida!*

Thank you very much.

NOTE: The President spoke at 10:32 a.m. In his remarks, he referred to Park Chul, president, Hankuk University of Foreign Studies; President Lee Myung-bak of South Korea; and Prime Minister Vladimir Vladimirovich Putin of Russia, in his capacity as President-elect of Russia.

Remarks Following a Meeting With President Dmitry Anatolyevich Medvedev of Russia in Seoul
March 26, 2012

President Medvedev. So I would like to start by saying, once again, that together with my friend and colleague Barack Obama, we had a very substantial discussion of different issues of our agenda of bilateral cooperation between the United States and Russia.

I told Barack that despite the fact that reset that has been largely debated over the past 3 years get different assessments, I still believe that it was an extremely useful exercise, and we probably enjoyed the best level of relations between the United States and Russia during those 3 years than ever during the previous decades. And we managed to achieve a lot in various areas. First and foremost, that was the New START Treaty that was signed. And we also managed to establish close cooperation on the most sensitive international issues.

And I would like to especially thank the U.S. President for his huge work and huge support in Russia's accession to the WTO. In my view, that was an extremely important topic, and I hope that we will be able to achieve similar successes in resolving remaining issues, such as the revoke of Jackson-Vanik amendment.

Lots remains to be done, of course, in terms of trade and economic relations. We need to bring them to the new level through increasing the volume of trade and raising the general level and pace of cooperation. And I believe that it would serve the interests of the U.S. companies and the U.S. citizens, especially now that the global economy is experiencing the turbulent times.

We, of course, as usual, discussed various international issues, including the most difficult ones, such as Syria. Yesterday I had a very good meeting with the Special Envoy of the U.N. Secretary General, Mr. Annan, and like I told the U.S. President, we believe that his mission is very good, and we hope that he will be able to reach good results and to somewhat appease, at least initially, the situation, and would help to establish communication because—between various public groups and forces that exist in Syria. And yesterday I expressed my every support to Mr. Annan.

Anyways, we need to make sure that we not end up in greater problems that we already have and that the threat of the civil war is averted, that it does not become reality, and that this mission would lead to dialogue between all the groups that exist in the country and government authorities.

Of course, we also spoke about the situation in the Middle East. We touched upon the Iranian nuclear program, the North Korean nuclear program, other sensitive issues, Afghanistan cooperation. So I guess we touched upon all main issues and gave all main positions.

Of course, we also spoke about the missile defense. I believe we still have time; time hasn't run out. And now we need to discuss and cooperate on various aspects on European missile defense. I believe such discussion could be more active. Now, in my view, time has come for discussions between technical aspects, and of course, we remain at our own positions, both the United States and Russian Federation. But I believe we still have time to agree on a balanced solution, and I believe that the good experience Barack and myself have gained while working on the START Treaty will help us and be very useful when finding solution to this very difficult problem.

And of course, Barack, I would like to take the opportunity to say how much I enjoyed the cooperation we had with you. And I believe that it really was the highlight of the previous years. And due to the high level of cooperation, we managed to resolve various complicated issues bilaterally—international agenda. And I hope that the same high level of our relations will remain between the United States of Russia—the United States of America and the Russian Federation when the new President starts—steps in office.

And I would like to—I already invited you to visit Russia. I understand that this year will be difficult for you since it's an election year. But still, I hope that you will be able to come. I already invited you to my hometown, St. Petersburg, so I would like to take the occasion to reiterate my invitation on behalf of myself and President-elect Vladimir Putin.

President Obama. Thank you. Well, first of all, let me just say that the last 3 years of my work with President Medvedev has been extremely productive. And he listed some of the achievements that has resulted from this work. The New START Treaty reduces our nuclear stockpiles in ways that can help create greater peace and security not just for our countries, but for the world and is consistent with our obligations under the Non-Proliferation Treaty.

Russia's ascension into the WTO can open up trade and commerce between our two countries that can create jobs and economic growth for both Russians and Americans. And as Dmitry mentioned, we think it's going to be very important for us to address Jackson-Vanik so that American businesses can fully take advantage of an open and liberalized Russian market.

It is true that there have been times where we have had to manage tensions between our countries, and that's to be expected. Obviously, there are always tensions between countries, and that's certainly true given the long history of the cold war between our two countries. But what I think we've been able to do is to ensure that rather than look backwards, we've been looking forwards.

Sorry, translator, I forgot you were there. [*Laughter*] I got on a roll.

Moving forward, we've got more work to do between our two countries. Dmitry identified some areas of continued friction, missile defense being an example. And what we've agreed to is to make sure that our teams, at a technical level, are in discussions about how some of these issues can be resolved.

The bilateral Presidential Commission that was chaired by Foreign Minister Lavrov and Secretary of State Clinton will be working actively around a number of the trade and commercial issues, not only with respect to WTO, but how we can more vigorously expand the kind of investment and the kind of cooperation on the economic front that can benefit both Russia and the United States.

On the international front, we agreed that, as two of the world's leading powers, it's absolutely critical that we communicate effectively and coordinate effectively in responding to a wide range of situations that threaten world peace and security.

So, on Syria, although there had been some differences over the last several months, we both agreed that we should be supportive of Kofi Annan's efforts to try to end some of the bloodshed that's taking place within Syria and move towards a mechanism that would allow for the Syrian people ultimately to have a representative and legitimate government that serves their interest.

On Iran, we agreed that the P–5–plus–1 talks with Iran that should be announced soon offer us an opportunity to resolve diplomatically the critical issue of ensuring that Iran is abiding by its international obligations that will allow it to rejoin the community of nations and have peaceful uses of nuclear energy while not developing nuclear weapons.

And with respect to North Korea, we are going to be both sending messages to North Korea that they should not go forward with this missile launch, which would violate existing U.N. Security Council resolutions. And our hope is, is that we can resolve these issues diplomatically.

So let me just say that at a time of great challenges around the world, cooperation between the United States and Russia is absolutely critical to world peace and stability. And I have to say that I could not have asked for a better partner in forging that strong relationship than Dmitry. I am confident that in his new role he is going to continue to have an outstanding influence in world affairs and help to continue to deepen and improve the relationship between our two countries.

I wish him all the best. And I would love to visit St. Petersburg. He is absolutely right that my next visit to Russia will undoubtedly be after my election. [*Laughter*]

Good luck, my friend.

NOTE: The President spoke at 1:01 p.m. at the Millennium Seoul Hilton hotel. In his remarks, he referred to former Secretary-General Kofi A. Annan of the United Nations, in his capacity as Joint U.N.-Arab League Special Envoy for Syria. President Medvedev spoke in Russian, and his remarks were translated by an interpreter.

Remarks Prior to a Meeting With President Nursultan Nazarbayev of Kazakhstan in Seoul
March 26, 2012

President Obama. Well, it is wonderful to see, once again, President Nazarbayev from Kazakhstan. And I want to first of all congratulate him on his leadership for the issues that are going to be discussed over the next 2 days.

Twenty years ago, Kazakhstan made a decision not to have nuclear weapons. And not only has that led to growth and prosperity in his own country, but he has been a model in efforts around the world to eliminate nuclear materials that could fall into the wrong hands. So I very much appreciate his leadership.

In fact, one of the major deliverables that will take place at this summit is a outstanding effort to deal with nuclear materials that were a carryover from the Soviet era. Working with Russia and the United States, Kazakhstan has been able to secure those materials, and that makes us all safer.

I know that we'll have an opportunity during this bilateral meeting to also discuss some of the other efforts that Kazakhstan has made when it comes to highly enriched uranium, plutonium, their efforts at helping to develop a international fuel bank that can lessen the need for countries to pursue their own enrichment capabilities.

And so across the board, Kazakhstan has been a key leader on these issues and is appropriately going to be featured during the next 2 days at this nuclear security summit.

The close relationship between our two countries extends beyond just the nuclear security issue, so this meeting will give us an opportunity to discuss the cooperation that we have built over the last several years with respect to Afghanistan and the help we've

365

received in supplying our troops and helping to assist the Afghan Government.

We obviously have commercial ties as well, and we'll be discussing how we can deepen those. I'll be interested in discussing with the President efforts to further expand democracy and human rights within Kazakhstan, which will help to lead to further growth and prosperity in the future.

And so I very much appreciate his leadership, his efforts. And I look forward to continuing to strengthen the relationship between our two countries.

President Nazarbayev. Well, I'm very grateful for this opportunity to participate in this important summit in Seoul. We are discussing a very crucial issue: nuclear security. And I am very grateful to you, Mr. President, for the invitation to participate at the Washington summit, and now we are here in Seoul to discuss a very important issue: nuclear security.

And, Mr. President, I support your call to all nations to struggle for a nuclear-free world, and we fully support the nuclear strategy of the United States. When you said that all the countries that support the Non-Proliferation Treaty will get the support of nuclear powers and will never be threatened by any nuclear state, and I think this is very important over the future.

You discussed in details—and your plan in details—the joint work that we carry out between our nations. And Kazakhstan 20 years ago was the first country to close its nuclear test site—in Semipalatinsk we voluntarily renounced our nuclear arsenal. And you know very well that at that time, on the territory of Kazakhstan, was 1,100 warheads were deployed on the intercontinental missiles.

And in the last years, we have worked closely—I mean, Russia, the United States, and Ka-

zakhstan—to demolish the infrastructure that was left over on the Polygon, and we did a lot to rehabilitate the part of the Kazakhstan territory that was radiated. And the people of Kazakhstan, who suffered a lot and who lost many lives in that tragedy, they appreciate that efforts very much.

And we worked very closely with the United States, and we have achieved a lot. We worked jointly on many projects. And about 20 billion U.S. dollars have been invested in the Kazakhstan economy so far. And 80 percent of all foreign investments that were directed in Central Asia ended up in Kazakhstan. And I always show this collaboration as a very shining and bright example of good collaboration. And I talk to all the nuclear powers and those who are threshold countries, and I talked to the leaders of Iran, and I explained that there can be better collaboration with the two countries will strive for peace.

And of course, we work very closely on struggling terrorism, on Afghanistan, and the issues of transportation and transit through the territory of Kazakhstan that we discussed 2 years ago are all settled and solved now.

And, Mr. President, we hope that the good and strong relations between us and the United States will strengthen further in the future, especially in economics and politics. And we're ready to work shoulder to shoulder on this particular issue of nuclear safety and in other—all of the issues that we believe that will involve our part of the world.

President Obama. Thank you, everybody.

NOTE: The President spoke at 2:27 p.m. at the Grand Hyatt Seoul hotel. President Nazarbayev spoke in Russian, and his remarks were translated by an interpreter.

Remarks Prior to a Meeting With President Hu Jintao of China in Seoul
March 26, 2012

President Hu. This is our first meeting this year, and our 11th meeting in the last 3 years and more. A month ago, Vice President Xi Jinping made a successful visit to the United States. I asked him to hand to you, Mr. President, my

reply to your earlier letter, and I want to thank the American side for the warm hospitality and thoughtful arrangements made for his visit.

Now I'd like to first listen to you, Mr. President.

President Obama. Well, Mr. President, first of all, I'd like to say, it is wonderful to see you again and your delegation. And I think that the fact that we have met 11 times during the course of my Presidency is an indication of the importance that both of us place on strong U.S.-China relations.

I think that—I am very pleased to hear that Vice President Xi had a wonderful visit. We very much enjoyed hosting him in the United States, and he did deliver your letter, which I appreciate very much.

I think this is an excellent opportunity for us to discuss a wide range of issues. First of all, the fact that we are at a nuclear security summit, following up on our discussions in Washington 2 years ago, shows the progress that the international community has made in preventing nuclear proliferation and making sure that we've secured nuclear materials. And I know that's in the interest of both the United States and China.

I think this is also an opportunity to build on the excellent cooperation and dialogue across all the dimensions of our relationship that we've been able to establish over the last 3 years. So I'm looking forward to discussing economic and commercial issues, how we can continue to expand trade and make sure that

there is strong mutual understanding about the potential benefits of commerce between our two nations, in accordance with international rules and norms.

It also gives us an opportunity to talk about a wide range of international issues. Obviously of great importance to us, and I know to you as well, the situation in North Korea, the situation in Iran. We both have an interest in making sure that international norms surrounding nonproliferation and preventing destabilizing nuclear weapons is very important. Issues like Sudan, where we both have an interest in ensuring peace and stability and development in a previously war-torn region of the world, the situation in the Middle East. In all of these issues, I think cooperation and coordination between the United States and China is very important, not only to the interest of our two countries, but to the interests of the world.

And so I'm looking forward, as always, to a constructive and frank and productive meeting that can ultimately benefit both the peoples of China and the peoples of the United States.

NOTE: The President spoke at 3:31 p.m. at the Coex Center. President Hu spoke in Chinese, and his remarks were translated by an interpreter.

Statement on the Presidential Election in Senegal
March 26, 2012

I congratulate Macky Sall on his victory in Senegal's Presidential elections. Domestic and international observers report that the election was carried out transparently, freely, and reflects the will of the Senegalese people.

I also recognize President Abdoulaye Wade for his leadership and friendship to the United States during his Presidency. I look forward to building similarly productive ties with President-elect Sall, while deepening the longstanding bonds between the United States and the Senegalese people.

Senegal has, through this election, reaffirmed its tradition as a leading example of good governance and democracy at work in Af-

rica and remains an example for its neighbors. The Government and people of Senegal have once again demonstrated their commitment to political expression through peaceful, democratic elections, making it harder for nondemocratic forces, near and far, to prevail. Today's results deepen hopes across the continent and around the world that the quest for human dignity cannot be denied and that Africa's democratic wave must continue.

The United States looks forward to maintaining its strong partnership and close engagement with the people and Government of Senegal to continue to strengthen democracy, peace, and prosperity in the region.

Message to the Congress Suspending Generalized System of Preferences Benefits to Argentina
March 26, 2012

To the Congress of the United States:

In accordance with section 502(f)(2) of the Trade Act of 1974, as amended (the "1974 Act") (19 U.S.C. 2462(f)(2)), I am providing notification of my intent to suspend designation of Argentina as a beneficiary developing country under the Generalized System of Preferences (GSP) program. Section 502(b)(2)(E) of the 1974 Act (19 U.S.C. 2462(b)(2)(E)) provides that the President shall not designate any country a beneficiary developing country under the GSP if such country fails to act in good faith in enforcing arbitral awards in favor of U.S.-owned companies. Section 502(d)(2) of the 1974 Act (19 U.S.C. 2462(d)(2)) provides that, after complying with the requirements of section 502(f)(2) of the 1974 Act (19 U.S.C. 2462(f)(2)), the President shall withdraw or suspend the designation of any country as a beneficiary developing country if, after such designation, the President determines that as the result of changed circumstances such country would be barred from designation as a beneficiary developing country under section 502(b)(2) of the 1974 Act.

Pursuant to section 502(d) of the 1974 Act, having considered the factors set forth in section 502(b)(2)(E), I have determined that it is appropriate to suspend Argentina's designation as a beneficiary country under the GSP program because it has not acted in good faith in enforcing arbitral awards in favor of U.S.-owned companies.

BARACK OBAMA

The White House,
March 26, 2012.

NOTE: The related proclamation is listed in Appendix D at the end of this volume.

Message to the Congress Extending Generalized System of Preferences Benefits to South Sudan
March 26, 2012

To the Congress of the United States:

In accordance with section 502(f)(1)(A) of the Trade Act of 1974, as amended (the "1974 Act") (19 U.S.C. 2462(f)(1)(A)), I am notifying the Congress of my intent to add the Republic of South Sudan (South Sudan) to the list of beneficiary developing countries under the Generalized System of Preferences (GSP) program. South Sudan became an independent nation on July 9, 2011. After considering the criteria set forth in section 502(c) of the 1974 Act (19 U.S.C. 2462(c)), I have determined that South Sudan should be designated as a GSP beneficiary developing country.

In addition, in accordance with section 502(f)(1)(B) of the 1974 Act (19 U.S.C. 2462(f)(1)(B)), I am providing notification of my intent to add South Sudan to the list of least-developed beneficiary countries under the GSP program. After considering the criteria set forth in section 502(c) of the 1974 Act, I have determined that it is appropriate to extend least-developed beneficiary developing country benefits to South Sudan.

BARACK OBAMA

The White House,
March 26, 2012.

NOTE: The related proclamation is listed in Appendix D at the end of this volume.

Remarks at the Opening Plenary Session of the Nuclear Security Summit in Seoul, South Korea
March 27, 2012

Thank you very much, President Lee, for welcoming us here today and for the extraordinary hospitality and accommodations that have been provided by the Republic of Korea. We are very grateful to you, and we are grateful to the Korean people for the outstanding leadership in bringing us here together in Seoul.

Like the G–20 summit 2 years ago, this gathering is a tribute to the nations that contribute to security and peace that's playing a leading role around the globe and that's taking its rightful place on the world stage. When I hosted the first Nuclear Security Summit 2 years ago in Washington, there were those who questioned whether our nations could summon the will to confront one of the gravest dangers of our time. In part because it involves a lot of technical issues, in part because the world was still grappling with a whole host of other issues like the economy and the global recession, there was some skepticism that we would be able to sustain an effort around this topic. But that's exactly what we've done.

We've agreed that nuclear terrorism is one of the most urgent and serious threats to global security. We agreed to the goal of securing the world's nuclear materials in 4 years. We committed ourselves to specific and concrete actions. And to get this done, we agreed a new effort of sustained and effective international cooperation was required, that we would need to create an architecture in which we could share best practices, help to enforce many of the commitments that we had already made, and continue to improve every aspect of this issue.

Over the past 2 years, the questions have been different: Would we back up our words with deeds? Would we sustain our cooperation? Today here in Seoul, we can answer with a resounding yes. We are fulfilling the commitments we made in Washington: We are improving security at our nuclear facilities; we are forging new partnerships; we are removing nuclear materials and, in some cases, getting rid of these materials entirely. And as a result, more of the world's nuclear materials will never fall into the hands of terrorists who would gladly use them against us.

Of course, what's also undeniable is that the threat remains. There are still too many bad actors in search of these dangerous materials, and these dangerous materials are still vulnerable in too many places. It would not take much—just a handful or so—of these materials to kill hundreds of thousands of innocent people. And that's not an exaggeration; that's the reality that we face.

And that's why what's required continues to be a serious and sustained effort, and why I'm so encouraged by the excellent participation today, which is, again, a testimony to President Lee's leadership. More nations have come to the table, this time more than 50, not to talk, but to take action. As a consequence of this summit, more commitments will be made, more real, tangible steps. As a consequence, more of our citizens will be safer from the danger of nuclear terrorism.

I think we all understand that no one Nation can do this alone. This is one of those challenges in our interconnected world that can only be met when we work as an international community. And what we did in Washington, what we're now doing in Korea, becomes part of a larger global architecture designed to reduce the dangers of nuclear weapons and nuclear terrorism, but also allows us, then, to more safely and effectively pursue peaceful uses of nuclear energy.

So again, I want to thank President Lee for his leadership. I want to thank all the leaders who are participating here today. I know people's schedules are extraordinarily busy. We've come a long way in a very short time, and that should encourage us. And that should not lead us to complacency, however; it should fortify our will as we continue to deal with these issues.

I believe we can maintain that will and that focus. I believe we must, because the security of the world depends on the actions that we take.

So, President Lee, thank you again.

NOTE: The President spoke at 9:22 a.m. at the Coex Center.

Remarks With President Nursultan Nazarbayev of Kazakhstan and President Dmitry Anatolyevich Medvedev of Russia and an Exchange With Reporters at the Nuclear Security Summit in Seoul
March 27, 2012

President Nazarbayev. Well, probably all of you know that Semipalatinsk nuclear test site was one of the largest nuclear test sites in the world, together with Nevada. And about 500 nuclear tests have been carried out on this test site, 70 of them in the open air.

And Polygon was closed by my first decree as the President of Kazakhstan 20 years ago, and since then, together with Russia and the United States, we have been working to rehabilitate the territory around the Semipalatinsk test site. And since 2004, we're able to rehabilitate from radiation about 3,000 square kilometers of that Polygon. The total polluted area is about 40,000 square kilometers. And as a result of tests in the past, about 1.5 million people have been radiated.

And this is a very good example of close collaboration when all three countries also worked on getting rid of the military infrastructure on that Polygon. And you probably know that about 100—1,100 warheads have been deployed on military missiles on the territory of the Polygon in military launching shafts. And we closed that also, together with the help of Russian and American partners. And we are very grateful, the people of Kazakhstan are very grateful for that assistance, and we hope that we'll be able to work together in the future for a safer world on nuclear nonproliferation.

President Obama. Well, I'm going to just make a very brief statement here. We wanted to do this brief appearance to highlight one of the most significant examples of what we've been doing through this Nuclear Security Summit and what our three countries have been able to accomplish through some painstaking cooperation over the last several years.

As President of Kazakhstan indicated, this was a major site for nuclear operations during the cold war. There was a lot of loose nuclear material that was vulnerable to potential smuggling, to potential infiltration. And as a consequence of extraordinary cooperation between our three countries—that actually predates my administration, but was accelerated as a consequence of this Nuclear Security Summit—we've been able to effectively lock down and secure all this vulnerable material.

So we have been able to do this in part because of the outstanding leadership of President Nazarbayev and the people of Kazakhstan. We've also been able to do it because the United States and Russia over the last several years have shown ourselves to have a mutual interest in making sure that nuclear materials are secured and that they do not fall into the wrong hands.

And so this kind of multilateral cooperation is being duplicated as a consequence of this Nuclear Security Summit. And it gives you a specific example of the kind of progress that we're making. We're going to need to make more progress over the next several years. But I am confident that we can actually meet the goal that we set in the first Washington summit, which is in 4 years to have made extraordinary progress in making sure that loose nuclear material is not vulnerable to smuggling or to potential terrorist plots.

President Medvedev. Summits are held not only to conduct meetings, not only to shake hands, not only to declare good goals, but it is also held to demonstrate examples, concrete examples, of cooperation. I believe that this is precisely one of such concrete examples.

From 2004, the three countries—United States, Kazakhstan, and Russia—have been cooperating to eliminate the remnants of the past activities within the territory of the Semipalatinsk test site. We were all aware of the threat coming from that test site. And at the moment, now we can state with confidence that all the threats have been liquidated and that the Semipalatinsk test site can now develop in a new capacity. The country of Kazakhstan can look into the future. So this is a—I believe that this is a good example of practical cooperation which should be highlighted.

I would like to thank my partners, in particular President of Kazakhstan Nazarbayev, for his proactive stance and for creating favorable conditions to accomplish those goals. The Russian Federation and the United States are precisely those countries which have special responsibility for ensuring nuclear security of the world. I believe that—and they managed to join efforts in this good example of cooperation.

Although we're aware that the situation we had was the result of the mindset of the past countries had, we managed to show this good example of cooperation, and such example, I believe, should be multiplied, should be reproduced, and should also lead other countries to ensure nuclear security.

President Obama. Thank you very much.

Russia-U.S. Relations/2012 Presidential and Congressional Elections/Missile Defense

Q. Mr. President, can I ask you quickly about the open mike? Can you clarify what you meant by having flexibility on missile defense in a second term, what you wanted to have passed on to Mr. Putin? And isn't it presumptuous to be talking about a second term?

President Obama. First of all, are the mikes on? [*Laughter*] Look, what I said yesterday, Ben [Ben Feller, Associated Press], is I think something that everybody in this room understands, which is——

[*At this point, an interpreter began translating President Obama's remarks.*]

President Obama. I'll just go ahead and then you can translate at the end.

Arms control is extraordinarily complex, very technical, and the only way it gets done is if you can consult and build a strong basis of understanding both between countries as well as within countries. And when you think about the New START Treaty that Dmitry and I were able to hammer out and ultimately get ratified, that was a painstaking 2-year process. I don't think it's any surprise that you can't start that a few months before a Presidential and congressional elections in the United States and at a time when they just completed elections in Russia and they're in the process of a Presidential transition where a new President is going to be coming in a little less than 2 months.

So it was a very simple point, and one that essentially I repeated when I spoke to you guys yesterday, which is that we're going to spend the next 9, 10 months trying to work through some of the technical aspects of how we get past what is a major point of friction—one of the primary points of friction between our two countries—which is this whole missile defense issue. And it involves a lot of complicated issues. If we can get our technical teams to clear out the underbrush, then, hopefully, in 2013, there's a foundation to actually make some significant progress on this and a lot of other bilateral issues.

So I think everybody understands that—if they haven't they haven't been listening to my speeches—I want to reduce our nuclear stockpiles. And one of the barriers to doing that is building trust and cooperation around missile defense issues. And so this is not a matter of hiding the ball; I'm on record. I made a speech about it to a whole bunch of Korean university students yesterday. I want to see us, over time, gradually, systematically, reduce reliance on nuclear weapons.

And as Dmitry said, the United States and Russia, because of our history and because we are nuclear superpowers, have a special obligation. That doesn't make it easy, because both countries are committed to their sovereignty and their defense.

371

And last point I'll make: The only way I get this stuff done is if I'm consulting with the Pentagon, if I'm consulting with Congress, if I've got bipartisan support. And frankly, the current environment is not conducive to those kinds of thoughtful consultations. I think the stories you guys have been writing over the last 24 hours is probably pretty good evidence of that. I think we'll do better in 2013.

All right. Thanks, guys.

NOTE: The President spoke at 12 p.m. at the Coex Center. In his remarks, he referred to Prime Minister Vladimir Vladimirovich Putin of Russia, in his capacity as President-elect of Russia. President Nazarbayev and President Medvedev spoke in Russian, and their remarks were translated by interpreters.

Remarks Prior to a Meeting With Prime Minister Syed Yousuf Raza Gilani of Pakistan in Seoul
March 27, 2012

President Obama. Well, I want to say how much I appreciate the opportunity to meet once again with Prime Minister Gilani and his delegation.

Obviously, the United States and Pakistan have a host of mutual interests. We're both interested in combating terrorism, both internationally and in our respective countries. We both are interested in economic development. We're both interested in nuclear security, as evidenced by our presence here today. And we have been working together, because we're both interested in a stable and secure Afghanistan and a stable and secure region that will benefit not only Pakistan, but also the entire world.

I want to express my appreciation to Prime Minister Gilani for the work that he's done in trying to strengthen the relationship between our two countries. There have been times—I think we should be frank—over the last several months where those relations have experienced strains. But I welcome the fact that the Parliament in Pakistan is reviewing, after some extensive study, the nature of this relationship. I think that it's important for us to get it right. I think it's important for us to have candid dialogue to work through these issues in a constructive fashion and a transparent fashion.

And my expectation is, is that as a consequence of the review that's taking place in Pakistan as well as the work that we're doing on the American side, that we can achieve the kind of balanced approach that respects Pakistan's sovereignty, but also it respects our concerns with respect to our national security and our needs to battle terrorists who have targeted us in the past.

I also want to express to the Prime Minister my appreciation for his recognition that it's in both of our interests and indeed in all of our interests to see an Afghan-led reconciliation process that needs to take place. And I appreciate the Prime Minister's statement in that regard.

And finally, I want to express my thanks for his participation in this conference, because I think that we all agree that given the threats that have been directed in Pakistan, the terrorism that has taken place on their own soil, and obviously our experiences with terrorism that we can't afford to have nonstate actors, terrorists, get their hands on nuclear weapons that could end up destroying our cities or harming our citizens.

So, Mr. Prime Minister, of course, I very much appreciate you being here. And please.

Prime Minister Gilani. Thank you so much. First of all, I want to thank Mr. President for sparing this opportunity to meet me and my delegation in Seoul.

And we are committed to fight against extremism and terrorism. It is in the interest of Pakistan for a stable, peaceful, prosperous, independent, sovereign Afghanistan. We want stability in Afghanistan. If there is a stability in Afghanistan, it's a stability in Pakistan, and peace for Afghanistan and Pakistan. We want to work together with you to have all the peace, prosperity, and progress of the whole world. And we want to work together.

I appreciate that you have said good words about Pakistan, that you want to respect the sovereignty of the country. So we—[*inaudible*]—together, and the parliamentary ses-

sion and we are—[*inaudible*]—to the Parliament.

President Obama. Safe travels.

Prime Minister Gilani. Thank you.

President Obama. Thank you, everybody.

NOTE: The President spoke at 5:16 p.m. at the Coex Center.

Remarks on Energy
March 29, 2012

Thank you very much. Everybody, please have a seat. Sorry we're running just a little bit behind, but I figured it's a great day to enjoy the Rose Garden.

Today Members of Congress have a simple choice to make: They can stand with the big oil companies, or they can stand with the American people.

Right now the biggest oil companies are raking in record profits, profits that go up every time folks pull up into a gas station. But on top of these record profits, oil companies are also getting billions a year—billions a year in taxpayer subsidies—a subsidy that they've enjoyed year after year for the last century.

Think about that. It's like hitting the American people twice. You're already paying a premium at the pump right now. And on top of that, Congress, up until this point, has thought it was a good idea to send billions of dollars more in tax dollars to the oil industry.

It's not as if these companies can't stand on their own. Last year, the three biggest U.S. oil companies took home more than $80 billion in profits. Exxon pocketed nearly $4.7 million every hour. And when the price of oil goes up, prices at the pump go up and so do these companies' profits. In fact, one analysis shows that every time gas goes up by a penny, these companies usually pocket another $200 million in quarterly profits. Meanwhile, these companies pay a lower tax rate than most other companies on their investments, partly because we're giving them billions in tax giveaways every year.

Now, I want to make clear, we all know that drilling for oil has to be a key part of our overall energy strategy. We want U.S. oil compa-

nies to be doing well. We want them to succeed. That's why under my administration, we've opened up millions of acres of Federal lands and waters to oil and gas production. We've quadrupled the number of operating oil rigs to a record high. We've added enough oil and gas pipeline to circle the Earth and then some. And just yesterday we announced the next step for potential new oil and gas exploration in the Atlantic.

So the fact is, we're producing more oil right now than we have in 8 years, and we're importing less of it as well. For 2 years in a row, America has bought less oil from other countries than we produce here at home for the first time in over a decade.

So American oil is booming. The oil industry is doing just fine. With record profits and rising production, I'm not worried about the big oil companies. With high oil prices around the world, they've got more than enough incentive to produce even more oil. That's why I think it's time they got by without more help from taxpayers who are already having a tough enough time paying the bills and filling up their gas tank. And I think it's curious that some folks in Congress, who are the first to belittle investments in new sources of energy, are the ones that are fighting the hardest to maintain these giveaways for the oil companies.

Instead of taxpayer giveaways to an industry that's never been more profitable, we should be using that money to double down on investments in clean energy technologies that have never been more promising: investments in wind power and solar power and biofuels; investments in fuel-efficient cars and trucks and energy-efficient homes and buildings. That's the future. That's the only way we're going to break this cycle of high gas prices that happen year after year after year as the economy is growing. The only time you start seeing lower gas prices is when the economy is doing badly. That's not the kind of pattern that we want to be in. We want the economy doing well, and people to be able to afford their energy costs.

And keep in mind, we can't just drill our way out of this problem. As I said, oil production here in the United States is doing very well, and it's been doing well even as gas prices are going up. Well, the reason is because we use more than 20 percent of the world's oil but we only have 2 percent of the world's known oil reserves. And that means we could drill every drop of American oil tomorrow, but we'd still have to buy oil from other countries to make up the difference. We'd still have to depend on other countries to meet our energy needs. And because it's a world market, the fact that we're doing more here in the United States doesn't necessarily help us because even U.S. oil companies, they're selling that oil on a worldwide market. They're not keeping it just for us. And that means that if there's rising demand around the world, then the prices are going to go up.

That's not the future that I want for America. I don't want folks like these back here and the folks in front of me to have to pay more at the pump every time that there's some unrest in the Middle East and oil speculators get nervous about whether there's going to be enough supply. I don't want our kids to be held hostage to events on the other side of the world.

I want us to control our own destiny. I want us to forge our own future. And that's why, as long as I'm President, America is going to pursue an all-of-the-above energy strategy, which means we will continue developing our oil and gas resources in a robust and responsible way.

But it also means that we're going to keep developing more advanced homegrown biofuels, the kinds that are already powering truck fleets across America.

We're going to keep investing in clean energy like the wind power and solar power that's already lighting thousands of homes and creating thousands of jobs. We're going to keep manufacturing more cars and trucks to get more miles to the gallon so that you can fill up once every 2 weeks instead of every week. We're going to keep building more homes and businesses that waste less energy so that you're in charge of your own energy bills.

We're going to do all of this by harnessing our most inexhaustible resource: American ingenuity and American imagination. That's what we need to keep going. That's what's at stake right now. That's the choice that we face. And that's the choice that's facing Congress today. They can either vote to spend billions of dollars more in oil subsidies that keep us trapped in the past, or they can vote to end these taxpayer subsidies that aren't needed to boost oil production so that we can invest in the future. It's that simple.

And as long as I'm President, I'm betting on the future. And as the people I've talked to around the country, including the people who are behind me here today, they put their faith in the future as well. That's what we do as Americans. That's who we are. We innovate. We discover. We seek new solutions to some of our biggest challenges. And ultimately, because we stick with it, we succeed. And I believe that we're going to do that again. Today the American people are going to be watching Congress to see if they have that same faith.

Thank you very much, everybody.

NOTE: The President spoke at 11 a.m. in the Rose Garden at the White House.

Remarks at an Obama Victory Fund 2012 Fundraiser in Burlington, Vermont
March 30, 2012

Thank you, everybody. Oh, it is good to be in Vermont. I had to come here because Michelle got such a reception here, and everybody was saying how popular she was and how much money she had raised and how everybody loved her, and—[*laughter*]—I was starting to feel a little—a little left out. [*Laughter*] So I said, I've got to go there too.

But part of the reason I had to come is because people like Jane and Bill and Charlie and Marie and others have just been such great friends for such a long time, and the enthusiasm that we received when I was still running, when I came here, was just extraordinary. And you've got a couple of outstanding Senators, a great Member of Congress, just a terrific delegation that has been on the right side of issues for a very long time. And so I just wanted to come up here and say thank you to the people of Vermont for having such good sense. Also, coming from Chicago, I thought it would be nice to enjoy just even a little taste of winter because I don't think it got below 50 degrees in Washington this entire year.

What I'm going to do is be very brief at the top so that I can spend most of my time answering questions.

Since Jane and I first met, and Charlie and I first met, and others, obviously this country has gone through an extraordinary journey: the worst financial crisis since the Great Depression, the worst economic crisis since the 1930s, millions of people losing their jobs, a housing market collapsing, changes internationally that very few of us could have imagined 3 or 4 or 5 years earlier. And so it's been a challenging time for America.

And yet one of the things that always gave me confidence was, as I traveled around the country, both first as a candidate and then as President, what I continually saw was the incredible resilience and strength and imagination of the American people. And so even during the darkest days of this recession, I always had confidence that America would bounce back. It was not a matter of if, it was a matter of when. And the question was, would we be able to pull the country together and move, not only to get us back to where we were before the financial crisis, but to solve these ongoing problems that we'd been putting off for decades.

And 3 years, 3½ years later, I'm here to report that we've made extraordinary progress.

We were losing 800,000 jobs a month the month I was sworn in. We've now seen over the last 2 years almost 4 million jobs created. The unemployment rate has started to tick down. We're seeing the strongest employment in manufacturing since the 1990s. Exports are on track to double the goal that we set. The economy is starting to get stronger, and businesses are starting to feel more confident.

In the meantime, those issues that so many of us were talking about during the election in 2008, we've started to address. So I said that I'd end the war in Iraq. We've ended it. I said that we would get a health care law that would provide near universal coverage so that people don't have to go bankrupt when they get sick in this country. We got it passed. We committed to ending "don't ask, don't tell." "Don't ask, don't tell" is history.

We said that we needed to help our students make sure that they can go to college, that they can afford it. And we took $60 billion that was going to the banks to subsidize them managing the student loan program, and now that money is going directly to students. And millions of students are getting higher Pell grants, or eligible for the first time, and we're on track to make sure that college is a lot more affordable for young people so that they can compete in this 21st-century economy.

And so not only have we been able to right the ship and get the banking system working again and make sure that the economy has an opportunity to grow, but we're also dealing with some of those underlying issues that had challenged us for a very long time, doubling fuel efficiency standards on cars, probably the most significant piece of environmental legislation in a very long time that could end up saving us billions of dollars and taking all kinds of carbon out of the atmosphere.

But I think all of us are here today because we know our job isn't finished. We've got a lot more to do. We still have to do more to make sure that people who don't have work can find work. We're going to have to do more to make sure that our housing system is working for everybody and that people can start recovering from the beating that they've taken with the decline in the real estate market.

We still have to have an energy policy that reflects both the short-term challenges that people are feeling, the pinch that they're feeling at the pump, but also the long-term challenges that we're facing in terms of energy independence and climate change.

We haven't reformed our immigration system yet. And we're a nation of laws and a nation of immigrants, and there's no reason why we shouldn't be able to reconcile those values, to have a system that's sensible and continues to replenish America with extraordinary talent from all around the world.

We've embarked on an extraordinary path to reform K-through-12 education through programs like Race to the Top, and we're encouraging innovation and accountability and making sure that teachers aren't teaching to the test, but instead are able to teach creatively and passionately. But we've got more work to do because there are still too many kids who are being shunted aside.

And on the foreign policy front, we've got to execute effective transition out of Afghanistan, leave a stable country, continue to press on those who would do us harm, and continue to forge the kind of diplomacy around the world that restores respect for America, but also ensures not only our own security, but also opportunity and well-being for folks who continue to suffer from extraordinary poverty around the world.

So we've still got huge challenges remaining, and we're going to have to figure out how to pay for everything that we do, which brings me to why in some ways this election, I think, is actually more important than 2008. In 2008, I was running against a candidate who believed in climate change, believed in immigration reform, believed in the notion of reducing deficits in a balanced way. We had some profound disagreements, but the Republican candidate for President understood that some of these challenges required compromise and bipartisanship.

And what we've witnessed lately is a fundamentally different vision of America and who

we are. It's an America that says—or it's a vision that says that America is about looking out for yourself, not for other people. It's an America that denies something like climate change, rejects it; that takes a position on immigration that would have been unthinkable in either party just a few years ago; that when it comes to figuring out how do we pay for the investments that we need to grow, basically says those of us who are doing best don't have to do a thing, and we will balance that budget on the backs of the poor and seniors, and at the expense of basic research and basic science and investments in clean energy and increasing the cost of student loans for students.

The recent budget that just passed the House, the budget that passed the House yesterday, if you did the math, essentially the only thing that would be left in the Federal Government would be defense; Social Security and the entitlement programs, although those would be diminished; interest on the national debt. That would be about it. You'd be looking at about 1 percent of the entire Federal budget devoted to everything else: education, environmental protection, science; those things that historically have made us an economic superpower, but also a country in which everybody has a fair shot, everybody does their fair share, and everybody is playing by the same set of rules.

And so, in some ways, this is going to be healthy for our democracy. I think it's going to be a clarifying election about who we are and what we stand for. But it's enormous. A lot is at stake in this election, and we're going to have to fight for it. We're not going to be complacent and be able to deliver on what we think is the right path for our kids and our grandkids and future generations.

And so I'm going to need your help. And in some ways, it may be a little harder because it has lost some of the novelty, right? When back in '08, it was cool to say: "Oh, you know, I'm supporting this guy Obama. You heard of him?" [*Laughter*] "Let me tell you about him." Now I'm old hat, I'm gray. [*Laughter*] But my determination is undiminished. My confidence in the core decency of the American people is undiminished. I believe we're on the right track. And Jane is right: I believe I'm going to get there. More importantly, I believe America is going to get there with your help.

Thank you very much, everybody.

NOTE: The President spoke at 1:04 p.m. at the Sheraton Burlington hotel. In his remarks, he referred to Jane Stetson, national finance chair, Democratic National Committee, and her husband E. William Stetson III; Charles F. Kireker, cofounder and senior adviser, Fresh Tracks Capital, L.P., and his wife Marie Kireker; and Sen. John S. McCain III, in his capacity as the 2008 Republican Presidential nominee. Audio was not available for verification of the content of these remarks.

Remarks at an Obama Victory Fund 2012 Fundraiser in Burlington
March 30, 2012

The President. Hello, Vermont! Oh, thank you! Oh, this is a good crowd here in Vermont! It is good to be at UVM. Go Catamounts! It is good to be in Vermont.

Now, out of all 50 States, Vermont has gone the longest without a Presidential visit. The last time a President stopped by was President Clinton in 1995. So we decided that today we are going to reset the clock.

I—couple of acknowledgements I want to make. First of all, give Jeanne a big round of applause for their introduction. You've got one of the best Governors in the country. And when flooding came and disaster struck, he was here every single day working on your behalf. And we couldn't be prouder of him—Peter Shumlin. We got two outstanding Senators, Patrick Leahy and Bernie Sanders. You've got an outstanding mayor-elect, Miro Weinberger.

Give it up for Grace Potter and the Nocturnals. I also want to thank Carolyn Dwyer and the entire host committee for helping to organize this unbelievable event.

And one last thing I want to do, I want to express my condolences to everybody who knew and loved Melissa Jenkins, because I know that some of the elected officials are going on to that funeral. This is a woman, by all accounts, who devoted her life to her community and helping to shape young minds. And I know that Vermont's heartbroken, so all we can do is live our lives in a way that pays tribute to hers, by looking out for her students and her son. And Michelle and I want to express our thoughts and prayers to everybody who knew her. So I know that's a tough situation.

Now, I'm here—[*applause*]—you know, maybe I should just quit while I'm ahead here. It's—[*laughter*]—I am going to take off my jacket, though. It's a little warm. The—I'm here not just because I need your help. I'm here because the country needs your help.

There were a lot of reasons that so many of you worked your hearts out for our campaign in 2008. It wasn't because it was going to be easy. It wasn't because it was a sure thing. When you decided to support a candidate named Barack Hussein Obama, that's not a guarantee of success. [*Laughter*] You didn't need a poll to know that might be some heavy sledding there. [*Laughter*]

The point is, you didn't join the campaign because of me. You joined it because we had a shared vision for America. It wasn't a vision where everybody is left to fend for themselves. It wasn't a vision where the rules are made just for the powerful. It was a vision of an America where everybody who works hard has a chance to get ahead—everybody.

That's the vision that we shared. That's the change that we believed in. And we knew it wasn't going to come easy; we knew it wouldn't come quickly. But we had confidence, we had faith in each other. We believed that when Americans make commitments to each other about a bold, generous vision for the country, that we can achieve it. There's no challenge we can't overcome.

And here's what I want to report: that in 3 years, because of what so many of you did in 2008, we've begun to see what change looks like. We've begun to see what change looks like.

Change is the first bill I signed into law, a law that says women deserve an equal day's pay for an equal day's work, because I want our daughters treated just like our sons.

Change is the decision we made to rescue an auto industry that was on the verge of collapse, even when some said let's let Detroit go bankrupt. One million jobs were at stake, so we weren't going to let that happen. And today, GM is back on top as the world's number-one automaker, reported the highest profits in a hundred years; 200,000 new jobs over the last 2½ years. The American auto industry is back, and it's making cars that are more fuel efficient. So that's helping the environment, even as we're putting people to work.

Change is the decision we made to stop waiting for Congress to do something about our oil addiction. That's why we finally raised our fuel efficiency standards. By the middle of the next decade, we will be driving American-made cars that get almost 55 miles to a gallon. Saves the typical family more than $8,000 at the pump. That's what change is.

Change is the fight we won to stop handing $60 billion in taxpayer giveaways to the banks who were processing student loans. We decided let's give those student loans directly to students, which meant we could make college more affordable to young people who need it. That's what change is. That happened because of you.

And yes, change is the health care reform that we passed after over a century of trying, reform that will finally ensure that in the United States of America, no one will go broke just because they get sick. Already, 2.5 million young people now have health insurance who didn't have it before because this law lets them stay on their parent's plan. Already, millions of seniors are paying less for their prescription drugs because of this law. Already, Americans can't be denied or dropped by their insurance companies when they need care the most. Already, they're getting preventive care that they didn't have before. That's happening right now.

Change is the fact that for the first time in history, you don't have to hide who you love in order to serve the country you love, because we ended "don't ask, don't tell."

Change is the fact that for the first time in 9 years, there are no Americans fighting in Iraq. We refocused our efforts on the terrorists who actually attacked us on 9/11. And thanks to the brave men and women in uniform, Al Qaida is weaker than it's ever been. Usama bin Laden is no more. We've begun to transition in Afghanistan to put them in the lead and start bringing our troops home from Afghanistan. That's what change is.

Now, none of this has been easy. We've had a little resistance from the other side. [*Laughter*] We've got more work to do. There are still too many Americans who are out there looking for work. There are still too many families who can barely afford to pay the bills or make the mortgage. We're still recovering from the worst economic storm in generations.

Audience member. Love you!

The President. Love you back!

But over the past 2 years, businesses have added nearly 4 million new jobs. Our manufacturers are creating jobs for the first time since the 1990s. Our economy is getting stronger. The recovery is accelerating. All of which means the last thing we can afford to do is to go back to the same policies that got us into the mess in the first place.

That's what the other side wants to do. They make no secret about it. They want to go back to the days where Wall Street played by its own rules. They want to go back to the day when insurance companies could do whatever they wanted to you. They want to go back to the days where—they want to continue to spend trillions of dollars on tax breaks for the wealthiest individuals in America, even if it means adding to the deficit or gutting education or gutting investments in clean energy or hurting Medicare.

Their philosophy is simple: You are on your own. You're on your own. If you are out of work, can't find a job, tough luck, you're on your own. If you don't have health care, that's your problem. You're on your own. If you're born into poverty, lift yourself up out of your own—with your own bootstraps, even if you don't have boots. You're on your own. They believe—that's their—that's how America has advanced. That's the cramped, narrow conception they have of liberty. And they are wrong. They are wrong.

In the United States of America, we are greater together than we are on our own. This country advances when we keep that basic American promise: If you work hard, you can do well enough to raise a family, own a home, send your kids to college, put a little away for retirement. And it doesn't matter who you are, where you come from, what you look like. That's what has created this extraordinary country of ours. That's what we're fighting for. That's the choice in this election.

This is not just your usual, run-of-the-mill political debate. This is the defining issue of our time, a make-or-break moment for the middle class. That's what we got to fight for.

We can go back to an economy that was built on outsourcing and bad debt and phony financial profits. Or we can build an economy that's built to last. An economy that's built on American manufacturing and American innovation and American energy and American workers who are trained and skilled and the values that make this country great: hard work and fair play and shared responsibility. That's the vision I believe in. That's what I'm fighting for.

We've got to make sure that the next generation of manufacturing takes root not in Asia, not in Europe, but in factories of Detroit and Pittsburgh and Cleveland. I don't want this Nation just to be known for buying and consuming things. I want us to build and sell things all around the world. I want us to stop rewarding businesses that ship jobs overseas, reward companies that are investing right here in the United States of America.

I want to make our schools the envy of the world. And by the way, that starts with the man or woman at the front of the classroom. A good teacher can increase the lifetime earnings of a classroom by over $250,000. A great teacher can help a child trapped in poverty dream and

then live beyond their circumstances. So I don't want folks in Washington to be bashing teachers. I don't want them to defend the status quo. I want us to give schools the resources they need to hire good teachers, reward great teachers. I want us to grant schools the flexibility to teach with creativity and passion and stop teaching to the test and replace teachers who aren't helping kids learn. That's what I want to see happen.

And when kids do graduate, the most daunting challenge can be the cost of college. When Americans owe more tuition debt than they do credit card debt, you know we've got a problem. Now, the first thing we got to do: Congress has to stop interest rates that are currently scheduled to go up in July on student loans, which will be a huge problem for a lot of young people. I've already asked Congress to do it. They haven't done it—shocking enough—they haven't done it so far. [*Laughter*] And colleges and universities have to do their part too to keep tuition from going up, because higher education cannot be a luxury. It is an economic imperative that every family in America should be able to afford.

An economy built to last is one that supports scientists and researchers and science. Whether we're talking about stem cell research or climate change, we don't need science deniers. We need people to understand that America has always succeeded because of our belief in science, our investment in research.

We've got to make sure the next great breakthrough in clean energy happens right here in the United States of America. We have been subsidizing oil companies for a hundred years now through taxpayer giveaways. I think it's time—I just talked about this yesterday—it's time to stop taxpayer giveaways to an oil industry that has been rarely more profitable. Let's double down on clean energy that has never been more promising: solar and wind and biofuels and energy efficiency, electric batteries. That's what we need to be investing in.

We've got to rebuild America. I want a—our businesses and our people to have access to the best roads and the best airports, faster high-speed rail, and Internet access. It's time for us to take the money we were spending at war, use half of it to pay down our debt, use the rest of it to start doing some nation-building right here at home.

And we've got to make sure that we've got a tax system that is actually fair. Part of that is something I call the Buffett rule. It's very simple: If you pay—if you are making more than a million dollars a year—not—I'm not saying you have a million dollars, I'm saying you're making a million dollars every year—then you shouldn't pay a lower rate than your secretary. That's a pretty simple proposition.

Now, if you make less than $250,000 a year, like 98 percent of American families, your taxes shouldn't go up, because right now folks are struggling still to dig themselves out of this incredible recession. But if you're making more than a million dollars a year, you can do a little more. This is not class envy. This is not class warfare. This is basic math. That's what this is.

Look, if somebody like me gets a tax break that they don't need and that the country can't afford, then one of two things are going to happen: Either it adds to our deficit, or we're taking something away from somebody else. That student now has to pay a higher interest rate on their student loan because we've got to make up the money somewhere. Or that senior has to start paying more for their Medicare because the money has to be made up somewhere. Or that veteran doesn't get the PTSD care that they needed after serving our country. Or a family that's struggling to get by maybe is getting less home heating oil assistance.

Look, there's no way of getting around that. Either folks like me are doing more, or somebody who can't afford it is getting less. And that's not right. That's not who we are. That's not what America is about.

I hear politicians talking about values in an election year. I hear a lot about that. Let me tell you about values. Hard work, personal responsibility, those are values. But looking out for one another, that's a value. The idea we're all in this together, I am my brother's keeper, I am my sister's keeper, that's a value. The idea that we think about the next generation and we're taking care of our planet, that's a value.

Each of us is only here because somebody, somewhere, felt responsibility, yes, to their families, but also to their fellow citizens, also to our country's future. That's the American story. The American story is not just about what we do on our own. Yes, we're rugged individualists, and we expect personal responsibility, and everybody out there has got to work hard and carry their weight. But we also have always understood that we wouldn't win the race for new jobs and businesses and middle class security if we were just applying some you're-on-your-own economics. It's been tried in our history, and it hasn't worked. It didn't work when we tried it in the decade before the Great Depression. It didn't work when we tried it in the last decade. We just tried this. What they're peddling has been tried. It did not work.

We know this from our own lives. If we attract some outstanding young person to become a teacher by giving them the pay and the support that they deserve, and that teacher goes on to educate the next Steve Jobs, well, we all benefit. We all do better. America rises. If we're providing faster Internet to rural America so that some small-business owner suddenly can sell his or her goods around the world, that's good for all of us. If we build a new bridge that saves a shipping company time and money, then workers and customers all around the country benefit. They do better. That's how America became an economic superpower.

This has not traditionally been a Democratic or a Republican idea. It was a Republican, Teddy Roosevelt, who called for a progressive income tax. It was Dwight Eisenhower who built the Interstate Highway System. The first Republican President, President Lincoln—who, by the way, couldn't win the nomination for the Republican primary right now, for the—[*laughter*]. He'd be—[*applause*]—in the middle of a civil war, helped to make the transcontinental railroad possible, the land-grant colleges, the National Academy of Scientists. He understood that we're in this together, we've got to make an investment in our futures. It was with the help of Republicans that FDR was able to give millions of returning heroes, including my grandfather, the chance to go to college through the GI bill.

And that same spirit of common purpose, it still exists today. Maybe it doesn't exist in Washington.

Audience member. It exists in Vermont.

The President. But out here in Vermont and all across America, it's there. It's there when you talk to folks on Main Street. It's there when you go to a town hall. It's there when you talk to members of our Armed Forces. It's there when you talk to people in their places of worship.

Our politics may be divided. But most Americans still understand that no matter where you come from, no matter who you are, we rise or fall together as one Nation, as one people. And that's what's at stake right now. That's what this election's about.

So I know we've gone through some tough years. And I know that for all the things we've done, we've still got so much undone. We—and sometimes the change we fought for hasn't always come as fast as we wanted. And when you see what's been going on in Washington, I know it's tempting sometimes to get discouraged, to kind of think, well, maybe change just isn't possible. Maybe it was an illusion. But I want you guys to recall, I did say back in 2008, real change, big change, it's hard. It takes time. It takes more than a single term and more than a single President. What it takes is ordinary citizens who are committed to keep fighting and to keep pushing and inching us closer and closer and closer to our country's highest ideals.

And you know something else I used to say in 2008, I said, I'm not a perfect man—Mi-

chelle will tell you that—and I'll never be a perfect President. But I made a promise to you then that I would always tell you what I believed and I would always tell you where I stood and I would wake up every single day fighting as hard as I know how for you. And I have kept that promise. I have kept that promise. I have kept that promise.

So if you're willing to keep pushing with me through all the obstacles, through all the naysayers; if you're willing to keep reaching for that vision of America that we all have talked about—that commitment you didn't just make to me or I made to you, but that we made to each other—I guarantee you change will come. If you're willing to work harder in this election than you did in the last one, I promise you change will come. If you're willing to knock on some doors and make some phone calls, I promise you change will come.

We will finish what we started in 2008. Fight with me, and press on with me, and we will remind the world once again just what America is all about.

God bless you, and God bless the United States of America.

NOTE: The President spoke at 2:25 p.m. at the University of Vermont. In his remarks, he referred to Jeanne A. Morrissey, president, J.A. Morrissey, Inc., who introduced the President; musician Grace Potter; Carolyn Dwyer, member, Vermont Democratic Party Executive Committee; and St. Johnsbury, VT, resident Melissa Jenkins, who was killed on March 25, and her son Ty.

Remarks at an Obama Victory Fund 2012 Fundraiser in South Portland, Maine
March 30, 2012

The President. Hello, Maine! Thank you! Thank you very much. Thank you! Well, it is good to be in South Portland, Maine!

Audience member. I love you!

The President. I love you! Thank you! It is wonderful to be here.

First of all, can everybody please give Richard a big round of applause for that great introduction. A couple other people I want to acknowledge. First of all, your outstanding Congresswoman, Chellie Pingree, is here. One of the great statesmen of our time, Senator

George Mitchell, in the house. From nearby Portland, Mayor Michael Brennan is here. And the Maine Finance Committee and everybody who helped put this together—what a wonderful event. And whoever arranged for the great weather, good job. The last time I was in Maine it was snowing—[*laughter*]—not surprisingly, and I love snow, but this is good too. [*Laughter*]

Now, let me say this, Maine. I am here today not just because I need your help. I'm here because the country needs your help. A lot of you worked really hard in 2008 in our campaign. And the reason you worked so hard wasn't because you thought it was going to be a cakewalk. When you decide to support a Presidential candidate named Barack Hussein Obama—[*laughter*]—then you know that this is not a sure thing. [*Laughter*]

The reason you guys worked so hard wasn't just because of me. It was because you shared a vision about what America is all about. You shared a vision about who we are as a people. And that vision said that we don't just leave people to fend for themselves. We don't just let the powerful play by their own rules. It was a vision of America where we're all in it together. Where everybody who works hard has the chance to get ahead, no matter what they look like, no matter where they come from, not just those at the very top, but everybody—that that was the recipe for American success.

That was the vision that we shared. That was the change we believed in. We knew it wouldn't be easy. We knew it wouldn't be quick. But when you think back over the last 3 years, I want you to know that because of what you did in 2008, we've begun to see what change looks like. We've begun to see it. We've begun to see it.

Change is the first bill I signed into law, a law that says a woman deserves an equal day's pay for an equal day's work. That's the kind of change we believed in.

Change is the decision that we made to rescue the American auto industry. There were a million jobs at stake. There were those who said let Detroit go bankrupt. We didn't do it, and today GM is back on top as the world's number-one automaker. And Detroit has never made better cars than it is today. With more than 200,000 new jobs over the last 2½ years, the American auto industry is back. And they're making better cars, and more fuel-efficient cars than ever before. That's what change is.

Change is the decision that we made to stop waiting for Congress to do something about our oil addiction and finally raise fuel efficiency standards on cars. And by the middle of the next decade, we're going to be driving American-made cars that get almost 55 miles a gallon, and that will save the typical family $8,000 at the pump over time. That's what change is. That happened because of you.

Change is the fight that we won to have $60 billion stop going to banks and instead go to lower interest rates for student loans and more help on Pell grants, so that our young people can get the college educations that they need to compete in the 21st century. That's what change is.

And yes, Maine, change is the health care reform that we passed after a century of trying, because we believe that in America, in this great country of ours, nobody should go bankrupt just because they get sick. And as a consequence of what you did, 2.5 million young people have health insurance now that didn't have it before because they're staying on their parents' plans. Millions of seniors are now paying less for prescription drugs. Insurance companies can't deny you coverage right at the time when you need it. People are getting preventive care that they weren't getting before. We're going to make sure the people with pre-existing conditions are finally able to get coverage. That's what change is. That happened because of what you guys did in 2008.

Change is the fact that for the first time in history, you don't have to hide who you love in order to serve the country that you love. We ended "don't ask, don't tell." Ended it.

And change is keeping another promise I made in 2008. For the first time in 9 years, we don't have any Americans fighting in Iraq. We refocused our efforts on the terrorists who actually attacked us on 9/11. And thanks to our brave men and women in uniform, Al Qaida is weaker than ever before and Usama bin Laden is no more. We've begun to transition in Afghanistan to put them into the lead. We are starting to bring our troops home. That's what change is. That happened because of you.

Now, Maine, nothing—none of this has been easy. And if you notice, we haven't gotten a lot of help from the other side. [*Laughter*] We've still got more work to do. I was listening to Richard tell his story, and he's absolutely right. That determination, that willingness to do whatever it takes, understanding that a job is not just a matter of money, it's also a matter of dignity and purpose and contributing to this country, that spirit of Richard's, that exists all across America.

But there are still a lot of folks who are still looking for work. We went through the worst financial crisis and the worst economic crisis in our lifetimes. And although we're starting to make progress, we still have too many families that are having trouble making the bills, too many folks still out of work. We're still recovering from this incredible storm.

But here's the good news. Over the last 2 years, businesses have added nearly 4 million new jobs. Our manufacturers are creating jobs for the first time since the nineties. Our economy is getting stronger. The recovery is accelerating. And that means the last thing we can afford to do right now is to go back to the very same policies that got us into this mess in the first place. Right?

But of course, that's exactly what the other side—all those folks who are running for this office—that's exactly what they're proposing. They don't make any secret about it. They want to go back to the days when Wall Street played by its own rules. They want to roll back health care so that insurance companies can jack up your rates whenever they want. They want to continue to spend trillions of dollars more on tax breaks for the wealthiest individuals, even if it means adding to the deficit, even if it means gutting things like education and basic research and clean energy and Medicare, all those things that help this economy grow.

Their philosophy is simple: You're on your own. That's their view that the only way the economy can grow is if you're out of a job, tough luck, figure it out on your own. If you don't have health care, too bad, you're on your own. If you're a senior having trouble paying your prescription drugs, that's not our problem. If you're a young person coming out of poverty, pull yourself up by your own bootstraps, even if you don't have boots. [*Laughter*] That's their vision.

And by the way, you look at their budget that the Republicans in the House of Representatives just passed, it's no exaggeration. They would gut things that we've always believed were the core of making America great: education, basic research in science, caring for the most vulnerable.

They are wrong. They are wrong in their vision of America. In the United States of America, we are greater on our own—we are greater together than we are on our own. In the United States of America, we believe in the basic promise that if you work hard, you can do well enough to raise your family and own a home and send your kids to college and put a little away for retirement.

That's the choice in this election: different visions of America. This is not just about another political debate. This is the defining issue of our time at a make-or-break moment for the middle class in this country: Who's going to be fighting for you? That's what this is about.

We can go back——

Audience members. Four more years! Four more years! Four more years!

The President. We can go back to what they're offering: an economy built on outsourcing and phony debt and phony financial profits. Or we can fight for an economy that works for everybody, an economy that's built to last, an economy built on American manufacturing and American science and American energy and American education that makes sure our kids have the skills they need. And the values that have always made this country great: hard work, everybody having a fair shot, everybody doing their fair share, everybody operating under the same set of rules, shared responsibility.

That's what we're fighting for. That's the kind of America we need to build.

I don't know about you, but I think we need to make sure the next generation of manufacturing, for example, takes root not in Asia, not in Europe. I want it to take place right here in Maine. I want it to take place in factories in Detroit and Pittsburgh and Cleveland. I don't want this Nation to be known just for buying and consuming things. I want it to be known for producing and inventing and selling stuff. That's how America was built. That's the kind of economy we've got to get back to.

And that's why it's time to stop rewarding businesses that ship jobs overseas. Let's start rewarding companies that create jobs right here in America. Let's give them tax breaks.

I want to make our schools the envy of the world. And we start to do that, not only are we putting more money into education, but we're also insisting on reform. And that starts with the man or woman at the front of the classroom. A good teacher can increase the lifetime earnings of a classroom by $250,000. A great teacher can inspire a kid who's trapped in poverty, trapped in their own circumstances, to shoot for something higher, to dream big.

So I don't want to hear folks in Washington just bashing teachers. I don't want them defending the status quo. Let's give schools the resources they need to hire good teachers and reward great teachers. Let's give schools the flexibility they need to teach with creativity and passion. We can stop teaching to the test. Replace teachers who aren't doing the job, but let's give them the power they need to inspire their students.

And when kids do graduate, right now they're having trouble financing their college educations. When Americans owe more in tuition debt than credit card debt, you know that's a problem. And that's why—coming up in July, by the way, if Congress doesn't do anything, the interest rates on student loans are going to go up, they're going to double.

That's a bad idea, which is why I've said, Congress, let's get moving. Now, they haven't done it yet. So you guys need to make sure that everybody understands how important this is.

And colleges and universities, they've got to do their part keeping tuition down. Because higher education can't be a luxury; it is an economic imperative that every family in America should be able to afford.

An economy built to last is one where we support scientists and research and science. Whether it's stem cell research or climate change, we want to make sure that the great medical breakthroughs happen here in the United States and that happens because we finance research. We want to make sure that the next breakthroughs in clean energy happen here in the United States. That happens because we support clean energy.

We have—we've subsidized oil companies for 100 years. And I think they're doing pretty good, last I checked. Every time you fill up a tank, they're doing just fine. So I think it's time to end 100 years of taxpayer giveaways to an industry that's never been more profitable. Let's double down on the clean energy industry that's never been more promising: solar power and wind power, biofuels.

And let's rebuild America. We're a nation of builders. You go to other countries, they've got newer airports, better rail lines. That's not who—America always had the best stuff. [*Laughter*] I want to make sure that our businesses have access to the newest roads and airports and the fastest railroads and Internet access for everybody. It's time for us to stop—look, let's take the money that we're no longer spending at war, use half of it to pay down our debt, use the other half to do some nation-building here at home. What do you think, Maine? I think it's time.

And when it comes to our deficit, when it comes to our fiscal situation, let's have a tax system that reflects everybody doing their fair share, doing their fair share. Some of you know I've proposed something called the Buffett rule. It's a pretty simple rule that Warren Buffett happens to endorse: If you make more than $1 million a year—I don't mean that you have $1 million, I mean every year, you're making more than $1 million—you should not pay a tax rate that's lower than your secretary's, which is what is happening for too many folks right now.

What I've said is, if you make $250,000 a year or less, like 98 percent of American families, then your taxes don't need to go up. Folks are still struggling. But if you're doing really well, you can do a little bit more. And when I say this, look, this is not class warfare, it's not class envy. This is just basic math. [*Laughter*] Because if somebody like me gets a tax break that I don't need and the country can't afford, then one of two things is going to happen. Either it adds to our deficit, or it takes something away from somebody else: that veteran who needs services for his PTSD after he served our country; that student that's trying to afford getting their college degree; that senior who's already having a tough time paying for their prescription drugs.

Why would we set up a system where I don't do anything and somebody who's in a tougher position has to bear the entire burden? That's not right. That's not who we are.

You know, I hear some of these other folks, some of these politicians talking about values during an election year. Well, let me tell you about values. Hard work is a value. Personal responsibility is a value. Looking out for one another is a value. The idea that I'm my brother's keeper, my sister's keeper, that's a value.

You and me, all of us, we're here just because somebody, somewhere, at some point, felt a responsibility not just to themselves, not even just to their own families, but they felt a responsibility to our fellow citizens, to our country's future.

I think about my own background. Somebody had the foresight to say, let's help people finance their college educations, and that's why my mother, a single mom, was able to get her degree even after she had me.

I think about—when you listen to Michelle talk about growing up, her and her brother, her dad, a blue-collar worker, her mom stayed at home and then went to work as a secretary, neither of them had a college degree. But Michelle talks about how there were always like after-school programs and sports programs and activities for kids, because somebody thought, you know what, let's make an investment in these kids so that they might have that ladder to opportunity, because that's how all of America grows.

Everybody here has a story like that. If it's not you, then it's your grandparents or your great-grandparents. We all have benefited because we didn't just think narrowly about the here and now and me; we thought about the future and us.

This is about what we can do together. We won't win the race for new jobs and new businesses and middle class security if we cling to this same old, worn-out, tired, you're-on-your-own economics that the other side is peddling. I mean, they act like we haven't tried it. We tried it. [*Laughter*] It was tried in the decades before the Great Depression. It didn't work then. It was tried in the last decade. It didn't work.

The idea that you would keep on doing the same thing over and over again, even though it's been proven not to work, that's a sign of madness. [*Laughter*] We've got to take this in a different direction.

And we know that from our own experience. Look, if we attract an outstanding young person to go into teaching because we're paying them well, we're giving them support, professional development, and they go on to teach the next Steve Jobs, that's good for all of us. If we provide faster Internet service to some rural part of Maine and there's some small business out there that suddenly has access to a worldwide market, that's good for the entire economy. If we build a new bridge that saves a shipping company time and money, well, workers and customers all over the country, they benefit.

And by the way, this has never been a Democratic or a Republican idea. The first Republican President, Lincoln, during—in the middle of a Civil War, he made investments in helping to forge the transcontinental railroad and started the American Academy of Sciences and land-grant colleges, because he wasn't just thinking about now, he was thinking about the greatness of this country in the future. Teddy Roosevelt called for a progressive income tax, a

Republican. Dwight Eisenhower built the Interstate Highway System. There were Republicans who helped FDR in Congress give millions of returning heroes, including my grandfather, the chance to go college on the GI bill.

So this is not a partisan idea. This is an American idea. And that same sense of common purpose exists today. It's alive and well. Maybe not in Washington—[*laughter*]—but here in Maine, all across America, on Main Streets and town halls, when you talk to our men and women in uniform, and you go to folks' places of worship, they understand this.

Our politics may be divided. But most Americans still understand that we've got a stake in each other. We're greater together. It doesn't matter what you look like, where you come from, we rise or fall as one Nation and one people. And that's what's at stake right now. That's what this election is about.

So I know it has been a tough few years. And for all the changes we've made, there are times where folks have gotten frustrated or discouraged, say things are so tough in Washington, so dysfunctional. Things just aren't happening as fast as they need to. And so it's understandable, it's tempting for some folks to just say, you know what, maybe the change we believed in is impossible. But I want to remind you, during the campaign I warned you this was going to be hard. Big change is hard. It takes time. It takes more than a year. It takes more than a single term. It takes more than a single President.

What it really requires is a committed citizenry who are willing to keep fighting and pushing, inching this closer—inching this country closer and closer to its highest ideals.

Michelle will tell you I'm not a perfect man. [*Laughter*] And I said that I wouldn't be a perfect President. But I made a promise in 2008. I said I'd always tell you what I think, I'd always tell you where I stood. And I said that I'd wake up every single day, fighting as hard as I know how for you. And I have kept that promise. I've kept that promise. I have kept that promise.

And so if you're willing to keep pushing with me and keep fighting with me, keep reaching for that vision that we believed in, then I promise you we won't just win another election, but we will finish what we started in 2008. And this country will be better for it. And we will remind the world just why it is that the United States of America is the greatest nation on Earth.

Thank you, everybody. God bless you. God bless the United States of America.

NOTE: The President spoke at 5:08 p.m. at Southern Maine Community College. In his remarks, he referred to Richard Schwartz, engineer, Kestrel Aircraft Co.; and former Sen. George J. Mitchell, Jr.

Remarks at an Obama Victory Fund 2012 Fundraiser in Portland, Maine
March 30, 2012

Thank you. Everybody, please have a seat. Have a seat.

Well, first of all, you want Karen and Bonnie having your back because you can tell that they're not going to take no for an answer. [*Laughter*] It is just a thrill to be here. I want to thank both of them. I also want to thank Bobby and Rob, because, like me, they don't shine quite as brightly as their spouses. [*Laughter*] But nevertheless, we are extremely fortunate to be improving our gene pool because of who we married.

A couple of other people I just want to acknowledge. First of all, your outstanding Members of Congress: Chellie Pingree is here; somebody who always is fighting for working people, Mike Michaud is here. One of the true statesmen in the history of American politics, George Mitchell is here. Your former Governor, John Baldacci is here. And one of the best SBA Administrators of all time, Karen Mills is in the house.

Now, I will confess that part of the reason I came here was Michelle just had too good a time. [*Laughter*] She came up here, and she came back, and she was all, "Oh, we had so much fun, and everybody was so nice, and they all thought I was so much better than you, and"—[*laughter*]—and I said, "Hold on, time out, time out." [*Laughter*] I said, "I got to get up there too."

I should point out, by the way, that during Michelle's birthday, I did the same thing: I brought a birthday cake and a check. [*Laughter*] So that's where they got the idea. [*Laughter*]

I could not be more grateful to all of you for just the extraordinary reception and hospitality. There are a lot of you who were involved in 2008, and a lot of you who have signed up for a second tour of duty here. And it's truly moving to me, and every time I've come to Maine, we have had this extraordinary reception. And people I think have not just been supportive financially, but more importantly, through organizing and knocking on doors and making phone calls, which has obviously been the hallmark of all our effort and dates back to my own history in politics.

I'm going to speak very briefly at the top because I want to save a lot of time for questions and answers and comments and advice. [*Laughter*]

We've gone through a tough 3 years, this country, as tough as any in our lifetime: the worst financial crisis since the Great Depression, the economic aftermath that left millions without work, a collapsed housing market. It's hard to remember sometimes how perilous things were when I was sworn in. The month I was sworn into office, we lost 800,000 jobs in that month alone. We had lost almost 4 million in the months before I took office. And then we would just keep on shedding jobs for the first few months that I was sworn in. The banks were locked up, so even blue-chip companies couldn't get credit. People, I think, genuinely thought that you might see a world financial meltdown. And nobody exactly knew where the bottom was. The stock market, by the way, was about half of what it is today.

And that meant we had to move fast to save the auto industry, to get the banks lending again, to make sure that State governments and local governments didn't have to lay off

even more teachers and first-responders and others that were providing vital services, but frankly, the States and local governments were having trouble being able to afford.

And we moved so fast that in some ways, people didn't fully appreciate the scope and magnitude of what got done in those first 6 months, that first year. Here's the good news: As you look back, from where we were to where we are now, over the last 2 years we've created almost 4 million jobs. We have the strongest manufacturing job growth since the 1990s. The auto industry is back, stronger than it was before. GM is once again the number-one auto company in the world, making profits that are higher than at any time in its 100-year history. We have seen the unemployment rate start ticking down. We're seeing companies hiring again, companies investing again. There's a sense that things have stabilized and that we can start getting back to where we were before this terrible storm.

But here's the thing. I ran for office not just to get back to the status quo; I ran for office—I ran for this office because we had not tended to a set of challenges that had been building up for decades. And that's why even as we were trying to right the ship and yank ourselves out of a potential depression, we did not take our eye off the commitments that I had made to you when I ran for office.

And that's why we fulfilled pledges to end "don't ask, don't tell," or to sign the Lilly Ledbetter act that ensures equal pay for equal work. That's why we followed through on commitments to invest in clean energy and doubled fuel efficiency standards on cars and trucks in an unprecedented fashion.

That's why we followed through on the commitment I made to make sure that people don't go bankrupt when they get sick and passed the Affordable Care Act. And already, you've got 2.5 million young people who have health insurance because of it. And already, everybody here who has insurance has protections that are more robust than the patient's bill of rights that had been debated in the 1990s and that had never gotten done. And seniors are benefiting from lower prescription drugs because of it. And small businesses are getting subsidies so that they can provide health insurance to their workers.

That's why we followed through and ended the war in Iraq. That's why we followed through and targeted Al Qaida. That's why, with Usama bin Laden gone and Al Qaida weakened, we've been able to start ramping down our involvement in Afghanistan and provide transition so that Afghans can take control of their own country. That's why we ended torture and we put our fight against terrorism on a legal footing. And that's why we worked to restore our respect around the world.

So, in addition to trying to stabilize the economy, we've tried to deal with issues like energy and health care and education, where we've made more strides in terms of reforming the system than probably the previous 30 years just in the last 3, making sure that college is more affordable. We've been focused on those things because those are the foundations for long-term growth, long-term sustainable growth that is inclusive, that says everybody gets a fair shot and everybody does their fair share and everybody plays by the same set of rules.

Now, in some ways, this election, then, becomes more important than 2008, not only to preserve the gains that had been made, but also to finish the task that we set ourselves—that we set for ourselves in 2008. Because we still have more work to do. We still have too many folks who are unemployed, which means that we've got to make sure that we've got a Tax Code that's incentivizing investment here in the United States, and we're enforcing our trade laws so that there's a level playing field, and we're training our workers to make sure that they can compete in this 21st-century globalized economy.

It means that we've got to sustain the work we've done making investments in research and development so that the breakthroughs in biotech or clean energy happen here in the United States.

It means that we have to preserve the gains we've made when it comes to respecting science. But it also means that when it comes to education, we've still got kids who are dropping out, unable to read, and they can't compete in this global economy. So we're going to have to do more work there.

It means we've got to invest in infrastructure. We used to have the best roads, the best bridges, the best rail lines. We don't anymore. And now is the time to rebuild America.

We still have to do more when it comes to energy, because as much progress as we've made over the last few years, the fact of the matter is, is that we still are importing too much oil and our economy is still subject to the whims of what happens in the Middle East. And our environment is still captive to our addiction to fossil fuels.

We've still got to reform an immigration system that's broken, because I believe we're a nation of laws and a nation of immigrants, and we can reconcile those two values, make this country stronger, because we continue to be a magnet for incredible talent from all around the world.

So the task before us still looms large. And the other side doesn't have answers to these questions. You don't see them debating how we improve our education system. You don't see them engaging in any serious way about how we're going to retrain our workers. There's not a conversation about how we restore manufacturing in this country.

They've got one message and that is, we're going to make sure that we cut people's taxes even more, so that by every objective measure our deficit is worse. And we will slash Government investments that have made this country great, not because it's going to balance the budget, but because it's driven by our ideological vision about how Government should be. That's their agenda, pure and simple.

And so we probably have not seen an election where the contrast is that sharp between the two parties as in this election. Keep in mind, when I ran in 2008, we had a Republican candidate who believed in climate change— [*laughter*]—who had worked on immigration reform, who had not ruled out the possibility that the wealthy might pay a little bit more as part of an overall package to reduce our deficit. But that's not what we have right now.

So there's a lot at stake. But the good news is, as I travel around the country, part of what sustained me each and every day—people sometimes ask, boy, you're working pretty long hours, and people are calling you pretty nasty names, and how do you put up with all that? And I tell them, in addition to having this remarkable family and having a rule of not watching television—[*laughter*]—what also sustains me is just the American people. When you go out there and you meet them, they're resilient. They're tough. They've got good sense. They have strong values.

And although this is a big, messy democracy and politics has always been contentious in this country, my confidence in the American people is undiminished. And my energy, my absolute certainty that we can be doing better and that if we follow the course that America is going to be in a stronger position today than it was 4 years ago, that determination is as strong as ever.

If you are just as determined and you're willing to work just as hard as we did 4 years ago, then we're going to win. And more importantly, we're going to make sure that this country is everything that it deserves to be.

Thank you very much, everybody. Thank you. Thank you.

NOTE: The President spoke at 7:04 p.m. at the Portland Museum of Art. In his remarks, he referred to Karen Harris, cochair, Obama for ME Finance Steering Committee, and her husband Robert G. Gips; Bonnie Porta, cochair, Obama for ME Finance Steering Committee, and her husband Robert C.S. "Bobby" Monks; former Sen. George J. Mitchell, Jr.; and Sen. John S. McCain III, in his capacity as the 2008 Republican Presidential nominee. Audio was not available for verification of the content of these remarks.

The President's Weekly Address
March 31, 2012

Over the last few months, I've been talking about a choice we face as a country. We can either settle for an economy where a few people do really well and everybody else struggles to get by, or we can build an economy where hard work pays off again, where everyone gets a fair shot, everyone does their fair share, and everyone plays by the same rules. That's up to us. Today I want to talk to you about the idea that everyone in this country should do their fair share.

Now, if this were a perfect world, we'd have unlimited resources. No one would ever have to pay any taxes, and we could spend as much as we wanted. But we live in the real world. We don't have unlimited resources. We have a deficit that needs to be paid down. And we also have to pay for investments that will help our economy grow and keep our country safe: education, research and technology, a strong military, and retirement programs like Medicare and Social Security.

That means we have to make choices. When it comes to paying down the deficit and investing in our future, should we ask middle class Americans to pay even more at a time when their budgets are already stretched to the breaking point? Or should we ask some of the wealthiest Americans to pay their fair share?

That's the choice. Over the last decade, we've spent hundreds of billions of dollars on what was supposed to be a temporary tax cut for the wealthiest 2 percent of Americans. Now we're scheduled to spend almost a trillion more. Today, the wealthiest Americans are paying taxes at one of the lowest rates in 50 years. Warren Buffett is paying a lower rate than his secretary. Meanwhile, over the last 30 years, the tax rates for middle class families have barely budged.

That's not fair. It doesn't make any sense. Do we want to keep giving tax breaks to the wealthiest Americans, folks like myself or Warren Buffett or Bill Gates, people who don't need them and never asked for them? Or do we want to keep investing in the things that will grow our economy and keep us secure? Because we can't afford to do both.

Now, some people call this class warfare. But I think asking a billionaire to pay at least the same tax rate as his secretary is just common sense. We don't envy success in this country. We aspire to it. But we also believe that anyone who does well for themselves should do their fair share in return so that more people have the opportunity to get ahead, not just a few.

That's the America I believe in. And in the next few weeks, Members of Congress will get a chance to show you where they stand. Congress is going to vote on what's called the Buffett rule: If you make more than a million dollars a year, you should pay at least the same percentage of your income in taxes as middle class families do. On the other end, if you make under $250,000 a year—like 98 percent of American families do—your taxes shouldn't go up. You're the ones struggling with the rising cost of everything from college tuition to groceries. You're the ones who deserve a break.

So every Member of Congress is going to go on record. And if they vote to keep giving tax breaks to people like me—tax breaks our country can't afford—then they're going to have to explain to you where that money comes from. Either it's going to add to our deficit, or it's going to come out of your pocket. Seniors will have to pay more for their Medicare benefits. Students will see their interest rates go up at a time when they can't afford it. Families who are scraping by will have to do more because the richest Americans are doing less.

That's not right. That's not who we are. In America, our story has never been about what we can do by ourselves, it's about what we can do together. It's about believing in our future and the future of this country. So tell your Members of Congress to do the right thing. Call them up, write them a letter, pay them a visit, and tell them to stop giving tax breaks to people who don't need them and start investing in the things that will help our economy grow and put people back to work.

That's how we'll make this country a little fairer, a little more just, and a whole lot stronger. Thanks.

NOTE: The address was recorded at approximately 4 p.m. on March 29 in the Library at the White House for broadcast on March 31. In the address, the President referred to Warren E. Buffett, chief executive officer and chairman, and Debbie Bosanek, assistant, Berkshire Hathaway Inc.; and William H. Gates III, chairman, Microsoft Corp. The transcript was made available by the Office of the Press Secretary on March 30, but was embargoed for release until 6 a.m. on March 31.

The President's News Conference With President Felipe de Jesus Calderon Hinojosa of Mexico and Prime Minister Stephen J. Harper of Canada
April 2, 2012

President Obama. Please have a seat. Good afternoon, everybody. It is my pleasure to welcome two great friends and partners, President Calderon of Mexico and Prime Minister Harper of Canada.

Now, I've worked with Stephen and Felipe on many occasions. We've joined our international partners from APEC to the G–20. From our last summit in Guadalajara, we remember Felipe's hospitality and that of the Mexican people, including some very good mariachi and——

President Calderon. Mexican food.

President Obama. ——some tequila, if I'm not mistaken. [*Laughter*] I can't reciprocate the music, but Felipe, Stephen and I are proud to welcome you here today.

President Calderon. Thank you.

President Obama. Between us, we represent nearly half a billion citizens, from Nunavut in the Canadian north to Chiapas in southern Mexico. In between, the diversity of our peoples and cultures is extraordinary. But wherever they live, they wake up every day with similar hopes: to provide for their families, to be safe in their communities, to give their children a better life. And in each of our countries, the daily lives of our citizens are shaped profoundly by what happens in the other two. And that's why we're here.

Today we focused on our highest priority: creating jobs and opportunity for our people. In the United States, our businesses have created nearly 4 million new jobs, confidence is up, and the economy is getting stronger. But with lots of folks still struggling to find work and pay the bills, we are doing everything we can to speed up the recovery. And that includes boosting trade with our two largest economic partners.

As President, I've made it a priority to increase our exports, and I'm pleased that our exports to Canada and Mexico are growing faster than our exports to the rest of the world. In fact, last year trade in goods with our two neighbors surpassed $1 trillion for the first time ever. This trade supports some 2.5 million American jobs, and I want more trade supporting even more jobs in the future.

So today Prime Minister Harper led us in a very good discussion about how our three countries can improve our competitiveness. We agreed to continue making our borders more efficient and more secure so it's faster and cheaper to travel and trade. We're expanding cooperation to create clean energy jobs and combat climate change, an area in which President Calderon and Mexico have been a real leader.

I'm pleased to announce that our three nations are launching a new effort to get rid of outdated regulations that stifle job creation. Here in the United States, our efforts to cut redtape and ensure smart regulations will help achieve savings and benefits to businesses, consumers, and our country of more than $100 billion. And we're already working to streamline and coordinate regulations with Canada and Mexico on a bilateral basis. So now our three nations are going to sit down together, go through the books, and simplify and eliminate more regulations that will make our joint economies stronger.

This is especially important, by the way, for our small and medium-sized businesses, which, when they start exporting, often start with Mexico and Canada. So this is going to help create jobs, and it's going to keep us on track to meet my goal of doubling U.S. exports.

More broadly, I reiterated my commitment to comprehensive immigration reform, which would be good for workers and good for business. I'm pleased that Canada and Mexico have also expressed an interest in joining the Trans-Pacific Partnership. Consultations with our TPP partners are now underway on how new members can meet the high standards of this trade agreement, which could be a real model for the world. And I very much appreciated President Calderon updating us on preparations for the next G–20 summit, which he will be hosting in June.

Our other major focus today was the security that our citizens deserve. Criminal gangs and narcotraffickers pose a threat to each of our nations, and each of our nations has a responsibility to meet that threat. In Mexico, President Calderon has shown great courage in standing up to the traffickers and cartels, and we've sped up the delivery of equipment and assistance to support those efforts.

Here in the United States, we've increased cooperation on our southern border and dedicated new resources to reducing the southbound flow of money and guns and to reduce the demand for drugs in the United States, which helps fuel—helped to fuel this crisis. And today each of us reaffirmed our commitment to meeting this challenge together, because that's the only way that we're going to succeed.

Beyond our borders, these cartels and traffickers pose an extraordinary threat to our Central American neighbors. So we're teaming up. Defense ministers from our three countries met last week as a group for the first time ever. And we're going to be coordinating our efforts more closely than ever, especially when it comes to supporting Central America's new strategy on citizen security, which will be discussed at the Summit of the Americas in Colombia next week.

So again, I want to thank Stephen and Felipe for being here. When I came to office, I pledged to seek new partnerships with our friends in the Americas, a relationship of equality and shared responsibility built on mutual interest and mutual respect. That's what we've done. And it wouldn't have been possible without the leadership and sense of purpose that these two outstanding leaders have brought to all our efforts, including our efforts today. As a result, I believe our nations and our citizens will be more secure, more prosperous, and in a better position to give their children the lives that they deserve.

So with that, let me turn it over to President Calderon.

President Calderon. Thank you, President Obama. Your Excellency, Mr. Barack Obama, President of the United States of America, Right Honorable Stephen Harper, Prime Minister of Canada, ladies and gentlemen of the press, Mr. Ambassadors, legislators, friends: First of all, I would like to thank President Barack Obama for his extraordinary hospitality and that of his Government in hosting this summit of the leaders of North America.

And briefly, I would also like to express on behalf of the Government of Mexico, the people of Mexico, my family, and my own behalf, my most sincere sympathies to the family and relatives of former President Miguel de la Madrid Hurtado for his lamentable death yesterday. Tomorrow we will be rendering homage to him in Mexico.

The reasons that—for which we are here today at this summit of the North American leaders with President Barack Obama and the Prime Minister of Canada, we've come through a work day that has been very fruitful and fluid with an exchange of opinions and progress to the benefit of our respective citizens.

I'm also very thankful to my two colleagues for the openness with which we have broached some very complex items on our working agenda. I recognize and value their enormous commitment to our common region.

The leaders of North America share a vision of a strong, solidary, safe, competitive region that is able to successfully face head on the challenges of today. We agree that our common challenges can only be faced together. And therein lays the importance of having dialogue, strong dialogue, amongst our three countries.

The data that President Obama has just given us is very important, that our trade has exceeded $1 trillion for the first time. And I think that that is not separate from a reality that has to be underscored. In this very complex world full of economic problems and severe crises, Canada, the United States, and Mexico are three countries that are growing right now and generating jobs today.

And that growth and those millions of jobs, many of them have to do precisely with the greatest trade exchanges that we have ever seen amongst these great nations. I would say that the potential of North America tied to these three countries is such that within our own nations we have a great deal to do to make the most of these opportunities for greater exchanges amongst our peoples.

As we've mentioned today, we have progressed on various fronts. For instance, we've advanced on the deregulation in our countries—in our own countries, as well as amongst our countries. We have progressed as well in harmonization of certain standards that facilitate trade. We've also progressed, in our case, on the bilateral relationship in border infrastructure. And all of this has led, of course, to the benefit of Canadian, Mexican, and American families.

In another line of ideas, I would also say that the three nations have renewed their decision to strengthen cooperation at the international level, particularly in issues as sensitive as the security of our citizens. We have reiterated the values upon which our societies were founded: democracy, liberty, justice, the respect for human rights. And today the political dialogue amongst us is perhaps stronger than ever.

We have renewed certain principles of our existence and of our challenges: the principle of shared responsibility, the exchange of information, and especially the strengthening of our institutions that has to be the guide of our cooperation.

Clearly, I expressed to President Obama and to Prime Minister Harper that the fight that Mexico is experiencing for a safer North America also requires a strengthening of national actions, amongst other things, to stop the traffic of weapons, to combat with greater strength money laundering, and of course, to reduce the demand for drugs that strengthens criminal organizations. I also expressed to President Obama and to Prime Minister Harper that Mexico recognizes that the commitment that they have undertaken to progress along those lines, it's also necessary to strengthen the regional security focus, and in order to do this, we need to include our neighbors and Central American partners, who are also facing serious problems and who need our solidarity. The three countries have agreed to establish a joint dialogue mechanism with the Central American Integration System, SICA, in support of the efforts undertaken by Central American nations to fight organized crime and in favor of regional security that benefits us all.

Of course, in this meeting, we have broached the topic of the regional economy. The leaders of North America agree that the United States, Canada, and Mexico must continue to delve deeper into our successful economic relationship so as to generate more jobs and greater well-being in all three countries.

Our governments recognize that it is absolutely necessary to continue to fully comply with the NAFTA, as well as to explore new means of strengthening regional competitiveness. And I am convinced that if we work together, we will become much more competitive than many areas of the world that we are competing with today.

Mexico's position is that the solution to the complex economic situation experienced by the world today is not a return to protectionist practices that only isolate countries, reduce competitiveness of economies, and send investment scurrying, but that part of the problem and the part of the investment that we need to see in the world economy is to see a

delving deeper into our economies and making the most of our advantages that show our economic complementarity in terms of investment, labor, technologies, natural resources. And only then will we be able to have success in a world that competes ferociously by regions.

The three countries have renewed our commitment to broaden the productive—the supply chains of the region that will be even more interconnected, supporting especially the small and medium-scale companies.

Mexican exports to the world represent 37 percent of—or have, rather, 37 percent of American content. In other words, so American exports are American exports, and they generate millions of jobs for the region. And in that lays the need to work even more in this region on a clear trilateral deregulation, for instance, in nanomaterials and emissions standards for some vehicles.

Today we also agreed to work in a coordinated fashion on actions that we will be adopting to modernize infrastructure and for border management. After 10 years—the last 2 years, we've seen three new border crossing areas between Mexico and the United States, after 10 years of not having seen one new route. And we continue to work in a coordinated fashion to make our border more dynamic so that it's a border of opportunities for progress on both sides of that border.

Tomorrow, here in Washington, our ministers of economy and of trade will be meeting within the framework of the Free Trade Commission of the NAFTA so as to continue to work towards achieving these objectives.

Today, we've seen that prosperity in the region depends on greater integration with full respect of our sovereignties in all fields. And in this context, I'd like to reiterate the interest of my country to join forces as soon as possible to the TPP, or the Trans-Pacific Partnership, and its negotiations. Because we know that Mexicans can contribute to a quick and successful conclusion of this project. If we join forces in this region where we see the greatest growth in the world, we will be generating benefits for our families, our workers, and also substantially improving the competitiveness of the three countries in this context.

We are convinced that the experience and participation of Mexico will enrich this free trade project of the latest generation that encompasses countries in Asia, Oceania, and America. Our country has a clear commitment to economic freedom. We even have the support of the private sector so as to enter into the TPP. We are a nation that believes in free trade as a true tool to foster growth and development, and we have acted as a result of this.

I would also like to thank the United States and Canada for renewing their support to Mexico and its presidency of G–20. As you know, in June of this year, Mexico will host the summit of the leaders of the G–20 in Los Cabos. We are convinced, over and above the topics that we will be dealing with there, that the complex international environment needs to be an opportunity so that the world can redefine its development models with a firm commitment to the well-being of peoples and the care for the environment.

Ladies and gentlemen, in this summit, the representatives of the United States, Canada, and Mexico have undertaken an open, constructive dialogue, just as corresponds to countries that share values. We've talked about the enormous challenges facing us so as to work together in a globalized world. And as a result, we will be working on building a new era that consolidates the right conditions for development in North America on the basis of a successful partnership, as we have seen so far today.

My dear President Obama, thank you for your hospitality.

President Obama. Prime Minister Harper.

Prime Minister Harper. Well, first of all, I'd like to begin by thanking you, Barack, for so graciously and so warmly—literally—hosting us here today. And I'd also like to begin by offering my sincere condolences to you, Felipe, and through you, to the people of Mexico on the passing of former President Miguel de la Madrid, who I gather had much to do with the NAFTA partnership that we enjoy today.

Canada places the highest value on the friendship and partnership among our three countries. We form one of the world's largest free trade zones, which has been of great benefit to all of our nations. We're also effective collaborators in the G–20 in responding to the challenges of the global recession and instability of these past few years.

As affirmed in our budget last week, our Government is focused on creating jobs, growth, and long-term prosperity for all Canadians.

I'm especially pleased that the United States has welcomed Canada's and Mexico's interest in joining the Trans-Pacific Partnership. We also had useful discussions on continued cooperation in managing our borders, streamlining regulation, securing global supply chains, and advancing clean energy.

In addition, we've announced a broadened plan for North American pandemic preparedness and a new North America-Central America dialogue on security to fight transnational organized crime.

Finally, we discussed the agenda for the upcoming Summit of the Americas in Colombia. Canada looks forward to continue to working with the United States and Mexico to promote democratic principles, regional stability, and market-based economic growth with our partners in the Western Hemisphere.

And once again, Barack and Felipe, I look forward to continuing our useful discussions in Cartagena.

President Obama. Outstanding.

All right, I think that we're going to take a question from each press delegation. So I'll start with Julianna [Julianna Goldman, Bloomberg News].

U.S. Influence Abroad/Health Care Reform

Q. Thank you, Mr. President. After last week's arguments at the Supreme Court, many experts believe that there could be a majority, a five-member majority, to strike down the individual mandate. And if that were to happen, if it were to be ruled unconstitutional, how would you still guarantee health care to the uninsured and those Americans who've become insured as a result of the law?

And then a question for President Calderon and Prime Minister Harper: Over the weekend, Governor Mitt Romney said that the U.S. used to promote free enterprise around the world, and he said, "Our President doesn't have the same feelings about American exceptionalism that we do, and I think over the last 3 or 4 years, some people around the world have begun to question that." So my question to the both of you is whether you think that American influence has declined over the last 3 to 4 years.

And, President Obama, if you'd like to respond to that too.

President Obama. Well, on the second part of your question, it's still primary season for the Republican Party. They're going to make a decision about who their candidate will be.

It's worth noting that I first arrived on the national stage with a speech at the Democratic Convention that was entirely about American exceptionalism and that my entire career has been a testimony to American exceptionalism. But I will cut folks some slack for now because they're still trying to get their nomination.

With respect to health care, I'm actually—continue to be confident that the Supreme Court will uphold the law. And the reason is because, in accordance with precedent out there, it's constitutional. That's not just my opinion, by the way; that's the opinion of legal experts across the ideological spectrum, including two very conservative appellate court justices that said this wasn't even a close case.

I think it's important—because I watched some of the commentary last week—to remind people that this is not an abstract argument. People's lives are affected by the lack of availability of health care, the inaffordability of health care, their inability to get health care because of preexisting conditions.

The law that's already in place has already given 2.5 million young people health care that wouldn't otherwise have it. There are tens of thousands of adults with preexisting conditions who have health care right now because of this law. Parents don't have to worry about their children not being able to get health care because they can't be prevented from getting health care as a consequence of a preexisting condition. That's part of this law.

Millions of seniors are paying less for prescription drugs because of this law. Americans all across the country have greater rights and protections with respect to their insurance companies and are getting preventive care because of this law.

So that's just the part that's already been implemented. That doesn't even speak to the 30 million people who stand to gain coverage once it's fully implemented in 2014.

And I think it's important, and I think the American people understand, and the—I think the Justices should understand that in the absence of an individual mandate, you cannot have a mechanism to ensure that people with preexisting conditions can actually get health care. So there's not only a economic element to this and a legal element to this, but there's a human element to this. And I hope that's not forgotten in this political debate.

Ultimately, I'm confident that the Supreme Court will not take what would be an unprecedented, extraordinary step of overturning a law that was passed by a strong majority of a democratically elected Congress. And I'd just remind conservative commentators that for years what we've heard is, the biggest problem on the bench was judicial activism or a lack of judicial restraint, that an unelected group of people would somehow overturn a duly constituted and passed law. Well, this is a good example. And I'm pretty confident that this Court will recognize that and not take that step.

Q. You say it's not an abstract conversation. Do you have contingency plans?

President Obama. I'm sorry. As I said, we are confident that this will be over—that this will be upheld. I'm confident that this will be upheld because it should be upheld. And again, that's not just my opinion, that's the opinion of a whole lot of constitutional law professors and academics and judges and lawyers who have examined this law, even if they're not particularly sympathetic to this particular piece of legislation or my Presidency.

President Calderon. Your question was a little local for me, and so I'm glad that the President of the United States answered it. But I would take advantage of this moment to say that after increasing the budget line for the folk insurance six-fold and after having built more than 1,000 new clinics in the country, we're getting close to reaching universal coverage of health care: full, free health care coverage for all people up to 18 years of age, including cancer coverage. Of the 120—112 million Mexicans, 106 million will have efficient, effective universal health care coverage.

So I would say that I would hope that one of the greatest economies in the world, such as the United States, could follow our example in achieving this, because it was a great thing.

Prime Minister Harper. Well, I don't think you really expect me to intervene in the U.S. Presidential election. Let me just say this. For Canada—and this is something that I think transcends governments in Canada or administrations here in the United States—for Canada, the United States is and always will be our closest neighbor, our greatest ally, and our best friend. And I believe that American leadership is at all times great and indispensable for the world.

And I think over the past few years we've done great things together in terms of the response both through the G–20 and bilaterally on the recession and the recovery. We had, under your leadership, Barack, that successful intervention in Libya. Our trade relationship is the biggest in the world and growing. And so I think it's been a tremendous partnership.

President Obama. Somebody from the Mexican press corps.

Gun Trafficking/Mexico's Presidential Election/Canada's Visa Program

Q. Good afternoon. For President Calderon, you were saying—you were referring to weapons. We'd like to know what President Obama said in terms of what's going to be done to stop the traffic of weapons.

And, President Obama, I'd like to know what plans your Government has in the Presidential election process in Mexico. What was

discussed in terms of the interviews with the candidates in Mexico City? And I'd also like to know, for the Government of the United States, there's a threat for the country in this sense on weapons, Mr. President. Weapons have come into the country. Are there military leaks of letting the arms come through? What's going to be done?

And for Prime Minister Harper, are—is the visa requirement going to be removed for Mexicans? Thank you.

President Obama. That's a lot of questions. [*Laughter*] Go ahead, go first.

President Calderon. My position on this subject is very clear, and I would repeat it here. Let me broach it from another angle. It's been shown that when there is an excessive, quick availability of weapons in any given society, there is an increase in violence and the murders that goes on many years afterwards.

This phenomenon took place in many places of Africa after their civil wars. We've seen it in El Salvador, Guatemala, in Eastern Europe, in Kosovo, in Bosnia. It's happened—it's taken place in many different areas of the world. And we sustain that the expiry of the assault weapons ban in the year 2004 coincided almost exactly with the beginning of the harshest period of violence we've ever seen.

During my Government, we have seized over 140,000 weapons in 4 years. And I think that the vast majority have been assault weapons: AK–57s, et cetera. And many, the vast majority of these weapons were sold in gun shops in the United States. Along the border of the U.S. and Mexico, there are approximately 8,000 weapons shops. If we do our accounts, that means that there are approximately nine weapons stores for each Walmart that exists in the United States and Mexico.

So a good deal of our discussion did touch upon this. But I recognize, at the same time, the administrative effort that's been undertaken, particularly by President Obama and his administration, so that the agencies for control of illegal actions curb this export of guns and weapons to Mexico. We've seen a much more active effort in this sense than in any other time in the past.

I have a great deal of respect for the U.S. legislation, especially the Second Amendment. But I know that if we don't stop the traffic of weapons into Mexico, also if we don't have mechanisms to forbid the sale of weapons, such as we had in the nineties, or for registry of guns, at least for assault weapons, then we are never going to be able to stop the violence in Mexico or stop a future turning of those guns upon the U.S.

So, if I am against the traffic of weapons in Mexico, I'm against the traffic of weapons anywhere, be that within any circumstance. The Government of Mexico will never be able to accept anything that has to do with opening this.

President Obama has been very clear on the position of his Government. We understand the work being done by the agencies to stop the criminals. But this cannot be an obstacle to the cooperation that we have to have amongst Mexico and the United States to stop these criminal activities that underlie this issue, which is one of the greatest obstacles and problems for Mexico.

I understand the internal problems from a political point of view in the United States, and I mentioned this publicly in Congress in the United States, and I said things exactly the way I believe them. I said them outright. There's a great deal of discrepancy between points of view. It's a very complex political issue. But it is very important to underscore it.

And I believe that's the only part of the question that I can answer, and I would say that what President Obama has already answered was very well done.

President Obama. Just very briefly, with respect to the Presidential elections in Mexico, Vice President Biden met with the candidates to express sentiments that are similar to the ones that Stephen just expressed here with respect to U.S. elections. And that is that the friendship between our three countries, the partnership between our three countries, extends beyond and is more fundamental than any particular party or any particular election. And that's the message we have to send with respect to Mexico.

I've had a excellent working relationship with Felipe. I expect to have an excellent working relationship with the next Mexican President, whoever that candidate may be, because the underlying common interests that we have economically, socially, culturally, the people-to-people relationship that we have is so important that it transcends partisan politics.

And with respect to the issue of guns, I've made very clear in every meeting that I've had with Felipe—and we've actually put into practice efforts to stop illegal gun trafficking north to south. It is a difficult task, but it's one that we have taken very seriously and taken some unprecedented steps. We will continue to coordinate closely with the Mexican Government because we recognize the toll that it's taken with respect to families and innocent individuals inside of Mexico.

And this is part of our broader comprehensive cooperation in weakening the grip of narcotrafficking within Mexico. And we recognize that we have a responsibility to reduce demand for drugs, that we have a responsibility to make sure that not only guns, but also bulk cash isn't flowing into Mexico. And I—obviously President Calderon takes very seriously his responsibilities to apply effective law enforcement within Mexico. And I think he's taken courageous steps to do that.

So we're going to keep on partnering together in order to continue to make progress on this very important issue.

Prime Minister Harper. You asked me about the visa requirement. The visa requirement is the really only effective means we have in Canada today to deal with large-scale bogus refugee claims under our refugee determination system.

Legislation that is being implemented—and in fact, there's legislation before Parliament to enhance those changes—that legislation will in the future, in years to come, will give us tools other than visa requirement to deal with that particular problem. But as of today that remains the only tool at our disposal.

President Obama. Okay. And finally from——

Prime Minister Harper. Yes. Mark Kennedy, Postmedia News.

Trans-Pacific Partnership/Narcotrafficking/Security Issues

Q. Hello, gentlemen. I have a couple of questions on two critical issues that you were discussing today, one on trade and one on crime. On trade, Prime Minister Harper, why is Canada's position at the negotiating table on the Trans-Pacific Partnership so important to Canada? And secondly, to get us there, to be a player, are you willing to give up as a precondition our supply management system?

And, President Obama, you said earlier that there needs to be high standards for a country to be there. I'm wondering whether you think, yet, Canada has met those high standards— whether you want us to drop our traditional supply management system.

And on crime, we in Canada read about the challenges that Mexico has on the drug cartels and the horrible violence that occurs down there. But perhaps it's possible that many Canadians, and perhaps even Americans, don't see it as affecting their lives, perhaps it doesn't affect their communities. So, on that issue, why do you three gentlemen think that a three-country coordinated approach is necessary to protect our citizens?

And, Prime Minister, I think you being the only person that can speak both English and French, if you can do that, please.

Prime Minister Harper. Sure. First of all, in response to the question on the Trans-Pacific Partnership, this is—our desire to be part of that negotiation is part of Canada's ambitious trade agenda. As you know, we are currently in negotiations with over 50 countries around the world, including the European Union and Japan and India. So this was obviously a logical extension of our desire, the desire of our Government to dramatically broaden our free trade relationships around the world.

Canada's position on Trans-Pacific Partnership is the same as our position in any trade negotiation. We expect to negotiate and debate all manner of issues, and we seek ambitious outcomes to free trade agreements. In those negotiations, of course, Canada will attempt to promote and to defend Canada's interest not just across the economy, but in individual sectors as well.

On the question of security, look, the security problems are—the security challenge, particularly around the drug trade, is a serious regional problem throughout our hemisphere that has real impacts. Not the kind of governance and security impacts we see maybe in Central America and the Caribbean and elsewhere—but has real, serious impacts on the health and safety of communities in our country as well. And as these criminal networks are transnational, it's important that our attempts to fight them be equally transnational. And that's why we work together on these initiatives.

President Obama. Well, with respect to the TPP, as is true of any process of arriving at a trade agreement, every country that's participating is going to have to make some modifications. That's inherent in the process, because each of our countries have their own idiosyncrasies, certain industries that have in the past been protected, certain practices that may be unique to that country, but end up creating disadvantages for businesses from other countries. And so it's a process of everybody making adjustments.

I don't think Canada would be unique in that. Are there areas where we'd like to see some changes in terms of Canadian practices? Of course. I assure you that Canada will have some complaints directed at us, and every member of the Trans-Pacific Partnership eventually would have to make some modifications in order to accommodate the larger interest of growing the overall economy and expanding trade and ultimately jobs. So I don't anticipate that there's something unique about Canada that wouldn't be true for any of the other aspirants to forming this Trans-Pacific Partnership.

With respect to the transnational drug trade, first and foremost, I think we should be concerned about what's happening in Mexico and Central America, because when you have innocent families and women and children who are being gunned down on the streets, that should be everybody's problem, not just our problem, not just their problem.

There's a sense of neighborly regard and concern that has to be part of our calculus and our foreign policy. But more practically, the United States shares a border with Mexico. If you have this kind of violence and the power of the drug trade as a whole expanding in countries that are so closely affiliated with us—in Central American countries—if you start getting a larger and larger space in which they have control over serious chunks of the economy, if they're undermining institutions in these countries, that will impact our capacity to do business in these countries. It could have a spillover effect in terms of our nationals who are living in those countries, tourists that are visiting these countries. It could have a deteriorating effect overall on the nature of our relationship. And that's something that we have to pay attention to.

And as I said, I think the Mexican Government has taken this very seriously at great cost to itself. We have an obligation to take it just as seriously, in part because we are the ultimate destination for a large chunk of this market.

And that—Stephen and I were trading notes—in places like the United States and Canada, this is not just an issue of—that traditionally was very urban. This is disseminated across our communities. And you go into rural communities and you've got methamphetamine sales that are devastating young and old alike, and some of that is originally sourced in Mexico. And so even in the remotest, most isolated parts of Canada or the United States, they're being impacted by this drug trade, and we've got to work cooperatively in order to deal with it.

President Calderon. And I'd like to look at it from another standpoint. The security of North America is absolutely tied to each of its member states. There cannot be full security in this country or in Canada or in Mexico if we do not have a system that actually enables the cooperation mechanisms to act in facing threats that have no borders, that are transnational by their very nature. And these are threats that are not just tied into drug trafficking, which is transnational of course.

And I'll give you two examples of success stories that I was mentioning this morning. One, the attempt to take to Mexico one of the children of Qadhafi—one of Qadhafi's children. This implied an international and very North American operation because it was headed up by a Canadian businesswoman who hired an American company, which hired, in turn, Mexican pilots and counterfeiters. And this multinational operation could have been—would not have been avoided without the international security mechanisms that we didn't have before, but that now we have.

Also, being able to avoid the assassination of the Saudi Ambassador here in Washington would not have been possible without the mechanisms and cooperation that we have today.

So thinking that what happens in Mexico doesn't have anything to do with the security of the citizens of this country or of any other citizen of North America is a mistake. We have to understand that we are all tied to one another.

Now, security, understood in the regional sense—in order to understand that, we have to understand where the greatest threats to security actually lay. The United States has a clear idea of its threat, of its security priorities, its threats of terrorism, of international terrorism, terrible attacks on the U.S. people. Another threat clearly is in the power of transnational organized crime, which I insist is not crime or organizations that are strictly Mexican in nature. They don't have a nationality, and they don't operate in just one country. They're probably operating right here in this city.

In Washington, for instance, the number of homicides per 100,000 inhabitants is higher by 10—more than 10 or 20 than the largest number in any of the big cities in Mexico. These are international organizations that have a growing destructive capacity, that act well beyond borders and threaten anyone, anywhere.

It is true, the efforts that we undertake clearly make it possible to contain that threat and to prevent it from acting in society—not just in the United States or Canada, but even in Mexico. And that explains why, for instance, despite the perception of my country, last year

23 million tourists came to our country by plane, plus another 7 million in cruise ships, plus another 50 million who crossed the border, the land borders.

So that's also why there are 2 million Mexicans living comfortably in Mexico, and many more living also here who came to visit us here and wanted to see us in the White House. And that's also why 1.6 million Canadians come to Mexico every year. So that's 5 percent of the Canadian population that travels to Mexico every year.

And that also explains why, despite the fact that a State such as Texas recommends that none of its young people should travel to anywhere in Mexico, that's why there are hundreds of thousands of young Texans who go to Mexico, enjoy it, and why we haven't seen one single incident with U.S. spring-breakers in Mexico this past spring, for instance.

Great concern, because these are multinational criminal organizations and the mechanisms, of course, to face them, to defeat them, have to be multinational. In addition to the solidarity—expressions of solidarity of President Obama, who says that he cannot stand aside from the expressions of threat that is facing a neighbor of his, that vulnerability from an institutional point of view in Mexico and Central America is an issue that also impacts and jeopardizes all of the citizens of North America.

President Obama. Thank you very much, everyone.

NOTE: The President's news conference began at 1:54 p.m. in the Rose Garden at the White House. In his remarks, the President referred to Judges Brett M. Kavanaugh and Laurence H. Silberman, U.S. Court of Appeals for the District of Columbia Circuit. President Calderon referred to former President Miguel de la Madrid Hurtado of Mexico, who died on April 1; Saadi Qadhafi, son of Col. Muammar Abu Minyar al-Qadhafi, former leader of Libya; and Saudi Arabia's Ambassador to the U.S. Adil al-Ahmad al-Jubayr. A reporter referred to Republican Presidential candidate former Gov. W. Mitt Romney of Massachusetts. President Calderon spoke in Spanish, and his remarks were translated by an interpreter.

Joint Statement by North American Leaders
April 2, 2012

We, the Leaders of North America, met today in Washington, DC to advance the economic well-being, safety, and security of the United States, Mexico, and Canada. Rooted in deep economic, historical, cultural, environmental, and societal ties, North American cooperation enhances our ability to face global challenges, compete in the international economy, and achieve greater prosperity. We reaffirm our commitment to further develop our thriving political and economic partnership with a consistent and strategic long-term vision, as progress on our common agenda directly benefits the peoples of our region.

Broad-based, sustainable economic growth and job creation remains our top priority. For the first time, in 2011 our total trilateral merchandise trade surpassed USD 1 trillion. Our integration helps maximize our capabilities and makes our economies more innovative and competitive globally. Working together, we strive to ensure that North American economic cooperation fosters gains in productivity for all of our citizens, enhancing our respective national and bilateral efforts to achieve that goal.

To that end, we pledge to introduce timely and tangible regulatory measures to enable innovation and growth while ensuring high standards of public health, safety, and environmental protection. We will continue to reduce transaction costs and improve the existing business environment. We have launched the U.S.-Mexico High-Level Regulatory Cooperation Council and the U.S.-Canada Regulatory Cooperation Council during the past two years, pursuing a shared objective that we commit to complement trilaterally in four sectors: certain vehicle emission standards, railroad safety, the Globally Harmonized System of Classification and Labeling of Workplace Chemicals, and aligning principles of our regulatory approaches to nanomaterials. This is particularly important to small- and medium-sized businesses, which are the engines of growth. By eliminating unnecessary regulatory differences, smaller businesses are better equipped to participate in an integrated North American economy. Success in these efforts opens the way to additional North American regulatory cooperation.

Continued North American competitiveness requires secure supply chains and efficient borders. We remain committed to achieving this through cooperative approaches. To this end, the United States and Mexico released the Declaration Concerning Twenty-first Century Border Management in May 2010 and the United States and Canada released the Beyond the Border Action Plan: A Shared Vision for Perimeter Security and Economic Competitiveness in December 2011. We are committed to the mutually-reinforcing goals of these important initiatives and to their full implementation. By also supporting the work of multilateral organizations to foster improved collaboration, integration, and standards, we better identify and interdict threats before they reach our borders, as well as expedite the legitimate movement of goods and people throughout North America in a more efficient, secure, and resilient manner. We also have instructed our trade and commerce ministers to identify sectors where we can deepen our regional cooperation through increased trade and investment.

As leading sources of innovation and creativity, our three countries are committed to the protection and enforcement of intellectual property rights (IPR). We commit to promote sound enforcement practices and an effective legal framework for IPR enforcement in the areas of criminal enforcement, enforcement at the border, civil and administrative actions, and distribution of IPR infringing material on the Internet consistent with the Anti-Counterfeiting Trade Agreement (ACTA), which the United States and Canada have recently signed. Mexico will continue to work on a comprehensive reform to its legal system to achieve the high standards pursued under ACTA.

Energy cooperation reduces the cost of doing business and enhances economic competitiveness in North America. We recognize the growing regional and federal cooperation in the area of *continental energy, including electricity generation* and interconnection and welcome increasing *North American energy trade*. We commit our governments to work with all stakeholders to deepen such cooperation to enhance our collective energy security, including the safe and efficient exploration and exploitation of resources. We support coordinated efforts to facilitate seamless energy flows on the interconnected grid and to promote trade and investment in clean energy technologies.

Enhanced electricity interconnection in the Americas would advance the goals of the Energy and Climate Partnership of the Americas to reduce energy poverty and increase the use of renewable sources of energy. We recognize Mexico's leadership in supporting inter-connections in Central America and reaffirm our support to bring affordable, reliable, and increasingly renewable power to businesses and homes in Central America and the Caribbean while opening wider markets for clean energy and green technology.

We pledge to continue our efforts to advance a lasting global solution to the challenge of climate change. We are pleased with the outcome of the climate conference in Durban, with respect to both operationalizing the Cancun agreements and laying the groundwork for a new legal agreement applicable to all Parties from 2020, support the activation of the Green Climate Fund, and underline the importance of climate finance and investment in the context of meaningful mitigation. We plan to work together, including through the Major Economies Forum on Energy and Climate, to secure a successful outcome at the 18th U.N. Framework Convention on Climate Change Conference of the Parties in Doha, Qatar. We continue to advance the transition to a clean energy economy and cooperate to reduce global rates of deforestation and land degradation. We also intend to deepen our trilateral cooperation and work with other interested partners to accelerate efforts aimed at reducing emissions of "short-lived climate pollutants," noting the recently launched Climate and Clean Air Coalition to Reduce Short-lived Climate Pollutants in which we are all actively engaged. Reducing our emissions of these substances, which include methane, black carbon, and many hydrofluorocarbons (HFCs), offers significant opportunities to reduce the rate of global warming in the near term, in the context of our broader efforts to address climate change, while also yielding many health, agricultural productivity, and energy security benefits.

As our societies and economies become more reliant on networked technology, we recognize the growing importance of an open, interoperable, secure, and reliable Internet. We reaffirm the importance of multi-stakeholder governance bodies for the Internet and underscore that fighting cybercrime is essential to promoting economic growth and international security. We recognize the seminal contribution of the Budapest Convention on Cybercrime, and believe the Convention should be adopted as widely as possible. To that end, we look forward to Canada's ratification and Mexico's completion of the necessary preparations for its signature of the Convention.

At the 2009 North American Leaders' Summit, we committed to build upon our successful coordinated response to the H1N1 pandemic, which stands as a global example of cooperation, to jointly prepare for future animal and pandemic influenza to enhance the health and safety of our citizens. Today we announce the culmination of that effort—the North American Plan for Animal and Pandemic Influenza (NAPAPI)—which provides a collaborative and multi-sectoral framework to strengthen our response to future animal and pandemic influenza events in North America and commit to its implementation.

All of our citizens are adversely affected by transnational organized crime. We commit to direct our national efforts and deepen our cooperation against all facets of this common challenge based on the principles of shared responsibility, mutual trust, and respect. We in-

tend to further share expertise and information and to cooperate in key areas such as countering arms trafficking and money laundering consistent with our laws and constitutions.

We are committed to strengthening security in the Americas through capacity building support. We intend to enhance our cooperation with our partners in Central America. In 2012, our governments will launch a consolidated Central America Integration System (SICA)-North America Security Dialogue to deepen regional security coordination and cooperation. We will remain actively engaged in the ongoing SICA-Group of Friends of Central America collaborative process, to align international assistance and programs supporting the implementation of the Central American Regional Security Strategy. We also welcome the recent High Level Hemispheric Meeting on Transnational Organized Crime, and recognize the relevance of closer collaboration and information sharing among all relevant national agencies.

We reiterate our commitment to Haiti and call upon Haitian political actors to work together and take concrete steps toward strengthening governance and the rule of law, which are fundamental to increased trade, investment, and long-term development and prosperity. We note the urgency and importance of parliamentary confirmation of a new government, and for that government to confirm the timeline for Senate and local elections. We also encourage Haiti to continue to pursue the development of the Haitian National Police so it can take full responsibility for Haiti's security.

To further strengthen nuclear security on the North American continent, we worked together, along with the International Atomic Energy Agency, to convert the fuel in Mexico's research reactor to low enriched uranium and provide new low enriched uranium fuel in exchange for the highly enriched uranium fuel, as pledged during the Washington Nuclear Security Summit in 2010 and announced at the Seoul Nuclear Security Summit in March 2012.

Our strengthened dialogue on priority issues in the North American agenda is reflected in the frequent formal and informal ministerial and technical meetings across a wide range of issues among our three countries, including the work of the NAFTA Free Trade Commission and the North American Commissions for Environmental Cooperation and for Labor Cooperation to continue to enhance our region's prosperity, protect the environment, and improve working conditions in North America. Taking into account our common security and defense challenges, such as transnational criminal organizations, as well as opportunities to strengthen cooperation in the field of disaster relief, we welcome the recent expansion of our ministerial-level dialogue through the North American Defense Ministers Meeting held March 26–27, 2012 in Ottawa.

As partners in the Americas, we are committed to work together within the Inter-American System and in the framework of the VI Summit of the Americas, to be held April 14–15 in Cartagena, Colombia. We fully support the Summit's theme of "Connecting the Americas: Partners for Prosperity." The Summit provides an opportunity to leverage the ties that connect the Americas to advance democratic, transparent, accountable governance that promotes inclusive, sustainable, market-based economic growth in the decade ahead. Deepening our shared interests and values will benefit the people of the Americas and bolster positive global engagement by countries from across the region. We pledge to work together to ensure the Summit strengthens a shared commitment to work in equal partnership toward these goals.

In light of the importance of the Americas to our collective economic wellbeing, we are committed to working together to advance the principles approved by the Inter-American Competitiveness Network in Santo Domingo and to support the Pathways to Prosperity initiative which underscores the importance of empowering small businesses; facilitating trade; building a modern work force; and developing stronger labor and environmental practices to encourage inclusive economic growth.

We also recognize the value of our common understandings on the major challenges faced by the world today, and acknowledge the importance of promoting growth and of preserving and deepening trade as keys to the global economic recovery. Canada and the United States support the efforts of the Mexican Presidency of the G–20 this year, and, together with Mexico, we commit ourselves to deepening our shared dialogue on economic governance therein, especially as we work to enhance North American competitiveness and prosperity. The Trans-Pacific Partnership (TPP) provides an opportunity to further deepen our trade relationship and create jobs. The United States welcomes Canada's and Mexico's interest in joining the TPP as ambitious partners.

President Obama and Prime Minister Harper welcome President Calderon's offer for Mexico to host the next North American Leaders' Summit.

NOTE: An original was not available for verification of the content of this joint statement.

Remarks at the Associated Press Luncheon and a Question-and-Answer Session
April 3, 2012

The President. Thank you very much. Please have a seat. Well, good afternoon, and thank you to Dean Singleton and the board of the Associated Press for inviting me here today. It is a pleasure to speak to all of you and to have a microphone that I can see. [*Laughter*] Feel free to transmit any of this to Vladimir if you see him. [*Laughter*]

Now, clearly, we're already in the beginning months of another long, lively election year. There will be gaffes and minor controversies, there will be hot mikes and Etch A Sketch moments. You will cover every word that we say, and we will complain vociferously about the unflattering words that you write, unless of course, you're writing about the other guy, in which case, good job. [*Laughter*]

But there are also big, fundamental issues at stake right now, issues that deserve serious debate among every candidate and serious coverage among every reporter. Whoever he may be, the next President will inherit an economy that is recovering, but not yet recovered, from the worst economic calamity since the Great Depression. Too many Americans will still be looking for a job that pays enough to cover their bills or their mortgage. Too many citizens will still lack the sort of financial security that started slipping away years before this recession hit. A debt that has grown over the last decade, primarily as a result of two wars, two massive tax cuts, and an unprecedented financial crisis, will have to be paid down.

And in the face of all these challenges, we're going to have to answer a central question as a nation: What, if anything, can we do to restore a sense of security for people who are willing to work hard and act responsibly in this country? Can we succeed as a country where a shrinking number of people do exceedingly well, while a growing number struggle to get by? Or are we better off when everyone gets a fair shot and everyone does their fair share and everyone plays by the same rules?

This is not just another run-of-the-mill political debate. I've said it's the defining issue of our time, and I believe it. It's why I ran in 2008. It's what my Presidency has been about. It's why I'm running again. I believe this is a make-or-break moment for the middle class, and I can't remember a time when the choice between competing visions of our future has been so unambiguously clear.

Keep in mind, I have never been somebody who believes that government can or should try to solve every problem. Some of you know my first job in Chicago was working with a group of Catholic churches that often did more good for the people in their communities than any government program could. In those same communities, I saw that no education policy,

however well crafted, can take the place of a parent's love and attention.

As President, I've eliminated dozens of programs that weren't working and announced over 500 regulatory reforms that will save businesses and taxpayers billions and put annual domestic spending on a path to become the smallest share of the economy since Dwight Eisenhower held this office, since before I was born. I know that the true engine of job creation in this country is the private sector, not Washington, which is why I've cut taxes for small-business owners 17 times over the last 3 years.

So I believe deeply that the free market is the greatest force for economic progress in human history. My mother and the grandparents who raised me instilled the values of self-reliance and personal responsibility that remain the cornerstone of the American idea. But I also share the belief of our first Republican President, Abraham Lincoln, a belief that, through Government, we should do together what we cannot do as well for ourselves.

That belief is the reason this country has been able to build a strong military to keep us safe and public schools to educate our children. That belief is why we've been able to lay down railroads and highways to facilitate travel and commerce. That belief is why we've been able to support the work of scientists and researchers whose discoveries have saved lives and unleashed repeated technological revolutions and led to countless new jobs and entire industries.

That belief is also why we've sought to ensure that every citizen can count on some basic measure of security. We do this because we recognize that no matter how responsibly we live our lives, any one of us, at any moment, might face hard times, might face bad luck, might face a crippling illness or a layoff. And so we contribute to programs like Medicare and Social Security, which guarantee health care and a source of income after a lifetime of hard work. We provide unemployment insurance, which protects us against unexpected job loss and facilitates the labor mobility that makes our economy so dynamic. We provide for

Medicaid, which makes sure that millions of seniors in nursing homes and childrens with disabilities are getting the care that they need.

For generations, nearly all of these investments—from transportation to education to retirement programs—have been supported by people in both parties. As much as we might associate the GI bill with Franklin Roosevelt or Medicare with Lyndon Johnson, it was a Republican, Lincoln, who launched the transcontinental railroad, the National Academy of Sciences, land-grant colleges. It was Eisenhower who launched the Interstate Highway System and new investment in scientific research. It was Richard Nixon who created the Environmental Protection Agency, Ronald Reagan who worked with Democrats to save Social Security. It was George W. Bush who added prescription drug coverage to Medicare.

What leaders in both parties have traditionally understood is that these investments aren't part of some scheme to redistribute wealth from one group to another. They are expressions of the fact that we are one Nation. These investments benefit us all. They contribute to genuine, durable economic growth.

Show me a business leader who wouldn't profit if more Americans could afford to get the skills and education that today's jobs require. Ask any company where they'd rather locate and hire workers: a country with crumbling roads and bridges or one that's committed to high-speed Internet and high-speed railroads and high-tech research and development?

It doesn't make us weaker when we guarantee basic security for the elderly or the sick or those who are actively looking for work. What makes us weaker is when fewer and fewer people can afford to buy the goods and services our businesses sell or when entrepreneurs don't have the financial security to take a chance and start a new business. What drags down our entire economy is when there's an ever-widening chasm between the ultrarich and everybody else.

In this country, broad-based prosperity has never trickled down from the success of a wealthy few. It has always come from the success of a strong and growing middle class. That's how a generation who went to college on the GI bill, including my grandfather, helped build the most prosperous economy the world has ever known. That's why a CEO like Henry Ford made it his mission to pay his workers enough so they could buy the cars that they made. That's why research has shown that countries with less inequality tend to have stronger and steadier economic growth over the long run.

And yet, for much of the last century, we have been having the same argument with folks who keep peddling some version of trickle-down economics. They keep telling us that if we'd convert more of our investments in education and research and health care into tax cuts—especially for the wealthy—our economy will grow stronger. They keep telling us that if we'd just strip away more regulations and let businesses pollute more and treat workers and consumers with impunity, that somehow we'd all be better off. We're told that when the wealthy become even wealthier and corporations are allowed to maximize their profits by whatever means necessary, it's good for America, and that their success will automatically translate into more jobs and prosperity for everybody else. That's the theory.

Now, the problem for advocates of this theory is that we've tried their approach on a massive scale. The results of their experiment are there for all to see. At the beginning of the last decade, the wealthiest Americans received a huge tax cut in 2001 and another huge tax cut in 2003. We were promised that these tax cuts would lead to faster job growth. They did not. The wealthy got wealthier. We would expect that. The income of the top 1 percent has grown by more than 275 percent over the last few decades to an average of $1.3 million a year. But prosperity sure didn't trickle down.

Instead, during the last decade, we had the slowest job growth in half a century. And the typical American family actually saw their incomes fall by about 6 percent, even as the economy was growing.

It was a period when insurance companies and mortgage lenders and financial institutions didn't have to abide by strong enough regulations or they found their ways around them. And what was the result? Profits for many of these companies soared. But so did people's health insurance premiums. Patients were routinely denied care, often when they needed it most. Families were enticed, and sometimes just plain tricked, into buying homes they couldn't afford. Huge, reckless bets were made with other people's money on the line. And our entire financial system was nearly destroyed.

So we've tried this theory out. And you would think that after the results of this experiment in trickle-down economics, after the results were made painfully clear, that the proponents of this theory might show some humility, might moderate their views a bit. You'd think they'd say, you know what, maybe some rules and regulations are necessary to protect the economy and prevent people from being taken advantage of by insurance companies or credit card companies or mortgage lenders. Maybe, just maybe, at a time of growing debt and widening inequality, we should hold off on giving the wealthiest Americans another round of big tax cuts. Maybe when we know that most of today's middle class jobs require more than a high school degree, we shouldn't gut education or lay off thousands of teachers or raise interest rates on college loans or take away people's financial aid.

But that's exactly the opposite of what they've done. Instead of moderating their views even slightly, the Republicans running Congress right now have doubled down and proposed a budget so far to the right it makes the "Contract With America" look like the New Deal. [*Laughter*] In fact, that renowned liberal, Newt Gingrich, first called the original version of the budget "radical" and said it would contribute to "right-wing social engineering." This is coming from Newt Gingrich.

And yet this isn't a budget supported by some small rump group in the Republican Party. This is now the party's governing platform. This is what they're running on. One of my potential opponents, Governor Romney, has said that he hoped a similar version of this plan from last year would be introduced as a bill on day one of his Presidency. He said that he's "very supportive" of this new budget, and he even called it "marvelous," which is a word you don't often hear when it comes to describing a budget. [*Laughter*] It's a word you don't often hear generally. [*Laughter*]

So here's what this "marvelous" budget does. Back in the summer, I came to an agreement with Republicans in Congress to cut roughly $1 trillion in annual spending. Some of these cuts were about getting rid of waste, others were about programs that we support, but we just can't afford given our deficits and our debt. And part of the agreement was a guarantee of another trillion in savings, for a total of about $2 trillion in deficit reduction.

This new House Republican budget, however, breaks our bipartisan agreement and proposes massive new cuts in annual domestic spending, exactly the area where we've already cut the most. And I want to actually go through what it would mean for our country if these cuts were to be spread out evenly. So bear with me. I want to go through this because I don't think people fully appreciate the nature of this budget.

The year after next, nearly 10 million college students would see their financial aid cut by an average of more than $1,000 each. There would be 1,600 fewer medical grants, research grants for things like Alzheimer's and cancer and AIDS. There would be 4,000 fewer scientific research grants, eliminating support for 48,000 researchers, students, and teachers. Investments in clean energy technologies that are helping us reduce our dependence on foreign oil would be cut by nearly a fifth.

If this budget becomes law and the cuts were applied evenly, starting in 2014, over 200,000 children would lose their chance to get an early education in the Head Start program. Two million mothers and young children would be cut from a program that gives them access to healthy food. There would be 4,500 fewer Federal grants at the Department of Justice and the FBI to combat violent crime, financial crime, and help secure our borders. Hundreds of national parks would be forced to close for part or all of the year. We wouldn't have the capacity to enforce the laws that protect the air we breathe, the water we drink, or the food that we eat.

Cuts to the FAA would likely result in more flight cancellations, delays, and the complete elimination of air traffic control services in parts of the country. Over time, our weather forecasts would become less accurate because we wouldn't be able to afford to launch new satellites. And that means Governors and mayors would have to wait longer to order evacuations in the event of a hurricane.

That's just a partial sampling of the consequences of this budget. Now, you can anticipate Republicans may say, well, we'll avoid some of these cuts, since they don't specify exactly the cuts that they would make. But they can only avoid some of these cuts if they cut even deeper in other areas. This is math. If they want to make smaller cuts to medical research, that means they've got to cut even deeper in funding for things like teaching and law enforcement. The converse is true as well. If they want to protect early childhood education, it will mean further reducing things like financial aid for young people trying to afford college.

Perhaps they will never tell us where the knife will fall, but you can be sure that with cuts this deep, there is no secret plan or formula that will be able to protect the investments we need to help our economy grow. This is not conjecture. I am not exaggerating. These are facts. And these are just the cuts that would happen the year after next.

If this budget became law, by the middle of the century, funding for the kinds of things I just mentioned would have to be cut by about 95 percent. Let me repeat that. Those categories I just mentioned we would have to cut by 95 percent. As a practical matter, the Federal budget would basically amount to whatever is left in entitlements, defense spending, and interest on the national debt, period. Money for these investments that have traditionally been supported on a bipartisan basis would be practically eliminated.

And the same is true for other priorities like transportation and homeland security and vet-erans programs for the men and women who have risked their lives for this country. This is not an exaggeration. Check it out yourself.

And this is to say nothing about what the budget does to health care. We're told that Medicaid would simply be handed over to the States. That's the pitch: Let's get it out of the central bureaucracy. The States can experiment. They'll be able to run the programs a lot better. But here's the deal the States would be getting. They would have to be running these programs in the face of the largest cut to Medicaid that has ever been proposed, a cut that, according to one nonpartisan group, would take away health care for about 19 million Americans—19 million.

Who are these Americans? Many are someone's grandparents who, without Medicaid, won't be able to afford nursing home care without Medicaid. Many are poor children. Some are middle class families who have children with autism or Down syndrome. Some are kids with disabilities so severe that they require 24-hour care. These are the people who count on Medicaid.

Then there's Medicare. Because health care costs keep rising and the baby boom generation is retiring, Medicare, we all know, is one of the biggest drivers of our long-term deficit. That's a challenge we have to meet by bringing down the costs of health care overall so that seniors and taxpayers can share in the savings.

But here's the solution proposed by the Republicans in Washington and embraced by most of their candidates for President: Instead of being enrolled in Medicare when they turn 65, seniors who retire a decade from now would get a voucher that equals the cost of the second cheapest health care plan in their area. If Medicare is more expensive than that private plan, they'll have to pay more if they want to enroll in traditional Medicare. If health care costs rise faster than the amount of the voucher—as, by the way, they've been doing for decades—that's too bad. Seniors bear the risk. If the voucher isn't enough to buy a private plan with the specific doctors and care that you need, that's too bad.

So most experts will tell you, the way this voucher plan encourages savings is not through better care at cheaper cost. The way these private insurance companies save money is by designing and marketing plans to attract the youngest and healthiest seniors—cherry-picking—leaving the older and sicker seniors in traditional Medicare, where they have access to a wide range of doctors and guaranteed care. But that, of course, makes the traditional Medicare program even more expensive and raise premiums even further.

The net result is that our country will end up spending more on health care, and the only reason the Government will save any money—it won't be on our books—is because we've shifted it to seniors. They'll bear more of the costs themselves. It's a bad idea, and it will ultimately end Medicare as we know it.

Now, the proponents of this budget will tell us we have to make all these draconian cuts because our deficit is so large, this is an existential crisis, we have to think about future generations, so on and so on. And that argument might have a shred of credibility were it not for their proposal to also spend $4.6 trillion over the next decade on lower tax rates.

We're told that these tax cuts will supposedly be paid for by closing loopholes and eliminating wasteful deductions. But the Republicans in Congress refuse to list a single tax loophole they are willing to close. Not one. And by the way, there is no way to get even close to $4.6 trillion in savings without dramatically reducing all kinds of tax breaks that go to middle class families: tax breaks for health care, tax breaks for retirement, tax breaks for homeownership.

Meanwhile, these proposed tax breaks would come on top of more than a trillion dollars in tax giveaways for people making more than $250,000 a year. That's an average of at least $150,000 for every millionaire in this country—$150,000.

Let's just step back for a second and look at what $150,000 pays for: a year's worth of prescription drug coverage for a senior citizen, plus a new school computer lab, plus a year of medical care for a returning veteran, plus a

medical research grant for a chronic disease, plus a year's salary for a firefighter or police officer, plus a tax credit to make a year of college more affordable, plus a year's worth of financial aid. A hundred fifty thousand dollars could pay for all of these things combined: investments in education and research that are essential to economic growth that benefits all of us. For $150,000, that would be going to each millionaire and billionaire in this country. This budget says we'd be better off as a country if that's how we spent it.

This is supposed to be about paying down our deficit? It's laughable.

The bipartisan Simpson-Bowles commission that I created—which the Republicans originally were for until I was for it—that was about paying down the deficit. And I didn't agree with all the details. I proposed about $600 billion more in revenue and 600 billion—I'm sorry, it proposed about $600 billion more in revenue and about 600 billion more in defense cuts than I proposed in my own budget. But Bowles-Simpson was a serious, honest, balanced effort between Democrats and Republicans to bring down the deficit. That's why, although it differs in some ways, my budget takes a similarly balanced approach: cuts in discretionary spending, cuts in mandatory spending, increased revenue.

This congressional Republican budget is something different altogether. It is a Trojan horse. Disguised as deficit reduction plans, it is really an attempt to impose a radical vision on our country. It is thinly veiled social Darwinism. It is antithetical to our entire history as a land of opportunity and upward mobility for everybody who's willing to work for it, a place where prosperity doesn't trickle down from the top, but grows outward from the heart of the middle class. And by gutting the very things we need to grow an economy that's built to last—education and training, research and development, our infrastructure—it is a prescription for decline.

And everybody here should understand that because there's very few people here who haven't benefited at some point from those investments that were made in the fifties and the sixties and the seventies and the eighties. That's part of how we got ahead. And now we're going to be pulling up those ladders up for the next generation?

So, in the months ahead, I will be fighting as hard as I know how for this truer vision of what the United States of America is all about. Absolutely, we have to get serious about the deficit. And that will require tough choices and sacrifice. And I've already shown myself willing to make these tough choices when I signed into law the biggest spending cut of any President in recent memory. In fact, if you adjust for the economy, the Congressional Budget Office says the overall spending next year will be lower than any year under Ronald Reagan.

And I'm willing to make more of those difficult spending decisions in the months ahead. But I've said it before, and I'll say it again: There has to be some balance. All of us have to do our fair share.

I've also put forward a detailed plan that would reform and strengthen Medicare and Medicaid. By the beginning of the next decade, it achieves the same amount of annual health savings as the plan proposed by Simpson-Bowles—the Simpson-Bowles commission, and it does so by making changes that people in my party haven't always been comfortable with. But instead of saving money by shifting costs to seniors, like the congressional Republican plan proposes, our approach would lower the cost of health care throughout the entire system. It goes after excessive subsidies to prescription drug companies. It gets more efficiency out of Medicaid without gutting the program. It asks the very wealthiest seniors to pay a little bit more. It changes the way we pay for health care, not by procedure or the number of days spent in a hospital, but with new incentives for doctors and hospitals to improve their results.

And it slows the growth of Medicare costs by strengthening an independent commission, a commission not made up of bureaucrats from Government or insurance companies, but doctors and nurses and medical experts and consumers, who will look at all the evidence and recommend the best way to reduce unneces-

sary health care spending while protecting access to the care that the seniors need.

We also have a much different approach when it comes to taxes, an approach that says if we're serious about paying down our debt, we can't afford to spend trillions more on tax cuts for folks like me, for wealthy Americans who don't need them and weren't even asking for them, and that the country cannot afford. At a time when the share of national income flowing to the top 1 percent of people in this country has climbed to levels last seen in the 1920s, those same folks are paying taxes at one of the lowest rates in 50 years. As both I and Warren Buffett have pointed out many times now, he's paying a lower tax rate than his secretary. That is not fair. It is not right.

And the choice is really very simple. If you want to keep these tax rates and deductions in place—or give even more tax breaks to the wealthy, as the Republicans in Congress propose—then one of two things happen: either it means higher deficits, or it means more sacrifice from the middle class. Seniors will have to pay more for Medicare. College students will lose some of their financial aid. Working families who are scraping by will have to do more because the richest Americans are doing less. I repeat what I've said before: That is not class warfare, that is not class envy, that is math.

If that's the choice that Members of Congress want to make, then we're going to make sure every American knows about it. In a few weeks, there will be a vote on what we've called the Buffett rule. Simple concept: If you make more than a million dollars a year—not that you have a million dollars—if you make more than a million dollars annually, then you should pay at least the same percentage of your income in taxes as middle class families do. On the other hand, if you make under $250,000 a year, like 98 percent of American families do, then your taxes shouldn't go up. That's the proposal.

Now, you'll hear some people point out that the Buffett rule alone won't raise enough revenue to solve our deficit problems. Maybe not, but it's definitely a step in the right direction. And I intend to keep fighting for this kind of balance and fairness until the other side starts listening, because I believe this is what the American people want. I believe this is the best way to pay for the investments we need to grow our economy and strengthen the middle class. And by the way, I believe it's the right thing to do.

This larger debate that we will be having and that you will be covering in the coming year about the size and role of Government, this debate has been with us since our founding days. And during moments of great challenge and change, like the ones that we're living through now, the debate gets sharper; it gets more vigorous. That's a good thing. As a country that prizes both our individual freedom and our obligations to one another, this is one of the most important debates that we can have.

But no matter what we argue or where we stand, we have always held certain beliefs as Americans. We believe that in order to preserve our own freedoms and pursue our own happiness, we can't just think about ourselves. We have to think about the country that made those liberties possible. We have to think about our fellow citizens with whom we share a community. We have to think about what's required to preserve the American Dream for future generations.

And this sense of responsibility to each other and our country, this isn't a partisan feeling. This isn't a Democratic or Republican idea. It's patriotism. And if we keep that in mind and uphold our obligations to one another and to this larger enterprise that is America, then I have no doubt that we will continue our long and prosperous journey as the greatest nation on Earth.

Thank you. God bless you. God bless the United States of America. Thank you.

Bipartisanship

Associated Press Chairman of the Board of Directors W. Dean Singleton. Thank you, Mr. President. We appreciate so much you being with us today. I have some questions from the audience, which I will ask. And I'll be more careful than I was last time we did this.

Republicans have been sharply critical of your budget ideas as well. What can you say to the Americans who just want both sides to stop fighting and get some work done on their behalf?

The President. Well, I completely understand the American people's frustrations, because the truth is that these are eminently solvable problems. I know that Christine Lagarde is here from the IMF, and she's looking at the books of a lot of other countries around the world. The kinds of challenges they face fiscally are so much more severe than anything that we confront, if we make some sensible decisions.

So the American people's impulses are absolutely right. These are solvable problems if people of good faith came together and were willing to compromise. The challenge we have right now is that we have on one side a party that will brook no compromise. And this is not just my assertion. I mean, we had Presidential candidates who stood on a stage and were asked, "Would you accept a budget package, a deficit reduction plan, that involved $10 of cuts for every dollar in revenue increases?" Ten-to-one ratio of spending cuts to revenue. Not one of them raised their hand.

Think about that. Ronald Reagan, who, as I recall, is not accused of being a tax-and-spend Socialist, understood repeatedly that when the deficit started to get out of control, that for him to make a deal he would have to propose both spending cuts and tax increases—did it multiple times. He could not get through a Republican primary today.

So let's look at Bowles-Simpson. Essentially, my differences with Bowles-Simpson were I actually proposed less revenue and slightly lower defense spending cuts. The Republicans want to increase defense spending and take in no revenue, which makes it impossible to balance the deficit under the terms that Bowles-Simpson laid out, unless you essentially eliminate discretionary spending. You don't just cut discretionary spending. Everything we think of as being pretty important—from education to basic science and research to transportation spending to national parks to environmental protection—we'd essentially have to eliminate.

I guess another way of thinking about this is—and this bears on your reporting—I think that there is oftentimes the impulse to suggest that if the two parties are disagreeing, then they're equally at fault and the truth lies somewhere in the middle, and an equivalence is presented, which is—reinforces, I think, people's cynicism about Washington generally. This is not one of those situations where there's an equivalence. I've got some of the most liberal Democrats in Congress who were prepared to make significant changes to entitlements that go against their political interests and who said they were willing to do it. And we couldn't get a Republican to stand up and say, we'll raise some revenue or even to suggest that we won't give more tax cuts to people who don't need them.

And so I think it's important to put the current debate in some historical context. It's not just true, by the way, of the budget. It's true of a lot of the debates that we're having out here.

Cap-and-trade was originally proposed by conservatives and Republicans as a market-based solution to solving environmental problems. The first President to talk about cap-and-trade was George H.W. Bush. Now you've got the other party essentially saying we shouldn't even be thinking about environmental protection; let's gut the EPA.

Health care, which is in the news right now: There's a reason why there's a little bit of confusion in the Republican primary about health care and the individual mandate since it originated as a conservative idea to preserve the private marketplace in health care while still assuring that everybody got covered, in contrast to a single-payer plan. Now, suddenly, this is some socialist overreach.

So, as all of you are doing your reporting, I think it's important to remember that the positions I'm taking now on the budget and a host of other issues, if we had been having this discussion 20 years ago or even 15 years ago, would have been considered squarely centrist positions. What's changed is the center of the Republican Party. And that's certainly true with the budget.

U.S. Influence Abroad/National Economy

Mr. Singleton. Mr. President, the managing director of the IMF did speak to us earlier today. She made an impassioned plea for continuation of United States leadership on global economic issues and underscored the need for a lower deficit and lower debt. How can we respond to that plea?

The President. Well, look, she's absolutely right. It's interesting, when I travel around the world at these international fora—and I've said this before—the degree to which America is still the one indispensable nation, the degree to which, even as other countries are rising and their economies are expanding, we are still looked to for leadership, for agenda-setting, not just because of our size, not just because of our military power, but because there is a sense that unlike most superpowers in the past, we try to set out a set of universal rules, a set of principles by which everybody can benefit.

And that's true on the economic front as well. We continue to be the world's largest market, an important engine for economic growth. We can't return to a time when by simply borrowing and consuming, we end up driving global economic growth.

I said this a few months after I was elected at the first G–20 summit. I said the days when Americans using their credit cards and home equity loans finance the rest of the world's growth by taking in imports from every place else, those days are over. On the other hand, we continue to be a extraordinarily important market and foundation for global economic growth.

We do have to take care of our deficits. I think Christine has spoken before, and I think most economists would argue as well, that the challenge when it comes to our deficits is not short-term discretionary spending, which is manageable. As I said before and I want to repeat, as a percentage of our GDP, our discretionary spending—all the things that the Republicans are proposing cutting—is actually lower than it's been since Dwight Eisenhower. There has not been some massive expansion of social programs, programs that help the poor, environmental programs, education programs. That's not our problem.

Our problem is that our revenue has dropped down to between 15 and 16 percent—far lower than it has been historically, certainly far lower than it was under Ronald Reagan—at the same time as our health care costs have surged and our demographics mean that there is more and more pressure being placed on financing our Medicare, Medicaid, and Social Security programs.

So, at a time when the recovery is still gaining steam and unemployment is still very high, the solution should be pretty apparent. And that is even as we continue to make investments in growth today—for example, putting some of our construction workers back to work rebuilding schools and roads and bridges or helping States to rehire teachers at a time when schools are having a huge difficulty retaining quality teachers in the classroom—all of which would benefit our economy, we focus on a long-term plan to stabilize our revenues at a responsible level and to deal with our health care programs in a responsible way. And that's exactly what I'm proposing.

And what we've proposed is let's go back, for folks who are making more than $250,000 a year, to levels that were in place during the Clinton era, when wealthy people were doing just fine, and the economy was growing a lot stronger than it did after they were cut. And let's take on Medicare and Medicaid in a serious way, which is not just a matter of taking those costs off the books, off the Federal books, and pushing them onto individual seniors, but let's actually reduce health care costs. Because we spend more on health care, with not as good outcomes, as any other advanced, developed nation on Earth.

And that would seem to be a sensible proposal. The problem right now is not the technical means to solve it. The problem is our politics. And that's part of what this election and what this debate will need to be about, is, are we, as a country, willing to get back to commonsense, balanced, fair solutions that encourage our long-term economic growth and stabilize our budget. And it can be done.

One last point I want to make, Dean, that I think is important, because it goes to the growth issue. If State and local government hiring were basically on par to what our current recovery—on par to past recoveries, the unemployment rate would probably be about a point lower than it is right now. If the construction industry were going through what we normally go through, that would be another point lower. The challenge we have right now—part of the challenge we have in terms of growth—has to do with the very specific issues of huge cuts in State and local government and the housing market still recovering from this massive bubble. And that are huge—those two things are huge headwinds in terms of growth.

I say this because if we, for example, put some of those construction workers back to work or we put some of those teachers back in the classroom, that could actually help create the kind of virtuous cycle that would bring in more revenues just because of economic growth, would benefit the private sector in significant ways. And that could help contribute to deficit reduction in the short term, even as we still have to do these important changes to our health care programs over the long term.

Health Care Reform

Mr. Singleton. Mr. President, you said yesterday that it would be unprecedented for a Supreme Court to overturn laws passed by an elected Congress. But that is exactly what the Court has done during its entire existence. If the Court were to overturn individual mandate, what would you do, or propose to do, for the 30 million people who wouldn't have health care after that ruling?

The President. Well, first of all, let me be very specific. We have not seen a Court overturn a law that was passed by Congress on a economic issue, like health care, that I think most people would clearly consider commerce; a law like that has not been overturned at least since *Lochner*. Right? So we're going back to the thirties, pre–New Deal.

And the point I was making is that the Supreme Court is the final say on our Constitution and our laws, and all of us have to respect it, but it's precisely because of that extraordinary power that the Court has traditionally exercised significant restraint and deference to our duly elected legislature, our Congress. And so the burden is on those who would overturn a law like this.

Now, as I said, I expect Congress—I expect the Supreme Court actually to recognize that and to abide by well-established precedence out there. I have enormous confidence that in looking at this law, not only is it constitutional, but that the Court is going to exercise its jurisprudence carefully because of the profound power that our Supreme Court has. As a consequence, we're not spending a whole bunch of time planning for contingencies.

What I did emphasize yesterday is there is a human element to this that everybody has to remember. This is not an abstract exercise. I get letters every day from people who are affected by the health care law right now, even though it's not fully implemented. Young people who are 24, 25, who say, you know what, I just got diagnosed with a tumor. First of all, I would not have gone to get a checkup if I hadn't had health insurance. Second of all, I wouldn't have been able to afford to get it treated had I not been on my parent's plan. Thank you and thank Congress for getting this done.

I get letters from folks who have just lost their job; their COBRA is running out. They're in the middle of treatment for colon cancer or breast cancer, and they're worried when their COBRA runs out, if they're still sick, what are they going to be able to do, because they're not going to be able to get health insurance.

And the point, I think, that was made very ably before the Supreme Court, but I think most health care economists who have looked at this have acknowledged, is there are basically two ways to cover people with preexisting conditions or assure that people can always get

coverage even when they have bad illnesses. One way is the single-payer plan: Everybody is under a single system, like Medicare. The other way is to set up a system in which you don't have people who are healthy, but don't bother to get health insurance, and then we all have to pay for them in the emergency room. That doesn't work, and so, as a consequence, we've got to make sure that those folks are taking their responsibility seriously, which is what the individual mandate does.

So I don't anticipate the Court striking this down. I think they take their responsibilities very seriously. But I think what's more important is for all of us, Democrats and Republicans, to recognize that in a country like ours—the wealthiest, most powerful country on Earth—we shouldn't have a system in which millions of people are at risk of bankruptcy because they get sick or end up waiting until they do get sick and then go to the emergency room, which involves all of us paying for it.

Mr. Singleton. Mr. President, you've been very, very generous with your time, and we appreciate very much you being here.

The President. Thank you so much, everybody. Thank you.

NOTE: The President spoke at 12:35 p.m. at the Washington Marriott Wardman Park hotel. In his remarks, he referred to Prime Minister Vladimir Vladimirovich Putin of Russia, in his capacity as President-elect of Russia; Republican Presidential candidates former Rep. Newton L. Gingrich and former Gov. W. Mitt Romney of Massachusetts; Erskine B. Bowles and Alan K. Simpson, Cochairs, National Commission on Fiscal Responsibility and Reform; Warren E. Buffett, chief executive officer and chairman, and Debbie Bosanek, assistant, Berkshire Hathaway Inc.; and Christine Lagarde, Managing Director, International Monetary Fund.

Remarks at the Easter Prayer Breakfast
April 4, 2012

The President. Good morning, everybody. Please, have a seat. Have a seat. Well, welcome to the White House. It is a pleasure to be with all of you this morning.

In less than a week, this house will be over-run by thousands of kids at the Easter Egg Roll. [*Laughter*] So I wanted to get together with you for a little prayer and reflection, some calm before the storm. [*Laughter*]

It is wonderful to see so many good friends here today. To all the faith leaders from all across the country—from churches and con-gregations large and small, from different de-nominations and different backgrounds—thank you for coming to our third annual Eas-ter Prayer Breakfast. And I'm grateful that you're here.

I'm even more grateful for the work that you do every day of the year: the compassion and the kindness that so many of you express through your various ministries. I know that some of you have joined with our Office of Faith-based and Neighborhood Partner-ships. I've seen firsthand some of the out-standing work that you are doing in your re-spective communities, and it's an incredible expression of your faith. And I know that all of us who have an opportunity to work with you draw inspiration from the work that you do.

Finally, I want to just express appreciation for your prayers. Every time I travel around the country, somebody is going around saying, "We're praying for you." [*Laughter*] "We've got a prayer circle going. Don't worry, keep the faith. We're praying." [*Laughter*] Michelle gets the same stuff. And that means a lot to us. It especially means a lot to us when we hear it from folks who, we know, probably didn't vote for me—[*laughter*]—and yet expressing ex-traordinary sincerity about their prayers. And it's a reminder not only of what binds us to-gether as a nation, but also what binds us to-gether as children of God.

Now, I have to be careful; I am not going to stand up here and give a sermon. It's always a bad idea to give a sermon in front of profes-sionals. [*Laughter*] But in a few short days, all of us will experience the wonder of Easter morning. And we will know, in the words of the Apostle Paul, "Christ Jesus . . . and Him crucified."

It's an opportunity for us to reflect on the triumph of the resurrection and to give thanks for the all-important gift of grace. And for me, and I'm sure for some of you, it's also a chance to remember the tremendous sacrifice that led up to that day and all that Christ en-dured, not just as a Son of God, but as a hu-man being.

For like us, Jesus knew doubt. Like us, Jesus knew fear. In the garden of Gethsemane, with attackers closing in around him, Jesus told His disciples, "My soul is overwhelmed with sor-row to the point of death." He fell to his knees, pleading with His Father, saying, "If it is possi-ble, may this cup be taken from me." And yet, in the end, He confronted His fear with words of humble surrender, saying, "If it is not possi-ble for this cup to be taken away unless I drink it, may Your will be done."

So it is only because Jesus conquered His own anguish, conquered His fear, that we're able to celebrate the resurrection. It's only be-cause He endured unimaginable pain that wracked His body and bore the sins of the world that He burdened—that burdened His soul that we are able to proclaim, "He is risen!"

So the struggle to fathom that unfathomable sacrifice makes Easter all the more meaningful to all of us. It helps us to provide an eternal per-spective to whatever temporal challenges we face. It puts in perspective our small problems relative to the big problems He was dealing with. And it gives us courage, and it gives us hope.

We all have experiences that shake our faith. There are times where we have questions for God's plan relative to us—[*laughter*]—but that's precisely when we should remember Christ's own doubts and eventually His own triumph. Jesus told us as much in the Book of John, when He said, "In this world you will have trouble." I heard an amen. [*Laughter*] Let me repeat. [*Laughter*] "In this world, you will have trouble."

Audience members. Amen!

The President. "But take heart!" [*Laughter*] "I have overcome the world." So we are here today to celebrate that glorious overcoming, the sacrifice of a risen Savior who died so that we might live. And I hope that our time together this morning will strengthen us individually, as believers and as a nation.

And with that, I'd like to invite my good friend, Dr. Cynthia Hale, to deliver our opening prayer. Dr. Hale.

NOTE: The President spoke at 9:43 a.m. in the East Room at the White House. In his remarks, he referred to Cynthia L. Hale, founding and senior pastor, Ray of Hope Christian Church in Decatur, GA.

Remarks on Signing the Stop Trading On Congressional Knowledge Act of 2012
April 4, 2012

Thank you. Please, have a seat, have a seat. Well, good morning, and welcome to the White House. I want to thank my outstanding Vice President, Joe Biden, for being here. And we are joined by Members of both parties in Congress who helped to get this bill to my desk. So I'm very grateful to them.

I want to recognize Congresswoman Louise Slaughter and wish her a speedy recovery. She broke her leg yesterday, so she can't be here in person. I think she'll be okay. But she first introduced the STOCK Act in 2006, and I know how proud she is to see this bill that she championed finally become law.

Lately, I've been talking a lot about the choices facing this country. We can settle for a country that—an economy where a shrinking number of people do exceedingly well, while a growing number struggle to get by. Or we can build an economy where everybody gets a fair shot, everybody is doing their fair share, and everybody plays by the same set of rules.

Now, that last part, the idea that everybody plays by the same rules, is one of our most cherished American values. It goes hand in hand with our fundamental belief that hard work should pay off and responsibility should be rewarded. It's the notion that the powerful shouldn't get to create one set of rules for themselves and another set of rules for everybody else.

And if we expect that to apply to our biggest corporations and to our most successful citizens, it certainly should apply to our elected officials, especially at a time when there is a deficit of trust between this city and the rest of the country. And that's why, in my State of the Union, I asked Members of the House and the Senate to send me a bill that bans insider trading by Members of Congress, and I said that I would sign it right away.

Well, today I am happy to say that legislators from both parties have come together to do just that. The STOCK Act makes it clear that if Members of Congress use nonpublic information to gain an unfair advantage in the market, then they are breaking the law. It creates new disclosure requirements and new measures of accountability and transparency for thousands of Federal employees. That is a good and necessary thing. We were sent here to serve the American people and look out for their interests, not to look out for our own interests.

So I'm very proud to sign this bill into law. I should say that our work isn't done. There's obviously more that we can do to close the deficit of trust and limit the corrosive influence of money in politics. We should limit any elected official from owning stocks in industries that they have the power to impact. We should make sure people who bundle campaign contributions for Congress can't lobby Congress, and vice versa. These are ideas that should garner bipartisan support. And they certainly have wide support outside of Washington. And it's my hope that we can build off today's bipartisan effort to get them done.

In the months to come, we're going to have plenty of debates over competing visions for this country that we all love: whether or not we invest in the things that we need to keep our country safe and to grow our economy so that it's sustained and lasting; whether or not we'll ask some of our wealthiest Americans to pay their fair share; how we're going to make sure that America remains a land of opportunity and upward mobility for all people who are willing to work. Those are all debates that I'm looking forward to having.

But today I want to thank all the Members of Congress who came together and worked to get this done. It shows that when an idea is right that we can still accomplish something on behalf of the American people and to make our Government and our country stronger.

So to the ladies and gentlemen who helped make this happen, thank you very much for your outstanding work. And with that, let me sign this bill.

NOTE: The President spoke at 11:56 a.m. in the South Court Auditorium of the Dwight D. Eisenhower Executive Office Building. S. 2038, approved April 4, was assigned Public Law No. 112–105.

Remarks on Signing the Jumpstart Our Business Startups Act
April 5, 2012

Thank you. Hello, everybody. Please, please have a seat. Good afternoon. I want to thank all of you for coming, and in particular, I want to thank the Members of Congress who are here today from both parties, whose leadership and hard work made this bill a reality.

One of the great things about America is that we are a nation of doers, not just talkers, but doers. We think big, we take risks, and we believe that anyone with a solid plan and a willingness to work hard can turn even the most improbable idea into a successful business. So ours is a legacy of Edisons and Graham Bells, Fords and Boeings, of Googles and of Twitters. This is a country that's always been on the cutting edge. And the reason is that America has always had the most daring entrepreneurs in the world.

Some of them are standing with me today. When their ideas take root, we get inventions that can change the way we live. And when their businesses take off, more people become employed because, overall, new businesses account for almost every new job that's created in America.

Now, because we're still recovering from one of the worst recessions in our history, the last few years have been pretty tough on entrepreneurs. Credit's been tight, and no matter how good their ideas are, if an entrepreneur can't get a loan from a bank or backing from investors, it's almost impossible to get their businesses off the ground. And that's why back in September, and again in my State of the Union, I called on Congress to remove a num-

ber of barriers that were preventing aspiring entrepreneurs from getting funding. And this is one useful and important step along that journey.

Here's what's going to happen because of this bill. For business owners who want to take their companies to the next level, this bill will make it easier for you to go public. And that's a big deal because going public is a major step towards expanding and hiring more workers. It's a big deal for investors as well because public companies operate with greater oversight and greater transparency.

And for startups and small businesses, this bill is a potential game changer. Right now you can only turn to a limited group of investors, including banks and wealthy individuals, to get funding. Laws that are nearly eight decades old make it impossible for others to invest. But a lot's changed in 80 years, and it's time our laws did as well. Because of this bill, startups and small business will now have access to a big new pool of potential investors, namely, the American people. For the first time, ordinary Americans will be able to go online and invest in entrepreneurs that they believe in.

Of course, to make sure Americans don't get taken advantage of, the websites where folks will go to fund all these startups and small businesses will be subject to rigorous oversight. The SEC is going to play an important role in implementing this bill. And I've directed my administration to keep a close eye as this law goes into effect and to provide me with regular updates. It also means that—to all the Members of Congress who are here today, I want to say publicly before I sign this bill—it's going to be important that we continue to make sure that the SEC is properly funded, just like all our other regulatory agencies, so that they can do the job and make sure that our investors get adequate protections.

This bill represents exactly the kind of bipartisan action we should be taking in Washington to help our economy. I've always said that the true engine of job creation in this country is the private sector, not the government. Our job is to help our companies grow and hire. That's why I pushed for this bill. That's why I know that the bipartisan group of legislators here pushed for this bill. That's why I've cut taxes for small businesses over 17 times. That's why every day I'm fighting to make sure America is the best place on Earth to do business.

Our economy has begun to turn a corner, but we've still got a long way to go. We've still got a lot of Americans out there who are looking for a job or looking for a job that pays better than the one that they've got. And we're going to have to keep working together so that we can keep moving the economy forward.

But I've never been more confident about our future. And the reason is because of the American people. Some of the folks beside me here today are a testimony to that. Day out—after day, they're out there pitching investors. Some meetings go well; some meetings don't go so well—that's true for me too. [*Laughter*] But no matter what, they keep at it. And who knows, maybe one of them or one of the folks in the audience here today will be the next Bill Gates or Steve Jobs or Mark Zuckerberg. And one of them may be the next entrepreneur to turn a big idea into an entire new industry. That's the promise of America; that's what this country is all about.

So, if these entrepreneurs are willing to keep giving their all, the least Washington can do is to help them succeed. I plan to do that now by proudly signing this bill.

Thank you very much, everybody.

NOTE: The President spoke at 2:36 p.m. in the Rose Garden at the White House. In his remarks, he referred to William H. Gates III, chairman, Microsoft Corp.; and Mark E. Zuckerberg, founder and chief executive officer, Facebook, Inc. H.R. 3606, approved April 5, was assigned Public Law No. 112–106.

Videotaped Remarks on the Observance of Passover
April 5, 2012

I'd like to wish a happy holiday to all those celebrating Passover.

The story of the Exodus is thousands of years old, but it remains as relevant as ever. Throughout our history, there are those who have targeted the Jewish people for harm, a fact we were so painfully reminded of just a few weeks ago in Toulouse. Just as throughout history, there have been those who have sought to oppress others because of their faith, ethnicity, or color of their skin.

But tomorrow night Jews around the world will renew their faith that liberty will ultimately prevail over tyranny. They will give thanks for the blessings of freedom, while remembering those who are still not free. And they will ask one of our life's most difficult questions: Once

we have passed from bondage to liberty, how do we make the most of all that God has given us?

This question may never be resolved, but throughout the years, the search for answers has deepened the Jewish people's commitment to repairing the world and inspired American Jews to help make our Union more perfect. And the story of that first Exodus has also inspired those who are not Jewish with common hopes and a common sense of obligation.

So this is a very special tradition, and it's one I'm proud to be taking part of tomorrow night at the fourth annual White House Seder. Led by Jewish members of my staff, we'll retell the story of the Exodus, listen to our youngest guest ask the four questions, and of course, look forward to a good bowl of matzo ball soup.

Michelle and I are proud to celebrate with friends here at home and around the world, including those in the State of Israel.

So, on behalf of the entire Obama family, *Chag Sameach*.

NOTE: The President's remarks were videotaped at approximately 4:05 p.m. on March 29 in the Library at the White House.

Remarks at an Obama Victory Fund 2012 Fundraiser
April 5, 2012

The President. Hello, everybody. Thank you. Thank you so much. Everybody, please have a seat. Thank you so much. Well, nice job, everybody. [*Laughter*] What an extraordinary event. It is wonderful to be here with so many old friends and new friends as well.

A couple of people I just want to say a special thank you to: first of all, somebody who is a class act and cares about working families, has been working so hard for so many years, first in the House, now our junior Senator from the great State of Maryland, Ben Cardin. Thank you. I also want to acknowledge somebody who is going to be critical to what's happening this year because he is going to be our host for the Democratic National Convention, the mayor of the great city of Charlotte, Anthony Foxx is in the house.

Now, it is good to see all of you.

Audience member. Good to see you!

The President. Well, thank you. [*Laughter*]

Obviously, I have, every once in a while, a little bit of time to reflect in between a few responsibilities as President—[*laughter*]—and coaching Sasha's basketball team—[*laughter*]—and making sure I'm doing what I'm told by my wife. And so I think back to the last 3 years. And I think back to all the work we did in 2008 and all the people who were involved in this remarkable journey that we've been on. And I'm reminded that, let's face it, back in 2008, the reason why you guys got involved and supported me was not because it was a sure thing. [*Laughter*] I was not the odds-on favorite. [*Laughter*] Whenever you support somebody named Barack Hussein Obama to run for President of the United States—[*laughter*]—you're betting on the underdog.

But the reason that so many of you put your heart and soul into the campaign, the reason that I decided to run, despite having a pretty young family and asking enormous sacrifices from them, was because we shared a vision about what America should be. We shared commitments to each other about who we are as a people and what we want to leave behind for our children and our grandchildren.

And that's what the campaign was about. It was about bringing about change not for change's sake, but bringing about change because there were certain values that we cared deeply about and we didn't see those values reflected in the policies of our Government. And we worried about the future.

Now, this was all before we knew that we were entering into the worst financial crisis and the worst economic crisis that any of us have seen in our lifetimes. We didn't understand that we would be losing 4 million jobs in the 6 months before I took office and another 4 million just in the few months after I took office, 800,000 jobs the month I was sworn in. We didn't realize the magnitude of the collapse of the housing industry and the possibility that we might dip into a great depression.

But we did understand that for too long, for too many people, the basic American compact, the basic idea that if you work hard, if you're responsible, if you're looking after your family, that you should be able to find a job that pays a living wage, and you should be able to have health insurance so that you don't worry about going bankrupt if somebody in your family gets sick, that you should be able to send your kids to college and aspire to higher heights than you ever achieved, that you should be able to retire with some dignity and respect. We understood that that basic compact for too many people felt like it was slipping away.

And so the vision we shared was an American where everybody gets a fair shot and everybody is doing their fair share and everybody is playing by the same set of rules. That's what we were fighting for that basic American promise.

And as we reflect back over the last 3 years, as tough a 3 years as this country has seen in a very long time, we understand that we've still got a lot of work to do. We're not there yet. But we can take some pride—you can take some pride—in knowing that because of the actions you took in 2008, we've brought about a lot of the change that we believed in.

Think about it. Change is the first legislation that I signed into law, the Lilly Ledbetter Act that has a very simple principle: Women should get paid an equal day's pay for an equal day's work, and our daughters should be treated just like our sons when it comes to the workplace. That's what change is. That happened because of you.

Because of you, we were able to save an auto industry and a million jobs that go with it, even when there were a whole bunch of people that were arguing that we should let Detroit go bankrupt. I wasn't about to let that happen. You weren't about to let that happen. And now GM is once again the number-one automaker in the world, seeing record profits. We've seen hundreds of thousands of folks hired back and the economies that are impacted by the auto industry strengthened all across the Midwest. That happened because of you.

And not only did we save the auto industry, but they're now making better cars. [*Laughter*] And along with it, we decided we weren't going to wait for Congress: We went ahead and doubled fuel efficiency standards on cars so that by the middle of the next decade every auto is going to be getting 55 miles per gallon, and that's going to save the average family $8,000 in their costs at the pump, not to mention all the carbon that's being taken out of the atmosphere so that we can potentially preserve this precious planet of ours. That happened because of you.

Because of you, you don't have to worry about who you love to serve the country you love, because we ended "don't ask, don't tell," as we committed to. That's what change is. Because of you we took $60 billion that were going to banks in the student loan program, we said, why don't we give that money directly to students. And so there are millions of young people who are getting more Pell grants or qualify for the first time and are able to finance college. That happened because of you.

Because of you, right now 2.5 million young people have health insurance that didn't have it before, and millions of seniors have seen lower prescription drug prices—because of you. And we are going to insure another 30 million people in this country, and we are making sure if you've got health insurance, that they can't drop you when you get sick, the strongest patient protection bill that we've ever seen when it comes to health care. That all happened because of you. That's what change is.

And change is keeping the promise—one of the promises I made in 2008. We ended the war in Iraq. And we refocused our attention on those who actually attacked us on 9/11. And Al Qaida is on its last legs, weaker than it's ever been. And Usama bin Laden is no longer around. And we are transitioning out of Afghanistan. And we've raised America's respect all around the world. That happened because of you.

So all this shouldn't make us complacent. We should not be satisfied. We didn't simply work that hard in 2008 just to clean up the mess that had been left. We got involved and engaged because we understood there were challenges that had been building up over decades that had to be attended to. And we've still got more work to do. The job is not done.

There are still way too many people all across this country that are desperately looking for work. I get letters from them every day, people who are well educated, people who don't have the education they need, but they want to work, and they are sending out résumés, they are pounding the pavement, and they are knocking on doors, and they're worried about their future.

There are folks who have a job, but are having trouble paying the bills, and maybe they've seen the value of their home drop by $10,000, $20,000, $100,000, and they don't know if they're ever going to be able to recover what they thought was their life savings.

We've got people who had decided they've got to forgo retirement, just completely change their plans, just so they can make sure that their children or their grandchildren can still afford college. And we've got young people who have gone to college and racked up a whole bunch of debt and aren't sure whether they can find a job that allows them to pay it off. There are still too many folks for whom that American promise is not yet a reality: good people, responsible people, patriotic people.

Now, understanding that we haven't finished the job yet should invigorate us. It should inspire us to work that much harder. But if that's not sufficient, then it's important to understand that the last thing that we can afford to do is go back to the same economic policies that got us into this mess in the first place, the same economic policies that have betrayed that American promise for too long. And that's exactly what the other side is proposing.

I gave a speech on Tuesday about the congressional budget that's been proposed by the Republicans in the House of Representatives, a budget that Governor Romney, who is the frontrunner in the Republican side, has embraced, said the budget was "marvelous," he said. [*Laughter*] And when you go through this budget, the vision that it portrays is of an America where everybody is fending for themselves, a few are doing very well at the top, and everybody else is struggling to get by.

And the Government is shrunk to the point where things that we take for granted as a society—as an advanced, responsible society—are gutted: education, science and research, early childhood education, caring for our environment, looking after our veterans, keeping up with our infrastructure, rebuilding our roads and our bridges so that they're safe, food safety laws, our capacity to enforce basic consumer protections. All of this is shrunk to the point of near invisibility.

And the rationale they provide is, well, the biggest crisis we face is the deficit, so we need to do something about it; we've got to make tough choices. They're absolutely right about that. Unfortunately, the vision that they're presenting adds to the deficit problem because they say they're going to cut more taxes for the wealthiest Americans after we have seen the tax rates for wealthy Americans go to below anyplace that they've been since I've been alive.

The contrast between visions in this election could not be more stark, because I believe that America is stronger when we're looking for one another. I believe in the free market. I believe that the private sector is the true generator of job growth. I believe that there are times where government doesn't have the answers, but like most previous Presidents, Democrat and Republican, I understand that we have a role in making sure that not just the powerful do well, but that everybody has got a shot.

I believe we have to make an investment in education because I know from my own life and from Michelle's life that we would not be where we were unless somebody had made an investment in us.

I believe in investing in basic research and science because I understand that all these extraordinary companies that are these enormous wealth generators, many of them would have never been there—Google, Facebook would not exist—had it not been for investments that we made as a country in basic science and research. I understand that makes us all better off.

I believe that it is part of our solemn responsibility to future generations that we look after this planet, that we make sure our air is clean and our water is clean, that we're not poisoning our kids.

I believe our economy does better—one of the things that has made our economy work so well is its transparency and its rule of law, and that consumers are protected, and we have some confidence, if we go into the store and we buy a product, that it's going to be safe.

We've set standards that allowed us not only to create a national market, but help to create an international market. We set the standard. That worked for us. That was good for business. It didn't weaken us.

I believe that in a society as wealthy as ours, we should have a commitment to our seniors and to the disabled. That's not a sign of weakness. That's not socialism. The idea that you want to care for people in our communities so our seniors don't have to plunge into poverty, that they have some modicum of security if they need health care, that a family that has been stricken by an illness doesn't have to worry if they're going to lose their home, that makes us stronger.

I believe in making sure that workers are able to work in a safe environment, that they get paid a decent wage, because I understand the same thing Henry Ford understood when he said, you know what, I want to make sure that my workers can afford to buy my cars. That broad-based prosperity, bottom-up economic growth is what sustains us. That's what I believe, and that's what you believe. And that's what animated our campaign in 2008.

So we are going to have a big, important debate in this country, and I cannot wait, because we have tried what they are selling. It's not like we didn't try it. We have tried what they're peddling, and it did not work. [*Laughter*] And we have been spending the last 3 years cleaning after some of that mess. And I don't want to have to do it again.

So we're going to keep on in a direction that has created 4 million jobs in the last 2 years. And we're going to keep on in a direction that has seen manufacturing in America coming back. And we're going to stay on the course that is helping us to double our exports so that we're not just known as a society that buys and consumes, but a society that creates and innovates and sells all around the world.

And we're going to continue to double down on education reform so that every young American knows that they can get the skills they need to succeed in this society. And we're going to produce American-made energy. And we're going to take an all-of-the-above strategy.

And we actually are seeing the highest oil production in this country in 8 years. Our imports have diminished below 50 percent, the lowest they've been in 13 years. So we're producing more oil. We're producing more gas. But we're also going to produce more clean energy: more wind and more solar and more biofuels. It's the smart thing to do. It's good for business. It's good for our environment. And I'm not going to cede those industries to other countries.

And we're going to continue on a course in foreign policy that maintains the strongest military on Earth, but also understands that we've got to have as powerful a diplomatic strategy, as powerful an economic strategy that we are exporting our values and upholding core ideas about how women are treated and how the young are treated and how minorities are treated, because that's part of what makes us special. That's part of what makes us exceptional.

So this is going to be a big debate. And it's going to be a fun debate—[*laughter*]—because it's always good to have the truth on your side. But it's not going to be easy. It's not going to be easy. We're going to have to work hard. There are a lot of folks out there still struggling. And there are a lot of folks who, understandably, seeing what goes on in Washington, sometimes lose heart, and they get cynical. Maybe some of you do sometimes.

You say to yourself, you know what, it just doesn't seem like things are on the level. It doesn't seem like people are thinking about me or my community. And they see the amounts of money that are being spent and the special interests that dominate and the lobbyists that always have access, and they say to themselves, maybe I don't count. They get discouraged. And that makes this tougher in some ways.

Back in 2008, being an Obama supporter, that was fresh and new, and I didn't have any gray hair. [*Laughter*] And this time, we're all a little older. We're a little wiser. Here is the thing I want to communicate to you though. That spirit that we're all in this together, that spirit that Abraham Lincoln understood and Teddy Roosevelt understood and Dwight Eisenhower understood—it wasn't just FDR and Johnson and Kennedy, because it's not a Democratic or a Republican idea, it's an American idea—that spirit may not always be evident in Washington, but it's still out there in the country.

You still see it in town halls. You still see it in churches or synagogues. You still see it in our amazing men and women in uniform. They still understand that we're stronger together than we can ever be on our own. They still understand an America in which everybody has a fair shot, no matter what you look like, no matter where you come from, no matter what your last name.

And so if we're energized, if we're determined, that core sense of decency and possibility and hope, it's still out there. But we have to make sure that we are determined. I used to say in 2008 that this wasn't going to be easy, I'm not a perfect man, I'm not going to be a perfect President. But I used to tell people, I'd always tell you what I thought, I'll always tell you where I stood, and I wake up every morning thinking about how I could work as hard as I could to make sure that every American had a

chance, every American felt that sense of possibility that I've lived out in my own life.

And I've kept that promise. I have kept that promise. And my hope is that you are willing to continue on this journey with me, that you're willing to work just as hard or harder than you did in 2008. Not just writing a check. I need you to get on the phone. I need you to knock on doors. I need some of you to do what you did last time: travel to other States and talk to your friends and your neighbors and your co-workers and fight back against the cynicism and answer the lies that may come up.

I am as determined—I am more determined than I was in 2008. I hope you are too. Because if you are, we will finish what we started, and we'll remind ourselves just why it is that this is the greatest country on Earth.

Thank you, everybody. God bless you. God bless America.

NOTE: The President spoke at 7:28 p.m. at the Mandarin Oriental hotel. In his remarks, he referred to Republican Presidential candidate former Gov. W. Mitt Romney of Massachusetts.

Remarks at the White House Forum on Women and the Economy
April 6, 2012

Thank you. Everybody, sit down, sit down. I was going to head over here earlier and they said, no, no, this place is full of women, and they're still settling down. [*Laughter*] I said, what do you mean settling down? What are they doing over there? Just creating havoc.

Welcome to the White House, everybody. It is a pleasure to be surrounded by so many talented, accomplished women. It makes me feel right at home. Although usually, I've got my wingman Bo with me. [*Laughter*]

I want to thank everybody who's made this forum on women and the economy possible. I thank Mika for helping moderate today and proving that, on your show every morning, that women really are the better half. [*Laughter*] Joe is not denying it. [*Laughter*] He's not denying it.

I want to thank the members of my Cabinet and administration who are participating today. And I want to thank all of you who've come today lending your time and your energy to the critical cause of broadening opportunity for America's women

Right now no issue is more important than restoring economic security for all our families in the wake of the greatest economic crisis since the Great Depression. And that begins with making sure everyone who wants a job has one. So we welcome today's news that our businesses created another 121,000 jobs last month and the unemployment rate ticked down. Our economy has now created more than 4 million private sector jobs over the past 2 years and more than 600,000 in the past 3 months alone. But it's clear to every American that there will still be ups and downs along the way and that we've got a lot more work to do.

And that includes addressing challenges that are unique to women's economic security, challenges that have been around since long before the recession hit. And that's why one of the first things I did after taking office was to create a White House Council on Women and Girls. I wanted to make sure that every agency across my administration considers the needs of women and girls in every decision we make. And today we're releasing a report on women and the economy that looks at women's economic security through all stages of life: from young women furthering their education and beginning their careers, to working women who create jobs and provide for their families, to seniors in retirement or getting ready for retirement.

There's been a lot of talk about women and women's issues lately, as there should be. But I do think that the conversation has been oversimplified. Women are not some monolithic bloc. Women are not an interest group. You shouldn't be treated that way. Women are over half this country and its workforce, not to mention 80 percent of my household, if you count my mother-in-law. [*Laughter*] And I always count my mother-in-law. [*Laughter*]

Every decision made by those of us in public life impacts women just as much as men. And this report you all have explains some of what we've done to try to lift up the lives of women and girls in this country. But I'd like to spend some time talking about why we've done what we've done.

For me, at least, it begins with the women who've shaped my life. I grew up the son of a single mom who struggled to put herself through school and make ends meet, had to rely on food stamps at one point to get us by. But she earned her education; she made it through with scholarships and hard work. And my sister and I earned our degrees because of her motivation and her support and her impact. I've told this story before: She used to wake me up before dawn when I was living overseas, making sure that I was keeping up with my American education, and when I'd complain, she'd

let loose with, "This is no picnic for me either, buster." [*Laughter*] And that's part of the reason why my sister chose to become a teacher.

When my mom needed help with us, my grandmother stepped up. My grandmother had a high school education. My grandfather got to go to college on the GI bill; my grandmother wasn't afforded those same opportunities even though she had worked on an assembly line, a bomber assembly line in World War II. Nevertheless, she got a job at a local bank, and she was smart and tough and disciplined, and she worked hard. And eventually, she rose from being a secretary to being vice president at this bank, and I'm convinced she would have been the best president that bank had ever seen if she had gotten the chance. But at some point, she hit the glass ceiling, and for a big chunk of her career, she watched other men that she had trained—younger men that she had trained—pass her up that ladder.

And then, there is the woman who once advised me at the law firm in Chicago where we met. [*Laughter*] Once—[*laughter*]—she gave me very good advice. That's why I decided to marry her. [*Laughter*] And once Michelle and I had our girls, she gave it her all to balance raising a family and pursuing a career—and something that could be very difficult on her, because I was gone a lot.

Once I was in the State legislature, I was teaching, I was practicing law, I'd be traveling, and we didn't have the luxury for her not to work. And I know when she was with the girls, she'd feel guilty that she wasn't giving enough time to her work. And when she was at work, she was feeling guilty she wasn't giving enough time to the girls. And like many of you, we both wished that there were a machine that could let us be in two places at once. And so she had to constantly juggle it and carried an extraordinary burden for a long period of time.

And then finally, as a father, one of my highlights of every day is asking my daughters about their day, their hopes, and their futures. That's what drives me every day when I step into the Oval Office: thinking about them. Every decision I make is all about making sure they and all our daughters and all our sons grow up in a country that gives them the chance to be anything they set their minds to, a country where more doors are open to them than were open to us.

So, when I think about these efforts, when we put together this Council on Women and Girls, this is personal. That's what is at the heart of all our efforts. These are the experiences, the prism through which I view these efforts. And that's what we mean when we say that these issues are more than just a matter of policy. And when we talk about these issues that primarily impact women, we've got to realize they are not just women's issues. They are family issues, they are economic issues, they are growth issues, they are issues about American competitiveness. They're issues that impact all of us.

Now, think about it. When women make less than men for the same work, that hurts families who have to get by with less and businesses who have fewer customers with less to spend. When a job doesn't offer amily leave to care for a new baby or sick leave to care for an ailing parent, that burdens men as well. When an insurance plan denies women coverage because of preexisting conditions, that puts a strain on emergency rooms, drives up costs of care for everybody. When any of our citizens can't fulfill the potential that they have because of factors that have nothing to do with talent, or character, or work ethic, that diminishes us all. It holds all of us back. And it says something about who we are as Americans.

Right now women are a growing number of breadwinners in the household. But they're still earning just 77 cents for every dollar a man does, even less if you're an African American or Latina woman. Overall, a woman with a college degree doing the same work as a man will earn hundreds of thousands of dollars less over the course of her career.

So closing this pay gap, ending pay discrimination, is about far more than simple fairness. When more women are bringing home the bacon, but bringing home less of it than men who are doing the same work, that weakens families, it weakens communities, it's tough on our kids, it weakens our entire economy.

Which is why the first bill I signed into law was the Lilly Ledbetter Act—the Fair Pay Act—to make it easier for women to demand fairness: equal pay for equal work. We're pushing for legislation to give women more tools to pay—to fight pay discrimination. And we've encouraged companies to make workplaces more flexible so women don't have to choose between being a good employee or a good mom.

More women are also choosing to strike out on their own. Today, nearly 30 percent of small-business owners are women. Their businesses generate $1.2 trillion last year. But they're less likely to get the loans that they need to start up or expand or to hire, which means they often have to depend on credit cards and the mounting debt that comes with them. And that's why, through some outstanding work by Karen Mills and the SBA and other parts of our administration, we've extended more than 16,000 new loans worth $4.5 billion to women-owned businesses—not to mention cut taxes for small businesses 17 times—so that more women have the power to create more jobs and more opportunity.

We're also focusing on making sure more women are prepared to fill the good jobs of today and tomorrow. Over the past decade, women have earned well over half of all the higher education degrees awarded in America. But once they get out of college, we still have a lot of ground to cover. Just 3 percent of Fortune 500 CEOs are women. Fewer than 20 percent of the seats in Congress are occupied by women. Is it possible that Congress would get more done if there were more women in Congress? [*Laughter*] Is that fair to say, Joe? I think it's fair to say. That is almost guaranteed. [*Laughter*]

And while women account for four in five degrees in areas like education—which is terrific because obviously, there's no profession that is more important than teaching—we also have to recognize that only two in five business degrees go to women; fewer than one in four engineering and computer science degrees go to women. They make up just 25 percent of the workforce in the science and technical fields. No unspoken bias or outdated barrier should ever prevent a girl from considering careers in these fields. When creativity is limited or ingenuity is discouraged, that hurts all of us. It denies America the game-changing products and world-changing discoveries we need to stay on top.

We've got to do more to encourage women to join these fields as well, make it easier to afford the education that's required to make it. Send a clear message to our daughters, which I'm doing every night: Math, science, nothing wrong with it, a lot right with it. We need you to focus. That's why our education reform, Race to the Top, has put a priority on science and technology and engineering and math education. It has rewarded States that took specific steps to ensure that all students—especially underrepresented groups like girls—have the opportunity to get excited about these fields at an early age. And we've helped more than 2.3 million more young women afford to pursue higher education with our increases in the Pell grants. That's good news.

Another example: health reform. It's been in the news lately. [*Laughter*] Because of the health reform law that we passed, women finally have more power to make their choices about their health care. Last year, more than 20 million women received expanded access to preventive services like mammograms and cervical cancer screenings at no additional cost. Nearly 2 million women enrolled in Medicare received a 50-percent discount on the medicine that they need. Over 1 million more young women are insured because they can now stay on their parent's plan. And later this year, women will receive new access to recommended preventive care like domestic violence screening and contraception at no additional cost. And soon, insurance companies will no longer be able to deny coverage based on preexisting conditions like breast cancer or charge women more just because they're women.

We don't know—we haven't gotten on the dry cleaning thing yet, though. I mean, I know that that's still—[*laughter*]—that's still frustrating, I'm sure. [*Laughter*]

So, when it comes to our efforts on behalf of women and girls, I'm proud of the accomplish-

ments that we can point to. Yes, we've got a lot more to do. But there's no doubt we've made progress. The policies we've put in place over the past 3 years have started to take hold. And what we can't do now is go back to the policies that got us into so many of the problems that we've been dealing with in the first place. That's what's at stake.

But when people talk about repealing health care reform, they're not just saying we should stop protecting women with preexisting conditions, they're also saying we should kick about a million young women off their parents' health care plans.

When people say we should get rid of Planned Parenthood, they're not just talking about restricting a woman's ability to make her own health decisions, they're talking about denying, as a practical matter, the preventive care, like mammograms, that millions of women rely on.

When folks talk about doing away with things like student aid that disproportionately help young women, they're not thinking about the costs to our future, when millions of young Americans will have trouble affording to go to college.

And when something like the Violence Against Women Act—a bill Joe Biden authored, a bill that once passed by wide bipartisan margins—is suddenly called to question, that makes no sense. I don't need to—[*applause*]—that's not something we should still be arguing about.

Now, I don't need to tell anybody here that progress is hard. Change can come slow. Opportunity and equality don't come without a fight. And sometimes you've got to keep fighting even after you've won some victories. Things don't always move forward. Sometimes they move backward if you're not fighting for them.

But we do know these things are possible. And all of you are proof to that. This incredible collection of accomplished women, you're proof of change. So is the fact that for the first time in history, young girls across the country can see three women sitting on the bench of the highest court in the land.

Or they can read about the extraordinary leadership of a woman who went by the title Madam Speaker. Or they can turn on the news and see that one of the most formidable Presidential candidates and Senators we ever had is now doing as much as anybody to improve America's standing abroad as one of the best Secretaries of State that we've ever known. And they can see that every single day, another 500 women, just like yourselves, take the helm of their own company right here in America and do their part to grab those doors of opportunity that they walked through and open them just a little bit wider for the next generation.

As long as I've got the privilege of being your President, we're going to keep working every single day to make sure those doors forever stay open and widen the circle of opportunity for all our kids. Thank you for what you do. Keep it up. God bless you. God bless the United States of America.

NOTE: The President spoke at 10:30 a.m. in the South Court Auditorium of the Dwight D. Eisenhower Executive Office Building. In his remarks, he referred to Mika Brzezinski and Joe Scarborough, cohosts, MSNBC's "Morning Joe" program; his mother-in-law Marian Robinson and sister Maya Soetoro-Ng; and House Democratic Leader Nancy Pelosi.

Statement on the Observance of Easter
April 6, 2012

This Sunday, Michelle and I will join Christians across the country and around the world to celebrate Easter and give thanks for the all-important gift of grace. Easter is a time to reflect on both Christ's suffering and ultimate triumph, as the anguish of the cross continues to give way to the victory of resurrection. So to all those celebrating with us, we extend our warmest Easter greetings and best wishes in the days ahead.

Statement on the 18th Anniversary of the Genocide in Rwanda
April 6, 2012

Eighteen years after the Rwandan genocide, we pause to reflect with horror and sadness on the 100 days in 1994 when 800,000 people lost their lives. The specter of this slaughter of mothers, fathers, sons, and daughters haunts us still and reminds the nations of the world of our shared responsibility to do all we can to protect civilians and to ensure that evil of this magnitude never happens again. The United States grieves with the Rwandan people, and we remember those whose lives were cut short. And as we do, we also recognize Rwanda's progress in moving beyond this horrible tragedy, the strides it has taken to improve the lives of its people, and its contributions to protecting civilians from other nations in U.N. peacekeeping missions around the world. The U.S. Government and the American people will continue to extend our friendship, partnership, and support to the Rwandan people as they seek to build a peaceful and prosperous future.

The President's Weekly Address
April 7, 2012

For millions of Americans, this weekend is a time to celebrate redemption at God's hand. Tonight Jews will gather for a second Seder, where they will retell the story of the Exodus. And tomorrow my family will join Christians around the world as we thank God for the all-important gift of grace through the resurrection of His Son and experience the wonder of Easter morning.

These holidays have their roots in miracles that took place thousands of years ago. They connect us to our past and give us strength as we face the future. And they remind us of the common thread of humanity that connects us all.

For me, and for countless other Christians, Easter weekend is a time to reflect and rejoice. Yesterday many of us took a few quiet moments to try and fathom the tremendous sacrifice Jesus made for all of us. Tomorrow we will celebrate the resurrection of a Savior who died so that we might live.

And throughout these sacred days, we recommit ourselves to following His example. We rededicate our time on Earth to selflessness and to loving our neighbors. We remind ourselves that no matter who we are or how much we achieve, we each stand humbled before an almighty God.

The story of Christ's triumph over death holds special meaning for Christians. But all of us, no matter how or whether we believe, can identify with elements of His story: the triumph of hope over despair, of faith over doubt; the notion that there is something out there that is bigger than ourselves.

These beliefs help unite Americans of all faiths and backgrounds. They shape our values and guide our work. They put our lives in perspective.

So to all Christians celebrating the resurrection with us, Michelle and I want to wish you a blessed and happy Easter. And to all Americans, I hope you have a weekend filled with joy and reflection, focused on the things that matter most.

God bless you, and may God bless the United States of America.

NOTE: The address was recorded at approximately 11:50 a.m. on April 6 in the Roosevelt Room at the White House for broadcast on April 7. The transcript was made available by the Office of the Press Secretary on April 6, but was embargoed for release until 6 a.m. on April 7.

Remarks at the White House Easter Egg Roll
April 9, 2012

The President. Good morning, everybody. How about Rachel Crow? Give her a big round of applause.

I want to wish everybody a wonderful Easter. And we are so thrilled that all of you could join us here today. My job is very simple: It is to introduce the powerhouse of the White House, the one truly in charge, as Malia, Sasha, and Bo all know, the First Lady of the United States, Michelle Obama.

The First Lady. Thank you, honey. My job is simple as well. I just want to officially welcome you all to the White House Easter Egg Roll. It is a beautiful day, perfect weather. We are so excited to have you all here. We've got a great set of activities planned for you. There's something for everyone. We're going to be over there doing a little egg roll. I think the President is going to try to beat a 3-year-old, which I hope he does not. [*Laughter*]

But we also have a wonderful yoga garden. We've got some storytime guests. We've got great readers here this year, as we do every year. You can get your face painted. We've got wonderful musical guests. Rachel was amazing, and she's a really sweet kid, which is more important. We've got wonderful athletes here. We've got Chris Evert—my gosh—and many, many others. The Harlem Globetrotters are here. You can do an obstacle course. We're going to be down at the kitchen learning how to do some healthy cooking with the—some of our celebrity chefs.

So it's a wonderful day, and I hope you all enjoy it. I hope you put on your comfortable shoes. We've got ours on, right, all the Obamas here.

So, on behalf of our family, I also want to wish you all a happy Easter and a happy Easter Egg Roll. So, in the theme of this year's Easter Egg Roll, let's go, let's play, let's move.

The President. Thank you, everybody. Have a great time. We'll see you down there.

NOTE: The President spoke at 10:46 a.m. on the South Lawn at the White House.

Remarks Following a Meeting With President Dilma Rousseff of Brazil
April 9, 2012

President Obama. Well, it gives me great pleasure to welcome to the Oval Office my good friend President Rousseff. This gives me an opportunity to return some of the extraordinary hospitality that I received when Michelle and our daughters and I had a chance to visit Brazil last year.

It gives me an opportunity as well to remark on the extraordinary progress that Brazil has made under the leadership of President Rousseff and her President—her predecessor, President Lula, moving from dictatorship to democracy, embarking on an extraordinary growth path, lifting millions of people out of poverty, and becoming not only a leading voice in the region, but also a leading voice in the world.

We've made enormous progress since we last met on our bilateral relationship. Our trade and investment is reaching record levels, which creates jobs and business opportunities in both countries. We have seen an extraordinary expansion of people-to-people contacts, including a unprecedented exchange of students around math and science and technology, where President Rousseff has shown incredible leadership. We are announcing defense cooperation of the sorts that we have not seen in the past.

And this meeting gives us an opportunity to also discuss a wide range of global issues, whether it's global economic growth, the situation in the Middle East, our work together on various multilateral platforms, as well as the progress that we've been able to make together in the Open Government Partnership that is increasing transparency, accountability, and reducing corruption, where the United States and Brazil were the initial cochairs, and now we're seeing countries all around the world eagerly involved and engaged in what can be a very important initiative.

Of course, we still have more work to do. We are consulting around the Summit of the Americas meeting this weekend to make sure that we are coordinating closely on issues of great importance like expanding educational exchanges, improving the cooperation between our countries on clean energy, dealing with issues like narcotrafficking, and citizen security issues that are so important to the region.

We have important progress to make on energy cooperation. Brazil has been a extraordinary leader in biofuels and obviously is also becoming a world player when it comes to oil and gas development. And the United States is not only a potential large customer to Brazil, but we think that we can cooperate closely on a whole range of energy projects together.

And both our governments are going to continue to work to make it easier to cultivate the friendships, the commerce, and interaction between the peoples of the United States and Brazil. For example, we have drastically cut down on visa wait times for Brazilian visitors to the United States and are opening up two new consulates. We want to continue to make progress on that front. We're going to have the opportunity to meet with business leaders from both Brazil and the United States to get their recommendations on how we can further enhance trade and investment relationships between our two countries.

So the good news is, is that the relationship between Brazil and the United States has never been stronger. But we always have even greater improvements that can be made. And I'm—feel very fortunate to have such a capable and farsighted partner as President Rousseff, so that not only Brazil and the United States, but the world can benefit from our deeper cooperation.

So welcome, Madam President. We're thrilled to have you here.

President Rousseff. I would like to say to all of you that this occasion has been very important for me to meet with President Obama, following our meeting last year in Brasilia. That first meeting in 2011 in Brazil, it proved very important in that it provided us with an opportunity for contacts with the First Lady Michelle and also with the children.

The U.S.-Brazil bilateral relations are, for Brazil, a very important relationship, not only from a bilateral, but also from a multilateral perspective. As regards the bilateral dimension of our agenda, Brazil and the United States have increasingly drawn closer ties in their trade links, while at the same time, expanding mutual investments.

Brazil's current investment level, direct investments in the United States currently account for 40 percent of the overall investments made by the United States in Brazil. All of these different fronts of our relationship have produced very substantial outcomes, but they also show that we remain current in our potentiality.

Both Brazil and the United States of America have strategic areas in which we can cooperate or, better said, where we can further deepen our existing cooperation. Take the energy sector, for example. Oil and gas pose a tremendous opportunity for further cooperation both as regards the supply of equipment and provision of services and also as regards a wider role in our trade relations.

Brazil and the United States are also partners in the biofuel arena. And I would like to welcome the recently announced reductions to ethanol tariffs. The field of energy efficiency, which is so very dear to President Obama, is yet another area to be highlighted for cooperation, and particularly renewable sources of energy and also technological evolution in the energy arena as regards to smart grids or networks.

Without a shadow of a doubt, there are also other areas of equal relevance, a number of— along which I would like to highlight, the areas of science, technology, and innovation, an area in which both business communities, the members of academia and governments have a high-profile role to perform. That is where our involvement in the Science Without Borders program is so very important. The program benefits Brazilian researchers and students who are given the opportunity to come to the United States to develop and conduct their studies here.

I would also like to publicly acknowledge the support we have received in all of those initiatives and also highlight the fact that Brazil feels it's very important the U.S.-run program titled 100,000 Strong. May I also highlight the opportunities available in areas such as the defense arena and also ship building, which holds significant opportunities for cooperation. And security is also another field for prosperous cooperation, without a shadow of a doubt.

Not only the government-led growth acceleration program, the PAC program, but also the upcoming World Soccer Cup in 2014 and the Olympics in 2016, provide extensive opportunities for investment and cooperation between Brazilian and U.S. businesses. I believe it is in our utmost interest to draw closer ties in our economic areas and also ensure a closer partnership in the field of innovation in particular.

Regarding the multilateral agenda, during this meeting we also covered and mentioned our concern regarding the international crisis, which has led to instability, low growth, and unemployment in several regions of the world. We also indicated that we acknowledged the role performed by central banks of different countries and, more particularly, in the recent past, the role of the European Central Bank, the role performed to the effect of ultimately preventing a liquidity crisis of substantial proportions, which would thus affect all countries adversely.

But I also voiced to President Obama Brazil's concern regarding the monetary expansion policies that ultimately mean that countries that have a surplus be able to strike a balance in those economic monetary expansion policies through fiscal policies that are ultimately based on expanding investments. Such expansionist monetary policies in and of themselves, in isolation regarding the fiscal policies, ultimately lead to a depreciation in the value of the currencies of emerging countries—rather, they lead to a depreciation in the value of the currency of developed countries, thus impairing growth outlooks in emerging countries.

It is our view that the role to be performed by the United States, against a backdrop and in an increasingly multilateral world, as we have seen—we believe the U.S. role is very important. The high degree of flexibility that is inherent to the United States economy plus the U.S. leadership in the fields of science, technology, and innovation in the United States, and at the same time, the democratic forces that are the founding elements of the U.S. nation mean that the role of the United States is indeed a key and very important role not only in containing the effects of the crisis, but also ensuring proper resumption of prosperity.

The BRICs countries currently account for a very substantial share of economic growth worldwide. But it is important to realize and bear in mind the resumption of growth in the medium-term future certainly involves a substantial resumption of growth in the U.S. economy. We very much welcome the major improvements that have been found in the U.S. economy in the recent past. And I am quite certain that that will very much be the emphasis in the next few months and years ahead under the capable leadership of President Obama.

Furthermore, we also discussed with President Obama the issues regarding the upcoming and fourth summit meeting of the Americas, which will be held next weekend in Cartagena, Colombia. The Summit of the Americas very much expresses the fact that Latin America is a growing continent and has grown by distributing income and engaging in a social inclusion or social mainstreaming process. But of course, the crisis does affect Latin American countries, not as strongly as in other regions of the world, but it does affect Latin America.

We will discuss in the upcoming summit meeting of the Americas how integration in the Americas can prove beneficial to Latin America and also how economic growth can only materialize if we introduce economic policies that

are targeted to strengthening our domestic markets by increasingly mainstreaming millions of Brazilians and, by extension, millions of Latin Americans, while also, of course, preventing the protectionist measures, particularly currency-related measures proved detrimental to our interests.

And a very important point on the agenda is to do with the concern we all have regarding the issue of drug trafficking and the violence it triggers. At the same time, we're keenly aware of the importance of Latin America in efforts to tackle drug trafficking. As I have consistently mentioned, I believe that when it comes to drug trafficking, we have to take a hard stance in fighting drug trafficking while addressing those that have fallen prey to—[*inaudible*]— thus becoming drug addicts.

I would also like to say that it is Brazil's view that the open government initiative meeting is very important. The upcoming meeting will be held on April 17 in Brasilia. It is by definition an interministerial meeting to be attended by the U.S. Secretary of State Hillary Clinton. The open government initiative was put forth initially by President Obama, and Brazil is a cochair in the forum. We believe that the open government policy is essential to ensuring the fight against corruption and ensure greater accountability, and also to ensure greater efficiency in government spending, in as much as one is able to improve the prospects for assessment and monitoring.

I believe all of those efforts also prove instrumental and greatly help enhance democracy in our countries and also to provide citizens with greater access to the information that is rightfully theirs. I'm quite certain that the ongoing cooperation efforts between Brazil and the United States, as well as our close relations and partnership, are indeed key to our both nations. But equally important for development at large in the 21st century, the kind of development that is ultimately to be marked by elements such as, for example, very much in line with the topic of the upcoming meeting—actually invited President Obama to attend the Rio+20 conference on sustainable development—and the key features we wish to work for includes economic growth, social inclusion, and environmental protection, which is tantamount to the very definition of sustainable development.

I would like to thank the President of the United States and also the American people for their very warm, brotherly, and friendly hospitality extended to me during this meeting today, to me and, of course, to my delegation.

Thank you very much.

NOTE: The President spoke at 1:17 p.m. in the Oval Office at the White House. In his remarks, he referred to former President Luiz Inacio Lula da Silva of Brazil. President Rousseff spoke in Portuguese, and her remarks were translated by an interpreter.

Joint Statement by President Obama and President Dilma Rousseff of Brazil
April 9, 2012

At the invitation of President Barack Obama, President Dilma Rousseff made an official visit to the United States on April 9, 2012 to discuss their countries' ongoing relationship on a broad range of bilateral, regional, and multilateral issues. The Leaders expressed satisfaction with the constructive and balanced partnership, based on the shared values and mutual trust that exist between their countries, the two largest democracies and economies in the Americas.

To form a U.S.-Brazil Partnership for the 21st Century, the Leaders reviewed the progress of major dialogues elevated to the Presidential-level in March 2011—the Economic and Financial Dialogue, the Global Partnership Dialogue, and the Strategic Energy Dialogue. To contribute to the 21st Century Partnership, the Presidents directed a new Defense Cooperation Dialogue between their two Defense Ministers that will also report regularly to the Presidents. They praised the work and acknowledged the importance of numerous other interactions and consultations between their two governments in enhancing bilateral cooperation.

They coincided on the importance of the contributions from civil society and the private sector to create the basis for a US-Brazil Partnership. The Presidents participated in the U.S.-Brazil CEO Forum, noting the important role that the private sector plays in the commercial relationship and welcomed the activities of the April 9, 2012 "US-Brazil Partnership for the 21st Century" conference in Washington focused on trade and investment, energy, innovation, competitiveness, and education.

The Leaders stressed that partnerships between state and local governments contribute to the fostering of friendship and understanding between their countries and to the advancing of shared national goals. They welcomed the signing of the Memorandum of Understanding to Support State and Local Cooperation, encouraging subnational entities to unite efforts to achieve goals in areas of mutual interest that complement the strengthening of U.S.-Brazil bilateral relations, such as trade and investment, economic opportunity, science, technology and innovation, social inclusion, environmental sustainability, and preparation for the 2014 FIFA World Cup, the 2016 Olympic and Paralympic Games and other megaevents.

The Leaders highlighted the important discussions that have taken place under the Economic and Financial Dialogue (EFD). The Presidents noted their satisfaction with the EFD's expanded focus on infrastructure and investment in both countries and welcomed the creation of a dialogue on investment under the Agreement on Trade and Economic Cooperation. The Leaders also noted the importance of the Commercial Dialogue and the Economic Partnership Dialogue between the two countries. President Obama announced the September 2012 trip of the President's Export Council to Brazil and President Rousseff stressed that high-level sectoral trade missions to the US will be organized, in areas such as foodservice, information technology, health and machinery.

President Rousseff underscored the importance of investment in infrastructure—

including in view of the upcoming 2014 FIFA World Cup and the 2016 Olympic and Paralympics Games—as well as in the energy sector, in particular the development of technology and productive capacity in Brazil.

They welcomed the growth of the U.S.-Brazil trade and investment relationship, illustrated by a record $74 billion in two-way trade in 2011. They further emphasized the importance of the mutual benefits of stimulating increased trade and investment. They reiterated their commitment to the multilateral trading system and to working together to ensure that the World Trade Organization contributes to global economic growth and job creation. The Presidents reaffirmed the commitment of both countries to advance trade in services and manufactured goods and to strengthen collaboration in agricultural policies, research, science-based sanitary and phytosanitary measures, as well as to strive, both in bilateral and multilateral fora, towards the removal of barriers to trade in agricultural products.

They highlighted education as an increasingly important strategic priority for strengthening and supporting all aspects of the U.S.-Brazil partnership, particularly science, technology, innovation, and competitiveness. Recognizing the economic advantages for both countries of increasing contact between Americans and Brazilians, the Presidents welcomed the momentum of and support for the U.S. 100,000 Strong in the Americas and the Brazilian Science Without Borders international exchange initiatives. They hailed the start of activities of the first group of students and researchers participating in Science Without Borders and look forward to welcoming thousands more students in both countries.

The Presidents welcomed the VII US-Brazil CEO Forum's support for the 100,000 Strong in the Americas and Science Without Borders initiatives, and their joint recommendations and commitment to enhanced engagement aimed at strengthening the business environment, increasing bilateral trade and investment, improving infrastructure, enhancing women's economic empowerment, encourag-

ing energy and aviation cooperation, and tracking progress toward these ends.

In the context of the EFD, the Presidents discussed greater collaboration in international financial institutions and as they look toward the G–20 Summit in Mexico to reduce global imbalances, promote financial stability and inclusion; and to create the conditions for strong, sustained, and balanced growth. They stressed the need to deepen the reform of the international financial institutions, which must reflect the new economic realities and, in this regard, underscored the importance of working together on quota and governance reforms in the IMF.

They welcomed the consolidation of the G20 as the highest forum for coordination of international economic policies and reaffirmed the G20 role in advancing measures to promote inclusive growth, job creation and overcoming global imbalances. They recommended that the two countries' senior representatives to the G20 continue to hold regular bilateral consultations. They noted the continued uncertainty present in the international economy while highlighting the important steps recently taken by European policymakers. They welcomed the continued signs of economic recovery in the United States. The Leaders also highlighted the opportunity for closer cooperation in the Multilateral Development Banks.

The Presidents noted the convergence of positions regarding the application of the "Emissions Trading System" (ETS) of the European Union, to international air transport. They further emphasized that issues related to international civil aviation emissions should be resolved multilaterally.

The Presidents underscored the importance of the upcoming United Nations Conference on Sustainable Development (Rio+20) in Brazil as an opportunity to promote sustainable development through innovation and broad stakeholder engagement. They emphasized the importance of broad participation in the High Level Segment of the Conference, on June 20–22, 2012. In support of this expanded collaboration, they recognized progress on mobilizing investments in smart and sustainable infrastructure in Rio de Janeiro and Philadelphia under the US-Brazil Joint Initiative on Urban Sustainability.

The Leaders praised the strengthening of US-Brazil dialogue on sustainable development and welcomed the adoption of an Environmental Protection Agency-Ministry of Environment Memorandum of Understanding, focused on environmental impact assessment, risk analysis, social inclusion and environmental justice. The leaders also praised the signing of a Memorandum of Understanding on Sustainable Housing and Urban Development to grow cooperative efforts and deepen learning exchange in the field of sustainable housing and urban development in support of the Energy and Climate Partnership of the Americas (ECPA).

They welcomed the outcomes of the 17th Conference of the Parties to the United Nations Framework Convention on Climate Change held in Durban, in December 2011, which reached a comprehensive and balanced result. They further highlighted the importance of the multilateral system in dealing with climate change through effective implementation of the outcomes from Durban.

The Leaders praised the signing of the Memorandum of Understanding on the Aviation Partnership, as well as progress made toward facilitating greater travel and tourism between their countries while maintaining and improving border security. They noted that the US-Brazil Aviation Partnership will promote bilateral cooperation in infrastructure, air transportation, and air traffic, which will contribute to growth, competitiveness and socioeconomic development in both countries. Areas of engagement may include exchanges of best practices, research and development, innovation, new technologies, sustainability, training, logistics, supply chains and other topics.

The Presidents reviewed the implementation of measures that facilitate the flow of tourists and business executives between the two countries. They committed to work closely together to satisfy the requirements of the of the US Visa Waiver Program and Brazil's applicable legislation to enable US and Brazilian citizens visa free travel. They discussed the "Global Entry" pilot-program and praised the efforts of both governments to facilitate travel, to the benefit of their respective citizens. President Obama recalled his directive to accelerate the U.S. ability to process visas by 40 percent in Brazil this year as well as the Department of State's recent announcement of its intent to open new consulates in Belo Horizonte and Porto Alegre.

They expressed their satisfaction with the advancement of a "Green-Lane" pilot-project on air cargo transportation, aimed at adopting a broad program of mutual recognition of authorized economic operators, to facilitate trade in goods between the two countries.

The Presidents welcomed the adoption of the Brazil-US Action Plan on Science and Technology Cooperation, which reflects the outcome of the March 2012 Joint Commission Meeting (JCM) on Science and Technology and highlighted the creation of a working group on innovation to explore the role of innovation in promoting competitiveness and job creation. The JCM also addressed cooperation in ocean science, technology and observation, disaster management, basic science, measurement standards, including for advanced biofuels, and the importance of access to Earth Observation data. They also welcomed the discussions during the III JCM on health, biomedicine and life sciences, women in science and nanotechnology.

The Leaders highlighted the importance of strengthening the bilateral space cooperation and instructed the appropriate agencies to examine the feasibility of developing joint space projects. They took note of the recent meeting in Brasilia of the Space Security Dialogue.

They highlighted the increasing importance of Internet and information and communication technologies (ICT)-related issues and the need to deepen discussion and expand cooperation between the U.S. and Brazil on issues so vital to their economies and societies. They noted with satisfaction the longstanding collaboration in those areas and welcomed the establishment of a new mechanism for consultations on issues such as Internet governance, Internet/ICT policy, and cyber security.

The Presidents spoke at length about global developments and welcomed the continued progress of the Global Partnership Dialogue (GPD). They welcomed the advancement of educational cooperation, scientific cooperation, and trilateral cooperation under the GPD. The Leaders noted their commitment to promote democracy, respect for human rights, cultural awareness, and social and economic inclusion around the world.

The Presidents concurred that just as other international organizations have had to change to be more responsive to the challenges of the 21st century, the United Nations Security Council (UNSC) also needs to be reformed, and expressed their support for a modest expansion of the Security Council that improves its effectiveness and efficiency, as well as its representativeness. President Obama reaffirmed his appreciation for Brazil's aspiration to become a permanent member of the Security Council and acknowledged its assumption of global responsibilities. The two leaders pledged to continue consultation and cooperation between the two countries to achieve the vision outlined in the UN Charter of a more peaceful and secure world.

In exchanging views on recent challenges in Africa and the Middle East, the Presidents underscored the importance of cooperative efforts to bring about the sustainable settlement of disputes that contribute to peace and stability. They expressed their commitment to support, as a matter of urgency, comprehensive and lasting multilateral solutions to today's pressing global issues and crises.

The Leaders reaffirmed their commitment to government transparency and accountability, as well as citizen engagement as key to strengthening democracy, human rights, and good governance, and preventing corruption. They celebrated their joint launch of the Open Government Partnership (OGP) in New York last September, praised the close collaboration between the two countries as co-chairs of the Partnership and discussed the upcoming OGP meeting in Brasilia, at which more than forty

new countries will issue National Action Plans that include concrete new commitments on fighting corruption, promoting transparency, and harnessing new technologies to empower citizens.

President Obama congratulated President Rousseff on Brazil's Freedom of Information Act, and its regional and global leadership role in engaging civil society and attracting a diverse set of countries to the second major high-level meeting. President Rousseff also congratulated President Obama on the U.S. implementation of its OGP plan, including the recent launch of Ethics.gov and the new Green Button initiative to ensure consumers have access to their own energy data.

The Leaders also reviewed and noted the progress of their countries' trilateral development cooperation in Latin America, the Caribbean, and Africa on issues ranging from food security, energy, agriculture, health, decent work, and humanitarian cooperation. They recalled their collaborative work and directed further efforts on trilateral food security cooperation. They welcomed the signing of an agreement on technical cooperation activities to improve food security in third countries.

They encouraged greater trilateral security cooperation and welcomed the recent launching of the pilot project for integrated monitoring system for surplus coca cultivation reduction in Bolivia.

The Presidents praised the cooperation fostered under the Joint Action Plan To Eliminate Racial and Ethnic Discrimination and Promote Equality in the areas of health, environmental justice, access to justice, education, and entrepreneurship in sports megaevents. They noted that as their economies grow, it is important that the benefits accrue to all sectors, including children and aged people and historically marginalized sectors such as women, people of African descent, indigenous peoples, people with disabilities, and LGBT people. They welcomed additional collaboration on LGBT issues in human rights multilateral fora. They also highlighted progress in bilateral cooperation for gender equality and advancement in the status of women, including efforts aimed at increasing women's political and economic participation in the fields of science and technology; as well as the prioritization of prevention and response to gender-based violence globally.

The Presidents reaffirmed the commitment of both countries to the conclusion of an effective international instrument in the World Intellectual Property Organization that ensures that copyright is not a barrier to equal access to information, culture, and education for visually impaired persons and persons with print disabilities.

They expressed their satisfaction with the positive effect of the dialogue regarding the Hague Convention on the Civil Aspects of International Child Abduction on the implementation of this instrument in Brazil and in the United States.

The Leaders expressed their support for the theme of the upcoming Summit of the Americas, "Connecting the Americas: Partners for Prosperity", which focuses on the role of physical integration, regional cooperation, poverty and inequalities, citizen security, disasters, and access to technologies as a means to achieve greater levels of development and overcome challenges in the Americas.

The Heads of State discussed the importance of continued economic progress and political stability in Haiti, to include the formation of a new government and timely elections. They underlined the achievements of the UN Stabilization Mission in Haiti (MINUSTAH) and encouraged the Government of Haiti (GOH) to work toward strengthening governance and the rule of law. They further encouraged Haiti to continue to pursue the development of the Haitian National Police. To spur new public-private partnerships for Haiti's energy sector, the Leaders committed to working with the GOH on developing and implementing its national energy plan, including its plans to modernize Haiti's electric utility and harness renewable energy sources, like the Artibonite 4C hydroelectric plant, to power Haiti's future development.

The Presidents noted the launch of the Strategic Energy Dialogue (SED) with significant interagency collaboration of both countries.

They underscored increased cooperation on oil and gas, biofuels, renewable energy and energy efficiency, science, and clean energy. Underscoring the importance of developing all of these key resources for global energy security, the Leaders directed their governments to seek greater opportunities to work with industry partners to help stabilize global oil and gas markets, increase access to energy, and enhance and promote the development and deployment of renewable, clean and low-carbon energy technologies.

The Leaders noted the importance of broader collaboration on oil and gas exploration; in particular the safe, clean, and efficient production of their countries' oil and gas reserves. They emphasized their commitment to provide opportunities that encourage companies to invest in production and to share their technology and their experience in ways that develop capacity in the oil and gas sector. They highlighted the importance of their governments and industries sharing information on best practices, including on unconventional gas development and through ongoing technical collaboration on deep-water oil and gas operations.

The Leaders committed to continue building on their countries' collaboration on bioenergy technology development and research, as well as sustainability; including for aviation biofuels and cooperation in third countries, such as Global Bioenergy Partnership capacity building in West Africa. They hailed the joint efforts that resulted in the conclusion of the first phase of viability studies for bioenergy production in third countries under the framework of the Memorandum of Understanding to Advance Cooperation on Biofuels.

The Presidents highlighted the importance of their regional cooperation on renewable energy through identification of potential financial resources from multilateral organizations. With regard to energy efficiency, they committed to support regional efforts to increase cooperation in the energy sector and further collaboration under the auspices of the Energy and Climate Partnership of the Americas.

As part of the Presidential Dialogues, the Leaders directed the establishment of a

Defense Cooperation Dialogue (DCD) and announced its first meeting on April 24 in Brazil. They noted the importance of the enhanced dialogue in enabling closer bilateral defense cooperation between their countries based on mutual respect and trust. They also observed the DCD will provide a forum for exchanging views and identifying opportunities for collaboration on defense issues around the globe.

They reiterated both countries' strong resolve to support international efforts towards nuclear non-proliferation, nuclear security, and disarmament, aiming to achieve the peace and security of a world without nuclear weapons. In this regard, they expressed support for the review cycle of the Treaty for the Non-Proliferation of Nuclear Weapons (NPT), and the

goals identified in the Action Plan adopted by the VIII NPT Review Conference, which includes the entry into force of the Comprehensive Nuclear-Test-Ban Treaty (CTBT), the beginning of negotiations on a treaty banning the production of fissile materials for nuclear weapons or other explosive purposes, and related initiatives. They decided to intensify bilateral and multilateral cooperation in the field of physical protection and nuclear safety, as well as the use of nuclear energy for peaceful purposes.

NOTE: The Office of the Press Secretary also released a Portuguese transcript of this joint statement. An original was not available for verification of the content of this joint statement.

Remarks at an Obama Victory Fund 2012 Fundraiser in Palm Beach Gardens, Florida
April 10, 2012

Thank you very much. The only title you forgot was husband of Michelle—[*laughter*]—father of Malia and Sasha and Bo. [*Laughter*]

I have to first of all thank Hansel and Paula for opening up their extraordinary home to us, and your wonderful hospitality. Please give them a big round of applause. Grateful for your friendship and grateful for your support.

A couple other people I want to acknowledge. First of all, your outstanding Senator from the great State of Florida, Bill Nelson is in the house. More importantly, his lovely wife Grace is in the house. And we also have Congresswoman and head of the DNC, Debbie Wasserman Schultz.

So I'm going to be very brief at the outset because I want to spend most of my time in conversation with you, take questions, get some comments, advice, tips. But let me just start off by saying it's undeniable we've gone through as tough a 3 years as we've seen in our lifetimes. I like to remind people that when I took office, that month we lost 800,000 jobs. We had lost 4 million jobs in the 6 months preceding me taking office. We lost another 6—

another 4 million jobs in the few months right after I took office. The housing market had collapsed. The banking system was locked up. And there was a very real threat that we would tip into a second Great Depression. And what that meant is we had to act quickly and boldly and, at times, in ways that weren't popular politically.

So the auto industry was on the verge of collapse, which would have meant the loss of a million jobs as well as an iconic industry in the United States that generations of middle class families had depended on. And we had to act quickly. And there were those who said let that industry go bankrupt. But we said that wouldn't be the right thing to do; it wouldn't be good for America long term.

We had to intervene in the banks in ways that got folks on the left and the right upset. But the fact of the matter is, is that finance is the lifeblood of industry, and had we not been able to unlock financing for large and small businesses alike, we would have seen more and more businesses close.

We had to pass a Recovery Act. And there were those who said, why are we going to be helping States keep teachers and police officers on the job, they should be able to handle it themselves. Why are we helping families on hard times by extending unemployment insurance? But what I tried to explain was that this was important not just for those individuals who get help, but it was important for the economy as a whole, because we had to make sure that there was enough aggregate demand out there, at a time when everybody was panicking, in order to keep the economy moving.

So a lot of tough decisions. But 3 years later, we can look back and say that we've made progress, that we're moving on the right track. Over the last 2 years, we've created over 4 million jobs, 600,000 just in the last quarter alone. The auto industry has come back. GM is now the number-one automaker again in the world, recorded the highest profits in its history. Across the board, we're seeing businesses large and small starting to hire again and feel a little more confident about the prospects of the economy.

Now, things are still tough out there, and we've still got a long ways to go, but there's no doubt that the economy is getting stronger, businesses are hiring again, the stock market is back. And the question then becomes, how do we build on what we've been able to do over the last several years to deal with some underlying problems that actually preceded the recession? Because I ran for office in 2008 not just to get back to the status quo; we had put off making some tough decisions for decades on issues that are of critical importance for America to be able to compete in the 21st century.

That's why we put so much effort into our education system and have prompted reforms in over 40 States who are now, from top to bottom, rethinking how they're training teachers, how they're hiring teachers, how they're holding schools accountable, how instead of teaching to the test, we're unleashing creativity and passion in the classroom, but also making sure that teachers and principals and students are accountable to success, and how are we going to finance college educations. We had a student loan system where billions of dollars were actually going to banks to manage loans that were federally guaranteed. We said let's just give them straight to students, and as a consequence we've opened up affordability for millions of students in need, because my goal is to make sure that once again we've got the highest college graduation rate of any country in the world.

That's why we took on energy. And Hansel mentioned—a model utility, what's going on down here Florida. Our goal has been that if we want to succeed in the 21st century, that we can't just depend on one source of energy and we certainly can't keep importing oil from some of the most volatile parts of the world.

And so what have we done? Over the last 3 years, because we've doubled fuel efficiency standards in cars, because we expanded clean energy investments like no previous administration, we've actually seen our oil imports decline to below 50 percent for the first time in 13 years. Oil production is still up. I know folks are still struggling with high gas prices, but we're moving in the right direction, where we can actually potentially achieve energy independence and put folks back to work in the process.

That's why we took on health care reform, not only because it's excusable to have 30 to 40 million people in a country as wealthy as ours potentially bankrupt every time somebody in their family gets sick, but also because it was breaking the bank for businesses and the Government and for individuals.

And even now, without the health care plan fully implemented, 2.5 million young people have health insurance who didn't have it before because they can stay on their parent's plan. And millions of seniors out there are getting discounts on their prescription drugs. And everybody can have preventive care as part of their insurance policies, including women getting the preventive care that they need in order to succeed, in order to be healthier.

And so the point is, is that our goal has not just been to make sure we didn't go into a depression, our goal is to—how do we build on the successes that are necessary for us to compete in this 21st-century economy that's going to be tougher than ever.

Now, we got an election coming up. I don't know if you guys are aware of that. [*Laughter*] And let me preface this by saying I'm a firm believer that whether you're a Democrat or a Republican, that you're a patriot, you care about this country, you love this country. And so I'm not somebody who, when we're in a political contest, suggests somehow that one side or the other has a monopoly on love of country.

But there are contrasting visions here. And this election will probably have the biggest contrast that we've seen maybe since the Johnson-Goldwater election, maybe before that. Because my vision, Bill Nelson's vision, the Democratic vision is one that says that free market is the key to economic growth, that we don't need to build Government just for the sake of expanding its reach, but there are certain things we have to do—whether it's investments in education or basic science and research or caring for the most vulnerable among us and creating an effective safety net—that we have to do, because we can't do it on our own, each of us individually. The same way that we don't have privatized fire services or police services or defense, well, there are some things that we've got to do together, that we do better together. And that's part of how we became an economic powerhouse.

And the Republicans in this race, they've got a fundamentally different idea. Their basic deal is that if they dismantle Government investments in infrastructure or clean energy research or education, if they give it all away in tax cuts to folks like me and some of you who don't need them and weren't even asking for them, that that somehow makes America stronger.

And I fundamentally disagree. That's not how our middle class got built. That's not what the GI bill was about. That's not what building the Hoover Dam or Golden Gate Bridge was all about. That's not what sending—as Bill knows better than anybody—a man to the Moon was all about. Our greatness as a nation has always been because we rise together and we have a broad-based prosperity, and we build a middle class where everybody who wants to work hard, everybody who's willing to put all their effort into it, they can make it, regardless of what they look like, where they come from, what their last name is.

That's our vision for America. That's what's at stake in this election. And I think for all the debate that takes place in Washington, the American people understand that. And that's why I'm confident we're going to win. But we're not going to win without your help. So everybody here is going to have to exhibit the same kind of enthusiasm and energy and passion as you did back in 2008.

I know I'm a little older and—[*laughter*]—hair is a little grayer. It may not be as fashionable to be on the Obama bandwagon as it was back then. But my determination is undiminished, and the need for your involvement is as important as ever. So, if all of you are willing to invest in the future the same way that our parents and our grandparents and our great-grandparents invested in the future, I'm confident America's best days are still ahead. But we're going to have to work for it. We're going to have to earn it. And that's what this election will be all about.

Thank you very much, everybody.

NOTE: The President spoke at 1:11 p.m. at the residence of Paula Tookes and Hansel E. Tookes II. Audio was not available for verification of the content of these remarks.

Remarks at Florida Atlantic University in Boca Raton, Florida
April 10, 2012

The President. Hello, Florida! Thank you! How is everybody doing today? Well, it is great to be back in Florida. It is great to be back in Boca. Great to be here at the home of the Fighting Owls.

I want to, first of all, thank Ayden not only for leading us in the Pledge of Allegiance, but also giving me great details about the burrowing owls. [*Laughter*] He explained it all to me. And then he told me he wants my job. [*Laughter*] And I explained to him that the Constitution requires you are 35 years old. [*Laughter*] So I will keep the seat warm for him for a few more years.

I want to thank Rebecca for that extraordinary performance. In addition to having an unbelievable singing voice, she wants to be a teacher—she is an English major—and we need great teachers out there, so we're very proud of her.

I want to thank your president, M.J. Saunders, the mayor of Boca Raton, Susan Whelchel, for hosting us here today. We've also got our outstanding Senator and former astronaut—which is very cool—Bill Nelson in the house. A wonderful Congressman, Ted Deutch is here. And my great friend, Congresswoman Debbie Wasserman Schultz is here. And you are here, which is very exciting. I am glad you guys came out. Now——

Audience member. We love you.

The President. I love you back. I do.

Now, look, guys, I know this is a busy time of year. Some of you are less than a month away from graduation. [*Applause*] Some seniors in the house. Pretty soon, you'll be closing the books at Wimberly for the last time. Maybe you'll be making that one last trip to the beach or Coyote Jack's. We'll be—you'll be picking up that diploma that you worked so hard for. Your parents will be there; they'll be beaming, full of pride. And then comes what folks call the real world.

Now, I actually think college is part of the real world. But obviously, there's a transition that will take place as you leave college. And some of you may go on to postgraduate degrees, but some of you are going to be out there looking for work. College is the single-most important investment you can make in your future. So I'm proud that you've made it and you've seen it through.

But I also know that the future can be uncertain. Now, we've gone through the 3 toughest years in our lifetimes, economically: worst financial crisis, worst economic crisis. Our economy is now recovering, but it's not yet where it needs to be. Too many of your friends and too many of your neighbors are still hurting out there. They're still looking for work. Too many of your families are still searching for that sense of security that started slipping away long before this recession hit.

Audience member. Amen. [*Laughter*]

The President. Got the amen corner here. [*Laughter*]

So, at a time like this, we've got to ask ourselves a central, fundamental question as a nation: What do we have to do to make sure that America is a place where, if you work hard, if you're responsible, that that hard work and that responsibility pays off? And the reason it's important to ask this question right now is because there are alternative theories.

There's a debate going on in this country right now: Could we succeed as a nation where a shrinking number of people are doing really, really well, but a growing number are struggling to get by? Or are we better off when everybody gets a fair shot and everybody does a fair share and everybody plays by the same set of rules?

That's what the debate in America is about right now. This is not just another run-of-the-mill gabfest in Washington. This is the defining issue of our time. This is a make-or-break moment for the middle class and everybody who's aspiring to get into the middle class. And we've got two very different visions of our future. And the choice between them could not be clearer.

Now, keep in mind, I start from the belief that Government cannot and should not try to solve every single problem that we've got. Government is not the answer to everything. My first job in Chicago, when I wasn't much older than most of you, was working with a group of Catholic churches on the South Side of Chicago in low-income neighborhoods to try to figure out how could we improve the schools, and how could we strengthen neighborhoods and strengthen families. And I saw that the work that some of these churches did did more good for people in their communities than any Government program could.

In those same communities, I saw that no education policy, no matter how well-crafted it is, no matter how well funded it is, can take the place of a parent's love and attention. And I also believe that since Government is funded by you that it has an obligation to be efficient and effective. And that's why we've eliminated dozens of programs that weren't working, announced hundreds of regulatory reforms to save businesses and taxpayers billions of dollars. We've put annual domestic spending on a path to become the smallest share of our economy since Eisenhower was in the White House, which is before I was born much less you being born. [*Laughter*]

I believe the free market is the greatest force for economic progress in human history. But here's the thing. I also agree with our first Republican President, a guy from my home State, a guy with a beard, named Abraham Lincoln. And what Lincoln said was that through our Government, we should do together what we cannot do as well for ourselves. That's the definition of a smart Government.

And that's the reason why we have a strong military, to keep us safe, because I suppose each of us could just grab whatever is around the house and try to defend our country, but we do better when we do it together. And we've got the best military in the history of the world, with the greatest men and women in uniform. We pay for that.

That's why we have public schools to educate our children. If we didn't have public schools, there would still be some families who would do very well. They could afford private schools or some would home-school. But there would be a lot of kids who would fall through the cracks. So we do that together.

It's one of the reasons that we've laid down railroads and highways. We can't build a highway for ourselves. We got to get our neighbors and our friends to say let's go build a road. That's why we supported the research and the technology that saved lives and created entire industries. The Internet, GPS, all those things were created by us together, not by ourselves.

It's the reason why we contribute to programs like Medicare and Medicaid and Social Security and unemployment insurance. Because we understand that no matter how responsibly we live our lives, we know that eventually we're going to get older. We know that at any point, one of us might face hard times or bad luck or a crippling illness or a layoff. And the idea that together we build this safety net, this base of support, that allows all of us to take risks and to try new things, and maybe try—get a new job—because we know that there's this base that we can draw on.

So these investments—in things like education and research and health care—they haven't been made as some grand scheme to redistribute wealth from one group to another. This is not some socialist dream. They have been made by Democrats and Republicans for generations, because they benefit all of us and they lead to strong and durable economic growth. That's why we've made these investments.

If you're here at FAU because you got financial aid or a student loan, a scholarship, which, by the way, was how I was able to help finance my college education. That's how Michelle got her college education. That doesn't just benefit you. It benefits whatever company might end up hiring you and profiting from your skills. If one of you goes on to become the next Steve Jobs or Mark Zuckerberg or one of you discovers the next medical breakthrough, think about all the people whose lives will be changed for the better. We made an investment in you; we'll get a return on the investment.

When we guarantee basic security for the elderly or the sick or those who are actively looking for work, that doesn't make us weak. What makes us weak is when fewer Americans can afford to buy the products that businesses are selling, when fewer people are willing to take risks and start their new business, because if it doesn't work out they worry about feeding their families. What drags our entire economy down is when the benefits of economic growth and productivity go only to the few, which is what's been happening for over a decade now, and gap between those at the very, very top and everybody else keeps growing wider and wider and wider and wider.

In this country, prosperity has never trickled down from the wealthy few. Prosperity has always come from the bottom up, from a strong and growing middle class. That's how a generation who went to college on the GI bill, including my grandfather, helped build the most prosperous economy that the world has ever known. That's why a CEO like Henry Ford made a point to pay his workers enough money so that they could buy the cars that they were building. Because he understood, look, there's no point in me having all this and then nobody can buy my cars. I've got to pay my workers enough so that they buy the cars, and that in turn creates more business and more prosperity for everybody.

This is not about a few people doing well. We want people to do well. That's great. But it's about giving everybody the chance to do well. That's the essence of America. That's what the American Dream is about. That's why immigrants have come to our shores, because the idea was, you know what, it doesn't matter what your name is, what you look like—you can be named Obama—[*laughter*]—you can still make it if you try.

And yet we keep on having the same argument with folks who don't seem to understand how it is that America got built. And let me just say, the folks that we have political arguments with, they're Americans who love their country. Democrats, Republicans, Independents, everybody, we all love this country. But there is a fundamental difference in how we think we move this country forward.

These folks, they keep telling us that if we just weaken regulations that keep our air or our water clean or protect our consumers, if we would just convert these investments that we're making through our Government in education and research and health care, if we just turned those into tax cuts, especially for the wealthy, then somehow the economy is going to grow stronger. That's the theory.

And here's the news: We tried this for 8 years before I took office. We tried it. It's not like we didn't try it. [*Laughter*] At the beginning of the last decade, the wealthiest Americans got two huge tax cuts, 2001, 2003. Meanwhile, insurance companies, financial institutions, they were all allowed to write their own rules or find their way around rules. We were told the same thing we're being told now: This is going to lead to faster job growth; this is going to lead to greater prosperity for everybody.

Guess what, it didn't. [*Laughter*] Yes, the rich got much richer. Corporations made big profits. But we also had the slowest job growth in half a century. The typical American family actually saw their incomes fall by about 6 percent even though the economy was growing, because more and more of that growth was just going to a few, and the average middle class American wasn't seeing it in their paychecks. Health care premiums skyrocketed. Financial institutions started making bets with other people's money that were reckless. And then our entire financial system almost collapsed. You remember that? It wasn't that long ago. I know you guys are young, but it was pretty recent. [*Laughter*]

Now, some of you may be science majors in here. I like that. We need more scientists, need more engineers. Now I was not a science major myself, but I enjoyed science when I was young. And if I recall correctly, if an experiment fails badly—[*laughter*]—you learn from that, right? Sometimes you can learn from failure. That's part of the data that teaches you stuff, that expands our knowledge. But you don't then just keep on doing the same thing over and over again. You go back to the drawing board. You try something different. But that's not what's been happening with these folks in Washington.

A lot of the folks who were peddling these same trickle-down theories—including Members of Congress and some people who are running for a certain office right now, who shall not be named—[*laughter*]—they're doubling down on these old broken-down theories. Instead of moderating their views even slightly, instead of saying, you know what, what we did really didn't work and we almost had a second Great Depression, and maybe we should try something different, they have doubled down.

They proposed a budget that showers the wealthiest Americans with even more tax cuts and then pays for these tax cuts by gutting investments in education and medical research and clean energy, in health care.

Now, these are the facts. If the cuts they're proposing are spread out evenly across the budget, then 10 million college students—including some of you—would see your financial aid cut by an average of more than $1,000 each.

Now, thousands of medical research grants for things like Alzheimer's and cancer and AIDS would be eliminated. Tens of thousands of researchers and students and teachers could lose their jobs. Our investments in clean energy that are making us less dependent on imported oil would be cut by nearly a fifth.

By the time you retire, instead of being enrolled in Medicare like today's seniors are, you'd get a voucher to pay for your health care plan. But here's the problem. If health care costs rise faster than the amount of the voucher, like they have been for decades, the rest of it comes out of your pockets. If the voucher isn't enough to buy a plan with the specific doctors and care that you need, you're out of luck. And by the middle of the next century—by the middle of this century, excuse me, by about 2050, at a time when most of you will have families of your own, funding for most of the investments I've talked about today would have been almost completely eliminated altogether.

Now, this is not an exaggeration. This is math. And when I said this about a week ago, the Republicans objected. They said, we didn't specify all these cuts. Well, right, you didn't because you knew that people wouldn't accept them. So you just gave a big number, and so what we've done is, we've just done the math. This is what it would it mean.

They say, well, we didn't specifically propose to cut student loans. Okay, if you don't cut student loans, then that means you've got to cut basic research even more. The money has got to come from somewhere. You can't give over $4 trillion worth of additional tax cuts, including to folks like me who don't need

them and weren't asking for them, and it just comes from some magic tree somewhere. [*Laughter*]

So, if you hear them saying, well, the President is making this stuff up. No, we're doing the math. If they want to dispute anything that I've said right now, they should show us specifically where they would make those cuts. They should show us. They should show us. Because, by the way, they're not proposing to cut defense, they're actually proposing to increase defense spending, so it's not coming out of there. So show me.

Look, America has always been a place where anybody who's willing to work and play by the rules can make it. A place where prosperity doesn't trickle down from the top, it grows from the bottom; it grows outward from the heart of a vibrant middle class.

And I believe that we cannot stop investing in the things that help create that middle class; that create real, long-lasting, broad-based growth in this country. And we certainly shouldn't be doing it just so the richest Americans can get another tax cut. We should be strengthening those investments. We should be making college more affordable. We should be expanding our investment in clean energy.

Now here's the other thing that the Republicans will tell you. They'll say, well, we've got to make all these drastic cuts because our deficit is too high. Our deficit is too high. And their argument might actually have a shred of credibility to it if you didn't find out that they wanted to spend $4.6 trillion on lower tax rates. I don't know how many of you are math majors, business majors, you can't pay down a deficit by taking in $4.6 trillion of less money, especially when you're denying that you're going to be making all these cuts. It doesn't add up. It doesn't make sense.

And keep in mind, more than a trillion dollars of the tax cuts they propose would be going to people who make more than $250,000 a year. That is an average of at least $150,000—again, we're just taking the numbers with the details they've given us and you spread it out—that averages to at least $150,000 for every millionaire, billionaire in the country. Each millionaire and billionaire, on average, would get $150,000. Some folks would get a lot more.

So we did some math of our own. We added up all the investments $150,000 could pay for. All right? So let's say a tax break that I might get that I really don't need—I've got—treated pretty well in this life. [*Laughter*] So right now I'm going to be okay. Malia, Sasha, they're going to be able to go to college. Michelle is doing fine. So understand what this means.

Here's what $150,000 means—$150,000, this is what each millionaire and billionaire would get, on average. This could pay for a tax credit that would make a year of college more affordable for students like you, plus a year's worth of financial aid for students like you, plus a year's worth of prescription drug savings for one of your grandparents, plus a new computer lab for this school, plus a year of medical care for a veteran in your family who went to war and risked their lives fighting for this country, plus a medical research grant for a chronic disease, plus a year's salary for a firefighter or police officer—$150,000 could pay for all of these things combined. Think about that.

So let me ask you, what's the better way to make our economy stronger? Do we give another $50,000 in tax breaks to every millionaire and billionaire in the country? Or should we make investments in education and research and health care and our veterans?

And I just want to emphasize again—look, I want folks to get rich in this country. I think it's wonderful when people are successful. That's part of the American Dream. It is great that you make a product, you create a service, you do it better than anybody else, that's what our system is all about. But understand, the share of our national income going to the top 1 percent has climbed to levels we haven't seen since the 1920s. The folks who are benefiting from this are paying taxes at one of the lowest rates in 50 years.

You might have heard of this, but Warren Buffett is paying a lower tax rate than his secretary. Now, that's wrong. That's not fair. And so we've got to choose which direction we want this country to go in. Do we want to keep giving those tax breaks to folks like me who don't

need them? Or give them to Warren Buffet? He definitely doesn't need them. [*Laughter*] Or Bill Gates? He's already said, "I don't need them." Or do we want to keep investing in those things that keep our economy growing and keep us secure? That's the choice.

And, Florida, I've told you where I stand. So now it's time for Members of Congress to tell you where they stand. In the next few weeks, we're going to vote on something called the Buffett rule, very simple: If you make more than $1 million a year—now, I'm not saying you have a million dollars, right? I'm not saying you saved up all your money and you made smart investments and now you've got your nest egg and you're preparing for retirement. I'm saying, you're bringing in a million bucks or more a year. Then, what the rule says is you should pay the same percentage of your income in taxes as middle class families do. You shouldn't get special tax breaks. You shouldn't be able to get special loopholes.

And if we do that, then it makes it affordable for us to be able to say for those people who make under $250,000 a year—like 98 percent of American families do—then your taxes don't go up. And we can still make those investments in things like student loans and college and science and infrastructure and all the things that make this country great.

And this is where you come in. This is why I came to see you. I mean, it's nice to see you. The weather is nice; you guys have been a wonderful audience. I learned about the burrowing owl. So there were all kinds of reasons for me to want to come down here. But one of the reasons I came was I want you to call your Members of Congress. I want you to write them an e-mail. I want you to tweet them. [*Laughter*] Tell them don't give tax breaks to folks like me who don't need them. Tell them to start investing in the things that will help the economy grow. Tell them if we want to bring down our deficit sensibly, then we've got to do it in a balanced way that's fair for everybody. Remind them who they work for. Tell them to do the right thing.

As I look out across this gymnasium, everybody here—from all different backgrounds, from all different parts of the country—each of us is here because somebody, somewhere, felt responsibility for other people. Our parents, obviously, our grandparents, great-grandparents, the sacrifices they made—some of them took enormous risks coming to this country with nothing because they wanted to give a better life to their kids and their grandkids. A lot of them did without so that you could benefit. But they weren't just thinking about their families. They were thinking about their communities. They were thinking about their country.

That's what responsibility means. It means that as you have greater and greater opportunity, then the scope of you being able to help more people and think about the future expands. And so you're not just thinking about yourself; you're thinking about your kids, your spouse, your family, your grandkids, your neighborhood, your State, your nation. You're thinking about the future.

And now it's our turn to be responsible. Now it's our turn to preserve the American Dream for future generations. Now it's our turn to rebuild, to make the investments that will assure our future, to make sure that we've got the most competitive workforce on Earth, to make sure that we've got clean energy that can help clean the planet and help fuel our economy.

It's our turn. It's our turn to rebuild our roads and our bridges and our airports and our ports. It's our turn to make sure that everybody here, every child born in whatever neighborhood in this country it is, that if they're willing to dream big dreams and put some blood, sweat, and tears behind it, they can make it.

I know we can do that. I know we can do it because of you. You're here because you believe in your future. You're working hard. Some of you are balancing a job or a family on the side.

You have faith in America. You know it's not going to be easy, but you don't give up. That's the spirit we need right now, because here in America, we don't give up. Here in America, we look out for one another. Here in America, we help each other get ahead. Here in America, we have a sense of common purpose. Here in America, we can meet any challenge. Here in America, we can seize any moment. We can make this century another great American century.

Thank you. God bless you. God bless the United States of America.

NOTE: The President spoke at 3:05 p.m. In his remarks, he referred to Ayden Maher and Rebecca Guillaume, students, and Mary Jane Saunders, president, Florida Atlantic University; Mark E. Zuckerberg, founder and chief executive officer, Facebook, Inc.; Warren E. Buffett, chief executive officer and chairman, and Debbie Bosanek, assistant, Berkshire Hathaway Inc.; and William H. Gates III, chairman, Microsoft Corp.

Remarks at an Obama Victory Fund 2012 Fundraiser in Hollywood, Florida
April 10, 2012

The President. Hello, Florida!

Audience member. We love you!

The President. I love you back.

It is good to be back in the Sunshine State. Well, there are some folks here I want to acknowledge. Everybody, have a seat. Relax. I've got a few things to say. [*Laughter*] First of all, your own Debbie Wasserman Schultz is in the house. Outstanding Members of Congress: Ted Deutch is here; Federica Wilson is here. Our Florida finance chair, Kirk Wagar is here.

Broward County finance chair, Andrew Weinstein is here.

The outstanding John Legend is in the house. John wanted me to sing a duet. I said no. [*Laughter*] Not tonight, but maybe if you practice a little bit. [*Laughter*] And I want to thank Gerri Ann for that wonderful introduction. Give her a big round of applause as well.

Now, I am here not just because the weather is really good. [*Laughter*] I'm not here just because there are a lot of great friends in the audience. And I'm not even here just because I need your help. I'm here because your country needs your help. A lot of you got involved in this campaign back in 2008. Some of you worked your hearts out. It wasn't, by the way, because you thought it was going to be easy. When you support a guy named Barack Hussein Obama for President—[*laughter*]—you're not looking at the oddsmakers. You don't need a poll to know that's not a sure thing. [*Laughter*]

You didn't join the campaign just because of me. This wasn't just about a candidate; this was about a vision that we shared for America, a vision that all of you shared. It wasn't a vision where people are left to fend for themselves and the most powerful can play by their own rules. It was a vision of America where everybody works hard, everybody is responsible, and everybody has a chance to get ahead, not just those at the very top. The notion that no matter where you come from, what you look like, what your last name is—Black, White, Hispanic, Asian, Native American, gay, straight, disabled or not—it doesn't matter, you've got a shot at the American Dream.

That's the vision we shared. That's the change that we believed in. And we knew it wasn't going to come easy. We knew it wouldn't come quickly. But we had confidence and faith in the American people and our capacity to bring about an America that was moving closer to our ideals. And you know what, in just a little over 3 years, because of what you did in 2008, we've started to see what change looks like.

Change is the first bill I signed into law that says women deserve an equal day's pay for an equal day's work. Our daughters should have the same opportunities as our sons. You made that happen.

Change is the decisions that we made to help prevent a second Great Depression, to rescue the American auto industry from collapse, even when some politicians were out there saying we should let Detroit go bankrupt. We had a million jobs on the line if we had let that happen. And I wasn't going to let that happen. And today, GM is back on top as the world's number-one automaker, making re-

cord profits, hiring back workers. More than 200,000 new jobs over the last 2½ years in the American auto industry, it is coming back. That happened because of you.

Change is the decision we made to stop waiting for Congress to do something about our oil addiction. We doubled fuel efficiency standards on cars and trucks. And by the middle of the next decade, we're going to be driving American-made cars that get almost 55 miles to a gallon, saves the typical family $8,000 at the pump. That happened because of you.

We decided let's stop handing out $60 billion in taxpayer giveaways to banks that were managing the student loan program, let's give the money directly to students. And because of you, millions of young people have gotten help affording college and being able to compete in this 21st-century economy. That happened because of your work back in 2008 and beyond.

Yes, change is health care reform that we passed after a century of trying, reform that says in the United States of America, the greatest country on Earth, nobody should go broke because they get sick. And because of that law, right now 2.5 million young people have health insurance that didn't have it before because they can stay on their parents' plans.

Right now millions of seniors are paying less for their prescription drugs. Right now every American has the assurance that they can't be denied coverage or dropped by their insurance company when they need care the most. And they can get preventive care, regardless of who they are, regardless of where you come from. That's what change is. That happened because of you.

Change is the fact that for the first time in our history you don't have to hide who you love to serve the country you love because we ended "don't ask, don't tell." It's over.

And change is keeping another promise I made in 2008: For the first time in 9 years there are no Americans fighting in Iraq. We've refocused our efforts on the terrorists who actually attacked us on 9/11. And because of our brave men and women, Al Qaida is back on its heels and Usama bin Laden is no more. That's what change is.

Now, we've——

Audience members. Four more years! Four more years! Four more years!

The President. It's actually 4½. [*Laughter*]

And we've begun to transition in Afghanistan to put Afghans in the lead, bring our troops home.

Record investments in clean energy, record investments in education, restoring science to its rightful place—well, none of this has been easy. And everybody here knows we've got a lot more work to do. There are still so many Americans out there that are still looking for work or trying to find a job that pays a little more, too many families who are barely able to pay the bills, homes underwater. We're still recovering from the worst economic crisis in generations.

But even on the economic front, over these last 2 years, we've seen businesses add more than 4 million new jobs, manufacturers creating jobs for the first time since the 1990s. The economy is getting stronger. The recovery is accelerating. And the last thing we can afford to do right now is to go back to the same, worn-out, tired, uninspired, don't-work policies that got us into this mess in the first place.

But of course, that's exactly what the other side wants to do. They make no bones about it. They don't make—they don't hide the ball. They want to go back to the days when Wall Street could play by its own rules. They've said, we want to roll back all the reforms that were put in place to protect consumers and make sure that we don't end up seeing taxpayer bailouts again. They want to go back to the days when insurance companies could deny you coverage or jack up premiums without reason. They want to spend trillions of dollars more on tax breaks for the very wealthiest of Americans, even if it means adding to the deficit, even if it means gutting things like education or clean energy or Medicare.

Their philosophy is simple: If we just let those who have done best keep on doing what they do, and everybody else is struggling to get by, somehow that's going to grow the economy.

They're wrong. In the United States of America we are greater together than we are on our own. We are better off when we keep that basic American promise: If you work hard, you can do well enough to raise a family, own a home, send your kids to college, put a little away for retirement.

And that's the choice in this election. This is not just your run-of-the-mill political debate. We have not seen a contrast like this in a long time. This is the defining issue of our time, this make-or-break moment for our middle class and all those who are fighting to get into the middle class. And are we going to stand with those folks who have been the backbone of economic growth in this country throughout our history?

We could go back to an economy built on outsourcing and bad debt and phony financial profits. Or we can fight for an economy that's built to last, an economy built on American manufacturing and American energy and skills for American workers and the values of everyday Americans of hard work and fair play and shared responsibility.

And I know—I know what side I am in that debate. I know what side I'm on in that debate. I think we've got to make sure that the next generation of manufacturing takes root not in Asia, not in Europe, takes root right here in the United States of America, right here in Florida, in Detroit, in Pittsburgh, in Cleveland. I don't want this Nation just to be known for what we buy and consume. I want us to be a nation known for what we produce and invent and sell all around the world. It's time to stop rewarding businesses that are shipping jobs overseas. Let's reward companies that are investing right here in the United States of America.

Let's make our schools the envy of the world. And that starts, by the way, with the men and women at the front of the classroom. You know, a good teacher can actually increase the lifetime earnings of a classroom by $250,000. A great teacher can inspire and plant that seed of possibility in a child, no matter how poor they are.

And that's why I don't like hearing folks just bashing teachers. I don't want them—I don't believe in just defending the status quo. I want schools to have the resources they need to keep good teachers on the job, reward the best ones, give schools the flexibility to teach with creativity and passion, stop teaching to the test. Give us a chance to train teachers that aren't doing a great job, get rid of those who are—we can create accountability in the system and high standards, but we've got to make sure that we're thinking about our kids first.

And when kids do graduate, the most daunting challenge ends up being the cost of college. Americans owe more in tuition debt than credit card debt right now, which means, by the way, Congress needs to stop the student interest—the interest rates on student loans from doubling, which is scheduled to happen in July.

And colleges and universities have to do their part. They've got to keep tuition from going up. And State legislatures need to keep their part by supporting higher education. This is not a luxury higher education; it is an economic imperative that every American should be able to afford.

An economy built to last is one where we support scientists and researchers that are trying to make the next breakthrough happen right here in the United States in biotech and nanotechnology and clean energy.

We've subsidized oil companies for a hundred years. It's time to end the hundred years of taxpayer giveaways for an industry that is plenty profitable, doing just fine, have more than enough incentive to keep on producing. Let's give it to clean energy industries that have never been more promising: solar and wind and biodiesel.

Let's rebuild America. I think about what was built in my grandparents' generation: Hoover Dam, Golden Gate Bridge, the Interstate Highway System. We've got to give our businesses the best access to the best roads and the best airports and the fastest railroads, faster Internet access. It's time for us to take some of that money that we spent on war, use half of it to pay down our debt, use the rest of it to do some nation-building here at home. We can put folks back to work right now rebuilding America.

[*At this point, the lights flickered.*]

Is there a little light show going on here? [*Laughter*] It's nice. [*Laughter*] Sort of a—it's a disco—disco rally. [*Laughter*] Somebody going to pull the roller skates out now? [*Laughter*] What's going on here?

And finally, we've got to make sure that we've got a tax system that reflects everybody doing their fair share. I just spoke about this earlier today. We have to reduce our deficit. It's a long-term challenge. And we've got to do it in a balanced way. We've made some very tough spending cuts. We're going to have to make some smart choices in terms of health reform. That's what's driving a lot of increased Government spending.

We've also got to make sure that revenues are there to pay for the things that are absolutely necessary for us to grow our economy, to maintain a basic safety net for our seniors and folks who are vulnerable.

Now, the other side, they've got a different idea. They want to decimate basic Government investments that historically have helped this economy grow and use it to finance tax cuts for the very wealthiest. And I've got a different idea. I say, let's follow what we call the Buffett rule: If you make more than a million dollars a year—I'm not saying you've got a million-dollar nest egg that you accumulated over the course of years saving for your retirement. I'm saying if you make a million dollars a year, then you shouldn't pay a lower tax rate than your secretary. That's common sense. That's not—they may call it class envy or—that's just being fair. And by doing that, that also allows us then to say to folks who are making $250,000 a year or less—like 98 percent of American families—that their taxes don't go up.

This is not class warfare. This is not about envy. We want Americans to be wealthy. We want them to be successful. But this is just basic math. Because if somebody like me, who is doing just fine, gets tax breaks I don't need and that the country can't afford, then one of two things is going to happen: either it gets added to our deficit—now, the other side say they care about the deficit; well, these tax cuts add to the deficit—or alternatively, you've got to take it away from somebody else, a student who's trying to pay for their college or a senior trying to get by with Social Security and Medicare or a veteran who needs some care after he or she has served this country with distinction or a family that's just trying to get by. That's not right. That's not who we are.

You know, when I hear politicians during an election year talk about values—well, what kind of values does that reflect? Hard work, that's a value. Responsibility, that's a value. Honesty, looking out for one another—I am my brother's keeper, I am my sister's keeper—that's a value. Our budget should reflect those values. Our politics should reflect those values.

Everybody here—look at this room, people from every conceivable background, every part of the country—everybody here, you're here because somebody, somewhere felt some responsibility not just for themselves, but for others. It started with your parents, grandparents. Some may have come to this country with nothing but wanted more opportunity for their kids; they worked on behalf of their family. They worked on behalf of their neighborhoods, their community. They worked on behalf of their country. They understood that the American story is not about just what you can do on your own. We're rugged individualists. We expect everybody to carry their own weight. But we also understand that what makes us great is what we can do together.

We won't win the race for new jobs and businesses, we won't restore middle class security with the same old you're-on-your-own economics. It doesn't work. It never worked. We tried it before the Great Depression, back in the twenties—didn't work. We tried it in the last decade. We were promised how this was going to unleash all this unbelievable economic growth. And what ended up happening? Sluggish job growth, wages and incomes flatlined for middle class families struggling to get by, and then culminated in the worst financial crisis we've seen since the 1930s. We tried it. Their theories don't work.

And most people understand this. They understand there's a different way to think about the economy and this journey we're on together. It says we've got a stake in each other's success. If we attract an outstanding teacher to the profession by paying them properly, by giving them the training they need, the professional development, and that teacher goes on to educate the next Steve Jobs, well, you know what, we all benefit. If we provide faster Internet service to rural America and then suddenly some store owner has access to a global market and they're selling goods and services and growing that business and hiring, that's good for all of us. If we build a bridge that cuts on commuting times and suddenly that shipping company is saving time and money, workers and customers, the whole country does better.

And this is not historically a Democratic or Republican idea. It was Republican Teddy Roosevelt who called for a progressive income tax. Dwight Eisenhower, Republican, built the Interstate Highway System. It was, with the help of Republicans in Congress, FDR who gave millions of returning heroes, including my grandfather, a chance to get ahead through the GI bill. Abraham Lincoln, first Republican President, helped to bind this country together through the transcontinental railroad, started the land-grant colleges, National Academy of Sciences. This is not just a Democratic idea.

And here's the good news: That spirit of common purpose, it still exists all across this country. Maybe not in Washington—[*laughter*]—but out in America, it's there. It's there when you talk to folks on Main Street, in town halls. It's there when you talk to our unbelievable members of our Armed Forces. It's there when you go to places of worship.

Our politics may be divided, but most Americans understand that we're greater together than we are apart, and that no matter where we come from, who we are, we rise or fall as one Nation. That's what's at stake in this election.

I know this has been a tough few years for America. We've seen a lot of stuff in these last 3 years, and I know that the change we fought for in 2008, as much as we've gotten done, we've got so much more to do. And there are times when change just doesn't come fast enough. I don't watch some of these cable news shows and all this sniping, but I imagine if you're sitting back, or, lord knows if you live in a swing State and you're watching these negative ads and, at a certain point, you must just step back and sort of say, maybe this change we believed in, maybe it's just not possible. It's tempting to be cynical and say you know what, this just is too hard.

So I'm here to remind you, I didn't say it was going to be easy. I told you real change, big change, takes time. These problems didn't build up overnight, and they're not going to be solved overnight. It will take more than a single term, more than a single President. What it takes is ordinary citizens. It takes folks like you who are committed to this larger project of making sure that America is constantly moving closer and closer to its highest ideals.

Back in 2008, I used to tell you, I'm not a perfect man, I will never be a perfect President. But I made a promise to everybody. I said, I will always tell you what I think; I'll tell you where I stand. And I told you I would wake up every single day fighting for you as hard as I know how. And I have kept that promise. I've kept that promise.

And so if you're willing to stick with me on this thing, if you're willing to keep pushing through the obstacles and knocking on doors and making phone calls and fighting for what is right, if you're willing to work even harder than we did in 2008, we will finish what we started. And we will remind the world just why it is that America is the greatest nation on Earth.

God bless you. God bless the United States of America.

NOTE: The President spoke at 5:50 p.m. at the Westin Diplomat Resort and Spa. In his remarks, he referred to Rep. Deborah Wasserman Schultz, chair, Democratic National Committee; Pompano Beach, FL, resident Gerri A. Bongiovanni-Capotosto; and musician John Legend.

Letter to Congressional Leaders on Continuation of the National Emergency With Respect to Somalia
April 10, 2012

Dear Mr. Speaker: (Dear Mr. President:)

Section 202(d) of the National Emergencies Act (50 U.S.C. 1622(d)) provides for the automatic termination of a national emergency unless, within 90 days prior to the anniversary date of its declaration, the President publishes in the *Federal Register* and transmits to the Congress a notice stating that the emergency is to continue in effect beyond the anniversary date. In accordance with this provision, I have sent to the *Federal Register* for publication the enclosed notice stating that the national emergency declared in Executive Order 13536 of April 12, 2010, is to continue in effect beyond April 12, 2012.

The fragile security situation and the persistence of violence in Somalia, and acts of piracy and armed robbery at sea off the coast of Somalia, which have repeatedly been the subject of United Nations Security Council resolutions, and violations of the Somalia arms embargo imposed by the United Nations Security Council, continue to pose an unusual and extraordinary threat to the national security and foreign policy of the United States. For these reasons, I have determined that it is necessary to continue the national emergency with respect to Somalia and related measures blocking the property of certain persons contributing to the conflict in Somalia.

Sincerely,

BARACK OBAMA

NOTE: Identical letters were sent to John A. Boehner, Speaker of the House of Representatives, and Joseph R. Biden, Jr., President of the Senate. The notice is listed in Appendix D at the end of this volume.

Remarks at an Obama Victory Fund 2012 Fundraiser in Golden Beach, Florida
April 10, 2012

Thank you, everybody. Well, first of all, let me thank Jeremy, who has been a friend for a long time. He supported me at a time when nobody could pronounce my name and had great faith, probably because I think we're both basketball fans and he was impressed with my knowledge, although his seats at games are generally better than mine. [*Laughter*]

And I want to thank Jeremy's family for taking the time to be here and his lovely mom and sisters. And Kirk Wagar, who has just been working so hard on my behalf not just this time out, but the previous time out, we appreciate you.

Debbie Wasserman Schultz, who is not only a outstanding Member of Congress and a great mom, but is also doing wonderful work on behalf of the DNC, we appreciate her. Thank you, Florida, for sending her into the national spotlight.

And Mayor Anthony Foxx, he is going to be our host in Charlotte, when we have our convention, and so we're glad that he's here as well.

And of course, I appreciate all of you. Some of you have been great friends in other venues, and we appreciate everything that you do.

I'm going to be very brief at the top because I want to spend most of my time answering questions and getting comments and thoughts from you. We've gone through 3 of the toughest years in our lifetimes: an economy that almost tipped into a Great Depression, an auto industry that almost went belly up, a banking system that froze, millions of people losing their jobs, a housing market that collapsed, a world economic crisis that began just a little bit before I was sworn into office. And we've been fighting to bring America back ever since.

The good news is we're making enormous progress on a whole range of fronts. The auto industry is back on its feet, selling cars. GM is making regular profits and is the number-one automaker again in the world, and they're making better cars. We've made progress in doubling fuel efficiency standards on cars that help

our environment and are reducing—is reducing our dependence on foreign oil. Actually, each year that I've been in office we've been importing less oil, even as the economy has become more productive and is growing: 4 million jobs over the last 2 years, the best manufacturing job growth since the 1990s, 600,000 jobs just in the last 3 months alone.

So we're making progress, but I think all of us understand that we've still got a lot more work to do, partly because we haven't fully recovered from the depths of this crisis. There are still too many people out there who are looking for work, there are still too many homes that are underwater—Florida, the economy here is still suffering from the headwinds of the housing market and its collapse. But partly because when we ran for office, when I ran for office in 2008, the goal wasn't just to get back to where we were in 2007. Because even then, even before the economic crisis had hit—the financial crisis had hit, we had seen a decade in which job growth was sluggish and incomes and wages for ordinary people didn't just flatline, they actually went down when you factored in inflation.

That sense of middle class security, the sense that if you worked hard you could get ahead, support a family, send your kids to college, retire with dignity and respect, that sense of security had been slipping away for too many people. And the goal in 2008 was to make those changes, to get rid of those obstacles, to reform systems that had had problems for decades so that middle class Americans and people who aspire to get in the middle class would once again have a chance. An economy that was characterized by everybody having a fair shot and everybody doing their fair share and everybody playing by the same set of rules, that's what we've been fighting for.

And that's why in addition to just dealing with the immediate crisis, in addition to dealing with two wars—ending one, transitioning in another—in addition to going after bin Laden and making sure that we degraded the Al

Qaida network, in addition to restoring America's respect in the world, in addition to all the things we've done in foreign policy, in crisis management, what we've tried to do is also make sure that we're dealing with those long-term barriers to economic growth and prosperity, broad-based prosperity.

So that means having an energy policy that emphasizes clean energy and solar and wind power and all those things that are going to allow us to stay at the cutting edge in the 21st century. It means reforming our education system—K–12, community colleges, and 4-year colleges and universities—so that we've got the best workforce in the world in this more competitive environment that we're in.

It means dealing with health care, not only to make sure that 30 million people get health care that didn't have it before so nobody is bankrupt when they get sick in this country, but also to start rationalizing the system so that it is more efficient, provides better care, lowers costs, is a good deal for everybody.

And it means making sure that we've got a budget, a tax system, that is fair so that you don't have Warren Buffett paying a lower tax rate than his secretary, so that we can lower the deficits and make investments that we need in the future generations—in rebuilding our infrastructure and investing in basic science and research, college loans for students—but doing so in a way that's paid for. And part of paying for it is, folks like me and many of you, making sure that we are doing our fair bit.

Now, the other side has a just fundamentally different view of these issues, and that's before we start talking about things like the courts and access to justice and women's rights and voting rights and a whole range of social concerns where, again, there is a—immigration—where there is a big contrast between what the other side is peddling and what I think is needed to make this country strong. So you're probably going to have as big a contrast in this election as we've seen in a very long time. And that means that we may have to work even harder than we did in 2008.

The good news is, I think the American people are on our side. I think the American people understand that this country is stronger when we come together and we're looking out for one another and we're thinking about the future and not just the next election. But they expect to see us fight for them. And that's what I intend to keep doing, with your help, for the next 4½ years.

So thank you very much, everybody. Thank you.

NOTE: The President spoke at 7:31 p.m. at the residence of Jeremy W. Alters. In his remarks, he referred to Nikki Rizzo, mother, and Kimberly Rizzo and Allison Salpeter, sisters, of Mr. Alters; and Kirk W.B. Wagar, Florida finance chair, and Rep. Deborah Wasserman Shultz, chair, Democratic National Committee. Audio was not available for verification of the content of these remarks.

Remarks on Tax Code Reform
April 11, 2012

Everybody, please have a seat. Thank you. Well, it's wonderful to see you——

[At this point, a baby started crying.]

——especially you. Oh, man, I know, having to listen to a speech. Yes. Aww.

Anyway, good morning everybody. It is wonderful to see you. Lately, we've been talking about the fundamental choice that we face as a country. We can settle for an economy where a shrinking number of people do very, very well, and everybody else is struggling to get by, or we can build an economy where we're rewarding hard work and responsibility, an economy where everybody has a fair shot and everybody is doing their fair share and everybody is playing by the same set of rules.

The people who have joined me here today are extremely successful. They've created jobs and opportunity for thousands of Americans. They're rightly proud of their success. They love the country that made their success possible, and most importantly, they want to make sure that the next generation—people coming up behind them—have the same opportunities that they had.

They understand, though, that for some time now, when compared to the middle class, they haven't been asked to do their fair share. And they are here because they believe there is something deeply wrong and irresponsible about that.

At a time when the share of national income flowing to the top 1 percent of people in this country has climbed to levels we haven't seen since the 1920s, these same folks are paying taxes at one of the lowest rates in 50 years. In fact, one in four millionaires pays a lower tax rate than millions of hard-working middle class households. And while many millionaires do pay their fair share, some take advantage of loopholes and shelters that let them get away with paying no income taxes whatsoever. And that's all perfectly legal under the system that we currently have.

You've heard that my friend Warren Buffett pays a lower tax rate than his secretary, because he's the one who's been pointing that out and saying we should fix it. The executives who are with me here today—not just behind me, but in the audience—agree with me. They agree with Warren. This should be fixed. They, in fact, have brought some of their own assistants to prove that same point: that it is just plain wrong that middle class Americans pay a higher share of their income in taxes than some millionaires and billionaires.

Now, it's not that these folks are excited about the idea of paying more taxes. This thing I've always made clear: I have yet to meet people who just love taxes. Nobody loves paying taxes. In a perfect world, none of us would have to pay any taxes. We'd have no deficits to pay down, and schools and bridges and roads and national defense and caring for our veterans would all happen magically.

We'd all have the money we need to make investments in the things that help us grow—investments, by the way, that have always been essential to the private sector's success as well.

Not just—they're not just important in terms of the people that directly benefit from these programs, but historically, those investments that we've made in infrastructure, in education, in science, in technology, in transportation, that's part of what has made us an economic superpower.

And it would be nice if we didn't have to pay for them, but this is the real world that we live in. We have real choices and real consequences. Right now we've got significant deficits that are going to have to be closed. Right now we have significant needs if we want to continue to grow this economy and compete in this 21st-century, hypercompetitive, technologically integrated economy. That means we can't afford to keep spending more money on tax cuts for wealthy Americans who don't need them and weren't even asking for them. And it's time we did something about it.

Now, I want to emphasize, this is not simply an issue of redistributing wealth. That's what you'll hear from those who object to a tax plan that is fair. This is not just about fairness. This is also about growth. This is also about being able to make the investments we need to succeed. And it's about we as a country being willing to pay for those investments and closing our deficits. That's what this is about.

Now next week, Members of Congress are going to have a chance to vote on what we call the Buffett rule. And it's simple: If you make more money, more than $1 million a year—not if you have $1 million, but if you make more than $1 million a year—you should pay at least the same percentage of your income in taxes as middle class families do. If, on the other hand, you make less than $250,000 a year, like 98 percent of American families do, your taxes shouldn't go up.

That's all there is to it. That's pretty sensible. Most Americans agree with me. So do most millionaires. One survey found that two-thirds of millionaires support this idea. So do nearly half of all Republicans across America.

So we just need some of the Republican politicians here in Washington to get on board with where the country is. I know that some prefer to run around using the same reflexive, false claims about wanting to raise people's taxes. What they won't tell you is the truth: that I've cut taxes for middle class families each year that I've been in office. I've cut taxes for small-business owners not once or twice, but 17 times.

As I said, for most of the folks in this room, taxes are lower than they've been, or as low as they've been, in 50 years. There are others who are saying, well, this is just a gimmick. It's—just taxing millionaires and billionaires, just imposing the Buffett rule, won't do enough to close the deficit. Well, I agree. That's not all we have to do to close the deficit. But the notion that it doesn't solve the entire problem doesn't mean that we shouldn't do it at all.

There are enough excuses for inaction in Washington. We certainly don't need more excuses. I'd just point out that the Buffett rule is something that will get us moving in the right direction towards fairness, towards economic growth. It will help us close our deficit, and it's a lot more specific than anything that the other side has proposed so far. And if Republicans in Congress were truly concerned with deficits and debt, then I'm assuming they wouldn't have just proposed to spend an additional $4.6 trillion on lower tax rates, including an average tax cut of at least $150,000 for every millionaire in America.

They want to go in the opposite direction. They want to double down on some of the inequities that already exist in the Tax Code. If we're going to keep giving somebody like me or some of the people in this room tax breaks that we don't need and we can't afford, then one of two things happens: Either you've got to borrow more money to pay down a deeper deficit, or you've got to demand deeper sacrifices from the middle class, and you've got to cut investments that help us grow as an economy.

You've got to tell seniors to pay a little bit more for their Medicare. You've got to tell the college student, we're going to have to charge you higher interest rates on your student loan or you're just going to get smaller student loans. You're going to have to tell that working family that's scraping by that they're going to

have to do more because the wealthiest of Americans are doing less.

That's not right. The middle class has seen enough of its security erode over the past few decades that we shouldn't let that happen. And we're not going to stop investing in the things that create real and lasting growth in this country just so folks like me can get an additional tax cut. We're not going to stop building first-class schools and making sure that they've got science labs in them. We're not going to fail to make investments in basic science and research that could cure diseases that harm people or create the new technology that ends up creating entire jobs and industries that we haven't seen before. In America, prosperity has never just trickled down from a wealthy few. Prosperity has always been built from the bottom up and from the heart of the middle class outward. And so it's time for Congress to stand up for the middle class and make our tax system fairer by passing this Buffett rule.

Let me just close by saying this: I'm not the first President to call for this idea that everybody has got to do their fair share. Some years ago, one of my predecessors traveled across the country pushing for the same concept. He gave a speech where he talked about a letter he had received from a wealthy executive who paid lower tax rates than his secretary and wanted to come to Washington and tell Congress why that was wrong. So this President gave another speech where he said it was "crazy"—that's a quote—that certain tax loopholes make it possible for multimillionaires to pay nothing, while a bus driver was paying 10 percent of his salary. That wild-eyed, socialist, tax-hiking class warrior was Ronald Reagan.

He thought that in America the wealthiest should pay their fair share, and he said so. I know that position might disqualify him from the Republican primaries these days—[laughter]—but what Ronald Reagan was calling for then is the same thing that we're calling for now: a return to basic fairness and responsibility, everybody doing their part. And if it will help convince folks in Congress to make the right choice, we could call it the Reagan rule instead of the Buffett rule.

But the choice is clear. This vote is coming up. I'm asking every American who agrees with me to call your Member of Congress or write them an e-mail, tweet them. Tell them to stop giving tax breaks to the wealthiest Americans who don't need them and aren't asking for them. Tell them to start asking everybody to do their fair share and play by the same rules so that every American who's willing to work hard has a chance at similar success, so that we're making the investments that help this economy grow, so that we're able to bring down our deficits in a fair and balanced and sensible way. Tell them to pass the Buffett rule. I'm going to keep on making this case across the country because I believe that this rule is consistent with those principles and those values that have helped make us this remarkable place where everybody has opportunity.

Each of us is only here because somebody somewhere felt responsibility not only for themselves, but also for their community and for their country. They felt a responsibility to us, to future generations. And now it's our turn to be similarly responsible. Now it's our turn to preserve that American Dream for future generations.

So I want to thank those of you who are here with me today. I want to thank everybody who's in the audience. And I want to appeal to the American people: Let's make sure that we keep the pressure on Congress to do the right thing.

Thank you very much, everybody.

NOTE: The President spoke at 10:25 a.m. in Room 430 of the Dwight D. Eisenhower Executive Office Building. In his remarks, he referred to Warren E. Buffett, chief executive officer and chairman, and Debbie Bosanek, assistant, Berkshire Hathaway Inc.

Remarks at the Port of Tampa in Tampa, Florida
April 13, 2012

Hello, Tampa! Well, it is great to be here in Tampa. Good to be in Florida. I just got a tour of this magnificent port. I was hoping to try out one of the cranes—[*laughter*]—Secret Service wouldn't let me. They don't let me have fun. They were more concerned about your safety than mine, though—[*laughter*]—they didn't want me messing anything up.

I want to thank David for that introduction. I want to thank Mayor Buckhorn for welcoming us to Tampa. I want to thank an outstanding Member of Congress, Kathy Castor, for joining us here today.

Now, if you guys have chairs, feel free to sit down; some of you do. I don't want you to feel—it's warm in here, we want you to—I don't want anybody dropping off. [*Laughter*] I've been talking a lot lately about the fundamental choice that we face as a country. We can either settle for a country where a shrinking number of people do really, really well, while a growing number are struggling to get by, or we can build an economy where everybody gets a fair shot and everybody is doing their fair share and everybody is playing by the same set of rules.

Now part of building that economy is making sure that we're not a country that's known just for what we buy and what we consume. After all, our middle class was built by workers who invented products and made products and sold products—the best in the world—all around the world. Our economy was thriving when shipping containers left ports like this packed with goods that were stamped with three proud words: Made in America. And those exports supported a lot of good-paying jobs in America, including right here in Florida.

That's the country I want us to be again. And that's why, 2 years ago, I set the goal of doubling American exports by the end of 2014. Today, with the trade agreements that I've signed into law, we're on track to meet that goal. Soon, there are going to be millions of new customers for American goods in South Korea, in Colombia, in Panama. Soon there will be new cars on the streets of Seoul that are imported from Detroit and Toledo and Chicago.

And that's progress. And I want to thank two key members of my Cabinet who are here today—Labor Secretary Hilda Solis is in the house and U.S. Trade Representative Ron Kirk—because they worked really hard to make this happen.

Now, one of the ways that we've helped American businesses sell their products around the world is by calling out our competitors, making sure they're playing by the same rules. For example, we've brought trade cases against China at nearly twice the rate as the last administration. We just brought a new case last month. And we've set up a trade enforcement unit that's designed to investigate any questionable trade practices taking place anywhere in the world. See, we're going to take action whenever other countries are skirting the rules, breaking the rules, and putting our workers and our businesses at an unfair position.

We're also going to make sure that you've got access to more customers. Ninety-five percent of the world's consumers live outside our borders. We want them buying our products. And I'm willing to go anywhere in the world to open up new markets for American businesses. In fact, that's what I'm going to be doing right after this visit to Tampa. I'm heading to Colombia to take part in the Summit of the Americas, which brings together leaders from the Caribbean and from North, South, and Central America.

Everybody here knows how critical this part of the world is to our economy and to creating jobs. A lot of the countries in the region are on the rise. In Latin America alone, over the past decade, tens of millions of people have stepped out of poverty and into the middle class. So they're now in a position to start buying American products. That means they've got more money to spend. We want them spending money on American-made goods, that American businesses can put more Americans back to work.

Now, the good news is, already our exports to the Western Hemisphere are up by 46 percent since 2009. I want to repeat that because that's obviously important to Tampa. Tampa is one of the biggest ports in the country and a lot

of the business being done here has to do with trade between us and Latin America. So the fact that it has gone up 46 percent since 2009 is a big deal for Tampa. In Florida, exports to this region are up nearly 30 percent. We now export more to the Western Hemisphere than to any other region in the world. And those exports support nearly 4 million U.S. jobs.

This is one of the most active trading relationships in the world and you see it up close here at the Port of Tampa. Every year, more than 2.5 million tons of fertilizer head out from here to farmers in the Caribbean and Central and South America. Engine oils that are produced not far from this port get shipped to countries throughout the hemisphere. Everything from recycled steel to animal feed gets sent from here to customers all across Latin America.

So, while I'm in Colombia talking with other leaders, I'm going to be thinking about you. I'm going to be thinking about how we can get more businesses like David's access to more markets and more customers in the region, because I want us selling stuff and I want to put more Americans back to work.

One of the new things that we're doing is launching something called the Small Business Network of the Americas. Obviously, a lot of the exports that leave from America to other places are big business, and that's great. We want our big corporations successful, selling products all around the world because we've got a lot of small businesses that are suppliers to those big business. But we also want our small and medium-sized businesses to have access to these markets. So this initiative is going to help our small businesses: Latino-owned businesses, women-owned businesses, African American-owned businesses. We want every business to be able to access these new markets, start exporting to these countries. So it'll make—this initiative will make it easier for them to get financing, it will link them up with foreign buyers who are interested in their products.

I've always said that the true engine of job creation in this country is the private sector, not Washington. Our job in Government is to help businesses grow and to hire, to create platforms for their success. That's one of the reasons I've cut taxes 17 times for small businesses. That's why I've fought to tear down barriers that were preventing entrepreneurs from getting funding. And that's why, yes, I've traveled around the world, opening new markets, so that American businesses can better compete in the global marketplace.

See, ultimately, this is what America is about. We're a nation of doers and a nation of builders. And we've never shied away from competition. We thrive on competition. If the global playing field is level, then America is going to win. So, as long as I'm President, I'm going to keep on doing everything I can to give our workers and our businesses the opportunity to succeed.

That's how we're going to make this recovery felt by all people. It's how we're going to make sure that we build not just from the top down, but from the bottom up and from the middle out. It's how we're going to make sure that everybody has a fair shot. It's how we're going to make sure that anybody who wants a job can find one, and anybody who wants to succeed and live out that American Dream has the opportunity to do so.

We've gone through 3 very tough years with this global financial crisis, worst crisis we've seen in a generation. And as I travel around the country and I talk to our workers and I talk to our businesses, you can't help but have confidence. We don't quit. We are resilient. We stay with it. We are the most inventive country in the world. We've got the best entrepreneurs in the world. We've got the best universities in the world. We've got the best research in the world. We've got the best infrastructure in the world, and we're going to keep on at it and make sure that the 21st century is the American century, just like the 20th century.

Thank you, everybody. God bless you.

NOTE: The President spoke at 1:12 p.m. In his remarks, he referred to David Hale, president, Tampa Tank Inc. and Florida Structural Steel; and Mayor Robert Buckhorn of Tampa.

The President's Weekly Address
April 14, 2012

One of the fundamental challenges of our time is building an economy where everyone gets a fair shot, everybody does their fair share, and everybody plays by the same set of rules.

And as many Americans rush to file their taxes this weekend, it's worth pointing out that we've got a tax system that doesn't always uphold the principle of everybody doing their part.

Now, this is not just about fairness. This is also about growth. It's about being able to make the investments we need to strengthen our economy and create jobs. And it's about whether we as a country are willing to pay for those investments.

In a perfect world, of course, none of us would have to pay any taxes. We'd have no deficits to pay down. And we'd have all the resources we needed to invest in things like schools and roads and a strong military and new sources of energy, investments that have always bolstered our economy and strengthened the middle class.

But we live in the real world, with real choices and real consequences. Right now we've got significant deficits to close. We've got serious investments to make to keep our economy growing. And we can't afford to keep spending more money on tax cuts for the wealthiest Americans who don't need them and didn't even ask for them.

Warren Buffett is one of the world's wealthiest men. But he pays a lower tax rate than his secretary. That's just the way the system is set up. In fact, one in four millionaires pays a lower tax rate than millions of hard-working middle class households.

As Warren points out, that's not fair and it doesn't make sense. It's wrong that middle class Americans pay a higher share of their income in taxes than some millionaires and billionaires.

Now, this week Members of Congress are going to have a chance to set things right. They get to vote on what we call the Buffett rule.

It's simple: If you make more than $1 million every year, you should pay at least the same percentage of your income in taxes as middle class families do. On the other hand, if you make less than $250,000 a year, like 98 percent of American families do, your taxes shouldn't go up.

That's all there is to it. It's pretty sensible. Most Americans support this idea. One survey found that two-thirds of millionaires do too. So do nearly half of all Republicans.

We just need some Republican politicians to get on board with where the country is. I know they'll say that this is all about wanting to raise people's taxes. They probably won't tell you that if you belong to a middle class family, then I've cut your taxes each year that I've been in office, and I've cut taxes for small-business owners 17 times.

But the thing is, for most Americans like me, tax rates are near their lowest point in 50 years. In 2001 and 2003, the wealthiest Americans received two huge new tax cuts. We were told these tax cuts would lead to faster job growth. Instead, we got the slowest job growth in half a century, and the typical American family actually saw its income fall.

On the flip side, when the most well-off Americans were asked to pay a little more in the 1990s, we were warned that it would kill jobs. Instead, tens of millions of jobs followed.

So we've tried this trickle-down experiment before. It doesn't work. And middle class families have seen too much of their security eroded over the past few decades for us to tell them they're going to have to do more because the wealthiest Americans are going to do less. We can't stop investing in the things that will help grow our economy and create jobs—things like education, research, new sources of energy— just so folks like me can get another tax cut.

So I hope you'll ask your Member of Congress to step up and echo that call this week by voting for the Buffett rule. Remind them that in America, prosperity has never just trickled down from a wealthy few. Prosperity has always been built by a strong, thriving middle class. That's a principle worth reaffirming right now.

Thanks. God bless you, and have a great weekend.

NOTE: The address was recorded at approximately 5:35 p.m. on April 12 in the Grand Foyer at the White House for broadcast on April 14. In the address, the President referred to Warren E. Buffett, chief executive officer and chairman, and Debbie Bosanek, assistant, Berkshire Hathaway Inc. The transcript was made available by the Office of the Press Secretary on April 13, but was embargoed for release until 6 a.m. on April 14.

Remarks at the CEO Summit of the Americas and a Question-and-Answer Session in Cartagena, Colombia
April 14, 2012

President Obama. Well, first of all, I want to thank President Santos and the people of Colombia for the extraordinary hospitality in the beautiful city of Cartagena. We're having a wonderful time. And usually when I take these summit trips, part of my job is to scout out where I may want to bring Michelle back later for vacation. So we'll make sure to come back sometime in the near future.

I want to acknowledge Luis Moreno of IDB, as well as Luis Villegas of the National Business Association of Colombia, for helping to set this up, and everybody who's participating.

As President Rousseff indicated, obviously, we've gone through some very challenging times. These last 3 years have been as difficult for the world economy as anything that we've seen in our lifetimes. And it is both a result of globalization, and it is also a result of shifts in technology. The days when we could think of each of our economies in isolation, those days are long gone. What happens in Wall Street has an impact in Rio. What happens in Bogota has an impact in Beijing.

And so I think the challenge for all of our countries, and certainly the challenge for this hemisphere, is how do we make sure that that globalization and that integration is benefiting a broad base of people, that economic growth is sustainable and robust, and that it is also giving opportunity to a growing, wider circle of people and giving businesses opportunities to thrive and create new products and new services and enjoy this global marketplace.

Now, I think the good news is this hemisphere is very well positioned in this global economy. It is remarkable to see the changes that have been taking place in a relatively short period of time in Latin and Central America and in the Caribbean. When you look at the extraordinary growth that's taken place in Brazil, first under President Lula and now under President Rousseff, when you think about the enormous progress that's been made here in Colombia under President Santos and his predecessor, what you see is that a lot of the old arguments on the left and the right no longer apply.

And what people are asking is, what works? How do we think in practical terms about delivering prosperity, training our people so that they can compete in the global economy? How do we create rule of law that allows businesses to invest with some sense of security and transparency? How do we invest in science and technology? How do we make sure that we have open and free trade at the same time as we're making sure that the benefits of free trade are distributed both between nations, but also within nations?

And the good news is, I think that, through various international organizations and organizations here within the hemisphere, we've seen enormous progress. Trade between the United States and Latin, Central—South America, Central America, and the Caribbean has expanded 46 percent since I came into office. Forty-six percent.

Before I came to Cartagena, I stopped in Tampa, Florida, which is the largest port in Florida. And they are booming and expanding.

And the reason is, is because of the enormous expansion of trade and commerce with this region. It's creating jobs in Florida, and it's creating jobs in Colombia, and it's creating jobs in Brazil and throughout the region. Businesses are seeing that if there—they have an outstanding product or an outstanding service, they don't have to restrict themselves to one market; they now have a regional market and ultimately a global market in which they can sell their goods and succeed.

A couple of things that I think will help further facilitate this productive integration: number one, the free trade agreement that we've negotiated between Colombia and the United States is an example of a free trade agreement that benefits both sides. It's a win-win. It has high standards—it's a high-standards agreement. It's not a race to the bottom, but rather it says each country is abiding by everything from strong rules around labor and the environment to intellectual property protection. And so I have confidence that as we implement this plan, what we're going to see is extraordinary opportunities for both U.S. and Colombian businesses.

So trade agreements of the sort that we have negotiated, thanks to the leadership of President Santos and his administration, I think point the way to the future.

In addition, I think there is the capacity for us to cooperate on problems that all countries face, and I'll take just one example, the issue of energy. All of us recognize that if we're going to continue to grow our economies effectively, then we're going to have to adapt to the fact that fossil fuels are a finite resource and demand is going up much faster than supply. There are also obviously significant environmental concerns that we have to deal with. So for us to cooperate on something like joint electrification and electric grid integration so that a country like Brazil that is doing outstanding work in biofuels or hydroenergy has the ability to export that energy, but also teach best practices to countries within the region, create new markets for clean energy throughout the region, which benefits those customers who need electricity, but also benefit those countries that are top producers of energy. That's another example of the kind of progress that we can make together.

On the education front, every country in the region recognizes that if we're going to compete with Asia, if we're going to compete with Europe, we've got to up our game. We have to make sure that we've got the best trained workers in the world, we've got the best education system in the world. And so the work that President Rousseff and I are doing together to try to significantly expand educational exchanges and send young people who are studying science and engineering and computer science to the United States to study if they're Brazilian, down to Brazil to study best practices in clean energy in Brazil, there's enormous opportunity for us to work together to train our young people so that this hemisphere is filled with outstanding entrepreneurs and workers and allows us to compete more effectively.

So there are a number of areas where I think cooperation is proceeding. Sometimes it's not flashy. I think that oftentimes in the press the attention in summits like this ends up focusing on where are the controversies. Sometimes those controversies date back to before I was born. [*Laughter*] And sometimes I feel as if in some of these discussions or at least the press reports we're caught in a time warp, going back to the 1950s and gunboat diplomacy and Yanquis and the cold war and this and that and the other. That's not the world we live in today.

And my hope is, is that we all recognize this enormous opportunity that we've got. And I know the business leaders who are here today, they understand it; they understand that we're in a new world and we have to think in new ways.

Last point I want to make. I think when you think about the extraordinary success in Brazil, the success in Colombia, a big piece of that is governance. You can't, I believe, have, over the long term, successful economies if you don't have some basic principles that are being followed: democracy and rule of law, human rights being observed, freedom of expression. And I think—and also personal security, the

capacity for people to feel as if they—if they work hard, then they're able to achieve and they have motivation to start a business and to know that their own work will pay off.

And I just want to compliment both Brazil and Colombia, coming from different political traditions, but part of the reason why you've seen sustained growth is governments have worked effectively in each country. And I think that when we look at how we're going to integrate further and take advantage of increased opportunity in the future, it's very important for us not to ignore how important it is to have a clean, transparent, open government that is working on behalf of its people.

And that's important to business as well. The days when a business feels good working in a place where people are being oppressed, ultimately, that's an unstable environment for you to do business. You do business well when you know that it's a well-functioning society and that there's a legitimate government in place that is going to be looking out for its people.

So I just want to thank both of my outstanding partners here. They're true leaders in the region. And I can speak, I think, for the United States to say that we've never been more excited about the prospects of working as equal partners with our brothers and sisters in Latin America and the Caribbean, because that's going to be the key to our success.

[*At this point, the discussion continued, and no transcript was provided. The discussion then continued as follows.*]

Narcotrafficking

MSNBC Reporter Chris Matthews. President Santos, I guess there are some issues in America—we have a very large Hispanic population. Ten percent of our electorate is going to be Hispanic in background. We are the second largest Spanish-speaking country in the world after Mexico. People have dual languages in the United States, of course, but there is so much Spanish speaking. You have the chance to sit next to President Obama now. Do you want to ask him about the ways you think the

United States could help your country in the drug war?

President Juan Manuel Santos Calderon of Colombia. Chris, don't you have a simpler question?

Mr. Matthews. Can we improve North-South relations generally speaking?

[*President Santos made remarks, and no transcript was provided. The discussion continued as follows.*]

President Obama. Do you want me to respond?

Mr. Matthews. Yes, sir.

President Obama. Well, this is a conversation that I've had with President Santos and others. Just as the world economy is integrated, so, unfortunately, the drug trade is integrated. And we can't look at the issue of supply in Latin America without also looking at the issue of demand in the United States.

And so whether it's working with President Santos or supporting the courageous work that President Calderon is doing in Mexico, I personally and my administration and, I think, the American people understand that the toll of narcotrafficking on the societies of Central America, Caribbean, and parts of South America are brutal and undermining the capacity of those countries to protect their citizens and eroding institutions and corrupting institutions in ways that are ultimately bad for everybody.

So this is part of the reason why we've invested, Chris, about $30 billion in prevention programs, drug treatment programs looking at the drug issue not just from a law enforcement and interdiction issue, but also from a public health perspective. This is why we've worked in unprecedented fashion in cooperation with countries like Mexico on not just drugs coming north, but also guns and cash going south.

This is one of the reasons why we have continued to invest in programs like Plan Colombia, but also now are working with Colombia, given their best practices around issues of citizen security, to have not just the United States, but Colombia provide technical assistance and training to countries in Central America and the Caribbean in finding ways that they can

duplicate some of the success that we've seen in Colombia.

So we're mindful of our responsibilities on this issue. And I think it is entirely legitimate to have a conversation about whether the laws in place are ones that are doing more harm than good in certain places.

I personally, and my administration's position, is that legalization is not the answer. That, in fact, if you think about how it would end up operating, that the capacity of a large-scale drug trade to dominate certain countries if they were allowed to operate legally without any constraint could be just as corrupting if not more corrupting then the status quo.

Nevertheless, I'm a big believer in looking at the evidence, having a debate. I think ultimately what we're going to find is, is that the way to solve this problem is both in the United States, us dealing with demand in a more effective way, but it's also going to be strengthening institutions at home.

You mentioned earlier, the biggest thing that's on everybody's minds—whether it's the United States, Canada, Brazil, Colombia, Jamaica—is, can I find a job that allows me to support my family and allows my children to advance and feel secure. And in those societies where you've got strong institutions, you've got strong business investment, you've got rule of law, you have a law enforcement infrastructure that is sound, and an economy that's growing, that country is going to be like a healthy body that is more immune than countries that have weak institutions and high unemployment, in which kids see their only future as participating in the drug trade because nobody has actually trained them to get a job with Google or Pepsi or start their own small business.

And so I think that it's important for us not to think that if somehow we look at the drug issue in isolation, in the absence of dealing with some of these other challenges—institutional challenges and barriers to growth and opportunity and the capacity for people to climb their way out of poverty—that we're going to be able to solve this problem. The drug issue in this region is, in some ways, a cause, but it's also, in some ways, an effect of some broader and underlying problems. And we as the United States have an obligation not only to get our own house in order, but also to help countries in a partnership to try to see if we can move in a better direction.

[The discussion continued, and no transcript was provided. The discussion then continued as follows.]

Global Economic Growth and Development

Mr. Matthews. Mr. President, do you want to respond? I think the question that seems to be apparent here in the last couple of days is, first of all, tremendous enthusiasm, and a zeitgeist here that's almost unusual in the world for positive optimism about the development in this part of the world. It's not like it was—just isn't the way it was we grew up with.

The challenge I think you just heard from the President of Brazil was the notion that Latin America is not interested in being our complementary economy anymore: the agricultural end while we do the industrial end; they do the provision of raw materials, and we do the finery—the finest and highest level high-tech work. How do we either respond to Brazil's demand, really, to be partners and rivals? They want to use our educational resources; they want to come north to learn how to compete with us, right, Madam President? You want to be equals. You want to learn everything we know, and then take it back and shove it at us, right? *[Laughter]* Isn't that it?

Well, anyway, that's the response. I'd ask you for your response. *[Laughter]*

President Obama. Chris, I'm not sure you're characterizing what President Rousseff said—*[laughter]*—but this is what happens when you get some of our U.S. political commentators moderating a panel. *[Laughter]* They try to stir up things that may not always be there. And Chris is good at it. He's one of the best. *[Laughter]*

But look, this is already happening. This is already happening. Brazil has changed, Colombia has changed, and we welcome the change. The notion somehow that we see this as a problem is just not the case, because if we've

got a strong, growing, prosperous middle class in Latin America, those are new customers for our businesses.

We want—Brazil is growing and that opportunity is broad-based, then suddenly they're interested in buying iPads, and they're interested in buying Boeing airplanes and—*[laughter]*.

President Dilma Rousseff of Brazil. Boeing—Embraer. *[Laughter]*

President Obama. I was just trying to see how she'd respond to that. *[Laughter]* But the point is, is that that's a market for us. So we in the United States should welcome not just growth, but broad-based growth, of the sort that President Rousseff described.

I'll give you just—I said I was in Tampa. All those containers that are coming in, they have, in some cases, commodities coming from Latin America, but they also have finished products that are coming in from Latin America. We have commodities that are going into Latin America that we're sending back on those containers, as well as finished products. And so this is a two-way street.

When I came into office, one of my first decisions was to say that the G–20 was not a temporary thing to respond to the world economic crisis, this should be the permanent forum for determining and coordinating direction in the world economy. And frankly, there were some folks who were members of the G–8 who were upset with me about that determination, but realistically, you can't coordinate world economic issues if you don't have China and Brazil and India and South Africa at the table—and Mexico. That's not possible.

So the world has changed. I think the United States and U.S. businesses stand to benefit from those changes. But it does mean that we have to adapt to that competitive environment. And all the advantages that President Rousseff mentioned we have as the United States—its flexibility, our scientific edge, our well-educated workforce, our top universities—those are the things that we continue to have to build and get better at. And that's true for every country here.

Every one of the businesses here are going to be making determinations about where you locate based on the quality of the workforce, how much investment you have to make in training somebody to handle a million-dollar piece of equipment. Do you feel as if your intellectual property is going to be protected? Do you feel as if there's a good infrastructure to be able to get your products to market? And so I think this is a healthy competition that we should be encouraging.

And what I've said at the first summit that I came to—Summit of the Americas that I came to was, we do not believe there are junior partners and senior partners in this situation. We believe there are partners. And Brazil is in many ways ahead of us on something like biofuels; we should learn from them. And does— if we're going to be trying to mount a regional initiative, let's make sure that Brazil is taking the lead. It doesn't have to be us in every situation.

Now, the flip side is—and I'll close with this—I think in Latin America, part of the change in mentality is also not always looking to the United States as the reason for everything that happens that goes wrong.

I was in an interview—several interviews yesterday. These were actually with Spanish-speaking television stations that have broadcast back in the United States. And the first interviewer said, why hasn't the United States done more to promote democracy in the region, because you've done a lot in the Arab Spring, but it seems as if you're not dealing with some of the problems here in Latin America. The next questioner said, why are you being so hard on Cuba and promoting democracy all the time? [*Laughter*] So—but that's an example, I think, of some of the challenges we face that are rooted in legitimate historical grievances. But it gets—it becomes a habit.

When it comes to economic integration and exchanges, I am completely sympathetic to the fact that there are challenges around monetary policy in developed and less developed countries. And Brazil, for example, has seen the real appreciate in ways that had been hurtful. I would argue a lot of that has to do with the failure of some other countries to engage in rebalancing, not the United States. But having said that, I think there's not a country in Latin America who doesn't want to see the United States grow rapidly because we're your major export market.

And so most of these issues end up being complicated issues. Typically, they involve both actions in the United States as well as actions in the other countries if we're going to optimize the kind of growth and prosperity and broad-based opportunity that both President Santos and President Rousseff have spoken about.

And the United States comes here and says: We're ready to do business. We are open to a partnership. We don't expect to be able to dictate the terms of that partnership, we expect it to be a negotiation based on mutual interest and mutual respect. And I think we're all going to benefit as a consequence of that.

[*The discussion continued, and no transcript was provided. The discussion concluded as follows.*]

Mr. Matthews. Thank you very much, President Rousseff, President Santos, and my President, President Obama. Thank you. It's been an honor.

NOTE: The President spoke at 10:43 a.m. in the Gran Salon Bolivar at the Hilton Cartagena Hotel. In his remarks, he referred to Luis Alberto Moreno, president, Inter-American Developmental Bank; Luis Carlos Villegas Echeverri, president, National Business Association of Colombia; former President Luiz Inacio Lula da Silva of Brazil; and former President Alvaro Uribe Velez of Colombia.

The President's News Conference With President Juan Manuel Santos Calderon of Colombia in Cartagena
April 15, 2012

President Santos. Good afternoon to you. I'd like to announce that we have had a bilateral meeting with President Obama and his team. This has been highly productive. Colombia and the U.S. have been successful partners in fighting against the drug trafficking, fighting against the terrorism, and in defending democracy.

In this meeting, we have made even more progress. Our countries have moved from being just good friends and partners to become real allies. We are allies in building a new world order. The world of the 20th century is behind; it is in the past. Now there is a new international reality, and we cannot simply be passive observers of this reality. Only joint work of those who share the ideals of freedom and democracy made sure a peaceful transition towards a better world. And we feel that we must work together.

We have talked with President Obama about bilateral problems and world problems, and we have also worked at the Security Council coordinating our positions. And we have been doing this—and we will do it at the G–20, where we will meet in a few months, and here in the summit, in this Summit of the Americas—and we have had very positive results. And I'm not only saying this as president of the summit, but most of the heads of state and government who were present said the same thing. And one of the reasons why it has been so successful was thanks to the presence of President Obama, who stayed here for 2 nights. And we discussed openly and candidly, and with respect and cordiality, all problems. Everything was discussed, and that was really appreciated by Latin America and the Caribbean in a very special fashion. So I'd like to thank you, President Obama. This was part of the success of the summit.

We all have the feeling that there are enormous opportunities to work together in a more integrated fashion. North and South America will be able to find the common denominators that will create synergies for the benefit of the North American and Latin American peoples.

In bilateral relations, I think that we have also made ways as never before, and I'd like to thank you, President Obama, for your permanent willingness and not only working with Colombia, but with Latin America. You said something that really touched us, and you—that was that you did not see Latin America as a problem or Latin Americans living in the U.S. as a problem, but the country—as a contribution, as a supplement to the dynamics that make the U.S. what they are today. And that has a lot of value. We would like to thank you for this. We would like to thank you, not only as Latin Americans who live south of Rio Grande, but those who live—the millions of Latin Americans who live in the U.S.

As for bilateral relations, finally, after working together for a long time in between two countries and their delegations, we can announce today that on May 15, precisely in 1 month, the new FTA with the U.S. will be enforced, which means that there will be thousands and millions of jobs created for the U.S. and Colombia. It is a dream we had for a lot of time. Since I was a Minister of Commerce 20 years ago, we were dreaming of having free trade with the U.S. And this has become a reality today, here in Cartagena, and right here where not so many years ago, about 10 to 12 years, the Plan Colombia was launched.

We were about to be considered a failed state. And today—thanks to the Plan Colombia and thanks to the U.S. and many others and thanks to you, President Obama, for your permanent support that you have always given us—today, we have a very strong democracy that is producing specific results for our peoples and that has been recognized by the world as a whole.

Number two, we also agreed with President Obama to work together so as to help Central American countries in fighting against organized crime and drug trafficking. The experience that we have gathered through Plan Colombia, together with the United States, is something that we have the obligation of sharing with our brothers in Central America who are going through difficult times. So that is a reason why we have decided to strengthen and improve joint assistance mechanisms for these countries.

Number three, we have agreed to work together so as to ensure energy interconnection of the whole continent. And this is something we discussed during the summit, but it concerns us very specifically here. Both the U.S. and Colombia may contribute to that interconnection. I am dreaming that at some point in time no individual living in the Americas will be out of this interconnection, because that will help us a lot in fighting against the poverty and for development.

Number four, we would like to thank the American Government for a decision, which is that as of now visas given to Colombians will be extended to 10 years, which is a proof of trust in the country. And we would like to thank you very much for this not only on behalf of the Government, but on behalf of the 46 million Colombians and the millions of Colombians who would love to go to the U.S.

And that is why I think that we are strengthening this wonderful relations that we have always had with the United States and with you personally, President Obama. You have not only an ally, but a friend. You can count on us. And let's continue working together. We've been able to attain many goals up to date, and I'm sure that we will be able to be more successful in the future.

So again, on behalf of these 46 million people in Colombia and all Latin Americans, thank you very much. Thank you very much for your interest. Thank you very much for coming to the summit and to this bilateral meeting. I think this has been a very important step forward in trying to work together in the Americas and the U.S. and Colombia. Thank you very much.

President Obama. Well, thank you, President Santos, for those warm words. Most of all, thank you and thanks to the First Lady and the

people of Colombia and Cartagena for your unbelievable hospitality. This is a beautiful city. And I'm going to do my best to bring Michelle and the girls back to come visit.

This will be remembered as a summit that brought the nations of our hemisphere closer together, and it will be remembered that we advanced the prosperity and the security and dignity of our peoples. And I believe it will be remembered that our progress was made possible in no small part by the outstanding commitment and leadership of President Santos and his team. So, Juan Manuel, *muchas gracias.*

As I said to my fellow leaders yesterday, there was a time not so long ago when few could have imagined holding a summit like this in Colombia. That we have and that the summit was such a success is a tribute to the remarkable transformation that's occurred in this Nation. There's a level of security that's not been seen in decades. Citizens are reclaiming their communities. The economy is growing, as you can see in the skylines of Cartagena and Bogota. Democratic institutions are being strengthened. In Colombia today, there's hope.

And this progress, once unthinkable, is a tribute to Colombian leaders, including President Santos. It's a testament to the extraordinary courage and sacrifices of Colombian security forces and the Colombian people. And now, as conflict begins to recede, this nation is embracing a new task: consolidating the gains it has won and building a just and durable peace that unlocks Colombia's incredible potential.

Today I pledged to President Santos that as Colombia forges its future, Colombia will continue to have a strong partner in the United States. When we met for the first time 2 years ago, we agreed to take the partnership between our two countries to a new level. This is part of my broader commitment in the Americas to seek partnerships of equality that are based on mutual interest and mutual respect. Here in Colombia and across the region, that's exactly what we've done. And today President Santos and I reviewed our progress and, I'm pleased to say, reached agreement on several new initiatives.

First, as has already been mentioned, we're moving ahead with our landmark trade agreement. In our meeting at the White House last year, we approved an action plan to ensure the protection of labor rights. We all know that more work still needs to be done, but we've made significant progress. And as a result, and given the actions taken by President Santos and the Colombian legislature, I can announce that the U.S.-Colombia Free Trade Agreement will enter into force next month on May 15.

As I've said before, this agreement is a win for both our countries. It's a win for the United States by increasing our exports by more than $1 billion, supporting thousands of U.S. jobs, and helping to achieve my goal of doubling U.S. exports. It's a win for Colombia by giving you even greater access to the largest market for your exports: the United States of America. And I'd add that this agreement is a win for our workers and the environment because of the strong protections it has for both, commitments that we are going to fulfill. So, President Santos, thank you for your partnership in getting this done.

Colombia's economic progress puts this nation on the path to join the ranks of developed nations. President Santos has made it a goal to seek membership in the Organisation for Economic Co-operation and Development. And today I can announce that when Colombia is ready to seek it, the United States will strongly support Colombia's candidacy for the OECD. Moreover, we will actively encourage other members of the OECD to join us in supporting Colombia's membership, which would be another symbol of Colombia's transformation.

Alongside our deeper economic cooperation, we're strengthening our security cooperation. The United States has been proud to stand with the Colombian people in their fight against a terrorist insurgency that took the lives of so many innocent civilians. I reaffirmed to President Santos that the United States will continue to stand with Colombia shoulder to shoulder as you work to end this conflict and build a just and lasting peace. And that in-

cludes supporting President Santos's very ambitious reform agenda, including reparations for victims and land reform. And this afternoon I look forward to joining President Santos as he presents land titles to two Afro-Colombian communities, advancing the vision of a Colombia that is just and equitable.

As Colombia grows stronger at home, it's increasingly playing a leadership role across the region, a third area where we're deepening our partnership. Colombia has shared its expertise in security by training police officers in countries from Latin America to Afghanistan. Today President Santos and I agreed that our two countries will work together to support our partners in Central America as they pursue a regional strategy to improve the security of their citizens.

And this is just one more example of how Colombia is contributing to security and peace beyond its borders, including as a current member of the U.N. Security Council. I want to take this opportunity to salute Colombian leadership, from supporting the recovery in Haiti to supporting sanctions against Iran, to standing up for the rights and freedoms of people in the Middle East and North Africa. And this week in Brazil, we'll join nations from around the world in advancing the open government that empowers citizens and makes governments more accountable.

Finally, I'm very pleased that we're deepening the ties between our peoples. As it now stands, visas for Colombians to visit the United States expire after 5 years. As was just mentioned, I'm announcing that these visas for Colombians will now be valid for 10 years, and this will make it easier for more Colombians to visit and experience the United States. And this is one more very tangible example of Colombia's transformation and the transformation in the relationship between our two countries.

So again, President Santos, thank you to you for your leadership. Thank you to the people of Cartagena and the people of Colombia for this outstanding summit and your great hospitality, the warmth that you've extended us and the other leaders who gathered here. It makes me very confident about Colombia's future.

465

Cuba/Falkland Islands

President Santos. Thank you. Thank you very much.

Well, there are some questions. I think, RCN TV, Juan Carlos, you have a question.

Q. Presidents, good afternoon. President Obama, today at the closing of the Summit of the Americas, there was great expectation because we never—you never came up with a document that would reflect a decision, and many people would say that Cuba and the Malvinas issue weren't taken up as they should have. Does this have to do in any way with the electoral environment, the electoral context in the United States?

And to President Santos, today that the State Department announced a new security plan for the region. What benefits do you see coming from this plan? Thank you very much.

President Obama. Well, first of all, what it reflects is a lack of consensus among those who participated in the summit. The issue of Cuba I've discussed before. Since I came into office, we have made changes to our Cuba policy. We've increased remittances that are permissible from Cuban Americans sending money to their families to help support them back home. We've increased travel by family members to Cuba. And we have discussed in the OAS the pathway whereby Cuba can fully participate in some of these regional forums. But the fact of the matter is, is that Cuba, unlike the other countries that are participating, has not yet moved to democracy, has not yet observed basic human rights.

I am hopeful that a transition begins to take place inside of Cuba. And I assure you that I and the American people will welcome the time when the Cuban people have the freedom to live their lives, choose their leaders, and fully participate in this global economy and international institutions.

We haven't gotten there yet. But as I indicated to President Santos and all the other leaders in—sitting around the table, we recognize that there may be an opportunity in the coming years, as Cuba begins to look at where it needs to go in order to give its people the kind of prosperity and opportunity that it needs, that it starts loosening up some of the constraints within that country. And that's something that we will welcome.

I'm not somebody who brings to the table here a lot of baggage from the past, and I want to look at all these problems in a new and fresh way. But I also deeply believe in those principles that are contained not just in the OAS charter, but in the United Nations Charter: that respect for individuals, respect for rule of law, respect for human rights that I think is part of the reason that we're seeing an incredible transformation here in Colombia.

And in terms of the Maldives [Malvinas][*] or the Falklands, whatever your preferred term, our position on this is that we are going to remain neutral. We have good relations with both Argentina and Great Britain, and we are looking forward to them being able to continue to dialogue on this issue. But this is not something that we typically intervene in.

President Santos. I would just like to repeat something that I said during the press conference this morning—early this afternoon, saying that the important thing of the summit is that we openly discussed all the issues—all issues. This didn't happen before. There were some issues that garnered agreement, others that didn't. We reached an agreement on the five fundamental issues that were identified from the very outset, and the discussion on other issues was an open, candid discussion. It was fully respectful and productive, I would say.

And that is what I—why I believe that in the aftermath of this summit, we will have a better understanding of these challenges. Some will be solved in the short term; others in the longer term. There are others that we will—naturally won't be able to resolve. But that is only natural. And summits such as these, where 33 countries participate, each one bringing to the table their own interests, each one bringing their own prism through which they look at things. But the positive thing is that we discuss

---

[*] White House correction.

these issues candidly and productively, a number of issues that were not even on the table before.

On the issue of security, with the United States, we have very close coordination, and perhaps we don't have this close relationship with any other country in the world. We have learned mutually from each other. They have helped us a great deal. As I said before, Plan Colombia was launched a few years ago. And it's not just the amount of money that was offered through Plan Colombia, it was the quality of the assistance. And to us, that was a very important step. And anything that we can do along that road to improve security in the United States and Colombia and to share our experiences will be more than welcome.

Cuba/U.S. Secret Service/Narcotrafficking

Q. Thank you, both of you. President Obama——

[*At this point, there was feedback from the microphone.*]

I'm a little close there. Following up on my Colombian colleague's question, could you address—he had referred to the electoral pressures that you face in the United States. Could you address the issue of how big Florida looms in terms of the United States policy towards Cuba?

And I wanted to ask quickly about—the issue that has sort of hung over this summit for the Americans is the controversy that involved members of the detail that is sworn to protect you. What did you—were you angry when you heard about this as you came here? And do you feel like there's any—this is indicative of any broader cultural problem within the Secret Service, such as a leading Republican Congressman suggested?

And President Santos—which, President Obama, you could also address this as well—I'm curious as to why you made drug trafficking such a prominent part of this summit when it could be argued that it detracted some from the attention you wanted to bring to the great

progress that Colombia has made on economic and security issues. Thank you.

President Obama. Well, first of all, my position on Cuba has been consistent. It hasn't wavered before I was elected for President the first time, it didn't change after I was elected for President, it hasn't changed now. So let me repeat, separate and apart from whatever electoral concerns you're describing: I want the people of Cuba, like people throughout this hemisphere, to have the opportunity to work, to raise their families, to start a business, to express themselves, to criticize their leaders—something that we in America take full advantage of—to replace them if they're not working, which presumably is the aspiration of, I think, most people throughout Latin America.

And as I indicated in an interview earlier, I am sometimes puzzled by the degree to which countries that themselves have undergone enormous transformations, that have known the oppression of dictatorship or have found themselves on the wrong side of a ruling elite and have suffered for it, why we would ignore that same principle here.

But, Jackie [Jackie Calmes, New York Times], as you know, I tend to be an optimistic person. And it is my hope that as Cuba looks at what's happening in countries like Colombia and Brazil and Chile and throughout the region, they're going to start saying to themselves, maybe there's a new path to take in the 21st century. And when that happens, they're going to have a welcome hand extended by the United States of America.

On the Secret Service, these men and women perform extraordinary service on a day-to-day basis protecting me, my family, U.S. officials. They do very hard work under very stressful circumstances and almost invariably do an outstanding job. And so I'm very grateful to the work that they do.

What happened here in Colombia is being investigated by the Director of the Secret Service. I expect that investigation to be thorough, and I expect it to be rigorous. If it turns out that some of the allegations that have been made in the press are confirmed, then of course, I'll be angry, because my attitude with respect to the Secret Service personnel is no different than what I expect out of my delegation that's sitting here. We're representing the people of the United States. And when we travel to another country, I expect us to observe the highest standards because we're not just representing ourselves, we're here on behalf of our people. And that means that we conduct ourselves with the utmost dignity and probity. And obviously, what's been reported doesn't match up with those standards. But again, I think I'll wait until the full investigation is completed before I pass final judgment.

The final point I'll make, just on the issue you raised with President Santos, about the issue of drug trafficking. I think it is wholly appropriate for us to discuss this issue because Colombia obviously has gone through a wrenching number of years dealing with this issue. It has been successful because of the courage and leadership not only of President Santos and his predecessors, but also because of Colombian security forces.

But you now have a number of countries in the region, in Central America and in the Caribbean, that are smaller, that have fewer resources, and are starting to feel overwhelmed. And obviously, we've been following what's been happening in Mexico and the violence that's been taking place there as a consequence of these narcotraffickers. So I think it wouldn't make sense for us not to examine what works and what doesn't and to constantly try to refine and ask ourselves, is there something we can do to prevent violence, to weaken these drug traffickers, to make sure that they're not peddling this stuff on our kids and they're not perpetrating violence and corrupting institutions in the region? And I thought it was a good and useful and frank discussion.

As I said a couple of days ago, Jackie, I'm not somebody who believes that legalization is a path to solving this problem. But I do think that we can constantly ask ourselves, are there additional steps we can take to be more creative? And are there ways that we can combine the law enforcement and interdiction approaches that we've successfully partnered with Colombia on with the public health ap-

proach that, I think, is important back home, making sure that we're trying to reduce demand, even as we try to choke off supply?

And so I'm looking forward to continuing to have that conversation. And based on the best evidence and the best ideas out there, hopefully, we can continue to strengthen these efforts.

President Santos. If I understood your question correctly, why—it is, why did we place drugs on the agenda when there are other more important things for the summit or things that we should highlight about our country, such as the progress that we've achieved economically and in strengthening our democracy?

The question is well put, but the answer is in your court. The media were the ones that placed such a high level of attention on this issue. I said many times in the interviews that I conducted before this summit, I said I don't want this issue to be the summit's issue; I have no interest in having this issue as the sole summit issue. This is one of many issues that some countries want to put on the table for negotiations.

And what I said before is that, fortunately, during this summit there were no issues that were left off the table, everything was open, and this was one of the issues that was discussed. We discussed it frankly, candidly. We heard positions from President Obama, from the United States, and positions from other countries. And they were all laid out on the table. And I think this is a positive step, and if we can find paths that will provide more effective and cheaper mechanisms to fight against drug trafficking and organized crime, well, let's work on that. But we—it was never our intention for this issue to be the issue of the summit.

Caracol Television.

President Obama's Visit to Colombia/Colombia-U.S. Relations/Trade

Q. President Obama, good afternoon. President Santos, good afternoon, sir. President Obama, you are the first U.S. President who comes to Colombia and stays 3 days, 2 nights, in the beautiful city of Cartagena. How should Colombia and the world interpret this gesture?

Is it an acknowledgment of the levels of security that we have here? Is it a gesture of trust in what President Santos has done? Or can we interpret it as a new phase beginning in relationships—the relations between two countries?

And, President Santos, there are small-businesspeople who are very concerned about the FTA. And what is your plan to deal with that, Mr. President?

President Obama. Well, I think the answer is all of the above. It is—this represents my confidence in the security of Colombia and the progress that's been made. It represents my confidence in President Santos and the work that we've done together, as a culmination of the efforts that we began when we first met a couple of years ago. It highlights the deliverables coming out of this summit, not just the free trade agreement, but all the other work that has been done, such as the increase in the length of visitor visas. And it is consistent with the approach that I indicated I would take when I first came into office when it comes to Latin America and Central America.

This is a fast-growing part of the world. It is our—one of our largest trading partners, the entire region. We have Colombian Americans, Americans who originate from the Dominican Republic, from Guatemala, from Mexico, who are constantly contributing to the vitality and the strength of the United States. And so there is a natural bond that already exists. And it's important that our governments build on that natural bond for the mutual benefit of both nations.

And my expectation is, is that we will continue to see the progress that's been made in this summit in subsequent meetings that we have with Colombia. And I think that Colombia increasingly, precisely because it went through difficult times over these last several years, can end up being a role model for a lot of countries around the region. Because they'll see: You know what, there's hope—even in the midst of violence, even in the midst of difficulty—there's the possibility of breaking through to the other side and achieving greater citizen security and greater prosperity.

And let me just mention, I know you asked the question of President Santos, but on the issue of small businesses, one of the things that I brought to the summit was a proposal that, I think, people are embracing throughout the region, and that is that we begin to focus more on small and medium-sized businesses, on women's businesses, making sure that the benefits of trade don't just go to the largest companies, but also go to smaller entrepreneurs and businesspeople.

Because in today's globalized world there's an opportunity for a small business or a medium-sized business to access a global marketplace and grow rapidly, and that means more jobs here in Colombia, and that means more jobs in the United States. So we don't want trade to just be taking place at this layer up here. We want it to be taking place at every level because we think that's going to be good for both our economies.

President Santos. You asked me about what contingency plan we had to help companies and people who were going to be adversely affected by the FTA. All free trade agreements have winners and they have losers, and in this case, we have many more winners than losers. Employment wins. We will create jobs in Colombia. We estimate that more than 500,000 jobs will be created. We will benefit economic growth. We will—we have estimated that between .5 and 1 percent will be added to our growth rate over the long term, and that will be translated into benefits for the economy—for the Colombians. And we estimate that everybody will benefit from this.

Obviously, there are some sectors that don't traditionally benefit. But small and medium enterprises can be the ones that benefit the most. That happened in Peru, for example, when the Peru-U.S. FTA—we saw a major uptick of the number of SMEs that benefited from this free trade agreement. We hope that that happens in Colombia as well, because thus far, Colombia has per capita exports which are very low. But we still have the great potential to bolster our free trade and our exports in those sectors that are vulnerable—which have been identified as vulnerable—are the focus of a series of policies and efforts that will help them weather the storm, to be transformed, to be more competitive, and to be able to face the competition that will open up with this new FTA. That has happened with every free trade agreement that has been signed in the past. What's important is that the final results yields more benefits than otherwise. And we have no doubts that in this case, it will have more benefits for everyone.

U.S. and Global Economy/Iran

Q. Thank you, sir. Yesterday the President of Brazil was talking about the importance not only of growing the economic pie, but making sure that it's divided more equitably. I wonder how you think that applies within the United States, where the idea of spreading the wealth around isn't always warmly greeted, and how, for example, with this free trade agreement, you make sure that the benefits are widely shared. And if I may, sir, on an unrelated topic, if I could get your reaction to the Prime Minister Netanyahu's comments that the P–5-plus-1 had given Iran a freebie with this additional time.

And for President Santos, what responsibility do you believe the countries of Latin America, especially those that have become more democratic, have for helping to bring Cuba into the democratic fold?

President Obama. The goal of any government should be to create security for its citizens and to give them opportunity to achieve prosperity and to pass that prosperity on to their kids. And I'm a strong believer that the free market is the best tool ever invented to create wealth.

But what's true in every country is that we always have to think about whether every single person is getting a fair shot, where they actually have opportunity. Is everybody doing their fair share to support the common efforts that are required to create a platform for growth? Is everybody playing by the same set of rules? And I think the history of the United States, the reason we became an economic superpower is because—not always perfectly, not always consistently, but better than any other

country on Earth—we were able to give opportunity to everybody. That's what the American Dream was all about.

So when we have debates now about our tax policy, when we have debates now about the Buffett rule that we've been talking about, where we say if you make a million dollars a year or more you shouldn't pay a lower tax rate than your secretary, that is not an argument about redistribution. That is an argument about growth. Because the history of the United States is we grow best when our growth is broad-based. We grow best when our middle class is strong. We grow best when everybody has opportunity. And that means that somebody who has a great idea and is selling a great product or service, we want them to get rich. That's great. But we also want to make sure that we as a society are investing in that young kid who comes from a poor family, who has incredible talent and might be able to get rich as well.

And that means we've got to build good schools, and we've got to make sure that that child can go to college. And we also want to make sure that we keep our scientific edge, and that means we've got to invest in basic research. And that means that we've got to have some basic safety net, because people are more willing to take risks that are required for the free market to work if they know that if they fall on hardship, if something happens, that there's still some floor that they can't fall beneath and that they'll be able to retire with some dignity and some respect.

And so one of the things that we're going to be talking about over the next several months as we debate the budget and Government spending and the proper role of Government, is just—I want everybody to remember, I'm going to say this repeatedly—this is not an argument about taking from A to give to B. This is not a redistributionist argument that we're making. We're making an argument about how do we grow the economy so that it's going to be prospering in this competitive 21st-century environment. And the only way we're going to do that is if people like me, who have been incredibly blessed, are willing to give a little bit back so that the next generation coming along can succeed as well. And the more people that succeed, the better off the country is going to be.

With respect to the Iranian talks, I've been very clear on this. Iran has violated U.N. Security Council resolutions. They're the only country that's a member of the Non-Proliferation Treaty, the NPT, that cannot convince the international community that they are abiding by the rules governing the NPT. And not just the United States, but the world community is now imposing some of the toughest sanctions that we've ever seen, and there are more to come. And it is my view that it would be contrary to the security interests of the United States and destabilizing for the world and the region, if Iran pursues, develops, obtains a nuclear weapon. So I've been very clear, and I've been talking about this quite a bit lately.

What I've also been clear about is that the best way to resolve this issue is diplomatically and my belief that we still have a window in which to resolve this conflict diplomatically. That window is closing, and Iran needs to take advantage of it. But it is absolutely the right thing to do for the U.S. Government, working in concert with the other permanent members of the Security Council, with Germany, with the rest of world community, to pursue this path.

Part of the reason we've been able to build a strong international coalition that isolates Iran around the nuclear issue is because the world has confidence that I've been sincere and my administration has been sincere about giving Iran an opportunity to pursue peaceful nuclear energy while foreclosing the pursuit of a nuclear weapon. That strengthens our hand. That's part of the reason why we've been able to execute on these strong sanctions. And we're going to keep on seeing if we make progress.

Now, the clock is ticking. And I've been very clear to Iran and to our negotiating partners that we're not going to have these talks just drag out in a stalling process. But so far, at least, we haven't given away anything other than the opportunity for us to negotiate and see if Iran comes to the table in good faith. And the notion that somehow we've given

something away or a freebie would indicate that Iran has gotten something. In fact, they've got some of the toughest sanctions that they're going to be facing coming up in just a few months if they don't take advantage of these talks. I hope they do.

Was there a—you guys ask too many questions. I start forgetting.

President Santos.

President Santos. Any foreign policy has a formula: Interests plus principles equals a foreign policy. So how do you combine these interests and principles, and how you defend those principles is what makes a foreign policy. In our case and in the case of many countries—countries that believe in freedom and democracy—we have the obligation to make sure that those principles are applied in every form possible and in every place possible.

But there are different formulas to defend and apply those principles as well. There are certain paths that are more effective than others. In some cases, sanctions may work. Generally, they don't, but they may work in some cases. In some other cases, it has been proven that sanctions are not the solution, and in these cases, we need to then pursue the defense of those principles through other ways.

And in our case, Colombia and other Latin American countries that believe in democracy and believe in freedom, we have the obligation to pursue those principles following the most effective paths. And I believe that that can yield the best results.

President Obama. Thank you very much, everybody.

President Santos. Muchas gracias.

NOTE: The President's news conference began at 4:30 p.m. in the Courtyard at La Casa de Huespedes Ilustres. In his remarks, the President referred to Maria Clemencia Rodriguez de Santos, wife of President Santos. A reporter referred to President Dilma Rousseff of Brazil; and Prime Minister Benjamin Netanyahu of Israel. President Santos and some reporters spoke in Spanish, and their remarks were translated by an interpreter.

Remarks at a Land Titling Event in Cartagena
April 15, 2012

Buenas tardes! It is a great honor to be here with President Santos, the First Lady, so many distinguished guests. I am especially thankful to all the children because they are sitting very still and well behaved, and I want to get lessons for my own children from the parents and teachers, because they're doing a great job here.

And I'm thrilled that—I'm thrilled we're joined by another champion of these communities, especially the education development of these beautiful children. So thank you, Shakira, for the wonderful work that you do.

This is a historic day, decades, even centuries in the making. For generations, many of you have lived on these lands, toiled these lands, raised your families on these lands. And now, from this day forward, you will at long last hold title to this land: La Boquilla and Basilio de Palenque.

And being here holds special meaning for me. Early in my Presidency, my family and I visited Ghana in West Africa. And we visited the historic Cape Coast Castle, and I'll never forget my two young daughters—the descendants of Africans and African Americans—looking out through the door of no return where so many Africans began their forced journey to this hemisphere.

Today we gather in a port city where so many of those Africans arrived in chains. Like their brothers and sisters in both our countries and across this hemisphere, they endured unimaginable cruelty. But in their suffering, which revealed man's capacity for evil, we also see the spirit of this day, man's capacity for good, for perseverance, for healing; the belief that we can overcome.

President Santos and I just took a tour of this magnificent cathedral dedicated to a man of faith who devoted his life to the least among us: San Pedro Claver—in the United States, Peter Claver. And in the United States, it was another man of faith, the Reverend Dr. Martin Luther King, who said that the arc of the moral universe is long, but it bends towards justice. And that's what's happening today.

Throughout my visit here in Colombia, I've spoken about the remarkable transformation that's underway in this country: more security, more prosperity, more hope. And this is a tribute to the perseverance of leaders like President Santos and you, the Colombian people. But we all understand that peace is not simply the absence of war. True and lasting peace has to be based on justice and dignity for every person.

And that's why today is so important. Giving you and so many Afro-Colombian communities title to this land is part of ending this nation's long conflict. It gives you a new stake in a new Colombia. Not far from here, your ancestors were bought and sold. Going forward, Colombia can realize its full potential by empowering all of its people, no matter what you look like or where you come from.

Both our nations have struggled to overcome a painful past. Both keep striving to fulfill our ideals of justice and equality. And I stand here today as President of the United States and you can stand here with title to the land, and that is proof that progress is possible.

And so when we look out to these children behind us, these beautiful children, they have a brighter future ahead of them. But that future will only be fulfilled if we're making investments in them every single day, as Shakira and the First Lady are working to do, as President Santos and I have to commit ourselves to do. But today is an important first step in creating that brighter future for them. And as you seek peace and prosperity and the dignity that all people deserve, I promise you, you will always have a strong and steady partner in the United States of America.

Muchas gracias.

NOTE: The President spoke at 6:09 p.m. in the Plaza San Pedro. In his remarks, he referred to Maria Clemencia Rodriguez de Santos, wife of President Juan Manuel Santos Calderon of Colombia; and musician Shakira Isabel Mebarak Ripoll. Audio was not available for verification of the content of these remarks.

Statement on Representative Edolphus Towns's Decision Not To Seek Reelection
April 16, 2012

As a veteran, teacher, minister, and Congressman, Edolphus Towns has dedicated his life to public service. In his 30 years representing the people of New York, Ed has fought tirelessly to improve the public health care system, strengthen consumer protections, and improve the public education system. He has served as chairman for the Congressional Black Caucus, the House Oversight and Government Reform Committee, and currently chairs the Congressional Social Work Caucus, which he created to provide a platform for over 600,000 social workers who positively impact the lives of the elderly, the disadvantaged, children, and veterans. Michelle and I join the people of New York in wishing Ed and his family all the best in the future.

Statement on the Selection of Jim Yong Kim as President of the World Bank
April 16, 2012

On behalf of the United States, I would like to offer my congratulations to Dr. Jim Yong Kim on his selection as the next President of the World Bank. I am confident that Dr. Kim will be an inclusive leader who will bring to the Bank a passion for and deep knowledge of development, a commitment to sustained economic growth, and the ability to respond to complex challenges and seize new opportunities. I appreciate the strong support offered to Dr. Kim from leaders around the world.

I am also pleased that this has been an open and transparent process and would like to take this opportunity to acknowledge the outstanding qualifications and commitment of the other two candidates. I look forward to working with Dr. Kim and our partners throughout the world in support of a strong and effective World Bank.

NOTE: The statement referred to World Bank President candidates Jose A. Ocampo and Ngozi Okonjo-Iweala.

Statement on Tax Code Reform
April 16, 2012

Tonight Senate Republicans voted to block the Buffett rule, choosing once again to protect tax breaks for the wealthiest few Americans at the expense of the middle class.

The Buffett rule is common sense. At a time when we have significant deficits to close and serious investments to make to strengthen our economy, we simply cannot afford to keep spending money on tax cuts that the wealthiest Americans don't need and didn't ask for. But it's also about basic fairness: It's just plain wrong that millions of middle class Americans pay a higher share of their income in taxes than some millionaires and billionaires. America prospers when we're all in it together and everyone has the opportunity to succeed.

One of the fundamental challenges of our time is building an economy where everyone gets a fair shot, everyone does their fair share, and everyone plays by the same rules. And I will continue to push Congress to take steps to not only restore economic security for the middle class and those trying to reach the middle class, but also to create an economy that's built to last.

Letter to the Speaker of the House of Representatives Transmitting Budget Amendments for Fiscal Year 2013
April 16, 2012

Dear Mr. Speaker:

I ask the Congress to consider the enclosed Fiscal Year (FY) 2013 Budget amendments for the Departments of Defense, Health and Human Services, Homeland Security, Housing and Urban Development, State and Other International Programs, as well as the Corps of Engineers. Also included is an amendment to a Government-wide general provision. These amendments will not increase the overall discretionary budget authority in my FY 2013 Budget.

In addition, this transmittal contains FY 2013 amendments for the Legislative Branch. As a matter of comity and per tradition, these appropriations requests for the Legislative Branch are transmitted without change.

These amendments are necessary to reflect correctly policies assumed in the FY 2013 Budget. The details of these amendments are set forth in the enclosed letter from the Acting Director of the Office of Management and Budget.

Sincerely,

BARACK OBAMA

Remarks on Energy Market Manipulation
April 17, 2012

Good morning, everybody. Lately, I've been speaking a lot about our need for an all-of-the-above strategy for American energy, a strategy that produces more oil and gas here at home, but also produces more biofuels and fuel-efficient cars, more solar power and wind power and other sources of clean, renewable energy.

This strategy is not just the right thing to do for our long-term economic growth; it's also the right way for us to reduce our dependence on foreign oil right now. It's the right way for us to put people to work right now. And ultimately, it's the right way to stop spikes in gas prices that we've put up [with]° every single year, the same kind of increases that we've seen over the past couple of months.

Obviously, rising gas prices means a rough ride for a lot of families. Whether you're trying to get to school, trying to get to work, do some grocery shopping, you have to be able to fill up that gas tank. And there are families in certain parts of the country that have no choice but to drive 50 or 60 miles to get to the job. So, when gas prices go up, it's like an additional tax that comes right out of your pocket.

That's one of the reasons we passed a payroll tax cut at the beginning of this year and then made sure it extended all the way through this year so that the average American is getting that extra $40 in every paycheck right now.

But I think everybody understands that there are no quick fixes to this problem. There are politicians who say that if we just drilled more then gas prices would come down right away. What they don't say is that we have been drilling more. Under my administration, America is producing more oil than at any time in the last 8 years. We've opened up new areas for exploration. We've quadrupled the number of operating rigs to a record high. We've added enough new oil and gas pipeline to circle the Earth and then some.

But, as I've said repeatedly, the problem is we use more than 20 percent of the world's oil and we only have 2 percent of the world's proven oil reserves. Even if we drilled every square inch of this country right now, we'd still have to rely disproportionately on other countries for their oil. That means we pay more at the pump every time there's instability in the Middle

---

° White House correction.

Photographic Portfolio

Overleaf: Speaking with Prime Minister Mario Monti of Italy by telephone aboard Air Force One, June 6.

Above left: Greeting U.S. troops at Bagram Air Base, Afghanistan, May 1.

Left: Chatting with students in the Blue Room at the White House before delivering remarks on college affordability, June 21.

Above: Holding Arianna Holmes, daughter of departing International Economic Affairs special assistant Angela Holmes, in the Oval Office at the White House, February 1.

Right: Transiting by helicopter from Kabul to Bagram Air Base, Afghanistan, with Gen. John R. Allen, USMC, commander, NATO International Security Assistance Force, Afghanistan, left, and U.S. Ambassador Ryan C. Crocker, right, May 1.

Left: Meeting with euro zone leaders on the Laurel Cabin patio during the Group of Eight (G–8) summit at Camp David, MD, May 19.

Below left: Conferring with President Hamid Karzai of Afghanistan during the NATO Summit in Chicago, IL, May 20.

Right: Watching as Hannah Wyman of Leominster, MA, demonstrates her science fair project in the Blue Room at the White House, February 7.

Below: Greeting veterans of the Tuskegee Airmen with Mrs. Obama in the East Garden Room prior to a screening of the film "Red Tails" at the White House, January 13.

Above: Hugging Rep. Gabrielle D. Giffords on the floor of the House Chamber prior to delivering the State of the Union Address at the U.S. Capitol, January 24.

Above left: Walking with Secretary of State Hillary Rodham Clinton at the Esperanza Resort in Cabo San Lucas, Mexico, June 18.

Left: Talking with a young woman during an impromptu visit to the Boys and Girls Club of Cleveland after a campaign event in Cleveland, OH, June 14.

Above right: Sitting on the Rosa Parks bus at the Henry Ford Museum in Dearborn, MI, April 18.

Right: Greeting workers at the One World Trade Center site in New York City, June 14.

Overleaf: Acknowledging applause following remarks on student loan interest rates at the Coors Events Center at the University of Colorado Boulder in Boulder, CO, April 24.

East or growing demand in countries like China and India.

That's what's happening right now. It's those global trends that are affecting gas prices. So, even as we're tackling issues of supply and demand, even as we're looking at the long term in terms of how we can structurally make ourselves less reliant on foreign oil, we still need to work extra hard to protect consumers from factors that should not affect the price of a barrel of oil.

That includes doing everything we can to ensure that an irresponsible few aren't able to hurt consumers by illegally manipulating or rigging the energy markets for their own gain. We can't afford a situation where speculators artificially manipulate markets by buying up oil, creating the perception of a shortage and driving prices higher, only to flip the oil for a quick profit. We can't afford a situation where some speculators can reap millions, while millions of American families get the short end of the stick. That's not the way the market should work. And for anyone who thinks this cannot happen, just think back to how Enron traders manipulated the price of electricity to reap huge profits at everybody else's expense.

Now, the good news is, my administration has already taken several actions to step up oversight of oil markets and close dangerous loopholes that were allowing some traders to operate in the shadows.

We closed the so-called Enron loophole that let traders evade oversight by using electronic or overseas trading platforms. In the Wall Street reform law, we said, for the first time, that Federal regulators will make sure no single trader can buy such a large position in oil that they could easily manipulate the market on their own. So I'd point out that anybody who's pledging to roll back Wall Street reform—Dodd-Frank—would also roll back this vital consumer protection along with it.

I've asked Attorney General Holder to work with Chairman Leibowitz of the Federal Trade Commission, Chairman Gensler of the Commodity Futures Trading Commission, and other enforcement agencies to make sure that acts of manipulation, fraud, or other illegal activity are not behind increases in the price that consumers pay at the pump.

So today we're announcing new steps to strengthen oversight of energy markets. Things that we can do administratively, we are doing. And I call on Congress to pass a package of measures to crack down on illegal activity and hold accountable those who manipulate the market for private gain at the expense of millions of working families. And be specific.

First, Congress should provide immediate funding to put more cops on the beat to monitor activity in energy markets. This funding would also upgrade technology so that our surveillance and enforcement officers aren't hamstrung by older and less sophisticated tools than the ones that traders are using. We should strengthen protections for American consumers, not gut them. And these markets have expanded significantly.

Chairman Gensler actually had a good analogy; he said, imagine if the NFL quadrupled the number of teams, but didn't increase the number of refs; you'd end up having havoc on the field and it would diminish the game. It wouldn't be fair. That's part of what's going on in a lot of these markets. So we have to properly resource enforcement.

Second, Congress should increase the civil and criminal penalties for illegal energy market manipulation and other illegal activities. So my plan would toughen key financial penalties tenfold and impose these penalties not just per violation, but for every day a violation occurs.

Third, Congress should give the agency responsible for overseeing oil markets new authority to protect against volatility and excess speculation, by making sure that traders can post appropriate margins, which simply means that they actually have the money to make good on their trades.

Congress should do all of this right away. A few weeks ago, Congress had a chance to stand up for families already paying an extra premium at the pump; congressional Republicans voted to keep spending billions of Americans' hard-earned tax dollars on more unnecessary subsidies for big oil companies. So here's a chance to make amends, a chance to actually do something that will protect consumers by increasing oversight of energy markets. That should be something that everybody, no matter their party, should agree with. And I hope Americans will ask their Members of Congress to step up.

In the meantime, my administration will take new executive actions to better analyze and investigate trading activities in energy markets and more quickly implement the tough consumer protections under Wall Street reform.

Let me close by saying none of these steps by themselves will bring gas prices down overnight. But it will prevent market manipulation and make sure we're looking out for American consumers. And in the meantime we're going to keep pursuing an all-of-the-above strategy for American energy to break the cycle of price spikes year after year. We are going to keep producing more biofuels, we're going to keep producing more fuel-efficient cars, we are go-

ing to keep tapping into every source of American-made energy.

And these steps have already helped put America on a path to greater energy independence. Our foreign—our dependence on foreign oil has actually decreased each year I've been in office, even as the economy has grown. America now imports less than half of the oil we use for the first time in more than a decade. So we are less vulnerable than we were, but we're still too vulnerable.

We've got to continue the hard, sustained work on this issue. And as long as I'm President, we're going to keep placing our bets on America's future: America's workers, America's technology, America's ingenuity, and American-made energy. That's how we're going to solve this problem once and for all.

Thank you very much, everybody.

NOTE: The President spoke at 11:27 a.m. in the Rose Garden at the White House.

Remarks Honoring the 2011 NASCAR Sprint Cup Series Champion
April 17, 2012

Thank you so much, everybody. Please, please have a seat. Welcome to the White House, and congratulations to Tony Stewart on his third Sprint Cup Championship. [*Applause*] You can give him a round of applause for that. It is great to have NASCAR back in Washington.

I want to thank Brian France and Mike Helton for their leadership. We've got some Members of Congress who are big racing fans who are here. We've got some of my staff who are big racing fans who are here. I also want to welcome the rest of the drivers who are with us, the best of the best right here. Thank you all for coming. We really appreciate it.

Now, full disclosure: I invited Tony here today because of what he did on the track. But I was also hoping he would give me some tips on the media, because he's got that quiet, reserved personality—[*laughter*]—and I was figuring I'd stay out of trouble if Tony gave me some advice on that.

It's good to see Number 14 on the South Lawn. Every year, I try to take a lap; nobody lets me do it. [*Laughter*] But I am still holding out hope that, at some point, I'm going to be able to get behind the wheel.

A few years ago, Jimmie Johnson showed up and showed me how to start one of these cars up, explained how everything worked. It was impressive. But what was even more impressive is he got in and got out dressed like he is now, and he did not rip his suit—[*laughter*]—which took some skill.

And I do want to acknowledge Jimmie because, even though his 5-year streak is over, I think we can all acknowledge he is one of the alltime greats. And I know he is itching to take the title back. So congratulations, Jimmie, on everything that you've done.

But this was Tony's year. And "Smoke" gave us one of the most dramatic finishes that we have ever seen. After barely making The Chase, Tony took off, winning an amazing four races in the postseason. And then came the final race in Miami, a must-win. Tony went all out. Twice he came from back of the pack, passing 118 cars, sometimes 3 wide. Tony said it felt like he passed half the State of Florida. But in the end, he hung on to take the checkered flag and win the championship with a tiebreaker.

And Tony himself acknowledged he didn't see it coming; nobody saw it coming. We've all heard about athletes who say they're going to do what it takes to win it all. But back in August, with the season winding down, Tony predicted he wouldn't be able to pull it off. In fact, he said that if he did end up winning the championship—this is a quote—"I'll declare I'm a total bumbling idiot." [*Laughter*] Here's your chance, Tony. [*Laughter*]

But I think Tony's hero, the great A.J. Foyt, put it best when he said the reason Tony won was because he drove the best race of his life, period. And he did it with the rest of these drivers on his tail.

I want to make special mention out of this outstanding group of Carl Edwards; he's also a member of my fitness council. Carl battled Tony down to the wire and came about as close as you can get without actually winning. And congratulations on all your unbelievable success as well. And I think everybody who saw Carl after the race, it was a great lesson in how you handle disappointment with grace and with class, and he's a outstanding representative for all of NASCAR.

And that's typical. Underneath the helmets, behind all the trash talking—and I notice it seems to be picking up quite a bit lately—these are some outstanding men. And it's true about the whole NASCAR organization. One thing especially I want to thank NASCAR for is the support that you guys have provided to our men and women in uniform. You give Active Duty soldiers, wounded warriors, veterans all a VIP experience at races. And Michelle had a chance to see that firsthand at the Homestead race last year. You look out for military families. You look out for Gold Star families. You make regular visits to Walter Reed to raise spirits there. And for you guys to give that much back to folks who have given so much to us as a country and help protect us and keep us safe is remarkable. So I want to thank all of you for what you do on behalf of our troops.

So congratulations again to Tony and his entire team. Thanks to everybody at NASCAR for what you do for our country. Thank you for not tearing up my grass—[*laughter*]—and best of luck in the season to come.

Thank you very much, everybody. Give them a big round of applause.

NOTE: The President spoke at 4:50 p.m. on the South Lawn at the White House. In his remarks, he referred to Brian France, chairman and chief executive officer, Mike Helton, president, and Anthony J. Foyt, Jr., former driver, NASCAR.

Remarks at Lorain County Community College in Elyria, Ohio
April 18, 2012

Thank you. Everybody, please have a seat. Well, hello, Ohio! It is good to be back here at Lorain. Last time I was here, I had an outstanding burger at Smitty's. [*Laughter*] I got my own Presidential football helmet at Riddell. I got a feeling I may need it between now and November. [*Laughter*]

It's also great to be back at Lorain Community College. I want to thank Bronson for that wonderful introduction. He is—I had a chance to meet Bronson and Andrea and Dave and Duane. And I just want Bronson's wife to know

that he gives her all the credit in the world. So, just in case you're watching—[*laughter*]—Gladys, he loves you to death.

I also want to thank your president, Dr. Roy Church, your mayor, Holly Brinda, for hosting us here today. I want to recognize my outstanding Secretary of Labor, Hilda Solis, in the house. And I want to thank all of you for coming.

I came here for a simple reason. In an economy that's still recovering from the worst financial crisis and the worst economic crisis of our lifetimes, the work that's going on here could not be more important. I meet business owners all the time who want to hire in the United States, but they can't always find the workers with the right skills. You've got growing industries in science and technology that have twice as many openings as we have workers who can do the job. That makes no sense: openings at a time when there's still a lot of Americans, including some on this stage, who are looking for work. So we've got to do a better job training more people for the skills that businesses are looking for.

When I met with manufacturers a while back, they said it's starting to make economic sense to bring jobs back to Ohio, to bring jobs back to Michigan, to bring jobs back to Illinois and Iowa and Indiana, because even if the labor costs are lower there, the workers are better here. And when you factor in transportation costs, a lot of times it makes sense to insource now, but that's only going to be true if we can make sure that we've got workers who have higher skills and can manage fancier machinery than folks in other places. And all that starts with community colleges like this one.

So I just had a chance to listen to four of your classmates and hear a little bit about how they got here, where they're headed. I talked to Duane, who was laid off at a packaging company, is now learning how to operate high-tech machinery. Andrea lost her job as an HR analyst, but she's now getting certified in the fast-growing field of electronic medical records. David, who in addition to being a truck driver for 23 years was also a marine, so we know he can do the job, he's here to retrain for a higher paying job. And you just heard from Bronson, who was laid off 2 years ago, and you heard what he said. He was in a dead end in his life, and this program, along with his wife—[laughter]—gave him an opportunity. So he's going to be learning hands-on machining over the next few weeks, after having already done some of the bookwork.

Now, I have to tell you, when I meet these folks, these folks inspire me, because a lot of them have gone through tough times. Andrea is still dealing with the aftermath of the flood that damaged her home. All of them have supportive family members. And it's hard being out of work. It's hard especially when you're midcareer, when you're having to change jobs. And the resilience they show and the determination they show, that's what America's about. That's our defining spirit. We don't quit.

And so the question now is, how do we make sure that all of America is expressing that spirit through making sure that everybody is getting a fair shot? Because that's going to be a major debate that we have in this country not just for the next few months, but for the next few years. Should we settle for an economy where a few people do really well and then a growing number are struggling to get by? Or do we build an economy where people like Duane and Andrea and David and Bronson, they've got a chance to get ahead, where there are ladders of opportunity, where everybody gets a fair shot and everybody does their fair share and everybody is playing by the same set of rules?

And this is not just another run-of-the-mill political debate. There's always chatter in Washington. Folks argue about whether the Sun rises in the east and whether it sets in the west—[laughter]—whether the sky is blue. There's always going to be arguments in Washington. But this one is different, because we're talking about the central challenge of our time. Right now we have two competing visions of our future, and the choice could not be clearer. And let me say, those folks on the other side, I am sure they are patriots, I'm sure they're sincere in terms of what they say. But their theory, I believe, is wrong.

See, I've never believed that government can or should try to solve every problem we've got. I believe that the free market is the greatest force for economic progress in human history. I agree that everybody has personal responsibility for their own lives. Everybody has got to work hard. Nothing is ever handed to us. But I also agree with our first Republican President—a guy named Abraham Lincoln—who said that, through government, we should do together what we cannot do as well on our own.

There's some things we don't do well on our own. That's why we've got a strong military to keep us safe. That's why we have fire departments, because we never know when we might have a fire in our house. That's why we've got public schools to educate our children. That's how we laid down railroads and highways and supported research and technology that's saved lives and helped create entire industries. That's why we have programs like Medicare and Social Security and unemployment insurance, because any one of us—I don't care how lucky you are, how rich you are, how blessed you are—you never know, you could face a layoff or a crippling illness or a run of bad luck or a tragedy.

Folks in Ohio know about that. Nothing is given. And that's why we're helping more community colleges like this one to become community career centers, so folks who are looking for a new job or a better paying job can learn the skills that businesses need right now. And that's good for all of us.

These—investing in a community college, just like investing in a new road or a new highway or broadband lines that go into rural communities, these investments are not part of some grand scheme to redistribute wealth. They've been made by Democrats and Republicans for generations because they benefit all of us. That's what leads to strong, durable economic growth. That's how America became an economic superpower. That's how we built the transcontinental railroad. That's why we've got the best universities and colleges in the world. That's why we have cutting-edge research that takes place here, and that then gets translated into new jobs and new businesses, because somebody did the groundwork. We created a foundation for those of us to prosper.

Somebody gave me an education. I wasn't born with a silver spoon in my mouth. Michelle wasn't. But somebody gave us a chance, just like these folks up here are looking for a chance.

When you take classes at a community college like this one and you learn the skills that you need to get a job right away, that does not just benefit you, it benefits the company that ends up hiring and profiting from your skills. It makes the entire region stronger economically. It makes this country stronger economically.

In this country, prosperity does not trickle down, prosperity grows from the bottom up. And it grows from a strong middle class out. That's how we grow this economy. And that's why I'm always confused when we keep having the same argument with folks who don't seem to remember how America was built. They keep telling us, well, if we just weaken regulations that keep our air and water clean and protect our consumers, if we just cut everybody's taxes and convert these investments in community colleges and research and health care into tax cuts, especially for the wealthy, that somehow the economy is going to get stronger and Ohio and the rest of the country will prosper. That's the theory.

Ohio, we tested this theory. Take a look at what happened in Ohio between 2000 and 2008. It's not like we didn't try it. And instead of faster job growth, we had the slowest job growth in half a century. Instead of broad-based prosperity, the typical American family saw their incomes fall by about 6 percent. Outsourcing, rampant, phony financial profits all over the place, and instead of strengthening our economy, our entire financial system almost collapsed. We spent the last 3½ years cleaning up after that mess. So their theory did not work out so well. Maybe they haven't been paying attention, but it didn't work out so well.

And instead of kind of stepping back and saying to themselves, well, maybe this didn't work so maybe we should try something different, they decided to double down. Instead of moderating their views even slightly, you now have Republicans in Washington and the ones running for President proposing budgets that shower the wealthiest Americans with even more tax cuts. Folks like me don't need them, weren't looking for them. And when you give somebody like me a tax cut, there are only two ways of paying for it: Either it adds to our deficit, meaning it's not paid for, or you end up—which is what they've proposed—gutting investments in education and medical research and clean energy and job training programs like this one.

If these cuts are spread out evenly, then 10 million college students, including some of you, would see your financial aid cut by an average of more than a thousand dollars each. Thousands of medical research grants for things like Alzheimer's and cancer and AIDS would be eliminated. Our investment in clean energy that are helping to break our dependence on foreign oil and are creating jobs here in Ohio would be cut by nearly a fifth. By the time you retire, Medicare would've been turned into a voucher system that likely would not cover the doctors or the care that you need; that would have to come out of your pocket. Job training programs like this one would be forced to cut back. Thousands of Americans would lose out on critical employment and training services. That's the truth.

When you ask the Republicans, "Well, what do you say about that?" they say, "Well, no, no, Obama is making this up, because we didn't specify which cuts we'd make." Well, the reason they didn't specify it is because they know folks wouldn't like it. [*Laughter*] But if you've got to cut a certain amount of money—and they've already said they're not going to cut defense spending, and they're going with their tax cuts—then you've got to go to all the other stuff that's left over, or else you're going to add to the deficit. That's just math. That's not theorizing on my part.

They'll tell you, "Well, we've got to do this because the deficit is so bad." The deficit is bad. We've got to deal with the deficit in a serious way, and that means all of us are going to have to make tough choices. But it's one thing to deal with the deficit in a way that is fair and asks everybody to do their fair share and dealing with the deficit as an excuse to do what you wanted to do anyway.

Their argument might fly if it weren't for the fact that they're also proposing to spend $4.6 trillion on lower tax rates on top of the 1 trillion they would spend on tax cuts for people making more than $250,000 a year or more. That's their priority. They want to give me more of a tax break. Now, I just paid taxes, so I'm—it's

not like I love paying taxes. [*Laughter*] But I can afford it. I don't need another tax break.

Right now companies can't find enough qualified workers for the jobs they need to fill. So programs like this one are training hundreds of thousands of workers with the skills that companies are looking for. And it's working. And it's going to help America grow. I've seen it. Here in Lorain County, 90 percent of people who graduate from this program have a job 3 months later—90 percent. That's a big deal. Why would we want to cut this program to give folks like me a tax cut that we don't need and that the country can't afford?

What's the better way to make our economy stronger: give more tax breaks to every millionaire and billionaire in the country, or make investments in education and research and health care and job training, make investments in Bronson and Duane and Andrea and David and put folks back to work? This is just common sense.

Understand, this is not a redistribution argument. This is not about taking from rich people to give to poor people. This is about us together making investments in our country so everybody has got a fair shot. And that will make all of us better off.

Now, on Monday, nearly every Republican in the Senate voted to block what's called the Buffett rule. Think about this. The Buffet rule says if you make a million dollars or more—I'm not saying you got a million dollars—let's say you're a small-businessperson, you saved, you worked, and after 10, 20, 30 years of working you finally saved up your little nest egg—that's not what I'm talking about. I'm saying you make a million dollars a year. And we said you should at least pay the same percentage in income tax as middle class families do, as a teacher or a bus driver. And by doing that, that helps us afford being to say to the 98 percent of families who make $250,000 a year or less, your taxes won't go up.

This was an idea that was supported by a strong majority of the American people, including nearly half of Republicans. The majority of millionaires supported it. And Senate Republicans didn't listen. They refused to even let it come up for a vote, refused to ask the wealthiest among us to do their fair share. Meanwhile, Republicans in the House just signaled their willingness to gut programs like this one that make a real difference in people's lives: thousands of middle class families or folks who are trying to get into the middle class.

And my point is the middle class has sacrificed enough over the last few decades. They're having enough trouble. And as I travel around the country, people aren't just concerned about their immediate circumstances. They're also concerned about our future. They're thinking how do we make sure that America stays ahead? How do we make sure that if somebody is willing to work hard, they can get ahead in this country?

And people understand Government is not all the answer, and if they see taxpayer money wasted, that makes them angry. They know the Government has got to be lean and mean and do smart things. But they also understand we can't stop investing in the things that are going to create real, lasting growth in this country. And we certainly can't do it just as an excuse to give me another tax cut. That's not who we are as a country. We're better than that.

Everybody here, we're here because somebody, somewhere, felt a sense of larger responsibility, not just to themselves, to their family, first of all, but then also to their community, also to their country. Maybe they served like Dave. Maybe they worked in a local charity. They understood—like my grandparents understood, like my mother understood, like Michelle's parents understood—that we do what we do not just for ourselves, but also for this larger project we call America. And now it's our turn to be responsible. Now it's our turn to make sure the next generation has the same opportunities that we do.

And I know we can do it. And the reason I know is because of the folks I had a chance to meet. It's because of you. You're working hard. You've haven't given up. You've gone through some struggles, but you're resilient. Ohio is a great example of the core strength and decency of the American people. You believe in our future. You believe in this country.

And if we work together in common purpose, I guarantee you we will make this an American century just like the 20th century was the American century.

Thank you. God bless you. God bless America.

NOTE: The President spoke at 2:36 p.m. In his remarks, he referred to Bronson Harwood, Andrea Ashley, David Palmer, and Duane Sutton, students, Lorain County Community College; and his mother-in-law Marian Robinson.

Remarks at an Obama Victory Fund 2012 Fundraiser in Dearborn, Michigan
April 18, 2012

The President. Hello, Michigan! How is everybody doing? It is good to be in Dearborn. It is good to be back in the Motor City!

A couple of people I want to acknowledge here. First of all, give it up for Jeff. Thank you so much for that outstanding introduction. Thank you, Jeff.

We've got Dearborn mayor—John O'Reilly is here; Wayne County Sheriff Benny Napoleon; Wayne County Commissioner Gary Woronchak. Although he is not here, he has done an outstanding job representing this district for longer than just about anybody—John Dingell. And John's wonderful wife Debbie is here. I want to thank Keith William Brown and Gary Bolda from the UAW. And I'm grateful that Cynthia and Edsel Ford II are here. Thank you so much.

And I'm glad all of you are here. This is a fantastic museum. I've got to bring the girls back here. I've got to check it out.

Audience member. [*Inaudible*]

The President. Look at this guy. I didn't mean to start a dialogue here. [*Laughter*]

Well, listen, I am here not just because I need your help, although I do. I'm here because the country needs your help. I see a lot of folks here who worked tirelessly on my 2008 campaign and, let's face it, you did not do it because you thought this was going to be a cakewalk. When you decide to support a candidate named Barack Hussein Obama, you know the odds are not necessarily in your favor. You didn't need a poll to tell you that wasn't going to be a sure thing. [*Laughter*]

But the point is you didn't get involved in this campaign just because of me. You did it because you were making a commitment to each other. You had a shared vision for America. It wasn't a vision where just a few were doing well and everybody else is left to fend for themselves and play by their own rules. It was a big, bold, generous vision of America where everybody who works hard has a chance to get ahead, not just those at the very top.

That's the vision we shared. That's the commitment you made to each other. And we knew it wasn't going to be easy. We knew the changes that we believed in wouldn't necessarily come quickly. But we understood that if we were determined, that we could overcome any obstacle; that we could meet any challenge. And in just 3 years, because of what you did in 2008, we've begun to see what change looks like. We've begun to see it.

Think about it. Change is the decision we made to rescue the American auto industry from collapse, when some politicians said let Detroit go bankrupt. There were 1 million jobs on the line, and fate—the fate of communities all across the Midwest was on the line, and we weren't going to let it happen. I placed my bets on American workers. Today, GM is back on top as the number-one automaker in the world. Chrysler is growing faster than any other car company. Ford is investing billions in plants and factories all across America, bringing thousands of jobs home—200,000 new jobs over the last 2½ years. The American auto industry is back. And that happened because of you. That happened because of you.

There are folks like Jeff all across the country and all across Michigan, all across Ohio and Indiana, and all across the Midwest. Because you had confidence in America's capacity to change, they were able to show just what they can do.

Change is the decision we made to stop waiting for Congress to do something about our oil addiction and finally raise fuel efficiency standards on cars. With the agreement of the auto industry, by the next—by the middle of the next decade, we will be driving American-made cars, better than ever, that get 55 miles to a gallon. That saves the typical family over $8,000 at the pump; helps the environment. That's what change is. That happened because of you.

Change is the first bill I signed into law.

Audience member. Lilly Ledbetter!

The President. Lilly Ledbetter, a law that says women deserve an equal day's pay for an equal day's work. Our daughters should have the same opportunities as our sons.

Change is the fight we won to stop handing out over $60 billion in taxpayer giveaways to banks who are managing the student loans—give that money directly to the students. And now you've got millions of students all across America who are benefiting with higher student loans, help—more help. That happened because of you. This young man right here mentioned it when I saw him behind stage.

Change is health care reform that we passed after a century of trying. Because of your commitment, here in the United States of America, nobody has to go broke because they get sick. Already 2.5 million young people have health insurance that didn't have it before, because this law lets them stay on their parent's plan. Millions of seniors, now paying less for their prescription drugs. It means Americans can no longer be denied or dropped by their insurance companies when they need care the most. And it means every American will be able to get health care, regardless of who you are, how much money you make. It doesn't matter if you've got a preexisting condition, you will be able to get coverage. That's what change is.

Change is the fact that for the first time in history, you don't have to hide who you love in order to serve the country you love, because we ended "don't ask, don't tell."

Change is the promise we made in 2008: For the first time in 9 years, there are no Americans fighting in Iraq. We have refocused our efforts on the terrorists who actually attacked us on 9/11. Al Qaida is weaker than it's ever been. Thanks to our amazing troops, Usama bin Laden no longer walks the face of this Earth. We have begun to transition out of Afghanistan. That's what change is.

None of this change would have happened if it weren't for you. And now we've got more work to do. We've got a lot more work to do. There's still too many Americans here in Michigan and all across the country that are out there looking for work. There's still too many Americans who have a tough time paying the bills or making the mortgage. We're still recovering from the worst economic crisis of our generation.

But the good news is, is that over the past 2 years, businesses have added over 4 million new jobs. Our manufacturers are creating jobs for the first time since the 1990s. Now we've got to keep it going. And the last thing we can afford to do is to go back to the very same policies that got us into this mess in the first place. That's part of what this election is all about.

You know we—that's what these other folks who are running for this office want to do. They make no secret about it. They want to roll back Wall Street reforms, so suddenly Wall Street is playing by its own rules again. They want to roll back health insurance reform; go back to the days when insurance companies could jack up your rates or deny you coverage without any reason. They want to spend trillions of dollars more on tax breaks for our wealthiest citizens, even if it means adding to the deficit, even if it means gutting student loan programs and education programs and clean energy, and making Medicare more expensive for seniors.

Their philosophy is, is that we're better off if a few are doing well at the top and everybody else is fending for themselves. And they're wrong. I have no doubt they love this country, but they're wrong about this.

In the United States of America, we have always been greater together than we are on our own. We're better off when we stick to that notion that if you work hard in this country—no matter where you come from, no matter what

you look like, no matter what your religious faith, if you work hard—if you believe in this country, you can do well enough to raise a family, own a home, send your kids to college, put a little away for retirement.

That idea—that's what's at stake. That's the choice in this election. This is not just another political debate. There's always going to be debating in Washington. I mean, they'll argue about anything. [*Laughter*] But this—this is real. This is a make-or-break moment for the middle class in this country and all those who are fighting to get into the middle class. Are we going to create those rungs on the ladder to opportunity, so that everybody has a shot?

We can go back to an economy that's built on outsourcing and bad debt and phony financial profits. That's what we saw before 2008. Or we can fight for an economy that's built to last, built on American manufacturing and American energy and skills for American workers, and the values that made this country great: hard work, fair play, shared responsibility.

You look at these amazing planes in this museum and cars in this museum, and you're reminded, part of what made us great is making stuff. And I want the next generation of manufacturing taking root not in Asia, not in Europe. I want it to happen right here in Detroit, right here in Michigan, in Pittsburgh, in Cleveland, in the United States of America. I don't want us to just be known for buying stuff from other countries: I want to invent and build and sell American products all around the world.

I want us to stop rewarding businesses that ship jobs overseas. I want to reward companies that are investing here, creating jobs in America. I want us to make sure that we've got the best schools in the world. And that means reform. It means properly funding our schools. It means looking out for the man or woman at the front of the classroom.

A good teacher can increase the lifetime earnings of a classroom by over $250,000. A great teacher can offer an escape from poverty for a child who thinks maybe they're bound by their circumstances but suddenly, that teacher helps them to raise their sights. So I don't want us defending the status quo, but I also don't want a bunch of folks in Washington bashing teachers. I want to give schools the resources they need to keep good teachers, to reward the best ones. I want to give schools the flexibility they need to teach with creativity and passion and stop teaching to the test and train teachers properly.

And those who can't make it, we understand they shouldn't be in the classroom. We want accountability, but we also want to make sure that we understand how important teaching is. Nothing is more important.

And when kids do graduate from high school, we've got to make college affordable. Americans already owe more tuition debt than credit card debt. That's one of the reasons Congress has to stop interest rates on student loans, which are scheduled to go up in July, if we don't do anything.

Audience members. Boo!

The President. Yes, that's not good. And then, colleges and universities have to do their part by keeping tuition from going up. And State legislatures have to step up and make sure that they're providing the support to higher education that's necessary. Higher education cannot be a luxury. Whether it's a 2-year program at a community college or a 4-year program or a postdoctorate program, it is not a luxury. It is an economic imperative. Every American family should be able to afford getting the skills they need to compete in this global economy. And that's what we're fighting for.

We need to be supporting scientists and researchers who are trying to make the next breakthrough in clean energy or biotech. I want clean energy to happen here in the United States. I want advanced batteries made here in the United States. I want electric cars made here in the United States. I want solar and wind power made here in the United States. We've been subsidizing oil companies with taxpayer giveaways for about 100 years now. It's time for us to double down on clean energy that has never been more promising.

And we need to build in America—roads, bridges, ports, airports, broadband lines— that's what this museum reminds us of, is what

it means to build. It's time we stop taking the money that we're spending at war—use half of it to pay down our debt, use the other half to do some nation building here at home. And when we talk about the deficit——

Audience member. We love you, Obama!

The President. I love you, baby. [*Laughter*] Thank you.

Audience member. We love you more! [*Laughter*]

The President. When we talk about the deficit, it's a real problem. It is something that we're going to have to address. We can't leave a bunch of unpaid bills for our kids and our grandkids. And so that means that we've got to make some tough decisions, get rid of programs that don't work to make that we can invest in programs that do. But we've also got to make sure that the tax system reflects everybody doing their fair share.

The Republicans in the Senate just rejected the Buffett rule; wouldn't let it come up for a vote. Simple idea that if you make more than a million dollars a year, you shouldn't pay a lower tax rate than your secretary. Now, the reason that's important is because if we abided by that rule, then we could say to folks what I have repeatedly said, which is, the 98 percent of Americans who make $250,000 a year or less, your taxes shouldn't go up. And that idea is not—it's not class warfare to say that somebody like me can afford to do a little bit more. It's just basic math.

If I get a tax break that I don't need and the country can't afford, then one of two things has to happen. Either it adds to the deficit because it's not paid for; that's what they've been doing. Or somebody else is going to have to shoulder the burden: a student who has to pay a higher rate on their student loan, a senior who has got to pay higher for their Medicare, a veteran who doesn't get the help that they need to deal with the aftermath of having fought for our freedoms, a family that's trying to get by. That's not right. That's not who we are.

And when I hear politicians talk about values, I agree: This campaign is, and should be, about values. Hard work, that's a value. Looking out for one another, that's a value. The idea that I am my brother's keeper, I am my sister's keeper, that's a value. That I have a commitment to something larger than myself.

Each of us is here—every one of us is here because somebody, somewhere——

Audience member. Made a sacrifice.

The President. ——made a sacrifice, was looking out for us. It starts with the family, but it extends beyond the family. You think about what—this museum was built because the Ford family and others said, you know what, this is important to the community that gave us so much. Our grandparents, our great-grandparents, immigrants, slaves—think about all the sacrifices they made not just to think about themselves, but to think about the country. Think about all our men and women in uniform making sacrifices because they believe that we are all in this together.

The American story has never been about just what we do on our own. We don't win the race for new jobs and new businesses and security and growth if it's just a you're-on-your-own economics. It doesn't work. And it's never worked. And we've tried it. We just finished trying it. Between 2000 and 2008, we tried what they're selling. It didn't work. Most sluggish job growth that we've seen, outsourcing, manufacturing deteriorating, and then it culminates in the worst crisis since the Great Depression. Why would we think that it would work now? [*Laughter*] Why would we want to go back to that?

We've all got a stake in each other's success. When an outstanding teacher is attracted to the profession, given the pay that she deserves, and then that teacher goes on to teach some talented kid, maybe of modest means, and that kid goes on to become the next Steve Jobs, we all benefit. If we provide faster Internet service and then it goes to a rural community and suddenly some small business has the chance to market to the world and is hiring more workers, that benefits everybody's bottom line. That benefits the entire economy. We build a new bridge that saves the shipping company time and money. You think about the research that led to the invention of the Internet and how much wealth has been created, but that came

out of our collective efforts. We all invested in that. That's how we grow.

This is not a Democratic idea or a Republican idea. This is an American idea. It was Teddy Roosevelt, a Republican, who called for a progressive income tax and Dwight Eisenhower, a Republican, who built the Interstate Highway System so all these outstanding cars from Michigan could have somewhere to go. It was a Republican in Congress that helped FDR give millions of returning heroes, including my grandfather, a chance to go to college under the GI bill. This is an American idea.

And you know that spirit still exists today. Maybe not in Washington, but out in the country, you go on Main Streets and town halls and VFW halls, you talk to the members of our Armed Forces, you go to our places of worship.

Our politics is divided, but most Americans, they still understand we're in this together. No matter where we come from, no matter what we look like, no matter what our last names are, we rise or fall as one Nation and as one people. And that's what's at stake right now. That's what this election is all about.

So let me just say, Michigan, I know these last 3½ years, 4 years, have been tough. I know there are times where we think change isn't happening as fast as we'd like. But—and I know that there's a tendency sometimes—and look at Washington and just say, you know what, it's easier being cynical. It's easier just—it's tempting to just say, maybe this isn't possible. But remember what we said during the last campaign. I said this was going to be hard. Change takes time. Sometimes it takes more than a year, it takes more than a single term. It takes more than a single President.

As I was walking in here, you've got a display of Abraham Lincoln, and then you've got the bus that Rosa Parks sat down in. It takes ordinary citizens to bring about change, who are committed to keep fighting and keep pushing and keep inching this country closer to our highest ideals.

That's why I need all of you. I need all of you. I said in 2008, I am not a perfect man, I will never be a perfect President. But what I promised you was that I would always tell you what I thought, I would always tell you where I stood, and I would wake up every single day fighting for you as hard as I know how. And I have kept that promise. I have kept that promise.

And if you're willing to keep pushing with me, to keep working on behalf of our higher ideals, there is nothing that will stop us. And we will finish what we started in 2008.

God bless you. God bless America.

NOTE: The President spoke at 5:34 p.m. at the Henry Ford Museum. In his remarks, he referred to Jeff Klayo, Local 1700 member, Keith W. Brown, Local 245 president, and Gary Bolda, Henry Ford Museum chairman, United Auto Workers; and Edsel B. Ford II, member of the Board of Trustees, Henry Ford Museum, and his wife Cynthia.

Statement on the Death of Dick Clark
April 18, 2012

Michelle and I are saddened to hear about the passing of Dick Clark. With "American Bandstand," he introduced decades' worth of viewers to the music of our times. He reshaped the television landscape forever as a creative and innovative producer. And of course, for 40 years, we welcomed him into our homes to ring in the new year. But more important than his groundbreaking achievements was the way he made us feel: as young and vibrant and optimistic as he was. As we say a final so long to Dick Clark, America's oldest teenager, our thoughts and prayers are with his family and friends, which number far more than he knew.

Remarks at an Obama Victory Fund 2012 Fundraiser in Bingham Farms, Michigan
April 18, 2012

Well, first of all, Denise and Jim, thank you for opening up this incredible home. They have been great friends. When I first met Denise, the fact that I was a Blackhawks fan—[*laughter*]—was incidental. But she right away lent us her support, and getting to know her has been just an incredible pleasure. And Jim, and your sons, thank you so much for helping to make this evening happen.

I want to thank Gerry Acker, I want to thank Barry Goodman for their great work. You've got an outstanding former Governor here, Jim Blanchard.

I want to thank Jalen Rose for—even though he did not pick the Bulls to win the Eastern Conference—[*laughter*]—I'm not sure I agree with his analysis, but he is a wonderful commentator and obviously is a great basketball player. And to have Willie Horton here is a great honor as well.

In smaller settings like this, what I love to do is not give a long speech, but just rather say a few things at the top and then just open it up for questions and comments. I just came from the Henry Ford Museum. What a spectacular museum. I had never been there before; it exceeded all expectation. I wanted to just go in there and roam around a bit, but they keep me on a schedule around here. [*Laughter*]

But part of what was remarkable is it captured so much of America's history, what makes this country exceptional, what makes us special. You had the ingenuity and the drive and the imagination of the Wright Brothers and Fords and all the inventors who helped to trigger this incredible economic superpower and to build this remarkable middle class that Michigan represents. And then it also had a range of displays about the long battle for freedom, to make sure that everybody was included in that American Dream. So I actually had the chance to sit in Rosa Parks's bus. I just sat there for a moment and pondered the courage and tenacity that is part of our very recent history, but is also a part of that long line of folks—sometimes nameless, oftentimes didn't make the history books—but who constantly insisted on their dignity, their stake in the American Dream.

Now, we've gone through 3½ very tough years, worst economic crisis since the Great Depression. When I came into office we were losing 750,000 jobs per month. Michigan had obviously been going through tough times for a decade or more, with outsourcing and plants closing and layoffs. The auto industry was buckling, on its knees, on the verge of not just conventional bankruptcy, but potentially a liquidation bankruptcy. And I think a lot of people weren't sure whether we were going to dip into a great depression.

And 3½ years later, we can look and say to ourselves that, in part because of the support of some of the folks in this room who helped not just propel me into office, but helped to give America a vision of what we could be, GM is now the number-one automaker in the world again, it's experience record profits, Chrysler is the faster growing auto company, is making investments in plants and equipment, and we've seen 200,000 auto workers hired back, back on the job. And that's just part of this steady process of economic healing that's led to 4 million jobs created in the last 2 years, businesses starting to invest again and the financial system stabilized and banks starting to lend again to not just businesses, but small—just like this and small businesses and consumers.

And so as we see the economy growing, it gives people some cautious sense of optimism. As I was at that museum, I reminded myself that when I ran for office in 2008, the goal wasn't just to get back to where we were in 2006 or 2005. We had gone through a decade in which job growth was sluggish and incomes and wages flatlined. The goal was to get back to that spirit that was reflected in that museum, where we are building again, and we are creating products that are the envy of the world and creating that sense of opportunity for people, where if they work hard they know that they can support a family, buy a home, send their kids to college, retire with dignity and respect, that sense that everybody, regardless of what they look like or where they come from, what

their last name is, that everybody has a fair shot and everybody is doing their fair share and everybody is playing by the same set of rules.

And we had a nice big event over at the museum. I told people, sometimes when you look at Washington you may not feel as if that spirit, that can-do spirit—that spirit of not just innovation and possibility, but also that spirit that everybody can take part in it—you might not feel that that's very evident in Washington. Because it just seems like folks in Washington are much more interested in ideological arguments and bickering.

But I tell you, as you travel around the country that spirit is still there. It's here in Michigan. It's in Ohio, where I just was. You see it in our men and women in uniform as they're defending our country around the world. You see it in our places of worship. That sense that we rise and fall together and that it makes sense for us to constantly be thinking not just about ourselves, but about others; not just about today, but about the next generation. That spirit is still out there. It's still out there.

And we captured that spirit in 2008. We've got to recapture it in 2012. And the stakes could not be higher, because the contrast between the two parties is going to be probably more pronounced in 2012 than it was in 2008. The other side has a very different vision. Yes, they're patriots; they care about the country. But their basic mission seems to be one in which a few folks are doing well at the top and everybody else is struggling to get by, but that's okay, that somehow that is a formula for growth.

We've got a different idea: that we believe in the free market, we believe in individual initiative, but we also believe in giving back and investing in schools so that everybody gets the education they need; investing in science and technology so that the great inventions that the marketplace takes advantage of are constantly happening here in the United States in our labs and our universities. We believe in creating the infrastructure that serves as a platform for economic growth. We believe in making sure that the vulnerable among us and our seniors have a basic safety net, because we never know

487

which one of us might at some point be stricken with an illness or suffer a layoff. And most of us in this room have somebody in their background who knows what it's like to fall on hard times and understand how important those safety nets are in order to get people back on their feet so they can succeed.

So we've got a lot at stake in this election. The good news is that I think we've got the truth on our side, and I think the values that we're going to be talking about over the next several months are not Democratic values or Republican values, they're American values. And I think people are going to be, once again, choosing a better future and our·best traditions. That's what we're going to be fighting

for. I'm glad you guys are on the team as I go out there and do that.

So thank you very much.

NOTE: The President spoke at 7:37 p.m. at the residence of Denise Ilitch and James Scalici. In his remarks, he referred to Sam Lites and Paul Scalici, sons of Ms. Ilitch and Mr. Scalici; Gerald H. Acker and Barry J. Goodman, senior partners, Goodman Acker, P.C.; Jalen A. Rose, former guard, University of Michigan men's basketball team; and Willie W. Horton, former left fielder and designated hitter, Major League Baseball's Detroit Tigers. Audio was not available for verification of the content of these remarks.

Remarks Honoring the 2011 NCAA Football Champion University of Alabama Crimson Tide
April 19, 2012

The President. Well, good afternoon, everybody. Have a seat. Have a seat. It is my pleasure to welcome the Alabama Crimson Tide back to the White House and congratulate them on winning their 14th national championship, their second in 3 years. Roll Tide.

I told Coach he's making this a habit. [*Laughter*] I'm also happy to see the best team in DC high school football in the house. Congratulations to the other Crimson Tide—Dunbar High School—on their city championship. Might have some recruits out here, Coach.

Now, we've got a lot of proud 'Bama fans here today. It is good to see Mayor Maddox of Tuscaloosa again. Mayor Bell of Birmingham is here, as well as Members of Congress, including several Alabama alums. I also want to recognize Alabama Director of Athletics Mal Moore and Interim University President Dr. Judy Bonner for their support of the best team in college football.

Now obviously, this is a team that knows something about adversity. It was 1 year ago next week that an F4 tornado carved a path right through the town of Tuscaloosa. I traveled down there 2 days later to see the devastation with the mayor and the Governor. And

I've got to tell you, I'd never seen anything like it.

And I remember something the mayor said that day. He said that when something like that happens, folks tend to forget all their petty differences. Things like politics, religion, race, when we're confronted with a tragedy of such magnitude, all that just fades away. We're reminded that all we have is each other. And if you need proof of that, just look how the Auburn community stepped up during that time of need.

The storm took the lives of 248 people, including 6 students. And it touched this team personally. Long snapper Carson Tinker's girlfriend lost her life in the storm. And a few weeks later, there was fresh grief for Aaron Douglas, an offensive lineman who passed away. So this became a team in every sense of the word. They remembered Aaron and those lost in the storm not just with their hearts, but on their helmets, with a houndstooth ribbon and the number 77.

And then they took to the field, they steamrolled opponent after opponent, they racked up an 8–0 record going into the rivalry game against LSU. Folks called it the "game of the century." The top two teams in the country, number 1 versus number 2, primetime national television. And it delivered. It was a defensive slugfest that wouldn't be settled until overtime. In the end, one team had to lose. And 'Bama gave up its only loss of the season.

Fortunately, they got a rematch. In the national championship game, the Tide not only beat the Tigers; they shut them out, the first in BCS championship game history. LSU earned just 5 first downs, crossed the midfield line only once, and were held to less than 100 yards.

And it wasn't just the defense that played lights out. Kicker Jeremy Shelley nailed a bowl-record five field goals. Heisman Trophy finalist Trent Richardson rushed for the only touchdown of the game in his usual fashion, like a boulder rolling downhill. Offensive lineman Barrett Jones summed it up pretty well when he said, "We felt like we were capable of dominating, and we did that."

So this team didn't just shatter records. I hear the championship trophy also took a bit of a spill—[*laughter*]—earlier this week.

So this was a fun season to watch, but it was also a deeply meaningful season for the Tide. And what's even more impressive is that these young men showed that success isn't about the individual, it's about the ability to work as a team. That's why senior linebacker Courtney Upshaw handed his defensive MVP award to his teammates, saying the whole defense deserved it.

That's why Coach became the first to win three BCS national championships, but he gave credit to his players' hard work and persistence. They played as a team because of what they had endured as a team. And so each victory was about more than getting to the title game; it was about the lives of these players and coaches that they'd carried with them and what they meant to each other.

Each of them found different ways to honor these memories. Coach Saban started a program called "13 for 30" that aims to rebuild 13 houses for families who lost theirs in the torna-

do. Strength coach Scott Cochran pitched in with players almost every Saturday helping families recover and rebuild. Courtney Upshaw raised $20,000 in relief funds for the impacted families. And Barrett Jones lugged a chainsaw around Tuscaloosa to remove tornado debris from homes and yards. So the Tide showed us what it takes to win as a team, but they also showed what it means to be a part of a larger community: to look out for one another, to help. And that makes them pretty special.

So I just want to say to all these outstanding men and all the staff, Coach and the entire Crimson Tide community, congratulations on an extraordinary season, and best of luck next season. Who knows, I may see you again.

Thank you.

[*At this point, University of Alabama Football Head Coach Nicholas L. Saban made brief remarks and presented the President with a game jersey.*]

The President. Now, that's a nice-looking jersey right there. [*Laughter*]

Mr. Saban. From the 2011 national champs. We would also like to give you a helmet over here. We certainly don't want to be responsible for any head injuries that the President might have. [*Laughter*]

The President. I was mentioning yesterday, I'm probably going to need a helmet between now and November. What do you think, Shelby? [*Laughter*] Huh? All right.

Mr. Saban. Well, good. Well, we really——

The President. Thank you so much.

Mr. Saban. We really appreciate the opportunity, and thank you so much for your time to honor our team. Thank you very much.

The President. Coach, I appreciate you.

NOTE: The President spoke at 2:27 p.m. on the South Lawn at the White House. In his remarks, he referred to Gov. Robert J. Bentley of Alabama; and Sen. Richard C. Shelby.

Statement on Holocaust Remembrance Day
April 19, 2012

On this Holocaust Remembrance Day, I join people of all faiths across the United States, in Israel, and around the world in paying tribute to all who suffered in the Shoah, a horrific crime without parallel in human history. We honor the memory of 6 million innocent men, women, and children who were sent to their deaths simply because of their Jewish faith. We stand in awe of those who fought back, in the ghettos and in the camps, against overwhelming odds. And in the year of the 100th anniversary of the birth of Raoul Wallenberg, we are humbled by the rescuers who refused to be bystanders to evil.

On this day and all days, we must do more than remember. We must resolve that "never again" is more than an empty slogan. As individuals, we must guard against indifference in our hearts and recognize ourselves in our fellow human beings. As societies, we must stand against ignorance and anti-Semitism, including those who try to deny the Holocaust. As nations, we must do everything we can to prevent and end atrocities in our time. This is the work I will advance when I join survivors and their families at the United States Holocaust Memorial Museum on Monday. This must be the work of us all as nations and peoples who cherish the dignity of every human being.

Remarks at the Wounded Warrior Project Soldier Ride Opening Ceremony
April 20, 2012

The President. Thank you so much. Well, good afternoon, everybody. Welcome to the White House. Thank you, Ric, for that introduction. More importantly, thank you for your service and for everything you do for our veterans and our wounded warriors.

And we've also got here today Senator Tom Udall and Congresswoman Corrine Brown with us. Thank you all for coming.

This is the fourth time we've had the Soldier Ride here in the South Lawn. And this year, you've already covered some ground: 34 miles over the last few days and another 24-mile ride tomorrow. So our job is to give you a break, maybe even a little extra fuel, and get you back on the road.

The reason I ask this group to stop by every year is because this is one of the most inspiring events that we have here at the White House. As Commander in Chief, I can't take sides, but I know the Army is represented here.

Audience members. Hooah!

The President. Navy's represented here.

Audience members. Navy!

The President. [*Laughter*] We've got some Air Force.

Audience members. Hooah!

The President. We've got some Marines in the house.

Audience members. Hooah!

The President. And we've got some Coast Guard.

Audience member. Hooah! [*Laughter*]

The President. And there's some folks here who don't wear a uniform, but who work just as hard and sacrifice just as much alongside you, and that's our outstanding military families in the house.

So this is a pretty diverse group, and I know you're all doing this ride for different reasons. Some of you may be athletes looking to get the competitive juices flowing again. Maybe some of you are trying to see how far you can push yourselves. Some of you are doing it for the camaraderie and the bond that comes when you work hard alongside people who know what you're going through. Maybe you're doing it to honor a loved one or a buddy. But all of you are here because you believe in living your lives to the fullest. You know that each of us has a responsibility to seize the opportunities we've been blessed with. You ride because you can, and you ride for those who can't. That's what this is all about.

And that's what inspired Chris Carney to hop on a bike and head across country on the first Soldier Ride 8 years ago to raise money and awareness for returning troops and wounded warriors. Chris came up with the idea working as a bartender in Long Island. And I have to say, it's better than most of the ideas that come out of bars. [*Laughter*] At least that's been my experience. [*Laughter*]

Today there are Soldier Rides all across the country. They serve as a reminder that all of us can do our part to serve the men and women who serve us. And I'm glad to see you're all decked out in the stars and stripes, because I want anybody who sees this ride to go by to know that they're in the presence of heroes.

Some of these guys I've had a chance to meet before. I first met Hospital Corpsman 3d Class Max Rohn when he was in the hospital recovering from a grenade attack in Fallujah that cost him his leg. And Max, I think, will admit he was in pretty rough shape at the time. But the next time I saw him, at a dinner that we hosted here recently for Iraq war veterans, Max had gained 80 pounds—or 40 pounds and was training for the upcoming Wounded Warrior Games. I offered him two dinners after he finished the first one kind of quick, and he readily accepted. [*Laughter*] After he finished the first dessert kind of quick, I offered him another one. He accepted that one too. I am positive it is the most anybody has ever eaten in the White House. [*Laughter*] And now he's ready to ride.

We've also got Captain Leslie Smith here today. Leslie lost her leg and her eyesight after serving in Bosnia, and this is her first time back on a bike. She's going to be riding in tandem alongside Meghan Speicher-Harris, who works with the Wounded Warrior Project. And it's good to have them both here.

And then there are the Schei brothers: Erik and Deven. When Erik enlisted in the Army, Deven made a promise that if anything bad ev-

er happened, he would finish what his brother started. And during his second tour in Iraq, Erik was shot in the head by a sniper. So Deven enlisted. And then 2 years ago, Deven was injured in Afghanistan. And now the two brothers ride a specially made tandem bike, with Deven leading the way. They're taking on this latest challenge just like they did every other one, together.

So these men and women, they're an inspiration. And it's also inspiring to meet the families behind them: the moms and dads and the brothers and sisters, the sons and daughters who are standing by their side through good times and bad. You're heroes too. And I know Michelle and I look forward to any time we get to spend with military families.

So I want to encourage everybody who sees these riders going by this weekend to go out and cheer and say thanks and salute and show your support. And as Commander in Chief, I promise to do everything I can to make sure that you guys get the care and the benefits that you deserve, that you've earned. All of you have served your country. That's why now it's time for the country to serve you. It's what you deserve, and here in America we take care of our own.

So to all the riders here today, we are proud of you. Your country is proud of you. And now I'm going to see how you guys do taking some laps around the South Lawn. But you got to do it on the horn. I don't want anybody cheating. [*Laughter*]

All right. On your marks, get set——

[*At this point, the President sounded a horn.*]

The President. Hey!

NOTE: The President spoke at 4:38 p.m. on the South Lawn at the White House. In his remarks, he referred to Secretary of Veterans Affairs Eric K. Shinseki; and Chris Carney, founder, Wounded Warrior Project Soldier Ride.

The President's Weekly Address
April 21, 2012

Hi. This week, I got the chance to sit down with some impressive students at Lorain County Community College in Ohio. One of them was a woman named Andrea Ashley. Two years ago, Andrea lost her job as an HR analyst. Today, she's getting certified in the fast-growing field of electronic medical records. Before enrolling at Lorain, Andrea told me she was looking everywhere trying to find a new job. But without a degree, she said that nobody would hire her.

Andrea's story isn't unique. I've met so many Americans who are out there pounding the pavement looking for work only to discover that they need new skills. And I've met a lot of employers who are looking for workers but can't find ones with the skills they're looking for.

So we should be doing everything we can to put higher education within reach for every American, because at a time when the unemployment rate for Americans with at least a college degree is about half the national average, it's never been more important. But here's the thing: It's also never been more expensive. Students who take out loans to pay for college graduate owing an average of $25,000. For the first time, Americans owe more debt on their student loans than they do on their credit cards. And for many working families, the idea of owing that much money means that higher education is simply out of reach for their children.

Now, in America, higher education cannot be a luxury. It's an economic imperative that every family must be able to afford. That's why next week I'll be visiting colleges across the country, talking to students about how we can make higher education more affordable and what's at stake right now if Congress doesn't do something about it. You see, if Congress doesn't act, on July 1 interest rates on some student loans will double. Nearly 7½ million students will end up owing more on their loan payments. That would be a tremendous blow. And it's completely preventable.

This issue didn't come out of nowhere. For some time now, I've been calling on Congress to take steps to make higher education more affordable: to prevent these interest rates from doubling, to extend the tuition tax credit that has saved middle class families millions of dollars, and to double the number of work-study jobs over the next 5 years.

Instead, over the past few years, Republicans in Congress have voted against new ways to make college more affordable for middle class families, and voted for huge new tax cuts for millionaires and billionaires, tax cuts that would have to be paid for by cutting things like education and job-training programs that give students new opportunities to work and succeed.

We cannot just cut our way to prosperity. Making it harder for our young people to afford higher education and earn their degrees is nothing more than cutting our own future off at the knees. Congress needs to keep interest rates on student loans from doubling, and they need to do it now.

This is a question of values. We cannot let America become a country where a shrinking number of people do really well, while a growing number of people struggle to get by. We've got to build an economy where everyone gets a fair shot, everyone does their fair share, and everyone plays by the same set of rules. That's how the middle class gets stronger. That's an economy that's built to last. And I'm not only going to take that case to college campuses next week; I'm going to take it to every part of the country this year. Thanks, and have a great weekend.

NOTE: The address was recorded at approximately 3:55 p.m. on April 20 in the East Room at the White House for broadcast on April 21. The transcript was made available by the Office of the Press Secretary on April 20, but was embargoed for release until 6 a.m. on April 21.

Letter to Congressional Leaders Reporting on the Executive Order Blocking the Property and Suspending Entry Into the United States of Certain Persons With Respect to Grave Human Rights Abuses by the Governments of Iran and Syria Via Information Technology
April 22, 2012

Dear Mr. Speaker: (Dear Mr. President:)

Pursuant to the International Emergency Economic Powers Act (50 U.S.C. 1701 *et seq.*) (IEEPA), I hereby report that I have issued an Executive Order (the "order") that takes additional steps with respect to the national emergencies declared in Executive Order 12957 of March 15, 1995, and relied on for additional steps in subsequent Executive Orders, and in Executive Order 13338 of May 11, 2004, as modified in scope and relied on for additional steps in subsequent Executive Orders.

I have determined that the commission of serious human rights abuses against the people of Iran and Syria by their governments, facilitated by computer and network disruption, monitoring, and tracking by those governments, and abetted by entities in Iran and Syria that are complicit in those governments' malign use of technology for those purposes, threaten the national security and foreign policy of the United States. Consistent with the vital importance of providing technology that enables the Iranian and Syrian people to freely communicate with each other and the outside world, as well as the preservation, to the extent possible, of global telecommunications supply chains for essential products and services to enable the free flow of information, the measures in the order are designed primarily to address the need to prevent entities located in whole or in part in Iran and Syria from facilitating or committing serious human rights abuses. To address this situation, the order takes additional steps with respect to the national emergencies described above.

The order blocks the property and interests in property, and suspends entry into the United States, of persons listed in the Annex to the order, as well as persons determined by the Secretary of the Treasury, in consultation with or at the recommendation of the Secretary of State:

- to have operated, or to have directed the operation of, information and communications technology that facilitates computer or network disruption, monitoring, or tracking that could assist in or enable grave rights abuses by or on behalf of the Government of Iran or the Government of Syria;

- to have sold, leased, or otherwise provided, directly or indirectly, goods, services, or technology to Iran or Syria likely to be used to facilitate computer or network disruption, monitoring, or tracking that could assist in or enable grave human rights abuses by or on behalf of the Government of Iran or the Government of Syria;

- to have materially assisted, sponsored, or provided financial, material, or technological support for, or goods or services to or in support of, the activities described above or any person whose property and interests in property are blocked pursuant to the order; or

- to be owned or controlled by, or to have acted or purported to act for or on behalf of, directly or indirectly, any person whose property and interests in property are blocked pursuant to the order.

I have delegated to the Secretary of the Treasury the authority, in consultation with the Secretary of State, to take such actions, including the promulgation of rules and regulations, and to employ all powers granted to the President by IEEPA, as may be necessary to carry out the purposes of the order.

All agencies of the United States Government are directed to take all appropriate measures within their authority to carry out the provisions of the order.

I am enclosing a copy of the Executive Order I have issued.

Sincerely,

BARACK OBAMA

NOTE: This letter was released by the Office of the Press Secretary on April 23. Identical letters were sent to John A. Boehner, Speaker of the House of Representatives, and Joseph R. Biden, Jr., President of the Senate. The Executive order is listed in Appendix D at the end of this volume.

Remarks at the United States Holocaust Memorial Museum
April 23, 2012

Good morning, everyone. It is a great honor to be with you here today. Of course, it is a truly humbling moment to be introduced by Elie Wiesel. Along with Sara Bloomfield, the outstanding director here, we just spent some time among the exhibits, and this is now the second visit I've had here. My daughters have come here. It is a searing occasion whenever you visit. And as we walked, I was taken back to the visit that Elie mentioned, the time that we traveled together to Buchenwald.

And I recall how he showed me the barbed-wire fences and the guard towers. And we walked the rows where the barracks once stood, where so many left this Earth, including Elie's father Shlomo. We stopped at an old photo: men and women lying in their wooden bunks, barely more than skeletons. And if you look closely, you can see a 16-year old boy, looking right at the camera, right into your eyes. You can see Elie.

And at the end of our visit that day, Elie spoke of his father. "I thought one day I will come back and speak to him," he said, "of times in which memory has become a sacred duty of all people of good will." Elie, you've devoted your life to upholding that sacred duty. You've challenged us all, as individuals, and as nations, to do the same, with the power of your example, the eloquence of your words, as you did again just now. And so to you and Marion, we are extraordinarily grateful.

To Sara, to Tom Bernstein, to Josh Bolten, members of the United States Holocaust Memorial Council, and everyone who sustains this living memorial, thank you for welcoming us here today. To the Members of Congress, members of the diplomatic corps, including Ambassador Michael Oren of Israel, we are glad to be with you.

And most of all, we are honored to be in the presence of men and women whose lives are a testament to the endurance and the strength of the human spirit, the inspiring survivors. It is a privilege to be with you on a very personal level. As I've told some of you before, I grew up hearing stories about my great uncle, a soldier in the 89th Infantry Division who was stunned and shaken by what he saw when he helped to liberate Ordruf, part of Buchenwald. And I'll never forget what I saw at Buchenwald, where so many perished with the words of *Sh'ma Yis'ra'eil* on their lips.

I've stood with survivors in the old Warsaw ghettos, where a monument honors heroes who said we will not go quietly, we will stand up, we will fight back. And I've walked those sacred grounds at Yad Vashem, with its lesson for all nations: The Shoah cannot be denied.

During my visit to Yad Vashem, I was given a gift, inscribed with those words from the Book of Joel: "Has the like of this happened in your days or in the days of your fathers? Tell your children about it, and let your children tell theirs, and their children the next generation." That's why we're here. Not simply to remember, but to speak.

I say this as a President, and I say it as a father. We must tell our children about a crime unique in human history. The one and only Holocaust—6 million innocent people, men, women, children, babies—sent to their deaths just for being different, just for being Jewish. We tell them, our children, about the millions of Poles and Catholics and Roma and gay people and so many others who also must never be forgotten. Let us tell our children not only how they died, but also how they lived: as fathers and mothers and sons and daughters and brothers and sisters who loved and hoped and dreamed just like us.

We must tell our children about how this evil was allowed to happen, because so many people succumbed to their darkest instincts and because so many others stood silent. Let us also tell our children about the Righteous Among the Nations. Among them was Jan Karski, a young Polish Catholic, who witnessed Jews being put on cattle cars, who saw the killings, and who told the truth, all the way to President Roosevelt himself.

Jan Karski passed away more than a decade ago. But today I'm proud to announce that this spring I will honor him with America's highest civilian honor, the Presidential Medal of Freedom.

We must tell our children. But more than that, we must teach them. Because remembrance without resolve is a hollow gesture. Awareness without action changes nothing. In this sense, "never again" is a challenge to us all to pause and to look within.

For the Holocaust may have reached its barbaric climax at Treblinka and Auschwitz and Belzec, but it started in the hearts of ordinary men and women. And we have seen it again, madness that can sweep through peoples, sweep through nations, embed itself. The killings in Cambodia, the killings in Rwanda, the killings in Bosnia, the killings in Darfur, they shock our conscience, but they are the awful extreme of a spectrum of ignorance and intolerance that we see every day, the bigotry that says another person is less than my equal, less than human. These are the seeds of hate that we cannot let take root in our heart.

"Never again" is a challenge to reject hatred in all of its forms, including anti-Semitism, which has no place in a civilized world. And today, just steps from where he gave his life protecting this place, we honor the memory of Officer Stephen Tyrone Johns, whose family joins us today.

"Never again" is a challenge to defend the fundamental right of free people and free nations to exist in peace and security, and that in-

cludes the State of Israel. And on my visit to the old Warsaw Ghetto, a woman looked me in the eye, and she wanted to make sure America stood with Israel. She said, "It's the only Jewish state we have." And I made her a promise in that solemn place. I said I will always be there for Israel.

So when efforts are made to equate Zionism to racism, we reject them. When international fora single out Israel with unfair resolutions, we vote against them. When attempts are made to delegitimize the State of Israel, we oppose them. When faced with a regime that threatens global security and denies the Holocaust and threatens to destroy Israel, the United States will do everything in our power to prevent Iran from getting a nuclear weapon.

"Never again" is a challenge to societies. We're joined today by communities who've made it your mission to prevent mass atrocities in our time. This museum's Committee of Conscience, NGOs, faith groups, college students, you've harnessed the tools of the digital age: online maps and satellites and a video and social media campaign seen by millions. You understand that change comes from the bottom up, from the grassroots. You understand—to quote the Task Force convened by this museum—"preventing genocide is an achievable goal." It is an achievable goal. It is one that does not start from the top, it starts from the bottom up.

It's remarkable—as we walked through this exhibit, Elie and I were talking as we looked at the unhappy record of the State Department and so many officials here in the United States during those years. And he asked, "What would you do?" But what you all understand is you don't just count on officials, you don't just count on governments, you count on people and mobilizing their consciences.

And finally, "never again" is a challenge to nations. It's a bitter truth: Too often, the world has failed to prevent the killing of innocents on a massive scale. And we are haunted by the atrocities that we did not stop and the lives we did not save.

Three years ago today, I joined many of you for a ceremony of remembrance at the U.S.

Capitol. And I said that we had to do "everything we can to prevent and end atrocities." And so I want to report back to some of you today to let you know that as President I've done my utmost to back up those words with deeds. Last year, in the first-ever Presidential directive on this challenge, I made it clear that "preventing mass atrocities and genocide is a core national security interest and a core moral responsibility of the United States of America."

That does not mean that we intervene militarily every time there's an injustice in the world. We cannot and should not. It does mean we possess many tools—diplomatic and political, and economic and financial, and intelligence and law enforcement and our moral suasion—and using these tools over the past 3 years, I believe—I know—that we have saved countless lives.

When the referendum in South Sudan was in doubt, it threatened to reignite a conflict that had killed millions. But with determined diplomacy, including by some people in this room, South Sudan became the world's newest nation. And our diplomacy continues, because in Darfur, in Abyei, in Southern Kordofan, and the Blue Nile, the killing of innocents must come to an end. The Presidents of Sudan and South Sudan must have the courage to negotiate, because the people of Sudan and South Sudan deserve peace. That is work that we have done, and it has saved lives.

When the incumbent in Cote d'Ivoire lost an election, but refused to give it up—give up power, it threatened to unleash untold ethnic and religious killings. But with regional and international diplomacy, and U.N. peacekeepers who stood their ground and protected civilians, the former leader is now in The Hague, and Cote d'Ivoire is governed by its rightful leader, and lives were saved.

When the Libyan people demanded their rights and Muammar Qadhafi's forces bore down on Benghazi, a city of 700,000, and threatened to hunt down its people like rats, we forged with allies and partners a coalition that stopped his troops in their tracks. And today, the Libyan people are forging their own

future, and the world can take pride in the innocent lives that we saved.

And when the Lord's Resistance Army led by Joseph Kony continued its atrocities in Central Africa, I ordered a small number of American advisers to help Uganda and its neighbors pursue the LRA. And when I made that announcement, I directed my National Security Council to review our progress after 150 days. We have done so, and today I can announce that our advisers will continue their efforts to bring this madman to justice and to save lives. It is part of our regional strategy to end the scourge that is the LRA and help realize a future where no African child is stolen from their family and no girl is raped and no boy is turned into a child soldier.

We've stepped up our efforts in other ways. We're doing more to protect women and girls from the horror of wartime sexual violence. With the arrest of fugitives like Ratko Mladic, charged with ethnic cleansing in Bosnia, the world sent a message to war criminals everywhere: We will not relent in bringing you to justice. Be on notice. And for the first time, we explicitly barred entry into the United States of those responsible for war crimes and crimes against humanity.

Now we're doing something more. We're making sure that the United States Government has the structures, the mechanisms to better prevent and respond to mass atrocities. So I created the first-ever White House position dedicated to this task. It's why I created a new Atrocities Prevention Board, to bring together senior officials from across our Government to focus on this critical mission. This is not an afterthought. This is not a sidelight in our foreign policy. The board will convene for the first time today, at the White House. And I'm pleased that one of its first acts will be to meet with some of your organizations, citizens, and activists who are partners in this work, who have been carrying this torch.

Going forward, we'll strengthen our tools across the board, and we'll create new ones. The intelligence community will prepare, for example, the first-ever National Intelligence Estimate on the risk of mass atrocities and genocide. We're going to institutionalize the focus on this issue. Across Government, alert channels will ensure that information about unfolding crises and dissenting opinions quickly reach decisionmakers, including me.

Our Treasury Department will work to more quickly deploy its financial tools to block the flow of money to abusive regimes. Our military will take additional steps to incorporate the prevention of atrocities into its doctrine and its planning. And the State Department will increase its ability to surge our diplomats and experts in a crisis. USAID will invite people and high-tech companies to help create new technologies to quickly expose violations of human rights. And we'll work with other nations so the burden is better shared, because this is a global responsibility.

In short, we need to be doing everything we can to prevent and respond to these kinds of atrocities, because national sovereignty is never a license to slaughter your people.

We recognize that, even as we do all we can, we cannot control every event. And when innocents suffer, it tears at our conscience. Elie alluded to what we feel as we see the Syrian people subjected to unspeakable violence, simply for demanding their universal rights. We have to do everything we can. And as we do, we have to remember that despite all the tanks and all the snipers, all the torture and brutality unleashed against them, the Syrian people still brave the streets. They still demand to be heard. They still seek their dignity. The Syrian people have not given up, which is why we cannot give up.

And so with allies and partners, we will keep increasing the pressure, with a diplomatic effort to further isolate Asad and his regime, so that those who stick with Asad know that they are making a losing bet. We'll keep increasing sanctions to cut off the regime from the money it needs to survive. We'll sustain a legal effort to document atrocities so killers face justice and a humanitarian effort to get relief and medicine to the Syrian people. And we'll keep working with the Friends of Syria to increase support for the Syrian opposition as it grows stronger.

Indeed, today we're taking another step. I've signed an Executive order that authorizes new sanctions against the Syrian Government and Iran and those that abet them for using technologies to monitor and track and target citizens for violence. These technologies should not empower—these technologies should be in place to empower citizens, not to repress them. And it's one more step that we can take toward the day that we know will come—the end of the Asad regime that has brutalized the Syrian people—and allow the Syrian people to chart their own destiny.

Even with all the efforts I've described today, even with everything that, hopefully, we have learned, even with the incredible power of museums like this one, even with everything that we do to try to teach our children about our own responsibilities, we know that our work will never be done. There will be conflicts that are not easily resolved. There will be senseless deaths that aren't prevented. There will be stories of pain and hardship that test our hopes and try our conscience. And in such moments, it can be hard to imagine a more just world.

It can be tempting to throw up our hands and resign ourselves to man's endless capacity for cruelty. It's tempting sometimes to believe that there is nothing we can do. And all of us have those doubts. All of us have those moments, perhaps especially those who work most ardently in these fields.

So, in the end, I come back to something Elie said that day we visited Buchenwald together. Reflecting on all that he had endured, he said: "We had the right to give up. We had the right to give up on humanity, to give up on culture, to give up on education, to give up on the possibility of living one's life with dignity, in a world that has no place for dignity." They had that right. Imagine what they went through. They had the right to give up. Nobody would begrudge them that. Who would question someone giving up in such circumstances?

But, Elie said, "We rejected that possibility, and we said, no, we must continue believing in a future." To stare into the abyss, to face the darkness and insist there is a future, to not give up, to say yes to life, to believe in the possibility of justice.

To Elie and to the survivors who are here today, thank you for not giving up. You show us the way. You show us the way. If you cannot give up, if you can believe, then we can believe. If you can continue to strive and speak, then we can speak and strive for a future where there's a place for dignity for every human being. That has been the cause of your lives. It must be the work of our Nation and of all nations.

So God bless you, and God bless the United States of America. Thank you very much. Thank you.

NOTE: The President spoke at 10 a.m. In his remarks, he referred to Nobel Prize winner, author, and Holocaust survivor Elie Wiesel and his wife Marion; Tom A. Bernstein, chairman, and Joshua R. Bolten, vice chairman, U.S. Holocaust Memorial Council; President Umar Hassan Ahmad al-Bashir of Sudan; President Salva Kiir Mayardit of South Sudan; former President Laurent Gbagbo and President Alassane Dramane Ouattara of Cote d'Ivoire; former Bosnian Serb army commander Ratko Mladic; and President Bashar al-Asad of Syria. He also referred to his great-uncle Charles Payne.

Remarks on Presenting the Commander in Chief's Trophy to the United States Air Force Academy Falcons
April 23, 2012

Well, good afternoon. Now, I heard last year, with this trophy on the line, Jon Davis said, "You don't get to meet the President every day." Today, you do. [*Laughter*]

Congratulations to the Fighting Falcons on winning their second straight and record 18th Commander in Chief Trophy last season. [*Applause*] There we go. I'm happy to meet you too. [*Laughter*] And welcome, everybody, to the White House.

Now, this trophy, which by the way is the biggest trophy—I give a lot of these out—[*laughter*]—this is the monster of all trophies here. This trophy has logged a lot of miles just jetting back and forth between Cadet Field House and the White House the past couple of years. And I'm looking forward to seeing it again when I visit Colorado Springs next month.

We are honored to be joined today by the Superintendent of the Air Force Academy, Lieutenant General Michael Gould, as well as Representative Mike McIntyre is in the house. To all the friends of Air Force football, congratulations on holding onto the title of gridiron supremacy in the Armed Forces.

Now, it was no easy feat for this team to make it here today. These guys faced a brutal

schedule, but they never backed down. As Coach Calhoun said, "This group had a warrior spirit in them." And they brought that fight to every game this season. They shut out New Mexico on the road. They brought home the Ram-Falcon Trophy with a decisive victory over Colorado State, a game that won them a bowl bid for a record-setting fifth straight year. They battled down to the wire against Toledo in an exciting Military Bowl, boldly going for the win with a 2-point conversion and falling just short. But I like that in you. [*Laughter*]

Even when they were dogged by injuries, this team pulled together when it mattered most. These guys toughed it out—toughed out a narrow overtime victory against Navy, with Alex Means blocking an extra point in overtime and Tim Jefferson barreling the last yard into the end zone with the game on the line. They stormed from behind to beat Army and secure this trophy with a third quarter that included two field goals, two touchdowns, a 2-point conversion, and two takeaways.

So this team had to fight hard this whole season. But the work paid off. The senior class standing behind me distinguished itself as one of the most talented in school history. Brady Amack and Jon Davis put together the sixth-ranking passing defense in the country. Asher Clark led the Nation's third-best rushing attack. Tim Jefferson will graduate as the winningest Air Force quarterback of all time and the first quarterback in service academy history to lead his team to four consecutive bowl games.

So these young men have a lot to be proud of. And if the past couple of seasons are any indication of what is to come, Coach Calhoun, we expect the Air Force will be back here this time next year. [*Laughter*] Now, I know Army and Navy will have something to say about that. [*Laughter*] But I know that the next year will take these young men from the Cadet Field House to pilot training, to air bases around the world, in defense of our country. Ultimately, these seniors understand that shutouts and bowl games and trophies are not nearly as important as the solemn obligation, the solemn oath that they will take in just a few weeks as the newest officers in the world's finest Air Force.

So, gentlemen, I have no higher privilege and no greater honor than serving as your Commander in Chief, and I look forward to joining you for that important ceremony.

Today we honor the success that these outstanding young men had on the playing field. And we look forward to their continuing excellence on behalf of the Nation. And, cadets, as you look to trade the proud uniform of your team for the proud uniform of your country, I want you to know that this country will stand by you and do everything possible to help you succeed and come home safe.

So God bless all those who serve, and God bless the United States of America, and God bless Air Force.

Thank you so much.

NOTE: The President spoke at 2:42 p.m. in the East Room at the White House. In his remarks, he referred to Jon Davis, defensive back, Alex Means, linebacker, Timothy Jefferson, Jr., quarterback, Brady Amack, linebacker, and Asher Clark, running back, U.S. Air Force Academy football team.

Statement on the Presidential Election in Timor-Leste
April 23, 2012

I congratulate Taur Matan Ruak on his victory in Timor-Leste's Presidential election and the people of Timor-Leste for successfully participating in a peaceful, free, and transparent election. I also recognize with deep appreciation President Jose Ramos Horta for his close friendship with the United States during his Presidency and look forward to continuing that productive relationship with Taur Matan Ruak.

Our partnership with Timor-Leste is fundamental and enduring. It is based on shared values of democracy, freedom, and human rights. The United States remains steadfast in its support of Timor-Leste's efforts to strengthen democratic institutions and consolidate peace and security in the country.

NOTE: The statement referred to President-elect Jose Maria "Taur Matan Ruak" Vasconcelos of Timor-Leste.

Statement on Department of Defense Initiatives To Combat Sexual Assault in the Military
April 23, 2012

I applaud the initiatives that Secretary of Defense Leon E. Panetta and General Martin Dempsey, the Chairman of the Joint Chiefs of

Staff, have announced to further combat sexual assault in the military. The men and women of the United States military deserve an environment that is free from the threat of sexual assault and in which allegations of sexual assault are thoroughly investigated, offenders are held appropriately accountable, and victims are given the care and support they need. Elevating these cases to a higher level of command review is a very important step. I believe that sexual assault has no place in our military. I thank Secretary Panetta and Chairman Dempsey and look forward to seeing continued progress on this important issue.

Remarks Honoring the National and State Teachers of the Year
April 24, 2012

The President. Wow, thank you, everybody. Thank you. Everybody, please have a seat. Have a seat. Welcome to the White House.

Before we get started, I want to recognize one of our greatest advocates for education and for teachers, our Secretary of Education, Arne Duncan, is here. Give him a big round of applause.

Now let's face it, a lot of important people visit the White House. [*Laughter*] But to young people in classrooms around the country, nobody is more important than the men and women that we honor here today, the State and National Teachers of the Year.

These are the kind of teachers who change lives forever. I wouldn't be here today if it were not for teachers like these who challenged me and pushed me and put up with me and inspired me and set me straight when they had to. And I think everybody here can say the exact same thing.

Teachers matter. That's why I often tell young people: If you want a guarantee that you're making a difference every single day, become a teacher. A teacher is the key to a child reaching their potential. And if we need more proof——

[*At this point, a baby chattered.*]

The President. Yes, it's true. [*Laughter*] Yes. She agrees. [*Laughter*]

And if we need more proof that teachers matter, all we've got to do is look around this room. I'm honored to be here with teachers like Gay Barnes, from Madison, Alabama, one of the four finalists for this award. There's Angela Wilson, who teaches children of military families at Vicenza Middle School in Italy. Not a bad place to hang out. [*Laughter*] There is Alvin Aureliano Davis, who teaches music in Florida.

And there is our 2012 National Teacher of the Year, Rebecca Mieliwocki, from Burbank, California. So give Rebecca a big round of applause. And this is Rebecca's crew right here—[*laughter*]—who are very proud. Auntie and cousins and—[*laughter*].

Rebecca Mieliwocki. My boss.

The President. Oh, boss. [*Laughter*] Even more important. [*Laughter*]

Now, you might say that teaching is in Rebecca's DNA, because both her parents taught in public schools. She saw how hard they worked, how much time and energy they devoted to their jobs, how much they gave to their students.

But when she was 18, of course, the last thing she wanted to be was a teacher. What teenager wants to do what their parents are doing? [*Laughter*] So, in college, she really rebelled and went to law school. [*Laughter*]

Now, she then tried a few different careers after that. After studying to become a lawyer, she went into publishing and floral design and event planning. But ultimately, she found herself drawn back to the classroom, and her students are so lucky that she did.

She's got high expectations for her seventh graders and for herself, but she also knows that school can be fun. And that fits a personality that she describes as "a 12-year-old goofball dying to get out." [*Laughter*] And I have to say, she was a little goofy when I met her. [*Laughter*] She was back there teasing me and asking Arne about our basketball games and stuff. [*Laughter*] You can tell she's just got a wonderful spirit.

And so in addition to everything they learn in her English class, Rebecca's students have had a chance to film their own adaptations of an O. Henry short story. They worked with a local writer to develop 5-minute plays, which professional actors then performed. Rebecca has led field trips to the science center, to the aquarium, to Chinatown, even the La Brea tar pits—that's a trip you really don't want to lose track of anybody. [*Laughter*] Only one kid? [*Laughter*] They never showed up that morning—[*laughter*]—I was wondering where they were. [*Laughter*]

Rebecca knows that education also is a responsibility that begins at home. So she hosts family nights to get parents involved. She sends home weekly parent memos so moms and dads know what's going on in school. She maintains a Facebook page for her class, where families can get information and updates 24/7.

And all this extra work makes a huge difference. When kids finish a year in Rebecca's class, they're better readers and writers than when they started. But even more than that, they know how important they are. And they understand how bright their futures can be. And they know that if they work at it, there's no limit to what they can achieve.

So Rebecca is the definition of "above and beyond." And so many teachers around the country are like her. She throws herself into her work for a simple reason: She knows that her students depend on her. And as she puts it, "Life is too short and too difficult to have anything less than the most engaged, enthusiastic teachers in schools." I couldn't agree more. And I know Arne couldn't agree more.

I also want to point something else out. Rebecca said in applying for this award, she said that in some ways it's harder than ever to be an educator. Even in the best of times, teachers are asked to do more with less. And today, with our economy still recovering from the worst recession since the Great Depression, States and communities have to stretch budgets tighter than ever.

So we've got a particular responsibility as elected officials in difficult times, instead of bashing teachers to support them. We should be giving States the resources to keep good teachers on the job and reward the best ones. And we should grant our educators the flexibility to teach with creativity and passion in the classroom and not just teaching to the test. And we should allow schools to replace teachers, who, even with the right resources and support, just aren't helping our kids to learn.

Because we've all got something at stake here. Our parents, our grandparents, they didn't build the world's most prosperous economy and the strongest middle class in the world out of thin air. It started with a world class education system. That was the foundation. And in the long run, no issue will have a bigger impact in our success as a country and the success of our citizens.

So, every day, when teachers like you put in long hours or dig into your own pockets to pay for school supplies or tweak lessons so they're even better than they were last year, you're not just serving your schools or your students, you're also serving your country. And you're helping to preserve the basic promise of America, that no matter who you are, where you come from, what you look like, what your last name is, you can succeed. You can make it if you try, if you put in the effort.

So, on behalf of the American people, thank you all for everything that you do. And congratulations. I'm going to present this spiffy looking award to Rebecca Mieliwocki.

NOTE: The President spoke at 10:11 a.m. in the East Room at the White House. In his remarks, he referred to Anita Schackman, former principal, Luther Burbank Middle School in Burbank, CA; and Bill and Sue Lipschultz, parents of Rebecca Mieliwocki.

Remarks at the University of North Carolina at Chapel Hill in Chapel Hill, North Carolina
April 24, 2012

The President. Thank you! Hello, North Carolina! What's up, Tar Heels?

Now, first of all, I want to thank Dominique for that unbelievable introduction. Wasn't she good? You can tell she will be an outstanding teacher.

Audience member. I love you, President Obama!

The President. I love you back. I do. Love North Carolina. I love North Carolina. I do. Every time I come down to this State, I just love it that much more. I said a while back, the thing about North Carolina is even the folks who don't vote for me are nice to me. [*Laughter*] I can't say that about everyplace. [*Laughter*]

Now, I want to issue a quick spoiler alert: Later today I am getting together with Jimmy Fallon—and the Dave Matthews Band—right here on campus. We're going to tape Jimmy's show for tonight, so I want everybody to tune in, make sure it has high ratings. [*Laughter*] It's a Dave Matthews fan right here.

We've got some wonderful people who are here who are doing a great job for you guys. First of all, your Governor, Bev Perdue, is in the house. Give her a big round of applause. Where's Bev? There she is. We've got your Congressman, Dave Price—Congressman David Price; Congressmen G.K. Butterfield; Congressman Brad Miller; your mayor, Mark Kleinschmidt; chancellor of UNC, Holden Thorp.

It is great to be back on the Lady Tar Heels' home court. This is an arena with some serious hoops history. I know the men's team used to play here back in the day. I just want to remind you right off the bat: I picked UNC to win it all in March Madness. Want to point out. And if Kendall hadn't gotten hurt—[*laughter*]—who knows where we might have been.

I saw McAdoo, by the way, at the airport. He came by and said hello, which I was excited. So I just want you to know I have faith in you guys.

Now, it's always good to begin with some easy applause lines, talk about the Tar Heels. [*Laughter*] But the reason I came to Chapel Hill today is to talk about what most of you do here every single day, and that's study, I assume. [*Laughter*] Higher education is the single most important investment you can make in your future. So I'm proud of all of you for doing what it takes to make that investment: for the long hours in the library—I hope—[*laughter*]—in the lab, in the classroom. This has never been more important.

Whether you're here at a 4-year college or university or you're at a 2-year community college, in today's economy, there's no greater predictor of individual success than a good education. Right now the unemployment rate for Americans with a college degree or more is about half the national average. The incomes of folks with a college degree are twice as high as those who don't have a high school diploma. A higher education is the clearest path into the middle class.

Now, I know that those of you who are about to graduate are wondering about what's in store for your future. Not even 4 years ago, just as the global economy was about to enter into freefall, you were still trying to find your way around campus. And you've spent your years here at a time when the whole world has been trying to recover, but has not yet fully recovered from the worst economic crisis since the Great Depression, the worst economic crisis in most of our lifetimes, and that includes your teachers.

Our businesses have added more than 4 million jobs over the past 2 years, but we all know there's still too many Americans out there looking for work or trying to find a job that pays enough to cover the bills and make the mortgage. We still have too many folks in the middle class that are searching for that security that started slipping away years before the recession hit.

So we've still got a lot of work to do to re-build this economy so that it lasts, so that it's solid, so that it's firm. But what I want you to know is that the degree you earn from UNC will be the best tool you have to achieve that basic American promise, the idea that if you work hard, you can do well enough to raise a family and own a home, send your own kids to college, put a little away for retirement. That American Dream is within your reach.

And there's another part of this dream, which is the idea that each generation is going to know a little bit more opportunity than the last generation. That our kids—I can tell you now as a parent, and I guarantee you, your parents feel this about you—nothing is more im-portant than your kid's success. You want them to do better than you did. You want them to shoot higher, strive more, and succeed beyond your imagination.

So keeping that promise alive is the defining issue of our time. I don't want this to be a country where a shrinking number of Ameri-cans are doing really, really well, but a growing number of people are just struggling to get by. That's not my idea of America. I don't want that future for you. I don't want that future for my daughters. I want this forever to be a coun-try where everybody gets a fair shot and every-body is doing their fair share and everybody is playing by the same set of rules. That's the America I know and love. That's the America within our reach.

I think back to my grandfather. He had a chance to go to college because this country decided every returning veteran of World War II should be able to afford it, should be able to go to college. My mother was able to raise two kids by herself because she was able to get grants and work her way through school. I am only standing here today, Michelle is only who she is today, because of scholarships and stu-dent loans. That gave us a shot at a great edu-cation. We didn't come from families of means, but we knew that if we worked hard we'd have a shot.

This country has always made a commit-ment to put a good education within the reach of all who are willing to work for it. That's what

makes us special. That's what made us an eco-nomic superpower. That's what kept us at the forefront of business and science and technolo-gy and medicine. And that's a commitment we have to reaffirm today in 2012.

Now, everybody will give lip service to this. You'll hear a lot of folks say, yes, education is important, it's important. [*Laughter*] But it re-quires not just words, but deeds. And the fact is, that since most of you were born, tuition and fees at America's colleges have more than doubled. And that forces students like you to take out a lot more loans. There are fewer grants. You rack up more debt. Can I get an "amen"?

Audience members. Amen!

The President. Now, the average student who borrows to pay for college now graduates with about $25,000 in student loan debt. That's the average; some are more. Can I get an "amen" for that?

Audience members. Amen!

The President. Yes, because some folks have more debt than that.

Audience member. Amen! [*Laughter*]

The President. Americans now owe more on their student loans than they do on their credit cards. And living with that kind of debt means that this generation is not getting off to the same start that previous generations, because you're already loaded up with debt. So that means you've got to make pretty tough choices when you are first starting out. You might have to put off buying a house. It might mean that you can't go after that great idea for a startup that you have, because you're still paying off loans. Maybe you've got to wait longer to start a family or save for retirement.

When a big chunk of every paycheck goes to-wards loan debt, that's not just tough on you, that's not just tough for middle class families, it's not just tough on your parents, it's painful for the economy, because that money is not go-ing to help businesses grow. I mean, think about the sooner you can start buying a house, that's good for the housing industry. The sooner you can start up that business, that means you're hiring some folks. That grows the economy.

And this is something Michelle and I know about firsthand. I just wanted everybody here to understand this is not—I didn't just read about this. [*Laughter*] I didn't just get some talking points about this. I didn't just get a policy briefing on this. Michelle and I, we've been in your shoes. Like I said, we didn't come from wealthy families.

So when we graduated from college and law school, we had a mountain of debt. When we married, we got poorer together. [*Laughter*] We added up our assets, and there were no assets. [*Laughter*] And we added up our liabilities, and there were a lot of liabilities, basically in the form of student loans. We paid more in student loans than we paid on our mortgage when we finally did buy a condo. For the first 8 years of our marriage, we were paying more in student loans than what we were paying for our mortgage. So we know what this is about.

And we were lucky to land good jobs with a steady income. But we only finished paying off our student loans—check this out, all right, I'm the President of the United States—we only finished paying off our student loans about 8 years ago. [*Laughter*] That wasn't that long ago. And that wasn't easy, especially because when we had Malia and Sasha, we're supposed to be saving up for their college educations, and we're still paying off our college educations.

So we have to make college more affordable for our young people. That's the bottom line. And like I said, look, not everybody is going to go to a 4-year college or university. You may go to a community college. You may go to a technical school and get into the workforce. And then, it may turn out that after you've had kids and you're 35, you go back to school because you're retraining for something new. But no matter what it is, no matter what field you're in, you're going to have to engage in lifelong learning. That's the nature of the economy today. And we've got to make sure that's affordable.

That's good for the country; it's good for you. At this make-or-break moment for the middle class, we've got to make sure that you're not saddled with debt before you even get started in life. Because I believe college isn't just one of the best investments you can make in your future, it's one of the best investments America can make in our future. This is important for all of us.

We can't price the middle class out of a college education. Not at a time when most new jobs in America will require more than a high school diploma. Whether it's at a 4-year college or a 2-year program, we can't make higher education a luxury. It's an economic imperative. Every American family should be able to afford it.

So that's why I'm here. Now, before I ask for your help, I've got something very specific I'm going to need you to do. But, North Carolina, indulge me. I want to briefly tell you what we've already done to help make college more affordable, because we've done a lot.

Before I took office, we had a student loan system where tens of billions of taxpayer dollars were going to banks, not students. They were processing student loan programs, except the student loans were federally guaranteed so they weren't taking any big risks, but they were still taking billions of dollars out of the system. So we changed it.

Some in Washington fought tooth and nail to protect the status quo, where billions of dollars were going to banks instead of students. And they wanted to protect that. They wanted to keep those dollars flowing to the banks.

One of them said—and I'm going to quote here because it gives you a sense of the attitudes sometimes we're dealing with in Washington—they said it would be "an outrage" if we changed the system so that the money wasn't going through banks and they weren't making billions of dollars of profits off of it. Said it was "an outrage."

And I said, no, the real outrage is letting these banks keep these subsidies without taking any risks while students are working two or three jobs just to get by. That's an outrage. [*Applause*] That's an outrage.

So we kept at it, we kept it at, we won that fight. Today, that money is going where it should be going—should have been going in the first place: It's going directly to students. We're bypassing the middleman. That means we can raise Pell grants to a higher level. More people are eligible. More young people are able to afford college because of what we did. Over 10 years, that's going to be $60 billion that's going to students that wasn't going to students before.

Now, then last fall, I acted to cap student loan payments faster, so that nearly 1.6 million students who make their payments on time will only have to pay 10 percent of their monthly income towards loans once they graduate. Now, this is useful—this is especially helpful for young people who decide, like Dominique, to become teachers, or maybe they go into one of the——

Audience member. Social work.

The President. ——social work or one of the helping professions. And they may not get paid a lot of money, but they've got a lot of debt. And so being able to cap how much per month you're paying as a percentage of your income gives you a little bit more security knowing you can choose that profession.

And then we wanted every student to have access to a simple fact sheet on student loans and financial aid, so you can have all the information you need to make your own choices about how to pay for college. And we set up this new consumer watchdog called the Consumer Financial Protection Bureau, and so they're now putting out this information. We call it "Know Before You Owe." "Know Before You Owe." It's something Michelle and I wish we had had when we were in your shoes because sometimes we got surprised by some of this debt that we were racking up.

So that's what we've done. But it's not enough just to increase student aid. We can't keep subsidizing skyrocketing tuition or we'll run out of money. And colleges and universities, they've got to do their part also to keep college costs down. So I've told Congress to steer Federal aid to those schools that keep tuition affordable, that provide good value, that serve their students well. And we've put colleges on notice: If you can't stop tuition from just going up every single year a lot faster than inflation, then funding you get from taxpayers, at least at the Federal level, will go down, be-cause we need to push colleges to do better and hold them accountable if they don't.

Now, public universities know well, and Governor Perdue knows well: States also have to do their part by making higher education a higher priority in their budgets. I know that Bev is fighting hard to make tuition affordable for North Carolina families. That's a priority for her. But last year, over 40 States cut their higher education spending. And these budget cuts have been among the largest factors in tuition increases at public colleges over the past decade. So we're challenging States to take responsibility. We told them, if you can find new ways to bring down the cost of college and make it easier for students to graduate, then we'll help you do it.

But I want everybody here, as you're thinking about voting, make sure you know where your State representative and your State senator stands when it comes to funding higher education. They've got to be responsible. They've got to be accountable as well to prioritize higher education.

All right. So helping more families, helping more young people afford a higher education, offering incentives for States and colleges and universities to keep their costs down, that's what we've been doing. Now Congress has to do their part.

They need to extend the tuition tax credit that we put in place back when I came into office. It's saving middle class families thousands of dollars. Congress needs to safeguard aid for low income students, like Pell grants, so that today's freshmen and sophomores knows that they'll be able to count on it. That's what Congress has to do. Congress needs to give more young people the chance to earn their way through college by doubling the number of work-study jobs over the next 5 years. That's what Congress needs to do.

And then there's one specific thing—and now this is where you come in—there's one specific thing that Congress needs to do right now to prevent the interest rates on student loans, Federal student loans, from shooting up and shaking you down. So this is where you come in. I want to explain this, so everybody listen carefully.

Five years ago, Congress cut the rate on Federal student loans in half. That was a good thing to do. But on July 1—that's a little over 2 months from now—that rate cut expires. And if Congress does nothing, the interest rates on those loans will double overnight.

So I'm assuming a lot of people here have Federal student loans. The interest rates will double unless Congress acts by July 1. And just to give you some sense of perspective: For each year that Congress doesn't act, the average student with these loans will rack up an additional thousand dollars in debt—an extra thousand dollars. That's basically a tax hike for more than 7 million students across America, more than 160,000 students here in North Carolina alone. Anybody here can afford to pay an extra thousand dollars right now?

Audience members. No! [*Laughter*]

The President. I didn't think so. So stopping this from happening should be a no-brainer. Helping more of our young people afford college, that should be at the forefront of America's agenda. It shouldn't be a Republican or a Democratic issue. This is an American issue.

The Stafford loans we're talking about, they're named after a Republican Senator. The Pell grants that have helped millions of Americans earn a college education, that's named after a Democratic Senator. When Congress cut those rates 5 years ago, 77 Republicans in the House of Representatives voted for it—along with a couple hundred Democrats—[*laughter*]—including the Democrats who are here.

So this shouldn't be a partisan issue. And yet the Republicans who run Congress right now have not yet said whether or not they'll stop your rates from doubling. We're 2 months away. Some have hinted that they'd only do it if we cut things like aid for low income students instead. So the idea would be, well, all right, we'll keep interest rates low if we take away aid from other students who need it. That doesn't make sense.

One Republican Congresswoman said just recently—I'm going to quote this because I

know you guys will think I'm making it up. [*Laughter*]

Audience member. We trust you. [*Laughter*]

The President. No, no, no. The—she said she had "very little tolerance for people who tell me they graduate with debt because there's no reason for that."

Audience members. Boo!

The President. I'm just quoting here. I'm just quoting. She said, students who rack up student loan debt are just sitting on their butts, having opportunity "dumped in your lap."

Audience members. Boo!

The President. I mean, I'm reading it here, so I didn't make this up. Now, can you imagine saying something like that? Those of you who have had to take out student loans, you didn't do it because you're lazy. You didn't do it lightly. You don't like debt. I mean, a lot of you, your parents are helping out, but it's tough on them. They're straining. And so you do it because the cost of college keeps going up and you know this is an investment in your future.

So if these folks in Washington were serious about making college more affordable, they wouldn't have voted for a budget that could cut financial aid for tens of millions of college students by an average of more than a thousand dollars.

They certainly wouldn't let your student loan rates double overnight. So when you ask them, well, why aren't you making this commitment? They say, well, we got to bring down the deficit. Of course, this is the deficit they helped run up over the past decade: didn't pay for two wars, didn't pay for two massive tax cuts. And now this is the reason why you want students to pay more?

They just voted to keep giving billions of dollars in taxpayer subsidies to big oil companies that are raking in record profits. They just voted to let millionaires and billionaires keep paying lower tax rates than middle class workers and their secretaries. They even voted to give an average tax cut of at least $150,000 to folks like me, the wealthiest Americans, a tax cut paid for by cutting things like education and job training programs that give students new opportunities to work and succeed.

Now, that's their priorities. And that doesn't make any sense. Do we want to keep tax cuts for the wealthiest Americans who don't need them and didn't ask for them, or do we want to make sure that they're paying their fair share? Do we want to keep subsidizing big oil, or do we want to make sure we're investing in clean energy? Do we want to jack up interest rates on millions of students, or do we want to keep investing in things that will help us and help them in the long term, things like education and science and a strong military and care for our veterans? We can't do both. We can't have it both ways. We've got to make a choice about what our priorities are.

You know, I've said this before, but I'm just going to keep on repeating it: In America, we admire success. We aspire to it. I want everybody to be rich. I want everybody to work and hustle and start businesses and study your tails off to get there. [*Laughter*] But America is not just about a few people doing well. America is about giving everybody a chance to do well: everybody—not just a few—everybody. That's what built this country. That's what the American Dream is all about.

A lot of us had parents or grandparents who said, maybe I can't go to college, but some day my son, he'll go to college, and I'll be so proud of him. A lot of us had parents or grandparents who said, maybe I can't start my own business, but maybe someday my daughter, she's going to start her own business, she's going to work for herself. A lot of us had parents or grandparents who said, I may be an immigrant, but I believe that this is a country where no matter what you look like and where you come from, no matter what your name is, you can make it if you try.

North Carolina, that's who we are. That's our values. That's what we're about. So no, "set your sights lower"—that's not an education plan. "You're on your own"—that's not an economic plan. We can't just cut our way to prosperity.

Previous generations made the investments necessary for us to succeed, to build a strong middle class, to create the foundation for America's leadership in science and technology and medicine and manufacturing. And now it's our turn. We've got to do the right thing. I want one of you to discover the cure for cancer or the formula for fusion or the next game-changing American industry. And that means we've got to support those efforts.

So, if you agree with me, I need your help. I need you to tell your Member of Congress, we're not going to set our sights lower. We're not going to settle for something less. Now, all of you are lucky, you already have three Congressmen who are on board. So don't—you don't need to call them. [*Laughter*] They're already doing the right thing. But I'm asking everyone else who's watching or following online, call your Member of Congress, e-mail them, write on their Facebook page, tweet them. We've got a hashtag. [*Laughter*] All right. Here's the hashtag for you to tweet them: #dontdoublemyrate. All right? Don't double my rate. I'm going to repeat that. The hashtag is #dontdoublemyrate. You tweet—everybody say it just so everybody remembers it.

Audience members. Don't double my rate.

The President. Don't double my rate—it's pretty straightforward.

Your voice matters. So stand up. Be heard. Be counted. Tell them now is not the time to double interest rates on your student loans. Now is the time to double down on smart investments to build a strong and secure middle class. Now is the time to double down on building an America that lasts.

Audience member. Absolutely!

The President. You—absolutely.

You and me, all of us here, every single one of us—we're here only because somebody, somewhere, felt responsibility not just for themselves, but they felt responsibility for something larger. It started with them feeling responsible for their families. So your parents sacrificed, your grandparents sacrificed to make sure you could succeed. But then they thought bigger than that. They thought about their neighborhood, they thought about their community, they thought about their country. Now——

Audience member. The planet.

The President. They thought about the planet. And now it's our turn to be responsible. It's our turn to keep that promise alive.

And no matter how tough these times have been, no matter how many obstacles that may stand in our way, I promise you, North Carolina, there are better days ahead. We will emerge stronger than we were before. Because I believe in you. I believe in your future. I believe in the investment you're making right here at North Carolina. That tells me that you share my faith in America's future. And that's what drives me every single day: your hopes, your dreams. And I'm not quitting now, because in America, we don't quit. We get each other's backs. We help each other get ahead.

And if we work together, we'll remind the world just why it is that America's the greatest nation on Earth.

Thank you, everybody. God bless you. God bless America.

NOTE: The President spoke at 1:13 p.m. at Carmichael Arena. In his remarks, he referred to Dominique N. Garland, student, University of North Carolina; James T. Fallon, Jr., host, NBC's "Late Night With Jimmy Fallon" program; Kendall Marshall, guard, and James M. McAdoo, forward, University of North Carolina men's basketball team; and Rep. Virginia A. Foxx.

Remarks During a Conference Call With College Reporters From Air Force One
April 24, 2012

Hey, everybody. Thanks for being on the call. And first of all, let me apologize if the connection sounds fuzzy. As was just mentioned, I'm joining you guys on Air Force One.

I'm just leaving North Carolina; I was at UNC–Chapel Hill. Now I'm on my way to the University of Colorado at Boulder. And tomorrow we're going to be at the University of Iowa in Iowa City. And what we're doing is going to schools to talk to students directly about the critical importance of the possibility that 7.4 million students with Federal student loans would see their interest rates double on July 1 unless Congress steps up and does what it needs to do.

I've always believed that we should be doing everything we can to help put higher education within reach for every single American student, because the unemployment rate for Americans with at least a college degree is about half the national average. And it's never been more important. Unfortunately, it's also never been more expensive. And most of you guys, I'm sure, have reported about this and know this: Students who take out loans to pay for college graduate owing an average of $25,000 a year. And I know what this is like,

because when Michelle and I graduated from college and law school, we had enormous debts, and it took us a lot of years to pay off. So that's probably why I feel this thing so personally.

For a lot of working families, the idea of owing that much money means higher education is simply out of reach for their children. And for the first time, now we've got Americans owing more debt on their student loans than they do on their credit cards.

The key point here is, is that in America, higher education can't be a luxury. It's an economic imperative that every family has got to be able to afford. We've already taken some important steps to make college more affordable. So, for example, we extended Pell grants to 3 million more students, and we signed a tax credit worth up to $10,000 to help middle class families cover the cost of tuition. We've eliminated a major expense for young people by allowing young adults to stay on their parents' health insurance plans until they're 26.

But there's clearly more work to be done. And that's why I'm going to colleges across the country. I want to talk to students right now about how we can make higher education more affordable and what's at stake right now if Congress doesn't do something about it.

So the key point I want to make: If Congress doesn't act on July 1, interest rates on Stafford loans, on student loans from the Federal Government, will double. Nearly 7½ million students will end up owing more on their loan payments. And that would be obviously a tremendous blow. And it's completely preventable.

And for some time now, I've been calling on Congress to take steps to make higher education more affordable, to prevent these interest rates from doubling, and to extend the tuition tax credit that has saved middle class families millions of dollars, but also, to double the number of work-study jobs over the next 5 years.

And instead, over the past few years, Republicans in Congress have voted against new ways to make college more affordable for middle class families, even while they're voting for huge tax cuts for millionaires and billionaires, tax cuts that, by the way, would have to be paid for by cutting things like education and job training programs that give students new opportunities to work and succeed.

So the bottom line here is, we can't just cut our way to prosperity. Making it harder for our young people to afford higher education, allowing them to earn their degrees, that's nothing more than cutting our own future off at the knees. And Congress has to keep interest rates on student loans from doubling, and they need to do it now.

And I have to say, from my perspective, this is a question of values. We can't let America become a country where a shrinking number of people are doing really well, a growing number of people struggle to get by, and you've got fewer ladders for people to climb into the middle class and to get opportunity. We've got to build an economy where everybody is getting a fair shot, everybody is doing their fair share, everybody is playing by the same set of rules. That's ultimately how the middle class gets stronger. And that's an economy that's built to last.

So I'm going to take this issue to every part of the country this year. I'm going to keep focusing on it until Congress passes legislation to keep interest rates low and to continue to give students the chance to get the college education they need for the jobs of today, but also for the jobs of tomorrow.

And part of the reason I wanted to be on this call is to let you know, very personally, I need your help on this. I need you all to tell your readers and your listeners why they've got to speak up, why they've got to speak out. Let Congress know that they need to do the right thing. And for those of you on Twitter, use the hashtag #dontdoublemyrate. That's #dontdoublemyrate.

Because we don't want Congress to double the interest rates on so many students. We need to reward hard work and responsibility. And part of that is keeping interest rates on students low—student loans low so more Americans get a fair shot at an affordable college education, the skills they need to find a good job, a clear path to the middle class that's not blocked by a mountain of debt. And the time to act is right now, and I'm going to need your help getting that message out.

So thanks so much to all of you for being on the call. And thanks for taking the time to shine a light on this important issue. And I know that our team is going to be on the phone call after I hang up. They can answer a bunch of specific details that you may have.

Talk to you soon. Bye-bye.

NOTE: The President spoke at 4:05 p.m. while en route to Boulder, CO.

Statement on Armenian Remembrance Day
April 24, 2012

Today we commemorate the *Meds Yeghern*, one of the worst atrocities of the 20th century. In doing so, we honor the memory of the 1.5 million Armenians who were brutally massacred or marched to their deaths in the waning days of the Ottoman Empire. As we reflect on the unspeakable suffering that took place 97 years ago, we join millions who do the same across the globe and here in America, where it is solemnly commemorated by our States, institutions, communities, and families. Through our words and our deeds, it is our obligation to keep the flame of memory of those who perished burning bright and to ensure that such dark chapters of history are never repeated.

I have consistently stated my own view of what occurred in 1915. My view of that history has not changed. A full, frank, and just acknowledgement of the facts is in all of our interests. Moving forward with the future cannot be done without reckoning with the facts of the past. The United States has done so many times in our own history, and I believe we are stronger for it. Some individuals have already taken this courageous step forward. We applaud those Armenians and Turks who have taken this path, and we hope that many more

will choose it, with the support of their governments, as well as mine.

Although the lives that were taken can never be returned, the legacy of the Armenian people is one of triumph. Your faith, courage, and strength have enabled you to survive and prosper, establishing vibrant communities around the world. Undaunted, you have preserved your patrimony, passing it from generation to generation. Armenian Americans have made manifold contributions to the vibrancy of the United States, as well as critical investments in a democratic, peaceful, and prosperous future for Armenia. The United States is proud of your heritage, and your contributions honor the memory of those who senselessly suffered and died nearly a century ago.

On this solemn day of remembrance, we stand alongside all Armenians in recalling the darkness of the *Meds Yeghern* and in committing to bringing a brighter future to the people of Armenia.

Remarks at the University of Colorado Boulder in Boulder, Colorado
April 24, 2012

The President. Hello, Boulder! How's it going, Buffaloes? Well, you guys are just happy because school is almost out, isn't it? [*Laughter*]

Please give Daniel a big round of applause for that great introduction. I just saw Daniel over at The Sink. I bought some pizza, and I heard a rumor that Robert Redford used to work there.

So that's just a sign. Always be nice to your server because you never know where they'll end up. [*Laughter*] I will say that I was shaking hands with folks outside, and a young woman, she got very excited and spilled yogurt on me. [*Laughter*] More hazardously, she spilled yogurt on the Secret Service, which you just— [*laughter*]—the agent just stood there, just looking at her. [*Laughter*]

I want to thank the chancellor of UC Boulder, Phil DiStefano. Give him a big round of applause for having me here today. We've got the Lieutenant Governor of Colorado, Joe

Garcia, in the house. And I want to thank you for being indoors when it is gorgeous outside.

Now, I've just come from the University of North Carolina at Chapel Hill. I was talking to another good-looking group of students. Jimmy Fallon and I taped his show there. Tonight, make sure to tune in. [*Laughter*] But we saved the primetime event for Boulder.

And I've come here to talk to you about what most of you are focused on every day, at least you're supposed to be, and that is studying and college. Look, college isn't just the best investment you can make in your future. It is the best investment that you can make in your country's future. I believe that.

And by the way, I just want to say, all of you who have seats, feel free to sit down, because it's hot in here, and I don't want folks dropping off. [*Laughter*] There you go, make yourself comfortable, take a load off.

So I'm proud of all of you for doing what it takes to make this investment in a college education because it has never been more important. In today's economy, there's no greater predictor of individual success than a good education. Right now the unemployment rate for Americans with a college degree or more is about half the national average. Their incomes are twice as high as those who don't have a high school diploma. Higher education, whether it's a 4-year college or 2 years at a community college, it's the clearest path we've got to the middle class.

Now, I know that those of you who are about to graduate—[*applause*]—you're pretty cheerful about that. I know those of you who are about to graduate sometimes are wondering what's in store for your future. Because not even 4 years ago, just as the global economy was about to enter into freefall, you were still trying to find your way around campus. And today, our economy is recovering, but it's not yet fully recovered from the worst financial crisis and economic crisis that we've experienced since the Great Depression.

Our businesses have added more than 4 million jobs over the past 2 years. But there are still too many Americans who are out there looking for a job or trying to figure out how to pay the bills and cover the mortgage. There are too many folks who still lack the basic security that has always been at the heart of the American promise, but has been slipping away for more than a decade now, even before the recession hit.

But here's the thing. I want all of you to know that the degree you earn from Colorado is going to be the best tool that you've got to achieve the American promise, by far. That basic idea that if you work hard—no matter where you come from, no matter what you look like, no matter what the circumstances of your birth—if you work hard, you can do well enough to raise a family and own a home, send your own kids to college, put a little bit away for retirement, that idea that each generation has a little more opportunity than the last.

I can tell you that now as a parent. When I look at Malia and Sasha—sometimes I coach Sasha's basketball games, and if she scores a basket, I am so excited compared to when I used to score a basket. [*Laughter*] It's the hope

that all your parents have for you, that your own kids will surpass you, that they're going to be able to shine as bright as they can imagine. And that's the dream that your parents have for you. And keeping that promise alive, that's the defining issue of our time.

Audience member. We believe in you!

The President. I believe in you.

And I don't want this to be a country where a shrinking number of Americans are doing really, really well while a growing number are struggling to get by. That's not the future I want for you. That's not the future I want for my daughters. I want this forever to be a country where everybody gets a fair shot, everybody is doing their fair share, everybody plays by the same set of rules. That's the America I know. That's the America I love.

It's a big and bold and generous America. It's not a cramped America. It's not an America that says, set your sights lower. And that's the America that's within our reach.

I think back sometimes to my own circumstances. My grandfather had the chance to go to college because this country decided that every returning veteran of World War II should be able to go to school. And then my mother was able to raise two kids by herself while she was going to school because she was able to get grants and work her way through school. And then I'm only standing here today, and Michelle is only where she is today, because scholarships and student loans gave us a shot at a great education.

We didn't come from well-to-do backgrounds. We didn't have famous families. But it wasn't just that we worked hard. It was also that somebody made an investment in us. That's what America did for us.

This country has always made a commitment to put a good education within the reach of everybody. Everybody who's willing to work for it, we've said, you know what, you've got a shot. That's what makes us special; that's what makes us exceptional. That's what kept us at the forefront of business and science and technology and medicine. And that's the commitment that we've got to reaffirm today. That's what we believe in.

But I don't need to tell all of you that it's gotten harder. Since most of you were born, tuition and fees at American colleges have more than doubled. And that forces students like you to take out more loans and rack up more debt. The average student who borrows to pay for college now graduates about $25,000 in student loan debt—not good. Americans now owe more on their student loans than they do on their credit cards.

And living with that kind of debt means some pretty tough choices when you're first starting out. It means putting off buying your first house. Or it means maybe you can't start up that business right away that you've got this great idea for.

When I was over at the Sink, I was talking to three business majors, and they all had these business ideas. But it's tougher if you've got all this loan that you're already thinking about the minute you get out of school. Maybe you've got to start a family a little bit later. It takes you a longer time to save for retirement. And when a big chunk of every paycheck goes towards loan debt, that's not just tough on you, it's not just tough on your families. It's painful for the whole economy because that's money that could be going into the economy and could be going into new businesses and could be helping businesses grow.

And I want to point out: Listen, I know about this firsthand. Michelle and I, we know about this firsthand. This is not something I read in a briefing book. [*Laughter*] This is not some abstract idea for us. We've been in your shoes. When we graduated from college and law school, we had a mountain of debt, both of us. That means when we got married, we got poorer together. We added our assets together, and they were zero. And then we added our liabilities together, and they were a lot. [*Laughter*]

We paid more for our student loans than we paid for our mortgage each month when we first bought our small condo in Chicago. And we were lucky to land good jobs with a steady income, but we only finished paying off our student loans about 8 years ago. Think about that. I'm the President of the United States, and so—[*laughter*]—so here I am, and we

were writing those checks every month. And that wasn't easy, especially when we had Malia and Sasha, because at that point, we're supposed to be saving for their college educations, and we're still paying off our—on our college educations. So I've been in your shoes. I know what I am talking about here. This is not something that I just read about.

So we've got to make college more affordable for you. We cannot price the middle class out of a college education. When most new jobs in America require more than a high school diploma, higher education—whether at a 4-year college, at a 2-year program—it can't be a luxury. It's an economic imperative for every family in America. And every family in America should be able to afford it. As long as those young people are willing to put in the work, as long as you're willing to study hard and take advantage of this opportunity, then we've got to make sure it's there for you.

So—now, I'm going to be asking for your help, but let me tell you what I've already done on this issue, Colorado, because I think it's important to know that we haven't just been talking the talk. We've been walking the walk to try to help make college more affordable.

Before I took office, we had a student loan system where tens of billions of taxpayer dollars were going to subsidize banks in the student loan program instead of going to students. So we changed it. We cut out the middleman. We said, why do we need the banks? They're not taking a risk. These are federally guaranteed loans. Let's give the money directly to students.

And I have to tell you, there were folks in Washington who fought us tooth and nail because they want to protect the status quo. One of them, when they heard that we wanted to take this business away from the banks, they said, this is "an outrage." But the real outrage was letting these banks keep these subsidies while students were working two or three jobs just to try to pay tuition. So we kept at it, and we kept at it, and we won that fight. And today, that money is going directly to where it should have been going in the first place, and that's helping millions of young people afford a college education.

And then last fall, I acted to cap student loan payments faster, so that nearly 1.6 million students who make their payments on time, they have the option of only paying 10 percent of their monthly income towards loans once they graduate. And that means if you decide to be a teacher or you decide to be a social worker or you're going into a profession that doesn't pay a lot of money, you still have that option because you know that your monthly payment will be manageable. And we want—[*applause*]. And that's important.

And then we decided we've got to make sure every student has access to a simple fact sheet on student loans and financial aid so you can have all the information you need to make intelligent choices on your own about how to pay for college. So some of you know we created this new Consumer Finance Protection Bureau. It's a watchdog for consumers. And one of their mandates is to focus on student loans. And so they've produced a website and fact sheets called "Know Before You Owe"— "Know Before You Owe"—which is something I wish Michelle and I knew about, wish we had had.

So we've done those steps to help provide you good information and to make sure that we've expanded access to Pell grants and student loans. But that's not enough. It's not enough just to increase student aid. We can't keep on subsidizing skyrocketing tuition, or we're just going to run out of money. We'll just run out of money.

So what I said to colleges and universities is, you got to get—you guys have to do your parts to keep costs down. And I've told Congress, steer Federal aid to those schools that keep tuition affordable and provide good value and serve their students well. We've put colleges on notice: If you can't show us that you're making every effort to keep tuition from going up, then funding from taxpayers will go down. You've got to make an effort. We've got to hold colleges accountable if they don't.

Of course, public universities like this one also understand that States have to do their part, State legislators have to do their part in making higher education a priority. Last year, over 40 States cut their higher education spending—not good. These budget cuts have been one of the biggest factors in your tuition going up. So we're challenging States to take responsibility. We told them, if you can bring—find new ways to bring down costs of college, make it easier for students to graduate, we'll help you do it.

So that's what we've already done. We've helped families, helped more young people afford a higher education. We're offering incentives to States and colleges and universities to keep costs down. And now, guess what, Congress has to do their part. Congress has to do their part.

They need to extend the tuition tax credit that we put in place when I first came into office that saves middle class families thousands of dollars. They need to safeguard aid for low-income students so that today's freshmen and sophomores know they're going to be able to count on it. Our Pell grants have to be there for students. They need to give more young people the chance to earn your way through college by doubling the number of work-study jobs over the next 5 years. And then there's something that they've got to do right now. They have to prevent the interest rates on Federal student loans from shooting up and shaking you down. And that's where you come in.

All right. Now, 5 years ago, Congress cut the rates on Federal student loans in half. That's 5 years ago. Not the current Congress, Congress 5 years ago. [*Laughter*] On July 1 of this year, 2 months from now, that rate cut expires. I want everybody to understand this. Interest rates on those loans will double overnight, starting on July 1, if Congress does not act. And for each year that Congress does not act, the average student with these loans is going to rack up an additional $1,000 in debt. So this is money out of your pocket. It's basically a $1,000 tax hike for more than 7 million students across America, almost 170,000 students here in Colorado alone.

Now, I just want to see a show of hands because I want to make sure I'm not misinformed here. How many of you can afford to pay an extra $1,000 right now? I didn't think so. So stopping this should be a no-brainer. Helping more of our young people afford college should be at the forefront of America's agenda. It shouldn't be a Democratic or a Republican issue. Think about it. This wasn't a partisan issue in the past. The Stafford loans, that's named after a Republican Senator. Pell grants, they're named after a Democratic Senator.

When——

Audience member. America!

The President. America. [*Laughter*] That's what we're supposed to be thinking about.

Look, when Congress cut these rates 5 years ago, 77 Republicans in the House of Representatives voted for it. Of course, a couple hundred Democrats voted for it, but that's okay. It was a bipartisan effort. Today, you've got Republicans who run for Congress, and they're not saying whether or not they're going to stop your rates from doubling. Some have hinted that they'd only do it if we cut things like aid for low-income students instead. So think about this. They'll say, we'll keep your rates low as long as we're messing with folks who need them even more. Does that make sense to you?

Audience members. No!

The President. I want to read a quote. This is from a Republican Congresswoman. I didn't really understand this. [*Laughter*] I'm quoting her. She said, very—she said that she has "very little tolerance for people who tell me they graduate with debt . . . because there's no reason for that." She said students who rack up student loan debt are just sitting on their butts, having opportunity "dumped in your lap."

You guys can Google her or what have you, but—[*laughter*]—now, think about that. Think about that. I can tell you, Michelle and I, we didn't take out loans because we were lazy. You didn't take out loans because you're lazy. You don't take out loans lightly. You don't say to yourself: "Man, this is great. I'm going to be really in debt. I'm thrilled." [*Laughter*] You did it because the cost of college kept on going up, and you're trying to graduate.

And if these guys were serious about making college more affordable, then they wouldn't be voting to cut financial aid in their budget; if you look at their budget, what it means is you're going to be cutting aid for 10 million college students by an average of more than 10—more than $1,000. They certainly wouldn't let student rates double overnight if they really cared about this issue.

They say that, well, we've got to do it because we've got to bring down the deficit. Now, first of all, these guys ran up the deficit. Remember, these are the same folks who voted in favor of two wars without paying for it and big tax cuts without paying for it. They just voted to keep billions of dollars of taxpayer subsidies to big oil companies who are raking in record profits. They just voted to let millionaires and billionaires keep paying low tax rates, lower tax rates than middle class workers. They just voted to give an average tax cut of at least $150,000 to the wealthiest Americans, folks like me who don't need it, weren't asking for it. And the way they pay for it is to cut things like education and job training that give students opportunities to work and succeed. So they can't be too serious about deficits.

I mean, do we want to keep tax cuts for the wealthiest Americans who don't need them, didn't ask for them, the country can't afford it? Or do we want to make sure that everybody pays their fair share and make sure that young people are able to afford to go to college?

Do we want to keep giving taxpayer giveaways to big oil, or do we want to invest in clean energy? And do we want to make sure that we're rebuilding this country, and make sure that we can keep interest rates on millions of students affordable? We need to be investing in the things that build America over the long term, things like education and science and caring for our veterans and a strong military. And we can't have it both ways. We've got to make choices.

In America, we admire success. We aspire to it. I want everybody here to do great, be rich, go out, start a business. That's wonderful. We work and we hustle. You study hard to get your degree because you believe in success and individual initiative. But America is not just about a few people doing well. America is about everybody having the chance to do well. That's what the American Dream is all about.

Some of us had parents or grandparents who said, maybe I can't go to college, but some day my son can go to college. Maybe I can't start my own business, but some day my daughter, she can start her own business. Maybe I'm an immigrant and I won't have every opportunity, but I believe that in this country, in this place—this is a place where no matter who you are or what you look like or where you come from or what your last name is, you can make it if you try. That's what America is about. That's who we are. That's who we are.

So let me just be clear here. We need to send a message to folks who don't seem to get this, that setting your sights lower, that's not an education plan. "You're on your own," that's not an economic plan. We can't just cut our way to prosperity.

Earlier generations made investments necessary to build a strong middle class. Somebody started this university. Somebody gave us a chance. Somebody made the investment in us, because they helped to forge America's leadership in things like science and technology and manufacturing. That's what previous generations did, and now it's our turn. Somebody here might be discovering the cure for cancer. Somebody here might be getting the formula for fusion. Somebody here might be inventing the next great American industry. But that's only going to happen if we understand that we're in this together.

And that's why I need your help. I'm asking everybody who's here and anybody who's watching, anybody who's following online, you need to send a message to your Member of Congress. Tell them you're not going to set your sights lower. Tell them you're not going to settle for something less. You call them, you e-mail them, you write on their Facebook page, tweet. [*Laughter*] We've got, actually, a hashtag that I want everybody to use: #dontdoublemyrate. It's pretty—everybody, I want you to repeat that.

Audience members. Don't double my rate.

The President. Don't double my rate.

Audience members. Don't double my rate.

The President. I asked students at North Carolina to do this earlier today, and they got it trending worldwide for a while. So let's see if you can do better, because we've got to keep the heat on. Your voice matters. You've got to stand up. You've got to be heard. You've got to be counted. You've got to tell them now is not the time to double your interest rates on student loans. Now is the time to double down on the investments in a strong and a secure middle class, and double down on an America that's built to last.

You, me, all of us, we're here because somebody, somewhere—starting with our parents or our grandparents or our great-grandparents—they made an investment not just in themselves, but in each other and in the future of our country. And now it's our turn. It's our turn to keep that promise alive.

And that's what drives me every single day. I used to—when I was running for this office, I said to people, look, I will not be a perfect man or a perfect President, but here's what I can do. I can work every single day as hard as I know how to make sure that you've got a chance, to make sure you can live out your hopes and your dreams. And I'm not about to quit now. We don't give up here in America. We get up. We get each other's back. We help each other get ahead. We work together.

And if you all are willing to join me, I guarantee you not only will we stop these interest rates from going up, but we're going to remind the rest of the world just why it is that America is the greatest nation on Earth.

God bless you. God bless the United States of America.

NOTE: The President spoke at 7:20 p.m. at the Coors Events Center. In his remarks, he referred to actor Robert Redford; Daniel Paiz and Kolbi Zerbest, students, University of Colorado Boulder; James T. Fallon, Jr., host, NBC's "Late Night With Jimmy Fallon" program; and Rep. Virginia A. Foxx. He also referred to his sister Maya Soetoro-Ng.

Remarks at the University of Iowa in Iowa City, Iowa
April 25, 2012

Hello, everybody. It is great to be back in Iowa City. I'm not going to give a long speech here. I just want to say thank you to all the people who are taking an interest in this important issue. I know we've got a lot of students here. Everybody cares about making sure you guys can pay for college in an affordable way, so that's what I'm going to be talking about.

But I just want to tell all of you I couldn't appreciate you more, taking the time to come out, and I hope that—how many seniors do we have here? [*Applause*] All right. Seniors, you've got just a few more weeks to go, so make sure to finish strong; don't goof off too much. [*Laughter*]

And I just want you to know that Iowa always feels like home to me because I spend so much time here. So all right, thank you, everybody. I'm going to shake some hands. Thanks, everybody.

NOTE: The President spoke at 1:19 p.m. Audio was not available for verification of the content of these remarks.

Remarks at the University of Iowa in Iowa City
April 25, 2012

The President. Hello, Hawkeyes! It is good to be back in Iowa! Can folks please give it up for Blake for that outstanding introduction? And I want to thank the University of Iowa Pep Band for firing everybody up.

There is some good hospitality here, and I should know. I spent a little time here in Iowa, spent a little time here in Iowa City. I'm glad that my hometown of Chicago will get to return the hospitality when your football team kicks off its season at Soldier Field.

I want to thank a couple guests. First of all, your Congressman, Dave Loebsack, is here; Attorney General Tom Miller; State Treasurer Mike Fitzgerald; your mayor, Matt Hayek; the president of the University of Iowa, Sally Mason.

So I have come to the University of Iowa to talk a little bit about you and some of the issues you guys are dealing with every single day. Now, I believe that college isn't just the best investment that you can make in your future, it's the best investment you can make in your country's future. And I'm proud of all of you for making that investment, because it's never been more important.

In today's economy, there's no greater predictor of individual success than a good education. That's at the top. Right now the unemployment rate for Americans with a college de-

gree or more is about half the national average. Their incomes are twice as high as those who don't have a high school diploma. A higher education is the single clearest path to the middle class.

I know that those of you who are about to graduate are wondering what's in store for your future. Because not even 4 years ago, just as the global economy was about to enter into freefall, you were still trying to find your way around campus, and now, 4 years later, you're looking at what it means when you leave this campus.

Now, the good news is, today our economy is recovering. That's the good news. But I'll be honest with you. It has not yet fully healed from the worst economic crisis since the Great Depression. Our businesses have added more than 4 million jobs over the past 2 years. But there's still a lot of Americans who are out there looking for a job or at least finding a job that pays the bills and helps cover the mortgage. There's still too many families who don't have that security, that basic middle class security that started slipping away even before this crisis hit.

But what I want all of you to know is that the degree you earn from Iowa will be the best tool you have to achieve that basic American promise, the idea that if you work hard, if you give it your all, if you're responsible, then you can do well enough to raise a family and own a home, send your own kids to college, put a little away for retirement. It's the idea that each generation is going to have a little more opportunity than the last. That's at the heart of the American Dream.

And I can tell you, as a parent now, when I see Malia and Sasha doing well, there's nothing more important to me. And that's true for American families everywhere, and it's the hope your parents have for you. That's the hope you'll have some day for your own kids. And keeping that promise alive is the defining issue of our time. I don't want this a country— I don't want this to be a country where a shrinking number of people are doing really, really well and then a growing number are barely able to get by. I don't want that future for you. I don't want it for my daughters. I don't want it for America.

I want this forever to be a country where everybody gets a fair shot and everybody's doing their fair share and everybody's playing by the same set of rules. That's the America I know, that's the America I love, and that's the America within our reach if we work for it.

And this is personal for me.

Audience member. We love you, Barack!

The President. I love you back. I love you guys, and I believe in you guys. That's the most important thing. I believe in you. And I believe in your future.

And I think about my own life. My grandfather had the chance to go to college because this country decided that every returning veteran of World War II should be able to afford it through the GI bill. My mom was a single mom—my dad wasn't around—and she raised two kids by herself with some help from my grandparents because she was able to get grants and work her way through school. And I'm only here today, and Michelle is only where she is today, because scholarships and student loans gave us a shot at a great education. That's how we succeeded.

And this country's always made a commitment to put a good education within the reach

of everybody who's willing to work for it. That's part of what made us special. That's what kept us at the forefront of business and science and technology and medicine. That's a commitment that we need to reaffirm today.

Now, here's the challenge we've got. Since most of you were born, tuition and fees at America's colleges have more than doubled. And that forces students like you to take out more loans and rack up more debt. The average student who borrows to pay for college now graduates with about $25,000 in student loan debt. And in this State, it's even higher. Americans now owe more on their student loans than they owe on credit cards.

And living with that debt means you've got to make some pretty tough choices. It might mean putting off buying a first home or chasing that great startup idea that you've got. Maybe you'll have to wait a little bit longer to start a family or save for retirement. And when a big chunk of every paycheck goes towards loan debt, that's not just tough on you, that's not just tough on middle class families. That's not good for our economy, because that money that could be going into businesses is going just to service debt.

And as I said, this is personal for me. I know something about this, because Michelle and I, we went through it. And it wasn't that long ago. We've been in your shoes. We didn't come from wealthy families. We needed loans and we needed grants to get our way through.

And that meant that when Michelle and I graduated from college and law school, we had a mountain of debt. When we got married, we got poorer together. [*Laughter*] Sort of, we combined our assets, and they were zero. [*Laughter*] And then we combined our liabilities, and they were a lot. [*Laughter*] So we ended up paying more for our student loans in the first few years that we were married than we paid on our mortgage each month when we finally bought a small condo. And we were lucky to land good jobs with a steady income, but we only finished paying off our student loans about 8 years ago. Think about that. I'm the President of the United States—[*laughter*]—it was only about 8 years ago that we finished paying off our student loans, so—[*applause*].

And let me tell you, it wasn't easy making those payments, because once we had Malia and Sasha, we're trying to save for their college education even as we're paying off our own college educations.

So this is personal. This is at the heart of who we are. We've got to make college more affordable for more young people. We can't put the middle class at a disadvantage. We can't price out folks who are trying to make sure that they not only succeed for themselves, but help the country succeed. We can't price the middle class out of a college education. Not when—we can't do it, especially when most new jobs in America will require more than a high school diploma. Higher education—whether it's at a 4-year institution or a 2-year program at a community college—it can't be a luxury. It's an economic imperative every family in America should be able to afford.

And before I came out here, I had a chance to meet not just with Blake, but with a number of other students, and we had a little roundtable. And the stories they told me were so familiar. One young man—single mom, she had lost her job. He was already about $30,000 in debt. He was only halfway through here at University of Iowa. Another young woman, her dad had been laid off at Maytag. They were trying to figure out how to make ends meet. She's about to graduate.

Now, what I told them is, you're making the right decision, because over the lifetime of earnings you will more than earn back this investment you're making. But making it more affordable would sure help. It would sure help.

Now, I'm going to have a specific request for you. I'm going to need your help, Iowa, but let me briefly tell you what we've already done to try to make college more affordable, because I'm not just interested in talking the talk, I want to walk the walk.

So, before I took office, we had a student loan system where tens of billions of taxpayer dollars were going to banks who were the middlemen on the Federal student loan program. So they were getting billions of dollars in prof-

its managing a loan program where they had no risk because it was all federally guaranteed loans. So we changed that.

And there were folks in Washington who fought tooth and nail to protect the status quo. One of them said it would be "an outrage" to change the system where banks are managing this thing. But the real outrage was letting them serve as middlemen and siphon off profits, while students were working two or three jobs just to get by. So we kept at it, and we fought, and we fought, and today, we don't have middlemen. That money is going directly where it should have been to—the first place. It's going to help more young people afford college.

And then last fall, I acted to cap student loan payments faster, so that nearly 1.6 million students who make their payments on time only have to pay 10 percent of their monthly income toward loans once they graduate, which means if you decide to become a teacher or a social worker or a guidance counselor, something that doesn't pay a lot of money, you can still afford to do it because you'll never have to pay more than 10 percent of your income in order to stay current on your loan.

And then, we decided, you know what, you guys need more information about this whole process. We want to have student—we want students to have a—access to a simple fact sheet on student loans and financial aid so you can have all the information you need to make your own choices about how to pay for college. So some of you know we set up this new Consumer Finance Protection Bureau to look out for consumers, and so they're now putting out a fact sheet called "Know Before You Owe." "Know Before You Owe," which is something Michelle and I could have used when we were in your shoes.

And then what we said was it's not enough just to increase student aid. We've also got to stop subsidizing skyrocketing tuition, or we'll run out of money. So the schools themselves have to keep their tuition lower. So we've challenged—[*applause*]—so we've put out the challenge to colleges and universities. And I've told Congress, steer Federal aid to those schools that are doing a good job keeping tuition affordable and providing good value and serving their students well. And we've put colleges on notice: If you can't stop tuition from skyrocketing, the funding you get from taxpayers is going to go down. We're going to put money into the schools that are doing a better job. And we're going to hold schools accountable.

Of course, as public universities like this one know, States and State legislators also have to do their part by making higher education a higher priority in their budgets. Last year, over 40 States cut their higher education spending.

Audience members. Boo!

The President. Yes, that's not good. [*Laughter*] These budget cuts are one of the biggest reasons why tuition goes up at public colleges and have been over the last decade. So we're challenging States: Take responsibility. If you can find new ways to bring down costs on college, make it easier for students to graduate, then we'll help you do it at the Federal level.

So that's what we've already done: helped more families, more young people afford a higher education, offer incentives to States and colleges and universities to keep costs down. That's what we've been doing. Now comes the tricky part: We got to get Congress to do their part. And that's where you come in.

There are a couple of things I'd like Congress to be doing this year. First, they need to extend the tuition tax credit that we put in place when I first came into office, because it's saving middle class families thousands of dollars. They get a tax break when they are helping their kids go to college. That's important.

Second, we need Congress to safeguard aid for low-income students so that today's freshmen and sophomores know they're going to be able to count on it. We've got to make sure the Pell grants are there for people who need them.

Number three, we've got to give more young people the chance to earn their way through college by doubling the number of work-study jobs over the next 5 years. That's an achievable goal.

And then, most immediately—and this is where I really need you guys—Congress needs to act right now to prevent interest rates on Federal student loans from shooting up and shaking you down. That's where you come in.

You see, 5 years ago, Congress cut the rates on Federal student loans in half. That was a good thing to do. But on July 1 of this year, which means about 2 months from now, that rate cut will expire. And if it expires, interest rates on these loans will double overnight. And for each year that Congress doesn't act, the average student with these loans will rack up an additional thousand dollars in debt. That's basically a thousand-dollar tax hike on more than 7 million students around America, including 250,000 students right here in Iowa.

Now, let me see if—I'll do a quick poll. This may be unscientific. How many people can afford to pay an extra thousand dollars right now?

Audience members. No!

The President. [*Laughter*] I don't think so. Stopping this from happening should be a no-brainer.

[*At this point, the President coughed.*]

The President. It makes me sick just thinking about it. [*Laughter*] Helping more young people afford college should be at the forefront of America's agenda. And it shouldn't be a Republican or Democratic issue. This is an American issue. The Stafford loans we're talking about were named after a Republican Senator; Pell grants named after a Democratic Senator. When Congress cut these rates 5 years ago, a majority of Democrats voted for it, but 77 Republicans in the House of Representatives voted for it too.

Now, the good news is, the Senate introduced a bill last night that would keep student loan rates from doubling. That's the good news. And what's also good news is some Republican Senators look like they might support it. And I'm ready to work with them to make it happen. That's good.

But I've got to tell you, the Republicans who run the House of Representatives have not yet said whether or not they'll stop your rates from doubling. And they've hinted that the only way they'd do it is if they cut things like aid for low-income students. So let me scratch my head there for a second. Think about that. We're going to help some students by messing with other students. That's not a good answer. How many people think that's a good answer?

Audience members. No!

The President. No, I didn't think so. One of these Members of Congress—I—you know, sometimes I like just getting these quotes, because I'm always interested in how folks talk about this issue. You've got one Member of Congress who compared these student loans—I'm not kidding here—to a "stage-three cancer of socialism."

Stage-three cancer? [*Laughter*] I don't know where to start. What do you mean? [*Laughter*] What are you talking about? Come on. Just when you think you've heard it all in Washington, somebody comes up with a new way to go off the deep end. [*Laughter*]

And then you've got the spokesman for the Speaker of the House who says, we're—meaning me, my administration—we're just talking about student loans to distract people from the economy. Now, think about that for a second. Because these guys don't get it. This is the economy. This is the economy. This is about your job security. This is about your future. If you do well, the economy does well. This is about the economy.

What economy are they talking about? You are the economy. If you've got skills, if you've got talents, if you're starting a business, if companies are locating here in Iowa because it's got a well-trained workforce, that's the economy. That's how we're going to compete. Making sure our next generation earns the best education possible is exactly America's business. Making sure that education is available to everybody and not just the few, that is America's business. Our future depends on it.

And then, some of them suggest that students like you have to pay more so we can help bring down the deficit. Now, think about that. These are the same folks who ran up the deficits for the last decade. They voted to keep giving billions of dollars in taxpayer subsidies to big oil companies who are raking in record profits. They voted to let millionaires and billionaires keep paying lower taxes than middle class workers. They voted to give folks like me, the wealthiest Americans, an average tax cut of at least $150,000, and that tax cut would be paid for by cutting things like education and job training programs that give students and workers opportunities to get what they need to succeed.

Now, does that make any sense? Does that some—sound like folks who are really concerned with the deficit?

Audience members. No!

The President. How can we want to maintain tax cuts for the wealthiest Americans who don't need them and weren't even asking for them? I don't need one. I needed help back when I was your age. I don't need help now. I don't need an extra thousand dollars or few thousand dollars. You do.

We need to make sure everybody pays their fair share. How can we continue to subsidize an oil industry that's making record profits instead of investing in things like clean energy that will help shape our future? Do we want to jack up interest rates on millions of students? Or do we want to keep investing in the things that help us in the long term, things like education and science and a strong military and care for our veterans? Because we can't have it both ways. We can't do all things on the cheap.

And one thing I want to be clear about, because when I talk like this, sometimes the other side, they get all hot and bothered, and they say, he's getting—he's engaging in class warfare. This isn't about class warfare. We want every American to succeed. That's the point. We—I want all of you to be rich. I want all of you to be successful. We aspire to it. That's what Americans do. We work and we hustle and we study and we take risks to succeed. And we don't expect a handout. But we also understand we're in this thing together and America is not about just a few people doing well, it's about everybody having a chance to do well. That's what the American Dream is all about.

You look at this auditorium, everybody who's here, you're here because somebody made a commitment to you. First, your parents. But it wasn't just your parents. It was the folks who decided, you know what, we're going to set up a public university. It was the folks who made a decision early on in this Republic that said we believe that all men are created equal, that everybody is endowed by their Creator with certain inalienable rights. Those were commitments that were made by previous generations to future generations.

So somebody here had a parent or a grandparent who said, maybe I can't go to college, but some day my son can. Maybe I can't start my own business, but someday I can picture my daughter starting her own business. Maybe I'm an immigrant, but I believe that this is the country, this is the place where no matter who you are, no matter what you look like, no matter where you come from, no matter what your last name is, you can make it if you try. That's what we believe.

That is what we believe. You and me, all of us, we're only here because someone, somewhere, felt a responsibility not just to themselves, but to this country's future. And now it's our turn to be responsible. Now it's our turn to keep that promise alive. That's where I need your help.

I'm asking everybody here, anybody who's watching, anybody who's following online, send your Member of Congress a message. Tell them you're not going to set your sights lower. Tell them you're not going to settle for something less. Call them, e-mail them, write on their Facebook page, tweet. [*Laughter*] We've got a hashtag: #dontdoublemyrate.

[*Laughter*] Don't double my rate. Don't double my rate.

We asked students at North Carolina, then at University of Colorado, to do this yesterday. They got it trending worldwide for a while. Let's see if you guys can do even better. See how the Hawkeyes can do. Because we've got to keep the heat on Congress until this gets done. And I need your help to do it. I need you to be heard. I need you to be counted.

Now is not the time to double the interest rates on our student loans. Now is not the time to double interest rates. Now is the time to double down on starting investments that build a strong and secure middle class. Now is the time to double down on building an America that's built to last.

If we work together, with clear eyes and a common purpose, I guarantee you we'll meet our challenges. We will rise to this moment. And the reason I know that is because I believe in you. I believe in you. And it's because of you that we will remind everybody just why it is that this is the greatest nation on Earth.

Thank you, Iowa. God bless you. God bless the United States of America.

NOTE: The President spoke at 1:28 p.m. at the Field House. In his remarks, he referred to Blake T. Anderson, Marissa L. Boles, Myranda L. Burnett, Jordan Garrison-Nickerson, and Martin J. Lopez, students, University of Iowa; Rep. Todd W. Akin; and Brendan Buck, Press Secretary for Speaker of the House of Representatives John A. Boehner.

Statement on Israeli Independence Day
April 26, 2012

Sixty-four years ago, the United States became the first country in the world to recognize the State of Israel, the realization of a modern day state in the historic homeland of the Jewish people. Since that momentous day, the special bond of friendship between the United States and Israel has grown stronger. Ours is a unique relationship founded on an unbreakable commitment to Israel's security and anchored by our common interests and deeply held values. These values continue to enlighten and guide our efforts as we work with Israel, as well as with others in the region, to confront shared challenges and to achieve a just and comprehensive peace based on a two-state solution that will usher in a future of peace, security, and dignity for the people of Israel and its neighbors.

Today, as Israelis celebrate their 64th Independence Day and their remarkable achievements over the past six decades, it gives me great pleasure to extend my best wishes and the best wishes of the American people to President Peres, Prime Minister Netanyahu, and the people of Israel.

Remarks at Fort Stewart, Georgia
April 27, 2012

Thank you. Hello, Fort Stewart! It is good to be here at Fort Stewart. First of all, how about the First Lady, Michelle Obama? Hooah! She is a tough act to follow. For the gentlemen out there who are not yet married, let me just explain to you, your goal is to improve your gene pool by marrying somebody who is superior to you. Isn't that right, General? [*Laughter*]

Listen, and as you just heard, when it comes to all of you—when it comes to our military, our veterans, your families—Michelle Obama and Jill Biden have your back. They are working tirelessly to make sure that our military families are treated with the honor and respect and support that they deserve. And I could not be prouder of all the efforts that they've been making on their behalf.

It's a privilege to hang out with some of America's finest. The "Dog Face Soldiers" of the 3d Infantry Division! Rock of the Marne! We've got a lot of folks in the house. We've got the Raider Brigade! We've got the Spartan Brigade! We've got the Vanguard Brigade! We've got the Provider Brigade! And we've got the Falcon Brigade!

Let me thank Major General Abrams and his beautiful wife Connie, for welcoming us. Abe is doing an incredible job carrying on his family's incredible tradition of service to our country. So we are grateful for him. Give him a big round of applause. I want to thank Command Sergeant Major Edd Watson and his beautiful wife Sharon.

I want to thank someone who's made it her life's mission to stand up for the financial security of you and your families, somebody who knows a little bit about military families and military service. And actually, this is a homecoming for her because she spent over 3 years when they were posted down here—Holly Petraeus is in the house. I want you guys to give her a big round of applause.

But most importantly, I want to thank all of you. I want to thank you for your service. I want to thank you for your sacrifice. I want to thank you for your unshakeable commitment to our country. You have worn the uniform with honor. You've performed heroically in some of the most dangerous places on Earth. You have done everything that has been asked of you, and more. And you have earned a special place in our Nation's history.

Future generations will speak of your achievements. They'll speak of how the 3d Infantry Division's "thunder run" into Baghdad signaled the end of a dictatorship and how you brought Iraq back from the brink of civil war. They'll speak of you and your service in Afghanistan and in the fight against Al Qaida, which you have put on the path to defeat.

And to the members of the Special Operations Forces community, while the American people may never know the full extent of your service, they will surely speak of how you kept our country safe and strong and how you delivered justice to our enemies.

So history will remember what you did, and so will we. We will remember the profound sacrifices that you've made in these wars. Michelle and I just had a few moments at the Warriors Walk, paying tribute to 441 of your fallen comrades, men and women who gave their last full measure of devotion to keep our Nation safe. And we will remember them. We will honor them, always. And our thoughts and prayers also go out to the troops from Fort Stewart who are serving so bravely right now as we speak in Afghanistan. And I know many of you will be deploying there too, so you know you're going to be in our thoughts and prayers.

Your generation—the 9/11 generation—has written one of the greatest chapters of military service that America has ever seen. But I know that for many of you, a new chapter is unfolding. The war in Iraq is over. The transition in Afghanistan is underway. Many of our troops are coming home, back to civilian life. And as you return, I know that you're looking for new jobs and new opportunities and new ways to serve this great country of ours.

And 3 years ago, I made your generation a promise: I said that when your tour comes to an end—when you see our flag, when you touch down on our soil—you'll be coming home to an America that will forever fight for you, just as you fought for us.

For me, as President, it's been a top priority. It's something I worked on as a Senator, when I served on the Veterans Affairs Committee. It's something I continue to this day. Since I took office, we've hired over 200,000 veterans to serve in the Federal Government.

We've made it easier for veterans to access all sorts of employment services. You just heard how Michelle and Jill have worked with businesses to secure tens of thousands of jobs for veterans and their families. And with support from Democrats and Republicans, we've put in place new tax credits for companies that hire veterans. We want every veteran who wants a job to get a job. That's the goal.

And those of you who want to pursue a higher education and earn new skills, you deserve that opportunity as well.

Like General Abrams's dad, my grandfather—the man who helped raise me—served in Patton's army. And when he came home, he went to school on the GI bill, because America decided that every returning veteran of World War II should be able to afford it. And we owe that same commitment to all of you.

So, as President, I've made sure to champion the post-9/11 GI bill. And with that bill and the tuition assistance program, last year we supported more than 550,000 veterans and 325,000 servicemembers who are pursuing a higher education. Because a higher education is the clearest path to the middle class. Now that's progress, but we've got more to do. We can't be satisfied with what we've already done, we've got more to do. We've got to make sure you've got every tool you need to make an informed decision when it comes to picking a school. And that's why Michelle and I are here today.

Right now it's not that easy. I've heard the stories. Some of you guys can relate; you may have experienced it yourselves. You go online to try and find the best school for military members or your spouses or other family members. You end up on a website that looks official. They ask you for your e-mail, they ask you for your phone number. They promise to link you up with a program that fits your goals. Almost immediately after you've typed in all that information, your phone starts ringing. Your inbox starts filling up. You've never been more popular in your life. All of these schools want you to enroll with them.

And it sounds good. Every school and every business should be out there competing for your skills and your talent and your leadership, everything that you've shown in uniform. But as some of your comrades have discovered, sometimes you're dealing with folks who aren't interested in helping you. They're not interested in helping you find the best program. They are interested in getting the money. They don't care about you; they care about the cash.

So they harass you into making a quick decision with all those calls and e-mails. And if they can't get you online, they show up on post. One of the worst examples of this is a college recruiter who had the nerve to visit a barracks at Camp Lejeune and enroll marines with brain injuries just for the money. These marines had injuries so severe some of them couldn't recall what courses the recruiter had signed them up for. That's appalling. That's disgraceful. It should never happen in America.

I'm not talking about all schools. Many of them—for-profit and nonprofit—provide quality education to our servicemembers and our veterans and their families. But there are some bad actors out there. They'll say you don't have to pay a dime for your degree, but once you register, they'll suddenly make you sign up for a high interest student loan. They'll say that if you transfer schools, you can transfer credits. But when you try to actually do that, you suddenly find out that you can't. They'll say they've got a job placement program when in fact, they don't. It's not right. They're trying to swindle and hoodwink you. And today, here at Fort Stewart, we're going to put an end to it. We're putting an end to it.

The Executive order I'm about to sign will make life a whole lot more secure for you and your families and our veterans and a whole lot tougher for those who try to prey on you. Here's what we're going to do.

First, we're going to require colleges that want to enroll members of our military or veterans or your families to provide clear information about their qualifications and available financial aid. You'll be able to get a simple fact sheet called "Know Before You Owe"—"Know Before You Owe." And it will lay out all the information that you need to make your own choices about how best to pay for college.

Second, we're going to require those schools to step up their support for our students. They need to provide a lot more counseling. If you've got to move because of a deployment or a reassignment, they've got to help you come up with a plan so that you can still get your degree.

Number three——

[At this point, the President sneezed.]

Excuse me. Number three—*[laughter]*.

Number three, we're going to bring an end to the aggressive and sometimes dishonest recruiting that takes place. We're going to up our oversight of improper recruitment practices. We're going to strengthen the rules about who can come on post and talk to servicemembers. And we're going to make it a lot easier for all of you to file complaints and for us to take action when somebody is not acting right.

This is about making sure you succeed, because when you succeed, our country succeeds. It's that simple. After all, at the end of World War II, so many Americans like my grandfather came home to new opportunities. Because of the original GI bill, by 1947, half of all Americans who enrolled in college were

veterans. And you know what, they did pretty well.

They rose to become Presidents and Supreme Court Justices and Nobel Prize winners. They went on to become scientists and engineers and doctors and nurses. Eight million Americans were educated under the original GI bill. And together, they forged the backbone of what would become the largest middle class that the world had ever seen. They built this country. They turned us into that economic superpower.

And we can do it again. We've faced tough times: gone through the worst recession since the Great Depression, two wars. But you know what, we've faced tough times before. And all of you know something that America should never forget: Just as you rise or fall as one unit, we rise or fall as one Nation. Just as you have each other's backs, what has always made America great is that we have each other's backs. Each of us is only here because somebody looked out for us. Not just our parents, but our neighbors and our communities and our houses of worship and our VFW halls. Each of us is here because we had a country that was willing to invest in things like community colleges and universities and scientific research and medicine and caring for our veterans. Each of us is only here because somebody, somewhere, had our backs.

This country exists because generations of Americans worked together and looked out for one other. Out of many, we are one. Those are the values we've got to return to. If we do, there's nothing this country cannot achieve. There's no challenge that's too great for us. There's no destiny beyond our reach. As long as we're joined in common purpose and common resolve, better days will always lie ahead, and we will remind everybody why the United States of America is the greatest country on Earth.

And as I look out at this sea of incredible men and women, it gives me confidence that our best days are still ahead.

God bless you. God bless our Armed Services. God bless the 3d Division. God bless the

United States of America. Thank you very much.

And now I'm going to sign this Executive order.

NOTE: The President spoke at 12:45 p.m. In his remarks, he referred to Jill T. Biden, wife of Vice President Joe Biden; Maj. Gen. Robert B. "Abe" Abrams, USA, commander, and CSM Edd Watson, USA, division command sergeant major, 3d Infantry Division; and Holly Petrae-us, wife of Gen. David H. Petraeus, USA (Ret.), Director, Central Intelligence Agency. He also referred to Executive Order 13607, which establishes principles of excellence for educational institutions serving servicemembers, veterans, spouses, and other family members. The Executive order is listed in Appendix D at the end of this volume. The transcript released by the Office of the Press Secretary also included the remarks of the First Lady.

Remarks at an Obama Victory Fund 2012 Fundraiser
April 27, 2012

Hello, everybody. Thank you. How's everybody doing? Good. Good afternoon. I want to thank my point guard Barbara for that wonderful introduction and for all the battles you have waged on behalf of America's women and America's families. And I want to thank all of you for being here today, for all the time and energy that you've been giving to our campaign. Everybody, feel free to sit. Just relax. I've got a few things to say. [*Laughter*]

It is always a pleasure to be surrounded by so many talented, accomplished women. It makes me feel right at home. [*Laughter*] Although, at least here I get a microphone— [*laughter*]—which levels the playing field a little bit. Bo and I, we try at dinner to try to get a word in.

Now, whether you have joined this cause in its earliest days or in recent months, I know you didn't join it just because of me. You did it because of the vision that we share for this country. It's not a vision of a country where a shrinking number of people do really well while a growing number barely get by. It's a vision for an America where everybody who works hard has the chance to get ahead, where everybody has a fair shot and everybody is doing their fair share and everybody plays by the same set of rules. That's the America we know and love. That's the America within our reach.

And right now no issue is more important than restoring economic security for all of our families. Today, our economy is recovering, but not yet recovered, from the worst crisis since the Great Depression. Our businesses have added more than 4 million jobs over the past 2 years. But too many Americans are still looking for a job that pays enough to cover the bills or the mortgage. Too many families are still searching for the middle class security that started slipping away years before the recession hit.

So we've got a lot of work to do. We've got to finish what we started. And I'm so grateful to have all of you in the Women's Leadership Forum on our team.

It's fair to say that there's been a bit of talk about women and women's issues so far this year. And I've said before, I want to repeat, I think it's been oversimplified. Women are not an interest group. Women shouldn't be treated that way. Women are half this country and half of its workforce. You're 80 percent of my household, if you count my mother-in-law, and I always count my mother-in-law. [*Laughter*]

So I've got a vested interest in making sure women do well. And I'm proud of what we've done on behalf of women across this country. I know you've heard a lot about that today. But I want you to know why we've done what we've done because there are values behind the policies.

And it begins, for me at least, with the women that have shaped my life. As some of you know, I grew up the son of a single mom who struggled to put herself through school and make ends meet, even relying on food stamps at one point to help us get by. But she earned her education, earned her Ph.D., started traveling around the world, helping women enter into the economy and make a little bit of money and gain a little bit of independence.

Through scholarships and hard work, she had the opportunity to give back. And she made sure that my sister and I were able to have those same opportunities. She used to wake me up before dawn to study, because we were living overseas for a time and she wanted to make sure I stayed up with my American schooling. I'd complain, and she'd let loose with, "This is no picnic for me either, buster." [*Laughter*] Because she had to go to work after she taught me lessons, and that's part of the reason why my sister Maya chose to become a teacher, seeing that example.

And when my mom needed help with us, my grandparents stepped up. And my grandmother, in particular, who had a high school education, worked during World War II on a bomber assembly line like Rosie the Riveter. And she didn't get a GI bill—unlike today's post-9/11 GI bill, it couldn't be transferred to family members—so she got jobs, and eventually, she got a job at a local bank.

And she worked hard and eventually made vice president, starting off as a secretary. And I'm convinced she could have been the best president that bank had ever seen, if she had gotten that chance. But she hit the glass ceiling like too many women in that generation did, and for the rest of her career, she'd watch men that she had once trained pass her by up that ladder. I think about her.

And then there's Michelle. Earlier this week, I visited a few colleges across the country as part of a battle to keep student loan rates from going up. And I spent some time on our own story, about how when Michelle and I got married, we both had loads of student debt from college and law school. So, when we teamed up together, we got poorer together. [*Laughter*]

We only finished paying off those loans about 8 years ago. And I bring this up because what I really want to point out is that every time I mentioned Michelle, the students cheered more loudly than they did for me. [*Laughter*] This is what happens.

But once Michelle and I had our girls, we gave it our all to balance raising a family and chasing a career. And it was tough on me, but let's face it, it was tougher on her. I was gone a lot. I know that when she was with the girls, she'd feel guilty that she wasn't giving enough time to work. And when she was at work, she'd feel guilty about not having enough time for the girls. And like many of you, I'm sure we both wished there was—there were a machine that would let us be in two places at once.

And then today, I think about these issues as a father, because the highlight of every day for me is asking my daughters about theirs. Their hopes and their futures, that's what drives me every single day when I step into the White House. Every decision I make is all about ensuring that all of our daughters and all of our sons grow up in a country that gives them the equal chance to be anything they set their minds to, a country where more doors are open to them than were open to us.

Those stories are what inform my work. Those women are what inspire me to do what I do. That's at the heart of everything that we've done. That's the lens through which I view all of this. And that's what we mean when we say that these issues are more than just a matter of policy, they're personal. They're not just women's issues, they're economic issues. They're family issues. They're America's issues. They impact all of us.

When women make less than men for the same work, that hurts families who have to get by with less and businesses who have fewer customers who can spend money there. When a job doesn't offer family leave to care for a new baby or sick leave to care for an ailing parent, that burdens all of us. It's not just a women's issue. When an insurance plan denies women coverage because of a preexisting condition, that puts a strain on emergency rooms and drives up the cost of care for everybody; it strains family budgets across America. When any of our citizens can't fulfill their potential because of factors that had nothing to do with talent or character or work ethic, that diminishes us as a country. It says something about who we are as Americans.

So when we started off with this administration, we were under no illusions that changing these things would be easy. We knew it wouldn't come quickly. But think about what's happened in 3 years, in large part because of you and the support that you've provided. We've started to see what change looks like.

It's been mentioned: Change is the first bill I signed into law, a law that says women deserve an equal day's pay for an equal day's work. A law that says our daughters should have the same opportunities as our sons. A law named for a courageous woman, Lilly Ledbetter, my dear friend, who is right here today. That's what change is, and it happened because of you.

Change is extending more than 16,000 new loans to women-owned businesses, cutting small-business taxes more than 18—17 times so that more women have the power to create new jobs and opportunity.

Change is education reform that does more to encourage young women to join fields like science and technology and engineering and math and increasing grants that have helped about 2.3 million more young women afford to go to college.

And yes, Barbara is absolutely right. Change is the health care reform we passed after a century of trying that finally gives women more power to make their own choices about their health care.

Last year, more than 20 million women received expanded access to preventive services like mammograms and cervical cancer screening at no additional cost. Nearly 2 million women enrolled in Medicare received a 50-percent discount on the medicine that they needed. Over 1 million more young women are insured because they can now stay on their parent's plan.

Soon, insurance companies will no longer be able to deny coverage based on preexisting conditions like breast cancer or charge women more just because they're women. And this year, women will receive new access to recommended preventive care like domestic violence screening and contraception at no additional cost. That's going to be happening.

This contraception fight in particular was illuminating. It was like being in a time machine. [*Laughter*] Republicans in Congress were going so far as to say an employer should be able to have a say in the health care decisions of its female employees. And I'm always puzzled by this. This is a party that says it prides itself on being rabidly antiregulation. These are folks who claim to believe in freedom from government interference and meddling. But it doesn't seem to bother them when it comes to women's health.

Now we've got Governors and legislatures across the river in Virginia, up the road in Pennsylvania, all across the country, saying that women can't be trusted to make your own decisions. They're pushing and passing bills forcing women to get ultrasounds, even if they don't want one. If you don't like it, the Governor of Pennsylvania said you can "close your eyes." It's a quote.

It's appalling. It's offensive. It's out of touch. And when it comes to what's going on out there, you're not going to close your eyes. Women across America aren't closing their eyes. As long as I'm President, I won't either. The days of male politicians controlling the health care decisions of our wives and our mothers and our daughters and our sisters that needs to come to an end.

And none of these fights have been easy. We've got to wage more fights and win them on these issues and many more. We've got more jobs to create, more students to educate, more clean energy to generate, more troops to bring home, more doors of opportunity to open for all our kids. The one thing we can't do—the one thing we can't afford to do right now is to go back to the very same policies that got us into this mess.

Of course, that's exactly what the other side has planned. And they make no secret about it. They want to go back to the days when Wall Street played by its own rules. They want to go back to the days when insurance companies could deny coverage or jack up premiums without a reason. A lot of them seem like they want to turn back the clock to the fifties or the forties or the thirties or maybe further back than that and close doors of opportunity that we thought we'd kicked open a long time ago, doors of opportunity to people who haven't made it quite yet.

Just look at some of the debates that we've already had this year. Instead of putting forward serious plans to help more Americans back to work, a lot of those folks in the other party have chosen to refight battles we settled long ago.

And I've heard some of them say, look, this is all just a big misunderstanding; they need to get their message out better when it comes to women. I don't think that's the problem. I think they're getting their message out just fine. We don't need to read between the lines in terms of what they're saying.

When folks talk about killing the health care reform that we passed, part of what they're saying is, is that women should pay more than men for the same health care coverage. They're saying we should stop protecting women with preexisting conditions. They're saying we should no longer let that 25-year-old daughter and more than a million other young women stay on their parents' health care plans.

When you talk about how marvelous your party's economic plan is, when you break down the numbers, what you're really saying is you want to pass massive new tax cuts for millionaires and billionaires, pay for them by gutting programs that, among other things, support low-income women and children and pregnant mothers and student aid for—that disproportionately helps young women.

When you say we should get rid of Planned Parenthood, you're not just talking about restricting a woman's ability to make her own health care decisions, you're talking about denying the preventive care like cancer screenings that millions of women rely on.

And when something like the Violence Against Women Act is actually up for debate, then we know something has gone haywire. That's something that should be beyond politics. This is a bill that my Vice President coauthored when he was in the Senate. It's a bill that once passed by wide bipartisan margins.

And it is a bill that we are going to renew. It is the right thing to do.

So the choice between going backward and moving forward has never been so clear. And as long as I'm President, we're going to keep moving forward. You can count on that. You don't have to take my word for it; you've got my signature on it. Because something like standing up for equal pay for equal work isn't something I've got to "get back to you on," it's the first law that I signed.

Progress is hard. Change can be slow. Opportunity, equality of opportunity, they don't come without a fight. And sometimes you got to fight to keep what you got.

But we know these things are possible. We know that because for the first time in history, young girls across the country can see three women sitting on the bench of the highest court in the land.

We know change is possible because they can read about the incredible leadership of a woman who went by the title Madam Speaker. They can turn on the news and see that one of the most formidable Presidential candidates ever is now doing as much as anyone to improve America's standing abroad as one of the best Secretary of States we've ever known.

These things are possible because earlier generations of Americans did their part to open up new doors of opportunity. And now it's our turn to open up these doors even wider. And what I want to say to all of you is if you're willing to keep pushing through all those obstacles with me, if you're willing to keep reaching for that vision of America that you hold in your hearts—that we hold in our hearts—change will come.

If you're willing to work even harder in this election than in the last one, I promise you we'll finish what we started in 2008. If you're willing to stick with me and fight with me and press on with me, I promise you we will remind everybody just why it is that America is still the greatest nation on Earth.

Thank you. God bless you. God bless the United States of America.

NOTE: The President spoke at 5:12 p.m. at the Walter E. Washington Convention Center. In his remarks, he referred to Sen. Barbara A. Mikulski; Lilly Ledbetter, former employee, Goodyear Tire and Rubber Company plant in Gadsden, AL; Gov. Thomas W. Corbett, Jr., of Pennsylvania; and House Democratic Leader Nancy Pelosi. He also referred to his mother-in-law Marian Robinson and sister Maya Soetoro-Ng.

Remarks at an Obama Victory Fund 2012 Fundraiser
April 27, 2012

Thank you. Everybody, please have a seat. It is wonderful to see you here, to be here. And I want to thank Debra for opening up this beautiful home on a lovely day and to then invite some of my best friends over to hang out. [*Laughter*]

A couple of other people I just want to mention very briefly. First of all, as somebody who is working tirelessly on our behalf each and every day, and we're so proud of her, our DNC chair, Debbie Wasserman Schultz, is here, accompanied by the adorable Shelby. Yay! And I want to say thank you to Jane Stetson, who has been such a dear friend, and is now chairing—cochairing our finance committee and doing just extraordinary work each and every day.

Typically, in these more intimate gatherings, what I like to do is to just make a few comments at the top and then make this a conversation. So we'll open it up, and you guys can ask questions, make comments, give me advice. I always get advice. [*Laughter*]

But obviously, we've gone through 3½ of the toughest years that this country has seen in my lifetime and most of yours: the worst financial crisis since the Great Depression, the worst economic crisis worldwide since the 1930s. The month I took office, we lost 750,000 jobs. The U.S. auto industry, the iconic industry that had helped to create our middle class, was on the verge of liquidation—at least two of the three of the Big Three auto firms.

We were in the midst of two wars. And I think there had been decades of issues that had been put off and put off—whether it was health care or energy or education—and a sense that somehow we could not get done what needed to get done to ensure that middle class families regained a sense of security, so that if they worked hard and they acted re-sponsibly, that they'd be able to afford a home and send their kids to college and retire with dignity and respect. That sense that we would be passing on a future for our children that was greater than ours.

That's what propelled me to run. And after 3½ years, we're nowhere near where we need to be yet. But think about the extraordinary progress that we've been able to make.

Over the last 3 months alone, 600,000 jobs created, 4 million jobs created over the last 2 years. We've been able to save an auto industry where GM is now the number-one automaker again in the world, saved probably a million jobs throughout the Midwest. Chrysler is back. And our auto industry is actually making better cars, cars that are being sold all around the world. Doubled fuel efficiency standards on cars, so that not only are we helping to save the planet, but we're saving people at the pump and helping to reduce our dependence on foreign oil so that it's below 50 percent for the first time in 13 years.

Passing health care reform that provides 30 million people, for the first time, the opportunity to get health insurance that didn't have it before. And it makes young people—it makes it possible for young people to stay on their parents' health insurance; 2.5 million young people already taking advantage of that. Preventive care, including mammograms and cervical cancer screenings for women, contraceptive care.

And not only is it helping families, but it's also help the country as a whole, because over time, what we're building into is a health care system that's going to be more efficient and provide better quality. And by the way, just yesterday or today Kaiser released a study showing that there's going to be over a billion dollars of rebates going out to millions of families all across America because of this law.

So whether it's what we've done on education with Race to the Top and helping to initiate school reform in more than 40 States; whether it's what we've done on clean energy—doubling the amount of energy that's coming from wind and solar and helping to build from scratch essentially an advanced battery industry that will be the future of automation—or the automotive industry for the future; whether it's the work that we've done not just to end the war in Iraq, but also to start transitioning our troops out of Afghanistan so that they can take greater responsibility in restoring that sense of respect for America around the world—on all these fronts, we've made enormous progress.

But we've got a lot more to do. I won't be satisfied until everybody can find a job that pays a living wage and allows them either to stay in the middle class, but also creates those ladders of opportunity into the middle class.

I'm not going to be satisfied until we once again have the best education system in the world and college is affordable for young people all across the country.

I'm not going to be satisfied not just with getting our troops home from Afghanistan, but making sure—as we talked about today down in Fort Stewart—that every single one of our veterans have the capacity to rebuild this country the same way my grandfather had and his generation had the capacity to rebuild the country when they came back from World War II.

So we've got a lot more work to do. And here's the good news. I think that when you look at the issues, when you look at where people stand in terms of making sure that everybody is getting a fair shot, everybody is doing their fair share, and everybody is playing by the same set of rules; when you look at how they feel about Wall Street reform or health care re-

form and break it down specifically—not, sort of, just the rhetoric that goes on out there, but do you believe that young people should be able to stay on their parents' health care plans, do you believe that seniors should be able to afford prescription drugs and get bigger discounts, do you believe that we should prevent reckless behavior on Wall Street, do you believe that we should have an all-of-the-above energy strategy—when you break down the issues, then people are on our side. They believe what we believe.

But understandably, things are tough, and they've grown cynical, and they see the mess that goes on in Washington and there's a temptation at a certain point to just say, oh, a plague on both their houses, nothing is getting done.

And so we're going to have to work harder this time than we did in '08. I always say, back in '08, I wasn't as gray, and it was kind of cool being an Obama supporter. [*Laughter*] And now I'm the President. [*Laughter*] I'm just saying—[*laughter*]—now we see the guy all the time, and he's kind of dinged up.

But I want you to know, my commitment, my sense of determination is undiminished. My confidence in the American people is undiminished. My hunger, my desire to help every one of those folks out there that is trying hard to carve out a life for themselves and their families, that hunger is undiminished.

So I'm going to work harder than I did—I—2008, and if you guys are willing to join me, then we're going to have 4 more years to be able to finish what we started. All right?

Thank you. Thank you.

NOTE: The President spoke at 6:19 p.m. at the residence of Debra L. Lee. In his remarks, he referred to Shelby Schultz, daughter of Rep. Deborah Wasserman Schultz; and Jane Stetson, national finance chair, Democratic National Committee. Audio was not available for verification of the content of these remarks.

The President's Weekly Address
April 28, 2012

On Friday, I traveled to Fort Stewart in Georgia to meet with soldiers from the 3d Infantry Division.

These men and women have fought with bravery and honor in some of the most dangerous places on the planet. Some of them didn't make it back. But those who did are now fighting a different kind of battle here at home. They're looking for new jobs, new opportunities, and new ways to serve.

For many, that means going back to school, and America has a long tradition of making sure our veterans and our men and women in uniform can afford to do that. After World War II, we helped a generation of Americans, including my grandfather, to go to school on the GI bill. Now, thanks to the 9/11 GI bill and the tuition assistance program, last year we supported more than half a million veterans and over 300,000 servicemembers who are pursuing a higher education.

And that's progress. But it's not enough to just help our veterans and servicemembers afford school. We need to make sure they have all the tools they need to make an informed decision when it comes to picking the right program.

The sad truth is, is that there are people out there who are less interested in helping our men and women in uniform get ahead and more interested in making a buck. They bombard potential students with e-mails and pressure them into making a quick decision. Some of them steer recruits towards high-interest loans and mislead them about credit transfers and job placement programs. One of the worst examples was a college recruiter who visited a marine barracks and enrolled marines with brain injuries so severe that some of them couldn't recall what courses the recruiter had signed them up for.

That's appalling. It's disgraceful. And even though the vast majority of schools do the right thing, we need to guard against the bad actors who don't.

That's why, on Friday, I signed an Executive order making life a whole lot more secure for our servicemembers, veterans, and their families, and a whole lot tougher for anyone who tries to prey on them.

We're making sure veterans and servicemembers get a simple fact sheet called "Know Before You Owe" that lays out all the information they need about financial aid and paying for college. We're requiring schools to offer counseling to help students finish their degree even if they have to move or deploy. And we're stepping up our efforts to fight dishonest recruiters by strengthening the rules about who can come on base and make it easier to file complaints.

When our men and women in uniform succeed, our country succeeds. They have our backs; now it's our turn to have theirs. And as long as I'm President, I'm going to make sure that anyone who serves this country gets every opportunity they deserve.

Thank you, and have a great weekend.

NOTE: The address was recorded at approximately 4 p.m. on April 27 in the Grand Foyer at the White House for broadcast on April 28. In the address, the President referred to Executive Order 13607, which is listed in Appendix D at the end of this volume. The transcript was made available by the Office of the Press Secretary on April 27, but was embargoed for release until 6 a.m. on April 28.

Remarks at the White House Correspondents' Association Dinner
April 28, 2012

The President. Thank you. Good evening, everybody. Good evening. I could not be more thrilled to be here tonight—[*laughter*]—at the White House Correspondents' Dinner. This is a great crowd. They're already laughing. It's terrific.

Chuck Todd, love you, brother. [*Laughter*] I'm delighted to see some of the cast members of "Glee" are here. [*Laughter*] And Jimmy Kimmel, it's an honor, man. [*Laughter*] What's so funny?

My fellow Americans, we gather during a historic anniversary. Last year at this time—in fact, on this very weekend—we finally delivered justice to one of the world's most notorious individuals.

[*At this point, a photograph of Trump Organization Chairman and Chief Executive Officer Donald J. Trump was shown.*]

Now, this year, we gather in the midst of a heated election season. And Axelrod tells me I should never miss a chance to reintroduce myself to the American people. So tonight this is how I'd like to begin: My name is Barack Obama. My mother was born in Kansas. My father was born in Kenya. And I was born, of course, in Hawaii. [*Laughter*]

[*The President winked at the audience.*]

In 2009, I took office in the face of some enormous challenges. Now, some have said I blame too many problems on my predecessor, but let's not forget that's a practice that was initiated by George W. Bush. [*Laughter*] Since then, Congress and I have certainly had our differences; yet, I've tried to be civil, to not take any cheap shots. And that's why I want to especially thank all the Members who took a break from their exhausting schedule of not passing any laws to be here tonight. [*Laughter*] Let's give them a big round of applause.

Despite many obstacles, much has changed during my time in office. Four years ago, I was locked in a brutal primary battle with Hillary Clinton. Four years later, she won't stop drunk-texting me from Cartagena. [*Laughter*]

Four years ago, I was a Washington outsider. Four years later, I'm at this dinner. Four years ago, I looked like this.

[*A photograph of the President during his 2008 election campaign was shown.*]

Today, I look like this. [*Laughter*]

[*A recent photograph of the President was shown.*]

And 4 years from now, I will look like this. [*Laughter*]

[*A photograph of actor Morgan Freeman was shown.*]

That's not even funny. [*Laughter*]

Anyway, it's great to be here this evening in the vast, magnificent Hilton ballroom, or what Mitt Romney would call a little fixer-upper. [*Laughter*] I mean, look at this party. We've got men in tuxes, women in gowns, fine wine, first-class entertainment. I was just relieved to learn this was not a GSA conference. [*Laughter*] Unbelievable. Not even the mindreader knew what they were thinking. [*Laughter*]

Of course, the White House Correspondents' dinner is known as the prom of Washington, DC, a term coined by political reporters who clearly never had the chance to go to an actual prom. [*Laughter*]

Our chaperone for the evening is Jimmy Kimmel, who is perfect for the job since most of tonight's audience is in his key demographic, people who fall asleep during "Nightline." [*Laughter*] Jimmy got his start years ago on "The Man Show." In Washington, that's what we call a congressional hearing on contraception. [*Laughter*]

And plenty of journalists are here tonight. I'd be remiss if I didn't congratulate the Huffington Post on their Pulitzer Prize. You deserve it, Arianna. There's no one else out there linking to the kinds of hard-hitting journalism that HuffPo is linking to every single day. [*Laughter*] Give them a round of applause. And you don't pay them. It's a great business model. [*Laughter*]

Even Sarah Palin is getting back into the game, guest hosting on the "Today" show, which reminds me of an old saying: What's the difference between a hockey mom and a pit bull? A pit bull is delicious. [*Laughter*] A little soy sauce—[*laughter*].

Now, I know at this point many of you are expecting me to go after my likely opponent, Newt Gingrich. [*Laughter*] Newt, there's still time, man. [*Laughter*] But I'm not going to do that. I'm not going to attack any of the Republican candidates. Take Mitt Romney. He and I actually have a lot in common. We both think of our wives as our better halves, and polls show, to a alarmingly insulting extent, the American people agree. [*Laughter*] We also both have degrees from Harvard; I have one, he has two. What a snob. [*Laughter*]

Of course, we've also had our differences. Recently, his campaign criticized me for slow jamming the news with Jimmy Fallon. In fact, I understand Governor Romney was so incensed he asked his staff if he could get some equal time on "The Merv Griffin Show." [*Laughter*] Still, I guess Governor Romney is feeling pretty good about things because he took a few hours off the other day to see "The Hunger Games." Some of you have seen it. It's a movie about people who court wealthy sponsors and then brutally savage each other until only one contestant is left standing. I'm sure this was a really great change of pace for him. [*Laughter*] I have not seen "The Hunger Games," not enough class warfare for me. [*Laughter*]

Of course, I know everybody is predicting a nasty election, and thankfully, we've all agreed that families are off limits. Dogs, however, are apparently fair game. [*Laughter*] And while both campaigns have had some fun with this, the other day I saw a new ad from one of these outside groups that, frankly, I think crossed the line. I know Governor Romney says he has no control over what his super PACs do, but can we show the ad real quick?

[*A video was shown.*]

The President. That's pretty rough—[*laughter*]—but I can take it, because my stepfather always told me, it's a boy-eat-dog world out there. [*Laughter*]

Now, if I do win a second term as President, let me just say something to all the—[*applause*]—let me just say something to all my conspiracy-oriented friends on the right who think I'm planning to unleash some secret agenda: You're absolutely right. [*Laughter*] So allow me to close with a quick preview of the secret agenda you can expect in a second Obama administration.

In my first term, I sang Al Green; in my second term, I'm going with Young Jeezy. [*Laughter*]

The First Lady. Yeah.

The President. Michelle said, "Yeah." [*Laughter*] I sing that to her sometimes. [*Laughter*]

In my first term, we ended the war in Iraq; in my second term, I will win the war on Christmas. [*Laughter*] In my first term, we repealed the policy known as "don't ask, don't tell"—[*applause*]—wait, though; in my second term, we will replace it with a policy known as "It's Raining Men." [*Laughter*] In my first term, we passed health care reform; in my second term, I guess I'll pass it again.

I do want to end tonight on a slightly more serious note. Whoever takes the oath of office next January will face some great challenges, but he will also inherit traditions that make us greater than the challenges we face. And one of those traditions is represented here tonight: a free press that isn't afraid to ask questions, to examine, and to criticize. And in service of that mission, all of you make sacrifices.

Tonight we remember journalists such as Anthony Shadid and Marie Colvin, who made the ultimate sacrifice as they sought to shine a light on some of the most important stories of our time. So whether you are a blogger or a broadcaster, whether you take on powerful interests here at home or put yourself in harm's way overseas, I have the greatest respect and admiration for what you do. I know sometimes you like to give me a hard time—and I certainly like to return the favor—[*laughter*]—but I never forget that our country depends on you. You help protect our freedom, our democracy, and our way of life.

And just to set the record straight, I really do enjoy attending these dinners. In fact, I had a lot more material prepared, but I have to get the Secret Service home in time for their new curfew. [*Laughter*]

Thank you very much, everybody. Thank you.

NOTE: The President spoke at 9:57 p.m. at the Washington Hilton hotel. In his remarks, he referred to Chuck Todd, chief White House correspondent, NBC News; James C. Kimmel, host, ABC's "Jimmy Kimmel Live!" program; David M. Axelrod, communications director of the President's 2012 election campaign; Republican Presidential candidate former Gov. W. Mitt Romney of Massachusetts and his wife Ann; Arianna Huffington, founder and editor in chief, the Huffington Post; former Gov. Sarah Palin of Alaska; Republican Presidential candidate Newton L. Gingrich; James T. Fallon, Jr., host, NBC's "Late Night With Jimmy Fallon" program; and musicians Al Green and Jay W. "Young Jeezy" Jenkins. He also referred to journalists Anthony Shadid, who died while on assignment in Syria on February 16, and Marie Colvin, who was killed while on assignment in Homs, Syria, on February 19.

Remarks at an Obama Victory Fund 2012 Fundraiser in McLean, Virginia
April 29, 2012

The President. Thank you so much. It's always good to be in Virginia.

To Dorothy, most of all—[*laughter*]—but also to this guy here, Terry—[*laughter*]—I want to thank the McAuliffe family for this incredible hospitality. Jack, we could not be prouder of you. You look sharp in whites, man. [*Laughter*] And to the whole family, it is a— I'm sure Terry and Dorothy feel the way Michelle and I feel about Malia and Sasha and the way Bill feels about—Bill and Hillary feel about Chelsea. There's nothing we do that's more important than raising our kids. And when we see outstanding young people like this, it gives us a lot of satisfaction.

A couple of other people I want to mention. It was already noted that the next U.S. Senator from the Commonwealth of Virginia, Tim Kaine, is here. I love Tim Kaine. One of the finest men I know and just a great friend and was a great Governor here, obviously.

You also have an outstanding Congressman in Jim Moran in the house. And I need to acknowledge—because some of you know I am a former State senator, so I never pass up the chance to introduce State senators—Barbara Favola is here, and this is her district, and we love State senators. Where's Barbara? She's over there somewhere. Good to see you, Barbara.

Well, you guys get two Presidents for one out of this event—[*laughter*]—which is a pretty good deal. [*Laughter*] And I was—as I was listening to President Clinton speaking, I was just thinking about the remarkable record that he was able to create during his Presidency and his singular capacity to be able to explain very difficult concepts in very understandable terms to the American people. A master communicator. But more importantly than his communication skills was, Bill Clinton understood at a time when, let's face it, the Democratic Party was a little bit lost, he understood what it meant to refocus not on ideology, not on abstractions, but focus on where people live, what they're going through day to day.

And early in our party in such a way that we were thinking about what has always been the central promise of America, the idea that if you work hard, if you play by the rules, if you're responsible, then you can live out that basic American promise: the idea that you can find a job that pays a decent living and buy a home and send your kids to school and not have to worry, if you get sick, that you might go bankrupt, and retire with dignity and respect.

And everything he did, all the years that he was in office, was designed to give people the tools to help fulfill that promise. And he did so to a remarkable degree. Terry mentioned the record.

And ever since that time, because of Bill Clinton's leadership, I think that when you look at the Democratic Party and what we've stood for, it has been squarely at the center of how the American people think and what they believe and is entirely consistent with some of our best traditions and our deepest values.

Now, as has been mentioned, when I came into office, obviously, we were experiencing the worst financial crisis since the Great Depression, the worst economic crisis since the Great Depression. The month I was sworn into office we lost 750,000 jobs, as I was taking the oath. We had lost 4 million jobs the 6 months prior, and we would lose another several million jobs before economic policies had a chance to take effect.

So a lot of what we've done over the last 3½ years has been designed just to right the ship to respond to crises: to make sure that Detroit didn't go under, to make sure that the banking system was no longer locked up, to make sure that small businesses could get loans and consumers could buy a home again or buy a car again, making sure that the system did not break down. And that took enormous amounts of energy and some pretty tough and difficult political decisions.

But I didn't run for President simply to get back to where we were in 2007. I didn't run for President simply to restore the status quo before the financial crisis. I ran for President because we had lost our way since Bill Clinton was done being President. And for almost a decade, what we had seen for ordinary families was a betrayal of that basic promise, that core American idea.

The economy in fits and starts grew between 2000 and 2008, but wages and incomes flatlined. Corporations were profitable, but ordinary people felt like they were working harder and harder just to get by. That sense of middle class security and the notion that successive generations would do better than the previous one, that felt like it was slipping away for too many people. That's why I ran for President in 2008, to restore that basic promise.

And that's why over the last 3½ years, in addition to dealing with immediate crises, what we've tried to do is make sure that we were finally dealing with some of those issues that had been put off and put off and put off, so that once again we could build an economy with a firm foundation, an economy built to last, an economy that would deliver for ordinary Americans, regardless of where they came from, what they looked like, what their last names were, that idea that you could make it here if you try.

And that's why we took on issues like health care reform, because as President Clinton said, the single most important thing to liberate our businesses, to make sure workers are getting raises, and to free ourselves from crippling debt both at the Federal level and at the State level was if we started having a more sensible health care system that provided better quality for lower cost.

And what we've been able to do as a consequence—if you look right now—2.5 million young people able to get health insurance because they're staying on their parent's plan; millions of seniors getting discounts on their prescription drugs that they weren't getting before; people being able to get preventive care, the best kind of care, instead of having to go to the emergency room; 30 million people who are going to be able to get health care who didn't have it before; people not having to worry if they've got a preexisting condition. And now we're seeing rebates all across the country, over a billion dollars in rebates to consumers, even as health care costs overall are going down.

On education, not only did we make college more affordable, taken $60 billion that was going to banks as middlemen in the student loan program, and we were able to cut out the middleman and send that money directly to young people so that now millions more young people are either eligible for Pell grants or getting higher Pell grants than they were before and are able to access a college education. We put in place a $10,000 tax credit for young people—or for their parents. [*Laughter*] I know you guys are sympathetic. [*Laughter*]

But we also started focusing on K–12 and how we're going to not just—[*applause*]—how we're going to get past this debate about reform or more money and say we need money and reform and let's reform those districts and those States and those schools that are doing the right thing and retaining outstanding teachers and developing them. And let's stop just teaching to the test. Let's make sure that teachers can teach with creativity and passion, but let's hold them accountable. And so with the help of Arne Duncan and the Secretary of Education, we are on track. Over 40 States now have adopted unprecedented reforms that are going to help us win the 21st century.

We refocused on manufacturing. And everybody has noted the fact that we helped to save Detroit, but here's the good news. Detroit is building better cars. [*Laughter*] Cars that folks want to drive. We're going to be getting 55 miles per gallon by the middle of the next decade, which will save the average driver $8,000 at the pump. And that's part of the reason why, actually, we are now consuming—less than 50 percent of our energy is imported, less than 50 percent of our oil is important. So there is an economic benefit; there is a security benefit.

But not only have we helped Detroit produce better cars, we've also created entire new industries. Advanced battery manufacturing: The key to electric cars is going to be who wins the race to make the best battery. And when we came into office, it looked like maybe 2 percent of the market was going to go to U.S. companies. Now it looks like it's going to be 40 percent, because of what we did. We are going to be winning the race for clean energy all across the board.

So whether it's our investments in clean energy, whether it's our reform of education, whether it's our reform of the health care system, whether it's making sure that Wall Street is operating by the same rules so we don't go through the same cycle that we did before, whether it's creating a Consumer Finance Protection Bureau that ensures people that aren't getting cheated in their financial transactions—what we've done is not just deal with crisis, but also try to play the long game and try to think what are the strategies, what are the investments that are going to help us grow over the long term, and what do we need to do to make sure that everybody gets a fair shot and everybody is doing their fair share and everybody is playing by the same set of rules.

Now, I joke sometimes with my staff, a lot of what we've done, a lot of what President Clinton did, there was a time when Republicans thought these were pretty good ideas. [*Laughter*] No, that's the truth. [*Laughter*] I mean, you can go back to the first Republican President, who comes from my home State, a guy named Abraham Lincoln, who built the first—helped to create the transcontinental railroad system and in the midst of civil war started the land-grant colleges and the National Academy of Sciences, understood the need to make investments in the future. That was not a foreign idea to the Republican Party.

There's Teddy Roosevelt, who thought it was a good idea to have a progressive income tax because he understood that the market works best—Teddy Roosevelt was no Socialist—[*laughter*]—but what he understood was, is that if you've got basic rules of the road in place and you've got equity in the tax system, then everybody can compete and people win based on the best ideas, not who they can prevent from competing. And you create platforms in which everybody can succeed. That was part of Republican ideas.

As recently as when President Clinton was President, when he tried to tackle health care, he had partners in the United States Senate and in the House on the Republican side who said, you know what, this is an idea that has to be tackled. We may not agree with you on every detail, but we understand that we can't keep on spending 18 percent of our GDP on health care and leave 30, 40 million people uninsured. That doesn't make sense.

And it used to be a guy like a Bob Dole or a Howard Baker, if they wanted to—you know, they were conservative, fiscal hawks—the idea was we were going to balance a budget, and they sure didn't like tax increases, but they understood if we're making cuts in spending, then we also need to pay for the kind of Government we want. And we're going to do a balanced approach to how we bring down deficits.

These were not just Democratic ideas, these were American ideas. And part of what's happened—[*applause*]—so part of what's happened is we now have a Republican Party that's unrecognizable. I've said this, and I meant it: Ronald Reagan could not get through a Republican primary in this election cycle—[*laughter*]—could not get through it. Here's a guy who raised taxes. That in and of itself would have rendered him unelectable in a Republican primary.

So I want to, when you're talking to your friends and your neighbors—I know everybody here knows some Republicans. [*Laughter*] You might be married to some, might have a mom and dad and whoever. [*Laughter*] And describe for them what it is that's at stake in this election.

When you've got a House Republican budget that would, on top of the Bush tax cuts for the wealthy, initiate an additional $4 trillion or $5 trillion in tax cuts that would be paid for by decimating everything that Bill Clinton talked about, everything that Terry McAuliffe talked about, everything I've been talking about, so that the nondefense side of the budget, other than Social Security would amount to less than 1 percent; historically, it's never been under 8 percent, even under Republican Presidents. And they're talking about taking this, everything—education, infrastructure, food safety, environmental protection, national parks, whatever it is that you conceive of as part of what we do together because we can't do it on our own—that would be reduced to less than 1 percent of the budget. It would basically be wiped out. That's not my opinion, that's what they're proposing.

And so it is impossible—taking their budget, taking their philosophy, taking their approach—to imagine how we compete with China on something like clean energy. It's impossible to imagine us being able to rebuild our roads, our bridges, our ports, our broadband lines. It's impossible for us to imagine being able to educate our kids effectively and to produce the number of engineers that we're going to need, the number of scientists we're going to need, the number of mathematicians that we're going to need.

So every election, Presidents will—or candidates will say this is the election that—this is a crossroads, this is the biggest election in histo-

ry. [*Laughter*] I'm sure back in 1988, 1989, every—you say this is—[*laughter*]—we need a bridge to the 21st century and all that. [*Laughter*] Every election is the most important election in our history. [*Laughter*]

But let me tell you: This one matters. [*Applause*] This one matters. [*Applause*] This one matters.

And that's before we start talking about foreign policy. Hillary and I, we've spent the last 3½ years cleaning up after other folks' messes. And by the way, we've got them—we're starting to get them pretty cleaned up. The war in Iraq is over. We're transitioning in Afghanistan. We've got the strongest allies we've ever seen. And Al Qaida is on the ropes. So we've done what we said we'd do.

But when you've got the leading contender, the presumptive nominee, on the other side suddenly saying our number-one enemy isn't Al Qaida, it's Russia—[*laughter*]. I don't make that up. [*Laughter*] I'm suddenly thinking, what—maybe I didn't check the calendar this morning. [*Laughter*] I didn't know we were back in 1975. [*Laughter*]

That's before I start talking about social issues that are at stake. You know something about that in Virginia, the kinds of nonsense that's been going on. But that's all across the country. When you have folks who talk about—want to repeal "don't ask"—repeal the repeal of "don't ask, don't tell." [*Laughter*] When you have folks who are talking about not just constraining women's reproductive health, but questioning things like contraception as part of our preventive care.

That's before I start talking about the fact that there are going to be some Supreme Court appointments probably, if you look actuarially, for the next President. There's so much at stake here.

So let me just close by saying this. I've overstayed my welcome. Dorothy is saying, golly, I'm trying to get these people out of this house. My lawn is all messed up. [*Laughter*]

Let me just say this, and I think Bill will agree with me. There's nothing more humbling, actually, than being President. It's a strange thing. Suddenly, you've got all the pomp and the circumstance, and you've got the helicopters, and you've got the Air Force One and—and the plane is really nice. [*Laughter*] It really is. I mean, Bill may not miss being President, but he misses that plane. [*Laughter*] Let's face it, he does. It's a great plane. And I'll miss it too. [*Laughter*]

Audience member. But not yet!

The President. But not yet. [*Laughter*]

But the reason it's humbling is because you wake up every morning and you know there are folks out there still hurting, especially in what we've been going through over the last 4 years. Yes, you get letters, or you talk to folks, and they've lost their job, or they've lost their home, or they thought they were going to retire, and suddenly, they realize they can't. Or it's a young person who has figured out, you know what, I've got to see if I can find work to help my family, even though I was planning to go to college. And every day, you know that there's just some portion of the country that are good and decent and working really hard and they're still having a tough time. And you want to just be able to help each one of those people, one by one, because they're deserving of it, because they represent what's best in America. And you know that at the end of the day, no matter how hard you work, there's still going to be some stuff left undone. And you also know that you're going to make mistakes and there are going to be times where your team makes mistakes. And so your mind doesn't rest, because you're constantly thinking, what else do I need to be doing?

But I'll tell you two things that keep me going. The first is—and I'm sure President Clinton agrees with this—you get no better vantage point of how wonderful the American people are than when you're President of the United States. And as you're traveling around the country, the resilience and the strength and the core decency of the American people inspire you. And you say to yourself, you know

what, no matter what we're going through right now, we're going to be okay. We're going to figure this out, because that's who we are and that's what we do. No matter how times—how tough times are, in fact, maybe especially when times are tough, we full together and we figure it out.

And the other thing that gets you through is—or at least gets me through is—I said back in 2008, I'm not a perfect man, and I will not be a perfect President; Michelle will confirm that. [*Laughter*] But I made a promise that I'd always tell people what I thought, I'd always tell people where I stood, and I'd always wake up every single day working as hard as I could on behalf of you. And that promise, I can say, I've kept. And I can look in the mirror and say that I've kept that promise.

And so if you're willing to join us and finish what we started in 2008 and continue what Bill Clinton was doing when he was President of the United States, and if you are willing to share that vision of what America can be, I guarantee you we won't just win this election, we're going to make sure that we remind this world of ours just why it is America is the greatest nation on Earth.

Thank you, everybody. God bless you. God bless the United States of America.

NOTE: The President spoke at 5:57 p.m. at the residence of Terence R. and Dorothy McAuliffe. In his remarks, he referred to Jack McAuliffe, son of Mr. and Mrs. McAuliffe; Chelsea Clinton, daughter of former President William J. Clinton and Secretary of State Hillary Rodham Clinton; former Sens. Robert J. Dole and Howard H. Baker, Jr.; and Republican Presidential candidate former Gov. W. Mitt Romney of Massachusetts. The transcript released by the Office of the Press Secretary also included the remarks of former President Clinton. Audio was not available for verification of the content of these remarks.

Remarks at the National Legislative Conference of the Building and Construction Trades Department of the AFL–CIO
April 30, 2012

The President. Thank you, guys. Everybody, take a seat. Well, thank you, Sean, for that outstanding introduction.

Audience members. Four more years! Four more years! Four more years!

The President. I'll take it!

Audience members. Four more years! Four more years! Four more years!

The President. Thank you. Thank you.

Well, it is good to be back among friends. The last time I was here we—was Saturday night. And they tell me I did okay. But I want to not only thank Sean for his extraordinary leadership, I want to acknowledge all the other presidents who are on stage for what they do each and every day on behalf of not just their members, but on behalf of all working people. I'm proud of that.

I want to thank my good friend Tim Kaine, who is here and is a friend of labor: the next United States Senator from the great Commonwealth of Virginia.

And obviously, we come here at a time where—I just want to repeat my condolences to everybody in the building and construction trades on the passing of Mark Ayers. Mark was a tremendous leader. He was a good friend. His commitment to the labor movement and to working people will leave a mark for years to come. And my thoughts and prayers are with his family. But I know that Sean is going to do an outstanding job, and we wish him all the best in his future endeavors. So congratulations.

So it's good to be back in front of all of you. It's always an honor to be with folks who get up every day and work real jobs—[*laughter*]—and every day fight for America's workers. You represent the latest in a long, proud line of men and women who built this country from the bottom up. That's who you are. It was workers like you who led us westward. It was workers like you who pushed us skyward. It was your predecessors who put down the hardhats and helped us defeat fascism. And when that was done, you kept on building: highways that we drive on and the houses we live in and the schools where our children learn. And you established the foundation of what it means to be a proud American.

And along the way, unions like yours made sure that everybody had a fair shake, everybody had a fair shot. You helped build the greatest middle class that we've ever seen. You believed that prosperity shouldn't be reserved just for a privileged few; it should extend all the way from the boardroom all the way down to the factory floor. That's what you believe.

Time and again, you stood up for the idea that hard work should pay off, responsibility should be rewarded. When folks do the right thing, they should be able to make it here in America. And because you did, America became home of the greatest middle class the world has ever known. You helped make that possible, not just through your organizing, but how you lived, looking after your families, looking out for your communities. You're what America is about.

And so sometimes, when I listen to the political debates, it seems as if people have forgotten American progress has always been driven by American workers. And that's especially important to remember today.

The last decade has been tough on everybody. But the men and women of the building and construction trades have suffered more than most. Since the housing bubble burst, millions of your brothers and sisters have had to look for work. Even more have had to struggle to keep the work coming in. And that makes absolutely no sense at a time when there is so much work to be done.

I don't have to tell you, we've got roads and bridges all over this country in desperate need of repair. Our highways are clogged with traffic. Our railroads are no longer the fastest in the world. Our skies are congested. Our airports are the busiest on the planet. All of this costs families and businesses billions of dollars a year. That drags down our entire economy.

And the worst part of it is that we could be doing something about it. I think about what my grandparents' generation built: the Hoover Dam, the Golden Gate Bridge, the Interstate Highway System. That's what we do: We build. There was a time where we would never accept the notion that some other country has better roads than us and some other country has better airports than us. I don't know about you, but I'm chauvinistic. I want America to have the best stuff. I want us to be doing the building, not somebody else. We should be having—[*applause*]—people should be visiting us from all over the world. They should be visiting us from all over the world and marveling at what we've done.

That kind of unbridled, can-do spirit, that's what made America an economic superpower. And now it's up to us to continue that tradition, to give our businesses access to the best roads and airports and high-speed rail and Internet networks. It's up to us to make sure our kids are learning in state-of-the-art schools. It's our turn to do big things. It is our turn to do big things.

But here's the thing: As a share of the economy, Europe invests more than twice what we do in infrastructure, China about four times as much. Are we going to sit back and let other countries build the newest airports and the fastest railroads and the most modern schools at a time when we've got private construction companies all over the world—or all over the country and millions of workers who are ready and willing to do that work right here in the United States of America?

American workers built this country, and now we need American workers to rebuild this country. That's what we need. It is time we take some of the money that we spend on wars, use half of it to pay down our debt, and then use the rest of it to do some nation-building right here at home. There is work to be done, there are workers ready to do it, and you guys can help lead the way.

Audience member. We can do it!

The President. We can do it. We've done it before. And the truth is, the only way we can do it on a scale that's needed is with some bold action from Congress. They're the ones with the purse strings. That's why, over the last year, I've sent Congress a whole series of jobs bills to put people to work, to put your members back to work. Again and again, I've said now is the time do this. Interest rates are low, construction workers are out of work, contractors are begging for work, and the work needs to be done. Let's do it. And time after time, the Republicans have gotten together, and they've said no.

I sent them a jobs bill that would have put hundreds of thousands of construction workers back to work repairing our roads, our bridges, schools, transit systems, along with saving the jobs of cops and teachers and firefighters, creating a new tax cut for businesses. They said no.

I went to the Speaker's hometown, stood under a bridge that was crumbling. Everybody acknowledges it needs to be rebuilt.

Audience member. Let him drive on it! [*Laughter*]

The President. You know, that—maybe he doesn't drive anymore. Maybe he didn't notice how messed up it was. [*Laughter*] They still said no.

There are bridges between Kentucky and Ohio where some of the key Republican leadership come from, where folks are having to do detours an extra hour, hour and a half drive every day on their commute because these bridges don't work. They still said no.

So then, I said, well, maybe they couldn't handle the whole bill in one big piece. Let's break it up. Maybe it was just too much for them. So I sent them just the part of the bill that would have created these construction jobs. They said no.

We're seeing it again right now. As we speak, the House Republicans are refusing to pass a bipartisan bill that could guarantee work for millions of construction workers. Already passed the Senate—ready to go—ready to put folks back to work. Used to be the most—the easiest bill to pass in Washington used to be getting roads and bridges built, because it's not like only Democrats are allowed to use these things. Everybody is permitted. [*Laughter*] Everybody needs them.

So this makes no sense. Congress needs to do the right thing. Pass this bill right away. It shouldn't be that hard. It shouldn't be that hard. Not everything should be subject to thinking about the next election instead of thinking about the next generation. Not everything should be subject to politics instead of thinking about all those families out there and all your membership that need work, that don't just support their own families, but support entire communities.

So we're still waiting for Congress. But we can't afford to just wait for Congress. You can't afford to wait. So where Congress won't act, I will. That's why I've taken steps on my own. That's why I've taken steps on my own and speeded up loans and speeded up competitive grants for projects across the country that will support thousands of jobs. That's why we're cutting through the redtape and launching a lot of existing projects faster and more efficiently.

Because the truth is, Government can be smarter. A whole bunch of projects at the State level sometimes are ready to go, but they get tangled up in all kinds of bureaucracy and redtape. So what we've said is, if there's redtape that's stopping a project and stopping folks from getting to work right now, let's put that aside.

Because the point is, infrastructure shouldn't be a partisan issue. Investments in better roads and safer bridges, these have never been made by just one party or another because they benefit all of us. They lead to a strong, durable economy. Ronald Reagan once said that rebuilding our infrastructure is "common sense"—"an investment in tomorrow that we need to make today." Ronald Reagan said that. That great Socialist, Ronald Reagan—[*laughter*]—couldn't get through a Republican primary these days.

The folks up on Capitol Hill right now, they seem to have exactly the opposite view. They voted to cut spending on transportation infrastructure by almost 30 percent. That means instead of putting more construction workers back on the job, they want to lay more off. Instead of breaking ground on new projects, they want to let existing projects grind to a halt. Instead of making the investments we need to get ahead, they're willing to let us all fall further behind.

Now, when you ask them, well, why are you doing this—other than the fact that I'm proposing it—[*laughter*]—they'll say it's because we need to pay down our deficit. And you know what? The deficit is a real problem. All of us recognize in our own lives and our own families, we try to live within our means. So we've got to deal with the debt, and we've got to deal with the deficit.

And their argument might actually fly if they didn't just vote to spend $4.6 trillion on lower tax rates—that's with a "t," trillion—on top of the $1 trillion they'd spend on tax cuts for people making more than $250,000 a year. So they're willing to spend over $5 trillion to give tax breaks to folks like me who don't need them and weren't even asking for them at a time when this country needs to be rebuilt. That gives you a sense of their priorities.

Think about that. Republicans in Congress would rather put fewer of you to work rebuilding America than ask millionaires and billionaires to live without massive new tax cuts on top of the ones they've already got.

Now, what do you think will make the economy stronger? Giving another tax break to every millionaire and billionaire in the country? Or rebuilding our roads and our bridges and our broadband networks that will help our businesses sell goods all around the world? It's pretty clear. This choice is not a hard one.

Of course, we need to bring down our deficits in the long term. But if we're smart about it, we also will be making and can afford to make the investments that will help our country and the American people in the short term. Not only will it put people back to work, but if the economy is growing—look, every time one of your members is on a job, that means they've got more money in their pockets. That means that they're going to the restaurant, and that restaurant owner suddenly is doing a little bit better. They're going to Home Depot to buy some stuff, and suddenly, Home Depot is doing a little bit better.

This is a no-brainer. And by the way, when everybody is doing better and the economy is growing, lo and behold, that actually helps to bring down the deficit, helps us pay off our debt. Previous generations understood this. Apparently, right now, Republicans disagree.

And what makes it worse—it would be bad enough if they just had these set of bad ideas, but they've also set their sights on dismantling unions like yours. I mean, if you ask them, what's their big economic plan in addition to tax cuts for rich folks, it's dismantling your unions. After all you've done to build and protect the middle class, they make the argument you're responsible for the problems facing the middle class. Somehow, that makes sense to them.

That's not what I believe. I believe our economy is stronger when workers are getting paid good wages and good benefits. That's what I believe. That's what I believe. I believe the economy is stronger when collective bargaining rights are protected. I believe all of us are better off when we've got broad-based prosperity that grows outwards from a strong middle class. I believe when folks try and take collective bargaining rights away by passing so-called right-to-work laws—that might also be called right-to-work-for-less laws—that's not about economics, that's about politics. That's about politics.

That's why we've reversed harmful decisions designed to undermine those rights. That's why we passed the Fair Pay Act to help stop pay discrimination. That's why we've supported Davis-Bacon. That's why we reversed the ban on project labor agreements, because we believe in those things as part of a strategy to rebuild America.

And as long as I'm your President, I'm going to keep it up. I am going to keep it up, because the right to organize and negotiate fair pay for hard work, that's the right of every American, from the CEO in the corner office all the way to the worker who built that office.

And every day, you're hearing from the other side, whether it's the idea that tax cuts for the wealthy are more important than investing for our future or the notion we should pursue antiworker policies in the hopes that somehow unions are going to crumble. It's all part of that same old philosophy—tired, wornout philosophy—that says if you've already made it, we'll protect you; if you haven't made it yet, well, tough luck, you're on your own.

That misreads America. That's not what America is about. The American story has never been about what we can do on our own. It's about what we do together. In the construction industry, nobody gets very far by themselves. I'm the first to admit—I've got to be careful here because I'm—just barely can hammer a nail into the wall. [*Laughter*] And my wife is not impressed with my skills when it comes to fixing up the house. Right now, fortunately, I'm in a rental, so I don't end up having to do a lot of work. [*Laughter*]

But here is what I know about the trades: If you've got folks who aren't pulling together, doing their own thing, things don't work. But if you've got enough people with the same goal, pulling in the same direction, looking at the same game plan, you can build something that will stand long after you're gone. That's how a Hoover Dam or a Golden Gate Bridge or a Empire State Building gets built, folks working together. We can do more together than we can do on our own.

That's why unions were built—understood workers on their own wouldn't have the same ability to look after themselves and their families as they could together. And what's true for you is true for America. We can't settle for a country where just a few people do really well and everybody else struggles to get by. We've got to build an economy where everybody has got a fair shot and everybody does their fair share and everybody plays by the same set of rules. We can't just cut our way to prosperity. We need to fight for an economy that helps everybody, one built on things like American education and American energy and American manufacturing and a kind of world-class infrastructure that makes it all possible.

Now, these have been some tough years we've been in. And I know a lot of your membership can get discouraged, and they can feel like nobody is looking out for them, and they can get frustrated and they—sure, it's easy to give up on Washington. I know that. But we've been through tougher times before. Your unions have been through tougher times before. And we've always been able to overcome it because we don't quit.

I know we can get there, because here in America we don't give up. We've been through tougher times before, and we've made it through because we didn't quit and we didn't throw in the towel. We rolled up our sleeves, we fired up our engines, and we remembered a fundamental truth about our country: Here in America, we rise or fall together as one Nation, as one people.

It doesn't matter where you come from, what you look like, what your last name is. It doesn't matter whether your folks came from Poland or came from Italy or came from Mexico. One people—strong, united, firing all cylinders—that's the America I know. That's the America I believe in. That's the America we can rebuild together.

So, if you're willing to join us in this project of rebuilding America, I want you to know—when I was running for this office, I told people I'm not perfect, not a perfect man. Michelle can tell you that—[*laughter*]—not a perfect President. But I made a promise, I'd always tell you where I stood. I'd always tell you what I thought, what I believed in. And most importantly, I would wake up every single day working as hard as I know how to make your lives a little bit better.

And for all that we've gone through over the last 3½, 4 years, I have kept that promise. I have kept that promise. And I'm still thinking about you. I'm still thinking about you, and I still believe in you. And if you join me, we'll remind the world just why it is that America is the greatest nation on Earth.

Thank you. God bless you. God bless the United States of America.

NOTE: The President spoke at 10:38 a.m. at the Washington Hilton hotel. In his remarks, he referred to Sean McGarvey, secretary-treasurer, Building and Construction Trades Department, AFL–CIO.

The President's News Conference With Prime Minister Yoshihiko Noda of Japan
April 30, 2012

President Obama. Please be seated. Good afternoon, everybody. It is a great pleasure to welcome Prime Minister Noda of Japan, one of America's closest allies in the Asia-Pacific region, but also around the world. And of course, one of the reasons that we enjoy such a strong alliance between our nations is because it's rooted in the deep friendship between our peoples. I've felt it in my own life, during my visits to Japan, including as a young boy. And we've seen that friendship on display very profoundly over the past year.

Last month, we marked the first anniversary of the Great East Japan Earthquake and tsunami and nuclear crisis that followed. All across Japan, people stopped and stood in silence at

2:46 p.m., the moment that the Earth shook. Mr. Prime Minister, on behalf of the American people, I want to say to you and the people of Japan, we continue to stand with you as well.

We stand with Japan in honoring the lost and the missing: 19,000 men, women, and children who will never be forgotten. We stand with you as you rebuild, what you, Mr. Prime Minister, have called "the rebirth of Japan." And we stand with Japan—in the Asia-Pacific and beyond—because even as it has focused on the hard work at home, Japan has never stopped leading in the world. It is a great tribute to the Japanese people and to leaders like Prime Minister Noda.

I'm told that over the past year many Japanese have found strength in what they call *kizuna*: the bonds of solidarity between friends and neighbors, bonds which cannot be broken. Mr. Prime Minister, the same could be said of the bonds between the United States and Japan. And today we welcome you in that spirit.

As President, I've worked to strengthen the ties between our two nations since my first days in office. And when Prime Minister Noda and I first met last September, we agreed to modernize our alliance to meet the needs of the 21st century. And, Mr. Prime Minister, I want to thank you for the personal commitment that you've brought to this effort. You've called the alliance with the United States Japan's greatest asset. And in our work together, we've seen your trademark determination and humility.

In fact, during our discussions today, the Prime Minister compared his leadership style to that of a point guard in basketball; he may not be the flashiest player, but he stays focused and gets the job done. He's brought that same sense of teamwork to our partnership, and it's helped make this visit a milestone in the history of our alliance.

I'm proud to announce that we have agreed to a new joint vision to guide our alliance and help shape the Asia-Pacific for decades to come. This is part of the broader effort I discussed in Australia last year in which the United States is once again leading in the Asia-Pacific.

First, we recognize that the U.S.-Japan alliance will remain the foundation of the security and prosperity of our two nations, but also a cornerstone of regional peace and security. As such, we reviewed the agreement that our governments reached last week to realign American forces in Japan. This reflects our effort to modernize America's defense posture in the Asia-Pacific with forces that are more broadly distributed, more flexible, and more sustainable. At the same time, it will reduce the impact on local communities like Okinawa.

Second, our joint vision commits us to deepening our trade and investment. We're already among each other's top trading partners, and our exports to Japan and Japanese companies here in the U.S. support more than 1 million American jobs. But there's more we can do, especially as we work to double U.S. exports. So I appreciate the Prime Minister updating me on his reform efforts in Japan, including liberalizing trade and playing a leading role in Asia-Pacific's economy. We instructed our teams to continue our consultation regarding Japan's interest in joining the Trans-Pacific Partnership, which would benefit both our economies and the region. And we agreed to deepen our cooperation on nuclear safety, clean energy, and cybersecurity to enhance our economic competitiveness.

Third, our joint vision lays out the future we seek in the Asia-Pacific: a region where international rules and norms are upheld, where nations contribute to regional security, where commerce and freedom of navigation is not impeded, and where disputes are resolved peacefully. As such, we continue our close consultations on the provocative actions of North Korea, which are a sign of weakness and not strength and only serve to deepen Pyongyang's isolation. And we discussed the changes underway in Burma and how our two nations can both reward progress there while encouraging more reforms that improve the lives of the Burmese people.

Fourth, our joint vision reaffirms our role as global partners bound by shared values and committed to international peace, security, and human rights. For example, our nations are the largest donors in Afghanistan. As we plan for the NATO summit in Chicago and the next phase of the transition in Afghanistan, Japan is planning for a donor conference to sustain development there.

I also want to take this opportunity to commend the Prime Minister and Japan for showing such strong leadership with regard to Iran's nuclear program. The regime in Tehran is now feeling the economic screws tighten, and one of the reasons is that countries like Japan made the decision to reduce oil imports from Iran. This is just one more example of how, despite challenging times at home, Japan has continued to serve as a model and a true global leader.

Finally, our joint vision commits us to deepening the ties between our peoples. This includes new collaborations between our scientists, researchers, and entrepreneurs to foster innovation. And it includes new exchanges that will bring thousands of our young people together, including high school students, to help Japanese communities rebuild after last year's disasters.

So again, Mr. Prime Minister, thank you for helping to revitalize our extraordinary alliance so that we enjoy even greater security and prosperity for both our countries. And I once again want to salute the people of Japan for the strength and the resilience and the courage that they've shown during this past year. More than ever, the American people are proud to call you a friend and honored to call you an ally.

And before I turn it over to the Prime Minister, I just want to warn the American press that the Prime Minister once considered himself a journalist, and instead, he became a judo expert. He is a black belt. [*Laughter*] So, if you get out of line—[*laughter*]—I've got some protection here. [*Laughter*]

Mr. Prime Minister.

Prime Minister Noda. Well, following President Obama forward, I, the point guard, Noda, will take up the microphone.

Now, this is the first visit to the United States by a Japanese Prime Minister in the context—the bilateral context since the change of Government took place in Japan. I wish to thank President Obama for the warm welcome and hospitality, as I know how busy he is with official duties.

I had a very good exchange of views with the President today on bilateral relations between Japan and the United States, the situation in the Asia-Pacific region, and various global challenges, among others. We were able to confirm from broader perspectives the present-day significance of the Japan-U.S. alliance and where the Japan-U.S. relations should be headed in the longer term.

The President just now spoke about his support, and I would like to take this opportunity to say thank you for all the unsparing support given by the Government and people of the United States, starting with Operation Tomodachi conducted by U.S. forces at the time of the Great East Japan Earthquake of last year.

Yesterday I met with the bereaved family—bereaved families of Taylor Anderson, who unfortunately passed away, but who took care of children until the very last moment following the Great East Japan Earthquake. I also met with representatives of the Fairfax County search and rescue team who, immediately following the earthquake, deployed in the disaster-affected region to help the people. So I was able to see—meet myself with these true friends of Japan.

Now, I have always held the conviction that our bilateral alliance is the lynchpin of Japan's diplomacy. And having had conversations with my—with U.S. friends yesterday only renewed my conviction that Japan-U.S. alliance must be unshakeable and in fact is unshakeable. Now, as one holding such conviction, I am particularly gratified that we're able to announce today a Japan-U.S. shared vision.

This document explicitly spells out the determination of Japan and the United States to fulfill their responsibilities and the roles in the interest of the peace and prosperity not only in the Asia-Pacific, but around the world by making full use of their respective capabilities and resources.

And this is my conviction as well. [*Inaudible*]—and arms buildup, and not to speak of the presence of D.P.R.K. In other words, major opportunities and challenges exist side by side in the region.

To cope with such conditions we are determined, as spelled out in the shared vision, to realize the new U.S. forces realignment plan in accordance with the Security Consultative Committee, or 2-plus-2, joint statement released the other day and to step up bilateral security and defense cooperation in a creative manner.

We also need to work with regional partners to build a multilayered network that is open, comprehensive, and building on international rules utilizing such frameworks as trilateral dialogues among Japan-U.S.-R.O.K. and Japan-U.S.-Australia, East Asia Summit, and APEC.

From this point of view, we shall also cooperate with China, which is an important partner.

It is also important that Japan and the United States cooperate to promote necessary rules-making in the areas of nontraditional threats such as terrorism, proliferation of weapons of mass destruction, and piracy, as well as human security and peace-building and development assistance: ocean, space, and cyberspace.

In the economic area, we shall deepen bilateral economic ties and fortify the growth and prosperity of the two countries through their promotion of economic integration in the Asia-Pacific region. And to this end, both our countries will work on regional trade and investment rules-making, with a view to building FTAAP, or the free trade area of the Asia-Pacific. From this vantage point as well, we shall advance consultations with a view to participating in the Trans-Pacific Partnership negotiations.

The shared vision also calls for the strengthening of energy cooperation. And we discussed in our meeting today expanding LNG exports from the United States to Japan.

Last, but not the least, as stated in the shared vision it is important to boost exchanges among next generation youth in the interest of the future of the Japan-U.S. alliance. We will further step up people-to-people exchanges among youth through such endeavors as Japan's Kizuna Project and U.S. Tomodachi Initiative.

Japan-U.S. alliance has reached new heights. Together with President Obama, I shall firmly advance these steps. I thank you.

President Obama. So we've got two questions on each side. We're going to start with Laura MacInnis of Reuters.

Chinese Activist Chen Guangcheng/Human Rights/North Korea

Q. President Obama, could you confirm whether the blind Chinese dissident Chen Guangcheng is under U.S. protection in Beijing? And how do you foresee that situation being resolved? Would the United States grant him asylum if he asked for it?

And, Prime Minister Noda, how likely do you think it is that North Korea will carry out a third nuclear test? How would Japan respond to such a test? And what would you like the U.S. to do to respond?

President Obama. Obviously, I'm aware of the press reports on the situation in China, but I'm not going to make a statement on the issue. What I would like to emphasize is that every time we meet with China, the issue of human rights comes up. It is our belief that not only is that the right thing to do because it comports with our principles and our belief in freedom and human rights, but also because we actually think China will be stronger as it opens up and liberalizes its own system.

We want China to be strong, and we want it to be prosperous. And we're very pleased with all the areas of cooperation that we've been able to engage in. But we also believe that that relationship will be that much stronger and China will be that much more prosperous and strong as you see improvements on human rights issues in that country.

I know it wasn't directed at me, but I'll just make a quick statement around North Korea. This was a topic of extensive discussion between myself and Prime Minister Noda. Our consultation throughout the failed missile launch was, I think, reflective of how important our alliance is not just to our two countries, but to the region as a whole. And what I've tried to do since I came into office is to make sure that the North Koreans understand that the old pattern of provocation that then gets attention and somehow insists on the world purchasing good behavior from them, that that pattern is broken.

And what we've said is, is that the more you engage in provocative acts, the more isolated you will become, the stronger sanctions will be in place, the more isolated you will be diplomatically, politically, and commercially. And so although we can't anticipate—and I don't want to hypothesize on what might happen in the coming months—I think Pyongyang is very clear that the United States, Japan, South Korea, other countries in the region are unified in insisting that it abide by its responsibilities, abide by international norms, and that they will not be able to purchase anything from further provocative acts.

Prime Minister Noda. With regard to North Korea, between myself and President Obama earlier we—with regard to the so-called launch of satellite—the missile launch—we share the view that it undermines the efforts of the various countries concerned to achieve resolution through dialogue.

Now, in the latest round of missile launch, they also conducted a nuclear test, which means that there is a great possibility they will conduct a nuclear test. And I believe the international community as a whole, together, will need to call for restraint on the part of D.P.R.K. And more specifically, I believe the measures incorporated in the recent U.N. Security Council chairman's statement need to be complied with. And among Japan, the U.S., and Korea, as well as China and Russia, we need to communicate with each other fully and also call—stress that China's role continues to be very important and cooperate with China while also maintaining close coordination with the United States. And we shared this view with President Obama.

And let me ask Mr. Imaichi of TBS, from Japan, to ask a question.

U.S. Military Installations in Japan

Q. Imaichi of TBS Television, and I have a question for both President Obama and Prime Minister Noda. How do you regard the Futenma relocation issue in the context of this joint statement, although you did not refer specifically to Futenma relocation? And the interim report on U.S. Forces Japan realignment leaves this question open to some extent. And what do you think of the possibility that Futenma Air Station ultimately will be relocated to a place other than Henoko as agreed between Japan and the United States?

Prime Minister Noda. Now, it is most meaningful that in the 2-plus-2 joint statement, as well as the summit meeting today, that we were able to confirm that our two countries will cooperate in the context of a deepening bilateral alliance towards the realization of the optimum U.S. force posture in the region and the reduction of burden on Okinawa, and we'll continue to work for an early resolution of this issue by taking into account the development of the—[*inaudible*]—date.

President Obama. The realignment approach that's being taken is consistent with the security interests of both Japan and the United States. We think we've found an effective mechanism to move this process forward in a way that is respectful of the situation in Okinawa, the views of residents there, but also is able to optimize the defense cooperation between our two countries and the alliance that's the linchpin not just of our own security but also security in the region as a whole.

So we're confident that we can move forward with an approach that realigns our base posture or our deployments, but also is continuing to serve the broad-based interests of our alliance as a whole.

And I want to thank publicly Prime Minister Noda for having taken such a constructive approach to an issue that has been lingering in our bilateral relationship for quite some time.

Christi Parson [Christi Parsons, Chicago Tribune].

Counterterrorism Efforts

Q. Thank you, Mr. President. We're coming up on the 1-year anniversary of the killing of bin Laden. I wonder if you would share some thoughts on that anniversary. And I also wanted to mention that your likely opponent says anybody would have made that call, "even Jimmy Carter." So I'm curious to see what you would say about that.

And, Mr. Prime Minister, if I may, on the same topic, you mentioned the international fight against terrorism in your opening remarks, and I wonder if you could reflect on President Obama's record here and if you think from an international perspective the U.S. is playing it right in marking this anniversary? Or if you think it—you might advise against excessive celebration?

President Obama. Well, let me make a couple of points. First of all, Christi, I hardly think that you've seen any excessive celebration taking place here. I think that people—the American people rightly remember what we as a country accomplished in bringing to justice somebody who killed over 3,000 of our citizens. And it's a mark of the excellence of our intelligence teams and our military teams, a political process that worked. And I think for us to use that time for some reflection to give thanks to those who participated is entirely appropriate, and that's what's been taking place.

As far as my personal role and what other folks would do, I'd just recommend that everybody take a look at people's previous statements in terms of whether they thought it was appropriate to go into Pakistan and take out bin Laden. I assume that people meant what they said when they said it. That's been at least my practice. I said that I'd go after bin Laden if we had a clear shot at him, and I did.

If there are others who have said one thing and now suggest they'd do something else, then I'd go ahead and let them explain it.

Prime Minister Noda. President Obama has been standing at the very forefront in the fight against terrorism, and I hold him in very high regard for that.

Now, although bin Laden has been killed, terrorism has not been rooted out, and I think continued efforts will be needed in cooperation with the United States. We also would like to continue all our efforts against terrorism. I think the forms of terrorism are being very diverse, amongst them, cyberterrorism, for example. This—[*inaudible*]—between Japan and the United States not just in the cyber—in the space and ocean, but we also decided to cooperate in cybersecurity as well. So, inclusive of all these, Japan and the United States shall work together to root out terrorism of all sorts.

Let me call on Takatsuka-san of Mainichi Shimbun.

China

Q. I'm Takatsuka with Mainichi Shimbun newspaper, and I would like to ask a question for Prime Minister Noda and President Obama.

There's no direct reference to China in this joint statement. What sort of exchange of views did you have on China in the context of working for stability in the Asia-Pacific connected with their advances in the oceans and also their military buildup? I wonder what sort of interlocution you had on the subject.

Prime Minister Noda. Let me answer first. As you correctly pointed out, the shared vision does not refer to any specific country, but we recognize China as a major partner in the region. And in our exchange of views, both of us, in fact, confirmed that viewpoint. China's development is an opportunity for the international community, for Japan, and for the Asia-Pacific.

Now, I explained in the meeting to President Obama that when I visited China last December, I broached to the Chinese leaders my six-point initiative, including confidence-building and cooperation in the East China Sea in order to further advance our mutually beneficial relationship based on common strategic interests, and that I'll work steadily to implement this.

I also told to the President that I wish to realize his strategic dialogue among Japan, U.S., and China. Now, EAS last year, we—where the view that was a success—and of course, ASEAN countries also participated in discussions that we need to seek a rules-based response for behavior from the Chinese. And we had these exchange of views.

President Obama. I think that I've said in the past and firmly believe that we welcome a peacefully rising China. And we have developed a very important strategic and economic dialogue with China. We think what they've accomplished in terms of lifting millions of people out of poverty is good for its own sake and it's also potentially good for the world and for the region.

As Prime Minister Noda and I noted, we do believe that as China continues to grow, as its influence continues to expand, that it has to be a strong partner in abiding by international rules and norms, whether those are economic norms like respecting intellectual property, whether these are norms of dispute resolution.

So, in maritime disputes, ensuring that small countries and large countries are both respected in international fora in resolving these issues; that across the board, we want China to be a partner with us in a set of international rules and norms that everybody follows. And I think as China makes that transition from a developing country into a major power, that it will see that over the long term it is in its interest as well to abide by these rules and norms.

And so all of our actions are not designed to in any way contain China, but they are designed to ensure that they are part of a broader international community in which rules, norms are respected, in which all countries can prosper and succeed.

Thank you very much, everybody.

NOTE: The President's news conference began at 2:16 p.m. in the East Room at the White House. In his remarks, Prime Minister Noda referred to Andy and Jeanne Anderson, parents, and Julia Anderson, sister, of Taylor Anderson, who died in Ishinomaki, Japan, in March 2011; David Barlow, captain, Keith Johnson, deputy chief, and Jennifer Massey, K–9 handler, Fairfax County Fire and Rescue Department; and U.S. Permanent Representative to the United Nations Susan E. Rice, in her capacity as President of the U.N. Security Council. A reporter referred to Republican Presidential candidate former Gov. W. Mitt Romney of Massachusetts. Prime Minister Noda and two reporters spoke in Japanese, and their remarks were translated by an interpreter.

Joint Statement by President Obama and Prime Minister Yoshihiko Noda of Japan—A Shared Vision for the Future
April 30, 2012

The U.S.-Japan Alliance is the cornerstone of peace, security, and stability in the Asia-Pacific region. This partnership has underwritten the dynamic growth and prosperity of the region for 60 years.

The strength of this Alliance, which was demonstrated during the Great East Japan Earthquake of 2011, is founded on the close bonds between our two nations and our people. These bonds will continue to anchor and sustain our partnership.

Japan and the United States share a commitment to democracy, the rule of law, open societies, human rights, human security, and free and open markets; these values guide us in our joint efforts to address the global challenges of our time.

The U.S.-Japan partnership continues to be defined by our enduring commitment to the maintenance of peace. Over the decades, our Alliance has steadily developed into a comprehensive partnership that contributes to peace and stability in the Asia-Pacific region, an important center for global economic growth, and beyond.

Japan and the United States pledge to fulfill our roles and responsibilities by utilizing the full range of capabilities to advance regional and global peace, prosperity and security. Our cooperation and dialogue extend to all levels and areas of government and the private sector.

To accomplish our shared vision for the future, we seek to further enhance our bilateral security and defense cooperation. We reaffirm the indispensability of the U.S.-Japan Alliance to the security of Japan, and to the peace, security, and economic prosperity of the Asia-Pacific region, which faces diverse challenges in a changing international environment. We will pursue our respective commitments, including the development of Japan's dynamic defense force under the 2010 National Defense Program Guidelines, and the U.S. strategic rebalancing to the Asia-Pacific with its efforts to achieve a more geographically distributed and operationally resilient force posture in the region. Our updated U.S. force realignment plan will further enhance the Alliance's ability to respond to a variety of contingencies in the region.

Japan and the United States are working with partners in the region to strengthen institutions and foster networks that are open, inclusive, and support internationally accepted rules and norms, including through fora such as the East Asia Summit (EAS) and APEC. This approach respects diversity in the region, while promoting mutual understanding, confidence, and transparency. Japan and the United States welcome all regional partners to make positive contributions to this process.

We face both conventional and emerging security threats, and commit to act together based on our 2011 Common Strategic Objectives in addressing global challenges such as terrorism, proliferation of weapons of mass destruction, and piracy. We pledge to work together to promote the rule of law, protect human rights, and enhance coordination on peacekeeping, post-conflict stabilization, development assistance, organized crime and narcotics trafficking, and infectious diseases. We must also work to protect and develop the tremendous potential of critical areas such as the high seas, space, and cyberspace, ensuring their use is responsible and rule-based.

We aim to enhance economic growth and prosperity for both our nations through bilateral economic harmonization and the promotion of regional economic integration. We will continue to seek ways to deepen our bilateral trade and investment ties and to promote cooperation on innovation, entrepreneurship, supply chain security, the Internet economy, and science and technology, as well as women's entrepreneurship and economic empowerment. We are also committed to working together to develop high standard trade and investment rules in the region and promote regional economic integration, consistent with the long-term objective of the APEC economies to develop a Free Trade Area of the Asia-Pacific (FTAAP). We will continue to advance our ongoing bilateral consultations on the Trans-Pacific Partnership (TPP), and further explore how bilateral economic harmonization and the promotion of regional economic integration could be achieved.

We also affirm our commitment to cooperating on energy, including the development of clean and renewable energy sources, peaceful, safe, and secure uses of nuclear energy, and on energy security. We share a mutual commitment to address the global impact of climate change.

The close bond between our people remains the greatest resource for our Alliance and for our shared vision of the future. To develop the strong ties between future generations of Japanese and American citizens, we commit to strengthening people-to-people connections at all levels through efforts such as the Kizuna Project and the TOMODACHI initiative. We pledge to increase the number of students and researchers attending one another's schools and universities and work together to facilitate greater travel and tourism.

In these areas and beyond, Japan and the United States of America are determined to expand our cooperation and further strengthen the Alliance in order to realize our shared vision for a future of peace and prosperity for all of our citizens and for the world.

NOTE: An original was not available for verification of the content of this joint statement.

Letter to Congressional Leaders Reporting on the Executive Order Prohibiting Certain Transactions With and Suspending Entry Into the United States of Foreign Sanctions Evaders With Respect to Iran and Syria
May 1, 2012

Dear Mr. Speaker: (Dear Mr. President:)

Pursuant to the International Emergency Economic Powers Act (50 U.S.C. 1701 *et seq.*) (IEEPA), I hereby report that I have issued an Executive Order (the "order") that takes additional steps with respect to the national emergencies declared in Executive Order 12957 of

March 15, 1995, as relied on for additional steps in subsequent Executive Orders; in Executive Order 13338 of May 11, 2004, as modified in scope and relied on for additional steps in subsequent Executive Orders; in Executive Order 12938 of November 14, 1994, as relied on for additional steps in subsequent Executive Orders; and in Executive Order 13224 of September 23, 2001, as relied on for additional steps in subsequent Executive Orders.

I have determined that efforts by foreign persons to engage in activities intended to evade U.S. economic and financial sanctions with respect to Iran and Syria undermine our efforts to address the national emergencies described above. To address this situation, the order takes additional steps with respect to those national emergencies.

The order authorizes the Secretary of the Treasury, in consultation with the Secretary of State, to impose specified measures on a foreign person upon determining that the foreign person:

- has violated, attempted to violate, conspired to violate, or caused a violation of any license, order, regulation, or prohibition contained in, or issued pursuant to, any Executive Order relating to the national emergencies declared in Executive Order 12957 of March 15, 1995, or in Executive Order 13338 of May 11, 2004, as modified in scope in subsequent Executive Orders;

- has violated, attempted to violate, conspired to violate, or caused a violation of any license, order, regulation, or prohibition contained in, or issued pursuant to, to the extent such conduct relates to property and interests in property of any person subject to United States sanctions concerning Iran or Syria, Executive Order 13382 of June 28, 2005, any Executive Order subsequent to Executive Order 13382 of June 28, 2005, that relates to the national emergency declared in Executive Order 12938 of November 14, 1994, or any Executive Order relating to the national emergency declared in Executive Order 13224 of September 23, 2001;

- has facilitated deceptive transactions for or on behalf of any person subject to United States sanctions concerning Iran or Syria; or

- is owned or controlled by, or is acting or purporting to act for or on behalf of, directly or indirectly, any person determined to meet the criteria set forth above.

The measures to be imposed on the foreign persons determined to meet one or more of these criteria are prohibitions on all transactions or dealings, whether direct or indirect, involving such persons, including any exporting, reexporting, importing, selling, purchasing, transporting, swapping, brokering, approving, financing, facilitating, or guaranteeing, in or related to (i) any goods, services, or technology in or intended for the United States, or (ii) any goods, services, or technology provided by or to United States persons, wherever located. The order also suspends entry into the United States of the foreign persons determined to meet the above criteria.

I have delegated to the Secretary of the Treasury the authority, in consultation with the Secretary of State, to take such actions, including the promulgation of rules and regulations, and to employ all powers granted to the President by IEEPA, as may be necessary to carry out the purposes of the order.

All agencies of the United States Government are directed to take all appropriate measures within their authority to carry out the provisions of the order.

I am enclosing a copy of the Executive Order I have issued.

Sincerely,

BARACK OBAMA

NOTE: Identical letters were sent to John A. Boehner, Speaker of the House of Representatives, and Joseph R. Biden, Jr., President of the Senate. Executive Order 13608 is listed in Appendix D at the end of this volume.

Remarks With President Hamid Karzai of Afghanistan on Signing the Strategic Partnership Agreement in Kabul, Afghanistan
May 2, 2012

[*President Karzai's remarks were joined in progress.*]

President Karzai. ——prosperity and peace for the people of Afghanistan.

Stability in Afghanistan and peace in Afghanistan—people will sleep, will be safe in their house, and also law-abiding citizens. Their life will be—will not threat their life by any forces. The people of Afghanistan in past three decades, they didn't have this, so now they want. This is the responsibility of Government of Afghanistan to fulfill the wishes of the people of Afghanistan to a better life, better future, and peace and prosperity and changing to reality for them.

For us, people of Afghanistan, as we know, this is a very important years in our life of our country and the people of Afghanistan. The people of Afghanistan want the transition Afghanistan before the 2014—end of—we will get all the responsibility to—and the end of—take the responsibility for the people of Afghanistan as one of our responsibility to—we have to take to—[*inaudible*].

With the—accepting this responsibility of this—all the forces who were in Afghanistan past 10 years, they worked with us, helped us, and support us—go back to their country. And of course, the people of Afghanistan will never forget their help and their support and also their relationship with this country. We will start a new start with this relationship, and we will continue with this relationship.

And, Mr. President, sir, I just want to say, and this—all the help and support the people of the United States and—to the people of Afghanistan did it, I thank you for that from the bottom my heart, sir. And I just—well, thank you. And also, we just want to thank you, sir, for the—all the—which is provide all the necessary to bring this strategic partnership for signing today—or tonight. And I just thank your—all your team, which is Ryan Crocker—Ambassador Crocker, General Allen. I thank

them for the hard work that with our team worked together. They were—very patiently worked together and continue this dialogue. Today we will see the result of this talking and communication. Today we sign it.

And I just want to thank you. I just ask you to, sir, to give your speech, sir. Thank you very much.

President Obama. President Karzai, leaders of the Afghan Government and society who are here, and most of all, to the Afghan people, thank you so much for welcoming me here today, especially in these beautiful surroundings.

I too want to thank Ambassador Ryan Crocker and National Security Adviser Spanta and their teams for the extraordinary work that brought about this day.

I've come to Afghanistan to mark a historic moment for our two nations, and to do so on Afghan soil. I'm here to affirm the bonds between our countries, to thank American and Afghans who have sacrificed so much over these last 10 years, and to look forward to a future of peace and security and greater prosperity for our nations.

Neither Americans nor the Afghan people asked for this war. Yet, for a decade, we've stood together to drive Al Qaida from its camps, to battle an insurgency, and to give the people of Afghanistan the possibility to live in peace and in dignity. The wages of war have been great for both our nations. But today, with the signing of the strategic partnership agreement, we look forward to a future of peace.

Together, we've made much progress. We've reached an agreement to transition detention facilities to Afghan control and to put Afghans in the lead on special operations. And today we're agreeing to a—to be long-term partners in combating terrorism and training Afghan security forces and strengthening democratic institutions and supporting development and protecting human rights of all Afghans. With this agreement, the Afghan people and the world should know that Afghanistan has a friend and a partner in the United States.

Mr. President, there will be difficult days ahead. But as we move forward with our transition, I'm confident that Afghan forces will grow stronger, the Afghan people will take control of their future. With this agreement, I am confident that the Afghan people will understand that the United States will stand by them, and they will know that the United States can achieve our goal of destroying Al Qaida and denying it a safe haven, but at the same time, we have the capacity to wind down this war and usher in a new era of peace here in Afghanistan.

Mr. President, I'm reminded of all who made the ultimate sacrifice in Afghanistan, including members of your own family. I pay tribute to those Afghans who have lost their lives alongside our men and women and sacrificed for their country. Of course, our hearts are heavy as we remember so many who have died in this war. I'm grateful that this agreement pays tribute to the sacrifices made by the American people here in Afghanistan.

As I've said before, the United States has not come here to claim resources or to claim territory. We came with a very clear mission: We came to destroy Al Qaida. And we have enormous respect for Afghan sovereignty and the dignity of the Afghan people. Together, we're now committed to replacing war with peace and pursuing a more hopeful future as equal partners.

To borrow words from this agreement, we "are committed to seeking a future of justice, peace, security, and opportunity." And I'm confident that although our challenges are not yet behind us, that the future before us is bright.

Thank you so much, Mr. President.

President Karzai. Thank you.

[*At this point, President Obama and President Karzai signed the agreement.*]

NOTE: The President spoke at 12 a.m. at the Presidential Palace. In his remarks, he referred to National Security Adviser Rangin Dadfar Spanta of Afghanistan. President Karzai referred to Gen. John R. Allen, USMC, commander, NATO International Security Assistance Force, Afghanistan. President Karzai spoke in Pashto and Dari, and his remarks were translated by an interpreter. A portion of these remarks could not be verified because the audio was incomplete.

Joint Statement—Enduring Strategic Partnership Agreement Between the United States of America and the Islamic Republic of Afghanistan
May 2, 2012

I. PREAMBLE

The Islamic Republic of Afghanistan ("Afghanistan") and the United States of America ("United States") have partnered closely since 2001 to respond to threats to international peace and security and help the Afghan people chart a secure, democratic, and prosperous future. As a result, Afghanistan is now on a path towards sustainable self-reliance in security, governance, economic and social development, and constructive partnership at the regional level.

The Parties express their appreciation for the November 2011 Traditional Loya Jirga, which declared: "Emphasizing the need to preserve the achievements of the past ten years, respect the Afghan Constitution, women's rights, freedom of speech, and taking into consideration the prevailing situation in the region, strategic cooperation with the United States of America, which is a strategic ally of the people and government of Afghanistan, is considered important in order to ensure political, economic and military security of the country. Signing a strategic cooperation document with the United States conforms with the national interest of Afghanistan and is of significant importance . . . When signing this document Afghanistan and the United States must be considered as two sovereign and equal countries", in accordance with the Charter of the United Nations.

Emphasizing their shared determination to further advance the Afghan people's desire for a stable and independent Afghan state, governed on the basis of Afghanistan's Constitution and shared democratic values, including respect for the fundamental rights and freedoms of all men and women, Afghanistan and the United States ("the Parties") commit to strengthen long-term strategic cooperation in areas of mutual interest, including: advancing peace, security, and reconciliation; strengthening state institutions; supporting Afghanistan's long-term economic and social development; and encouraging regional cooperation. Recognizing the continued relevance of their commitments at the 2010 London and Kabul Conferences, as well as the 2011 Bonn Conference, the Parties affirm their resolve to strengthen Afghanistan's institutions and governance capacity to advance such areas of long-term strategic cooperation.

Cooperation between Afghanistan and the United States is based on mutual respect and shared interests—most notably, a common desire for peace and to strengthen collective efforts to achieve a region that is economically integrated, and no longer a safe haven for al-Qaeda and its affiliates.

Afghanistan and the United States go forward in this partnership with confidence because they are committed to seeking a future of justice, peace, security, and opportunity for the Afghan people.

Respect for the sovereignty and equality of states constitutes the foundation of this partnership.

Respect for the rule of law, as well as the sound and transparent adherence to Afghanistan's Constitution and all other operative laws, reinforces its foundation. The Parties reaffirm their strong commitment to the sovereignty,

independence, territorial integrity and national unity of Afghanistan.

Accordingly, the Parties agree to the following:

II. PROTECTING AND PROMOTING SHARED DEMOCRATIC VALUES

1. The Parties agree that a strong commitment to protecting and promoting democratic values and human rights is a fundamental aspect of their long-term partnership and cooperation.

2. Underscoring the central importance of the values and principles of the Afghan Constitution, Afghanistan reaffirms its strong commitment to inclusive and pluralistic democratic governance, including free, fair, and transparent elections in which all the people of Afghanistan participate freely without internal or external interference. Reaffirming its commitments made at the 2011 Bonn Conference, Afghanistan shall strengthen and improve its electoral process.

3. Afghanistan reaffirms its commitment to protecting human and political rights under its Constitution and international obligations, including the International Covenant on Civil and Political Rights. In this regard, Afghanistan shall strengthen the integrity and capacity of its democratic institutions and processes, including by taking tangible steps to further the efficiency and effectiveness of its three branches of state, within its unitary system of government, and supporting development of a vibrant civil society, including a free and open media.

4. Afghanistan reaffirms its commitment to ensuring that any kind of discrimination and distinction between citizens of Afghanistan shall be forbidden, and ensuring the rights and freedoms that are guaranteed to all Afghans under Afghan law and the Afghan Constitution. Consistent with its Constitution and international obligations, Afghanistan shall ensure and advance the essential role of women in society, so that they may fully enjoy their economic, social, political, civil and cultural rights.

III. ADVANCING LONG-TERM SECURITY

1. The Parties reaffirm that the presence and operations of the U.S. forces in Afghanistan since 2001 are aimed at defeating al-Qaeda and its affiliates. The Parties acknowledge the great sacrifices and suffering that the Afghan people have endured in the struggle against terrorism and the continued threats to their desire for peace, security and prosperity. The Parties also pay tribute to the sacrifices made by the people of the United States in this struggle.

2. In order to strengthen security and stability in Afghanistan, contribute to regional and international peace and stability, combat al-Qaeda and its affiliates, and enhance the ability of Afghanistan to deter threats against its sovereignty, security, and territorial integrity, the Parties shall continue to foster close cooperation concerning defense and security arrangements, as may be mutually determined.

    a. The Parties' respective obligations under this Agreement, and any subsequent arrangements, are without prejudice to Afghan sovereignty over its territory, and each Party's right of self-defense, consistent with international law.

    b. The Parties shall, subject to their internal procedures, initiate negotiations on a Bilateral Security Agreement. Negotiations should begin after the signing of this Strategic Partnership Agreement, with the goal of concluding within one year a Bilateral Security Agreement to supersede the *Agreement regarding the Status of United States Military and Civilian Personnel of the U.S. Department of Defense Present in Afghanistan in connection with Cooperative Efforts in Response to Terrorism, Humanitarian, and Civic Assistance, Military Training and Exercises, and Other Activities* (2003), and other such related agreements and understandings that are mutually determined to be contrary to the provisions of the Bilateral Security Agreement.

    c. The conduct of ongoing military operations shall continue under existing frameworks, which include the *Memorandum of Understanding on the Transfer of U.S. Detention Facilities* (2012) and the *Memorandum of Understanding on the Afghanization of Special Operations* (2012), until superseded by the Bilateral Security Agreement or other arrangements, as mutually determined. This obligation is without prejudice to the status, commitments, and understandings of those frameworks, until superseded as noted above.

3. To help provide a long-term framework for mutual security and defense cooperation, the United States shall designate Afghanistan a "Major Non-NATO Ally."

4. The Parties underscore their strong support for Afghan efforts towards peace and reconciliation.

    a. The necessary outcomes of any peace and reconciliation process are for individuals and entities to: break ties with al-Qaeda; renounce violence; and abide by the Afghan Constitution, including its protections for all Afghan women and men.

    b. Afghanistan affirms that in all state actions and understandings with regard to peace and reconciliation, it shall uphold the values of the Afghan Constitution.

5. Beyond 2014, the United States shall seek funds, on a yearly basis, to support the training, equipping, advising, and sustaining of the Afghan National Security Forces (ANSF), so that Afghanistan can independently secure and defend itself against internal and external threats, and help ensure that terrorists never again encroach on Afghan soil and threaten Afghanistan, the region, and the world.

    a. Such support should: (1) help build appropriate capabilities reflecting the evolving nature of mutually-recognized threats to Afghan stability; (2) support efforts to help the Afghan State attain a sustainable security structure; and (3) strengthen the capacity of security institutions of Afghanistan.

b. A U.S-Afghanistan Working Group on Defense and Security, established under the framework of this Agreement, shall undertake regular assessments of the level of threat facing Afghanistan, as well as the country's security and defense requirements, and make specific recommendations about future cooperation in this field to the Bilateral Commission.

c. Assistance to the ANSF should have the goal of being consistent with NATO standards and promote interoperability with NATO forces.

d. The Parties further call on NATO member states to sustain and improve Afghan security capabilities beyond 2014, by taking concrete measures to implement the *Declaration by NATO and the Government of the Islamic Republic of Afghanistan on an Enduring Partnership* concluded at the November 2010 NATO Lisbon Summit.

6. Afghanistan shall provide U.S. forces continued access to and use of Afghan facilities through 2014, and beyond as may be agreed in the Bilateral Security Agreement, for the purposes of combating al-Qaeda and its affiliates, training the Afghan National Security Forces, and other mutually determined missions to advance shared security interests.

a. The United States emphasizes its full respect for the sovereignty and independence of Afghanistan. It reaffirms its commitment to the *Inteqal* framework, and a transition to full Afghan security responsibility. It further reaffirms that it does not seek permanent military facilities in Afghanistan, or a presence that is a threat to Afghanistan's neighbors.

b. The United States further pledges not to use Afghan territory or facilities as a launching point for attacks against other countries.

c. The nature and scope of the future presence and operations of U.S. forces in Afghanistan, and the related obligations of Afghanistan and the United States, shall be addressed in the Bilateral Security Agreement.

7. The Parties shall enhance information and intelligence sharing to counter common threats, including terrorism, narcotics trafficking, organized crime, and money laundering.

8. The Parties also underscore their support to improve regional security cooperation and coordination. The Parties affirm that the production, trafficking, and consumption of illicit narcotics poses a major threat to ensuring security and the formation of a licit Afghan economy, as well as to regional security and a healthy world. They are determined to cooperate in Afghanistan, the region, and the world to eliminate this threat.

9. Recognizing that the stability of Afghanistan would contribute to the development and stability of South-Central Asia, the United States affirms that it shall regard with grave concern any external aggression against Afghanistan. Were this to occur, the Parties shall hold consultations on an urgent basis to develop and implement an appropriate response, including, as may be mutually determined, political, diplomatic, economic, or military measures, in accordance with their respective constitutional procedures.

IV. REINFORCING REGIONAL SECURITY AND COOPERATION

1. The Parties agree on the importance of Afghanistan having cooperative and friendly relations with its neighbors, and emphasize that such relations should be conducted on the basis of mutual respect, non-interference, and equality. They call on all nations to respect Afghanistan's sovereignty and territorial integrity, and to refrain from interfering in Afghanistan's internal affairs and democratic processes.

2. With a view to the importance of regional cooperation for the consolidation of security in the region, the Parties shall undertake earnest cooperation with the countries of the region,

regional organizations, the United Nations, and other international organizations on mutually recognized threats, including: terrorist networks; organized crime; narcotics trafficking; and money laundering.

3. To enhance regional stability and prosperity, the Parties shall further cooperate in restoring Afghanistan's historic role as a bridge connecting Central and South Asia and the Middle East by:

    a. building on and facilitating implementation of existing and future regional initiatives, including transit and trade agreements;

    b. strengthening border coordination and management between Afghanistan and its neighbors;

    c. expanding linkages to regional transportation, transit, and energy networks through the realization of projects, including infrastructure, throughout Afghanistan; and

    d. mobilizing international support for regional investments that facilitate Afghanistan's integration with the region.

V. SOCIAL AND ECONOMIC DEVELOPMENT

1. The Parties agree that developing Afghanistan's human and natural resources is crucial to regional stability, sustainable economic growth, and Afghanistan's recovery from more than three decades of war and that Afghanistan will have special, significant and continuing fiscal requirements that cannot be met by domestic revenues in the years following Transition. In this regard, the United States reaffirms its commitment made at the 2011 Bonn Conference to directing financial support, consistent with the Kabul Process, towards Afghanistan's economic development, helping Afghanistan address its continuing budget shortfall to secure the gains of the last decade, make Transition irreversible, and become self-sustaining.

2. In the economic sphere:

    a. The Parties shall pursue consolidation and growth of a market economy, and

long-term cooperation for Afghanistan's sustainable economic growth, taking into consideration Afghanistan's Constitution, as well as its historical and social realities.

    b. Noting Afghanistan's priorities, the United States shall help strengthen Afghanistan's economic foundation and support sustainable development and self-sufficiency, particularly in the areas of: licit agricultural production; transportation, trade, transit, water, and energy infrastructure; fostering responsible management of natural resources; and building a strong financial system, which is needed to sustain private investment.

    c. To encourage trade and private sector development, the Parties shall undertake common efforts to increasingly use the Generalized System of Preferences. Further, to encourage investment, the United States intends to mobilize the Overseas Private Investment Corporation, U.S. Export-Import Bank, and U.S. Trade and Development Agency to encourage U.S. private sector activity in Afghanistan. Afghanistan shall augment its support for the development of its private sector through the relevant Afghan institutions.

    d. The Parties affirm their strong desire that the Afghan people should be the primary beneficiaries of Afghanistan's mineral wealth. The United States shall therefore support Afghanistan's efforts to govern its natural wealth through an accountable, efficient, effective and transparent framework that builds upon and surpasses international best practices.

3. In the social sphere, the Parties shall undertake sustainable joint efforts to help Afghanistan develop its human capacity through:

    a. access to and enhancing the quality of education, including higher education and vocational training in key areas for all Afghans; and

b. access to basic health services and specialized care, including for women and children.

4. The Parties underscore the crucial importance of the fight against corruption.

　a. The Parties shall fight decisively against all forms of corruption.
　b. The Parties shall devise mechanisms to enhance aid effectiveness and avoid corruption through improved procurement practices, transparency, and accountability.
　c. Afghanistan shall strengthen its anticorruption institutions, and revise and enforce its laws, as necessary, in accordance with its national and international obligations.
　d. Afghanistan further shall safeguard and enhance the Afghan financial system by implementing recommendations from the Financial Action Task Force Asia Pacific Group (FATF/APG) regarding anti-money laundering and combating terrorist financing.

5. The United States and Afghanistan shall continue their cooperation to promote Afghanistan's development, including annual U.S. social and economic assistance to Afghanistan commensurate with the strategic importance of the U.S.-Afghan partnership.

　a. To achieve this goal, the United States shall seek on a yearly basis, funding for social and economic assistance to Afghanistan. The United States also supports Afghanistan's efforts to encourage international investment and support for the Afghan private sector, which is crucial to developing a secure, prosperous, peaceful Afghanistan and region.
　b. Building on its commitments at the 2010 Kabul and London Conferences ("the Conferences"), the United States reiterates its commitment to channel at least 50 percent of such economic and social assistance to Afghanistan through Afghan government budgetary mecha-

nisms. The Parties shall periodically review this commitment, through the Afghanistan-United States Bilateral Commission, established under this Agreement, with the goal of increasing the percentage of assistance channeled through Afghan Government budgetary mechanisms beyond 2012.
　c. The United States also reaffirms its 2010 Kabul Conference commitment to progressively align its development assistance behind Afghan National Priority Programs, as mutually determined by both Parties, with the goal of achieving 80 percent of alignment by the end of 2012. The United States agrees that any development assistance not aligned is to be fully transparent and consulted with the Government of Afghanistan.
　d. These commitments are contingent upon the Afghan government establishing mechanisms and demonstrating agreed-upon progress to ensure financial transparency and accountability, increasing budget expenditures, improving revenue collection, enhancing public financial management systems, and other mutually determined measures of performance and progress, including those committed at the Conferences.

6. The Parties shall strengthen the longstanding relations between their people and civil societies through a range of efforts, including youth and women's initiatives, and cooperation between their universities and institutions of higher education.

7. The United States shall promote exchanges and related activities, which may include initiatives such as the Fulbright Program and International Visitor Leadership Program.

8. The Parties also shall cooperate to support Afghan cultural institutions, and preservation of cultural heritage.

VI. STRENGTHENING AFGHAN INSTITUTIONS AND GOVERNANCE

1. The Parties shall cooperate towards improving the human capacity of Afghanistan's

crucial government institutions. U.S. assistance to Afghanistan should be based on the priorities of the Afghan Government and mutually identified needs.

2. Afghanistan shall improve governance by increasing the responsiveness, and transparency of Afghan executive, legislative, and judicial institutions so that they better meet the civil and economic needs of the Afghan people. It shall promote efficiency and accountability at all levels of the government, consistent with Afghan law, and ensure that they provide services according to fair and objectively applied procedures and consistent with national standards for minimum service delivery.

3. The United States shall support the Afghan Government in strengthening the capacity, self-reliance, and effectiveness of Afghan institutions and their ability to deliver basic services.

4. The Parties shall work cooperatively to eliminate "parallel structures," including Provincial Reconstruction Teams and District Stabilization Teams consistent with the *Inteqal* framework.

VII. IMPLEMENTING ARRANGEMENTS AND MECHANISMS

1. To advance cooperation and monitor progress towards implementing this Agreement, the Parties shall establish an Afghanistan-United States Bilateral Commission and associated implementation mechanisms.

    a. The Commission shall be chaired by the respective foreign ministers of Afghanistan and the United States, or their designees, and meet semi-annually in Kabul and/ Washington on a rotational basis.

      i. Preexisting bilateral forums, such as the Afghanistan-United States Bilateral Security Consultative Forum, shall be incorporated into the framework of this new structure.

    b. A Joint Steering Committee shall guide and report to Ministers on the work of standing expert working groups formed to implement this Agreement.

      i. These working groups shall be chaired by relevant ministers, or their designees, and are to constitute a forum for regular, senior-level consultations on issues of mutual concern. These issues include, but are not limited to, advancing long-term security, promoting social, democratic, and economic development, and strengthening Afghan institutions and governance.

    c. The Joint Steering Committee should also convene regularly to assess common threats and discuss regional issues of mutual concern.

2. Through the Bilateral Commission, Parties should establish mutually determined levels of support and assistance.

3. Afghanistan and the United States may enter into further arrangements or agreements, as necessary and appropriate, to implement this Agreement, subject to the relevant laws and regulations of both Parties.

VIII. FINAL PROVISIONS

1. This Agreement shall enter into force when the Parties notify one another, through diplomatic channels, of the completion of their respective internal legal requirements necessary for the entry into force of this Agreement. It shall remain in force until the end of 2024. Upon mutual written agreement of the Parties, six months prior to the expiration of the Agreement, it may be renewed for a mutually agreed period. This Agreement may be amended or terminated by mutual written agreement of both Parties at any time, and either Party may provide written notice to the other of its intent to terminate this Agreement, which shall be effective one year after the date of such notification.

2. All actions taken under this Agreement shall be consistent with the Parties' respective commitments and obligations under international law. Cooperation under this Agreement is subject to the relevant laws and regulations of the respective Parties, including applicable appropriations laws.

3. Any disputes with respect to implementation of this Agreement shall be settled through diplomatic consultations between the Parties.

Signed in duplicate by the Presidents of the Islamic Republic of Afghanistan and the United States of America on this 2nd day of the month of May, in the year 2012, in the city of Kabul, in the Pashto, Dari and English languages, each text being equally authentic.

For the
United States of America:

BARACK OBAMA

For the
Islamic Republic of Afghanistan:

HAMID KARZAI

Remarks at Bagram Air Base, Afghanistan
May 2, 2012

The President. How's everybody doing tonight?

Audience members. Hooah!

The President. Hooah!

It is good to be back here with all of you. I've got a few acknowledgments I've got to make before I say what I've got to say. First of all, somebody who has served our country with the kind of distinction that doesn't happen a lot, somebody who has been a leader for you and a leader for our country for a very long time—give your commander, General John Allen, a big, big round of applause.

We also have somebody who is John's partner on the civilian side and has made extraordinary sacrifices, first in Iraq, now in Afghanistan—Ambassador Ryan Crocker is here. Please give him a big round of applause.

All right, now, let me just see if I've got this right. We've got the 1st Infantry Division in the house. We've got the 455th Air Expeditionary Wing. We've got the Task Force Muleskinner. We've got the 101st Army Field Sustainment Brigade. We've got Task Force Paladin in the house. And we've got Task Force Defender in the house. And we've got me in the house.

Audience members. Eighty-second!

The President. Eighty-second. Eighty-second in the house—82d in the house. You know, somebody is going to be in trouble that they didn't have 82d on here. Anybody else I'm missing?

Audience members. [*Inaudible*]

The President. There you go. All right. I love all of you.

Now listen, I'm not going to give a long speech. I'm going to have the opportunity to address the Nation from Bagram just in a little bit, and it's going to be broadcast back home during primetime. So all I want to do is just say thank you.

The sacrifices all of you have made, the sacrifices your families make every single day are what make America free and what make America secure. And I know that sometimes, out here, when you're in theater, it's not clear whether folks back home fully appreciate what's going on. And let's face it, a lot of times it's easier to get bad news on the news than good news.

But here's the good news, and here's part of the reason that I'm here. I just finished signing a strategic partnership agreement with Afghanistan that signals the transition in which we are going to be turning over responsibility for Afghan security to the Afghans. We're not going to do it overnight. We're not going to do it irresponsibly. We're going to make sure that the gains, the hard-fought gains that have been made are preserved. But the reason we're able to do that is because of you. The reason that the Afghans have an opportunity for a new tomorrow is because of you. And the reason America is safe is because of you.

We did not choose this war. This war came to us on 9/11. And there are a whole bunch of folks here, I'll bet, who signed up after 9/11.

We don't go looking for a fight. But when we see our homeland violated, when we see our fellow citizens killed, then we understand what we have to do. And because of the sacrifices now of a decade, and a new greatest generation, not only were we able to blunt the Taliban momentum, not only were we able to drive Al Qaida out of Afghanistan, but slowly and systematically, we have been able to decimate the ranks of Al Qaida. And a year ago, we were able to finally bring Usama bin Laden to justice.

That could have only happened because each and every one of you, in your own way, were doing your jobs. Each and every one of you—without a lot of fanfare, without a lot of fuss—you did your jobs. No matter how small or how big, you were faithful to the oath that you took to protect this Nation. And your families did their job supporting you and loving you and remembering you and being there for you.

And so, together, you guys represent what is best in America. And you're part of a long line of those who have worn this uniform to make sure that we are free and secure, to make sure that those of us at home have the capacity to live our lives. And when you're missing a birthday or you're missing a soccer game or when you're missing an anniversary, and those of us back home are able to enjoy it, it's because of you.

And I'm here to tell you, everybody in America knows that. And everybody in America appreciates it. And everybody in America

honors it. And when the final chapter of this war is written, historians will look back and say, not only was this the greatest fighting force in the history of the world, but all of you also represented the values of America in an exemplary way.

I could not be prouder of you. And I want you to understand, I know it's still tough. I know the battle is not yet over. Some of your buddies are going to get injured, and some of your buddies may get killed. And there's going to be heartbreak and pain and difficulty ahead. But there's a light on the horizon because of the sacrifices you've made. And that's the reason why for Michelle and me, nothing is more important than looking after your families while you're here. And I want everybody here to know that when you get home, we are going to be there for you when you're in uniform, and we will stay there for you when you're out of uniform. Because you've earned it; you've earned a special place in our hearts. And I could not be prouder to be your Commander in Chief.

God bless you, and God bless the United States of America. Now I want to shake some hands.

NOTE: The President spoke at 1:21 a.m. In his remarks, he referred to Gen. John R. Allen, USMC, commander, NATO International Security Assistance Force, Afghanistan; and U.S. Ambassador to Afghanistan Ryan C. Crocker.

Address to the Nation on United States Military Operations in Afghanistan From Bagram Air Base
May 2, 2012

Good evening from Bagram Air Base. This outpost is more than 7,000 miles from home, but for over a decade, it's been close to our hearts. Because here in Afghanistan, more than half a million of our sons and daughters have sacrificed to protect our country.

Today I signed a historic agreement between the United States and Afghanistan that defines a new kind of relationship between our

countries, a future in which Afghans are responsible for the security of their nation and we build an equal partnership between two sovereign states, a future in which war ends and a new chapter begins.

Tonight I'd like to speak to you about this transition. But first, let us remember why we came here. It was here, in Afghanistan, where Usama bin Laden established a safe haven for his terrorist organization. It was here, in Afghanistan, where Al Qaida brought new recruits, trained them, and plotted acts of terror. It was here, from within these borders, that Al Qaida launched the attacks that killed nearly 3,000 innocent men, women, and children.

And so, 10 years ago, the United States and our allies went to war to make sure that Al Qaida could never again use this country to launch attacks against us. Despite initial success, for a number of reasons, this war has taken longer than most anticipated. In 2002, bin Laden and his lieutenants escaped across the border and established safe haven in Pakistan. America spent nearly 8 years fighting a different war in Iraq. And Al Qaida's extremist allies within the Taliban have waged a brutal insurgency.

But over the last 3 years, the tide has turned. We broke the Taliban's momentum. We built strong Afghan security forces. We devastated Al Qaida's leadership, taking out over 20 of their top 30 leaders. And 1 year ago, from a base here in Afghanistan, our troops launched the operation that killed Usama bin Laden. The goal that I set to defeat Al Qaida and deny it a chance to rebuild is now within our reach.

Still, there will be difficult days ahead. The enormous sacrifices of our men and women are not over. But tonight I'd like to tell you how we will complete our mission and end the war in Afghanistan.

First, we've begun a transition to Afghan responsibility for security. Already, nearly half of the Afghan people live in places where Afghan security forces are moving into the lead. This month, at a NATO summit in Chicago, our coalition will set a goal for Afghan forces to be in the lead for combat operations across the country next year. International troops will continue to train, advise, and assist the Afghans, and fight alongside them when needed. But we will shift into a support role as Afghans step forward.

As we do, our troops will be coming home. Last year, we removed 10,000 U.S. troops from Afghanistan. Another 23,000 will leave by the end of the summer. After that, reductions will continue at a steady pace, with more and more of our troops coming home. And as our coali-

tion agreed, by the end of 2014, the Afghans will be fully responsible for the security of their country.

Second, we are training Afghan security forces to get the job done. Those forces have surged and will peak at 352,000 this year. The Afghans will sustain that level for 3 years and then reduce the size of their military. And in Chicago, we will endorse a proposal to support a strong and sustainable long-term Afghan force.

Third, we're building an enduring partnership. The agreement we signed today sends a clear message to the Afghan people: As you stand up, you will not stand alone. It establishes the basis for our cooperation over the next decade, including shared commitments to combat terrorism and strengthen democratic institutions. It supports Afghan efforts to advance development and dignity for their people. And it includes Afghan commitments to transparency and accountability and to protect the human rights of all Afghans: men and women, boys and girls.

Within this framework, we'll work with the Afghans to determine what support they need to accomplish two narrow security missions beyond 2014: counterterrorism and continued training. But we will not build permanent bases in this country, nor will we be patrolling its cities and mountains. That will be the job of the Afghan people.

Fourth, we're pursuing a negotiated peace. In coordination with the Afghan Government, my administration has been in direct discussions with the Taliban. We've made it clear that they can be a part of this future if they break with Al Qaida, renounce violence, and abide by Afghan laws. Many members of the Taliban—from foot soldiers to leaders—have indicated an interest in reconciliation. The path to peace is now set before them. Those who refuse to walk it will face strong Afghan security forces, backed by the United States and our allies.

Fifth, we are building a global consensus to support peace and stability in South Asia. In Chicago, the international community will express support for this plan and for Afghanistan's future. And I have made it clear to its neighbor Pakistan that it can and should be an equal partner in this process in a way that respects Pakistan's sovereignty, interests, and democratic institutions. In pursuit of a durable peace, America has no designs beyond an end to Al Qaida safe havens and respect for Afghan sovereignty.

As we move forward, some people will ask why we need a firm timeline. The answer is clear: Our goal is not to build a country in America's image or to eradicate every vestige of the Taliban. These objectives would require many more years, many more dollars, and most importantly, many more American lives. Our goal is to destroy Al Qaida, and we are on a path to do exactly that. Afghans want to assert their sovereignty and build a lasting peace. That requires a clear timeline to wind down the war.

Others will ask, why don't we leave immediately? That answer is also clear: We must give Afghanistan the opportunity to stabilize. Otherwise, our gains could be lost, and Al Qaida could establish itself once more. And as Commander in Chief, I refuse to let that happen.

I recognize that many Americans are tired of war. As President, nothing is more wrenching than signing a letter to a family of the fallen or looking into the eyes of a child who will grow up without a mother or father. I will not keep Americans in harm's way a single day longer than is absolutely required for our national security. But we must finish the job we started in Afghanistan and end this war responsibly.

My fellow Americans, we've traveled through more than a decade under the dark cloud of war. Yet, here in the predawn darkness of Afghanistan, we can see the light of a new day on the horizon. The Iraq war is over. The number of our troops in harm's way has been cut in half, and more will soon be coming home. We have a clear path to fulfill our mission in Afghanistan, while delivering justice to Al Qaida.

This future is only within reach because of our men and women in uniform. Time and again, they have answered the call to serve in distant and dangerous places. In an age when so many institutions have come up short, these Americans stood tall. They met their responsibilities to one another and to the flag they serve under. I just met with some of them and told them that as Commander in Chief, I could not be prouder. And in their faces, we see what is best in ourselves and our country.

Our soldiers, our sailors, our airmen, marines, coastguardsmen, and civilians in Afghanistan have done their duty. Now we must summon that same sense of common purpose. We must give our veterans and military families the support they deserve and the opportunities they have earned. And we must redouble our efforts to build a nation worthy of their sacrifice.

As we emerge from a decade of conflict abroad and economic crisis at home, it's time to renew America. An America where our children live free from fear and have the skills to claim their dreams, a united America of grit and resilience, where sunlight glistens off soaring new towers in downtown Manhattan and we build our future as one people, as one Nation.

Here in Afghanistan, Americans answered the call to defend their fellow citizens and uphold human dignity. Today we recall the fallen and those who suffered wounds, both seen and unseen. But through dark days, we have drawn strength from their example and the ideals that have guided our Nation and led the world: a belief that all people are treated equal and deserve the freedom to determine their destiny. That is the light that guides us still.

This time of war began in Afghanistan, and this is where it will end. With faith in each other and our eyes fixed on the future, let us finish the work at hand and forge a just and lasting peace.

May God bless our troops, and may God bless the United States of America.

NOTE: The President spoke at 4:01 a.m.

Remarks at a Cinco de Mayo Celebration
May 3, 2012

Hola, hola! Gracias y bienvenidos. I am honored to welcome you to Cinco de Mayo at the White House. Even though it's only *tres de Mayo*. We just like to get the fiesta started early around here. [*Laughter*]

It is a pleasure to be joined by so many Latinos and Latinas and those who wish they were Latino and Latina. [*Laughter*] I knew you wouldn't miss an opportunity for great music and dancing at the White House, especially with the outstanding Ballet Folklorico from Georgetown University. Give them a big round of applause.

Our great friend Ambassador Arturo Sarukhan and his lovely wife Veronica are here. I'm honored to welcome Hispanic Americans serving at every level of my administration, including Secretary of Labor Hilda Solis. I want to recognize Charlie Gonzalez, chairman of the Congressional Hispanic Caucus. As all of you know, Charlie's birthday is on Cinco de Mayo, so don't forget to wish him a *feliz cumpleaños*.

Finally, thank you to the White House Hispanic Summit steering committee for your hard work to engage thousands of Latino leaders across the country this year. Good job. Your work demonstrates that this celebration is all about pride in the heritage and contributions of Hispanics in all aspects of American life.

Cinco de Mayo marks a singular moment in Mexican history. Exactly 150 years ago, General Zaragoza and his ragtag band of patriots made a brave stand against the invading forces of a world-renowned European army. Sounds familiar. And the story goes that after these heroic citizens and soldiers beat the odds and turned back the invaders, General Zaragoza found time to sit down and write a brief note to the war minister. He celebrated the glory of the national army, noting that they never turned their backs. And today we honor their valor.

When the news of the Mexican victory at Puebla reached this house, this country was in the midst of its own struggles. But soon after, the U.S. lent assistance to help Mexico definitively expel the French from their land. And ever since, the United States and Mexico have lived intersecting and overlapping histories. Our two countries share the ties of history and *familia* and values and commerce and culture. And today, we are more united than ever in friendship and in common purpose.

Right now there are more than 50 million Americans of Latino descent, one sixth of our population. You're our neighbors, our coworkers, our family, our friends. You're starting businesses. You're teaching in classrooms. You're defending this country. You're driving America forward.

And for our part, we know that securing our future depends on making sure that all Americans have the opportunity to reach their potential. And that's why we've worked hard over the last 3½ years to create jobs, to make sure you get the care you need when you get sick, to make college affordable for everybody, to ensure that no matter where you are, where you come from, what you look like, what your last name is—even if it's Obama—[*laughter*]—you can make it if you try.

These are victories for Latinos, but they're, more importantly, victories for America. We could not have come this far without you. Of course, there is still plenty of unfinished business, including fixing our broken immigration system. And it is long past the time that we unleash the promise of all our young people and make the "DREAM Act" a reality.

A lot of you remember, over a year ago, we brought the "DREAM Act" to a vote in Congress, thanks to the hard work of many of you. And it passed the House and a majority of votes in the Senate. Unfortunately, we had some on the other side of the aisle that got together and blocked it. But we didn't come this far just to let partisan politics stand in our way.

So we're going to keep fighting for this commonsense reform, not just because hundreds of thousands of talented young students depend on it, but because ultimately, America depends on it. "No" is not an option. I want to sign the "DREAM Act" into law. I've got the pens all ready. I'm willing to work with anybody who is serious to get this done and to achieve bipartisan, comprehensive immigration reform that solves this challenge once and for all.

It's worth remembering, America is and always will be a nation of immigrants. We are richer because of the men and women and children who have come to our shores and joined our Union. So, as we mark Cinco de Mayo, on both sides of the border, we pay tribute to our shared heritage and our future partnership.

We honor what brings us together. We are mothers and fathers of a great generation, and we're going to keep on making sure that our sons and daughters have every opportunity to realize the American Dream. That's what drives me every day. That's what I know drives a lot of you. And I look forward for us making future progress together.

So with that, let's party. Let's have a good time. *Feliz Cinco de Mayo.*

Thank you, everybody. God bless you.

NOTE: The President spoke at 5:12 p.m. in the Rose Garden at the White House. In his remarks, he referred to Mexico's Ambassador to the U.S. Arturo Sarukhan Casamitjana and his wife Pilar Veronica Valencia Fedora.

Statement on World Press Freedom Day
May 3, 2012

On this World Press Freedom Day, the United States honors the role of a free press in creating sustainable democracies and prosperous societies. We pay special tribute to those journalists who have sacrificed their lives, freedom, or personal well-being in pursuit of truth and justice.

Over 60 years after the Universal Declaration of Human Rights proclaimed the right of every person "to seek, receive and impart information and ideas through any media and regardless of frontiers," that right remains in peril in far too many countries.

While this year has seen some positive developments, like the release of journalists along with hundreds of other political prisoners in Burma, arbitrary arrests and detentions of journalists continue across the globe. As we condemn recent detentions of journalists like Mazen Darwish, a leading proponent of free speech in Syria, and call for their immediate release, we must not forget others like blogger Dieu Cay, whose 2008 arrest coincided with a mass crackdown on citizen journalism in Vietnam, or journalist Dawit Isaak, who has been held incommunicado by the Eritrean Government for over a decade without formal charge or trial.

Threats and harassment, like that endured by Ecuadorian journalist Cesar Ricaurte and exiled Belarusian democratic activist Natalya Radzina, and indirect censorship, including through restrictions on freedom of movement like those imposed on Cuban blogger Yoani Sanchez, continue to have a chilling effect on freedom of expression and the press. We call on all governments to protect the ability of journalists, bloggers, and dissidents to write and speak freely without retribution and to stop the use of travel bans and other indirect forms of censorship to suppress the exercise of these universal rights.

In some cases, it is not just governments threatening the freedom of the press. It is also criminal gangs, terrorists, or political factions. No matter the cause, when journalists are intimidated, attacked, imprisoned, or disappeared, individuals begin to self-censor, fear replaces truth, and all of our societies suffer. A culture of impunity for such actions must not be allowed to persist in any country.

This year, across the Middle East, North Africa, and beyond, the world witnessed not only these perils, but also the promise that a free press holds for fostering innovative, successful, and stable democracies. On this World Press Freedom Day, we call upon all governments to seize that promise by recognizing the vital role of a free press and taking the necessary steps to create societies in which independent journalists can operate freely and without fear.

Remarks in a Discussion With Students and Parents at Washington-Lee High School in Arlington, Virginia
May 4, 2012

[*The President's remarks were joined in progress.*]

The President. What I'm going to be talking about today is obviously financing college educations. And I tell a story about how both Michelle and I, we had to rely on student loans and grants and scholarships to get through college and law school, and we still had a huge amount of debt after we graduated. It paid off, it's a great investment, but obviously, we're pretty sympathetic to the challenges that families go through in terms of financing.

And so I just wanted to get a sense—all of you are going to be taking out Stafford loans. And two things I wanted to get a sense of— number one, I'm assuming that a doubling of the interest rates is not helpful to you, but feel free to talk about that. I also wanted to get a sense of how it was to apply for them, because one of the things Arne and I and others in the administration have talked about is how do you simplify the process just to make it a little bit easier for people. Because I know that—and based on your chuckle, it sounds like that's something that we need to do. But—anybody want to start?

Secretary of Education Arne Duncan. How was the financial aid form itself? Was that scary? Was it easy? Was it hard?

Student Rina Castaneda. Pretty easy. It was kind of like filling out a college application, so that made it really easy. Fast, so it pretty much did it all for you.

The President. Oh, good.

Secretary Duncan. That's what I like to hear. Other folks—filling out the FAFSA?

Student Brendan Craig. It was pretty easy.

Secretary Duncan. It used to be really, really tough, and we worked with the IRS to simplify that. I was scared to partner with the IRS—[*laughter*]—but they did a great, great job. The form itself used to be a barrier to going on. So what was your sense on it?

Student Amirah Delwin. I did it in my college summit class, and my teacher helped me with it.

Secretary Duncan. How was it?

Ms. Delwin. It was easy.

The President. Good. Parents, how are you feeling about this whole college cost thing?

Parent Tim Craig. Well, Brendan is my third one in school right now, and I have one more that will be coming up, so four.

The President. So you're a pro. [*Laughter*]

Tim Craig. Yes. [*Laughter*] We go through that every year.

The President. And how about you? Do you have other kids who are—you've got to be thinking about?

Parent Kezia Truesdale. Yes, I have one— two that are in community college now, and so then she's going to go on to a 4-year university. But for Amirah, she is going straight to a 4-year university, and the cost is a lot more than community college. So we're looking at all our options: grants, scholarships, and definitely the Stafford loans.

The President. Just to be able to afford it. So it's a big chunk to handle.

How about you?

Parent Elma Molina. Well, Rina is my first one to go to college. I have two more; they're small right now. One is in third grade, and my last one is almost pre-K.

The President. Okay, so you've got things spaced out a little bit. That's good.

Well, there are two things that we're focused on. One is obviously keeping loan rates low. The second thing, though, is to actually try to lower college cost itself. And we've met with colleges and universities—the inflation rate on college has actually gone up faster than health care, which is pretty hard to do.

And some of it is not actually the fault of the universities. If it's a State school, the State legislatures across the country have been cutting back on the support for public colleges and universities. And the only way these colleges a lot of times can make it up is by raising tuition. They've got higher health care costs that they have to deal with. But some of it is, I think, a lack of creativity in terms of thinking about how do you keep costs down. All of you guys, when you get to school, you're going to have to think about making sure that you're not loading up yourselves with a lot of debt unnecessarily.

Everybody here is going to be living in dorms?

Students. Yes.

The President. And eating ramen noodles or—[*laughter*]? But I think you guys are in a good position because in addition to being able to take out student loans and having parents who are obviously interested and engaged in the process, what we're trying to do is to, through a variety of channels, provide more information to students so that they can plan ahead about what their debt loads might be when they graduate. And that's something that, frankly, when we were going to school we didn't really have a good idea. And a lot of kids ended up being surprised by how much things——

Secretary Duncan. Knowing 4-year costs, knowing the loan repayments. We're trying to do some things to reduce loan repayments at the back end—something called income-based repayment, IBR, you can take a look at. But helping the front end, know what your costs are, more transparency, and help at the back end. So we're trying to do all those things. As the President said, push States to invest and push colleges to be reasonable. These are tough times, and don't get carried away, and a lot of colleges are doing it well; some aren't. So we're trying to challenge them as well.

The President. So the—but overall, it sounds like you guys are all set. I'm excited for you.

[*At this point, the discussion continued, and no transcript was provided.*]

NOTE: The President spoke at 11:35 a.m.

Remarks at Washington-Lee High School in Arlington
May 4, 2012

The President. Hello, Generals! Hello, Virginia! Well, let me first of all say, following Amirah is kind of tough. [*Laughter*] She is really good. Give her a big round of applause for the great introduction. There are a couple of other people I want to introduce who are here today. First of all, my Secretary of Education, Arne Duncan, is here. Give him a round of applause. Your Congressman, Jim Moran, is here.

And before we came out, I had a chance to meet with Amirah and her mom, but also a couple other of your classmates. Brendan Craig is here, and his dad, and also Rina Castaneda and her mom. Let me just say, they represented you really well. Those were three impressive seniors. Thanks for hanging out with me on a Friday. I know that you're happy not because I'm here. There are seniors in the crowd—[*applause*]—and you're excited about graduating. I know the juniors are excited to get the seniors—[*applause*]—they're excited to get the seniors out so they'll be at the top of the heap.

You've got prom coming up. I guess you've already got your dress all picked out, huh? Yes. [*Laughter*] All right. You've got final exams. You've got a great summer coming up. And then, more than 90 percent of this year's seniors from this school are going to some sort of postsecondary education, whether it is a 4-year college, community college, vocational. That makes us proud. That is a testament to your principal, who is doing a great job. So we're very proud of him. Thank you.

Now, I know a lot of you—certainly a lot of your parents—are focused on how you're going to pay for college. And that's what I was talking to your classmates and some of your parents about. That's why I'm here. But first, I want to say something about the economy that we're going to be working to rebuild for you. Because not only do we want you to have a good education, we want to make sure that you're getting a job after you graduate.

Now, this morning, we learned that our economy created 130,000 private sector jobs in April and the unemployment rate ticked down again. So, after the worst economic crisis since the Great Depression, our businesses have now created more than 4.2 million new jobs over the last 26 months, more than 1 million jobs in the last 6 months alone.

So that's the good news. But there are still a lot of folks out of work, which means that we've got to do more. If we're going to recover all the jobs that were lost during the recession, and if we're going to build a secure economy that strengthens the middle class, then we're going to have to do more. And that's why, next week, I'm going to urge Congress, as they start getting back to work, to take some actions on some commonsense ideas, right now, that can accelerate even more job growth. That's what we need, and my message to Congress is going to be, just saying no to ideas that will create new jobs is not an option. There's too much at stake for us not to all be rowing in the same direction. And that's true for you, and that's true for your parents.

Now, that's in the short term. But in the long run, the most important thing we can do for our economy is to give all of you and all Americans the best education possible. That's the most important thing we can do. That means helping our schools hire and reward the best teachers, and you've got some great teachers here. That means stepping up our focus on math and science, something I tell Malia and Sasha every day. [*Applause*] You're solid on math? Okay, I like to hear that. [*Laughter*] That means giving more Americans the chance to learn the skills that businesses are looking for right now. And in the 21st century, it also means higher education cannot be a luxury; it is an economic imperative that every American should be able to afford.

Now, my grandfather had the chance to go to college because this country decided that every returning veteran of World War II should be able to afford it. And on a bipartisan basis, the GI bill was created that allowed him to go to college. My mother was able to raise two kids by herself because she was also able to get grants and loans to work her way through school. Michelle and I are only where we are because scholarships and student loans gave us a shot at a great education. We didn't come from a wealthy background, but this country gave us a chance at a good education.

This country has always made a commitment to put a good education within the reach of everybody who is willing to work for it. That's what makes us special. That's the kind of investment in our own people that helped us lead the world in business and science and technology and medicine. That's what made us an economic superpower.

But unfortunately, since you guys were born—which doesn't seem that long ago to me—[*laughter*]—maybe it does to you—the cost of going to college has more than doubled. And that means students have to take out more loans. It's now to the point where the average student who borrows to pay for college graduates with about $25,000 worth of debt—$25,000. And Americans now owe more for their student loans than they do on their credit cards.

Now, I want to give you guys some relief from that debt. I don't want you to start off life saddled with debt. And I don't want your parents to be taking on so much debt as well. Because when you start off already owing a lot of money graduating from school it means making a lot of really tough choices, like maybe waiting longer to buy a house or to start a family or to chase that career that you really want.

And like I said, Michelle and I know about this. We graduated from college and law school with a truckload of student loan debt. We got married, and together, we got poorer. [*Laughter*] After we graduated, we were lucky enough to land good jobs, so it was still a great investment for us to go to college and law school. But we only finished paying off our student loans about 8 years ago. And I know some of your teachers here probably can relate. When we should have been starting to save up for Malia's and Sasha's college educations, we were still paying off our educations.

So we can't price the middle class out of a higher education. We've got to make college more affordable. And that's why we fixed a broken student loan system that was giving tens of billions of dollars to big banks, and we said, let's use that money to help more people afford college. That's why we strengthened aid for low-income students. That's why we fought to set up a new, independent consumer watchdog agency that's now working with every student and their parents to access a simple fact sheet on student loans and financial aid, so you can make your own choices, the best choices, about how to pay for college. We call it "Know Before You Owe." Know before you owe.

But making college more affordable isn't something Government can or should do alone. I was mentioning to your classmates, we're talking to colleges and universities about doing their part. And I've told Congress to steer Federal aid to schools that keep tuition affordable and provide good value and serve their students well. If colleges and universities can't stop their costs from going up, then the funding they get from taxpayers, that—it should go down. We should steer it to the schools that are really giving students the best deal.

And States have to do their part by making higher education a higher priority in their budgets. Last year, over 40 States cut their higher education spending. These cuts have been among the largest drivers of public college tuition increases over the past decade. So we've told States, if you can find new ways to bring down the cost of college and make it easier for students to graduate, then we're going to help you do it, which is good news.

Now, Congress also has to do its part. Right now that means preventing the interest rates on Federal student loans from doubling, which would make it harder for you to pay for college next year. The three classmates of yours that I met, they're all getting Stafford loans to help

pay for college. And these Stafford loans right now have a very low interest rate, because 5 years ago Congress cut the rate for these student loans in half. That was a good idea. It made college more affordable. But here's the bad news.

Audience member. Uh-oh.

The President. Uh-oh. [*Laughter*] On July 1, less than 2 months from now, that rate cut expires, and interest rates on those loans will double overnight.

Audience members. Boo!

The President. That's not good. For each year that college doesn't act, the average student with these Stafford loans will rack up an additional thousand dollars in debt. That's like a thousand-dollar tax hike for more than 7 million students across America.

Now, let me ask, is that something that you can afford if you're going to college?

Audience members. No!

The President. You guys shouldn't have to pay an extra thousand dollars just because Congress can't get its act together. This is something—this should be a no-brainer. This is something that we need to get done.

So the good news is, the Senate will vote next week on a bill that would keep student loan rates from doubling. And some Republican Senators look like they might support it. I'm ready to work with them to make it happen. But unfortunately, rather than find a bipartisan way to fix this problem, the House Republicans are saying they're only going to prevent these rates from doubling if they can cut things like preventive health care for women instead. So——

Audience members. Boo!

The President. That's not good. We shouldn't have to choose between women having preventive health care and young people keeping their student loan rates low.

Some of the Republicans in the House are coming up with all sorts of different reasons why we should just let these rates double. One of them compared student loans to a "stage-three cancer of socialism," whatever that means. I don't know. [*Laughter*] Another warned that this is all about giving you a "free college education," which doesn't make sense because, of course, loans aren't free; you've got to pay them back. The spokesman for the Speaker of the House said that we were—meaning me—we're just talking about student loans to distract folks from the economy. Now, this makes no sense, because this is all about the economy. Making sure our young people can earn the best possible education, that's one of the best things we can do for the economy. Making sure college is available to everyone and not just a few at the top, that's one of the best things we can do for our economy.

And I don't think it's fair when they suggest that students like you should pay more so we can bring down deficits that they helped to run up over the past decade. They just voted—[*applause*]—we've got to do something about our deficits. We paid for two wars with a credit card, debt that you're going to have to pay off. We gave two tax cuts to folks that don't need it and weren't asking for it. They—the Republicans in the House just voted to keep giving billions of taxpayer dollars every year to big oil companies raking in record profits. They just voted to let millionaires and billionaires keep paying lower tax rates than middle class workers. They even voted to give an average tax cut of at least $150,000 to every millionaire in America. And they want you to pay an extra thousand dollars a year for college.

Audience members. Boo!

The President. No, no, that doesn't make sense. In America, we admire success. We aspire to it. I was talking to folks—Rina wants to study business, and I'm confident she's going to be really wealthy some day and the—[*applause*]—we want all of you to work and hustle and study your tails off and achieve your dreams. But America is not just about protecting a few people who are doing well. America is about giving everybody a chance to do well. That's what makes us strong. That's what the American Dream is all about. Everybody here, you're only here, you're only succeeding because somebody, somewhere, felt a responsibility not just to themselves, not even just to their own families, but to the country as a whole. And now it's our turn to be responsible.

It's our turn to keep that promise alive for the next generation.

So if you agree with me, then I need all of you—I see a lot of cell phones here and a lot of—[*laughter*]—all kinds of stuff. [*Laughter*] I want you to send a message to Congress. Tell them, "Don't double my rate." You should—"don't double my rate." You should call them, you should e-mail them, write on their Facebook page, tweet them. [*Applause*] Tweet them. Teach your parents how to tweet. [*Laughter*] And there's a—use the hashtag #dontdoublemyrate. Don't double my rate. [*Applause*] Don't double it. I asked some students at the University of North Carolina and the University of Colorado and the University of Iowa to do this last week, and they got it trending worldwide for a while. So there were, of course—there were more of them than there were of you. I had Jimmy Fallon's help. [*Laughter*]

But what I do expect from each of you on this and every other issue that you come to care about, I want you guys to realize your voice makes a difference. Your voice matters. I know sometimes it seems like it doesn't, but I guarantee you, Members of Congress, they pay attention. And if they start getting a lot of folks telling them they care deeply about something, it changes their mind. Sometimes, it changes their vote. Don't let anybody tell you otherwise.

It doesn't matter how old you are, what you look like, where you come from, or how much you have, your voice can make a difference. So tell Congress now is not the time to double your interest on your student loans. Now is the time to double down on our smart investments in building a strong and secure middle class. Now is the time to double down on building an America that lasts. And if we work together, I guarantee you, we'll meet our challenges.

When I met your classmates, when I look out at your faces, it gives me confidence about our future. I believe in you. And I believe you're going to do great things. And I believe your generation will remind the world just why it is America is the greatest nation on Earth.

Thank you, everybody. God bless you.

NOTE: The President spoke at 11:53 a.m. In his remarks, he referred to Amirah Delwin, student, Washington-Lee High School, and her mother Kezia Truesdale; Tim Craig, father of student Brendan Craig; Elma Molina, mother of student Rina Castaneda; Gregg Robertson, principal, Washington-Lee High School; Reps. Todd W. Akin and W. Joseph Walsh; Brendan Buck, press secretary for Speaker of the House of Representatives John A. Boehner; and James T. Fallon, Jr., host, NBC's "Late Night With Jimmy Fallon" program. He also referred to his sister Maya Soetoro-Ng.

Remarks Honoring the NCAA Men's Basketball Champion University of Kentucky Wildcats
May 4, 2012

The President. Thank you. Come on over here, Coach. Thank you very much. Thank you so much. Everybody, have a seat. Have a seat. Have a seat. Welcome to the White House, and congratulations to the Kentucky Wildcats on your eighth national championship. Eighth national champ—that's not bad. [*Laughter*] That's not bad. Although, this is the first in 14 years. [*Laughter*]

Now, this was the fourth year that I filled out my bracket on ESPN. And what I've learned is that if I make the right picks, I look like a genius. But if things go the other way, then a team like Kentucky gets to come to my house and remind me in person that I was wrong. [*Laughter*] So it is a double-edged sword.

Of course, I knew Kentucky was good. I had them in the championship game. But in the end, I thought, these—they got all these freshmen. These guys are too young. [*Laughter*] And keep in mind, at this time last year, three of the Wildcats' five starters were still in high school. Michael Kidd-Gilchrist couldn't even vote yet. [*Laughter*]

But let's face it, sometimes talent triumphs experience. And sometimes, a bunch of young players, even if they're used to being big fishes in their ponds, even if they've never played together before, they can buy into a system, they understand the concept of team, and they do something special right away. And that's exactly what happened in Kentucky.

Of course, a lot of credit for that goes to their outstanding coach, Coach Calipari. My understanding is, when he recruited these players, Coach started off by asking them some simple questions: Do you want to win a national title? The answer was yes, apparently. [*Laughter*] Can you do it by yourself? The answer was no. He took a roster with six former All-Americans and got them to do something even more impressive, and that was share the ball. So you had six players average double figures in points this year; nobody averaged more than nine shots a game. If you didn't play defense, you didn't play.

And as a result, the Wildcats started winning. At one point, they won 24 straight. And they spent the final 8 weeks of the season ranked number one. They cruised through the tournament, trailed for less than 10 minutes total, before beating Kansas in front of 70,000 fans at the Super Dome. So that's a pretty good run.

Most importantly, though, they did it as a team. And nobody, I think, was a better example of that than Anthony Davis, who—everybody kept on remarking on it. Nobody has ever seen somebody who didn't have a lot of field goals and yet still controlled the game. Still ended up being the most valuable player: racked up 16 rebounds, 6 blocks, 3 steals. That doesn't count all the intimidation factor—[*laughter*]—that the other team had to go through. Of course, that's what happens when you grow 8 inches between your sophomore and senior years of high school. In fact, he has grown an inch since he got to the White House. [*Laughter*] His pants are already like this. [*Laughter*] Just got a new suit, you know, and his—[*laughter*].

When Anthony needed help, Doron Lamb stepped up, dropping 22 points in the biggest game of his career. First off the bench, Darius Miller, who became the first player in Kentucky history to be named Mr. Basketball, win a State championship in high school and win a national title with the Wildcats. I'm pretty sure Coach Cal is right that if Darius decides to run for Governor, he'll do all right in Kentucky. [*Laughter*] I also want to congratulate Darius and Eloy Vargas for getting their diplomas on Sunday. That's worth a big round of applause.

And I want to congratulate them for doing their share of community service in the Lexington community, from packing backpacks full of food for kids who don't have enough to raising money for tornado victims.

So these guys do it all. Everybody's got to take a good look now, because a whole bunch of these guys are going on to the NBA. Who knows, one of them might end up here in Washington. We'll take him.

Coach Cal is back on the recruiting trail, and if the next group of Wildcats is anything like this one, then I might see them again sometime soon.

So congratulations again to all the fans, to all the faculty, to all the—everybody who helps to make Kentucky such an outstanding university. Most of all, congratulations to the team and to Coach Calipari.

Head Coach John V. Calipari. Thank you very much. Mr. President, on behalf of the Big Blue Nation, the Commonwealth of Kentucky, we are honored and humbled to be here. This team, when they won that championship on that court in New Orleans, they were jumping up and down not saying: "We did it! We won!"

They were saying: "We're going to the White House! We're going to the White House!" [*Laughter*] Because they wanted to meet you.

As a member of our team, I'd like our seniors, Darius Miller, to give you his number-one jersey that he wore for 4 years.

The President. That's great.

Coach Calipari. Eloy Vargas has a ball that he—the team has signed, and the young—[*applause*]. There's the number-one jersey.

The President. That's a good-looking jersey right there.

Coach Calipari. And the young guy from your home city of Chicago——

The President. Chicago! [*Laughter*]

Coach Calipari. ——would like to present you with the 2012 National Championship ring, and I might say, it is the first.

The President. Hold that up. Look at that. That's all right. That's beautiful, man. Fantastic. Well, this is some nice gear. [*Laughter*] I have to say, by the way, after the game, I called the coach and the team, and I mentioned to Anthony that I had actually been to his school, a small charter school in Chicago, when I was still a Senator. And I had spoken to the kids there, and he told me, yes, I was there. [*Laughter*] But I didn't recognize him. He looked a little different apparently 4 years ago. So what a wonderful set of gifts. I appreciate that.

NOTE: The President spoke at 5:03 p.m. in the East Room at the White House. In his remarks, he referred to Michael Kidd-Gilchrist, Anthony Davis, and Eloy Vargas, forwards, and Doron Lamb and Darius Miller, guards, University of Kentucky men's basketball team.

The President's Weekly Address
May 5, 2012

This week, I traveled to Afghanistan to thank our troops serving far from home and to sign a historic agreement that will help us complete our mission and end the war.

As Commander in Chief, nothing is more humbling or inspiring than the chance to spend some time with our troops. At Bagram

Air Base, I visited with some of our outstanding men and women in uniform. I thanked them for their extraordinary service. And I let them know that America honors their sacrifice.

Because of their bravery and dedication, the tide of war has turned in Afghanistan. We've broken the Taliban's momentum. We've built strong Afghan security forces. We've devastated Al Qaida's leadership. And 1 year ago, our troops launched the operation that killed Usama bin Laden. The goal that I set to defeat Al Qaida and deny it a chance to rebuild is within reach.

Because of the progress we've made, I was able to sign an historic agreement between the United States and Afghanistan that defines a new kind of relationship between our countries: a future in which Afghans are responsible for the security of their nation and we build an equal partnership between two sovereign states, a future in which the war ends and a new chapter begins.

The enormous sacrifices of our men and women in uniform are not over, but many of our troops are already coming home. Last year, we removed 10,000 U.S. troops from Afghanistan; another 23,000 will leave by the end of the summer. As our coalition agreed, by the end of 2014, the Afghans will be fully responsible for the security of their country. And this is as it should be, because after more than a decade of war, it's time to focus on nation-building here at home.

As a new greatest generation returns from overseas, we must ask ourselves: What kind of country will they come back to? Will it be a country where a shrinking number of Americans do really well while a growing number barely get by? Or will it be a country where everyone gets a fair shot, everyone does their fair share, and everyone plays by the same set of rules, a country with opportunity worthy of the troops who protect us?

America has answered this question before. My grandfather, a veteran of Patton's army, got the chance to go to college on the GI bill. My grandmother, who worked on a bomber assembly line, was part of a workforce that turned out the best products on Earth. They contributed to a story of success that every American had the chance to share in: the basic American promise that if you worked hard, you could do well enough to raise a family, own a home, send your kids to college, and put a little away for retirement.

Keeping that promise alive is the defining issue of our time. But it means making responsible choices.

I don't think we should prioritize things like more tax cuts for millionaires while cutting the kinds of investments that build a strong middle class. That's why I've called on Congress to take the money we're no longer spending at war, use half of it to pay down our debt, and use the other half to rebuild America.

Because we've got more jobs to create, more students to educate, more clean energy to generate, more entrepreneurs with the next great idea, just looking for their shot at success. We've got to invest in things like education and medical research. We've got to build newer and faster transportations and communications networks. And we've got to secure the care and benefits our veterans have earned, so that we serve them as well as they've served us.

Every time I have the privilege of meeting with our troops, I'm struck by their courage, their commitment, their selflessness, and their teamwork. They have something to teach us. Recovering from the worst economic crisis since the Great Depression is a work in progress, but if we follow their example, then I have no doubt we will preserve the promise of this country, protect the freedoms we cherish, and leave for our children an America that's built to last.

God bless you, and have a great weekend.

NOTE: The address was recorded at approximately 2:05 p.m. on May 4 in the Map Room at the White House for broadcast on May 5. The transcript was made available by the Office of the Press Secretary on May 4, but was embargoed for release until 6 a.m. on May 5.

Remarks at an Obama Victory Fund 2012 Fundraiser in Columbus, Ohio
May 5, 2012

The President. Hello, Ohio! It is good to be back in Ohio! Right before I came out, somebody happened to give me a buckeye for good luck.

Audience member. I love you!

The President. I love you back! Now, before I begin, I want to say thank you to a few people who are joining us here today. Your mayor, Michael Coleman, is here. Former Governor Ted Strickland is here. Senator Sherrod Brown is in the house. An American hero, John Glenn is with us.

And I want to thank so many of our neighborhood team leaders for being here today. You guys will be the backbone of this campaign. And I want the rest of you to join a team or become a leader yourself, because we are going to win this thing the old-fashioned way: door by door, block by block, neighborhood by neighborhood.

Ohio, 4 years ago, you and I began a journey together. I didn't run, and you didn't work your hearts out, just to win an election. We came together to reclaim the basic bargain that built the largest middle class and the most prosperous nation on Earth.

We came together because we believe that in America, your success shouldn't be determined by the circumstances of your birth. If you're willing to work hard, you should be able to find a good job. If you're willing to meet your responsibilities, you should be able to own a home, maybe start a business, give your children the chance to do even better, no matter who you are or where you come from or what you look like or what your last name is.

We believe the free market is one of the greatest forces for progress in human history, that businesses are the engine of growth, that risk takers and innovators should be rewarded. But we also believe that at its best, the free market has never been a license to take whatever you want, however you can get it, that alongside our entrepreneurial spirit and our rugged individualism, America only prospers when we meet our obligations to one another and to future generations.

We came together in 2008 because our country had strayed from these basic values. A record surplus was squandered on tax cuts for people who didn't need them and weren't even asking for them. Two wars were being waged on a credit card. Wall Street speculators reaped huge profits by making bets with other people's money. Manufacturing left our shores. A shrinking number of Americans did fantastically well, while most people struggled with falling incomes, rising costs, the slowest job growth in half a century.

It was a house of cards that collapsed in the most destructive crisis since the Great Depression. In the last 6 months of 2008, even as we were campaigning, nearly 3 million of our neighbors lost their jobs. Over 800,000 more were lost in the month I took office alone.

It was tough. But I tell you what, Ohio, the American people are tougher. All across this country, people like you dug in. Some of you retrained. Some of you went back to school. Small-business owners cut back on expenses, but did everything they could to keep their employees. Yes, there were setbacks. Yes, there were disappointments. But we didn't quit. We don't quit. Together, we're fighting our way back.

When some wanted to let Detroit go bankrupt, we made a bet on American workers, on the ingenuity of American companies. And today, our auto industry is back on top of the world. Manufacturers started investing again, adding jobs for the first time since the 1990s. Businesses got back to the basics, exports surged. And over 4 million jobs were created in the last 2 years, more than 1 million of those in the last 6 months alone. Are we satisfied?

Audience members. No!

The President. Of course not. Too many of our friends and family are still out there looking for work. The housing market is still weak, deficits are still too high, States are still laying off teachers, first-responders. This crisis took years to develop, and the economy is still facing headwinds. And it will take sustained, persistent effort—yours and mine—for America to fully recover. That's the truth. We all know it.

But we are making progress. And now we face a choice. Now we face a choice, Ohio.

Audience member. We love you, Barack Obama!

Audience members. Aww!

The President. [*Laughter*] Thank you. Now we face a choice. For the last few years, the Republicans who run this Congress have insisted that we go right back to the policies that created this mess. But to borrow a line from our friend Bill Clinton, now their agenda is on steroids. This time, they want even bigger tax cuts for the wealthiest Americans. This time, they want even deeper cuts to things like education and Medicare and research and technology.

This time, they want to give banks and insurance companies even more power to do as they please. And now, after a long and spirited primary, Republicans in Congress have found a nominee for President who has promised to rubber stamp this agenda if he gets the chance.

Ohio, I tell you what: We cannot give him that chance. Not now. Not with so much at stake. This is not just another election. This is a make-or-break moment for the middle class, and we've been through too much to turn back now.

We have come too far to abandon the change we fought for these past few years. We have to move forward to the future we imagined in 2008, where everyone gets a fair shot and everyone does their fair share and everyone plays by the same rules. That's the choice in this election, and that's why I'm running for a second term as President of the United States.

Governor Romney is a patriotic American who has raised a wonderful family, and he has much to be proud of. He's run a large financial firm, and he's run a State. But I think he has drawn the wrong lessons from those experiences. He sincerely believes that if CEOs and wealthy investors like him make money, the rest of us will automatically prosper as well.

When a woman in Iowa shared the story of her financial struggles, he responded with economic theory. He told her, "Our productivity equals our income." Well, let me tell you something. The problem with our economy isn't that the American people aren't productive enough; you've been working harder than ever. The challenge we face right now—the challenge we've faced for over a decade—is that harder work hasn't led to higher incomes. It's that bigger profits haven't led to better jobs.

Governor Romney doesn't seem to get that. He doesn't seem to understand that maximizing profits by whatever means necessary—whether through layoffs or outsourcing or tax avoidance or union-busting—might not always be good for the average American or for the American economy.

Why else would he want to spend trillions more on tax cuts for the wealthiest Americans? Why else would he propose cutting his own taxes while raising them on 18 million working families? Why else would he want to slash the investments that have always helped the economy grow, but at the same time, stop regulating the reckless behavior on Wall Street that helped the economy crash?

Somehow, he and his friends in Congress think that the same bad ideas will lead to a different result. Or they're just hoping you won't remember what happened the last time we tried it their way.

Well, Ohio, I'm here to say that we were there, we remember, and we are not going back. We are moving this country forward.

Look, we want businesses to succeed. We want entrepreneurs and investors rewarded when they take risks, when they create jobs and grow our economy. But the true measure of our prosperity is more than just a running tally of every balance sheet and quarterly profit report. I don't care how many ways you try to explain it: Corporations aren't people. People are people.

We measure prosperity not just by our total GDP, not just by how many billionaires we produce, but how well the typical family is doing, whether they can go as far as their dreams and hard work will take them.

And we understand that in this country, people succeed when they have a chance to get a decent education and learn new skills, and by the way, so do the businesses that hire them or the companies that they start.

We know that our economy grows when we support research into medical breakthroughs and new technologies that lead to the next Internet app or lifesaving drug.

We know that our country is stronger when we can count on affordable health insurance and Medicare and Social Security, when we protect our kids from toxic dumping and mercury pollution, when there are rules to make sure we aren't taken advantage of by credit card companies and mortgage lenders and financial institutions. And we know these rules aren't just good for seniors or kids or consumers; they're good for business too. They're part of what makes the market work.

Look, we don't expect government to solve all our problems, and it shouldn't try. I learned from my mom that no education policy can take the place of a parent's love and affection. As a young man, I worked with a group of Catholic churches who taught me that no poverty program can make as much of a difference as the kindness and commitment of a caring soul. Not every regulation is smart. Not every tax dollar is spent wisely. Not every person can be helped who refuses to help themselves.

But that's not an excuse to tell the vast majority of responsible, hard-working Americans, "You're on your own," that unless you're lucky enough to have parents who can lend you money, you may not be able to go to college; that even if you pay your premiums every month, you're out of luck if an insurance company decides to drop your coverage when you need it most.

That's not how we built America. That's not who we are. We built this country together. [*Applause*] We built this country together.

We built railroads and highways, the Hoover Dam, the Golden Gate Bridge together. We sent my grandfather's generation to college on the GI bill together. We instituted a minimum wage and worker safety laws together. Together, we touched the surface of the Moon, unlocked the mystery of the atom, connected the world through our own science and imagination. We did these things together, not because they benefited any particular individual or group, but because they made us all richer. Because they gave us all opportunity. Because they moved us forward together, as one people, as one Nation.

That's the true lesson of our past, Ohio. That's the right vision for our future. And that's why I'm running for President.

I'm running to make sure that by the end of the decade, more of our citizens hold a college degree than any other nation on Earth. I want to help our schools hire and reward the best teachers, especially in math and science. I want to give 2 million more Americans the chance to go to community colleges and learn the skills that local businesses are looking for right now. In the 21st century, higher education can't be a luxury. It is an economic imperative that every American should be able to afford. That's the choice in this election. That's why I'm running for President.

I'm running to make sure the next generation of high-tech manufacturing takes root in places like Columbus and Cleveland and Pittsburgh and Richmond. I want to stop rewarding businesses that ship jobs and profits overseas and start rewarding companies that create jobs right here in the United States of America. That's the choice in this election.

I'm running so that we can keep moving towards a future where we control our own energy. Our dependence on foreign oil is at its lowest point in 16 years. By the middle of the next decade, our cars will average nearly 55 miles per gallon. Thousands of Americans have jobs right now because the production of renewal energy in this country has nearly doubled in just 3 years.

So now is not the time to cut these investments to pay for another $4 billion giveaway to the oil companies. Now is the time to end the subsidies for an industry that's rarely been more profitable. Let's double down on a clean energy future that's never been more promising—for our economy and for our security and for the safety of our planet. That's why I'm running for President. That's the choice in this election, Ohio.

For the first time in 9 years, there are no Americans fighting in Iraq. Usama bin Laden is no longer a threat to this country. Al Qaida is on the path to defeat. And by 2014, the war in Afghanistan will be over.

America is safer and more respected because of the courage and selflessness of the United States Armed Forces. And as long as I'm Commander in Chief, this country will care for our veterans and serve our veterans as well as they've served us. Because nobody who fights for this country should have to fight for a job or a roof over their heads when they come home.

My opponent said it was "tragic" to end the war in Iraq. He said he won't set a timeline for ending the war in Afghanistan. I have, and I intend to keep it. After a decade of war that's cost us thousands of lives and over a trillion dollars, the Nation we need to build is our own. I will use half of what we're no longer spending on war to pay down the deficit and the other half to repair our roads and our bridges, our runways, and our wireless networks. That's the choice in this election, to rebuild America.

I'm running to pay down our debt in a way that's balanced and responsible. After inheriting a trillion-dollar deficit, I signed $2 trillion of spending cuts into law. And now I want to finish the job by streamlining Government and cutting more waste and reforming our Tax Code so that it is simpler and fairer and asks the wealthiest Americans to pay a little bit more.

My opponent won't tell us how he'd pay for his new, $5 trillion tax cut, a tax cut that gives an average of $250,000 to every millionaire in this country. But we know the bill for that tax cut will either be passed on to our children or it will be paid for by a whole lot of ordinary Americans. That's what we know. And I refuse to let that happen again.

I refuse to pay for another millionaire's tax cut by eliminating medical research projects into things like cancer and Alzheimer's disease. I refuse to pay for another tax cut by kicking children off of Head Start programs or asking students to pay more for college or eliminating health insurance for millions of poor and elderly and disabled Americans on Medicaid.

And as long as I'm President of the United States, I will never allow Medicare to be turned into a voucher that would end the program as we know it. We will not go back to the days when our citizens spent their golden years at the mercy of private insurance companies. We will reform Medicare, not by shifting the cost of care to seniors, but by reducing the spending that isn't making people healthier. That's what's at stake in this election. That's what's at stake, Ohio.

On issue after issue, we can't afford to spend the next 4 years going backward. America doesn't need to refight the battles we just had over Wall Street reform and health care reform. On health care reform, here is what I know: Allowing 2.5 million young people to stay on their parent's health insurance plan, that was the right thing to do. Cutting prescription drug costs for seniors, that was the right thing to do. I will not go back to the days when insurance companies had unchecked power to cancel your policy or deny your coverage or charge women differently from men. We're not going back there. We're going forward.

We don't need another political fight about ending a woman's right to choose or getting rid of Planned Parenthood or taking away access to affordable birth control. I want women to control their own health choices, just like I want my daughters to have the same opportunities as your sons. We are not turning back the clock. We are moving forward.

We're not returning to the days when you could be kicked out of the United States military just because of who you are or who you love. That would be wrong for our national security, and it would be a betrayal of our values.

This should be the last election where multimillion-dollar donations speak louder than the voices of ordinary citizens. We need more checks on lobbyists and special interests, not less.

We're not going to eliminate the EPA. We're not going to roll back the bargaining rights that generations of workers fought for. It's time to stop denying citizenship to responsible young people just because they're the children of undocumented immigrants. This country is at its best when we harness the God-given talents of every individual, when we hear every voice, when we come together as one American family, striving for the same dream.

That's what we're fighting for. That's what we're fighting for, Ohio: a bold America, a competitive America, a generous America, a forward-looking America, where everybody has a chance to make of their life what they will. That's what made us the envy of the world. That's what makes us great. That's why I'm running again for President of the United States.

And that is why I need your help. Ohio, this election will be even closer than the last. Too many of our friends, too many of our neighbors are still hurting because of this crisis. I've heard from too many people wondering why they haven't been able to get one of the jobs that have been created, why their home is still under water, why their family hasn't yet been touched by the recovery.

The other side won't be offering these Americans a real answer to these questions. They won't offer a better vision or a new set of ideas. But they will be spending more money than we've ever seen before on negative ads—on TV, on radio, in the mail, on the Internet—ads that exploit people's frustrations for my opponent's political gain. Over and over again, they'll tell you that America is down and out, and they'll tell you who to blame and ask if you're better off than you were before the worst crisis in our lifetime.

We've seen that play before. But you know what? The real question—the question that will actually make a difference in your life and in the lives of your children—is not just about how we're doing today. It's about how we'll be doing tomorrow.

Will we better off if more Americans get a better education? That's the question. Will we better off if we depend less on foreign oil and more on our own ingenuity? That's the question. Will we better off if we start doing some nation-building right here at home? That's the question. Will we be better off if we bring down our deficit without gutting the very things we need to grow? When we look back 4 years from now or 10 years from now or 20 years from now, won't we be better off if we have the courage to keep moving forward?

That's the question in this election. [*Applause*] That's the question in this election. And the outcome is entirely up to you. Now, sure, we'll have to contend with even more negative ads, with even more cynicism and nastiness and sometimes just plain foolishness. There will be more of that than we saw in the last campaign.

But if there is one thing that we learned in 2008, it's that nothing is more powerful than millions of voices calling for change. When enough of you knock on doors, when you pick up phones, when you talk to your friends, when you decide that it's time for change to happen, guess what? Change happens. Change comes to America.

And that's the spirit we need again. If people ask you what this campaign is about, you tell them it's still about hope. You tell them it's still about change. You tell them it's still about ordinary people who believe that in the face of great odds, we can make a difference in the life of this country.

Because I still believe, Ohio. I still believe that we are not as divided as our politics suggest. I still believe that we have more in common than the pundits tell us, that we're not Democrats or Republicans, but Americans first and foremost. I still believe in you, and I'm asking you to keep believing in me. I told you in 2008 that I wasn't a perfect man, and I would never be a perfect President. But I promised that I would always tell you what I thought. I would always tell you where I stood. And I would wake up every single day fighting for you as hard as I know how.

And I have that kept that promise. I have kept that promise, Ohio. And I will keep it so long as I have the honor of being your President. So if you're willing to stick with me, if you're willing to fight with me and press on with me, if you're willing to work even harder in this election than you did in the last election, I guarantee you, we will move this country forward.

We will finish what we started. We are still fired up. We are still ready to go. And we are going to remind the world once more just why it is that the United States of America is the greatest nation on Earth.

Thank you. God bless you. God bless the United States of America.

NOTE: The President spoke at 1:05 p.m. at the Value-City Schottenstein Center. In his remarks, he referred to former Sen. John H. Glenn, Jr.; former President William J. Clinton; and Republican Presidential candidate former Gov. W. Mitt Romney of Massachusetts. The transcript released by the Office of the Press Secretary also included the remarks of the First Lady.

Remarks at an Obama Victory Fund 2012 Fundraiser in Richmond, Virginia
May 5, 2012

The President. Hello, Virginia! What do you think about Michelle Obama? I hate following her, she is too good. And she looked good too, didn't she? Yes, she does. I'm just saying, she looked pretty good. How's it going, VCU?

Well, before I begin, there are a few people that I want to thank for joining us here today. First of all, your mayor Dwight Jones is here. Representative Bobby Scott is in the house. Your former Governor Tim Kaine is here. And a guy that, I gather, is pretty popular in these parts, Coach Shaka Smart is in the house. When I saw Coach backstage, he said, "I just want you to know, we're going to be coming to the White House just like that Kentucky team came this week." And he wasn't smiling. [*Laughter*]

I also want to thank so many of our neighborhood team leaders for being here today. You guys will be the backbone of this campaign. And I want the rest of you to join a team or become a leader yourself, because we are going to win this thing door by door, block by block, neighborhood by neighborhood.

Audience member. We love you, Barack!

The President. I love you back. Love Virginia. Virginia, 4 years ago, you and I began a journey together. I didn't run, and you did not work your hearts out, just to win an election. We came together to reclaim the basic bargain that built the largest middle class and the most prosperous nation on Earth.

We came together because we believe that in America, your success shouldn't be determined by the circumstances of your birth. If you're willing to work hard, you should be able to find a good job. If you're willing to meet your responsibilities, you should be able to own a home, maybe start a business, give your kids the chance to do even better, no matter who you are, no matter where you come from, no matter what you look like, no matter what your last name is.

We believe the free market is one of the greatest forces for progress in human history, that businesses are the engine of growth, and that risk takers and innovators should be rewarded. But we also believe that at its best, the free market has never been a license to take whatever you want, however you can get it. We've understood that alongside our entrepreneurial spirit, our rugged individualism, America only prospers when we meet our obligations to one another and to future generations.

We came together in 2008 because our country had strayed from these basic American values. A record surplus was squandered on tax cuts for people who didn't need them and weren't even asking for them. Two wars were being waged on a credit card. Wall Street speculators reaped huge profits by making bets with other people's money. Manufacturing left our shores. A shrinking number of Americans did fantastically well, while most people struggled with falling incomes and rising costs and the slowest job growth in half a century.

And in 2008, that house of cards collapsed in the most destructive crisis since the Great Depression. In the last 6 months of that year, even as we campaigned, nearly 3 million of our neighbors lost their jobs. Over 800,000 more were lost in the month I took the oath of office. And it was tough. It was tough here in Virginia. It was tough all across the country.

But the American people are tougher. All across America, people like you dug in. Folks like you fought back. Some of you retrained. Some of you went back to school. Small-business owners cut back on expenses, but did everything they could to keep their employees. And sure, there were setbacks. There have been disappointments. But we didn't quit. We don't quit. Together, we are fighting our way back. [*Applause*] Together, we're fighting our way back.

When some wanted to let Detroit go bankrupt, we made a bet on American workers, on the ingenuity of American companies. And today, our auto industry is back on top of the world. Manufacturers started investing in America again, adding jobs for the first time since the 1990s. Businesses got back to basics, exports surged, and over 4 million jobs were created in the last 2 years, more than 1 million of those in the last 6 months alone. Now, does this make us satisfied?

Audience members. No!

The President. Of course not. Too many of our friends and family are still looking for work. The housing market is still weak, deficits are still too high. States are still laying off teachers and first-responders. This crisis took years to develop, and the economy is still facing a bunch of headwinds. So it's going to take sustained, persistent effort—yours and mine—for America to fully recover, for us to be where we need to be. That's the truth. We all know it.

But, Virginia, I'm here to tell you we are making progress. And now we face a choice. For the last few years, the Republicans who run this Congress have insisted that we go right back to the policies that created this mess in the first place.

But it gets worse, because to borrow a line from our friend Bill Clinton, now their agenda is on steroids. This time, they want even bigger tax cuts for the wealthiest Americans. This time, they want even deeper cuts to things like education and Medicare and research and

technology. This time, they want to give banks and insurance companies even more power to do as they please.

And now, after a long and spirited primary, Republicans in Congress have found a champion. They have found a nominee for President who has promised to rubberstamp this agenda if he gets a chance. But, Virginia, I tell you what, we can't give him the chance. Not now. Not with so much at stake. This isn't just another election. This is a make-or-break moment for America's middle class. We've been through much to turn back now. We've come too far to abandon the change we fought for these past few years. Virginia, we've got to move forward to the future that we imagined in 2008. We've got to move forward to that future where everyone gets a fair shot and everyone does their fair share and everyone plays by the same rules. That's the choice in this election. And that's why I'm running for a second term as President of the United States of America.

Now, Governor Romney is a patriotic American. He's raised a wonderful family, and he has much to be proud of. He's run a large financial firm, and he's run a State. But I think he's drawn the wrong lessons from these experiences. He sincerely believes that if CEOs and wealthy investors like him make money, the rest of us will automatically prosper as well.

When a woman in Iowa shared the story of her financial struggles, he responded with economic theory. He told her, "Our productivity equals our income." Well, let me tell you something, Virginia, the problem with our economy is not that the American people aren't productive enough; you've never been working harder in your lives. You're working harder than ever. The challenge we face right now—the challenge we've faced for over a decade—is that harder work hasn't led to higher incomes. It's that bigger profits haven't led to better jobs.

And Governor Romney doesn't seem to get that. He doesn't seem to understand that maximizing profits by whatever means necessary—whether through layoffs or outsourcing or tax avoidance or union-busting—might not always be good for the average American or for our economy.

I mean, why else would he want to spend trillions more on tax cuts for the wealthiest Americans? Why else would he propose cutting his own taxes while raising them on 18 million working families? Why else would he want to slash the investments that have always helped the economy grow, while at the same time stopping regulations of the reckless behavior on Wall Street that helped make the economy crash?

Somehow, he and his friends in Congress think that the same bad ideas will lead to a different result. Or they're just hoping that you won't remember what happened the last time we tried it their way. Virginia, I'm here to say that we were there, we remember, and we're not going back. We're moving this country forward. We remember.

Look, we want businesses to succeed. We want entrepreneurs and investors rewarded when they take risks, when they create jobs and grow our economy. But the true measure of our prosperity is more than just a running tally of every balance sheet and quarterly profit report. I don't care how many ways you try to explain it: Corporations aren't people. People are people.

We measure prosperity not just by our total GDP, not just by how many billionaires we produce, but how well is the typical family doing, whether they can go as far as their dreams and hard work will take them.

We understand that in this country, people succeed when they have the chance to get a decent education and learn new skills. And by the way, so do the businesses that hire those people or the companies that those people start.

We know that our economy grows when we support research into medical breakthroughs and new technologies that lead to the next Internet app or lifesaving drug.

We know that our country is stronger when we can count on affordable health care and Medicare and Social Security, when we protect our kids from toxic dumping and mercury pollution, when there are rules to make sure we aren't taken advantage of by credit card companies or mortgage lenders or financial institutions. These rules aren't just good for seniors or kids or consumers. They're good for business. They're good for the marketplace. They're good for America.

Look, we don't expect Government to solve all our problems, and it shouldn't try. I learned from my mom that no education policy can take the place of a parent's love and attention and sometimes getting in your face and telling you what you need to do. As a young man, I worked with a group of Catholic churches who taught me that no poverty program can make as much difference as the kindness and commitment of a caring soul. Not every regulation is smart. Not every tax dollar is spent wisely. Not every person can be helped who refuses to help themselves.

That's what we believe. People have to make an effort. People have to try hard. But that's not an excuse to tell the vast majority of responsible, hard-working Americans, "You're on your own," that unless you're lucky enough to have parents who can lend you the money, you may not be able to go to college; that even if you pay your premiums every month, you're out of luck if an insurance company decides to drop your coverage when you need it most.

That's not how we built America. That's not who we are. We built this country together. We built railroads and highways, the Hoover Dam, the Golden Gate Bridge together. We sent my grandfather's generation to college on the GI bill together. We instituted a minimum wage and worker safety laws together. Together, we touched the surface of the Moon, unlocked the mystery of the atom, connected the world through our own science and our own imaginations. We did these things not because they benefited any particular group or individual, but because they made us all richer, because they gave us all opportunity, because they moved us forward together, as one Nation, as one people.

That's the lesson of our past. That's the right vision for our future. And that's why I'm running for President of the United States of America.

I'm running to make sure that by the end of this decade, more of our citizens hold college degrees than any other nation on Earth. I want to help our schools hire and reward the best teachers, especially in math and science. I want to give 2 million more Americans the chance to go to community colleges and learn the skills that local businesses are looking for right now. Because in the 21st century, a higher education can't be a luxury; it's an economic imperative that every American should be able to afford. And that's the choice in this election. That's why I'm running for President.

I'm running to make sure the next generation of high-tech manufacturing takes root in places like Richmond and Columbus and Cleveland and Pittsburgh. I want to stop rewarding businesses that ship jobs and profits overseas. I want us to reward companies that create jobs right here in the United States of America. That's the choice in this election.

I'm running so that we keep moving towards a future where we control our own energy. Our dependence on foreign oil is at its lowest point in 16 years. By the middle of the next decade, our cars will average nearly 55 miles per gallon. That will save you money. Thousands of Americans have jobs because the production of renewable energy in this country—solar, wind, biofuels—it's nearly doubled in just 3 years.

So now is not the time to cut these investments to pay for another $4 billion giveaway to the oil companies. Now is the time to end the subsidies for an industry that has rarely been more profitable. Let's double down on a clean energy future that's never been more promising for our economy and our security and for the safety of our planet. That's why I'm running, Virginia. That's the choice in this election.

For the first time in 9 years, there are no Americans fighting in Iraq. Usama bin Laden is no longer a threat to this country. Al Qaida is on the path to defeat. And by 2014, the war in Afghanistan will be over. America is safer and more respected because of the courage and selflessness of the United States Armed Forces, a lot of them from Virginia. A lot of folks right here in Virginia, putting on that uniform, serving on our behalf. And as long as I'm Com-

mander in Chief, this country will care for our veterans and serve our veterans as well as they've served us, because nobody who serves, nobody who fights for this country should have to fight for a job or a roof over their heads when they come back home.

My opponent has different ideas. My opponent has a different view. He said it was—and I quote—"tragic" to end the war in Iraq. He said he won't set a timeline for ending the war in Afghanistan.

Well, I have, and I intend to keep to that timeline. After a decade of war that's cost us thousands of lives and over a trillion dollars, the nation we need to build is right here, right here at home. So we're going to use half of what we're no longer spending on war to pay down the deficit, and we will use the other half to repair our roads and our bridges and our airports and our wireless networks. That's the choice in this election. That's why I'm running for President.

I am running to pay down our debt in a way that's balanced and responsible. We inherited a trillion-dollar deficit. The other side doesn't like to be reminded of this. But that's okay. I signed $2 trillion of spending cuts into law. And now I want to finish the job by streamlining Government and cutting more waste and reforming our Tax Code so that it's simpler and that it's fairer and that it asks the wealthiest Americans to pay a little bit more.

Now, my opponent has a different view. He won't tell us how he'd pay for his new, $5 trillion tax cut—$5 trillion—a tax cut that gives an average of $250,000 to every millionaire in the country. But even if he won't disclose the details of how he's going to pay for it, we know the bill for that tax cut will either be passed on to our children or it will be paid for by a whole lot of you, a whole lot of ordinary Americans.

And, Virginia, I refuse to let that happen again. I refuse to let that happen again. I refuse to pay for another millionaire's tax cut by eliminating medical research projects on things like cancer and Alzheimer's. I refuse to pay for another tax cut by kicking children off of the Head Start program or asking students to pay more for college or eliminating health insurance for millions of poor and elderly and disabled Americans on Medicaid. We're not going to do that.

As long as I'm President of the United States, I will never allow Medicare to be turned into a voucher that would end the program as we know it. We're not going to go back to the days when our citizens spent their golden years at the mercy of private insurance companies. We will reform Medicare, not by shifting the cost of care to seniors, but by reducing the spending that isn't making people healthier. That's the right way to do it. And that's what's at stake, Virginia. On issue after issue, we just can't afford to spend the next 4 years going backwards.

America doesn't need to refight the battles we just had over Wall Street reform and health care reform. And by the way, on health care reform, here's what I know: Allowing 2.5 million young people to stay on their parents' health insurance, that was the right thing to do. Cutting prescription drug costs for seniors, that was the right thing to do. We're not going back to the days when insurance companies had unchecked power to cancel your policy or deny you coverage or charge women differently than men. We're not going back to that.

We certainly don't need another political fight about ending a woman's right to choose or getting rid of Planned Parenthood or taking away access to affordable birth control. I want women to control their own health choices, just like I want my daughters to have the same opportunities as your son. We're not turning back the clock.

We're not returning to the days when you could be kicked out of the United States military just because of who you are and who you love. We're not going back to that. That would be wrong for our national security. It would be a betrayal of our values. It's not going to happen on my watch.

This should be the last election where multimillion-dollar donations speak louder than the voices of ordinary citizens. We need more checks on special interests and lobbyists, not fewer checks on them.

We're not going to eliminate the EPA. We're not going to roll back the bargaining rights of generations of workers. And it's time to stop denying citizenship to responsible young people just because they're the children of undocumented workers. This country is at its best when we harness the God-given talents of every individual, when we hear every voice, when we come together as one American family, striving for that same dream.

That's what we're fighting for: a bold America, a competitive America, a forward-looking America, where everybody has the chance to make of their life what they will. That's what made us the envy of the world. That's what makes us great. That's why I'm running again for President of the United States.

And, Virginia, that's why I need your help. This election will be even closer than the last. Too many of our friends and neighbors are still hurting because of this crisis. I've heard from too many people wondering why they haven't been able to get one of the jobs that have been created, why their home is still underwater, why their family hasn't yet been touched by the recovery.

The other side won't be offering these Americans any real answers to those questions. They won't be offering a better vision. They won't be offering new ideas. But what they will do is spend more money than we've ever seen before, all on negative ads—on TV and radio, in the mail, on the Internet, probably tweeting a few negative ads out there somewhere—ads that exploit people's frustration for my opponent's political gain. And over and over again, they will tell you that America is down and out, and they'll tell you who to blame.

And they'll ask if you're better off than you were before the worst crisis of our lifetime. We've seen the play before. We know what to expect. But you know what, the real question—the question that will actually make a difference in your life and in the lives of your children—is not just about how we're doing today, it's about how we'll be doing tomorrow.

Will we be better off if more Americans get a better education? Will we better off if we depend less on foreign oil and more on our own ingenuity? Will we be better off if we start doing some nation-building at home? Will we be better off if we bring down our deficits in a balanced, responsible way without gutting the very things that we need to grow? When we look back 4 years from now or 10 years from now or 20 years from now, won't we be better off if we have the courage to keep moving forward?

That's the question in this election. And that outcome is entirely up to you. We're going to have to contend with even more negative ads, with even more cynicism, more nastiness, sometimes just plain foolishness. It will be worse than we saw in the last campaign. We know because we've seen some of the foolishness over the last 3½ years.

But if there's one thing we learned in 2008, it's that nothing is more powerful than millions of voices calling for change. When enough of you knock on doors and enough of you pick up the phone, when enough of you are talking to your friends and your coworkers, when you decide that it's time for change to happen, guess what? Change happens. Change comes to America.

Virginia, that's the spirit we need again. If people ask you what's this campaign about, you tell them it's still about hope. You tell them it's still about change. You tell them it's still about ordinary people who believe in the face of great odds that we can make a difference in the life of this country. You tell them.

Because I still believe, Virginia. I still believe that we're not as divided as our politics suggest. I still believe we still have more in common than the pundits tell us, that we're not Democrats or Republicans first, but we are Americans first and foremost.

I still believe in you, and I'm asking you to keep believing in me. I told you in 2008 that I wasn't a perfect man, and I will never be a perfect President. But I promised you then that I would always tell you what I thought. I would always tell you where I stood. And I would wake up every single day fighting for you as hard as I know how.

And I have kept that promise. I have kept that promise. And I will keep it so long as I have the honor to be your President. So if you're willing to stick with me and fight with me and press on with me, if you're willing to work even harder in this election than in the last election, I guarantee you, we will move this country forward. We will finish what we started. We're still fired up. We're still ready to go. And we're going to remind the world once more why it is that the United States of America is the greatest nation on Earth.

Thank you. God bless you, and God bless the United States of America.

NOTE: The President spoke at 5:05 p.m. at Virginia Commonwealth University. In his remarks, he referred to former President William J. Clinton; and Republican Presidential candidate former Gov. W. Mitt Romney of Massachusetts. The transcript released by the Office of the Press Secretary also included the remarks of the First Lady.

Remarks at the University at Albany in Albany, New York
May 8, 2012

Hello, New York! Thank you. Thank you so much. Everybody, please have a seat. It is great to be back in Albany. It is wonderful to be with all of you here today.

And I want to thank Governor Cuomo not only for the outstanding introduction, but also for the extraordinary leadership that he's showing here in the great State of New York. Please give him a big round of applause. He is doing outstanding work.

I also want to thank Mayor Jennings, who's here. Give the mayor a big round of applause. Don't be shy. We've got Chancellor Zimpher—we appreciate very much. Dr. Kaloyeros—I want to make sure I say that right, folks mess up my name all the time—[*laughter*]—Kaloyeros for hosting us here today. We've got a couple Members of Congress here—Paul Tonko, and also, Representative Chris Gibson is here. And all of you are, and I'm happy about that. Yes.

So it is wonderful to be here at the University of Albany NanoCollege. This is one of the only colleges in the world dedicated to nanotechnology. And it's a incredible complex. But you're working on particles as small as an atom, and you're doing it in rooms that are 10,000 times cleaner than a hospital operating room, which is very impressive, since "clean" is not usually a word I associate with college students. [*Laughter*] Maybe things have changed since I was in school.

Now, the reason I came here today is because this school——

[At this point, an audience member sneezed.]

The President. ——bless you—[*laughter*]—and this community represents the future of our economy. Right now some of the most advanced manufacturing work in America is being done right here in upstate New York. Cutting-edge businesses from all over the world are deciding to build here and hire here. And you've got schools like this one that are training workers with the exact skills that those businesses are looking for.

Now, we know the true engine of job creation in this country is the private sector; it's not Washington. But there are steps we can take as a nation to make it easier for companies to grow and to hire, to create platforms of success for them, everything from giving more people the chance to get the right training and education to supporting new research projects into science and technology. In fact, there was a substantial investment made here; I was talking to Governor Cuomo about the investment his father made here to help get this center started.

There are things we can do to make sure that if you're willing to work hard and meet your responsibilities, you can find a job, own a home, maybe start a business, and most importantly, give your kids a chance to do even better than you did. And that's something we believe has to be available to everybody, no matter where you come from, no matter what you look like. We can make a difference. And at this make-or-break moment for America's

middle class, there's no excuse for inaction. There's no excuse for dragging our feet. None.

Now, over the last few years, there are certain steps that I've been able to take on my own to help spur the kind of innovation that we're seeing here and also to help the overall economy grow. So we announced a new policy several months back that will help families refinance their mortgages, save up to a—to thousands of dollars a year. We sped up loans and competitive grants for new projects all across the country so thousands of construction workers can get back on the job. We simplified the student loan process to help roughly 5.8 million students like the students here save money on repayments.

So these are some steps that the administration's been able to take on its own. But the truth is, the only way we can accelerate the job creation that takes place on a scale that is needed is bold action from Congress.

Because of the Recovery Act, because of all the work we've done, we've created over 4 million jobs over the last 2 years. We've created hundreds of thousands of jobs each month over the last several months. So we're making progress, but everybody knows we need to do more. And in order to do that, we're going to need some more action from Congress. Democrats and Republicans have to come together. And they've shown that they can do it. I mean, they did some important work. They passed tax cuts for workers, approved trade deals to open up new markets for American products. We reformed our patent system to make it easier for innovative ideas to come to market. Those are all good things. But the size of the challenges we face requires us to do more.

So, back last September, I sent Congress a jobs bill that included all sorts of policies that we knew would help grow our economy and put more Americans back to work. That wasn't just my opinion, that wasn't just the opinion of Democrats. It was the opinion of independent, nonpartisan experts, economists who do this for a living and analysts on Wall Street who evaluate what's going to really make the economy grow. And the one big piece that we were able to get done was make sure that we didn't see payroll tax go up and people get 40 bucks taken out of their paychecks each time.

But most of it didn't get done in Congress. Just about every time we put these policies up for a vote, the Republicans in Congress got together and they said no. They said no to putting hundreds of thousands of construction workers back on the job repairing our roads and our bridges and our schools and our transit systems. No to a new tax cut for businesses that hire new workers. No to putting more teachers back in our classrooms, more cops back on the beat, more firefighters back to work. And this is at a time when we know one of the biggest drags on our economy has been layoffs by State and local governments. That's true all across the country.

And it's worth noting, by the way—this is just a little aside—after there was a recession under Ronald Reagan, government employment went way up. It went up after the recessions under the first George Bush and the second George Bush. So each time there was a recession with a Republican President, compensated—we compensated by making sure that government didn't see a drastic reduction in employment.

The only time government employment has gone down during a recession has been under me. So I make that point just so you don't buy into this whole bloated government argument that you hear. And frankly, if Congress had said yes to helping States put teachers back to work and put the economy before our politics, then tens of thousands of more teachers in New York would have a job right now. That is a fact. And that would mean not only a lower unemployment rate, but also more customers for businesses.

Now, I know this is an election year. But it's not an excuse for inaction. Six months is plenty of time for Democrats and Republicans to get together and do the right thing, taking steps that will spur additional job creation right now. Just saying no to ideas that we know will help our economy isn't an option. There's too much at stake. We've all got to pull in the same direction.

So even if Republicans are still saying no to some of the bigger proposals we made in the jobs act, there are some additional ideas that could help people get to work right now and that they haven't said no to yet, so I'm hoping they say yes. And they're simple ideas. They're the kinds of things that, in the past, have been supported by Democrats and Republicans. These are traditionally ideas that have had bipartisan support. They won't have as big of an impact as rebuilding our infrastructure or helping States hire back teachers, but together, all of these ideas will do two things: They'll grow the economy faster; they'll create more jobs.

So today I'm announcing a handy, little to-do list—[*laughter*]—that we've put together for Congress. You can see it for yourselves at whitehouse.gov. It's about the size of a Post-it note, so every Member of Congress should have time to read it—[*laughter*]—and they can glance at it every so often. And you, hopefully, will just be checking off the list, just like when Michelle gives me a list, I check it off. [*Laughter*] Each of the ideas on this list will help accelerate our economy and put people back to work—not in November, not in next year, but right now.

All right, so I'm going to go through the list. First, Congress needs to help the millions of Americans who have worked hard, made their mortgage payments on time, but still have been unable to refinance their mortgages with these historically low rates. This would make a huge difference for the economy.

Families could save thousands of dollars, and that means they got more money in their pocket, which means they can either build their equity back up on their homes or they go out and use that money to do things like helping to—their kids finance a college education. So Congress should give those responsible homeowners a chance to refinance at a lower rate. We estimate they'd save at least $3,000 a year. So that's on our to-do list. It's not complicated.

Second, if Congress fails to act soon, clean energy companies will see their taxes go up and they could be forced to lay off employees. In fact, we're already hearing from folks who produce wind turbines and solar panels and a lot of this green energy that they're getting worried because there's uncertainty out there. Congress hasn't renewed some of the tax breaks that are so important to this industry. And since I know that the other side in Congress have promised they'll never raise taxes as long as they live, this is a good time to keep that promise when it comes to businesses that are putting Americans to work and helping break our dependence on foreign oil. So we should extend these tax credits. That's on the to-do list. That's number two.

Number three, Congress should help small-business owners by giving them a tax break for hiring more workers and paying them higher wages. We believe small businesses are the engine of economic growth in this country. We should not hold them to a situation where they may end up having to pay higher taxes just by hiring more workers. We should make it easier for them to succeed. So that's on our to-do list. That's number three.

Number four, Congress should help our veterans returning from Iraq and Afghanistan find a good job once they come home. Our men and women in uniform have served this country with such honor and distinction. A lot of them come from upstate New York. Now it's our turn to serve them. So we should create a veterans job corps that helps them find work as cops and firefighters, employees at our national parks. That's on our to-do list.

And then the last item, the fifth item, which bears especially on what's going on here, the last item on our congressional to-do list is something that will help a lot of you in particular. You know better than anybody that technology has advanced by leaps and bounds over the last few decades. And that's a great thing. Businesses are more productive; consumers are getting better products for less. But technology has also made a lot of jobs obsolete. Factories where people once thought they'd retire suddenly left town. Jobs that provided a decent living got shipped overseas. And the result's been a lot of pain for a lot of communities and a lot of families.

There is a silver lining to all this though. After years of undercutting the competition, now it's getting more expensive to do business in places like China. Wages are going up. Shipping costs are going up. And meanwhile, American workers are getting more and more efficient. Companies located here are becoming more and more competitive. So for a lot of businesses, it's now starting to make sense to bring jobs back home.

And here in the tri-city area, you've got companies like IBM and GlobalFoundries that could have decided to pack up and move elsewhere, but they chose to stay in upstate New York because it made more sense to build here and to hire here. You had more to offer—got some of the best workers in the world, you got an outstanding university.

Now I want what's happening in Albany to happen all across the country, places like Cleveland and Pittsburgh and Raleigh. I want to create more opportunities for hard-working Americans to start making things again and selling them all over the world stamped with those proud words: Made in America. That's the goal.

So the good news is, we're already starting to see it happen. American manufacturers are creating jobs for the first time since the late 1990s. And that's good for you, but it's also good for the businesses that supply the materials you use. It's good for the construction workers who build the facilities you work in. It's good for communities, where people are buying more houses and spending more money at restaurants and stores. Everybody benefits when manufacturing is going strong.

So you've heard about outsourcing. Today, more and more companies are insourcing. One recent study has found that half of America's largest companies are thinking of moving their manufacturing operations from China back to the United States of America. That's good news. Because even when we can't make things cheaper than other countries because of their wage rates, we can always make them better. That's who we are. That's what America is all about.

So this brings me back to our to-do list. What we need to do now is to make it easier for more companies to do the right thing, and one place to start is our Tax Code. At the moment, companies get tax breaks for moving factories, jobs, and profits overseas. They can actually end up saving on their tax bill when they make the move. Meanwhile, companies that choose to stay here are getting hit with one of the highest tax rates in the world. That doesn't make sense.

And politicians from both parties have been talking about changing it for years, so I've put forward my own plan to make it right in the long term. But in the short term, before we completely rework the Tax Code, before we've done a full-blown tax reform, at the very least what we can do right away is stop rewarding companies who ship jobs overseas and use that money to cover moving expenses for companies that are moving jobs back here to America. So we're putting that on Congress's to-do list. This should—this is something simple to do. We shouldn't wait. We should get it done right now.

So that's the fifth item. That's all on our to-do list. Not trying to overload Congress here. [*Laughter*]

So, over the next few weeks, I'm going to be taking about this to-do list when I'm on the road. I'm going to be talking about all the things that Congress can do right now to boost our economy and accelerate even more job growth. Of course, it's not enough just to give them the list; we've also got to get them to start crossing things off the list. And that's where all of you come in.

I'm going to need you to pick up the phone, write an e-mail, tweet, remind your Member of Congress we can't afford to wait until November to get things done. Tell them now is the time to help more Americans save money on their mortgages, time for us to invest more in clean energy and small businesses, it's time for us to help more veterans find work, and it's time to make it easier for companies to bring jobs back to America. It's the right thing to do.

Now, I'm cheating a little bit. I said that was my to-do list. There actually is one other thing they've got to do. Before they do anything else, Congress needs to keep student loan rates

from doubling for students who are here and all across the country. That has to happen by January 1 [July 1]° or rates on Stafford loans double. These young people are nodding their heads. They don't like that. They've heard about this. [*Laughter*]

And we need to pass a transportation bill that guarantees almost a million construction workers can stay on the job. So—[*applause*].

The good news is both parties say they want to make this happen. We've done this before. So Congress just needs to work out the details. Don't let politics get in the way. Get this done before July 1. Those bills should be passed right now.

So I'm cheating a little bit. There are actually seven items on the to-do list. [*Laughter*] But two of them are old business, and folks have already said they want to get them done.

Albany, we've got a long way to go if we're going to make sure everybody who wants a job can find one and every family can feel that sense of security that was the essence of America's middle class experience. But we can't just go back to the way things used to be. We've got to move forward to an economy where everybody gets a fair shot, everybody is doing their fair share, everybody plays by the same set of rules.

And that's what you guys are doing here in Albany. You're investing in your future. You're not going backwards, you're going forward. With your help, I know we can get there, because here in America, we don't give up. We keep moving. We look out for one another. We pull each other up. That's who we are. And if we work together with common purpose, I've got no doubt we can keep moving this country forward and remind the world just why it is the United States of America is the greatest nation on Earth.

Thank you so much, everybody. God bless you. God bless America.

NOTE: The President spoke at 1:24 p.m. at the College of Nanoscale Science and Engineering. In his remarks, he referred to Gov. An-

---

° White House correction.

drew M. Cuomo of New York, and his father, former Gov. Mario M. Cuomo; Mayor Gerald D. Jennings of Albany, NY; Nancy L. Zimpher, chancellor, State University of New York; and

Alain E. Kaloyeros, senior vice president and chief executive officer, College of Nanoscale Science and Engineering, University at Albany, State University of New York.

Remarks at the Asian Pacific American Institute for Congressional Studies Annual Gala
May 8, 2012

The President. Thank you. Everybody, please, please, have a seat. Have a seat. You're making me blush. [*Laughter*] *Mahalo!*

Audience members. Mahalo!

The President. Thank you so much. Thank you, Norm, for that kind introduction. More importantly, thank you for your lifetime of distinguished service to our country. I want to thank all the Members of Congress who are with us, including two people who are fighting hard every day on behalf of every member of this community: Judy Chu and Mike Honda. Give them a big round of applause.

Now, I am thrilled to be here tonight because all of you hold a special place in my heart. When I think about Asian Americans and Pacific Islanders, I think about my family: my sister Maya; my brother-in-law Konrad, who's in the house somewhere—I don't know where Konrad is; my nieces Suhaila and Savita. I think about all the folks I grew up with in Honolulu, as part of the—[*applause*].

Audience member. Aloha! [*Laughter*]

The President. ——as part of the Hawaiian *ohana.* I think about the years I spent in Indonesia. So for me, coming here feels a little bit like home. This is a community that helped to make me who I am today. It's a community that helped make America the country that it is today.

So your heritage spans the world. But what unites everyone is that in all of your families you have stories of perseverance that are uniquely American. Some of you—those from Hawaii or the Pacific Islands—live where your family has lived for generations and your story is in part, about keeping alive treasured native traditions. But for others, your story starts with ancestors who at some point left behind every-

thing they knew to seek the promise of a new land. Maybe the story traces back a century and a half, to the laborers who risked their lives to connect our coasts by rail. Maybe it begins with one of the hundreds of thousands of immigrants who, decades ago, made the tough journey to Angel Island.

Maybe the story starts with your parents. Or maybe it starts with you. But here's the thing. No matter when it began, no matter where it began, your stories are about someone who came here looking for new opportunities not merely for themselves, but for their children and for their children's children and for all generations to come.

Few of them had money. A lot of them didn't have belongings. But what they did have was an unshakeable belief that this country, of all countries, is a place where anybody can make it if they try.

Now, many of them faced hardship, many of them faced ridicule, many of them faced racism. Many were treated as second-class citizens, as people who didn't belong. But they didn't give up. They didn't make excuses. They kept forging ahead. They kept building up America. They kept fighting for America, like Danny Inouye, who's here. They were trailblazers. Danny, who was my Senator most of my life. [*Laughter*] Love that man.

But they were trailblazers like Dalip Singh Saund, a young man from India who, in 1920, came to study agriculture, stayed to become a farmer, and took on the cause of citizenship for all people of South Asian descent. And once Dalip earned his own citizenship, he stepped up to serve the country he loved, and became the first Asian American elected to the Congress.

They were pioneers like my former Congresswoman Patsy Mink, who was not only the first Asian American woman elected to Congress, but the author of title IX, which has changed the playing field for all of our girls.

And then there's the story of a young Japanese American boy, just 10 when his family was forced from their home and taken hundreds of miles away to an internment camp. For 3 years, they lived in that camp, but when that boy got home, he didn't turn his back on America, he devoted his life to America. In his words, he pledged "to speak out for the underrepresented and to pick up on those issues that weren't being carried by others." And as the first Asian American to ever serve in a President's Cabinet, Norm Mineta made good on that pledge.

So think about how proud all those previous generations would be to see this room, to see how far this community has come. Asian Americans, Pacific Islanders are now the inventors and entrepreneurs keeping our country on the cutting edge, the business men and women at the helm of some of our most successful industries, leaders in every aspect of American life: in science and medicine, in education, in sports, in the arts, in our Armed Forces, in our Government, and in our courts. In fact, over the past 3 years, we have more than doubled the number of Asian Americans on the Federal bench.

Just yesterday Jacqueline Nguyen became the first Asian American woman to get confirmed as a Federal appellate judge. Where's Jacqueline? She's here tonight. There she is. You didn't bring your robe though. [*Laughter*] That's pretty cool. [*Laughter*] And we're so proud to have her along with another appellate judge I appointed, Denny Chin. He's here. Where's Denny? There he is, back there. So we thank them for their service.

Whether your heritage stems from South Asia or East Asia, from my native Hawaii or the Pacific Islands, whether you're first generation——

Audience member. Woo-hoo!

The President. These Hawaiians here. [*Laughter*] What's up with that?

Audience members. Woo-hoo! [*Laughter*] Aloha!

The President. Whether you are first generation or the fifth, you're helping to build a better America.

And I know it can be tempting, given the success that's on display here tonight, for people to buy into the myth of the "model minority" and glance over the challenges that this community still faces. But we have to remember there's still educational disparities like higher dropout rates in certain groups, lower college enrollment rates in others. There's still economic disparities like higher rates of poverty and obstacles to employment. There are health disparities like higher rates of diabetes and cancer and hepatitis B. Those who are new to America, many still face language barriers. Others, like Vincent Chin, who we lost three decades ago, have been victims of horrible hate crimes, driven by the kinds of ignorance and prejudice that are an affront to everything America stands for.

So those are real problems, and we can't ignore them. And if we're going to do a better job addressing them, then we first have to stop grouping everybody just in one big category. Dozens of different communities fall under the umbrella of the Asian Americans and Pacific Islanders, and we have to respect that the experiences of immigrant groups are distinct and different. And your concerns run the gamut.

That's something that Washington needs to understand better. And that's why I reestablished the White House Initiative on Asian Americans and Pacific Islanders, so that we could better identify specific issues within specific communities. Many of those Commissioners are here. I want to thank them for the great job that they're doing.

And so we're making a difference on that front and on many other fronts. When we stepped up support for America's small businesses, we stepped up support for this community, providing over $7 billion in loans for small businesses owned by Asian Americans and Pacific Islanders. When we passed health care reform, we put in place new mechanisms to get better data about health disparities. Because of that law, nearly 3 million Asian Americans and Pacific Islanders are going to receive expanded and preventive coverage through private insurance, and nearly 1 million are receiving free preventive services through Medicare.

So some of the things that matter to this community are things that matter to every community, like making sure that a woman earns an equal day's pay for an equal day's work, or ending "don't ask, don't tell" so that nobody has to hide who they love to serve the country they love, or enacting education reform so that every child has access to good schools and higher education, or caring for our veterans because it's our duty to serve them as well as they have served us.

That's what this country is about. That's what we've always been about. We've gone through some tough years because of this extraordinary recession and we've still got a long way to go. But we will get there. We will arrive at that destination where every child born in America, regardless of race, creed, color, is going to have a chance. We're going to do that together, because in this country, we look out for each other. We fight for each other. If somebody is suffering through injustice or inequality, we take up their cause as if it was our own. That's the story of America. And that's certainly the story of this community.

In the midst of World War II, when the son of Japanese immigrants, Gordon Hirabayashi, ignored the curfews and refused transfer to an internment camp, when he was jailed for his defiance, when he later appealed his convic-

tion and took his case all the way to the Supreme Court, he understood that he was fighting for something larger than himself. And he once said: "I never look at my case just as a Japanese American case. It's an American case, with principles that affect the fundamental human rights of all Americans." And while Gordon is no longer with us, later this year, I'll award him the Presidential Medal of Freedom, the highest civilian award America has to offer. Because he reminds us that each of us is only who we are today because somebody, somewhere, felt a sense of responsibility, not just to themselves, but to their family and their communities and to this country that we all love.

So tonight we honor the trailblazers who came before. But we also celebrate the leaders yet to come, all the young people who are here tonight. Together, it's our turn to be responsible for the future. It's our turn to make sure the next generation has more opportunities than we did. It's our turn to make sure that no matter who you are, no matter where you came from, no matter what you look like, America forever remains the place where you can make it if you try.

Thank you, everybody. God bless you. God bless the United States of America.

NOTE: The President spoke at 5:46 p.m. at the Ritz-Carlton hotel. In his remarks, he referred to former Secretary of Transportation Norman Y. Mineta. He also referred to his sister Maya Soetoro-Ng, her husband Konrad Ng, and their daughters Suhaila and Savita.

Statement on the Retirement of Senator Richard G. Lugar
May 8, 2012

As a friend and former colleague, I want to express my deep appreciation for Dick Lugar's distinguished service in the United States Senate. While Dick and I didn't always agree on everything, I found during my time in the Senate that he was often willing to reach across the aisle and get things done. My administration's efforts to secure the world's most dangerous weapons has been based on the work that Sena-

tor Lugar began, as well as the bipartisan cooperation we forged during my first overseas trip as Senator to Russia, Ukraine, and Azerbaijan. Senator Lugar comes from a tradition of strong, bipartisan leadership on national security that helped us prevail in the cold war and sustain American leadership ever since. He has served his constituents and his country well, and I wish him all the best in his future endeavors.

Message to the Congress on Continuation of the National Emergency With Respect to the Actions of the Government of Syria
May 9, 2012

To the Congress of the United States:

Section 202(d) of the National Emergencies Act, 50 U.S.C. 1622(d), provides for the automatic termination of a national emergency, unless, within 90 days prior to the anniversary date of its declaration, the President publishes in the *Federal Register* and transmits to the Congress a notice stating that the emergency is to continue in effect beyond the anniversary date. In accordance with this provision, I have sent to the *Federal Register* for publication the enclosed notice stating that the national emergency with respect to the actions of the Government of Syria declared in Executive Order 13338 of May 11, 2004, as modified in scope and relied upon for additional steps taken in Executive Order 13399 of April 25, 2006, Executive Order 13460 of February 13, 2008, Executive Order 13572 of April 29, 2011, Executive Order 13573 of May 18, 2011, Executive Order 13582 of August 17, 2011, Executive Order 13606 of April 22, 2012, and Executive Order 13608 of May 1, 2012, is to continue in effect beyond May 11, 2012.

While the Syrian regime has reduced the number of foreign fighters bound for Iraq, the regime's own brutality and repression of its citizens who have been calling for freedom and a representative government endangers not only the Syrian people themselves, but could yield greater instability throughout the region. The Syrian regime's actions and policies, including obstructing the Lebanese government's ability to function effectively, pursuing chemical and biological weapons, and supporting terrorist organizations, continue to pose an unusual and extraordinary threat to the national security, foreign policy, and economy of the United States. For these reasons, I have determined that it is necessary to continue in effect the national emergency declared with respect to this threat and to maintain in force the sanctions to address this national emergency.

In addition, the United States condemns the Asad regime's use of brutal violence and human rights abuses and calls on the Asad regime to step aside and immediately begin a transition in Syria to a political process that will forge a credible path to a future of greater freedom, democracy, opportunity, and justice. The United States will consider changes in the composition, policies, and actions of the Government of Syria in determining whether to continue or terminate this national emergency in the future.

BARACK OBAMA

The White House,
May 9, 2012.

NOTE: The notice is listed in Appendix D at the end of this volume.

Remarks at PBS's "Burt Bacharach and Hal David: The Library of Congress Gershwin Prize for Popular Song In Performance at the White House"
May 9, 2012

Good evening, everybody. Well, thank you all for joining us tonight to honor a legendary songwriting duo: Burt Bacharach and Hal David.

I want to start by thanking the outstanding artists who are here to pay tribute to Burt and Hal. They have just been extraordinary.

I'd also like to thank Dr. James Billington of the Library of Congress and the outstanding team of producers for their hand in making tonight's wonderful evening possible.

And finally, I want to say a word about someone who is missing tonight. Even though Hal cannot be here with us, this celebration is for him. And we're happy that his lovely wife Eunice David is here to receive his award—this award on his behalf.

The Gershwin Prize is named for one of the great American songwriting duos of all time. And it's fitting that tonight's award is being presented to another.

Burt and Hal first met at Famous Music in the Brill Building in New York. Burt had come a long way from his days of hoping to be a football player—[*laughter*]—as well as a musical career. And Hal had taken his wordsmithing from the pages of New York newspapers to the frontlines of big band. Soon, the football player and the journalist started writing songs, and they struck gold in 1957 with Marty Robbins singing "The Story of My Life."

What began as an occasional collaboration in the late fifties quickly became a partnership that produced dozens of Top 40 hits. There was even a span of 10 years during the 1960s and seventies when a week rarely went by without one of their songs being on the Billboard charts.

Burt and Hal racked up Grammys and Oscars and have been honored by numerous lifetime achievement awards. And today, more than 55 years after their first songs hit the airwaves, these guys have still got it. Alicia Keys and John Legend are recording their songs.

Burt is appearing on "American Idol" and "Dancing with the Stars." [*Laughter*] And in 2004, Burt and Hal worked with Twista, Kanye West, and Jamie Foxx to get back to number one with a slow jam medley. So these guys can work with anybody. [*Laughter*]

Like the Gershwin brothers, Burt and Hal have never been limited to one genre or even one generation. Burt once said that all he looks for in writing a good melody is "to write something that I like." Hal agreed, saying, "We just tried to write with as much integrity as we could." Above all, they stayed true to themselves. And with an unmistakable authenticity, they captured the emotions of our daily lives: the good times, the bad times, and everything in between. And they've lived their lives on their own terms, and they've taught Americans of all ages to embrace their individual stories, even as we move forward together.

So tonight, on behalf of a grateful nation, it is my privilege to present the Nation's highest prize for popular music to two kings of songwriting, Burt Bacharach and Hal David.

NOTE: The President spoke at 8:45 p.m. in the East Room at the White House. In his remarks, he referred to musician Carl T. "Twista" Mitchell.

Remarks at an Obama Victory Fund 2012 Fundraiser in Seattle, Washington
May 10, 2012

The President. All right! Give it up for Libby!

Libby Blume. Hello. Thank you very much for coming. We're all very honored. I'm Libby. I'm the youngest of the Blumes. And I'm very, very proud to present the President of the United States of America.

The President. Yay! Yay! Nice job!

Thank you. Libby knows the key to good public speaking: Be brief. [*Laughter*] That always makes people happy.

I just want to thank the entire Blume family—especially Libby—but in addition to Bruce and Ann, their other kids, Max, Rebecca, Jacob, and Scooter, for opening up this extraordi-

nary home to us and for their friendship. I'm so grateful to you guys.

Thanks for whoever is in charge of the weather. [*Laughter*] I've been told this is typical Seattle weather. [*Laughter*] But I've been here before so—[*laughter*].

What I'm going to do is actually be pretty brief at the top because what I'd really enjoy is just answering questions and getting comments and kind of hearing what you guys are thinking about.

We've been through an extraordinary period in American history: worst financial crisis, worst economic crisis since the Great Depression. When you think about the Blume family growing up, what a lot of this younger generation has seen is hardship and recession and people being laid off of work. And yet the good news is that America is full of incredibly resilient, wonderful, decent people who have been willing to buckle down and work through these difficult times, and as a consequence, the country, I think, is on a path of great strength and great promise.

We've seen more than 4 million jobs created over the last 2 years, more than 800,000 just in the last 4 months alone; the greatest increase in manufacturing employment since the 1990s, a lot of that having to do with an auto industry that has surged back after a period of time when a lot of us thought that they might go under. Here in this region, the last time I was in Seattle—I think it was the last time—we had a chance to visit Boeing, which is as good of a symbol of American ingenuity and American promise, and I teased the CEO there that I deserve a gold watch because we've been selling a lot of planes all around the world. [*Laughter*]

And so slowly, in fits and starts, the economy is getting stronger, and businesses are starting to invest again. And in fact, you're starting to see companies that had moved to places like China recognizing: Why would we abandon the largest market in the world? Wages are going up in China and workers are getting more productive here; let's start bringing companies and businesses back.

We've still got headwinds. Europe is still in a difficult state, partly because they didn't take some of the decisive steps that we took early on in this recession. Gas prices are still pinching a lot of folks. The housing market is still very weak all across the country. But the good news is that we have weathered the storm and are in a position now to make sure that the 21st century is the American century just like the 20th century was.

But in order to do that, we've got to make good choices. And when I ran in 2008, I did not run just to get the country back to where it was before the crisis, because there had been problems that had been building for decades. And so the question was, were we finally going to take on some of these core challenges that

had been holding us back for far too long? And that's the reason why, even as we were trying to manage the auto bailout, even as we were trying to deal with the banks and the fact that credit was locked up, even as we were trying to make sure that we could immediately put people back to work, we were also looking at what are the long-term things that are going to make a big difference in the life of this country?

That's why we took on health care. And I am very proud of the fact that you got 2.5 million young people who have health insurance because they can stay on their parents' plans right now that didn't have it before and 30 million who stand to get it over the next couple of years.

That's the reason why we took on energy. And not only have we increased traditional energy in this country—oil and gas—but we're looking at the energies sources of the future and have doubled clean energy investment and raised fuel efficiency standards, doubling fuel efficiency standards on cars, which will not only end up saving about $8,000 for the average consumer over the life of a car, but is going to take huge amounts of carbon out of the atmosphere and is part of what's contributing to some of the lowest levels of oil imports that we've seen in years, which obviously has national security implications.

It's the reason why we took on education. And in addition to investing in reform at the K-through-12 level, we're also making sure that every young person has access to a college education and rechanneled money that was going to banks in the student loan program, tens of billions of dollars that are now going directly to students in the form of Pell grants. And now we've got a little more work to do to make sure that interest on their student loans don't double on July 1.

That's why we made investments during the Recovery Act to rebuild our roads and our bridges and our ports, but also to start looking at things like high-speed rail and new broadband lines into rural areas that didn't have them before. Because the fact is that, historically, America grows not just because a few folks are doing well, but because we create a platform where everybody can succeed. Anybody who's working hard, everybody who's willing to put in the time and the effort and the energy, anybody who's got a new idea, no matter what they look like, no matter where they come from, they can succeed. And through their success, we all succeed.

And we're huge admirers of individual initiative, and we insist on individual responsibility, but we also recognize, this country succeeds together, not apart. And that is going to be probably the biggest theme in this election, because we've got another party on the other side that just has a fundamentally different view about how to make sure that America succeeds. I think they're patriotic folks. I think they care about this country. But I also think that they have a very narrow vision that says, if I'm doing well, then it's up to everybody else to figure their own way.

And that's certainly not the reason I'm here. I'm here because my grandfather, after coming back from World War II, was able to study on the GI bill. I'm here because my mother, a single mom, was able to get scholarships and grants to help her make her way through school. Michelle and I are where we are today because, although we came from very modest backgrounds, we got some of the best education in the world.

When I hear people talk about the free enterprise system and entrepreneurship, I try to remind them, you know, all of us made that investment in DARPA that helped to get the Internet started; so there's no Facebook, there's no Microsoft, there's no Google if we hadn't made this common investment in our future.

And that's what we're going to be debating. There are going to be a lot of ups and downs and a lot of other issues, but the fundamental issue is going to be, do we believe that we grow together, or do we believe that "you're on your own" is a better model for how we advance not just our interests, but the future of our children?

Now, we've still got a lot of work to do. And the reason I'm running is because there's a lot of unfinished business. Still too many people out of work, and there's some things we could be doing right now to put construction workers back to work rebuilding America. There are things we could be doing right now to invest in science and technology to make sure we maintain a cutting edge.

We haven't done as much on energy and climate change as we need to do. And so continuing to push for the kinds of work that a company like McKinstry is doing, making sure that we have energy-efficient buildings and companies and universities and hospitals and schools all across the country. We could reduce our consumption of energy by about 20 percent just by making these simple investments, and we haven't done that yet. We've made progress, but we've got more work to do.

We've still got to reform an immigration system that is broken and make sure that young people who are raised in this country with our kids, that they're treated as the Americans that they are and they're given an opportunity to serve and make of themselves what they will, because that's also part of our tradition.

We're a great country because what binds us together isn't just what we look like or our last names, but we share a creed. And if you believe in America, then you can be part of it.

So we're going to have a whole lot of work to do over the next 5 years, and I'm not going to be able to get there on my own. I practice what I preach. In the same way that I don't think a society is successful on its own, well, my campaign is not successful on its own. Back in 2008, we didn't succeed because of me, we succeeded because of you, because all of you made a common commitment to a common vision of what America should be.

And I'm hoping that you're willing to continue with me on this always fascinating journey. [*Laughter*] Thank you.

NOTE: The President spoke at 1 p.m. at the residence of Bruce M. and Ann S. Blume. In his remarks, he referred to W. James McNerney, Jr., president and chief executive officer, Boeing Co.

Remarks at an Obama Victory 2012 Fundraiser in Seattle
May 10, 2012

The President. Thank you very much. The—[*applause*]—it's good to be back in Seattle.

A few people I want to acknowledge. First of all, please give a big round of applause to Sue for that unbelievable story, the great introduction, her incredible courage. She is just a—she's a—just a wonderful person. And I was saying backstage as I was listening, she's the kind of story that you don't read about in the papers. That's a story I'd like to read about: somebody overcoming so many challenges, doing the right thing. And I could not be prouder to have her introduce me.

A couple of other folks that are here today that I want to acknowledge: your outstanding Governor, Chris Gregoire; your outstanding Lieutenant Governor, Brad Owen is here; one of the best United States Senators in the country, Patty Murray's in the house; former U.S. Representative and soon-to-be Governor, Jay Inslee is here.

I want to thank King County Executive Dow Constantine; my—a terrific friend, former King County executive and somebody who did great work for us at HUD in Washington, Ron Sims; State party chair Dwight Pelz; and of course, somebody who I just love and I'm just such a huge fan of because he's a great person in addition to being a great musician, Dave Matthews.

Audience member. I love you!

The President. [*Laughter*] I love you too. So, Seattle, I'm here not just because I need your help—although I do; you'll hear more about that. I'm here because your country needs your help.

Now, there was a reason why so many of you worked your hearts out in 2008. And it wasn't because you thought it would be easy. You did support a candidate named Barack Hussein Obama. The odds are rarely in your favor in that situation. [*Laughter*] You didn't need a poll to tell you that might not be a sure thing.

You did not join the campaign because of me. You came together—we came together—because of a shared vision. We came together

to reclaim that basic bargain that built the largest middle class and the most prosperous nation on Earth.

We came together because we believed that in America, your success shouldn't be determined by the circumstances of your birth. If you're willing to work hard, you should be able to find a good job. If you're meeting your responsibilities, you should be able to own a home, maybe start a business. You should be able to give your kids the chance to do even better than you, no matter who you are, no matter where you come from, no matter what you look like, no matter what your last name, no matter who you love.

And so we came together. This wasn't just about me. This was you guys making a commitment to each other to try to bring about change because our country had strayed from these basic values. We'd seen a record surplus that was squandered on tax cuts for people who didn't need them and weren't even asking for them. Two wars were being waged on a credit card. Wall Street speculators reaped huge profits by making bets with other people's money. Manufacturing was leaving our shores. A shrinking number of Americans did fantastically well, but a lot more people struggled with falling incomes and rising costs and the slowest job growth in a century.

So it was a house of cards, and it collapsed in the most destructive, worst crisis that we've seen since the Great Depression. And sometimes people forget the magnitude of it, you know? And you saw some of that, I think, in the video that was shown. Sometimes I forget. In the last 6 months of 2008, while we were campaigning, nearly 3 million of our neighbors lost their jobs; 800,000 lost their jobs in the month that I took office. And it was tough. But the American people proved they were tougher. So we didn't quit. We kept going. Together, we fought back.

When my opponent said we should just let Detroit go bankrupt, we made a bet on American workers, on the ingenuity of American companies, and today our auto industry is back on top of the world.

We saw manufacturers start to invest in America again, consistently adding jobs for the first time since the 1990s. Businesses got back to basics, created over 4 million jobs in the last 26 months, more than 1 million of those in the last 6 months alone.

So we're making progress. Are we satisfied? Of course not. Too many of our friends, too many of our family are still out there looking for work. Too many homes are still underwater. Too many States are still laying off teachers and first-responders. A crisis this deep didn't happen overnight, and we understand it won't be solved overnight. We've got more work to do. We know that.

But here's what else we know: that the last thing we can afford is a return to the policies that got us here in the first place. Not now. Not with so much at stake. We've come too far to abandon the changes that we fought for these past few years. We've got to move forward, to the future that we imagined in 2008, where everybody gets a fair shot and everybody is doing their fair share and everybody plays by the same rules. That's the choice in this election. And, Seattle, that's why I'm running for a second term as President of the United States of America.

Now, my opponent in this election, Governor Romney, he's a patriotic American. He's raised a wonderful family. He should be proud of the great personal success he's had as the CEO of a large financial firm. But I think he's drawn the wrong lessons from those experiences. He actually believes that if CEOs and the wealthiest investors like him get rich, that the rest of us automatically do too. [*Laughter*]

When a woman in Iowa shared the story of her financial struggles, he gave an answer right out of an economics textbook. He said, "Our productivity equals our income," as if the only reason people can't pay their bills is because they're not productive enough.

Well, that's not what's going on. Most of us who have spent some time talking to people understand that the problem isn't that the American people aren't working hard enough, aren't productive enough; you've been working harder than ever. The challenge we face right now—the challenge we've faced for over a decade—is that harder work isn't leading to higher incomes. Bigger profits haven't led to better jobs.

What Governor Romney does not seem to get is that a healthy economy doesn't just mean maximizing your own profits through massive layoffs or busting unions. You don't make America stronger by shipping jobs or profits overseas. When you propose cutting your own taxes while raising them on 18 million families, that's not a recipe for economic growth.

And by the way, there's nothing new of these—about these ideas. I—you know, I'm just starting to pay a little more attention to this campaign here, and—[*laughter*]—I keep on waiting for them to offer up something new. But it's just the same old stuff. [*Laughter*] It's the same agenda that they have been pushing for years. It's the same agenda that they implemented when they were last in charge of the White House, although, as Bill Clinton pointed out a few weeks ago, this time their agenda is on steroids. [*Laughter*] This time they want even bigger tax cuts for the wealthiest Americans. This time they want even deeper cuts to things like education and Medicare and research and technology. This time they want to give banks and insurance companies even more power to do as they please.

Now, somehow they think that these same bad ideas will lead to different results than they did the last time, or they're hoping you won't remember what happened the last time when we tried their bad ideas. [*Laughter*]

Well, I'm here to say, Seattle, that we were there. We remember. We're not going back there. We're moving this country forward. We're moving forward. We're moving forward.

Look, we don't expect government to solve all our problems, and it shouldn't try to solve all our problems. I learned from my mom that no education policy can take the place of a parent's love and attention and occasionally getting in your face. [*Laughter*] As a young man, I worked with a group of Catholic churches who taught me that no poverty program can make as much of a difference as the kindness and commitment of a caring soul. Not—[*applause*].

And, Democrats, we have to remember some things. Not every regulation is smart. Not every tax dollar is spent wisely. Not every person can be helped who refuses to help themselves. We believe in individual responsibility. But that's not an excuse to tell the vast majority of responsible, hard-working Americans—folks like Sue, who've done all the right things— "you're on your own." That if you're—have the misfortune, like most people do, of having parents who may not be able to lend you all the money you need for college, that you may not be able to go to college. That even if you pay your premiums every month, you're out of luck if an insurance company decides to drop your coverage when you need it most.

That's not who we are. That's not what built this country. That's not reflective of what's best in us. We built this country together. We built railroads and highways. We built the Hoover Dam and the Golden Gate Bridge. We built those things together. We sent my grandfather's generation to college on the GI bill, together. We did these things not because they benefited any particular individual, any particular group; we did these things because we were building a platform for everybody to be able to succeed. We were creating the conditions for everybody to be able to succeed. These things made us all richer. They gave us all opportunity. They moved us all together, all forward, as one Nation and as one people.

And that's the true lesson of our past. We love the free market. We believe in rewarding entrepreneurship and risk. But when I hear my opponent and some of these folks talk as if somehow nobody had anything to do with the success of these businesses and our entrepreneurs, I have to remind them that we—we the people—invested in creating the Internet that allowed Microsoft and Google and Facebook to thrive. There's not a business in this country that's not benefiting from roads and bridges and airports, the investments we make together. Every time we've got a kid who's getting a great education in a public school and able to go to get an outstanding education at a public

university, we're contributing to the possibilities of the free market succeeding. And that's the right vision for our future. That's the reason I'm running for President, because I believe in that vision. I believe in that vision.

I'm running to make sure that by the end of this decade, more of our citizens hold college degrees than any other nation on Earth. I want that to happen here in America. I want to help our schools hire and reward the best teachers, especially in math and science. I want to give 2 million more Americans the chance to go to community colleges and learn the skills that local businesses are looking for right now, because that's what we need in the 21st century. Higher education can't be a luxury. Education is a—higher education is an imperative that every American should be able to afford, not just for young people, but for midcareer folks who have to retrain, have to upgrade their skills. That's the choice in this election. That's why I'm running for President.

I'm running to make sure that the next generation of high-tech manufacturing takes root in places like Seattle and Cleveland and Pittsburgh and Charlotte. I want to stop rewarding businesses that ship jobs and profits overseas. I want to reward companies that are creating jobs here in the United States of America. That's the choice in this election.

I'm running so that we can——

Audience member. [*Inaudible*]

The President. I am running so that we can keep moving forward to a future where we control our own energy. Our dependence on foreign oil is at the lowest point it's been in 16 years. Because of the actions we took, by the middle of the next decade our cars will average nearly 55 miles per gallon. Thousands of Americans have jobs because the production of renewable energy in this country has nearly doubled in just 3 years.

So now's not the time to cut these investments to pay for $4 billion a year in giveaways to the oil companies. Now's not—now's the time to end subsidies for an industry that's just doing fine on its own. Let's double down on clean energy that's never been more promising for our economy and for our security and for the safety of our planet. That's why I'm running, Seattle, and that's the choice in this election.

For the first time in 9 years, there are no Americans fighting in Iraq. Usama bin Laden is no longer a threat to this country. Al Qaida is on the path to defeat. And by 2014, the war in Afghanistan will be over.

America is safer and it's more respected because of the courage and selflessness of our diplomats and our intelligence officers, but most of all, because of the United States Armed Forces.

And as long as I'm Commander in Chief, this country will care for our veterans, and we will serve our veterans as well as they've served us, because no one who fights for this country should have to fight for a job or a roof over their heads when they come home.

My opponent has a different view. He said it was "tragic" to end the war in Iraq. He says he won't set a timeline for ending the war in Afghanistan. I have set a timeline, and I intend to keep it. After a decade of war that's cost us thousands of lives, that's cost us over a trillion dollars, the nation we need to build is our own.

So we're going to use half of what we're no longer spending on war to pay down the deficit, and we're going to invest the rest in research and education and repairing our roads and our bridges and our runways and our wireless networks. That's the choice in this election.

And I'm running to pay down our debt in a way that is balanced and a way that's responsible. After inheriting a trillion-dollar deficit, I signed 2 trillions of dollars of spending cuts into law. And now I want to finish the job responsibly and properly, streamlining Government, cutting more waste—there's still more there to be had—but also reforming our Tax Code so that it's simpler and fairer and it asks the wealthiest Americans to pay a little bit more.

My opponent won't tell us how he'd pay for his new, $5 trillion tax cut, a tax cut that gives an average of $250,000 to every millionaire in the country. So we may not know the details, but we know the bill for that tax cut will either be passed on to our children, or it's going to be paid by a whole lot of ordinary Americans. And I refuse to let that happen again.

We're not going to pay for another millionaire's tax cut by eliminating medical research projects into things like ovarian cancer or Alzheimer's. I refuse to pay for another tax cut by kicking children out of Head Start programs or asking students to pay more for college or eliminating health insurance for millions of poor and elderly and disabled Americans on Medicaid.

And as long as I'm President of the United States, I'm not going to allow Medicare to be turned into a voucher that would end the program as we know it. We'll reform Medicare, not by shifting costs to seniors, but by reducing the spending that isn't making people healthier. There are ways of doing it that preserve this program that is so vital to so many people.

So, Seattle, that's what's at stake. There's a lot at stake. On issue after issue, we can't afford to spend the next 4 years going backwards.

America doesn't need to refight the battles we just had over Wall Street reform or health care reform. Listen to Sue. Here's what I know: Allowing 2.5 million young people to stay on their parent's health insurance plan, that was the right thing to do. Cutting prescription drug costs for seniors, right thing to do. We're not going back to the days when insurance companies had unchecked power to cancel your policy or deny you coverage or charge women differently from men. We're not going back. We're going forward.

We don't need another political fight about ending a woman's right to choose or getting rid of Planned Parenthood or taking away access to affordable birth control. I want women to control their own health choices. That's—[*applause*]—just like I want my daughters to have the same economic opportunities as your sons. We're not going to turn back the clock. We're not turning back the clock.

We're not returning to the days when you could be kicked out of the United States military just because of who you are and who you love. We're moving this country forward. We are moving forward to a country where every American is treated with dignity and with respect. And here in Washington, you'll have the chance to make your voice heard on the issue of making sure that everybody, regardless of sexual orientation, is treated fairly. You will have a chance to weigh in on this. We are a nation that treats people fairly. We're not going backwards. We're not going backwards. We're going forwards. We're going forward. We're going forward, where everybody—everybody—is treated with dignity and respect.

We will not allow another election where multimillion-dollar donations speak louder than the voices of ordinary citizens.

It's—[*applause*]—and it's time to stop denying citizenship to responsible young people just because they're children of undocumented immigrants. This country is at its best when we harness the God-given talents of every individual, when we hear every voice, when we come together as one American family—Black, White, Hispanic, Asian, Native American, gay, straight, disabled—everybody striving for the same dream. That's what we're fighting for. That's why I ran for President. That's why I'm running again for President. That's why I need your help.

You know, Seattle, this election is actually going to be, I—even closer than the last. And the reason for that is too many of our friends and neighbors, they're still hurting because of this crisis. And they see what's going on in Washington, and they don't like it, and so there's just a frustration level there that will express itself in the election.

And I hear from too many people who are wondering why they haven't been able to get one of the jobs that have been created. Because even if jobs have been created, until you got a job, that jobs report doesn't mean much. They're wondering why their home is still underwater or why their family hasn't been touched by the recovery. So there's still a lot of work to be done. And folks are just—they get so frustrated about Washington.

And as I said, the other side, they're not going to—the other side will not be offering these Americans a real answer to their questions. They're not offering a better vision. They're not offering a new set of ideas. Every-

body knows that. There's nothing you've heard from them where you say, man, I didn't think of that. [*Laughter*] Now, that's fresh. That's new. Maybe that will work. [*Laughter*] That's not what's going on here.

What they will be doing is spending more money than we've ever seen before on negative ads, ads that exploit people's frustration for some short-term political gain. Over and over again, they'll tell you America is down and out. America is not working. They'll say, are you better off than you were, without mentioning that their frame of reference is before the worst crisis in our lifetime.

We've seen this play before. And here's the thing: The real question, the question that we have to answer, the question that will actually make a difference in your life and the lives of your children and the lives of your grandchildren, it's not just about how we're doing today. It's about how we're doing tomorrow and the next day and the day after that.

Will we be better off if more Americans get a better education? Will we be better off if we reduce our dependence on foreign oil? Will we be better off if we start doing some nation-building here at home? Will we be better off if we're investing in clean energy? Will we be better off if we ask the wealthiest Americans to pay for—their fair share? Will we be better off if we invest in new research and science and technology?

When we look back 4 years from now or 10 years from now or 20 years from now, won't we be better off if we have the courage to keep moving forward? That's the question in this election. That's the question in this election. And that outcome is entirely up to you. You'll have to contend with even more negative ads, with more cynicism, more nastiness, sometimes just plain foolishness. [*Laughter*]

But if there's one thing that we learned the last time around, one thing we learned in 2008, there is nothing more powerful than millions of voices calling for change. When you knock on doors, when you pick up the phone, when you talk to your friends, when you decide it's time for change to happen, guess what? Change happens. Change comes to America. And that's the spirit that we need again.

If people ask you what this campaign is about, you tell them it's still about hope. You tell them it's still about change. You tell them it's still about ordinary people who believe that in the face of great odds, we can make a difference in the life of this country.

Because I still believe, Seattle. I still believe. I still believe we're not as divided as our politics suggest. I still believe that we have more common ground than the pundits tell us. I believe we're not Democrats or Republicans first; I think we're Americans first. I still believe in you. I still believe in you, and that's why I'm asking you to still believe in me. I told you in 2008 that I wasn't a perfect man—maybe Michelle told you. [*Laughter*] And I won't be a perfect President. But I promised back when I was running that first time that I'd always tell you what I thought, and I'd always tell you

where I stood, and I'd wake up every single day fighting as hard as I know how for you.

And, Seattle, I've kept that promise. I have kept that promise, and I will keep it as long as I have the honor of being your President. So if you're willing to stick with me, if you're willing to fight with me, if you're willing to work even harder this election than the last one, I guarantee you we will move this country forward. We will finish what we started.

I'm still fired up. I'm still ready to go. And we will show the world why it is that the United States of America is the greatest nation on Earth.

Thank you, everybody. God bless you.

NOTE: The President spoke at 3 p.m. at the Paramount Theatre. In his remarks, he referred to Kenmore, WA, resident Suzanne Black; Republican Presidential candidate former Gov. W. Mitt Romney of Massachusetts; and former President William J. Clinton.

Remarks at an Obama Victory Fund 2012 Fundraiser in Studio City, California
May 10, 2012

The President. Thank you, everybody. Please, everybody have a seat. What a extraordinary evening. It is wonderful to be with all of you.

A couple of people I want to acknowledge: First of all, your outstanding mayor, Antonio Villaraigosa, is in the house. Where's Antonio? Right here. Also the Congressman of this district, somebody who knows foreign policy as well as anybody in Congress and who has just shown extraordinary leadership on so many issues, Congressman Howard Berman is here.

I want to thank Jeffrey not just for this evening, but for his tenacious support and advocacy since we started back in 2007. He has just consistently been there for me through thick and through thin. Sometimes, the 2008 campaign gets romanticized, and everybody says how perfect it was, and I have to remind them, no, I was there. [*Laughter*] And the only person I don't have to remind is Jeffrey, because he was there through all the ups and downs. And occasionally, he would call and say,

"Barack, I don't think things are working the way they're supposed to." [*Laughter*] But no matter where we were and what phase we were in, in that campaign, he stuck with us. And over the last 3½ years, he's remained just an extraordinary friend.

So, Jeffrey, thank you for everything you've done.

And then I want to thank Clooney for letting us use his basketball court. [*Laughter*] This guy has been talking smack about his basketball game—[*laughter*]—ever since I've known him. And we've actually known each other a while. It was wonderful, walking through the house, and the famous "Hope" poster from the 2008 campaign—people don't realize that the photograph of me is actually me sitting next to George. Because George had come into DC to advocate on behalf of Darfur and to make sure that we were doing the right thing for so many people who were going through such horrific events, and we struck up a friendship. And this is the first time that George Clooney has ever been photoshopped out of a picture. [*Laughter*] Never happened before. [*Laughter*] Never happened before, will never happen again. [*Laughter*]

But the wonderful thing is the artist actually sent George—some of you have seen this—a print with my picture and his picture right next to each other with the same—in the same format. Why he said at the bottom, "Dope and Hope," I don't know. [*Laughter*] I don't think that's fair. That's not fair. [*Laughter*] That's not right. It ain't right. [*Laughter*]

But look, I cannot take credit for this. Jeffrey can take some credit. But let's face it, we raised a lot of money because everybody loves George. [*Laughter*] They like me; they love him. [*Laughter*] And rightfully so. Not only is he an unbelievable actor, but he is one of those rare individuals who is at ease with everybody, seems to just occupy a constant state of grace, and uses his extraordinary talents on behalf of stuff that's really important. And he takes time to actually figure out the facts and the issues. And so we couldn't be prouder, George. Thank you. And I couldn't be prouder of him as a friend.

I see a lot of familiar faces in the audience, and I'm going to be joining each of you at your table, so I'm not going to take a long time to talk up here.

As Jeffrey said, we've gone through 3½ extraordinary years, as tough as anything that we've experienced in our lifetimes. It turns out, though, the American people are tougher. So yes, we lost almost 8 million jobs during the crisis in 2007, 2008, 4 million before I took office, 800,000 the day I was sworn in—or the month that I was sworn in. The auto industry was brought to its knees, the banking system locked up, even as we were still in the midst of two wars and extraordinary terrorist threats from abroad.

And yet, despite all this, the American people are pulling through. And one of the great privileges of being President is you travel around the country and everyday there's an affirmation of how decent and how strong and how caring the American people are. They're not always paying attention to the babble in Washington. They don't have the time to read big briefing books on the latest ideas for Medicare reform. But they have good instincts about what's right and what's true. And it's those instincts and it's that resilience that really has enabled this country to weather an extraordinary storm.

And I've had the great privilege of seeing people in communities all across the country pull together, keep businesses open so that they don't have to lay off their employees, folks who are out of work supporting each other in places of worship and in community centers, raising their kids, making sure that they're getting off to a good start.

And as a consequence, we're now at a place where we've created 4 million jobs in the last 2 years, 800,000 in the last 6 months—or few months alone, almost a million actually in the last 6 months. GM is the number-one automaker in the world, and not only that, but they're actually making good cars and that people are buying. The banking system has worked through a lot of these issues, and slowly, things are coming back.

But as Jeffrey said, we still have so much work to do. There's still so many people out there who are hurting, too many folks who are looking for work, too many people whose homes are underwater, too many communities that aren't sure about the future, that are anxious. Even if they're doing okay, they're anxious about whether the future is going to be better for their kids and for their grandkids.

And so I always remind people that in 2008, I did not just run to get back to where we were in 2007. The crisis in a lot of ways was a manifestation of what had been going on for a decade or more: a sense in which a few of us were doing really well, but that that fundamental American promise that if you worked hard, no matter what you looked like, where you came from, what your last name was, who you loved, that you could make it if you tried; that everybody had a fair shot and everybody did their fair share and everybody played by the same rules. Those basic values had been dissipating for a decade or more.

And so that's the reason why over the last 3½ years, even as we've managed crisis, even as we've ended a war and are in the process of ending another one, even as we went after Al Qaida and have decimated the ranks of their leadership, even as we got the auto industry back to a place where it can now compete internationally and we unlocked the financial system so that businesses and families could get financing again—even as we did all those things, we kept our eye on the basic promise of our 2008 campaign.

That's why we worked on health care reform, not because it was popular, but because it was right. And as a consequence, 30 million people will have health insurance that didn't have it before. That's why we did Wall Street reform, not because it was easy or popular, but because it was right, because we can't have a system in which the recklessness of a few can bring down an entire economy.

That's why we have taken on education, sometimes offending folks in our own party because the status quo of some communities where half the kids are dropping out and only 1 out of 10 are reading at grade level. We can't compete doing that.

That's why we've doubled clean energy. That's why we doubled fuel efficiency standards on cars. That's why we've invested in science and research. That's why projects all across the country have been built, putting construction workers back to work. All of this has been in pursuit of the goal that we originally talked about in 2008, and that was creating an America where everybody had a shot, where we create a platform where if you are willing to work hard, you can make it.

And that requires us to do things together. And we're not finished. We've got a lot more work. And as we look forward towards this next campaign, the choice between the path that I've set for this country and that of my opponent could not be starker, and the stakes couldn't be higher. And I won't run through the differences in all the issues. What it comes down to is they have a different vision about how America works.

See, I think we work best when we're all in it together, when we've all got a stake in each other. And I've said this before: I believe that—Malia and Sasha are the most magical girls in the world. I don't worry about them. But I think their lives will be better if every child in America has opportunity and a good education and can go to college without worrying about being loaded up with tens of thousands of dollars' worth of debt. That will be a stronger America for them.

And Michelle and I—people have commented on the fact that I've got gray hair now. There was a blog post about look how wrinkly Obama is getting. [*Laughter*] It was sort of distressing. [*Laughter*] George doesn't have to go through these things. [*Laughter*]

Actor George T. Clooney. Look at me!

The President. I like that in you, brother. [*Laughter*]

But Michelle and I will be okay after this is all done. But our lives are better if, when I'm walking down the street and I see some elderly couple holding hands and they're walking through a park, I know, you know what, they've got Medicare that they can count on and they've got Social Security that they can count on. They're going to be able to pay the bills and enjoy their retirement.

I remind people when folks talk about the free market, you won't find a bigger advocate for the free market than me, but I also understand the free market works when we've got rules so that folks who are engaging in fair dealing and providing good products and good customer service, that they're not being undercut by folks who are cutting corners and cheating and bilking consumers.

And I'm reminded—I just came from Seattle; I told a roomful of folks, some of whom work for Microsoft, Bill Gates is a genius, Steve Jobs is a genius, Mark Zuckerberg, amazing what they've accomplished. But the Internet doesn't exist unless all of us together make an investment in something called DARPA that helped develop the Internet. That was a common enterprise that created this platform for success for everybody.

The other side has got a different view. Their attitude is, you're on your own. If you're a kid born in a poor neighborhood in L.A., tough luck, you're on your own. If you're a senior citizen who, because of bad luck, got laid off, or the company ended up dissolving without your pension being vested, tough luck, you didn't plan well enough. That's not the America I believe in. That's not the America you believe in.

And obviously, yesterday we made some news, but the truth is it was a logical extension of what America is supposed to be. It grew directly out of this difference in visions: Are we a country that includes everybody and gives everybody a shot and treats everybody fairly, and is that going to make us stronger? Are we welcoming to immigrants? Are we welcoming to people who aren't like us? Does that make us stronger? I believe it does.

And so that's what's at stake. Now, I will just close by saying that this is going to be harder than it was the last time. This is going to be harder than it was the last time, not only because I'm older and grayer and your "Hope" posters are dog eared and—[*laughter*]. You know, 2008 in some ways was lightning in a bottle. That's not going to be replicated. And we shouldn't expect it to; I've been President for 3½ years. But part of the reason it's going to be harder is because folks are still hurting out there and those frustrations with Washington and the nonsense they see on the news is making them more cynical than they were in 2008.

So we're going to have to fight against cynicism and a belief that maybe things can't happen and maybe the game is rigged, what's the point. That's what we're going to be fighting against this time.

And that means we're going to have to work harder. That means we're going to have to be more determined. That means that that passion that we brought to bear in 2008 is going to have to express itself maybe not in such flashy form, it's going to have to be steady, but we're going to have to keep those fires burning all the way through November and beyond. Because I'm not interested in just winning the election, I'm also interested in making sure that we can finish what we started in 2008. We've still got a lot of work to do.

So bottom line is, I still believe in the American people, and I still believe in you. And I hope you still believe in me. Because I'm as determined as I've ever been to make sure that this country stays on the right path. We're moving forward; we're not going backwards.

Thank you, everybody.

NOTE: The President spoke at 7:30 p.m. at the residence of George T. Clooney. In his remarks, he referred to Jeffrey Katzenberg, chief executive officer, DreamWorks Studios; graphic artist Shepard Fairey; William H. Gates III, chairman, Microsoft Corp.; and Mark E. Zuckerberg, founder and chief executive officer, Facebook, Inc.

Remarks in Reno, Nevada
May 11, 2012

Well, good afternoon, everybody. And thank you for arranging a beautiful day. This is just a spectacular afternoon, and I'm thrilled to be here.

We all know how difficult these past few years have been for this country, but especially for this State. After the worst recession in our lifetimes—a crisis that followed the collapse of the housing market—it's going to take a long time for the economy to fully recover. More time than any of us would like. But there are

plenty of steps that we can take to speed up the recovery right now. There are things we can do right now to help create jobs and help restore some of the financial security that too many families have lost.

Now, I have to say that there are a few too many Republicans in Congress who don't seem to be as optimistic as we are. They think that all we can do are try the things that have been done in the past, things that they've tried in the past. So they want to cut more taxes, especially for the wealthiest Americans. They want to cut back on the rules that we put in place for banks and financial institutions. They've said that they want to let the housing market hit bottom and just hope for the best. That's it. We've heard those ideas before. That's their economic agenda. And I'll be honest with you, I don't buy it. I think they're wrong.

We've tried their ideas for nearly a decade and they didn't work. And I refuse to sell this country short by going back to the exact same ideas that helped to get us in this mess in the first place. Our goal is to build an economy where hard work and responsibility are rewarded, where you can find a good job, make a good wage, own your own home, maybe start a business, send your kids to college. Hopefully, their lives will be even better than ours. That's what I wish for Malia and Sasha, and I know you guys feel the same way who have kids.

And that's where we need to go. I've been pushing Congress to help us get there by passing a few commonsense policies that we're convinced will make a difference. We even made a handy to-do list for Congress so they can just check them off. It's a list like Michelle gives me. [*Laughter*] I know Paul is familiar with that list. He gets it from Val.

Now, there are only five things on this list, because I don't want to overload Congress with too much at once. But they're ideas that will help create jobs and build a stronger economy right now.

So first up on the list: It makes absolutely no sense that we actually give tax breaks to companies that ship jobs and factories overseas. That doesn't make any sense at all. So we told Congress it's time to end tax breaks for companies that ship jobs overseas and use that money to cover moving expenses for companies that bring jobs back to America.

Second, instead of just talking about job creators, Congress should help small businesses and help small-business owners, who create most of the new jobs in America. So we want to give them a tax break for hiring more workers and paying them higher wages.

The third thing on our to-do list: Congress should extend tax credits that are set to expire

for our clean energy companies. These businesses are putting folks to work here in this state of Nevada. Last time I was here, in fact, I went to see a huge solar plant—solar energy plant. A lot of folks are working both in the construction of it and maintaining it. That's happening all across the country. And so we've got to make sure that we are helping those folks, because that helps us break our dependence on foreign oil. Over the long term that will help drive down gas prices and it puts people to work right now. It's the right thing to do.

Fourth, Congress should create a veterans jobs corps so that we can help communities hire returning heroes—our veterans—as cops and firefighters and employees at national parks, because nobody who fights for this country should ever have to come home and fight for a job or fight for a roof over their heads.

All right, so that's four, which brings me to the fifth. The fifth thing on the list—and that's why I'm here today—I'm calling on Congress to give every responsible homeowner the chance to save an average of $3,000 a year by refinancing their mortgage. It's a simple idea. It makes great sense. And I know it will have an impact.

Last October, I was in Clark County, where I announced new steps to help responsible homeowners refinance their homes. And at the time, Congress wasn't willing to act, so we did. We went ahead and did what we could do administratively, without a new law being passed. And as a result, Americans who were previously stuck in high interest loans have been able to take advantage of these lower rates. And they've been able to save thousands of dollars every year.

And it turns out that two of those people are your neighbors, Paul and Valerie Keller. So I just had a chance to visit with Paul and Valerie and look at their beautiful home and check out the grill out back. [*Laughter*] Valerie says Paul is a pretty good cook, so I'm going to take her word for it.

The Kellers have lived in this house for 14 years. Val works nearby, helping secure loans for farmers and ranchers. Paul is a retired electrical contractor who started a family business with their son. Last year, with mortgage rates at historic lows, the Kellers decided it would make sense for them to refinance. They thought it would be easy, since they're current on their mortgage; they make their payments on time. So this is an example of responsible homeowners doing the right thing.

But when they tried to refinance, they were told they couldn't do it. Because the Kellers' house, like thousands of others in this State and probably some of the neighbors here, their house is underwater, which means that the price is currently lower than what they owe on it. So they were hit—you were hit—with a historic drop in housing prices, which caused the value of homes in their neighborhood to plummet. And a lot of banks, historically, have said, well, we're not going to refinance you if your home is underwater.

Now, luckily, the Kellers saw my announcement that I had made down in Clark County. So I'm assuming it must have been Val because whenever something smart is done, it's usually the wife in the house. [*Laughter*]

So they called their lender and within a few months—within 90 days—they were able to refinance under this new program that we set up. Their monthly mortgage bill has now dropped $240 dollars a month and that means every year they're saving close to $3000.

Now, Val says that they've been talking to some of their neighbors—maybe some of you are here today—and you're saying, well, that sounds like a pretty good idea. And a lot of folks across the country recognize this is a smart thing to do not only for homeowners, but for our economy, because if Paul and Val have an extra $240, $250 a month, then they might spend it on the local business. They might go to a restaurant a little more often. They might spoil their grandkids even more. [*Laughter*] And that means more money in the economy and businesses do better and slowly home prices start rising again. So it makes sense for all of us.

And the good news is, since I've made this announcement, refinancing applications have gone up by 50 percent nationwide and 230 percent here in Nevada alone. That's the good news. People are taking advantage of this. That's what we want to see.

But here's the only catch—and this is where you come in, because you're going to have to pressure Congress—the pool of folks who can refinance right now, when their homes are underwater, is still too small. The reason the Kellers were able to refinance is because the only thing that we could do without congressional action was to give opportunities for refinancing for folks with a Government-backed loan—an FHA-backed loan. But in order to expand that opportunity, we want to include everybody, people whose mortgages aren't Government-backed. And in order to do that, we've got to have Congress move.

There's absolutely no reason why they can't make this happen right now. If they started now, in a couple of weeks, in a month, they could make every homeowner in America who is underwater right now eligible to be able to refinance their homes—if they're making their payments, if they're responsible, if they're doing the right thing. And think about all those families saving $3,000 on average a month [year].° That's a huge boost to our economy. And for some of you who are underwater, you might say, "Instead of spending that money I can plow that back into equity in my home and build that back up," which would further strengthen housing prices here in Nevada and around the country.

So it's the right thing to do. There's already a bill in the works. It's supported by independent, nonpartisan economists. It's supported by industry leaders. Congress should pass it right now.

And let me just say this—maybe there are some Members of Congress watching—if you need some motivation to make this happen, then you should come to Reno and you should visit with folks like the Kellers. I'm not saying the Kellers want all these Members of Con-

---

° White House correction.

gress up in their house. [*Laughter*] It's bad enough having me and Secret Service in there. [*Laughter*] But at least they—they probably wouldn't mind saying hello and talking to them here in front of their house. [*Laughter*] But they should talk to people whose lives are better because of the action that we took.

All over the country, there are people just like Paul and Val, folks just like you, who are doing everything they can to do the right thing: to meet their responsibilities, to look after their families, to raise their kids right, give them good values. You're not looking for a handout. You just want to make sure that somebody is looking out for you, and that when you do the right thing, that you're able to keep everything that you've worked for. That's what folks are looking for and that's what they expect from Washington: to put the politics aside and the electioneering aside and just do what's right for people.

The President's Weekly Address
May 12, 2012

We all know the past few years have been difficult for this country. After the worst recession of our lifetimes, it's going to take longer than any of us would like for the economy to fully recover. But there are plenty of steps we can take to speed up the recovery. There are things we can do right now to help create jobs and restore some of the financial security that so many families have lost.

Now, the other side isn't so optimistic. They think all we can do is cut taxes, especially for the wealthiest Americans, and go back to letting banks and corporations write their own rules again. That's their plan.

But I think they're wrong. We tried their ideas for nearly a decade, and it didn't work out so well. We can't go back to the same policies that got us into this mess. We've got to move forward. We need to build an economy where hard work and responsibility are rewarded, where you can find a good job, own

So I need all of you, and everybody who's watching, to push Congress on their to-do list. Nag them until they actually get it done. We need to keep moving this country forward. Send them an e-mail, tweet them, write them a letter if you're old-fashioned like me. [*Laughter*]

But communicate to them that this will make a difference. It's one small step that will help us create the kind of economy that all Americans deserve. And that's an economy that's built to last, an economy where everybody has a fair shot, everybody gets a fair share, everybody is playing by the same set of rules. That's what made us great in the past. That's what's going to make us great in the future.

All right. Thank you, everybody. God bless you. God bless America. And give Paul and Val a big round of applause.

NOTE: The President spoke at 12 p.m. at the residence of Paul and Valerie Keller.

your own home, maybe start a businesses, and give your kids the chance to do even better.

That's where we need to go. And I've been pushing Congress to help us get there by passing a few commonsense policies that would make a difference. Democrats and Republicans have already done some important work together, from passing tax cuts for workers, to opening up new markets for American products, to reforming our patent system. But now we need to do more.

That's why we made Congress a handy to-do list, just like the kind I get from Michelle. It's short, but each of the ideas on this list will help create jobs and build a stronger economy right now.

First, Congress should stop giving tax breaks to companies that ship jobs overseas and use that money to cover moving expenses for companies that bring jobs back to America.

Second, Congress should help the millions of Americans who have worked hard and made their mortgage payments on time refinance their mortgages at lower rates and save at least $3,000 a year.

Third, Congress should help small-business owners by giving them a tax break for hiring more workers and paying them higher wages. Small businesses are the engine of economic growth in this country. We shouldn't be holding them back; we should be making it easier for them to succeed.

Fourth, if Congress fails to act soon, clean energy companies will see their taxes go up and could be forced to lay off employees. These companies are putting Americans to work and helping break our dependence on foreign oil. Congress should extend these tax credits.

And finally, Congress should help our veterans returning from Iraq and Afghanistan by creating a veterans' job corps. Our men and women in uniform have served this country with honor. Now it's our turn to serve them.

So that's Congress's to-do list. But now we need them to start crossing things off. I need you to call your Members of Congress, write them an e-mail, tweet, and let them know we can't afford to wait any longer to get things done. Tell them now is the time to take steps we know will grow our economy and create jobs.

You're working harder. You're meeting your responsibilities, and your representatives in Washington should do the same. Let's push Congress to do the right thing. Let's keep moving this country forward together.

Thanks, and have a great weekend.

NOTE: The address was recorded at approximately 9:15 a.m. on May 11 in the Stardust Room at the Beverly Hilton hotel in Beverly Hills, CA, for broadcast on May 12. The transcript was made available by the Office of the Press Secretary on May 11, but was embargoed for release until 6 a.m. on May 12.

Remarks at a Ceremony Honoring the National Association of Police Organizations TOP COPS
May 12, 2012

The President. Thank you, everybody. Please, please, have a seat.

Well, welcome to the White House. It is wonderful to be with all of you. It is especially good to be with somebody who has been fighting on behalf of law enforcement all his life. Everywhere I go, in every community, people see the track record and the legacy of Joe Biden's work when it comes to looking after law enforcement. And so I just want to thank my Vice President, who has shown leadership in this administration to make sure you guys have what you need.

My Secretary of Homeland Security, Janet Napolitano, is here. She does outstanding work. The Director of the Office of National Drug Control Policy, and a longtime police officer, Gil Kerlikowske, is here. Give Gil a big round of applause. Representative John Conyers is here. And of course, I want to welcome the leaders of the National Association of Police Organizations, including your president, Tom Nee. Tom told me he just had a new granddaughter.

National Association of Police Organizations President Thomas J. Nee. Grandson.

The President. Grandson. What's his name?

Mr. Nee. Nicholas Joseph.

The President. Nicholas Joseph. So give him a round of applause for that.

You know, I look forward to this event each and every year, because it's a chance to say thank you. Every day, hundreds of thousands of law enforcement officers keep our neighborhoods safe, and frankly, they don't ask for a lot. They don't ask for a lot of credit. They don't go to work planning to be heroes. They just do their jobs.

But when you put on that badge, you assume a special responsibility. And every time you put it on, you never know if this day will be the day that you've spent your entire career training for, the day when just doing your job and being a hero are exactly the same thing. For the men and women standing behind me, America's TOP COPS, that day came. And when it did, they were ready. They didn't flinch. They didn't back off. There are people who are alive today only because of their courage.

I had a chance to just shake each one of these individuals' hands and express my appreciation to them personally. They're a pretty humble group. Some of them will tell you they don't deserve to be called heroes; they're entitled to their opinion. [*Laughter*] I disagree with them. I think they are. What else do you call a team that takes down a deranged gunman and saves countless lives? Or a unit that flies a helicopter into dangerous winds and pulls off a daring nighttime rescue? Or an officer who, after being shot three times, switches her gun from her right hand to her left, so that she can return fire until backup arrives?

I guarantee you that when the bullets were flying, when lives were on the line, these men and women weren't thinking about bravery. They weren't thinking of themselves. Instead, they were looking out for their fellow officers and for the civilians that they swore to protect. And when they return home, they'll go back to being just another member of the team.

But they've earned this moment. Today we celebrate 34 extraordinary individuals, and we recognize the sacrifices they and their fellow officers make. Some of our TOP COPS are still recovering from gunshot wounds. I'm sure that many are, even now, thinking of a partner or a teammate who fell in the line of duty.

So we honor their memories today. We honor all those who have put their lives on the line in order to protect their fellow citizens, even if they were complete strangers. I hope that we also pledge to learn something from the exam-ple that they set. Because while most of us will never be asked to run straight into a hail of bullets or chase down an armed suspect on foot, we also have responsibilities to meet.

For those of us in elected office, that includes helping States and cities to keep first-responders on the job. It includes supporting cutting-edge tools they need, from a high-speed public safety broadband network to a new generation of mobile apps.

Even as we do everything we can to support men and women like our TOP COPS, and to make police work safer and more effective, we do have to recognize that one thing will never change. Our safety will always depend on the quiet heroism of ordinary Americans, like the ones that we recognize today. We will be forever in debt to those who wear the badge, to men and women with a deep sense of duty and a willingness to serve and sacrifice on our behalf. And I think these individuals don't mind me saying that they are representative of the sacrifices and that quiet courage that exists among law enforcement officers all across the country, and their families, because I know the strains of families in such a difficult job is significant as well. And those families, those of you who are here today, we want to say thank you to you as well.

So again, to the 2012 TOP COPS, thank you for everything you do. God bless you and your families, and God bless the United States of America. All right.

NOTE: The President spoke at 11:13 a.m. in the Rose Garden at the White House. The transcript released by the Office of the Press Secretary also included the remarks of Vice President Joe Biden. The related proclamation of May 14 is listed in Appendix D at the end of this volume.

Statement on the Security Transition in Afghanistan
May 13, 2012

I welcome President Karzai's announcement today of the third tranche of areas to transition to Afghan security lead, which is an important step forward in our effort to achieve our objectives in Afghanistan. As transition proceeds in these areas, nearly 75 percent of the population of Afghanistan will be living in provinces, districts, and villages where Afghan forces are leading. The Afghan National Security Forces are strengthening their capacity as we remain on track to meet our goal of having the Afghan Government fully responsible for security across the country by the end of 2014.

A week from now, world leaders will gather at the NATO summit in Chicago to discuss how we can effectively advance the transition process as our forces move from combat to a support role and demonstrate our enduring support for the Afghan Government and Afghan National Security Forces. I look forward to meeting with President Karzai and my fellow leaders in Chicago to discuss these critical steps that will strengthen Afghan sovereignty while responsibly winding down the war.

Commencement Address at Barnard College in New York City
May 14, 2012

The President. Please, please have a seat. Thank you. Thank you, President Spar, trustees, President Bollinger. Hello, class of 2012! Congratulations on reaching this day. Thank you for the honor of being able to be a part of it.

There are so many people who are proud of you—your parents, family, faculty, friends—all who share in this achievement. So please give them a big round of applause. To all the moms who are here today, you could not ask for a better Mother's Day gift than to see all of these folks graduate.

I have to say, though, whenever I come to these things, I start thinking about Malia and Sasha graduating, and I start tearing up and—[*laughter*]—it's terrible. I don't know how you guys are holding it together. [*Laughter*]

I will begin by telling a hard truth: I'm a Columbia College graduate. [*Laughter*] I know there can be a little bit of a sibling rivalry here. [*Laughter*] But I'm honored nevertheless to be your commencement speaker today, although I've got to say, you set a pretty high bar, given the past 3 years. Hillary Clinton, Meryl Streep, Sheryl Sandberg, these are not easy acts to follow.

But I will point out Hillary is doing an extraordinary job as one of the finest Secretaries of State America has ever had. We gave Meryl the Presidential Medal of Arts and Humanities. Sheryl is not just a good friend, she's also one of our economic advisers. So it's like the old saying goes: Keep your friends close and your Barnard commencement speakers even closer. There's wisdom in that. [*Laughter*]

Now, the year I graduated—this area looks familiar—[*laughter*]—the year I graduated was 1983, the first year women were admitted to Columbia. Sally Ride was the first American woman in space. Music was all about Michael and the moonwalk. [*Laughter*] We had the Walkman——

Audience member. Do it! [*Laughter*]

The President. No, no moonwalking. [*Laughter*] No moonwalking today. [*Laughter*]

We had the Walkman, not iPods. Some of the streets around here were not quite so inviting. [*Laughter*] Times Square was not a family destination. [*Laughter*] So I know this is all ancient history. Nothing worse than commencement speakers droning on about bygone days. [*Laughter*] But for all the differences, the class of 1983 actually had a lot in common with all of you. For we too were heading out into a world at a moment when our country was still recovering from a particularly severe economic recession. It was a time of change. It was a time of uncertainty. It was a time of passionate political debates.

You can relate to this because just as you were starting out finding your way around this campus, an economic crisis struck that would claim more than 5 million jobs before the end of your freshman year. Since then, some of you have probably seen parents put off retirement, friends struggle to find work. And you may be looking toward the future with that same sense of concern that my generation did when we were sitting where you are now.

Of course, as young women, you're also going to grapple with some unique challenges, like whether you'll be able to earn equal pay for equal work, whether you'll be able to balance the demands of your job and your family, whether you'll be able to fully control decisions about your own health.

And while opportunities for women have grown exponentially over the last 30 years, as young people, in many ways you have it even tougher than we did. This recession has been more brutal, the job losses steeper. Politics seems nastier, Congress more gridlocked than ever. Some folks in the financial world have not exactly been model corporate citizens. [*Laughter*]

No wonder that faith in our institutions has never been lower, particularly when good news doesn't get the same kind of ratings as bad news anymore. Every day you receive a steady stream of sensationalism and scandal and stories with a message that suggest change isn't possible, that you can't make a difference, that you won't be able to close that gap between life as it is and life as you want it to be.

My job today is to tell you, don't believe it. Because as thing—as tough as things have been, I am convinced you are tougher. I've seen your passion, and I've seen your service. I've seen you engage, and I've seen you turn out in record numbers. I've heard your voices amplified by creativity and a digital fluency that those of us in older generations can barely comprehend. I've seen a generation eager, impatient even, to step into the rushing waters of history and change its course.

And that defiant, can-do spirit is what runs through the veins of American history. It's the lifeblood of all our progress. And it is that spirit which we need your generation to embrace and rekindle right now.

See, the question is not whether things will get better; they always do. The question is not whether we've got the solutions to our challenges; we've had them within our grasp for quite some time. We know, for example, that this country would be better off if more Americans were able to get the kind of education that you've received here at Barnard, if more people could get the specific skills and training that employers are looking for today.

We know that we'd all be better off if we invest in science and technology that sparks new businesses and medical breakthroughs, if we developed more clean energy so we could use less foreign oil and reduce the carbon pollution that's threatening our planet.

We know that we're better off when there are rules that stop big banks from making bad bets with other people's money; when insurance companies aren't allowed to drop your coverage when you need it most or charge women differently from men. Indeed, we know we are better off when women are treated fairly and equally in every aspect of American life, whether it's the salary you earn or the health decisions you make.

We know these things to be true. We know that our challenges are eminently solvable. The question is whether, together, we can muster the will—in our own lives, in our common institutions, in our politics—to bring about the changes we need. And I'm convinced your generation possesses that will. And I believe that the women of this generation—that all of you—will help lead the way.

Now, I recognize that's a cheap applause line when you're giving a commencement at Barnard. [*Laughter*] It's the easy thing to say. But it's true. It is—in part, it is simple math. Today, women are not just half this country, you're half its workforce. More and more women are outearning their husbands. You're more than half of our college graduates and master's graduates and Ph.D.'s. So you've got us outnumbered. [*Laughter*]

After decades of slow, steady, extraordinary progress, you are now poised to make this the century where women shape not only their own destiny, but the destiny of this Nation and of this world.

But how far your leadership takes this country, how far it takes this world, well, that will be up to you. You've got to want it. It will not be handed to you. And as someone who wants that future—that better future—for you and for Malia and Sasha, as somebody who's had the good fortune of being the husband and the father and the son of some strong, remarkable women, allow me to offer just a few pieces of advice. That's obligatory. [*Laughter*] Bear with me.

My first piece of advice is this: Don't just get involved. Fight for your seat at the table. Better yet, fight for a seat at the head of the table.

It's been said that the most important role in our democracy is the role of citizen. And indeed, it was 225 years ago today that the Constitutional Convention opened in Philadelphia and our Founders, citizens all, began crafting an extraordinary document. Yes, it had its flaws, flaws that this Nation has strived to protect [perfect]° over time. Questions of race and gender were unresolved. No woman's signature graced the original document, although we can assume that there were founding mothers whispering smarter things in the ears of the Founding Fathers. I think that's almost certain.

What made this document special was that it provided the space—the possibility—for those who had been left out of our charter to fight their way in. It provided people the language to appeal to principles and ideals that broadened democracy's reach. It allowed for protest and movements and the dissemination of new ideas that would repeatedly, decade after decade, change the world, a constant forward movement that continues to this day.

Our Founders understood that America does not stand still. We are dynamic, not static. We look forward, not back. And now that new doors have been opened for you, you've got an obligation to seize those opportunities.

You need to do this not just for yourself, but for those who don't yet enjoy the choices that you've had, the choices you will have. One reason many workplaces still have outdated policies is because women only account for 3 percent of the CEOs at Fortune 500 companies. One reason we're actually refighting long-settled battles over women's rights is because women occupy fewer than one in five seats in Congress.

Now, I'm not saying that the only way to achieve success is by climbing to the top of the corporate ladder or running for office. Although, let's face it, Congress would get a lot more done if you did. [*Laughter*] That I think we're clear about. But if you decide not to sit yourself at the table, at the very least you've got to make sure you have a say in who does. It matters.

Before women like Barbara Mikulski and Olympia Snowe and others got to Congress, just to take one example, much of federally funded research on diseases focused solely on their effects on men. It wasn't until women like Patsy Mink and Edith Green got to Congress and passed title IX, 40 years ago this year, that we declared women too should be allowed to compete and win on America's playing fields. Until a woman named Lilly Ledbetter showed up at her office and had the courage to step up and say, you know what, this isn't right, women aren't being treated fairly, we lacked some of the tools we needed to uphold the basic principle of equal pay for equal work.

So don't accept somebody else's construction of the way things ought to be. It's up to you to right wrongs. It's up to you to point out injustice. It's up to you to hold the system accountable and sometimes upend it entirely. It's up to you to stand up and to be heard, to write and to lobby, to march, to organize, to vote. Don't be content to just sit back and watch.

Those who oppose change, those who benefit from an unjust status quo, have always bet on the public's cynicism or the public's complacency. Throughout American history, though, they have lost that bet, and I believe they will this time as well. But ultimately, class of 2012, that will depend on you. Don't wait for the person next to you to be the first to speak up for what's right. Because maybe, just maybe, they're waiting on you.

Which brings me to my second piece of advice: Never underestimate the power of your example. The very fact that you are graduating, let alone that more women now graduate from college than men, is only possible because earlier generations of women—your mothers, your grandmothers, your aunts—shattered the myth that you couldn't or shouldn't be where you are.

° White House correction.

I think of a friend of mine who's the daughter of immigrants. When she was in high school, her guidance counselor told her, you know what, you're just not college material. You should think about becoming a secretary. Well, she was stubborn, so she went to college anyway. She got her master's. She ran for local office, won. She ran for State office, she won. She ran for Congress, she won. And lo and behold, Hilda Solis did end up becoming a secretary. [*Laughter*] She is America's Secretary of Labor.

So think about what that means to a young Latina girl when she sees a Cabinet Secretary that looks like her. Think about what it means to a young girl in Iowa when she sees a Presidential candidate who looks like her. Think about what it means to a young girl walking in Harlem right down the street when she sees a U.N. Ambassador who looks like her. Do not underestimate the power of your example.

This diploma opens up new possibilities, so reach back, convince a young girl to earn one too. If you earned your degree in an area where we need more women, like computer science or engineering, reach back and persuade another student to study it too. If you're going into fields where we need more women, like construction or computer engineering, reach back, hire someone new. Be a mentor. Be a role model.

Until a girl can imagine herself, can picture herself as a computer programmer or a combatant commander, she won't become one. Until there are women who tell her, ignore our pop culture obsession over beauty and fashion and focus instead on studying and inventing and competing and leading, she'll think those are the only things that girls are supposed to care about. Now, Michelle will say, nothing wrong with caring about it a little bit. [*Laughter*] You can be stylish and powerful too. That's Michelle's advice.

And never forget that the most important example a young girl will ever follow is that of a parent. Malia and Sasha are going to be outstanding women because Michelle and Marian Robinson are outstanding women. So understand your power, and use it wisely.

My last piece of advice—this is simple, but perhaps most important: Persevere. Persevere. Nothing worthwhile is easy. No one of achievement has avoided failure—sometimes catastrophic failures. But they keep at it. They learn from mistakes. They don't quit.

You know, when I first arrived on this campus, it was with little money, fewer options. But it was here that I tried to find my place in this world. I knew I wanted to make a difference, but it was vague how, in fact, I'd go about it. [*Laughter*] I—but I wanted to do my part to shape a better world.

So, even as I worked after graduation in a few unfulfilling jobs here in New York—I will not list them all—[*laughter*]—even as I went from motley apartment to motley apartment, I reached out. And I started to write letters to community organizations all across the country. And one day, a small group of churches on the South Side of Chicago answered, offering me work with people in neighborhoods hit hard by steel mills that were shutting down and communities where jobs were dying away.

The community had been plagued by gang violence, so as—once I arrived, one of the first things we tried to do was to mobilize a meeting with community leaders to deal with gangs. And I'd worked for weeks on this project. We invited the police, we made phone calls, we went to churches, we passed out flyers. The night of the meeting, we arranged rows and rows of chairs in anticipation of this crowd. And we waited, and we waited. And finally, a group of older folks walked in to the hall and they sat down. And this little old lady raised her hand and asked, "Is this where the bingo game is?" [*Laughter*] It was a disaster. Nobody showed up. My first big community meeting, nobody showed up.

And later, the volunteers I worked with told me, that's it, we're quitting. They'd been doing this for 2 years even before I had arrived. They had nothing to show for it. And I'll be honest, I felt pretty discouraged as well. I didn't know what I was doing. I thought about quitting. And as we were talking, I looked outside and saw some young boys playing in a vacant lot across the street. And they were just throwing rocks up at a boarded building. They had nothing better to do—late at night, just throwing rocks. And I said to the volunteers: "Before you quit, answer one question. What will happen to those boys if you quit? Who will fight for them if we don't? Who will give them a fair shot if we leave?"

And one by one, the volunteers decided not to quit. We went back to those neighborhoods, and we kept at it, and we registered new voters, and we set up afterschool programs, and we fought for new jobs and helped people live lives with some measure of dignity. And we sustained ourselves with those small victories. We didn't set the world on fire. Some of those communities are still very poor. There are still a lot of gangs out there. But I believe that it was those small victories that helped me win the bigger victories of my last 3½ years as President.

And I wish I could say that this perseverance came from some innate toughness in me. But the truth is, it was learned. I got it from watching the people who raised me. More specifically, I got it from watching the women who shaped my life.

I grew up as the son of a single mom who struggled to put herself through school and make ends meet. She had marriages that fell apart, even went on food stamps at one point to help us get by. But she didn't quit. And she earned her degree and made sure that, through scholarships and hard work, my sister and I earned ours. She used to wake me up when we were living overseas—wake me up before dawn to study my English lessons. And when I'd complain, she'd just look at me and say, "This is no picnic for me either, buster." [*Laughter*]

And my mom ended up dedicating herself to helping women around the world access the money they needed to start their own businesses; she was an early pioneer in microfinance. And that meant, though, that she was gone a lot, and she had her own struggles trying to figure out balancing motherhood and a career. And when she was gone, my grandmother stepped up to take care of me.

She only had a high school education. She got a job at a local bank. She hit the glass ceiling and watched men she once trained promoted up the ladder ahead of her. But she didn't quit. Rather than grow hard or angry each time she got passed over, she kept doing her job as best as she knew how and ultimately ended up being vice president at the bank. She didn't quit.

And later on, I met a woman who was assigned to advise me on my first summer job at a law firm. And she gave me such good advice that I married her. [*Laughter*] And Michelle and I gave everything we had to balance our careers and a young family. But let's face it, no matter how enlightened I must have thought myself to be, it often fell more on her shoulders when I was traveling, when I was away. I know that when she was with our girls, she'd feel guilty that she wasn't giving enough time to her work, and when she was at her work, she'd feel guilty she wasn't giving enough time to our girls. And both of us wished we had some superpower that would let us be in two places at once. But we persisted. We made that marriage work.

And the reason Michelle had the strength to juggle everything and put up with me and eventually the public spotlight was because she too came from a family of folks who didn't quit. Because she saw her dad get up and go to work every day even though he never finished college, even though he had crippling MS. She saw her mother, even though she never finished college, in that school, that urban school, every day making sure Michelle and her brother were getting the education they deserved. Michelle saw how her parents never quit. They never indulged in self-pity, no matter how stacked the odds were against them. They didn't quit.

Those are the folks who inspire me. People ask me sometimes, who inspires you, Mr. President? Those quiet heroes all across this country—some of your parents and grandparents who are sitting here—no fanfare, no articles written about them, they just persevere. They just do their jobs. They meet their responsibilities. They don't quit. I'm only here because of them. They may not have set out to change the world, but in small, important ways, they did. They certainly changed mine.

So whether it's starting a business or running for office or raising a amazing family, remember that making your mark on the world is hard. It takes patience. It takes commitment. It comes with plenty of setbacks, and it comes with plenty of failures.

But whenever you feel that creeping cynicism, whenever you hear those voices say you can't make a difference, whenever somebody tells you to set your sights lower, the trajectory of this country should give you hope. Previous generations should give you hope. What young generations have done before should give you hope. Young folks who marched and mobilized and stood up and sat in, from Seneca Falls to Selma to Stonewall, didn't just do it for themselves; they did it for other people.

That's how we achieved women's rights. That's how we achieved voting rights. That's how we achieved workers' rights. That's how we achieved gay rights. That's how we've made this Union more perfect.

And if you're willing to do your part now, if you're willing to reach up and close that gap between what America is and what America should be, I want you to know that I will be right there with you. If you are ready to fight for that brilliant, radically simple idea of Amer-

ica that no matter who you are or what you look like, no matter who you love or what God you worship, you can still pursue your own happiness, I will join you every step of the way.

Now more than ever, America needs what you, the class of 2012, has to offer. America needs you to reach high and hope deeply. And if you fight for your seat at the table and you set a better example and you persevere in what you decide to do with your life, I have every faith not only that you will succeed, but that, through you, our Nation will continue to be a beacon of light for men and women, boys and girls, in every corner of the globe.

So thank you. Congratulations. God bless you. God bless the United States of America.

NOTE: The President spoke at 1:28 p.m. on the South Lawn at Columbia University. In his remarks, he referred to Debora L. Spar, president, Barnard College; Lee C. Bollinger, president, Columbia University; actor and National Medal of Arts recipient Meryl Streep; Sheryl K. Sandberg, chief operating officer, Facebook, Inc.; and Lilly Ledbetter, former employee, Goodyear Tire and Rubber Company plant in Gadsden, AL; and U.S. Permanent Representative to the United Nations Susan E. Rice. He also referred to his mother-in-law Marian Robinson, sister Maya Soetoro-Ng, and brother-in-law Craig M. Robinson.

Remarks at an Obama Victory Fund 2012 Fundraiser in New York City
May 14, 2012

Thank you! Well, it is wonderful to be with all of you. There are a couple of special acknowledgements I want to make. First of all, I just want to thank Ricky Martin for being here today. Those of you who haven't caught "Evita" yet, go out there. I'm sure there's still tickets available. [*Laughter*] But you know that he's going to be spectacular in it. And I'm so grateful for him stepping out and being willing to support me in this way.

I want to thank Donald and Shelley Rubin for not only making this extraordinary event possible, but all that they've done for the civic

life of New York. Please give them a big round of applause.

I want to thank Raj Goyle, who helped to put this together. And he's got two beautiful daughters, one of whom he's still holding like this, and it's—[*laughter*]—it reminds me of when Malia and Sasha were like this, and now they're like this. [*Laughter*] But I want to thank Raj for this.

Your outstanding attorney general, Eric Schneiderman, is in the house, so please give him a big round of applause as well.

So we've been busy. [*Laughter*] We've got a few things to do here. I'm here to ask for your help, but I'm also here because your country needs your help. When we ran 4 years ago, I think we all understood that the campaign wasn't just about me. It was about the commitment we made to each other to make sure that this country lived up to the meaning of its creed. The idea that all of us, if we worked, if we tried, we could make it here in America, regardless of what we look like, where we came from, who we loved, what our surnames were; the notion that those basic values of responsibility and hard work, of giving back, of that that's what built this country and we built it together. And we felt like we had lost some of those core values.

When I was first elected, we were looking backwards at a decade of manufacturing moving overseas and the middle class struggling with flat wages and flat incomes, even though the cost of everything from college to health care had been skyrocketing. We had seen recklessness by some on Wall Street, almost bringing the economy to its knees, an auto industry that was on the verge of collapse, a foreign policy that had not gained us the kind of respect that we needed in the world and had cost us over a trillion dollars.

And so we understood we had a lot of work to do. And the month that I took office we were losing 800,000 jobs that month, and we had already lost 4 million, and we'd lose another 3 million after that. And so these have been tough times. It's been tough times for the country, tough times for a lot of families all across America.

But the good news is the American people have proven to be tougher. And so for all the challenges that we've gone through, we have seen families across America willing to cut back on things they didn't need, to make sure that they were looking after their kids and doing the things that they did need to do. There were some people who had to go back and retrain because the industries that they were in were no longer operating at that same capacity. We've seen businesses that had to scale back, but did everything they could to keep their workers.

And because of all these individuals efforts and, frankly, some tough, but good decisions that we made early on, we're weathering this storm and we've seen the country start to come back. Four million jobs created over the last 2 years alone. Just in the last 6 months, over a million jobs. The auto industry all the way back, so that GM is now once again the biggest carmaker in the world and producing better cars, because we doubled fuel efficiency standards on cars so that by the middle of the next decade everybody is going to be getting 55 miles a gallon, and that will save the average family about $8,000. And we'll be taking a whole bunch of carbon out of the atmosphere so that we can make sure that all these wonderful kids who are in attendance are inheriting a planet that hasn't been wrecked because we didn't take the proper decisions.

We've doubled our production of clean energy, even as our oil production is higher and our imports of oil from other countries are lower.

We ended the war in Iraq as promised, and we're now winding down the war in Afghanistan.

And so we've done a lot over these last 3½ years to make sure that the country was able to manage through this crisis that we have not seen in our lifetimes before. But we—I did not just run and you didn't just support me just to get back to the status quo. And we know that there are still families out there that are having a tough time, people whose homes are still underwater. We still know that there are too many children all across America who don't have the kind of opportunities that we want them to have and that America needs them to have.

And so we now come to this point this election where the American people are going to have a choice, and this choice is going to be as important as any choice that we've made in a very long time; in some ways, more important than 2008, because we've got a very clear contrast this time.

John McCain believed in climate change and believed in immigration reform. On some issues, there was a sense of independence. What we've got this time out is a candidate who said he'd basically rubber stamp a Republican Congress who wants us to go backwards and not forwards on a whole range of issues.

They've got an economic theory that basically says the only way to grow the economy is to slash everybody's taxes further, especially the wealthiest Americans, to dismantle Government in so many ways. And that somehow, if everybody—the most powerful in our society are left to do whatever it is that they want, that somehow we're going to be better off.

And we've just got a completely different vision about how America has succeeded. And it's rooted in fact and it's rooted in history. [*Laughter*] It's based on what we've seen, because the ideas that they're putting forward have been tried. We tried them between 2000 and 2008, and it resulted in the most sluggish job growth that we've ever seen, resulted in all kinds of phony financial profits and debt, and resulted in the worst financial crisis and economic crisis we've seen since the 1930s. So we—it's not as if they're offering any new ideas. They're basically saying you're on your own, and when everybody is on their own, somehow we're better off.

And we've got a contrasting vision that says we are stronger together, that America was built together, that all of us have responsibilities, that we thrive in a free market where risk takers and innovators are rewarded for taking a bet, taking a chance. But we also understand that we grew because we made a decision at some point we were going to have public schools where every kid—immigrants who showed up here in New York City fleeing wars in Europe—that they could come here and suddenly go into a public school and learn and end up winning Nobel Prizes and starting Fortune 500 companies. That was how we built this country.

We built this country around the idea that everybody should have access to a great college education. And so as a consequence, we set up—President Lincoln, the first Republican President, set up land-grant colleges all across this country, where the kid of a farmer could suddenly go and learn something new and all

of us would become more productive because of it.

This country was built because together we built the Hoover Dam and the Golden Gate Bridge and the Interstate Highway System. That's how we sent a man to the Moon, that's how the Internet was invented, because we did these things together.

My grandfather went to college on the GI bill because we understood that that would help make everybody rich. We didn't do those things just because it was good for one group or one individual. We did it because we understood that when everybody has got a shot, no matter what you look like, no matter where you come from, we all do better. And that's what's at stake in this election. Those are the contrasting visions. And we know which direction this country needs to go in.

This is a country that needs to invest in clean energy because we don't need to be subsidizing big oil companies to the tune of $4 billion a year. We need to double down on solar and wind and biofuels that are going to help reduce our dependence on foreign oil and clean up our environment. We know that it's important for us to make sure that young people are able to afford to go to college—everybody, not just some.

We know that we have to invest in science and technology and stem cell research and all the things that can help lead to amazing medical and scientific breakthroughs. We know that we've got to rebuild this country, which is why I want to spend half of the money that we're saving on wars we're no longer fighting to build our roads and our bridges and our airports.

And we also know that if we're going to restore a sense of middle class security, that we've got to make sure that we're rewarding businesses that are investing here in the United States, not businesses that are shipping jobs overseas. We know these things.

And we can do it. And we can do it in a balanced way. And one of the big arguments we're going to have over the next 4 or 5 months is, how do we pay for stuff? And I happen to believe that it makes sense for us to make these investments to make sure that Social Security and Medicare are still there for the next generation, to make sure that we're not kicking poor kids and people with disabilities and seniors who don't have any other means off of Medicaid just to balance our budgets. I think that I can afford to pay a little bit more, and frankly, some of the people in this room can afford to pay a little bit more, so that we can bring down our debts in a responsible way: cutting out waste, cutting out programs that don't work anymore, but also making sure that everybody is paying their fair share.

And at root, so much of this has to do with a belief that not only are we all in this together, but all of us are equal in terms of dignity and in terms of respect, and everybody deserves a shot. So part of what we've been spending a lot of time doing is just making sure that those ideals that we profess are made real.

The first bill I signed, the Lilly Ledbetter Act—a simple proposition—equal pay for equal work. I don't want my daughters treated differently than my sons. That's the reason why we're fighting for comprehensive immigration reform, because I believe that a child who's here, raised with our kids, playing with our kids, has as much talent as our kids, the notion that somehow they would not have the capacity, the ability to proclaim themselves Americans and to fulfill their American Dream, that's not who we are and that's not what we're about.

The announcement I made last week about my views on marriage equality, same principle. The basic idea: I want everybody treated fairly in this country. We have never gone wrong when we expanded rights and responsibilities to everybody. That doesn't weaken families, that strengthens families. It's the right thing to do.

On each and every one of these issues, there is a fundamental difference between the candidates. And when we passed health care reform, we did it because a country this wealthy, we shouldn't have 30 million people without health insurance. That's not an efficient way to go. We shouldn't have people showing up at emergency rooms that we end up having to pay for indirectly because we couldn't give them

preventive care. I don't want women being charged more than men for their ailments. That's not right. I want to make sure that seniors who have been paying into Medicare, that they've got Medicare that they can count on in their golden years. And we've got to make some changes, but we're not going to voucherize that program.

So I'm—it's been said that this election is going to be about values, and I absolutely agree. It's about the economic values we have, about the values that I believe are what makes America so special: the idea that everybody gets a fair shot, everybody does their fair share, everybody plays by the same set of rules. So everything we do—from Wall Street reform, making sure that banks aren't taking risks with other people's money that taxpayers may have to end up bailing out later, to repealing DOMA, to getting the "DREAM Act" passed, to investing in our schools, to rebuilding manufacturing in America—all of these things are designed to make sure that we're restoring middle class security for all those folks out there that are struggling for their small portion of the American Dream.

And the good news is, I think the American people are on our side on this. When you ask them specifically about all these issues, they ultimately choose the vision that I'm presenting over the one that the other side is presenting. The only thing that's holding us back is the fact that things are still tough out there. There are still too many people without work, and there are still too many people who are struggling to get by even if they've got work.

And what's also going to make this a very close race is the fact that you've got special interests and these super PACs that are spending money on negative ads in unprecedented ways. And their message is going to be very simple: You know what, you're frustrated, you're dissatisfied, and it's Obama's fault. You can boil down the message. [*Laughter*] That's—we were traveling around trying to prevent a doubling of student loan rates, and the Republicans said, he's trying to distract from the economy. Well, now, the last I checked, making sure our kids got a good education and weren't loaded down with debt, that had something to do with our economy. But what they really meant was, this distracts from our basic argument that you're frustrated and it's Obama's fault. [*Laughter*] And they will spend hundreds of millions of dollars trying to drill that home.

But I'm not worried. And the reason I'm not worried is because of you, because I believe that if we are getting our message out effectively, if we are describing not only what we've done over the last 3½ years, not only the 2½ million young people who have health insurance who wouldn't otherwise have it because they can stay on their parent's plan, not just everything that we've done to make sure that we're changing the rules on things like people being able to visit their loved ones in hospitals, not just everything that we've done in terms of restoring the auto industry, but when we describe what we plan to do for the future, if we can get that message out effectively, I believe we'll win. But more importantly, the country will win.

But I'm going to need all of you. This is going to be a tough race. It is going to be a tight race. Nobody should be taking this for granted, especially when I come to New York sometimes people go around and say, I don't know anybody who is not supporting you, Barack. [*Laughter*] I say, you live in Manhattan, man. [*Laughter*]

This is going to be a challenging race. But we can win as long as all of you are activated, as long as all of you are motivated, as long as you're doing everything you can, not just mak-

ing phone calls, not just raising money, but I want folks out hitting the streets, knocking on doors, talking to your family, talking to your friends.

In 2008, a lot of people were skeptical, but we showed them that when ordinary folks are motivated, they can't be stopped. When they decide it's time for change to happen, change happens. And that's going to happen this time as well.

I used to say in 2008, I'm not a perfect man, and I'm not going to be a perfect President, but I'd always tell you what I thought, I always would tell you where I stood, and I'd work every single day—every day I would wake up thinking about how I could make your lives better and making sure that every kid out there has the same kind of amazing possibilities that Malia and Sasha have. And that promise I've kept.

So I still believe in you. I hope you still believe in me. And if you do, I'm absolutely positive we're going to win this election.

Thank you, everybody. God bless you. God bless America.

NOTE: The President spoke at 4:40 p.m. at the Rubin Museum of Art. In his remarks, he referred to musician and actor Ricky Martin; philanthropists Donald and Shelley Rubin; former Kansas State Rep. Rajeev K. Goyle; Sen. John S. McCain III, in his capacity as the 2008 Republican Presidential nominee; and Republican Presidential candidate former Gov. W. Mitt Romney of Massachusetts.

Remarks at an Obama Victory Fund 2012 Fundraiser in New York City
May 14, 2012

Thank you. Well, first of all, let me thank Tony and Amie for hosting us here today. Describing what it's like to have people move furniture out of six of your rooms—[*laughter*]—and I've been assured that it will all be put back where it was. [*Laughter*]

I want to thank all of you for being here. And frankly, because this is a nice, intimate setting, I'm not going to spend a lot of time talking at the top; I want to spend most of the

time answering your questions, taking your comments, having a conversation.

I tell you though, I couldn't make the argument too much better than Tony just made it. When I ran in 2008, it was based on the premise that America was built on the idea that anybody can make it if they try, that everybody gets a fair shot, everybody does their fair share, everybody plays by the same rules. And that idea had been slipping away for too long. So you'd seen a decade of sluggish job growth, incomes and wages had flatlined even as the cost of health care and college were going up. And the question was, how do we restore that sense of balance?

Now, this is all before we had a sense that we were going to be experiencing the worst financial crisis and the worst economic crisis in our lifetimes. And over the last 3½ years, obviously, we have had extraordinary challenges, challenges unlike any that we've seen. And there are a lot of folks still hurting out there: a lot of people who are still looking for work or underemployed, a lot of folks whose homes are still underwater, a lot of people who are fearful or anxious about the future.

But we've made progress. The good news is, is that over the last 2 years, we've created more than 4 million jobs, a million jobs in the last 6 months—close to the last 6 months alone. We have been able to restore the greatness of the U.S. auto industry at a time when a lot of folks thought it would liquidate. We've doubled clean energy production. We've been able to start seeing manufacturing come back to our shores in a way that a lot of people hadn't anticipated. The financial system, although it is still healing, is in obviously much better shape than it was back in 2007, 2008.

So we've made some progress. Now, the reason I'm running is we haven't made enough yet. We still have a long way to go. And this election is going to present as stark a choice in terms of visions for the future as any election that we've seen in a very long time. I believe that the free market is the greatest wealth generator ever devised by man, and it's at the heart, at the core, of who we are. I think risk takers and innovators should be rewarded. I think all of us benefit from the freedom of free enterprise.

But if you look at our history, what we also realize is that what makes our markets work and what allows us then to go out and pursue our individual dreams is that there are some things we've done in concert. There are some things that we've done as a common enterprise: making sure that our schools are teaching our kids the skills that they need to compete in a new economy; making certain that we're investing in science and research so that the next medical breakthrough or the next great business idea takes root right here in the United States; making sure we're investing in roads and bridges and airports and broadband lines and wireless networks that allow—that provide a platform for businesses and individuals to succeed; and making sure that we've got basic rules of the road in place so that the markets function in a transparent, clear way so that small investors have confidence if they invest on Wall Street they're not going to get bilked by somebody who has more information than them; that we make sure that our financial system is stable and that we're not going to tip over into a situation where, because of somebody's miscalculation or sometimes just because of panic, suddenly, the whole system is at risk; making sure that we have a basic safety net so that seniors who have worked all their lives can count on Social Security and Medicare; that the most vulnerable among us are cared for through programs like Medicaid; and making sure that something like health care is not the luxury of a few, but is something that if people are playing by the rules and working hard, they can count on, and they don't have to worry about losing their home because their child gets sick.

And in this campaign, what's going to be tested is whether that view which says, yes, we believe in individual initiative and we believe in risk-taking and we believe in markets and entrepreneurship, but we also believe in doing some things together, because all of us prosper from that, whether that's a better idea. Or the better idea is just, everybody is on their own, we slash taxes more for those of us who have been incredibly fortunate and blessed by this system, slowly those rungs on the ladder to upward mobility start to fray; people are left to fend for themselves. There is a theory that that somehow is going to unleash the kind of growth that we imagine for this country. And my argument is, is that we tried it and it doesn't work. It's not good for the markets. It's not good for business. It's not good for consumers. It's not good for our kids. It's not good for our future.

And that's ultimately what this election is going to be about. When you cut through all the other stuff—there's going to be a lot of noise and a lot of day-to-day skirmishes and arguing—but ultimately, it's going to come down to, whose vision do you believe? And I think we've got the facts and the evidence on our side. And the fact that you're all here today tells me that you're interested in that same kind of vision, one in which our kids succeed, but you know what, other people's kids succeed too. Because I think that will be a better America and a better world for our kids as well.

This is going to be a tough election. This is going to be a close election precisely because there are folks out there who are still hurting. But I'm pretty confident that if we work hard, if we stay true to that vision, that it's the one that the American people believe in as well.

So I'm grateful for your help. I'm looking forward to your questions. And I hope you are ready to get to work. All right, thank you.

NOTE: The President spoke at 5:56 p.m. at the residence of Amie and Hamilton E. "Tony" James. The transcript was released by the Office of the Press Secretary on May 15. Audio was not available for verification of the content of these remarks.

Remarks at the National Peace Officers Memorial Service
May 15, 2012

Please have a seat. Thank you so much. Thank you, Chuck, for that very kind introduction. Chuck is a proud police officer, he's the proud parent of a police officer, and he has dedicated his life to law enforcement and their families. So I want to thank him for his extraordinary service.

I want to recognize the entire Fraternal Order of Police and its leadership, including Jim Pasco, for all your work on behalf of those who wear the badge. I'd like to recognize FOP Auxiliary President Linda Hennie, all the members of the FOP Auxiliary, Members of Congress including Speaker Boehner, Congressman Hoyer, and Senator Leahy, as well as members of my administration. And most of all, I want to acknowledge and thank the families of those who have fallen.

As Scripture tells us, "Blessed are the peacemakers, for they shall be called sons of God." Blessed are the peacemakers, for they shall be called sons of God.

Our country's law enforcement officers use force when they have to. They are well armed, and they are well trained. But they never forget that theirs is a mission of peace. Their job is to keep the peace, to allow all of us to enjoy peace in our neighborhoods and for our families. And today, with heavy hearts, we honor

those who gave their lives in the service of that mission. Their families are in our thoughts and prayers, as we remember the quiet courage of the men and women we have lost.

These are officers like Detective John Falcone, of Poughkeepsie, New York. In February, Detective Falcone responded to a "shot fired" call on Main Street. And when he arrived on the scene, he saw a man holding a gun with one hand and a small child with the other.

In a situation like that, every instinct pushes us towards self-preservation. But when the suspect fled, still holding the child, Detective Falcone didn't think twice. He took off in pursuit, and tragically, in the struggle that followed, he was shot and killed. He is survived by his parents.

But there's another survivor as well: a 3-year-old child who might not be alive today had it not been for the sacrifice of a hero who gave his life for another.

This willingness to risk everything for a complete stranger is extraordinary. And yet, among our Nation's law enforcement officers, it is also commonplace. Last summer, the North Platte River was running high near Douglas, Wyoming. When a teenage girl got caught in the current, Deputy Bryan Gross, of the Converse County Sheriff's Office, jumped in after her.

The girl was eventually pulled from the water, but Deputy Gross was swept away. And he is survived by his wife Amy. Today we remember a man who swore to protect his neighbors and who kept that promise no matter what the cost.

I suspect that at that moment, Deputy Gross wasn't trying to be a hero, he was just doing his job. You can find that bravery, the courage to do your duty, day in and day out, in so many officers across our country.

One of those officers was Deputy Sheriff Suzanne Hopper, from Clark County, Ohio. Deputy Hopper was known as the go-to person in her department, no task was too large or too small.

And on New Year's Day 2011, Deputy Hopper arrived at a crime scene and began a preliminary investigation, just as she had done many times during her 12 years of service. But as she was photographing evidence, a man opened the door of his trailer and fired at her with his shotgun, killing her. And today we remember not just a fine officer, but a wife, a mother, and a stepmother.

Like all those we honor today, Deputy Hopper is also survived by the fellow officers who she meant so much to and who meant so much to her. Last week, her childhood friend, Sergeant Kris Shultz, posted her flag at a memorial in Ohio. He made a promise in her memory. He said, "To honor her, we will keep going and continue to do what we've done, no matter how hard it is at times."

We will keep going. There is no pledge that better honors the memory of those we have lost. And there are no memories—there are no words that better capture the unbreakable spirit of those who wear the badge.

Because even in the face of tragedy, I know that so many of you will return home and continue to do what you have always done. Some of you will kiss your husbands or wives good-bye each morning and send them out the door not knowing what might happen that day. Some of you are children and parents, sisters and brothers, whose pride is mixed with worry.

And of course, there are the officers themselves. Every American who wears the badge knows the burdens that come with it: the long hours and the stress, the knowledge that just about any moment could be a matter of life or death. You carry these burdens so the rest of us don't have to.

And this shared sense of purpose brings you together, and it brings you to our Nation's Capital today. You come from different States and different backgrounds and different walks of life, but I know that you come here as a community: one family, united by a quiet strength and a willingness to sacrifice on behalf of others.

The rest of us can never fully understand what you go through, but please know that we hold you in our hearts, not just today, but always. We are forever in your debt. And it is on behalf of all of us—the entire American people—that I offer my thoughts, my prayers, and my thanks.

May God shine a light upon the fallen and comfort the mourning. May He protect the peacemakers who protect us every day. And may He bless, now and forever, the United States of America.

NOTE: The President spoke at 11:25 a.m. at the U.S. Capitol. In his remarks, he referred to K. Charles Canterbury, Jr., national president, and James O. Pasco, Jr., executive director, Fraternal Order of Police; Kenneth C. Canterbury II, son of Mr. Canterbury; and Margaret Falcone and John M. Falcone, Sr., parents of Detective John M. Falcone, Jr. The related proclamation of May 14 is listed in Appendix D at the end of this volume.

Remarks Honoring the 2011 Major League Soccer Champion L.A. Galaxy
May 15, 2012

Thank you. Everybody, please have a seat. Have a seat. Well, welcome to the White House, everybody. And congratulations to the L.A. Galaxy on your third MLS Cup, number three.

Before we start, I want to acknowledge an L.A. native and my outstanding Secretary of Labor—I don't know how her game is, but she's a fan—Hilda Solis is here. We've got some proud members of the California delegation of the House of Representatives who are here. We're thrilled to have them.

I'm not going to flatter myself by assuming these cameras are for me. [*Laughter*] I want to thank the Galaxy for letting me share in the spotlight. The truth is, in America, most professional soccer players have the luxury of being able to walk around without being recognized, but not these guys. This is the Miami Heat of soccer. And together, they—[*laughter*]—together they represent one of the most talented lineups that MLS has ever seen.

You've got Robbie Keane, alltime leading scorer of the Irish national team. Cousin of mine. [*Laughter*] Robbie arrived halfway through last season, scored his first goal in the first 21 minutes of his first game. His teammates were so happy to have him that they filled his locker with what they called the pleasures of Ireland: Guinness, Baileys, and Irish Spring. [*Laughter*] Hopefully, Robbie has broadened their horizons a little bit since then.

We also have a young up-and-comer on the team, a guy named David Beckham. [*Laughter*] I have to say I gave David a hard time. I said half his teammates could be his kids. [*Laughter*] We're getting old, David, although you're holding up better than me.

Last year, at the age of 36, David had his best year in MLS, leading the team with 15 assists. He did it despite fracturing his spine halfway through the season, injuring his hamstring the week before the championship game. He is tough. In fact, it is a rare man who can be that tough on the field and also have his own line of underwear. [*Laughter*] David Beckham is that man. [*Laughter*]

And then, there's the captain, Landon Donovan, who has done more for American soccer than just about anybody. Landon's eye for the net, his will to win are legendary, and once again, he stepped up when his teammates needed him most.

After going undefeated at home last season, the Galaxy was struggling in the cold and rainy championship match. But then, in the 72d minute, David headed the ball to Robbie, who made the perfect pass to Landon, who chipped in the game winner. And that set off an all-night celebration in L.A., although my understanding is that David had to get up for carpool duty at 8 a.m.—[*laughter*]—so his day was ending a little early.

So the big names came through in the clutch, but they didn't do it alone. For a group with so much firepower, this team shone on defense, recording 17 shutouts. They were led by two local guys, Omar Gonzalez—give it up—[*applause*]—and A.J. DeLaGarza, who won a national championship at Maryland. Now they've got another title to their résumés.

And of course, a lot of credit goes to Coach Bruce Arena. He took this team from worst to first in just 4 years. And I want to take this opportunity to apologize to Bruce. When I called to congratulate him on winning the Cup, the team was in Indonesia; it was in the middle of the night. Thank you for taking my call and acting like you actually wanted to talk to me. [*Laughter*]

So everyone who's a part of this club—the staff, the players, the fans back in L.A.—together, you pulled off one of the toughest feats in team sports: You lived up to the hype. You combined star power, hard work; it paid off. And I also want to thank you for doing a little Q&A with some of the younger players after we're done. As a soccer dad, I know you've inspired a lot of kids. And today you're giving them an experience that they will never forget.

So again, give a big round of applause to the L.A. Galaxy. Congratulations. Best of luck this season.

NOTE: The President spoke at 2:12 p.m. in the East Room at the White House. In his remarks, he referred to Robbie Keane, forward, David Beckham and Landon Donovan, midfielders, and Omar Gonzalez and A.J. DeLaGarza, defenders, L.A. Galaxy.

Statement on the Reauthorization of the Export-Import Bank of the United States
May 15, 2012

I'm pleased that Members of Congress from both parties have come together to reauthorize the Export-Import Bank. This important step will help American businesses create jobs here at home and sell their products around the world, all at no cost to taxpayers.

Last year marked the highest level of financing in the Bank's 77-year history, as they supported thousands of U.S. companies, hundreds of thousands of jobs, and brought us closer to the goal I set of doubling our Nation's exports by the end of 2014. Over the last several months, I've met with business leaders here in Washington, visited workers at companies like Boeing, and urged Congress to reauthorize the Bank to keep building on this progress. And I'm glad to see it get done.

Now Congress needs to keep going. Last week, I proposed several commonsense ideas that will help small businesses, reward companies that bring jobs back to America, invest in clean energy and veterans, and help responsible homeowners save money on their mortgages. Congress should continue to do the right thing by acting on proposals we know will grow our economy and create jobs. In the meantime, I look forward to signing this bill into law.

Remarks During a Discussion With Small-Business Owners
May 16, 2012

Well, listen, what I just want to say to the reporters who are here: You've got three small businesses who are outstanding examples of American entrepreneurship, whether it's food services, retail, construction. All across the country, you're seeing examples of folks who have confidence in the economy and have confidence in America, and it's their ingenuity and their hard work that's allowed them to be successful.

But organizations like the SBA have also made a difference, because sometimes private financing isn't willing to take a chance on a couple of young guys who have an idea about starting a great hoagie shop. Sometimes, it may be that a smaller business like a construction business, where it's relatively capital intensive, is going to have difficulty competing with some of the larger companies in terms of buying the equipment that they need.

And so actions by Congress and good execution by the Small Business Administration can make a big difference in helping these folks. See, it's not going to do it for them, it's not going to make up for bad service or a bad product, but when you've got a great service or a great product and people are willing to work really hard, then action by Government and the SBA can help give them a hand up and get them started.

And this is the reason why we think it's so important for Congress to act right now. The economy is recovering, but we've still got a long way to go. Too many folks are still out of work. We've got some headwinds: the situation in Europe and still a difficult housing market.

And so we want to sustain momentum. And one of the ways that we can sustain momentum is for Congress to take some actions right now—even though it's election season, even though there's gridlock, even though there's partisanship—take some actions right now that would really make a difference. And we've put together a handy to-do list; it's very short. I've been talking about it over the last couple of weeks.

One of the items on that to-do list would be to provide tax breaks for companies like these that are hiring new employees or raising the wages and salaries of their existing employees. Either way, what that does is it gives them an incentive as their expanding to say: Maybe we hire an extra 2 people; maybe we hire an extra 3 people; maybe we hire an extra 10 people.

And they will have additional resources to continue to grow and to continue to expand. It's something that in the past has been an idea that garnered support from Democrats and Republicans. There's no reason why we shouldn't act on that right now, the same way that we should be allowing all families to refinance, because if they've got an extra $3,000 in their pocket, then they can buy more hoagies or go shop for some outstanding organic foods.

And it's the same reason why all the other items on the to-do list could really make a difference. For example, some of these small businesses may be interested in hiring a veteran, and we've already done a lot of work on veterans hiring. A lot of the items on the to-do list is a veterans job corps that could potentially put some veterans who are coming back from Iraq and Afghanistan to work rebuilding America.

So my message to Congress—and I'm going to have a chance to see the congressional leadership when I get back to the White House; I'm going to offer them some hoagies while they're there—is let's go ahead and act to help build and sustain momentum for our economy. There will be more than enough time for us to campaign and politick, but let's make sure that we don't lose steam at a time when a lot of folks like these are feeling pretty optimistic and are ready to go.

All right. Thank you, everybody.

NOTE: The President spoke at 10:44 a.m. at Taylor Gourmet delicatessen. In his remarks, he referred to Casey Patten and David Mazza, owners, Taylor Gourmet. Audio was not available for verification of the content of these remarks.

Remarks on Presenting Posthumously the Medal of Honor to Specialist Leslie H. Sabo, Jr.
May 16, 2012

The President. Please be seated. Thank you, General Rutherford. Good afternoon, everyone. We gather today to present the Medal of Honor for valor above and beyond the call of duty. In so doing we celebrate the soldier, the life that produced such gallantry, Specialist Leslie H. Sabo, Jr.

Today is also a solemn reminder that when an American does not come home from war, it is our military families and veterans who bear that sacrifice for a lifetime. They are spouses, like Rose Mary, who all these years since Vietnam still displays in her home her husband's medals and decorations. They are siblings, like Leslie's big brother George, who carries the childhood memories of his little brother tagging along at his side. And they are our veterans, like the members of Bravo Company, who still speak of their brother Les with reverence and with love.

Rose, George, Bravo Company, more than a hundred family and friends, Michelle and I are honored to welcome you to the White House.

The Medal of Honor is the highest military decoration that America can bestow. It reflects the gratitude of the entire Nation. So we're joined by Members of Congress and leaders from across our Armed Forces, including Secretary of Defense Leon Panetta; Vice Chairman of the Joint Chiefs Sandy Winnefeld; from the Army, Secretary John McHugh and Chief of Staff General Ray Odierno; and from the Marine Corps, the Commandant, General Jim Amos.

We're honored to be joined by Vietnam veterans, including recipients of the Medal of Honor. And we're joined by those who have carried on Les's legacy in our time, in Iraq and Afghanistan, members of the 101st Airborne Division, the legendary Screaming Eagles.

This gathering of soldiers, past and present, could not be more timely. As a nation, we've ended the war in Iraq. We are moving towards an end to the war in Afghanistan. After a decade of war, our troops are coming home. And this month, we'll begin to mark the 50th anniversary of the Vietnam war, a time when, to our shame, our veterans did not always receive the respect and the thanks they deserved, a mistake that must never be repeated. And that's where I want to begin today, because the story of this Medal of Honor reminds us of our sacred obligations to all who serve.

It was 1999, around Memorial Day, and a Vietnam vet from the 101st was at the National Archives. He was doing research for an article. And there, among the stacks, an archivist brought him a box. And he took off the lid. And inside, he found a file, marked with the name "Leslie H. Sabo, Jr." And there it was, a proposed citation for the Medal of Honor. And so this Vietnam veteran set out to find answers. Who was Leslie Sabo? What did he do? And why did he never receive that medal? Today, four decades after Leslie's sacrifice, we can set the record straight.

I just spent some time with Rose and George and the Sabo family. Last week marked 42 years since Les gave his life. This soldier, this family, has a uniquely American story. Les was actually born in Europe, after World War II, to a family of Hungarian refugees. And as the Iron Curtain descended, they boarded a boat for America and arrived at Ellis Island, past the Statue of Liberty. They settled in the steel town of Ellwood City, Pennsylvania. Les's father worked hard, pulled his family into the middle class. And when Les was a teenager, the family went to the county courthouse together, raised their hands and became proud American citizens.

They say that Les was one of the nicest guys you'd ever want to meet. He loved a good joke. He loved to bowl. He could have given me some tips. [*Laughter*] Rose says he was pretty good looking too. That's what I hear.

He'd do anything for anybody. And when George went to college, Les looked after their mom. When George went to night school, Les helped care for his three young sons. When Les fell in love with Rose—who couldn't wait to start a life together—he slipped the ring on her finger, right there in his car, while stopped at a red light. [*Laughter*] And as he headed out for Vietnam, he stopped at a shop and ordered some flowers for his mom, for Mother's Day, and for Rose, for her birthday.

For Les and Bravo Company, those early months of 1970 were a near constant battle, pushing through jungles and rice paddies in their heavy packs, enduring incredible heat and humidity, the monsoon rains that never seemed to stop, an enemy that could come out of nowhere and then vanish just as fast. For his bravery in battle, Les earned the respect of his comrades. And for his family, he wrote home every chance he could.

When American forces were sent into Cambodia, Bravo Company helped lead the way. They were moving up a jungle trail. They entered a clearing. And that's when it happened—an ambush. Some 50 American soldiers were nearly surrounded by some 100 North Vietnamese fighters. Said Les's comrades, "The enemy was everywhere"—in bunkers, behind trees, up in the trees, shooting down. And they opened up on them.

And Les was in the rear, and he could have stayed there. But those fighters were unloading on his brothers. So Les charged forward and took several of those fighters out. The enemy moved to outflank them. And Les attacked and drove them back. Ammo was running low. Les ran across a clearing to grab more. An enemy grenade landed near a wounded American. Les picked it up and he threw it back. And as that grenade exploded, he shielded that soldier with his own body.

Throughout history, those who have known the horror of war, and the love behind all great sacrifice, have tried to put those emotions into words. After the First World War, one soldier wrote this: "They are more to me than life, these voices, they are more than motherliness and more than fear; they are the strongest, most comforting thing there is anywhere: they are the voices of my comrades."

Those were the voices Leslie Sabo heard that day: his comrades, pinned down, at risk of being overrun. And so, despite his wounds, despite the danger, Leslie did something extraordinary. He began to crawl straight toward an enemy bunker, its machine guns blazing. Those who were there said the enemy zeroed in with everything they had. But Les kept crawling, kept pulling himself along, closer to that bunker, even as the bullets hit the ground all around him.

And then, he grabbed a grenade and he pulled the pin. It's said he held that grenade and didn't throw it until the last possible moment, knowing it would take his own life, but knowing he could silence that bunker. And he did. He saved his comrades who meant more to him than life.

Leslie Sabo left behind a wife who adored him, a brother who loved him, parents who cherished him, and family and friends who admired him. But they never knew. For decades, they never knew their Les had died a hero. The fog of war and paperwork that seemed to get lost in the shuffle meant this story was almost lost to history.

And so today we thank that Vietnam vet who found Les's files in the Archives and who was determined to right this wrong—that's Tony Mabb, who joins us here today. Where's Tony? Tony, thank you.

We salute Les's buddy, George Koziol, who, wounded in his hospital bed, first drafted the citation we'll hear today and who spent the last years of his life fighting to get Les the recognition that he deserved.

And most of all, we salute the men who were there in that clearing in the jungle. More than two dozen were wounded. Along with Les, seven other soldiers gave their lives that day. And those who came home took on one last mission, and that was to make sure America would honor their fallen brothers. They had no idea how hard it would be or how long it would take.

Instead of being celebrated, our Vietnam veterans were often shunned. They were called many things, when there was only one thing that they deserved to be called, and that was American patriots. In 2 weeks, on Memorial Day, Michelle and I will join our Vietnam veterans and their families at the wall to mark the 50th anniversary of their service. It will be another chance for America to say to our Vietnam veterans what should have been said when you first came home: You did your job; you served

with honor; you made us proud. And here today, as I think Les would have wanted it, I'd ask the members of Bravo Company to stand and accept the gratitude of our Nation.

So yes, this Medal of Honor is bestowed on a single soldier for his singular courage. But it speaks to the service of an entire generation and to the sacrifice of so many military families. Because, you see, there is one final chapter to this story.

You'll recall that as he shipped out to Vietnam, Les stopped at that flower shop. Well, the day he gave his life was Mother's Day. And on that day the flowers he had ordered arrived for his mom. And the day he was laid to rest was the day before Rose's birthday. And she received the bouquet he had sent her, a dozen red roses. That's the kind of guy—the soldier, the American—that we celebrate today.

Les's mother and father did not live to see this day. But in his story we see the shining values that keep our military strong and keep America great. We see the patriotism of families who give our Nation a piece of their heart: their husbands and wives, their sons and their daughters. And we see the devotion of citizens who put on the uniform, who kiss their families goodbye, who are willing to lay down their lives so that we can live ours in peace and in freedom.

No words will ever be truly worthy of their service. And no honor can ever fully repay their sacrifice. But on days such as this we can pay tribute. We can express our gratitude. And we can thank God that there are patriots and families such as these. So, on behalf of the American people, please join me in welcoming Rose for the reading of the citation.

[At this point, Maj. Gary Marlowe, USAF, Air Force Aide to the President, read the citation, and the President presented the medal. Following the presentation, Brig. Gen. Donald L. Rutherford, USA, Army Chief of Chaplains, said a prayer.]

The President. I want to thank everybody for their attendance. Please give another round of applause to the Sabo family. I hope that

627

everybody enjoys the reception. I hear the food is pretty good around here. [*Laughter*]

God bless you. God bless our troops. God bless the United States of America.

NOTE: The President spoke at 3:26 p.m. in the East Room at the White House. In his remarks, he referred to Rose Mary Sabo-Brown, widow of Spc. Sabo.

Message to the Congress on Blocking Property of Persons Threatening the Peace, Security, or Stability of Yemen
May 16, 2012

To the Congress of the United States:

Pursuant to the International Emergency Economic Powers Act (50 U.S.C. 1701 *et seq.*) (IEEPA), I hereby report that I have issued an Executive Order (the "order") declaring a national emergency with respect to the unusual and extraordinary threat to the national security and foreign policy of the United States posed by the actions and policies of certain members of the Government of Yemen and others to threaten Yemen's peace, security, and stability.

The order does not target the entire country of Yemen or its government, but rather targets those who threaten the peace, security, or stability of Yemen, including by obstructing the implementation of the agreement of November 23, 2011, between the Government of Yemen and those in opposition to it, which provides for a peaceful transition of power that meets the legitimate demands and aspirations of the Yemeni people for change, or by obstructing the political process in Yemen. The order provides criteria for the blocking of property and interests in property of persons determined by the Secretary of the Treasury, in consultation with the Secretary of State, to:

- have engaged in acts that directly or indirectly threaten the peace, security, or stability of Yemen, such as acts that obstruct the implementation of the agreement of November 23, 2011, between the Government of Yemen and those in opposition to it, which provides for a peaceful transition of power in Yemen, or that obstruct the political process in Yemen;

- be a political or military leader of an entity that has engaged in the acts described above;

- have materially assisted, sponsored, or provided financial, material, or technological support for, or goods or services to or in support of, the acts described above or any person whose property and interests in property are blocked pursuant to the order; or

- be owned or controlled by, or to have acted or purported to act for or on behalf of, directly or indirectly, any person whose property and interests in property are blocked pursuant to the order.

The designation criteria will be applied in accordance with applicable Federal law including, where appropriate, the First Amendment to the United States Constitution.

I have delegated to the Secretary of the Treasury, in consultation with the Secretary of State, the authority to take such actions, including the promulgation of rules and regulations, and to employ all powers granted to the President by IEEPA as may be necessary to carry out the purposes of the order. All agencies of the United States Government are directed to take all appropriate measures within their authority to carry out the provisions of the order.

I am enclosing a copy of the Executive Order I have issued.

BARACK OBAMA

The White House,
May 16, 2012.

NOTE: The Executive order is listed in Appendix D at the end of this volume.

Statement on the Death of Donna Summer
May 17, 2012

Michelle and I were saddened to hear about the passing of Donna Summer. A five-time Grammy Award winner, Donna truly was the Queen of Disco. Her voice was unforgettable, and the music industry has lost a legend far too soon. Our thoughts and prayers go out to Donna's family and her dedicated fans.

Statement on the Nomination of Derek J. Mitchell To Be the United States Ambassador to Burma
May 17, 2012

Today marks the beginning of a new chapter in the relationship between the United States and Burma. Since I announced a new U.S. opening to Burma in November, President Thein Sein, Aung San Suu Kyi, and the people of Burma have made significant progress along the path to democracy. The United States has pledged to respond to positive developments in Burma and to clearly demonstrate America's commitment to the future of an extraordinary country, a courageous people, and universal values. That is what we are doing.

Today I am nominating our first U.S. Ambassador to Burma in 22 years, Derek Mitchell, whose work has been instrumental in bringing about this new phase in our bilateral relationship. We also are announcing that the United States will ease its bans on the exportation of financial services and new investment in Burma. Opening up greater economic engagement between our two countries is critical to supporting reformers in Government and civil society, facilitating broad-based economic development, and bringing Burma out of isolation and into the international community.

Of course, there is far more to be done. The United States remains concerned about Burma's closed political system, its treatment of minorities and detention of political prisoners, and its relationship with North Korea. We will work to establish a framework for responsible investment from the United States that encourages transparency and oversight and helps ensure that those who abuse human rights, engage in corruption, interfere with the peace process, or obstruct the reform process do not benefit from increased engagement with the United States. We will also continue to press for those who commit serious violations of human rights to be held accountable. We are also maintaining our current authorities to help ensure further reform and to retain the ability to reinstate selected sanctions if there is backsliding.

Americans for decades have stood with the Burmese people in their struggle to realize the full promise of their extraordinary country. In recent months, we have been inspired by the economic and political reforms that have taken place, Secretary Clinton's historic trip to Naypyidaw and Rangoon, the parliamentary elections, and the sight of Aung San Suu Kyi being sworn into office after years of struggle. As an iron fist has unclenched in Burma, we have extended our hand and are entering a new phase in our engagement on behalf of a more democratic and prosperous future for the Burmese people.

NOTE: The statement referred to Member of Parliament and National League for Democracy Leader Aung San Suu Kyi of Burma.

Message to the Congress on Continuation of the National Emergency With Respect to Burma
May 17, 2012

To the Congress of the United States:

Section 202(d) of the National Emergencies Act (50 U.S.C. 1622(d)) provides for the automatic termination of a national emergency unless, within 90 days prior to the anniversary date of its declaration, the President publishes in the *Federal Register* and transmits to the Congress a notice stating that the emergency is to continue in effect beyond the anniversary date. In accordance with this provision, I have sent to the *Federal Register* for publication the enclosed notice stating that the national emergency with respect to Burma that was declared on May 20, 1997, is to continue in effect beyond May 20, 2012.

The Burmese government has made progress in a number of areas including releasing hundreds of political prisoners, pursuing cease-fire talks with several armed ethnic groups, and pursuing a substantive dialogue with Burma's leading pro-democracy opposition party. The United States is committed to supporting Burma's reform effort, but the situation in Burma continues to pose an unusual and extraordinary threat to the national security and foreign policy of the United States. Burma has made important strides, but the political opening is nascent, and we continue to have concerns, including remaining political prisoners, ongoing conflict, and serious human rights abuses in ethnic areas. For this reason, I have determined that it is necessary to continue the national emergency with respect to Burma and to maintain in force the sanctions that respond to this threat.

BARACK OBAMA

The White House,
May 17, 2012.

NOTE: The notice is listed in Appendix D at the end of this volume.

Message to the Senate Transmitting the Chile-United States Taxation Convention
May 17, 2012

To the Senate of the United States:

I transmit herewith, for the advice and consent of the Senate to their ratification, the Convention between the Government of the United States of America and the Government of the Republic of Chile for the Avoidance of Double Taxation and the Prevention of Fiscal Evasion with Respect to Taxes on Income and Capital, signed in Washington on February 4, 2010, with a Protocol signed the same day, as corrected by exchanges of notes effected February 25, 2011, and February 10 and 21, 2012, and a related agreement effected by exchange of notes (the "related Agreement") on February 4, 2010. I also transmit for the information of the Senate the report of the Department of State, which includes an Overview of the proposed Convention, the Protocol, and related Agreement.

The proposed Convention, Protocol, and related Agreement (together "proposed Treaty") would be the first bilateral income tax treaty between the United States and Chile. The proposed Treaty contains comprehensive provisions designed to address "treaty shopping," which is the inappropriate use of a tax treaty by residents of a third country, and provides for a robust exchange of information between the tax authorities in the two countries to facilitate the administration of each country's tax laws.

I recommend that the Senate give early and favorable consideration to the proposed Treaty and give its advice and consent to the ratification thereof.

BARACK OBAMA

The White House,
May 17, 2012.

Message to the Senate Transmitting the Protocol Amending the Convention on Mutual Administrative Assistance in Tax Matters
May 17, 2012

To the Senate of the United States:

I transmit herewith, for the advice and consent of the Senate to its ratification, the Protocol Amending the Convention on Mutual Administrative Assistance in Tax Matters, done at Paris on May 27, 2010 (the "proposed Protocol"), which was signed by the United States on May 27, 2010. The existing Convention on Mutual Administrative Assistance in Tax Matters, done at Strasbourg on January 25, 1988, entered into force for the United States on January 4, 1995 (the "existing Convention"). I also transmit, for the information of the Senate, the report of the Department of State, which includes an Overview of the proposed Protocol.

The proposed Protocol amends the existing Convention in order to bring it into conformity with current international standards on exchange of information, as reflected in the Organization for Economic Co-operation and Development's (OECD) Model Tax Convention on Income and Capital and the current U.S. Model Income Tax Convention. Furthermore, it updates the existing Convention's rules regarding the confidentiality and permitted uses of exchanged tax information, and opens the existing Convention to adherence by countries other than OECD and Council of Europe members. The Protocol entered into force on January 6, 2011, following ratification by five parties to the existing Convention.

I recommend that the Senate give early and favorable consideration to the proposed Protocol and give its advice and consent to its ratification.

BARACK OBAMA

The White House,
May 17, 2012.

Message to the Senate Transmitting the Convention on the Law Applicable to Certain Rights in Respect of Securities Held With an Intermediary
May 17, 2012

To the Senate of the United States:

With a view to receiving the advice and consent of the Senate to ratification, I transmit herewith the Convention on the Law Applicable to Certain Rights in Respect of Securities Held with an Intermediary (the "Convention"), done at The Hague on July 5, 2006, and signed by the United States on that same day. The report of the Secretary of State, which includes an Overview of the proposed Convention, is enclosed for the information of the Senate.

The United States supported the development of the Convention, which provides uniform rules for determining the law applicable to certain rights in commercial transactions involving investment securities held through intermediaries (such as brokers, banks, and other financial institutions). The Convention incorporates modern commercial finance methods already market-tested in the United States through the Uniform Commercial Code. It would ensure that countries that become party to this Convention would also apply those methods. The Convention, once in force, would improve the functioning of investment securities markets, reduce uncertainty in cross-border commerce, and reduce national and cross-border systemic risk.

The Department of the Treasury, the U.S. Securities and Exchange Commission, the Commodities Futures Trading Commission, and the New York Federal Reserve Bank support ratification by the United States of this Convention, as do key private sector associations. I recommend, therefore, that the Senate give early and favorable consideration to the Convention and give its advice and consent to its ratification.

BARACK OBAMA

The White House,
May 17, 2012.

Message to the Senate Transmitting the Convention on the Rights of Persons with Disabilities
May 17, 2012

To the Senate of the United States:

I transmit herewith, for advice and consent of the Senate to its ratification, the Convention on the Rights of Persons with Disabilities, adopted by the United Nations General Assembly on December 13, 2006, and signed by the United States of America on June 30, 2009 (the "Convention"). I also transmit, for the information of the Senate, the report of the Secretary of State with respect to the Convention.

Anchored in the principles of equality of opportunity, nondiscrimination, respect for dignity and individual autonomy, and inclusion of persons with disabilities, the Convention seeks to promote, protect, and ensure the full and equal enjoyment of all human rights by persons with disabilities. While Americans with disabilities already enjoy these rights at home, U.S. citizens and other individuals with disabilities frequently face barriers when they travel, work, serve, study, and reside in other countries. The rights of Americans with disabilities should not end at our Nation's shores. Ratification of the Disabilities Convention by the United States would position the United States to occupy the global leadership role to which our domestic record already attests. We would thus seek to use the Convention as a tool through which to enhance the rights of Americans with disabilities, including our veterans. Becoming a State Party to the Convention and mobilizing greater international compliance could also level the playing field for American businesses, who already must comply with U.S. disability laws, as well as those whose products and services might find new markets in countries whose disability standards move closer to those of the United States.

Protection of the rights of persons with disabilities has historically been grounded in bipartisan support in the United States, and the principles anchoring the Convention find clear expression in our own domestic law. As described more fully in the accompanying report, the strong guarantees of nondiscrimination and equality of access and opportunity for persons with disabilities in existing U.S. law are consistent with and sufficient to implement the requirements of the Convention as it would be ratified by the United States.

I recommend that the Senate give prompt and favorable consideration to this Convention and give its advice and consent to its ratification, subject to the reservations, understandings, and declaration set forth in the accompanying report.

BARACK OBAMA

The White House,
May 17, 2012.

Remarks at the Symposium on Global Agriculture and Food Security
May 18, 2012

Please have a seat. Thank you. Well, good morning, everybody. Thank you, Catherine Bertini and Dan Glickman and everyone at the Chicago Council. We were originally going to convene, along with the G–8, in Chicago. But since we're not doing this in my hometown, I wanted to bring a little bit of Chicago to Washington. [*Laughter*] It is wonderful to see all of you. It is great to see quite a few young people here as well. And I want to acknowledge a good friend. We were just talking backstage; he was my inspiration for singing at the Apollo. [*Laughter*] Bono is here, and it is good to see him.

Now, this weekend at the G–8, we'll be represented by many of the world's largest economies. We face urgent challenges: creating jobs, addressing the situation in the euro zone, sustaining the global economic recovery. But even as we deal with these issues, I felt it was also important, also critical to focus on the urgent challenge that confronts some 1 billion men, women, and children around the world: the injustice of chronic hunger, the need for long-term food security.

So tomorrow at the G–8, we're going to devote a special session to this challenge. We're launching a major new partnership to reduce hunger and lift tens of millions of people from poverty. And we'll be joined by leaders from across Africa, including the first three nations to undertake this effort and who join us here today. I want to acknowledge them: Prime Minister Meles of Ethiopia, President Mills of Ghana, and President Kikwete of Tanzania. Welcome.

I also want to acknowledge President Yayi of Benin, chair of the African Union, which has shown great leadership in this cause. And two of our leaders in this effort: USAID Administrator—every time I meet him, I realize that I was an underachiever in my thirties—[*laughter*]—Dr. Raj Shah is here; and the CEO of the Millennium Challenge Corporation, Daniel Yohannes.

Now, this partnership is possible because so many leaders in Africa and around the world have made food security a priority. And that's why, shortly after I took office, I called for the international community to do its part. And at the G–8 meeting 3 years ago in L'Aquila, in Italy, that's exactly what we did, mobilizing more than $22 billion for a global food security initiative.

After decades in which agriculture and nutrition didn't always get the attention they deserved, we put the fight against global hunger where it should be, which is at the forefront of global development. And this reflected the new approach to development that I called for when I visited Ghana, hosted by President Mills, and that I unveiled at the last summit on the Millennium Development Goals.

It's rooted in our conviction that true development involves not only delivering aid, but also promoting economic growth: broad-based, inclusive growth that actually helps nations develop and lift people out of poverty. The whole purpose of development is to create the conditions where assistance is no longer needed, where people have the dignity and the pride of being self-sufficient.

You see our new approach in our promotion of trade and investment, of building on the outstanding work of the African Growth and Opportunity Act. You see it in the global partnership to promote open government, which empowers citizens and helps to fuel development, creates the framework, the foundation for economic growth.

You see it in the international effort we're leading against corruption, including greater transparency so taxpayers receive every dollar they're due from the extraction of natural resources. You see it in our Global Health Initiative, which instead of just delivering medicine is also helping to build a stronger health system, delivering better care and saving lives.

And you see our new approach in our food security initiative, Feed the Future. Instead of simply handing out food, we've partnered with countries in pursuit of ambitious goals: better nutrition to prevent the stunting and the death of millions of children, and raising the incomes of millions of people, most of them farmers. And the good news is we're on track to meet our goals.

As President, I consider this a moral imperative. As the wealthiest nation on Earth, I believe the United States has a moral obligation to lead the fight against hunger and malnutrition and to partner with others.

So we take pride in the fact that, because of smart investments in nutrition and agriculture and safety nets, millions of people in Kenya and Ethiopia did not need emergency aid in the recent drought.

But when tens of thousands of children die from the agony of starvation, as in Somalia, that sends us a message we've still got a lot of work to do. It's unacceptable. It's an outrage. It's an affront to who we are.

So food security is a moral imperative, but it's also an economic imperative. History teaches us that one of the most effective ways to pull people and entire nations out of poverty is to invest in their agriculture. And as we've seen from Latin America to Africa to Asia, a growing middle class also means growing markets, including more customers for American exports that support American jobs. So we have a self-interest in this.

It's a moral imperative, it's an economic imperative, and it is a security imperative. For we've seen how spikes in food prices can plunge millions into poverty, which in turn can spark riots that cost lives and can lead to instability. And this danger will only grow if a surging global population isn't matched by surging food production. So reducing malnutrition and hunger around the world advances international peace and security, and that includes the national security of the United States.

Perhaps nowhere do we see this link more vividly than in Africa. On the one hand, we see Africa as an emerging market. African economies are some of the fastest growing in the world. We see a surge in foreign investment. We see a growing middle class, hundreds of millions of people connected by mobile phones, more young Africans online than ever before. There's hope and some optimism. And all of this has yielded impressive progress: for the first time ever, a decline in extreme poverty in Africa; an increase in crop yields; a dramatic drop in child deaths. That's the good news, and in part, it's due to some of the work of the people in this room.

On the other hand, we see an Africa that still faces huge hurdles: stark inequalities, most Africans still living on less than $2 a day, climate change that increases the risk of drought and famine. All of which perpetuates stubborn barriers in agriculture, in the agricultural sector, from the bottlenecks in infrastructure that prevent food from getting to market to the lack of credit, especially for small farmers, most of whom are women.

I've spoken before about relatives I have in Kenya who live in villages where hunger is sometimes a reality, despite the fact that African farmers can be some of the hardest working people on Earth. Most of the world's unused arable land is in Africa. Fifty years ago, Africa was an exporter of food. There is no reason why Africa should not be feeding itself and exporting food again. There is no reason for that.

So that's why we're here. In Africa and around the world, progress isn't coming fast enough. And economic growth can't just be for the lucky few at the top, it's got to be broad based, for everybody, and a good place to start is in the agricultural sector. So even as the world responds with food aid in a crisis—as we've done in the Horn of Africa—communities can't go back just to the way things were, vulnerable as before, waiting for the next crisis to happen. Development has to be sustainable, and as an international community, we have to do better.

So here at the G–8, we're going to build on the progress we've made so far. Today I can announce a new global effort we're calling a New Alliance for Food Security and Nutrition. And to get the job done, we're bringing together all the key players around a shared commitment. Let me describe it.

Governments, like those in Africa, that are committed to agricultural development and food security, they agree to take the lead, building on their own plans by making tough reforms and attracting investment. Donor countries, including G–8 members and international organizations, agree to more closely align our assistance with these country plans. And the private sector—from large multinationals to small African cooperatives, your NGOs, and civil society groups—agree to make concrete and continuing commitments as well, so that there is an alignment between all these sectors.

And I know some have asked, in a time of austerity, whether this New Alliance is just a way for governments to shift the burden onto somebody else. I want to be clear: The answer is no. As President, I can assure you that the United States will continue to meet our responsibilities, so that even in these tough fiscal times, we will continue to make historic investments in development. And by the way, we're going to be working to end hunger right here in the United States as well. That's—that will continue to be a priority.

We'll continue to be the leader in times of crisis, as we've done as the single largest donor of aid in the Horn of Africa and as we focus on the drought in the Sahel. That's why I've proposed to continue increasing funds for food security. So I want to be clear: The United States will remain a global leader in development in partnership with you. And we will continue to make available food—or emergency aid. That will not change. But what we do want to partner with you on is a strategy so that emergency aid becomes less and less relevant as a consequence of greater and greater sustainability within these own countries.

That's how development is supposed to work. That's what I mean by a new approach that challenges more nations, more organizations, more companies, more NGOs, challenges individuals—some of the young people who are here—to step up and play a role. Because government cannot and should not do this alone. This has to be all hands on deck.

And that's the essence of this New Alliance. So G–8 nations will pledge to honor the commitments we made in L'Aquila. We must do what we say, no empty promises. And at the same time, we'll deliver the assistance to launch this new effort. Moreover, we're committing to replenish the very successful Global Agricultural and Food Security Program. That's an important part of this overall effort.

Next, we're going to mobilize more private capital. Today I can announce that 45 companies—from major international corporations to African companies and cooperatives—have pledged to invest more than $3 billion to kick off this effort. And we're also going to fast-track new agricultural projects so they reach those in need even quicker.

Third, we're going to speed up the development and delivery of innovation—better seeds, better storage—that unleash huge leaps in food production. And we're going to tap that mobile phone revolution in Africa so that more data on agriculture—whether it's satellite imagery or weather forecasts or market prices—are put in the hands of farmers so they know where to plant and when to plant and when to sell.

Fourth, we're joining with the World Bank and other partners to better understand and manage the risks that come with changing food prices and a changing climate, because a change in prices or a single bad season should not plunge a family, a community, or a region into crisis.

And finally, we're going to keep focusing on nutrition, especially for young children, because we know the effects of poor nutrition can last a lifetime: It's harder to learn, it's harder to earn a living. When there is good nutrition, especially in those thousand days during pregnancy up to the child's second birthday, it means healthier lives for that child and that mother. And it's the smart thing to do because better nutrition means lower health care costs and it means less need for assistance later on.

That's what we're going to do. We're going to sustain the commitments we made 3 years ago, and we're going to speed things up. And we're starting with these three countries—

Tanzania, Ghana, and Ethiopia—precisely because of their record in improving agriculture and food security.

But this is just the beginning. In the coming months, we'll expand to six countries. We'll welcome other countries that are committed to making tough reforms. We'll welcome more companies that are willing to invest. We're going to hold ourselves accountable; we'll measure results. And we'll stay focused on clear goals: boosting farmers' incomes and, over the next decade, helping 50 million men, women, and children lift themselves out of poverty.

And I know there are going to be skeptics; there always are. We see heartbreaking images—fields turned to dust, babies with distended bellies—and we say it's hopeless and some places are condemned to perpetual poverty and hunger. But the people in this room disagree. I think most of the American people disagree. Anyone who claims great change is impossible, I say look at the extraordinary successes in development.

Look at the Green Revolution, which pulled hundreds of millions of people out of poverty. Look at microfinance, which has empowered so many rural poor, something my mother was involved with. Look at the huge expansion of education, especially for girls. Look at the progress we've made with vaccines—from smallpox to measles to pneumonia to diarrhea—which have saved the lives of hundreds of millions. And of course, look at the global fight against HIV/AIDS, which has brought us to the point where we can imagine what was

once unthinkable, and that is the real possibility of an AIDS-free generation.

Moreover, we are already making progress in this area right now. In Rwanda, farmers are selling more coffee and lifting their families out of poverty. In Haiti, some farmers have more than doubled their yields. In Bangladesh, in the poorest region, they've had their first-ever surplus of rice. There are millions of farmers and families whose lives are being transformed right now because of some of the strategies that we're talking about. And that includes a farmer in Ethiopia who got a new loan, increased production, hired more workers. And he said: "This salary changed my life. My kids can now go to school."

And we start getting the wheel turning in the direction of progress. We can do this. We're already doing it. We just need to bring it all together. We can unleash the change that reduces hunger and malnutrition. We can spark the kind of economic growth that lifts people and nations out of poverty. This is the new commitment that we're making. And I pledge to you today that this will remain a priority as long as I am United States President. Thank very much. God bless you. Thank you. God bless America.

NOTE: The President spoke at 10:08 a.m. at the Ronald Reagan Building and International Trade Center. In his remarks, he referred to Catherine A. Bertini and Daniel R. Glickman, cochairs, Symposium on Global Agriculture and Food Security; and musician and activist Paul D. "Bono" Hewson.

Remarks Following a Meeting With President François Hollande of France
May 18, 2012

President Obama. Well, it is my great pleasure to welcome President Hollande to the United States, to the Oval Office, and this evening to Camp David.

We all watched the remarkable election, and I offered him hardy congratulations and assured him that the friendship and alliance between the United States and France is not only of extraordinary importance to me,

but is deeply valued by the American people.

I was interested, when I was reading the President's biography, that he actually spent some time in the United States in his youth, studying American fast food. And although he decided to go into politics, we'll be interested in his opinions of cheeseburgers in Chicago. [*Laughter*]

I also warned him that now that he's President, he can no longer ride a scooter in Paris. I know because I've tried with the Secret Service, and they don't let me do it. [*Laughter*]

Obviously, we have had a lot to talk about. Much of our discussion centered on the situation in the euro zone. And President Hollande and I agree that this is an issue of extraordinary importance not only to the people of Europe, but also to the world economy. And we're looking forward to a fruitful discussion later this evening and tomorrow with the other G–8 leaders about how we can manage a responsible approach to fiscal consolidation that is coupled with a strong growth agenda.

We also discussed the situation in Afghanistan, in anticipation of our NATO meeting in Chicago on Saturday and Sunday. And we agreed that even as we transition out of a combat phase in Afghanistan that it's important that we sustain our commitment to helping Afghans build security and continue down the path of development.

We also identified the issues of Iran and Syria, the transition that's taking place in countries like Egypt and Tunisia as topics of critical importance. And we'll be devoting extensive time to those issues throughout the G–8 meeting.

France has shown great leadership on these issues. And as I indicated to President Hollande, when the United States and France, along with our other key allies, make up our minds to stand firm on the side of democracy and freedom and development, that enormous progress can be made.

So I'm grateful to President Hollande for being willing to come here so shortly after his election and the formation of his Government. He's gotten off to a very strong start. And I hope that he will find my administration and the American people strong partners in delivering prosperity not only to the people of France, but helping to provide peace and security throughout the world.

President Hollande. I wanted my first visit outside Europe to be to the United States in order to meet President Obama. The Camp David G–8 summit, as well as the meeting in

Chicago, was an outstanding opportunity, and I would like to thank President Obama for taking that opportunity to allow us to have a long conversation together.

This is the first time that we meet and not the last one. There will be many other opportunities for as long as possible. But it was important for me, on this occasion, to reaffirm the importance of the relationship between France and the United States.

Through history, we lived together some important events. We've had our differences, but we always manage to overcome them because of that strong link between our two countries. We also share some common causes: freedom, democracy. This is the reason why our history, our culture go back together a long way. And we managed to go through these differences when necessary and have these ties that mean that when France and the U.S. come together, we can make progress.

I discussed the main topics with President Obama, including the economy and the fact that growth must be a priority at the same time as we put in place some fiscal compacts to improve our finances. And on growth, President Obama was able to acknowledge shared views, so that we can progress.

I also insisted on the Greece—the euro zone situation and our concerns regarding Greece. And we share the same views: the fact that Greece must stay in the euro zone and that all of us must do what we can to that effect. There will be elections in Greece, and we wanted to send a message to that effect to the Greek people.

Our economies depend on one another. What happens in Europe has an impact on the U.S. and vice versa. So we are related, and the more coherent we are, the more efficient we can be.

We also discussed Afghanistan, and I reminded President Obama that I made a promise to the French people to the effect that our combat troops would be withdrawn from Afghanistan by the end of 2012. That being said, we will continue to support Afghanistan in a different way. Our support will take a different format, and all of that will be done in good understanding with our allies within ISAF. And so we will continue and comply with our commitment to that country and supply and support, as I said, in a different way.

We will discuss that further in Chicago. And I'm pretty sure that we will find the right means so that our allies can continue with their mission, and at the same time, I can comply to the promise I made to the French people.

[At this point, the interpreter mistranslated the remarks and was corrected by President Hollande.]

Interpreter. And regarding Iraq, again we found——

President Hollande. Iran.

Interpreter. Regarding Iran, we again noted that we share views and that we could start negotiations, but that being said, with the required firmness that Iran doesn't get the nuclear capability—military capability.

[President Hollande continued his remarks.]

President Hollande. Regarding Syria and Arab Spring countries, we talked about the Deau-ville Partnership. And here again, I said that we would comply with our commitments.

What was important to say today is that, as to our responsibilities, France and the U.S. are countries that have an impact on the destiny of the world, but we are great in friendship, cohesion, and partnership. France is an independent country and cares about its independence, but in all friendship with the United States of America. So it is with that friendship and with that independence that we can be both the most efficient when it comes to dealing with the current challenges.

And I would like to thank President Obama for the knowledge he has of my life before I took office. I will say nothing against cheeseburgers, of course. And as to my own vehicle, the one I used to have until I took office, I hope that I will not have to use it in a while. *[Laughter]*

President Obama. I just want to remember that cheeseburgers go very well with french fries. *[Laughter]*

NOTE: The President spoke at 12:35 p.m. in the Oval Office at the White House. President Hollande spoke in French, and his remarks were translated by an interpreter.

Message to the Congress on Continuation of the National Emergency With Respect to the Stabilization of Iraq
May 18, 2012

To the Congress of the United States:

Section 202(d) of the National Emergencies Act (50 U.S.C. 1622(d)) provides for the automatic termination of a national emergency unless, within 90 days prior to the anniversary date of its declaration, the President publishes in the *Federal Register* and transmits to the Congress a notice stating that the emergency is to continue in effect beyond the anniversary date. In accordance with this provision, I have sent the enclosed notice to the *Federal Register* for publication continuing the national emergency with respect to the stabilization of Iraq. This notice states that the national emergency with respect to the stabilization of Iraq

declared in Executive Order 13303 of May 22, 2003, as modified in scope and relied upon for additional steps taken in Executive Order 13315 of August 28, 2003, Executive Order 13350 of July 29, 2004, Executive Order 13364 of November 29, 2004, and Executive Order 13438 of July 17, 2007, is to continue in effect beyond May 22, 2012.

Obstacles to the orderly reconstruction of Iraq, the restoration and maintenance of peace and security in the country, and the development of political, administrative, and economic institutions in Iraq continue to pose an unusual and extraordinary threat to the national security and foreign policy of the United States. Accordingly, I have determined that it is necessary to continue the national emergency with respect to this threat and maintain in force the measures taken to deal with that national emergency.

Recognizing positive developments in Iraq, my Administration will continue to evaluate Iraq's progress in resolving outstanding debts and claims arising from actions of the previous regime, so that I may determine whether to further continue the prohibitions contained in Executive Order 13303 of May 22, 2003, as amended by Executive Order 13364 of November 29, 2004, on any attachment, judgment, decree, lien, execution, garnishment, or other judicial process with respect to the Development Fund for Iraq, the accounts, assets, and property held by the Central Bank of Iraq, and Iraqi petroleum-related products, which are in addition to the sovereign immunity accorded Iraq under otherwise applicable law.

BARACK OBAMA

The White House,
May 18, 2012.

NOTE: The notice is listed in Appendix D at the end of this volume.

The President's Weekly Address
May 19, 2012

For the past 3½ years, we've been fighting our way back from an historic economic crisis, one caused by breathtaking irresponsibility on the part of some on Wall Street who treated our financial system like a casino. Not only did that behavior nearly destroy the financial system, it cost our economy millions of jobs, hurt middle class families, and left taxpayers holding the bag.

Since then, we've recovered taxpayer dollars that were used to stabilize troubled banks. And we've put in place Wall Street reform with smarter, tougher, commonsense rules that serve one primary purpose: to prevent a crisis like that from ever happening again. And yet, for the past 2 years, too many Republicans in Congress and an army of financial industry lobbyists actually have been waging an all-out battle to delay, defund, and dismantle Wall Street reform.

Recently, we've seen why we can't let that happen. We found out that a big mistake at one of our biggest banks resulted in a $2 billion loss. While that bank can handle a loss of that size, other banks may not have been able to. And without Wall Street reform, we could have found ourselves with the taxpayers once again on the hook for Wall Street's mistakes.

That's why it's so important that Members of Congress stand on the side of reform, not against it, because we can't afford to go back to an era of weak regulation and little oversight, where excessive risk-taking on Wall Street and a lack of basic oversight in Washington nearly destroyed our economy. We can't afford to go back to that brand of you're-on-your-own economics. Not after the American people have worked so hard to come back from this crisis.

We've got to keep moving forward. We've got to finish the job of implementing this reform and putting these rules in place.

These new rules say that if you're a big bank or financial institution, you now have to hold more cash on hand so that if you make a bad decision, you pay for it, not the taxpayers.

You have to write out a living will that details how you'll be winding down if you do fail. The new law takes away big bonuses and paydays from failed CEOs, while giving shareholders a say on executive salaries.

And for the first time in our Nation's history, we have in place a consumer watchdog whose sole job is to look out for working families by protecting them from deceptive and unfair practices.

So, unless you run a financial institution whose business model is built on cheating consumers or making risky bets that could damage the whole economy, you have nothing to fear from Wall Street reform. Yes, it discourages big banks and financial institutions from making risky bets with taxpayer-insured money. And it encourages them to do things that actually help the economy, like extending loans to entrepreneurs with good ideas, to middle class families who want to buy a home, to students who want to pursue a higher education.

That's what Wall Street reform is all about, making this economy stronger for you. And we're going to keep working to recover every job lost to the recession, to build an economy where hard work and responsibility are once again rewarded, to restore an America where everyone has a fair shot, everyone does their fair share, and everyone plays by the same rules.

I believe the free market is one of the greatest forces for progress in human history, that businesses are the engine of growth, that risk takers and innovators should be celebrated.

But I also believe that at its best, the free market has never been a license to take whatever you want, however you can get it. Alongside our entrepreneurial spirit and rugged individualism, America only prospers when we meet our obligations to one another and to future generations.

If you agree with me, let your Member of Congress know. Tell them to spend less time working to undermine rules that are there to protect the economy and spend more time actually working to strengthen the economy.

Thanks, and have a great weekend.

NOTE: The address was recorded at approximately 6:05 p.m. on May 16 in the Foyer at the White House for broadcast on May 19. The transcript was made available by the Office of the Press Secretary on May 18, but was embargoed for release until 6 a.m. on May 19.

Remarks Prior to a Working Session With Group of Eight Leaders at Camp David, Maryland
May 19, 2012

All right, everybody, listen up. First of all, I want to welcome all the leaders here. The press, you're welcome as long as you don't break anything. [*Laughter*]

This is, by the way, the largest gathering ever of international leaders at Camp David, and I'm glad that we could arrange for good weather. Last night we had a chance to discuss some core issues that affect our common security. And I want to say that we are unified when it comes to our approach with Iran. I think all of us agree that Iran has the right to peaceful nuclear power, but that its continuing violations of international rules and norms and its inability thus far to convince the world community that it is not pursuing the weaponization of nuclear power is something of grave concern to all of us.

We are hopeful about the discussions that will be taking [place]° in Baghdad, but all of us are firmly committed to continuing with the approach of sanctions and pressure in combination with diplomatic discussions. And our hope is, is that we can resolve this issue in a peaceful fashion that respects Iran's sovereignty and its rights in the international community, but also recognizes its responsibilities.

We had a discussion about Syria. And we all believe that a peaceful resolution and political transition in Syria is preferable. We are all deeply concerned about the violence that's taking place there and the loss of life. We are supportive of the Annan plan, but we agreed—and I expect this will be reflected in our communique—that the Annan plan has to be fully implemented and that a political process has to move forward in a more timely fashion to resolve that issue.

We also had a chance to discuss the situation in North Korea. All of us agree that North Korea is violating its international obligations and that there is a path for them to rejoin the inter-

---

° White House correction.

national community, but that path is not going to be—or that objective will not be achieved if they continue with the provocative actions that they have shown over the last several months.

And on a brighter note, we had the opportunity to discuss Burma, and all of us are hopeful that the political process and transition—transformation that is beginning to take place there takes root. Many of us have taken action to open up trade and investment with Burma for the first time in many years, and we have had discussions with the leadership there. Our hope is, is that this process will continue, and we're going to do everything that we can to encourage that process.

Finally, we had a brief discussion around the issue of women's empowerment, where we agreed that both when it comes to economic development and when it comes to peace and security issues, empowering women to have a seat at the table and get more engaged and more involved in these processes can be extraordinarily fruitful. And this is something that we will also be introducing during the G–20.

So I want to thank all the leaders, despite the fact that at least those coming from across the Atlantic ended up staying up, I guess, until 6 in the morning their time. The discussions were very fruitful. This morning we're going to be spending a lot of time on economic issues. Obviously, the euro zone will be one topic, and

all of us are absolutely committed to making sure that both growth and stability, and fiscal consolidation, are part of a overall package that all of us have to pursue in order to achieve the kind of prosperity for our citizens that we're looking for.

We'll also be talking about uncertainty in the energy markets and how we can help to resolve some of those issues. And we'll be spending some time talking about development in the Middle East, North Africa, and our capacity to sustain economic development in Afghanistan. Obviously, in Chicago, during the NATO meeting, we'll spend more time talking about security matters, but here we want to make sure that we recognize the need for Afghanistan to be able to sustain a development agenda moving forward as we begin to transition out of war.

So again, I want to thank all the leaders for being here. So far, this has been a frank and useful conversation, and it gives me great optimism about our ability to meet these challenges in the future.

All right. Thank you very much, everybody.

NOTE: The President spoke at 9:24 a.m. In his remarks, he referred to former Secretary-General Kofi A. Annan of the United Nations, in his capacity as Joint U.N.-Arab League Special Envoy to Syria.

Joint Statement by Group of Eight Leaders on the Global Economy
May 19, 2012

Our imperative is to promote growth and jobs.

The global economic recovery shows signs of promise, but significant headwinds persist.

Against this background, we commit to take all necessary steps to strengthen and reinvigorate our economies and combat financial stresses, recognizing that the right measures are not the same for each of us.

We welcome the ongoing discussion in Europe on how to generate growth, while maintaining a firm commitment to implement fiscal consolidation to be assessed on a structural ba-

sis. We agree on the importance of a strong and cohesive Eurozone for global stability and recovery, and we affirm our interest in Greece remaining in the Eurozone while respecting its commitments. We all have an interest in the success of specific measures to strengthen the resilience of the Eurozone and growth in Europe. We support Euro Area Leaders' resolve to address the strains in the Eurozone in a credible and timely manner and in a manner that fosters confidence, stability and growth.

We agree that all of our governments need to take actions to boost confidence and nurture recovery including reforms to raise productivity, growth and demand within a sustainable, credible and non-inflationary macroeconomic framework. We commit to fiscal responsibility and, in this context, we support sound and sustainable fiscal consolidation policies that take into account countries' evolving economic conditions and underpin confidence and economic recovery.

To raise productivity and growth potential in our economies, we support structural reforms, and investments in education and in modern infrastructure, as appropriate. Investment initiatives can be financed using a range of mechanisms, including leveraging the private sector. Sound financial measures, to which we are committed, should build stronger systems over time while not choking off near-term credit growth. We commit to promote investment to underpin demand, including support for small businesses and public-private partnerships.

Robust international trade, investment and market integration are key drivers of strong sustainable and balanced growth. We underscore the importance of open markets and a fair, strong, rules-based trading system. We will honor our commitment to refrain from protectionist measures, protect investments and pursue bilateral, plurilateral, and multilateral efforts, consistent with and supportive of the WTO framework, to reduce barriers to trade and investment and maintain open markets. We call on the broader international community to do likewise. Recognizing that unnecessary differences and overly burdensome regulatory standards serve as significant barriers to trade, we support efforts towards regulatory coherence and better alignment of standards to further promote trade and growth.

Given the importance of intellectual property rights (IPR) to stimulating job and economic growth, we affirm the significance of high standards for IPR protection and enforcement, including through international legal instruments and mutual assistance agreements, as well as through government procurement processes, private-sector voluntary codes of best practices, and enhanced customs cooperation, while promoting the free flow of information. To protect public health and consumer safety, we also commit to exchange information on rogue internet pharmacy sites in accordance with national law and share best practices on combating counterfeit medical products.

NOTE: An original was not available for verification of the content of this joint statement.

Joint Statement by Group of Eight Leaders on Global Oil Markets
May 19, 2012

There have been increasing disruptions in the supply of oil to the global market over the past several months, which pose a substantial risk to global economic growth. In response, major producers have increased their output while drawing prudently on excess capacity. Looking ahead to the likelihood of further disruptions in oil sales and the expected increased demand over the coming months, we are monitoring the situation closely and stand ready to call upon the International Energy Agency to take appropriate action to ensure that the market is fully and timely supplied.

NOTE: An original was not available for verification of the content of this joint statement.

Remarks at the Group of Eight Summit in Camp David, Maryland
May 19, 2012

Good afternoon, everybody. It has been a great pleasure to host the leaders of some of the world's largest economies here at Camp David. I think the surroundings gave us an opportunity to hold some intimate discussions and make some genuine progress.

For the past 3 years, our nations have worked together and with others first to rescue a global economy from freefall, then to wrestle it back to a path of recovery and growth. Our progress has been tested at times by shocks like the disaster in Japan, for example. Today, it's threatened once again by the serious situation in the euro zone.

As all the leaders here today agreed, growth and jobs must be our top priority. A stable, growing European economy is in everybody's best interests, including America's. Europe is our largest economic partner. Put simply, if a company is forced to cut back in Paris or Madrid, that might mean less business for manufacturers in Pittsburgh or Milwaukee. And that might mean a tougher time for families and communities that depend on that business.

And that's why, even as we've confronted our own economic challenges over the past few years, we've collaborated closely with our European allies and partners as they've confronted theirs. And today we discussed ways they can promote growth and job creation right now, while still carrying out reforms necessary to stabilize and strengthen their economies for the future.

We know it is possible in part based on our own experience here. In my earliest days in office, we took decisive steps to confront our own financial crisis, from making banks submit to stress tests to rebuilding their capital, and we put in place some of the strongest financial reforms since the Great Depression.

At the same time, we worked to get our own fiscal house in order in a responsible way. And through it all, even as we worked to stabilize the financial sector and bring down our deficits and debt over the longer term, we stayed focused on growing the economy and creating jobs in the immediate term.

Of course, we still have a lot of work to do. Too many of our people are still looking for jobs that pay the bills. Our deficits are still too high. But after shrinking by nearly 9 percent the quarter before I took office, America's economy has now grown for almost 3 consecutive years. After losing hundreds of thousands of jobs a month, our businesses have created more than 4 million jobs over the past 26 months. Exports have surged and manufacturers are investing in America again.

And this economic growth then gives us more room to take a balanced approach to reducing our deficit and debt, while preserving our investments in the drivers of growth and job creation over the long term: education, innovation, and infrastructure for the 21st century.

Europe's situation, of course, is more complicated. They've got a political and economic crisis facing Greece, slow growth and very high unemployment in several countries. And what's more, when they want to decide on a way to move forward, there are 17 countries in the euro zone that need to come to an agreement. We recognize that, and we respect that.

But the direction the debate has taken recently should give us confidence. Europe has taken significant steps to manage the crisis. Individual countries and the European Union as a whole have engaged in significant reforms that will increase the prospects of long-term growth. And there's now an emerging consensus that more must be done to promote growth and job creation right now in the context of these fiscal and structural reforms. That consensus for progress was strengthened here at Camp David.

Today we agreed that we must take steps to boost confidence and to promote growth and demand while getting our fiscal houses in order. We agreed upon the importance of a strong and cohesive euro zone and affirmed our interest in Greece staying in the euro zone while respecting its commitments. Of course, we also recognized the painful sacrifices that the Greek people are making at this difficult time, and I know that my European colleagues will carry forward these discussions as they prepare for meetings next week.

The leaders here understand the stakes. They know the magnitude of the choices they have to make and the enormous political, economic, and social costs if they don't. In addition to our G–8 meeting, it was—I was able to talk to them individually over the last 2 days, and I reaffirmed that Europe has the capacity to meet its challenges, and America is not only confident in their ability to meet their challenges, but we are supportive of their efforts.

This morning I updated you on the progress we made last night in our discussion of security issues. And today, following our discussion of the economy, we also made progress on a range of other important challenges. We discussed the importance of pursuing an all-of-the-above strategy for energy security in a safe and sustainable way. Leaders agreed to join a new U.S.-led coalition to address climate change, in part by reducing short-lived pollutants. And in the face of increasing disruptions in the supply of oil, we agreed that we must closely monitor global energy markets. Together, we stand ready to call upon the International Energy Agency to take action to ensure that the market remains fully and timely supplied.

We also announced a new alliance on food security with African leaders and the private sector as part of an effort to lift 50 million people out of poverty over the next decade. We discussed our support for a sustainable Afghan

economy as we wind down the war, and we reaffirmed our support for the democratic transitions underway in the Middle East and North Africa.

So I'm very pleased that we were able to make some important progress here at Camp David, and we're going to keep at it. Tomorrow we begin our NATO summit in my hometown of Chicago, where we'll discuss our plans to responsibly end the war in Afghanistan. Next week, European leaders will gather to discuss their next steps on the euro zone. Next month, we'll all have the chance to continue this collaboration at the G–20 in Mexico. And I look forward to building on this progress in promoting economic recovery in the weeks and months to come.

Thank you very much, everybody. I hope you've enjoyed the great views and the great weather.

NOTE: The President spoke at 6:04 p.m. in the Aspen Lodge.

Remarks Following a Meeting With President Hamid Karzai of Afghanistan and an Exchange With Reporters in Chicago, Illinois
May 20, 2012

President Obama. It is a great pleasure to welcome President Karzai to my hometown of Chicago after he extended hospitality to me during my visit to Kabul recently. During that trip to Afghanistan, we were able to finalize the strategic partnership agreement that reflects a future in which two sovereign nations—the United States and Afghanistan—are operating as partners to the benefit of our countries' citizens, but also for the benefit of peace and security and stability in the region and around the world.

I want to thank President Karzai for his cooperation, and his delegation's hard work in helping us to achieve the strategic partnership agreement. And the NATO summit is going to be largely devoted to ratifying and reflecting the broad consensus that so many of our partners and ISAF members have agreed to; one in which we are working with the Afghans over

the next several years to achieve a complete transition to Afghan lead for Afghan security, one in which we continue to provide support for the Afghan National Security Forces that have made excellent progress over the last several years, and also painting a vision post-2014 in which we have ended our combat role, the Afghan war as we understand it is over, but our commitment to friendship and partnership with Afghanistan continues.

And so the strategic partnership agreement, this NATO summit, are all part and parcel of a shared vision that we have in which Afghanistan is able to transition from decades of war to a transformational decade of peace and stability and development. And so I just want to stress my appreciation for the hard work that President Karzai has done. I think he recognizes the enormous sacrifices that have been made by the American people and, most profoundly, by American troops, as well as the troops of our other coalition partners. We recognize the hardship that the Afghan people have been through during these many, many years of war. Both of us recognize that we still have a lot of work to do, and there will be great challenges ahead. The loss of life continues in Afghanistan; there will be hard days ahead. But we're confident that we are on the right track, and what this NATO summit reflects is that the world is behind the strategy that we've laid out.

Now it's our task to implement it effectively. And I believe that we can do so, in part because of the tremendous strength and resilience of the Afghan people. I think they desperately want peace and security and development. And so long as they're reflecting that resilience and that hope for a better future, they will have a friend in the United States of America.

So, President Karzai, welcome. I am confident this will be a productive NATO summit, and I'm looking forward to continuing to work to implement the plans that we've laid out.

President Karzai. Great. Thank you, Mr. President. We have had a good meeting today in which Afghanistan reaffirmed its commitment to the transition process and to the completion of it in 2013 and the completion of withdrawal of our partners in 2014, so that Afghanistan is no longer a burden on the shoulder of our friends in the international community, on the shoulders of the United States and our other allies.

Afghanistan, indeed, Mr. President, as you very rightly put it, is looking forward to an end to this war and a transformational decade in which Afghanistan will be working further for institution building and the development of sounder governance in the country and a better economy, where the Afghans will be taking steady steps towards self-reliance in all aspects of life, that Afghanistan will be collecting its own revenues.

But in the meantime, that the world community, in particular the United States and our allies in NATO and ISAF, will be with us to make sure that we take steady and strong steps and are back while you are making those steps towards 2024, when Afghanistan will be largely defending itself and providing for itself.

Mr. President, the partnership that we signed a few weeks ago in Kabul has turned a new page in our relations. And the new page is a page of two sovereign countries working together for the mutual interests: peace and security and in all other areas of concentration.

Mr. President, I'm bringing to you and to the people of the United States the gratitude of the Afghan people for the support that your taxpayers' money has provided Afghanistan over the past decade and for the difference that it has made to the well-being of the Afghan people, to our education and health and the building of the Afghan Government.

Mr. President, Afghanistan is fully aware of the task ahead and of what Afghanistan needs to do to reach the objectives that we all have of a stable, peaceful, and self-reliant Afghanistan.

In the meantime, until then, thank you for your support.

President Obama. Thank you, Mr. President. Thank you. Thank you so much.

International Assistance to Afghanistan

Q. Mr. President, will you get the financial support needed to hit that $4.1 billion? Are you confident about that?

President Obama. We'll have a press conference.

Q. Okay, thanks.

NOTE: The President spoke at 11:57 a.m. at McCormick Place convention center. A portion of these remarks could not be verified because the audio was incomplete.

Remarks Prior to a Meeting With Secretary General Anders Fogh Rasmussen of the North Atlantic Treaty Organization in Chicago
May 20, 2012

President Obama. Well, I just want to not only welcome Secretary General Rasmussen to my hometown of Chicago—my understanding is he's already enjoyed some of the sights, and we were hearing about him jogging along the lake, appreciating the outstanding views and the skyline—but more importantly, I want to thank him for his extraordinary leadership.

Secretary General Rasmussen arrived in this post during one of most challenging times that NATO has faced. He has guided us through some very rocky times, and I think the results of this NATO summit are reflective of his extraordinary leadership.

At this summit, we anticipate not only ratifying the plan for moving forward in Afghanistan—a transition process that will bring the war to an end at the end of 2014 and put Afghans in the lead for their own security—but we're also going to be talking about the progress that we've made in expanding NATO's defense capabilities, ensuring that every NATO member has a stake and is involved and integrated in our mutual defense efforts.

And we're going to have an opportunity to talk about the partnerships that NATO has been able to set up with like-minded countries around the world and find ways that we can deepen and engage those partners to help to promote security and peace around the world.

All this has happened because of Secretary General Rasmussen's leadership. I'm very proud of the work that he's done. I think it's going to be reflected in the success of this summit. And on behalf of the American people, we want to say thank you.

Secretary General Rasmussen. Thank you very much. Mr. President, I would like to thank you very much for your strong leadership, for your dedication to our alliance. America has always been a source of strength and inspiration in NATO, and I'm very pleased that we can hold our 25th summit in your home city, Chicago.

Chicago has always been a place where Europeans and North Americans have come together. And now, we have come together to reaffirm the unbreakable bond between us.

I look very much forward to a successful summit, and I would like to take this opportunity to thank all those who have worked so hard to make this summit a success. And I would like to thank the people of Chicago for their great hospitality.

President Obama. All right. Thank you so much, everybody.

NOTE: The President spoke at 12:52 p.m. at McCormick Place convention center.

Remarks at the North Atlantic Council Meeting in Chicago
May 20, 2012

Thank you very much, Mr. Secretary General Anders, I want to take this opportunity on behalf of all of us to thank you for your outstanding leadership over these past 3 years. And I want to begin by welcoming each and every one of you to my hometown. I hope everybody has enjoyed themselves. I understand some took a architectural boat tour, some have run along the lakefront. Chicago is a great place, and we look forward to having you back again.

As Anders mentioned, so many people here in Chicago trace their roots back to NATO countries. So it's especially fitting that Chicago is the first American city outside of Washington, DC, ever to host a NATO summit. Given the moment of silence we just observed, I also want to take the opportunity to salute Admiral Stavidris, General Abrial, General Allen, and all of our men and women who are serving in uniform on our behalf, and especially those who are serving today in Afghanistan.

For over 65 years, our alliance has been the bedrock of our common security, our freedom, and our prosperity. And though the times may have changed, the fundamental reason for our alliance has not. Our nations are stronger and more prosperous when we stand together. In good times and in bad, our alliance has endured; in fact, it has thrived, because we share an unbreakable commitment to the freedom and security of our citizens.

We've seen this from the cold war to the Balkans, from Afghanistan to Libya. And that's the spirit that we need to sustain here in Chicago, and with an alliance that is focused squarely on the future.

When we last met in Lisbon, we agreed to a bold plan of action to revitalize the alliance and ensure that we have the tools that are required to confront a changing and uncertain strategic landscape. Here, at this session, we can reaffirm our article 5 commitment to our collective defense and to investing in the defense capabilities and new technologies that meet our collective security needs.

In these difficult economic times, we can work together and pull our resources. NATO is a force multiplier, and the initiatives we will endorse today will allow each of our nations to accomplish what none of us could achieve alone. We can all be proud that in Lisbon we committed, and now in Chicago we are delivering.

Over the next 2 days, we'll meet—first as allies and then with President Karzai and our international partners—to chart the next phase of the transition in Afghanistan. Just as we've sacrificed together for our common security, we will stand together, united, in our determination to complete this mission.

And finally, I look forward to our meeting with NATO's neighbors and our partners around the world who have been so critical to NATO operations, as in Afghanistan and Libya. It will be another reminder that NATO is truly a hub of a network of global security partners. There is nothing else like it on Earth.

So again, thank you, Mr. Secretary General, for your outstanding leadership. Thank you to all my fellow leaders and friends who are here. Welcome to Chicago. I'm confident that the next 2 days are going to help to sustain and strengthen the strongest and most successful alliance that the world has ever known.

NOTE: The President spoke at 2:15 p.m. at McCormick Place convention center. In his remarks, he referred to Secretary General Anders Fogh Rasmussen of the North Atlantic Treaty Organization; Adm. James G. Stavidris, USN, Supreme Allied Commander, Europe; Gen. Stephane Abrial, French Air Force, NATO Supreme Allied Commander Transformation; Gen. John R. Allen, USMC, commander, NATO International Security Assistance Force, Afghanistan; and President Hamid Karzai of Afghanistan.

Remarks at the International Security Assistance Force Meeting on Afghanistan in Chicago
May 21, 2012

Well, good morning, everyone. And for those who are joining us for the first time, welcome to Chicago. I was just hearing from a few folks who are not NATO members that they had fun on the town last night. Hopefully, no stories in the press. [*Laughter*]

We come together as 50 nations—NATO allies and partners—that make up the International Security Assistance Force in Afghani-

stan. I want to welcome the presence of President Karzai, as well as officials from central Asia and Russia, nations that have an important perspective and that continue to provide critical transit for ISAF supplies.

The presence of so many leaders and nations illustrates once again that this is a truly international mission, and that's because the region and the world have a profound interest in an Afghanistan that is stable, that is secure, and that is not a source of attacks on other nations. And today, as always, our thoughts are with our brave forces who are serving in this vital mission.

Two years ago, in Lisbon, our nations agreed on a framework for transition in Afghanistan that would allow us to responsibly wind down the war. We agreed that this transition to Afghan lead for security would begin in 2011 and that it would conclude in 2014. At the same time, we said that we would seek a long-term partnership with Afghanistan and the Afghan people.

Over the past 2 years, we've made important progress. Our forces broke the Taliban's momentum, more Afghans are reclaiming their communities, Afghan security forces have grown stronger, and the transition that we agreed to in Lisbon is well underway.

This past week, we saw more progress. We very much welcome President Karzai's announcement of the third group of areas to begin transition. This means that 75 percent of the Afghan people live in areas where Afghan forces will be moving into the lead.

Today we'll decide the next phase of the transition, the next milestone. We'll set a goal for Afghan forces to take the lead for combat operations across the country in 2013—next year—so that ISAF can move to a supporting role. This will be another step toward Afghans taking full lead for their security as agreed to by 2014, when the ISAF combat mission will end.

Today is also an opportunity to ensure our hard-worn—hard-won progress is preserved. The strategic partnership agreement that President Karzai and I signed in Kabul ensures that as Afghans stand up, they will not stand alone. Today we can agree on NATO's long-term relationship with Afghanistan beyond 2014, including our support of Afghan security forces.

So we have a lot of work to do. Again, I want to thank all of my fellow leaders and our partners for being here. Our nations and the world have a vital interest in the success of this mission. And I am confident, because of the leadership represented here as well as the leadership of our outstanding armed forces, that we can advance that goal today and responsibly bring this war to an end.

NOTE: The President spoke at 9:24 a.m. at McCormick Place convention center. In his remarks, he referred to President Hamid Karzai of Afghanistan.

The President's News Conference in Chicago
May 21, 2012

The President. Good afternoon, everybody. Let me begin by saying thank you to my great friend Rahm Emanuel, the mayor of the city of Chicago, and to all my neighbors and friends, the people of the city of Chicago, for their extraordinary hospitality and for everything that they've done to make this summit such a success. I could not be prouder to welcome people from around the world to my hometown.

This was a big undertaking, some 60 world leaders, not to mention folks who were exercising their freedom of speech and assembly, the very freedoms that our alliance are dedicated to defending. And so it was a lot to carry for the people of Chicago, but this is a city of big shoulders. Rahm, his team, Chicagoans proved that this world-class city knows how to put on a world-class event.

And partly, this was a perfect city for this summit because it reflected the bonds between so many of our countries. For generations, Chicago has welcomed immigrants from around the world, including an awful lot of our NATO allies. And I'd just add that I have lost track of the number of world leaders and their delegations who came up to me over the last day and a half and remarked on what an extraordinarily beautiful city Chicago is. And I could not agree more.

I am especially pleased that I had a chance to show them Soldier Field. I regret that I was not able to take in one of the Crosstown Classics, although I will note that my teams did okay. Now—White Sox fan in the back. [*Laughter*] Right on.

Now, as I said yesterday, NATO has been the bedrock of common security, freedom, and prosperity for nearly 65 years. It hasn't just endured; it has thrived because our nations are stronger when we stand together. We saw that, of course, most recently in Libya, where NATO afforded capabilities that no one else in the world could match.

As President, one of my top foreign policy priorities has been to strengthen our alliances, including NATO, and that's exactly what we've done. Two years ago in Lisbon, we took action in several areas that are critical to the future of our alliance. And we pledged that in Chicago we would do more. Over the last 2 days, we have delivered.

First, we reached agreement on a series of steps to strengthen the alliance's defense capabilities over the next decade. In keeping with the strategic concept we agreed to in Lisbon and in order to fulfill our article 5 commitment to our collective security, we agreed to acquire a fleet of remotely piloted aircraft, drones, to strengthen intelligence, surveillance, and reconnaissance. We agreed to continue air patrols over our Baltic allies, which reflects our unwavering commitment to collective defense. We also agreed on a mix of conventional nuclear missile and missile defense forces that we need, and importantly, we agreed on how to pay for them, and that includes pooling our resources in these difficult economic times.

We're moving forward with missile defense and agreed that NATO is declaring an interim capability for the system. America's contribution to this effort will be a phased adaptive approach that we're pursuing on European missile defense. And I want to commend our allies who are stepping up and playing a leadership role in missile defense as well. Our defense radar in Turkey will be placed under NATO control. Spain, Romania, and Poland have agreed to host key U.S. assets. The Netherlands will be upgrading radars. And we look forward to contributions from other allies. Since this system is neither aimed at nor undermines Rus-

sia's strategic deterrent, I continue to believe that missile defense can be an area of cooperation with Russia.

Second, we're now unified behind a plan to responsibly wind down the war in Afghanistan, a plan that trains Afghan security forces, transitions to the Afghans, and builds a partnership that can endure after our combat mission in Afghanistan ends. Since last year, we've been transitioning parts of Afghanistan to the Afghan National Security Forces and that has enabled our troops to start coming home. Indeed, we're in the process of drawing down 33,000 U.S. troops by the end of this summer.

Here in Chicago, we reached agreement on the next milestone in that transition. At the ISAF meeting this morning, we agreed that Afghan forces will take the lead for combat operations next year, in mid-2013. At that time, ISAF forces will have shifted from combat to a support role in all parts of the country. And this will mark a major step toward the goal we agreed to in Lisbon, completing the transition to Afghan lead for security by the end of 2014 so that Afghans can take responsibility for their own country and so our troops can come home.

This will not mark the end of Afghanistan's challenges, obviously, or our partnership with that important country. But we are making substantial progress against our core objective of defeating Al Qaida and denying it safe haven, while helping the Afghans to stand on their own. And we leave Chicago with a clear roadmap. Our coalition is committed to this plan to bring our war in Afghanistan to a responsible end.

We also agreed on what NATO's relationship with Afghanistan will look like after 2014. NATO will continue to train, advise and assist, and support Afghan forces as they grow stronger. And while this summit has not been a pledging conference, it's been encouraging to see a number of countries making significant financial commitments to sustain Afghanistan's progress in the years ahead. Today the international community also expressed its strong support for efforts to bring peace and stability to South Asia, including Afghanistan's neighbors.

Finally, NATO agreed to deepen its cooperation with partners that have been critical to alliance operations, as in Afghanistan and Libya. Today's meeting was unprecedented. Our 28 allies, joined by 13 nations from around the world—Europe, the Middle East, North Africa, and Asia—each of these countries has contributed to NATO operations in different ways: military, political, financial. And each wants to see us do more together. To see the breadth of those countries represented in that room is to see how NATO has truly become a hub of global security.

So again, I want to thank all my fellow leaders. I think the bottom line is that we are leaving Chicago with a NATO alliance that is stronger, more capable, and more ready for the future. As a result, each of our nations—the United States included—is more secure, and we're in a stronger position to advance the security and prosperity and freedom that we seek around the world.

So with that, I'm going to take a couple of questions, and I'm going to start with Julie Pace of AP [Associated Press]. Where's Julie? There she is.

Pakistan

Q. Thank you, Mr. President. You've said that the U.S. can't deal with Afghanistan without also talking about Pakistan. And yet there has been little public discussion at this summit about Pakistan's role in ending the war. In your talks with President Zardari today, did you make any progress in reopening the supply lines? And if the larger tensions with Pakistan can't be resolved, does that put the NATO coalition's gains in Afghanistan at risk?

The President. Well, keep in mind my discussion with President Zardari was very brief, as we were walking into the summit, and I emphasized to him what we have emphasized publicly as well as privately. We think that Pakistan has to be part of the solution in Afghanistan; that it is in our national interest to see a Pakistan that is democratic, that is prosperous, and that is stable; that we share a common enemy in the extremists that are found not only in Afghanistan, but also within Pakistan; and that

we need to work through some of the tensions that have inevitably arisen after 10 years of our military presence in that region.

President Zardari shared with me his belief that these issues can get worked through. We didn't anticipate that the supply line issue was going to be resolved by this summit. We knew that before we arrived in Chicago, but we're actually making diligent progress on it.

And I think ultimately everybody in the alliance, all of ISAF, and most importantly, the people of Afghanistan and Pakistan understand that neither country is going to have the kind of security, stability, and prosperity that it needs unless they can resolve some of these outstanding issues and join in common purpose with the international community in making sure that these regions are not harboring extremists. So I don't want to paper over real challenges there. There is no doubt that there have been tensions between ISAF and Pakistan, the United States and Pakistan over the last several months. I think they are being worked through both military and diplomatic channels.

But ultimately, it is in our interest to see a successful, stable Pakistan, and it is in Pakistan's interest to work with us and the world community to ensure that they themselves are not consumed by extremism that is in their midst. And so we're going to keep on going at this. And I think every NATO member, every ISAF member is committed to that.

Hans Nichols [Bloomberg News]. Where is Hans?

2012 Presidential Election

Q. Yes, thank you, Mr. President. Yesterday your friend and ally Cory Booker said that an ad that you released, that your campaign released, was nauseating. And it alleged that Romney at Bain Capital was, quote, "responsible for job losses at a Kansas City steel mill." Is that your view, that Romney is personally responsible for those job losses? Will comments from Booker and your former auto czar Steve Rattner that have criticized some of these advertisements call on you to pull back a little bit? And generally, can you give us your sense—three part, Mr. President——

The President. [*Inaudible*]

Q. Could you give us your sense of just what private equity's role is in stemming job losses as they seek a return on investment for their investors? Thank you.

The President. Well, first of all, I think Cory Booker is an outstanding mayor. He is doing great work in Newark and obviously helping to turn that city around. And I think it's important to recognize that this issue is not a, quote, "distraction." This is part of the debate that we're going to be having in this election campaign about how do we create an economy where everybody from top to bottom, folks on Wall Street and folks on Main Street, have a shot at success, and if they're working hard and they're acting responsibly, that they're able to live out the American Dream.

Now, I think my view of private equity is that it is set up to maximize profits. And that's a healthy part of the free market. That's part of the role of a lot of businesspeople. That's not unique to private equity. And as I think my representatives have said repeatedly, and I will say today, I think there are folks who do good work in that area. And there are times where they identify the capacity for the economy to create new jobs or new industries, but understand that their priority is to maximize profits. And that's not always going to be good for communities or businesses or workers.

And the reason this is relevant to the campaign is because my opponent, Governor Romney, his main calling card for why he thinks he should be President is his business experience. He is not going out there touting his experience in Massachusetts. He is saying, I'm a business guy, and I know how to fix it. And this is his business.

And when you're President, as opposed to the head of a private equity form—firm, then your job is not simply to maximize profits. Your job is to figure out how everybody in the country has a fair shot. Your job is to think about those workers who get laid off and how are we paying for their retraining. Your job is to think about how those communities can start creat-

ing new clusters so that they can attract new businesses. Your job as President is to think about how do we set up a equitable tax system so that everybody is paying their fair share that allows us then to invest in science and technology and infrastructure, all of which are going to help us grow.

And so if your main argument for how to grow the economy is, I knew how to make a lot of money for investors, then you're missing what this job is about. It doesn't mean you weren't good at private equity, but that's not what my job is as President. My job is to take into account everybody, not just some. My job is to make sure that the country is growing, not just now, but 10 years from now and 20 years from now.

And so to repeat: This is not a distraction. This is what this campaign is going to be about—is, what is a strategy for us to move this country forward in a way where everybody can succeed? And that means I've got to think about those workers in that video just as much as I'm thinking about folks who have been much more successful.

Q. Just for—[*inaudible*]—is Romney personally responsible for those 750 job losses?

The President. What I would say is that Mr. Romney is responsible for the proposals he is putting forward for how he says he is going to fix the economy. And if the main basis for him suggesting he can do a better job is his track record as the head of a private equity firm, then both the upsides and the downsides are worth examining.

Hold on a second. Alister Bull [Reuters].

Greece/Global Economy

Q. Thank you, Mr. President. I'd like to take you back to not this summit, but the one you hosted at Camp David a couple of days ago and whether you feel that you can ensure—assure investors there are contingency plans in place to cope, if Greece leaves the euro, to prevent a Lehman-like shock to the U.S. and the global economy?

The President. We had an extensive discussion of the situation in the euro zone, and obviously, everybody is keenly interested in getting that issue resolved.

I'm not going to speculate on what happens if the Greek choose to exit because they've got an election and this is going to be an important debate inside of Greece. Everybody who was involved in the G–8 summit indicated their desire to see Greece stay in the euro zone in a way that's consistent with the commitments that it's already—that have already been made. And I think it's important for Greece, which is a democracy, to work through what their options are at a time of great difficulty.

I think we all understand, though, what's at stake. What happens in Greece has an impact here in the United States. Businesses are more hesitant to invest if they see a lot of uncertainty looming across the Atlantic because they're not sure whether that's going to mean a further global slowdown. And we're already seeing very slow growth rates and in fact contraction in a lot of countries in Europe. So we had an extensive discussion about how do we strengthen the European project, generally, in a way that does not harm world economic growth, but instead moves it forward.

And I've been clear, I think, in—not just this week, but over the last 2 years about what I think needs to be done. We've got to put in place firewalls that ensure that countries outside of Greece that are doing the right thing aren't harmed just because markets are skittish and nervous.

We've got to make sure that banks are recapitalized in Europe so that investors have confidence. And we've got to make sure that there is a growth strategy to go alongside the need for fiscal discipline, as well as a monetary policy that is promoting the capacity of countries—like a Spain or an Italy—that have put in place some very tough targets and some very tough policies to also offer their constituencies a prospect for the economy improving, job growth increasing, incomes expanding, even if it may take a little bit of time.

And the good news was, you saw a consensus across the board, from newly elected President Hollande to Chancellor Merkel, to other members of the European community, that that balanced approach is what's needed right now. They're going to be meeting this week to try to advance those discussions further. We've offered to be there for consultation to provide any technical assistance and work through some of these ideas in terms of how we can stabilize the markets there.

Ultimately, what I think is most important is that Europe recognizes this euro project involves more than just a currency. It means that there's got to be some more effective coordination on the fiscal and the monetary side and on the growth agenda. And I think that there was strong intent there to move in that direction. Of course, they've got 17 countries that have to agree to every step they take. So I think about my one Congress, then I start thinking about 17 congresses, and I start getting a little bit of a headache. It's going to be challenging for them.

The last point I'll make is, I do sense greater urgency now than perhaps existed 2 years ago or 2½ years ago. And keep in mind, just for folks here in the States, when we look backwards at our response in 2008 and 2009, there was some criticism because we had to make a bunch of tough political decisions.

In fact, there's still criticism about some of the decisions we made. But one of the things we were able to do was to act forcefully to solve a lot of these problems early, which is why credit markets that were locked up started loosening up again. That's why businesses started investing again. That's why we've seen job growth of over 4 million jobs over the last 2 years. That's why corporations are making money, and that's why we've seen strong economic growth for a long time.

And so acting forcefully, rather than in small, bite-sized pieces and increments, I think, ends up being a better approach, even though obviously we're still going through challenges ourselves. I mean, some of these issues are ones that built up over decades.

All right? Stephen Collinson [Agence France-Presse]. Where's Stephen?

Yemen

Q. Thank you, Mr. President. As you at this summit try to continue the work of stopping Afghanistan from reverting to its former role as a terrorist haven, terrorists today in Yemen massacred a hundred soldiers. Are you concerned that despite U.S. efforts, Yemen seems to be slipping further into anarchy? And what more can the U.S. do to slow that process?

The President. We are very concerned about Al Qaida activity and extremist activity in Yemen. A positive development has been a relatively peaceful political transition in Yemen, and we participated diplomatically along with Yemen's neighbors in helping to lead to a political transition, but the work is not yet done.

We have established a strong counterterrorism partnership with the Yemeni Government, but there's no doubt that in a country that is still poor, that is still unstable, it is attracting a lot of folks that previously might have been in the FATA before we started putting pressure on them there. And we're going to continue to work with the Yemeni Government to try to identify AQAP leadership and operations and try to thwart them. That's important for U.S. safety. It's also important for the stability of Yemen and for the region.

But I think one of the things that we've learned from the Afghanistan experience is for us to stay focused on the counterterrorism issue, to work with the Government, to not overextend ourselves, to operate smartly in dealing with these issues. And it's not unique to Yemen, by the way. I mean we've got similar problems in Somalia, what's happening now in Mali and the Sahel. And so this is part of the reason why not only is NATO important, but these partnerships that we're establishing is important, because there are going to be times where these partners have more effective intelligence operations, more diplomatic contacts, et cetera, in some of these parts of the world where the state is a little wobbly and you may see terrorists attempting to infiltrate or set up bases.

Yes, I'm going to call on Jake Tapper [ABC News] because, Jake, Jay Carney told me that you've been talking to some of our troops in Afghanistan. And since so much of the topic of this summit has been on Afghanistan, obviously, none of this would be working were it not for the extraordinary sacrifices that they're making, so——

U.S. Military Operations in Afghanistan

Q. Thanks, Mr. President. I appreciate it. I put out an invitation for some troops and their families that I know, and I'll just give you two or three of them. "Mr. President, if this handoff and withdrawal prove premature, what plans are in place for dealing with an Afghanistan that's fallen apart or is possibly again under Taliban rule?" And I'll just do one more. "Do you feel that the reporting you receive from the Pentagon fully represents what the on-ground commanders assess? Is there any disconnect between what leaders feel the public and President want to hear versus what is actually occurring on the ground?" These are from troops I've met who served in Nuristan Province.

The President. Let me take the second question first. I mean, I think that one of the things that I emphasize whenever I'm talking to John Allen or the Joint Chiefs or any of the officers who are in Afghanistan is, I can't afford a whitewash. I can't afford not getting the very best information in order to make good decisions. I should add, by the way, that the danger a lot of times is not that anybody is purposely trying to downplay challenges in Afghanistan. A lot of times, it's just the military culture is, we can get it done. And so their thinking is, how are we going to solve this problem? Not, boy, why is this such a disaster? That's part of the reason why we admire our military so much and we love our troops, because they've got that can-do spirit.

But I think that we have set up a structure that really tries to guard against that. Because even in my White House, for example, I've got former officers who have been in Afghanistan, who I will send out there as part of the national security team of the White House—not simply the Pentagon—to interact and to listen and to go in and talk to the captains and the majors

653

and the corporals and the privates to try to get a sense of what's going on.

And I think the reports we get are relatively accurate in the sense that there is real improvement. In those areas where we've had a significant presence, you can see the Taliban not having a foothold, that there is genuine improvement in the performance of Afghan National Security Forces.

But the Taliban is still a robust enemy. And the gains are still fragile, which leads me then to the second point that you've made in terms of a premature withdrawal. I don't think that there is ever going to be an optimal point where we say, this is all done, this is perfect, this is just the way we wanted it, and now we can wrap up all our equipment and go home. This is a process, and it's sometimes a messy process, just as it was in Iraq.

But think about it: We've been there now 10 years. We are now committing to a transition process that takes place next year, but the full transition to Afghan responsibility is almost 2 years away. And the Afghan security forces themselves will not ever be prepared if they don't start taking that responsibility.

And frankly, the large footprint that we have in Afghanistan over time can be counterproductive. We've been there 10 years. And I think no matter how much good we're doing and how outstanding our troops and our civilians and diplomats are doing on the ground, 10 years in a country that's very different, that's a strain not only on our folks, but also on that country, which at a point is going to be very sensitive about its own sovereignty.

So I think that the timetable that we've established is a sound one, it is a responsible one. Are there risks involved in it? Absolutely. Can I anticipate that over the next 2 years there are going to be some bad moments along with some good ones? Absolutely.

But I think it is the appropriate strategy whereby we can achieve a stable Afghanistan that won't be perfect; we can pull back our troops in a responsible way, and we can start rebuilding America and making some of the massive investments we've been making in Afghanistan here back home, putting people back

to work, retraining workers, rebuilding our schools, investing in science and technology, developing our business climate.

So—but there are going to be challenges. The one thing that I'm never doubtful about is just the amazing capacity of our troops and their morale. When I was in Bagram just a couple of weeks ago, the fact that you still have so much determination and stick-to-it-ness and professionalism, not just from our troops, but from all our coalition allies, all of ISAF, is a testament to them. It's extraordinary. And we are very proud of them.

All right, the—since I am in Chicago, even though my Press Secretary told me not to do this, I am going to call on a Chicagoan to ask a Chicago question.

Jay [Jay Levine, CBS 2].

North Atlantic Treaty Organization Summit in Chicago, Illinois

Q. Mr. President.

The President. Good to see you. How you been?

Q. Good to see you too, Mr. President, and good to see you in Chicago. Chicagoans look at you standing there with Chicago, Chicago, Chicago, on the wall behind you. There is an undeniable——

The President. [*Inaudible*]

Q. ——sense of pride. In your view, how did reality match up to fantasy in welcoming the world leaders to Chicago? And did the demonstrators in any way on the streets undermine your efforts, Mayor Emanuel's efforts, to project the image of Chicago you would have liked to have seen?

The President. I have to tell you, I think Chicago performed magnificently. Those of us who were in the summit had a great experience. If you talk to leaders from around the world, they love the city. Michelle took some of the spouses down to the South Side to see the Comer Center, where wonderful stuff is being done with early education. They saw the Art Institute.

I was just talking to David Cameron. I think he's sneaking off and doing a little sightseeing before he heads home. I encouraged everybody to shop. I want to boost the hometown economy. We gave each leader a "Bean"—a small model—for them to remember, as well as a football from Soldier Field. Many of them did not know what to do with it. [*Laughter*] So people had a wonderful time, and I think the Chicagoans that they interacted with couldn't have been more gracious and more hospitable. So I could not have been prouder.

Now, I think with respect to the protesters, as I said, this is part of what NATO defends, is free speech and the freedom of assembly. And frankly, to my Chicago press, outside of Chicago, folks really weren't all that stressed about the possibility of having some protesters here, because that's what—part of what America is about. And obviously, Rahm was stressed, but he performed wonderfully, and the Chicago police, Chicago's finest, did a great job under some significant pressure and a lot of scrutiny.

The only other thing I'll say about this is thank you to everybody who endured the traffic situation. Obviously, Chicago residents who had difficulties getting home or getting to work or what have you, that's—what can I tell you, that's part of the price of being a world city.

But this was a great showcase. And if it makes those folks feel any better, despite being 15 minutes away from my house, nobody would let me go home. I was thinking I would be able to sleep in my own bed tonight. They said I would cause even worse traffic. So I ended up staying in a hotel, which contributes to the Chicago economy. [*Laughter*]

Thank you, everybody.

NOTE: The President's news conference began at 3:26 p.m. at the South Building. In his remarks, the President referred to Republican Presidential candidate former Gov. W. Mitt Romney of Massachusetts; President François Hollande of France; Chancellor Angela Merkel of Germany; White House Press Secretary James F. "Jay" Carney; Gen. John R. Allen, USMC, commander, NATO International Security Assistance Force, Afghanistan; and Prime Minister David Cameron of the United Kingdom. He also referred to the Federally Administered Tribal Areas (FATA) of Pakistan; and Al Qaida in the Arabian Peninsula (AQAP).

Commencement Address at Joplin High School in Joplin, Missouri
May 21, 2012

Thank you, everybody. Please have a seat. A few people I want to acknowledge. First of all, you have an outstanding Governor in Jay Nixon, and we are proud of all the work that he's done. I want to acknowledge Senator Claire McCaskill, who is here; Representative Billy Long; your mayor, Melodee Colbert-Kean; somebody who doesn't get a lot of attention, but does amazing work all across the country, including here in Joplin, the head of FEMA, the Administrator, Craig Fugate, who spent an awful lot of time here helping to rebuild.

Superintendent Huff, Principal Sachetta, to the faculty, the parents, the family, friends, the people of Joplin, and most of all the class of 2012, congratulations on your graduation, and thank you for allowing me the honor of playing a small part in this special day.
a diploma in his hand. It took Lantz Hare, who

Now, the job of a commencement speaker primarily is to keep it short. Chloe, they've given me more than 2 minutes. [*Laughter*] But the other job is to inspire. But as I look out at this class and across this city, what's clear is that you're the source of inspiration today, to me, to this State, to this country, and to people all over the world.

Last year, the road that led you here took a turn that no one could have imagined. Just hours after the class of 2011 walked across this stage, the most powerful tornado in six decades tore a path of devastation through Joplin that was nearly a mile wide and 13 long. In just 32 minutes, it took thousands of homes and hundreds of businesses and 161 of your neighbors, friends, and family. It took a classmate, Will Norton, who had just left this auditorium with should have received his diploma next year.

And by now, I expect that most of you have probably relived those 32 minutes again and again: where you were; what you saw; when you knew for sure that it was over; the first contact, the first phone call you had with somebody you loved; the first day that you woke up in a world that would never be the same.

And yet the story of Joplin isn't just what happened that day. It's the story of what happened the next day and the day after that and all the days and weeks and months that followed. As your city manager, Mark Rohr, has said, the people here chose to define the tragedy "not by what happened to us, but by how we responded."

Class of 2012, that story is yours. It's part of you now. As others have mentioned, you've had to grow up quickly over the last year. You've learned at a younger age than most of us that we can't always predict what life has in store. No matter how we might try to avoid it, life surely can bring some heartache, and life involves struggles. And at some point, life will bring loss.

But here in Joplin, you've also learned that we have the power to grow from these experiences. We can define our lives not by what happens to us, but by how we respond. We can choose to carry on. We can choose to make a difference in the world. And in doing so, we can make true what's written in Scripture, that "tribulation produces perseverance; and perseverance, character; and character, hope."

Of all that's come from this tragedy, let this be the central lesson that guides us, let it be the lesson that sustains you through whatever challenges lie ahead.

As you begin the next stage in your journey, wherever you're going, whatever you're doing, it's safe to say you will encounter greed and selfishness and ignorance and cruelty and sometimes just bad luck. You'll meet people who try to build themselves up by tearing others down. You'll meet people who believe that looking after others is only for suckers.

But you're from Joplin, so you will remember, you will know, just how many people there are who see life differently, those who are guided by kindness and generosity and quiet service.

You'll remember that in a town of 50,000 people, nearly 50,000 more came in to help the weeks after the tornado, perfect strangers who've never met you and didn't ask for anything in return.

One of them was Mark Carr, who drove 600 miles from Rocky Ford, Colorado, with a couple of chainsaws and his three little children. One man traveled all the way from Japan, because he remembered that Americans were there for his country after last year's tsunami, and he wanted the chance, he said, "to pay it forward." There were AmeriCorps volunteers who have chosen to leave their homes and stay here in Joplin until the work is done.

And then there was the day that Mizzou's football team rolled into town with an 18-wheeler full of donated supplies. And of all places, they were assigned to help out on Kansas Avenue. [*Laughter*] I don't know who set that up. [*Laughter*] And while they hauled away washing machines and refrigerators from the debris, they met a woman named Carol Mann, who had just lost the house she lived in for 18 years. And Carol didn't have a lot. She works part-time at McDonald's. She struggles with seizures, and she told the players that she had even lost the change purse that held her lunch money. So one of them, one of the players, went back to the house, dug through the rubble, and returned with the purse with $5 inside.

And Carol's sister said: "So much of the news that you hear is so negative. But these boys renewed my faith that there are so many good people in the world."

That's what you'll remember, because you're from Joplin.

You will remember the half-million-dollar donation that came from Angelina Jolie and some up-and-coming actor named Brad Pitt. [*Laughter*] But you'll also remember the $360 that was delivered by a 9-year-old boy who organized his own car wash. You'll remember the school supplies donated by your neighboring towns, but maybe you'll also remember the brand new laptops that were sent from the

United Arab Emirates, a tiny country on the other side of the world.

When it came time for your prom, makeup artist Melissa Blayton organized an effort that collected over a thousand donated prom dresses, FedEx kicked in for the corsages, Joplin's own Liz Easton, who had lost her home and her bakery in the tornado, made a hundred—or 1,500 cupcakes for the occasion. They were good cupcakes. [*Laughter*]

There are so many good people in the world. There is such a decency, a bigness of spirit, in this country of ours. And so, class of 2012, you've got to remember that. Remember what people did here. And like that man who came all the way from Japan to Joplin, make sure in your own life that you pay it forward.

Now, just as you've learned the goodness of people, you've also learned the power of community. And you've heard from some of the other speakers how powerful that is. And as you take on the roles of coworker and business owner, neighbor, citizen, you'll encounter all kinds of divisions between groups, divisions of race and religion and ideology. You'll meet people who like to disagree just for the sake of being disagreeable. [*Laughter*] You'll meet people who prefer to play up their differences instead of focusing on what they have in common, where they can cooperate.

But you're from Joplin, so you will always know that it's always possible for a community to come together when it matters most. After all, a lot of you could have spent your senior year scattered throughout different schools, far from home. But Dr. Huff asked everybody to pitch in so that school started on time, right here in Joplin. He understood the power of this community, and he understood the power of place.

And so these teachers worked extra hours, coaches put in extra time. That mall was turned into a classroom. The food court became a cafeteria, which maybe some of you thought was an improvement. [*Laughter*] And yes, the arrangements might have been a little noisy and a little improvised, but you hunkered down. You made it work together. You made it work together.

That's the power of community. Together, you decided this city wasn't about to spend the next year arguing over every detail of the recovery effort. At the very first meeting, the first town meeting, every citizen was handed a Post-it note and asked to write down their goals and their hopes for Joplin's future. And more than a thousand notes covered an entire wall and became the blueprint that architects are following to this day. I'm thinking about trying this with Congress, give them some Post-it notes. [*Laughter*]

Together, the businesses that were destroyed in the tornado decided they weren't about to walk away from the community that made their success possible, even if it would have been easier, even if it would've been more profitable to go someplace else. And so today, more than half the stores that were damaged on the Range Line are up and running again. Eleven more are planning to join them. And every time a company reopens its doors, people cheer the cutting of a ribbon that bears the town's new slogan: "Remember, rejoice, and rebuild." That's community.

I've been told, class of 2012, that before the tornado, many of you couldn't wait to leave here once high school was finally over. So student council president Julia Lewis—where is Julia? She's out here somewhere. [*Laughter*] She is too embarrassed to raise her hand. I'm quoting you, Julia. She said: "We never thought Joplin was anything special"—now that's typical with teenagers; they don't think their parents are all that special either—[*laughter*]—"but seeing how we responded to something that tore our community apart has brought us together. Everyone has a lot more pride in our town." So it's no surprise then that many of you have decided to stick around and go to Missouri Southern or go to colleges or community colleges that aren't too far away from home.

That's the power of community. That's the power of shared effort and shared memory. Some of life's strongest bonds are the ones we forge when everything around us seems broken. And even though I expect that some of you will ultimately end up leaving Joplin, I'm

657

pretty confident that Joplin will never leave you. The people who went through this with you, the people who you once thought of as simply neighbors or acquaintances, classmates, the people in this auditorium tonight, you're family now. They're your family.

And so my deepest hope for all of you is that as you begin this new chapter in your life, you'll bring that spirit of Joplin to every place you travel, to everything you do. You can serve as a reminder that we're not meant to walk this road alone, that we're not expected to face down adversity by ourselves. We need God. We need each other. We are important to each other, and we're stronger together than we are on our own.

And that's the spirit that has allowed all of you to rebuild this city, and that's the same spirit we need right now to help rebuild America. And you, class of 2012, you're going to help lead this effort. You're the ones who will help build an economy where every child can count on a good education. You're the one that's going to make sure this country is a place where everybody who is willing to put in the effort can find a job that supports a family. You're the ones that will make sure we're a country that controls our own energy future, where we lead the world in science and technology and innovation. America only succeeds when we all pitch in and pull together, and I'm counting on you to be leaders in that effort, because you're from Joplin, and you have already defied the odds.

Now, there are a lot of stories here in Joplin of unthinkable courage and resilience over the last year, but still there are some that stand out, especially on this day. And by now, most of you know Joplin High's senior Quinton Anderson; look, he is already looking embarrassed. Somebody is talking about him again. But, Quinton, I'm going to talk about you anyway, because in a lot of ways, Quinton's journey has been Joplin's journey.

When the tornado struck, Quinton was thrown across the street from his house. The young man who found Quinton couldn't imagine that Quinton would survive his injuries. Quinton woke up in a hospital bed 3 days later.

And it was then that his sister Grace told him that both their parents had been lost in the storm.

So Quinton went on to face over 5 weeks of treatment, including emergency surgery. But he left that hospital determined to carry on, to live his life, to be there for his sister. And over the past year, he's been a football captain who cheered from the sidelines when he couldn't play. He worked that much harder so he could be ready for baseball in the spring. He won a national scholarship as a finalist for the high school football "Rudy" awards. He plans to study molecular biology at Harding University this fall.

Quinton has said that his motto in life is "always take that extra step." And today, after a long and improbable journey for Quinton, and for Joplin and for the entire class of 2012, that extra step is about to take you towards whatever future you hope for and whatever dreams you hold in your hearts.

Yes, you will encounter obstacles along the way. I guarantee you will face setbacks and you will face disappointments. But you're from Joplin, and you're from America. And no matter how tough times get, you'll always be tougher. And no matter what life throws at you, you will be ready. You will not be defined by the difficulties you face, but by how you respond, with grace and strength and a commitment to others.

Langston Hughes, poet, civil rights activist who knew some tough times, he was born here in Joplin. In a poem called "Youth," he wrote:

> We have tomorrow
> Bright before us
> Like a flame.
> Yesterday
> A night-gone thing,
> A sun-down name.
> And dawn-today. Broad arc above the
> road we came.
> We march.

To the people of Joplin and the class of 2012, the road has been hard and the day has been long, but we have tomorrow, so we march. We march together, and you're leading the way, because you're from Joplin. Congratulations.

May God bless you. May God bless the class of 2012. May God bless the United States of America.

NOTE: The President spoke at 8:40 p.m. in the Leggett & Platt Athletic Center at Missouri Southern State University. In his remarks, he referred to C.J. Huff, superintendent, Joplin Schools; Kerry Sachetta, principal, and Chloe Hadley, senior class president, Joplin High School; Caleb, Colton, and Jordan Carr, children of Rocky Ford, CO, resident Mark Carr; Patricia Williams, aunt of Joplin, MO, resident Carol Mann; volunteer Toyshia Muto; actress Angelina Jolie; and George Zevin, who organized a car wash for Joplin schools.

Commencement Address at the United States Air Force Academy in Colorado Springs, Colorado
May 23, 2012

The President. Thank you so much. Please be seated. Good morning, everybody!

Audience members. Good morning!

The President. It is wonderful to be at the United States Air Force Academy on such a spectacular day, and it is a privilege to join you in honoring the class of 2012.

I want to thank Secretary Donley for his introduction, but more importantly, for his leadership. Generals Gould, Clark, and Born; Academy faculty and staff; the Governor, Hickenlooper; Members of Congress; distinguished guests, ladies and gentlemen—I especially want to acknowledge a graduate of this Academy who has kept our Air Force strong through a time of great challenge, a leader I've relied on and for whom today is his final commencement as Chief of Staff, General Norton Schwartz. Norty, Suzie, we could not be prouder of you, and we are grateful for 39 years of extraordinary service to our Nation. And although he is not with us today, I'm proud to have nominated another Academy graduate, General Mark Welsh, as the next Chief of Staff.

Now, this is my second visit to the Academy. I was here in the summer of 2008, and you were getting ready to head out to Jacks Valley. So I was proud to be here when you began this journey, and I thought I'd come back and help you celebrate at the end. [*Laughter*] It's great to be back at a school that has produced so many of the airmen I've known as President.

Every day, I rely on outstanding Academy graduates who serve at the White House. Some of you know that photo from the Situation Room on the day we delivered justice to bin Laden. You can see, right next to me, a great leader of our Special Operations forces, General Brad Webb.

Last month, I was able to present the Commander in Chief Trophy to Coach Calhoun and the Fighting Falcons for the second straight year, a record 18th time. And of course, every time I step on Air Force One, I count on Academy graduates like my pilot today, Colonel Scott Turner. Now, I was going to tell you a joke about Scott, but he's my ride home. [*Laughter*] So I'm going to have to keep it to myself.

Cadets, you distinguished yourselves as leaders before you ever stepped foot on the Terrazzo. And when you arrived, I know your upper classmen gave you quite a welcome. They let you experience the joy of the "Beast," the pleasure of "Recognition." They made you experts on filling out forms. I only ask that you resist the temptation to rate my speech: "fast, neat, average, friendly, good, good." [*Laughter*]

But you survived. In you, we see the values of integrity and service and excellence that will define your lives. And I know you couldn't have made it without the love and support of your moms and dads and brothers and sisters and grandmas, grandpas, aunts, uncles, cousins. So give them all a big round of applause.

659

This Academy is one of the most demanding academic institutions in America. And you have excelled. I'm told you have set at least three Academy records: the largest number of graduates ever to go directly on to graduate school; the largest number of female graduates in Academy history. You will follow in the footsteps of General Janet Wolfenbarger, who I was proud to nominate as the first female four-star general in Air Force history.

And of course, your final and perhaps most impressive distinction: breaking the world's record for the largest game of dodgeball. Three thousand participants, 30 hours, I didn't know that was possible. [*Laughter*] Of course, you are also the class that snuck into the Superintendent's office and moved all the furniture into your dorm rooms, which does bring me to some important business. In keeping with longstanding tradition, I hereby grant amnesty to all cadets serving restrictions and confinements for minor offenses. Of course, I leave it up to General Gould to define "minor." [*Laughter*]

Cadets, this is the day you finally become officers in the finest Air Force in the world. Like generations before you, you'll be charged with the responsibility of leading those under your command. Like classes over the past 10 years, you graduate in a time of war, and you may find yourselves in harm's way. But you will also face a new test, and that's what I want to talk to you about today.

Four years ago, you arrived here at a time of extraordinary challenge for our Nation. Our forces were engaged in two wars. Al Qaida, which had attacked us on 9/11, was entrenched in their safe havens. Many of our alliances were strained, and our standing in the world had suffered. Our economy was in the worst recession since the Great Depression. Around the world and here at home, there were those that questioned whether the United States still had the capacity for global leadership.

Today, you step forward into a different world. You are the first class in 9 years that will graduate into a world where there are no Americans fighting in Iraq. For the first time in your lives, and thanks to Air Force personnel who did their part, Usama bin Laden is no longer a threat to our country. We've put Al Qaida on the path to defeat. And you are the first graduates since 9/11 who can clearly see how we'll end the war in Afghanistan.

So what does all this mean? When you came here 4 years ago, there were some 180,000 American troops in Iraq and Afghanistan. We've now cut that number by more than half. And as more Afghans step up, more of our troops will come home while achieving the objective that led us to war in the first place, and that is defeating Al Qaida and denying them safe haven. So we aren't just ending these wars, we are doing so in a way that makes us safer and stronger.

Today we pay tribute to all our extraordinary men and women in uniform for their bravery, for their dedication. Those who gave their lives in Iraq and Afghanistan to make this progress possible, including 16 graduates of this Academy, we honor them. We will always honor them.

For a decade, we have labored under the dark cloud of war. And now, we can see a light, the light of a new day on the horizon. So the end of these wars will shape your service, and it will make our military stronger. Ten years of continuous military operations have stretched our forces and strained their families. Going forward, you'll face fewer deployments. You'll have more time to train and stay ready. That means you'll be better prepared for the full range of missions you face.

And ending these wars will also ensure that the burden of our security no longer falls so heavily on the shoulders of our men and women in uniform. As good as you are, you can't be expected to do it alone. There are many sources of American power: diplomatic, economic, and the power of our ideals. And we've got to use them all. And the good news is, today we are.

Around the world, the United States is leading once more. From Europe to Asia, our alliances are stronger than ever. Our ties with the Americas are deeper. We're setting the agenda in the region that will shape our long-term security and prosperity like no other: the Asia-Pacific.

We're leading on global security: reducing our nuclear arsenal with Russia, even as we maintain a strong nuclear deterrent; mobilizing dozens of nations to secure nuclear materials so they never fall into the hands of terrorists; rallying the world to put the strongest sanctions ever on Iran and North Korea, which cannot be allowed to threaten the world with nuclear weapons.

We are leading economically, forging trade pacts to create new markets for our goods, boosting our exports, stamped with three proud words: Made in America. We're expanding exchanges and collaborations in areas that people often admire most about America: our innovation, our science, our technology.

We're leading on behalf of human dignity and on behalf of freedom: standing with the people of the Middle East and North Africa as they seek their rights; preventing a massacre in Libya with an international mission in which the United States and our Air Force led from the front.

We're leading global efforts against hunger and disease. And we've shown our compassion, as so many airmen did, in delivering relief to our neighbors in Haiti when they were in need and to our Japanese allies after the earthquake and tsunami.

Because of this progress, around the world there is a new feeling about America. I see it everywhere I go, from London and Prague to Tokyo and Seoul, to Rio and Jakarta. There's a new confidence in our leadership. And when people around the world are asked, which country do you most admire, one nation comes out on top: the United States of America.

Of course, the world stage is not a popularity contest. As a nation, we have vital interests, and we will do what is necessary always to defend this country we love, even if it's unpopular. But make no mistake: How we're viewed in the world has consequences for our national security and for your lives.

See, when other countries and people see us as partners, they're more willing to work with us. It's why more countries joined us in Af-ghanistan and Libya. It's why nations like Australia are welcoming our forces who stand side by side with allies and partners in the South Pacific. It's why Uganda and its African neighbors have welcomed our trainers to help defeat a brutal army that slaughters its citizens.

I think of the Japanese man in the disaster zone who, upon seeing our airmen delivering relief, said, "I never imagined they could help us so much." I think of the Libyans who protected our airman when he ejected over their town because they knew America was there to protect them. And in a region where we've seen burning of American flags, I think of all the Libyans who were waving American flags.

Today, we can say with confidence and pride the United States is stronger and safer and more respected in the world, because even as we've done the work of ending these wars, we've laid the foundation for a new era of American leadership. And now, cadets, we have to build it. We have to build on it. You have to build on it.

Let's start by putting aside the tired notion that says our influence has waned or that America is in decline. We've heard that talk before. During the Great Depression, when millions were unemployed and some believed that other economic models offered a better way, there were those who predicted the end of American capitalism. Guess what: They were wrong. We fought our way back. We created the largest middle class in history and the most prosperous economy the world has ever known.

After Pearl Harbor, some said, the United States has been reduced to a third-rate power. Well, we rallied. We flew over the Hump and took island after island. We stormed the beaches and liberated nations. And we emerged from that war as the strongest power on the face of the Earth.

After Vietnam and the energy crisis of the 1970s, some said America had passed its high point. But the very next decade, because of our fidelity to the values we stand for, the Berlin Wall came tumbling down and liberty prevailed over the tyranny of the cold war.

As recently as the 1980s, with the rise of Japan and the Asian Tigers, there were those who said we had lost our economic edge. But we retooled. We invested in new technologies. We launched an information revolution that changed the world.

After all this, you would think folks understand a basic truth: Never bet against the United States of America. And one of the reasons is that the United States has been, and will always be, the one indispensable nation in world affairs. It's one of the many examples of why America is exceptional. It's why I firmly believe that if we rise to this moment in history, if we meet our responsibilities, then—just like the 20th century—the 21st century will be another great American century. That's the future I see. That's the future you can build.

I see an American century because we have the resilience to make it through these tough economic times. We're going to put America back to work by investing in the things that keep us competitive: education and high-tech manufacturing, science and innovation. We'll pay down our deficits, reform our Tax Code, and keep reducing our dependence on foreign oil. We need to get on with nation-building here at home. And I know we can because we're still the largest, most dynamic, most innovative economy in the world. And no matter what challenges we may face, we wouldn't trade places with any other nation on Earth.

I see an American century because you are part of the finest, most capable military the world has ever known. No other nation even comes close. Yes, as today's wars end, our military and our Air Force will be leaner. But as Commander in Chief, I will not allow us to make the mistakes of the past. We still face very serious threats. As we've seen in recent weeks, with Al Qaida in Yemen, there are still terrorists who seek to kill our citizens. So we need you to be ready for the full range of threats. From the conventional to the unconventional, from nations seeking weapons of mass destruction to the cell of terrorists planning the next attack, from the old danger of piracy to the new threat of cyber, we must be vigilant.

And so, guided by our new defense strategy, we'll keep our military and our Air Force fast and flexible and versatile. We will maintain our military superiority in all areas: air, land, sea, space, and cyber. And we will keep faith with our forces and our military families.

And as our newest veterans rejoin civilian life, we will never stop working to give them the benefits and opportunities that they have earned, because our veterans have the skills to help us rebuild America, and we have to serve them as well as they have served us.

I see an American century because we have the strongest alliances of any nation. From Europe to Asia, our alliances are the foundation of global security. In Libya, all 28 NATO allies played a role, and we were joined by partners in the air from Sweden to the Gulf States. In Afghanistan, we're in a coalition of 50 allies and partners. Today, Air Force personnel are serving in 135 nations, partnering, training, building their capacity. This is how peace and security will be upheld in the 21st century: more nations bearing the costs and responsibilities of leadership. And that's good for America. It's good for the world. And we're at the hub of it, making it happen.

I see an American century because no other nation seeks the role that we play in global affairs and no other nation can play the role that we play in global affairs. That includes shaping the global institutions of the 20th century to meet the challenges of the 21st. As President, I've made it clear: The United States does not fear the rise of peaceful, responsible emerging powers, we welcome them. Because when more nations step up and contribute to peace and security, that doesn't undermine American power, it enhances it.

And when other people in other countries see that we're rooting for their success, it builds trust and partnerships that can advance our interests for generations. It makes it easier to meet common challenges, from preventing the spread of nuclear weapons to combating climate change. And so we seek an international order where the rights and responsibilities of all nations and peoples are upheld and where countries thrive by meeting their obligations and they face consequences when they don't.

I see an American century because more and more people are reaching toward the freedoms and values that we share. No other nation has sacrificed more—in treasure, in the lives of our sons and daughters—so that these freedoms could take root and flourish around the world. And no other nation has made the advancement of human rights and dignity so central to its foreign policy. And that's because it's central to who we are as Americans. It's also in our self-interest because democracies become our closest allies and partners.

Sure, there will always be some governments that try to resist the tide of democracy, who claim theirs is a better way. But around the world, people know the difference between us. We welcome freedom to speak, to assemble, to worship, to choose your leaders. They don't. We welcome the chance to compete for jobs and markets freely and fairly. They don't. When fundamental human rights are threatened around the world, we stand up and speak out. And they don't.

We know that the sovereignty of nations cannot strangle the liberty of individuals. And so we stand with the student in the street who demands a life of dignity and opportunity. We stand with women everywhere who deserve the same rights as men. We stand with the activists unbowed in their prison cells and the leaders in parliament who's moving her country towards democracy. We stand with the dissident who seeks the freedom to say what he pleases and the entrepreneur who wants to start a business without paying a bribe and all those who strive for justice and dignity. For they know, as we do, that history is on the side of freedom.

And finally, I see an American century because of the character of our country, the spirit that has always made us exceptional. That simple yet revolutionary idea, there at our founding and in our hearts ever since, that we have it in our power to make the world anew, to make the future what we will. It is that fundamental faith, that American optimism, which says no challenge is too great, no mission is too hard. It's the spirit that guides your class: "Never falter, never fail."

That is the essence of America, and there's nothing else like it anywhere in the world. It's what's inspired the oppressed in every corner of the world to demand the same freedoms for themselves. It's what's inspired generations to come to our shores, renewing us with their energy and their hopes. And that includes a fellow cadet, a cadet graduating today, who grew up in Venezuela, got on a plane with a one-way ticket to America, and today is closer to his dream of becoming an Air Force pilot: Edward Camacho. Edward said what we all know to be true: "I'm convinced that America is the land of opportunity."

You're right, Edward. That is who we are. That's the America we love: always young, always looking ahead to that light of a new day on the horizon. And, cadets, as I look into your eyes as you join that long blue line, I know you will carry us even farther and even higher. And with your proud service, I'm absolutely confident that the United States of America will meet the tests of our time. We will remain the land of opportunity. And we will stay strong as the greatest force for freedom and human dignity that the world has ever known.

May God bless you. May God bless the class of 2012, and may God bless the United States of America.

NOTE: The President spoke at 10:29 a.m. In his remarks, he referred to Lt. Gen. Michael C. Gould, USAF, Superintendent, Brig. Gen. Richard M. Clark, USAF, commandant of cadets, and Brig. Gen. Dana H. Born, USAF, dean of the faculty, U.S. Air Force Academy; Gov. John W. Hickenlooper of Colorado; Suzanne Schwartz, wife of Gen. Norton A. Schwartz, USAF; and Troy Calhoun, head coach, U.S. Air Force Academy football team.

Remarks at an Obama Victory Fund 2012 Fundraiser in Denver, Colorado
May 23, 2012

The President. Hello, Denver! Thank you. Thank you so much. Everybody, please have a seat if you got a seat, just so the folks back there can—[*laughter*]. It is good to be back in Denver. Can everybody please give Tami a wonderful round of applause for that great introduction.

There are some special guests here. You've heard from a bunch of them. I just want to acknowledge them, because they are outstanding public servants. First of all, one of the best Governors and one of the funniest Governors in the country, give it up for John Hickenlooper. One of the finest Lieutenant Governors—and according to Hickenlooper, and he's right, somebody much cooler than the Governor—the Lieutenant Governor, Joe Garcia, is here.

Your outstanding mayor, Michael Hancock's in the house. Diana DeGette, great Congresswoman, is in the house. Jared Polis is here. And Ed Perlmutter is in the house. We've also got national cochair John Register here, and the former mayor of Denver, Wellington Webb, in the house.

Plus, all of you are in the house, and I can tell you're fired up. We had some folks to get you fired up.

Audience member. Ready to go!

The President. And ready to go.

Audience member. Si, se puede!

The President. Now—si, se puede. That too.

All right. Now, I'm here not just because I need your help, although I do need your help. [*Laughter*] I'm here because the country needs your help. Four years ago, we came together to reclaim the basic values that built this country, that built the largest middle class and the most prosperous economy in the world. And we came together because we believe that in America, your success shouldn't be determined by the circumstances of your birth. If you're willing to work hard, you should be able to find a good job. If you're willing to meet your responsibilities, you should be able to own a home, maybe start a business, give your kids a chance to do better than you did, no matter who you are, no matter where you came from, no matter what you look like, no matter who you love.

And the reason we came together in 2008, it wasn't—this wasn't about me. This was about us. We believed that the country was straying from these basic values. We had a record surplus that had been squandered on tax cuts for people who didn't need them and weren't even asking for them, two wars being waged on a credit card. Washington speculators were reaping huge profits by making bets with other people's money. Manufacturing was leaving our shores. So a shrinking number of Americans were doing fantastically well, while the vast majority—a growing number—were struggling to get by. Falling incomes, rising costs, the slowest job growth in a century, that's what we were confronting.

And it was all a house of cards that collapsed in the most destructive crisis since the Great Depression. And just to give people a sense of perspective: In the last 6 months of 2008, even while we were campaigning, nearly 3 million of our neighbors lost their jobs; 800,000 lost their jobs the month I was sworn into office.

So it was tough. But the good news is, Americans proved to be tougher. We don't quit. We keep on going. And together, we began to fight our way back.

There were those who said we should let Detroit go bankrupt, but we met—we made a bet on the American worker, on the ingenuity of American companies, and now the auto industry is back on top of the world and manufacturing is starting to invest in America again. We've seen American manufacturing adding jobs for the first time since the 1990s.

Business got back to basics. On the way over, the Governor and a couple of the Congressmen and I were talking about small businesses. And all those folks who were taking a chance, maybe they failed the first time, maybe even the second time, and then during this recession they were doing everything they had, maybe sometimes not taking any money out of the business themselves so they could keep their workers, who depended on those jobs, on the job. And it's because of folks like that that we've created over 4 million jobs in the last 26 months, more than 1 million of those in the last 6 months alone.

Now, we're not satisfied. We're not satisfied when so many of our friends and family are still looking for work. We're not satisfied when neighbors have homes underwater. We're not satisfied when there are young people who are still looking for opportunity, States are still facing severe budget crunches, teachers are still being laid off, first-responders. A crisis this deep will not be solved overnight. Anybody who says it will aren't telling you the truth. We've got more work to do. And we know that.

But we also know that the last thing we can afford to do after we've started to make progress, as we're starting to turn the corner, is a return to the policies—the very same policies—that got us into this mess in the first place. Not now. Not with so much at stake. We have come too far to abandon the change that we fought for over these past years. We're not going to make it happen.

We have to move forward, to the future we imagined in 2008, where everybody gets a fair shot, everybody's doing their fair share, everybody's playing by the same set of rules. And that's the choice in this election. That's the reason I'm running for a second term as President of the United States of America.

Now, my opponent in this election, Governor Romney, is a patriotic American. He's raised a wonderful family. He should be proud of the great personal success he's had as the CEO of a large financial firm. But I think he's drawn the wrong lessons from his experience, because his working assumption is, if CEOs and wealthy investors like him get rich, then the rest of us automatically will too.

When—there was a woman in Iowa who shared her stories of financial struggles, and he gave her an answer right out of an economic textbook. He said, "Our productivity equals our income." And the notion was that somehow the reason people can't pay their bills is because they're not working hard enough. If

they got more productive, suddenly their incomes would go up. Well, those of us who've spent time in the real world—[*laughter*]—know that the problem isn't that the American people aren't productive enough; you've been working harder than ever. The challenge we face right now, and the challenge we've faced for over a decade, is that harder work has not led to higher incomes and bigger profits at the top haven't led to better jobs.

And what Governor Romney doesn't seem to get is that a healthy economy doesn't just mean a few folks maximizing their profits through massive layoffs or busting unions. You don't make America stronger by shipping jobs and profits overseas. When you propose cutting your own taxes while raising them on 18 million working families, that's not a recipe for broad-based economic growth. And——

Audience member. We need you, Barack!

The President. ——it's true.

Audience members. Yeah!

The President. You know, I—and I need you! Look——

Audience member. You got me! [*Laughter*]

The President. There is nothing new about these ideas. It's the same old stuff they've been peddling for years. Though Bill Clinton pointed this out a few weeks ago: This time their agenda is on steroids. [*Laughter*] They want even bigger tax cuts for the wealthiest Americans. They want even deeper cuts to things like education and Medicare and research and technology. They want to give banks and insurance companies even more power to do as they please.

Governor Romney says that his 25 years in the private sector gives him a special understanding of how the economy works. Now, if that's true, I got to ask, why is he running around with the same bad ideas that brought our economy to collapse this last time out? I mean, either he thinks that they're going to lead to a different result this time, or he's hoping you won't remember what happened the last time. [*Laughter*] And I'm here to say we were there—[*laughter*]—we remember. We're not going back. We're moving forward. That's why I'm running for President again.

Now, understand, we don't expect government to solve all our problems, and it shouldn't try. I learned from my mom, no education policy can take the place of a loving, attentive, and sometimes somewhat stern parent. [*Laughter*] When I was a young community organizer, I was working with Catholic churches, and they taught me that no government program can make as much of a difference as kindness and commitment on the part of neighbors and friends. Not every regulation is smart. Not every tax dollar is spent wisely. Your Governor, your mayor, your President, all of us are constantly looking for ways to make government smarter and to upgrade what we've been doing. A lot of the stuff we're doing now we were doing back in the thirties, forties, fifties, and sixties. We need to change some of this stuff.

So we can't just be defending the status quo, we want to transform it, including how government works. Not every person can be helped who refuses to help themselves. But that's not an excuse to tell the vast majority of responsible, hard-working Americans, you're on your own; that unless you're lucky enough to have parents who can lend you money, you may not be able to go to college; that even if you pay your premiums every month, you may be out of luck if an insurance company decides to drop your coverage right when you need it most.

That's not who we are. That's not how we built America. We built this country together. We built railroads and highways and the Hoover Dam and the Golden Gate Bridge together. We sent my grandfather's generation back to college on the GI bill together. We didn't do these things because it was going to be just good for one person or just one group. We did it because we understood, you know what, if my neighbor, my friend, my colleague, my coworker, if they're getting a good education, then my business, my company, my community will thrive. All of us will do better.

If we invest in building roads and bridges, all of us will do better. It will make all of us richer. All of us will have opportunity. Those previous generations understood, we move forward together, as one Nation and as one people. That's the true lesson of our past. And that's the right vision for our future. That's why I'm running for President.

I'm running to make sure that by the end of this decade, more of our citizens hold a college degree than any other nation on Earth. I want to make sure our schools are hiring and rewarding the best teachers, especially in math and science. I want to give 2 million more Americans the chance to go to community colleges and learn the skills that local businesses are looking for right now.

Higher education isn't a luxury, it's an economic imperative that every American should be able to afford. That's the choice in this election.

I'm running to make sure that the next generation of high-tech manufacturing takes place in Denver and Cleveland and Pittsburgh and Charlotte. I don't want to reward businesses that are investing, creating jobs overseas. I want to reward them for investing right here in Colorado, creating jobs right here in the United States of America. That's the choice in this election.

I'm running so that we can have control over our energy future. Our dependence on foreign oil is at its lowest point in 16 years. And by the middle of the next decade, our cars will average nearly 55 miles per gallon. Thousands of Americans have jobs because of the production of renewable energies here in Colorado and all across the country. And your Governor and your mayors have been leaders in this. Your congressional delegation, they understand now is not the time to cut these investments to pay for $4 billion a year in giveaways to the oil companies. Now's the time to end those subsidies on an industry that's rarely been more profitable. And let's invest in the future, let's invest in energy that has rarely been more promising for our economy and our security and the safety of our planet.

That's why I'm running, Denver. That's the choice in this election.

For the first time in 9 years, there are no Americans fighting in Iraq. Usama bin Laden is no longer a threat to this country, and Al Qaida is on the path to defeat. We just came out of a NATO summit in Chicago in which all the countries participating, an international coalition, said the war in Afghanistan will end on 2014. It will be over, and we'll—we are going to be starting to bring our troops home. And we're going to do it in a way that is responsible and allows Afghans to take a greater lead for their own security.

America is safer and more respected because of the courage and the selflessness of the U.S. Armed Forces. I was just at the Air Force Academy, shaking 1,100 hands—[*laughter*]—giving 1,100 salutes. And as long as I am Commander in Chief, this country will care for our veterans. We will care and serve our veterans the way they've served us, because no veteran should have to fight for a job when they come home or fight for a roof over their heads.

That's why we're so proud we're building that VA hospital right here in Denver. And our congressional delegation helped to make that happen.

My opponent has different ideas. He said it was "tragic" to end the war in Iraq, won't set a timeline for ending the war in Afghanistan. I have set a timeline. Our coalition partners and the Afghans agree with me. I intend to keep it. After a decade of war that's cost us thousands of lives and over a trillion dollars, the nation we need to build is our own. We're going to use half of what we're no longer spending on the war to pay down our deficit, use the other half to invest in education and research and wireless networks and smart grids and broadband lines and new runways. And that's the choice in this election.

And I'm running to pay down our debt in a way that is balanced and responsible. After inheriting a $1 trillion deficit, I signed $2 trillion of spending cuts into law. My opponent won't admit it, but it's been starting to appear in places—real liberal outlets like the Wall Street Journal—[*laughter*]—since I've been President, Federal spending has risen at the lowest pace in nearly 60 years. Think about that. Think about that.

I'd just point out that it always goes up least under Democratic Presidents. This other side, I don't know how they've been bamboozling

folks into thinking that they are the responsible, fiscally disciplined party. They run up these wild debts, and then when we take over, we got to clean it up. And they point and say, look how irresponsible they are. Look at the facts. Look at the numbers.

And now I want to finish the job. I want to finish the job in a balanced way. Yes, we're going to streamline Government. There's more waste to be cut. We can reform our Tax Code so that it's simpler and fairer, but so that it also asks the wealthiest Americans to pay a little bit more.

And let me say, my opponent, he won't tell us how he'd pay for his new $5 trillion tax cut. Now, this is a tax cut that gives an average of $250,000 to every millionaire in the country. This is on top of the Bush tax cuts. This is more. [*Laughter*] So I'd get more. I don't need more. And we know that the tax bill—or the bill for this tax cut, it's going to come from two places. Either it's passed on to our children, or it will pay—be paid for by a whole lot of ordinary Americans.

And we're not going to let that happen again. We're not going to let another millionaire's tax cut get paid for by eliminating medical research projects into things like cancer or Alzheimer's. We're not going to pay for another tax cut by kicking more kids out of Head Start programs or asking students to pay more for college or eliminating health insurance for millions of poor and elderly and disabled Americans on Medicaid. And I'm not going to allow Medicare to be turned into a voucher that would end the program as we know it. We're not going to do that. We'll reform Medicare, not by shifting the cost of care to seniors, but by reducing the spending that isn't making people healthier.

So that's what's at stake. On issue after issue, we can't afford to spend the next 4 years going backwards. We don't need to refight the battles over Wall Street reform; we just saw how much it's needed. We don't need to refight the battle over health care reform; Tami told you why it's needed. We've got 2.5 million young people who are on their parent's plan right now because of that bill, have health insurance who wouldn't otherwise have it. Millions of seniors who are seeing their prescription drug prices lower because it was the right thing to do. We're not going to go back to days when the insurance companies had unchecked power to cancel your policy or deny your coverage or charge women differently than men. We're not going back there.

We certainly don't need another political fight about ending a woman's right to choose or get rid of Planned Parenthood or taking away affordable birth control. I want women to control their own health choices, just like I want my daughters to have the same opportunities as your sons. We're not turning back the clock. We won't do that.

We're not going back to the days when you could be kicked out of the United States military because of who you are and who you love. We're moving forward to a country where every American is treated with dignity and respect and equality. That's what we're moving towards.

We need to put an end to another election where multimillion-dollar donations speak louder than the voices of ordinary citizens.

We need to move forward so that we can stop denying citizenship to responsible young people just because they're the children of undocumented immigrants. This is a country that is at its best when we harness the God-given talents of every individual, when we hear every voice, when we come together as one American family, and we're striving for the same dream.

That's what we're fighting for. That's why I'm running for President. That's why I need your help. This election will be closer than the last one. People don't remember the last election was close. [*Laughter*] We're going to have to contend with even more negative ads, even more cynicism and nastiness, and just plain foolishness. But the outcome of the election is ultimately going to depend on all of you.

Audience member. We'll just have to work harder!

The President. That's exactly right. [*Laughter*] Because if there's one thing I learned in 2008, there's nothing more powerful than millions of voices calling for change. When you guys are knocking on doors, when you're picking up phone call—phones and calling your friends and talking to your neighbors and your coworkers, when you decide it's time for change to happen, well, guess what, it happens. Change comes to America. And that's the spirit we need again. That's the spirit we need again.

I took some pictures with some folks before I came out here, and one of the first pictures I took was with a couple of gentlemen—these two right here—90 years old. They were U.S. Olympians in 1938, with Jesse Owens, their friend. [*Applause*] They can get up. They can stand up; these gentlemen right here—[*applause*]—1938. Think about that; 1938—'48, excuse me. I'm sorry. I'm making them even older—[*laughter*]—1948.

And so we were talking about all the changes they've seen, everything that's happened in their lifetimes. And I was just imagining what the world looked like then and, because in part of the example they set, what the world looks like now. And then, one of my last pictures—in fact, the last picture I took was with a baby—where's Barrett—who was drooling on my—[*laughter*]—there he is right there. All right, so I got the drool all over me, all over me—[*laughter*]. Now—and I started imagining what the world will look like for him 50 years from now and all the changes he's going to see.

And those stories are bound together. That little baby, these two handsome gentlemen, they're part of that same story of who we are as Americans, and they understand that we're bound together. And if people ask you what this campaign is about, you tell them it's about these gentlemen and it's about that baby. [*Laughter*] You tell them it's about hope. You tell them it's still about change. You tell them it's still about ordinary people who believe in each other, who believe we have more in common than anything that drives us apart, who believe that in the face of great odds, we can make a difference in the life of this country.

I still believe. I believe—I am absolutely convinced—we're not as divided as our politics suggest right now. I still believe we've got more in common than the pundits tell us.

We're not Democrats or Republicans first; we're Americans first. That's what I believe.

And so you should all know I still believe in you, and I'm asking you to believe in me. Because, as I told you in 2008, I'm not a perfect man, and I'll never be a perfect President, but I told you I'd always tell you what I thought, I'd always tell you where I stood, and I'd always wake up every single day fighting as hard as I can for you. And I have kept that promise. And I will keep that promise as long as I have the honor of being your President.

So if you'll fight with me and stick with me and march with me and press with me, if you're willing to work even harder this time than the last time, we'll move this country forward. We will finish what we started. We'll re-mind the world again why the United States of America is the greatest nation on Earth.

Thank you, Denver. God bless you. God bless America.

NOTE: The President spoke at 3:45 p.m. at the Hyatt Regency Denver hotel. In his remarks, he referred to Mancos, CO, resident Tami Graham; Reps. Jared Polis and Edwin G. Perlmutter; John Register, national cochair, Obama for America; Republican Presidential candidate former Gov. W. Mitt Romney of Massachusetts; former President William J. Clinton; W. Harrison Dillard and Herbert P. Douglas, Jr., members, 1948 U.S. Olympic team; and Bennett Dodge, infant son of R. Stanton Dodge, executive vice president, Dish Network, and his wife Lindsey.

Remarks at an Obama Victory Fund 2012 Fundraiser in Atherton, California
May 23, 2012

The President. Thank you, everybody. Please, please have a seat.

Well, let me start out by just saying that the Goldman family and Doug and Lisa, they have had my back from the get-go. At a time when a lot of people had no idea who I was, they stepped up and were enormous supporters, along with some of the people in this room. They've been great friends. Even though the boys here beat me in air hockey—[*laughter*]—they haven't rubbed it in, except for when I show up and they have an air hockey table here. [*Laughter*] But they've just been extraordinary supporters, and I could not thank them more for everything that they've done. So please give them another round of applause.

I want to thank David Crosby and Graham Nash for providing some wonderful music. It's not every day you get Rock and Roll Hall of Famers strumming the guitar for you. So we really appreciate them. And they've been wonderful supporters as well. We really appreciate that.

I want to thank Don Cheadle for helping to frame the debate here. And Don has been a terrific friend as well. I'm not going to talk about the basketball game we had a couple of weeks ago. [*Laughter*] We're not going to say anything about it.

Actor Don Cheadle. Thank you.

The President. Nothing. [*Laughter*]

And I want to thank all of you for being here.

Now, in these kinds of settings, I try not to give a long speech. What I'd like to do is just make some very brief remarks at the top, because I want to save as much time as possible just for questions, for comments, for advice. I always get advice at these things so—[*laughter*]—I'm sure this crowd will not be shy.

But as has already been said, we've gone through 3½ of the toughest years in our lifetimes. It wasn't just the 800,000 jobs a month that we were losing. We had lost 3 million jobs before I was even sworn into office. We had lost 8 million before our economic policies had a chance to take effect. And we've still got a long way to go here in California and all across the country. There are a lot of folks who are hurting, people are out of work or underemployed, people whose homes are $100,000 underwater and have no sense of how they'll ever get out from under the debts that they've accumulated. There are an awful lot of young people here who are extraordinarily talented, but don't see a path or a vision for the future. So our work is not done.

The good news, though, is that we're beginning to steer that ship in the right direction. We've set a path and a target and a direction where this is again a country where everybody gets a fair shot, everybody does their fair share, everybody plays by the same set of rules. A lot of that has to do with making sure that every kid in this country is getting a good education. And I could not be prouder of the work that we've done on education reform.

A lot of it has to do with making sure that higher education is not a luxury. And it's not just 4-year colleges. We need more engineers, we need more scientists, we need more Stanford grads, but we also need folks who are going to community colleges and are able to get the skills and the training that they need in order to compete for jobs the 21st century.

We're making progress when it comes to science and innovation and all the investments that we've been making to try to make sure that we retain the edge that made us into an economic superpower. We've started to rebuild our infrastructure, not just the infrastructure of the past, not just roads and bridges, but also smart grids and high-speed rail.

We're starting to make progress when it comes to advanced manufacturing, bringing jobs back here to the United States of America. And our exports have surged. We're opening up markets all across the world. And it turns out that America continues to have the best workers and the best businesses in the world. We just have to get organized, and we're starting to do so.

Health care continues to be an extraordinary challenge, but we're starting to see the impact of the health care bill. And young people, 2.5 million young people who are able to stay on their parent's plan because of the health care bill, millions of seniors who are seeing reductions in the cost of their prescription drugs. And ultimately, 30 million people who right now are showing up at the emergency room are going to have the chance for affordable, decent health care coverage. And in the process,

we're rationalizing the system, so that we start driving down costs.

We've doubled fuel efficiency standards on cars. We have doubled the amount of clean energy that we're producing. We've still got a long way to go to have the kind of energy strategy that we need. But we actually have seen our imports of foreign oil drop down under 50 percent, the lowest that it's been in 15 years. And through not only the production of clean energy, but massive investments in energy efficiency, we've got a chance to get control of our energy future in a way that is good for our economy, good for our national security, and is good for our environment. And we can start tackling climate change in a serious way and lead the world on that issue.

It's been mentioned that we ended the war in Iraq. We're in the process of ending the war in Afghanistan. And in the process, we're also restoring respect for this country all around the world. I had a chance to speak to 1,100 cadets who were graduating from the Air Force Academy this afternoon—this morning. And I told them, don't buy this whole notion that America's influence is declining in the world, because the truth is, as we travel everywhere, we continue to be the agenda setters. Folks continue to look to us to help shape international rules and norms that allow us to tackle things like terrorism or climate change or poverty and development. We continue to be the one indispensible nation. And because we project it with our values and our ideals and restored a sense of rule of law, people are paying attention, people are listening, and people are hungry for our leadership.

So the strides that we've made over the last 3½ years have been extraordinary, but we've still got a long way to go. We've got a lot of work to do. We may not even finish it in 5 years, but I certainly need 5 more years to get us locked in on where we need to go.

And that's where all of you come in. A lot of people here have made a lot of sacrifices to put me in this office. And you've continued to help inform and guide a lot of my thinking on a lot of important issues. But I tell you, we're not done. And as much noise as there is out there—and those of you who follow this stuff and you're reading blogs and watching cable TV and it feels like the sky is falling—let me tell you, when you get out into the country, this is a country full of decent people who believe in America and are generous and kind and tolerant.

You know, I gave one commencement this week before I went to the Air Force Academy; it was the high school graduation at Joplin High. Now, you'll recall this is a town that had been devastated by a tornado, and the kids ended up going to high school in a mall, and they ended up eating at the food court there for lunch, which they thought was an improvement. [*Laughter*] But to see the faces of these young people and their parents, and all they had been through—there was a young man who had lost both his parents in the tornado, had been thrown and was out for 3 days. When he finally woke up, he had to go through 5 weeks of rehabilitation, and he had to look after a sister. And he was graduating this year and going on to college. And when you talk to a young man like that and he says, "I know it's not easy, but I don't quit," that captures who we are and what we're about.

And that's been displayed—that resilience and that strength has been displayed—over the last 3½ years, just like it's been displayed over the last 300 years. And that's not fading. That's as strong as it's ever been. And that's what inspires me. That's what makes me as determined now, more determined now than I was in 2008.

So I hope you have that same determination, because I intend to win this things, and I intend to keep on changing this country.

So thank you. Thank you. Thank you, guys.

NOTE: The President spoke at 8:03 p.m. at the residence of Douglas E. and Lisa M. Goldman. In his remarks, he referred to Jason E. and Matthew W. Goldman, sons of Mr. and Mrs. Goldman; and Quinton Anderson, student, Joplin High School in Joplin, MO, and his sister Grace. The transcript was released by the Office of the Press Secretary on May 24.

Remarks at an Obama Victory Fund 2012 Fundraiser in Redwood City, California
May 23, 2012

The President. How's it going, Redwood City? Thank you very much. Thank you. Thank you, guys. Well, it is good to be back in California.

A couple of people I just want to acknowledge. First of all, your mayor, Alicia Aguirre; give her a big round of applause—she's here. And please give it up for Ben Harper for performing tonight.

Now, you guys can have a seat. I'm going to be talking for a while. [*Laughter*] It is good to see all of you. Are you having fun tonight?

Well, listen, I'm here not just because I need your help—although I do need your help. I'll get to that in a second. But I'm here because your country needs your help.

Now, 4 years ago, we came together because we wanted to reclaim the basic bargain that had built the largest middle class and the most prosperous nation on Earth. We shared a belief that in America, your circumstances shouldn't be determined—or your success shouldn't be determined by the circumstances of your birth, right? We—and you can see that in Redwood City—people from every background, from every corner not just of the country, but of the world.

This represents that idea that if you're willing to work hard, you should be able to create a life for yourself and your family, find a good job. If you're willing to meet your responsibilities, you should be able to own a home and maybe start a business, strike out with a new idea, send your kids to a good school, give them a chance to do even better than you, no matter who you are, no matter where you come from, no matter what you look like, no matter who you love.

So that's why we did all this in 2008. This wasn't a commitment you made because of me. This was a commitment you made to each other, because you felt that the country had strayed from some of those basic values.

We watched a record surplus that was squandered on tax cuts for folks who didn't need them and weren't asking for them. We saw two wars being waged on a credit card. We saw speculation in the financial sector, reaping huge profits for a few folks who were making bets with other people's money, but it was a flimsy kind of success. Manufacturing left our shores. A shrinking number of Americans did really, really well, but a growing number saw falling incomes and stagnant job growth and rising costs for everything from college to health care.

And so we had strayed from those values. And we built a house of cards. It ended up collapsing in the worst economic crisis since the Great Depression: lost 3 million jobs while we were campaigning; 800,000 jobs lost the month I took office.

And it's been tough. But it turns out the American people were tougher. We don't quit. We don't give up. We keep on going. Together, we fought back. We fought our way back. When some said, you know what, we should just let Detroit go bankrupt, we made a bet on American workers and American innovators and American companies, and today, the auto industry is back on top of the world.

Manufacturers are starting to invest in America again, adding jobs for the first time consistently since the nineties. Businesses got back to basics. Small-business owners, entrepreneurs, they hung on, made it work, kept on their employees where they could—created over 4 million jobs in the last 26 months, more than 1 million in the last 6 months alone.

Now, we're not satisfied. We've got a lot more to do. Not when so many of our friends and family are still out of work. Not when so many homes are still underwater. Not when so many States are still laying off teachers and first-responders.

This crisis—a crisis this deep—didn't happen overnight, and it's not going to be solved overnight, so we've got more work to do. We know that. And that's why this year is so important. Because we know the last thing we can afford to do is to go back to the very same policies that got us into this mess in the first place. Not now. Not with so much at stake. We've come too far to abandon the changes that we've fought for, for the last few years.

We've got to move forward and not backwards, forward to what we imagined in 2008: a country where everybody has got a fair shot and everybody is doing their fair share and everybody is playing by the same set of rules. And that's the choice in this election, and that's why I'm running again for President of the United States.

Audience members. Four more years! Four more years! Four more years!

The President. Now, you know we're starting to get into election season here. [*Laughter*] You know, I've still got my day job, and so I'm—[*laughter*]—I'm working hard solving problems. But I've got to pay attention to what the other side is up to. [*Laughter*]

And my opponent in this election, Governor Romney, he's a patriotic American. He's raised a wonderful family. He should be proud of the great personal success he's had. [*Laughter*] No, I mean, he has been extraordinarily successful at the financial firm that he helped put together. But I think he's drawn the wrong lessons from these experiences. He seems to believe that if CEOs and wealthy investors like him are getting rich that the rest of us automatically do too.

Now, we believe in the free market. We believe in risk-taking and innovation. This whole area is built on risk-taking and innovation. But we also understand that it doesn't happen in a vacuum. It happens because of outstanding schools and universities. It happens because of a well-regulated financial market. It happens because we have extraordinary infrastructure. It happens for a whole host of reasons.

But Governor Romney doesn't seem to understand that. So, when a woman in Iowa shared the story of her financial struggles, he sounded like he was talking out of a textbook. He said, well, our productivity equals our income. Well, the implication was the only reason that somebody might be in financial hardship is because they're not productive enough, they're not working hard enough.

But I have to tell you, those of us who have spent a lot of time talking to a lot of Americans have come to realize the problem isn't the American people aren't productive enough. Our productivity is actually higher than it's ever been. You've been working harder than ever. The challenge right now, the challenge we've faced for over a decade, is that harder work for too many people doesn't lead to higher incomes, and bigger profits don't necessarily lead to better jobs.

And so what Governor Romney and my opponents don't seem to understand is that a healthy economy doesn't just mean maximizing the profits of some. That's important. That's part of our free market, but not if it's purchased at the cost of massive layoffs, not if your main strategy is busting unions. You don't make America stronger just by shipping jobs and profits overseas. You don't create an environment where everybody has got a fair shot if you're gutting all those investments that help to create a platform for everybody's success. You don't create economic growth when you propose cutting your own taxes while raising them on 18 million working families. That's not a recipe for broad-based economic growth.

Of course, the fact is there's nothing new about these ideas. They've been peddling this stuff for years. Although, as Bill Clinton said a few weeks ago, this time their agenda is on steroids. But it's not new. They want bigger tax cuts for the wealthiest Americans. They want even deeper cuts for things like education and Medicare and research and technology. They want to give banks and insurance companies even more power to do as they please and gut and strip out regulations that help protect consumers.

But that's not new. That was tried, remember? The last guy did all this. [*Laughter*] Governor Romney, well, he is saying, well, my 25 years in private sector gives me a special understanding of how our economy works. Well, if that's true, why is he peddling the same bad

ideas that brought our economy to the brink of collapse? Most good businesspeople I know, if something doesn't work, they do something different. So he must either think that there's going to be a different result, or he's hoping you don't remember what happened the last time we tried it his way.

I'll tell you what, I remember. You remember. We were there. And we're not going back to that. We're moving this country forward. Now, you're going to be hearing a bunch of stuff during the course of this campaign. Of course, you've been hearing it for the last 3½ years. They started saying it the day after I took office—actually the day I took office. [*Laughter*] So let's be clear. We don't expect government to solve all our problems. It shouldn't try. I learned from my mom there is no education policy that by itself can take the place of a parent's love and attention, and sometimes a stern rebuke.

My first job as a community organizer was with Catholic churches who taught me the power of kindness and commitment to others in neighborhoods. Not everything in government works. Not every regulation is smart. Not every tax dollar is spent wisely. Not every person can be helped who refuses to help themselves. And the fact is, is that a bunch of the stuff that we do in government is outdated and has to be streamlined. And we've been focused on everything from making sure that they don't use rotary phones anymore to—[*laughter*]. I'm exaggerating. [*Laughter*]

But there is all kinds of reorganization and streamlining that has to be done, because we want government to have the same customer service mentality that the best businesses do. We want folks to have that same sense of efficiency and effectiveness.

But that's different from telling the vast majority of responsible, hard-working Americans, you're on your own; that unless you're lucky enough to have parents who can lend you the money, you may not be able to go to college; that even if you pay your premiums every month, you're out of luck if an insurance company decides to drop your coverage when you need it most. That's not who we are. That's not how America was built.

We built this country together. We built railroads and highways, the Hoover Dam and the Golden Gate Bridge together. We sent my grandfather's generation to college on the GI bill together. We went to the Moon together. The entire structure for the Internet we built together. All the stuff that's going on here can be traced back to investments we made together that then gave the opportunity, created the platform for Google and Facebook and you name it, because we understood that there are some things that we have to do together.

And we didn't do it for some particular group or individual. We understood that stuff made us all richer. It gave us all opportunity. We move forward together, as one Nation and as one people. And that's the true lesson of our past. That's the right vision for our future. That's why I'm running again for President of the United States.

I'm running to make sure that by the end of this decade, more of our citizens hold college degrees than any other nation on Earth. I want more engineers. I want more scientists. I want our schools to be able to hire and reward the best teachers, especially in math and science. I want to give 2 million more Americans the chance to go to community colleges and learn the skills that local businesses need so that workers can compete in the 21st century. Higher education is not a luxury, it is a necessity of this new global economy and everybody should be able to afford it. Everybody should be able to get that chance. That's the choice in this election. That's why I'm running for President.

I'm running to make sure the next generation of high-tech innovation takes place right here, in Silicon Valley, in Cleveland, and in Pittsburgh and Charlotte and Chicago. I want to stop rewarding businesses that ship jobs and profits overseas. I want to reward companies that are investing and creating jobs here in the United States. And that's the choice in this election.

I want to keep moving towards a future where we control our own energy. Our depen-

dence on foreign oil is at its lowest point in 16 years. We have doubled clean energy investments. We have raised fuel efficiency standards so the cars will be getting 55 miles a gallon. Thousands of Americans have jobs because of the investments we're making in things like advanced battery manufacturing. That's our future.

And imagine what we could keep on doing if we weren't spending $4 billion a year on subsidies for the oil companies, and we were investing that in clean energy, we were investing it in energy efficiency. It is time for us to end subsidies for a mature industry that's rarely been more profitable. Let's double down on the clean energy future that's never been more promising for our economy and for our security and for the safety of our planet and doing something about climate change.

We can make a difference. That's our future. That's our choice. And that's why I'm running for reelection—because we still have more work to do.

For the first time in 9 years, we have no Americans fighting in Iraq. Usama bin Laden is no longer a threat to this country. Al Qaida is on the path to defeat. And by 2014, the war in Afghanistan will be over.

America is safer and stronger and more respected around the world because of the courage and selflessness of the U.S. Armed Forces, because of their outstanding service. And as long as I'm Commander in Chief, this country will care for our veterans and serve our veterans as well as they've served us. They shouldn't have to fight for a job when they come home. They shouldn't be fighting homelessness when they come home. We need to look after them. That's what we've done for the last 3½ years. And I want to keep on doing it as long as I'm President of the United States of America.

And this is another place where my opponent has different ideas. He said ending the war was "tragic"—in Iraq. He won't set a timeline for ending the war in Afghanistan. I have, and I intend to keep it. It's the right thing to do for our country, because after a decade of war that's cost us thousands of lives and over a trillion dollars, the nation we need to build is our own.

We will end this war responsibly. We will use half of what we're no longer spending to cut our deficit. We'll use the rest to do some rebuilding right here in research and education, in building new runways and wireless networks. That's the choice in this election.

Audience member. [*Inaudible*]—loves you! [*Laughter*]

The President. Well, I love you too. Thank you.

And by the way, look—we're going to pay down our debt in a way that is balanced and responsible. I inherited a trillion-dollar deficit; I signed $2 trillion in spending cuts. My opponents won't admit it because it runs contrary to, I guess, the only argument they have, but since I've been President, Federal spending has actually risen at the lowest pace in nearly 60 years. It—usually it takes a Democrat to fix these problems after they have run up the tab.

And so we're going to finish the job. Yes, by streamlining Government and cutting more waste. But we also need to reform our Tax Code so it's simpler and fairer and so it asks folks like me—the wealthiest Americans—just to pay a little more.

And my opponent won't—he's proposed a $5 trillion tax cut on top of the Bush tax cut. This gives an average of $250,000 to every millionaire in the country. And although he won't detail how he's going to pay for it, I can tell you, either it's going to be passed on to our kids, or you're going to have to pay for it. A whole lot of ordinary Americans will have to pay for it.

And I refuse to let that happen. We're not going to have another millionaires tax cut paid for by eliminating medical research for cancer and Alzheimer's, another tax cut paid for by kicking kids out of Head Start programs or asking students to pay more for college or eliminating health insurance for millions of poor, elderly, disabled Americans on Medicaid. We're not going to voucherize our Medicare system.

We are going to reform Medicare and Medicaid, but we'll do it the right way, which is to stop spending money on things that don't make people healthier, actually reduce costs, don't

just shift them on to seniors, don't just shift them off to folks who can't afford it. That's the right way to do it. And that's what's at stake.

On issue after issue, these guys want to go backwards. America doesn't want to spend the next 4 years refighting the battles we just had over Wall Street reform. We're just seeing now how necessary it still is to just provide some basic rules for the road. We don't want to refight the battles of health care. We've got 2.5 million young people on their parent's health insurance plan. That was the right thing to do. Millions of seniors saving on their prescription drugs, that was the right thing to do. We're not going to go back to a time when insurance companies could just drop your coverage or cancel your policy or charge women more than men. We're not going back to that.

We don't need another political fight about ending a woman's right to choose or getting rid of Planned Parenthood or taking away access to affordable birth control. I want women to control their own health care choices, just like I want my daughters to have the same opportunities as my sons. We're not rolling back the clock.

We're not going back to the days when the U.S.—when somebody could be kicked out of the military just because of who you are and who you love. We're not going there. We're moving forward to a country where everybody is treated with dignity and respect. That's what we're moving towards.

And we're not going to enshrine a system where elections are determined because you can write a $10 million check, drowning out the voices of other citizens. We're not going to go—we're not going to give up on the notion that it makes no sense for us to deny citizenship to responsible young people who want to start a business here or work here, to contribute to this country, to serve their country, just because their parents might have been undocumented. That doesn't make sense. This country is best when we harness the God-given talents of every individual and we hear every voice and we come together as one American family, striving for the same American Dream.

That's what we're fighting for. That's why I'm running for President. That's why I need your help.

Audience members. Four more years! Four more years! Four more years!

The President. Now, let me tell you, this election is going to be tougher than the last. We've got more negative ads, more undisclosed spending.

Audience member. Super PACs.

The President. More super PACs. [*Laughter*] Didn't even know what those—there weren't super PACs last time we ran. And the atmosphere of cynicism and nastiness and sometimes just plain foolishness seems to ratchet up each cycle.

But ultimately, the outcome of this election is going to be up to you. I'll work hard. Michelle is out there. We're going after this thing. But if there's one thing we learned in 2008, no matter what the other side throws at us, when there are millions of voices calling for change, when you knock on enough doors and make enough phone calls and talk to your friends and neighbors, and when you decide it's time for change to happen, guess what, change happens. And that's the spirit that we're going to need again, only more so.

If people ask you what this campaign is about, you tell them it's still about hope. You tell them it's still about change. You tell them it's still about ordinary people who believe in the face of great odds that we can make a difference in the life of this country.

I still believe that. I still believe our politics isn't as divided as our politics suggest. I still believe that we've got more in common than the pundits tell us we do. We're not Democrats or Republicans first, we're Americans first. And I see it all across the country, wherever I travel: north, south, east, west, big cities, small towns. There's a core decency and practicality and common sense in the American people that makes me so determined to get this thing done.

I still believe in you, and I hope you still believe in me. Because I told you in 2008, I may not be a perfect man, and I'm not a perfect President, but I'll always tell you what I think and where I stand. And I wake up every single day thinking about you and how I can make your lives better and your kids' lives better. And if you stick with me, if you march with me and campaign with me and work as hard as you did the last time, we're going to finish what we started in 2008. We're going to finish what we started in 2008. We're going to get this country moving. We're going to be going forward and remind the entire world just why it is the United States is the greatest nation on Earth.

Thank you, everybody. God bless you.

NOTE: The President spoke at 9:45 p.m. at the Fox Theatre. In his remarks, he referred to Republican Presidential candidate former Gov. W. Mitt Romney of Massachusetts; and former President William J. Clinton. The transcript was released by the Office of the Press Secretary on May 24.

Remarks at TPI Composites, Inc., in Newton, Iowa
May 24, 2012

Hello, Iowa! Well, it is good to be back in Newton! It's been a while. It's good to be back in Iowa. It's brought back memories of a lot of driving. [*Laughter*] And I just had a great tour of this facility. By the way, if people have chairs, feel free to sit down. [*Laughter*] Some of you may not have seats, but I want to make everybody comfortable. But don't worry, I'm not going to talk that long. I didn't want to give that impression.

I just had a wonderful tour of this facility. And I was telling some of the folks, we couldn't take the helicopter in because the winds were too strong, so you are definitely in the right business. [*Laughter*] Obviously, there's some wind power here in Iowa that we want to tap.

I want to thank Quinton for the terrific introduction, for sharing his story. Give Quinton a big round of applause. Quinton was telling my team, this is the first time he's ever spoken in public, but he looked like a pro to me.

I want to thank your mayor, Mayor Allen, for welcoming us here today. I also want to thank Representative Dave Loebsack for being here. Give Dave a big round of applause. And I know he had to leave early, but I just want to acknowledge somebody you know well, our outstanding Secretary of Agriculture, Tom Vilsack. Tom was instrumental in helping transform Newton, and he's still got your back. He is still fighting every single day for every single person in this town, but all across rural America. And so we're very proud of him.

Now, we all know how difficult these past few years have been for the country. Iowa has actually done a little better than some other States, but it's still been tough. And after the worst recession of our lifetimes, it's going to take some time for the economy to fully recover, more time than a lot of us would like. And we're still facing some headwinds, like the situation in Europe right now, which is having an impact on our economy.

But while there's certain economic developments we can't control, there are a bunch of things that we can control. There are plenty of steps that we can take right now—steps that we must take right now—to speed up this recovery and to create jobs and to restore some of the financial security that a lot of families have lost. It's within our control to do all of that right now. But here's the thing—[*applause*]. It's true, we can make that difference.

The challenge we've got is that too many folks aren't on the same page. We've got too many of my dear Republican friends in Congress that have been standing in the way of some steps that we could take that would make a difference at the moment. Either they say they don't want to do anything at all or they don't want to do it before the election or they want to double down on some of the policies that didn't work and helped to get us into this mess in the first place.

And Newton knows something about that, because Newton lost manufacturing. Newton lost Maytag. A lot of the trends that we had seen even before the financial crisis hit, hit Newton first. And so when you hear somebody say we should cut more taxes, especially for the wealthiest Americans, well, Newton, you've been there, and you've done that. We did that: 2000, 2001, 2003. When you hear people say that we should cut back more on the rules we put in place for banks and financial institutions to avoid another taxpayer bailout, well, we tried that. When people say that we should just wait until the housing market hits bottom and hope that it comes back, hope for the best, well, that's not an answer for people. That doesn't make sense.

We've tried at lot of these ideas for nearly a decade. It did not work. We saw manufacturing moving offshore. We saw a few people do very well, but too many families struggling just to get by, all before the financial crisis hit. And the financial crisis made it worse. So we can't go backwards. We've got to move forward. We've got to build an economy where hard work and responsibility pay off, where you can find a good job and own your own home, maybe start your own businesses, give your kids a chance for a better future. That's the American way. That's who we are.

So I've been pushing Congress to help us get there by passing a few commonsense policies that would strengthen the economy and put more folks to work right now. We even made a handy to-do list that they can check off. It's just like the to-do list Michelle gives me, a honey-do list. [*Laughter*] There are only five things on it, on this to-do list, but these are all things we could get done before the election. We don't have to wait until then. There are some things that we should put ahead of politics and one of them is making sure that the economy is moving forward and the recovery is moving forward.

And like I said, I kept it simple. There are just five things. I didn't want to overload Congress with too much at once. [*Laughter*] But these are all ideas that will make a difference right now, and we shouldn't wait for an election to get them done.

So, first up on the list, it makes no sense that we're actually still giving tax breaks to companies that ship jobs and factories overseas. That doesn't make sense at all. That doesn't make any sense. So what I've asked Congress to do is end tax breaks for companies that are shipping jobs overseas, use that money to cover the moving expenses for companies that are bringing jobs back to the United States of America. That's a commonsense approach.

Second, we've asked Congress to give every responsible homeowner—folks who have been making their mortgage payments—the opportunity to save an average of $3,000 a year by refinancing their mortgage and taking advantage of these historically low rates. The problem is, a lot of folks are having trouble refinancing if their home is underwater, if it's less—worth less than their mortgage, and sometimes banks have been pulling back a little bit. We want to make it easier for people to refinance. So that's the second thing because that will create—that will put more money in the economy for everybody. And if you've got an extra $3,000 in your pocket, then you'll go shopping, you'll go out to a restaurant, suddenly, there's a lot more money circulating and the economy gets stronger. So that's the second thing.

Two weeks ago, I was in Reno, Nevada, with a family; they got a chance to refinance because of some steps that we had already taken administratively. And it's making a huge difference in their lives. And we want all families to have that same opportunity.

Third thing, instead of just talking about job creators—you always hear—every Member of Congress has said, we've got to help the job creators. Okay, let's help them. Congress should help small-business owners who create most of the new jobs in America—small-business owners. So what we want to do is give them a tax break for hiring more workers and for paying them higher wages. Give them an incentive to say, you know what, if on the margins maybe I'm thinking about hiring that extra person, if I get a tax break it makes that person a little bit cheaper to hire, and that can put more of our neighbors and friends back to work. So that's a commonsense idea.

Fourth thing, we have done a whole lot to make sure that those men and women who have served us in Iraq and Afghanistan, that we

are serving them as well as they've served us, treating them with honor and respect that they have earned when they come home. So we put together the post-9/11 GI bill so they're able to go back and get some training and skills. We've mobilized the private sector to hire more veterans and given the private sector incentives to hire more veterans.

But there's another thing we can do. Congress should create what we're calling a veterans jobs corps, so that we can help communities across America put our returning heroes back to work as police officers and firefighters and park rangers. Nobody who fought for our country overseas should have to fight for a job when they come back home. We've still got too much unemployment among our veterans.

So those are four simple things. And the fifth thing is the reason why I'm here today. The fifth item on my to-do list: I'm calling on Congress to extend tax credits that are set to expire at the end of the year for clean energy companies like TPI. Let's not wait. Let's do it now.

Many of you know the story of what's happening here better than I do, but I just want to remind you how far we've come. Shortly after I took office, I came to Newton—some of you remember—and we unveiled an all-of-the-above energy strategy for America. We said let's produce more oil and gas, but let's also produce more biofuels, let's produce more fuel-efficient cars, let's produce more solar and wind power and other sources of clean, renewable energy. And I came to Newton because Newton is helping to lead the way when it comes to building wind turbines.

And since then, our dependence on foreign oil has gone down every single year that I've been in office—every single year. America is now producing more domestic oil than any time in the last 8 years. But we're also producing more natural gas, and we're producing more biofuels than any time in our history. And that's good for the Iowa economy. We're laying the foundation for some of our Nation's first offshore wind farms. And since I became President, America has nearly doubled the use of renewable energy, like solar power and wind power. We've nearly doubled it.

So this country is on the path towards more energy independence. And that's good for everybody. It's good for people's pocketbooks, it's good for the environment, it's good for our national security. We don't want our economy dependent on something that happens on the other side of the world. We don't want every time there's a scare about war or some regime change in the Middle East that suddenly everybody here is getting socked and the whole economy is going down.

And the best thing is, in the process, we're also putting thousands of Americans back to work, because the more we rely on American-made energy, the less oil we buy from other countries, the more jobs we create here at home, the more jobs we create here in Iowa.

So let's look at the wind industry. It's so important to Iowa. This industry, thanks in large part to some very important tax credits, has now taken off. The State of Iowa now gets nearly 20 percent of all your electricity from wind—20 percent. Overall, America now has enough wind capacity to power 10 million homes. So this is an industry on the rise. And as you know, it's an industry that's putting people to work. You know this firsthand. There are more wind power jobs in Iowa than any other State. That's a big deal.

And one of these modern windmills has more than 8,000 different parts, everything from the towers and the blades to the gears, to the electrical switches. And it used to be that almost all these parts were imported. Today, more and more of these parts are being made here in America—right here. We used to have just a few dozen manufacturing facilities attached to the wind industry. Today, we have nearly 500 facilities, in 43 States, employing tens of thousands of American workers—tens of thousands.

So we're making progress. And you know it better than anybody. I mean, when I was talking to Quinton and Mark and a whole bunch of the other folks who are working here, they reminded me of the experience of working at Maytag and putting your heart and soul into a company and making a great product, and then suddenly having that company leave, and how hard that was for families and how hard it was for the community. But folks made the transition.

And now, when you look at what's happening here—700 to 800 jobs, over $30 million being put back into the community—this gives folks hope. It gives people opportunity. I met some folks who have been in manufacturing for 30 years, but I also met a couple of young folks who were just getting started. And that's what we're looking for. Nobody wants a handout. Nobody wants to get something for nothing. But if we've got a chance to create energy and create value and put people back to work, why wouldn't we do that?

So I'm here today because, as much progress as we've made, that progress is in jeopardy. If Congress doesn't act, those tax credits that I mentioned—the ones that helped build up the wind industry, the ones that helped to bring all these jobs to Newton—those tax credits will expire at the end of the year if Congress doesn't do anything.

If Congress doesn't act, companies like this one will take a hit. Jobs will be lost. That's not a guess, that's a fact. We can't let it happen. And keep in mind that—and this is something Congress needs to understand—Dave Loebsack understands it, but I want every Member of Congress to understand it. These companies that are putting in orders for these amazing blades, they're making plans now. They're making decisions now. So, if they're cutting back on their orders, if they're not confident that the industry is going to be moving at a fast clip and they start reducing orders here, that affects you. You can't wait for 6 months. You can't wait for 8 months. You can't wait for a year to get this done. It's got to be done now.

So this is a simple thing on Congress's to-do list: extend these tax credits. Do it now. Every day they don't act, business grows more concerned that they will not be renewed. They're worried demand for their products is going down, so they start thinking twice about expanding, more cautious about making new investments. They start looking overseas. I was talking to your CEO. We got an opportunity to branch out, but we want to branch out by making the stuff here and then sending it there. We don't want to branch out by sending the jobs and the investments over there, and then shipping it back to America. That doesn't make sense. One company that had plans to invest a hundred million dollars to build a wind manufacturing plant in Arkansas—and create hundreds of jobs—put those plans on hold.

And by the way, this should not be a partisan issue. There are several Republican Governors—including the Governor of this State—who are calling on Congress to act. There are Members of Congress in both Chambers and on both sides of the aisle—including your two Senators—who support these tax credits. And that doesn't happen much in Washington where Democrats and Republicans say they agree on something. So, if you agree, why haven't we gotten it done yet?

This is not just an issue, by the way, for the wind industry. Some of America's most prominent companies—from Starbucks to Campbell's Soup—they're calling on Congress to act, because they use renewable energy.

Sometimes when I think about Washington and Congress—and I know some of you think the same way—I don't get it. I understand why we wouldn't get something done if we really disagree on something. And there are some big disagreements: They want to make big cuts to pay for more big tax cuts for the wealthy. I disagree with that. I think we should have a balanced approach: cut waste, but make sure that everybody is paying their fair share. An issue like that, maybe it can't get settled before an election, because they just have a different approach. I understand that. But this, everybody says they agree to or at least a lot of people agree to it.

So I'm going to need your help. I need you to get involved. I need you to help get this done. I need everybody here in Newton, and I mean everybody—I don't just mean folks who work at TPI—anybody who's watching, every-body here in Iowa, pick up the phone, send an e-mail, send a tweet, tell Congress, let's do the right thing. Tell Congress the story of Newton. Tell folks why it's so important to this community. Tell them we've come too far to turn back now.

It used to be Newton was known for building washers and dryers, used to be Newton was known for Maytag. And obviously, they were a big employer, thousands of people working in the area. But back in 2007 when they closed down the operations here, that was a major blow. And everybody here, if you don't—if you weren't affected personally by it, you were affected indirectly: your friends, your neighbors. Folks like Quinton were forced to start all over again, and he didn't give up. You didn't give up. You kept pushing ahead. Some of you had to retrain. Pretty soon after one industry had left, another showed up. Some of the facilities that Maytag closed were reopened. So a lot of folks who used to build washers and dryers, now they're part of the future, building an industry that's going to make America stronger. That's the story of Newton. That's the story of America.

So yes, we're facing tough times, but we're getting through them. We're getting through them together, because in this country, just like in Newton, we don't give up. We keep moving. We keep moving forward. And if we work together with a common purpose, we will get this economy back on track and remind everybody why America is the greatest country on Earth.

Thank you, everybody. God bless you. God bless America. Thank you.

NOTE: The President spoke at 4:30 p.m. In his remarks, he referred to Quinton Gearhart, employee, Mark Parriott, general manager, and Steven C. Lockard, president and chief executive officer, TPI Composites, Inc.; Mayor Charles Allen of Newton, IA; Reno, NV, residents Paul and Valerie Keller; and Gov. Terry E. Branstad of Iowa.

Remarks to an Overflow Crowd at an Obama Victory Fund 2012 Fundraiser in Des Moines, Iowa
May 24, 2012

The President. Hello, Iowa! How's it going, Des Moines? Well, it is good to be back in my home away from home.

Now, I've got to give a long speech in there, so I'm not going to give a long speech here. But what I do want to just say to all of you is——

Audience member. I love you!

The President. I love you back.

You know, this journey started in Iowa, and that's why we're going to be spending a lot of time in Iowa this time round. Because when I go around the country and I talk about how decent folks are and responsible they are, and everybody wants a fair shot and everybody is willing to do their fair share and everybody is playing by the same set of rules, I'm talking about the people of Iowa as a great example of what America is all about.

So we're going to have a lot of work to do. We've gone through some tough times. The economy has been tough. We still have friends and neighbors who are out of work. We still have too many folks whose home values have dropped, small businesses that are still struggling. So we're going to have to keep on moving. We've got to push forward. We can't go backwards.

And these other folks, they want to go back to the same stuff that got us into this mess in the first place, and we're not going to do that. We want to move forward. We're not going backwards.

So how many of you are ready to work? Because it's going to take some work this time.

This is going to take some work. This is going to be harder this time than it was the last time. But Iowa is full of hard-working folk. And there's something about Iowa: When I come here, I want to work even harder.

So I just want to say thank you to all the team members, team leaders, everybody who's out there knocking on doors, making phone calls, talking to your neighbors, talking to your friends, talking to your uncle or aunt who somehow still thinks the other side knows what they're talking about—[*laughter*]—and you've got to help them see the light. You just keep at it.

And the last thing I'll say is this. Even though all these folks are spending all this millions of dollars of money on negative ads—that's going to keep on because of these super PACs and all that stuff—nothing is more important than ordinary people standing up: standing up for our values, standing up for what America is all about. So don't think that these folks can beat us. If you're out there, you're going to beat them. And we're going to bring this country together and get things moving in the right direction.

Thank you, everybody. God bless you. God bless America.

NOTE: The President spoke at 6:54 p.m. in the Susan Knapp Amphitheater at the Iowa State Fairgrounds. Audio was not available for verification of the content of these remarks.

Remarks at an Obama Victory Fund 2012 Fundraiser in Des Moines
May 24, 2012

The President. Hello, Iowa! I don't know about you, but I'm feeling fired up! I am definitely ready to go! Definitely ready to go. We just had a chance to talk to the folks in the overflow, and before that, we were in Newton. And I was just telling my team, there's something

about coming to Iowa, it just gets me going! It's my home away from home. Just love this place! Even just all those long drives. [*Laughter*] Seeing all that corn makes me feel good.

So listen, I want to thank a couple of Iowa friends of mine. First of all, your outstanding former Governor and now outstanding Secretary of Agriculture, Tom Vilsack is in the house. Your mayor, Frank Cownie, is here; your Congressman, Leonard Boswell; your attorney general and one of my campaign cochairs, Tom Miller; your State treasurer and one of my earliest supporters, Mike Fitzgerald.

And I also want to thank some folks who've been keeping us fired up from the very beginning, the Isiserettes, who are in the house. We were talking about when we had the J-J dinner, we were all going in together, and the Isiserettes were at the front, and Michelle and I were dancing—she was dancing, I was trying to dance. [*Laughter*]

So it's good to be back. It's good to be back among friends. It's good to be seeing all of you. You know, 4 or 5 years ago, it was you who kept us going when a lot of pundits in Washington had written us off. You remember that. It was on your front porches, it was in your backyards where our movement for change began.

Audience member. We love you, Mr. President!

The President. I love you back.

Audience members. Four more years! Four more years! Four more years!

The President. You know, it was here where we came together to reclaim the basic bargain that built the largest middle class and the most prosperous nation on Earth. We believe that in America success shouldn't be determined by the circumstances of your birth. If you're willing to work hard, you should be able to find a good job. If you're willing to meet your responsibilities, you should be able to own a home, maybe start a business. You should be able to give your children a better chance than you had, no matter where you came from, no matter what you look like, no matter who you love. That's what we believe.

And we came together in 2008 because you could tell that our country—or at least the leadership in Washington—had strayed away from these basic values. We had a record surplus that had been squandered on tax cuts for folks who didn't need them and weren't even asking for them. Two wars had been waged on a credit card. Wall Street speculators were

reaching huge profits, making bets with other people's money, but it was destabilizing our financial system. Manufacturing was moving offshore. A shrinking number of Americans were doing fantastically well, but a whole lot of people were struggling with falling incomes and rising costs and the slowest job growth in half a century.

And it was a house of cards, and we sensed that. And then right in the middle of the campaign we saw the most destructive crisis since the Great Depression. In the last 6 months of 2008, while we were still campaigning, nearly 3 million of our neighbors lost their jobs; 800,000 lost their jobs the month I was sworn in. Hadn't seen anything like it since the Great Depression.

And so it was tough. But it turned out Americans were tougher. Folks in Iowa were tougher. We don't quit. We keep going. And together, we're fighting our way back.

So, when some said we should just let Detroit go bankrupt, we put our money on American workers and the ingenuity of American companies. And today, plants are adding new workers and new shifts, and the American auto industry is firing on all cylinders. Our manufacturers started investing in America again; first time we consistently added manufacturing jobs since the 1990s.

Businesses started getting back to the basics, creating over 4 million new jobs in the last 26 months, more than 1 million in the last 6 months alone. Here in Iowa, farmers, food producers, manufacturers, renewable energy producers, they're all driving new job growth, showing the resilience and strength of our rural economies.

Now, are we satisfied? Of course not. We've still got friends out there, and family, who are looking for work. All across America there are homes that are still underwater, too many small businesses still struggling to get financing. States are still laying off teachers and first-responders.

This was a deep crisis; it didn't happen overnight. And we never thought it was going to be solved overnight. We know we have more work to do. But we also know that the last thing we can afford to do is to return to the very same policies that got us into this mess in the first place. Not now. Not with so much at stake. We have come too far to abandon the change that we fought for over these past few years. We've got to move forward. We can't go backward. We've got to move forward.

That's the choice in this election. And that's why I'm running for a second term as President of the United States: to move this country forward.

Now, my opponent in this election, Governor Romney, is a patriotic American. He's raised a wonderful family. He should be proud of the great personal success he's had as a CEO of a large financial firm. There are plenty of good and honest people in that industry, and there's an important, creative role for it in the free market.

But Governor Romney has made his experience as a financial CEO the entire rationale of his candidacy for President. Now, he doesn't really talk about what he did in Massachusetts. But he does talk about being a business guy. Right? He says this gives him a special understanding of what it takes to create jobs and grow the economy, even if he's unable to offer a single new idea about how to do that. No matter how many times he's asked about it, he says he knows how to do it. So I think it's a good idea to look at the way he sees the economy.

Now, the main goal of a financial firm like Governor Romney's is not to create jobs. And by the way, the people who work at these firms will tell you that's not their goal. Their main goal is to create wealth for themselves and their investors. That's part of the American way. That's fine.

Sometimes, jobs are created in that process. But when maximizing short-term gains for your investors rather than building companies that last is your goal, then sometimes it goes the other way: workers get laid off, benefits disappear, pensions are cut, factories go dark. In some cases, companies are loaded up with debt, not to make the companies more productive, not to buy new equipment to keep them at the cutting edge, but just to pay investors. Companies may go bankrupt as a result. Tax-

payers may be on the hook to help out on those pensions. Investors walk off with big returns, and working folks get stuck holding the bag.

Now, that may be the job of somebody who's engaged in corporate buyouts. That's fine. But that's not the job of a President. That's not the President's job. There may be value for that kind of experience, but it's not in the White House.

See, the job of a President is to lay the foundation for strong and sustainable broad-based growth, not one where a small group of speculators are cashing in on short-term gains. It's to make sure that everybody in this country gets a fair shake, everybody gets a fair shot, everybody is playing by the same set of rules.

When you're the President, your job is to look out for the investor and the worker, for the big companies and the small companies, for the health of farmers and small-business people and the nurse and the teacher. You're supposed to be thinking about everybody and the health of the middle class and what the future is going to hold for our kids. That's how I see the economy.

Of course, the worldview that Governor Romney gained from his experience as a financial CEO explains something. It explains why the last time he visited these very same fairgrounds, he famously declared that corporations are people. "Human beings, my friends"—that's what he said. That's what he called them: "Human beings, my friends."

It also explains why, when a woman right here in Iowa shared the story of her financial struggles, he gave her an answer out of an economics textbook. He said, "Our productivity equals our income." Well—as if she'd have an easier time making it if she would just work harder.

Now, let me tell you something. We believe in the profit motive. We believe that risk takers and investors should be rewarded. That's what makes our economy so dynamic. But we also believe everybody should have opportunity. We believe—[*applause*]—we think everybody who makes the economy more productive or a company more productive should benefit.

And the problem with our economy isn't that the American people aren't productive enough; you're working harder than ever. Productivity is through the roof. It's been going up consistently over the last decade. The challenge we face right now, the challenge we've faced for over a decade, is that harder work hasn't led to higher incomes. Bigger profits haven't led to better jobs. And you can't solve that problem if you can't even see that it's a problem.

And he doesn't see it's a problem. And so this experience explains why he is proposing the exact same policies that we already tried in the last decade, the very policies that got us into this mess. He sincerely believes that if CEOs and wealthy investors are getting rich, then the wealth is going to trickle down and the rest of us are going to do well too. And he is wrong.

You don't build a strong economy by proposing more tax cuts for corporations that ship jobs and profits overseas. But that's his plan. You don't build a strong economy by repealing the rules that are designed to prevent another taxpayer bailout of Wall Street banks. But that's what he pledges to do, roll those things back. You don't build a strong economy by offering another budget-busting tax cut skewed to the wealthiest Americans, while raising taxes on 18 million working families. But that's what he's proposing.

And then, he and his folks, they've got the nerve to go around saying they're somehow going to bring down the deficit. Economists who have looked at his plan say it would swell our deficits by trillions of dollars, even with the drastic cuts he's called for in things like education and agriculture and Medicare, even with the drastic cuts to the basic research and technology that have always been the strength of the American economy. He promises to do that on day one. We don't need that. That's a vision that's going backwards. We're going forwards.

We're going forward. We're not going to double down on the same bad ideas that we've tried over the last decade. It's not as if we haven't tried these things. We tried them. They didn't work. We're not going to listen to folks who argue that somehow this time it's going to be different. I'm here to tell you we were there when we tried them. We remember. We're not going back. We're moving this country forward.

And I want to make clear here, it's not like Democrats don't have work to do. We've got work to do. Government—we have to acknowledge government can't solve all our problems, and it shouldn't try. I learned from my mom no education policy can take the place of a parent's love and attention, and sometimes a scolding when you didn't do your homework. As a young man, when I was working as a community organizer with Catholic churches, they taught me no poverty program can make as much of a difference as neighbors coming together and working together with kindness and commitment.

Not every regulation is smart, not every tax dollar is spent wisely, not every person can be helped who refuses to help themselves. But that's not an excuse to tell the vast majority of hard-working, responsible Americans they're on their own; that unless you're lucky to have parents who can lend you the money, you may not be able to go to college; that even if you pay your premiums every month, you may be out of luck if an insurance company decides to drop your coverage just when you need it most.

That's not who we are, Iowa. That's not how we built America. We built this country together. The Hoover Dam, the Golden Gate Bridge, GI bill, the Moon landing, the Internet, we did those things together. Not to make some small group rich, not to make—help any single individual, but because we knew that if we made those investments it would provide a framework, a platform for everybody to do well, for everybody to succeed. That's the true lesson of our past. That's the right vision for our future. And that's why I'm running for President of the United States.

I'm running to make sure that by the end of this decade, more of our citizens hold a college degree than any other nation on Earth. I want to help our schools hire and reward the best teachers, especially in math and science. I want to give 2 million more Americans the chance to go to community colleges and learn skills that local businesses are looking for right now. Higher education can't be a luxury; it is a necessity, and I want everybody to be able to afford it. That's the choice in this election. That's why I'm running for President.

I'm running to make sure the next generation of high-tech innovation and manufacturing takes root in places like Des Moines and Newton and Waterloo. I want to stop rewarding businesses that ship jobs and profits overseas. I want to reward companies that are creating jobs and bringing jobs back here to the United States of America. That's the choice in this election.

I'm running so we can keep moving forward to a future where we control our own energy. Our dependence on foreign oil is at the lowest point it's been in 16 years. By the middle of the next decade, our cars will average nearly 55 miles per gallon. Thousands of Americans have jobs—including here in Iowa—because the production of renewable energy has nearly doubled in just 3 years in this country.

Now is not the time to cut these investments just to keep giving billions in tax giveaways to oil companies. They've never been more profitable. Now is the time to double down on biofuels and solar and wind, clean energy that's never been more promising for our economy and our security and for the safety of the planet. That's the choice in this election, Iowa.

You know, for the first time in 9 years, there are no Americans fighting in Iraq. Usama bin Laden is no longer a threat to this country. Al Qaida is on the path to defeat, and by 2014, the war in Afghanistan will be over.

And all this was made possible because of the courage and selflessness of our men and women in uniform, which is why, on Memorial Day, we're going to remember them. And I'm going to actually be talking especially about our Vietnam vets. Because they weren't honored the way they were supposed to when they came home, and we're not going to make that mistake again. So, as long as I'm Commander in Chief, this country will care for our veterans and serve them as well as they've served us. Because no one who fights for this country

should have to fight for a job, or a roof over their heads when they come home. That's why I'm running for President.

My opponent has got a different view. He said it was "tragic" to end the war in Iraq. He won't set a timeline to end the war in Afghanistan. And I have and I intend to keep it, because after a decade of war that's cost us thousands of lives and over a trillion dollars, the nation we need to build is our own. So I want to use—[*applause*]—so we're going to use half of what we're no longer spending on war to pay down our deficit and the rest to invest in education and research, to repair our roads and bridges, our runways, our wireless networks. That's the choice in this election, Iowa.

I'm running to pay down our debt in a way that's balanced and responsible. Now, I know Governor Romney came to Des Moines last week; warned about a "prairie fire of debt." That's what he said: "Prairie fire." [*Laughter*] But he left out some facts. His speech was more like a cow pie of distortion. [*Laughter*] I don't know whose record he twisted the most, mine or his. [*Laughter*]

Now, listen, the debt and the deficit are serious problems, and it is true that the depth of the recession added to the debt. A lot more folks were looking for unemployment insurance. A lot fewer folks were paying taxes because they weren't making money, so that added to the debt. Our efforts to prevent it from becoming a depression—helping the auto industry, making sure that not as many teachers were laid off—all those things added to the debt.

But what my opponent didn't tell you was that Federal spending since I took office has risen at the slowest pace of any President in almost 60 years. By the way, what generally happens—what happens is, the Republicans run up the tab, and then we're sitting there and they've left the restaurant, and then they point and—"Why did you order all those steaks and martinis?" [*Laughter*] What he did not also tell you was that after inheriting a trillion-dollar deficit, I signed $2 trillion of spending cuts into law.

685

So now I want to finish the job: yes, by streamlining Government—we've got more work to do; yes, by cutting more waste, but also by reforming our Tax Code so that it is simpler and fairer and so that it asks the wealthiest Americans to pay a little bit more.

Oh, by the way, something else he didn't mention, something else he didn't tell you: He hasn't told you how he'd paid for a new $5 trillion tax cut which includes a 25-percent tax cut for nearly every millionaire in the country. Five trillion in new tax cuts: That is like trying to put out a prairie fire with some gasoline.

So we're not going to do that. I refuse to let that happen to our country. We're not going to pay for another millionaire's tax cut by eliminating medical research that's helping people with cancer and Alzheimer's disease. We're not going to pay for it by shortchanging farmers in rural America. We're not going to pay for it by kicking some kids out of Head Start or asking students to pay more for college or eliminating health insurance for millions of poor and elderly and Americans on disabilities who are all on Medicaid.

And as long as I'm President, we're not going to allow Medicare to be turned into a voucher that would end the program as we know it. We're going to reform Medicare not by shifting the cost of care to seniors; that's easy to do, but it's wrong. We're going to reform it by reducing the actual costs of health care, reducing the spending that doesn't make people healthier. That's the right thing to do. That's what at stake, Iowa. That's why I'm running for reelection.

On issue after issue, we can't afford to spend the next 4 years just going backwards. We don't need to refight the battle we just had over Wall Street reform. That was the right thing to do. We've seen how important it is. We don't need to refight the battle we just had over health care reform. Having 2.5 million young people stay on their parents' health insurance, that was the right thing to do. Cutting prescription drug costs for seniors, right thing to do. We're not going to go back to the days when insurance companies had unchecked power to cancel your policies or deny you coverage or charge women differently than men. We're not going back to that.

We don't need another political fight about ending a woman's right to choose or getting rid of Planned Parenthood or taking away affordable birth control. We don't need that. I want women to control their own health choices, just like I want my daughters to have the same economic opportunities as my sons. We're not turning back the clock. We're not going backwards.

We're not going back to the days when you could be kicked out of the military just because of who you are and who you love. We're moving forward as a country, where everybody is treated with dignity and respect—moving forward.

We're not going to just stand back while $10 million checks are speaking louder than the voices of ordinary citizens in our elections. We recognize that's a problem.

And it's time to stop denying citizenship to responsible young people just because they're the children of undocumented immigrants. Look, you know what, this country is at its best when we harness the God-given talents of every individual, when we hear every voice, when we come together as one American family all striving for the same American Dream. That's what we're fighting for. That's why I'm running for a second term. That's why I need your help.

You know, let me say this, this election is going to be even closer than the last one. And by the way, the last one was close. People don't remember, it was close. Everybody remembers Grant Park. It was close. We're going to have to contend with even more negative ads. We've got these super PACs and shadowy special interests, like the ones you've been bombarded with. You guys just got hit here in Iowa. We'll have to overcome more cynicism and nastiness and just some plain foolishness even more than we did the last time.

But the outcome of this election, it's entirely up to you. I'm going to be working hard. Michelle is out there working hard. But there's one thing we learned in 2008: There's nothing more powerful than millions of voices calling for change.

Michelle and I, we were talking the other night over dinner, and I told her we were coming back to Iowa, and she said something—it's absolutely true—she said, I remember back in the first campaign, we would be reading all these news reports and watching the news, and everything looked terrible and everybody was counting us out. And then I'd come to Iowa, and I'd see what was going on on the ground, and I'd be meeting people and talking to people. It wasn't necessarily that it was a sure thing that we were going to win. But what was being reflected out there, that wasn't what was happening here. That wasn't what ordinary folks were thinking.

So she just stopped watching TV or at least the news part of it. She still watches HGTV and some other things—"Dancing With the Stars." [*Laughter*] But this place taught us that not that we're always right, not that we don't make mistakes, but that there's just a core decency and strength and resilience to the American people, and that ultimately, the conversations that are going around on kitchen tables and at the VFW hall and in churches, that those conversations aren't what's reflected in the cable news.

And so when I look out at this crowd, all these different faces—different ages, different races, different faiths—I'm reminded of that. And when enough of you knock on enough doors and pick up enough phones and talk to your friends or your neighbors and your co-workers—and you're doing it respectfully and you're talking to folks who don't agree with you, you're talking to people who are good people, but maybe they don't have all the information—when you make that happen, when you decide it's time for change to happen, you know what, change happens. Change comes to America.

It's always easier to be cynical. It's always easier to say nothing can change, especially after we've gone through such a tough time. And despite all the changes we've made, despite all the good things we've done, things are still tough. And so the other side, they are going to try and play on that sense that, well, things aren't perfect, Congress is still arguing, the poli-

tics is still polarized. But you're the antidote to that. And that's the spirit we need again.

So, if people ask you what this campaign is about, you tell them, yes, it's still about hope. It is still about change. It's still about ordinary folks who believe that in the face of great odds, we can make a difference in the life of this country. Don't let them tell you different.

You proved it in 2008. Without you—I look around this place, I see folks who were out there knocking on doors and making things happen—I would not have had the privilege of being your President. You were the first ones to make this country believe we could still come together around a common purpose. And I still believe that today.

I still believe that we're not as divided as our politics suggest. I still believe we have more in common than the experts tell us. I still believe we're not Democrats or Republicans first, we are Americans first. I still believe in you. And I want you to keep believing in me.

Some of you remember—because I've spent a lot of time here, I used to go around and I would tell you—I warned you, and if you weren't listening, Michelle would tell you, I'm not a perfect man, and I wouldn't be a perfect President. But what I told you was, I promised you I would always tell you what I thought and I'd always tell you where I stood, even when it politically wasn't convenient. And I would wake up every single day, fighting as hard as I know how for you and your families and your children's future.

And, Iowa, I have kept that promise. I have kept that promise, and I will keep it as long as I have the honor of being your President. So if you're willing to stick with me and fight with me and press on with me, and if you're willing to work even harder than you did the last time, we will move this country forward and we will finish what we started. And we'll remind the world just why it is America is the greatest nation on Earth.

God bless you. God bless America.

NOTE: The President spoke at 7:10 p.m. in the Paul R. Knapp Animal Learning Center at the Iowa State Fairgrounds. In his remarks, he referred to Republican Presidential candidate former Gov. W. Mitt Romney of Massachu-setts. He also referred to Jefferson-Jackson dinners, Democratic Party fundraising events.

The President's Weekly Address
May 26, 2012

This weekend, folks across the country are opening up the pool, firing up the grill, and taking a well-earned moment to relax. But Memorial Day is more than a 3-day weekend. In town squares and national cemeteries, in public services and moments of quiet reflection, we will honor those who loved their country enough to sacrifice their own lives for it.

This Memorial Day, Michelle and I will join Gold Star families, veterans, and their families at Arlington National Cemetery. We'll pay tribute to patriots of every generation who gave the last full measure of devotion, from Lexington and Concord to Iraq and Afghanistan.

Later that day, we'll join Vietnam veterans and their families at the Vietnam Veterans Memorial—the wall. We'll begin to mark the 50th anniversary of the Vietnam war. It's another chance to honor those we lost at places like Hue, Khe Sanh, Da Nang, and Hamburger Hill. And we'll be calling on you, the American people, to join us in thanking our Vietnam veterans in your communities.

Even as we honor those who made the ultimate sacrifice, we reaffirm our commitment to care for those who served alongside them, the veterans who came home. This includes our newest generation of veterans, from Iraq and Afghanistan. We have to serve them and their families as well as they have served us: by making sure that they get the health care and benefits they need, by caring for our wounded warriors and supporting our military families, and by giving veterans the chance to go to college, find a good job, and enjoy the freedom that they risked everything to protect.

Our men and women in uniform took an oath to defend our country at all costs, and today, as members of the finest military the world has ever known, they uphold that oath with dignity and courage. As President, I have no higher honor than serving as their Commander in Chief. But with that honor comes a solemn responsibility, one that gets driven home every time I sign a condolence letter or meet a family member whose life has been turned upside down.

No words can ever bring back a loved one who has been lost. No ceremony can do justice to their memory. No honor will ever fill their absence.

But on Memorial Day, we come together as Americans to let these families and veterans know they are not alone. We give thanks for those who sacrificed everything so that we could be free. And we commit ourselves to upholding the ideals for which so many patriots have fought and died.

Thank you, God bless you, and have a wonderful weekend.

NOTE: The address was recorded at approximately 12:55 p.m. on May 25 in the Map Room at the White House for broadcast on May 26. The transcript was made available by the Office of the Press Secretary on May 25, but was embargoed for release until 6 a.m. on May 26. The related proclamation of May 25 is listed in Appendix D at the end of this volume.

Remarks at a Memorial Day Ceremony in Arlington, Virginia
May 28, 2012

Thank you very much. Please be seated. Good morning, everybody. Thank you, Secretary Panetta, for your introduction and for your incredible service to our country. To General Dempsey, to Major General Linnington, Kathryn Condon, Chaplain Berry, all of you who are here today—Active Duty, veterans, family and friends of the fallen—thank you for allowing me the privilege of joining you in this sacred place to commemorate Memorial Day.

These 600 acres are home to Americans from every part of the country who gave their lives in every corner of the globe. When a revolution needed to be waged and a Union needed to be saved, they left their homes and took up arms for the sake of an idea. From the jungles of Vietnam to the mountains of Afghanistan, they stepped forward and answered the call. They fought for a home they might never return to; they fought for buddies they would never forget. And while their stories may be separated by hundreds of years and thousands of miles, they rest here, together, side by side, row by row, because each of them loved this country, and everything it stands for, more than life itself.

Today we come together as Americans to pray, to reflect, and to remember these heroes. But tomorrow this hallowed place will once again belong to a smaller group of visitors who make their way through the gates and across these fields in the heat and in the cold, in the rain and the snow, following a well-worn path to a certain spot and kneeling in front of a familiar headstone.

You are the family and friends of the fallen, the parents and children, husbands and wives, brothers and sisters by birth and by sacrifice. And you too leave a piece of your hearts beneath these trees. You too call this sanctuary home.

Together, your footsteps trace the path of our history. And this Memorial Day, we mark another milestone. For the first time in 9 years, Americans are not fighting and dying in Iraq. We are winding down the war in Afghanistan, and our troops will continue to come home. After a decade under the dark cloud of war, we can see the light of a new day on the horizon.

Especially for those who've lost a loved one, this chapter will remain open long after the guns have fallen silent. Today, with the war in Iraq finally over, it is fitting to pay tribute to the sacrifice that spanned that conflict.

In March of 2003, on the first day of the invasion, one of our helicopters crashed near the Iraqi border with Kuwait. On it were four marines: Major Jay Aubin, Captain Ryan Beaupre, Corporal Brian Kennedy, and Staff Sergeant Kendall Waters-Bey. Together, they became the first American casualties of the Iraq war. Their families and friends barely had time to register the beginning of the conflict before being forced to confront its awesome costs.

Eight years, 7 months, and 25 days later, Army Specialist David Hickman was on patrol in Baghdad. That's when his vehicle struck a roadside bomb. He became the last of nearly 4,500 American patriots to give their lives in Iraq. A month after David's death—the days before the last American troops, including David, were scheduled to come home—I met with the Hickman family at Fort Bragg. Right now the Hickmans are beginning a very difficult journey that so many of your families have traveled before them, a journey that even more families will take in the months and years ahead.

To the families here today, I repeat what I said to the Hickmans: I cannot begin to fully understand your loss. As a father, I cannot begin to imagine what it's like to hear that knock on the door and learn that your worst fears have come true. But as Commander in Chief, I can tell you that sending our troops into harm's way is the most wrenching decision that I have to make. I can promise you, I will never do so unless it's absolutely necessary, and that when we do, we must give our troops a clear mission and the full support of a grateful nation.

And as a country, all of us can and should ask ourselves how we can help you shoulder a burden that nobody should have to bear alone. As we honor your mothers and fathers, your sons and daughters, we have given—who have given their last full measure of devotion to this country, we have to ask ourselves how can we support you and your families and give you some strength?

One thing we can do is remember these heroes as you remember them: not just as a rank or a number or a name on a headstone, but as Americans, often far too young, who were guided by a deep and abiding love for their families, for each other, and for this country.

We can remember Jay Aubin, the pilot, who met his wife on an aircraft carrier, and told his mother before shipping out, "If anything happens to me, just know I'm doing what I love."

We can remember Ryan Beaupre, the former track star, running the leadoff leg, always the first one into action, who quit his job as an accountant and joined the Marines because he wanted to do something more meaningful with his life.

We can remember Brian Kennedy, the rock climber and lacrosse fanatic, who told his father 2 days before his helicopter went down that the marines he served alongside were some of the best men he'd ever dealt with, and they'd be his friends forever.

We can remember Kendall Waters-Bey, a proud father, a proud son of Baltimore, who was described by a fellow servicemember as "a light in a very dark world."

And we can remember David Hickman, a freshman in high school when the war began, a fitness fanatic who half-jokingly called himself Zeus, a loyal friend with an infectious laugh.

We can remember them. And we can meet our obligations to those who did come home, and their families who are in the midst of a different, but very real battle of their own.

To all our men and women in uniform who are here today, know this: The patriots who rest beneath these hills were fighting for many things—for their families, for their flag—but above all, they were fighting for you. As long as I'm President, we will make sure you and your loved ones receive the benefits you've earned and the respect you deserve. America will be there for you.

And finally, for all of you who carry a special weight on your heart, we can strive to be a nation worthy of your sacrifice, a nation that is fair and equal, peaceful, and free, a nation that weighs the cost of every human life, a nation where all of us meet our obligations to one another and to this country that we love. That's what we can do.

As President, I have no higher honor and no greater responsibility than serving as Commander in Chief of the greatest military the world has ever known. And on days like this, I take pride in the fact that this country has always been home to men and women willing to give of themselves until they had nothing more to give. I take heart in the strength and resolve of those who still serve, both here at home and around the world. And I know that we must always strive to be worthy of your sacrifice.

God bless you. God bless the fallen. God bless our men and women in uniform, and may God bless the United States of America.

NOTE: The President spoke at 11:39 a.m. in the Memorial Amphitheater at Arlington National Cemetery. In his remarks, he referred to Gen. Martin E. Dempsey, USA, Chairman, Joint Chiefs of Staff; Maj. Gen. Michael S. Linnington, USA, commanding general, and Col. Steven L. Berry, USA, command chaplain, Joint Force Headquarters-National Capital Region and Military District of Washington; Kathryn A. Condon, Executive Director, Army National Military Cemeteries; Rhonda Aubin, wife, and Nancy Chamberlain, mother, of Maj. Jay T. Aubin, USMC; and Mark D. Kennedy, father of Cpl. Brian M. Kennedy, USMC. The related proclamation of May 25 is listed in Appendix D at the end of this volume.

Remarks Commemorating the 50th Anniversary of the Vietnam War
May 28, 2012

Good afternoon, everybody. Chuck, thank you for your words and your friendship and your life of service. Veterans of the Vietnam war, families, friends, distinguished guests: I know it is hot, but you are here to honor your loved ones. And Mi-

chelle and I could not be more honored to be here with you.

It speaks to the complexity of America's time in Vietnam that, even now, historians cannot agree on precisely when the war began. American advisers had served there and died there as early as the mid-fifties. Major combat operations would not begin until the mid-sixties. But if any year in between illustrated the changing nature of our involvement, it was 1962.

It was January, in Saigon. Our Army pilots strapped on their helmets and boarded their helicopters. They lifted off, raced over treetops carrying South Vietnamese troops. It was a single raid against an enemy stronghold just a few miles into the jungle, but it was one of America's first major operations in that faraway land.

Fifty years later, we come to this wall, to this sacred place, to remember. We can step towards its granite wall, reach out, touch a name. Today is Memorial Day, when we recall all those who gave everything in the darkness of war so we could stand here in the glory of spring. And today begins the 50th commemoration of our war in Vietnam. We honor each of those names etched in stone: 58,282 American patriots. We salute all who served with them, and we stand with the families who love them still.

For years, you've come here to be with them once more. And in the simple things you've left behind—your offerings, your mementos, your gifts—we get a glimpse of the lives they led: the blanket that covered him as a baby; the baseball bat he swung as a boy; a wedding ring; the photo of the grandchild he never met; the boots he wore, still caked in mud; the medals she earned, still shining. And of course, some of the things left here have special meaning, known only to the veterans: a can of beer, a packet of M&Ms, a container of SPAM, an old field ration—still good, still awful. [*Laughter*]

It's here we feel the depth of your sacrifice. And here we see a piece of our larger American story. Our Founders, in their genius, gave us a task. They set out to make a more perfect Union. And so it falls to every generation to carry on that work: to keep moving forward, to overcome a sometimes painful past, to keep striving for our ideals.

And one of the most painful chapters in our history was Vietnam, most particularly, how we treated our troops who served there. You were often blamed for a war you didn't start, when

you should have been commended for serving your country with valor. You were sometimes blamed for misdeeds of a few, when the honorable service of the many should have been praised. You came home and sometimes were denigrated, when you should have been celebrated. It was a national shame, a disgrace that should have never happened. That's why here today we resolve that it will not happen again.

And so a central part of this 50th anniversary will be to tell your story as it should have been told all along. It's another chance to set the record straight. That's one more way we keep perfecting our Union: setting the record straight. And it starts today. Because history will honor your service, and your names will join a story of service that stretches back two centuries.

Let us tell the story of a generation of servicemembers—every color, every creed, rich, poor, officer, and enlisted—who served with just as much patriotism and honor as any before you. Let's never forget that most of those who served in Vietnam did so by choice; so many of you volunteered. Your country was at war, and you said, "Send me." That includes our women in Vietnam, every one of you a volunteer. Those who were drafted, they too went and carried their burden. You served; you did your duty.

You persevered though some of the most brutal conditions ever faced by Americans in war: the suffocating heat; the drenching monsoon rains; an enemy that could come out of nowhere and vanish just as quickly; some of the most intense urban combat in history and battles for a single hill that could rage for weeks. Let it be said: In those hellholes like Briarpatch and the Zoo and the Hanoi Hilton, our Vietnam POWs didn't simply endure; you wrote some of the most extraordinary stories of bravery and integrity in the annals of military history.

As a nation, we've long celebrated the courage of our forces at Normandy and Iwo Jima, the Pusan Perimeter and Heartbreak Ridge. So let us also speak of your courage at Hue and Khe Sanh, at Tan Son Nhut and Saigon, from Hamburger Hill to Rolling Thunder. All too often it's forgotten that you, our troops in Vietnam, won every major battle you fought in.

When you came home, I know many of you put your medals away, tucked them in a drawer or in a box in the closet. You went on with your lives, started families and pursued careers. A lot of you didn't talk too much about your service. As a consequence, this Nation has not always fully appreciated the chapter of your lives that came next.

So let us also tell a story of a generation that came home, and how, even though some Americans turned their back on you, you never turned your back on America. Like generations before you, you took off the uniform, but you never stopped serving. You became teachers and police officers and nurses, the folks we count on every single day. You became entrepreneurs, running companies and pioneering industries that changed the world. You became leaders and public servants, from town halls to Capitol Hill, lifting up our communities, our States, our Nation.

You reminded us what it was like to serve, what it meant to serve. Those of you who stayed in uniform, you rose through the ranks, became leaders in every service, learned from your experience in Vietnam, and rebuilt our military into the finest force that the world has ever known. And let's remember all those Vietnam veterans who came back and served again in the wars in Iraq and Afghanistan. You did not stop serving.

Even as you succeeded in all these endeavors, you did something more—maybe the most important thing you did—you looked after each other. When your Government didn't live up to its responsibilities, you spoke out, fighting for the care and benefits you had earned, over time, transforming the VA. And of course, one of these Vietnam veterans is now our outstanding Secretary of Veterans Affairs, Ric Shinseki.

You looked after one another. You cared for one another. People weren't always talking about PTSD at the time. You understood it, and you were there for each other. Just as importantly, you didn't just take care of your own; you cared for those that followed. You made it

your mission to make sure today's troops get the respect and support that all too often you did not receive.

Because of you, because our Vietnam veterans led the charge, the post-9/11 GI bill is helping hundreds of thousands of today's veterans go to college and pursue their dreams. Because of you, because you didn't let us forget, at our airports, our returning troops get off the airplane, and you are there to shake their hands. Because of you, across America, communities have welcomed home our forces from Iraq. And when our troops return from Afghanistan, America will give this entire 9/11 generation the welcome home they deserve. That happened in part because of you.

This is the story of our Vietnam servicemembers, the story that needs to be told. This is what this 50th anniversary is all about. It's another opportunity to say to our Vietnam veterans what we should have been saying from the beginning: You did your job. You served with honor. You made us proud. You came home, and you helped build the America that we love and that we cherish.

So here today it must be said, you have earned your place among the greatest generations. At this time, I would ask all our Vietnam veterans, those of you who can stand, to please stand, all those already standing, raise your hands, as we say those simple words which always greet our troops when they come home from here on out: Welcome home. Welcome home. Welcome home. Thank you. We appreciate you. Welcome home.

Today we're calling on all Americans and every segment of our society to join this effort. Everybody can do something. Five decades removed from a time of division among Americans, this anniversary can remind us of what we share as Americans. That includes honoring our Vietnam veterans by never forgetting the lessons of that war.

So let us resolve that when America sends our sons and daughters into harm's way, we will always give them a clear mission, we will always give them a sound strategy, we will give them the equipment they need to get the job done, we will have their backs. We will resolve that leaders will be candid about the risks and about progress and have a plan to bring our troops home with honor.

Let us resolve to never forget the costs of war, including the terrible loss of innocent civilians, not just in Vietnam, but in all wars. For we know that while your sacrifice and service is the very definition of glory, war itself is not glorious. We hate war. When we fight, we do so to protect ourselves because it's necessary.

Let's resolve that in our democracy, we can debate and disagree, even in a time of war. But let us never use patriotism as a political sword. Patriots can support a war; patriots can oppose a war. And whatever our view, let us always stand united in support of our troops, who we've placed in harm's way. That is our solemn obligation.

Let's resolve to take care of our veterans as well as they've taken care of us: not just talk, but actions. Not just in the first 5 years after a war, but the first five decades. For our Vietnam veterans, this means the disability benefits for diseases connected to agent orange. It means job opportunities and mental health care to help you stand tall again. It means ending the tragedy of veterans' homelessness, so that every veteran who has fought for America has a home in America. You shouldn't have to fight for a roof over your heads when you fought on behalf of the country that you love.

And when an American does not come back—including the 1,666 Americans still missing from the Vietnam war—let us resolve to do everything in our power to bring them home. This is our solemn promise to mothers like Sarah Shay, who joins us today—93 years old—who has honored her son, Major Donald Shay, Jr., missing in action for 42 years. There she is. Sarah, thank you for your courage. God bless you.

This is the promise we're fulfilling today to the Meroney family of Fayetteville, Arkansas. Forty-three years after he went missing, we can announce that Army Captain Virgil Meroney III is coming home, and he will finally rest in peace.

Some have called this war era a scar on our country, but here's what I say. As any wound heals, the tissue around it becomes tougher, becomes stronger than before. And in this sense, finally, we might begin to see the true legacy of Vietnam. Because of Vietnam and our veterans, we now use American power smarter, we honor our military more, we take care of our veterans better. Because of the hard lessons of Vietnam, because of you, America is stronger than before.

And finally, on this anniversary and all the years to come, let us remember what binds us as one people. This is important for all of us, whether you fought in the Vietnam war or fought against it, whether you were too young to be shaped by it. It is important that our children understand the sacrifices that were made by our troops in Vietnam, that for them, this is more than just a name in history books. It's important that we know the lesson of a gift once left at this memorial.

It was towards the end of the day, and most of the tourists and visitors had departed. And there it was: a football helmet, black with white stripes, and a wristband. And with them was a handwritten note. And it was from a young man, still in high school. And mind you, this was more than two decades after Vietnam. That high school student was born years after the war had already ended. But in that short, handwritten note he captured the reverence— the bonds between generations—that bring us here today.

The letter began, "Dear Vietnam Veterans, here are two things from me to you that I think you should have." He explained that it was his helmet from midget football and his wristband from his senior year. So today I want to close with the words he wrote:

"In these two pieces of equipment, I was allowed to make mistakes, correct them, grow and mature as a person. However, that was on my battlefield. You didn't get the chance to do that on your battlefield. Some of you were forced to grow up too fast; all of you died too soon. We do have many things in common, though. We both have pride, heart and determination. I'm just sorry you guys had to learn those qualities too fast. That is why I'm giving you what I grew up with. You are true heroes and you will never be forgotten."

That's from a high school kid, born decades after the end of the war. And that captures the spirit that this entire country should embrace.

Veterans, families of the Vietnam war, I know the wounds of war are slow to heal. You know that better than most. But today we take another step. The task of telling your story continues. The work of perfecting our Union goes on. And decades from now, I hope another young American will visit this place and reach out and touch a name. And she'll learn the story of servicemembers—people she never met, who fought a war she never knew—and in that

moment of understanding and of gratitude and of grace, your legacy will endure. For you are all true heroes, and you will all be remembered.

May God bless you. May God bless your families. May God bless our men and women in uniform, and may God bless these United States of America.

NOTE: The President spoke at 2:27 p.m. at the Vietnam Veterans Memorial on the National Mall. In his remarks, he referred to former Sen. Charles T. Hagel. The related proclamation of May 25 is listed in Appendix D at the end of this volume.

Remarks on Presenting the Presidential Medal of Freedom
May 29, 2012

The President. Thank you very much. Everybody, please have a seat, and welcome to the White House. It is an extraordinary pleasure to be here with all of you to present this year's Medals of Freedom. And I have to say, just looking around the room, this is a packed house, which is a testament to how cool this group is. [*Laughter*] Everybody wanted to check them out.

This is the highest civilian honor this country can bestow, which is ironic, because nobody sets out to win it. No one ever picks up a guitar or fights a disease or starts a movement, thinking, "You know what, if I keep this up, in 2012, I could get a medal in the White House from a guy named Barack Obama." [*Laughter*] That wasn't in the plan.

But that's exactly what makes this award so special. Every one of today's honorees is blessed with an extraordinary amount of talent. All of them are driven. But we could fill this room many times over with people who are talented and driven. What sets these men and women apart is the incredible impact they have had on so many people, not in short, blinding bursts, but steadily, over the course of a lifetime.

Together, the honorees on this stage, and the ones who couldn't be here, have moved us with their words, they have inspired us with

their actions, they've enriched our lives, and they've changed our lives for the better. Some of them are household names; others have labored quietly out of the public eye. Most of them may never fully appreciate the difference they've made or the influence that they've had, but that's where our job comes in. It's our job to help let them know how extraordinary their impact has been on our lives. And so today we present this amazing group with one more accolade for a life well led, and that's the Presidential Medal of Freedom.

So I'm going to take an opportunity—I hope you guys don't mind—to brag about each of you, starting with Madeleine Albright.

Usually, Madeleine does the talking. [*Laughter*] Once in a while, she lets her jewelry do the talking. [*Laughter*] When Saddam Hussein called her a "snake," she wore a serpent on her lapel—[*laughter*]—the next time she visited Baghdad. When Slobodan Milosevic referred to her as a "goat," a new pin appeared in her collection.

As the first woman to serve as America's top diplomat, Madeleine's courage and toughness helped bring peace to the Balkans and paved the way for progress in some of the most unstable corners of the world. And as an immigrant herself—the granddaughter of Holocaust victims who fled her native Czechoslovakia as a child—Madeleine brought a unique perspective to the job. This is one of my favorite stories. Once, at a naturalization ceremony, an Ethiopian man came up to her and said, "Only in America can a refugee meet the Secretary of State." And she replied, "Only in America can a refugee become the Secretary of State." [*Laughter*] We're extraordinarily honored to have Madeleine here. And obviously, I think it's fair to say I speak for one of your successors who is so appreciative of the work you did and the path that you laid.

It was a scorching hot day in 1963, and Mississippi was on the verge of a massacre. The funeral procession for Medgar Evers had just disbanded, and a group of marchers was throwing rocks at a line of equally defiant and heavily-armed policemen. And suddenly, a White man in shirtsleeves, hands raised, walked towards the protestors and talked them into going home peacefully. And that man was John Doar. He was the face of the Justice Department in the South. He was proof that the Federal Government was listening. And over the years, John escorted James Meredith to the University of Mississippi. He walked alongside the Selma-to-Montgomery march. He laid the groundwork for the Civil Rights Act of 1964 and the Voting Rights Act of 1965. In the words of John Lewis, "He gave [civil rights workers] a reason not to give up on those in power." And he did it by never giving up on them. And I think it's fair to say that I might not be here had it not been for his work.

Bob Dylan started out singing other people's songs. But, as he says, "There came a point where I had to write what I wanted to say, because what I wanted to say, nobody else was writing." So, born in Hibbing, Minnesota, a town, he says, where "you couldn't be a rebel—it was too cold"—[*laughter*]—Bob moved to New York at age 19. By the time he was 23, Bob's voice, with its weight, its unique, gravelly power, was redefining not just what music sounded like, but the message it carried and how it made people feel. Today, everybody from Bruce Springsteen to U2 owes Bob a debt of gratitude. There is not a bigger giant in the history of American music. All these years

later, he's still chasing that sound, still searching for a little bit of truth. And I have to say that I am a really big fan. [*Laughter*]

In the 1960s, more than 2 million people died from smallpox every year. Just over a decade later, that number was zero—2 million to zero, thanks, in part, to Dr. Bill Foege. As a young medical missionary working in Nigeria, Bill helped develop a vaccination strategy that would later be used to eliminate smallpox from the face of the Earth. And when that war was won, he moved on to other diseases, always trying to figure out what works. In one remote Nigerian village, after vaccinating 2,000 people in a single day, Bill asked the local chief how he had gotten so many people to show up. And the chief explained that he had told everyone to come see—to "come to the village and see the tallest man in the world." [*Laughter*] Today, that world owes that really tall man a great debt of gratitude.

On the morning that John Glenn blasted off into space, America stood still. For half an hour, the phones stopped ringing in Chicago police headquarters, and New York subway drivers offered a play-by-play account over the loudspeakers. President Kennedy interrupted a breakfast with congressional leaders and joined 100 million TV viewers to hear the famous words, "Godspeed, John Glenn." The first American to orbit the Earth, John Glenn became a hero in every sense of the word, but he didn't stop there serving his country. As a Senator, he found new ways to make a difference. And on his second trip into space at age 77, he defied the odds once again. But he reminds everybody, don't tell him he's lived a historic life. He says, "Are living." He'll say, "Don't put it in the past tense." He's still got a lot of stuff going on.

George Hirabayashi knew what it was like to stand alone. As a student at the University of Washington, Gordon was one of only three Japanese Americans to defy the Executive order that forced thousands of families to leave their homes, their jobs, and their civil rights behind and move to internment camps during World War II. He took his case all the way to the Supreme Court, and he lost. And it would be another 40 years before that decision was reversed, giving Asian Americans everywhere a small measure of justice. In Gordon's words, "It takes a crisis to tell us that unless citizens are willing to standup for the [Constitution], it's not worth the paper it's written on." And this country is better off because of citizens like him who are willing to stand up.

Similarly, when Cesar Chavez sat Dolores Huerta down at his kitchen table and told her they should start a union, she thought he was joking. She was a single mother of seven children, so she obviously didn't have a lot of free time. But Dolores had been an elementary schoolteacher and remembered seeing children come to school hungry and without shoes. So, in the end, she agreed, and workers everywhere are glad that she did. Without any negotiating experience, Dolores helped lead a worldwide grape boycott that forced growers to agree to some of the country's first farm worker contracts. And ever since, she has fought to give more people a seat at the table. "Don't wait to be invited," she says, "step in there." And on a personal note, Dolores was very gracious when I told her I had stolen her slogan, "*Si, se puede*"—"Yes, we can." [*Laughter*] Knowing her, I'm pleased that she let me off easy because Dolores does not play. [*Laughter*]

For years, Jan Karski's students at Georgetown University knew he was a great professor; what they didn't realize was he was also a hero. Fluent in four languages, possessed of a photographic memory, Jan served as a courier for the Polish resistance during the darkest days of World War II. Before one trip across enemy lines, resistance fighters told him that Jews were being murdered on a massive scale and smuggled him into the Warsaw Ghetto and a Polish death camp to see for himself. Jan took that information to President Franklin Roosevelt, giving one of the first accounts of the Holocaust and imploring to the world to take action. It was decades before Jan was ready to tell his story. By then, he said: "I don't need courage anymore. So I teach compassion."

Growing up in Georgia in the late 1800s, Juliette Gordon Low was not exactly typical. She flew airplanes. She went swimming. She experimented with electricity for fun. And she recognized early on that in order to keep up with the changing times, women would have to be prepared. So, at age 52, after meeting the founder of the Boy Scouts in England, Juliette came home and called her cousin and said: "I've got something for the girls of Savannah, and all of America, and all the world. And we're going to start it tonight!" A century later, almost 60 million Girl Scouts have gained leadership skills and self-confidence through the organization that she founded. They include CEOs, astronauts, my own Secretary of State. And from the very beginning, they have also included girls of different races and faiths and abilities, just the way that Juliette would have wanted it.

Toni Morrison, she is used to a little distraction. As a single mother working at a publishing company by day, she would carve out a little time in the evening to write, often with her two sons pulling on her hair and tugging at her earrings. Once, a baby spit up on her tablet so she wrote around it. [*Laughter*] Circumstances may not have been ideal, but the words that came out were magical. Toni Morrison's prose brings us that kind of moral and emotional intensity that few writers ever attempt. From "Song of Solomon" to "Beloved," Toni reaches us deeply, using a tone that is lyrical, precise, distinct, and inclusive. She believes that language "arcs toward the place where meaning might lie." The rest of us are lucky to be following along for the ride.

During oral argument, Justice John Paul Stevens often began his line of questioning with a polite, "May I interrupt?" or "May I ask a question?" You can imagine the lawyers would say, "Okay"—[*laughter*]—after which he would, just as politely, force a lawyer to stop dancing around and focus on the most important issues in the case. That was his signature style: modest, insightful, well-prepared, razor-sharp. He is the third longest serving Justice in the history of the Court. And Justice Stevens applies—applied, throughout his career, his clear and graceful manner to the defense of individual rights and the rule of law, always favoring a pragmatic solution over an ideological one. Ever humble, he would happily comply when unsuspecting tourists asked him to take their picture in front of the Court. [*Laughter*] And at his vacation home in Florida, he was John from Arlington, better known for his world-class bridge game than his world-changing judicial opinions. Even in his final days on the bench, Justice Stevens insisted he was still "learning on the job." But in the end, we are the ones who have learned from him.

When a doctor first told Pat Summitt she suffered from dementia, she almost punched him. When a second doctor advised her to retire, she responded, "Do you know who you're dealing with here?" [*Laughter*] Obviously, they did not. As Pat says: "I can fix a tractor, mow hay, plow a field, chop tobacco, fire a barn, and call the cows. But what I'm really known for is winning." In 38 years at Tennessee, she racked up 8 national championships, more than 1,000 wins; understand, this is more than any college coach, male or female, in the history of the NCAA. And more importantly, every player that went through her program has either graduated or is on her way to a degree. That's why anybody who feels sorry for Pat will find themselves on the receiving end of that famous glare, or she might punch you. [*Laughter*] She's still getting up every day and doing what she does best, which is teaching. "The players," she says, "are my best medicine."

Our final honoree is not here, Shimon Peres, the President of Israel, who has done more for the cause of peace in the Middle East than just about anybody alive. I'll be hosting President Peres for a dinner here at the White House next month, and we'll be presenting him with his medal and honoring his incredible contributions to the State of Israel and the world at that time. So I'm looking forward to welcoming him. And if it's all right with you, I will save my best lines about him for that occasion.

So these are the recipients of the 2012 Medals of Freedom. And just on a personal note, I had a chance to see everybody in the back. What's wonderful about these events for me is so many of these people are my heroes individually. I know how they impacted my life.

I remember reading "Song of Solomon" when I was a kid and not just trying to figure out how to write, but also how to be and how to think. And I remember in college listening to Bob Dylan and my world opening up because he captured something that—about this country that was so vital. And I think about Dolores Huerta, reading about her when I was starting off as an organizer.

Everybody on this stage has marked my life in profound ways. And I was telling, somebody like Pat Summitt, when I think about my two daughters, who are tall and gifted, and knowing that because of folks like Coach Summitt they're standing up straight and diving after loose balls and feeling confident and strong, then I understand that the impact that these people have had extends beyond me. It will continue for generations to come. What an extraordinary honor to be able to say thank you to all of them for the great work that they have done on behalf of this country and on behalf of the world.

So it is now my great honor to present them with a small token of our appreciation.

[*At this point, Lt. Cmdr. Tiffany Hill, USN, Navy Aide to the President, read the citations, and the President presented the medals.*]

The President. Can everybody please stand and give a rousing applause to our Medal of Freedom winners?

Well, we could not be prouder of all of them. We could not be more grateful to all of them. You have had an impact on all of us, and I know that you will continue to have an impact on all of us. So thank you for being here. Thank you for putting yourself through White House ceremonies—[*laughter*]—which are always full of all kinds of protocol.

Fortunately, we also have a reception afterwards. I hear the food around here is pretty good. [*Laughter*] So I look forward to all of you having a chance to stay and mingle, and again, thank you again, to all of you.

NOTE: The President spoke at 3:45 p.m. in the East Room at the White House. In his re-marks, he referred to Rep. John R. Lewis; and H. Ford Morrison, son of Toni Morrison.

Remarks on Signing the Export-Import Bank Reauthorization Act of 2012
May 30, 2012

Thank you very much. Everybody, please have a seat. Have a seat. I want to begin by recognizing the Members of Congress who are here today. All of them did outstanding work on this legislation. I in particular want to thank Steny Hoyer, Congresswoman Mahoney, and—as well as Congressman Miller, who helped to make this day possible. Their leadership, their hard work made this bill a reality.

We've talked a lot recently about the fundamental choice that we face as a country. America can either settle for an economy where just a few are doing well and a lot of folks are struggling to get by, or we can build the kind of economy where everybody is getting a fair shot and everybody is doing their fair share and everybody is playing by the same rules.

And part of building that broad-based economy with a strong middle class is making sure that we're not just known as a nation that consumes. We've got to be a nation that produces, a nation that sells. Our middle class was created by workers who made and sold the best products in the world. Our communities and our economy have always done better when we shipped more goods than anybody else, stamped with that phrase: Made in America. And I want us to be that nation again. I want us to be that nation in perpetuity.

Two years ago, I set a goal of doubling American exports over 5 years. Today, with the trade agreements that we've signed into law, with the help of some of these same Members of Congress, we're making historic progress. Soon, there are going to be millions of new customers for our goods and services in Korea, in Colombia, and Panama. That way, even though we got some Hyundais over here, we're also going to have some Chryslers and Fords and Chevys in Seoul that are imported from Detroit and Toledo and Chicago.

So I'm going to go anywhere I can in the world to create new markets for American goods. And we're also not going to stand by when our competitors aren't following the rules. We've brought trade cases against China at nearly twice the rate of the previous administration. We've set up a trade enforcement unit to investigate unfair trade practices that are taking place anyplace—anywhere in the world. Anytime other countries skirt the rules or put our workers and our businesses in an unfair position, we're going to take action.

We're also making sure that American businesses have better access to the 95 percent of the world's consumers who live beyond our shores. And that's why the bipartisan bill that I'm about to sign is so important. By reauthorizing support for the Export-Import Bank, we're helping thousands of businesses sell more of their products and services overseas, and in the process, we're helping them create jobs here at home. And we're doing that at no extra cost to the taxpayer.

Over the past few years, I've met with a lot of business leaders and a lot of workers across America, from companies like Boeing to Dow Chemical to smaller companies that are also interested in accessing foreign markets. And they've told me how critical support from the Ex-Im Bank has been in competing more effectively in the global marketplace. As the head of the bank, we owe our thanks to Fred Hochberg, who is here on stage, for doing such an outstanding job.

Just to give you a couple examples, Boeing relied on support from the Ex-Im Bank to strike a deal selling more than 200 planes to one of the fastest growing airlines in the world. And that translates into thousands of jobs here in the United States. As long as our global competitors are providing financing for their exports, we've got to do the same. So I'm glad that Congress got this done. I'm grateful to members of both parties who came together and put the interests of the American people first.

Now we've got to do more. Obviously, the world economy is still in a delicate place because of what's going on in Europe and the fact that some of the emerging countries have been slowing down. It is absolutely critical for us to make sure that we are full speed ahead.

I've been traveling around the country talking about a to-do list for Congress with some commonsense ideas that historically have had bipartisan support to help continue growth and job creation. And just like the bill I'm about to sign, those policies can help strengthen the economy and put more folks back to work. We shouldn't have to wait until an election to do some of this business.

A couple of points. Number one, it still makes no sense for us to be giving tax breaks to companies that are shipping jobs and factories overseas. The great news is there are a lot of companies that are now thinking about insourcing and moving jobs back to the United States. We are more competitive than ever. Our workers are more productive than ever. We want to help provide incentives for folks to make those decisions. So it's time for Congress to take tax breaks away that allow for deductions moving jobs overseas and instead cover moving expenses for companies that are interested in bringing jobs back to America.

Number two, Congress should give every responsible homeowner the opportunity to save an average of $3,000 a year by refinancing their mortgage. We're starting to see a little bit of stabilizing in some of the housing markets around the country, but that continues to be a significant drag on our economy. But when families are able to take advantage of these historically low rates, it makes a difference. It puts money in their pockets, or it may help them rebuild some of their equity. It gives them more confidence, and the housing market stabilizes further.

We've done everything that we can do administratively to help some portion of homeowners around the country refinance. But every responsible homeowner in America should have this—a chance to save money. That's not just good, by the way, for the housing industry. That's good for all businesses, because it means consumers are going to be out there with a little extra money in their pockets.

Number three, Congress still has the opportunity to do more to help small-business owners, who create most of the new jobs in America. So we want to give them a tax break for hiring more workers and providing those workers higher wages.

Fourth, Congress should extend the tax credits for clean energy companies that are set to expire at the end of the year. This is something that a lot of Members, both Democrats and Republicans, should be able to appreciate, because wind power, solar power, biofuels, those aren't partisan issues, that's a job sector that is growing across the country. But right now there is too much uncertainty because we haven't gone ahead and locked down some of these tax credits.

These companies are putting folks back to work and they're helping us break our dependence on foreign oil. There are Members, again, of both parties that support these tax credits. And tens of thousands of jobs are at stake. So I think it's very important for us to make sure that we move forward on that.

Fifth—and I'm going to speak to this on Friday—Congress should create a veterans job corps so we can put our returning heroes back to work as cops and firefighters and park rangers. We just observed Memorial Day, an extraordinarily moving Memorial Day. We were down at the Vietnam Veterans Memorial commemorating 50 years since that difficult and challenging war. And one thing we learned from that was that we've got to treat our heroes with the respect and dignity that they have earned.

And our veterans are some of the most highly trained, highly educated, highly skilled workers we've got. These are Americans who want to keep serving now that they're back. So we've got to make sure when they come home, they come home to new jobs and new opportunities. So there are a number of things that my administration can do on our own, and we're going to keep on doing them, but it gets a whole lot easier if we get some help from Congress. And this is a great example, a great model of what can happen.

America has come through some tough times together, and it's going to take more time than any of us would like to get to a place where all of us have fully recovered from the worst recession in our lives. There will continue to be hurdles and there will continue to be some headwinds that we can't fully control. But there are plenty of things that we can control, and there's plenty of solutions within our reach. There are steps that we can take right now to speed up this recovery, to help create jobs, to restore some of the financial security that families have lost. It's within our control to do the right thing and do it now.

So my message to Congress is thank you and congratulations on authorizing Ex-Im Bank to continue on its extraordinary mission. We've got more work to do. I hope this ends up being a model for the kind of progress that we can make in the months to come and the years to come. So with that, it is my great pleasure to sign this bill into law.

NOTE: The President spoke at 11:35 a.m. in the East Room at the White House. In his remarks, he referred to Rep. Gary G. Miller. He also mistakenly referred to Rep. Carolyn McCarthy as "Congresswoman Mahoney." H.R. 2072, signed May 30, was assigned Public Law No. 112–122.

Remarks at a Reception Celebrating Jewish American Heritage Month
May 30, 2012

Thank you. Well, welcome to the White House, everybody. I hope you're having fun. [*Applause*] Excellent.

I want to recognize Ambassador Michael Oren and thank him for his work representing our great friend, the State of Israel. I want to recognize and thank all the Members of Congress and the members of my administration who are here today. I want to thank our musical guests, Rak Shalom. I was just meeting with all of them back there, they said they did quite a few numbers. And they were outstanding, I know.

This year, we celebrate Jewish Heritage Month—Jewish American Heritage Month—and we're also commemorating an important anniversary. A hundred and fifty years ago, General Ulysses Grant issued an order known as General Orders No. 11 that would have expelled Jews "as a class" from what was then known as the military Department of the Tennessee. It was wrong. Even if it was 1862, even if official acts of anti-Semitism were all too common around the world, it was wrong and indicative of an ugly strain of thought.

But what happened next could have only taken place in America. Groups of American Jews protested General Grant's decision. A

Jewish merchant from Kentucky traveled here, to the White House, and met with President Lincoln in person. After their meeting, President Lincoln revoked the order, one more reason why we like President Lincoln. [*Laughter*]

And to General Grant's credit, he recognized that he had made a serious mistake. So, later in his life, he apologized for this order, and as President, he went out of his way to appoint Jews to public office and to condemn the persecution of Jews in Eastern Europe.

Today we have a few documents on display; maybe some of you saw them when you walked in. There are two letters of protest from Jewish organizations to President Lincoln. There is President Lincoln's handwritten reply saying that he had taken action. And there is a receipt for the donation that President Grant made to the Adas Israel synagogue here in Washington, when he attended a service there in 1876.

So together, these papers tell a story, a fundamentally American story. Like so many groups, Jews have had to fight for their piece of the American dream. But this country holds a special promise: that if we stand up for the traditions we believe in and in the values that we share, then our wrongs can be made right, our

Union can be made more perfect, and our world can be repaired.

Today, it's our turn, our generation's turn, and you guys, your generation's turn. You're younger than us. [*Laughter*] We got some later generations here in the front. We're the ones who have to stand up for our shared values. Here at home, we have to rebuild an America where everybody gets a fair shot and everybody is doing their fair share and everybody is playing by the same rules.

Beyond our borders, we have to stand alongside our friends who share our commitment to freedom and democracy and universal rights, and that includes, of course, our unwavering commitment to the State of Israel and its security and the pursuit of a just and lasting peace.

It's no secret that we've got a lot of work to do, but as your traditions teach us, while we are not obligated to finish the work, neither are we free to desist from that work.

So today we don't just celebrate all that American Jews have done for our country, we also look toward the future. And as we do, I know that those of you in this room, but folks all across this country will continue to help perfect our Union, and for that, I am extraordinarily grateful.

God bless you. God bless America.

NOTE: The President spoke at 5:17 p.m. in the East Room at the White House. The related proclamation of May 2 is listed in Appendix D at the end of this volume.

Remarks on the Unveiling of the Official Portraits of Former President George W. Bush and First Lady Laura Bush
May 31, 2012

Well, good afternoon, everybody. Thank you, Fred, for that introduction. To President George H.W. Bush and Barbara, to all the members of the Bush family who are here, it is a great privilege to have you here today. And to President and Mrs. Bush, welcome back to the house that you called home for 8 years.

The White House is many things at once: It's a working office; it's a living museum; it's an enduring symbol of our democracy. But at the end of the day, when the visitors go home and the lights go down, a few of us are blessed with the tremendous honor to actually live here.

I think it's fair to say that every President is acutely aware that we are just temporary residents. We're renters here. We're charged with the upkeep until our lease runs out. But we also leave a piece of ourselves in this place. And today, with the unveiling of the portraits next to me, President and Mrs. Bush will take their place alongside men and women who built this country and those who worked to perfect it.

It's been said that no one can ever truly understand what it's like being President until they sit behind that desk and feel the weight and responsibility for the first time. And that is true. After 3½ years in office, and much more gray hair, I have a deeper understanding of the challenges faced by the Presidents who came before me, including my immediate predecessor, President Bush.

In this job, no decision that reaches your desk is easy. No choice you make is without costs. No matter how hard you try, you're not going to make everybody happy. I think that's something President Bush and I both learned pretty quickly. [*Laughter*]

And that's why, from time to time, those of us who have had the privilege to hold this office find ourselves turning to the only people on Earth who know the feeling. We may have our differences politically, but the Presidency transcends those differences. We all love this country. We all want America to succeed. We all believe that when it comes to moving this country forward, we have an obligation to pull together. And we all follow the humble, heroic example of our first President, George Washington, who knew that a true test of patriotism is the willingness to freely and graciously pass the reins of power on to somebody else.

701

That's certainly been true of President Bush. The months before I took the oath of office were a chaotic time. We knew our economy was in trouble, our fellow Americans were in pain, but we wouldn't know until later just how breathtaking the financial crisis had been. And still, over those 2½ months, in the midst of that crisis, President Bush, his Cabinet, his staff, many of you who are here today, went out of your ways—George, you went out of your way—to make sure that the transition to a new administration was as seamless as possible.

President Bush understood that rescuing our economy was not just a Democratic or a Republican issue, it was a American priority. I'll always be grateful for that.

The same is true for our national security. None of us will ever forget where we were on that terrible September day when our country was attacked. All of us will always remember the image of President Bush standing on that pile of rubble, bullhorn in hand, conveying extraordinary strength and resolve to the American people, but also representing the strength and resolve of the American people.

And last year, when we delivered justice to Usama bin Laden, I made it clear that our success was due to many people in many organizations working together over many years, across two administrations. That's why my first call, once American forces were safely out of harm's way, was to President Bush. Because protecting our country is neither the work of one person nor the task of one period of time. It's an ongoing obligation that we all share.

Finally, on a personal note, Michelle and I are grateful to the entire Bush family for their guidance and their example during our own transition. George, I will always remember the gathering you hosted for all the living former Presidents before I took office, your kind words of encouragement. Plus, you also left me a really good TV sports package. I was—[*laughter*]—I use it.

Laura, you reminded us that the most rewarding thing about living in this house isn't the title or the power, but the chance to shine a spotlight on the issues that matter most. And the fact that you and George raised two smart, beautiful daughters—first, as girls visiting their grandparents and then as teenagers preparing to head out into the world—that obviously gives Michelle and I tremendous hope as we try to do the right thing by our own daughters in this slightly odd atmosphere that we've created.

Jenna and Barbara, we will never forget the advice you gave Sasha and Malia as they began their lives in Washington. They told them to surround themselves with loyal friends, never stop doing what they love, to slide down the banisters occasionally—[*laughter*]—to play sardines on the lawn, to meet new people and try new things, and to try to absorb everything and enjoy all of it. And I can tell you that Malia and Sasha took that advice to heart. It really meant a lot to them.

One of the greatest strengths of our democracy is our ability to peacefully and routinely go through transitions of power. It speaks to the fact that we've always had leaders who believe in America and everything it stands for above all else; leaders and their families who are willing to devote their lives to the country that they love.

This is what we'll think about every time we pass these portraits, just as millions of other visitors will do in the decades and, perhaps, even the centuries to come. I want to thank John Howard Sanden, the artist behind these beautiful works, for his efforts. And on behalf of the American people, I want to thank most sincerely President and Mrs. Bush for their extraordinary service to our country.

And now I'd like to invite them on stage to take part in the presentation.

NOTE: The President spoke at 1:31 p.m. in the East Room at the White House. In his remarks, he referred to Frederick J. Ryan, Jr., chairman, White House Historical Association; and former Presidents Jimmy Carter and William J. Clinton. The transcript released by the Office of the Press Secretary also included the remarks of former President George W. Bush, former First Lady Laura Bush, and First Lady Michelle Obama.

Remarks at the Honeywell International Inc. Manufacturing Facility in Golden Valley, Minnesota
June 1, 2012

The President. Hello, Golden Valley! It is good to be back in Minnesota. It is good to see your Governor, Mark Dayton, here. On the way over we were talking about making sure the Vikings were staying. Now, that's a hard thing for a Bears fan to do. [*Laughter*] But I was rooting for the Vikings sticking around here, and the Governor did a great job.

Audience member. We were praying.

The President. You were praying too, huh? [*Laughter*] Absolutely. Prayer never hurts. It helps.

You got two outstanding Senators, Amy Klobuchar and Al Franken. Your mayor, Shep Harris, is here. Outstanding congressional delegation in the house, give them a big round of applause. And I thought Ryan was really good, so give him a big round of applause. He's a natural.

Now, one of the last times I was here was last August. We took a bus tour around the State. I needed a little "Minnesota nice." [*Laughter*] I stopped for some pie in Zumbrota. I held a town hall in Cannon Falls. Amy and Al were there. I think Al ate my pie, in fact. [*Laughter*] And I spent a lot of time talking with folks who'd spent the past couple years making their way through a tough economy.

And today, we're still fighting our way back from the worst economic crisis since the Great Depression. The economy is growing again, but it's not growing as fast as we want it to grow. Our businesses have created almost 4.3 million new jobs over the last 27 months, but as we learned in today's jobs report, we're still not creating them as fast as we want. And just like this time last year, our economy is still facing some serious headwinds. We had high gas prices a month, 2 months ago, and they're starting to come down, and they were spiking, but they're still hitting people's wallets pretty hard. That has an impact. And then, most prominently, most recently, we've had a crisis in Europe's economy that is having an impact worldwide, and it's starting to cast a shadow on our own as well. So we've got a lot of work to do before we get to where we need to be. And all these factors have made it even more challenging to not just fully recover, but also lay the foundation for an economy that's built to last over the long term.

But that's our job. From the moment we first took action to prevent another depression, we knew the road to recovery would not be easy. We knew it would take time. We knew there would be ups and downs along the way. But we also knew if we were willing to act wisely and boldly, and if we were acting together, as Americans, if we were willing to keep at it, if we were willing to roll up our sleeves and never quit, then we wouldn't just come back, we'd come back stronger than ever. That was our belief. And that continues to be my belief.

We will come back stronger, we do have better days ahead, and that is because of all of you. That's because of all of you. I'd place my bets on American workers and American businesses any day of the week. You've been fighting through this tough economy with resilience and grit and innovation. Honeywell is a great example of a company that's doing outstanding work, and I want to acknowledge Dave Cote here who has been serving on my Jobs Council and doing a lot of great work.

That's why our auto industry has come roaring back. It's why manufacturing is consistently adding jobs for the first time since the 1990s. All that is happening because of you. Everybody here plays by the rules. You work hard. You meet your responsibilities. And you deserve leaders who do the same, leaders who will stand shoulder to shoulder with you and do everything possible to strengthen the middle class and move this economy forward. That's what you deserve.

Look, we can't fully control everything that happens in other parts of the world: disturbances in the Middle East, what's going on in

703

Europe. But there are plenty of things we can control here at home. There are plenty of steps we can take right now to help create jobs and grow this economy.

Now, let me give you a couple examples. I sent Congress a jobs bill last September full of the kinds of bipartisan ideas that would have put our fellow Americans back to work and helped reinforce our economy against some of these outside shocks. I sent them a plan that would have reduced the deficit by $4 trillion in a way that is balanced, that pays for the job-creating investments we need by cutting unnecessary spending, but also by asking the wealthiest Americans to pay a little more in taxes.

And I'll give them a little bit of credit: Congress has passed a few parts of that jobs bill, like a tax cut that's allowing working Americans to keep more of your paychecks every week. That was important. I appreciated it. But Congress has not acted on enough of the other ideas in that bill that would help make a difference and help create jobs right now. And there's no excuse for it. Not when there are so many people out there still looking for work. Not when there are still folks out there struggling to pay their bills. It's not lost on anybody that it's an election year. I understand that; I've noticed.

Audience members. Four more years! Four more years! Four more years!

The President. [*Laughter*] But we've got responsibilities that are bigger than an election. We've got responsibilities to you.

So my message to Congress is: Now is not the time to play politics. Now is not the time to sit on your hands. The American people expect their leaders to work hard no matter what year it is. The economy still isn't where it needs to be. There are steps that could make a difference right now, steps that can also serve as a buffer in case the situation in Europe gets any worse.

So right now Congress should pass a bill to help States prevent more layoffs, so we can put thousands of teachers and firefighters and police officers back on the job. Layoffs at the State and local levels have been a chronic problem for our recovery, but it's a problem we can fix.

Congress should have passed a bill a long time ago to put thousands of construction workers back on the job rebuilding our roads and our bridges and our runways. Since the housing bubble burst, no sector has been hit harder than the construction industry, and we've got all this stuff that needs fixed. Remember that bridge here in Minnesota? So this is a problem we can fix. Let's do it right away.

Instead of just talking about job creators, Congress should give small-business owners a tax break for hiring more workers and paying them higher wages. We can get that done. We can get it done right now. Let's not wait.

Right now Congress should give every responsible homeowner the opportunity to save an average of $3,000 a year by refinancing their mortgage. We've got historically low rates right now. I was with a family n Reno, Nevada, a couple weeks ago. They got a chance to refinance—even though their home was underwater—put that money back in their pockets because we had taken some steps as an administration to make that available for those who have mortgages held by Government agencies like the FHA or a Government guarantee. But not everybody has those kinds of mortgages. I want everybody to have those same opportunities.

I assume there are some folks here who could use $3,000 a year. Let's get that done right now. That means there are going to be— if you have $3,000 a year extra, that helps you pay down your credit cards. That helps you go out and buy some things that your family needs, which is good for business. Maybe somebody will be replacing some thingamajig for their furnace. [*Laughter*] They've been putting that off. But if they've got that extra money, they might just go out there and buy that thing. Right? [*Laughter*]

Right now Congress needs to extend the tax credits for clean energy manufacturers that are set to expire at the end of this year. I was talking to Dave Cote. The issue of energy efficiency and everything we need to do to shift away from dependence on foreign oil, we're making huge progress. We're actually importing less oil than any time in the last 8 years. We're down under 50 percent, but we can do more.

And these clean energy companies, they're hiring folks. They're helping us break dependence on foreign oil. It's part of a package of stuff that Honeywell is doing a lot of work on. But almost 40,000 jobs are on the line if these tax credits expire. Why would anyone in Congress walk away from those jobs? We need to pass those tax credits right now. We need to pass them right now.

It's long past time we started encouraging what a lot of companies have been doing lately, which is bringing jobs back to this country. And some of them are coming to Minnesota. The Governor and I were talking in the car about some companies coming back—Red Bull, right? Coming back. But let's give more incentive. It's time for Congress to end tax breaks for companies that ship jobs overseas. Let's use that money to cover moving expenses for companies that are bringing jobs back to America. That would make a difference right now.

So those are all steps that we could be taking to strengthen the economy, to provide us some insurance if the situation overseas starts getting worse so we can control our own destiny, keep this recovery moving forward.

Which brings me to the last thing Congress should do to help businesses create jobs—that's why I'm here at Honeywell today. I believe that no one who fights for this country should ever have to fight for a job when they come home. And for Congress, that means creating a veterans job corps so we can put our returning heroes back to work as cops and firefighters, on projects that protect our public lands and resources. And they should do it right now. They should do it right now. But if we're going to serve our veterans as well as they've served us, we've got to do even more.

We just observed Memorial Day, which makes us think about the extraordinary sacrifices so many make. But we've got to make sure we translate words into action. We can't just be in a parade, can't just march. We also have to deliver for our veterans.

Over the past three decades—over the past decades, rather, more than 3 million service-members have transitioned back to civilian life. And now that the war in Iraq is over and we're starting to wind down the war in Afghanistan, over a million more of those outstanding heroes, they're going to be joining this process of transition back into civilian life over the next few years.

Now, just think about the skills these veterans have acquired at an incredibly young age. Think about the leadership they've learned, 25-year-olds, 26-year-olds leading platoons into unbelievably dangerous situations, life-or-death situations. Think about the cutting-edge technologies they've mastered. Their ability to adapt to changing and unpredictable situations, you can't get that stuff from a classroom.

I mean, these kids, these men, these women, they've done incredible work, and that's exactly the kind of leadership and responsibility that every business in America should be wanting to attract, should be competing to attract. That's the kind of talent we need to compete for the jobs and the industries of the future. These are the kinds of Americans that every company should want to hire.

And that's why, here at Honeywell, you've made it a mission to hire more veterans. And let me say, Dave is incredibly patriotic, loves his veterans, but this—Honeywell is doing this not just because it feels good. They're doing it because it's good for business, because veterans make outstanding workers. So today I'm taking executive action that will make it easier for a lot of companies to do the same thing.

I've told the story before of a soldier in the 82d Airborne who served as a combat medic in Afghanistan, saved lives over there, earned a Bronze Star for his actions. But he came home, here to Minnesota—met him on our way to Cannon Falls. When he first came home, he couldn't even get a job as a first-responder. Think about it. This guy is out there taking care of troops who are wounded in action, couldn't initially get a job. So then, he took classes through the post-9/11 GI bill—classes that he could have taught—[*laughter*]—just so he could qualify for the same duties at home that he had performed every day at the war.

Let me tell you something. If you can save a life on the battlefield, you can save a life in an ambulance. If you can oversee a convoy or millions of dollars of assets in Iraq, you can help manage a supply chain or balance its books here at home. If you can maintain the most advanced weapons in the world, if you're an electrician on a Navy ship, well, you can manufacture the next generation of advanced technology in our factories like this one. If you're working on complex machinery, you should be able to take those skills and find a manufacturing job right here, right here at home.

But unfortunately, a lot of returning heroes with advanced skills like these, they don't get hired simply because they don't have the civilian licenses or certifications that a lot of companies require. At the same time, I hear from business leaders all the time who say they can't find enough workers with the skills necessary to fill open positions. Eighty percent of manufacturers say this, according to one survey. So think about it. We got all these openings and all these skilled veterans looking for work, and somehow they're missing each other. That doesn't make any sense. So that's where executive action comes in. That's where we're going to fix it.

Today I'm proud to announce new partnerships between the military and manufacturing groups that will make it easier for companies to hire returning servicemembers who prove they've earned the skills our country needs. Soldiers, sailors, marines, airmen, coastguardsmen, if they've got skills in machining or welding or weapons maintenance, for example, you'll have a faster track to good-paying manufacturing jobs. Servicemembers with experience in logistics or maintenance on the frontlines, they'll have a faster track to jobs in those fields here at home.

I've also directed the Department of Defense to establish a new Task Force charged with finding new opportunities for servicemembers to use the skills they've learned in the military to gain the relevant industry credentials—the civilian certifications and licenses—so that it doesn't cost them and they don't necessarily have to go back to school for 3 years and take out a whole bunch of student loans when, potentially, they could do it quicker, more inexpensively, and get on the job faster. We're talking about jobs in manufacturing, in health care, in IT, in logistics, for first-responders, so that returning combat medic that I spoke about, he doesn't have to prove himself over and over again.

So this Task Force's first action is going to create opportunities for up to 126,000 servicemembers to gain the industry-recognized certifications for high-demand manufacturing jobs like the jobs right here at this plant at Honeywell. This builds on the Skills for America's Future partnership that we launched last year with the National Association of Manufacturers to provide 500,000 community college students with industry-recognized credentials that will help them secure good manufacturing jobs.

And all of this builds on the steps we've already taken to make sure our returning heroes come home able to share in the opportunities that they have defended. Because when our men and women sign up to become a soldier, a sailor, an airman, marine, coastguardsman, they don't stop being a citizen. When they take off that uniform, their service to this Nation doesn't stop. Think about previous generations. Well, today's veterans are the same. When they come home, they're looking to continue serving America however they can. And at a time when America needs all hands on deck, they've got the skills and the strength to help lead the way.

Our Government needs their patriotism and their sense of duty. That's why I ordered the hiring of more veterans by the Federal Government; we've hired more than 200,000 so far.

Our economy needs their outstanding talent. That's why I pushed hard last year for tax breaks for businesses that hire unemployed veterans and wounded warriors. And I'm proud to say that both parties in Congress came together to get that part done.

That's why we launched free personalized job services—job search services through the Veterans Gold Card program and an online Veterans Job Bank to help veterans find jobs that meet their talents. And by the way, if there are any veterans here who need those services, you can find that at whitehouse.gov/vets. And then, later this month, the VA will hold a jobs fair in Detroit where 12,000 more opportunities will be available to veterans.

And that's also why I challenged business leaders to hire 100,000 post-9/11 veterans and their spouses by the end of next year. Because don't forget our military families; they're serving alongside our veterans. Michelle and Jill Biden—that's Michelle Obama and Jill Biden—[*laughter*]—just in case you were curious. [*Laughter*] You might not know which Michelle I was talking about. [*Laughter*] They're leading this effort with respect to military families, nationally—it's called Joining Forces—to mobilize all of us to support today's military families and their veterans.

And so far, the good news is participating businesses have hired more than 70,000 veterans. And they've pledged to hire 175,000 more in the coming years. And I want to thank Honeywell not only for being an active partner in this initiative, but right here, Honeywell has hired 900 veterans over the past year, and for employing 65 veterans just here at Golden Val-

ley. So give them a big round of applause. Proud of them. Proud of them.

Standing up for our veterans, this is not a Democratic responsibility, it's not a Republican responsibility, it's an American responsibility. It's an obligation of every citizen who enjoys the freedom that these heroes defended. So we've got to meet our obligations today just like folks here at Honeywell are doing.

And as Commander in Chief, I want all of our servicemembers and veterans to know we are forever grateful for your service and your sacrifice. Just like you fought for us, we'll keep fighting for you—for more jobs, more security, for the opportunity to keep your families strong—because you'll help us keep America on top in the 21st century. We're going to keep fighting, just as you did, to show just why it is that the United State of America is the greatest nation on Earth.

God bless you. God bless America.

NOTE: The President spoke at 12:18 p.m. In his remarks, he referred to Ryan Sullivan, employee, Honeywell's Golden Valley manufacturing facility, who introduced the President; David M. Cote, chairman and chief executive officer, Honeywell International Inc.; Reno, NV, residents Paul and Valerie Keller; Spc. Nicholas Colgin, USA, 82d Airborne Division; and Jill T. Biden, wife of Vice President Joe Biden.

Remarks at an Obama Victory Fund 2012 Fundraiser in Minneapolis, Minnesota
June 1, 2012

The President. Thank you. Well, it is good to be back in Minnesota. I want to, first of all, say thank you to your outstanding Governor, Mark Dayton. We are proud of him. I had the extraordinary honor of serving with Mark when I first arrived in the Senate, and I know he's really sorry not to still be in the Senate. [*Laughter*] But he did a great job then, and he's doing a great job now, because he's passionate about people and wanting to make sure that they have opportunity. And so we're really grateful to him. And I know you guys are very pleased

that the Vikings are staying here in Minnesota. [*Laughter*] That is a priority.

I don't know—is R.T. still here? Your mayor was here a while—he was. I love him too, so just—[*laughter*]—you let him know that. R.T. is one of my dearest friends. He was actually part of the "draft Obama" movement, a very early supporter. Even before I was a supporter, or Michelle was a supporter, R.T. was a supporter. [*Laughter*] So I love him.

It is wonderful to be back here and to see the great work that Mark's doing and R.T. and your Senators and your congressional delegation.

As Mark mentioned, we've gone through, these past 3½, 4 years, as tough a period in our country's history as anything in our lifetime, certainly anything since the 1930s. And we're not out of the woods yet. We've still got work to do. There's still far too many people than we want who are out there looking for work, too many people whose homes are still underwater. But as Mark indicated, what we have tried to do for the last 3½, 4 years is just to make dogged progress, to just be persistent, to just stay at it.

And because of that, we were able to ensure that we didn't plunge into a full-blown depression when we first came into office. We were able to make sure that the financial system stabilized. People forget, the month that I took office we had lost 800,000 jobs in that month alone——

[*At this point, a baby cried.*]

The President. Yes, it was terrible! [*Laughter*] And we had lost 3 million jobs even before I was inaugurated. And so slowly, by making sure that the Recovery Act allowed teachers and firefighters to stay on the job, by making sure the projects all across the country got started to rebuild our roads and our bridges and projects that needed to get done, by making sure that everybody had a little more money in their pockets with tax cuts for the middle class—98 percent of workers—because of all those steps, the economy started to stabilize.

And then it started to move forward, and businesses started to invest again. And we made a commitment to double our exports. And so suddenly people were thinking about not just how much we consume, but what do we produce, what do we make, which is at the heart of who we are as Americans. How can we continue to innovate? How can we continue to adapt to this rapidly changing global economy?

So we're not there yet, but the good news is, we've made enormous strides over these last 3½ years. But the reason that some of you worked so hard back in 2008, the reason I decided to run for office, wasn't just to deal with the immediate crisis. It was also to address problems that had been lingering for decades that we hadn't taken care of. For decades, we had had a health care system that was broken and getting more and more expensive, providing less and less quality care to everybody, and was becoming increasingly unaffordable, not just for individual families, but also for businesses and for our Government.

For decades, we hadn't had an energy policy. So not only were we polluting the planet, but we were also finding ourselves sending billions of dollars to other countries because of our dependence on foreign oil.

For decades, we had seen manufacturing leave our shores and losing the competition when it came to trade around the world. For decades, our education system was working really well for a few, but for a lot of our young people, they weren't being equipped with the skills that they needed to compete.

And so what we've been fighting for is not just to right the ship short term, it's also to make sure that over the long term we're building an economy that can last, an economy with a firm foundation.

That's why we tackled health care, so that we can make sure that 30 million people are able to get access to insurance, but also so that we can start bending the cost curve because that's the primary contributor to our deficit.

That's why we took on education and said we're going to give more money in exchange for more reform, making schools accountable, but also making sure we're not just teaching to the test, making sure that we're unleashing the creativity and all the possibilities of good teachers working with inspired students.

That's why we made sure that college was more affordable, and we took tens of billions of dollars that were previously going to banks and made sure that that money was going directly to our students to help them pay for college education.

That's why we invested in clean energy so that we've actually doubled clean energy production in this country. And while oil and gas production are up higher than they've been in 8 years, our dependence on foreign oil is actually down as low as we've seen in almost a decade—under 50 percent—and we were able to get a doubling of fuel efficiency standards on cars, which means that sometime halfway in the next decade we're going to have cars that get 55 miles to a gallon, and everybody's car will get 55 miles to a gallon. And that's going to save consumers thousands of dollars, but it's also going to make sure that we're taking a whole bunch of carbon out of the atmosphere.

So, on each of these fronts, what we've tried to do is deal with the immediate challenges in front of us, but also think long term.

Now, throughout this process, the other side's had a different vision. My hope, when I came into office, was that we would have Republicans and Democrats coming together because the Nation was facing extraordinary challenges. It turns out that wasn't their approach, to put it mildly. [*Laughter*] Their approach, in part, was that if we can beat Obama, then that should be our primary focus. But there was also a philosophical difference, because their vision is one in which if a few are doing very well at the top, then that's somehow good for everybody. And what I tried to point out to them was that throughout our history, when we've done well, the reason we became an economic superpower was because we created a platform where everybody can succeed, where everybody is getting a fair shot and everybody is doing their fair share and everybody is playing by the same rules.

And so a lot of the tussles that we've had over the last 3½ years have had to do with this difference in vision, and it will be coming to a head in this election. We're going to have as stark a contrast as we've seen in a very long time between the two candidates. I mean, 2008 was a significant election, obviously. But John McCain believed in climate change. [*Laughter*] John believed in campaign finance reform. He believed in immigration reform. I mean, there were some areas where you saw some overlap.

In this election, the Republican Party has moved in a fundamentally different direction. The center of gravity for their party has shifted. And so things that we used to be able to take for granted, it's been more difficult to take for granted over the last 3½ years.

And let's just take one example: deficit reduction. We have a significant long-term debt that has to be dealt with. Now, our top priority should be putting people to work right now, because if our economy is growing faster, that actually will help reduce the deficit. But there's no doubt that it's unsustainable for us to keep on having health care costs in Medicare and Medicaid go up 6, 8, 10 percent, when the overall inflation rate and growth rate are coming in lower. That's a recipe for long-term disaster.

So what we've said is, look, let's cut out waste, let's streamline programs, let's reorganize Government where we can. Let's end the war in Iraq. Let's wind down the war in Afghanistan. Let's use some of those savings for deficit reduction. Let's tackle Medicare and Medicaid in an intelligent way that preserves this critical social safety net, but also achieves significant savings. And let's ask those of us who've been most fortunate, just to pay a little bit more. And if we put that package together, we can achieve $4 trillion of savings and we can pay right now to rebuild our roads and our bridges and rehire some teachers and grow the economy right now. We can package that together to make progress.

And we couldn't get them to take yes for an answer, because, ideologically, the notion of billionaires and millionaires paying a little bit more in taxes didn't adhere to the philosophy that they've been fighting for over the last several years.

Now, I believe that if we're successful in this election—when we're successful in this election—that the fever may break, because there's a tradition in the Republican Party of more common sense than that. My hope and my expectation is that after the election, now that it turns out the goal of beating Obama doesn't make much sense because I'm not running again—[*laughter*]—that we can start getting some cooperation again and we're not going to have people raising their hands and saying—or refusing to accept a deal where there's $10 of cuts for every dollar of tax increases, but that people will accept a balanced plan for deficit reduction.

My expectation is, is that we can get a highway transportation bill done that puts people back to work right now and rebuilds our infrastructure to succeed over the long term.

My hope and expectation is, is that they'll recognize we need immigration reform because we're a nation of laws and a nation of immigrants. And it actually is better for our economy, and by the way, it saves us money if all those folks who are working underground are above ground and paying taxes. It's actually good for our economy.

My expectation is, is that if we can break this fever, that we can invest in clean energy and energy efficiency, because that's not a partisan issue, that's a sensible approach to making sure that our economy is going forward and we have control over it over the long term.

So, so much is at stake in this election. And Minnesota is going to be important, and all of you are going to be critically important to that process. This is going to be a very close race. It's not a close race actually because the other side has a whole bunch of great ideas—they don't. [*Laughter*] They are just churning out the same ideas that we saw in the decade before I took office: the same ideas, the same you're-on-your-own philosophy, the same tax cuts and deregulation agenda that helped get us into this mess in the first place. But it's going to be close because there are a lot of folks out there who are still having a tough time and the economy is still fragile.

And right now our biggest challenge is the situation not here in the United States, but coming overseas. I mean, Europe is having a significant crisis, in part because they haven't taken as many of the decisive steps as were needed to deal with the challenge. And that's weakening Asia, and that means it's harder for our exporters. All this stuff makes a difference in a global economy.

So it's going to be close. And that means that we're going to have to be working just as hard and we have to be just as passionate, we have to be just as committed, just as excited as we were the last time.

Now, admittedly, I'm grayer now. [*Laughter*] And so—and I've been President for a while, so you know, you're never as cool as you were that first time. [*Laughter*] Right? But I tell you, I am still so absolutely convinced in America's future. I travel a lot around the world, and when you ask folks where they look to for leadership, it is still the United States of America.

When they think about what country embodies universal aspirations, they still talk about the United States of America. And there is not a country on Earth that wouldn't trade places with us, because we still have the best workers in the world. We still have the best universities in the world. We still have the best scientists and the best innovation in the world. We've got the best free market and the most dynamic entrepreneurs in the world.

Ironically, the—some of the very things that the Republicans don't like are part of what makes our free market so strong, because the rules we put in place for transparency and accountability and consumer protection means our products are better and our investments are safer. And that's the reason why money rushes here when we've got problems all around the world—is precisely because there are rules in place that everybody is supposed to abide by.

And so we've got all the tools to make the 21st century an American century just like the 20th century was. And the question is, are we going to seize it? And that's where all of you come in. This little guy who has been eating his feet the whole time I've been talking—[*laughter*]—when I think about why I ran for office, I think about Malia and Sasha.

Audience member. Henry.

The President. ——and Henry. [*Laughter*] And what's your name?

Audience member. Dmitry.

The President. Dmitry. I think about them and what kind of country are we leaving for them.

The truth is, probably, our kids in this restaurant are going to be okay. We've been incredibly blessed, most of us. We've been incredibly lucky. But the quality of their lives will also depend on whether every other child in America has got a shot, whether they're doing well, whether they feel invested in the American Dream.

Now, it doesn't do us any good if our kids are succeeding, but the environment is ruined. They can't protect themselves from that. It's not going to do much good if they're doing very well, but they're having to drive on dilapidated roads and bridges and their airports don't work and broadband lines are better someplace else and innovation has taken place somewhere else. I don't want them ever to have to think about moving to someplace else to have more opportunity. That's what we fight for.

So I used to say, back in 2008, I'm not a perfect man, and I won't be a perfect President. But I promised I would always tell people what I thought, I'd always tell people where I stood, and I would fight as hard as I could to make sure that Henry and Malia and Sasha and Dmitry and our kids have a better future. And I've kept that promise.

And the reason I've been able to keep that promise is because I get a chance in this job to meet Americans from every walk of life, and I travel all across the country. And what I said in that first speech I made on the national stage I still believe, which is: Black, White, Asian, Hispanic, Native American, gay, straight, disabled or not, we're one people. And the decency and strength and resilience of the American people, it comes shining through every place I go: in VFW halls, in a small business, in teachers who I meet, and firefighters and our incredible men and women in uniform.

This is a country full of good people who want to do the right thing, and they deserve a government who reflects that decency. That's what we've tried to give them, and that's what we're going to keep on giving them for the next 5 years.

So thank you very much, everybody. Thank you.

NOTE: The President spoke at 1:37 p.m. at the Bachelor Farmer restaurant. In his remarks, he referred to Mayor Raymond T. Rybak, Jr., of Minneapolis, MN; and Sen. John S. McCain III, in his capacity as the 2008 Republican Presidential nominee.

Letter to Congressional Leaders Transmitting a Report Regarding the Waiver of Sanctions Against North Korea
June 1, 2012

Dear _____:

Pursuant to section 1405 of the Supplemental Appropriations Act, 2008 (Public Law 110–252) (the "Act"), and in order to keep the Congress fully informed, I am providing the enclosed report prepared by my Administration. This report includes information related to the issuance of any waivers under the authority of section 1405 of the Act of certain sanctions against North Korea and to certain other matters relating to North Korea.

Sincerely,

BARACK OBAMA

NOTE: Identical letters were sent to Daniel K. Inouye, chairman, and W. Thad Cochran, vice chairman, Senate Committee on Appropriations; Carl M. Levin, chairman, and John S. McCain III, ranking member, Senate Committee on Armed Services; John F. Kerry, chairman, and Richard G. Lugar, ranking member, Senate Committee on Foreign Relations; Harold Rogers, chairman, and Norman D. Dicks, ranking member, House Committee on Appropriations; Howard P. "Buck" McKeon, chairman, and Adam Smith, ranking member, House Committee on Armed Services; and Ileana Ros-Lehtinen, chair, and Howard L. Berman, ranking member, House Committee on Foreign Affairs.

Letter to Congressional Leaders Transmitting Designations Under the Kingpin Act
June 1, 2012

Dear _____:

This report to the Congress, under section 804(a) of the Foreign Narcotics Kingpin Designation Act, 21 U.S.C. 1903(b)(1) (the "Kingpin Act"), transmits my designations of the following three foreign individuals as appropriate for sanctions under the Kingpin Act and reports my direction of sanctions against them under the Act:

Naser Kelmendi (Bosnia and Herzegovina)
Sayed Wazir Shah (Afghanistan)
Jose Antonio Soto Gastelum (Mexico)

Sincerely,

BARACK OBAMA

NOTE: Identical letters were sent to Carl M. Levin, chairman, and John S. McCain III, ranking member, Senate Committee on Armed Services; Max S. Baucus, chairman, and Orrin G. Hatch, ranking member, Senate Committee on Finance; John F. Kerry, chairman, and Richard G. Lugar, ranking member, Senate Committee on Foreign Relations; Patrick J. Leahy, chairman, and Charles E. Grassley, ranking member, Senate Committee on the Judiciary; Dianne Feinstein, chair, and Saxby C. Chambliss, vice chairman, Senate Select Committee on Intelligence; Howard P. "Buck" McKeon, chairman, and Adam Smith, ranking member, House Committee on Armed Services; Ileana Ros-Lehtinen, chair, and Howard L. Berman, ranking member, House Committee on Foreign Affairs; Lamar S. Smith, chairman, and John J. Conyers, Jr., ranking member, House Committee on the Judiciary; Mike Rogers, chairman, and C.A. Dutch Ruppersberger, ranking member, House Permanent Select Committee on Intelligence; and Dave Camp, chairman, and Sander M. Levin, ranking member, House Committee on Ways and Means.

Remarks at an Obama Victory Fund 2012 Fundraiser in Chicago, Illinois
June 1, 2012

The President. Hey, Chicago! Thank you. Ah, it is good to be back home. I am sleeping in my bed tonight. I'm going to go into my kitchen; I might cook something for myself. [*Laughter*] Putter around in the backyard a little bit. It's good being home. White House is nice, but I'm just leasing. [*Laughter*]

I—it is so good to see so many great friends. But I just have to point out the person who introduced me. He was one of the best Chiefs of Staff that you could ever want to have. He would be in the White House at 5 or 6; he'd leave there at 7 or 8. He'd take work home with him. He'd be there on the weekends, sacrifices, all the stuff that he did. But as good as he was at being a Chief of Staff, I have never seen him happier than he is as Mayor of the City of Chicago.

He loves Chicago. He loves its people. He loves its institutions. He loves its kids. And so all the work that he is doing on behalf of making the schools better and streamlining government and making things work in every part of the city and not just some parts of the city, that's all reflective—all that energy, all that pent-up energy—[*laughter*]—that's reflective of his love of the city. So I just wanted to give—everybody to give a big round of applause to an outstanding Mayor, Rahm Emanuel.

So I'm here because not only do I need your help, but your country needs your help. So some of you have known me since I was running for the State senate. There were folks who saw me lose a congressional race and saw me win a U.S. Senate race. And I know you, and I know your values, and I know what you care about. And as much as we may have had friendships and relationships—and that's part of the reason you supported me in 2008—the election 4 years ago wasn't just about me; it wasn't about one person. It was about our commitments to each other. It was about core, basic beliefs we had in America and America's future.

We believed that everybody should have a fair shot and everybody should do their fair share and everybody should play by the same set of rules. We believed that if you're willing to work hard, if you're willing to take responsibility, if you're willing to be part of a community, then it doesn't matter what you look like, where you come from, what your last name is, who you love, the bottom line is that you should be able to make it in America. That's what this city is all about. That's reflective of this city. You've got surnames from everywhere in Chicago—not just Obamas—because this has been a magnet for people who say, if I work hard, I can make it.

Audience member. I love you, Obama.

Audience members. Aww.

The President. Hi. [*Laughter*] One of my younger friends was there.

And that's why we came together in 2008, because we felt as if, for a decade, those values were being betrayed or at least we weren't living up to them. We had seen a surplus turned into a deficit—massive deficits—because folks got tax cuts who didn't need them and weren't even asking for them, two wars run on a credit card, first time in our history where we cut taxes while sending young men and women off to fight.

We had seen an economic system that was dependent on financial speculation and frankly a lot of recklessness. We had seen manufacturing move overseas. We became known as the country that was consuming things. We were the engine of the world economy because of what we bought on credit cards or on home equity loans, instead of what we had previously been known as, a country that made things and sold them all around the world with those three proud words: Made in America.

And all this came tumbling down in a financial crisis that really began to happen just as we were still in the midst of the campaign. So, before I took office, we had lost 3 million jobs. The month I took office, we lost 800,000 jobs, 8 million all told before our economic policies had a chance to take effect. And so we had to make a series of tough decisions quickly. We had to make sure that an iconic auto industry was saved. We had to make sure that the banking system was stabilized. We had to make sure that teachers' layoffs were minimized and States got some help and middle class families got tax cuts.

And because of those decisions, we were able to stabilize the economy and begin to grow again, because we had faith in the American people. Most of those decisions weren't easy. We knew we'd be subject to political criticism, but they were the right thing to do for our country. And despite all the noise and the misinformation and the obfuscation and bamboozling—[*laughter*]—that you hear, what we did worked to help make sure that the economy began to grow again, so that we have now seen over 2 years of the economy growing and jobs being produced, more than 4 million jobs produced, over 800,000 produced just this year alone.

Now, here's the thing, though: We're not where we need to be. We're not there yet. We saw that in today's jobs report. Yes, a lot of that is attributable to Europe and the cloud that's coming over from the Atlantic, and the whole world economy is—has been weakened by it. And it's having an impact on us. But beyond that, we still know too many of our friends and family who are out of work. And there are too many folks whose homes are still underwater, too many people still struggling to pay the bills, too many kids still locked out of opportunity.

And when we embarked on this journey in 2008, it wasn't just to get back to where we were before the financial crisis. The idea was to start fixing things in a more fundamental way: to make sure that every child in America gets a good education, to make sure people aren't bankrupt when they get sick, to make sure we've actually got an energy policy that works for this country, to make sure we're still a nation of innovators, to build an economy that lasts and that allows middle class families to get a sense of security again. That's what we were fighting for.

And we've got more work to do. On that front, we've got more work to do. We are not satisfied. As proud as we are of the work that we've gotten done, we've still got miles to go on this journey.

Now, what makes this year so important is because we've got a contrast this time that we may not have seen in American politics in quite some time. Even the last time we ran, we had a Republican candidate who—I had some profound disagreements with him, but he acknowledged the need for immigration reform and acknowledged the need for campaign finance reform, acknowledged the need for policies that would do something about climate change.

Now what we've got is not just a nominee, but a Congress and a Republican Party, that have a fundamentally different vision about where we need to go as a country. Look, I believe they love this country. The nominee, he's achieved great personal success, seems to have a wonderful family. God bless them. But the vision that he has for this country, like the vision that Republicans in Congress have for this country, is exactly the vision that got us into this mess in the first place. Except, as Bill Clinton said a few weeks ago, it's on steroids this time. [*Laughter*]

They don't have a new idea about how to move the country forward. They're just regurgitating all the old ideas: We want more tax cuts for some of the wealthiest individuals. We want to cut back further on things like education and transportation and the basic investments that have allowed America to succeed. They want to further roll back—to pay for the tax cuts—our core social safety net of Medicare and Medicaid. They want to strip away regulations that we fought to put in place to make sure, for example, that we don't have the same kind of financial crisis on Wall Street that we just went through. They want to strip it all away.

Their basic philosophy is, if a few folks are doing really, really well, and we strip away whatever restraints on how the market operates to protect consumers and to make sure that everybody gets a chance and everybody can start a small business or everybody can be out there and compete and succeed, that if we just let everybody be on their own, that somehow we're going to be better off. And that is a fundamental misreading of American history. That is not how Chicago became a great city. That's not how Illinois became a great State. That's not how America became a great nation.

We're a nation of rugged individualists with an entrepreneurial spirit. We believe in rewarding risk takers and innovators, but we also believe that we're all in this together. We also believe that when we make investments together in quality public schools, then those kids who are being educated are going to be the workers of the future and the business leaders of the future, and we will all be richer for it. We will all benefit. So it's worth us making that investment.

As I was coming down the lakefront today and thinking about Daniel Burnham and "make no little plans," we understand that when we build our infrastructure and great roads and railways and, in the 21st century, broadband lines and wireless and high-speed rail, that that's what helped drive us as an economic superpower.

When we make investments in research and science, so that the Government gets involved and suddenly, there's an Internet, that creates a platform for all kinds of private industry, all sorts of wealth creation, all sorts of opportunity. We don't do it for one individual, for one group; we do it for everybody.

The same way that together we paid for firefighting and police departments and national defense, there are some things we do better together. That's what we've always understood, and that is what has made this country great.

And so the choice in this election is going to be between a vision that didn't work during 2000 to 2008, didn't work right before the Great Depression. We've gone through periodic spasms of this: the Gilded Age, Roaring

Twenties. We've seen this philosophy before. But the good thing is usually we come to our senses. [*Laughter*] We realize, you know what, that's not the way our democracy is built. That's not how this country's built. And that's the vision that we're going to have to confront and address in this election.

Now, the good news is when you cut through the noise, if you just ask people, it turns out most people agree with this, the things that we've already done. When you ask people, you know what, is it a good idea to make sure that we have more teachers in the classroom, people say, absolutely. When we tell them, you know what, taking tens of billions of dollars that were going to the banks in the student loan program, cutting out the middleman, and giving that money directly to students so that college was more affordable, is that a good idea? Absolutely.

Does it make sense for us to double fuel efficiency standards on cars, so that a decade from now every car is going to be getting 55 miles per gallon, so that even though our oil production is higher than it's been in the last 8 years and imports of foreign oil have actually dropped, we've also doubled clean energy so that we are starting to control our energy future and be able to do something about climate change? Is that a good idea? People say, yes.

When we tell people, you know what, manufacturing's coming back—seeing more jobs in manufacturing than at any time since the 1990s, not just in the auto industry—and companies are starting to say, you know what, it makes sense for us to reinvest in America again because America has still got the best market and the best workers, why not bring some jobs home? We're starting to see that happen. And so when you ask people, does it make sense for us to stop giving tax breaks to companies that are shipping jobs overseas, let's give those tax breaks to companies to help with their moving expenses to bring jobs back to America, they say, that's a good idea, we agree.

And when we say to people, doesn't it make sense for us to make sure that young people can stay on their parent's health insurance plan until they're 26 and make our seniors' prescrip-

tion drug plans more affordable and make sure that everybody is guaranteed preventive care and women are able to get preventive care and make determinations about their own health, people say, yes, that's a good idea. And we tell them, well, that's my health care bill. [*Laughter*]

So the good news is that the majority of the American people share our vision. They believe that we have to work hard, each of us. We have to take responsibility, each of us, for our families, for ourselves, for our neighborhoods, for our communities. They understand government can't solve every problem and it shouldn't try. They understand that not everybody can be helped if they're not willing to help themselves. They understand that not every regulation is a smart one and not every dollar of government money is well spent. They want lean and smarter government, the kind of government that Rahm's providing here in Chicago. They understand that—those things.

But they also say, you know what, I've got obligations to something bigger. I've got obligations to the next generation. I've got obligations to the future. That's worth fighting for. That's worth fighting for.

And nowhere do we see it more than in our men and women in uniform. Now, I talked today about a—one more initiative that I'm trying to push Congress to create a veterans jobs corps, so that all these young men and women, now that we've ended the war in Iraq and are starting to wind down the war in Afghanistan, that anybody who fought for this country doesn't have to fight for a job when they come home or fight for a roof over their heads when they come home.

But in our troops, we see that spirit, that sense of common purpose, and that sense of mission and that sense of sacrifice. But everybody feels that to some degree. We just have to tap into it. We know that is right, not just right for the country, but right for ourselves. Because I don't want to live in a country where all we're doing is thinking about ourselves, where we're not thinking about future generations.

Now, when you make this argument, by the way, to the other side, what they'll say is,

"We're thinking about the future; that's why we have to do something about these deficits." That's what they'll—"out-of-control Government spending." And I smile, and I say, you are absolutely right. We've got to get Government spending and our deficits and our debt under control, which is why I signed a trillion dollars—$2 trillion worth of tax cuts in this last plan. It's the reason why Government spending has gone up at a slower rate under my administration than any administration since Dwight Eisenhower.

But I say, you know what, if you're really serious about deficit reduction, then why don't we get together? We'll build on the cuts we've already made. We'll work with you to see if there are some additional waste and streamlining and Government organization we can do. We'll look at health care costs in Medicare and Medicaid, which are the main drivers of the deficit. And if—as long as we're not voucherizing that program like you guys have proposed, and as long as we're keeping that basic commitment we make to folks in their golden years, as long we're keeping that intact, I'm happy to work with you.

But here's just one thing. I think somebody like myself, I should pay a little bit more in taxes, because I don't want us to be cutting student loans to young people or Medicaid for a disabled child or shortchanging our veterans for the care they need when they come home. I don't want that, because I don't need that tax cut big enough. I don't need it bad enough. And you know what, it turns out most millionaires and billionaires don't need it either. They're doing just fine. Their tax rates are lower than they've been in 50 years.

And what we've proposed is simply, well, let's go back to the rates under the last Democratic administration, when we created 22 million jobs. It didn't seem to be a problem for job creators then. Why is it a problem for job creators now? What happened? What happened?

So we put forward plans. Here's $4 trillion that we can reduce our deficit in a balanced way that protects the investments we need for growth and helps our middle class. I haven't gotten any takers so far on that side. [*Laugh-*

ter] Actually, there are a number of Republicans who think it's a good idea to have a balanced approach like this, but they're out of office now. [*Laughter*]

So don't tell me that you're interested in the future, but you're not willing to make just an iota of sacrifice, a little bit of modification of your ideology in order to secure that future. And if you look at Mr. Romney's plan, he's got $5 trillion worth of additional tax cuts on top of the Bush tax cuts, and he hasn't identified how that they'd be paid for. He says, "Well, we'll close some loopholes." Well, which loopholes? "I don't know." [*Laughter*]

I mean, we put forward a detailed budget. Here, here's how we can do it. Haven't gotten any takers so far. So don't buy that song and dance about, yes, we're concerned about future generations, but you don't think Warren Buffet can pay a dime more in taxes in order to support that future? So that's the debate we're going to be having over the next several months. It's a critical debate about the economy.

There are a lot of other issues out there. I believe that we've got to have comprehensive immigration reform. We're a nation of laws and a nation of immigrants. My opponent has a different view. I believe we did the right thing in repealing "don't ask, don't tell" and that we have to fight for a future of fairness and equality in this country under the law. My opponent has a different view. I think I did the right thing in ending the war in Iraq and in setting a timeline for getting out of Afghanistan. My opponent has a different view.

So there are going to be a whole bunch of issues to fuss about. But the central one, about how we build an economy that works for everybody, that's the one I want everybody to pay attention to. But this is going to be a close race. And the reason it's going to be a close race is we've gone through a tough 4 years on top of a tough decade for a lot of families before that, and folks feel worn out.

And if you don't have a job, you don't care that there have been 4 million jobs created. You're still waiting for yours. If your house is $100,000 underwater, the fact that the housing market's beginning to stabilize isn't satisfactory. You're still trying to figure out how you dig yourself out of a hole.

And that's going to make it tough. And frankly, it makes it easier for the other guys, because the other side, all they've got to do is just say, you know what, you're frustrated, things aren't where they need to be, and it's Obama's fault. And if they can spend hundreds of millions of dollars promoting that argument, then they don't have to come up with answers. They don't have to come up with a credible plan. They figure they can surf folks' frustrations all the way to the White House.

We've seen this game before. We've just never seen this much money behind the game. So the question then for us is going to end up being, well, how badly do we believe in what we say we believe in? How hard are we willing to fight for the future that we say we want for our kids and our grandkids?

The one thing I learned in 2008—traveling all across the country, starting in Iowa—was for all the cynicism and negativity and phony issues and sometimes outright lies that passed for political campaigns, when a group of ordinary citizens say, we want to bring change to our country, we want to make this work for everybody, when voters start talking to each other and making commitments to each other, not just to a candidate, but to an idea, change happens. That's what you showed me last time.

And so this time, we're going to have to be more determined and we're going to have to make those same commitments. I told people back in 2008, I said, I'm not a perfect man and I won't be a perfect President. But I promise you this: I will always tell you what I think, and I'll always tell you where I stand. And I'll wake up every single day just working as hard as I can to make your lives a little better. And you know what, I've kept that promise. I've kept that promise.

I still believe in you. I still believe in the American people. I still believe in the American idea. And if you still believe in me and if you are willing to knock on some doors and make some phone calls and get out there and get working and fight to finish what we started in 2008, we will not just win an election, we will continue down a path of glory for this country and remind the entire world just why it is that America is the greatest nation on earth.

Thank you, everybody. God bless you. God bless the United States of America.

NOTE: The President spoke at 6:27 p.m. at the Chicago Cultural Center. In his remarks, he referred to Sen. John S. McCain III, in his capacity as the 2008 Republican Presidential nominee; Republican Presidential candidate former Gov. W. Mitt Romney of Massachusetts; and Warren E. Buffett, chief executive officer and chairman, Berkshire Hathaway Inc.

Remarks at an Obama Victory Fund 2012 Fundraiser in Chicago
June 1, 2012

Well, I can follow a lawyer, but following a poet—[*laughter*]—that's hard.

I'm so grateful to Chaka and Tracey and their beautiful daughters for opening up this great home. I want to acknowledge somebody who is doing outstanding work on behalf of Illinois families every single day, your Governor, Pat Quinn, who's here today. Good job, Pat.

It's nice to be back on the South Side. For some reason, they didn't—whoever organized this didn't understand the geography of Chicago, because—[*laughter*]—we came south, now I'm going to have to go back north. [*Laughter*]

And then I go home back south. [*Laughter*] See, we could have just kept on going. [*Laughter*] But it's good to be home, and it's good to see so many good friends, and I appreciate all the new ones.

It is true Chaka and I have know each other for a long time. The first time we met, he was still a young up-and-comer. Now he's a big ship—[*laughter*]—now he's a big ship in the deep ocean, so—[*laughter*]. But not only has he not gotten any gray hair, whereas I have—[*laughter*]—but he hasn't changed in terms of his graciousness and his character. And so we're just really appreciative of the friendship that we had.

Usually in intimate settings like this, I don't like to give a long speech. I'd rather have a conversation with everybody, have a chance to answer questions, take comments. So let me just say a few things at the top.

First of all, obviously, we've gone through an extraordinary time over the last 4 years, worst financial crisis since the Great Depression: a worldwide contraction, the locking up of the financial markets, businesses—even blue-chip companies—not being able to finance themselves, consumers getting hammered, the housing market crashing. And so we had to make a series of decisions very quickly at the beginning of my administration.

And we, for the most part, made the right decisions. They weren't always popular, but because of those decisions, the auto industry came roaring back. Because of those decisions, suddenly, credit started flowing again. Because of those decisions, we were out there exporting goods once again all around the world. Because of those decisions, the ship was righted and we started growing again and started producing jobs again. And we've now seen over 4 million jobs created over the last couple of years, and we've seen, just in the last 6 months alone, over 800,000 jobs created. Strongest manufacturing job growth since the 1990s.

And so there's a sense, even with a disappointing jobs report today because of what's happening in Europe—and we're now a global economy; it's integrated. So, when something happens across the Atlantic or across the Pacific, it gives us a shock. Despite all that, though, we're moving in the right direction. But we're not moving as fast as we could be. And more importantly, the reason I ran, and the reason a lot of you support me, wasn't just to get back to the status quo, it was to address the underlying challenges that had prevented us from creating an economy that, on a sustained basis, is providing security and hope and promise for people who were willing to work hard: middle class families who want to live out that dream of being able to buy a home and raise a family and send their kids to college and make sure

that they're doing even better than their—than they were.

And that's the reason why, even as we've done all this work to try to get the economy moving in the right direction—in fits and starts, as frustrating as it sometimes has been—what we've also tried to do is think about the future: Where are we going? And that's the reason why we doubled fuel efficiency standards on cars and doubled the production of clean energy, even as we were increasing the production of oil and gas, because we want to make sure that we've got control of our energy future. That's going to be critical to our success.

That's the reason we decided to double exports, because we don't want to just be a country that consumes things, we want to be a country that sells things.

That's the reason why we invested so heavily in education reform. And some great work's being done in Illinois. But all across the country, over 40 States have engaged in some unprecedented reforms looking for results. And that's the reason why we made college more accessible by greatly increasing the access to student loans and Pell grants, making sure that young people have the ability to train themselves for the skills they need for the 21st century.

That's the reason why we did health care reform, because not only was health care killing families, but it was also just the biggest single factor in driving our deficits and a huge strain on American businesses that were making us less competitive. And so I could not be prouder of the fact that 30 million people are going to have access to health care who didn't have it before. And young people already are able to stay on their parent's plan. And seniors are seeing discounts for their prescription drugs that are making a difference in their quality of life.

And on the international scene, because, as I said, we don't live—just to continue the nautical theme—[*laughter*]—no country is an island. [*Laughter*] Well, some countries are islands, but we're not. [*Laughter*] The world's interconnected. And so we had a goal of righting the ship of foreign policy, regaining respect around the world, strengthening our alliances, ending the war in Iraq, phasing down the war in Afghanistan, going after Al Qaida in a way that was smart so that not only did we get bin Laden, but also we've weakened Al Qaida to the point where it's much more difficult for them to threaten our homeland or our allies.

So that's a lot of work for a relatively short period of time. But we've got so much more work to do. And that's where we're going to need your help. This is going to be a close election; it's going to be a tight election. I'm absolutely confident that the agenda we have to further expand clean energy and to invest in science and technology, in balancing our deficits and reducing our debt in a balanced way, in making sure that we keep Wall Street reform that will prevent the kinds of shenanigans

that got us into this mess in the first place, and making sure that we maintain health care reform that is providing, for example, preventive care for women—I want to make sure that stays in place, that we're implementing it effectively, because that's going to be part of how we create an economy that lasts for everybody, not just for a few.

But in order to do it, we're going have to want it; we're going to have to fight for it. And we proved in 2008 that when people come together, they can't be stopped. That's what we're going to do in 2012 as well.

So thank you very much, everybody.

NOTE: The President spoke at 7:35 p.m. at the residence of Chaka M. and Tracey Patterson.

Remarks at an Obama Victory Fund 2012 Fundraiser in Chicago
June 1, 2012

Thank you, everybody. Thank you. Well, first of all, it is just good to be home. And it is good to be back with so many close friends.

Jim was in some ways being modest, because he talked about supporting me for my Presidential race, but like so many of you here—like folks like John and Neil and other folks in this room—actually, the Crown family, from the grandpas all the way to the grandkids, they supported me when I ran for State senate, supported me when I lost a congressional race, supported me when I won my Senate race, and then supported me in my run for the Presidency. These guys have been friends for a really long time. And Michelle and I love them to death, and to see how remarkable their children have turned out, watching them grow up, is a great thing to see. So please give the Crowns a big round of applause. They—[*applause*]—wonderful friends.

So I am not going to give a long speech. This really is family. You guys know me. You don't need to hear a lot of speechmaking. What I want to do is mostly answer questions and entertain ideas and comments from you. But what I do want to just say briefly is both what

this campaign's going to be about and why it's going to be so important.

There are going to be a lot of issues involved because we have probably as sharp a contrast between two candidates as we've seen in a very long time, substantively. I feel very strongly we've got to have comprehensive immigration reform. We should—we're a nation of laws and a nation of immigrants. Governor Romney has a different view. I care very deeply about women's health issues. Governor Romney thinks differently about those issues. I very much believe that the environment and making sure that we're protecting it for the next generation is consistent not just with Democratic traditions, but with traditions dating back to Teddy Roosevelt, a Republican. Mr. Romney disagrees with me.

So there are going to be a whole set of issues to debate. But the essence of this campaign is going to be about the economy. It's going to be about how do we create an economy that works for everybody, that is dynamic, that is competitive, that meets the challenges of the 21st century and provides a platform where everybody who's willing to work hard can succeed. And I mean everybody—whatever their background, race, gender, surname, faith—that if you're willing to apply yourself and do everything it takes to follow your dream, that you can make it in this country.

And not everybody is going to make it like a Lester Crown or a Neil Bluhm, but you should be able to find a job that pays a living wage and buy a home and send your kids to college and imagine that they're going to do better than you did and have some sense of security after a lifetime of labor.

And the big challenge is not just since this financial crisis, but for a decade before that people felt that that basic compact was slipping away, that basic security was being lost, that rewards weren't matching up to effort and responsibility. And so that is going to be the essence of the debate: Who's got a vision for how we make sure that the next generation of Americans, as well as this generation of Americans, can succeed if they're responsible and they're working hard.

Now, obviously, so much of that debate is going to be clouded by the fact that we've had an unprecedented crisis, something we haven't seen at least since the 1930s. And today's job report reminds us that for all the progress we've made, the world economy is integrated and it's still fragile: too many people still out of work, too many folks still have homes underwater, too many people are still struggling to pay the bills, too many people are still struggling with debt.

But the truth is, is that the steps we took back in 2009 and 2010 have helped to stabilize this economy. It is growing. We've created more than 4 million jobs, more than 800,000 in the last few months alone. And if, as we work with other countries in Europe—but also in Asia—to try to restore a sense of stability for the world economy, then I have no doubt that we can continue on a path of growth. But that alone is not enough.

And so the debate is going to have to extend beyond just how do we solve immediate crises. It's going to be how do we make sure that every child is getting the kind of education they need in the 21st century. It's going to be how we continue to make progress on energy inde-

pendence and clean energy that's important for our economy, but also for our environment. How are we going to make sure that we are reducing the costs of health care while improving the quality of health care, because we are still spending 17 or 18 percent of our GDP on health care. Other countries spend 11 and 12 percent, and they're still getting better outcomes. And I believe that the health care bill that we passed is pushing us in the right direction, but we're going to have more work to do on that front.

We're going to have to debate how to reduce our deficit in a way that still allows us to make the investments we need to grow and make sure that everybody is paying their fair share, doing their part. We're going to have to talk about how we rebuild our infrastructure and our broadband lines and our wireless and all the things that we need that provide a platform for success and how are we investing in basic research and development.

And on each of these questions there's just a fundamentally different vision between myself and Governor Romney. I think he's a patriotic American. He's had great personal success, which we applaud, and he seems to have a wonderful family. But his recipe for how you grow an economy in a way that allows everybody to prosper, that's broad based and lasting, is basically a retread of ideas that we tried before I came into office and didn't work and in fact haven't worked for most of our history.

And so that's what the debate's going to be about. And there are going to be all kinds of distractions over the next 5 months, but I cannot wait to have that debate. And I want the American people to hear it, with great clarity, because if they understand the choices involved, I'm absolutely convinced we're going to win. And as a consequence, I'm absolutely convinced that the 21st century is going to be the American Century just like the 20th.

All right, thanks. Thank you, guys.

NOTE: The President spoke at 9 p.m. at the residence of Paula and James S. Crown. In his remarks, he referred to John W. Rogers, Jr., chairman, chief executive officer, and chief investment officer, Ariel Investments; Neil G. Bluhm, cofounder, JMB Realty Corp., and managing principal, Walton Street Capital;

Lester Crown, chairman, Henry Crown and Co.; and Republican Presidential candidate former Gov. W. Mitt Romney of Massachusetts.

The President's Weekly Address
June 2, 2012

Today I'm at one of Honeywell's manufacturing facilities in Golden Valley, Minnesota, where I just announced a step that will make it easier for companies to hire returning servicemembers who have the skills our country needs right now. It's another part of our effort to make sure that no American who fights for this country abroad has to fight for a job when they come home. That's why businesses like Honeywell are answering our challenge to hire 100,000 post-9/11 veterans and their spouses by the end of next year. That's why I've directed the Government to hire over 200,000 veterans so far, because our economy needs their tremendous talent and because millions of Americans are still looking for a job.

Right now this country is still fighting our way back from the worst economic crisis since the Great Depression. The economy is growing again, but it's not growing as fast as we'd like. Our businesses have created almost 4.3 million new jobs over the last 27 months, but as we learned in this week's jobs report, we're not creating them fast enough. And just like last year at this time, our economy faces some serious headwinds. Gas prices are starting to come down again, but when they spiked over the last few months, it hit people's wallets pretty hard. The crisis in Europe's economy is casting a shadow on our own. And all of this makes it even more challenging to fully recover and lay the foundation for an economy that's built to last.

But from the moment we first took action to prevent another depression, we knew the road to recovery wouldn't be easy. We knew it would take time, that there would be ups and downs along the way. But we also knew that if we were willing to act wisely and boldly and together, if we were willing to keep at it and never quit, we'd come back stronger.

Nothing has shaken my faith in that belief. We will come back stronger, we do have better days ahead, and it's because of you. I'd place my bet on American workers and American businesses any day of the week. You're the reason our auto industry has come roaring back. You're the reason manufacturing is hiring at its fastest pace since the 1990s. You work hard. You play by the rules. And what you deserve are leaders who will do the same, who will do whatever it takes to fight for the middle class and grow this economy faster. Because while we can't fully control everything that happens in other parts of the world, there are plenty of things we can control here at home. There are plenty of steps we can take right now to continue to create jobs and grow this economy.

I sent Congress a jobs bill last September full of the kinds of bipartisan ideas that would have put our fellow Americans back to work and helped reinforce our economy against those outside shocks. I sent them a plan that would have reduced the deficit by $4 trillion in a way that's balanced, that pays for the job-creating investments we need by cutting unnecessary spending and asking the wealthiest Americans to pay a little more in taxes.

Since then, Congress has only passed a few parts of that jobs bill, like a tax cut that's allowing working Americans to keep more of your paycheck every week. And that's important, but Congress hasn't acted on enough of the other ideas in that bill that would make a difference and help create jobs right now. There's no excuse for that. Not when so many people are still looking for work. Not when so many people are still struggling to pay the bills.

So my message to Congress is, let's get to work.

Right now Congress should pass a bill to help States prevent more layoffs so we can put thousands of teachers and firefighters and police officers back on the job. Congress should have passed a bill a long time ago to put thousands of construction workers back on the job rebuilding our roads and our bridges and our runways. Instead of just talking a good game about job creators, Congress should give small-business owners a tax break for hiring more workers and paying them higher wages. Let's get all that done.

Right now Congress should give every responsible homeowner the opportunity to save an average of $3,000 a year by refinancing their mortgage. Next week, there's a vote in Congress on a bill that would give working women the tools they need to demand equal pay for equal work. Ensuring paycheck fairness for women should be a no-brainer, and they need to pass that bill.

Right now Congress also needs to extend tax credits for clean energy manufacturers that are set to expire at the end of the year so that we don't walk away from 40,000 good jobs that are being created. And it's long past time for Con-

gress to end the tax breaks for companies that ship jobs overseas and use that money to cover moving expenses for companies that are bringing jobs back to America.

It's not lost on anybody that this is an election year. But we've got responsibilities that are bigger than an election. We've got responsibilities to you. With so many people struggling to get by, now is not the time to play politics. Now is not the time for Congress to sit on its hands. The American people expect their leaders to work hard, no matter what year it is. That's what I intend to do. And I expect Democrats and Republicans to join me.

NOTE: The address was recorded at approximately 12:35 p.m. on June 1 at the Honeywell International Inc. manufacturing facility in Golden Valley, MN, for broadcast on June 2. The transcript was made available by the Office of the Press Secretary on June 1, but was embargoed for release until 6 a.m. on June 2.

Remarks During a Conference Call on Wage Equality
June 4, 2012

Hey, guys, thanks for joining the call. As Valerie just said, and I know everybody has been talking about, tomorrow Congress is going to have a chance to vote on the "Paycheck Fairness Act." I don't have to tell you how much this matters to families across the country. All of you are working day in, day out, to support the basic principle, equal pay for equal work.

And we've made progress. But we've got a lot more to do. Women still earn just 70 [77]° cents for every dollar a man earns. It's worse for African American women and Latinas. Over the course of her career, a woman with a college degree is going to earn hundreds of thousands of dollars less than a man who is doing the same work.

So at a time when we're in a make-or-break moment for the middle class, Congress has to step up and do its job. If Congress passes the

"Paycheck Fairness Act," women are going to have access to more tools to claim equal pay for equal work. If they don't, if Congress doesn't act, then women are still going to have difficulty enforcing and pressing for this basic principle.

And we've got to understand, this is more than just about fairness. Women are the breadwinners for a lot of families, and if they're making less than men do for the same work, families are going to have to get by for less money for childcare and tuition and rent, small businesses have fewer customers. Everybody suffers.

So that's why we moved forward with the Lilly Ledbetter Fair Pay Act. That's why I established a National Equal Pay Task Force to help crack down on violations of equal pay laws. Earlier this year, the Department of La-

---

° White House correction.

bor announced the winners of a national competition for equal pay apps that give women interactive tools and key information to help them determine if they're getting paid fairly.

So we're going to be releasing this afternoon a formal administration policy message supporting the "Paycheck Fairness Act," and we're going to call on Congress to do the right thing. But let's face it. Congress is not going to act because I said it's important; they're going to act because you guys are making your voices heard. So Senators have to know you're holding them accountable. Everything that they're going to be hearing over the next 24 hours can make a difference in terms of how they vote.

We've got a long way to go, but we can make this happen, and together, we can keep moving forward. So let's make sure hard work pays off, responsibility is rewarded.

I appreciate everything you guys do. And I'm going to turn over the call to Cecilia Munoz, who is going to describe the "Paycheck Fairness Act" in more detail. All right?

Thanks, everybody. Bye-bye.

NOTE: The President spoke at 12:15 p.m. in the Oval Office at the White House. In his remarks, he referred to Senior Adviser to the President Valerie B. Jarrett, in her capacity as Chair of the White House Council on Women and Girls; and Cecilia Munoz, Director, Domestic Policy Council.

Remarks at an Obama Victory Fund 2012 Fundraiser in New York City
June 4, 2012

Thank you, everybody. No need to—thank you so much. Thank you. Please, please.

Well, first of all, to the Lasry family, to Marc and Cathy, all the kids—particularly Alex, who had been working with Valerie Jarrett for a while and now is off to business school—I just want to thank them for their extraordinary friendship. They have been great supporters and great friends for a really, really long time. And so to open up their beautiful home to us and offer such great hospitality, I can't be more grateful.

To President Bill Clinton—as usual, he pretty much summed it up. [*Laughter*] So I don't have to add too much—don't want to guild the lily here.

Nobody has a better grasp and understanding of the issues than this man. He spent 8 years guiding this country through, initially, some difficult times and then ushered in one of the greatest booms that we've seen, a recipe of stable, steady growth in which everybody participated, growth that started from the bottom up and from the middle class out.

And everybody did well, including those at the top, because—in part, because of President Clinton's background. He understood what it takes to grow this economy, that there's

just extraordinary talent all across the country. In little places in Arkansas and little apartment buildings in Hawaii and—[*laughter*]—there are folks out there who are eager to live out that American Dream and create new businesses and new opportunities. And just about everybody here, somewhere in their lives they've known that when we work together we can't be stopped. And that's what's at stake in this election, as Bill said.

I want to spend most of my time answering questions, but part of what I'm going to be doing over the next several weeks is just clarifying for people the choice involved, because we have a fundamental choice. And the truth is it's an argument that dates back to Bill Clinton's Presidency. As you will recall, you didn't get a lot of cooperation out of those Republicans in Congress either. [*Laughter*]

And the basic issue is: After World War II, we arrived at a basic consensus in this country; it was a rough consensus between Republicans and Democrats, and there was a spectrum there, but everybody understood that the market was the best generator of wealth and opportunity that we had ever seen. It was understood that America's business was business, that Government is not the ultimate source of our wealth and our freedom. But what we also understood was that there were certain investments we had to make to create a platform for opportunity for everybody.

And so among Democrats and Republicans there was a belief in a basic social safety net. And there was a belief that regulations wouldn't inhibit, necessarily, economic growth, they could actually advance them. Because the reason we had the best capital markets in the world was people trusted our capital markets, and they believed in disclosure, and they believed in transparency and openness and accountability. And so small investors and large investors said, you know what, let's put our money in America.

And people from Richard Nixon to George H.W. Bush understood that if we have smart environmental regulations, that can actually create opportunity. And if we have good consumer regulations, that actually helps America's brand because people can trust our products and trust our services.

And there was an understanding we're going to make an investment in education, whether the GI bill or opening up more and more opportunity for a college education and making sure that we're investing in our—the crown jewel of America's economy, our colleges and our universities, because we understood that that's where innovation comes from and ultimately that's going to create opportunity.

And we understood whether we were going to make investments in the Interstate Highway System or in DARPA that ultimately that would inure to the benefit of the marketplace.

And we understood that we had to pay for it. The notion was this stuff wasn't going to be free. It used to be the argument between Democrats and Republicans was, what's the best way to pay for it? But we understood that ultimately these were investments worth making. And there were times where Democrats got a little excessive. We had a little too much faith in Government, a little too much faith in regulation, and there was a corrective mechanism. And Bill Clinton helped to correct some of our excesses.

And we understood not every Government program is going to work, and we understood that not every regulation should be command-and-control, top down; that a lot of times the market might provide—if we provide the proper incentives, the market might come up with better solutions for how we were going to solve some of these vexing problems.

But over the last 15 years, the last 20 years, that consensus has broken down. If you look at what the Republican Party today represents—we haven't moved that much. If you've compared—there's a reason why Jack Lew was the OMB Director under Bill Clinton and he was my OMB Director and now my Chief of Staff. Jack hasn't changed that much. [*Laughter*] He's gotten a little grayer. [*Laughter*] Our basic policies haven't shifted. We've responded to new information and new circumstances.

What's changed is the Republican Party. They have gone from a preference for market-based solutions to an absolutism when it comes to the marketplace, a belief that all regulations are bad; that Government has no role to play; that we shouldn't simply be making sure that we balance the budget, we have to drastically shrink Government and eliminate those commitments that have ensured a middle class had a chance to succeed and to thrive for several generation.

And so if you look at Paul Ryan's budget or you look at Governor Romney's proposals, what they're talking about is something that is fundamentally different from our experience in growing this economy and creating jobs. And so that's going to be the central issue in this campaign. And we're going to do everything we can to clarify that choice.

The good news is, the American people, I think, agree with us. The challenge is that things have been very tough for people for the last 3, 4, 5, 10 years. And when things are tough, you're willing to try just about anything even if you've seen it before. And so what we have to do is to make sure that we're constantly getting a clear message out about how we intend to grow the middle class, how we're going to create jobs, and how our positions are squarely in the center of America's traditions.

We're not the ones who changed. And the track record that Bill Clinton mentioned is one that I'm extraordinarily proud of. But as important as the work that we've done over the last 3½ years has been, this is actually an election that's going to set the stage for what we do over the next 20 or the next 30. And I want the American people to understand that.

But I think precisely because we're right on these issues, I think we're going to win this election. We're just going to make—we're going to have to just make sure that we get our message out effectively. And that means help from all of you.

So I'm grateful for all of you being here, and I'm looking forward to hitting the campaign trail hard. And luckily, I'll have some pretty good companions along the way.

Thank you.

NOTE: The President spoke at 5:24 p.m. at the residence of Marc and Cathy Lasry. In his remarks, he referred to Alexander Lasry, son of Mr. and Mrs. Lasry; former President George H.W. Bush; Rep. Paul D. Ryan; and Republican Presidential candidate former Gov. W. Mitt Romney of Massachusetts. The transcript released by the Office of the Press Secretary also included the remarks of former President William J. Clinton. Audio was not available for verification of the content of these remarks.

Remarks at an Obama Victory Fund 2012 Fundraiser in New York City
June 4, 2012

The President. Hello, New York! Thank you! Well, thank you, everybody. Thank you. Thank you so much. Thank you. Everybody, have a seat.

Audience members. Four more years!

The President. Thank you. I plan on getting 4 more years, because of you.

Let me just say some thank-yous at the front here. First of all, you've got an outstanding attorney general. Please give Eric Schneiderman a big round of applause. He is doing the right thing on behalf of consumers and working people all across this great State and having an influence all across the country.

I want to thank my dear friend Jon Bon Jovi, who has been a great supporter for a long, long time. I have to say that the only thing worse than following Jon is following Jon and Bill Clinton. [*Laughter*]

I want to acknowledge—Congresswoman Carolyn Maloney is here. Where is Carolyn? Thank you, Carolyn. Party Chair Jacobs, thanks for the great work you've done. I want to thank all of you who helped to make this event possible tonight.

And most of all, I want to thank the guy behind me here.

President Clinton and I had a chance to talk over dinner before we came out, and we talk about a lot of things. We talk about basketball. [*Laughter*] We talk about our daughters, and agree that you can't beat daughters. Sons who are out there, we love you too—[*laughter*]—but I'm just saying, we bond on that front. We both agree that we have improved our gene pool because we married outstanding women.

But whatever the topic, whatever the subject, what I was reminded of as I was talking to President Clinton is just how incredibly passionate he is about this country and the people in it. You don't talk to Bill without hearing at least 30 stories about extraordinary Americans who are involved in clean energy or starting a whole new project to teach kids math or figuring out how to build some new energy-efficient building or you name it. And it's that passion and connection that he has to the American people that is infectious. And it's a curiosity and a love for people that is now transforming the world.

So I could not be prouder to have called him President. I could not be prouder to know him as a friend. And I could not be more grateful for him taking the time to be here tonight. And I thank him for putting up with a very busy Secretary of State. [*Laughter*]

Now, the reason I'm here tonight is not just because I need your help. It's because the country needs your help. If you think about why we came together back in 2008, it wasn't about me. It wasn't even necessarily just about the Democratic Party. It was about a common set of values that we held dear, a set of beliefs that we had about America, a belief that if you're willing to work hard, in this country you should be able to make it. You should be able to find a job that pays a living wage. You should be able to own a home, send your kids to college, retire with dignity and respect, not go bankrupt when you get sick; that everybody in this country—regardless of what you look like, where you come from, whether you're Black, White, gay, straight, Hispanic, disabled, not—doesn't matter, if you're willing to put in the effort this is a place where you make dreams happen. And by you putting in that effort, not only do you do well for yourself but you build the country in the process.

And we had seen that those values were eroding, a sense that that bedrock compact that we make with each other was starting to diminish. We had seen a surplus—a historic surplus—wasted away on tax cuts for folks who didn't need them and weren't even asking for them. Suddenly surpluses turned to deficits. We had seen two wars fought on a credit card. We had seen a recklessness of a few almost bring the entire system to collapse.

And there was a sense that, although a few of us were doing really, really well, that you had a growing number of folks who were struggling just to get by no matter how hard they worked.

So what we set out to do in 2008 was reclaim that basic American promise. And it wasn't easy, and many of you who supported me, certainly you guys didn't do it because it was easy. When you support a guy named Barack Hussein Obama for the Presidency you know that's not a sure thing. [*Laughter*] But you did it because you sensed that the country was ready for change.

Now, we didn't know at the time—we knew that there had been a decade of problems, that since this man had left office we had been going in the wrong direction. We didn't realize how this would culminate in the worst financial crisis since the Great Depression. As Bill said, the month I was sworn in, 800,000 jobs lost. We had lost 3 million before the election had even taken place.

But we didn't give up. We didn't quit, because that's not what the American people do. And so all across this country, you had folks who just dug in. They focused on what was necessary. And I do believe we implemented the right policies. When folks said that we should let Detroit go bankrupt, we said, no, we're not going to let over a million jobs go. We're not going to let an iconic industry waste away.

And so we brought workers together and management, and now GM is back on top, and we've seen more growth in the U.S. auto industry and more market share than we've seen in a very, very long time. And manufacturing is coming back. Even though that decision wasn't popular, we made the right decision.

We made the right decision in starting to free up credit again so that companies could borrow and small businesses could keep their doors open. We made the right decision when it came to ensuring that all across this country, States got help to keep teachers and firefighters and police officers on the job. We made the right decision in making sure that we used this opportunity to rebuild big chunks of America: our roads and our bridges and our rail lines.

So we made a lot of good policy decisions. But the reason we came back is ultimately because of the American people, because of their resilience and their strength. They made it happen. They decided, you know what, maybe I'll retrain for school. A small business decided, I'm going to keep my doors open even though it's very hard to make payroll right now.

One of the great privileges of being President is you go to every corner of the country and you see people from every walk of life, and it makes you optimistic about the American people. Even over these last 3½ years, as tough as things have been, it made me more optimistic about the American people, that we have all the ingredients for success.

It's because of them that we've seen more than 4 million jobs created, more than 800,000 jobs just this year alone. It's because of them that we're seeing more manufacturing jobs coming back than any time since the 1990s.

But—and this is where you come in—all that work that we've done, all that effort, that stands to be reversed because we've had an opposition that has had a fundamentally different vision of where we should take America. They had it from the day I was sworn in. They made a determination that politics would trump what was needed to move this country forward. And they have tried to put sand in the gears in Congress ever since.

And now they've got a nominee who is expressing support for an agenda that would reverse the progress we've made and take us back to the exact same policies that got us into this mess in the first place. And the reason we're here today is because we're not going back. We're going forward. We have worked too hard and too long to right the ship and move us in the right direction. We're not going backwards, we're going forwards. That's what we're doing, New York. And we're going to do it with your help.

Now, the reason that they think they may be able to pull this off is because things are still tough. There are a lot of folks still hurting out there; too may folks still looking for work, too many people whose homes are still underwater. So we know we've got more to do. That's why I'm running again, because our job isn't finished yet. And this election in some ways is going to be even more consequential than 2008, because the choices are going to be starker this time.

Keep in mind, when I ran in 2008, I was running against a Republican who believed in climate change, believed in immigration reform, believed in campaign finance reform, had some history of working across the aisle. We had profound disagreements, but even during the midst of the financial crisis there was an agreement of the need for action to create jobs and create growth early.

We don't have that this time. My opponent, Governor Romney, is a patriotic American. He has seen enormous financial success, and God bless him for that. He has got a beautiful fami-

ly. But his vision of how you move this country forward is what Bill Clinton said, the same agenda as the previous administration, except on steroids. So it's not enough just to maintain tax cuts for the wealthy, we're going to double tax cuts. We're going to do even more of the same. It's not enough just to roll back the regulations that we put in place to make sure that, for example, the financial system is transparent and working effectively so we don't have taxpayer bailouts anymore, we're going to do even more to eliminate regulations that have kept our air clean and our water clean and protected our kids for 20, 30 years.

When you look at the budget that they've put forward, they're not just talking about rolling back Obamacare; they're talking about rolling back the New Deal. [*Laughter*] And that's not an exaggeration.

And so there's an enormous amount at stake. And we're going to have to make sure that in this election, we are describing clearly what's at stake. And we shouldn't be afraid of this debate, because we've got the better argument. We have got the better argument.

It's not just a matter of being able to say the change that we brought about in lifting the auto industry back, that's something we're proud of. It's not just the 4.3 million jobs. It's not just the fact that 2.5 million young people have health insurance that didn't have it before. It's not just the fact that, as a consequence of our policies, millions of young people are getting Pell grants and have the capacity to go to college who didn't have it before. It's not just the track record I've amassed over the last 3½ years that I am proud of. But it's also the fact that when you look at our history, America has not grown, it has not prospered, it has not succeeded with a philosophy that says you're all on your own.

That's not how we built this country. The reason we became an economic superpower is because for all our individual initiative, all our entrepreneurship, all our belief in personal responsibility, despite all those things, what we've also understood is there's certain things we do better together. Creating a public school system that works so that everybody gets educated, we understand that.

The first Republican President understanding we built a transcontinental railroad to stitch this country together—he understood that there's certain things we do better together. Investments in the National Academy of Sciences, investment in land-grant colleges, Eisenhower building the Interstate Highway System, my grandfather and his generation going to college on the GI bill, building the Hoover Dam, building the Golden Gate Bridge, these things we did together. And it created a platform where everybody had a chance, everybody got a fair shot, everybody did their fair share, everybody played by the same rules.

If you look at our history, the reason why we have the best capital markets in the world, the reason why Wall Street is the center of finance—because we had rules in place that made us the most transparent, where investors could trust if they put their money there, they weren't going to be cheated. You had a strong SEC. You had FDIC. You had an entire infrastructure that allowed our capital markets to thrive. That's been a strength, not a weakness.

Throughout our history, there have been certain things that we have to do together. And what was true in the past is true now as well. So that's what's at stake in this election. I'm not going to go back to the days when suddenly our young people can't afford to go to college just to pay for tax cuts for me and Bill Clinton.

We're not going to go back to the day where 30 million people can't get health insurance despite working two jobs, where young people can't stay on their parent's policies or seniors suddenly find prescription drugs more expensive again. We're not going to go back to the days when suddenly women don't have preventive care or we eliminate funding for Planned Parenthood. We're not going back to those days. I want my daughters to have the same opportunities as our sons. And I want our women to have the same ability to control their health care decisions as anybody else. We're not going backwards.

We're not going to go back to the days when you couldn't serve in our military and at the same time admit who it is that you loved. We're moving forward with an agenda of dignity and respect for everybody.

We're not going to go back to the days when folks thought somehow there was a conflict between economic growth and looking after our environment and good stewardship for the next generation. We're not going back to those days.

But we're going to have to fight for it. This is not going to be an easy race. Because of the *Citizens United* decision, we're seeing hundreds of millions of dollars spent all across this country—unprecedented numbers. We haven't seen this kind of spending. There's never been this amount of negative spending before. There was a brief—a newspaper just printed, somebody had evaluated negative ads—70 percent of our ads have been positive; 70 percent of their ads have been negative. And I suspect that ratio could become even more pronounced as the weeks go by.

And as I said, folks out there are still anxious and they're still scared about the future. And so what the other side is counting on is fear and frustration; that that in and of itself is going to be good enough, because they're sure not offering any new ideas. All they're offering is the same old ideas that didn't work then and won't work now.

Even when it comes to their big issue of deficits and debt, as President Clinton just mentioned, the truth is, is that the two Presidents over the last 30 years, 40 years, who've had the lowest increases in Government spending, you're looking at them right here. They're on this stage. They are on this stage.

And the agenda that we've put forward—which says, let's put people to work right now rebuilding our roads and our bridges and putting teachers back in the classroom to accelerate growth now, at the same time as we couple it with long-term spending restraint—that's a recipe that works. We've seen it work before. We saw it work in the nineties. There's no reason why it wouldn't work now. And that will allow us to make sure that we can still invest in our future.

As I travel around the world—and I know President Clinton does, as well—you talk to people; nothing gets me more frustrated when I hear, sometimes, reports in the press about America's decline, because around the world there's nobody who wouldn't trade places with us. We've got the best universities, the most productive workers, the best entrepreneurs, the best scientists. We've got all the ingredients we need to make it work. Now we just need the best politics. Now we just need the best politics. And that's what this election is going to be all about.

So the bottom line is this: All of you, you're going to have to work not just as hard as we did in 2008, we're going to need you to work harder. One of the things we learned in 2008 is for all the negative ads, for all the rough-and-tumble of politics, for all the distortions and just plain nonsense that you sometimes hear, when folks come together, when citizens come together and insist that it's time for a change, guess what, change happens.

And what was true then is just as true now. And I want you guys to know that it is true that my hair is grayer. I haven't quite caught up to Bill yet—[*laughter*]—but I'm getting there. Those of us who have this awesome privilege of holding this office, we end up showing a few dings and dents along the way. That's inevitable. But I am more determined now than I was in 2008. I am more inspired by America now than I even was then, because I've seen more of this country, and I've seen its strength and I've seen its passion. I've seen what's possible.

I've seen the changes we've already brought. And it shouldn't make us complacent, but it should make us confident about the changes that we can bring about in the future. It means that we're going to be able to do even more to double clean energy. It means we're going to be able to do even more to bring back manufacturing. We're going to be able to do more to

put people back to work. We're going to be able to make sure that we're a nation of laws and a nation of immigrants.

All those things on our checklist that we haven't yet gotten done, we will get done. But we're only going to get it done because of you. I'm only going to get it done because of you.

You know, I used to say that I'm not a perfect man—Michelle will tell you—and I'll never be a perfect President. No President is. But I promised you I would always tell you what I thought, I'd always tell you where I stood, and I'd wake up every single day just thinking about how I can make the lives of the American people a little bit better, and I'd work as hard as I knew how to make that happen. And I have kept that promise. I have kept that promise because I still believe in you. And I hope you still believe in me.

Because if you're willing to join me this time out, and knock on doors, and make phone calls, and get out there and talk to your friends and talk to your neighbors, I promise you we will finish what we started in 2008. We will not go backward. We will go forward. And we will remind the entire world just why it is the United States of America is the greatest nation on Earth.

Thank you, New York. I love you. God bless you. God bless America.

NOTE: The President spoke at 8:40 p.m. at the Waldorf-Astoria Hotel. In his remarks, he referred to musician Jon Bon Jovi; Secretary of State Hillary Rodham Clinton, wife, and Chelsea Clinton, daughter, of former President William J. Clinton; Jay S. Jacobs, chairman, New York State Democratic Party; Sen. John S. McCain III, in his capacity as the 2008 Republican Presidential nominee; and Republican Presidential candidate former Gov. W. Mitt Romney of Massachusetts. The transcript released by the Office of the Press Secretary also included the remarks of former President Clinton.

Remarks at an Obama Victory Fund 2012 Fundraiser in New York City
June 4, 2012

Thank you. It is good to be back on Broadway! But before I get to this unbelievable opening act—[*laughter*]—let me thank my producer. That's usually what you do when you're on Broadway. [*Laughter*] Margo Lion has been such a great friend of mine for so long. Bill, during the campaign, she—Margo set up, I think, a couple of these.

And for all those who performed tonight, I could not be more grateful and more appreciative. Many of you have put in a lot of time and effort, not just this time out, but last time out. And it is just a great joy to be with all of you. But Margo especially, I just want to give her a public acknowledgment because she has been a great friend.

Before we get to the some of the more serious items, I do want to just share a quick story about Margo. Shortly after I had been elected—Bill can relate to this—the Secret Service bubble shrinks and it starts really clamping down. And the thing that you miss most when you're President—extraordinary privilege, and really nice plane and all kinds of stuff—[*laughter*]—but suddenly, not only have you lost your anonymity, but your capacity to just wander around and go into a bookstore or go to a coffee shop or walk through Central Park.

So I was saying, it was a beautiful day, and I had just been driving through Manhattan, and I saw Margo. And I said, you know, I just desperately want to take a walk through Central Park again and just remember what that feels like. But the problem is, obviously, it's hard to do now. And so my idea has been to see if I was—if I got a disguise—[*laughter*]—could I pull this off. [*Laughter*]

And so Margo thought about it, and about a week later I got this fake moustache—[*laughter*]—that I guess she got from one of the makeup artists on Broadway. And I tried it on, and I thought it looked pretty good. [*Laughter*] But when I tested this scheme with the Secret Service, they said it didn't look good enough. [*Laughter*]

But I kept it. I have kept this moustache just in case in the second term I—[*laughter*]. So if you—so if a couple years from now you see a guy with big ears and a moustache—[*laughter*]—just pretend you don't know who it is. Just look away. Eating a hotdog, you know. [*Laughter*] Going through the—[*inaudible*]—you know.

I want to thank Bill Clinton—not only for the extraordinary support that he's shown tonight and the support he's showing throughout this campaign, not only for the fact that he is as good at breaking down what's at stake at any given moment in our history, his inexhaustible energy and knowledge, the work that he's doing around the world on behalf of folks in need, but I also want to thank him for his legacy. Because in many ways Bill Clinton helped to guide the Democratic Party out of the wilderness and to lay the groundwork for a sensible, thoughtful, commonsense, progressive agenda that is important to remember at this moment.

When many of us came together in 2008, we came together not just because of me. In fact, folks weren't sure whether I was going to win. When you support a guy named Barack Hussein Obama, the odds are always—[*laughter*]—a little long. But we came together because of a shared commitment we made to each other as American citizens, a basic compact that defines this country, that says if you're willing to work hard, if you're willing to take responsibility, then there's nothing you can't accomplish. It doesn't matter where you come from, what you look like, whether you're Black, White, Hispanic, Asian, Native American, gay, straight, able, disabled—it doesn't matter—that you've got a stake in this country. You've got a claim on this country. And if you're willing to work hard, you can make it if you try in the United States of America.

And in 2008, we understood that that compact seemed like it was eroded. A few people were doing very well, but more and more people seemed to be struggling to get by. We had squandered a surplus on tax cuts for folks who didn't need them and weren't even asking for them. We had paid for two wars on a credit card. Because we hadn't enforced basic rules of the marketplace, we saw more and more of our economy built on speculation and financial schemes that were inherently unstable. And it all came crashing down in the worst crisis that we've seen in our lifetimes.

But part of the reason why we understood both what was possible and what had been lost was because of our memories of Bill Clinton's tenure as President, and our recognition that there's no contradiction between growing an economy and making sure that everybody is taking part. In fact, that's how you grow an economy, is because you're giving everybody a shot and everybody is doing their fair share and everybody is playing by the same set of rules.

We had seen, we understood there's no contradiction between economic growth and caring for our environment; that, in fact, if we make smart investments in clean energy, that's an entire industry of the future that can put people back to work.

We understood that there wasn't a contradiction between being fiscally responsible, but also making sure that kids got Head Start, kids could go to college, and we were investing in basic science and basic research. This wasn't some fantasy of ours. This wasn't some pie in the sky, wild imaginings. We'd seen it. We knew it was possible. And that's what we fought for.

Of course, we didn't know at the time that we were going to see this incredible crisis: 3 million jobs lost in the 6 months before the election and 800,000 lost the month I was sworn into office.

But here's one thing we understood. The campaign taught us this: the incredible resilience and the incredible strength of the American people. And so part of what allowed us to fight our way out of this hole was some tough decisions that we made: to save the auto industry even when some people said, let's let Detroit go bankrupt, and getting management and workers together to save over a million jobs.

And now GM is back on top. The American auto industry is making better cars than ever.

We made tough decisions to make sure that credit was flowing again to businesses large and small, and they could keep their doors open and start hiring again and make investments again in the future. And we've seen over 4 million jobs created. We've seen more manufacturing jobs created at any time since the 1990s.

And so in part, the reason that we have been weathering this storm was because of some tough policies, but the right policies. But a lot of it just had to do with the resilience of the American people. They don't give up. They don't quit. So some 55-year-old gets laid off and they decide, you know what, I'm going to back to school. I'm going to get myself retrained to find the job of the future. I'm not giving up. A small-business owner, they patch together whatever money they can to keep their doors open and to make sure that they can keep their employees on, even if it means maybe they don't get paid for a while, even if it means that the owner of that business is having to scrimp. That's how much they care about their employees.

Folks decided, you know what, we were going to retire at 65, but maybe we're going to have to work an extra 5 years because I'm going to make sure my child or my grandchild gets to go to college. All kinds of decisions like that made all across America.

And so after this incredible crisis, America is moving in the right direction. We're not there yet; we're not where we need to be. There are still too many people out there who are looking for work, too many homes that are still underwater, too many kids in poverty who still don't see prospects for the future. But we started to right the ship, and we've moving in the direction that we imagined in 2008.

And that is why this election in a lot of ways is even more important than the last one. Because as hard as we've worked over the last 4 years, as much as we've done to start rebuilding a country that's not built on how much we consume or some sort of Ponzi schemes, but built on what we're producing and what we're making, and the skills of our people, and the ingenuity of our scientists, and the risk-taking of our entrepreneurs—after all that work that we've done, the last thing we're going to do is to go back to the very same policies that got us into this mess in the first place. We're not going backwards. We're not going backwards, New York. We intend to go forwards. And that's why I'm running for a second term as President of the United States of America. We're not going back.

We're not going back to a set of policies that say you're on your own. And that's essentially the theory of the other side. George Romney—wrong guy. [*Laughter*] Governor Romney—he was a good Governor. [*Laughter*] Governor Romney is a—he's a patriotic American. He's had great success in his life, and he's raised a beautiful family. But he has a theory of the economy that basically says, if I'm maximizing returns for my investors, for wealthy individuals like myself, then everybody is going to be better off.

He was in Iowa talking to a woman, and she was describing her financial struggles, and his response was out of an economic textbook. He said, "Productivity equals income." [*Laughter*]

Now, I guess in the aggregate, technically—right—this is a coherent argument. But the implication was somehow that this woman, or others who are struggling out there, they're not productive enough.

Well, let me tell you, actually, America has become incredibly productive. People are working harder than ever. We've got some of the most productive workers in the world. The problem is not that we aren't productive enough; the problem is that productivity has not translated for far too many people into higher incomes. The problem is that profits haven't translated into jobs and investment in this country.

We believe in the marketplace. We believe in entrepreneurship and rewarding risk-taking. But what we also understand is that our economy works best—America became an economic superpower—because we created a platform where everybody could succeed. And we set up rules of the road that made the market work for everybody and gave consumers confidence that they weren't going to be bilked and gave investors confidence that if you're a small investor, you're not some insider, you still have a chance buying a stock.

And we understood that if we're investing in things like a Hoover Dam or DARPA—the research and development arm of our military that ended up producing things like the Internet or GPS—that that, in fact, would be good for everybody.

We understand that when my grandfather's generation came back from fighting in World War II and they had a chance to go to college on the GI bill, that wasn't just good for one individual, it wasn't just good for one group. That was good for everybody. We all became richer together.

And that's the lesson that Mr. Romney and the Republicans in Congress don't seem to understand, they don't seem to get. But look at our history. Ironically, the first Republican President understood it. Abraham Lincoln understood it. That's why in the middle of a Civil War he was still building a transcontinental railroad and starting land-grant colleges and starting the National Academy of Sciences, because he understood that ultimately there are some things we do better on our own. Not every Government program works, not everybody can [be]° helped who doesn't want to be helping themselves. All of us have responsibilities.

And I learned early on that no matter how much money you pour into the schools, nothing replaces the love and attention and occasional scoldings from a parent. I learned as a community organizer that no government program can substitute for the caring and passion of neighbors and communities. But I also understood, and you understand and Americans understand, that when we've done great things in this country, we've done them together. We've done them together. And that's what's at stake in this election.

° White House correction.

And we're not going back to this other theory. I'm not going to go back to a time when if you got sick, you had no recourse and you potentially could go bankrupt. I'm not going to go back to a time when 2.5 million young people can't get health insurance or can't stay on their parent's plan or 30 million people who are working maybe two jobs can't afford to buy health insurance and end up in an emergency room just because they can't get sick and aren't getting preventive care. We're not going to go back to that.

We're not going to go back to a time when—we're not going to refight the battles about whether or not we need to make some basic reforms on Wall Street so that taxpayers don't have to bail out folks after they've made irresponsible or reckless bets. That's not good for our financial markets. We're not going to refight that battle.

We're not going to go back to a time when manufacturing is all moving offshore. We want to bring companies onshore. I want to give tax breaks to companies that are investing in jobs investment here in the United States, not shipping jobs overseas. We don't need to go back to policies like that.

We're not going to go back to a time when our military could expel somebody because of who they loved. We believe in everybody being treated fairly and equally and respecting everybody's rights. We're not going to go backwards. We're going forwards.

We don't need to go back to a foreign policy that thinks the measure of our security is everything we do, we do on our own. We've been able to restore respect and collaboration and our alliances have never been stronger, partly because I've got a pretty good Secretary of State.

But—[*applause*]—and that's how we ended the war in Iraq. And that's how we're starting to transition out of Afghanistan. And that's how we brought Usama bin Laden to justice. And we're not going to go backwards on policies that make America stronger.

We're not going to go back to the days when somehow women couldn't get the preventive care that they need. We don't need a situation where women aren't controlling their own health care choices. We don't need to eliminate Planned Parenthood. I want my daughters to have the same opportunities as my sons. That's part of what America is about. We're not turning back the clock. We're not going backwards.

And we can afford the investments we need to grow. We can afford to make sure that every kid has a chance to go to college and they're going to a decent school and they're graduating.

We can afford to rebuild our roads and our bridges and our airports and our broadband lines and high-speed rail and putting people back to work. We can afford—in fact, we can't afford not to invest in the science and research that's going to keep us at the cutting edge.

We're not going to throw millions of people off the Medicaid rolls, folks who are disabled or poor, seniors who are relying on it. We're not going to voucherize Medicare. We're going to responsibly reduce this deficit. You know, two Presidents over the last 30 years that have actually reduced the pace of the growth in Government spending happen to be on this stage right here. They happen to be the two Democrats.

So we have to get our deficit and debt under control. We've got to do it in a responsible way, cut out programs we don't need. I've already signed a trillion dollars in cuts that have already been made, another trillion that are slated to be made. But we're also going to ask folks who can afford it like the two of us to pay a little bit more—and some of you too, so don't chuckle—[*laughter*]—to pay a little bit more so that we can afford the things that will help us grow. That's the right recipe. That's what made us an economic superpower. And that's the policy that we're going to pursue.

Now, here's the good news. The American people, on the issues, when presented with the facts, they actually agree with us. Now, it's hard sometimes getting the facts out. There's a lot of bugs on the windshield. [*Laughter*] Sometimes you've got to—[*laughter*]—so you got to get those wipers going pretty hard sometimes. It's not always clear. [*Laughter*]

But when folks know the facts, when they're given a choice—and that's what this election is about, every election is about a choice—when given a choice between a vision that says we're going to have a balanced approach to deficit reduction, and we're going to continue to make investments in things like clean energy and fuel efficiency and science and innovation and education and rebuilding our infrastructure, versus another $5 trillion worth of tax cuts that would give the average millionaire and billionaire an additional $250,000 a year in tax breaks, people agree with us.

On issue after issue, if you give them a fair presentation, no spin on the ball, the majority of the country—not just Manhattan—[*laughter*]—the majority of the country agrees with us. Which is why the other side isn't—they're not presenting anything new. As Bill said the other day, this is the same old stuff, just on steroids. [*Laughter*] Just more of. More tax cuts for the wealthy. We're not just going to reduce regulation, we're going to cripple EPA. And people aren't buying that. They don't really think that that's going to work.

The only reason that this is going to be a close election is because people are still hurting. The situation in Europe is slowing things down. We've been prevented from, for example, the plans that I've put forward repeatedly to Congress to say, let's give States more help so they don't have to lay off more teachers. Let's—now interest rates have never been lower. Literally, the Government can—basically people will pay us to lend us money—[*laughter*]—and there would never be a better time for us to start making investments that could put construction workers back to work all across the country.

But that's not something Congress, so far, has been willing to do. Though we're going to keep on putting pressure on them over these next few months because we don't have time just to wait for an election to do something.

But folks are still hurting. And this has been a long slog for people. And sometimes when things are tough you just say, well, you know what, I'll just keep on trying something until

something works. And that's compounded by $500 million in super PAC negative ads that are going to be run over the course of the next 5 months that will try to feed on those fears and those anxieties and that frustration.

That's basically the argument the other side is making. They're not offering anything new, they're just saying, things are tough right now and it's Obama's fault. You can pretty much sum up their argument. There's no vision for the future there. There's no imagination. I mean, somebody is going to have to explain to me how repealing Obamacare and throwing 30 million people back to a situation where they don't have health care, somehow that's an economic development agenda. [*Laughter*] Nobody has really explained that to me.

So it's going to be a tough election. But 2008 was tough too. And what you all taught me was that when Americans are willing to come together and make a commitment to each other, when they have a vision about what's possible and they commit to it, and they join together and they work for it, when they decide—when you decide—that change is going to happen, guess what, change happens. Change happens.

And so I may be a little grayer than I was the last time I was on Broadway. Going to need to get Margo to send me something to do something—do something about that. As President Clinton will tell you, you go through some dings and dents in this job. But I tell you what. I'm more determined than I've ever been. I'm more determined than I've ever been to finish what we started.

I used to say back in 2008, I'm not a perfect man, and haven't been and won't be a perfect President. Nobody is. But what I told you was I'd always tell you what I thought, I'd always tell you where I stood, and I'd wake up every single morning fighting as hard as I knew how to make life better for the American people. And I have kept that promise. I have kept that promise, Broadway. I have kept that promise.

I still believe in you. I hope you still believe in me. I hope you still believe. If people ask you what this campaign is about, you tell them it's still about hope and it's still about change. And if you're willing to knock on some doors and make some phone calls and talk to your friends and neighbors and work just as hard as you did in 2008, we will finish what we started and remind the world why it is America is the greatest nation on Earth.

Thank you. God bless you. God bless America.

NOTE: The President spoke at 9:54 p.m. at the New Amsterdam Theatre. In his remarks, he referred to Margo Lion, Cochair, President's Committee on the Arts and the Humanities; and Republican Presidential candidate former Gov. W. Mitt Romney of Massachusetts. The transcript released by the Office of the Press Secretary also included the remarks of former President William J. Clinton.

Statement on Senate Action on Paycheck Fairness Legislation
June 5, 2012

This afternoon Senate Republicans refused to allow an up-or-down vote on the "Paycheck Fairness Act," a commonsense piece of legislation that would strengthen the Equal Pay Act and give women more tools to fight pay discrimination. It is incredibly disappointing that in this make-or-break moment for the middle class, Senate Republicans put partisan politics ahead of American women and their families. Despite the progress that has been made over the years, women continue to earn substantially less than men for performing the same work. My administration will continue to fight for a woman's right for equal pay for equal work, as we rebuild our economy so that hard work pays off, responsibility is rewarded, and every American gets a fair shot to succeed.

NOTE: The statement referred to S. 3220.

Remarks at an Obama Victory Fund 2012 Fundraiser in San Francisco, California
June 6, 2012

Willie Mays, everybody, the "Say Hey Kid." Thank you so much, everybody. Everybody, have a seat.

First of all, it is true that they provide me with this really nice plane in this job. [*Laughter*] But as cool as Air Force One is, it is much, much cooler when Willie Mays is with you on the plane. [*Laughter*] I am so grateful to him for his support, but more importantly—he mentioned, obviously, the history that was made with my election. The fact is, is that we don't make that history unless there are people like Jackie Robinson and Willie Mays, who helped to lay the groundwork for a more inclusive America. And so we could not be prouder of him, and he could not be more gracious.

A couple of other people I want to acknowledge. Your outstanding Governor of the great State of California, Jerry Brown; there he is. Your equally dynamic Lieutenant Governor, Gavin Newsom, is in the house. The wonderful mayor of San Francisco, Ed Lee, give him a big round of applause.

I want to thank Clint and Janet Reilly for hosting us here today. We are in their spot, and we are very grateful. You can give them a round of applause.

And we've got a guy who I guess is a little bit of a carpetbagger here today. [*Laughter*] He is former chairman of the DNC, former Governor of Virginia, now running for the United States Senate in Virginia, but is also one of my dearest friends. This was the first guy outside of Illinois, the first elected official outside of Illinois to endorse my candidacy for President. And we made that announcement together in Richmond, the seat of the former Confederacy. And this was at a time when Barack Hussein Obama was not favored to win. [*Laughter*] And so he is a man of character. And I would urge all of you to get to know his incredible track record and support his terrific efforts in Virginia. Please give Tim Kaine a big round of applause.

So it is good to be back in San Francisco. I've noticed I've been getting very good weather in San Francisco. [*Laughter*] I don't know if Ed or Gavin or somebody is arranging this, but it's always spectacular to be here among so many friends, a lot of people who supported me in the past.

I'm here not just because I need your help, but because the country needs your help. And when we came together in 2008, like Tim, you didn't do it because you thought I was necessarily the odds on favorite. But we came together, because there was a sense that those core values that we hold dear, the things that make America special—the values that helped to expand opportunity for people from every walk of life and from all over the world—that those values had eroded a little bit, that they weren't being observed in Washington the way we'd like them to be.

We had seen surpluses turned into yawning deficits because of tax cuts for people who didn't need them and weren't even asking for them. We had seen two wars fought on a credit card. We had seen an economy that was increasingly built on financial speculation as opposed to us making stuff, and manufacturing was consistently moving offshore. And we'd gotten a sense that for a few people things were going really well, but an expanding number of Americans were having more and more trouble getting by, with the cost of everything from health care to college education skyrocketing, even as wages and incomes were flat.

And so there was the sense that the core of the American Dream, the idea that anybody can make it if they try, regardless of what they look like, where they come from, who they love—that everybody has a stake, everybody has a piece in this exceptional, extraordinary country—that that was slipping away from too many people.

Now, we didn't know at the time that we were going to be facing the worst economic crisis in most of our lifetimes. We had already

lost $4 million jobs before I sworn in, and we'd lose 800,000 jobs the month I was sworn in. But we understood what was at stake. And what we also understood was the incredible strength and resilience of the American people.

And so, we made some tough policy decisions. We did some things that weren't always popular. There were those who said, let Detroit go bankrupt. But we made our bet on the American worker and American businesses. And now GM is back on top and the American auto industry is actually hiring again.

We helped stabilize the financing system and made sure that small businesses were getting loans and teachers and firefighters, police officers could stay on the job. But part of the reason that we've been able to weather this storm is just because the American people are tough. And the tougher the times, the tougher they get.

So one of the privileges of being President is you travel all around the country and you meet the small-business owner who kept their business open and their employees on their payroll, even if it meant that for a year or two they weren't making any money, they weren't taking anything home. That's how important those workers were to them.

Or you'll meet the 55-year-old who got laid off of their job, had been working on an assembly line all their lives and now suddenly had to retrain, and then going back and discovering how much they enjoyed working in the health care sector, caring for people who really needed care.

You saw all across the country people buckle down and make adjustments and businesses getting back to basics. And because of the extraordinary talents and gifts and resilience of the American people, we've been able to create more than 4.3 million jobs since we started growing this economy together; over 800,000 in the last few months alone. We've been able to make sure that manufacturing is growing faster than at any time since the 1990s.

We've been able to stabilize the situation. But we also understand that a lot of folks are still hurting out there, that too many people's homes are still underwater, and that too many people who want to work—even if they've got a job—aren't working full time or don't have the benefits that they need to make sure that they can care for their families.

And that's why, in some ways, 2012 is even more important than 2008. Because for all the extraordinary work we've been able to do over the last 3½ years, we're not where we need to be yet. We've got to finish what we started. And that's why I'm running again for President of the United States of America.

Now, it's also important because we probably won't see another election that presents a greater contrast between the parties and between the candidates. When I ran in 2008, I was running against a guy who I had a lot of disagreements with, but he believed in climate change, he believed in campaign finance reform, he believed in immigration reform. The character of the party and the Republicans in Congress had fundamentally shifted.

What are they offering? They're offering not just the Bush tax cuts, but an additional $5 trillion in tax cuts for folks who don't need them oftentimes. And we know it will blow up the deficit, but their theory is—Governor Romney's theory, the Republican leadership in Congress's theory—is that the economy grows best when we are all on our own, when the market is king, and regulations are stripped away and people can do what they please.

And we deeply believe in the free markets, and we deeply believe in risk-takers and innovators being rewarded. And there's no place that innovates like northern California. But we all recognize that the way America became great, the way it became an economic superpower, is because, for all our individual initiative, for all our rugged individualism, there were some things that we do better together.

We understand that we've got to make investments in making sure that every child can learn. And that's why we created public schools and great public universities and colleges. And we understand that's not just good for those kids, it's not just good for our kids; it's good for everybody if we've got the most highly skilled, highly trained workforce in the world.

It's the reason we built amazing infrastructure—the Hoover Dam or the Golden Gate Bridge—because we understood that that creates jobs not just for the folks who build it, but creates a platform for success for generations to come. It's the reason why we invest in things like DARPA that helps to create the Internet. No individual might have made that investment, but because together we made that investment, entire new industries have been formed. We understand that there are some things we do better together, and that's the reason why America became the singular economic power that it's become.

So there are two fundamentally contrasting visions. And I have to tell you that there was a time when there was a consensus between Democrats and Republicans. Republicans might want slightly lower taxes and slightly less spending, Democrats might be more concerned about certain social investments, but there was a general consensus that all of us had to think not just about ourselves, but about the good of the country and the future. And that's changed on the other side.

And you see it in this campaign, and you see it in the behavior of the current Congress. You see it when they, as I said before, suggest that the way to balance a budget is to cut taxes further—$5 trillion for folks who don't need it—and then, presumably, eliminate $5 trillion worth of basic medical research, $5 trillion of Head Start programs or Pell grants for young people, or the kind of infrastructure that will help us—broadband lines and high-speed rail—that will help lead us into the 21st century; that potentially makes Medicare a voucher program so that the costs of health care are shifted onto seniors as opposed to us trying to reduce the cost of health care for everybody.

And so we are going to be facing a fundamental choice. And I want this to be a fulsome debate. I want the American people to hear exactly what they're getting if the other side prevails, and what they're going to be getting if I prevail. Because I've been pretty clear about what I believe, and we've implemented a whole bunch of stuff which is reflective of the values that I think have made this country great.

People ask me sometimes, well, how does this campaign compare to 2008? I say, if somebody asks you, you tell them it's still about hope and change. And if you want to know what change is, change is the first bill that I signed into law that said—the Lilly Ledbetter law that says an equal day's work deserves an equal day's pay and that our daughters should be treated the same way as our sons.

Change is making sure that not only are we attracting manufacturing back to our shores, but we're investing in advanced manufacturing—in areas like advanced battery technology or solar energy or wind power—that will not only usher in tens of thousands, hundreds of thousands of new jobs all across America, but are also going to make sure that we are passing on to our kids and our grandkids the kind of planet that they deserve.

That's why we doubled fuel efficiency standards on cars, which means that in the middle of the next decade cars are going to be getting 55 miles a gallon, taking a whole bunch of carbon out of the atmosphere and saving everybody $8,000 for the life of their car. That's what change looks like.

Change is us saying we're going to stop funneling tens of billions of dollars of taxpayer money to banks for running the student loan program. Let's just give that money directly to students, so that millions more young people are getting Pell grants and reducing the burden of debt that they have when they go to college, because we want to make sure that America continues to have the best educated workforce in the world. That's what change is. That's what we've done.

Change is making sure that, yes, we passed a health care bill so that 30 million Americans won't be worried about going bankrupt in case they get sick. And now we've got 2.5 million young people who are on their parents' insurance because of this law and millions of seniors who are seeing lower costs for their prescription drugs because of this law. And everybody is able to get preventive care, and women are no longer being charged more than men for it.

And they can't drop you from coverage just when you need it most. That's what change is.

Change is ending the war in Iraq and winding down the war in Afghanistan and reestablishing respect for America around the world. That doesn't make us less tough. Because of our efforts, bin Laden is no longer a threat to America, Al Qaida is on its heels. And we've done it the right way, in a focused way that abides by rule of law.

And so we have evidence of the possibility of change. We've seen it over the last 3½ years. But we're not there yet. We've got more to do. We've got more to do to make sure that college is affordable. We've got more to do to continue to reform our education system, K–12, so that we're producing more scientists and engineers and mathematicians and that every young person has a chance to succeed.

We've got to implement health care reform and make sure that the benefits for families all across the country aren't stripped away. We don't need to reargue that battle. By the way, the last 2 years—recent reports show the last 2 years, health care inflation has gone up at a slower rate than any time in the last 15 years, in part because we're starting to change how health care is delivered.

We're going to have to make more progress on clean energy. We've doubled clean energy production over the last 3½ years. We've got to do more to make sure that we are the most energy efficient country in the world. And we can do it. If we start retrofitting our buildings, if we start investing in new clean technologies, if we change the incentive structures for businesses, there's no reason why we can't not only grow our economy faster, but also reduce pollution quicker and put hundreds of thousands more people back to work.

We've still got to rebuild—we've got to rebuild our infrastructure in this country. Now is the time to do it. We've got deferred maintenance on everything. And we've got a whole bunch of construction workers out of work, and essentially you can borrow zero percent. [*Laughter*] Why wouldn't we go ahead and get that done now? That would boost economic growth now and it would lay the groundwork for economic growth for decades to come. We still need to do that.

We've still got work to do to make sure that our veterans are served as well as they have served us. I want to make sure that every single veteran who comes home from Iraq or Afghanistan, that they don't have to fight for a job or a roof over their heads here in the United States of America after they fought for us. That's work we still have to do.

We've got to make sure that women still have the capacity to control their own health care decisions. We're not going backwards on that. We're not getting rid of Planned Parenthood.

We're not going to let anybody roll back the decision that says our military cannot be denied the opportunity for service to your country just because of who you love. We're not refighting that battle. We are moving forward to fight a battle that says everybody deserves respect, everybody deserves dignity.

We've got more work to do to make sure that in America everybody has got a fair shot, everybody does their fair share, and everybody is playing by the same rules.

And that's where you come in. As much as I appreciate the extraordinary staff I have in the White House and all of the various agencies, I know that the only reason I've gotten this privilege is because of you and the work that you've done. And this is going to be a tough race, precisely because the economy is not where it needs to be yet. There are still a lot of folks out there who are struggling. There's still frustration. There's still fear and anxiety about the future. I think it's fair to say that, whether in Virginia or Iowa or North Carolina or California, all across the country there are a lot of folks who are still wondering, are we going to be able to fully deliver that promise of a country that is thriving and has an economy that's built to last, where if you work hard and you're responsible, you can make it.

And the other side, they don't have any new ideas. As Bill Clinton said a couple weeks ago, they're just offering more of the same on steroids. [*Laughter*] And because they don't have any new ideas, what they will do is spend $500,

$700, a billion dollars on negative ads, and their simple message will be: This is somebody else's fault, and that's enough reason for you to vote for us. And if we don't answer them, that can work.

So we're going to have to work hard. But the good news is that what you taught me in 2008 was that when ordinary people come together, when they decide—neighbors, friends, coworkers, partners, families—when folks come together and say, you know what, we see a vision out there, we see a direction for this country, we know what's right, we know what's fair, we know what's just, and we're willing to fight for it, we're willing to make phone calls and we're willing to knock on doors and we're willing to talk to people, even if you know that they may not agree with us, we're willing to get organized and have our voices heard—when that happens, despite all the negativity and all the cynicism and all the countervailing forces, guess what, change happens. America is transformed. And what was true then is going to be true this time out.

I used to tell people—some of you remember this—during the campaign in 2008, I'm not a perfect man, and I won't be a perfect President. But I can make you a promise that I'll always tell you what I think, I'll always tell you where I stand, and I'll wake up every single day fighting as hard as I know how for you. Every morning I'll wake up and every evening I'll go to bed thinking about how do I make sure that the American people, that they've got a little bit better shot to fulfill their dreams. And I've kept that promise.

And what's allowed me to keep that promise is because, as I've traveled all across this country over the last 4 or 5 years, I'm never disappointed by the American people. I'm always amazed by how good and decent they are. I still believe in you. I hope you still believe in me. And if you do, and if we're willing to work for it and show the same determination we did in 2008, I guarantee you we will finish what we started. This economy will keep moving. And we'll remind the world just why it is the United States of America is the greatest nation on Earth.

Thank you, everybody. God bless you. God bless America.

NOTE: The President spoke at 2:28 p.m. at the Julia Morgan Ballroom. In his remarks, he referred to Willie H. Mays, Jr., assistant to the president and former center fielder, Major League Baseball's San Francisco Giants; Clin-ton Reilly, founder and owner, Clinton Reilly Holdings, and his wife Janet; Sen. John S. Mc-Cain III, in his capacity as the 2008 Republican Presidential nominee; Republican Presidential candidate former Gov. W. Mitt Romney of Massachusetts; and former President William J. Clinton. Audio was not available for verification of the content of these remarks.

Statement on the Death of Ray D. Bradbury
June 6, 2012

For many Americans, the news of Ray Bradbury's death immediately brought to mind images from his work, imprinted in our minds, often from a young age. His gift for storytelling reshaped our culture and expanded our world. But Ray also understood that our imaginations could be used as a tool for better understanding, a vehicle for change, and an expression of our most cherished values. There is no doubt that Ray will continue to inspire many more generations with his writing, and our thoughts and prayers are with his family and friends.

Remarks at an Obama Victory Fund 2012 Fundraiser in Beverly Hills, California
June 6, 2012

The President. Thank you.

Audience members. Four more years! Four more years! Four more years!

The President. Thank you so much, everybody. Everybody, have a seat. You're going to make me blush. [*Laughter*]

A couple people I want to acknowledge this evening. First of all, your outstanding mayor, Antonio Villaraigosa, is here. The wonderful attorney general of the great State of California, Kamala Harris, is in the house. Speaker John Perez is here.

I want to thank my wonderful friend who accepts a little bit of teasing about Michelle beating her in pushups—[*laughter*]—but I think she claims Michelle didn't go all the way down. [*Laughter*] That's what I heard. I just want to set the record straight—Michelle outdoes me in pushups as well. [*Laughter*] So she shouldn't feel bad. She's an extraordinary talent and she's just a dear, dear friend, Ellen DeGeneres. Give Ellen a big round of applause. I want to thank, in addition, an outstanding talent, Daren Criss. Give Daren—[*applause*]. President of the United States. It was an ex-

The event cochairs, Dana Perlman and Barry Karas. Yay!

And most of all, I want to thank Vito, not simply for that introduction, but for a lifetime of service and a lifetime of sacrifice. As I think about Vito's story and his career, the lives he's saved, the limbs he may have saved, I'm reminded that day that we signed the law repealing "don't ask, don't tell." And what was most moving was not just those in active service who were there in that auditorium to witness that history being made. It wasn't just the extraordinary warmth that people expressed towards Admiral Mullen, who I think showed extraordinary courage in helping to guide the Pentagon to the right place on that issue. But it was also seeing all these veterans, some of them 60, 65, serving in Vietnam, some in the Korean war, who were there, and thinking about all those years in which the wholeness of their life had not been fully acknowledged, that they had to live divided from themselves. And to see the tears streaming down the faces of some of them, that's as good as it gets when you're traordinary privilege to be there.

And what Vito's story and the stories of those who were in that auditorium remind us of is—obviously, I could not be prouder of the work that we've done on behalf of the LGBT community. From the work we did to facilitate hospital visitations to ending the HIV/AIDS ban, to the work we did to pass the Matthew Shepard law, to repealing "don't ask, don't tell," to all the administrative work that's been done by agencies to make sure that folks are fully recognized is something that I'm personally very proud of.

But what Vito's story also reminds us of is that the fight for equality and justice on behalf of the LGBT community is just part of a broader fight on behalf of all Americans. It's part of our history of trying to make this Union a little bit more perfect. The experiment that started well over 200 years ago, the genius of the Founders was a recognition that through this Declaration of Independence and our Constitution, that it would give the opportunity for people—even if those documents weren't perfect, even if the political structures were imperfect—it would give us as citizens the chance to fight to make it more perfect.

And so in successive waves, the history, the scope of this country has always been to further broaden the meaning of citizenship to include more and more people, to give better and better expression to our highest aspirations, to make the country more fair and more just and more equal. That's what wars were fought about. That's what the civil rights movement was about. That's what the women's movement was all about. That's what the workers' movement was all about, this constant progression to include more and more people in the possibility of the American Dream. And so this is just one more step in that journey that we've taken as a nation.

And it doesn't always go in a straight line; it goes in zigs and zags. And there are times where the body politic takes a wrong turn, and there are times where there are folks who are left out. But what makes America exceptional is that, eventually, we get it right. What Dr. King called the arc of the moral universe, it bends towards justice. That's what makes

America different. That's what makes America special.

And so when we came together back in 2008—and there are a lot of folks here who were fierce supporters even when nobody could pronounce my name—[*laughter*]—you guys, you didn't get involved because you thought it was a sure thing. The reason you got involved in this movement for change was those values of fairness and inclusion and opportunity that all of us have benefited from felt like they were being betrayed, that Washington wasn't living up to those values and those ideals.

And so we made a commitment to each other. That campaign wasn't just about me; it was about us. It was about the American people recognizing that we had taken a wrong turn, taking surpluses to deficits because of tax cuts for folks who didn't need them and weren't even asking for them, fighting two wars on a credit card. We had seen an economy that was very good for a few but more and more people were struggling just to get by, just to keep up. And it all came crashing down in the worst recession in our lifetimes.

And so even before the election, we understood that we had a lot more work to do, that we had to recapture that sense of possibility and fairness; the notion that anybody in America can make it if they try; that if you're willing to work hard and take responsibility, that you can buy a home, start a business, raise a family, not have to worry about going bankrupt because you get sick; send your kids to college so that they can do even better than you can, and that that opportunity is available for everybody, regardless of what you look like or where you come from, what your last name is, who you love.

That's what we were fighting for in 2008. And we didn't know at the time that we were going to have this extraordinary recession and that 4 million jobs would be lost before I was even sworn in and 800,000 jobs would be lost the month I took office.

And so it's been a challenge and it's been a struggle for a lot of Americans all across the country. The good news is, it turns out that Americans are tougher than tough times.

Americans are tougher than tough times. And so small businesses kept their doors open and kept folks on payroll, even if it meant that the owner of the small business wasn't pulling any salary in for a year or two, living off savings or credit cards. It turns out that the 55-year-old who lost their job in an assembly plant, they were willing to go get trained and find a new job in a high-tech industry or working as a nurse or some new door opened.

There were those who said we should let Detroit go bankrupt, but because we made a bet on American workers and American businesses, GM is back on top and the American auto industry has recovered. Businesses got back to the basics, so that we've created more than 4 million jobs, more jobs in manufacturing than any time since the 1990s, 800,000 jobs just this year alone.

And so we've made progress. And I keep a little checklist in my desk at the Oval Office. I've got a to-do list. [*Laughter*] And every so often, I take a look at it and I say, you know what, we're doing okay.

The Lilly Ledbetter law that makes sure that we get equal pay for equal work—check. Doubling fuel economy standards on cars to make sure that not only consumers are saving money and we're reducing imports of foreign oil, but we're also helping to save the environment—check.

Making sure that young people can go to college, rechanneling tens of billions of dollars that were being used—that were going to banks as middlemen for the student loan program, saying let's just pay the students directly, let's give that money directly to them, so that millions of kids out there are getting Pell grants and having lower debt totals, opening up college opportunity so that we'll once again be number one in the world in the percentage of college graduates—check.

Making sure that 30 million Americans have access to affordable health care and 2.5 million young people can stay on their parent's plan and seniors get discounts on their prescription drugs and preventive care is there for everybody and women can control their own health care choices—check.

Ending the war in Iraq—check. Beginning the transition in Afghanistan, going after Al Qaida, defeating Usama bin Laden—check. We've got some stuff done these last 3½ years, with relatively modest cooperation from the other side. [*Laughter*] I think that's a fair characterization. [*Laughter*]

But here's the thing. A lot of people are still hurting out there. Unemployment is still too high. A lot of folks still have homes underwater. People who were lucky enough to have work, a lot of them have trouble making ends meet. A lot of young people, they're still burdened by debt. Parents are still worried about how to pay for college and their own retirement. We've made enormous progress, but we didn't come together in 2008 just to get back to where we were in 2007, right? We made a commitment consistent with that commitment I talked about at the beginning of my remarks, that commitment to widen opportunity for everybody, everybody getting a fair shot, everybody doing their fair share, everybody playing by the same set of rules.

And on that task we've still got a lot more work to do. We've got to make sure that America has an energy policy that works. We're producing a lot more oil and a lot more natural gas, but we've got to invest in solar and wind and biodiesel, to continue to reduce our dependence on foreign oil, to do something about climate change, while at the same time creating hundreds of thousands of jobs. That's work that remains to be done.

We've still got to reform a broken immigration system, because we're a nation of laws and a nation of immigrants. And it makes no sense for us to exclude extraordinary talent who could be starting businesses and contributing to the growth and competitiveness of the United States of America. We've still got to do that.

We've still got a lot more work to do to attract jobs back to the United States. The good news is, is that companies are starting to recognize there are no workers that are more productive than U.S. workers. Some of them are starting to relocate. We've got to make sure we've got a Tax Code that rewards companies that are creating jobs here instead of shipping jobs overseas. That's a priority.

We've got to make sure that our education system is working for every child, whether in East L.A. or South Side of Chicago or Anacostia or some rural town in Iowa. We've got to make sure that every kid is getting the education they need in math and in science and technology, that they can afford to go to college without breaking the bank.

We still have more work to do internationally. We have restored our respect around the world in our alliances, but we can do more.

And so, in some ways, this election is going to be more important than the last one. We've got to consolidate the great work that we've done, but we've also got to win a basic contest of ideas between us and the other side.

Mr. Romney is a patriotic American who has experienced great success in his life and seems to have a beautiful family, but his idea—similar to the idea of Republicans in Congress, about how we grow the economy, how we make sure everybody gets a fair shot—is very different. His basic idea is, you know what, if those of us at the top are doing really well then everybody else presumably will benefit too. [*Laughter*] And so it's not enough just to continue the Bush tax cuts; we've going to tack on another $5 trillion worth of tax cuts.

And we say we're concerned about the deficit, but if we're willing to blow a hole through the deficit like that, the only way to make it up is then to cut out all those things that we have done together as a nation to make us stronger: investments in research and development and science, investments in infrastructure, investments in helping kids go to college, investments in taking care of our veterans, making sure that if you're disabled or you're a poor child or you're a senior citizen that you've got a basic baseline where you can live with dignity and respect and get the help that you need.

I don't think that's how you grow an economy. That's not the history of what's made us great. The history of what's made us great is us doing certain things together. We love the free market and we love risk-taking and we love folks getting rich. But we also believe in public

schools, because that helps make us an economic superpower. We believe in investing in the Hoover Dam and the Golden Gate Bridge, because that gave us a platform for success. We believe in investing in research that created the Internet, so that all those companies could be created. We believe in doing some things together, because it works for all of us.

So there's a fundamentally different vision about what's going on. And a lot of this debate is going to be about the economy, but also obviously there's a different vision about how we create an inclusive America. I refused to let anybody reimpose a law that would force Vito back into the shadows when he is serving on our behalf and our safety and our security. That's not something I will tolerate. So we're going to have a lot of work to do.

The good news is, I'm convinced that the American people share those values I talked about at the beginning of my remarks, those values that built this country. People aren't paying attention to the day-to-day stuff that goes on in Washington. It all just seems cynical and negative and dysfunctional. [*Laughter*] Right? They're not going—listening to the back-and-forth, the tit-for-tat. And they're anxious. They're anxious. Even if they're doing pretty well themselves, they're anxious about the future of their country. They're anxious about the prospects for their kids, whether their kids will have a better life than they did. And that anxiety can be tapped into.

You're going to see hundreds of millions of dollars of negative ads because the other side is not offering anything new. The same old stuff, the same stuff—the same set of ideas that helped get us into this mess in the first place, they're just regurgitating them all over again. But what they're going to do is they're going to say, well, you know what, you're still not satisfied, and it's Obama's fault. That's the essence of their campaign. It's very easy to put on a bumper sticker. [*Laughter*] "It's Obama's Fault." [*Laughter*]

And so we're going to have to work through that. And because there are a lot of folks who are still hurting out there this will be a very close election. Not because people buy what they're selling, but just because a lot of folks have given up feeling that anything is going to make their lives better. But the thing we discovered in 2008 is when people come together, when Americans come together—neighbors, friends, coworkers, spouses, lovers—when folks come together and say it's time for a change, change happens.

I go home to Hawaii a lot, and—every Christmas—and we usually stay right near the Kaneohe Marine Base, which is a beautiful piece of real estate that the Marine Corps got somehow. [*Laughter*] And they let me work out at the gym there. And it's actually pretty depressing working out with marines because they're all 2-percent body fat—[*laughter*]—and they're benching 500 pounds and stuff. But they tolerate me because I'm their Commander in Chief, so—[*laughter*].

So, last time we were back, I was working out, and during the course of a week, probably four marines came up and said, thank you for ending "don't ask, don't tell." It's meant so much to me, it's meant so much to my spouse, meant so much to my partner. The day before I was leaving, one marine came up—young man—and he says—he was very fit—[*laughter*]—first of all, he said to me, "You're not doing that exercise right"—[*laughter*]—"sir." He said "sir." [*Laughter*]

But then he said: "I can't tell you how much it means to me that you repealed 'don't ask, don't tell.' It really made me proud of our country." And I said: "I appreciate that. Was this something that you'd been wrestling with for a while?" And I imagined him dealing with his partners, similar to the stories that Vito told. He said: "No, sir, I'm not gay. It was important to me because I've had friends in my

unit that were, and I know how much that tore them up, and I didn't think it was right. And I think we're a better Marine Corps because they can be who they are and serve our country. And these are just outstanding marines that I've been proud to call a friend."

And I tell that story so that if anybody out there asks you what this campaign is about, you tell them it's still about hope and change. You tell them I still believe in the American people, in the innate goodness of this country. I still believe in that vision where we all come together, that out of many, we are one. And there are more things we have in common than things that drive us apart.

And if you remember that and you're willing to work just as hard or harder this time as you did the last time, we'll finish what we started. We will win this election. And we will remind the world just why it is that the United States of America is the greatest nation on Earth.

God bless you. God bless the United States of America.

NOTE: The President spoke at 7 p.m. at the Beverly Wilshire hotel. In his remarks, he referred to Mayor Antonio R. Villaraigosa of Los Angeles, CA; Rep. John A. Perez, speaker, California State Assembly; comedian and talk show host Ellen DeGeneres; actors Darren Criss and Barry Karas; Dana Perlman, cochairman, Lesbian, Gay, Bisexual, Transsexual Leadership Council of the Democratic National Committee; Col. Vito Imbasciani, State surgeon, California Army National Guard; Adm. Michael G. Mullen, USN (Ret.), former Chairman, Joint Chiefs of Staff; and Republican Presidential candidate former Gov. W. Mitt Romney of Massachusetts.

Remarks at an Obama Victory Fund 2012 Fundraiser in Beverly Hills
June 6, 2012

The President. Thank you so much, everybody. First of all, I just want to thank Ryan and David for opening up this incredible home and arranging perfect weather. We are grateful to you for your hospitality.

I want to also acknowledge John Emerson, who is here, and has been just a great friend, and worked on my behalf for a very, very long time and helped to pull this thing together.

I will not be singing tonight.

Audience members. Aww.

The President. I'm just saying. [*Laughter*] But usually in these kinds of settings where I've got a few friends, I like to spend most of my time in a conversation, as opposed to giving a long speech. So I'm just going to make a few brief remarks at the top.

I just came from a wonderful event over at the Wilshire—or the Hilton—I'm not sure which. [*Laughter*] Here's what happens—because you go through the kitchens—[*laughter*]—of all these places and so you never are quite sure where you are. [*Laughter*] But I was telling folks, many of you got involved in the campaign back in 2008, and you did so not because you thought electing Barack Obama was a sure thing. Generally people named Barack Hussein Obama are not sure things in Presidential races. [*Laughter*] The reason some of you got involved is because I think you understood that there are a set of values that make this country extraordinary, that make this country exceptional.

It's not just our military might or the size of our economy. It has to do with a set of ideas, a creed, that started more than 200 years ago, when a band of colonists decided that they had a different idea about self-governance and they had an idea that said everybody is created equal and everybody can participate and each of us, if we're willing to work hard and take responsibility, can take our lives as far as our dreams will take us.

And those documents that they issued were not perfect, and the society in which they lived wasn't perfect. But they created this space where, through successive generations, we could continually broaden the scope of opportunity to more and more people and include more and more people as citizens and recognize each other as part of this American story.

And so through civil wars and civil rights and women's rights and workers' rights, there's been this constant battle so that more and more people can take part. And that's made us all stronger. That's made us all richer. And it's made us this beacon for the rest of the world.

And the sense was back in 2008 that maybe we had lost our way, because history doesn't always move in a straight line, and so there are times where we go sideways and even times where we step back. And we looked and we said we've seen a surplus squandered on tax cuts for folks who didn't need them and weren't even asking for them. We've seen two wars paid on a credit card. We've seen an economy that has done very well for a few, but has made it tougher and tougher for ordinary folks to get by. This was all before the financial crisis, before we knew what was going to happen when Lehmans collapsed.

And so we had a sense, we can do better than this. But the America we believe in is one where everybody has a shot—everybody has a fair shot and everybody does their fair share and everybody is playing by the same set of rules, and if you're willing to put your all into it, you can find a job or start a business and buy a home and send your kids to college, and they're going to do even better than you can. And nobody is excluded from it. It doesn't matter what you look like, where you come from, what your last name is, who you love.

That's what we were fighting for in 2008. And now we've gone through a very difficult period in our history, the toughest economy—I'm looking around the room—that any of us have lived through. And the good news is it turns out the American people are tougher than tough times, and so we have bounced back. And we made some very tough decisions to save the auto industry and to stabilize the financial system and keep teachers in the classroom. And America is coming back.

We've seen more than 4 million jobs created—800,000 this year alone—and manufacturing stronger than it's been since the 1990s and a whole lot of progress has been made. But we've still got a lot more work to do. And that's why, hopefully, you're here tonight, because you recognize that that journey we started in 2008 is not finished.

We've made sure that 30 million people can get health insurance who didn't have it before and that 2.5 million young people can stay on their parent's health insurance plans and preventive care is in place and women can control their own health care choices.

We have signed the Lilly Ledbetter Act that says equal pay for equal work, because I want my daughters treated the same way your sons are.

We have doubled fuel efficiency standards on cars and doubled the amount of clean energy to make sure that we're not only creating jobs and reducing dependence on foreign oil, but making sure that we're also saving the planet in the process and doing something about climate change.

We've changed the education system in remarkable ways all across the country, made it easier for young people to go to college. Millions of young people are getting scholarships now or loans or grants that they weren't getting before.

So we made a lot of progress, but we've still got a lot of work to do. We still have an immigration system that is broken. We still have an economy where too many people are out of work and homes are underwater. And there is a fundamental contrast between our vision of where America needs to go and where the other side needs to go—the other side wants to take this country.

And this is going to be a close election, because people are still frustrated and a lot of folks are still hurting. And the other side happens to have these super PACs that spend $500 million on negative ads and feed into people's anxieties and their frustrations.

But the good news is that those ideals I talked about at the beginning, that's what the American people believe in. They're not always paying attention to what's going on in Washington, and it seems so negative and dysfunctional, a lot of times folks just tune it out. But when you offer them a choice, a vision that says we're all in this together; and we're going to make investments so that every child can get an education; and we're going to rebuild America so we've got the kind of infrastructure and broadband lines and high-speed rail that will keep us an economic superpower; and we're going to invest in clean energy so that we further reduce our dependence on foreign oil; and we're going to do it in a balanced way, so we're asking those of us who have been most

successful to do a little bit more so that other folks can come up behind us and succeed just like we did—when you give them that choice, they know what the right answer is.

And so the key in 2012 is going to be how bad do we want it? Are we willing to fight for it, fight for that vision with even greater determination than we did in 2008?

And I told a story at the last event, I go back to my birthplace—and I had a birth certificate for this—[*laughter*]—once a year. And we usually stay near a Marine base. And it's depressing working out at the gym at the Marine base because the marines all have 2-percent body fat and can bench 500 pounds—[*laughter*]—and they make you feel bad.

This past winter, while I'd be working out, folks would come up to me and they would say, you know what, Mr. President, I just wanted to say how much I appreciate you repealing "don't ask, don't tell," because I'd been serving as a marine for 5 years, for 10 years. There have been times where I haven't been able to have my partner see me off as I'm being deployed. And for you to acknowledge me not just as a soldier, but somebody who is a full citizen and equal participant in the life of this country, really makes a difference.

And I was telling folks at the hotel that after about four of these, the last day, a young man came up—and first, he pointed out that I wasn't doing the exercise right. [*Laughter*] And then he said, "I want to thank you for repealing 'don't ask, don't tell.'" And I was anticipating a similar story. And so I asked him, "Well, what kind of struggles have you been through being gay in uniform?" He says: "No, sir, I'm not gay. I want to thank you because I've had friends who were gay who were great marines. And it always embarrassed me that somehow—even though it didn't matter to any of us in the unit—they had to pretend to be something they weren't. And this will make us better marines and this will make us stronger as a country."

And that spirit is why I'm running for a second term, because I believe that's the essence of who we are as a country. That's what makes us special. That's what we're fighting for.

That's why I appreciate you guys being on board, because I want to finish what we started in 2008. All right, thanks. Thank you.

NOTE: The President spoke at 8:09 p.m. at the residence of Ryan Murphy and David Miller.

In his remarks, he referred to John Emerson, president, Capital Group Private Client Services. The transcript was released by the Office of the Press Secretary on June 7. Audio was not available for verification of the content of these remarks.

Remarks at an Obama Victory Fund 2012 Fundraiser in View Park, California
June 7, 2012

Thank you, everybody. Everybody, sit down. Make yourselves comfortable. In fact, it's warm out here. Gentlemen, feel free to take off your jackets. [*Laughter*] I'm going to. There you go. That's what's called an Executive order. [*Laughter*]

I want to thank Jo Ann and Charles for hosting us in their extraordinary home. You can give them a big round of applause. I want to thank our event cochairs: Nicole and Clarence Avant, Lorna Johnson, Kerman Maddox, Candace and Steve McKeever, Cookie Parker, and Danielle Smith.

I want to thank all of you for being here on this spectacular Los Angeles day. I'm glad some of you brought your children, your young people, which is great to see, although it doesn't seem like they were arguing that much about getting out of one of the last days of school. I don't know how many excuse notes I'm going to have to write. [*Laughter*]

Michelle says hi. The girls, they're in the mindset that school is almost done. We're trying to keep them focused, telling them to run through the tape, don't start slacking off too early. And Bo says hi as well. [*Laughter*]

Now, I'm here not just because I need your help, but I'm here because the country needs your help. When we came together—and so many of you were supporters back in 2008, and a lot of you got on this bandwagon before people could even pronounce my name properly—we came together not just to support me, not just to support an individual. The idea was that we were making a commitment to each other, that there were a set of values and ideals, there were a set of principles that we believed in as Americans that date back to the founding of this country.

This did not begin as a perfect Union, but the charter of this country, our Declaration of Independence, our Constitution, spoke to the possibility of perfecting the Union. There were those who were excluded. There were those who were not considered full citizens. But there was this idea at the core of America that can be expressed very simply, which is, in this country you should be able to make it if you try, if you're willing to work hard, if you're willing to take responsibility, that everybody can make it, regardless of what they look like or where they come from, what faith they hold or who they love, that everybody should be able to make it in this country if they try.

Now, there were a lot of struggles to fulfill that promise. There was a war fought and the civil rights movement and the women's rights movement and a workers' movement. But the trajectory of this country has always been, we're going to expand more and more opportunity to more and more people and promote dignity and respect and justice and equality and fairness for more and more people. That's been the trajectory of this country. That's the reason I can stand here today as President of the United States, because of the extraordinary work that was done in the past.

And what we recognized in 2008 was, as much progress as had been made, it seemed like we were taking a wrong turn, that we were not being true to those ideals that everybody can make it. So we had a surplus turned into a deficit because of tax cuts for folks who didn't need them and weren't even asking for them. We had two wars fought on a credit card. A few people were doing really well, but more and more folks were struggling to get by as costs of everything from health care to sending your kid to college were skyrocketing. And people's incomes and wages were flatlining, and job growth was stagnant, and manufacturing was moving offshore. And so we came together to affirm and assert that we were going to restore that basic sense that in America everybody gets a fair shot and everybody does their fair share and everybody plays by the same set of rules.

Now, we didn't know at the time that I started running that we would end up experiencing the worst financial crisis in our lifetimes. We didn't know that we were losing 4 million jobs even as I was still campaigning, lose 800,000 the month that I took office. But we understood that we were going to have to try to work as hard as we could to bring about change that was desperately needed to fulfill this country's promise.

And so yes, we've gone through 3½ years of very difficult times. I had to make a bunch of decisions that weren't always popular. But we made the right decisions. Because it turns out that the American people are tougher than tough times. So, when some folks said we should let Detroit go bankrupt, we said, we're not going to let that happen; we're going to save more than a million jobs. And right now GM is the number-one automaker in the world once again, and Detroit is coming back better than ever.

All across the country, we put people back to work rebuilding our roads and our bridges and our infrastructure and made sure that teachers and firefighters and police officers could stay on the job. We stabilized the financial system. We made sure that loans were starting to flow again to small businesses and businesses started getting back to basics. And as a consequence, we've now created over 4 million jobs over the last couple of years, more than 800,000 this year alone, more jobs in the manufacturing sector than any time since the 1990s.

Because of the resilience and the grit of the American people all across this country, we're starting to see progress again. We're starting to move in the right direction again.

But—and here's the reason I'm here today—we're not finished. We've got more work to do. This journey is not over. There are still too many folks out there who are hurting, who are desperate for a job, but can't find one. Folks who have seen their homes lose value, $100,000 underwater, don't know what it will mean for themselves, for their future. Too many young people who still are trying to go to college and having a tough time affording it. So, despite all the work that we've done, we've still got more work to do.

And we've got an election that in some ways is going to be more critical than 2008 because the other party has gone in a direction that is contrary to those values that we fought for in 2008. You know, Governor Romney is a patriotic American, and he's got a beautiful family, and he's been very successful. But along with this Republican Congress, they've got a vision that doesn't say we work together; it says everybody is on their own. It says, if you don't have health care, tough luck, you're on your own, figure it out. It says, if you were a child born into poverty, pull yourself up by your own bootstraps, even if you don't have boots. [*Laughter*] You're on your own.

It's a vision that basically believes that the answer to every question are more tax cuts for the wealthiest, the most powerful; the fewest regulations that protect consumers or keep our air and water clean or make sure that workers are treated fairly; and that somehow, if Government isn't doing anything, then the country is automatically going to be better.

Now, it would be one thing if we hadn't tried this. [*Laughter*] But we tried it. Remember there was a previous administration. We tried this whole recipe, and it didn't work. And the idea that we—after all the progress we fought for, everything that we've done over the last 3½ years—that we'd go back to the very same policies that got us into this mess in the first place, I don't think so. We are not going to let it happen. And that's the reason why I'm running for a second term as President of the United States of America. We're not going backwards. We're going forwards. We are going forward. We're moving forward.

And everything that we've accomplished, everything that we've accomplished with outstanding Members of Congress like Karen Bass, who's here today, by the way—give Karen a big round of applause; we love Karen—everything that we've accomplished should give us confidence not only that we can win this election, but that we can keep progress going.

I keep a checklist in my desk of stuff I said I was going to do, a little to-do list. This is separate from Michelle's to-do list. [*Laughter*] She's got her own to-do list. I check both of them every day. Said that we would make sure that 30 million Americans get health care—check. We got that done, 2.5 million young people who are on their parents' health insurance plans right now. I had a gentleman, while we were taking photos, come up and say, boy, that's really helping me because my daughter, she needed health care. And think about if somebody who can afford to come here today got helped, imagine what that means for a whole bunch of families all across the country. Imagine what that means.

Doubled fuel efficiency standards on cars so that by the next—by the middle of the next decade, you're going to see cars getting 55 miles per gallon. That's not only good for your pocketbook, it's helping reduce our dependence on foreign oil, and it's saving the environment in the process.

We took tens of billions of dollars that were going to banks, subsidizing them through the student loan program, we said, let's take that money, let's give it directly to students. And as a consequence, we've gotten millions of people who are now getting opportunities for Pell grants and reducing their loan burden as a consequence of the work that we did.

We said, in a country that is constantly expanding opportunity, it does not make sense for patriotic Americans doing outstanding work not to be able to serve the country they love just because of who they love. And so we ended "don't ask, don't tell," an expression of our values and our ideals.

War in Iraq—over. Afghanistan—in transition. Al Qaida—on the ropes. Bin Laden—gone.

All that progress that we've made, it shouldn't make us complacent, but it should give us confidence that if we're willing to work hard, we can bring about more changes, more things that help ordinary families, so that if you're working hard out there, you can find a job, you can pay a mortgage, send your kids to college, retire with some dignity and some respect. That's what folks are looking for.

The American people, they're not—they don't have wild expectations. They understand that government can't solve every problem, and it shouldn't try. They recognize that they've got to take responsibility for making sure their children are instilled with a love of knowledge and taking school seriously. They understand that not everybody can be helped if they don't want to be helped. They're not looking for a handout, but they are looking for a hand up. They are looking for a shot, an opportunity. And so we've got more work to do on a whole range of fronts.

We've got more work to do to make sure that manufacturing and good jobs continue to come back onshore. Instead of giving tax breaks to companies that ship jobs overseas, we want to give companies tax breaks that are investing here in the United States of America and creating jobs for our folks back home.

We've got more work to do. For all the work we've done improving our schools—and we have made historic transformations. Forty States have initiated, because of our Race to the Top program, major reforms that focus on learning, K through 12, improving teacher performance.

We've still got more work to do. There are still schools right here in Los Angeles and all across the country where half the kids are dropping out before they graduate. One out of 10 are reading at grade level. So we've got to make investments, not just investments in money, although it does involve money, but also investments in reform, to make sure that there is not a child in America who is not equipped when they graduate to compete in this global economy.

And it also means making sure that they can afford to go to college. And if they're not going to a 4-year college or university, they can go to a 2-year college or university, but get the skills that they need. And there are programs out there that work. We know they work. The question is if we can scale them up to make sure that everybody has access to them.

We've got to implement health care reform. We've got to implement Wall Street reform to make sure we don't see another taxpayer-funded bailout. I don't want to have to go through that again.

And we've got to balance our fiscal situation in a responsible way. And this is going to be a major debate that comes up next year. The other side, they're always talking about debt and deficits, which I find interesting since they're always the ones who run up the debt and the deficits, say we don't care about deficits, until Democrats get into office, and suddenly, they see religion. [*Laughter*]

But now you've got a Presidential candidate on the other side and a Republican Congress that says not only do we want to renew the Bush tax cuts for the wealthiest Americans, we want to double down with $5 trillion more worth of tax cuts. And when they do try to explain how it would be paid for, when you do the math, what it comes down to is they would eliminate investments in science and technology that have made us an economic superpower, investments in our infrastructure that allow us to move goods and services and people around the world and make us competitive. They want to eliminate investments in education at the precise time when we've got to be investing in our young people's education.

If you implemented their budget, you could not afford anything outside of defense, Social Security, interest on the national debt, and Medicare. Everything else would be fundamentally wiped out. Now, we think deficits and debt are important. But we think that the way to do it is, yes, eliminate programs that don't work, reform our health system not by shifting cost to seniors, but by reducing costs and improving quality of care. But also, let's ask those of us who can do a little bit more to do a little bit more.

For us to go back to the tax rates under Bill Clinton for folks who are millionaires or billionaires, that's not asking too much. That's consistent with the idea that everybody does their fair share. That is something that has made this country great and is something that we still believe.

So there are a lot of reasons why this election is important. There are probably going to be some additional Supreme Court appointments. We've got the other side saying that they'd defund Planned Parenthood. I believe that women's health should be in the control of women. I think a program like Medicaid, we can't just slash it in ways that make children and the disabled and our seniors more vulnerable. I'm not going to allow them to roll back progress that we've made on health care. We're going to have to make sure that we keep the gains that we've made on things like student loans.

So there are all kinds of reasons why this election is important. But I want to tell you, this election is also going to be close though. And the reason it's going to be close is not because the other side has good ideas. They don't. [*Laughter*] It's not because they've got new ideas, because as Bill Clinton said the other day, this is the just the same old thing they've been peddling for the last 20 years, it's just on steroids." [*Laughter*]

The reason it's going to be close is because there are still folks out there who are hurting. There are still folks out there who are having a tough time. And that means that as frustrated as they are, if they're receiving $500 million worth of negative ads from these super PACs, then people start wondering, well, maybe nothing can work in Washington. Maybe that "change we can believe in," maybe it couldn't happen.

The other side is not going to provide new ideas, but they will try to tap into people's frustrations about a very difficult period in our history. And so we're going to have to work through the cynicism and the negativity and the just plain nonsense that we've become accustomed to during political campaigns. It will just be funded at a higher level than we've ever seen before.

Here is the thing that makes me confident though: What you taught me in 2008 was that when folks get together, when citizens get together, when ordinary people get together and decide it's time for change to happen, you know what, change happens. Change happens when you make a commitment and you're talking to your friends and your neighbors, and suddenly, young people are getting engaged and involved again in the life of this country and people are knocking on doors and making phone calls and talking about the issues and getting informed. When that happens, it can't be stopped. It doesn't matter how much money the other side spends. It doesn't matter how much misinformation is out there: The truth shall out.

And I expect that's going to happen this time. I understand some people, when they take pictures with me, they show me—pictures that we took 4 years ago together, they want me to sign them. And it's generally just a reminder of how old I'm getting. [*Laughter*] I'm all gray and dinged up—[*laughter*]—bruised and battered. But I want everybody here to know that I am more determined now than I have ever been. I have more confidence in the American people than ever before. Because when I travel around the country and I meet a single mom who has raised some wonderful child who has now gone to college, and she never got more than a high school education. And she is seeing him graduate, and she tells us, that's what all that work was for. Or I meet a small-business owner who didn't lay off his workers even during really tough times and

didn't take a salary himself because he understood a lot of families were being supported at that time. When I meet our troops who just serve us with such professionalism and dignity and patriotism and never complain. All across the country you travel and you're just reminded how decent the American people are, how good they are, how right their instincts are.

I still believe in the American people, and so I hope you still believe in me. I told you when I was running in 2008, I'm not a perfect man, and I am not a perfect President. But I told you, I'd always tell you what I thought, I'd always tell you where I stood, and I'd always, every day, wake up working as hard as I knew how to make your lives a little bit better. And you know what, I have kept that promise. I have kept that promise.

And so if you're willing to stick with me on this and knock on some more doors and make some more phone calls and work even harder this time than you did the last time, then we won't just win an election, but we will finish what we started. Everybody will have a shot in this country. And we'll remind the world just why it is that the United States of America is the greatest nation on Earth.

Thank you, everybody. God bless you. God bless America.

NOTE: The President spoke at 10:18 a.m. at the residence of Jo Ann and Charles O. Quarles. In his remarks, he referred to Republican Presidential candidate former Gov. W. Mitt Romney of Massachusetts; and former President William J. Clinton. Audio was not available for verification of the content of these remarks.

Remarks at the University of Nevada, Las Vegas, in Las Vegas, Nevada
June 7, 2012

The President. Thank you so much. If you've got a chair, go ahead and sit down. You can make yourself comfortable. [*Laughter*] If you don't, you're out of luck, just stay there. It is great to be back in Nevada. I want everybody to give Gorge a big round of applause for that introduction. I want to thank all the students

for coming out here on a nice summer afternoon; some of you might be at Capriotti's or someplace, you know—[*laughter*]—but instead you're here with us.

Audience member. You look great!

The President. Thank you. Thank you, I'll tell Michelle you said so.

Audience member. We love her too!

The President. And I love you back. Thank you. So I'm here today at UNLV, home of the Runnin' Rebels, to talk about what a lot of you folks are thinking about every day. Now, keep in mind, we're in Vegas. So, in Vegas, you can bet on just about anything. [*Laughter*] But what the students here have bet on is themselves. They've bet on themselves. By earning your degree, you've decided to make the best possible investment in your future and in the future of America. And I'm proud of all of you for making that investment, because it's never been more important.

In today's economy, the single best predictor of success, by far, is a good education. And the statistics prove it. The unemployment rate for Americans with a college degree or more is about half the national average. Their incomes are twice as high as those with only a high school diploma. A higher education is the clearest path to the middle class.

And rebuilding the middle class is what we've been all about. I don't have to tell folks in Nevada that we're recovering from a crisis that cost millions of middle class jobs. When that housing bubble burst, it hit people really hard.

But we're also fighting back from a long-term trend that has cost working families all across the country that sense of security. So our job is not just to get people back to work; our job is to build an economy where hard work pays off.

So I want more people to be able to make the investment you're making. I want to make it easier for more students like you to earn a degree without shouldering a mountain of debt, because even though education—a college education is still a great investment, the burden of debt is serious, and it's hard on folks just as they're starting off in life. I don't want to be a country where a shrinking number of people are doing really, really well and then a growing number are barely able to get by.

I want everybody in America to get a fair shot. I want everybody to do their fair share. I want everyone to play by the same rules. That's the America I know. That's the America I believe in. That's the America we're trying to build for you, for my children, for future generations.

Audience member. Thank you, President Obama!

The President. You're welcome. Now look, the fact is—again, I don't have to tell folks in Nevada—we're still going through this process of recovery from that crisis. And we've taken some tough steps together. And the good news is, our economy is growing again, but we need it to grow faster. Businesses have created almost 4.3 million new jobs over the last 27 months. But to recover all the jobs that were lost in that recession, we've got to have them come back faster.

The truth is, the recovery has seen stronger job growth than what happened during the last recession a decade ago. But the problem is, the hole we have to fill is a lot deeper. The global aftershocks are much greater. We're already seeing it. Just like last year around this time, our economy has been facing some serious headwinds. You've got the lingering effects of the spring spike in gas prices. You remember that. It's still tough on a lot of folks' wallets. You've got the situation in Europe.

But from the moment we first took action when I came into office to make sure that we did not go into a freefall depression, we knew that all—recovering all the jobs that were lost during the recession was going to take some time. And we knew there would be ups and downs along the way. What we also knew though was if we acted wisely and we acted together, if we didn't quit, we'd come back stronger. We would do more than just get back to where we were; we would build an economy that would last for the long term.

And, Las Vegas, I still believe that. I believe we will come back stronger. We have better days ahead, and it's because of people like you. It's because of folks like you. I'm inspired when I hear folks like Gorge putting in long hours working and taking summer classes. Some older students who are retaining—[*applause*]—there you go. I don't know, you don't look that old to me. [*Laughter*] But folks deciding to go back to school—retrain yourself for a new job, the jobs of the future.

So you're working hard. You're playing by the rules. You deserve to have leaders who are going to do the same, leaders who will take action, leaders who will do whatever it requires to fight for the middle class and grow the economy faster. We may not fully control everything that happens in other parts of the world, but there are plenty of things we can do right here in the United States to strengthen the economy further. There are plenty of steps we can take right now to help create jobs and grow this economy faster.

So let me just give you some examples. Last September, I sent to Congress a jobs bill full of the kinds of ideas that, historically, Republicans and Democrats have supported. If they had taken all the steps I was pushing for back in September, we could have put even more Americans back to work. We could have sliced through these headwinds more easily.

Now since then, in fairness, Congress has passed a few parts of that jobs bill. They passed a payroll tax cut that's put more money in every working person's paycheck right now. That's good news. We thank them for it. But they haven't acted fast enough on the other ideas that economists, independent economists—not me, but folks who study this stuff for a living—say could have put over a million more people to work. Now, there's no excuse for that. When so many people are still out there pounding the pavement and sending out résumés, so many families are doing whatever it takes to pay the bills, Congress can't just sit on their hands.

So my message to Congress is let's get to work. Let's get to work. I know this is an election year. That's not lost on me. [*Laughter*] But at this make-or-break moment for America's middle class, we can't afford to have Congress take 5 months off. You've got to keep working. You're not suddenly just sitting around not doing anything. You should expect the same thing from your representatives in Washington, right?

So there are a bunch of things that Congress can do right now. Let me tick a few off. At a time when our businesses have created more

than 4 million new jobs, unfortunately, State and local governments have lost 450,000 jobs. That's been one of the biggest problems in our economy is all the layoffs happening at the State and local level: cops, teachers, firefighters all being laid off.

Now, those folks provide vital services. They protect us. They're teaching our kids. Congress should pass a bill like I've asked them to do to help States like Nevada put Americans—those Americans who are doing outstanding service on behalf of our communities—put those folks back on the job right now. That's something we can do.

Number two, we know that the housing bubble burst. Here in Nevada, the construction industry got killed, right? So I told Congress months ago, let's pass a bill to put hundreds of thousands of construction workers and contractors back to work rebuilding America, rebuilding roads and bridges and new schools for rising populations and—[*applause*]. That's good for the economy now; it's good for the economy later. There's no excuse for Congress to just shrug its shoulders. Let's get it done.

The housing bubble that burst and helped cause this whole mess is still a major drag on the economy. Right now Congress should pass the changes necessary to give every responsible homeowner the opportunity to save an average of $3,000 a year by refinancing their mortgage at today's historically low interest rates.

I mean, think about it. If you're a homeowner and you live here in this State, your house very well may be underwater and so it's hard for you to refinance. We did, through an Executive order, a plan that allows those of you whose mortgages are guaranteed by FHA to refinance, but we've got to have Congress to take additional steps to reach everybody, to reach even more homeowners.

These are folks who are paying their mortgage every month, but can't refinance because your home is underwater. And let me tell you, I was up in Reno last month, met a family. They had refinanced through the program that we set up, and they're getting an extra

$250,000 a month. And that makes a difference. How many people here could use an extra $250 a month? And that's good for everybody; that's good for everybody's economy, because if you've got that extra money in your pocket, you might help—that might help rebuild some equity in your home or you might go spend it on textbooks or a new computer, and the entire economy gets stronger. So let's give every responsible family that chance.

Instead of—all right, here's another thing. Instead of just talking about job creators, Congress should put their money where their mouth is. Give small-business owners a tax break for hiring more workers and for paying higher wages.

And then, with all the veterans that are coming back from Iraq and Afghanistan, let's make some special efforts there. We should create what we're calling a veterans job corps, because no one who fights for this country should ever have to fight for a job when they come home.

Right now Congress needs to extend the tax credits for clean energy manufacturers. Those tax credits are set to expire at the end of the year. Nearly 40,000 good jobs are at stake, making solar panels and wind turbines and lowering our dependence on foreign oil. So, instead of giving tax breaks—billions of tax breaks to oil companies that are making a whole lot of money and don't need help—let's double down on a clean energy industry that's rarely been more promising. And you're seeing it right here in Nevada. There's a lot of sunshine out here. [*Laughter*] We can turn that into electricity and put people back to work in the process. Let's make that happen.

And while we're at it, it's past time for Congress to stop giving tax breaks that ship jobs overseas. Give tax breaks to companies that are bringing jobs back to the United States of America, that are investing right here.

All right, so these are all things we're pushing Congress to do before they go on vacation. [*Laughter*] But the number one thing Congress should do for you, UNLV, right now, is to stop interest rates on student loans from doubling at the end of the month.

The clock is running out. You know, in today's economy, higher education can't be a luxury. It's an economic necessity. Everybody should be able to afford it. But over the last 20 years, the cost of college has more than doubled. It's gone up faster than everything else, even faster than health care costs. We're at a point where the average student who borrows to pay for college graduates with $26,000 in student loan debt. And let's face it, some folks graduate with more than that: 50, 75, even a hundred. Together, Americans owe more on their student loans than they do on their credit cards.

And all that debt, that means folks making really tough choices. It may mean waiting longer to buy a house or starting a family or taking that job that you really want, because it doesn't pay enough. And by the way, Michelle and I know something about this. We did not come from wealthy families. We graduated from college and law school, and we had a whole lot of debt. And when we got married, we got poorer together. [*Laughter*] We sort of added our liabilities together. [*Laughter*]

Of course, look, we were lucky enough to land good jobs. But even with those great jobs that we had, we only finished paying off our student loans about 8 years ago. Now, think about that. I'm the President of the United States—[*laughter*]—it was only about 8 years ago that I finished paying off my student loans. So I know what a lot of you are going through. I've been there. I have done that. When the girls were first born and we were starting to save up for their college education, we were still paying for our own college educations. [*Laughter*]

And we can do better than that. I don't want that future for young people. So that's why my administration has already taken a bunch of steps. We fixed a broken student loan system that was giving tens of billions of dollars to big banks and said, let's give that money directly to students—use that money to afford college. That's why we strengthened aid, like Pell grants for low-income students. That's why we set up a new consumer watchdog agency called the Consumer Finance Protection Bureau, and it's now working with the Department of Education to give students and their parents access to a simple fact sheet on student loans and financial aid, because everybody has got to be well informed. We call it "Know Before You Owe"—"Know Before You Owe." [*Laughter*] Don't be surprised, 2 weeks from graduation, you look up, and whap! You just got hit upside the head. Know before you owe.

On Tuesday, college presidents from across the country came together. They agreed to provide clear information about costs, financial aid, and loan repayments to all incoming students starting next year. So that's good news, all right?

But we've got more to do. So today I've directed my Education Secretary and my Treasury Secretary to make it easier for millions of students with Federal loans to afford their loan payments. And that includes some of you. This is a program that more people need to know about. And we're going to start doing more advertising about this because this is really important. For those of you who are still in school, you're about to graduate, as long as you make your monthly payments on time—all right, so pay your bills on time—we will cap the payments you have to make on your student loans at 10 percent of your discretionary income once you graduate—10 percent. And this is a big deal, because no matter what career you choose—if you decide you're going to be a teacher or you're going to be a social worker or you're going to go into public service or the nonprofit sector—you'll still be able to stay current on your loans.

So these are all the things we've already done. But understand, this isn't going to make much of a difference if the costs—underlying costs of college keep going up faster than everything else. So everybody has got to do their part. Colleges and universities, they need to do their part. I've told Congress, let's steer Federal aid to schools that are doing a good job keeping tuition affordable and provide good value and serve their students well. If you're getting Federal student loans, colleges and universities, you shouldn't just be loading up a whole bunch of debt on your students. You've got to

figure out how are you working to make sure that they can afford their education.

States have a role to play. I see some of my buddies from the State legislature here. Right now the amount of money that State and local governments invest in their college students is at a 25-year low; spending a lot of money on prisons, spending a lot of money on other stuff, but we're not spending enough to make sure that tuition stays affordable. That's one of the reasons that tuition has gone up so fast.

If States can find smart new ways to keep costs down and make it easier for more students to graduate, then we're going to help them do it. So everybody has got to do their part: colleges, universities, the States, my administration, and yes, Congress. Congress has got to do their part.

I warned over a month ago—I even went on Jimmy Fallon to say this—if Congress doesn't act by the end of this month, by July 1, interest rates on Federal student loans will double overnight. That means the average student with those loans—including 8,000 students right here at UNLV—will rack up an additional $1,000 in debt. That's like a $1,000 tax hike for more than 7 million students. How many people can afford to pay an extra $1,000 if you're a student just because Congress can't get its act together? That makes no sense. This is a no-brainer.

So I just said to Congress, get this done. Get it done. Get it done. This is not complicated. Last month, Democrats in the Senate put forward a plan that would have kept these low rates in place, wouldn't have added a dime to the deficit. The Senate Republicans got together; they blocked it. They said, no. House Republicans voted to keep your rates down only if we agreed to cut things like preventive health care for women. So that's not a smart thing to do.

There are folks on the other side who are coming up with all sorts of reasons why we should just go ahead and let these rates double. One of them compared these student loans to a "stage-three cancer of socialism." I don't know what that means exactly. [*Laughter*] The idea—my grandfather went to school on the

GI bill. There's a long tradition of us helping people get a good education, because they know—we know that it makes everybody richer. It makes our entire country more competitive and stronger.

Some of these folks in Congress, they were saying we're just talking about student loans to distract from the economy. I guess they don't get this is the economy. Helping you get the skills that businesses are looking for, that's one of the best things we can do for the economy. Making college affordable, that's one of the best things we can do for the economy. Putting opportunity within the reach of everybody, no matter what you look like or where you come from, that's what America is about. But these guys say that students like you should pay more, so we can bring down the deficit they say.

Now, keep in mind, they ran up this deficit for over a decade. Now they want to cut loans to students while giving tax breaks to oil companies and folks like me who don't need tax breaks. They voted to let millionaires and billionaires keep paying lower taxes than middle class workers. They voted to give an average tax cut of at least $150,000 to every millionaire in America, but they want you to pay an extra $1,000 a year for college. It doesn't make any sense. It's wrong. It's wrong.

Look, here in America, we admire success. That's why a lot of you are going to school. We work and study for it. And if folks aren't willing to help themselves, we can't help them. But America is about more than just protecting folks who have already done well. It's about giving everybody a chance to do well. It's about hard work and responsibility being rewarded. It's about everybody having the chance to get ahead and then reach back and help somebody behind you so that everybody has a chance.

That's what makes us strong. That's what makes us strong.

So, if you agree with me, I need your help. Some of these folks in Congress are a little stubborn. So I need your help. You've got to tell Congress, don't double my rate. Call them up, e-mail them, post on their Facebook wall, tweet them. [*Laughter*] We've got a hashtag: #dontdoublemyrate. Don't double my rate.

Never forget that your voice matters. I know sometimes it seems like Washington isn't listening. And frankly, Congress sometimes isn't. But we're talking about issues that have a real impact on your lives, real impact on your futures. Making education more affordable, that's real. Making homes more affordable, making it a little easier for you to make your mortgage payments, that's real. Building an economy that works for everybody, that's real.

So I need you all to stand up. I need you to be heard. Tell Congress now is not the time to double the interest rates on your student loans. Now is the time to double down on the middle class. Now is the time to build an America that lasts. Now is the time to work together, to put people back to work and strengthen our housing market and help our veterans. Let's get this done.

Let's remind the world why the United States of America is the greatest nation on earth. Thank you, Las Vegas. God bless you. God bless America.

NOTE: The President spoke at 12:53 p.m. in the Cox Pavilion. In his remarks, he referred to Gorge Henriquez, student, University of Nevada, Las Vegas; Reno, NV, residents Paul and Valerie Keller; and James T. Fallon, Jr., host, NBC's "Late Night With Jimmy Fallon" program.

Remarks on the National Economy and an Exchange With Reporters
June 8, 2012

The President. Good morning. I just want to say a few words about the economy, and then I will take some of your questions.

Today, we're fighting back from the deepest economic crisis since the Great Depression.

After losing jobs for 25 months in a row, our businesses have now created jobs for 27 months in a row, 4.3 million new jobs in all. The fact is, job growth in this recovery has been stronger than in the one following the last recession a decade ago. But the hole we have to fill is much deeper, and the global aftershocks are much greater. That's why we've got to keep on pressing with actions that further strengthen the economy.

Right now one concern is Europe, which faces a threat of renewed recession as countries deal with a financial crisis. Obviously, this matters to us because Europe is our largest economic trading partner. If there's less demand for our products in places like Paris or Madrid, it could mean less businesses—or less business for manufacturers in places like Pittsburgh or Milwaukee.

The good news is, there is a path out of this challenge. These decisions are fundamentally in the hands of Europe's leaders, and fortunately, they understand the seriousness of the situation and the urgent need to act. I've been in frequent contact with them over the past several weeks, and we know that there are specific steps they can take right now to prevent the situation there from getting worse.

In the short term, they've got to stabilize their financial system. And part of that is taking clear action as soon as possible to inject capital into weak banks. Just as important, leaders can lay out a framework and a vision for a stronger euro zone, including deeper collaboration on budgets and banking policy. Getting there is going to take some time, but showing the political commitment to share the benefits and responsibilities of a integrated Europe will be a strong step.

With respect to Greece, which has important elections next weekend, we've said that it is in everybody's interest for Greece to remain in the euro zone while respecting its commitments to reform. We recognize the sacrifices that the Greek people have made, and European leaders understand the need to provide support if the Greek people choose to remain in the euro zone. But the Greek people also need to recognize that their hardships will likely be worse if they choose to exit from the euro zone.

Over the longer term, even as European countries with large debt burdens carry out necessary fiscal reforms, they've also got to promote economic growth and job creation. As some countries have discovered, it's a lot harder to rein in deficits and debt if your economy isn't growing. So it's a positive thing that the conversation has moved in that direction and leaders like Angela Merkel and François Hollande are working to put in place a growth agenda alongside responsible fiscal plans.

The bottom line is, the solutions to these problems are hard, but there are solutions. The decisions required are tough, but Europe has the capacity to make them. And they have America's support. Their success is good for us. And the sooner that they act, and the more decisive and concrete their actions, the sooner people and markets will regain some confidence, and the cheaper the costs of cleanup will be down the road.

In the meantime, given the signs of weakness in the world economy, not just in Europe, but also some softening in Asia, it's critical that we take the actions we can to strengthen the American economy right now.

Last September, I sent Congress a detailed jobs plan full of the kind of bipartisan ideas that would have put more Americans back to work. It had broad support from the American people. It was fully paid for. If Congress had passed it in full, we'd be on track to have a million more Americans working this year. The unemployment rate would be lower. Our economy would be stronger.

Of course, Congress refused to pass this jobs plan in full. They did act on a few parts of the bill, most significantly, the payroll tax cut that's putting more money in every working person's paycheck right now. And I appreciate them taking that action. But they left most of the jobs plan just sitting there. And in light of the headwinds that we're facing right now, I urge them to reconsider. Because there are steps we can take right now to put more people back to work. They're not just my ideas, they're not just Democratic ideas, they're ideas that independent, nonpartisan economists believe would make a real difference in our economy.

Keep in mind that the private sector has been hiring at a solid pace over the last 27 months. But one of the biggest weaknesses has been State and local governments, which have laid off 450,000 Americans. These are teachers and cops and firefighters. Congress should pass a bill putting them back to work right now, giving help to the States so that those layoffs are not occurring.

In addition, since the housing bubble burst, we've got more than a million construction workers out of work. There's nothing fiscally responsible about waiting to fix your roof until it caves in. We've got a lot of deferred maintenance in this country. We could be putting a lot of people back to work rebuilding our roads, our bridges, some of our schools. There's work to be done; there are workers to do it. Let's put them back to work right now.

The housing market is stabilizing and beginning to come back in many parts of the country. But there are still millions of responsible homeowners who've done everything right, but still struggle to make ends meet. So, as I talked about just a few weeks ago, let's pass a bill that gives them a chance to save an average of $3,000 a year by refinancing their mortgage and taking advantage of these historically low rates. That's something we can do right now. It would make a difference.

Instead of just talking a good game about job creators, Congress should give the small-business owners that actually create most of the new jobs in America a tax break for hiring more workers.

These are ideas that, again, have gotten strong validation from independent, nonpartisan economists. It would make a difference in our economy. And there's no excuse for not passing these ideas. We know they can work.

Now, if Congress decides, despite all that, that they aren't going to do anything about this simply because it's an election year, then they should explain to the American people why. There's going to be plenty of time to debate our respective plans for the future. That's a debate I'm eager to have. But right now people in this town should be focused on doing everything we can to keep our recovery going and keeping our country strong. And that requires some action on the part of Congress. And so I would urge them to take another look at some

of the ideas that have already been put forward.

And with that, I'm going to take a couple of questions. And I'm going to start with Caren Bohan, who is with Reuters, but as we all know, is about to go get a fancy job with National Journal. [*Laughter*] And we're very proud of her. So congratulations to you, Caren. You get the first crack at me.

Economic Stabilization Efforts in Europe/National Economy

Q. Thank you very much, Mr. President. Could you tell the American people what role the United States is playing in the European debt crisis? And also, do you think European leaders have a handle on what's needed to stem the crisis? And finally, you talked about a number of ideas that you've already put forth to shield the American economy. Do you plan to give a speech or lay out additional ideas now that the crisis is really escalating?

The President. Well, a couple of things. First of all, the situation in Europe is not simply a debt crisis. You've got some countries like Greece that genuinely have spent more than they're bringing in, and they've got problems. There are other countries that actually were running a surplus and had fairly responsible fiscal policies, but had weaknesses similar to what happened here with respect to their housing market or the real estate markets, and that has weakened their financial system. So there are a bunch of different issues going on in Europe. It's not simply a debt crisis.

What is true is, is that the markets getting nervous have started making it much more expensive for them to borrow, and that then gets them on a downward spiral.

We have been in constant contact with Europe over the last—European leaders over the last 2 years, and we have consulted with them both at the head of Government and head of state level. I frequently speak to the leaders not only at formal settings like the G–8, but also on the telephone or via videoconference. And our economic teams have gone over there to consult.

As I said in my opening remarks, the challenges they face are solvable. Right now their focus has to be on strengthening their overall banking system—much in the same way that we did back in 2009 and 2010—making a series of decisive actions that give people confidence that the banking system is solid, that capital requirements are being met, that various stresses that may be out there can be absorbed by the system. And I think that European leaders are in discussions about that and they're moving in the right direction.

In addition, they're going to have to look at how do they achieve growth at the same time as they're carrying out structural reforms that may take 2 or 3 or 5 years to fully accomplish. So countries like Spain and Italy, for example, have embarked on some smart structural reforms that everybody thinks are necessary—everything from tax collection to labor markets to a whole host of different issues—but they've got to have the time and the space for those steps to succeed. And if they are just cutting and cutting and cutting, and their unemployment rate is going up and up and up, and people are pulling back further from spending money because they're feeling a lot of pressure, ironically, that can actually make it harder for them to carry out some of these reforms over the long term.

So I think there's discussion now about, in addition to sensible ways to deal with debt and government finances, there's a parallel discussion that's taking place among European leaders to figure out how do we also encourage growth and show some flexibility to allow some of these reforms to really take root.

Now, keep in mind that this obviously can have a potential impact on us because Europe is our largest trading partner. The good news is, is that a lot of the work we did back in 2009 and 2010 have put our financial system on a much more solid footing. Our insistence of increasing capital requirements for banks means that they can absorb some of the shocks that might come from across the Atlantic. Folks in the financial sector have been monitoring this carefully and, I think, are prepared for a range of contingencies.

But even if we weren't directly hit in the sense that our financial system still stayed solid, if Europe goes into a recession, that means we're selling fewer goods, fewer services, and that is going to have some impact on the pace of our recovery. So we want to do everything we can to make sure that we are supportive of what European leaders are talking about. Ultimately, it is a decision that they've got to make, in terms of how they move forward towards more integration, how they move forward in terms of accommodating the needs for both reform and growth.

And the most important thing, I think, we can do is make sure that we continue to have a strong, robust recovery. So the steps that I've outlined are the ones that are needed. We've got a couple of sectors in our economy that are still weak. Overall, the private sector has been doing a good job creating jobs. We've seen record profits in the corporate sector.

The big challenge we have in our economy right now is State and local government hiring has been going in the wrong direction. You've seen teacher layoffs, police officers, cops, firefighters being laid off. And the other sector that's still weak has been the construction industry. Those two areas we've directly addressed with our jobs plan. The problem is that it requires Congress to take action, and we're going to keep pushing them to see if they can move in that direction. Okay?

Jackie Calmes [New York Times]. Where did Jackie go? She was—there she is.

Economic Stabilization Efforts in Europe

Q. Thank you, Mr. President. I'd like to ask you a couple—about what a couple of other people have said about Europe. And one is that I'd like to know if you agree with former President Bill Clinton, who said in the past week that the Europeans' policies that you've described here today are much like those of the Republicans in this country—politics of austerity that would take us in the same direction as Europe—if you agree with that. The Republicans, for their part, have said that you're simply blaming the Europeans for problems that have been caused by your own policies. So I'd like you to respond to both of those. And also, tell us precisely how much time you personally spend on the European situation.

The President. Any other aspects to the question? [*Laughter*]

Q. I do have more questions. [*Laughter*]

Q. Is she going to National Journal? [*Laughter*]

The President. First of all, in terms of the amount of time I spend, look, I think it's fair to say that over the last 2 years I'm in consistent discussions with European leadership and consistent discussions with my economic team.

This is one of the things that's changed in the world economy over the last two or three decades, is that this is a global economy now, and what happens anywhere in the world can have an impact here in the United States. Certainly, that's true after the kind of trauma that we saw in 2008 and 2009.

And if you think about the situation in Europe, they're going through a lot of the things that we went through back in 2009, 2010, where we took some very decisive action. The challenge they have is they've got 17 governments that have to coordinate; 27 if you count the entire European Union, not just the euro zone. So imagine dealing with 17 Congresses instead of just one. That makes things more challenging.

But what we've tried to do is to be constructive, to not frame this as us scolding them or telling them what to do, but to give them advice, in part based on our experiences here in having stabilized a financial situation effectively. And ultimately, though, they're going to have to make a lot of these decisions, and so what we can do is to prod, advise, suggest. But ultimately, they're going to have to make these decisions.

Now, in terms of characterizing the situation over there, what is absolutely true—this is true in Europe, and it's true here in the United States—is that we've got short-term problems and long-term problems. And the short-term problems are: How do we put people back to work? How do we make the economy grow as rapidly as possible? How do we ensure that the recovery gains momentum?

Because if we do those things, not only is it good for the people who find work, not only is it good for families who are able to pay the bills, but it actually is one of the most important things we can do to reduce deficits and debt. It's a lot easier to deal with deficits and debt if you're growing, because you're bringing in more revenue and you're not spending as much because people don't need unemployment insurance as much; they don't need other programs that are providing support to people in need because things are going pretty good.

Now, that's true here in the United States, and that's true in Europe. So the problem, I think, President Clinton identified is that if, when an economy is still weak and a recovery is still fragile, that you resort to a strategy of "let's cut more"—so that you're seeing government layoffs, reductions in government spending, severe cutbacks in major investments that help the economy grow over the long term—if you're doing all those things at the same time as consumers are pulling back because they're still trying to pay off credit card debt, and there's generally weak demand in the economy as a whole, then you can get on a downward spiral where everybody is pulling back at the same time. That weakens demand, and that further crimps the desire of companies to hire more people. And that's the pattern that Europe is in danger of getting into.

Some countries in Europe right now have an unemployment rate of 15, 20 percent. If you are engaging in too much austerity too quickly, and that unemployment rate goes up to 20 or 25 percent, then that actually makes it harder to then pay off your debts. And the markets, by the way, respond in—when they see this kind of downward spiral happening, they start making a calculation, well, if you're not growing at all, if you're contracting, you may end up having more trouble paying us off, so we're going to charge you even more. Your interest rates will go up. And it makes it that much tougher.

So I think that—what we want both for ourselves, but what we've advised in Europe as well is a strategy that says let's do everything can to grow now, even as we lock in a long-term plan to stabilize our debt and our deficits and start bringing them down in a steady, sensible way.

And by the way, that's what we proposed last year; that's what's proposed in my budget. What I've said is, let's make long-term spending cuts; let's initiate long-term reforms; let's reduce our health care spending; let's make sure that we've got a pathway, a glide path to fiscal responsibility, but at the same time, let's not underinvest in the things that we need to do right now to grow. And that recipe of short-term investments in growth and jobs with a long-term path of fiscal responsibility is the right approach to take for, I think, not only the United States, but also for Europe. Okay?

National Economy

Q. What about the Republicans saying that you're blaming the Europeans for the failures of your own policies?

The President. The truth of the matter is that, as I said, we've created 4.3 million jobs over the last two—27 months, over 800,000 just this year alone. The private sector is doing fine. Where we're seeing weaknesses in our economy have to do with State and local government, oftentimes, cuts initiated by Governors or mayors who are not getting the kind of help that they have in the past from the Federal Government and who don't have the same kind of flexibility as the Federal Government in dealing with fewer revenues coming in.

And so if Republicans want to be helpful, if they really want to move forward and put people back to work, what they should be thinking about is, how do we help State and local governments and how do we help the construction industry. Because the recipes that they're promoting are basically the kinds of policies that would add weakness to the economy; would result in further layoffs, would not provide relief in the housing market, and would result, I think, most economists estimate, in lower growth and fewer jobs, not more.

All right. David Jackson [USA Today].

National Security/Classified Information

Q. Thank you, sir. There are a couple of books out with, essentially, details about national security issues. There are reports of terrorist kill lists that you supervised, and there are reports of cyber attacks on the Iranian nuclear program that you ordered. Two things. First of all, what's your reaction of this information getting out in public? And secondly, what's your reaction to lawmakers who accuse your team of leaking these details in order to promote your reelection bid?

The President. Well, first of all, I'm not going to comment on the details of what are supposed to be classified items. Second, as Commander in Chief, the issues that you've mentioned touch on our national security, touch on critical issues of war and peace, and they're classified for a reason, because they're sensitive and because the people involved may, in some cases, be in danger if they're carrying out some of these missions. And when this information, or reports, whether true or false, surface on the front page of newspapers, that makes the job of folks on the frontlines tougher, and it makes my job tougher, which is why since I've been in office, my attitude has been zero tolerance for these kinds of leaks and speculation.

Now, we have mechanisms in place where if we can root out folks who have leaked, they will suffer consequences. In some cases, it's criminal—these are criminal acts, when they release information like this. And we will conduct thorough investigations, as we have in the past.

The notion that my White House would purposely release classified national security information is offensive. It's wrong. And people, I think, need to have a better sense of how I approach this office and how the people around me here approach this office.

We're dealing with issues that can touch on the safety and security of the American people, our families, or our military personnel, or our allies. And so we don't play with that. And it is a source of consistent frustration, not just for my administration, but for previous administrations, when this stuff happens. And we will continue to let everybody know in Government, or after they leave Government, that they have certain obligations that they should carry out.

But as I think has been indicated from these articles, whether or not the information they've received is true, the writers of these articles have all stated unequivocally that they didn't come from this White House. And that's not how we operate.

Q. Are there leak investigations going on now? Is that what you're saying? Of these stories?

The President. What I'm saying is, is that we consistently, whenever there is classified information that is put out into the public, we try to find out where that came from. All right?

Okay? Thank you very much, everybody. Thank you.

NOTE: The President spoke at 10:40 a.m. in the James S. Brady Press Briefing Room at the White House. In his remarks, he referred to Chancellor Angela Merkel of Germany; and President François Hollande of France.

Remarks Following a Meeting With President Benigno Aquino III of the Philippines and an Exchange With Reporters
June 8, 2012

President Obama. Well, it is a great pleasure to welcome President Aquino to the Oval Office and to the White House.

I had the opportunity to spend a lot of time with him, most recently during my Asia trip, when we met most recently in Bali. And at that time, we discussed how important the U.S.-Philippine relationship was, the historic ties, the 60 years of a mutual defense treaty, the extraordinary links between Filipino Americans that have brought our two countries so closely together. And we pledged to work on a whole host of issues that would continue to strengthen and deepen the relationship for the 21st century.

We talked about how we could work on security issues, on economic issues, on people-to-people exchanges, and on a whole host of regional issues. And I just want to thank President Aquino for his excellent cooperation, because we've made a great deal of progress since that time.

On economic issues, the Philippines is the recipient of a Millennium Challenge grant that is helping to foster greater development and opportunity within the Philippines. We have a partnership for growth that is working on how we can make sure that we are structuring a relationship of expanding trade and commerce between our two countries.

I want to congratulate President Aquino for the work that he's done on the Open Government Partnership, which is consistent with his campaign to root out corruption that can facilitate greater economic development within the Philippines.

And on security and military issues, we've had discussions about how we can continue to consult closely together, engage in training together, work on a range of regional issues together, all of which is consistent with the announced pivot by the United States back to Asia and reminding everybody that, in fact, the United States considers itself and is a Pacific power.

Throughout all these exchanges and all the work that we've done, I've always found President Aquino to be a thoughtful and very helpful partner. And I think that as a consequence of the meeting today in which we discussed not only military and economic issues, but also regional issues—for example, trying to make sure that we have a strong set of international norms and rules governing maritime disputes in the region—that I'm very confident that we're going to see continued friendship and strong cooperation between our two countries.

So, Mr. President, thank you for visiting.

President Aquino. Thank you.

President Obama. We are very proud of the friendship between our two countries, and we look forward to continuing in the future.

President Aquino. Yes. Thank you very much. Well, on our part, I would like to thank President Obama for all the support that the U.S. has given us in our quest to really transform our society. Ours is a shared history, shared values, and that's why America is just one of two that we have strategic partnerships with.

Today's meeting has really even deepened and strengthened a very long relationship we have, especially as we face the challenges that are before both our countries in the current situation.

And again, we'd like to thank them for all the expressions of support that even now has led to the resolution of situations within our part of the world.

Thank you.

President Obama. All right. Thank you, everybody.

U.S. Economy

Q. Mr. President, Mitt Romney says you're out of touch for saying the private sector is doing fine. What's your response?

President Obama. Listen, it is absolutely clear that the economy is not doing fine. That's the reason I had the press conference. That's why I spent yesterday, the day before yesterday, this past week, this past month, and this past year talking about how we can make the economy stronger.

The economy is not doing fine. There are too many people out of work. The housing market is still weak and too many homes underwater. And that's precisely why I asked Congress to start taking some steps that can make a difference.

Now, I think if you look at what I said this morning and what I've been saying consistently over the last year, we've actually seen some good momentum in the private sector. We've seen 4.3 million jobs created—800,000 this year alone—record corporate profits. And so that has not been the biggest drag on the economy.

The folks who are hurting, where we have problems and where we can do even better, is small businesses that are having a tough time getting financing. We've seen teachers and police officers and firefighters who've been laid off, all of which, by the way, when they get laid off spend less money buying goods and going to restaurants and contributing to additional economic growth. The construction industry is still very weak, and that's one of the areas where we've still seen job losses instead of job gains.

So if we take the steps that I laid out to make sure that we're not seeing teacher layoffs and we're not seeing police officer layoffs, and we're providing small businesses with additional financing and tax breaks for when they hire or if they're giving raises to their employees; if we refinance housing—or allow homeowners to refinance so they've got an extra $3,000 in their pocket so that they can spend money and contribute to further economic growth; if we're making sure that we're rebuilding, work that has to be done anyway, deferred maintenance on roads and bridges that could put construction back—workers back to work—all those things will strengthen the economy and independent economists estimate it would create an additional million jobs.

Now, you can't give me a good reason as to why Congress would not act on these items other than politics, because these are traditionally ideas that Democrats and Republicans have supported. So let me be as clear as I can be. The economy needs to be strengthened. That's why I had a press conference.

I believe that there are a lot of Americans who are hurting right now, which is what I've been saying for the last year, 2 years, 3 years, what I've been saying since I came into office. And the question then is what are we going to do about it? And one of the things that people get so frustrated about is that instead of actually talking about what would help, we get wrapped up in these political games. That's what we need to put an end to.

So the key right now is for folks to—what I'm interested in hearing from Congress and Mr. Romney is what steps are they willing to take right now that are going to make an actual difference. And so far, all we've heard are additional tax cuts to the folks who are doing fine, as opposed to taking steps that would actually help deal with the weaknesses in the economy and promote the kind of economic growth that we would all like to see.

All right. Thank you very much, everybody.

NOTE: The President spoke at 2:48 p.m. in the Oval Office at the White House. In his remarks, he referred to Republican Presidential candidate former Gov. W. Mitt Romney of Massachusetts.

Remarks Honoring the 2012 Super Bowl Champion New York Giants
June 8, 2012

Hello, everybody! Well, I—everybody, please have a seat. Welcome to the White House, and congratulations to the Super Bowl Champion New York Giants.

We've got some Members of Congress and members of my administration who are here today and rabid Giants fans. I want to also recognize the Maras and the Tisches, as well as, of course, Head Coach Tom Coughlin and General Manager Jerry Reese. They have built this team into one of the NFL's most outstanding franchises. So we are very proud of them.

Now, I know for some of you, this is just, welcome back. [*Laughter*] You guys have been through this drill before. The last time the Giants were here was in 2008. A lot of folks thought that team didn't have a chance to win a Super Bowl. They ended up winning with a circus catch in the fourth quarter, MVP performance by Eli Manning, a come-from-behind win over the Patriots. So this is all starting to sound kind of like déjà vu all over again.

But every season's different, and last year's Giants were obviously a special bunch, not just because of where they ended up, but because of how they got there. Every team has to deal with injuries to the players. Not many teams have to deal with a late hit on the head coach. [*Laughter*] You saw that Jets game.

Now, Coach Coughlin reminds everybody, he did not go down. That's a tough guy, and you can see that toughness reflected in everybody else on this team. The Giants took a whole bunch of hits this season, but they never went down. From day one, they followed a simple motto: Finish. Finish the play. Finish the game. Finish the season.

And after week 15, sitting at 7–7, they knew that every game was a playoff game. But the players, the coaches, the staff, the owners, they didn't quit. They believed in each other. And they kept winning, all the way to Indianapolis.

The night before the Super Bowl, they watched a highlight reel set to Justin Tuck's good-luck song, "In the Air Tonight." I don't know about a little Phil Collins before a big game. [*Laughter*] I may try that before a big meeting with Congress.

But apparently it worked. Next night, Eli Manning led the way, earned his second Super Bowl MVP. So I would just advise the sportswriters out there, the next time Eli says he thinks he's a elite quarterback, you might just want to be quiet. [*Laughter*]

Eli wasn't alone, of course. Justin Tuck got to the QB, Victor Cruz scored and salsaed, Mario Manningham kept his feet inbounds for the biggest catch of his life. Nobody was perfect, but everybody did their job. And when the Patriots' Hail Mary hit the ground, the Giants were Super Bowl champions. Of course, the fans back home went crazy.

Now, people from New York and New Jersey don't fall for just anybody. It's a tough crowd, let's face it. You've got to earn their respect. They're never completely satisfied, and you've got to earn it both on and off the field. And that's exactly what the Giants did. From fighting childhood obesity—Michelle likes that—to wrapping up leftover food for homeless shelters to working with the Make-A-Wish Foundation to bring kids to practices and games, Big Blue supports the folks who support them.

They've certainly earned the respect of folks like Ray Odierno who's here, who is obviously one of our greatest warriors and one of our greatest soldiers, because this team is always there for our men and women in uniform. This is a New York Giants tradition that goes back to World War II. Back in World War II, Wellington Mara served in the United States Navy, so this is a long tradition here.

And these guys have made it clear that no matter who you root for on Sundays, if you're a veteran, the New York Giants are on your team. Whether it's setting up tickets to games or inviting folks to practices, the Giants never forget the men and women who risk everything to protect our freedom. And I especially want to thank and congratulate Coach Coughlin on receiving the Army's Outstanding Civilian Service Award. That's a great honor.

By the way, we've got some wounded warriors here today. Let's give them all a big round of applause. Having these folks here today, seeing how much the Giants means to them is a reminder of how important sports and foot-

ball can be, but it's also a reminder that there are some things that are more important than football, and the Giants know that. They finished strong, they won six straight games with everything on the line, they made a difference in the lives of those around them. But most importantly, they did it not just on Sunday, but every week.

So again, I want to congratulate the New York Giants. Good luck this season. It looks like we've got somebody singing for you. [*Laughter*] That's how happy everybody is.

Give the New York Giants a big round of applause.

NOTE: The President spoke at 3:09 p.m. on the South Lawn at the White House. In his remarks, he referred to Justin Tuck, defensive end, Victor Cruz, wide receiver, and Mario Manningham, former wide receiver, New York Giants; and Gen. Raymond T. Odierno, USA, Chief of Staff, U.S. Army. He also referred to the Mara and Tisch families, owners, New York Giants franchise.

The President's Weekly Address
June 9, 2012

This week, I spent some time talking with college students about how we can make higher education more affordable. And one of the things I told them was how proud I was that they were making that investment in themselves, because in today's economy, the best predictor of success is a good education.

That's not just true for our individual success; it's also true for America's success. New jobs and new businesses will take root wherever they can find the most highly educated, highly skilled workers. And I want those workers to be American workers. I want those good-paying, middle class jobs to take root right here.

So it should concern everybody that right now, all across America, tens of thousands of teachers are getting laid off. In Pennsylvania alone, there are 9,000 fewer educators in our schools today than just a year ago. In Ohio, the number is close to 7,000. And nationwide, over

the past 3 years, school districts have lost over 250,000 educators. Think about what that means for our country. When there are fewer teachers in our schools, class sizes start climbing up, our students start falling behind, and our economy takes a hit.

The point is, teachers matter. One study found that a good teacher can increase the lifetime income of a classroom by over $250,000. A great teacher can change the course of a child's life. So the last thing our country needs is to have fewer teachers in our schools.

Now, I know States are still going through some tough times. I realize that every Governor is dealing with limited resources and many face stark choices when it comes to their budgets.

But that doesn't mean we should just stand by and do nothing. When States struggle, it's up to Congress to step in and help out. In 2009 and in 2010, we provided aid to States to keep hundreds of thousands of teachers in the classroom. But we need to do more. That's why a critical part of the jobs bill that I sent to Congress back in September was to help States prevent even more layoffs and rehire even more teachers who had lost their jobs. Of course, months later, we're still waiting on Congress to act.

When it comes to this recovery, we can't fully control everything that happens in other parts of the world. But there are plenty of things we can control. There are plenty of steps we can take right now to strengthen our economy. Putting teachers back in our kids' classrooms is one of those steps. There's no excuse for inaction. You work hard. Your leaders should too, especially at this make-or-break moment for the middle class.

I know this is an election year. But some things are bigger than an election. Some things are bigger than politics. So I hope you'll join me in telling Congress to do the right thing, to get to work, and to help our teachers back in the classroom. We can't afford to wait any longer.

Thanks and have a great weekend.

NOTE: The address was recorded at approximately 4:05 p.m. on June 8 in the Grand Foyer at the White House for broadcast on June 9. The transcript was made available by the Office of the Press Secretary on June 8, but was embargoed for release until 6 a.m. on June 9.

Remarks at an Obama Victory Fund 2012 Fundraiser in Owings Mills, Maryland
June 12, 2012

Thank you, everybody. Everybody, please have a seat. Well, it is wonderful to be with all of you. Let me begin by thanking our hosts, Josh and Genine. Thank you so much for opening up this extraordinary home—and their gorgeous daughters who are doing all wonderful things. I was telling Josh, you cannot beat daughters. No offense, sons, but—[*laughter*]—I'm just saying, when you've got wonderful daughters, it puts a smile on your face. But thank you so much for your hospitality.

You guys benefit from having one of the best Governors in the country. Please give Martin O'Malley a big round of applause. Absolutely. An outstanding Lieutenant Governor, classmate of mine at Harvard, although he was a little younger than me, Anthony Brown. Two wonderful allies, great friends, great champions on behalf of working people not just here in Maryland, but all across the country: Barbara Mikulski is here, the senior Senator, and Ben Cardin in the house. We've got the wonderful Congressman—I loved his dad; he's doing just a great job following in his footsteps—John Sarbanes is here. And the outstanding mayor of Baltimore, Stephanie Rawlings-Blake is in the house.

And of course, all of you are here, and we're very pleased with that. I'm going to be very brief, because usually what I want to do in a setting like this is to take questions and provide comments or get advice.

But let me just say briefly, building on what Martin said, we've gone through the toughest economy and the toughest financial crisis in our lifetimes. What we've seen not just here in the United States, but worldwide, is something that we haven't seen since the thirties. And we've still got a long way to go. There are a lot of folks out there who are hurting—a lot of folks who are looking for work or are underemployed, a lot of folks whose homes are underwater—and we've been reading over the last several days about, because of the plunge in housing prices, the loss of that wealth that a lot of families are experiencing. It's put enormous strains on people all across the country, including here in Maryland.

But what we have been able to do over the last 3½ years, after a decade in which we had been moving in the wrong direction, is to begin to point towards a trajectory where here in this country, everybody is getting a fair shot, everybody is doing their fair share, everybody is playing by the same set of rules; trying to restore those core values here in America where if you work hard, you can make it, regardless of where you come from, what you look like, you have a chance if you act responsibly and you're willing to put in some sweat equity to make it here in America.

That's what the rescue of the auto industry was all about, recognizing that if you place a bet on American workers and American ingenuity, and people start cooperating, that we could once again be number one. And we're seeing GM now the number-one automaker in the work and the U.S. auto industry not only back on its feet, but producing cars that people want to buy all around the world.

It's what we're seeing in clean energy, where we've now doubled clean energy production since I came into office. The progress that we've been able to make with respect to making sure that businesses have markets all around the world so that we're not just known as a country that buys things, but we're also a country that's selling stuff. And we're well on track to double our exports since I came into office, because I want once again for products made in the United States to be known around the world as the best products that are available.

So we've been able to right the ship a little bit. We're moving in the right direction, but this election in many ways is going to be more consequential than 2008, because for all the changes that we've been able to achieve—equal pay for equal work legislation, reversing "don't ask, don't tell," health care legislation that gives 2.5 million young people the ability to stay on their parents' health care plans and gives 30 million people the opportunity to get affordable insurance for the first time, Wall Street reforms that are able to make sure that we don't go through another taxpayer bailout of our banking system like we did that last time. Despite all that work, we're going to need another term to make sure that we consolidate these gains and we lock in the kind of progress that we need to ensure that America's middle class is growing again.

And the reason this election is so important is because you'll never see a sharper contrast

between the two parties in the vision that they have for where this country needs to go.

You've got a party that, at this point, its only recipe for success is another $5 trillion worth of tax cuts on top of the Bush tax cuts that—by every independent analyst who's looked at it—would actually make a our debt and our deficits much worse, or alternatively, would lead to us slashing the kinds of investments that are required for us to grow over the long term: investments in basic science and research and development that have been made us an economic superpower; investments in education, because we know that in the 21st century, those countries that have the best trained workers are going to be the most successful; investments we make in our basic infrastructure—our roads, our bridges, broadband lines, wireless networks; investments we make in ensuring that people who've worked all their lives can retire with dignity and respect, things like Medicare and Social Security.

And so there's going to be a very stark choice in terms of how we deal with our debt and our deficits, how we grow an economy, how we invest in our people to make sure that the next generations succeeds.

And the good news is, is that the American people generally agree with our vision. I mean, if you just put in front of them issue after issue and you present the Democratic approach and the Republican approach, we win. The challenge is, because folks are still hurting right now, the other side feels that it's enough for them to just sit back and say things aren't as good as they should be, and it's Obama's fault. I mean, you can pretty much put their campaign on a tweet and have some characters to spare. [*Laughter*]

And that's why your involvement, your contributions, your investment in this election, your willingness to talk to your friends and your neighbors and your coworkers and to help mobilize the same kind of energy on the ground that we had last time is going to be so important. And it's going to be important not just for this Presidential election, but it's going to be important to make sure that we retain control of the Senate. It's going to be important for us to be able to take the House.

But the one last thought I want to leave you with is a sense of optimism about how solvable our problems are. It's become fashionable to talk about how America can't recover from these kinds of challenges. You know what, that's what they've said throughout our history. They've always underestimated the resilience and the strength of the American people. And we've been through tougher times before.

And I, as you might imagine, spend a lot of time traveling all around the world. There's not a country that wouldn't trade places with us. If you look at, as tough as things have been, the pace at which we've grown, the accessibility of solutions to our fiscal problems relative to what's happening in Europe, for example, what's required is not out of reach.

It will require some tough choices. Most of all, it requires those on Capitol Hill to work across party lines to achieve some basic solutions. But we are poised to make sure that the 21st century is the American century, just like the 20th century was. It's going to require some work though, and this election is going to help determine it.

So I hope you guys are ready to go. I hope you are still fired up. I am just as determined as I've ever been, and I'm looking forward to this campaign.

So thank you. Thank you. Thank you so much.

NOTE: The President spoke at 1:23 p.m. at the residence of Joshua E. and Genine M. Fidler. In his remarks, he referred to former Sen. Paul S. Sarbanes. Audio was not available for verification of the content of these remarks.

Remarks at an Obama Victory Fund 2012 Fundraiser in Baltimore, Maryland
June 12, 2012

The President. Hello, hello, hello! How's it going, Maryland? How's it going, Baltimore? Well, it is good to be in Baltimore, home of what may end up being rivals with the White Sox: the Orioles. [*Laughter*] I hear you guys are—the Orioles are having a pretty good season, I got to admit. They're doing all right.

It is wonderful to see all of you. A couple of people I just want to acknowledge. First of all, one of the finest Governors we have in this country, Martin O'Malley is in the house. Your Lieutenant Governor, Anthony Brown, is here. Two of the outstanding leaders of the United States Senate: the senior Senator, although young at heart, Barbara Mikulski is here. And the junior Senator, but wiser than his years—[*laughter*]—Ben Cardin is here.

You've got an outstanding congressional delegation: Donna Edwards, John Sarbanes, Elijah Cummings. You've got Mayor Stephanie Rawlings-Blake in the house. And I want to give a big round of applause—because it's not easy to do—I want to give Anna, who spoke before the Governor, give her a big round of applause, because she did an outstanding job.

Oh, it wasn't on my card—Dutch is here. Give it up. Sorry, brother, didn't see you. He's doing a great job. This is an outstanding congressional delegation.

Now, I am here today not just because I need your help, although I do. But I'm here because the country needs your help. A lot of you got involved in our campaign in 2008, and we came together not because of me; we came together because all of us shared the feeling that we needed to reclaim the basic bargain that built this country, that created the biggest middle class that the world had ever seen.

We came together because of a shared belief that in America, your success should not be determined by the circumstances of your birth. If you're willing to work hard, if you're willing to take responsibility, you should be able to own a home. You should be able to send your kids to college. You shouldn't be bankrupt when you get sick. You should be able to retire with dignity and respect. No matter who you are, no matter where you come from, no matter what you look like, no matter who you love, no matter what your faith, here in America you should be able to make it if you try. That's why we came together.

And back in 2008, we had a sense that Washington had strayed away from these basic values. Think about it. We had a record surplus that was squandered on tax cuts for people who didn't need them and weren't even asking for them; two wars fought on a credit card; Wall Street speculation reaping huge profits for a few while manufacturing was leaving our shores and a shrinking number of people were doing fantastically well, but more and more people had to get by with falling incomes even while the cost of everything from college to health care was skyrocketing.

We saw the slowest job growth in half a century in the decade before I took office. And then it all culminated in a house of cards that collapsed in the most destructive financial crisis since the Great Depression. In the last 6 months of 2008, while we were campaigning, our friends and neighbors lost nearly 3 million jobs. Over 800,000 more were lost the month I was sworn in.

So, even as we were in Grant Park that night celebrating, as much hope and possibility as we felt on that cold day in January on the National Mall, we knew we had our work cut out for us. And so we had to take action—bold, swift action, and sometimes it wasn't popular—to prevent another depression. And we understood that the road to recovery would not be easy. We knew it would take time. We knew there would be ups and downs. We knew there would be plenty of stubborn opposition along the way. But we knew—we also knew this: If we were willing to act wisely and with unity, and if we were persistent and we stayed at it, if we were willing to roll up our sleeves, if we were determined not to quit, then we could come back stronger than before. And I still believe that.

Nothing has shaken my faith in that belief. In fact, the American people continually confirm it for me. Because they are strong and they are resilient, I know America will come back stronger, and I know our better days are ahead of us.

And I believe that because of you. You guys give me faith. It's been tough, but the American people are tougher. And so while some people were saying, let's go ahead and let Detroit go bankrupt, we said let's make our bet on the American worker and on American businesses. And as Governor O'Malley said, GM is number one again, and we are coming back stronger than before.

We had small-business owners that I had a chance to meet who would describe for me how they——

Audience members. We love you, Mr. President!

The President. I love you too. I love you back. [*Laughter*]

But small-business owners who would decide, you know what, I'm not going to lay off my workers, even though it means I don't have to take a salary this year, or because I know that families are depending on me. We don't quit. We keep going. You saw people who had been laid off from their jobs, and at the age of 50 or 55, they go back and retrain for a new job at a new industry. Don't quit. With grit and resilience and innovation, we're fighting our way back.

And so just like we didn't let Detroit go bankrupt—not only did we save the auto industry, but we're actually seeing better cars made, which allows our auto industry to be on top of the world once again—doubling fuel efficiency standards on cars so that you'll get 55 miles a gallon in the next decade. That will save the average family $8,000 during the life of a car. So not only did we prevent liquidation, we're actually coming back stronger than before.

The same is true when it came to manufacturing. Manufacturing is now hiring at a faster pace, investing in America again, consistently adding jobs for the first time since the 1990s. Businesses starting to get back to basics, the private sector creating nearly 4.3 million new jobs in the last 27 months, over 800,000 jobs just this year alone.

Now, does this make us satisfied? No. Not when we've got so many folks who are still out there looking for work. Not when so many homes are still underwater. Not when so many States are still laying off teachers and first-responders.

This crisis did not happen overnight; it will not be solved overnight. The fact is, job growth in this recovery has been stronger than the one following the last recession a decade ago. We've recovered more effectively than most other advanced nations. But the hole we have to fill is deep. The global aftershocks are great. And that's why we've got to keep pressing with actions that further strengthen this recovery. We've got more work to do. We know that.

Now, what we also understand is the last thing we can do is return to the very policies that got us into this mess in the first place. Not now. Not with so much at stake, Baltimore. We have come too far to abandon the change that we fought for these past 4 years. We've got to move forward to the future we imagined where everybody is getting a fair shot and everybody is doing their fair share and everybody is playing by the same rules.

And that's the choice in this election. And that's why I'm running for a second term as President of the United States of America. We've got more work to do.

Now, my opponent in this election, Governor Romney, is a patriotic American. He's raised a wonderful family. He should be proud of the personal success he achieved as the head of a large financial firm. But I think he's—he has drawn the wrong lessons from these experiences. He seems to believe that if CEOs and wealthy investors like him are doing well, the rest of us automatically do well.

Audience member. No way!

The President. When a woman shared the story of her financial struggles in Iowa, he gave her an answer out of an economic textbook. He said, "Well, our productivity equals our income." And the implication was, is that people are having trouble paying the bills because they're not productive enough or working hard enough.

Well, those of us who've spent time in the real world know that the problem is not the American people aren't productive enough. You've been working harder than ever. The challenge we're facing is that for over a decade, harder work hasn't led to higher incomes. Bigger profits at the top haven't led to better jobs across the board. You can't solve that problem if you can't even see it. [*Laughter*]

Now, what a lot of current Republicans don't seem to get is that a healthy economy doesn't just mean you're maximizing your own profits through massive layoffs or busting unions. You don't make America stronger by shipping jobs and profits overseas. When Governor Romney or the Republicans controlling the House of Representatives propose cutting taxes for folks who don't need them while raising them on 18 million working families, that's not a recipe for economic growth.

And by the way, there's nothing new about these ideas. This is the same old stuff they have been peddling for years. [*Laughter*] Although, as Bill Clinton pointed out the other day, this time their agenda is on steroids. [*Laughter*] They want even bigger tax cuts for the wealthiest Americans. They want even deeper cuts to things like education and Medicare and research and technology. They want to give banks and insurance companies even more power to do as they please.

Audience members. No!

The President. And so when I hear Governor Romney say his 25 years in the private sector gives him a special understanding of how the economy works, my question is: Why are you running with the same bad ideas that brought our economy to the brink of disaster?

I mean, either he believes that it will lead to a different result this time—although there's no evidence of that—or he's hoping you won't remember just what happened the last time we tried those bad ideas. And we're here to say we remember, and we're not going back there. We're moving this country forward.

I want to be clear. We don't expect government to solve all our problems, and it shouldn't try to solve all our problems. I learned from my mother that no education policy is more important than your parents nagging you—[*laughter*]—and making—and giving you the love and attention and scoldings you need——

Audience member. Thanks, Mom.

The President. Thanks, Mom. [*Laughter*] Absolutely.

My first job—or one of my first jobs out of college—was working with a group of Catholic churches who taught me no poverty program can make as much of a difference in people's lives as the kindness and commitment and engagement of a caring neighbors and caring friends. And not every regulation is smart. Not every tax dollar is spent wisely. And not every person can be helped who refuses to help themselves.

But that's not an excuse to tell the vast majority of responsible, hard-working Americans—many of whom are struggling—you're on your own; that unless you are lucky to have parents who can afford to lend you money, you may not be able to go to college; that even if you pay your premiums every month, the insurance company may decide to drop your coverage when you need it most and you're out of luck. That's not who we are. That's not what built America.

We built this country together. We built railroads and highways and the Hoover Dam and the Golden Gate Bridge. We built those things together. We sent my grandfather's generation to college on the GI bill, including my grandfather. We did that together. We didn't do these things—making investments in research that ultimately led to the Internet or GPS or all these things that created platforms for private businesses to succeed—we didn't do these things for one particular individual or one particularly group. We did it because we understood this will make us all richer. If we've got great public schools and great public universities, and we're making these investments in outstanding infrastructure, that's good for everybody. Everybody can succeed. It moved us together as one Nation and as one people.

And that's the lesson—the true lesson of our past. That's the right vision for our future. That's why I'm running again for President of the United States.

You know, I'm running to make sure that by the end of this decade, most—more of our citizens hold college degrees than any nation on Earth. I want to help our schools hire and reward the best teachers, especially in math and science. I want to give 2 million more Americans the chance to go to community colleges and learn the skills that local businesses are looking for right now. In the 21st century, higher education cannot be a luxury; it is an economic imperative that every American should be able to afford. And we're going to make that happen. That's the choice in this election. That's why I'm running for President.

I want to make sure the next generation of high-tech manufacturing takes root in Baltimore and Cleveland and Pittsburgh. I want to stop rewarding businesses that ship jobs overseas. I want to start rewarding companies that are creating jobs and investing right here in Maryland, right here in the United States of America. That's the choice in this election.

I'm running because I want us to keep moving towards a future where we control our own energy. Our dependence on foreign oil is at its lowest point in 16 years. As I said, we doubled fuel efficiency standards on cars, with cooperation from workers and management, which is why our cars will average nearly 55 miles per gallon. Thousands of Americans have jobs because the production of renewable energy in this country has doubled in just 3 years.

Now is not the time to cut these investments out, especially when we're giving $4 billion away to oil companies every year. Now is the time to end those subsidies to an industry that's already profitable, double down on clean energy that has never been more promising for our economy and our security and for the safety of our planet. That's why I'm running for President. That's the choice in this election.

For the first time in 9 years, there are no Americans fighting in Iraq. Bin Laden is no longer a threat to this country. Al Qaida is on the path to defeat. By 2014, the war in Afghanistan will be over. So there is a foreign policy dimension to this election.

America is safer and more respected because of the courage and the selflessness of the United States Armed Forces. And as long as I'm Commander in Chief, with the help of this outstanding congressional delegation, this country will care for our veterans and serve our veterans as well as they've served us. Nobody who fights for this country should have to fight for a job or a roof over their heads when they come home. There's just a difference between me and the other guy on this issue.

My opponent says it was "tragic" to end the war in Iraq. He won't set a timeline to end the war in Afghanistan. I have set that timeline. I intend to keep it, because after a decade of war that's cost us thousands of lives and over a trillion dollars, the nation we need to build is our own. So I want to use half of what we're no longer spending on war to pay down our deficit. I want to invest the rest in education and research. I want us to repair our bridges and our roads, our runways, our wireless networks. And that's the choice in this election.

I want to pay down our debt in a way that is balanced and responsible. I love listening to these guys give us lectures about debt and deficits. [*Laughter*] I inherited a trillion-dollar deficit. [*Laughter*] We had a surplus; they turned it into a deficit, built in a structural deficit that extends for decades. And——

Audience member. And then, they blamed you! [*Laughter*]

The President. Isn't that something?

So we inherited a trillion-dollar deficit. We signed $2 trillion of spending cuts into law. I laid out a detailed plan for a total of $4 trillion in deficit reduction. My opponent won't admit it, but even when you account for the steps we took to prevent a depression and jump-start the economy, all right? So you include the Recovery Act, all the stuff we did to help States like Maryland make sure that they didn't have to lay folks off, and put people back to work, even if you take that into account, spending under my administration has grown more slowly than under any President in 60 years.

So this notion that somehow we caused the deficits is just wrong. [*Laughter*] It's just not true. And anybody who looks at the math will tell you it's not true. And if they start trying to give you a bunch of facts and figures suggesting that it's true, what they're not telling you is, is that they baked all this stuff into the cake with those tax cuts and a prescription drug plan that they didn't pay for and the war. So all this

stuff is baked in, with all the interest payments for it.

It's like somebody goes to a restaurant, orders a big steak dinner, martini all that stuff, and then just as you're sitting down, they leave—[*laughter*]—and accuse you of running up the tab. That's what they do. I am not making this up. [*Laughter*] I mean, press, go back, check, take a look at the numbers.

So we've made tough cuts, and we've proposed additional work that we can do—streamlining Government, cutting more waste, reforming our Tax Code so it's simpler and fair, but also so that it asks the wealthiest Americans—folks like me—to pay a little bit more.

Now, in contrast, my opponent, he's proposed a new $5 trillion tax cut on top of the Bush tax cuts. This includes a 25-percent tax cut for nearly every millionaire in the country. Now, he won't detail how he's going to pay for this, but the bill for this tax cut will either be passed on to our children, or it's going to be paid for by you, a whole lot of ordinary Americans. And I refuse to let that happen again.

I refuse to pay for another millionaire's tax cut by eliminating medical research on projects that could help cure cancer or Alzheimer's. I refuse to pay for another tax cut by kicking kids off of Head Start programs or asking students to pay more for college or eliminating health insurance for millions of poor and elderly and disabled Americans who rely on Medicaid.

I'm not going to allow Medicare to be turned into a voucher that would end the program as we know it. We're going to reform Medicare not by shifting costs to seniors, but by reducing the spending that isn't making people healthier. There are ways to do this that don't but the burden on seniors. That's what's at stake, Baltimore.

And on issue after issue, we cannot afford the next 4 years going backward. We need forward, not backwards. We need better, not worse. America doesn't need to refight the battles we just had over Wall Street reform and health care reform.

Let me tell you something. Allowing 2.5 million young people to stay on their parent's health insurance plan, that was the right thing to do. Cutting prescription drug costs for seniors, right thing to do. We're not going to go back to the days when insurance companies could cancel your policy or deny you coverage or charge women differently than men. We're not going back there.

We don't need another political fight about ending a woman's right to choose, or getting rid of Planned Parenthood, taking away access to affordable birth control. I want women to control their own health choices, just like I want my daughters to have the same opportunities as your sons.

Working with Barbara Mikulski and others, we want to—I want to sign the "Paycheck Fairness Act" into law so women can fight for fair pay. We're not turning back the clock. We want to go forward.

We need to put an end to elections where multimillion-dollar donations speak louder than the voices of ordinary citizens.

We're not going back to the days when you could be kicked out of the United States military just because of who you are and who you love. We're moving forward to a country where we treat everybody fairly and everybody equally, with dignity and respect. And here in Maryland, thanks to the leadership of committed citizens and Governor O'Malley, you have a chance to reaffirm that principle in the voting booth in November. It's the right thing to do.

It's time to stop denying citizenship to responsible young people just because they're children of undocumented immigrants. You know, this country is at its best when we harness the God-given talents of every individual, when we hear every voice, when we come together as one American family and we're all striving for the same American Dream. That's what we're fighting for. That's why I'm running for President. And that's why I need your help.

Maryland, this election is going to be even closer than the last one. We're going to have to contend with even more negative ads, more cynicism, more foolishness than we saw in the last campaign. But the outcome of this election, ultimately, it's up to you. That's one thing we learned in 2008. There's nothing more powerful than millions of voices calling for

change. When you knock on enough doors, and pick up a phone and talk to enough neighbors and friends, when you decide it's time for change to happen, guess what: change happens. Change comes to America.

And that's the spirit we need again. So, if people ask you, what's this campaign about, you tell them it's still about hope. You tell them it's still about change. You tell them it's still about ordinary people who believe that in the face of great odds, we can make a difference in the life of this country.

I still believe that. I believe this country is not as divided as our politics suggest. We've got more in common than the pundits tell us. I believe we're not Democrats or Republicans first, we're Americans first. Most of all, I still believe in you. And I want you to keep believing in me. You know, I——

Audience members. Yes, we do! Yes, we do! Yes, we do!

Audience members. Four more years! Four more years! Four more years!

The President. I told you in 2008 I wasn't a perfect man. Michelle told you too. [*Laughter*] And I told you I'd never be a perfect President. But I promised you I would always tell you what I thought and I'd always tell you where I stood. And most of all, I told you I'd wake up every single day fighting as hard as I knew how on your behalf to make your life a little bit better. And I have kept that promise. And I will keep it as long as I have the honor of serving as your President.

So, if you're willing to stick with me and fight with me and press on, if you're willing to work even harder than we did in 2008, I guarantee you we will move this country forward. We will finish what we started. And we'll remind the world just why it is the United States of America is the greatest nation on Earth.

God bless you. God bless America. Thank you.

NOTE: The President spoke at 3:30 p.m. at the Hyatt Regency Baltimore hotel. In his remarks, he referred to Anna Hosain, volunteer, Obama for America; Rep. C.A. "Dutch" Ruppersberger; and Republican Presidential candidate former Gov. W. Mitt Romney of Massachusetts.

Remarks to the Science Leadership Academy's Graduating Class in Philadelphia, Pennsylvania
June 12, 2012

Hello, everybody! Thank you. Thank you so much. Everybody, have a seat. Have a seat. Well, this is so exciting to have a chance to see all of you. Congratulations on your graduation. I know I kind of messed up graduation a little bit, but it turned out that it was beautiful yesterday. So we had this all planned out. [*Laughter*] We knew there was going to be sun yesterday; it's a little cloudier today. We wanted to make sure you guys looked good in your caps and gowns and didn't get too wet.

Listen, I just want to say to all of you how incredibly proud I am of the work that you guys have accomplished, because some of you may have heard—in between studying, you may have listened to a speech that I've given or remarks that I've made in the past—the nation that excels in science and math and technology, that's going to be the nation that rises to the top in the 21st century. Almost everything we do is based on our capacity to innovate. And America became a economic superpower because we were constantly able to tap into the incredible talents and ingenuity of young people like you who decided, why can't we fly? Why can't we cure diseases? Why can't we make sure that the energy that we use is able to make life a little bit better and a little bit easier for people?

And so throughout our history, we've constantly had innovators who have been able to not only excel in basic science and basic research, but have then been able to translate it into practical things that we now take for granted. And obviously, there was a pretty good scientist here in Philadelphia named Benjamin Franklin, who was able to tool around with kites and keys and all kinds of stuff before he helped to write our Constitution. So you've got a pretty good legacy, here in Philadelphia, of innovation.

And the fact that, as I look around this auditorium, we are tapping into the talents of everybody—women as well as men, folks from every ethnic group, every background—that's also this incredible strength for the United States, because innovation, brainpower does not discriminate by gender or race or faith or background. Everybody has got the capacity to create and improve our lives in so many ways.

So you guys are representative of the future. This is a great postcard for what America is all about. And as you take your next steps—I'm assuming that everybody here is going to some sort of post–high school education, everybody here is going to be going to college, and some of you are going to continue beyond college. I just want you to know that you are going to be succeeding not just for yourself, and that's important—your parents are going to want you to have a job, so they're very pleased about the fact that you're taking a path that is almost assured to provide you with extraordinary opportunities in the future—but you're also going to be making a difference for the country as a whole.

So my expectation is, is that somebody in this auditorium is going to figure out new sources of energy that help not only make us more energy independent, but also deals with problems like climate change. There is somebody in this room who's going to help make sure that we are defeating diseases like Alzheimer's or cancer. There is somebody in this room who is going to help revolutionize our agricultural sector or our transportation sectors or will invent some entire new industry that we don't even know about yet.

And the pace of change these days is so rapid; I'm reminded when I talk to Malia and Sasha that when Sasha was born, most people weren't on the Internet, and now she knows more about it than I do. And so in many ways your youth, and the fact that you've come of age in this new Information Age, gives you an enormous advantage over old fogies like us.

So the bottom line is, we're proud of you. You are going to succeed. You're well on your way. The last thing I'd ask of you, even as you focus on your chosen field and you are moving forward, is to make sure that you also give back, that for a lot of you in your neighborhoods there may not be as many kids who are interested in math and science. And you need to make sure that wherever you have the opportunity, you're mentoring and serving as a good role model to the next generation coming up behind you.

For the women who are here, a lot of you know that historically we haven't had as many women in math and science and engineering fields. So, as you succeed, hopefully, you're going to go back and mentor some people and encourage them to get involved in these fields as well. If you do that then I have extraordinary optimism for the future. And I think that not only will you succeed, but you're going to help your country succeed as well.

So thank you very much, everybody. Appreciate you. Thank you.

NOTE: The President spoke at 5:50 p.m. at the Franklin Institute.

Remarks at an Obama Victory Fund 2012 Fundraiser in Philadelphia
June 12, 2012

Hello! Thank you! How's it going Philadelphia? Well, it is good to be back in Philadelphia. It is good to be among so many good friends, including Benjamin Franklin, one of my favorite Founders. [*Laughter*] I have to admit, I had to restrain myself because this is such an amazing facility, and just wandering around, I started reading about all kinds of American history and that the Dead Sea Scrolls were here. [*Laughter*] Staff was saying, Mr. President, you have some other stuff that you have to do.

There are a couple of acknowledgments that I want to make. First of all, you've got one of the best mayors in the country, Mayor Michael Nutter is here. You've got a couple of the finest Members of Congress in Bob Brady and Chaka Fattah. And you've got somebody here who's been one of my dearest friends and one of my favorite people who has always had my back, and he and I share a lot in common. We're both—we both pretend to play basketball, even though we're way too old. [*Laughter*] We both married up and we both have extraordinary daughters. He happens also to be one of the best Members of the Senate that we have. Bob Casey is in the house.

So I'm here not just because I need your help, although I do. I'm here because the country needs your help. When you think back to 2008, a lot of you were involved in that campaign. You didn't get involved because you thought Barack Obama was the odds-on favorite to become President of the United States. Let's face it. That was a long shot. The reason we came together was because we shared a belief in the basic bargain that built this country: the idea that if you're willing to work hard, if you're willing to take responsibility, that in this country you can make it; that you can find a job that pays a living wage and you can save and buy a home. You can send your kids to college so they do even better than you did. You can retire with some dignity and some respect. The idea that no matter where you come from, no matter what you look like, no matter what your faith, no matter who you love, that in America you can make it if you try.

It's that idea that builds the broadest middle class in the history of the world—and that was and has been the strength of America, the backbone of America—is that everybody had a shot. And we felt back in 2008 that those ideals were being lost, that we had taken a wrong turn. We had taken a surplus left behind by President Clinton and turned it into deficits as far as the eye could see, not because we invested in our economic future, but because we gave tax cuts to folks who didn't need them and weren't even asking for them. We put two wars on a credit card. Our economy increasingly was built on financial speculation and a housing bubble. Manufacturing was leaving our shores.

And although a few people were doing really, really well, that broad-based middle class that built this country, that was the essence of this country, found themselves—you found yourselves—in a situation where wages, incomes were flatlining and job growth was the most sluggish it had been in 50, 60 years and the cost of everything from health care to college education kept on going up and up and up. And it all culminated in the worst financial crisis since the Great Depression. Three million jobs lost in the 6 months before I took office, while we were campaigning, 800,000 jobs lost the month that I was sworn into office.

And so we had to make a series of tough decisions and decisive decisions and quick decisions, and we had to do it without much help from the other side. But the thing that gave me confidence throughout was what I had learned about the American people as I traveled all across the country—and it is a great privilege just running for President and obviously a greater privilege being President because you meet Americans from every walk of life and they show you their grit and they show you their determination. And it turns out Americans are tougher than any tough times.

And so when some people said we should let Detroit go bankrupt, we decided, no, we're going to make a bet on the American worker and American industry. And because of the actions that we took, GM is back on top, and we're seeing the auto industry rehiring and producing better cars than ever. We helped to stabilize the financial system so small businesses could get help again and get credit and financing flowing again. Businesses got back to basics, and we created 4.3 million jobs over the last 27 months, 800,000 this year alone.

So we've made progress. And the reason we made progress was in part because of our policies, but in part because Americans everywhere figured out how they were going to respond. And so you had small-business owners who decided, I'm not going to lay off these workers because their families are counting on their jobs, that maybe I'll take out less this year, maybe I won't even pay myself a salary this year so I can keep my doors open.

And you had folks who were laid off at the age of 45 or 50, and they decided, you know what, I'm not just going to give up, I'm going to

retrain, and I'm going to find a job for the future, even if it means I'm sitting in a classroom with kids who are my kid's age. All across the country people made tough decisions, but they were determined to move forward because, Americans, we don't quit. We don't quit.

And so we can say that we are in a stronger position, we are moving in a better direction, than when I took office. Now, does that mean that I'm satisfied? Does that mean we are satisfied? Absolutely not. Because we have too many friends and neighbors who are still out of work. We know too many people whose homes are still underwater, too many folks who still have too much trouble paying the bills at the end of the month. These problems that we've got, they weren't created overnight, and we never thought they'd be solved overnight. But we understand where we need to go. We understand we've got to keep moving forward. And we understand that the last thing we need is to go back to the very same policies that got us into this mess in the first place.

And let me tell you something: That is all the other side is offering. That's all they're offering. Governor Romney is a patriotic American, he's got a lovely family, and he should be proud of his personal success. But his ideas are just retreads of stuff that we have tried and that have failed. Bill Clinton described it well the other day; he said, they want to do the same thing, just on steroids. [*Laughter*]

If you really pay attention—and one of our jobs during this election is to get folks to pay attention to what the other side is actually offering—then it boils down to deeper tax cuts for the wealthiest Americans, $5 trillion in tax cuts on top of the Bush tax cuts, an average of a 25-percent tax cut for millionaires all across the country, and the elimination of regulations that would make sure that Wall Street doesn't engage in the kind of behavior that resulted in this crisis, that would roll back the kinds of progress we've made making sure insurance companies can't drop you when you get sick, that would roll back environmental and worker protection and consumer protections that we have been working on not just during my administration, but for the last 30, 40 years. And that's it. That's the essence of what they're offering.

And I guess he thinks either it would result in a different outcome than it did when we just tried this 10 years ago, or he and the Republican Congress are counting on the notion that we forgot how it turned out. [*Laughter*] We didn't forget. We remember. We're not going back. We're moving forward, and that's why I'm running for a second term as President of the United States of America.

I'm running to make sure that we keep bringing manufacturing and industry back to Philadelphia, back to Pittsburgh, back to Pennsylvania, back to Ohio. I want to stop giving tax breaks for companies that are shipping jobs overseas. I want those tax breaks to go to companies that are investing right here in the United States of America.

I'm running to make sure that we continue on a path of providing the best education possible for every single one of our children and make sure that we've got the highest rates of college graduates of any country on Earth, because that's going to be the future. We took a student loan program where tens of billions of dollars were being funneled to banks as middlemen in the student loan program, we said, why don't we just give that money directly to students. And as a consequence, we've got millions of students who are benefiting from higher Pell grants; more kids are eligible. We're able to make sure that we can cap the amount of money that folks have to pay back each month on their student loans, because we recognized that a higher education cannot be a luxury. You can't just count on the fact that your parents are paying for your college education. A lot of kids need help. And that's good for the country. We're not going backwards on that, we're going to keep moving forward.

I'm running because I want to continue to see America be the best innovator in the world. When you think about Benjamin Franklin—I just had a chance to talk to these outstanding students from a science and leadership academy who graduated. There are some of them over there, or at least some teachers. And I told them, what's America about? We've been

about technology and discovery and invention, dating back to this guy. [*Laughter*]

That's how we became an economic superpower. So the notion that we would now shortchange our investments in science and basic research, the possible cures for cancer or Alzheimer's or the clean energy that can make sure that we're doing something about climate change and saving money for families—that's not the answer, rolling back those investments. We've got to move forward. We're not going to move backwards. That's why I'm running for President of the United States again.

I'm running because I want us to continue to build this country. We are a nation of builders. The mayor and I were talking as we were driving from the airport about all the projects, all the infrastructure, all the folks being put back to work making Philadelphia a more attractive place for people to do business.

And all across the country, I want us to rebuild our roads and our bridges, our airports. I want us to build broadband lines and high-speed rail and wireless networks so that we have the platform for businesses to succeed all across this country. That's why I'm running for President. We're not going backwards. I want to put people back to work rebuilding America.

I'm running because I believe in America's energy future. Since I've been President, oil production, up, natural gas production, up, oil imports, down under 50 percent. So we have focused on traditional sources of energy, but we've also doubled fuel efficiency standards on cars. We've also doubled the production of clean energy. I want us to control our own energy future, and we can put people back to work in the process. And that's why I'm running for President of the United States of America, because I believe we can achieve that.

And I'm running for President because I want to do something about our debt and our deficits in a balanced and responsible way. And that is as sharp a contrast as we've got between my approach and what Republicans are peddling right now. And I think this is worth focusing on. They think somehow they've got a winner on this issue. Let's talk about the facts here.

Remember, when the last Democratic President was in office, we had a surplus. By the time I got into office, we had a $1 trillion deficit because of tax cuts that weren't paid for, two wars that weren't paid for, a prescription drug plan that was not paid for. We had baked into the cake structural deficits that were made even worse by the financial crisis.

And so for these folks suddenly to get religion—[*laughter*]—and say, man, deficits and Government spending—when they ran up the tab and are trying to pass off the bill to me—[*laughter*]—listen, let me tell you something. Even after you factor in all the work that we did to prevent us from slipping into a depression, the pace of growth of Government spending is lower under my administration than it has been in the last 50 years.

The two Presidents with the least growth in Government spending in the modern era happen to be two Democrats named Barack Obama and Bill Clinton. It wasn't the other guys. And now you've got Mr. Romney proposing a $5 trillion tax cut. And he doesn't detail how it would be paid for, but if you go through the possibilities, then one of two things: either it's not paid for, in which case, that's $5 trillion that's piled on top of the debt we already have, passed onto the next generation, or it's going to come from middle class families all across this country. Those are the only two possibilities.

And I'm running for President because we're not going to let that happen. We are not going to allow another millionaires' tax cut to result in cuts in basic research and science, and cuts in Head Start programs, and less help to States and cities who are putting folks back to work. We're not going to have poor and disabled and seniors who rely on Medicaid having to bear the brunt for another millionaires' tax cut. We're not going to voucherize Medicare.

We've got to do something about the debt and deficits, and the way to do it is by making sure that, yes, we go after waste in Government. Not every Government program works. Not every proposal or program or policy the Government offers is ideal. But what we do

have to make sure of is that we do it in a balanced way. So, even as we're paring back on things that don't work—and I've already signed $2 trillion of cuts into law already and have proposed $2 trillion in additional deficit reduction—even as we're making sensible cuts, even as we're reforming our health care system to make sure that the dollars we pay actually make us healthier, what we're not going to do is to make the most vulnerable people in our society, as well as the middle class, shoulder the burden. We're going to ask those like myself who are best equipped to help to do their fair share because that's part of the American bargain. Everybody gets a fair shot. Everybody does their fair share. Everybody plays by the same set of rules.

That's what we mean when we say we're going forward. We're not going to relitigate Wall Street reform. That was the right thing to do. We're not going to relitigate health care reform. It was the right thing to do; 2.5 million young people who can stay on their parent's plan and now have health insurance who didn't otherwise have it. That was the right thing to do. Millions of seniors getting discounts on their prescription drugs, that was the right thing to do. Health care prevention and women being able to control their own health care decisions, that was the right thing to do. We're not going backwards, we're going forward.

In 2008, I said I'd end the war in Iraq. I ended it. In 2008, I said we'd go after Al Qaida. And bin Laden is no longer a threat to this country and Al Qaida is on its heels. We are transitioning in Afghanistan, and by 2014, we have set a timeline, that war will be over. And we are going to use the savings that we get from ending these wars. Half of it will go to deficit reduction; the other half, we'll put to work rebuilding America, because this is the nation we need to build. That's what I mean when I say we're moving forward.

We're not going to go back to the days when you couldn't serve in the military just because of who you love. "Don't ask, don't tell" was bad for America's security, and it was wrong, and we believe in the fairness and dignity and equality of all people. We're moving forward. We're not going backwards.

We want to move forward and make sure that elections aren't just about $10 million checks being written by folks who have vested interests in maintaining the status quo. We want to move forward to make sure that we're creating an immigration system that reflects our tradition as a nation of laws and a nation of immigrants. Look, we are at our best when every voice is heard, when everybody has a stake. And that's not just a Democratic tradition. That is an American tradition. That's a tradition started by folks like Benjamin Franklin. That's the essence of our creed.

If you look at our history, when we've made progress we've done it together. That's how this country got built. That's how my grandfather's generation was educated on a GI bill. That's how we built the Hoover Dam. That's how we sent a man to the Moon. We believe in individual initiative and the free market. We believe in entrepreneurs and risk takers being rewarded. We love folks getting rich—[*laughter*]—that's part of America's success.

But we also understand there are some things we do together as a nation. That's the true lesson of our history. And that's the choice that we face in this election.

Now, let me tell you, this election is going to be close, because folks have gone through a tough time. And no matter how many times you tell them, well, we avoided a whole bunch of really bad stuff, if you don't have a job, if your house is still underwater, if you haven't seen your income go up in a decade, you're still frustrated. You're still concerned about your kid's future. And rightly so.

And the other side, they don't have any new ideas. I am telling you, I want you all to pay attention over the next 5 months and see if they're offering a single thing that they did not try when they were in charge, because you won't see it. It will be the same stuff. The same okeydoke. [*Laughter*] But you know what they do have is they'll have $500 million worth of negative ads. And they will tap into and feed into cynicism and a sense of frustration. And

they'll try to direct blame. That's a campaign they know how to run.

The thing is, though, what you guys taught me in 2008 was when Americans, when citizens decide to come together, when they say, it's time for change, when they start talking to their neighbors and their friends and they're really starting to pay attention in terms of who's saying what and asking themselves, how do we move this country forward, when you decide change needs to happen, guess what, it happens. It happens.

And so I have never been more convinced about the strength and the dignity of the American people. I've never been more convinced about our prospects for the future, and the reason is because of you.

As I travel all across this country, the American people constantly give me hope. They constantly give me cause for optimism. I still believe in you. And I told you back in 2008 that I wouldn't be—I wasn't a perfect man. Michelle would tell you that. [*Laughter*] And I wouldn't—I'd never be a perfect President, but I did say I'd always tell you what I thought and I'd always tell you where I stood. And I promised you I would wake up every single day thinking about how I can work as hard as I know how, to make your lives a little bit better and to make the lives of future generations a little bit better. And you know what? I've kept that promise.

And so I hope you still believe in me. And if you're ready to go out there and work, if you're ready to join me and make phone calls and knock on doors, talk to your friends and talk to your neighbors, if you're willing to work even harder than you did in 2008, we'll finish what we started. We will move this country forward, and we'll remind the world just why it is the United States of America is the greatest nation on Earth.

Thank you, everybody. God bless you. God bless America.

NOTE: The President spoke at 7:30 p.m. at the Franklin Institute. In his remarks, he referred to Republican Presidential candidate former Gov. W. Mitt Romney of Massachusetts.

Remarks at an Obama Victory Fund 2012 Fundraiser in Philadelphia
June 12, 2012

Thank you. Everybody, please have a seat. First of all, let me just thank David for all of his extraordinary efforts. There are a lot of long-time, hardcore supporters in this room, but David has been tireless, and Ruth has put up with him in support of my campaign back when people couldn't pronounce my name. And so I just couldn't be more grateful to them, and I just want to acknowledge all your leadership on this.

I also want to acknowledge a couple of other extraordinary leaders—your outstanding mayor, Michael Nutter, who is here. One of my best friends in Washington or anywhere, Bob Casey is in the house. He's around here somewhere. And we have with us soon-to-be attorney general of the great State of Pennsylvania, Kathleen King [Kane],° who is here.

And all of you are here. And so because you are here I don't want to spend a lot of time giving a long speech—I just gave one—and many of you have had the chance to hear me in larger settings before. I want to take advantage of this more intimate setting so that we can have more of a conversation.

Those numbers David provided are a good starting point for what this election is all about. I am very proud of the record and what we've done in this administration during as challenging a time as we've experienced in this country's history. But this election ultimately is also going to be about where we go from here, because as much progress as we've made, we've still got a lot of work to do. There's still too many people who are out of work, too many homes underwater, and middle class families still don't have confidence that the future for their kids and their grandkids are going to be brighter than their futures have been.

And so the question in this election is going to be, whose vision is more likely to create that basic bargain, to affirm that basic bargain that made America the economic superpower and the greatest country on Earth? And that bargain says that if you work hard in this country, regardless of what you look like, where you come from, what faith you hold, who you love, that you can make it if you try.

The question in this election is going to be, whose vision is most likely to lead us back to a point where economic growth is strong and is steady and is broad based so that people who are willing to take initiative and work hard can succeed; that we're not just a nation of consumers, but we're a nation of producers; that we're not just importing, but we're exporting; that we're a magnet for good, well-paying, middle class jobs in this society?

And the choices in this election could not be starker. I said before, back in 2008, I had some strong disagreements with John McCain, but there were certain baselines that we both agreed on. We both agreed on things like immigration reform. We agreed on the existence of climate change. We agreed on the need to control campaign finance spending.

This time out, across the board, there is just a fundamental disagreement, a difference of vision in terms of where we want to go. And Governor Romney's vision is pretty much in sync with the vision of the House Republican Party right now, and it can be described basically with two ideas. One is that we need to slash taxes even more, particularly for the wealthiest, most successful among us. And two, we need to eliminate any kind of regulations, whether consumer or worker regulations or environmental regulations, that in any way impede the free market from operating however it will.

And the vision that I'm presenting in this campaign is consistent with what we talked about in 2008, and what I'm going to continue to talk about, and that we put into practice over the last 3½ years, and that says: Government can't solve every one of our problems, and it shouldn't try; that there are some Government programs that don't work and should be end-

---

° White House correction.

ed; and there are some things that have to be done at a local level, but there are also some things that we have to do together.

We have to invest in an education system that ensures we have the strongest, most skilled workforce on Earth. We have to invest together in things like basic research and science to ensure that we continue to innovate. Together, we've got to make sure that we continue to build the infrastructure for the 21st century, whether it's basics like roads and bridges, or it's things like broadband lines and improved Internet access and the kinds of things that will ensure that we're a platform for success for businesses coming from all around the world.

Together, we've got to make sure that we reduce our debt and our deficit in a balanced way, where everybody is doing their fair share, so that we're not just relying on cuts to programs for the vulnerable or for our kids, but we're also asking those of us who have been incredibly blessed to be born in this country, for us to give a little back and to think about the future.

And that's really what this election is going to come down to: Whose vision is more consistent with our history and those moments when we've been most successful as a country? And I think history is on our side and the facts are on our side. When you think of recent history, when did we grow fastest? It was when Bill Clinton decided we're going to raise taxes a little bit, close our deficit in a responsible way, make investments in the future. Prior to that, when did we grow fastest? In the postwar consensus, when the middle class was getting a decent wage and we began to invest in our infrastructure and our schools and our public colleges and universities and basic research and basic

science and things like environmental protection and worker safety laws. Those didn't impede our growth, they accelerated our growth.

And so I am looking forward to having this debate, and it's a debate that this country needs to have. Because I know a lot of folks are frustrated by gridlock. Well, the reason we've got gridlock is there is just an honest disagreement about how we need to move this country forward. And I'm looking forward to taking that debate to the American people. And the good news is, I think the American people agree with us. They're not following, as David said, the ups and downs, the ins and outs of this campaign. But they do have a sense of what's true, and they have pretty good instincts about what works. And they're not persuaded that an economy built on the notion that everybody here is on their own is somehow going to result in a stronger, more prosperous America.

So our job is just to make sure that we get that message out, that the facts are presented fairly, that we push back against misinformation. But if we can just have a straight, honest, clear debate about the choices presented, then not only are we going to win this election, but more importantly, we're going to keep this country moving forward.

So thank you very much, everybody.

NOTE: The President spoke at 8:34 p.m. at Fels Planetarium. In his remarks, he referred to David L. Cohen, executive vice president, Comcast Corp., and his wife Rhonda; Sen. Robert P. Casey, Jr.; Sen. John S. McCain III, in his capacity as the 2008 Republican Presidential nominee; and Republican Presidential candidate former Gov. W. Mitt Romney of Massachusetts. Audio was not available for verification of the content of these remarks.

Remarks at Kenny's BBQ Smoke House
June 13, 2012

[*The President's remarks were joined in progress.*]

——these guys are also young fathers, and they're doing a great job. He's got four kids.

He's got two. And Michelle and I have been working a lot with military families, trying to support them. When these guys are deployed, sometimes they're leaving the family behind, and we want to make sure they get support.

And then the reason the two older gentlemen are here is, as I was mentioning, barbershops are where a lot of men still come, and we want to work with them—we want to work with barbershops to figure out how we can get better information to fathers about resources that are available to them, where they can find job training programs, they can find support groups for fathers. Because the more information we're getting out there to folks about how they can take responsibility for their kids, make sure that they're in their child's lives, help support their mother even if they're not living with the mother—it makes a huge difference.

It turns out that with the father being involved, the kids are less likely to do drugs, they're less likely to—girls are less likely to have teen pregnancy. And so that message is something that we want to make sure gets out there. And barbershops are a good place to do it, so—because that's where everybody has to come, right?

So the—although I was teasing these guys, cutting their hair wouldn't be that complicated. [*Laughter*] You just take a—[*laughter*]. Isn't that right? I was just saying you got to give these guys a discount if they come in for a haircut, because that will only take 5 minutes. [*Laughter*]

So all right, guys, thank you. Let—we're going to eat in peace now.

NOTE: The President spoke at 12:26 p.m. In his remarks, he referred to 1st Lt. William Edwards, USA, and his children David, Jacob, Elana, and Luke; Capt. Joubert Paulino, USA, and his children Jonah and Julia; and barbers Otis Gamble and Nurney Mason of Washington, DC.

Remarks on Presenting the Presidential Medal of Freedom to President Shimon Peres of Israel
June 13, 2012

Good evening, everybody. Please have a seat. On behalf of Michelle and myself, welcome to the White House on this beautiful summer evening.

The United States is fortunate to have many allies and partners around the world. Of course, one of our strongest allies, and one of our closest friends, is the State of Israel. And no individual has done so much over so many years to build our alliance and to bring our two nations closer as the leader that we honor tonight, our friend Shimon Peres.

Among many special guests this evening we are especially grateful for the presence of Shimon's children—Zvia, Yoni, and Chemi—and their families. Please rise so we can give you a big round of applause.

We have here someone representing a family that has given so much for peace, a voice for peace that carries on with the legacy of her father Yitzhak Rabin, and that's Dalia. We are grateful to have you here. Leaders who've helped ensure that the United States is a partner for peace—and in particular, I'm so pleased to see Secretary Madeleine Albright, who is here this evening; and one of the great moral voices of our time and an inspiration to us all, Professor Elie Wiesel.

The man, the life that we honor tonight is nothing short of extraordinary. Shimon took on his first assignment in Ben-Gurion's Haganah, during the struggle for Israeli independence in 1947, when he was still in his early twenties. He ran for President of Israel, and won, when he was 83. [*Laughter*]

By the way, I should mention that I just learned that his son-in-law is also his doctor. And I asked for all his tips. [*Laughter*]

Shimon has been serving his nation, and strengthening the bonds between our two nations, for some 65 years, the entire life of the State of Israel. Ben-Gurion and Meir, Begin and Rabin, these giants of Israel's founding generation now belong to the ages. But tonight we have the rare privilege in history, and that's to be in the presence of a true founding father.

Shimon, you have never stopped serving. And in 2 months, we'll join our Israeli friends in marking another milestone, your 89th birthday.

Now, I think Shimon would be the first to tell you that in the ups and downs of Israeli politics, he has been counted out more than once. But in him we see the essence of Israel itself, an indomitable spirit that will not be denied. He's persevered, serving in virtually every position: in dozens of Cabinets, some two dozen ministerial posts, Defense Minister, Finance Minister, Foreign Minister three times—try that, Madeleine—[*laughter*]—and now, the ninth President of Israel. And I think President Clinton would agree with me on this: Shimon Peres is the ultimate "comeback kid." [*Laughter*]

And he's still going—on Facebook, on YouTube—[*laughter*]—connecting with young people, looking to new technologies, always facing tomorrow. Recently, he was asked, "What do you want your legacy to be?" And Shimon replied, "Well, it's too early for me to think about it." [*Laughter*]

Shimon, you earned your place in history long ago. And I know your work is far from done. But tonight is another example of how it's never too early for the rest of us to celebrate your legendary life.

Shimon teaches us to never settle for the world as it is. We have a vision for the world as it ought to be, and we have to strive for it. Perhaps Shimon's spirit comes from what he calls the Jewish "dissatisfaction gene." [*Laughter*] "A good Jew," he says, "can never be satisfied." There is a constant impulse to question, to do even better. So too with nations, we must keep challenging ourselves, keep striving for our ideals, for the future that we know is possible.

Shimon knows the necessity of strength. As Ben-Gurion said, "An Israel capable of defending herself, which cannot be destroyed, can bring peace nearer." And so he's worked with every American President since John F. Kennedy. That's why I've worked with Prime Minister Netanyahu to ensure that the security cooperation between the United States and Israel is closer and stronger than it has ever been,

because the security of the State of Israel is non-negotiable, and the bonds between us are unbreakable.

Of course, Shimon also knows that a nation's security depends not just on the strength of its arms, but upon the righteousness of its deeds, its moral compass. He knows, as Scripture teaches, that we must not only seek peace, but we must pursue peace. And so it has been the cause of his life: peace, security, and dignity for Israelis and Palestinians and all Israel's Arab neighbors. And even in the darkest moments, he's never lost hope in, as he puts it, "a Middle East that is not a killing field, but a field of creativity and growth."

At times, some have seen his hope and called Shimon Peres a dreamer. And they are right. Just look at his life. The dream of generations, after 2,000 years, to return to Israel, the historic homeland of the Jewish people, Shimon lived it. The dream of independence, a Jewish State of Israel, he helped win it. The dream of an Israel strong enough to defend itself, by itself, against any threat, backed by an ironclad alliance with the United States of America, he helped build it.

The dream of making the desert bloom, he and his wife Sonya were part of the generation that achieved it. The dream of the high-tech Israel we see today, he helped spark it. That historic handshake on the White House lawn, he helped to create it. That awful night in Tel Aviv, when he and Yitzhak sang a song for peace, and the grief that followed, he guided his people through it. The dream of democracy in the Middle East and the hopes of a new generation, including so many young Arabs, he knows we must welcome it and nurture it.

So yes, Shimon Peres—born in a *shtetl* in what was then Poland, who rose to become President of Israel—he is a dreamer. And rightly so. For he knows what we must never forget: With faith in ourselves and courage in our hearts, no dream is too big, no vision is beyond our reach.

And so it falls on each of us—to all of us—to keep searching, to keep striving for that future that we know is possible, for the peace our children deserve.

And so it is a high honor for me to bestow this statesman, this warrior for peace, America's highest civilian honor, the Presidential Medal of Freedom. And I'd ask you to please join me in welcoming President Peres to the presentation.

[*At this point, Lt. Cmdr. John F. McCarthy, USCG, Coast Guard Aide to the President, read the citation, and the President presented the medal.*]

Before inviting remarks from President Peres, I'd like to conclude by inviting you all to join me in a toast, with the words that Shimon spoke when he accepted the Peace Prize in Oslo:

"From my earliest youth, I have known that while one is obliged to plan with care the stages of one's journey, one is entitled to dream, and keep dreaming, of its destination. A man may feel as old as his years, yet as young as his dreams."

Shimon, to all our friends here tonight and to our fellow citizens across America and Israel, may we never lose sight of our destination. Shalom, and may we always be as young as our dreams.

[*A toast was offered.*]

L'chaim. Cheers.

I have one last order of business to attend to. Before I ask our recipient to come to the stage—while I began my remarks, I was not yet sure whether one more—or two more guests of honor had arrived. I think it would be entirely appropriate at this point for us also to acknowledge two people who have constantly sought to achieve peace, not only in the Middle East, but all around the world—one of them happens to be traveling a lot these days on my behalf—[*laughter*]—and I am extraordinarily grateful to them. Shimon, I know that you're pleased to have two very dear friends to help celebrate this evening: President Bill Clinton and our outstanding Secretary of State, Hillary Clinton.

Ladies and gentlemen, President Shimon Peres.

NOTE: The President spoke at 7:12 p.m. in the East Room at the White House. In his remarks, he referred to Zvia and Raphael Walden, daughter and son-in-law, and Yoni and Nehemia "Chemi" Peres, sons, of President Peres; former Secretary of State Madeleine K. Albright; and Nobel Prize winner, author, and Holocaust survivor Elie Wiesel. The transcript released by the Office of the Press Secretary also included the remarks of President Peres.

Remarks at Cuyahoga Community College in Cleveland, Ohio
June 14, 2012

The President. Thank you! Thank you, everybody. Good afternoon, everybody. It is great to be back in Cleveland. It is great to be back here at Cuyahoga Community College.

I want to, first of all, thank Angela for her introduction and sharing her story. I know her daughter is very proud of her; I know her daughter is here today. So give her a big round of applause. I want to thank your president, Dr. Jerry Sue Thornton. And I want to thank some Members of Congress who made the trip today: Representative Marcia Fudge, Representative Betty Sutton, and Representative Marcy Kaptur.

Now, those of you who have a seat, feel free to sit down. [*Laughter*]
Audience member. We love you!
The President. Thank you.
Audience members. Four more years! Four more years! Four more years!
The President. Thank you.
So, Ohio, over the next 5 months, this election will take many twists and many turns. Polls will go up, and polls will go down. There will be no shortage of gaffes and controversies that keep both campaigns busy and give the press something to write about. You may have heard, I recently made my own unique contribution

to that process. [*Laughter*] It wasn't the first time; it won't be the last. [*Laughter*]

And in the coming weeks, Governor Romney and I will spend time debating our records and our experience, as we should. But though we will have many differences over the course of this campaign, there's one place where I stand in complete agreement with my opponent: This election is about our economic future.

Yes, foreign policy matters. Social issues matter. But more than anything else, this election presents a choice between two fundamentally different visions of how to create strong, sustained growth, how to pay down our long-term debt, and most of all, how to generate good, middle class jobs so people can have confidence that if they work hard, they can get ahead.

Now, this isn't some abstract debate. This is not another trivial Washington argument. I have said that this is the defining issue of our time, and I mean it. I said that this is a make-or-break moment for America's middle class, and I believe it. The decisions we make in the next few years on everything from debt and taxes to energy and education will have an enormous impact on this country and on the country we pass on to our children.

Now, these challenges are not new. We've been wrestling with these issues for a long time. The problems we're facing right now have been more than a decade in the making. And what is holding us back is not a lack of big ideas. It isn't a matter of finding the right technical solution. Both parties have laid out their policies on the table for all to see. What's holding us back is a stalemate in Washington between two fundamentally different views of which direction America should take. And this election is your chance to break that stalemate.

At stake is not simply a choice between two candidates or two political parties, but between two paths for our country. And while there are many things to discuss in this campaign, nothing is more important than an honest debate about where these two paths would lead us.

Now, that debate starts with an understanding of where we are and how we got here.

Long before the economic crisis of 2008, the basic bargain at the heart of this country had begun to erode. For more than a decade, it had become harder to find a job that paid the bills, harder to save, harder to retire, harder to keep up with rising costs of gas and health care and college tuitions. You know that; you lived it.

During that decade, there was a specific theory in Washington about how to meet this challenge. We were told that huge tax cuts, especially for the wealthiest Americans, would lead to faster job growth. We were told that fewer regulations, especially for big financial institutions and corporations, would bring about widespread prosperity. We were told that it was okay to put two wars on the Nation's credit card, that tax cuts would create enough growth to pay for themselves. That's what we were told. So how did this economic theory work out?

For the wealthiest Americans, it worked out pretty well. Over the last few decades, the income of the top 1 percent grew by more than 275 percent to an average of $1.3 million a year. Big financial institutions, corporations saw their profits soar. But prosperity never trickled down to the middle class.

From 2001 to 2008, we had the slowest job growth in half a century. The typical family saw their incomes fall. The failure to pay for the tax cuts and the wars took us from record surpluses under President Bill Clinton to record deficits. And it left us unprepared to deal with the retirement of an aging population that's placing a greater strain on programs like Medicare and Social Security.

Without strong enough regulations, families were enticed, and sometimes tricked, into buying homes they couldn't afford. Banks and investors were allowed to package and sell risky mortgages. Huge, reckless bets were made with other people's money on the line. And too many from Wall Street to Washington simply looked the other way.

For a while, credit cards and home equity loans papered over the reality of this new economy, people borrowed money to keep up. But the growth that took place during this time period turned out to be a house of cards. And in the fall of 2008, it all came tumbling down with a financial crisis that plunged the world into the worst economic crisis since the Great Depression.

Here in America, families' wealth declined at a rate nearly seven times faster than when the market crashed in 1929. Millions of homes were foreclosed. Our deficit soared. And 9 million of our citizens lost their jobs: 9 million hard-working Americans who had met their responsibilities, but were forced to pay for the irresponsibility of others.

In other words, this was not your normal recession. Throughout history, it has typically taken countries up to 10 years to recover from financial crises of this magnitude. Today, the economies of many European countries still aren't growing, and their unemployment rate averages around 11 percent.

But here in the United States, Americans showed their grit and showed their determination. We acted fast. Our economy started growing again 6 months after I took office, and it has continued to grow for the last 3 years.

Our businesses have gone back to basics and created over 4 million jobs in the last 27 months—more private sector jobs than were created during the entire 7 years before this crisis—in a little over 2 years.

Manufacturers have started investing in America again, including right here in Ohio. And across America, we've seen them create almost 500,000 jobs in the last 27 months, the strongest period of manufacturing job growth since 1995.

And when my opponents and others were arguing that we should let Detroit go bankrupt, we made a bet on American workers and the ingenuity of American companies. And today, our auto industry is back on top of the world.

But let's be clear: Not only are we digging out of a hole that is 9 million jobs deep, we're digging out from an entire decade where 6 million manufacturing jobs left our shores; where costs rose, but incomes and wages didn't; and where the middle class fell further and further behind.

So recovering from the crisis of 2008 has always been the first and most urgent order of business, but it's not enough. Our economy won't be truly healthy until we reverse that much longer and profound erosion of middle class jobs and middle class incomes.

So the debate in this election is not about whether we need to grow faster or whether we need to create more jobs or whether we need to pay down our debt. Of course, the economy isn't where it needs to be. Of course, we have a lot more work to do. Everybody knows that. The debate in this election is about how we grow faster and how we create more jobs and how we pay down our debt. That's the question facing the American voter. And in this election, you have two very different visions to choose from.

Governor Romney and his allies in Congress believe deeply in the theory that we tried during the last decade: the theory that the best way to grow the economy is from the top down. So they maintain that if we eliminate most regulations, if we cut taxes by trillions of dollars, if we strip down Government to national security and a few other basic functions, then the power of businesses to create jobs and prosperity will be unleashed, and that will automatically benefit us all.

That's what they believe. This is their economic plan. It has been placed before Congress. Governor Romney has given speeches about it, and it's on his website. So, if they win the election, their agenda will be simple and straightforward. They have spelled it out: They promise to roll back regulations on banks and polluters, on insurance companies and oil companies. They'll roll back regulations designed to protect consumers and workers. They promise to not only keep all of the Bush tax cuts in place, but add another $5 trillion in tax cuts on top of that.

Now, an independent study says that about 70 percent of this new, $5 trillion tax cut would go to folks making over $200,000 a year. And folks making over a million dollars a year would get an average tax cut of about 25 percent.

Now, this is not my opinion. This is not political spin. This is precisely what they have proposed.

Now, your next question may be, how do you spend $5 trillion on a tax cut and still bring down the deficit? Well, they tell us they'll start by cutting nearly a trillion dollars from the part of our budget that includes everything from education and job training to medical research and clean energy.

Now, I want to be very fair here. I want to be clear. They haven't specified exactly where the knife would fall. But here's some of what would happen if that cut that they've proposed was spread evenly across the budget: 10 million college students would lose an average of $1,000 each in financial aid; 200,000 children would lose the chance to get an early education in the Head Start program. There would be 1,600 fewer medical research grants for things like Alzheimer's and cancer and AIDS, 4,000 fewer scientific research grants, eliminating support for 48,000 researchers, students and teachers.

Now, again, they have not specified which of these cuts they choose from. But if they want to make smaller cuts to areas like science or medical research, then they'd have to cut things like financial aid or education even further. But either way, the cuts to this part of the budget would be deeper than anything we've ever seen in modern times.

Not only does their plan eliminate health insurance for 33 million Americans by repealing the Affordable Care Act, according to the independent Kaiser Family Foundation, it would also take away coverage from another 19 million Americans who rely on Medicaid, including millions of nursing home patients and families who have children with autism and other disabilities. And they proposed turning Medicare into a voucher program, which will shift more costs to seniors and eventually end the program as we know it.

But it doesn't stop there. Even if you make all the cuts that they've proposed, the math still doesn't allow you to pay for a new, $5 trillion tax cut and bring down the deficit at the same time. So Mr. Romney and his allies have told us we can get the rest of the way there by reforming the Tax Code and taking away certain tax breaks and deductions that, again, they ha-

ven't specified. They haven't named them, but they said we can do it.

But here's the problem: The only tax breaks and deductions that get you anywhere close to $5 trillion are those that help middle class families afford health care and college and retirement and homeownership. Without those tax benefits, tens of millions of middle class families will end up paying higher taxes. Many of you would end up paying higher taxes to pay for this other tax cut.

And keep in mind that all of this is just to pay for their new $5 trillion tax cut. If you want to close the deficit left by the Bush tax cuts, we'd have to make deeper cuts or raise middle class taxes even more.

This is not spin. This is not my opinion. These are facts. This is what they're presenting as their plan. This is their vision. There is nothing new, just what Bill Clinton has called the same ideas they've tried before, except on steroids. [*Laughter*]

Now, I understand I've got a lot of supporters here, but I want to speak to everybody who's watching who may not be a supporter, may be undecided, or thinking about voting the other way. If you agree with the approach I just described, if you want to give the policies of the last decade another try, then you should vote for Mr. Romney.

Audience members. Boo!

The President. Now, like I said, I know I've got supporters here. No, no, you should vote for his allies in Congress.

Audience members. No!

The President. You should take them at their word, and they will take America down this path. And Mr. Romney is qualified to deliver on that plan. [*Laughter*] No, he is. I'm giving you an honest presentation of what he's proposing.

Now, I'm looking forward to the press following up and making sure that you know I'm not exaggerating.

I believe their approach is wrong. And I'm not alone. I have not seen a single independent analysis that says my opponent's economic plan would actually reduce the deficit. Not one. Even analysts who may agree with parts of his economic theory don't believe that his plan would create more jobs in the short term. They don't claim his plan would help folks looking for work right now.

In fact, just the other week, one economist from Moody's said the following about Mr. Romney's plan—and I'm quoting here—"On net, all of these policies would do more harm in the short term. If we implemented all of his policies, it would push us deeper into recession and make the recovery slower."

That's not my spin. That's not my opinion. That's what independent economic analysis says.

As for the long term, remember that the economic vision of Mr. Romney and his allies in Congress was tested just a few years ago. We tried this. Their policies did not grow the economy. They did not grow the middle class. They did not reduce our debt. Why would we think that they would work better this time?

We can't afford to jeopardize our future by repeating the mistakes of the past, not now, not when there's so much at stake.

I've got a different vision for America. I believe that you can't bring down the debt without a strong and growing economy. And I believe you can't have a strong and growing economy without a strong and growing middle class.

This has to be our north star: an economy that's built not from the top down, but from a growing middle class, that provides ladders of opportunity for folks who aren't yet in the middle class.

You see, we'll never be able to compete with some countries when it comes to paying workers lower wages or letting companies do more polluting. That's a race to the bottom that we should not want to win. Because those countries don't have a strong middle class; they don't have our standard of living.

The race I want us to win—the race I know we can win—is a race to the top. I see an America with the best educated, best trained workers in the world, an America with a commitment to research and development that is second to none, especially when it comes to new sources of energy and high-tech manufac-

turing. I see a country that offers businesses the fastest, most reliable transportation and communication systems of anywhere on Earth.

I see a future where we pay down our deficit in a way that is balanced, not by placing the entire burden on the middle class and the poor, but by cutting out programs we can't afford and asking the wealthiest Americans to contribute their fair share.

That's my vision for America: education, energy, innovation, infrastructure, and a Tax Code focused on American job creation and balanced deficit reduction.

This is the vision behind the jobs plan I sent Congress back in September, a bill filled with bipartisan ideas that, according to independent economists, would create up to 1 million additional jobs if passed today.

This is the vision behind the deficit plan I sent to Congress back in September, a detailed proposal that would reduce our deficit by $4 trillion through shared sacrifice and shared responsibility.

This is the vision I intend to pursue in my second term as President, because I believe——

Audience members. Four more years! Four more years! Four more years!

The President. Because I believe if we do these things, if we do these things, more companies will start here and stay here and hire here and more Americans will be able to find jobs that support a middle class lifestyle.

Understand, despite what you hear from my opponent, this has never been a vision about how Government creates jobs or has the answers to all our problems. Over the last 3 years, I've cut taxes for the typical working family by $3,600. I've cut taxes for small businesses 18 times. I have approved fewer regulations in the first 3 years of my Presidency than my Republican predecessor did in his. And I'm implementing over 500 reforms to fix regulations that were costing folks too much for no reason.

I've asked Congress for the authority to reorganize the Federal Government that was built for the last century. I want to make it work for the 21st century, a Federal Government that is leaner and more efficient and more responsive to the American people.

I've signed a law that cuts spending and reduces our deficit by $2 trillion. My own deficit plan would strengthen Medicare and Medicaid for the long haul by slowing the growth of health care costs, not shifting them to seniors and vulnerable families. And my plan would reduce our yearly domestic spending to its lowest level as a share of the economy in nearly 60 years.

So no, I don't believe the Government is the answer to all our problems. I don't believe every regulation is smart or that every tax dollar is spent wisely. I don't believe that we should be in the business of helping people who refuse to help themselves. But I do share the belief of our first Republican President, from my home State—Abraham Lincoln—that through government, we should do together what we cannot do as well for ourselves.

That's how we built this country, together. We constructed railroads and highways, the Hoover Dam and the Golden Gate Bridge. We did those things together. We sent my grandfather's generation to college on the GI bill, together. We instituted a minimum wage and rules that protected people's bank deposits, together.

Together, we touched the surface of the Moon, unlocked the mystery of the atom, connected the world through our own science and imagination.

We haven't done these things as Democrats or Republicans. We've done them as Americans.

As much as we might associate the GI bill with Franklin Roosevelt or Medicare with Lyndon Johnson, it was a Republican—Lincoln—who launched the transcontinental railroad, the National Academy of Sciences, land-grant colleges. It was a Republican—Eisenhower—who launched the Interstate Highway System and a new era of scientific research. It was Nixon who created the Environmental Protection Agency, Reagan who worked with Democrats to save Social Security and who, by the way, raised taxes to help pay down an exploding deficit.

Yes, there have been fierce arguments throughout our history between both parties about the exact size and role of Government,

some honest disagreements. But in the decades after World War II, there was a general consensus that the market couldn't solve all of our problems on its own; that we needed certain investments to give hard-working Americans skills they needed to get a good job and entrepreneurs the platforms they needed to create good jobs; that we needed consumer protections that made American products safe and American markets sound.

In the last century, this consensus, this shared vision, led to the strongest economic growth and the largest middle class that the world has ever known. It led to a shared prosperity.

It is this vision that has guided all my economic policies during my first term as President, whether in the design of a health care law that relies on private insurance or an approach to Wall Street reform that encourages financial innovation, but guards against reckless risk-taking. It's this vision that Democrats and Republicans used to share that Mr. Romney and the current Republican Congress have rejected in favor of a no-holds-barred, government-is-the-enemy, market-is-everything approach.

And it is this shared vision that I intend to carry forward in this century as President, because it is a vision that has worked for the American middle class and everybody who's striving to get into the middle class.

Let me be more specific. Think about it. In an age where we know good jobs depend on high skills, now is not the time to scale back our commitment to education. Now is the time to move forward and make sure we have the best educated, best trained workers in the world.

My plan for education doesn't just rely on more money or more dictates from Washington. We're challenging every State and school district to come up with their own innovative plans to raise student achievement. And they're doing just that. I want to give schools more flexibility so that they don't have to teach to the test and so they can remove teachers who just aren't helping our kids learn.

But look, if we want our country to be a magnet for middle class jobs in the 21st century, we also have to invest more in education and training. I want to recruit an army of new teachers and pay teachers better and train more of them in areas like math and science.

I have a plan to give 2 million more Americans the chance to go to community colleges just like this one and learn the skills that businesses are looking for right now. I have a plan to make it easier for people to afford a higher education that's essential in today's economy.

And if we truly want to make this country a destination for talent and ingenuity from all over the world, we won't deport hard-working, responsible young immigrants who have grown up here or received advanced degrees here. We'll let them earn the chance to become American citizens so they can grow our economy and start new businesses right here instead of someplace else.

Now is not the time to go back to a greater reliance on fossil fuels from foreign countries. Now is the time to invest more in the clean energy that we can make right here in America.

My plan for energy doesn't ignore the vast resources we already have in this country. We're producing more oil than we have in over a decade. But if we truly want to gain control of our energy future, we've got to recognize that pumping more oil isn't enough.

We have to encourage the unprecedented boom in American natural gas. We have to provide safe nuclear energy and the technology to help coal burn cleaner than before. We have to become the global leader in renewable energy: wind and solar and the next generation of biofuels, in electric cars and energy-efficient buildings.

So my plan would end the Government subsidies to oil companies that have rarely been more profitable. Let's double down on a clean energy industry that has never been more promising. And I want to put in place a new clean energy standard that creates a market for innovation, an approach that would make clean energy the profitable kind of energy for every business in America.

With growing competition from countries like China and India, now is not the time for America to walk away from research and devel-opment. Now is the time to invest even more so that the great innovations of this century take place in the United States of America so that the next Thomas Edison, the next Wright Brothers is happening here, in Ohio or Michigan or California.

My plan to encourage innovation isn't about throwing money at just any project or new idea. It's about supporting the work of our most promising scientists, our most promising researchers and entrepreneurs.

My plan would make the R&D tax credit permanent. But the private sector can't do it alone, especially when it comes to basic research. It's not always profitable in the short term. And in the last century, research that we funded together through our tax dollars helped lay the foundation for the Internet and GPS and Google and the countless companies and jobs that followed. The private sector came in and created these incredible companies, but we, together, made the initial investment to make it possible.

It's given rise to miraculous cures that have reduced suffering and saved lives. This has always been America's biggest economic advantage: our science and our innovation. Why would we reverse that commitment right now when it's never been more important?

At a time when we have so much deferred maintenance on our Nation's infrastructure—schools that are crumbling, roads that are broken, bridges that are buckling—now is not the time to saddle American businesses with crumbling roads and bridges. Now is the time to rebuild America.

So my plan would take half the money we're no longer spending on war, let's use it to do some nation-building here at home. Let's put some folks to work right here at home.

My plan would get rid of pet projects and Government boondoggles and bridges to nowhere. But if we want businesses to come here and to hire here, we have to provide the highways and the runways and the ports and the broadband access, all of which move goods and products and information across the globe.

My plan sets up an independent fund to attract private dollars and issue loans for new construction projects based on two criteria: how badly are they needed and how much good will they do for the economy.

And finally, I think it's time we took on our fiscal problems in an honest, balanced, responsible way. Everybody agrees that our deficits and debt are an issue that we've got to tackle. My plan to reform the Tax Code recognizes that Government can't bring back every job that's been outsourced or every factory that's closed its doors. But we sure can stop giving tax breaks to businesses that ship jobs overseas and start rewarding companies that create jobs right here in the United States of America: in Ohio, in Cleveland, in Pennsylvania.

And if we want to get the deficit under control—really, not just pretending to during election time—[*laughter*]—not just saying you really care about it when somebody else is in charge, and then you don't care where you're in charge. If you want to really do something about it, if you really want to get the deficit under control without sacrificing all the investments that I've talked about, our Tax Code has to ask the wealthiest Americans to pay a little bit more, just like they did when Bill Clinton was President, just like they did when our economy created 23 million new jobs, the biggest budget surplus in history, and a lot of millionaires to boot.

And here's the good news: There are plenty of patriotic, very successful Americans who'd be willing to make this contribution again.

Look, we have no choice about whether we pay down our deficit. But we do have a choice about how we pay down our deficit. We do have a choice about what we can do without, and where our priorities lie.

I don't believe that giving someone like me a $250,000 tax cut is more valuable to our future than hiring transformative teachers or providing financial aid to the children of a middle class family.

I don't believe that tax cut is more likely to create jobs than providing loans to new entrepreneurs or tax credits to small-business owners who hire veterans. I don't believe it's more likely to spur economic growth than investments in clean energy technology and medical research, or in new roads and bridges and runways.

I don't believe that giving someone like Mr. Romney another huge tax cut is worth ending the guarantee of basic security we've always provided the elderly and the sick and those who are actively looking for work.

Those things don't make our economy weak. What makes our economy weak is when fewer and fewer people can afford to buy the goods and services our businesses sell. Businesses don't have customers if folks are having such a hard time.

What drags us all down is an economy in which there's an ever-widening gap between a few folks who are doing extraordinarily well and a growing number of people who, no matter how hard they work, can barely make ends meet.

So Governor Romney disagrees with my vision. His allies in Congress disagree with my vision. Neither of them will endorse any policy that asks the wealthiest Americans to pay even a nickel more in taxes. It's the reason we haven't reached a grand bargain to bring down our deficit, not with my plan, not with the Bowles-Simpson plan, not with the so-called Gang of Six plan.

Despite the fact that taxes are lower than they've been in decades, they won't work with us on any plan that would increase taxes on our wealthiest Americans. It's the reason a jobs bill that would put 1 million people back to work has been voted down time and time again. It's the biggest source of gridlock in Washington today.

And the only thing that can break the stalemate is you. You see, in our democracy, this remarkable system of government, you, the people, have the final say.

This November is your chance to render a verdict on the debate over how to grow the economy, how to create good jobs, how to pay down our deficit. Your vote will finally determine the path that we take as a nation, not just tomorrow, but for years to come.

When you strip everything else away, that's really what this election is about. That's what is at stake right now. Everything else is just noise. Everything else is just a distraction.

From now until then, both sides will spend tons of money on TV commercials. The other side will spend over a billion dollars on ads that tell you the economy is bad; that it's all my fault; that I can't fix it because I think government is always the answer, or because I didn't make a lot of money in the private sector and don't understand it, or because I'm in over my head, or because I think everything and everybody is doing just fine. That's what the scary voice in the ads will say. That's what Mr. Romney will say. That's what the Republicans in Congress will say.

Well, that may be their plan to win the election, but it's not a plan to create jobs. It's not a plan to grow the economy. It's not a plan to pay down the debt. And it's sure not a plan to revive the middle class and secure our future.

I think you deserve better than that.

At a moment this big—a moment when so many people are still struggling—I think you deserve a real debate about the economic plans we're proposing.

Governor Romney and the Republicans who run Congress believe that if you simply take away regulations and cut taxes by trillions of dollars, the market will solve all of our problems on its own. If you agree with that, you should vote for them. And I promise you they will take us in that direction.

I believe we need a plan for better education and training and for energy independence and for new research and innovation, for rebuilding our infrastructure, for a Tax Code that creates jobs in America and pays down our debt in a way that's balanced. I have that plan. They don't.

And if you agree with me—if you believe this economy grows best when everybody gets a fair shot, and everybody does their fair share, and everybody plays by the same set of rules— then I ask you to stand with me for a second term as President.

In fact, I'll take it a step further. I ask, you vote for anyone else—whether they're Democrats, Independents, or Republicans—who share your view about how America should grow.

I will work with anyone of any party who believes that we're in this together, who believes that we rise or fall as one Nation and as one people. Because I'm convinced that there are actually a lot of Republicans out there who may not agree with every one of my policies, but who still believe in a balanced, responsible approach to economic growth and who remember the lessons of our history and who don't like the direction their leaders are taking them.

And let me leave you with one last thought. As you consider your choice in November, don't let anybody tell you that the challenges we face right now are beyond our ability to solve.

It's hard not to get cynical when times are tough. And I'm reminded every day of just how tough things are for too many Americans. Every day I hear from folks who are out of work or have lost their home. Across this country, I meet people who are struggling to pay their bills or older workers worried about retirement or young people who are underemployed and burdened with debt. I hear their voices when I wake up in the morning, and those voices ring in my head when I lay down to sleep. And in those voices, I hear the echo of my own family's struggles as I was growing up, and Michelle's family's struggles when she was growing up, and the fears and the dashed hopes that our parents and grandparents had to confront.

But you know what, in those voices I also hear a stubborn hope and a fierce pride and a determination to overcome whatever challenges we face. And in you, the American people, I'm reminded of all the things that tilt the future in our favor.

We remain the wealthiest nation on Earth. We have the best workers and entrepreneurs, the best scientists and researchers, the best colleges and universities. We are a young country with the greatest diversity of talent and ingenuity drawn from every corner of the globe. So yes, reforming our schools, rebuilding our infrastructure will take time. Yes, paying down our debt will require some tough choices and shared sacrifice. But it can be done. And we'll be stronger for it.

And what's lacking is not the capacity to meet our challenges. What is lacking is our politics. And that's something entirely within your power to solve. So this November, you can remind the world how a strong economy is built, not from the top down, but from a growing, thriving middle class.

This November, you can remind the world how it is that we've traveled this far as a country, not by telling everybody to fend for themselves, but by coming together as one American family, all of us pitching in, all of us pulling our own weight.

This November, you can provide a mandate for the change we need right now. You can move this Nation forward. And you can remind the world once again why the United States of America is still the greatest nation on Earth.

Thank you. God bless you. God bless the United States of America. Thank you.

NOTE: The President spoke at 2:02 p.m. In his remarks, he referred to North Olmsted, OH, resident Angela Schafer and her daughter Megan; Republican Presidential candidate former Gov. W. Mitt Romney of Massachusetts; Mark M. Zandi, chief economist, Moody's Analytics; Erskine B. Bowles and Alan K. Simpson, Cochairs, National Commission on Fiscal Responsibility and Reform; and Sens. Saxby C. Chambliss, Thomas A. Coburn, G. Kent Conrad, Michael D. Crapo, Richard J. Durbin, and Mark R. Warner.

Statement on Senate Confirmation of Maria del Carmen Aponte as the United States Ambassador to El Salvador
June 14, 2012

Ambassador Mari Carmen Aponte has been a highly effective advocate for the United States in El Salvador, earning respect from across the political spectrum, from civilians and military leaders, and from public and private officials. As an honest broker, she has helped advance programs and policies to enhance citizen security in El Salvador, while weakening transnational crime links that affect our own national security. Ambassador Aponte has also been a strong voice for democratic governance throughout the region. She should have never been forced to leave her post. I am grateful to Ambassador Aponte for her service and for the hard work that took place alongside our partners in the U.S. Senate, in particular Majority Leader Harry Reid and Senator Robert Menendez, to achieve her confirmation. Today's vote is a testament to the value of perseverance and a reminder that our national security must be bigger than politics and that Congress can still do the right thing. I look forward to continuing to work with Ambassador Aponte to build on our partnership with the people of El Salvador and advance our partnerships throughout the Americas.

Letter to Congressional Leaders on Continuation of the National Emergency With Respect to the Actions and Policies of Certain Members of the Government of Belarus and Other Persons To Undermine Belarus Democratic Processes or Institutions
June 14, 2012

Dear Mr. Speaker: (Dear Mr. President:)

Section 202(d) of the National Emergencies Act (50 U.S.C. 1622(d)) provides for the automatic termination of a national emergency unless, within 90 days prior to the anniversary date of its declaration, the President publishes in the *Federal Register* and transmits to the

Congress a notice stating that the emergency is to continue in effect beyond the anniversary date. In accordance with this provision, I have sent to the *Federal Register* for publication the enclosed notice stating that the national emergency and related measures blocking the property of certain persons undermining democratic processes or institutions in Belarus are to continue in effect beyond June 16, 2012.

In 2011, the Government of Belarus continued its crackdown against political opposition, civil society, and independent media. The government arbitrarily arrested, detained, and imprisoned citizens for criticizing officials or for participating in demonstrations; imprisoned at least one human rights activist on manufactured charges; and prevented independent media from disseminating information and materials. These actions show that the Government of Belarus has taken additional steps backward in the development of democratic governance and respect for human rights.

The actions and policies of certain members of the Government of Belarus and other persons to undermine Belarus democratic processes or institutions, to commit human rights abuses related to political repression, and to engage in public corruption continue to pose an unusual and extraordinary threat to the national security and foreign policy of the United States. For this reason, I have determined that it is necessary to continue the national emergency declared to deal with this threat and the related measures blocking the property of certain persons.

Sincerely,

BARACK OBAMA

NOTE: Identical letters were sent to John A. Boehner, Speaker of the House of Representatives, and Joseph R. Biden, Jr., President of the Senate. The notice is listed in Appendix D at the end of this volume.

Remarks at an Obama Victory Fund 2012 Fundraiser in New York City
June 14, 2012

The President. Well, first of all, to Sarah Jessica and her whole crew—[*laughter*]—Matthew apparently had a show he had to run off to—but for them to let us crash their house, Secret Service tromping all over the place, is incredibly generous. And they've been great friends. Sarah Jessica is doing all kinds of stuff with our Arts and Humanities Council, and she has been a great leader and champion on behalf of the arts. And we could not thank her more for everything that she's done. So please give her a big round of applause.

To Anna, who has been just a great friend, and I think this is—she is working really hard here in New York, but she actually was in Chicago as well, making things happen on our behalf. So thank you, Anna, for everything that you do.

Now, I recognize that most of you are here to see Michelle. [*Laughter*] I understand. I have been there before. I always explain I rank fifth in the hierarchy in the White House. [*Laughter*] There's Michelle, my mother-in-

law, the two girls, Bo—so that actually makes it six—[*laughter*]—in terms of star wattage. People come to the White House, first they ask, where's Michelle? They ask, where are the girls? And then they say, where's Bo? [*Laughter*] But that's okay. See, that's how you're thinking too, isn't it? [*Laughter*] It makes sense to you.

But I do want to say—I don't get a chance to say this a lot publicly—some of you know that Michelle had some skepticism about a life in politics. I think that's well known. And so the grace and the strength and the poise and the warmth that she has brought to an extraordinarily difficult task as First Lady and still being the best mom imaginable couldn't make me prouder. And so I'm very pleased she's here. And this is sort of our date night, so—[*applause*].

Now, because this is an intimate setting I usually don't give a long speech, and I already gave a long speech today. So what I'd rather do is spend most of my time taking questions and getting comments and advice. I usually get some advice. That's one of the things about the President—[*laughter*]—you have advisers everywhere. But let me just say a few things at the top.

In 2008, when we came together, it was because we had a sense that some of the core values, the basic bargain that had made this country the extraordinary place it is had been betrayed, or at least misplaced. We had a country in which folks who didn't need them were getting tax cuts that exploded the deficit. We had two wars that were placed on a credit card. We had an economy that was doing very well for a few, but for a huge number of people—and a growing number of people—meant harder work for less pay, lower incomes, more stress.

And Michelle and I, I think, embody the essence of an America in which, if you are willing to work hard, if you're willing to take responsibility not just for your own life, but for your community and your family, your neighborhood, that you can make it in this country, regardless of what you look like, where you come from, who you love, what your faith. And that basic bargain, that dream, felt like it was eroding. So that's why I ran in 2008, and that's why a lot of you supported me in 2008.

What we didn't know was that we would end up experiencing the worst financial crisis since the Great Depression: 9 million people ultimately losing their jobs, millions of homes in foreclosure, people having a harder and harder time just making ends meet.

And the good news is that because of the incredible resilience of the American people—and one of the great privileges of being President is you travel all across the country and you meet people from every walk of life—the good news is, because of their resilience, we've begun to come back.

So we've created more than 4 million jobs over the last 27 months, 800,000 this year alone. We were able to stabilize the financial system. Manufacturing started coming back. Sometimes we had to make some tough choices like bailing out the auto industry. But because we had faith in those workers and we had faith in American ingenuity, GM is now back

on top and—[*applause*]—that's worth applauding. Yes, why not? Why not? James has been dying to—he wanted to fire up the crowd a little bit.

Audience member. He knows how to applause line.

The President. Absolutely. And that was a good one, right on cue. [*Laughter*]

But there are still a lot of people hurting out there. We have not come all the way back. And with what's happening in Europe and what's happening around the globe, the economy is fragile. And we have to remind ourselves of how much more we have to do not just to get back to where we were before the crisis hit, but how do we get back to that core American ideal in which everybody has a shot: everybody has a fair shot, everybody is doing their fair share, and everybody is playing by the same set of rules.

And so, even as we try to address the crisis—that was our first order of business—what we also tried to do was slowly begin a process of reforming our institutions so that we can build a strong middle class and give a ladder of opportunity for people who are trying to get into the middle class.

That's why we passed health care reform. That's the reason why we made sure that we reformed our financial system so we wouldn't go through the kind of crisis that we did in 2008. That's why we reformed our student loans system so millions of students have a better chance of going to college. That's why we invested in science and research, because we understand that's how we're going to be able to compete over the long term in this very competitive economy.

And that's why I'm running for a second term, because our work is not yet done. We still have to put more people back to work. We still have to rebuild America. We still have to reform our immigration system to make sure that incredibly talented young people who grew up here, who understand themselves as Americans, but may have been brought here with parents who didn't have papers, that those kids have a chance to contribute, start businesses, and thrive and do all the things that remind us this is a nation of immigrants as well as a nation of laws.

We've got to make sure that health care gets implemented. Having ended the war in Iraq, we have to now make sure that we're dealing with a transition in Afghanistan that's responsible, but ends the war by 2014. We have to continue to restore respect for America around the world, because we observe rule of law and we've eliminated torture and we've once again reached out to countries on the basis of our ideals and our values and not just our incredible military. And we've got to take care of our veterans who have fought for us and are now coming home, because they shouldn't have to fight for a job after they fought for us.

So we've got a huge amount of work to do. And the speech that I gave today focused on the fact that we've still got a choice. We've got as fundamental a choice this time out as we've had maybe in 30, 40, 50 years.

In some ways, this election is more important than 2008, because in 2008, as much as I disagreed with Mr. McCain, he believed in climate change. He believed in campaign finance reform. He believed in immigration reform. And now what we have is a Republican nominee and a Republican Party that has moved fundamentally away from what used to be a bipartisan consensus about how you build an economy; that has said our entire agenda is based on cutting taxes even more for people who don't need them and weren't asking for them, slashing our commitment to things like education or science or infrastructure or a basic social safety net for seniors and the disabled and the infirm; that wants to gut regulations for polluters or those who are taking advantage of consumers.

So they've got a very specific theory about how you grow the economy. It's not very different from the one that actually got us into this mess in the first place. And what we're going to have to do is to present very clearly to the American people that choice. Because ultimately, you guys and the American people, you're the tie-breaker; you're the ultimate arbiter of which direction this country goes in. Do

we go in a direction where we're all in this together and we share in prosperity, or do we believe that everybody is on their own and we'll see how it plays out?

And I am absolutely convinced in my gut that we are in this together and that for all the differences that you hear about in the news and on cable, there is still a lot more that we have in common than what drives us apart. And I think our ideas are ones that the American people believe in.

But we're going to have to fight for it, because the American people are tired. They've gone through a very tough economy. They're still having a tough time. And that's why this election is going to be close. Because at a certain point, the other side is going to spend $500 million with a very simple message, which is: You're frustrated, you're disappointed, and it's the fault of the guy in the White House. And that's a—it's an elegant message. It happens to be wrong, but it's crisp. You can fit it on a bumper sticker.

And so we're going to have to work hard in this election. We're going to have to work harder than we did in 2008. But the good news is, from those travels around the country, I will tell you people remain hopeful, they remain resilient, and ultimately, they prefer our vision of the future. So we've just got to present it to them and go out and win an election, and then we're going to have to spend 4 more years doing a lot of work.

And I want you to know, despite the fact that my hair is a little grayer than it was—[*laughter*]—when I started on this journey, I've never been more determined and more convinced about the importance of our cause.

Thank you, everybody. Thank you.

NOTE: The President spoke at 8:05 p.m. at the residence of Sarah Jessica Parker and Matthew Broderick. In his remarks, he referred to Anna Wintour, editor in chief, American Vogue magazine; James W. Broderick, son of Ms. Parker and Mr. Broderick; Sen. John S. McCain III, in his capacity as the 2008 Republican Presidential nominee; and Republican Presidential candidate former Gov. W. Mitt Romney of Massachusetts. He also referred to his mother-in-law

Marian Robinson. Audio was not available for verification of the content of these remarks.

Remarks at an Obama Victory Fund 2012 Fundraiser in New York City
June 14, 2012

Thank you so much. Well, it is wonderful to see all of you.

Let me begin my thanking a couple of folks who preceded me. First of all, the most important person, the true star of the Obama family—along with Malia, Sasha, and Bo—the First Lady of the United States, Michelle Obama. This is what qualifies as date night in the Obama household. [*Laughter*]

I also want to thank Mariah Carey for performing this evening. We are grateful to her. Appreciate you. And somebody who can sing pretty good too, but also just is incredibly passionate about issues and ideas, and I'm so grateful for her friendship, Alicia Keys.

So I think the way we're going to do this tonight is I want to actually spend some time in conversation with you, so we're going to do some Q&A later, and I'm going to just give a few brief remarks at the top.

I was in Cleveland earlier today at Cuyahoga Community College. This is obviously a region that has been struggling, not just since 2008, but has been struggling for over a decade. And I described to them what was at stake in this election and explained that there is one area where I and my opponent completely agree, and that is that, as important as foreign policy is, as proud as I am to have ended the war in Iraq and made sure that we were providing the resources to go after Al Qaida and take out bin Laden, and the transition that we're working on in getting our troops home from Afghanistan, as important as social issues are, the crux of this campaign is going to be about the economy.

Because when we came together in 2008, part of what compelled me to run and part of what I think brought a lot of people to support me was a belief in a basic bargain that here in America, no matter what you look like, no matter where you come from, no matter who you love, no matter what your faith, if you are will-

ing to work hard you should be able to make it. Not everybody will experience extraordinary monetary success, but you should be able to find a good job and make a good home and educate your kids so that they can achieve more than you ever dreamed of and retire with some dignity and some respect—the notion that if you show responsibility for yourself and your life, that you can succeed.

And it was that basic bargain that built the greatest middle class in history. It's what made us an economic superpower. It wasn't the idea that the economy grew from the top down; it was the idea that it grew out from the middle, all kinds of people contributing, coming together, sharing in prosperity and sharing in responsibility not only for this generation, but for the next generation.

And the sense was in 2008 that we had lost touch with those values and those ideals. We had squandered a surplus and turned it into deficits by giving tax cuts to folks who didn't need them and weren't even asking for them, two wars paid on a credit card. Manufacturing increasingly left our shores. A lot of our economic growth was built on debt and speculation. And we didn't know at the time when I started to run that we would end up with that entire house of cards collapsing and the result would be the worst financial crisis and the worst economic crisis in our lifetimes.

We've spent 3½ years working diligently—and when I say "we," I don't just mean my administration, I mean the American people all across this country—working to recover from that crisis. We've created more than 4 million jobs over the last 27 months—more jobs than were created in the entire 7 years preceding my Presidency, 800,000 jobs just this year alone. But we lost 9 million jobs.

We rebuilt and gave the opportunity for workers and businesses to begin to rebuild the auto industry and have started to see manufacturing grow again for the first time since the 1990s. But we lost 6 million jobs in the decade before as manufacturing moved offshore.

We were able to stabilize the financial system. But millions of people all across the country saw their homes suddenly lose 10, 20, 30 percent of their value. And so as a consequence, we saw actually more wealth lost in that short span of time than was lost during the Depression.

And so as much as we've done over the last 3½ years, we've got a lot more work to do, because the hole that was dug was so deep. And what this election is going to come down to is where do we go from here? Because I have a fundamentally different vision about where we need to take this country than my opponent.

And so all the gridlock in Washington, all the stalemate, all the questions as to why, for example, my jobs bill that I proposed that the economists said would create a million jobs hasn't passed, or the $4 trillion in deficit reduction that I proposed hasn't gotten done, part of it is politics. Part of it is the party that's not in the White House wanting to block a President who's in the White House. But part of it has to do with just a different conception of how we grow the economy.

Mr. Romney and his congressional allies believe that if we not only extend the tax cuts that were passed under the previous administration, but also an addition $5 trillion—giving a lot of folks in this room big tax cuts—that that will somehow grow the economy faster. That if we strip away regulations on polluters or protections that are offered to consumers or workers, that that will unleash the marketplace. That's the essence of their prescription.

Their analysis is, is that Government is the problem, and if we just prune it back to a few basics like national security and break it up and give it back in the form of tax cuts—particularly for the wealthiest Americans—that we will grow faster. And they will deliver on that vision if Mr. Romney is elected and Republicans control the Congress.

So I don't necessarily question their sincerity, but I do question their understanding of how we built America. Because throughout most of our postwar era, the way we grew America was understanding that the market was the most powerful wealth generator in history, that we had a entrepreneurial culture and we rewarded risk takers and innovators, but we also understood there were some things we had to do together to make sure everybody had a shot, to make sure that everybody did their fair share, to make sure that everybody was playing by the same rules.

And so we created public schools and public universities because we understood all of us would succeed if every talented kid had a chance to get a great education. And yes, that cost money, and we couldn't do it on our own. We had to do it together.

And we understood that businesses are going to thrive if we've got great infrastructure, so we built railroads and highways and ports and airports, telecommunications lines, because we recognized that businesses have to move services and goods and information. And the faster we can do it, the more efficiently we can do it, the more all of us benefit.

And we understood that if we invest in science and technology——

[At this point, a cellular phone rang.]

Whose phone is that? *[Laughter]* I'm just impressed because it was a really loud ring. *[Laughter]* That if we invested in science and technology, that wasn't necessarily something that we could do on our own, and it might not always be profitable for the private sector, but because of those investments, we laid the foundation for the Internet and GPS and medical breakthroughs, which then the private sector was able to take advantage of and commercialize and create jobs and businesses all across America.

We understood that if we set up some rules of the road for our capital markets, small investors, and others would be more likely to put their money in because they figured they weren't getting cheated, which gave us the strongest capital markets in the world. We understood that if we put in place consumer protections and safety standards, that the American brand, our products people would have confidence in. And we couldn't do those things on our own; we had to do them together.

The Hoover Dam, the Golden Gate Bridge, the GI bill, those things weren't bad for the marketplace. Those things facilitated the marketplace. It helped create our wealth.

And so in this election, we are going to have a choice: Do we continue with that vision, which, by the way, used to have adherence not just in the Democratic Party, but also in the Republican Party. This used to be a postwar consensus. There would be arguments about how big government, how small government, but there was a basic understanding that there were some things we do better together.

And so the reason I'm running is because I want to continue that tradition. That will provide us the kind of foundation we need to grow.

And you've got on the other side a basic argument that says government is the enemy; the market for everything, that's the solution to our problems. And I'm not exaggerating here. As I pointed out in my speech today, if you look at what it would mean to provide an additional $5 trillion tax cut, the only way to pay for it without just exploding the deficit would be to cut out 20 percent of that part of the budget that includes education, includes basic research—just about everything except Medicare, Social Security, national defense would be cut—20 percent.

That doesn't get you $5 trillion, though, so you'd then also have to raise taxes in one way or another on the middle class in order to pay for it. And that doesn't deal with the existing deficit; that's just the $5 trillion deficit that would be created if we have these additional tax cuts.

If you roll back the health care bill that we passed, it's estimated that millions of people will not have health insurance and then millions more if we carry out what's been proposed in terms of cutting Medicaid: vulnerable kids, kids with autism or disabilities, or folks in nursing homes.

Now, I understand the argument the other side is making. The problem is, is that we tried

it just a few years ago. And it was exactly that theory that led to sluggish economic growth, sluggish job growth, huge deficits, and ultimately resulted in a financial crash. So the question is why would we think that it would work now? What evidence do we have that this theory would make sense?

But that's the great thing about democracy: You can present a plan even if it doesn't make sense. [*Laughter*] And you can make your argument for it. But the point I tried to make today—and this is what we're going to be doing over the next 5 months—is I want absolute clarity on the part of the American people about which way we're going.

I believe in making sure that we're investing in clean energy, in solar and wind, because I think that will create jobs and I think it's good for our national security and I think it will reduce our dependence on foreign oil and I think it's good for climate change. Mr. Romney disagrees. I want to have that debate.

I believe we have to invest in education at the K-through-12 level. We're going to reform the system, but we also have to hire new teachers, pay them better, hold them accountable, but stop teaching to the test. And yes, that's going to require some resources. Mr. Romney wants to cut back on those resources. I want to have that debate.

I believe we have to rebuild America, and we should rebuild America right now. We've got trillions of dollars in deferred maintenance that we're going to at some point have to replace unless we intend to become a second-rate power. And we could put thousands of people to work doing it right now here in New York and all across the country. Mr. Romney disagrees. I want to have that debate.

I want to reduce the deficit, but I want to do it in a balanced way. I think everybody should do their fair share and we shouldn't balance it on the backs of folks who are the most vulnerable when we can afford to do a little bit more. Mr. Romney has a different theory, and I want to have that debate.

So let me just close by saying this. Over the next 5 months, you won't be seeing a lot of ads because, frankly, Manhattan is not a battleground

State. [*Laughter*] But out in those battleground States, they will be seeing not just millions of dollars of ads, but potentially over a billion dollars of negative ads. And the message will be very simple: The economy is not where it needs to be, and it's Obama's fault. That's their message. There are no new ideas; there's no new proposals. What they're promising is what Bill Clinton called the same policies as the last time except on steroids. [*Laughter*] But you know people are anxious, and they've gone through a really tough time, and sometimes, just making an argument that feeds into that dissatisfaction can be enough.

So this will be a close election. The good news is, I believe we are right. I believe the American people understand that what made this country great was not a fend-for-yourself economy, but one in which all of us feel a sense of buy-in and all of us feel a sense of obligation and commitment, a sense of citizenship. And what we also learned in 2008 is that when the American people decide something is right and something is true, regardless of all the money and all the cynicism and all the nonsense that

passes for political campaigns these days—and that we always have to guard against getting sucked into because we're just in this muddy field—despite all that, the American people decide what's right and what's true, they can change the country.

That's the bet we made in 2008; that's the bet I'm making now. And I hope you are ready to work just as hard as you did 4 years ago, because in many ways this election is even more important. And if you do, then I think I'll have 4 more years to finish the job.

Thank you.

NOTE: The President spoke at 11 p.m. at the Plaza Hotel. In his remarks, he referred to Republican Presidential candidate former Gov. W. Mitt Romney of Massachusetts; and former President William J. Clinton. The transcript was released by the Office of the Press Secretary on June 15 and also included the remarks of the First Lady. Audio was not available for verification of the content of these remarks.

Remarks on Immigration Reform and an Exchange With Reporters
June 15, 2012

The President. Good afternoon, everybody. This morning Secretary Napolitano announced new actions my administration will take to mend our Nation's immigration policy to make it more fair, more efficient, and more just, specifically for certain young people sometimes called "DREAMers."

Now, these are young people who study in our schools, they play in our neighborhoods, they're friends with our kids, they pledge allegiance to our flag. They are Americans in their heart, in their minds, in every single way but one: on paper. They were brought to this country by their parents—sometimes even as infants—and often have no idea that they're undocumented until they apply for a job or a driver's license or a college scholarship.

Put yourself in their shoes. Imagine you've done everything right your entire life—studied hard, worked hard, maybe even graduated at the top of your class—only to suddenly face the

threat of deportation to a country that you know nothing about, with a language that you may not even speak.

That's what gave rise to the "DREAM Act." It says that if your parents brought you here as a child, you've been here for 5 years, and you're willing to go to college or serve in our military, you can one day earn your citizenship. And I have said time and time and time again to Congress that—send me the "DREAM Act," put it on my desk, and I will sign it right away.

Now, both parties wrote this legislation. And a year and a half ago, Democrats passed the "DREAM Act" in the House, but Republicans walked away from it. It got 55 votes in the Senate, but Republicans blocked it. The bill hasn't really changed. The need hasn't changed. It's still the right thing to do. The only thing that has changed, apparently, was the politics.

Now, as I said in my speech on the economy yesterday, it makes no sense to expel talented young people, who, for all intents and purposes, are Americans—they've been raised as Americans, understand themselves to be part of this country—to expel these young people who want to staff our labs or start new businesses or defend our country simply because of the actions of their parents or because of the inaction of politicians.

In the absence of any immigration action from Congress to fix our broken immigration system, what we've tried to do is focus our immigration enforcement resources in the right places. So we prioritized border security, putting more boots on the southern border than at any time in our history. Today, there are fewer illegal crossings than at any time in the past 40 years. We focused and used discretion about whom to prosecute, focusing on criminals who endanger our communities rather than students who are earning their education. And today, deportation of criminals is up 80 percent. We've improved on that discretion carefully and thoughtfully. Well, today we're improving it again.

Effective immediately, the Department of Homeland Security is taking steps to lift the shadow of deportation from these young people. Over the next few months, eligible individuals who do not present a risk to national security or public safety will be able to request temporary relief from deportation proceedings and apply for work authorization.

Now, let's be clear: This is not amnesty; this is not immunity. This is not a path to citizenship. It's not a permanent fix. This is a temporary stopgap measure that lets us focus our resources wisely while giving a degree of relief and hope to talented, driven, patriotic young people. It is——

Daily Caller reporter Neil Munro. [Inaudible]

The President. ——the right thing to do.

Mr. Munro. ——foreigners over American workers.

The President. Excuse me, sir. It's not time for questions, sir.

Mr. Munro. No, you have to take questions.

The President. Not while I'm speaking.

Precisely because this is temporary, Congress needs to act. There is still time for Congress to pass the "DREAM Act" this year, because these kids deserve to plan their lives in more than 2-year increments. And we still need to pass comprehensive immigration reform that addresses our 21st-century economic and security needs, reform that gives our farmers and ranchers certainty about the workers that they'll have; reform that gives our science and technology sectors certainty that the young people who come here to earn their Ph.D.'s won't be forced to leave and start new businesses in other countries; reform that continues to improve our border security and lives up to our heritage as a nation of laws and a nation of immigrants.

Just 6 years ago, the unlikely trio of John McCain, Ted Kennedy, and President Bush came together to champion this kind of reform. And I was proud to join 23 Republicans in voting for it. So there's no reason that we can't come together and get this done.

And as long as I'm President, I will not give up on this issue, not only because it's the right thing to do for our economy—and CEOs agree with me—not just because it's the right thing to do for our security, but because it's the right thing to do, period. And I believe that eventually enough Republicans in Congress will come around to that view as well.

I believe that it's the right thing to do because I've been with groups of young people who work so hard and speak with so much heart about what's best in America, even though I knew some of them must have lived under the fear of deportation. I know some have come forward, at great risks to themselves and their futures, in hopes it would spur the rest of us to live up to our own most cherished values. And I've seen the stories of Americans in schools and churches and communities across the country who stood up for them and rallied behind them, and pushed us to give them a better path and freedom from fear, because we are a better nation than one that expels innocent young kids.

And the answer to your question, sir—and the next time I'd prefer you let me finish my statements before you ask that question—is this is the right thing to do for the American people——

Mr. Munro. [*Inaudible*]

The President. I didn't ask for an argument. I'm answering your question.

Mr. Munro. I'd like to——

The President. It is the right thing to do——

Mr. Munro. [*Inaudible*]

The President. ——for the American people. And here's why——

Mr. Munro. ——high unemployment——

The President. Here's the reason: because these young people are going to make extraordinary contributions and are already making contributions to our society.

I've got a young person who is serving in our military, protecting us and our freedom. The notion that in some ways we would treat them as expendable makes no sense. If there's a young person here who has grown up here and wants to contribute to this society, wants to maybe start a business that will create jobs for other folks who are looking for work, that's the right thing to do. Giving certainty to our farmers and our ranchers, making sure that in addition to border security, we're creating a comprehensive framework for legal immigration, these are all the right things to do.

We have always drawn strength from being a nation of immigrants, as well as a nation of laws, and that's going to continue. And my hope is that Congress recognizes that and gets behind this effort.

All right. Thank you very much.

Mr. Munro. What about American workers who are unemployed while you import foreigners?

NOTE: The President spoke at 2:09 p.m. in the Rose Garden at the White House. In his remarks, he referred to former President George W. Bush.

Remarks at a Reception Honoring Lesbian, Gay, Bisexual, and Transgender Pride Month
June 15, 2012

Well, welcome to the White House, everybody. We are glad all of you could join us today. I want to thank the Members of Congress and the members of my administration who are here, including our friends who are doing outstanding work every day: John Berry, Nancy Sutley, Fred Hochberg.

Now, each June since I took office, we've gathered to pay tribute to the generations of lesbian, gay, bisexual, and transgender Americans who devoted their lives to our most basic ideals: equality not just for some, but for all. Together, we've marked major milestones like the 40th anniversary of the Stonewall riots, when a group of brave citizens held their ground against brutal discrimination. Together, we've honored courageous pioneers who, decades ago, came out and spoke out, who challenged unjust laws and destructive prejudices. Together, we've stood resolute, unwavering in our commitment to advance this movement and to build a more perfect Union.

Now, I've said before that I would never counsel patience, that it wasn't right to tell you to be patient any more than it was right for others to tell women to be patient a century ago or African Americans to be patient a half century ago. After decades of inaction and indifference, you have every reason and right to push, loudly and forcefully, for equality. But 3 years ago, I also promised you this: I said that even if it took more time than we would like, we would see progress, we would see success, we would see real and lasting change. And together, that's what we're witnessing.

For every person who lost a loved one at the hand of hate, we ended a decade of delay and finally made the Matthew Shepard Act the land of the law. For every person with HIV who was treated like an outcast, we lifted the HIV entry ban. And because of that important step, next month, for the first time in more than two decades, the International AIDS Conference will be held right here in the United States.

For every American diagnosed with HIV who couldn't get access to treatment, we put forward a National HIV/AIDS Strategy, because who you are should never affect whether you get life-extending care. Marjorie Hill, the head of the Gay Men's Health Crisis, is here. GMHC has saved so many lives, and this year they are celebrating their 30th anniversary. So I want to give them and all these organizations who work to prevent and treat HIV a big round of applause. Give it up for Marjorie and everybody else.

For every partner or spouse denied the chance to comfort a loved one in the hospital, to be by their side at their greatest hour of need, we said, enough. Hospitals that accept Medicare or Medicaid, and that is most of them, now have to treat LGBT patients just like any other patient. For every American denied insurance just for being lesbian, gay, bisexual, or transgender, we passed health insurance reform, which will ban that kind of discrimination.

We've expanded benefits for same-sex partners of Federal employees, prohibited discrimination on the basis of gender identity for workers in the Federal Government. We've supported efforts in Congress to end the so-called Defense of Marriage Act. And as we wait for that law to be cast aside, we've stopped defending its constitutionality in the courts.

We've put forward a strategy to promote and protect the rights of LGBT communities all over the world, because, as Secretary Clinton said back in December, gay rights are human rights.

And of course, last year we finally put an end to "don't ask, don't tell" so that nobody would ever have to ever again hide who they love in order to serve the country they love. And I know we've got some military members who are here today. I'm happy to see you with your partners here. We thank you for your service. We thank your families for their service, and we share your joy at being able to come with your spouses or partners here to the White House with your Commander in Chief.

Now, we know we've got more to do. Americans may feel more comfortable bringing their partners to the office barbecue, but we're still waiting for a fully inclusive "Employment Non-Discrimination Act." Congress needs to pass that legislation so that no American is ever fired simply for being gay or transgender.

Americans may be able to serve openly in the military, but many are still growing up alone and afraid, picked on, pushed around for being different. And that's why my administration has worked to raise awareness about bullying. And I know—I just had a chance to see Lee Hirsch, the director of "Bully," who is here. And we thank him for his work on this issue.

I want to acknowledge all the young leaders here today who are making such a big difference in their classrooms and in their communities. And Americans may be still evolving when it comes to marriage equality, but—[*laughter*]—but as I've indicated personally, Michelle and I have made up our minds on this issue. And we believe that same-sex couples should be treated equally.

So we still have a long way to go, but we will get there. We'll get there because of all of you. We'll get there because of all of the ordinary Americans who, every day, show extraordinary courage. We'll get there because of every man and woman and activist and ally who is moving us forward by the force of their moral arguments, but more importantly, by the force of their example.

And as long as I have the privilege of being your President, I promise you, you won't just have a friend in the White House, you will have a fellow advocate for an America where, no matter what you look like or where you come from or who you love, you can dream big dreams and dream as openly as you want.

Thank you. God bless you. God bless America.

NOTE: The President spoke at 5:16 p.m. in the East Room at the White House.

Letter to Congressional Leaders on the Deployment of United States Combat-Equipped Armed Forces
June 15, 2012

Dear Mr. Speaker: (Dear Mr. President:)

I am providing this supplemental consolidated report, prepared by my Administration and consistent with the War Powers Resolution (Public Law 93–148), as part of my efforts to keep the Congress informed about deployments of U.S. Armed Forces equipped for combat.

MILITARY OPERATIONS AGAINST AL-QA'IDA, THE TALIBAN, AND ASSOCIATED FORCES AND IN SUPPORT OF RELATED U.S. COUNTERTERRORISM (CT) OBJECTIVES

Since October 7, 2001, the United States has conducted combat operations in Afghanistan against al-Qa'ida terrorists, their Taliban supporters, and associated forces. In support of these and other overseas operations, the United States has deployed combat equipped forces to a number of locations in the U.S. Central, Pacific, European, Southern, and Africa Command areas of operation. Previously such operations and deployments have been reported, consistent with Public Law 107–40 and the War Powers Resolution, and operations and deployments remain ongoing. These operations, which the United States has carried out with the assistance of numerous international partners, have degraded al-Qa'ida's capabilities and brought an end to the Taliban's leadership of Afghanistan.

United States Armed Forces are now actively pursuing and engaging remaining al-Qa'ida and Taliban fighters in Afghanistan. The total number of U.S. forces in Afghanistan is approximately 90,000, of which more than 70,000 are assigned to the North Atlantic Treaty Organization (NATO)-led International Security Assistance Force (ISAF) in Afghanistan. In accordance with June 2011 Presidential guidance, the Department of Defense remains on track to achieve a Force Management Level of 68,000 U.S. forces by the end of this summer. After that, reductions will continue at a steady pace.

The U.N. Security Council most recently reaffirmed its authorization of ISAF for a 12-month period until October 13, 2012, in U.N. Security Council Resolution 2011 (October 12, 2011). The mission of ISAF, under NATO command and in partnership with the Government of the Islamic Republic of Afghanistan, is to prevent Afghanistan from once again becoming a safe haven for international terrorists. Fifty nations, including the United States and all 28 NATO Allies, contribute forces to ISAF. These forces, including U.S. "surge" forces deployed in late 2009 and 2010, broke Taliban momentum and trained additional Afghan National Security Forces (ANSF). The ANSF are now increasingly assuming responsibility for security on the timeline committed to at the 2010 NATO Summit in Lisbon by the United States, our NATO allies, ISAF partners, and the Government of Afghanistan.

United States Armed Forces are detaining in Afghanistan approximately 2,748 individuals under the Authorization for the Use of Military Force (Public Law 107–40) as informed by the laws of war. On March 9, 2012, the United States signed a Memorandum of Understanding with the Afghan government under which the United States is to transfer Afghan nationals detained by U.S. forces in Afghanistan to the custody and control of the Afghan government within 6 months. Efforts are underway to accomplish such transfers in a safe and humane manner.

The combat-equipped forces, deployed since January 2002 to Naval Base, Guantanamo Bay, Cuba, continue to conduct secure detention operations for the approximately 169 detainees at Guantanamo Bay under Public Law 107–40 and consistent with principles of the law of war.

In furtherance of U.S. efforts against members of al-Qa'ida, the Taliban, and associated forces, the United States continues to work with partners around the globe, with a particular focus on the U.S. Central Command's area of responsibility. In this context, the United States has deployed U.S. combat-equipped forces to assist in enhancing the CT capabilities of our friends and allies, including special operations and other forces for sensitive operations in various locations around the world.

In Somalia, the U.S. military has worked to counter the terrorist threat posed by al-Qa'ida and al-Qa'ida-associated elements of al-Shabaab. In a limited number of cases, the U.S. military has taken direct action in Somalia against members of al-Qa'ida, including those who are also members of al-Shabaab, who are engaged in efforts to carry out terrorist attacks against the United States and our interests.

The U.S. military has also been working closely with the Yemeni government to operationally dismantle and ultimately eliminate the terrorist threat posed by al-Qa'ida in the Arabian Peninsula (AQAP), the most active and dangerous affiliate of al-Qa'ida today. Our joint efforts have resulted in direct action against a limited number of AQAP operatives and senior leaders in that country who posed a terrorist threat to the United States and our interests.

The United States is committed to thwarting the efforts of al-Qa'ida and its associated forces to carry out future acts of international terrorism, and we have continued to work with our CT partners to disrupt and degrade the capabilities of al-Qa'ida and its associated forces. As necessary, in response to the terrorist threat, I will direct additional measures against al-Qa'ida, the Taliban, and associated forces to protect U.S. citizens and interests. It is not possible to know at this time the precise scope or the duration of the deployments of U.S. Armed Forces necessary to counter this terrorist threat to the United States. A classified annex to this report provides further information.

MILITARY OPERATIONS IN IRAQ

The United States completed its responsible withdrawal of U.S. forces from Iraq in December 2011, in accordance with the 2008 Agreement Between the United States of America and the Republic of Iraq on the Withdrawal of United States Forces from Iraq and the Organization of Their Activities during Their Temporary Presence in Iraq.

MILITARY OPERATIONS IN CENTRAL AFRICA

In October and November 2011, U.S. military personnel with appropriate combat equipment deployed to Uganda to serve as advisors to regional forces that are working to apprehend or remove Joseph Kony and other senior Lord's Resistance Army (LRA) leaders from the battlefield, and to protect local populations. The total number of U.S. military personnel deployed for this mission, including those providing logistical and support functions, is approximately 90. United States forces are working with select partner nation forces to enhance cooperation, information-sharing and synchronization, operational planning, and overall effectiveness. Elements of these U.S. forces have deployed to forward locations in the LRA-affected areas of the Republic of South Sudan, the Democratic Republic of the Congo, and the Central African Republic to enhance regional efforts against the LRA. These forces, however, will not engage LRA forces except in self-defense. It is in the U.S. national security interest to help our regional partners in Africa to develop their capability to address threats to regional peace and security, including the threat posed by the LRA. The United States is pursuing a comprehensive strategy to help the governments and people of this region in their efforts to end the threat posed by the LRA and to address the impacts of the LRA's atrocities.

MARITIME INTERCEPTION OPERATIONS

As noted in previous reports, the United States remains prepared to conduct maritime interception operations on the high seas in the areas of responsibility of each of the geographic combatant commands. These maritime operations are aimed at stopping the movement, arming, and financing of certain international terrorist groups, and also include operations aimed at stopping proliferation by sea of weapons of mass destruction and related materials. Additional information is provided in the classified annex.

HOSTAGE RESCUE OPERATIONS

As noted to you in my report of January 26, 2012, at my direction, on January 24, 2012, U.S. Special Operations Forces conducted a successful operation in Somalia to rescue Ms. Jessica Buchanan, a U.S. citizen who had been kidnapped by individuals linked to Somali pirate groups and financiers.

MILITARY OPERATIONS IN EGYPT

Approximately 693 military personnel are assigned to the U.S. contingent of the Multinational Force and Observers, which have been present in Egypt since 1981.

U.S.-NATO OPERATIONS IN KOSOVO

The U.N. Security Council authorized Member States to establish a NATO-led Kosovo Force (KFOR) in Resolution 1244 on June 10, 1999. The original mission of KFOR was to monitor, verify, and, when necessary, enforce compliance with the Military Technical Agreement between NATO and the then-Federal Republic of Yugoslavia (now Serbia), while maintaining a safe and secure environment. Today, KFOR deters renewed hostilities in cooperation with local authorities, bilateral partners, and international institutions. The principal military tasks of KFOR forces are to help maintain a safe and secure environment and to ensure freedom of movement throughout Kosovo.

Currently, 23 NATO Allies contribute to KFOR. Seven non-NATO countries also participate. The United States contribution to KFOR is approximately 817 U.S. military personnel out of the total strength of approximately 6,401 personnel, which includes a temporarily deployed Operational Reserve Force.

I have directed the participation of U.S. Armed Forces in all of these operations pursuant to my constitutional and statutory authority as Commander in Chief (including the authority to carry out Public Law 107–40 and other statutes) and as Chief Executive, as well as my constitutional and statutory authority to conduct the foreign relations of the United States. Officials of my Administration and I communicate regularly with the leadership and other Members of Congress with regard to these deployments, and we will continue to do so.

BARACK OBAMA

NOTE: Identical letters were sent to John A. Boehner, Speaker of the House of Representatives, and Daniel K. Inouye, President pro tempore of the Senate.

The President's Weekly Address
June 16, 2012

Over the last few weeks, I've been talking a lot about America's economic future. I've told you how I believe we should go about creating strong, sustained growth; how we should pay down our long-term debt in a balanced way; and most of all, what we should do right now to create good, middle class jobs so people who work hard can get ahead.

This isn't some abstract debate or trivial Washington argument. I've said that this is the defining issue of our time, and I mean it. I've said that this is a make-or-break moment for the middle class, and I believe it. The decisions we make over the next few years will have an enormous impact on the country we live in, and the one we pass on to our children.

Right now we're still fighting our way back from the worst economic crisis since the Great Depression. The economy is growing again, but it's not growing fast enough. Our businesses have created 4.3 million new jobs over the last 27 months, but we're not creating them fast enough. And we're facing some pretty serious headwinds, the effects of the recent spike in gas prices to the financial crisis in Europe.

But here's the thing: We have the answers to these problems. We have plenty of big ideas and technical solutions from both sides of the aisle. That's not what's holding us back. What's holding us back is a stalemate in Washington.

Last September, I sent Congress a jobs bill full of the kinds of bipartisan ideas that could have put over a million Americans back to work and helped bolster our economy against outside shocks. I sent them a plan that would have reduced our deficit by $4 trillion in a balanced way that pays for the investments we need by cutting unnecessary spending and by asking the wealthiest Americans to pay a little bit more in taxes.

Since then, Congress has passed a few parts of that jobs bill, like a tax cut that's allowing working Americans to keep more of your paycheck every week. But on most of the ideas that would create jobs and grow our economy, Republicans in Congress have not lifted a finger. They'd rather wait until after the election in November. Just this past week, one of them said, "Why not wait for the reinforcements?" That's a quote, and you can bet plenty of his colleagues are thinking the same thing.

I think that's wrong. This isn't about who wins or loses in Washington. This is about your jobs and your paychecks and your children's future. There is no excuse for Congress to stand by and do nothing while so many families are struggling, no reason whatsoever.

And right now Congress should pass a bill to help States put thousands of teachers and firefighters and police officers back on the job. They should have passed a bill a long time ago.

to put thousands of construction workers back to work rebuilding our roads and bridges and runways. And instead of just talking about job creators, they should give small-business owners a tax break for hiring more workers and paying them higher wages.

Right now Congress should give every responsible homeowner the opportunity to save an average of $3,000 a year by refinancing their mortgage. They should extend tax credits for clean energy manufacturers so we don't walk away from 40,000 good jobs. And instead of giving tax breaks to companies who ship jobs overseas, Congress should take that money and use it to cover moving expenses for companies that are bringing jobs back to America. There is no reason to wait.

So you see, every problem we face is within our power to solve. What's lacking is our politics. I need you to remind your Members of Congress why you sent them to Washington in the first place. Tell them to stop worrying about the next election and start worrying about the next generation. I'm ready to work with anyone—Republican, Democrat, or Independent—who is serious about moving this country forward. And I hope Members of Congress will join me.

Thanks, and have a great weekend.

NOTE: The address was recorded at approximately 4:25 p.m. on June 15 in the Map Room at the White House for broadcast on June 16. In the address, the President referred to Rep. James D. Jordan. The transcript was made available by the Office of the Press Secretary on June 15, but was embargoed for release until 6 a.m. on June 16.

Statement on the Death of Crown Prince Nayif bin Abd al-Aziz Al Saud of Saudi Arabia
June 16, 2012

It was with great regret that I learned of the passing of Crown Prince Nayif bin Abd al-Aziz Al Saud of Saudi Arabia. For decades, Crown Prince Nayif served as Minister of the Interior

and dedicated himself to the security of Saudi Arabia, as well as security throughout the region. Under his leadership, the United States and Saudi Arabia developed a strong and effective partnership in the fight against terrorism, one that has saved countless American and Saudi lives. Crown Prince Nayif also strongly supported the broader partnership between our two countries begun by his late father, King

Abd al-Aziz Al Saud, and President Roosevelt in their historic meeting in 1945. On behalf of the American people, I would like to offer my deepest condolences to King Abdallah, the royal family, and the people of Saudi Arabia.

Remarks Following a Meeting With President Felipe de Jesus Calderon Hinojosa of Mexico in Los Cabos, Mexico
June 18, 2012

President Calderon. Good morning, Mr. President, President Barack Obama, President of the United States; distinguished members of the delegations, and distinguished members of media. Thank you for being with us today.

First, I would like to say that it is very important for me to be able to share great news with you. But before doing that, I would like to thank personally, and on behalf of the Mexican nation, President Barack Obama for his valuable decision by executive order to give an opportunity for young people who were not born in the United States but who arrived in that great Nation before they were 16 years of age, or who are studying in university, or who have served in the United States Armed Forces, for them not to be deported for at least a period of 2 years, so this is a clear and certain situation for them.

We believe that this is very just. It's a humanitarian action. And it's an unprecedented action in our opinion. And in this sense, Mr. President, we would like to thank you for the valor and courage that you had in implementing this action. I am sure that many, many families in the United States of America are thankful to you as well.

I'd also like to inform you that President Barack Obama and I have had a very fruitful meeting. We have touched upon issues of great relevance for the success of the G–20 summit. But there's one topic of the greatest importance that we'd like to share with you, and that is that the United States, together with the other eight countries that make up the TPP—the Trans-Pacific Partnership—have welcomed Mexico for it to join the negotiations of this initiative.

The Trans-Pacific Partnership is an expansion of the trade agreement that was known initially as P–4, and that began in 2006 by Brunei, Chile, New Zealand and Singapore. And this commercial trade initiative was added into by Australia, the United States, Malaysia, Peru, and Vietnam afterwards. So this is one of the free trade initiatives that's most ambitious in the world and would foster integration of the Asia-Pacific region, one of the regions with the greatest dynamism in the world. And this region negotiating the TPP represents 26—of the world's GDP, 15 percent of exports and 12 of imports.

But most importantly, at this time of recession in some areas of the world, of a slowdown in others, the TPP, or Trans-Pacific Partnership, perhaps represents the greatest potential area of growth in an entire decade. So this is a great piece of news for Mexicans because it implies jobs and economic growth for at least the next two decades.

So the invitation that is made to Mexico by these nine nations to join the negotiations of the TPP also recognizes Mexico's efforts in trade and reaffirms Mexico's weight within the new economic and international financial context.

The fact that President Barack Obama has communicated to me that Mexico is being invited to join this negotiation is a sample of the solidarity of our relationships and the joint, or shared, responsibility that President Obama has taken on in our bilateral agenda, as well as issues of competitiveness and greater trade. Better and more trade is more jobs and growth for Mexicans, more growth and jobs for the United States as well.

So it's very important for Mexico to join this process. I know that other nations want to join the TPP, and I hope that they'll be able to do that soon. Clearly, current members of the TPP have recognized the possibilities of what this means and the contribution to the Mexican economy being part of this process.

Our business sector has welcomed this initiative, and I'd like to thank that sector for supporting the Mexican Government in entering into this. And I'm sure that this will imply a great deal of jobs for us. In short, I believe that the TPP and the United States' support for Mexico's joining the initiative opens a door to Mexico in the 21st century in terms of trade integration. And I'm sure that the negotiations that we will be undertaking in the next months will be beneficial for Mexico, beneficial for the United States, and beneficial in general for all of the countries who have a coast on the Pacific. And this will be enable us to have further economic growth and prosperity as a result.

Thank you very much, Mr. President, for both things: for the humanitarian action that you undertook this week, as well as for the support to Mexico in this matter.

President Obama. Well, thank you very much. Let me begin by thanking President Calderon and the Mexican people for their extraordinarily gracious hospitality in this beautiful setting. We are confident that this will be a very productive summit thanks to all the organization and efforts that have been made by you.

On the bilateral relationship, I think that because of the work that we've done together, Mr. President, the bonds that were already so strong between our two countries have become stronger. And the Trans-Pacific Partnership negotiations that you just referred to are a good example.

We are obviously two of our most important trading partners to each other, but we both recognize that growth is going to take place in the Asia-Pacific region. We are part of that network of nations that are growing and dynamic. And for us now to be able to create a high standards trade agreement that further increases job opportunities, commercial opportunities,

investment opportunities, I think will benefit citizens in both our countries that are eager to compete and to be able to prosper in a global market.

And you have personally shown significant courage and hard work in being able to join these negotiations. We appreciate your administration's efforts. We think it will be good for Mexico; we think it will be good for the United States; and we think it will be good for the region as well.

With respect to the summit, obviously, we are going to be very busy over the next day and a half. The world is concerned about the slowing of growth that has taken place. A lot of attention has been centered on Europe. Now is the time, as we've discussed, to make sure that all of us join to do what's necessary to stabilize the world financial system, to avoid protectionism, to ensure that we are working hand in hand to both grow the economy and create jobs while taking a responsible approach long term and medium term towards our fiscal structures.

I think the election in Greece yesterday indicates a positive prospect for not only them forming a government, but also them working constructively with their international partners in order that they can continue on the path of reform and do so in a way that also offers the prospects for the Greek people to succeed and prosper.

And we are going to be working under your leadership with our European partners and with all countries to make sure that we're contributing so that the economy grows, the situation stabilizes, confidence returns to the markets, and most importantly, we're giving our people the chance if they work hard to succeed and do well.

And from everything that we've seen, your leadership on this summit I think will help us take one important step in a series of steps that are going to be required to continue to improve global economic prospects.

So I just want to thank you for all your leadership and your friendship. I want to thank all the members of your administration. I remember hosting one of these G–20s, and I know that as much work as it is for us, it's even more work for them. So we appreciate that very much.

President Calderon. Thank you.

President Obama. Thank you, Mr. President.

NOTE: The President spoke at 9:39 a.m. at the American Grand Los Cabos Resort. President Calderon spoke in Spanish, and his remarks were translated by an interpreter. President Calderon's opening remarks could not be verified because the audio was incomplete.

Remarks Following a Meeting With President Vladimir Vladimirovich Putin of Russia in Los Cabos
June 18, 2012

President Putin. Mr. President, this has been our second meeting. I remember our lengthy meeting we had in Moscow.

Today we had a very meaningful and subject-oriented discussion. We've been able to discuss issues pertaining to security. We discussed bilateral economic relations. In this regard, I'd like to thank you for the support rendered to Russia with her accession to the World Trade Organization. I am positive this will help to further develop the economic relations between our two countries, to promote creation of jobs in both countries.

We also discussed international affairs, including the Syrian affair. From my perspective, we've been able to find many commonalities pertaining to all of those issues. And we'll now further develop our contacts both on a personal level and on the level of our experts involved.

You visited the Russian Federation 3 years ago. Now, welcome again. I invite you to visit Moscow.

President Obama. Thank you very much, Mr. President.

We, in fact, did have a candid, thoughtful, and thorough conversation on a whole range of bilateral and international issues. Over the last 3 years, the United States and Russia have been able to make significant progress on a wide range of issues, including the New START Treaty, the 123 Agreement, the work we've done on Russia's accession to the WTO, and setting up a Presidential process whereby issues of trade and commerce, science, technology are all discussed at a much more intensive level.

We agreed that we need to build on these successes, even as we recognize that there are going to be areas of disagreement, and that we can find constructive ways to manage through any bilateral tensions. In particular, we discussed the need to expand trade and commercial ties between the United States and Russia, which are still far below where they should be. And I emphasized my priority of having Congress repeal Jackson-Vanik, provide permanent trade relations status to Russia, so that American businesses can take advantage of the extraordinary opportunities now that Russia is a member of the WTO.

We discussed a range of strategic issues, including missile defense, and resolved to continue to work through some of the difficult problems involved there.

I thanked the President and the Russian people for the work they've done with us on the Northern Distribution Network that is vital to providing supplies and resources to our brave troops who are still in Afghanistan.

We emphasized our shared approach when it comes to the Iranian situation, as members of the P–5-plus-1. We agreed that there's still time and space to resolve diplomatically the issue of Iran's potential development of nuclear weapons, as well as its interest in developing peaceful nuclear power.

And finally, as Mr. President mentioned, we discussed Syria, where we agreed that we need to see a cessation of the violence, that a political process has to be created to prevent civil war and the kind of horrific deaths that we've seen over the last several weeks. And we pledged to work with other international actors including the United Nations, Kofi Annan, and all interested parties in trying to find a resolution to this problem.

Mr. President, I look forward to visiting Russia again, and I look forward to hosting you in the United States.

Thank you, everybody.

NOTE: The President spoke at 12:42 p.m. at the Esperanza Resort. In his remarks, he referred to former Secretary-General Kofi A. Annan of the United Nations, in his capacity as Joint U.N.-Arab League Special Envoy to Syria. He also referred to the Jackson-Vanik amendment to the Trade Act of 1974, which places restrictions on normalized trade relations between the U.S. and Russia and other countries of the former Soviet Union based on their economic structure and emigration policies. President Putin spoke in Russian, and his remarks were translated by an interpreter.

Joint Statement by President Barack Obama and President Vladimir Vladimirovich Putin of Russia
June 18, 2012

The United States of America and the Russian Federation confirm our commitment to strengthening close and cooperative relations for the benefit of the peoples of our countries, international peace, global prosperity, and security. In recent years, we have laid a solid foundation for expanding our bilateral interaction in a variety of areas. Today we agree to continue this work guided by the principles of the rule of law, respect for human rights, equality, and mutual respect.

One of the key tasks on our shared agenda is the expansion of trade and investment relations, which should foster mutual economic growth and prosperity. To this end, we have agreed to prioritize the expansion and diversification of our bilateral trade and investment through nondiscriminatory access to our markets based on international rules.

An important step in this direction is Russia's accession to the World Trade Organization (WTO), which has become possible thanks to our joint efforts. In order for WTO rules and mechanisms to apply to our bilateral trade, the Obama Administration is working closely with the U.S. Congress to terminate, as soon as possible, application of the Jackson-Vanik Amendment with respect to Russia and extend Permanent Normal Trade Relations to the Russian Federation. The United States has also welcomed and offered its support to Russia's pursuit of membership in the Organization for Economic Cooperation and Development (OECD).

Nuclear arms control and non-proliferation remain a special responsibility for the United States and Russia as the two states with the world's largest nuclear weapons arsenals. We reiterate our strong support for the Treaty on the Non-Proliferation of Nuclear Weapons and our shared goal of universal adherence to and compliance with that Treaty and the International Atomic Energy Agency's comprehensive safeguards, consistent with the Treaty's Article III, and with the Additional Protocol. We recognize the achievements made through the Nuclear Security Summits, including the removal and elimination of nuclear materials, minimization of the civilian use of highly enriched uranium, and worldwide improvements in a nuclear security culture.

We are continuing research on the feasibility of converting research reactors in the United States and Russia to low-enriched uranium fuel. We agree to redouble bilateral efforts to improve nuclear security, counter nuclear smuggling, and combat nuclear terrorism, as well as to facilitate the beginning of negotiations at the Conference on Disarmament on a fissile material cutoff treaty that will halt production of fissile materials for use in nuclear weapons and other nuclear explosive devices, within the framework of a balanced program of work at the Conference. We will strive for the early entry into force of the Comprehensive Nuclear Test-Ban Treaty.

As a priority, we intend to successfully implement the New START Treaty, and to continue our discussions on strategic stability. Despite differences in assessments, we have agreed to continue a joint search for solutions to challenges in the field of missile defense.

The pursuit of international peace and security remains a priority for the United States and Russia, recognizing how much we have to gain by working together to overcome the main challenges of this century. While recognizing Iran's right to the peaceful uses of nuclear energy, we agree that Iran must undertake serious efforts aimed at restoring international confidence in the exclusively peaceful nature of its nuclear program. To this end, Tehran must fully comply with its obligations under the relevant UN Security Council and IAEA Board of Governors resolutions, and cooperate with the International Atomic Energy Agency for the expedited resolution of all remaining issues. Our common goal remains a comprehensive negotiated settlement based on the principles of a step-by-step approach and reciprocity, and we look forward to constructive engagement with Iran through the P5+1 process, including the latest round of talks taking place in Moscow on June 18–19.

We urge North Korea to come into compliance with all the relevant directives of the UN Security Council and fulfill its commitments under the Joint Statement by China, the DPRK, the Republic of Korea, Russia, the U.S., and Japan of September 19, 2005. We count on the DPRK not to commit acts that would escalate tensions on the Korean peninsula. As partners in the Six-Party talks, we are prepared to continue the joint efforts to achieve verifiable denuclearization on the Korean peninsula in accordance with the Joint Statement of September 19, 2005.

We agree to cooperate bilaterally and multilaterally to solve regional conflicts. In order to stop the bloodshed in Syria, we call for an immediate cessation of all violence and express full support for the efforts of UN/League of Arab States Joint Special Envoy Kofi Annan,

including moving forward on political transition to a democratic, pluralistic political system that would be implemented by the Syrians themselves in the framework of Syria's sovereignty, independence, unity, and territorial integrity. We are united in the belief that the Syrian people should have the opportunity to independently and democratically choose their own future.

The need for a just, lasting, and comprehensive peace in the Middle East has never been more apparent, and we will continue working with our Quartet partners to advance peace efforts on the basis of the Quartet statements of September 23, 2011, and April 11, 2012, and to strengthen the Palestinian Authority's ability to meet the full range of civil and security needs of the Palestinian people, both now and in a future state.

The United States and Russia continue to face a common threat from al Qaeda and other terrorist groups operating in and around Afghanistan. We recognize that this is a pivotal time for international efforts to strengthen security and promote economic development in Afghanistan, as well as to counter the narcotics threat. With the successful implementation of bilateral and multilateral transit arrangements, Russia has made a significant contribution to international efforts to promote stability in Afghanistan.

We reiterate that the process leading to reconciliation must be truly Afghan-led and Afghan-implemented. Reconciliation must include, as integral parts, a commitment to a sovereign, stable, and unified Afghanistan, breaking ties to al Qaeda, ending violence, and accepting the Afghan Constitution, including its human rights provisions, notably the rights of women. We will explore opportunities to strengthen the Northern Distribution Network, to bolster regional security, and to expand cooperation as we fight terrorism and narcotics trafficking, taking advantage of the capabilities of the Collective Security Treaty Organization and the NATO-Russia Council to enhance law-enforcement training for the region.

The United States of America and the Russian Federation intend to increase cooperation in addressing the world drug problem, so as to radically reduce production and consumption of illicit drugs, as affirmed by resolutions of the UN General Assembly and the UN Commission on Narcotic Drugs. We are ready to continue active support of efforts undertaken by the international community to counteract illicit production and illegal trafficking and consumption of drugs.

The United States of America and the Russian Federation are committed to furthering our multifaceted cooperation to counter terrorism. Both our nations face persistent and evolving domestic and transnational terrorist threats, including from terrorists based in North Africa, the Middle East, the Horn of Africa, Afghanistan, and Pakistan. Acknowledging the global character of these challenges, we reaffirm our readiness for further joint work to implement the UN's Global Counterterrorism Strategy, the UN Security Council resolutions and statements on terrorism, as well as to utilize other applicable international counterterrorism instruments, including counterterrorism sanctions regimes introduced by the UN Security Council with respect to al Qaeda and the Taliban.

The United States and Russia affirm our intent to work together to ensure the long-term success of the recently launched Global Counterterrorism Forum and continue to interact on various multilateral platforms, including the G–8 Roma/Lyon Group, the Asia Pacific Economic Cooperation (APEC) Forum, the ASEAN Regional Forum, and the Organization for Security and Cooperation in Europe (OSCE). We will continue to work together to counter financial support for terrorism, disrupt the possible connections between terrorist networks and criminal groups, prevent the spread of violent extremism, and improve transportation security, including by concluding bilateral agreements in this field.

An important role in strengthening U.S.-Russian relations belongs to the Presidential Commission, created in July 2009, which coordinates our bilateral cooperation on the widest range of issues from strategic stability, energy and space, fighting terrorism and illegal drug trafficking and consumption—to public health, agriculture, the environment, civil society, and cultural and educational exchanges. We are pleased to announce a new Working Group on Military-Technical Cooperation. U.S.-Russian cooperation has been growing in the global fight against malaria.

This year we together celebrate the 200th anniversary of Fort Ross in California, which was founded by Russian settlers and underscores the historic ties between our countries. In order to give our bilateral relations a new quality, we intend to pay special attention to broadening contacts between our peoples and societies, including by liberalizing the visa regime. We welcome steps to bring into force the U.S.-Russian Agreement on Simplifying Visa Formalities, signed in 2011, which should make two-way travel by American and Russian tourist and business travelers easier. We also commit to work together to ensure the rights and protections of adopted children. This will be facilitated by bringing into force and implementing the bilateral adoptions agreement signed last year.

The United States of America and the Russian Federation will only be able to achieve positive new results by acting together for the purpose of strengthening the democracy, security, and prosperity of the American and Russian peoples, and by solving other complex challenges confronting our countries and the international community.

NOTE: An original was not available for verification of the content of this joint statement.

Joint Statement by President Barack Obama, President Vladimir Vladimirovich Putin of Russia, and President François Hollande of France on the Nagorno-Karabakh Conflict
June 18, 2012

We, the Presidents of the OSCE Minsk Group Co-Chair countries—France, the Russian Federation, and the United States of America—are united in our resolute commitment to a peaceful settlement of the Nagorno-Karabakh conflict. The parties to the conflict should not further delay making the important decisions necessary to reach a lasting and peaceful settlement. We regret that the Presidents of Azerbaijan and Armenia did not take the decisive steps that our countries called for in the joint statement at Deauville on May 26, 2011. Nevertheless, the progress that has been achieved should provide the momentum to complete work on the framework for a comprehensive peace.

We call upon the leaders of Armenia and Azerbaijan to fulfill the commitment in their January 23, 2012 joint statement at Sochi to "accelerate" reaching agreement on the Basic Principles for a Settlement of the Nagorno-Karabakh Conflict. As evidence of their political will, they should refrain from maximalist positions in the negotiations, respect the 1994 ceasefire agreement, and abstain from hostile rhetoric that increases tension. We urge the leaders to be guided by the principles of the Helsinki Final Act—particularly those relating to the non-use of force or the threat of force,

territorial integrity, and equal rights and self-determination of peoples—and the elements of a settlement outlined in our countries' statements at L'Aquila in 2009 and Muskoka in 2010.

Military force will not resolve the conflict and would only prolong the suffering and hardships endured by the peoples of the region for too long. Only a peaceful, negotiated settlement can allow the entire region to move beyond the status quo toward a secure and prosperous future.

Our countries will continue to work closely with the sides, and we call upon them to make full use of the assistance of the Minsk Group Co-Chairs as mediators. However, peace will depend ultimately upon the parties' willingness to seek an agreement based on mutual understanding, rather than one-sided advantage, and a shared vision of the benefits that peace will bring to all their peoples and to future generations.

NOTE: The joint statement referred to President Ilham Aliyev of Azerbaijan; and President Serzh Sargsian of Armenia. An original was not available for verification of the content of this joint statement.

Statement on the Selection of Prince Salman bin Abd al-Aziz Al Saud as Crown Prince and Deputy Prime Minister of Saudi Arabia
June 18, 2012

I congratulate King Abdallah and the Saudi people on the selection of Prince Salman bin Abd al-Aziz Al Saud as Crown Prince and Deputy Prime Minister of the Kingdom of Saudi Arabia. As governor of Riyadh and then Minister of Defense, Crown Prince Salman has served his country with dedication and honor over the past five decades. I had the pleasure of receiving him at the

White House this April and know that he is a man of deep faith who is committed to improving the lives of the people of Saudi Arabia and to the security of the region. The United States looks forward to continuing our strong relationship with Crown Prince Salman in his new capacity as we deepen the longstanding partnership between the United States and Saudi Arabia.

Message to the Congress on Continuation of the National Emergency With Respect to North Korea
June 18, 2012

To the Congress of the United States:

Section 202(d) of the National Emergencies Act (50 U.S.C. 1622(d)) provides for the automatic termination of a national emergency unless, within 90 days prior to the anniversary date of its declaration, the President publishes in the *Federal Register* and transmits to the Congress a notice stating that the emergency is to continue in effect beyond the anniversary date. In accordance with this provision, I have sent to the *Federal Register* for publication the enclosed notice stating that the national emergency declared in Executive Order 13466 of June 26, 2008, expanded in scope in Executive Order 13551 of August 30, 2010, and addressed further in Executive Order 13570 of April 18, 2011, is to continue in effect beyond June 26, 2012.

The existence and risk of proliferation of weapons-usable fissile material on the Korean Peninsula, and the actions and policies of the Government of North Korea that destabilize the Korean Peninsula and imperil U.S. Armed Forces, allies, and trading partners in the region continue to constitute an unusual and extraordinary threat to the national security, foreign policy, and economy of the United States. For these reasons, I have determined that it is necessary to continue the national emergency with respect to these threats and maintain in force the measures taken to deal with that national emergency.

BARACK OBAMA

The White House,
June 18, 2012.

NOTE: The notice is listed in Appendix D at the end of this volume.

Message to the Congress on Continuation of the National Emergency With Respect to the Risk of Nuclear Proliferation Created by the Accumulation of Weapons-Usable Fissile Material in the Territory of the Russian Federation
June 18, 2012

To the Congress of the United States:

Section 202(d) of the National Emergencies Act (50 U.S.C. 1622(d)) provides for the automatic termination of a national emergency unless, within 90 days prior to the anniversary date of its declaration, the President publishes in the *Federal Register* and transmits to the Congress a notice stating that the emergency is to continue in effect beyond the anniversary date. In accordance with this provision, I have sent to the *Federal Register* for publication the enclosed notice stating that the emergency declared in Executive Order 13159 of June 21, 2000, with respect to the risk of nuclear proliferation created by the accumulation of a large volume of weapons-usable fissile material in the territory of the Russian Federation is to continue beyond June 21, 2012.

It remains a major national security goal of the United States to ensure that fissile material removed from Russian nuclear weapons pursuant to various arms control and disarmament agreements is dedicated to peaceful uses, subject to transparency measures, and protected from diversion to activities of proliferation concern. The accumulation of a large volume of weapons-usable fissile material in the territory of the Russian Federation continues to pose an unusual and extraordinary threat to the national security and foreign policy of the United States. For this reason, I have determined that it is necessary to continue the national emergency declared with respect to the risk of nuclear proliferation created by the accumulation of a large volume of weapons-usable fissile material in the territory of the Russian Federation and maintain in force these emergency authorities to respond to this threat.

BARACK OBAMA

NOTE: The notice is listed in Appendix D at the end of this volume.

Remarks Prior to a Meeting With President Hu Jintao of China in Los Cabos, Mexico
June 19, 2012

President Obama. I just want to say that it's a great pleasure once again to have this bilateral meeting with President Hu.

Over the last several years, as a consequence of not only extensive one-on-one meetings, but also because of the outstanding work that our teams have done through the Strategic and Economic Dialogue, we have been able to really create a new model for practical, constructive, and comprehensive relations between our two countries.

Obviously, as two of the largest economies in the world, much of our focus has been on increasing trade and commerce between our two countries in a way that creates mutual benefits, and we have made significant progress in not only our bilateral relations, but also in helping to manage through some very difficult economic crises.

We've also been able to cooperate on a range of regional issues relating to the Asia-Pacific region, but also with respect to conflict and security challenges around the world.

In the wake of the G–20, this will be a good opportunity for us to recap the work that both China and the United States have to do to sustain global economic growth and to make sure that we are creating jobs and opportunity for our citizens.

And I'm also looking forward to having the opportunity to discuss some immediate issues that the world confronts. We need to discuss Iran, North Korea, and the challenges of curbing nuclear proliferation. This will also give us an opportunity to discuss the situation in Syria and to arrive at a cooperative approach that can end the bloodshed there and lead to the kind of legitimate government that I think we all hope for.

So once again, I want to thank President Hu for his leadership both in the G–20 and in helping to nurture the kind of cooperative relationship that we've developed, and I look forward very much to our discussion.

President Hu. I'm delighted to meet with you, Mr. President, again. It's already our 12th meeting. In March this year, you and I had very good talks in Seoul, Korea, and over the past 3 months, the working teams of both countries have been working in real earnest to follow through with the important agreement you and I reached. And we have made new progress in developing a cooperative partnership between China and the United States.

Building a good, stable, and productive China-U.S. relationship is in the fundamental mutual interest of our two countries and our two peoples and also contributes to peace and development of the world.

China is willing to work together with the United States to remain firmly committed to building a cooperative partnership. We are willing to work with the United States to continue enhance mutual trust and cooperation, appropriately handle disagreements and the sensitive issues, and continue to move forward with this cooperative partnership on a sustained, steady, and sound course.

I highly appreciate the important role played by President Obama in promoting the growth of this relationship. I believe that the talks we are going to have are going to be conducted in a sincere, friendly, and productive manner.

President Obama. Thank you.

NOTE: The President spoke at 4:09 p.m. at the Convention Center. President Hu spoke in Chinese, and his remarks were translated by an interpreter.

The President's News Conference in Los Cabos
June 19, 2012

The President. I want to begin by thanking my good friend and partner, President Calderon, and the people of Los Cabos and Mexico for their outstanding hospitality and leadership. Mexico is the first Latin American country to host a G–20 summit, and this has been another example of Mexico playing a larger role in world affairs, from the global economy to climate change to development.

Since this is my last visit to Mexico during President Calderon's time in office, I want to say how much I've valued Felipe's friendship and the progress that we've made together over the past several years. And building on the spirit here at Los Cabos, I'm absolutely confident that the deep ties between our countries will only grow stronger in the years to come.

Now, over the past 3 years, these G–20 summits have allowed our nations to pull the global economy back from a free fall and put us back on the path of recovery and growth. In the United States, our businesses have created jobs for 27 months in a row—more than 4 million jobs in all—and our highest priority continues to be putting people back to work even faster.

Today, we recognize that there are a wide range of threats to our ongoing global economic recovery and growth. But the one that's received the most focus obviously and that is having a significant impact on the United States as well as globally is the situation in Europe. As our largest trading partner, slower growth in Europe means slower growth in American jobs. So we have a profound interest in seeing Europe prosper. That's why I've been consulting closely with my European counterparts during this crisis, as we've done here at Los Cabos.

I do think it's important to note, however, that most leaders of the euro zone, the economies are not part of the G–20. The challenges facing Europe will not be solved by the G–20

or by the United States. The solutions will be debated and decided, appropriately, by the leaders and the people of Europe.

So this has been an opportunity for us to hear from European leaders on the progress they're making and on their next steps, especially in the wake of the election in Greece, and because they're heading into the EU summit later this month. It's also been a chance for the international community, including the United States—the largest economy in the world, and with our own record of responding to financial crises—to stress the importance of decisive action at this moment.

Now, markets around the world as well as governments have been asking if Europe is ready to do what is necessary to hold the euro zone together. Over the last 2 days, European leaders here in Cabos have made it clear that they understand the stakes and they pledged to take the actions needed to address this crisis and restore confidence, stability, and growth. Let me just be a little more specific.

First, our friends in Europe clearly grasp the seriousness of the situation and are moving forward with a heightened sense of urgency. I welcome the important steps that they have already taken to promote growth, financial stability, and fiscal responsibility. I'm very pleased that the European leaders here said that they will take all necessary measures to safeguard the integrity and stability of the euro zone, to improve the functioning of the financial markets. And this will contribute to breaking the feedback loop between sovereigns and banks and make sovereign borrowing costs sustainable.

I also welcome the adoption of the fiscal compact and its ongoing implementation, assessed on a structural basis, together with a growth strategy, which includes structural reforms.

G–20 leaders all supported Europe working in partnership with the next Greek Government to ensure that they remain on a path to reform and sustainability within the euro zone. Another positive step forward was the euro zone's commitment to work on a more integrated financial architecture, including banking supervision, resolution, and recapitalization, as well as deposit insurance. Also, in the coming days, Spain will lay out the details of its financial support request for its banks restructuring agency, providing clarity to reassure markets on the form and the amount and the structure of support to be approved at the earliest time.

It's also positive that the euro zone will pursue structural reforms to strengthen competitiveness in deficit countries and to promote demand and growth in surplus countries to reduce imbalances within the euro area.

And finally, I welcome the fact that Europe is determined to move forward quickly on measures to support growth and investment including by completing the European single market and making better use of European funds.

Of course, Europe is not, as I said, the only source of concern when it comes to global growth. The G–20 also agreed that reversing the economic slowdown demands a renewed focus on growth and job creation.

As the world's largest economy, the best thing the United States can do is to create jobs and growth in the short term, even as we continue to put our fiscal house in order over the long term. And as part of that effort, we've made significant progress in advancing our trade agenda. This is an essential to promoting growth, innovation and jobs in the United States.

Here in Los Cabos, we announced important steps towards closer integration with three of our major trading partners. Both Mexico and Canada have been invited to join the Trans-Pacific Partnership negotiations, which is an ambitious 21st-century trade agreement that will now include 11 countries. And this agreement holds enormous opportunities to boost trade in one of the world's fastest growing regions.

Even as we build this new framework for trade in the Asia-Pacific, we're also working to expand our trade with Europe. So today the United States and the European Union agreed to take the next step in our work towards the possible launching of negotiations on an agreement to strengthen our already very deep trade and investment partnership.

In addition, and in keeping with our commitments at the last G–20 in Cannes, we agreed that countries should not intervene to hold their currencies at undervalued levels and that countries with large surpluses and export-oriented economies needed to continue to boost demand.

So, in closing, I'd note that with Mexico's leadership, we continue to make progress across a range of challenges that are vital to our shared prosperity, from food security to green economic growth that combats climate change, from financial education and protection for consumers to combating corruption that stifles economic growth, and in strengthening financial regulation to creating a more level playing field. All of this happened in large part because of the leadership of President Calderon. I want to thank him, and I want to thank my fellow leaders for their partnership as we work very hard to create jobs and opportunity that all of our citizens deserve.

So with that, I'm going to start with Ben Feller of AP [Associated Press].

Economic Stabilization Efforts in Europe/U.S. Economy

Q. Thank you very much, Mr. President. We're all hearing a lot of encouraging promises about what Europe plans to do, but can you assure us that those actions, if they're able to come together on them, will actually do anything to create jobs in America this year? And if Europe is not able to rally in a big way pretty quickly, do you think that will cost you the election?

The President. Well, first of all, I think that what I've heard from European leaders during the course of these discussions is they understand the stakes. They understand why it's important for them to take bold and decisive action. And I'm confident that they can meet those tests.

Now, I always show great sympathy for my European friends because they don't have to deal with one Congress; they have to deal with 17 Parliaments, if you're talking about the euro zone. If you're talking about the European Union, you're talking about 27. And that means that sometimes, even after they've conceived of approaches to deal with the crisis, they have to work through all the politics to get it done. And markets are a lot more impatient.

And so what I've encouraged them to do is to lay out a framework for where they want to go in increasing European integration, in resolving the financial pressures that are on sovereign countries. Even if they can't achieve all of it in one full swoop, I think if people have a sense of where they're going, that can provide confidence and break the fever. Because if you think about Europe, look, this remains one of the wealthiest, most productive regions of the world. Europe continues to have enormous strengths: a very well educated, productive workforce. They have some of the biggest, best run companies in the world. They have trading relationships around the world. And all of these problems that they're facing right now are entirely solvable, but the markets, when they start seeing potential uncertainty, show a lot more risk aversion, and you can start getting into a negative cycle.

And what we have to do is it to create a positive cycle, where people become more confident, the markets settle down, and they have the time and the space to execute the kinds of structural reforms that not only Europe, but all of us are having to go through, in balancing the need for growth, but also dealing with issues like debt and deficits. And I'm confident that over the next several weeks, Europe will paint a picture of where we need to go, take some immediate steps that are required to give them that time and space. And based on the conversations that I've had here today and the conversations that I've had over the last several

months, I'm confident that they are very much committed to the European project.

Now, all this affects the United States. Europe as a whole is our largest trading partner. And if fewer folks are buying stuff in Paris or Berlin, that means that we're selling less stuff made in Pittsburgh or Cleveland. But I think there are a couple of things that we've already done that help. The financial regulatory reforms that we passed means that our banks are better capitalized. It means that our supervision and our mechanisms for looking at trouble spots in our financial system are superior to what they were back in 2008. That's an important difference. But there's still some more things we can do.

And the most important thing we can do is something that I've already talked about. If Congress would act on a jobs plan that independent economists say would put us on the path of creating an extra million jobs on top of the ones that have already been created—putting teachers back in the classroom, putting construction workers back on the job rebuilding infrastructure that badly needs to be rebuilt—all those things can make a significant difference. And given that we don't have full control over what happens in Europe or the pace at which things happen in Europe, let's make sure that we're doing those things that we do have control over and that are good policy anyway.

2012 Presidential Election

Q. [*Inaudible*]
The President. I think it's fair to say that any—all these issues, economic issues, will potentially have some impact on the election. But that's not my biggest concern right now. My biggest concern is the same concern I've had over the last 3½ years, which is folks who are out of work or underemployed or unable to pay the bills, what steps are we taking that potentially put them in a stronger position. And I've consistently believed that if we take the right policy steps, if we're doing the right thing, then the politics will follow. And my mind hasn't changed on that.

Jeff Mason, Reuters. Where's Jeff?

Situation in Syria

Q. Thank you, sir. My question is about Syria. Did President Putin of Russia indicate any desire on Russia's part for Asad to step down or to leave power? And did you make any tangible progress in your meetings with him or with Chinese President Hu in finding a way to stop the bloodshed there?

The President. Right. Well, these were major topics of conversation in both meetings. And anybody who's seen scenes of what's happening in Syria I think recognizes that the violence is completely out of hand, that civilians are being targeted, and that Asad has lost legitimacy. And when you massacre your own citizens in the ways that we've seen, it is impossible to conceive of a orderly political transition that leaves Asad in power.

Now, that doesn't mean that that process of political transition is easy. And there's no doubt that Russia, which historically has had a relationship with Syria, as well as China, which is generally wary of commenting on what it considers to be the internal affairs of other countries, are and have been more resistant to applying the kind of pressure that's necessary to achieve that political transition.

We had a very candid conversation. I wouldn't suggest that at this point the United States and the rest of the international community are aligned with Russia and China in their positions, but I do think they recognize the grave dangers of all-out civil war. I do not think they condone the massacres that we've witnessed. And I think they believe that everybody would be better served if Syria had a mechanism for ceasing the violence and creating a legitimate government.

What I've said to them is that it's important for the world community to work with the United Nations and Kofi Annan on what a political transition would look like. And my hope is, is that we can have those conversations in the coming week or two and that we can present to the world, but most importantly, to the Syrian people, a pathway whereby this conflict can be resolved.

But I don't think it would be fair to say that the Russians and the Chinese are signed on at this point. I think what is fair to say is that they recognize that the current situation is grave; it does not serve their interests; it certainly does not serve the interests of the Syrian people. And where we agree is that if we can help the Syrian people find a path to a resolution, all of us would be better off.

But it's my personal belief—and I shared this with them—that I don't see a scenario in which Asad stays and violence is reduced. He had an opportunity with the Annan plan. They did not fulfill their side of the deal. Instead we saw escalation and murder of innocent women and children. And at this point, we have the international monitors that were sent in having to leave because of this violence that's being perpetrated. And although you'll hear sometimes from some commentators that the opposition has engaged in violence as well, and obviously, there's evidence of that, I think it's also fair to say that those haunting images that we saw in places like Hom were the direct result of decisions made by the Syrian Government and ultimately Mr. Asad is responsible.

Q. Did either of them talk about Syria without Asad?

The President. We had an intensive conversation about it. If you're asking me whether they signed on to that proposition, I don't think it would be fair to say that they are there yet. But my—I'm going to keep on making the argument, and my expectation is, is that at some point there's a recognition that it's hard to envision a better future for Syria while Asad is still there.

Julianna Goldman [Bloomberg News].

Economic Stabilization Efforts in Europe

Q. Thank you, Mr. President. One of Mitt Romney's economic advisers recently wrote in a German publication that your recommendations to Europe and to Germany in particular reveal ignorance of the causes of the crisis, and he said that they have the same flaws as your own economic policies. I want to get your response to that and also to follow up on Ben's question. Europe has been kicking the can down the road for years, so why are you any more convinced that we won't see another 3-month fix emerge out of Brussels at the end of the month?

The President. Well, first of all, with respect to Mr. Romney's advisers, I suggest you go talk to Mr. Romney about his advisers. I would point out that we have one President at a time and one administration at a time, and I think traditionally the notion has been that America's political differences end at the water's edge. I'd also suggest that he may not be familiar with what our suggestions to the Germans have been. And I think sometimes back home there is a desire to superimpose whatever ideological arguments are taking place back home on to a very complicated situation in Europe.

The situation in Europe is a combination of things. You've got situations where some countries did have undisciplined fiscal practices, public debt. You had some countries like Spain whose problems actually arose out of housing speculation and problems in the private sector that didn't have to do with public debt.

I think that there's no doubt that all the countries in Europe at this point recognize the need for growth strategies inside of Europe that are consistent with fiscal consolidation plans. And by the way, that's exactly what I think the United States should be thinking about. The essence of the plan that I presented back in September was how do we increase growth and jobs now while providing clarity in terms of how we reduce our deficit and our debt, medium and long term.

And I think that's the right recipe generally, not just for us, but across the board.

You had a second question. What was it?

Q. Why are you—[*inaudible*]?

The President. Why am I confident? Well, look, I don't want to sound Pollyannish here. Resolving the issues in Europe is difficult. As I said, there are a lot of players involved. There are a lot of complexities to the problems, because we're talking about the problems of a bunch of different countries at this point. Changing market psychology is very difficult. But the tools are available. The sense of urgen-

cy among the leaders is clear. And so what we have to do is combine that sense of urgency with the tools that are available and bridge them in a timely fashion that can provide markets confidence. And I think that can be done.

Hopefully, just to give an example, when Spain clarifies exactly how it intends to draw down and utilize dollars—or not dollars, but euros to recapitalize its banking system, given that it's already got support from other European countries, given that the resources are available, what's missing right now is just a sense of specifics and the path whereby that takes place. When markets see that, that can help build confidence and reverse psychology.

So there are going to be a range of steps that they can take. None of them are going to be a silver bullet that solves this thing entirely over the next week or 2 weeks or 2 months. But each step points to the fact that Europe is moving towards further integration rather than breakup and that these problems can be resolved and points to the underlying strength in Europe's economies.

These are not countries that somehow at their core are unproductive or dysfunctional; these are advanced economies with extraordinarily productive people. They've got a particular challenge that has to do with a currency union that didn't have all the best bells and whistles of a fiscal or a monetary union, and they're catching up now to some of those needs. And they just need the time and the space to do it. In the meantime, they've got to send a strong signal to the market, and I'm confident they can do that.

All right. Thank you very much, everybody.

NOTE: The President's news conference began at 5:47 p.m. at the Convention Center. In his remarks, the President referred to President Bashar al-Asad of Syria; former Secretary-General Kofi A. Annan of the United Nations, in his capacity as Joint U.N.-Arab League Special Envoy for Syria; and Republican Presidential candidate former Gov. W. Mitt Romney of Massachusetts. The transcript was released by the Office of the Press Secretary on June 20.

Statement on the Observance of Juneteenth
June 19, 2012

On this day in 1865, 2 years after President Lincoln signed the Emancipation Proclamation, word finally reached the people of Galveston, Texas, that the Civil War was over. All enslaved men, women, and children were now free.

Though it would take decades of struggle and collective effort before African Americans were granted equal treatment and protection under the law, Juneteenth is recognized by Americans everywhere as a symbolic milestone in our journey toward a more perfect Union.

With the recent groundbreaking of the first Smithsonian museum dedicated to African American history and culture and the dedication of a monument to Dr. Martin Luther King, Jr., on the National Mall, this Juneteenth offers another opportunity to reflect on how far we've come as a nation. And it's also a chance to recommit ourselves to the ongoing work of guaranteeing liberty and equal rights for all Americans.

Statement on World Refugee Day
June 20, 2012

On this World Refugee Day, the United States joins the international community in recognizing the nearly 15 million refugees worldwide, and millions more internally displaced people. We honor the dignity, courage, and determination of these men, women, and children who have fled persecution and violence in their homelands and the commitment and generosity of the countries and organizations that provide them protection and assistance during this difficult time.

While we work to promote lasting peace and stability and human rights around the world so that these refugees may one day return to their countries in safety and dignity, we know that for some voluntary return may not be possible.

For these refugees, social, economic, and legal integration in their country of asylum not only provides opportunities for them to begin rebuilding their lives, but also for the contribution of their knowledge, talents, and skills to be fully realized. Americans know the benefits of these valuable contributions firsthand. Since 1975, we have welcomed more than 3 million refugees from all over the world and continue to lead the world in refugee resettlement.

Together with the Office of the United Nations High Commissioner for Refugees and the international community, we are committed to protecting the world's refugees, mitigating their suffering, and working to help find ways for them to live in dignity and peace.

Remarks on Education Reform
June 21, 2012

The President. Thank you. Everybody, have a seat. Well, it is good to see all of you.

Audience member. We love you!

The President. I love you guys back. [*Laughter*] I have to say, the—I don't know about the choice of music coming in here, though. [*Laughter*] I love my Marine Band, but this is kind of a young demographic for the piano cocktail hour. [*Laughter*]

are much more dressed up than usually when I

So some of the most fun I've had as President is when I get a chance to talk with you—college students—about the importance of earning a higher education in today's economy. And I'll admit that the East Room isn't as rowdy as Carmichael Arena at UNC or—we got any UNC folks here in the house? There we go. Coors Center at CU Boulder—any—no? Okay. [*Laughter*] I have to say that most of you see you in your own natural habitats.

But our message today is serious. Right now the unemployment rate for Americans with a college degree or more is about half the national average. They earn twice as much as those who don't have a high school diploma. So, whether it's at a 4-year college or a community college or a technical program, some form of higher education, something beyond high school has never been more important. It's the surest path to finding a good job, earning a good salary, making it into the middle class.

And at the same time, over the last two decades, the cost of college has doubled—it's actually more than doubled. And that means—and I don't have to tell you, because you're probably tallying it up right now—the cost for you to take out loans has increased, and you are more likely to rack up more debt. The average student who borrows to pay for college now graduates with about $26,000 of debt from their student loans. Americans as a whole now owe more on student loans than they do on their credit cards. And that is wrong, because we cannot afford to price the middle class and folks who aspire to go into the middle class, we can't price them out of the college education market. We can't stand by when millions of young people are already saddled with debt just as you're starting off.

Your parents, your grandparents, oftentimes they were in a position where when they got that first job, the first thing they're thinking about is, how do I save to buy a home and start a family? And if you're already dealing with a big bunch of debt before you even get started, that's a problem. And it's mind-boggling that we've had this stalemate in Washington that threatens to make the situation even worse.

So the reason you're all here, the reason all these fine-looking young people behind me are here is that in just over a week the interest rates on Federal student loans are scheduled to double. I've been talking about this now for what, a month and a half, 2 months, 3 months, 5 months? I've lost track. We've been talking about it for a long time. If Congress does not get this done in a week, the average student with Federal student loans will rack up an ad-

ditional $1,000 in debt over the coming year. If Congress fails to act, more than 7 million students will suddenly be hit with the equivalent of a $1,000 tax hike. And that's not something that you can afford right now.

Now, as I said, if this warning sounds familiar, we've been talking about this for months. Congress has had the time to fix this for months. It's part of the reason why everybody here looks impatient. This issue didn't come out of nowhere; it's been looming for months. But we've been stuck watching Congress play chicken with another deadline. So we're 9 days away from thousands of American workers having to walk off their job because Congress hasn't passed a transportation bill. We're 10 days away from nearly 7.5 million students seeing their loan rates double because Congress hasn't acted. This should be a no-brainer. It should not be difficult. It should've gotten done weeks ago.

Now, the good news is, there are folks in Congress trying to do the right thing. Last month, Democrats in the Senate put forward a plan that would have kept these rates in place without adding a dime to the deficit. Unfortunately, Senate Republicans got together and blocked it. Over in the House, the Republicans said they'd keep these rates down only if we agreed to cut things like preventive health care for women, which obviously wouldn't fix the problem, but would create a new problem.

This is—even as they were voting in lockstep for an economic plan that would cut financial aid for 9 million college students by an average of $1,000 and give a $150,000 tax cut to wealthy Americans. So I recognize that there's been some effort to change the subject from this rate hike.

One Congressman warned that this is all about giving college students "free college education"—which doesn't make much sense, because the definition of a loan is it's not free—[*laughter*]—you have to pay it back. Others have said we're just talking about student loans to distract from the economy. That doesn't make much sense because this is the economy.

This is all about the economy. This is all about whether or not we are going to have the best trained, best educated workforce in the world. That improves our economy. And higher education cannot be a luxury reserved just for a privileged few. It's an economic necessity for every family, and every family should be able to afford it.

So you guys, during this period when you've been in college have been some of the toughest economic times since the 1930s, and there are still a lot of challenges ahead globally. And we can't control every economic headwind that we face, but this is something we can control. This is something we can do something about. Stopping student rates from doubling at the end of the month is something we can do right now to make a difference in the lives of all the American people.

There's still 10 days for Congress to do the right thing. I understand that members of both parties say they want to get this done, and there are conversations taking place, but they haven't done it yet. And we've got to keep the pressure on.

That's where all of you come in. Over the past few months, there are so many students and parents who have been working hard to shine a light on this issue. You've rallied on campuses, in your communities. You've called, you've e-mailed, you've tweeted your representatives in Washington. So you've played your part in making sure your voice is heard and your democracy is responsive.

My main message is, as you guys embark on this day of action, I want to make sure you keep this going. Don't stop until it's actually done. There is nothing more powerful than millions of voices that are calling for change, and all of your voices can make a difference. So keep telling Congress to do what's right, to get this done. Tell them now is not the time to double interest rates on your student loans. Tell them to double down on an investment in a strong and secure middle class, and that means your education. Tell them now is the time to double down on an America where everybody who works hard has a fair shot at success.

And for those who are not here and are watching, if you tweet, use the hashtag #dontdoublemyrate—[*laughter*]—don't double my rate. But I tell you, when I look out at this group right here, you give me confidence in America. You make me optimistic, not only because you're getting a great education, but also because all of you are participating and making sure that this democracy works the way it's supposed to. We need outstanding engineers, and we need outstanding nonprofit leaders, and we need outstanding entrepreneurs, but we also need outstanding citizens. And that's what you guys are displaying by your presence and your activities.

So keep it up. Let's get this done. Thanks, everybody.

NOTE: The President spoke at 1:36 p.m. in the East Room at the White House. In his remarks, he referred to Rep. W. Joseph Walsh.

Statement on the Resignation of John E. Bryson as Secretary of Commerce
June 21, 2012

Last night I accepted the resignation of John Bryson as Secretary of the Department of Commerce. I want to extend my deepest thanks and appreciation to John for his service over the past months and wish him and his family the very best.

As Secretary, John fought tirelessly for our Nation's businesses and workers, helping to

bolster our exports and promote American manufacturing and products at home and abroad. John has proven himself an effective and distinguished leader throughout his career in both the public and private sectors, from his success in the business world to his work leading on issues in the renewable energy industry. I am grateful that he brought that invaluable experience and expertise to my administration and am pleased that he has agreed to continue supporting our efforts to strengthen the economy and create good jobs by serving as a member of my Export Council going forward.

I am confident that Dr. Rebecca Blank will serve the American people well as Acting Secretary and that the Commerce Department staff will continue their tireless work putting forward policies that help our workers and businesses compete.

Remarks at the National Association of Latino Elected and Appointed Officials Annual Conference in Orlando, Florida
June 22, 2012

The President. Gracias! Thank you so much. Thank you. Everybody, please have a seat. Ah, it is good to be back at NALEO. *Que placer estar aqui con tantos amigos.* It is wonderful to see a lot of good friends from all across the country. It is nice to be at Disney World. This is now the second time I've come to Disney World without my daughters. They are not happy with me. [*Laughter*]

I want to thank Secretary Solis for the introduction and for her hard work. She is one of the best Labor Secretaries we have ever had, and she is thinking about you each and every day. I want to thank Sylvia and Arturo for their outstanding leadership. Arturo, happy early birthday. I will not sing, don't worry. [*Laughter*] Welcome to the other side of the hill. [*Laughter*]

And it is especially good to have Ambassador Mari Carmen Aponte here with us. We are very proud of her. When the Senate refused to confirm Mari, I sent her to El Salvador anyway—[*laughter*]—because I knew she was going to do an outstanding job. And she has. And I'm glad to see the Senate finally confirmed her last week. So she's now official.

Last but not least, I want to thank all of you. It's always nice to get out of Washington. It's nice to get a little Florida sunshine. But it's especially nice to see folks who have devoted themselves to serving their communities and their country, who've dedicated themselves to making people's lives just a little bit better each and every day, at every level: school board, State legislatures, county boards. You guys are where the rubber hits the road. And I've had a chance to see many of you in your lo-

cal communities and hear the stories of all your efforts and all your hopes and all your dreams and also some of your frustrations and the hardships that are taking place.

Yesterday your featured speaker came here and said that the election in November isn't about two people. It's not about being a Republican or a Democrat or an Independent. It is about the future of America. And while we've got a lot of differences, he and I, on this point I could not agree more. This is about America's future. The defining issue of our time is whether we carry forward the promise that has drawn generations of immigrants to our shores from every corner of the globe, sometimes at great risk, men and women drawn by the promise that no matter who you are, no matter what you look like, no matter where you come from, no matter what your last name, this is a place where you can make it if you try. This is a place where you can make it if you try.

And whether our ancestors arrived on the *Mayflower* or were brought here on slave ships, whether they signed in at Ellis Island or they crossed the Rio Grande, their diversity has not only enriched this country, it helped build the greatest economic engine the world has ever known.

Hungry people, striving people, dreamers, risk-takers. People don't come here looking for handouts. We are a nation of strivers and climbers and entrepreneurs, the hardest working people on Earth. And nobody personifies these American values, these American traits, more than the Latino community. That's the essence of who you are.

All we ask for is that hard work pays off, that responsibility is rewarded, so that if these men and women put in enough effort, they can find a good job, own their own home, send their kids to college, let their kids dream even bigger, put away a little bit for retirement, not go bankrupt when you get sick.

And I ran for this office because for more than a decade, that dream had been slipping away from too many Americans. Before I even took office, the worst economic crisis of our lifetimes pushed it even further from reach, particularly for a lot of Latino communities, which had already faced higher unemployment and higher poverty rates.

So the question is not whether we need to do better. Of course, the economy isn't where it needs to be. Of course, there's still too many who struggle. We've got so much more work to do. But the question is: How do we make the economy grow faster? How do we create more jobs? How do we create more opportunity? The question is: What vision are we going to stand up for? Who are we going to fight for?

That's what we have to decide right now. That's what this election's about. Who are we fighting for? What vision of America do we believe in?

If America is about anything, it's about passing on even greater opportunity to our children. It's about education. And that's why I expanded Pell grants, which will give an additional 150,000 children in the Latino community a chance to go to college. That's why I've invested in our community colleges, which are a gateway to a good job for so many Hispanic Americans, Americans of every stripe.

That's why schools in almost every State, some in the toughest neighborhoods around, have answered our challenge to raise their standards for teaching and learning—not by teaching to a test, but by expanding creativity and improving curriculums and focusing more on kids who are hardest to reach so that we give every child a fighting chance. That's part of the vision of America that we believe in.

In this country, we believe that if you want to take a risk on a new idea, you should have the chance to succeed. And you shouldn't have

to have wealthy parents in order to be successful. Latino-owned businesses have been the fastest growing small businesses, and we've cut their taxes 18 times. We've expanded new loans and new credit so they can grow and they can hire. That's the vision we believe in.

In America, we believe you shouldn't go broke because you get sick. Hard-working people out there—sometimes two jobs, three jobs—still don't have health insurance. If you did have health insurance, insurance companies were able to discriminate against certain patients. That was wrong. It was wrong to let insurance companies just jack up premiums for no reason and to have millions of working Americans uninsured, with the Latino community having the highest rate of uninsured of any community in the country.

So, after a century of trying, we finally passed reform that will make health care affordable and available for every American. That was the right thing to do. That was the right thing to do. That was the right thing to do.

Now, we're not done yet. We've got more to do. We need to put more good teachers in our classrooms. We need to get colleges and universities to bring down the cost of tuition to make it more affordable for more young people.

We need to invest in new research and innovation, especially new sources of energy and high-tech manufacturing. We need to put people back to work rebuilding our roads and our highways and our runways. Construction jobs can have a huge ripple effect in communities all across the country. And nobody knows it better than State and local officials. You know the difference it makes. And with the housing bubble bursting, we've got tens of thousands of construction workers just ready and eager to get to work.

We need to give families in hard-hit housing markets like Florida and Nevada the chance to refinance and save $3,000 a year on their mortgage. That's good for those families. It's good for the housing market. It's good for the surrounding community. There's no reason why Congress hasn't already done it.

Instead of just talking a big game about "job creators," we should give small-business owners a tax break for hiring more workers or for paying higher wages. Instead of rewarding companies that ship jobs overseas, we should take that money and use it to cover moving expenses for companies who are bringing jobs back to America.

On almost every issue of concern to your community, to every community, what's holding us back isn't a lack of big ideas. It's not a lack of technical solutions. By now just about every policy and proposal has been laid out on the table. What's holding us back is a stalemate, a stalemate in Washington between two fundamentally different views of which direction we should go.

The Republicans who run Congress, the man at the top of their ticket, they don't agree with any of the proposals I just talked about. They believe the best way to grow the economy is from the top down. So they want to roll back regulations and give insurance companies and credit card companies and mortgage lenders even more power to do as they please. They want to spend $5 trillion on new tax cuts, including a 25-percent tax cut for every millionaire in the country. And they want to pay for it by raising middle class taxes and gutting middle class priorities like education and training and health care and medical research.

And that's it. That's it. That's their economic plan. When they tell you they can do better, that's their idea of doing better. When they tell you they know how to fix the economy, that's exactly how they plan to do it. And I think they're wrong. I think they're wrong.

In this country, prosperity has never come from the top down. It comes from a strong and growing middle class and creating ladders of opportunity for all those who are striving to get into the middle class. It comes from successful, thriving small businesses that over time grow into medium-size and then large businesses.

We don't need more top-down economics. What we need is a better plan for education and training and energy independence and innovation and infrastructure that can rebuild America. What we need is a Tax Code that en-courages companies to create jobs and manufacturing here in the United States and, yes, asks the wealthiest Americans to help pay down the deficit. That's what's needed.

And what's also needed is immigration reform that finally lives up to our heritage as a nation of laws and as a nation of immigrants and continues the American story of renewal and energy and dynamism that's made us who we are.

I mean, think about it. You and I both know one of America's greatest strengths has always been our ability to attract talented, hard-working people who believe in this country, who want to help make it stronger. That's what keeps us young. That's what keeps us dynamic and energized. That's what makes us who we are.

But our current immigration system doesn't reflect those values. It allows the best and brightest to study here, but then tells them to leave, start companies somewhere else. It punishes immigrants and businesses who play by the rules and fails to address the fact that there are too many who don't. It separates families, and it denies innocent young people the chance to earn an education or serve in the uniform of the country they love.

Now, once again, the problem is not the lack of technical solutions. We know what the solutions are to this challenge. Just 6 years ago, an unlikely trio—John McCain, Ted Kennedy, President Bush—came together to champion comprehensive immigration reform. I, along with a lot of Democrats, were proud to join 23 Senate Republicans in voting for it. Today, those same Republicans have been driven away from the table by a small faction of their own party. It's created the same kind of stalemate on immigration reform that we're seeing on a whole range of other economic issues. And it's given rise to a patchwork of State laws that cause more problems than they solve and are often doing more harm than good.

Now, this makes no sense. It's not good for America. And as long as I am President of the United States, I will not give up the fight to change it.

In the face of a Congress that refuses to do anything on immigration, I've said that I'll take action wherever I can. So my administration has been doing what we can, without the help in Congress, for more than the last—for more than 3 years now. And last week, we took another step. On Friday, we announced that we're lifting the shadow of deportation from deserving young people who were brought to this country as children.

We should have passed the "DREAM Act" a long time ago. It was written by members of both parties. When it came up for a vote a year and a half ago, Republicans in Congress blocked it. The bill hadn't changed. The need hadn't changed. The only thing that had changed was politics. The need had not changed. The bill hadn't changed—written with Republicans. The only thing that had changed was politics. And I refused to keep looking young people in the eye, deserving young people in the eye, and tell them, tough luck, the politics is too hard.

I've met these young people all across the country. They're studying in our schools. They're playing with our children, pledging allegiance to our flag, hoping to serve our country. They are Americans in their hearts, in their minds. They are Americans through and through, in every single way but on paper. And all they want is to go to college and give back to the country they love. So lifting the shadow of deportation and giving them a reason to hope—that was the right thing to do. It was the right thing to do.

It's not amnesty. It falls short of where we need to be: a path to citizenship. It's not a permanent fix. This is a temporary measure that lets us focus our resources wisely while offering some justice to these young people. But it's precisely because it's temporary, Congress still needs to come up with a long-term immigration solution, rather than argue that we did this the wrong way or for the wrong reasons.

So to those who are saying Congress should be the one to fix this—absolutely. For those who say we should do this in a bipartisan fashion—absolutely. My door has been open for 3½ years. They know where to find me. [*Laughter*]

I've said time and again: Send me the "DREAM Act." I will sign it right away. And I'm still waiting to work with anyone from either party who is committed to real reform. But in the meantime, the question we should consider is this: Was providing these young people with the opportunity for a temporary measure of relief the right thing to do?

Audience members. Yes!

The President. I think it was. It's long past time that we gave them a sense of hope.

Now, your speaker from yesterday has a different view. In his speech, he said that when he makes a promise to you, he'll keep it. Well, he has promised to veto the "DREAM Act," and we should take him at his word. I'm just saying. [*Laughter*]

And I believe that would be a tragic mistake. You do too.

On all these issues—on the investments we need to grow the middle class and leave a better future for our kids, on deficit reduction that's fair and balanced, on immigration reform, on consumer financial protection so that people aren't exploited, whether at a payday loan shop or if they're sending remittances back to their families—on all these issues, Washington's got a long way to go to catch up with the rest of the country.

The whole idea behind the "DREAM Act," after all, was inspired by a music teacher in Illinois. She decided to call her Senator, Dick Durbin, when she discovered that one of her own students was forced to live in the shadows. But even as that idea fell prey to gridlock and game-playing in Washington, it gained momentum in the rest of the country: from every student who marched and organized to keep their classmates from being deported; from every parent who discovered the truth about the child down the street and chose to stand up for them, because these are all our kids; for every American who stood up and spoke out across the country because they saw a wrong and wanted it to be righted, who put their shoulder to the wheel and moved us a little closer toward justice.

That's what's always moved us forward. It doesn't start in Washington. It starts with a million quiet heroes who love their country and believe they can change it.

We all have different backgrounds. We all have different political beliefs. The Latino community is not monolithic; the African American community is not all of one mind. This is a big country. And sometimes, in tough times, in a country this big and busy, especially during a political year, those differences are cast in a bright spotlight.

But I ran for this office because I am absolutely convinced that what binds us together has always proven stronger than what drives us apart. We are one people. We need one another. Our patriotism is rooted not in race, not in ethnicity, not in creed; it is based on a shared belief in the enduring and permanent promise of America.

That's the promise that draws so many talented, driven people to these shores. That's the promise that drew my own father here. That's the promise that drew your parents or grandparents or great-grandparents, generations of people who dreamed of a place where knowledge and opportunity were available to anybody who was willing to work for it, anybody who was willing to seize it. A place where there was no limit to how far you could go, how high you could climb.

They took a chance. And America embraced their drive and embraced their courage—said, "Come, you're welcome." This is who we are.

Every single day I walk into the Oval Office, every day that I have this extraordinary privilege of being your President, I will always remember that in no other nation on Earth could my story even be possible. That's something I celebrate.

That's what drives me, in every decision I make, to try and widen the circle of opportunity, to fight for that big and generous and optimistic country we inherited, to carry that dream forward for generations to come. Because when I meet these young people, all throughout communities, I see myself. Who knows what they might achieve? I see my daughters and my nieces and my nephews. Who knows what they might achieve if we just give them a chance?

That's what I'm fighting for. That's what I stand for.

This fight will not always be easy. It hasn't always been easy. It will not happen overnight. Our history has been one where that march towards justice and freedom and equality has taken time. There will always be plenty of stubborn opposition in the way that says: "No, you can't. No, you shouldn't. Don't even try."

But America was built by people who said something different, who said, "Yes, we can," who said, "*Si, se puede.*" And as long as I have the privilege of being your President, I will be alongside you, fighting for the country that we together dream of.

God bless you. Thank you, NALEO. God bless the United States of America.

NOTE: The President spoke at 1:43 p.m. at the Walt Disney World Resort. In his remarks, he referred to Sylvia R. Garcia, president, and Arturo Vargas, executive director, National Association of Latino Elected and Appointed Officials; Republican Presidential candidate former Gov. W. Mitt Romney of Massachusetts; and Tereza Lee, doctoral student, Manhattan School of Music.

Remarks at an Obama Victory Fund 2012 Fundraiser in Tampa, Florida
June 22, 2012

The President. Hello, Tampa! Oh, it is good to be back in Tampa, Florida! I was so fired up, I missed a stair. [*Laughter*] I couldn't wait to get out here. Well, how's everybody doing today?

Couple of people I want to acknowledge. First of all, the outstanding mayor of your fair city, Bob Buckhorn's in the house. Florida's own, the chairwoman of the Democratic National Committee, Debbie Wasserman Shultz is here. And the chair of the Florida Democratic Party, Rod Smith is in the house.

And all of you are here.

Audience members. Fired up! Ready to go!

The President. Well——

Audience members. Fired up! Ready to go! Fired up! Ready to go! Fired up! Ready to go!

The President. Thank you.

Listen, Tampa, I'm here not only because I need your help. But I'm also here because the country needs your help. For the past 3 years, we've been battling our way back from the worst economic crisis since the Great Depression. Not only are we digging out of a hole that's 9 million jobs deep, we're digging out of an entire decade where manufacturing left our shores; where costs rose, but incomes weren't going up; where middle class families fell further and further behind. It was a decade where two wars and trillions of dollars in tax cuts were put on our Nation's credit card, turning a record surplus into record deficits.

Now, today, our economy is growing again, but it needs to grow faster. Our businesses have created over 4 million jobs in the last 27 months. But we need to create more, and they need to pay better. I signed a law that will reduce our deficit by $2 trillion, but we've got to do more work on our deficit. One of the most urgent tasks is recovering from this immediate crisis, but the economy won't be truly healthy until we reverse that much longer erosion of the middle class, until we restore the basic American bargain that says if you work hard in this country, you can get ahead and own a home and send your kids to college and retire with dignity and respect.

Now, here's the thing, Florida. What's holding us back from meeting these challenges is not the lack of good ideas, it's not the lack of technical solutions. By now, just about every policy and proposal has been laid out there on the table. What is holding us back is a stalemate between two fundamentally different views in Washington about which direction we should go in.

This isn't just one of the run-of-the-mill political arguments you hear about in Washington sometimes. This is the defining issue of our time. We're in a make-or-break moment for the middle class. And the next President and the next Congress will face a set of decisions— on the economy and on the deficit and on tax-es—that will have an enormous impact on this country not just today, but the country that we pass on to our children.

And you know what, the outcome of this decision, this choice, is entirely up to you. It's up to you: the people of Tampa, the people of Florida, the American people.

Now, Governor Romney and his allies——

Audience members. Boo!

The President. They're patriotic Americans. They've got wonderful families. But they believe that we should go back to the top-down economics of the last decade.

Audience members. No!

The President. They figure that if we simply eliminate regulations and cut taxes by trillions of dollars, then the market will solve all of our problems.

You see? You heard that? [*Laughter*] I'm just saying.

No, wait, wait, that's their argument. They argue that if we help corporations and wealthy investors maximize their profits by whatever means necessary—whether through layoffs or outsourcing or union-busting—that it will automatically translate into jobs and prosperity that benefit all of us. That's their theory. That's their theory.

But I believe they're wrong. I think they're wrong. I believe we should do everything we can to help our entrepreneurs succeed. I want our companies to be as profitable as they can be. But that alone is not enough. Because the central challenge we face right now, the challenge that we've faced for over a decade, is that bigger profits haven't led to better jobs. Bigger profits haven't led to higher incomes.

And the reason is, in this country, in America, prosperity has never come from the top down; it comes from a strong and growing middle class and all those people who are striving and working to get into the middle class. It comes from successful, thriving small businesses that grow into medium-sized businesses and then large businesses.

We don't need more top-down economics. What we need is some middle-class-out economics, some bottom-up economics. We need a plan for better education and for better training, for energy independence, for innovation, for infrastructure that can rebuild America. What we need is a Tax Code that encourages companies to create jobs and manufacturing here in the United States and that asks the wealthiest Americans to help pay down our deficit, to do their fair share.

Tampa, that's the way forward. That's where I want to take this country over these next 4 years. And that's why I'm running for a second term as President of the United States.

Audience members. Four more years! Four more years! Four more years!

The President. Now, listen, there's no mystery about where the other side will take us if they win the election. I mean, their economic plan has been voted on in Congress. Governor Romney has it right there on his website. So look, first, they promise to roll back all kinds of regulations on banks and polluters and insurance companies and oil companies.

Audience members. Boo!

The President. That's part of—first part of their plan. Second part of their plan: They don't just want to keep all the Bush tax cuts in place, the ones for the wealthiest Americans, they want to keep those in place; then, they want to add another $5 trillion in tax cuts on top of that——

Audience members. Boo!

The President. ——including a 25-percent tax cut for every millionaire in the country.

Audience members. Boo!

The President. Now, I can tell this is a sophisticated group, so—[*laughter*]—so you might be wondering, how do they spend $5 trillion on new tax cuts and then, with a straight face, say that their plan would reduce the deficit? How do they do that? This is a good question. Now—well, let me tell you. They start by proposing a trillion dollars in cuts to things like education and training and medical research and clean energy.

Audience members. No!

The President. But that's not enough. That's only a trillion dollars; they've got all this—4 trillion to go. So then, they propose eliminating health care for about 50 million Americans.

Audience members. No!

The President. And then, they propose turning Medicare into a voucher program. But, you know what, that's still not enough. So, as it was reported in the newspaper just this week, they'll also have to raise taxes on the middle class by taking away tax deductions for everything from health care to college to retirement to homeownership.

Audience members. Boo!

The President. And that could cost some families thousands of dollars. So think about that. To pay for another $250,000 tax cut for the average millionaire, they want you to foot the bill.

Audience members. Boo!

The President. Let me see a show of hands: Is there anybody here who can afford to pay thousands of dollars to give people like me and Mr. Romney another tax cut?

Audience members. No!

The President. Come on, go ahead and raise your hand. Don't be shy. [*Laughter*]

Now, look, that's their entire economic plan. That's it. When Mr. Romney tells us he's some sort of financial wizard who can fix our economy, that's how he intends to do it.

And Bill Clinton has pointed out that this Republican agenda, it's nothing new. It's nothing more than the same thing we tried during the last administration, except on steroids. [*Laughter*]

Now, here's the thing. I have not seen a single nonpartisan expert say that the other side's economic plan would actually reduce the deficit in the long term. I haven't seen a single independent economist say it would create jobs in the short term. In fact, one said it would push us even deeper into recession.

But, you know what, if people still think their plan sounds like a good idea——

[*At this point, a baby cried.*]

The President. See? Somebody is depressed about this plan. They're hearing about it—[*laughter*]—I know, it's heartbreaking. [*Laughter*]

But if somebody out there thinks that's a good idea, if they want to give the policies of the last decade another try, then they should vote for Mr. Romney. That's how our democracy works. They should reelect the Republicans who've been running for Congress. That's what our democracy is all about. And together, Mr. Romney and a Republican Congress will take America back down this path that we've tried and didn't work the last time.

But if you believe we need a better plan, if you believe we need a middle class plan that grows our economy and shrinks our deficit, then we need to win this election. We need to move this country forward.

Despite what you'll hear from the other side, my plan isn't based on some belief that Government has the answer to all our problems. Over the last 3 years, I've cut taxes for the typical working family by $3,600. I've cut taxes for small businesses 18 times. I want a Government that is leaner and smarter, one that's designed for the 21st century, more responsive to the American people.

So look, I don't believe every regulation is smart or that every tax dollar is spent wisely. I don't believe that we should be in the business of helping people who refuse to help themselves. But I do share the belief of our first Republican President, a guy from my home State named Abraham Lincoln, who said that through Government, we should do together what we can't do as well for ourselves.

That's how we built this country, together. Sure, Democrats and Republicans have always disagreed on certain policies and programs. But throughout our history, at least our modern history, there's been a shared belief that, yes, we're a great market economy, but the market can't solve all its problems on our own.

So that's why FDR worked with Republicans and Democrats to send a generation of returning veterans to college on the GI bill, an investment that led to the largest middle class, the most prosperous economy in our history. They understood that people succeed when they have a chance to get a decent education and learn new skills and the businesses that hire those people benefit as well and the companies they start benefit as well. That was not just a Democratic belief, that was an American belief.

President Eisenhower, a Republican, he launched the Interstate Highway System and a new generation of scientific research. He understood that for companies to grow and hire, they need access to the best transportation and the fastest communication, the most cutting-edge innovation.

Ronald Reagan worked with Democrats to save Social Security and pay down the deficit by, yes, asking the wealthiest Americans to pay a little bit more in taxes. They understood that our economy is stronger when we don't balance our budget on the backs of middle class and poor Americans. We do it best when everybody does their fair share.

So Governor Romney and the Republican leaders in Congress, they've rejected what used to be this bipartisan tradition. They've opted for top-down, on-your-own economics that has never succeeded in this country. And I've got a different view. I have an economic plan based on the shared vision that's always worked for America's middle class and all those striving to get there, a plan focused on education and energy and innovation and infrastructure and a Tax Code that is fair and responsible. That's how we're going to build this country. That's why I'm running for President of the United States.

So first, we're going to make sure that every American has a chance to get the skills and training that today's jobs require. I—my plan would recruit an army of new teachers, pay them better, hire more teachers in areas like math and science. I want to give 2 million more Americans the chance to go to community colleges like this one and learn skills that local businesses are looking for right now. I want to make higher education affordable for every American who's willing to work for it, not just by offering more loans and financial aid, but also by getting schools to hold down the cost of college tuition.

Second, under my plan, we're going to move towards a future where we control our own energy. That's something that's good for our economy, good for our environment, good for our national security. So we need to end Government subsidies to oil companies; they're making a lot of money on their own. Let's double down on clean energy that's never been more promising, on wind power and solar power, biofuels and fuel-efficient cars. I want to put in place a new standard that makes clean energy the profitable kind of energy for every business in America.

Number three, we're going to make sure the United States of America is the best place on Earth for innovation and science and discovery. So my plan would give companies a permanent tax credit for research and development that they do here in America. We'll double down on public research that laid the foundation for the Internet and GPS and Google and all the companies and jobs that followed. That's who we are. We are innovators. We create things. We don't just buy things from other countries. We create things here in America and build them here in America.

And then, we're going to take half the money we're no longer spending on war, and we're going to use it to do some nation-building here at home. If we want businesses to thrive here, we got to put people back to work rebuilding our roads and our runways, our wireless networks, our ports. And what I'm pushing for is an independent fund that will attract private dollars and issue loans for new construction projects just based on two criteria: how badly are they needed and how much good will they do for the economy. We don't need bridges to nowhere. We need bridges to help businesses move goods and services and people all across the country and all around the world.

And fifth, we're going to reduce our deficit by $4 trillion. I have a detailed plan. We'll cut spending we can't afford. We'll strengthen programs like Medicare for the long haul. We can reform our Tax Code in a way that is fair and responsible, which, by the way, means let's stop giving tax breaks to businesses that ship jobs and factories overseas. Let's reward companies that create jobs in manufacturing right here in the United States of America.

Now, Mr. Romney disagrees with this. Today it was reported in the Washington Post that the companies his firm owned were "pioneers" in the outsourcing of American jobs to

places like China and India. Pioneers. Let me tell you, Tampa, we do not need an outsourcing pioneer in the Oval Office. We need a President who will fight for American jobs and fight for American manufacturing. That's what my plan will do. That's why I'm running for a second term as President of the United States.

Audience members. Four more years! Four more years! Four more years!

The President. And look, to get our deficit under control without sacrificing all the investments I've talked about—everything that we need to grow the economy—my plan, yes, will ask the wealthiest Americans to pay a little bit more, just like they did when Bill Clinton was President, just like they did when our economy created 23 million new jobs and the biggest budget surplus in history and a whole lot of millionaires to boot. And there are—look, there are plenty of patriotic, very successful Americans who'd be willing to make this contribution again because they believe in this country.

So this is about choices. I don't believe that giving millionaires and billionaires a $250,000 tax cut is more valuable to our future than hiring transformative teachers or providing financial aid to kids who need it to go to college. I don't believe that kind of tax cut is more likely to create jobs than providing loans to new entrepreneurs or tax credits to small businesses who hire veterans. I don't think it's more likely to spur economic growth than our investments in clean energy and medical research, in building new roads and bridges and expanding our ports and our runways.

So Governor Romney disagrees with my vision. And his allies in Congress disagree with my vision. Neither of them will endorse any policy that asks the wealthiest Americans to pay even a nickel more in taxes. Not a penny more. It's the reason—that's the reason we haven't reached an agreement on how to reduce our deficit. That's the reason my jobs bill that would put a million more people back to work has been voted down by Republicans in Congress time and time again. It is the biggest source of gridlock in Washington and has been over the last 3 years.

So, Tampa, here's the thing. Only you can break that stalemate. In this election, you have the final say about where we go. After a decade of war that's cost us thousands of lives and over a trillion dollars, you can decide whether we keep our brave men and women in Afghanistan indefinitely, like Mr. Romney wants to do, or whether we stick to the timeline that will finally bring our troops home.

You can decide—did something just fall down there? [*Laughter*] That's why we need infrastructure, right there.

You can decide whether we're going to have another political fight about ending a woman's right to choose and getting rid of Planned Parenthood and taking away access to birth control. Or you can decide that women should control their own health care choices.

You can decide: You choose whether to refight the battles we just had over financial reform and health care reform. Or you can decide that ending taxpayer bailouts of Wall Street banks was the right thing to do and that allowing 3 million young people to stay on their parent's health insurance plan is the right thing to do and that preventing insurance companies from discriminating against people with preexisting conditions is the right thing to do. You can decide.

You can decide whether we're going back to the days when you could be kicked out of the United States military just because of who you are and who you love.

You can decide whether it's time to stop denying citizenship to responsible young people just because they're the children of undocumented immigrants.

You can decide that this is—becomes the last election where multimillion-dollar donations that are undisclosed somehow speak louder than the voices of ordinary citizens.

So you know what, Tampa, this is up to you. This is up to you. From now until November, the other side will spend more money than we have ever seen in the history of the Republic. And all that money is going to be spent on ads telling you that the economy is bad, it's all my fault, and I can't fix it because Government is always the answer, according to me. [*Laugh-*

ter] Or because I didn't make a lot of money in the private sector, or because I'm in over my head, or because I think everybody's doing just fine. [*Laughter*] They will have ad after ad after ad, and all of them will have scary voices. [*Laughter*] They'll have pictures of me looking all old and—[*laughter*]—broke down. You've seen those ads. You've seen them. That's what Mr. Romney's going to say. That's what the Republicans in Congress will say.

And that may be their plan to win an election, but it's sure not a plan to create jobs. It's not a plan to grow the economy. It's not a plan to pay down the debt. It's not a plan to restore the middle class and restore the American Dream.

You deserve better than that. At such a big moment in our history, at a time when so many people are struggling, you deserve a real debate about the economic plans we're proposing. And then, make a choice: If there's anybody who believes the best way to grow our economy and create jobs is eliminating regulations and cutting $5 trillion worth of taxes, they should vote for Governor Romney and the Republicans who run Congress. God bless them.

Audience members. No!

The President. Because those folks—because that's what they're proposing. They are more than qualified to take us in that direction.

But if you believe we need a plan for education and energy and innovation and infrastructure, if you believe this economy grows best when everybody's got a fair shot and everybody does their fair share and everybody's playing by the same rules, if you believe that everybody should be able to succeed if they're working hard, no matter where they come from or what they look like, what their last name is or who they love, then I ask that you stand with me for a second term as President of the United States. I——

Audience members. Four more years! Four more years! Four more years!

The President. You know—in fact, I ask everybody—I want you guys—vote for anybody else—Democrat, Independent, or Republican—who shares this belief in how we grow an economy that is good for everybody and not just some. I will work with anybody of any party who believes that we're in this together, who believes that we rise or fall as one Nation and one people.

Don't let anybody tell you we lack the capacity to meet our challenges. We're Americans. The only thing lacking right now is our politics. And we can solve that. That's what your vote is for.

So I need you to hit the doors. I need you to make some phone calls. I need you to register your friends, get your family members going. Get on Facebook, get on Twitter.

I know since the last time I ran that my hair is a little grayer—[laughter]—and I know that we've been through some tough times together. But I promised you back in 2008 that I would always tell you what I thought and I'd always tell you where I stood. And I promised you that I would wake up every single day thinking about you and fighting for you. And, Tampa, I have kept that promise. I have kept that promise. I still believe in you. I need you to still believe in me.

And if we're out there working together, we can finish what we started and remind the world how a strong economy is built and why the United States of America is the greatest nation on Earth.

God bless you. God bless America.

NOTE: The President spoke at 4:18 p.m. at Hillsborough Community College. In his remarks, he referred to Republican Presidential candidate former Gov. W. Mitt Romney of Massachusetts.

Letter to Congressional Leaders on Continuation of the National Emergency With Respect to the Western Balkans
June 22, 2012

Dear Mr. Speaker: (Dear Mr. President:)

Section 202(d) of the National Emergencies Act (50 U.S.C. 1622(d)) provides for the automatic termination of a national emergency unless, within 90 days prior to the anniversary date of its declaration, the President publishes in the *Federal Register* and transmits to the Congress a notice stating that the emergency is to continue in effect beyond the anniversary date. In accordance with this provision, I have sent to the *Federal Register* for publication the enclosed notice stating that the Western Balkans emergency is to continue in effect beyond June 26, 2012.

The crisis constituted by the actions of persons engaged in, or assisting, sponsoring, or supporting (i) extremist violence in the Republic of Macedonia and elsewhere in the Western Balkans region, or (ii) acts obstructing implementation of the Dayton Accords in Bosnia, United Nations Security Council Resolution 1244 of June 10, 1999, in Kosovo, or the Ohrid Framework Agreement of 2001 in Macedonia, that led to the declaration of a national emergency on June 26, 2001, in Executive Order 13219, and to the amendment of that order in Executive Order 13304 of May 28, 2003, has not been resolved. The acts of extremist violence and obstructionist activity outlined in Executive Order 13219, as amended, are hostile to U.S. interests and continue to pose an unusual and extraordinary threat to the national security and foreign policy of the United States. For these reasons, I have determined that it is necessary to continue the national emergency declared with respect to the Western Balkans and maintain in force the sanctions to respond to this threat.

Sincerely,

BARACK OBAMA

NOTE: Identical letters were sent to John A. Boehner, Speaker of the House of Representatives, and Joseph R. Biden, Jr., President of the Senate. The notice is listed in Appendix D at the end of this volume.

The President's Weekly Address
June 23, 2012

Over the past 3 years, we've been clawing our way back from the worst economic crisis of our lifetimes. And we know it will take longer than any of us would like to fully recover all the jobs and savings that have been lost. But there are things we can do right now to help put people back to work and make life a little easier for middle class families.

For months, I've been pushing Congress to help us along by passing commonsense policies that would make a difference. Democrats and Republicans have already done some important work together, like passing a tax cut that's allowing working Americans to keep more of their paychecks every week. But Congress has refused to act on most of the other ideas in my jobs plan that economists say could put a million more Americans back to work.

There's no excuse for this kind of inaction. Right now we are 7 days away from thousands of American workers having to walk off the job because Congress hasn't passed a transportation bill. We are 8 days away from nearly 7½ million students seeing their loan rates double because Congress hasn't acted to stop it.

This makes no sense. We know that one of the most important things we can do for our economy is to make sure that all Americans get the best education possible. Right now the unemployment rate for Americans with a college degree or more is about half the national average. Their incomes are twice as high as those who don't have a high school diploma. So if we know that a higher education is the clearest path to the middle class, why would we make it harder to achieve?

So much of America needs to be repaired right now. Bridges are deteriorating after years of neglect. Highways are choked with congestion. Transportation delays cost Americans and businesses billions of dollars every year. And there are hundreds of thousands of construction workers who have never been more eager to get back on the job. So why would we let our transportation funding run out? This is a time when we should be doing everything in our power—Democrats and Republicans—to keep this recovery moving forward.

My administration is doing its part. On Friday, Secretary of Transportation Ray LaHood announced $500 million in competitive grants for States and communities that will create construction jobs on projects like road repair and port renovation. And that's an important step, but we can't do it all on our own.

The Senate did their part. They passed a bipartisan transportation bill back in March. It had the support of 52 Democrats and 22 Republicans.

Now it's up to the House to follow suit: to put aside partisan posturing, end the gridlock, and do what's right for the American people.

It's not lost on any of us that this is an election year, but we've got responsibilities that are bigger than an election. We answer to the American people, and they are demanding action. Let's make it easier for students to stay in college. Let's keep construction workers rebuilding our roads and bridges. And let's tell Congress to do their job. Tell them it's time to take steps that we know will create jobs now and help sustain our economy for years to come.

NOTE: The address was recorded at approximately 5:05 p.m. on June 21 in the East Room at the White House for broadcast on June 23. The transcript was made available by the Office of the Press Secretary on June 22, but was embargoed for release until 6 a.m. on June 23.

Remarks at an Obama Victory Fund 2012 Fundraiser in Durham, New Hampshire
June 25, 2012

The President. Hello, New Hampshire! Hello, Durham! Thank you. Thank you so much. Thank you, everybody. It is great to be back in New Hampshire.

A couple of people I want to acknowledge. First of all, wasn't Scott outstanding? Give Scott a big round of applause for his introduction. I want to thank Todd Allen, who is the principal here at Oyster River High School, and I want to thank our outstanding Senator from New Hampshire, Jeanne Shaheen. And I want to thank all of you.

I know it's a little warm in here. [*Laughter*] That's okay. That's okay. It is wonderful to be back. And I just have so many good memories here in New Hampshire, and I see some familiar faces and folks who were with me when people were still figuring out how to pronounce my name. [*Laughter*]

Audience member. We love you!

The President. I love you guys back. I really do.

Now, I am back here in New Hampshire not just because I need your help—although I do—but more importantly, I'm here because your country needs your help.

In 2008, we came together to reclaim the basic bargain that built this country, the basic ideal of this country, the thing that created the largest middle class, the most prosperous nation in the history of the world. We came together because we believe that in America, your success shouldn't be determined by the circumstances of your birth.

If you are willing to work—here in the United States of America, if you are willing to work hard, you should be able to find a good job. If you're willing to meet your responsibilities, you should be able to take care of your family and own a home, maybe start a business, give your kids a better chance than you had, no matter who you are, no matter where you come from, no matter what you look like, no matter who you love. That's what we believe. That's what America is about.

That's why we came together. That's why so many of you got involved in 2008. It wasn't because you thought my election was a sure thing. When you support a guy named Barack Obama—[*laughter*]—you know that's not a guarantee. But we shared that common sense of what America has been, and is, and must be for the future.

I ran for this office because for more than a decade, that basic bargain, that profound American Dream had been slipping away from too many people. Before I took office, the worst economic crisis of our lifetime made it even worse.

So, Durham, the debate in this election is not whether we need to do better. Everybody understands that our economy isn't where it needs to be. There are too many people out there who are struggling, too many folks out of work, too many homes that are still underwater. Of course, we need to do better. The debate is not whether; it is how. How do we grow the economy faster? How do we create more jobs? How do we pay down our debt? How do we reclaim that central American promise that no matter who you are, you can make it here if you try?

And this is not just the usual run-of-the-mill political argument. This is not the usual Washington chatter. There's a lot of that. But this, this is the defining issue of our time. This is a make-or-break moment for our middle class and folks who are aspiring to get into the middle class. The next President and the next Congress will face a set of decisions—on the economy, on deficits, on taxes—that will have a profound impact, not only on the country we live in today, but the country that we pass on to our kids.

And here's why you're so important, because what's holding us back from meeting the challenges we face is not the lack of big ideas, it's not the lack of technical solutions. Just about every policy and proposal, by now, has been put on the table; everybody knows what the options are. What's holding us back is a stalemate in Washington between two fundamentally different visions of which direction we should go.

And, New Hampshire, this election is your chance to break the stalemate. This election is your chance to move this country forward instead of seeing it go backwards. That's why I'm here. That's why I need your help.

Audience members. Four more years! Four more years! Four more years!

The President. Governor Romney and his allies in Congress, they believe—they have a certain idea about how they would proceed if they're in power. They think that we should go back to the top-down economic policies of the last decade.

They believe that if we eliminate regulations and we cut taxes by trillions of dollars, that the market will solve all of our problems on its own. They argue that if we help corporations and wealthy investors maximize their profits by whatever means necessary—whether it's through layoffs or outsourcing or whatever steps it takes to maximize those profits—that that automatically translates into jobs and prosperity for you.

Now, just last week, it was reported that Governor Romney's old firm owned companies that were pioneers in the business of outsourcing American jobs to places like China and India. Now——

Audience members. Boo!

The President. So yesterday his advisers were asked about this and they tried to clear this up by telling us there's actually a difference between "outsourcing" and "offshoring." [*Laughter*] That's what they said. You cannot make this stuff up. [*Laughter*]

Now, what Governor Romney and his advisors don't seem to understand is this: If you're a worker whose job went overseas, you don't need somebody trying to explain to you the difference between outsourcing and offshoring. You need somebody who's going to wake up every single day and fight for American jobs and investment here in the United States. That's what you need. That's why I'm running.

Unlike Governor Romney, I want to close the outsourcing loophole in our Tax Code. I want to give tax breaks to companies who create jobs and manufacturing here in New Hampshire, here in the United States of America.

But what's important to understand is Governor Romney's commitment to outsourcing is not just part of his record, it's part of an overall economic vision that he and Republicans in Congress want to implement if they win this election.

Audience member. Hell no! [*Laughter*]

The President. And look, their plan is pretty simple. It's been voted on in Congress. It's right there on Governor Romney's website. First of all, they promise to roll back all kinds of regulations on banks and polluters and insurance companies and oil companies.

Audience members. Boo!

The President. So that's step number one. And then, second, they promise not only to keep all of the Bush tax cuts in place—not just the ones for the middle class, but for everybody, for the wealthiest Americans—but they also then want to add another $5 trillion in tax cuts on top of that, including a 25-percent tax cut for every millionaire in the country.

Audience members. Boo!

The President. Now, you may be wondering—because I can tell—[*laughter*]—you're scratching your head here—you may be wondering how do they spend $5 trillion on new tax cuts and still keep a straight face when they say that their plan would reduce our deficit? This is a good question. Well, they say that they'll start by proposing $1 trillion in cuts to things like education and training——

Audience members. No!

The President. ——and medical research and clean energy. But that's only $1 trillion. They've got $5 trillion that they want to pay for, right? So that's not enough. So they also propose eliminating health care for about 50 million Americans and turning Medicare into a voucher program.

Audience members. Boo!

The President. But that's still not enough. Still haven't gotten to the $5 trillion yet. So then, they'll also have to raise taxes on the middle class by taking away tax benefits for every-thing from health care to college to retirement to homeownership, and this could cost some families thousands of dollars.

So think about this. To pay for another $250,000 tax cut for the average millionaire, they're going to ask you to foot the bill.

Audience member. We can't afford it!

The President. I figure you can't afford it. [*Laughter*] Is there anybody here who can afford to pay thousands of dollars to give folks like Mr. Romney or me another tax cut?

Audience members. No!

The President. Unfortunately, that is their entire economic plan. That's it. When Mr. Romney tells us he's some sort of financial wizard who can fix our economy, that's exactly how he intends to do it.

Now, there may be some people—in fact, I know there are some people—who think this kind of plan is a good idea. They want to give the policies of the last decade another try. And if they do, they should vote for Mr. Romney. They should reelect the Republicans who've been running Congress. Together, they will take America back down this path that we tried.

I believe they're wrong. I believe their policies were tested, and they failed. And that—my belief is not just based on some knee-jerk partisan reaction. It's based on the fact that we tried it. And you look at our economic history. In this country, prosperity has never come from the top down. It comes from a strong and growing middle class. It comes from success-ful, thriving small businesses.

We don't need more top-down economics. What we need is a better plan for education and training and energy independence and in-frastructure and innovation that rebuilds America. What we need is a Tax Code that en-courages companies to create jobs and manu-facturing here in the United States and that asks the wealthiest Americans to pay a little bit more to help pay down our deficit.

Listen, we don't expect Government to solve all our problems, and it shouldn't try to solve all our problems. And I learned from my mom, no education policy can take the place of

a parent's love and attention and sometimes scolding. [*Laughter*] As a young man, I worked with a group of Catholic churches who taught me that no poverty program can make as much of a difference as the kindness and commit-ment and involvement of caring neighbors and friends and fellow parishioners.

Over the last 3 years, I cut taxes for the typi-cal working family by $3,600. I cut taxes for small businesses 18 times. I don't believe every regulation is smart, or that every tax dollar is spent wisely. I don't believe we should be in the business of helping people who refuse to help themselves. But let me tell you what I do believe.

I share the belief of our first Republican President, Abraham Lincoln, that through gov-ernment, we should do together what we can-not do as well for ourselves.

And that's how we built this country, togeth-er. We built railroads and highways, and the Hoover Dam and the Golden Gate Bridge. We did that together. We did big things together. We sent my grandfather's generation to college on the GI bill. We did that together.

We invented amazing scientific technologies and medical breakthroughs because we invest-ed in basic research and science. We did those things together. We didn't do those things for any particular individual, any particular group, but we understood that by making these com-mon investments, everybody would have the platform, everybody would have the capacity to do better. It would make us all richer—togeth-er. It gave all of us opportunity—together.

We moved forward together, as one Nation and as one people. And that is the right lesson for our future. That's why I'm running for a second term as President of the United States, because I want us all to move forward—to-gether.

Audience members. Four more years! Four more years! Four more years!

The President. I'm running to make sure that every American has a chance to get the skills and training that today's jobs require. My plan would recruit an army of new teachers, pay those teachers better. I want to hire more teachers in areas like math and science. I want to give 2 million more Americans the chance to go to community colleges and learn the skills that local businesses are looking for right now. And I want to make higher education affordable for every American who's willing to work for it, not just by offering more loans and financial aid, but by holding down the costs of a college tuition.

A college education can't be a luxury. It's a vital necessity for everybody. It may not be a 4-year college; it may be a 2-year college, it may be a technical school, but everybody is going to need the skills they need to compete. And that's the choice in this election. That's why I'm running for President.

Now, I'm running so that we have a future where we control our own energy, and that's good for our economy, our security. It's good for our environment. So my plan would end Government subsidies to oil companies that are making plenty of profits. Let's double down on clean energy: wind power and solar power, next generation of biofuels, fuel-efficient cars. That's the choice in this election.

I'm running to make sure that the United States of America is the best place on Earth for innovation and discovery, which is why my plan would give companies a permanent tax credit for research and development that they do here in America, and we double down on the public research that's helped lay the foundation for the Internet and GPS and Google, and the countless companies and jobs that follow.

I'm running so that after a decade of war, we can start doing some nation-building here at home. So we've ended the war in Iraq. We are transitioning in Afghanistan. My plan would take half the money we're no longer spending on war, use it to put people back to work rebuilding our roads and our runways and our ports and our wireless networks. That's the choice in this election.

I'm running so that we can reduce our deficit in a responsible way, by $4 trillion, doing it in a balanced, responsible way——

Audience member. The way it was done before.

The President. The way it was done before. I put forward a detailed plan. It will cut spend-

ing we can't afford. And there's some programs that don't work—we can eliminate that money—strengthen programs like Medicare for the long haul, reform our Tax Code so that the wealthiest Americans pay a little bit more, just like they did when Bill Clinton was President; just like they did when our economy created 23 million new jobs.

I mean, think about it, we created 23 million new jobs, the biggest budget surplus in history—and by the way, we produced a lot of millionaires too. There's no contradiction here. And there are plenty of patriotic, successful Americans, a lot of business leaders, a lot of folks who'd be willing to make this contribution again if they were asked to help pay down the deficit and they saw it as part of a responsible, balanced plan.

This is about choices. I don't believe that giving millionaires and billionaires a $250,000 tax cut is going to do more for our future than hiring transformative teachers or providing financial aid to the children of middle class families. I don't believe a poorly designed tax cut like that is more likely to create jobs than providing loans to new entrepreneurs or tax credits to small businesses who hire veterans. I don't think it's more likely to spur economic growth than investments in clean energy and medical research, and new roads and bridges and runways.

Audience member. Eldercare.

The President. Or eldercare.

So Governor Romney, he fundamentally disagrees with my vision. That's what elections are about. His allies in Congress disagree with my vision. Neither of them will endorse any policy that asks the wealthiest Americans to pay even a nickel more in taxes.

That's the reason we haven't reached an agreement on our deficit. It's the reason my jobs bill that would put more than 1 million people back to work has been voted down by Republicans in the Congress again and again and again. It's been the biggest source of gridlock in Washington for the last 3 years.

And, New Hampshire, the only thing that can break this stalemate is you—in you. In this election, on every single challenge that we face, you've got the final say. That's the amazing thing about our democracy.

You can decide whether we keep our brave men and women in Afghanistan indefinitely, like Mr. Romney wants to do, or whether we stick to the timeline that I've set to finally bring our troops home. That's up to you.

You can decide that instead of restricting access to birth control or defunding Planned Parenthood, we should make sure that in this country, women control their own health care choices. That's up to you.

You can decide whether we keep Wall Street reform; whether ending taxpayer bailouts for Wall Street banks was the right thing to do; whether preventing insurance companies from discriminating against people who are sick is the right thing to do; whether over 3 million young people being able to stay on their parent's health insurance plan is the right thing to do.

You can decide whether or not we go back to the days when you could be kicked out of the United States military just because of who you are and who you love. You can decide whether or not it's time to stop denying citizenship to responsible young people just because they're the children of undocumented workers—who have been growing up with our kids and want to contribute to this country.

It's going to be up to you whether we continue seeing these elections where multimillion-dollar donations, one person writing a $10 million check—whether that speaks louder than the voices of ordinary citizens. It's all up to you.

This is going to be a close election. And from now until November, the other side will spend more money than at any time in American history. And almost all of it will be on ads that tell you the economy is bad—it's all Obama's fault. He can't fix it because he thinks government is always the answer; because he doesn't have the experience of making a lot of money in the private sector; or because he is in over his head; or because he thinks everything is just fine. That's what the scary voices in the ads will tell you over and over and over again. That's what Mitt Romney will say. That's what

the Republicans in Congress will say. And I give them credit. They have a lot of message discipline. They just repeat over and over and over again the same thing. Doesn't matter if it's true, they'll just keep on repeating. That's what they do.

But, you know what, that may be a plan to win the election; it's sure not a plan to create jobs. It's not a plan to grow the economy. It's not a plan to pay down our debt. It's not a plan to revive the middle class and restore the American Dream.

So, Durham, if you believe we need a plan for education and energy, for infrastructure and innovation; if you believe that our economy grows best when everybody has a fair shot and everybody is doing their fair share and everybody is playing by the same set of rules, then I'm going to need you to stand with me as I run for a second term as President. I'm going to need you. The country is going to need you.

And here in New Hampshire, I know you guys have a tradition—a lot of Independents out here. Listen, I'm asking you, vote for anybody else—Democrat, Independent, Republican—anybody who shares your views about how this country should move forward. I will work with anyone of any party who believes that we are in this together, that we rise or fall as one Nation and as one people.

It's fashionable right now for people to be cynical. We go in cycles like this, and right now a lot of people are saying, oh, America is doing terribly and this and that, and what are we going to do. Let me tell you something. There's no problem out there, no challenge we face, that we do not have the capacity to solve. We are Americans, and we are tougher than whatever tough times may bring us. And what's lacking right now is our politics. What's lacking right now is that some of the worst impulses in our politics have been rewarded. And that's something entirely within your power to solve.

And in 2008, we made a commitment to each other. We said, together, we can bring about change, even against opposition, even against all kinds of nonsense going on in the campaigns. What we saw, what we witnessed, was that when Americans as citizens come together, nothing can stop them.

And I made a commitment to you. I said, you know what, I'm not going to be a perfect President. I'm not a perfect man—Michelle can tell you that. [*Laughter*] But you know what I did say? I said—some of you may remember this—I said I will always tell you where I stand, I will always tell you what I think, what I believe. And I will wake up every single day, fighting as hard as I can for you, fighting as hard as I know how for American families who are out there working hard, who are out there striving, who are doing what they're supposed to be doing.

And, you know what, New Hampshire, I've kept that promise, because I still believe in you. I believe in the American people. And I

need you to keep believing in me. I need you to hit some doors and make some phone calls and register your friends. Talk to your neighbors. Get on Facebook. Get on Twitter. Let's get to work. Let's finish what we started. Let's remind the world how a strong economy is built, and remind them why America is the greatest nation on Earth.

Thank you, everybody. God bless you. God bless America.

NOTE: The President spoke at 2:34 p.m. at Oyster River High School. In his remarks, he referred to Windham, NH, software developer Scott Baetz; and Republican Presidential candidate former Gov. W. Mitt Romney of Massachusetts.

Statement on the United States Supreme Court Ruling on Arizona's Illegal Immigration Enforcement Legislation
June 25, 2012

I am pleased that the Supreme Court has struck down key provisions of Arizona's immigration law. What this decision makes unmistakably clear is that Congress must act on comprehensive immigration reform. A patchwork of State laws is not a solution to our broken immigration system, it's part of the problem.

At the same time, I remain concerned about the practical impact of the remaining provision of the Arizona law that requires local law enforcement officials to check the immigration status of anyone they even suspect to be here illegally. I agree with the Court that individuals cannot be detained solely to verify their immigration status. No American should ever live under a cloud of suspicion just because of what they look like. Going forward, we must ensure that Arizona law enforcement officials do not enforce this law in a manner that undermines the civil rights of Americans, as the Court's decision recognizes. Furthermore, we will continue to enforce our immigration laws by focusing on our most important priorities like border security and criminals who endanger

our communities and not, for example, students who earn their education, which is why the Department of Homeland Security announced earlier this month that it will lift the shadow of deportation from young people who were brought to the United States as children through no fault of their own.

I will work with anyone in Congress who's willing to make progress on comprehensive immigration reform that addresses our economic needs and security needs and upholds our tradition as a nation of laws and a nation of immigrants. And in the meantime, we will continue to use every Federal resource to protect the safety and civil rights of all Americans and treat all our people with dignity and respect. We can solve these challenges not in spite of our most cherished values, but because of them. What makes us American is not a question of what we look like or what our names are. What makes us American is our shared belief in the enduring promise of this country and our shared responsibility to leave it more generous and more hopeful than we found it.

Letter to Congressional Leaders on Blocking Property of the Government of the Russian Federation Relating to the Disposition of Highly Enriched Uranium Extracted From Nuclear Weapons
June 25, 2012

Dear Mr. Speaker: (Dear Mr. President:)

Pursuant to section 204(b) of the International Emergency Economic Powers Act (IEEPA), 50 U.S.C. 1703(b), I hereby report that I have exercised my authority to declare a national emergency to deal with the threat posed to the United States by the risk of nuclear proliferation created by the accumulation in the Russian Federation of a large volume of weapons-usable fissile material.

In Executive Order 13159 of June 21, 2000, the President found that this same risk constituted an unusual and extraordinary threat to the national security and foreign policy of the United States and declared a national emergency to deal with that threat. The United States and the Russian Federation had entered into a series of agreements that provide for the conversion of highly enriched uranium (HEU) extracted from Russian nuclear weapons into low enriched uranium (LEU) for use in commercial nuclear reactors. There were concerns that payments due to the Russian Federation under these agreements may be subject to attachment, garnishment, or other judicial process, in the United States, which could put implementation of such agreements at risk. In Executive Order 13159, the President therefore ordered blocked all property and interests in property of the Government of the Russian Federation directly related to the implementation of the HEU Agreements so that it would be protected from the threat of attachment, garnishment, or other judicial process.

In the Executive Order I have issued today, I find that the risk of nuclear proliferation created by the accumulation in the Russian Federation of a large volume of weapons-usable fissile material continues to constitute an unusual and extraordinary threat to the national security and foreign policy of the United States. I therefore declared a national emergency to address this threat and to continue the blocking of all property and interests in property of the Government of the Russian Federation directly related to the implementation of the HEU Agreements.

A major national security goal of the United States is to ensure that fissile material removed from Russian nuclear weapons pursuant to various arms control and disarmament agreements is dedicated to peaceful uses, subject to transparency measures, and protected from diversion to activities of proliferation concern. The United States and the Russian Federation entered into an international agreement in February 1993 to deal with these issues as they relate to the disposition of HEU extracted from Russian nuclear weapons (the "HEU Agreement"). The HEU Agreement provides for 500 metric tons of HEU to be converted to LEU over a 20-year period. This is the equivalent of 20,000 nuclear warheads.

Additional agreements were put in place to effectuate the HEU Agreement, including agreements and contracts on transparency, on the appointment of executive agents to assist in implementing the agreements, and on the disposition of LEU delivered to the United States (collectively, the "HEU Agreements"). Under the HEU Agreements, the Russian Federation extracts HEU metal from nuclear weapons. That HEU is oxidized and blended down to LEU in the Russian Federation. The resulting LEU is shipped to the United States for fabrication into fuel for commercial reactors.

The HEU Agreements provide for the Russian Federation to receive money and uranium hexafluoride in payment for each shipment of LEU converted from the Russian nuclear weapons. The money and uranium hexafluoride are transferred to the Russian Federation executive agent in the United States.

The executive branch and the Congress have previously recognized and continue to recognize the threat posed to the United States national security from the risk of nuclear proliferation created by the accumulation of weapons-usable fissile material in the Russian Federation. This threat is the basis for significant programs aimed at Cooperative Threat Reduction and at controlling excess fissile material. The HEU Agreements are essential tools to accomplish these overall national security goals. The Congress has repeatedly demonstrated support for these agreements.

Payments made to the Russian Federation pursuant to the HEU Agreements are integral to the operation of this key national security program. Uncertainty surrounding litigation and the possible attachment, garnishment, or other judicial process that could impede these payments could lead to a long-term suspension of the HEU Agreements, which creates the risk of nuclear proliferation. This is an unacceptable threat to the national security and foreign policy of the United States.

Accordingly, I have concluded that all property and interests in property of the Government of the Russian Federation directly related to the implementation of the HEU Agreements should remain protected from the threat of attachment, garnishment, or other judicial process. I have, therefore, exercised my authority and issued an Executive Order that provides:

- except to the extent provided in regulations, orders, directives, or licenses that may be issued pursuant to the order, or that were issued pursuant to Executive Order 13159 of June 21, 2000, all property and interests in property of the Government of the Russian Federation directly related to the implementation of the HEU Agreements that are in the United States, that hereafter come within the United States, or hereafter come within the possession or control of any United States persons, including any foreign branch, are blocked and may not be

transferred, paid, exported, withdrawn, or otherwise dealt in;

- unless licensed or authorized pursuant to the order, any attachment, judgment, decree, lien, execution, garnishment, or other judicial process is null and void with respect to any property or interest in property blocked pursuant to the order; and

- that all heads of departments and agencies of the United States Government shall continue to take all appropriate measures within their authority to further the full implementation of the HEU Agreements.

The effect of this Executive Order is limited to property that is directly related to the implementation of the HEU Agreements. Such property will be clearly defined by the regulations, orders, directives, or licenses that will be issued pursuant to this Executive Order. I have delegated to the Secretary of the Treasury, in consultation with the Secretary of State, the authority to take such actions, including the promulgation of rules and regulations, and to employ all powers granted to the President by IEEPA as may be necessary to carry out the purposes of the order. All agencies of the United States Government are directed to take all appropriate measures within their authority to carry out the provisions of the order.

I am enclosing a copy of the Executive Order I have issued.

Sincerely,

BARACK OBAMA

NOTE: Identical letters were sent to John A. Boehner, Speaker of the House of Representatives, and Joseph R. Biden, Jr., President of the Senate. The Executive order is listed in Appendix D at the end of this volume.

Letter to Congressional Leaders on the Designation of Irving A. Williamson as Chair of the United States International Trade Commission
June 25, 2012

Dear Mr. Speaker: (Dear Mr. President:)

Consistent with the provisions of 19 U.S.C. 1330(c)(1), this is to notify the Congress that I have designated Irving A. Williamson as Chair of the United States International Trade Commission for the term expiring June 16, 2014.

Sincerely,

BARACK OBAMA

NOTE: Identical letters were sent to John A. Boehner, Speaker of the House of Representatives, and Joseph R. Biden, Jr., President of the Senate.

Remarks at an Obama Victory Fund 2012 Fundraiser in Boston, Massachusetts
June 25, 2012

The President. Hello, Boston! Thank you, Boston. Thank you. Please, everybody, have a seat. Oh, it is—*[laughter]*.

Audience members. Four more years! Four more years! Four more years!

The President. Thank you. Well, it is good to be back in Boston. Good to be back in Massachusetts.

I want to make some acknowledgments here. First of all, you've got one of the finest Governors in the country in Deval Patrick. You've got one of the finest mayors in the country in the Tom Menino. You've got an outstanding State auditor in Suzanne Bump.

And I just want to thank Elizabeth for that introduction and let you know how lucky all of you are to have a chance to vote for her in the next election. Nobody fought harder for Wall Street reform—the reform that is now law and protecting consumers all across the country—than Elizabeth, reform that will end taxpayer bailouts, make sure folks aren't being taken advantage of by mortgage lenders and credit card companies. She has been a fierce advocate, since before I knew her, for the middle class. She has been advocating on core issues that matter to families her entire career. She is going to be an outstanding Senator from Massachusetts, and everybody here has got to turn out for her.

I want to thank Miri Ben-Ari for her outstanding talent. We appreciate her appearing here today. I will not sing today, even though—*[laughter]*—when I'm in Symphony Hall, I'm tempted. I am tempted, but—*[laughter]*—can't do it. We have some serious business to attend to. [*Laughter*]

I also want to acknowledge former Governor Michael Dukakis, who is here, and his lovely wife Kitty. And finally, "Bos," I just want to say thank you for Youkilis.

Audience members. Boo!

The President. I'm just saying. He's going to have to change the color of his "sox."

Audience members. Boo!

The President. I didn't think I'd get any "boos" out of here, but—*[laughter]*—I guess I shouldn't have—I should not have brought up baseball. I understand. My mistake.

Audience members. Boo!

The President. My mistake. You've got to know your crowd. [*Laughter*]

Audience member. We still love you! [*Laughter*]

The President. Now, Boston, I'm here not just because I need your help—although I do. I'm here because the country needs your help.

Now, in 2008, we came together not just to support a candidate—it wasn't just about me. When you support a guy named Barack Obama, you're not doing it because you

845

thought it was a sure thing. [*Laughter*] The reason we came together in 2008 was because we had a shared vision about what's best in this country. We wanted to reclaim the basic bargain that made America what it is, that built the largest middle class in history, that built the most prosperous nation on Earth, that compact that binds us together as a people. That binds us together as citizens. We believed that in America, your success shouldn't be determined by the circumstances of your birth.

We believed that if you worked hard, you should be able to find a good job; if you meet your responsibilities, you should be able to support your family and own a home, maybe start a business, give your kids opportunities you could not have imagined, no matter who you are, no matter what you look like, no matter where you come from, no matter who you love, no matter what your last name is.

It's that basic bargain that allowed Michelle and I to succeed. It's that basic bargain that took a young kid from the South Side of Chicago to become the Governor of the Commonwealth. It's that basic bargain that brought a lot of your parents or grandparents or great-grandparents to these shores from countries where that ideal didn't take root. And it was that basic bargain, that simple dream, that we understood had been slipping away for too many Americans.

We'd gone through a decade in which surpluses were turned into deficits, in which two wars were fought on a credit card, in which a few people were doing very well but more and more people were having trouble just getting by, no matter how hard they worked, all of which culminated in the worst financial crisis of our lifetimes. And after that crisis, that dream seemed even more tattered, even more frayed.

And so we went to work. And over the last 3½ years, step by step, we've tried to rebuild the foundations of that dream, making sure that we reformed our financial system so that reckless bets didn't always bring down our economy; making sure that people who are out there working hard don't have to worry about being bankrupt just because somebody in their fami-

ly gets sick; making sure that young people are able to get the assistance they need to go to college and make something that approximates their dreams.

And because of the incredible resilience and the incredible hard work, the toughness of the American people, we've begun to see progress: created over 4 million jobs over the last 3½ years, 800,000 in the last few months alone. When some were saying let's go ahead and let Detroit go bankrupt, we bet on the American worker and American industries. And today, the U.S. auto industry is back on top and getting stronger.

But what we also understand is, is that there are way too many people out there who are still struggling, too many people whose homes are underwater, too many small businesses that are still finding it hard to get financing and keep their doors open.

And so the debate in this election is not whether we have more work to do. Of course, the economy is not where it needs to be. Of course, there are too many folks still struggling. Of course, we need to do better. These challenges were built up over years. They weren't created overnight; they weren't going to be solved overnight. But the debate in this election is how do we grow the economy faster? How do we create more jobs? Moving forward, how do we create more opportunity? How do we pay down our debt? How do we reclaim that basic bargain that makes America the greatest nation on Earth? How do we do it?

And this is not just your usual run-of-the-mill Washington Beltway argument, this is the defining issue of our time. It is a make-or-break moment for our middle class, and the next President and the next Congress will be setting the course on the economy, on deficits, on taxes, not just for today, not just for tomorrow, but the next decade, the next two. This election will have an enormous impact on the country we live in today, but more importantly, it's going to have an impact on the country we pass on to our children.

Now, what's holding us back from meeting these challenges—as much progress as we've made—what's holding us back still is not a lack of big ideas, it's not a lack of technical solutions. All the options are out there; everybody knows them. What's holding us back is a stalemate in Washington between two fundamentally different visions of which direction we should go.

And this election is your chance to break that stalemate. This election is your chance to move this country forward. This is your choice.

And let's be clear about what these choices are. Mr. Romney and his allies in Congress, they've got a very particular theory about how you grow the economy. They believe we should go back to the top-down economic policies of the last decade. You can sum them up fairly simply. They believe that if we eliminate regulations and cut taxes by trillions of dollars, that will free up the marketplace and will solve all our problems. That's the essence of their argument. They argue if we help corporations and wealthy investors maximize their profits by whatever means necessary—whether through layoffs or outsourcing or union-busting—that that will automatically translate into jobs and prosperity that benefit all of us. That's their theory.

And that's not an exaggeration. Just last week, it was reported that Governor Romney's old firm owned companies that were pioneers—this is not my phrase, but how it was described in the report—"pioneers" in the business of outsourcing American jobs to places like China and India. Yesterday his advisers tried to clear this up by telling us that there was a difference between "outsourcing" and "offshoring." [*Laughter*] Seriously. You can't make that up. [*Laughter*]

And what Mr. Romney and his advisors don't seem to understand is this: If you're a worker whose job went overseas, you really don't need somebody explaining you the difference between outsourcing and offshoring. [*Laughter*] What you need is somebody who is going to wake up every day fighting to make sure that investments and jobs are happening here in Massachusetts and here in the United States of America. That's what you need.

And let me be clear. We all believe in the free market. We all believe that risk takers and

entrepreneurs need to be rewarded. It's that dynamism that built this country. But we also believe in shared prosperity. I want to close the outsourcing loophole in our Tax Code. I want to give tax breaks to companies who create jobs and manufacturing right here in the United States of America.

And this particular commitment to outsourcing isn't just part of his record, it's part of an overall economic theory that Republicans in Congress want to implement if they win this election. It's been voted on in Congress. It's right there on Governor Romney's website. They promise to roll back all kinds of regulations on banks and polluters, insurance companies, oil companies. They don't want to just keep all of the Bush tax cuts in place, including tax cuts for folks who don't need them and weren't even asking for them; they want to add another $5 trillion in tax cuts on top of that, including a 25-percent tax cut for every millionaire in this country.

Now, you may be wondering, how do they spend $5 trillion on new tax cuts and still keep a straight face when they say that their plan would reduce the deficit? This is a good question that you're asking yourselves. [*Laughter*] Boston has a lot of smart people in it. [*Laughter*] And I'm sure that we probably have some MIT grads here. See, math majors, they're thinking $5 trillion, all right, how does that add up?

Well, they start by proposing a trillion dollars in cuts to things like education and training, medical research, clean energy. But that's only a trillion dollars, so that's not enough. So then, they propose eliminating health care for about 50 million Americans and converting Medicare into a voucher program. But that's still not enough. So then, they also have to effectively raise taxes on the middle class by taking away tax deductions for everything from health care, college, retirement, homeownership, which could cost families thousands of dollars.

Now, this is on their websites; they voted on these plans. That's the entirety of their economic approach. That's it. There's nothing new there. We've tried this, by the way. When Mr.

Romney tells us that he is some sort of financial wizard who can fix our economy, this is how he intends to do it.

Now, if you're a person who thinks this plan sounds like a good idea, if we want to try the same policies that we just implemented in the last decade and did not work, those folks should vote for Mr. Romney. They should reelect the Republicans who have been running this Congress. And together, I promise you, this is the path they'll take America down. They're more than qualified to do it. [*Laughter*]

But I believe their policies have been tested, and their policies have failed. And that's because in this country, prosperity hasn't come from the top down. It's come from a strong and growing middle class. It's come from people striving to get into that middle class. It's come from successful, thriving small businesses that turned into medium-sized businesses and large businesses. It comes from consumers who are seeing enough income and wage increases that they can afford to buy great products and services from businesses, and the entire economy grows.

We do not need more top-down economics. We need a plan for better education and training so that our young people can take advantage of the marketplace; for energy independence and innovation and infrastructure. And we need a Tax Code that encourages companies to create jobs here in the United States and a Tax Code that asks the wealthiest Americans to help pay down our deficit. That's what we need. That's what we need.

There's nothing radical about that vision. That's the vision that built this country. It was part of what used to be a bipartisan consensus. We don't expect government to solve all our problems. This notion that somehow there's been some heavy tilt to the left on the part of the Democratic Party, over the last 3 years, I cut taxes for the typical working family by $3,600. I cut taxes for small businesses 18 times, eliminated billions of dollars in regulations that didn't make sense and weren't making people healthier or safer.

I don't believe we should be in the business of helping people who refuse to help themselves. I don't think government can solve every problem. But I do share this basic belief with our first Republican President, Abraham Lincoln, who said that through government we should do together what we cannot do as well for ourselves: that there is a place for us to work on the common good, that there's a common good that we invest in together.

That's how we built this country together. We built railroads and highways together. We built the Hoover Dam and the Golden Gate Bridge together. We sent my grandfather's generation to college on the GI bill together. We invented—we invested in basic science that led to unimaginable discoveries. We did those things together. Because we understood it made us all better off. It gave us all opportunity because it created a platform where everybody could succeed.

If you were willing to work hard, you could succeed, in part, because we had great schools and we had built great roads and we had a system in place that made sure that investors weren't cheated when they put money into the stock market and bank deposits were guaranteed and polluters didn't run wild. All those things made us, together, better off and allowed us to succeed as one people, as one Nation.

That's the true lesson of our past. That is the right vision for our future. And, Boston, that is why I'm running for a second term as President of the United States, because I want to move that vision forward. [*Applause*] I want to move that vision forward.

I'm running to make sure that every American has a chance to get the skills and training that today's jobs require. I want to recruit an army of new teachers. I want to pay them better. I want to hire more in areas like math and science. I want to give 2 million more Americans the chance to go to community colleges and learn the skills that local businesses are looking for right now. And I want to make higher education affordable for every American who's willing to work for it—not just by offering more loans and financial aid, but by bringing down the cost of college tuition—because this is no longer an economic luxury. Every young American needs the skills and the training to succeed in the 21st-century economy.

Boston understands this. Massachusetts understands this. That's what we're fighting for. That's the choice in this election. That's why I'm running for President of the United States.

I'm running so that we have a future where we control our own energy. That's good for our economy, it's good for our national security, it's good for our planet. We need to end subsidies for oil companies that are making plenty of money on their own and double down on a clean energy industry that's never been more promising: in wind power and solar power and biofuels and fuel-efficient cars.

I'm running to make sure that the United States becomes—continues to be the best place on Earth for innovation and discovery.

I'm proud that I kept the promise I made to you in 2008: We have ended the war in Iraq. We are transitioning out of Afghanistan.

So I want to start doing some nation-building here at home. I want to take half the money we're no longer spending on war, use it to put people back to work rebuilding our roads, rebuilding our runways, rebuilding our ports, building wireless networks, building high-speed rail, investing more in research, investing more in science, all those ingredients that made us an economic superpower. That's the choice in this election.

I'm running because we need to reduce our deficit, we need to manage our debt, and so I've put forward a plan: $4 trillion of deficit reduction that is balanced and responsible, that allows us to cut spending we can't afford, strengthens programs like Medicare for the long haul, and yes, reforms our Tax Code so that the wealthiest Americans pay a little bit more.

And just as Mr. Romney's theories and the Republicans in Congress, their theories, have been tested, well, my theories have been tested as well, because that Tax Code that I described happened to be the Tax Code that was around when Bill Clinton was President, and we created 23 million new jobs, the biggest budget surplus in history. We created a whole lot of mil-

lionaires to boot. Businesses did just fine. And you know there are plenty of patriotic, successful Americans all across the country—I meet them every day—who'd be willing to make this contribution again because they understand there is such a thing as the common good. They understand that we're in this thing together.

Mr. Romney disagrees with this vision. His allies in Congress disagree with this vision. Neither of them will endorse any policy that asks the wealthiest Americans to pay even a nickel more in taxes. That's the reason why we haven't reached an agreement to lower our deficits. That's the reason my jobs bill that independent economists say would put 1 million more people back to work has been voted down time and time again. It's the biggest source of gridlock in Washington for the last 3 years.

Which brings me back to where I started. The only way we're going to break that gridlock is through you. Very rarely do you see such a stark choice in an election, with so much at stake. On every challenge we face, you have the final say about where do we go from here.

You can decide whether we keep our brave men and women in Afghanistan indefinitely, as Mr. Romney proposes, or whether we stick to the timeline that I established that allows us to finally bring our troops home. That's your decision.

You can decide whether we should restrict access to birth control or defund Planned Parenthood, or we can make a decision that in this country, women control their own health choices. That's a decision for you to make.

You can decide whether ending taxpayer bailouts of Wall Street banks was the right thing to do; whether protecting consumers from unscrupulous practices—like Elizabeth fought for—whether that's the right thing to do; whether preventing insurance companies from discriminating against people who are sick is the right thing to do; or allowing over 3 million young people to stay on their parent's health insurance plan, whether that's the right thing to do; or bringing down prescription drugs costs for seniors was the right thing to do.

I think it was the right thing to do. I know it was the right thing to do. And it's your choice whether we keep moving forward.

You can decide whether we go back to the days where you could be kicked out of the United States military just because of who you are or who you love. I know where I stand on this.

You can decide whether it's time to stop denying citizenship to responsible young people just because they were brought here as children of undocumented immigrants. I know where I stand on this. I know the choice I make.

And you can decide whether we continue to have elections where multimillion-dollar donations, $10 million checks speak louder than the voices of ordinary citizens.

Audience members. No!

The President. This is going to be up to you. This election will be close. It will be close because there are a lot of folks who are still going through a tough time. And even if they don't buy what the other side is selling, it's hard [not hard]° in this environment sometimes for people to feel discouraged, for cynicism to creep in.

And the other side, they feed on that. They will spend more money than we have ever seen in American history, and their message is very simple. They will just tell you that the economy is not where it needs to be, the economy is bad, and it's all my fault. [*Laughter*] They'll tell you, Obama can't fix it because he thinks Government is always the answer; or because he didn't make a lot of money in the private sector so he's in over his head; or because Obama thinks everything is—everybody is doing just fine. You'll just hear those messages over and over and over again. Scary voices in the ads. [*Laughter*] Flashing at you. [*Laughter*] That's what Mr. Romney will say. That's what the Republicans in Congress will say.

And I understand their approach. I mean, it's a plausible plan to win an election. But it's not a plan to create jobs. It's not a plan to grow the economy. It's not a plan to give all the people I meet around the country who are working

so hard and struggling every day, it's not a plan to give them a handle on achieving their dreams. It's not a plan to rebuild our middle class.

And ultimately, that's what we have to have. We've got to have a plan that goes back to that basic bargain that we were fighting for in 2008, that basic compact between citizens that says, I've got a stake in your success. And that kid over in Dorchester who didn't have all the opportunities, or in South Boston who didn't have all the chances that I had, you know what, I've got a stake in his success. I think I'll be better off, my kids will be better off, if that kid gets an education.

That sense that you know what, I don't put on a hard hat every day when I go to work, but if I'm seeing the skyline rising and those construction workers out there building, you know somehow that's going to make my life better. It's going to help secure the future of my kids and my grandkids.

And if I see an elderly couple strolling through the park and they're holding hands and I know that they've got the security and dignity of a retirement that eases their anxieties, yes, that makes me feel better about my country. It's good for my life.

We are not there yet. This is hard work. It's always been hard. Progress in this country has always been hard. It's never come easy. There have been episodes, moments in our history where it looked easy, but it always involved struggle. And what we started in 2008, I never promised you it was going to be easy. I told you then I wasn't a perfect man and I wouldn't be a perfect President. But what I told you was also that I promised you that every single day, I would tell you what I thought, I would tell you where I stood, and I'd wake up in the morning and I'd go to bed at night thinking about how I could make your lives better. I would fight for you as hard as I could.

And I've kept that promise. I've kept that promise, Boston. I believe in you. And if you believe in me, and if you agree with me about how we've got to give everybody a fair shot and

---

° White House correction.

we want everybody to do their fair share and we want everybody to play by the same rules, then I need you to stand with me for a second term as President.

I need you to knock on doors with me. I need you to make phone calls with me. I want all of you to understand that if you share this belief—and I believe a vast majority of the American people do—and in fact, I think there are Republicans out there who do. [*Laughter*] They just can't admit it right now. [*Laughter*] I'll work with anyone of any party who believes that we are in this together and believes that we will rise and fall as one Nation, as one people. That's what we're fighting for right now.

Don't let anybody tell you we don't have the capacity to solve our challenges. We do. We've got the opportunities. We are Americans, and we've never shied away from these kinds of fights. But we've got to fix our politics, and you guys are the ones who are going to help fix it.

So I hope you're ready. I hope you're ready. I hope you're still fired up. And if anybody asks you what this campaign is about, you tell them it's still about hope, and it is still about change, and we're going to finish what we started in 2008. We're going to move this country forward and remind the world why America is the greatest nation on Earth.

Thank you, everybody. God bless you. God bless America.

NOTE: The President spoke at 7:41 p.m. at Symphony Hall. In his remarks, he referred to Massachusetts senatorial candidate Elizabeth Warren; musician Miri Ben-Ari; Kevin E. Youkilis, infielder, Major League Baseball's Chicago White Sox, who was traded from the Boston Red Sox on June 24; and Republican Presidential candidate former Gov. W. Mitt Romney of Massachusetts.

Remarks at an Obama Victory Fund 2012 Fundraiser in Weston, Massachusetts
June 25, 2012

The President. Thank you. You don't need to stand up again. No, you already did that. Come on, come on. Thank you, everybody. Thank you so much.

Let me, first of all, thank Doug and Judi and George and Lizbeth. What a spectacular evening. You guys could not be more gracious. And if this is the first time you've done this, you're actually quite good at this. [*Laughter*] So just want to let you know that you're doing fine. [*Laughter*] Really.

A couple other people who are here: As was mentioned, Rob Barber has been an extraordinary friend for many, many years, and so we thank him for all of his support. We've also got somebody who I met when I was still running for the U.S. Senate and has been a wonderful friend all these years, your treasurer, Steve Grossman, is here. Where is Steve? There he is.

And finally, let me just say that somebody who I genuinely consider a brother—I don't mean that in the vernacular. [*Laughter*] I mean somebody who—when I think about people who I admire, I care about, who I just

think is good people and who articulates a vision of what this country should be as well as anybody in this country, it's your Governor, Deval Patrick. I love the guy. Thank you, Deval Patrick.

So some of you were at Symphony Hall, and I had a chance to give a long speech. And what I'd like to do tonight—take advantage of the fact that we have an intimate setting—I'm not going to give a long speech at the front end. What I'd rather do is have a conversation, answer your questions, take some comments.

But let me just say at the top that many of you were involved in the election in 2008, and in some ways, when I talk to my political team about—and reminisce about—2008, it was like lightening in a bottle. It captured a spirit and an energy and an electricity that was spectacular. And I couldn't be prouder of the campaign we ran in 2008.

But, in some ways, this election is more important than 2008. In some ways, the stakes are higher. Because back in 2008, there was some overlap between Democrats and Republicans on some important issues. The nominee from the other party believed in climate change, believed in campaign finance reform, believed in immigration reform. And what we've seen in the face of probably the worst financial crisis and economic crisis of our lifetimes is that the Republican Party has moved in a fundamentally different direction, so that on every issue we have fundamental choices that are at stake that will determine not just how we do tomorrow or the next day, but for the next 10 years or the next 20 years.

And I've said this before, and I believe it: This is a make-or-break moment for who we are as a country and the values that we live by. And I think it's a make-or-break moment for the middle class in this country or everybody who is aspiring to get into the middle class.

Obviously, we're still recovering from the financial crisis and the economic crisis, and there are a lot of people who are still out of work and a lot of homes that are still underwater and a lot of businesses that are still struggling. But for a decade before that crisis, what we had seen was that the basic bargain that built this country, that allowed so many of us to be successful—the notion that if you work hard, no matter who you are, where you come from, what you look like, who you love, you can make it; that if you're responsible and you look after your family and you apply yourself, you can support a family and have a home and send your kids to college so they can do better than you ever imagined—that basic compact had been eroding, so that job growth had been more sluggish in the previous decade than any time in the previous 50 years, and a few people were doing extraordinarily well, but for more and more people it was a struggle just to keep up.

And it was papered over for a while through debt and home equity loans and credit cards, but that was a house of cards that all came tumbling down. And so even as we work on the immediate task of putting people back to work and getting the economy growing faster, we've got this underlying challenge that we have to meet. And that is, how do we get back to an economy that is built to last and where everybody has got a fair shot and everybody is doing

their fair share and everybody is playing by the same set of rules?

And in answering that question, we've got two fundamentally different visions: one vision that essentially can be summed up as get rid of all regulations and cut taxes for another $5 trillion, a top-down approach to economic growth; and I've got a different vision that says we are entrepreneurs and rugged individualists and we don't expect to help people who don't want to help themselves, but we also believe in a common good.

And we believe in things like a public education system and colleges and universities that give everybody a chance to succeed. And we believe in investing in science and technology so that these extraordinary discoveries can then be used to create entire industries and provide opportunity for more and more people.

And we believe in creating a great infrastructure so businesses can move people and products and services seamlessly throughout our global economy. And we believe in a Tax Code that is fair and balanced, in which success is rewarded, but in which we also are paying for those investments that allow us to pass on a great country to the next generation.

And we believe in an energy program that taps into American energy, but also makes sure that we're taking care of our environment and we're not subject to the whims of what happens in some country in the Middle East at any given moment.

And we believe in American manufacturing, not because manufacturing is going to be as central to today's economy as it was back in the 1950s, but when we make things and produce things and sell things around the world, there is a basic strength to our economy that ripples everywhere and gives more and more the chance to get ahead, just as the auto industry did for two or three generations, which is exactly why we had to intercede to make sure that they succeeded.

So, on each of these issues about the economy, there are profound, fundamental differences. And we had a stalemate in Washington now for 3 years. And you, the American voter, is going to have to break that stalemate.

Now, that's before we start getting into foreign policy, where my opponent thinks that it is tragic that I ended the war in Iraq the way I did or that resists setting a timeline for getting out of Afghanistan.

That doesn't capture the differences we have on things like women's health, where my opponent wants to end funding for Planned Parenthood or restrict access to birth control.

It doesn't capture the differences we have on something like "don't ask, don't tell." I think if you love this country, it shouldn't matter who you love, you should be able to serve.

The Supreme Court, immigration reform, environmental protection—you name it, there's a fundamental choice involved.

So this is going to be a close election. Not because people are particularly persuaded by the argument the other side is making; it's the same old argument they've been making for the last 30, 40 years. It's going to be close because people are scared and frustrated and there are a lot of folks who are still out of work and the economy is still tough. And the other side is spending more money than we've ever seen before, trying to tap into those anxieties. They're betting they don't have to offer much; they just say things aren't good and it's Obama's fault.

The good news is that as I've traveled around the country over the last several years, what I've realized is, that core decency and strength and common sense of the American people, it wins out in the end. When folks are mobilized and activated, and when we're out there speaking truth, over time it breaks through. It wins out.

But it doesn't happen automatically. It happens because of effort. It happens because of determination. And although it is true that I'm a little grayer now than I was when I met some of you the first time—[*laughter*]—my determination is undiminished. I am as fired up as I ever was. And I hope you're ready to go.

Thanks. Thank you.

NOTE: The President spoke at 9:34 p.m. at the residence of Douglas S. and Judith Krupp. In his remarks, he referred to George D. Krupp, chief executive officer and senior partner, Berkshire Group, and his wife Lizbeth; Robert C. Barber, partner, Looney & Grossman LLP; State Treasurer and Receiver General Steven Grossman of Massachusetts; Sen. John S. McCain III, in his capacity as the 2008 Republican Presidential nominee; and Republican Presidential candidate former Gov. W. Mitt Romney of Massachusetts. Audio was not available for verification of the content of these remarks.

Remarks at an Obama Victory Fund 2012 Fundraiser in Atlanta, Georgia
June 26, 2012

The President. Hello, Atlanta! Hello, hello! Thank you so much. It is good to see everybody here, back in Atlanta.

Couple of people I want to acknowledge. First of all, your outstanding mayor, Mr. Kasim Reed, is in the house. Former Governor Roy Barnes is in the house. I want to thank all the members of the host committee who made this such an extraordinary event. And then I've got to give a special shout-out to one of my favorite people. He's a little bit of a troublemaker—[*laughter*]—he's a little bit irascible. [*Laughter*] But he is a man of God, and he's a man of the people, and he has been a great friend to

me for a very long time. So give it up for Reverend Joseph Lowery. Love that man.

So, Atlanta, I am here not just because I need your help—although I do—but I'm here because your country needs your help.

Back in 2008, we came together because we believed in a basic bargain that built this country, the basic idea that in America, your life is not determined by the circumstances of your birth; the idea that here in America, if you are willing to work hard, then you can find a job that pays a living wage, that you can care for your family, that you can have a home, that you can send your kids to college and allow them to have experiences and opportunities you didn't even dream of, that you can retire with dignity and respect. That basic American idea that if you take responsibility for your own life, that you can go as far as your dreams can take you and it doesn't matter what you look like, where you come from, what your last name is, who you love. That basic American idea that you can make it if you try.

And for almost a decade, we had seen that dream that built the largest middle class in history and the most successful economy in history, we had seen that dream slipping away. We had watched surpluses turned into deficits. We had seen two wars fought on a credit card. We had seen a few people at the top do really, really well while more and more folks were struggling to get by, dealing with higher costs of health care, higher costs of education, but weren't seeing higher salaries or higher incomes. And this was all before the worst financial crisis in our lifetimes struck and the worst economic crisis in our lifetimes hit.

And so over the last 3½ years, that journey that we began, it's been tough sometimes. We've had a steep mountain to climb. But slowly and surely, the American people have proved, once again, that they are tougher than tough times. There were folks who said, let's let Detroit go bankrupt. We said, let's invest in American workers and American businesses, and now the American auto industry is back on top.

All across the country, folks who lost their jobs, they went back to school, retrained for the industries of the future. All across the country, small businesses hung on, no matter how tough it was; kept folks on payroll, even if the owner sometimes couldn't take a salary, because they understood that families were depending on them. And over time, what we've seen is steady progress and steady movement. More than 4 million jobs created over the last 27 months, more than 800,000 created just in the last few months alone.

But of course, we understand we had a big hole that was created by that crisis. And it's going to take more than just a few months or a few years to dig our way out of that hole, be-

cause this is a challenge that's existed for over a decade now. And we recognize there's still too many of our friends who don't have work and too many of our family members whose homes are underwater, too many folks struggling. We've got more work to do. We understand we've got so much more work to do.

And the question is not whether we need to put more folks back to work or whether we need to see the economy growing faster or whether we need to bring down our debt, the question is how do we do it. The question is how do we do it.

And in this election, all of you have the opportunity to choose between two fundamentally different visions of how you grow America, two fundamentally different visions about who we are as a people and what makes this Nation great. On one side you've got Mr. Romney and his allies in Congress——

Audience members. Boo!

The President. Mr. Romney is a patriotic American. He's got a beautiful family. He's been very successful in his life. [*Laughter*] But—no, he has. But his basic vision is one in which if wealthy investors like him and folks at the very top are freed up from any kind of regulations, if they are maximizing their profits, even if it means polluting more or offshoring jobs or avoiding taxes or busting unions— whatever the strategies—if they're doing well, then everybody else is automatically doing well. That's their view.

And that's basically their economic plan. I'm not making this up. It's on the—Mr. Romney's website. Members of Congress have put forward this plan. They voted for this plan. Their basic idea is we're going to eliminate regulations on everything, we are going to provide a $5 trillion tax cut on top of the Bush tax cuts for the wealthiest Americans, and we're just going to let the market take care of the rest. And the presumption is that everybody here, everybody around the country, will share in this newfound prosperity.

Now, I don't doubt that they will execute this plan if they get elected. Here is the problem: We tried it. We tried it very recently, and it didn't work. That kind of top-down economics has never worked. That's not how this country was built. It's good for a few, but it doesn't create that broad-based middle class and folks having ladders to get into the middle class that made this country great.

And so we've got an alternative vision, because I believe we're all in it together. I've got a vision that says the way we're going to grow our economy and put people back to work is to make sure every child in America has the best education possible. I've got a vision that says the way we grow our economy is by making sure that we're bringing manufacturing back to the United States. I've got a vision that says the way we build our economy is to rebuild America—our roads, our bridges, our runways, our ports, our airports—putting people back to work. I've got a vision that says we'll grow our economy if we control our own energy sources so we're not dependent on what happens in the Middle East. And that's why we got to double down on clean energy: wind power and solar power. And I've got a vision that says we grow best when our Tax Code makes sure that the wealthiest Americans are paying a little bit more in order to bring down our debt.

It's the basic idea that everybody gets a fair shot and everybody does their fair share and everybody plays by the same set of rules. That's my vision for America. And just like their vision has been tested, my vision's been tested as well. When you look at the history of this country, the way we emerged as an economic superpower was doing it together.

My grandfather's generation was educated on the GI bill. We did that together. We made a common investment in the common good. The Hoover Dam, the Golden Gate Bridge, the Interstate Highway System—we did those things together, because we understood everybody would be more successful if we were making those common investments that gave each of us the capacity to do well.

Abraham Lincoln, the first Republican President, said it pretty well. He said, we should do for ourselves what we do best for ourselves, but we should also do together those things that we do better together. And so we made investments in science and technology, inventing

the products that led to the Internet and GPS and Google and amazing medical breakthroughs. We did that because together, through our Government, we made these investments in basic research.

We did all these things throughout our history not because they were good for one particular person, not because they were good for one particular group, but because they were good for all of us. Because we understood we rise and fall as one people, as one Nation.

That's my vision for America. That's what I've been fighting for, for the last 3½ years. That's why I'm running for a second term as President of the United States of America.

Audience members. Four more years! Four more years! Four more years!

The President. So let me break this down just a little bit more specifically, just because I want everybody to understand. Let's look for a moment at Mr. Romney's—the specifics of his plan. I already indicated to you he wants to roll back regulations for polluters and for insurance companies and for the big banks, wants to get rid of the Wall Street reform that we did to make sure that we don't have any more taxpayer bailouts. All right, so that's one big part of his plan. Then he's got this plan to cut taxes by another $5 trillion. All right? So what this would mean would be the average millionaire would see their taxes go down by 25 percent.

Now, you may be wondering, how is it that he can talk about cutting taxes by $5 trillion and, at the same time, say he's going to reduce our deficit. Because they always talk about the deficit and how terrible it is and we've got to get control of the deficit and the debt, and this—we can't pass this on to the next generation. All right, so you're going to cut $5 trillion, giving folks like me or Mr. Romney a tax break. How do the numbers work?

Well, what Mr. Romney says, first of all, is we'll cut a trillion dollars out of that portion of the Federal budget that finances everything from education to Head Start to health care to environmental protection to consumer protection—all the things we think of—food safety, you name it. A trillion dollars gets cut out of that, which means that a lot of people suddenly will not have the protections they were counting on. A lot of folks around the country won't be getting services that we think are part of what makes America great.

All right? But that's only $1 trillion, so that doesn't get you everywhere you need to go. So then, the next step would be to have tens of millions of people no longer have health insurance.

Audience members. No!

The President. He'd roll back the Affordable Care Act, and he'd block-grant Medicaid in such a way where vulnerable people all across the country, folks who may be disabled, folks—seniors who are relying on those services—that would be eliminated.

But that doesn't pay for $5 trillion. That's not enough. So then, what they'd have to do is eliminate a whole bunch of deductions that middle class families count on to keep their taxes low. And so what this adds up to is essentially you—your family, your friends, middle class people all across the country—would end up seeing higher taxes to pay for tax cuts for Mr. Romney and me.

Audience member. It ain't right.

The President. It ain't right. [*Laughter*]

It—[*applause*]—now, that's not a recipe for economic growth. That's not going to make us stronger. That's not going to make our young people more educated. It's not going to make us more competitive in this global economy.

So what I've said is, no, here is what we need to do. We need to invest more in education. I want to hire more teachers, especially in math and science. I want 2 million more people to have access to community colleges to get the skills and the training they need to get jobs from local businesses right now. I want to make college more affordable so young people don't have as much debt when they graduate. That's my vision for how we're going to move forward.

I want to stop giving subsidies to oil companies that have never been more successful, never made more profits. I want to take that money and give subsidies to clean energy, to the energy of the future that's never been more promising—fuel-efficient cars and solar power and wind power, biodiesel—putting folks back to work creating homegrown energy, so we're less dependent on foreign oil.

I want to invest in science and technology all across the country, because that's always been what's maintained our cutting edge.

And then, as you know, I promised in 2008 I would end the war in Iraq. We ended it. We're phasing down the war in Afghanistan. And I want to take half of those savings, pay down the deficit, and take the other half and let's start doing some nation-building right here at home, putting folks back to work rebuilding our infrastructure all across the country.

I want to change our Tax Code, because I'm tired of seeing us give tax breaks to companies that ship jobs overseas. I want to give tax breaks to companies that are investing right here in Georgia, right here in Atlanta, right here in the United States of America.

There was an article the other day in the Washington Post about how Mr. Romney's former firm—this is what gave him all this amazing success—was a "pioneer" in offshoring jobs to China and India. And when they were asked about it, some of his advisers explained, no, there's a difference between offshoring and outsourcing. [*Laughter*] I'm not kidding, that's what they said. Those workers who lost their jobs, they didn't understand the difference.

But the point is, we don't need somebody who's a pioneer in offshoring or outsourcing. We need a President in the White House who's going to, every single day, be fighting to bring jobs back to the United States, do some insourcing, put folks back to work here.

And on this Tax Code, as I said, I do not think that a $250,000 tax break for me or Mr. Romney—he'd get a little more, he's got more—[*laughter*]—more than I do—I don't think that's more important than us hiring outstanding teachers. I don't think that's more important than us sending broadband lines into rural areas of Georgia and all across the country so that folks have access to the Internet. I don't think that's going to help our economy grow more than us investing in cures for Alzheimer's or cancer.

I want to bring down the deficit in a responsible, balanced way. I've already put forward a plan—$4 trillion in deficit reduction—spending cuts for things that we don't need, strengthen Medicare and our health care system so that we get a better bang for our buck, and asking the wealthiest to pay a little bit more. And you know what, when you talk to folks around the country, successful Americans, they want to do a little more. If it's done right, they want to contribute to making America stronger.

Now, that vision—the good news is, is when you ask people, item by item, between these two visions, the American people have a sense of what makes sense. They prefer our vision. But this is still going to be a close election because the economy is still tough and folks are still frustrated. And what that means is that you're going to have more money spent in this election than ever before by the other side on negative ads. And their message will be simple. They'll say, the economy's bad and it's Obama's fault. [*Laughter*] They suffer a little bit of amnesia so they don't remember all the stuff that happened before I was sworn into office, but that's going to be their message.

And because times are tough, and because they're spending these ungodly sums, it's going to be close. But here's the thing that all of you taught me from 2008: When the American people decide that something is important, when ordinary citizens come together and they talk to their neighbors, they talk to their friends, they talk to their coworkers, they start getting organized, they knock on doors, they make phone calls, amazing things happen. Change happens.

No matter how much money is spent on the other side, when people are engaged and involved and they understand that our core values and who we are and what we're giving to the next generation is at stake, the American people fight for what's right.

And the American people understand that we're not going to make progress by going backwards. We need to go forwards. They understand we don't need to refight this battle over health care. It's the right thing to do that we've got 3 million young people who are on their parents' health insurance plans that didn't have it before. It's the right thing to do to give seniors discounts on their prescription drugs. It's the right thing to do to give 30 million Americans health insurance that didn't have it before.

They want to go forward. They understand it's the right thing to do to make sure that we don't have to bail out Wall Street again, that we've got some basic regulations to protect our consumers from unscrupulous lenders or mortgage brokers. They understand that. They don't want to go backwards.

They don't want to go back to the days when women had a tough time getting access to birth control or Planned Parenthood's getting defunded. They want women to have control over their own health care choices. They don't want to go backwards.

They don't want to go back to the days when you might not be able to fight for the country you love just because of who you love. They don't want "don't ask, don't tell" reinstated. They don't want to go backwards to a day when young people who, as children, were brought to the United States and were raised with our kids and went to school with our kids—are our kids, are Americans through and through in everything except the papers—that somehow they should be sent away instead of contributing to the United States of America. They don't want to go back to that.

So I have faith in the American people. I know when we started this journey back in 2008, I didn't have all this gray hair. [*Laughter*]

Audience member. It looks good! It looks good!

The President. But from traveling all across the country, my faith, my conviction in the strength and resilience and the goodness and decency of the American people, it is restored every single day. I have so much confidence that, even when we occasionally take the wrong turn, eventually, the road straightens out. We follow that right path. I truly believe this is a blessed country.

And so we'll see some cynicism and negativism and foolishness during the course of this campaign. [*Laughter*] This campaign will have its ups, and it will have its downs. But I remind you of what I said in 2008: I'm not a perfect man, and I'll never be a perfect President. But I told you I'd always tell you what I thought, I'd always tell you what I believed, and most importantly, I told you I'd wake up every single day and fight as hard as I knew how for you, that I'd fight as hard as I knew how for all those folks who are doing the right thing out there, all those people who kept the faith with this country. And you know what, I've kept that promise. I have kept that promise.

I believe in you. I hope you still believe in me. I hope you're ready to stand. I hope you're ready to fight. I hope you're ready to go out there and knock on some doors and make some phone calls, talk to your friends and talk to your neighbors and get them to the polls. And if you do, we will finish what we started in 2008. And we will rebuild this economy and rebuild our middle class. And we will remind the world just why it is that we are the greatest nation on Earth.

God bless you. God bless the United States of America.

NOTE: The President spoke at 1:07 p.m. at the Westin Peachtree Plaza hotel. In his remarks, he referred to civil rights activist Joseph E. Lowery; and Republican Presidential candidate former Gov. W. Mitt Romney of Massachusetts.

Remarks at an Obama Victory Fund 2012 Fundraiser in Miami Beach, Florida
June 26, 2012

The President. Hello, Miami! Thank you. It is good to be back in Miami.

Now, let me just, first of all, recognize a few people who are here. First of all, wasn't Maytee wonderful? Give her a big round of applause. She is an example of what this campaign is all about. And I could not be prouder to have folks like her involved every single day, out there in the grassroots, making a difference. So all of you who are out there volunteering, knocking on doors, making phone calls, I love you and I'm grateful to you.

A couple of other people I want to acknowledge: First of all, outstanding Congresswoman and DNC Chair Debbie Wasserman Schultz is in the house. We love Debbie. My Florida finance chair, Kirk Wagar, is here. Abigail and F.J. Pollak did a great job—thank you. I want to thank Enrique Santos for emceeing. Somebody who has become just a great friend and an extraordinary person and also sings and dances pretty good, Marc Anthony.

Finally, it would be incomplete if I did not congratulate the city of Miami for having the world champion Miami Heats here in town. You guys earned it. And since one of my favorite people is Alonzo Mourning, who's here, and Tracy Mourning, I just want to give them a special shout-out. Alonzo looks like he can still

play. [*Laughter*] Hasn't aged a bit—unbelievable. I'm getting all gray, and he just looks the same. [*Laughter*] Except he doesn't have that flattop. [*Laughter*]

Now, Miami, I'm here not just because I need your help—although I do, and I will get to that.

Audience member. I love you!

The President. I love you back.

But I'm mainly here because your country needs your help.

Back in 2008, we came together to reclaim the basic bargain that built this country, the essence of America, what created the largest middle class and the most prosperous economy on Earth. We came together because we believed that in America, your success shouldn't be determined by the circumstances of your birth. If you're willing to work hard, you should be able to find a good job. If you're willing to meet your responsibilities, you should be able to own a home, maybe start a business, give your children a chance to do even better than you did, no matter who you are, no matter what you look like, no matter where you came from, no matter what your last name, no matter who you love. That is the promise of America.

And we came together in 2008 because we felt that basic bargain, that simple dream was slipping away for too many people, and it had been for a decade. We'd gone through a decade where manufacturing was leaving our shores and a surplus had turned to a deficit; a few folks were doing really well but more and more people were struggling to get by, no matter how hard they worked. And the costs of health care and college were going up and up and up; people were borrowing with credit cards and home equity loans to try to maintain their standard of living, but it just got harder and harder. And all this culminated in the worst economic crisis that we've seen in our lifetimes. And because of that crisis, that dream felt like it was even farther away.

Now, the good news is the American people are tougher than tough times. And over the last 3½ years we've fought back. And when some said let's let Detroit go bankrupt, we believed in the American worker and we believed in American manufacturing, and now Detroit is back on top, and we are selling cars all over the world. People who lost their jobs went back and got retrained—maybe a 50-year-old sitting back in a classroom in a community college and suddenly finding an entire new career opening up to him. Small businesses, through the SBA, were able to get some financing and keep their doors open and keep their payrolls and make sure that the families who depended on that business were still able to succeed.

Now, we've still got a long way to go. We lost 9 million jobs in that recession. And although we've created more than 4 million since I've taken office and 800,000 in the last few months alone, this has been a steep climb. And we understand from our friends and our neighbors, in our own lives, how much more work we have to do. Too many folks out there still without a job; too many people here in Florida still seeing their homes underwater. So we understand how much work we have left.

But the debate in this election is not whether we need to do better. Everybody understands the economy is not where it needs to be. A lot of folks are still struggling; we've got to do better. The debate in this election, though, is about how do we do better. How do we grow our economy faster? How do we create more good jobs? How do we pay down our debt? How do we reclaim that basic bargain and rebuild our middle class that has made us the greatest nation on Earth? That's the question in this election. That's the choice in this election.

And this is not a manufactured debate. This is not one of those Washington Beltway insider arguments that don't mean anything. This is the defining issue of our time. It's a make-or-break moment for the middle class, but also for all those folks who still aspire to the middle class, who are still trying to climb into a life of security for their families. The next President, the next Congress, is going to face a set of decisions on the economy and on deficits and on taxes that will have an enormous impact not just on our country today, but on the country that we pass on to the next generation.

And understand that what's holding us back from meeting these challenges is not the lack of technical solutions; it's not the lack of big ideas. What's holding us back right now is we've got a stalemate in Washington. We've got a stalemate between two fundamentally different views, two fundamentally different visions of where this country should go.

And you know who's going to break that stalemate? You. You're going to break that stalemate. This election is your chance to move this country forward and make sure it does not go backwards.

So let me just break down this choice, because I want everybody to be very clear about it. Governor Romney and his allies believe that we should go back to the top-down economics of the last decade.

Audience members. No!

The President. They believe that if we eliminate regulations and we cut taxes by trillions of dollars, we just leave the market alone, that everybody will prosper. They argue that if we help corporations and wealthy investors maximize their profits by whatever means necessary—whether it means layoffs or outsourcing or union-busting or whatever means are available—that that will automatically translate into jobs and prosperity that benefit everybody.

Last week it was reported Governor Romney's old firm owned companies that, according to this article, were pioneers in the business of outsourcing American jobs to places like China and India. And yesterday his advisers were asked about this, and they tried to clear it up by explaining that there's actually a difference between outsourcing and offshoring. [*Laughter*] I'm not making that up. You can't make something like that up. [*Laughter*]

Now, if you're a worker whose job just went overseas, you really aren't looking for somebody to explain to you the difference between offshoring and outsourcing. What you need is somebody who's going to wake up every single day fighting for your job, fighting for American jobs. That's what you want.

You want somebody who will close the outsourcing loopholes in our Tax Code. You want somebody who will give tax breaks to companies that create jobs in manufacturing here in the United States, not ship them overseas.

And the reason this is relevant is because this is part of their overall economic vision, an overall economic plan that he and the Republicans in Congress share and they will implement if they are elected. And it's there for all to see it; they've put it on the table. It's been voted on in Congress. It's right on Governor Romney's website. They're going to roll back all kinds of regulations on banks and polluters and insurance companies and oil companies. That's part one of the plan.

Part two of the plan is not only to keep all the Bush tax cuts in place, including for the wealthiest Americans, but also add another $5 trillion in tax cuts on top of that, which includes a 25-percent tax cut for every millionaire in the country.

Audience members. Boo!

The President. Now, you may be wondering—because I can tell this is a smart crowd—[*laughter*]—how do they spend $5 trillion on new tax cuts and then claim that their plan would reduce the deficit? That's a good question.

They start by proposing a trillion dollars in cuts to things like education and training and medical research and clean energy— $1 tril-

lion out of that part of the budget that is helping to make us more competitive. But that's not enough. They also proposed eliminating health care for about 50 million Americans and turning Medicare into a voucher program.

But that's still not enough. It still doesn't get you to 5 trillion. So they'll also then have to eliminate deductions, which effectively will raise taxes on the middle class by taking away tax benefits for everything from health care, college, retirement, homeownership. So that could cost middle class families thousands of dollars.

That's their entire economic plan. That's it. So, when Mr. Romney says he's some financial wizard who can fix our economy, that's exactly how he intends to do it.

Now, there are folks out there who think this plan sounds like a good idea. They want to give the policies of the last decade another try. And if so, they should vote for Mr. Romney. They should reelect the Republicans who have been running Congress. Together, they will take America down this path. They are more than qualified to do it. They will do it. Take them at their word, they will do it. [*Laughter*]

But you and I remember how it worked out the last time we tried this philosophy. These policies have been tested, and they have failed. And the reason is because there's another vision out there for America, the one I believe in, the one you believe in. A vision that says prosperity never comes from the top down; it comes from a strong and growing middle class and all those strivers who are fighting to get into the middle class and successful, thriving small businesses that become medium-sized businesses and big businesses.

We don't need more top-down economics. We need a plan for better education and training and energy independence and innovation and new infrastructure, and we need a Tax Code that encourages companies to keep jobs here in the United States and asks wealthy Americans to help pay down our deficit. That's what we need. That's what we're fighting for. And that's why I'm running for a second term as President of the United States of America.

Audience members. Four more years! Four more years! Four more years!

The President. Listen, listen. Miami, we do not expect Government to solve all our problems. This notion that somehow all we believe in are Government solutions, look at the record. Over the last 3 years, I cut taxes for the typical working family by $3,600. Cut taxes for small businesses 18 times. Eliminated billions of dollars of regulations that don't make sense, aren't making people safer or healthier. I don't believe we should be in the business of helping people who refuse to help themselves. I believe in individual responsibility.

I believe no education program is going to be better than parents doing their job at making sure that kids are instilled with a love of learning. But I do share the belief of our first Republican President, a guy named Abraham Lincoln, that through our Government we should do together what we can't do as well for ourselves.

The belief that we are a team, that's how we built this country—together. We built railroads and highways, the Hoover Dam, the Golden Gate Bridge, the Interstate Highway System, the transcontinental rail. We built those things together. We sent my grandfather's generation to college on the GI bill. We did that together. We made investments in sending a man to the Moon and helping to create the Internet. We did those things together.

We did those things because there is such a thing as a common good. There's the understanding that these investments we make, make us all richer. They give us all opportunity. We don't do it just for one person or for one group. We understand that we move forward as one Nation and as one people. That's the lesson of our past. That's the right vision for our future. That's why I'm running for a second term as President of the United States. I believe in that vision. I believe in it.

I'm running to make sure that every American, every young person has a chance to get the skills and training that today's jobs require. And that's why we want to recruit an army of new teachers and pay them better and hire them in areas like math and science and give 2 million more Americans the chance to go to community colleges to upgrade their skills to get the jobs that local businesses are looking for right now.

That's why we want to make higher education affordable for every young person who's willing to work for it, not just by offering loans and grants, but also by getting schools to hold down their college tuition. It's the right thing to do. That's the choice in this election, and that's why I'm running for President.

I want us to be in control of our own energy future. That's good for our economy, our security. It's good for our planet. That's why we need to end Government subsidies for oil companies that are already making a lot of money. Let's double down on investments in clean energy, in solar and wind and biodiesel and fuel-efficient cars. That will be good for all of us.

I want to make sure that America continues to be the best place for innovation and discovery. It's why we need to continue investing in research and development. And after a decade of war, it's time for us to start doing some nation-building here at home.

I ended the war in Iraq, as I promised. We are winding down the war in Afghanistan. I want to take half the money we're no longer spending on war and put it to use putting people back to work rebuilding our roads and our runways and our ports and our wireless networks. That's the choice in this election.

The other side will say, well, we can't afford to do all that; deficits, debt, that's our problem. Well, I put forward a plan that will reduce our deficit by $4 trillion in a way that's balanced and responsible, a detailed plan that cuts spending we can't afford—and there's waste in Government programs that don't work—that also strengthens programs like Medicare for the long haul and reforms our Tax Code so that the wealthiest Americans pay a little more.

And by the way, that approach—just like their approach has been tested, our approach has been tested, because that formula of a Tax Code that is balanced and fair is what produced those surpluses under Bill Clinton. It's what got our economy creating 23 million new jobs. It's what got the engines of our economy moving. And by the way, it was good for business. We created a lot of millionaires and a lot of billionaires during those times, because they had a lot of customers for their services and their products. And there are a lot of patriotic, successful Americans—including here tonight—who would be willing to do a little bit more for their country because they understand the concept of a common good. They understand we're in it together.

Now, Governor Romney disagrees with my vision. That's what democracy's all about: We choose. His allies in Congress disagree with my vision. They've got a different approach. Neither of them will endorse any policy that asks folks like me or Marc Anthony—[*laughter*]—to pay even a nickel more in taxes. That's the reason we haven't reached an agreement on our deficit. It's the reason my jobs bill that independent economists say would put an additional million people back to work has been voted down time and time again. It's the biggest source of gridlock in Washington these last 3 years.

And the folks who can break this stalemate are you. You can decide. On every challenge we face, you get the final say. That's how our democracy works. You can decide. You can decide whether we decide to keep our brave men and women in Afghanistan indefinitely, as Mr. Romney wants to do, or whether we stick to the timeline that I set that will finally bring our troops home. That will be your decision.

You can decide whether or not we go back to restricting access to birth control or defunding Planned Parenthood, or whether you believe that women in America should control their own health choices. That will be your decision.

You can decide whether we should roll back Wall Street regulations that we put in place to prevent taxpayer bailouts and to protect consumers. You can decide whether it makes sense, as Mr. Romney wants to do, to roll back the reforms that we put in place that prevent insurance companies from discriminating against people who are sick.

I believe it's the right thing to do. I believe health reform was the right thing to do. I believe it was right to make sure that over 3 million young people can stay on their parent's health insurance plan. I believe it was right to provide more discounts for seniors on their prescription drugs. I believe it was right to make sure that everybody in this country gets decent health care and is not bankrupt when they get sick. That's what I believe. But it's up to you. You decide.

It's your decision whether we go back to the days when you could be kicked out of the U.S. military just because of who you are and who you love. I believe ending "don't ask, don't tell" was the right thing to do.

You can decide whether or not it makes sense to stop denying the opportunity of responsible young people: to allow them to stay here and prosper here and get educated here, just because they're the children of undocumented immigrants. They are Americans through and through, except for their papers. I believe it was the right thing to do. But ultimately, it's up to you.

And you know what, you can also decide whether we're going to continue to have elections decided by multimillion-dollar donations instead of the voices of ordinary citizens.

Audience members. Boo!

The President. This is going to be a close election. It's going to be close because there are a lot of folks still struggling out there. But it's also going to be close because the other side will spend more money than at any time in United States history on negative ads that have a very simple message. They'll say the economy's bad and it's all my fault. [*Laughter*] That will be their message. I mean, they'll have variations to the same theme. They'll say, well, he can't fix it because he thinks Government's always the answer, or he can't fix it because he didn't make a lot of money in the private sector, or he's in over his head, or he thinks everybody's doing just fine.

That's what the scary voices in the ads will be saying. That's what Mitt Romney will say. That's what the Republicans in Congress will say. And since you are in a battleground State, you will hear this a lot.

And I understand it's a theory to win an election. It's sure not a plan to create jobs. It's not a plan to grow our economy. It's not a plan to restore the American Dream.

And so ultimately, the question for all of you is how much are you willing to fight for this? If you agree with me and if you believe this economy grows best when everybody gets a fair shot and everybody does their fair share and everybody is playing by the same set of rules, if you believe in the common good, if you believe we're a team, if you believe we do best when we work together, then I'm going to need you. And I'm going to need you to go out there and work hard.

And by the way, this is not a Democratic idea or a Republican idea. You vote for anybody—Republican, Democrat, Independent— anybody who shares these values and shares this vision, because there was a time when Republicans would express these same values and these same visions. And I think there are a lot of Republicans and Independents out there who recognize that we can't go back to you're-on-your-own economics, that don't believe we should just tell the young person who can't afford college, you're on your own, or tell somebody who's working hard, but doesn't have health care, tough luck.

But it's going to require us to work hard. It's going to require us to have faith. In 2008, I used to tell you, in the height of all the excitement, I would remind people I'm not a perfect man, and I said I'd never be a perfect President. But what I said was—I made a promise. I said I'd always tell you where I stood and I'd always tell you what I believed and I would work as hard as I could, as hard as I knew how, every single day, every minute of every day, for

you. That I would be thinking about you and I'd be fighting for you and advocating for you, for all those folks out there all across the country who know what struggle is, but also know what it means to overcome struggle.

And I've kept that promise. I've kept that promise because my faith in the American people is undiminished. And as I travel across the country, I see your decency and I see your strength and I see your resilience, and I am inspired. And so I am just as determined as I ever have been.

I believe in this country, and I believe in you. And if you still believe in me, I'm going to need you to stand with me in this election and get on the phone and knock on doors and talk to your friends and talk to your neighbors. And we are going to fight, and we are going to struggle, and we're going to finish what we started in 2008 and remind the world just why it is that America is the greatest nation on Earth.

God bless you. God bless the United States of America.

NOTE: The President spoke at 8:01 p.m. at the Fillmore Miami Beach at the Jackie Gleason Theater. In his remarks, he referred to Medley, FL, resident Maytee Lopez, who introduced the President; Frederick J. Pollak, president and chief executive officer, TracFone Wireless, Inc., and his wife Abigail, who hosted a campaign fundraiser at their Miami Beach, FL, residence earlier in the evening; radio host Enrique Santos; Alonzo Mourning, former center, National Basketball Association's Miami Heat, and his wife Tracy; and Republican Presidential candidate former Gov. W. Mitt Romney of Massachusetts.

Statement on National HIV Testing Day
June 27, 2012

National HIV Testing Day highlights the importance of HIV testing and the fight against HIV/AIDS. Of the over 1.1 million Americans living with HIV, more than 200,000 are unaware of their infection and may unknowingly be transmitting the virus to others. Knowing

your HIV status is a vital step toward accessing life-extending treatment for HIV, and thanks to ongoing research, that treatment is more effective than ever.

In July 2010, my administration released the National HIV/AIDS Strategy, which emphasizes the goals of reducing infections, improving health outcomes, and reducing HIV-related health disparities. Two years into its implementation, the Strategy continues to focus Federal, State, and local efforts on improving the delivery of HIV/AIDS services, including expanding outreach, testing, linkage to care, and treatment.

Testing remains a special priority, and thanks to quick and accurate tests, finding out your HIV status has never been easier. The Affordable Care Act now requires many health insurance plans to provide recommended preventive health services with no out-of-pocket costs, giving millions of Americans better access to HIV testing. Another CDC program, the Expanding Testing Initiative, has conducted 2.8 million tests in its first 3 years. Together, these and other efforts will help prevent new infections and ensure that people living with HIV lead healthy lives, moving us towards our goal of an AIDS-free generation.

Joint Statement by President Obama and Crown Prince Mohammed bin Zayed Al Nahyan of Abu Dhabi, Deputy Supreme Commander of the Armed Forces of the United Arab Emirates
June 27, 2012

The United States and United Arab Emirates remain deeply committed to close consultation and cooperation to promote peace and stability in the Gulf region and broader Middle East. In their meeting at the White House today, President Obama and Crown Prince Mohammed bin Zayed Al-Nuhayan reviewed the full range of regional security issues including Iran, Syria, terrorism, and energy security.

The President and Crown Prince discussed the ongoing negotiations with Iran on its nuclear program and the three Gulf islands whose sovereignty is disputed between the UAE and Iran. They called upon Iran to meet its international obligations under the Nuclear Nonprolilferation Treaty and relevant United Nations Security Council and International Atomic Energy Agency Board of Governors resolutions. They also called for a peaceful resolution of the islands' status, regarding which the United States strongly supports the UAE's initiative to resolve the issue through direct negotiations, the International Court of Justice, or another appropriate international forum.

Both the President and Crown Prince expressed the urgent need to implement the Annan plan to prevent further bloodshed in Syria and their support for a transition plan that would meet the legitimate aspirations of the Syrian people. Noting the profound changes taking place in other countries in the Middle East, they called on governments and citizens alike to avoid violence, advance tolerance, and protect human rights-particularly the rights of women. They highlighted the importance of reforms that support accountable governance, increase civic participation, and promote economic opportunities, especially for young people.

The President and Crown Prince pledged to sustain the two countries' joint counter-terrorism and security initiatives in the region. They discussed programs to counter violent extremism and the ideological roots of terrorism, and welcomed the upcoming launch in October in Abu Dhabi of the new Center for Countering Violent Extremism, a project supported by both countries and the international community.

The President and Crown Prince reaffirmed their commitment to strong bilateral defense cooperation to enhance regional security and deter any threat of aggression against the UAE. They identified a number of mechanisms to continue to deepen this cooperation, including more joint exercises and training, improved combined planning, and future defense equipment sales. They noted their appreciation that the militaries of the two governments had worked together in multiple coalition operations, including in Desert Storm, Kosovo, Afghanistan, and Libya. They discussed transition plans for Afghanistan, where UAE Special Forces units have been deployed for 10 years as part of broader coalition military and humanitarian stabilization efforts. They pledged to enhance multilateral cooperation on regional security issues through the U.S.-Gulf Cooperation Council Strategic Cooperation Forum.

On energy security, the Crown Prince outlined the UAE's ongoing initiatives to reduce price volatility and ensure reliable supplies to world markets at prices that support global economic growth. The President and Crown Prince discussed the importance of protecting critical shipping lanes against threats of aggression, terrorism, and piracy. The President congratulated the Crown Prince on the announcement of the opening of a new 1.5 million bpd oil pipeline that crosses the UAE, thus allowing energy supplies to bypass the Strait of Hormuz, and also expressed his appreciation for the UAE's efforts in the field of renewable energy.

The President and Crown Prince welcomed their countries' strong bilateral economic, cultural, and social ties, noting that the UAE is one of the largest trading partners of the United States in the Middle East. The President thanked the UAE for hosting the Global Entrepreneurship Summit this December in Dubai, and reaffirmed U.S. support for encouraging broad-based economic growth and opportunity in the region. The President also noted with appreciation the significant investment by the UAE in the United States, including in a semiconductor manufacturing facility in upstate New York scheduled to open later this year.

NOTE: An original was not available for verification of the content of this joint statement.

Remarks at the Congressional Picnic
June 27, 2012

The President. Hello, everybody!

Audience members. Hello!

The President. Now, you don't have to worry, I will not be singing. We have professionals for that. [*Laughter*] But on behalf of Michelle and myself, I just want to say welcome. We have a perfect day for a picnic. It is spectacular.

We want to thank, as usual, our outstanding Marine Band. They can play anything at any time. And we're so grateful for their service to our country. Obviously, that goes to all our men and women in uniform. And today is a great day for us to acknowledge everything they do to provide our liberty and way of life.

I want to say a special welcome not only to the Members of Congress, but most importantly, to their families, because Michelle reminds me every day how difficult it is to be married to a politician. [*Laughter*] And the sacrifices that all of you make—the birthday parties that get missed or the soccer games that you're late to, the travel that keeps you away from your loved ones—all of that obviously is in service of our country, and you guys are serving alongside those of us who hold elective

office. So we're thrilled that you have at least one day where you got a chance to be together in Washington and nobody is arguing.

So that also just reminds me that for all the political differences that are sometimes expressed in this town, we are first and foremost Americans, not Democrats or Republicans. And I think all of us want to make sure that during extraordinarily challenging times for this country that we constantly keep that in mind. That's what the people who sent us here are expecting. And I know that each of us in our own way are hopeful that, because of the work that we do here, we pass on something a little better and a little brighter to our kids and our grandkids.

And so I'm looking forward to continuing to work with you. I'm glad I see some folks here in shorts—[*laughter*]—and some Hawaiian shirts. And so everybody is dressed appropriately for a picnic. If you still have your tie on, take it off. [*Laughter*] Make sure to enjoy the barbecue, enjoy the music. And——

The First Lady. Go see the garden.

The President. Go see the garden if you want.

And we are going to be coming down on this rope line, and I want to be able to shake everybody's hands. I warn you in advance that because the line is long, it's going to be hard for us to pose for individual pictures for everybody. The exceptions that we make are kids who are 12 and under. How about that? That's going to be our cutoff. So, little kids, if you want a picture, I don't mind. I can't say no to little kids. You bigger folks, you're just going to get a handshake and maybe a kiss if—[*laughter*]—unless you haven't shaved, in which case—so anyway, everybody have a wonderful time.

God bless you. God bless America.

NOTE: The President spoke at 7:12 p.m. on the South Lawn at the White House.

Remarks on the United States Supreme Court Ruling on the Patient Protection and Affordable Care Act
June 28, 2012

Good afternoon. Earlier today the Supreme Court upheld the constitutionality of the Affordable Care Act, the name of the health care reform we passed 2 years ago. In doing so, they've reaffirmed a fundamental principle that here in America, in the wealthiest nation on Earth, no illness or accident should lead to any family's financial ruin.

I know there will be a lot of discussion today about the politics of all this, about who won and who lost. That's how these things tend to be viewed here in Washington. But that discussion completely misses the point. Whatever the politics, today's decision was a victory for people all over this country whose lives will be more secure because of this law and the Supreme Court's decision to uphold it.

And because this law has a direct impact on so many Americans, I want to take this opportunity to talk about exactly what it means for you.

First, if you're one of the more than 250 million Americans who already have health insurance, you will keep your health insurance; this law will only make it more secure and more affordable. Insurance companies can no longer impose lifetime limits on the amount of care you receive. They can no longer discriminate against children with preexisting conditions. They can no longer drop your coverage if you get sick. They can no longer jack up your premiums without reason. They are required to provide free preventive care like checkups and mammograms, a provision that's already helped 54 million Americans with private insurance. And by this August, nearly 13 million of you will receive a rebate from your insurance company because it spent too much on things like administrative costs and CEO bonuses, and not enough on your health care.

There's more: Because of the Affordable Care Act, young adults under the age of 26 are able to stay on their parents' health care plans, a provision that's already helped 6 million young Americans. And because of the Affordable Care Act, seniors receive a discount on their prescription drugs, a discount that's already saved more than 5 million seniors on Medicare about $600 each.

All of this is happening because of the Affordable Care Act. These provisions provide commonsense protections for middle class families, and they enjoy broad popular support. And thanks to today's decision, all of these benefits and protections will continue for Americans who already have health insurance.

Now, if you're one of the 30 million Americans who don't yet have health insurance, starting in 2014 this law will offer you an array of quality, affordable, private health insurance plans to choose from. Each State will take the lead in designing their own menu of options, and if States can come up with even better ways of covering more people at the same quality and cost, this law allows them to do that too. And I've asked Congress to help speed up that process and give States this flexibility in year one.

Once States set up these health insurance marketplaces, known as exchanges, insurance companies will no longer be able to discriminate against any American with a preexisting health condition. They won't be able to charge you more just because you're a woman. They won't be able to bill you into bankruptcy. If you're sick, you'll finally have the same chance to get quality, affordable health care as everyone else. And if you can't afford the premiums, you'll receive a credit that helps pay for it.

Today the Supreme Court also upheld the principle that people who can afford health insurance should take the responsibility to buy health insurance. This is important for two reasons. First, when uninsured people who can afford coverage get sick and show up at the emergency room for care, the rest of us end up paying for their care in the form of higher premiums. And second, if you ask insurance companies to cover people with preexisting conditions, but don't require people who can afford it to buy their own insurance, some folks might wait until they're sick to buy the care they need, which would also drive up everybody else's premiums.

That's why, even though I knew it wouldn't be politically popular and resisted the idea when I ran for this office, we ultimately included a provision in the Affordable Care Act that people who can afford to buy health insurance should take the responsibility to do so. In fact, this idea has enjoyed support from members of both parties, including the current Republican nominee for President.

Still, I know the debate over this law has been divisive. I respect the very real concerns that millions of Americans have shared. And I know a lot of coverage through this health care debate has focused on what it means politically.

Well, it should be pretty clear by now that I didn't do this because it was good politics. I did it because I believed it was good for the country. I did it because I believed it was good for the American people.

There's a framed letter that hangs in my office right now. It was sent to me during the health care debate by a woman named Natoma Canfield. For years and years, Natoma did everything right. She bought health insurance. She paid her premiums on time. But 18 years ago, Natoma was diagnosed with cancer. And even though she'd been cancer-free for more than a decade, her insurance company kept jacking up her rates, year after year. And despite her desire to keep her coverage—despite her fears that she would get sick again—she had to surrender her health insurance and was forced to hang her fortunes on chance.

I carried Natoma's story with me every day of the fight to pass this law. It reminded me of all the Americans, all across the country, who have had to worry not only about getting sick, but about the cost of getting well.

Natoma is well today. And because of this law, there are other Americans—other sons and daughters, brothers and sisters, fathers and mothers—who will not have to hang their fortunes on chance. These are the Americans for whom we passed this law.

The highest Court in the land has now spoken. We will continue to implement this law. And we'll work together to improve on it where we can. But what we won't do—what the country can't afford to do—is refight the political battles of 2 years ago or go back to the way things were.

With today's announcement, it's time for us to move forward, to implement and, where necessary, improve on this law. And now is the time to keep our focus on the most urgent challenge of our time: putting people back to work, paying down our debt, and building an economy where people can have confidence that if they work hard, they can get ahead.

But today I'm as confident as ever that when we look back 5 years from now or 10 years from now or 20 years from now, we'll be better off because we had the courage to pass this law and keep moving forward.

Thank you. God bless you, and God bless America.

NOTE: The President spoke at 12:15 p.m. in the East Room at the White House. In his remarks, he referred to Republican Presidential candidate former Gov. W. Mitt Romney of Massachusetts; and Medina, OH, resident and

health care reform advocate Natoma A. Canfield.

Remarks During a Tour of Wildfire Damage and an Exchange With Reporters in Colorado Springs, Colorado
June 29, 2012

The President. First of all, I want to say to Mayor Bach, Governor Hickenlooper, and the congressional delegation, but most importantly, all the guys on the ground who have been fighting this fire: We are so grateful to see the extraordinary coordination that's taking place between the State, Federal, municipal, all the agencies—everybody tried to put everything they got into this thing.

This has been a devastating early fire season for Colorado. This community obviously is heartbroken by the loss of homes. We're lucky because of the quick action that's been taken, that we haven't seen a lot of loss of life. But for those families who have lost everything—their possessions, who have been displaced—our thoughts and prayers are with them.

What I've said is, is that the Federal Government is going to do everything we can to coordinate assistance, not just short term, but long term. In fact, one of the good things that we've been seeing is some innovative ways in which some military assets have been deployed alongside the traditional assets that are used in these fire fights.

So we're going to have a long way to go before all these fires are put out. We need a little bit of help from Mother Nature. But I hope that people all across the country recognize that when challenges like this happen, all of us come together as one American family. And we're seeing similar disasters, some of the flooding in Florida. Obviously, we've been seeing tornadoes and other natural threats. But what always is inspiring to me is whenever I come to these communities, the strength, the resilience, the degree to which people are willing to work together, it's a reminder of what is the most important aspect of this country, and

that is its people and the way that we are willing to get each other's backs.

And so I just want say again, Mr. Mayor, you did an outstanding job. Governor, as always, you're on top of things. And I think I speak for the congressional delegation in saying the Federal Government will continue to do everything we can to help coordinate relief. But we've still got a ways to go before these fires are out.

Q. What do you think when you see just this stuff right here?

The President. Well, what's remarkable is obviously how devastating these fires are. Once they hit a house and they take root, it is very difficult for anybody to imagine the kind of devastation and how quickly it happens.

And obviously, what's also tragic is, is that the nature of these fires, you can have a house that is perfectly fine on one side and then another house that's completely destroyed on the other. But because of those outstanding firefighters that we just saw, three of those homes were saved. And for those three families, those folks are heroes.

And when you think about 18-hour days and the kind of effort that these guys are putting in, and the danger that they're putting themselves under, it's a testament to our Forest Service and our firefighters. And we just got to make sure that we are giving them the best equipment, all the resources that they need. But what we can't give them is their courage. They bring that to the table from the start.

NOTE: The President spoke at 1:03 p.m. in the Mountain Shadows residential neighborhood. In his remarks, he referred to Mayor Stephen G. Bach of Colorado Springs, CO.

Remarks to Firefighters and First-Responders in Colorado Springs
June 29, 2012

[*The President's remarks were joined in progress.*]

———just to say thank you. I know that everybody here has been working nonstop. We just had a chance to see one of the subdivisions that have been obviously devastated by the course of this fire. But we also had a chance while we were there to thank some guys who were on the site who had just saved three homes.

And what I told the press earlier, in natural disasters like this, the Federal Government, our job is to provide all the resources possible. What we've been seeing is unprecedented coordination between Federal, State, and local resources and personnel.

I want to thank the mayor, Mayor Bach, as well as Governor Hickenlooper for the great work they've been doing. We've been doing some unusual stuff using military assets for the first time in a different kind of way to help leverage some of the resources that you guys already have.

But the main thing I said was no matter how much equipment you have, no matter how many resources are provided, we don't provide you with the courage and professionalism and stick-to-it-ness that all of you guys show every single day. So I want you to know that not only is this community grateful for your work, but the country is grateful for your work. And I want you to know that we're going to stay on it. The job is obviously not done yet, but the country has got your back. And just remember, each and every day, despite all the sacrifices—and what I got to assume is some pretty weary bodies—that you got a lot of people out there who are grateful and families whose lives are going to be better because of what you do every day.

So thank you very much. And with that, all I want to do is go shake some hands and say I appreciate you.

Thank you, guys.

NOTE: The President spoke at 1:20 p.m. at Fire Station 9. In his remarks, he referred to Mayor Stephen G. Bach of Colorado Springs, CO. Audio was not available for verification of the content of these remarks.

Remarks Following a Tour of Wildfire Damage in Colorado Springs
June 29, 2012

Well, we just had a chance to tour some of the damage that's been done by this devastating fire. I've had a chance to thank Mayor Bach, as well as Governor Hickenlooper, and the entire congressional delegation; members of the fire service—the Forest Service, as well as local fire officials have gotten a full briefing.

I think what you see here is an example of outstanding coordination and cooperation between Federal, State, and local agencies. We have been putting everything we have into trying to deal with what's one of the worst fires that we've seen here in Colorado. And it's still early in the fire season, and we still got a lot more work to do. But because of the outstanding work that's been done, because of not only the coordination, but also some unprecedented arrangements that have been made with military resources combined with the civil resources, we're starting to see progress.

Obviously, as you saw in some of these subdivisions, the devastation is enormous. And our thoughts and prayers go out to all the families who have been affected.

One of the things that I've tried to emphasize is that whether it's fires in Colorado or flooding in the northern parts of Florida, when natural disasters like this hit, America comes together. And we all recognize that there, but for the grace of God, go I. We've got to make sure that we have each other's backs. And that spirit is what you're seeing in terms of volunteers, in terms of firefighters, in terms of Government officials. Everybody is pulling together to try to deal with this situation.

Now, as I said, we're not completely out of the woods yet. These folks, some of them have been working 18-hour days, 20-hour days, trying to make sure that these fires get put out. They're going to be carefully monitoring the situation; ultimately, they're going to need a little bit of help from Mother Nature in order to fully extinguish these fires.

In the meantime, some lessons are being learned about how we can mitigate some of these fires in the future, and I know that the mayor and Governor and other local officials are already in those conversations. It means that, hopefully, out of this tragedy, some long-term planning occurs, and it may be that we can curb some of the damage that happens the next time, even though you obviously can't fully control fires that are starting up in these mountains.

Last point I just want to make, and that is that we can provide all the resources, we can make sure that they're well coordinated, but as I just told these firefighters, what we can't do is to provide them with the courage and the determination and the professionalism, the heart

that they show when they're out there battling these fires.

When we had a chance onsite to see some guys who had just saved three homes in a community that had been devastated, for those families, the work and the sacrifice of those firefighters means the world to them, and they are genuine heroes.

And so we want to just say thank you to all the folks who have been involved in this. We're proud of you. We appreciate what you do each and every day. And so for folks all around the country, I hope you are reminded of how important our fire departments are, our Forest Service is. Sometimes they don't get the credit that they deserve until your house is burning down or your community is being threatened. And you have to understand they're putting their lives at risk to save us and to help us. We've got to make sure that we remember that 365 days a year, not just when tragedies like this strike.

Thank you very much, everybody.

NOTE: The President spoke at 1:35 p.m. at Fire Station 9. In his remarks, he referred to Mayor Stephen G. Bach of Colorado Springs, CO.

Message to the Congress Suspending Generalized System of Preferences Benefits to Gibraltar and the Turks and Caicos Islands
June 29, 2012

To the Congress of the United States:

In accordance with section 502(f)(2) of the Trade Act of 1974, as amended (the "1974 Act") (19 U.S.C. 2462(f)(2)), I am providing notification of my intent to terminate the designations of Gibraltar and the Turks and Caicos Islands as beneficiary developing countries under the Generalized System of Preferences (GSP) program. Section 502(e) of the 1974 Act (19 U.S.C. 2462(e)) provides that if the President determines that a beneficiary developing country has become a "high income" country, as defined by the official statistics of

the International Bank for Reconstruction and Development (i.e., the World Bank), then the President shall terminate the designation of such country as a beneficiary developing country for purposes of GSP, effective on January 1 of the second year following the year in which such determination is made.

Pursuant to section 502(e) of the 1974 Act, I have determined that it is appropriate to terminate Gibraltar's designation as a beneficiary developing country under the GSP program, because it has become a high income country as defined by the World Bank. Accordingly,

Gibraltar's eligibility for trade benefits under the GSP program will end on January 1, 2014.

In addition, pursuant to section 502(e) of the 1974 Act, I have determined that it is appropriate to terminate Turks and Caicos Islands' designation as a beneficiary developing country under the GSP program, because it has become a high income country as defined by the World Bank. Accordingly, Turks and Caicos Islands' eligibility for trade benefits un-der the GSP program will end on January 1, 2014.

BARACK OBAMA

The White House,
June 29, 2012.

NOTE: The related proclamation is listed in Appendix D at the end of this volume.

Message to the Congress Extending Generalized System of Preferences Benefits to Senegal
June 29, 2012

To the Congress of the United States:

In accordance with section 502(f)(1)(B) of the Trade Act of 1974, as amended (the "1974 Act") (19 U.S.C. 2462(f)(1)(B)), I am notifying the Congress of my intent to add the Republic of Senegal (Senegal) to the list of least-developed beneficiary developing countries under the Generalized System of Preferences program. After considering the criteria set forth in section 502(c) of the 1974 Act (19 U.S.C. 2462(c)), I have determined that it is appropriate to extend least-developed beneficiary developing country benefits to Senegal.

BARACK OBAMA

The White House,
June 29, 2012.

NOTE: The related proclamation is listed in Appendix D at the end of this volume.

The President's Weekly Address
June 30, 2012

Hi, everybody. I'm here in Colorado Springs, visiting some of the devastating fires that have been taking place over the last several days. As many of you have been watching on television, entire communities are under threat. And we had a chance to tour some of the devastation that had been taking place in some of the subdivisions here.

Firefighters are working 18 hours a day, around the clock, trying to make sure that they get this blaze under control. We've got volunteers who are out here who are making sure that these firefighters have the food and the water and all the resources that they need. And we've been engaging in some unprecedented coordination between Federal, State, and local communities to try to bring this fire under control.

And one of the things I've done here, in addition to saying thank you to these firefighters, is to let them know that all of America has their back. One of the things that happens—whether it's a fire here in Colorado, or a tornado in Alabama or Missouri, or a flood or a hurricane in Florida—one of the things that happens here in America is when we see our fellow citizens in trouble and having difficulty, we come together as one American family, as one community. And you see that spirit and you see that strength here in Colorado Springs, where people are working together, promising each other to rebuild. We've got to make sure that we are there with them every step of the way, even after this fire is put out.

So for those of you who can provide some help, you should get on the online site of

American Red Cross. They're very active in this community, and you can make your contributions there. We're going to continue to make sure that the Federal Emergency Management Agency, the Forest Service, our military and National Guard, and all the resources that we have available at the Federal level are brought to bear in fighting this fire.

This is a good reminder of what makes us Americans. We don't just look out for ourselves, we look out for each other. And one of the things that I told these firefighters is that we can provide them all the resources they need, but only they provide the courage and the discipline to be able to actually fight these fires. And it's important that we appreciate what they do, not just when our own communities are struck by disaster. It's important that we remember what they do each and every single day and that we continue to provide support to our first-responders, our emergency management folks, our firefighters, our military—everybody who helps secure our liberty and our security each and every day.

So, America, I hope you guys remember the folks during these times of need. I know this is a little bit unusual. We don't usually do weekly addresses like this, but I thought it was a good opportunity for us to actually focus attention on a problem that's going on here in Colorado Springs. We never know when it might be our community that's threatened, and it's important that we're there for them.

All right, thank you very much.

NOTE: The address was recorded at approximately 9:45 a.m. on June 29 at Fire Station 9 in Colorado Springs, CO, for broadcast on June 30. The transcript was made available by the Office of the Press Secretary on June 29, but was embargoed for release until 6 a.m. on June 30.

Appendix A—Digest of Other White House Announcements

The following list includes the President's public schedule and other items of general interest announced by the Office of the Press Secretary and not included elsewhere in this book.

January 1

In the morning, in Kailua, HI, the President had an intelligence briefing.

January 2

In the morning, the President had an intelligence briefing.

In the afternoon, the President, Mrs. Obama, and their daughters Sasha and Malia returned to Washington, DC, arriving the following morning.

The White House announced that the President will travel to Cleveland, OH, on January 4.

January 3

In the morning, in the Oval Office, the President and Vice President Joe Biden had an intelligence briefing. Then, also in the Oval Office, he met with his senior advisers.

In the afternoon, in the Private Dining Room, the President and Vice President Biden had lunch. Later, in the Oval Office, they met with Secretary of Defense Leon E. Panetta.

January 4

In the morning, in the Oval Office, the President and Vice President Joe Biden had an intelligence briefing. Then, he traveled to Cleveland, OH.

In the afternoon, outside the home of William and Endia Eason, the President greeted local residents. Later, he returned to Washington, DC.

The White House announced that the President will travel to the Pentagon in Arlington, VA, on January 5.

The White House announced that the President will welcome the 2011 National Basketball Association Champion Dallas Mavericks to the White House on January 9.

The President announced the recess appointment of Richard A. Cordray as Director of the Consumer Financial Protection Bureau.

The President announced the recess appointments of Sharon Block, Terence F. Flynn, and Richard F. Griffin, Jr., as members of the National Labor Relations Board.

January 5

In the morning, in the Oval Office, the President and Vice President Joe Biden had an intelligence briefing. Then, he traveled to Arlington, VA. Later, he returned to Washington, DC.

In the afternoon, in the State Dining Room, the President met with his Council of Advisers on Science and Technology. Later, in the Oval Office, he and Vice President Biden met with Secretary of the Treasury Timothy F. Geithner.

January 6

In the morning, in the Oval Office, the President had a telephone conversation with King Abdullah II of Jordan to discuss the Middle East peace process. Then, also in the Oval Office, he and Vice President Joe Biden had an intelligence briefing.

In the afternoon, at the Scion restaurant, the President had lunch with Bill Blackwelder of Fayetteville, NC, Val Grossmann of Westminster, CO, Kathie Toigo of Yerington, NV, and Scott Zoebisch of Atlanta, GA, winners of a contest held by his reelection campaign.

The White House announced that the President will meet with his Council on Jobs and Competitiveness at the White House on January 17.

The President declared a major disaster in Massachusetts and ordered Federal aid to supplement Commonwealth and local recovery efforts in the area affected by a severe storm and snowstorm on October 29 and 30, 2011.

January 7

The White House announced that the President will host the White House Insourcing American Jobs Forum on July 11.

January 8

In the morning, the President had a telephone conversation with Rep. Gabrielle D. Giffords to discuss a candlelight vigil being held in honor of the victims of the January 8, 2011, shootings in Tucson, AZ.

January 9

In the morning, in the Oval Office, the President had a telephone conversation with Prime Minister Portia Simpson-Miller of Jamaica to congratulate her on her election victory and discuss Jamaica-U.S. relations. Then, he and Vice President Joe Biden had an intelligence briefing. Later, also in the Oval Office, he met with his senior advisers.

In the afternoon, in the Private Dining Room, the President and Vice President Biden had lunch. Later, in the Oval Office, the President met with Matthew Ritsko, winner of the 2011 Securing Americans Value and Efficiency (SAVE) Award.

In the evening, at the Jefferson hotel, the President attended a roundtable discussion with campaign supporters.

The White House announced that the President will welcome the 2011 World Series Champion St. Louis Cardinals to the White House on January 17.

January 10

In the morning, in the Oval Office, the President and Vice President Joe Biden had an intelligence briefing. Then, also in the Oval Office, he met with his senior advisers.

In the afternoon, in the Oval Office, the President and Vice President Biden met with Secretary of Defense Leon E. Panetta.

During the day, in the Oval Office, the President met with Minister of Foreign Affairs Saud al-Faysal bin Abd al-Aziz Al Saud of Saudi ia to discuss Saudi ia-U.S. relations.

The White House announced further details on the White House Insourcing American Jobs Forum to be held on January 11.

The White House announced that the President with welcome King Abdullah II of Jordan to the White House on January 17.

The President announced his intention to appoint Nancy E. Soderberg as Chairperson of the Public Interest Declassification Board.

The President announced his intention to appoint Elizabeth R. Parker as a member of the Public Interest Declassification Board.

The President announced his intention to appoint Peter H. Bell and Jack M. Brandt as members of the President's Committee for People With Intellectual Disabilities.

The President announced that he has named Cecilia Munoz as Director of the White House Domestic Policy Council.

January 11

In the morning, in the Oval Office, the President and Vice President Joe Biden had an intelligence briefing.

In the afternoon, in the Oval Office, the President met with actors Brad Pitt and Angelina Jolie to discuss their advocacy on human rights issues. Later, he traveled to Chicago, IL, where he visited his campaign headquarters and met with campaign volunteers and staffers.

During the day, in the Oval Office, the President met with National Economic Council Director Eugene B. Sperling, Special Assistant to the President for Manufacturing Policy Jason Miller, and Senior Policy Adviser Jacob Leibenluft.

In the evening, the President returned to Washington, DC.

January 12

In the morning, the President had a telephone conversation with Prime Minister Benjamin Netanyahu of Israel to discuss the Middle East peace process. He also had a telephone conversation with Head Coach Nicholas L. Saban of the University of Alabama football team to congratulate him on his team's victory in the BCS Championship.

The President announced the designation of the following individuals as members of a Presidential delegation to attend the Inauguration of Otto Perez Molina as President of Guatemala in Guatemala City, Guatemala, on January 14:

Aaron S. Willams (head of delegation);
Arnold A. Chacon;
Mary L. Landrieu; and
Mark Feierstein.

January 13

In the morning, in the Oval Office, the President had a telephone conversation with Prime Minister Recep Tayyip Erdogan of Turkey to discuss democracy efforts, security issues, and economic development in the Middle East and the situations in Iraq, Syria, and Iran. Then, he met with Secretary of the Treasury Timothy F. Geithner.

In the afternoon, at the Jefferson hotel, the President attended an Obama Victory Fund 2012 fundraiser. Then, he returned to the White House, where, in the Oval Office, he met with Secretary of State Hillary Rodham Clinton. Later, in the Family Theater, he and Mrs. Obama hosted a screening of the film "Red Tails" for members of the Tuskegee Airmen, cast, and crew.

The White House announced that the President and Mrs. Obama will welcome the 2011 World Series Champion St. Louis Cardinals to the White House on January 17.

The White House announced that the President will host the 2011 Stanley Cup Champion Boston Bruins to the White House on January 23.

The President announced the designation of the following individuals as members of a Presidential delegation to attend the Inauguration of Ellen Johnson Sirleaf as President of Liberia in Monrovia, Liberia, on January 16:

Hillary Rodham Clinton (head of delegation);
Linda Thomas-Greenfield;
Christopher A. Coons;
Johnnie Carson;
Melanne Verveer;
Donald Steinberg;
Carrie Hessler-Radelet;
Carter F. Ham; and
Grant T. Harris.

January 16

In the evening, at the John F. Kennedy Center for the Performing Arts, the President and Mrs. Obama attended the "Let Freedom Ring" celebration in honor of Martin Luther King, Jr.

January 17

In the morning, in the Oval Office, the President and Vice President Joe Biden had an intelligence briefing. Then, also in the Oval Office, he met with his senior advisers.

In the afternoon, in the Private Dining Room, the President and Vice President Biden had lunch. Later, in the Oval Office, they met with Secretary of Defense Leon E. Panetta.

The White House announced that the President will welcome President Mikheil Saakashvili of Georgia to the White House on January 30.

The White House announced that the President will travel to Lake Buena Vista, FL, on January 19.

The President announced that he has designated Jeffrey D. Zients as Acting Director of the Office of Management and Budget.

January 18

In the morning, in the Oval Office, the President had an intelligence briefing.

In the afternoon, in the Oval Office, the President participated in a credentialing ceremony for newly appointed Ambassadors to the U.S. Then, also in the Oval Office, he met with Secretary of the Treasury Timothy F. Geithner.

In the evening, in the East Room, the President hosted a reception for the U.S. Conference of Mayors.

During the day, the President had a telephone conversation with Prime Minister Stephen J. Harper of Canada to convey his administration's decision on the Keystone XL Pipeline project and to discuss Canada-U.S. relations. He also met with White House Counsel Kathryn Ruemmler in the Oval Office.

January 19

In the morning, the President traveled to Lake Buena Vista, FL. While en route aboard

Air Force One, he met with Mayor John H. "Buddy" Dyer, Jr., of Orlando, FL.

In the afternoon, the President traveled to New York City.

In the evening, the President returned to Washington, DC.

January 20

In the morning, in the Oval Office, the President met with Secretary of State Hillary Rodham Clinton. Then, also in the Oval Office, he had a telephone conversation with Chairman of the Supreme Council of the Armed Forces Field Marshal Mohamed Hussein Tantawi of Egypt to discuss Egypt's transition to democracy and Egyptian-U.S. relations.

In the afternoon, at the Jefferson hotel, the President attended an Obama Victory Fund 2012 fundraiser. Later, in the Oval Office, he met with his senior advisers.

January 23

In the morning, in the Oval Office, the President and Vice President Joe Biden had an intelligence briefing.

During the day, the President had a telephone conversation with Suzanne P. Paterno, wife, and Joseph V. "Jay" Paterno, Jr., son, of former Pennsylvania State University football Head Coach Joseph V. Paterno to express his condolences for Coach Paterno's death. Also during the day, in the Oval Office, he met with Director of Speechwriting Jonathan E. Favreau to prepare for his State of the Union Address.

In the evening, the President was briefed by Homeland Security and Counterterrorism Adviser John O. Brennan on developments concerning American aid worker Jessica Buchanan and Danish aid worker Poul Hagen Thisted, held captive in Somalia since October 2011. Following the briefing, he authorized a rescue mission.

The White House announced that the President will welcome Prime Minister Mario Monti of Italy to the White House on February 9.

The White House announced that the President will travel to Cedar Rapids, IA, Phoenix, AZ, and Las Vegas, NV, on January 25.

The White House announced that the President will travel to Cambridge, MD, on January 27.

The President announced his intention to nominate Tony Clark to be a Commissioner of the Federal Energy Regulatory Commission.

The President announced his intention to nominate Erin C. Conaton to be Under Secretary for Personnel and Readiness at the Department of Defense.

The President announced his intention to nominate Scott H. DeLisi to be Ambassador to Uganda.

The President announced his intention to nominate Deborah S. Delisle to be Assistant Secretary for Elementary and Secondary Education at the Department of Education.

The President announced his intention to nominate Tracey A. Jacobson to be Ambassador to Kosovo.

The President announced his intention to nominate James J. Jones to be Assistant Administrator for Toxic Substances at the Environmental Protection Agency.

The President announced his intention to nominate Frank Kendall III to be Under Secretary for Acquisition, Technology, and Logistics at the Department of Defense.

The President announced his intention to nominate James N. Miller, Jr., to be Under Secretary for Policy at the Department of Defense.

The President announced his intention to nominate Marietta S. Robinson to be a Commissioner of the Consumer Product Safety Commission.

The President announced his intention to nominate Adam E. Sieminski to be Administrator of the Energy Information Administration at the Department of Energy.

The President announced his intention to nominate J. Christopher Stevens to be Ambassador to Libya.

The President announced his intention to nominate Linda Thomas-Greenfield to be Director General of the Foreign Service at the Department of State.

The President announced his intention to nominate Constance B. Tobias to be Chairman of the Board of Veterans' Appeals.

The President announced his intention to nominate Pamela A. White to be Ambassador to Haiti.

The President announced his intention to nominate Jessica L. Wright to be Assistant Secretary for Reserve Affairs at the Department of Defense.

The President announced his intention to appoint Eldar Shafir as a member of the President's Advisory Council on Financial Capability.

The President announced his intention to appoint Robert J. Stevens as a member of the Advisory Committee for Trade Policy and Negotiations.

The President announced his intention to appoint Kimberlydawn Wisdom as a member of the Advisory Group on Prevention, Health Promotion, and Integrative and Public Health.

The President announced that he has nominated Robert E. Bacharach to be a judge on the U.S. Court of Appeals for the Tenth Circuit.

The President announced that he has nominated William J. Kayatta, Jr., to be a judge on the U.S. Court of Appeals for the First Circuit.

The President announced that he has nominated Michael A. Shipp to be a judge on the U.S. District Court for the District of New Jersey.

January 24

Throughout the day, the President received updates from Homeland Security and Counterterrorism Adviser John O. Brennan on the mission to rescue American aid worker Jessica Buchanan and Danish aid worker Poul Hagen Thisted from captivity in Somalia.

In the evening, the President was informed that Ms. Bucahanan and Mr. Thisted had been successfully rescued. Later, at the U.S. Capitol, following the State of the Union Address, he had a telephone conversation with Ms. Buchanan's father John Buchanan to inform him of her rescue.

The White House announced that the President will travel to Denver, CO, and Detroit, MI, on January 26.

The White House announced that the President will travel to Ann Arbor, MI, on January 27.

January 25

In the morning, the President traveled to Cedar Rapids, IA. Upon arrival, he traveled to Conveyor Engineering & Manufacturing, where he toured the new design and production facility and met with employees.

In the afternoon, the President traveled to Chandler, AZ.

In the evening, at Intel Corporation Ocotillo Campus, the President taped an interview with Maria Elena Salinas of Univision's "Noticiero" program for later broadcast. Later, he traveled to Las Vegas, NV. Upon arrival, he traveled to the Element Las Vegas Summerlin hotel, where he remained overnight.

January 26

In the morning, at the Element Las Vegas Summerlin hotel, the President taped a telephone interview with Frankie Darcell of WMXD in Detroit, MI, for later broadcast. Then, he traveled to UPS Las Vegas South, where he taped separate interviews with Diane Sawyer of ABC's "World News With Diane Sawyer" program and Rosana Romero of KBLR in Las Vegas, NV, for later broadcast.

In the afternoon, the President traveled to Buckley Air Force Base, CO. Later, he taped separate telephone interviews with Maria Rozman of KDEN in Denver, CO, and Paul W. Smith of WJR in Detroit, MI, for later broadcast. Then, he traveled to Detroit, MI.

In the evening, upon arrival in Detroit, he traveled to the Sheraton Detroit Metro Airport hotel, where he remained overnight.

January 27

In the morning, the President traveled to Ann Arbor, MI. Later, he traveled to Cambridge, MD.

In the afternoon, the President returned to Washington, DC. Later, in the Oval Office, he and Vice President Joe Biden met with Secretary of State Hillary Rodham Clinton.

In the evening, in the Oval Office, the President met with former President George H.W.

Bush and former Gov. John E. "Jeb" Bush of Florida.

The President announced his intention to nominate Michael P. Botticelli to be Deputy Director of the Office of National Drug Control Policy.

The President announced his intention to nominate Christy L. Romero to be Special Inspector General for the Troubled Asset Relief Program.

The President announced his intention to appoint Alex Mehran as a member of the Board of Directors of the Presidio Trust.

January 28

In the evening, at the Capital Hilton hotel, the President and Mrs. Obama attended the Alfalfa Club dinner.

January 30

In the morning, in the Oval Office, the President had an intelligence briefing, followed by a meeting with his senior advisers.

In the afternoon, in the East Room, the President and Mrs. Obama hosted a reception for the diplomatic corps.

In the evening, in the Roosevelt Room, the President participated in an interview with YouTube and Google+ participants.

The White House announced that the President will travel to Falls Church, VA, on February 1.

January 31

In the morning, in the Oval Office, the President had an intelligence briefing.

In the afternoon, in the Oval Office, the President met with Secretary of Defense Leon E. Panetta.

The White House announced that the President will host the White House Science Fair on February 7.

February 1

In the morning, in the Oval Office, the President had an intelligence briefing. Then, he traveled to Falls Church, VA. Later, he returned to Washington, DC.

In the afternoon, in the Oval Office, the President met with his senior advisers.

The President declared a major disaster in Utah and ordered Federal aid to supplement State and local recovery efforts in the area struck by a severe storm on November 30 and December 1, 2011.

The President declared a major disaster in Alabama and ordered Federal aid to supplement State and local recovery efforts in the area struck by severe storms, tornadoes, straight-line winds and flooding on January 22 and 23.

February 2

In the afternoon, in the Oval Office, the President met with his senior advisers. Then, in the Private Dining Room, he and Vice President Joe Biden had lunch. Later, in the Oval Office, he had separate meetings with Secretary of State Hillary Rodham Clinton and Secretary of the Treasury Timothy F. Geithner.

The President announced that he has nominated Stephanie Marie Rose to be a judge on the U.S. District Court for the Southern District of Iowa.

The President announced that he has nominated Michael P. Shea to be a judge on the U.S. District Court for the District of Connecticut.

The President announced that he has nominated Jamie A. Hainsworth to be U.S. marshal for the District of Rhode Island.

The President announced that he has nominated Louise W. Kelton to be U.S. marshal for the Middle District of Tennessee.

The President declared a major disaster in Alaska and ordered Federal aid to supplement State and local recovery efforts in the area affected by a severe storm from November 15 through 17, 2011.

February 3

In the morning, in the Oval Office, the President and Vice President Joe Biden had an intelligence briefing, followed by a meeting with his senior advisers. Later, he traveled to Arlington, VA.

In the afternoon, the President returned to Washington, DC. Later, at the Jefferson hotel, he attended an Obama Victory Fund 2012 fundraiser.

The White House announced that the President will welcome Prime Minister David Cameron of the United Kingdom to the White House on March 13 and 14.

The White House released further details on the White House Science Fair to be held on February 7.

The President announced his intention to nominate Jeremiah O. Norton to be a member of the Board of Directors of the Federal Deposit Insurance Corporation.

The President announced his intention to nominate Bill Bair to be Assistant Attorney General for the Antitrust Division at the Department of Justice.

The President announced his intention to nominate Marcilynn A. Burke to be Assistant Secretary for Land and Mineral Management at the Department of the Interior.

The President announced his intention to nominate Joseph G. Jordan to be Administrator for Federal Procurement Policy at the Office of Management and Budget.

The President announced his intention to nominate John R. Norris to be a Commissioner of the Federal Emergency Regulatory Commission.

The President announced his intention to nominate Heidi Shyu to be Assistant Secretary of the Army for Acquisition, Logistics, and Technology.

The President announced his intention to appoint Milton Irvin and George B. Walker, Jr., as members of the President's Board of Advisers on Historically Black Colleges and Universities.

February 5

In the afternoon, in the Blue Room, the President taped an interview with Matt Lauer of NBC's "Today" program for later broadcast.

February 6

In the afternoon, in the Oval Office, the President had an intelligence briefing, followed by a meeting with his senior advisers.

The White House released further details on the White House Science Fair to be held on February 7.

The White House announced that the President and Mrs. Obama will host a dinner honoring U.S. servicemembers who served in Iraq on February 29.

February 7

In the morning, in the Oval Office, the President and Vice President Joe Biden had an intelligence briefing, followed by a meeting with senior advisers. Later, in the State Dining Room, he viewed projects exhibited at the White House Science Fair.

In the afternoon, in the Private Dining Room, the President and Vice President Biden had lunch. Later, in the Oval Office, they met with Secretary of Defense Leon E. Panetta.

During the day, the President had a telephone conversation with New York Giants Head Coach Tom Coughlin to congratulate him on his team's victory in Super Bowl XLVI.

The White House announced that the President will welcome Prime Minister Helle Thorning-Schmidt of Denmark to the White House on February 24.

The White House announced that the President will welcome President Dilma Rousseff of Brazil to the White House on April 9.

February 8

In the morning, in the Oval Office, the President had an intelligence briefing, followed by a meeting with his senior advisers.

In the afternoon, the President traveled to Nationals Park, where he attended a Democratic Senate Caucus retreat. Later, in the Oval Office, he and Vice President Biden met with Secretary of State Hillary Rodham Clinton. Then, in the Situation Room, he met with his national security team to discuss the situations in Afghanistan and Pakistan.

February 9

In the morning, in the Oval Office, the President had an intelligence briefing.

The White House announced that the President will travel to Annandale, VA, on February 13.

The White House announced that the President will award the 2011 National Medal of

Arts and National Humanities Medal on February 13.

February 10

In the morning, in the Oval Office, the President and Vice President Joe Biden had an intelligence briefing. Then, in the South Court Auditorium of the Dwight D. Eisenhower Executive Office Building, he dropped by a briefing with leaders of The Arc organization for people with intellectual and developmental disabilities.

In the afternoon, at the Jefferson hotel, the President attended an Obama Victory Fund 2012 fundraiser.

The White House released further details on the President's awarding of the 2011 National Medal of Arts and National Humanities Medal on February 13.

The President announced his intention to nominate William P. Doyle to be a Commissioner of the Federal Maritime Commission.

The President announced his intention to nominate Richard A. Lidinsky, Jr., to be Chairman of the Federal Maritime Commission.

The President announced his intention to nominate James M. Demers and Naomi A. Walker to be members of the Board of Directors of the Overseas Private Investment Corporation.

The President announced his intention to nominate Katharina G. McFarland to be Assistant Secretary for Acquisition at the Department of Defense.

The President announced his intention to nominate Kenneth Merten to be Ambassador to Croatia.

The President announced his intention to appoint David Kotelchuck and Loretta R. Valerio as members of the Advisory Board on Radiation and Worker Health of the Centers for Disease Control and Prevention.

The President announced his intention to appoint Karen L. Jefferson as a member of the National Historical Publications and Records Commission for the National Archives and Records Administration.

The President announced his intention to appoint Martin C. Faga and William H. Leary as members of the Public Interest Declassification Board for the National Archives and Records Administration.

February 12

The White House announced that the President will travel to Milwaukee, WI, on February 15.

February 13

In the morning, in the Oval Office, the President had an intelligence briefing. Then, he traveled to Annandale, VA. Later, he returned to Washington, DC, arriving in the afternoon.

During the day, in the Oval Office, the President had a telephone conversation with Prime Minister David Cameron of the United Kingdom to discuss the situations in Syria, Somalia, and Afghanistan, the economic situation in Europe, preparations for the London Conference on Somalia on February 23, and the Prime Minister's official visit to Washington, DC, on March 13 and 14.

The White House announced that the President will travel to Everett, WA, on February 17.

February 14

In the morning, in the Oval Office, the President had an intelligence briefing, followed by a meeting with his senior advisers.

In the afternoon, in the Diplomatic Room, the President taped separate television interviews with Paula Francis of KLAS in Las Vegas, NV, Amanda Davis of WAGA in Atlanta, GA, Keith Cate of WFLA in Tampa, FL, and Paul Cameron of WBTV in Charlotte, NC, for later broadcast. Later, in the Oval Office, he met with Secretary of Defense Leon E. Panetta.

In the evening, the President and Mrs. Obama traveled to Alexandria, VA, where, at Vermilion Restaurant, they had dinner. Later, they returned to Washington, DC.

February 15

In the morning, in the Oval Office, the President and Vice President Joe Biden had an intelligence briefing. Later, he traveled to Milwaukee, WI.

In the afternoon, the President toured the Master Lock Co. manufacturing plant and met with employees. Later, he traveled to Los Angeles, CA.

During the day, the President had separate telephone conversations with Sen. Benjamin L. Cardin and Rep. Christopher Van Hollen to discuss the ongoing negotiations over legislation to extend the payroll tax cut.

The White House announced that the President will deliver remarks at the groundbreaking ceremony for the Smithsonian National Museum of African American History and Culture in Washington, DC, on February 22.

February 16

In the morning, the President traveled to Coronoa del Mar, CA. Later, he traveled to San Francisco, CA, arriving in the afternoon.

In the afternoon, at the Great Eastern restaurant, the President visited with patrons and ordered lunch.

The President announced the designation of the following individuals as members of a Presidential delegation to attend a ceremony elevating Archbishop Timothy M. Dolan and Archbishop Edwin F. O'Brien to the College of Cardinals in at the Holy See (Vatican City) on February 18: Miguel H. Diaz (head of delegation); and Kenneth F. Hackett.

The President announced his intention to nominate Erica L. Groshen to be Commissioner of Labor Statistics at the Department of Labor.

The President announced his intention to nominate Jeffrey D. Levine to be Ambassador to Estonia.

The President announced his intention to nominate C. Peter Mahurin to be a member of the Board of Directors of the Tennessee Valley Authority.

The President announced his intention to nominate Maj. Gen. John Peabody, USA, to be President of the Mississippi River Commission.

The President announced that he has nominated Jill A. Pryor to be a judge on the U.S. Court of Appeals for the Eleventh Circuit.

The President announced that he has nominated Elissa F. Cadish to be a judge on the U.S. District Court for the District of Nevada.

The President announced that he has nominated Paul W. Grimm to be a judge on the U.S. District Court for the District of Maryland.

The President announced that he has nominated Mark E. Walker to be a judge on the U.S. District Court for the Northern District of Florida.

February 17

In the morning, the President traveled to Everett, WA, where he toured the Boeing Co. production facility and met with employees.

In the afternoon, the President traveled to Medina, WA. Then, he traveled to Bellevue, WA. Later, he returned to Washington, DC, arriving in the evening.

The President announced his intention to nominate Makila James to be Ambassador to Swaziland.

The President announced his intention to nominate Richard B. Norland to be Ambassador to Georgia.

The President announced his intention to nominate Carlos Pascual to be Assistant Secretary for Energy Resources at the Department of State.

The President announced his intention to nominate Mark A. Pekala to be Ambassador to Latvia.

The President announced his intention to appoint David C. Lizarraga and Ronald L. Phillips as members of the Community Development Advisory Board.

The President announced his intention to appoint Charles Shively as U.S. Alternate Commissioner of the Kansas-Oklahoma Arkansas River Commission.

The President announced his intention to appoint Earnie Gilder as U.S. Commissioner of the Kansas-Oklahoma Arkansas River Commission.

The President announced his intention to appoint Gary W. Loveman and Denise Morrison as members of the President's Export Council.

The President announced his intention to appoint Amy Gutmann as Chair of the Presidential Commission for the Study of Bioethical Issues.

The President announced his intention to appoint James W. Wagner as Vice Chair of the Presidential Commission for the Study of Bioethical Issues.

The President announced his intention to appoint David M. Strauss as Chairman of the Advisory Committee to the Pension Benefit Guaranty Corporation.

February 20

In the morning, the President had a telephone conversation with President Hamid Karzai of Afghanistan to discuss regional support for Afghan-led reconciliation efforts, the recent Afghanistan-Pakistan-Iran trilateral meetings in Islamabad, Pakistan, and Afghanistan-U.S. relations.

The White House announced that the President will travel to Miami, FL, on February 23.

February 21

In the morning, in the Oval Office, the President and Vice President Joe Biden had an intelligence briefing. Then, he had a telephone conversation with Chancellor Angela Merkel of Germany to discuss economic stabilization efforts in Europe, global financial markets, and the upcoming Group of Eight (G–8) summit. Later, also in the Oval Office, he met with his senior advisers.

In the afternoon, in the Private Dining Room, the President and Vice President Biden had lunch. Later, in the Oval Office, they met with Secretary of Defense Leon E. Panetta.

February 22

In the afternoon, in the East Room, the President and Mrs. Obama hosted a reception in honor of the groundbreaking of the Smithsonian Institution's National Museum of African American History and Culture.

February 23

In the morning, the President traveled to Coral Gables, FL, arriving in the afternoon.

In the afternoon, the President traveled to Pinecrest, FL.

In the evening, the President traveled to Orlando, FL. Later, he returned to Washington, DC.

February 24

In the morning, in the Oval Office, the President had an intelligence briefing, followed by a meeting with his senior advisers. Later, in the Dwight D. Eisenhower Executive Office Building, he participated in a meeting of the Democratic Governors Association.

The White House announced that the President has named David P. Agnew to be Director of Intergovernmental Affairs.

February 25

In the afternoon, the President had a telephone conversation with Gen. John R. Allen, USMC, commander, NATO International Security Assistance Force, Afghanistan, to discuss the situation in Afghanistan and the deaths of two U.S. servicemembers.

February 27

In the morning, in the Oval Office, the President and Vice President Joe Biden had an intelligence briefing. Then, also in the Oval Office, he met with his senior advisers.

In the afternoon, in the Oval Office, the President and Vice President Biden met with Secretary of the Treasury Timothy F. Geithner. Later, at the Jefferson hotel, he attended an Obama Victory Fund 2012 fundraiser.

The White House announced that the President will travel to Nashua, NH, on March 1.

The White House announced that the President will welcome Prime Minister David Cameron of the United Kingdom to the White House on March 14.

February 28

In the morning, in the Oval Office, the President and Vice President Joe Biden had an intelligence briefing.

In the afternoon, in the Private Dining Room, the President and Vice President Biden had lunch. Later, in the Oval Office, they met with Secretary of Defense Leon E. Panetta.

February 29

In the morning, in the Oval Office, the President and Vice President Joe Biden had an intelligence briefing.

In the afternoon, in the Private Dining Room, the President and Vice President Biden had lunch with congressional leaders to discuss the national economy and job creation.

During the day, the President taped an interview with ESPN's Bill Simmons for later broadcast.

The President announced that he has nominated Brian J. Davis to be a judge on the U.S. District Court for the Middle District of Florida.

The President announced that he has nominated John E. Dowdell to be a judge on the U.S. District Court for the Northern District of Oklahoma.

March 1

In the morning, in the Oval Office, the President had an intelligence briefing. Later, he traveled to Nashua, NH, arriving in the afternoon

In the afternoon, the President toured Nashua Community College. Later, he traveled to New York City.

In the evening, the President returned to Washington, DC.

The White House announced that the President will welcome President John Evans Atta Mills of Ghana to the White House on March 8.

March 2

In the morning, in the Oval Office, the President and Vice President Joe Biden had an intelligence briefing. Later, also in the Oval Office, they met with Secretary of State Hillary Rodham Clinton.

In the afternoon, the President had a telephone conversation with Georgetown University law student Sandra K. Fluke to offer his support and express his disappointment regarding comments made about her in the media following her February 29 testimony before the House Democratic Steering and Policy Committee on student health insurance coverage of contraceptive services.

Later in the afternoon, the Presdient traveled to Bethesda, MD, where, at Walter Reed

National Military Medical Center, he met with wounded U.S. military personnel and their families and presented Purple Hearts to eight servicemembers. Then, he returned to Washington, DC.

The President announced his intention to nominate Edward M. Alford to be Ambassador to Gambia.

The President announced that he as nominate Peter W. Bodde to be Ambassador to Nepal.

The President announced his intention to nominate Piper A.W. Campbell to be Ambassador to Mongolia.

The President announced his intention to appoint Rye Barcott and Christie L. Gilson as members of the J. William Fulbright Foreign Scholarship Board.

The President declared a major disaster in Oregon and ordered Federal aid to supplement State and local recovery efforts in the area affected by a severe winter storm, flooding, landslides, and mudslides from January 17 through 21.

March 3

During the day, the President was briefed by Federal Emergency Management Agency Administrator W. Craig Fugate on severe weather and tornadoes affecting the South and Midwest. Then, he had separate telephone conversations with Gov. Mitchell E. Daniels, Jr., of Indiana, Gov. Steven L. Beshear of Kentucky, and Gov. John R. Kasich of Ohio to express his condolences for the loss of life due to severe weather and tornadoes and offer Federal assistance for recovery efforts.

March 5

In the morning, in the Oval Office, the President met with his senior advisers.

In the afternoon, in the State Dining Room, the President had lunch with Prime Minister Benjamin Netanyahu of Israel and U.S. and Israeli delegations. Later, in the Oval Office, he had separate meetings with Secretary of the Treasury Timothy F. Geithner and Secretary of Defense Leon E. Panetta.

The White House announced that the President will travel to Mount Holly, NC, on March 7.

The White House announced that the President will travel to Petersburg, VA, on March 9.

The White House announced that the President will travel to New York City on May 14.

The White House announced that the President will travel to Joplin, MO, on May 21.

The White House announced that the President will travel to Colorado Springs, CO, on May 23.

The President declared a major disaster in Washington and ordered Federal aid to supplement State and local recovery efforts in the area struck by a severe winter storm, flooding, landslides, and mudslides from January 14 through 23.

March 6

In the morning, in the Oval Office, the President had an intelligence briefing.

In the afternoon, in the East Room, the President met with wounded warriors, after which he signed the prosthetic arm of Sgt. Carlos Evans, USMC. Later, at the Jefferson hotel, he attended an Obama Victory Fund 2012 fundraiser.

The White House announced that the President will travel to Houston, TX, on March 9.

The President declared a major disaster in Kentucky and ordered Federal aid to supplement Commonwealth and local recovery efforts in the area struck by severe storms, tornadoes, straight-line winds, and flooding from February 29 through March 3.

March 7

In the morning, in the Roosevelt Room, the President met with Prime Minister Abd al-Rahim al-Keeb of Libya to discuss the situation in Libya and Libya-U.S. relations. Later, he traveled to Mount Holly, NC.

In the afternoon, the President toured the Daimler Trucks North America manufacturing plant and met with employees. Later, he returned to Washington, DC. Then, in the East Room, he met with students from the U.S. Senate Youth Program.

March 8

In the morning, in the Situation Room, the President had a videoconference with President Hamid Karzai of Afghanistan to discuss the situation in Afghanistan, the transition of security operations to Afghan forces, and Afghanistan-U.S. relations. Later, in the Oval Office, he had an intelligence briefing.

In the afternoon, in the Oval Office, the President met with White House Chief of Staff Jacob J. "Jack" Lew, National Economic Council Director Eugene B. Sperling, and Council of Economic Advisers Chairman Alan B. Krueger. Later, at the Boundary Road restaurant, he and Mrs. Obama had dinner with Regina Newkirk of Nashville, TN, Cathleen Loringer of Wauwatosa, WI, and Judy Glassman of Cambridge, MA, winners of a contest held by his reelection campaign.

March 9

In the morning, in the Oval Office, the President had an intelligence briefing. Then, he traveled to Petersburg, VA. While en route aboard Air Force One, he had a telephone conversation with Prime Minister Vladimir Vladimirovich Putin of Russia to congratulate him on his victory in the recent Presidential election and discuss Russia-U.S. relations.

In the afternoon, upon arrival in Petersburg, the President toured the Rolls-Royce Crosspointe manufacturing plant and met with employees. Later, he traveled to Houston, TX.

In the evening, the President returned to Washington, DC.

The White House announced that the President and Prime Minister David Cameron of the United Kingdom will travel to Dayton, OH, on March 13.

The President announced his intention to nominate Arthur Bienenstock to be a member of the National Science Board for the National Science Foundation.

The President announced his intention to nominate Paula Gangopadhyay, Luis Herrera, and Suzanne E. Thorin to be members of the National Museum and Library Services Board.

The President announced his intention to nominate Dorothea-Maria "Doria" Rosen to be Ambassador to Micronesia.

The President announced his intention to nominate Katherine C. Tobin to be a Governor of the Board of Governors of the U.S. Postal Service.

The President announced his intention to appoint Sonny Ramaswamy as Director of the National Institute of Food and Agriculture at the Department of Agriculture.

The President announced that he has appointed Todd Park as U.S. Chief Technology Officer.

The President declared a major disaster in Indiana and ordered Federal aid to supplement State and local recovery efforts in the area struck by severe storms, straight-line winds, and tornadoes from February 29 through March 3.

March 11

In the morning, the President was informed by members of his national security team of the shootings in Panjwai, Afghanistan.

In the afternoon, the President was briefed by National Security Adviser Thomas E. Donilon, Deputy National Security Adviser Denis R. McDonough, and Special Assistant to the President for Afghanistan and Pakistan Douglas E. Lute on the shootings in Panjwai, Afghanistan. Then, he had a telephone conversation with President Hamid Karzai of Afghanistan and expressed his shock and sadness over the reported killing and wounding of Afghan civilians by a U.S. servicemember and extended his condolences to the Afghan people.

March 12

In the morning, in the Oval Office, the President had an intelligence briefing. Later, in the Cabinet Room, he taped separate interviews with Marc Brown of KABC in Los Angeles, CA, Karen Leigh of KCNC in Denver, CO, Terri Gruca of KVUE in Austin, TX, John Bachman of WHO in Des Moines, IA, Greg Warmoth of WFTV in Orlando, FL, Rob Braun of WKRC in Cincinnati, OH, Adriana Arevalo of KINC in Las Vegas, NV, and Jon Delano of KDKA in Pittsburgh, PA, for later broadcast.

In the afternoon, in the Roosevelt Room, the President met with officers of the National League of Cities.

March 13

In the morning, in the Oval Office, the President had an intelligence briefing, followed by a meeting with his senior advisers. Later, in the Dwight D. Eisenhower Executive Office Building, he met with 2012 Intel Science Talent Search student finalists.

In the afternoon, the President and Prime Minister David Cameron of the United Kingdom, traveled to Dayton, OH, where, at the University of Dayton Arena, they attended an NCAA men's basketball championship game. During halftime, they taped an interview with Clark Kellogg of CBS Sports for later broadcast.

In the evening, the President and Prime Minister Cameron returned to Washington, DC.

The White House announced that the President will travel to Largo, MD, on March 15.

March 14

In the morning, in the Oval Office, the President had a bilateral meeting with Prime Minister David Cameron of the United Kingdom. Then, in the Cabinet Room, he and Vice President Joe Biden had an expanded meeting with Prime Minister Cameron.

In the afternoon, the President had a telephone conversation with President Lee Myung-bak of South Korea to welcome the entry into force of the U.S.-Korea Free Trade Agreement on March 15 and thank President Lee for South Korea's cooperation in implementing the agreement.

In the evening, on the North Portico, the President and Mrs. Obama greeted Prime Minister Cameron and his wife Samantha upon their arrival for a state dinner and reception. Then, on the Grand Staircase, they participated in a photographic opportunity with Prime Minister Cameron and Mrs. Cameron.

The President announced that he has appointed Grant Colfax as Director of the Office of National AIDS Policy.

March 15

In the morning, the President traveled to Largo, MD.

In the afternoon, the President traveled to Clinton, MD, where, at the Texas Ribs and BBQ restaurant, he had lunch with Sen. Benjamin L. Cardin and visited with patrons. Then, he returned to Washington, DC. Later, in the Oval Office, he met with Secretary of the Treasury Timothy F. Geithner. Then, also in the Oval Office, he met with his senior advisers.

March 16

In the morning, the President had a telephone conversation with President Hamid Karzai of Afghanistan to congratulate him and his wife Zeenat on the birth of their daughter. They also discussed the transfer of full security responsibility to Afghan forces by the end of 2014, ongoing negotiations concerning the Afghanistan-U.S. memorandum of understanding, and the upcoming NATO summit in Chicago, IL. Later, he traveled to Chicago, IL.

In the afternoon, at the Palmer House Hilton hotel, the President attended a campaign event. Later, he traveled to Atlanta, GA.

In the evening, the President returned to Washington, DC, arriving the following morning.

The White House announced that the President will welcome Prime Minister Enda Kenny of Ireland to the White House on March 20.

The White House announced that the President will welcome Prime Minister Stephen J. Harper of Canada and President Felipe de Jesus Calderon Hinojosa to the White House on March 20.

The White House announced that the President will travel to Boulder City, NV, Carlsbad, NM, Cushing, OK, and Columbus OH, on March 21 and 22.

The White House announced that the President has named Brian P. McKeon to be Deputy Assistant to the President, Executive Secretary and Chief of Staff of the National Security Staff.

The President announced his intention to nominate Mark L. Asquino to be Ambassador to Guinea.

The President announced his intention to nominate Derek H. Chollet to be Assistant Secretary of Defense for International Security Affairs.

The President announced his intention to nominate Kathleen H. Hicks to be Principal Deputy Under Secretary for Policy at the Department of Defense.

The President announced his intention to nominate Susanna Loeb to be a member of the Board of Directors of the National Board of Education Sciences.

The President announced his intention to nominate Edward W. Brehm to be a member of the Board of Directors of the African Development Foundation.

The President declared a major disaster in Tennessee and ordered Federal aid to supplement State and local recovery efforts in the area struck by a severe winter storm and flooding from February 29 through March 2.

The President declared a major disaster in West Virginia and ordered Federal aid to supplement Sate and local recovery efforts in the area struck by sever winter storms, flooding, mudslides, and landslides from February 29 through March 5.

March 17

In the afternoon, at the Dubliner restaurant and Irish pub, the President celebrated St. Patrick's Day with his cousin Henry Healy and Ollie Hayes, owner of a pub in Moneygall, Ireland.

March 19

In the morning, in the Oval Office, the President had an intelligence briefing, followed by a meeting with his senior advisers. Later, also in the Oval Office, he had a telephone conversation with President Mahmoud Abbas of the Palestinian Authority to discuss the Middle East peace process.

In the afternoon, in the Oval Office, the President met with Secretary of State Hillary Rodham Clinton. Later, at the W Washington DC hotel, he attended a campaign event.

During the day, the President had a telephone conversation with President Juan Manuel Santos Calderon of Colombia to discuss the upcoming Summit of the Americas, implementation of the U.S.-Colombia Free Trade Agreement, and the Colombian Action Plan Related to Labor Rights.

The White House announced that the President will travel to Boulder City, NV, and Oklahoma City, OK, on March 21.

The White House announced that the President will travel to Cushing, OK, and Columbus, OH, on March 22.

March 20

In the morning, in the Oval Office, the President had an intelligence briefing. Then, also in the Oval Office, he and Vice President Joe Biden met with Prime Minister Enda Kenny of Ireland.

In the afternoon, in the Oval Office, the President and Vice President Biden met with Secretary of Defense Leon E. Panetta.

The White House announced that the President will travel to Maljamar, NM, on March 21.

March 21

In the morning, the President traveled to Boulder City, NV. While en route aboard Air Force One, he had a telephone conversation with President Nicolas Sarkozy of France to express his condolences for the loss of life and injuries in the terrorist attack in Toulouse. Upon arrival in Boulder City, he toured the Copper Mountain Solar 1 facility with John A. Sowers, vice president of operations, and Kevin Gillespie, director of operations, Sempra U.S. Gas and Power LLC.

In the afternoon, the President traveled to Maljamar, NM.

In the evening, the President traveled to Oklahoma City, OK. Upon arrival, he traveled to the Sheraton Oklahoma City hotel, where he remained overnight.

The President announced that he has nominated John S. Leonardo to be U.S. attorney for the District of Arizona.

The President announced that he has nominated Rainey R. Brandt to be a judge on the Superior Court of the District of Columbia.

The President announced that he has appointed Michael B. Filler, David J. Holway, and H.T. Nguyen as members of the National Council on Federal Labor-Management Relations.

March 22

In the morning, the President traveled to Stillwater, OK.

In the afternoon, the President traveled to Columbus, OH, where, at Ohio State University, he toured the Center for Automotive Research and spoke with engineering students. Later, he returned to Washington, DC, arriving in the evening.

In the evening, in the East Room, the President hosted a reception for Greek Independence Day.

The President declared a major disaster in West Virginia and ordered Federal aid to supplement State and local recovery efforts in the area struck by severe storms, flooding, mudslides, and landslides beginning on March 15 and continuing.

March 23

In the morning, in the Oval Office, the President had an intelligence briefing, followed by a meeting with his senior advisers.

During the day, in the Situation Room, the President had a briefing on his upcoming visit to South Korea.

The White House announced that the President will meet with Prime Minister Syed Yousuf Raza Gilani of Pakistan in Seoul, South Korea, on March 27.

March 24

In the morning, the President traveled to Seoul, South Korea, arriving the following morning.

March 25

In the morning, upon arrival in Seoul, South Korea, the President traveled the Grand Hyatt Seoul hotel, where he met with his senior advisers. Later, he traveled to Camp Bonifas. While en route, he met with U.S. Ambassador to South Korea Sung Kim.

In the afternoon, the President traveled to Observation Post Ouellette, where he received a briefing from Lt. Col. Edward J. Taylor, USA, battalion commander, U.N. Command Security Battalion—Joint Security Area, and Lt. Col. Yoon Bong-hee, South Korean Army, and viewed the Korean demilitarized zone. Later, he returned to the Grand Hyatt Seoul.

In the evening, at the Spring House in the Blue House complex, the President had dinner with President Lee Myung-bak of South Korea. Later, he returned to the Grand Hyatt Seoul, where he remained overnight.

March 26

In the evening, at the Coex Center in Seoul, the President attended a welcoming ceremony. Later, at the Spring House in the Blue House complex, he participated in a working dinner with Nuclear Security Summit leaders.

The President announced the designation of the following individuals as members of a Presidential delegation to attend the state funeral of King George Tupou V in Nuku'alofa, Tonga, on March 27: Frankie A. Reed (head of delegation); Anthony M. Babauta; and Duane D. Thiessen.

The President announced his intention to nominate Brett H. McGurk to be U.S. Ambassador to Iraq.

The President announced his intention to nominate Michele J. Sison to be U.S. Ambassador to Sri Lanka and the Maldives.

March 27

In the morning, at the Coex Center, the President attended a plenary session of the Nuclear Security Summit. Later, he participated in the official Nuclear Security Summit heads of delegation photograph.

In the afternoon, at the Coex Center, the President attended a Nuclear Security Summit working lunch. Then, he attended a summit plenary session.

During the day, the President met with President Viktor Yanukovych of Ukraine to discuss Ukraine's complete removal of highly enriched uranium from its territory and other nuclear material security efforts.

In the evening, the President returned to Washington, DC.

The President announced his intention to nominate James C. Miller III to be a Governor of the Board of Governors of the U.S. Postal Service.

The President announced his intention to nominate Michael P. Huerta to be Administrator of the Federal Aviation Administration at the Department of Transportation.

The President announced his intention to nominate the following individuals to be members of the Board of Directors of the Legal Services Corporation:

Robert J. Grey, Jr.;
John G. Levi;
Laurie I. Mikva;
Martha L. Minow; and
Gloria Valencia-Weber.

March 29

In the morning, in the Oval Office, the President had an intelligence briefing.

In the afternoon, on the White House Basketball Court, the President taped an interview with Clark Kellogg of CBS Sports for later broadcast.

The President announced his intention to nominate Yvonne B. Burke to be Director of the Amtrak Board of Directors.

The President announced his intention to nominate Patricia K. Falcone to be Associate Director for National Security and International Affairs at the Office of Science and Technology Policy.

The President announced his intention to nominate Douglas M. Griffiths to be U.S. Ambassador to Mozambique.

The President announced his intention to nominate Maria R. Jackson to be a member of the National Council on the Arts.

The President announced his intention to appoint Marc H. Morial as a member of the President's Advisory Council on Financial Capability.

The President announced his intention to appoint Karyn L. Stockdale as a member of the Board of Directors of the Valles Caldera Trust.

The President announced that he has nominated Patrick A. Miles, Jr., to be U.S. attorney for the Western District of Michigan.

The President announced that he has nominated Danny C. Williams, Sr., to be U.S. attorney for the Northern District of Oklahoma.

The President announced that he has nominated Patrick J. Wilkerson to be a U.S. marshal for the Eastern District of Oklahoma.

March 30

In the morning, the President traveled to Burlington, VT. While en route aboard Air Force One, he met with Sen. Patrick J. Leahy.

In the afternoon, the President traveled to Portland, ME.

In the evening, the President returned to Washington, DC.

The President announced the designation of the following individuals as members of a Presidential delegation to attend the Inauguration of Macky Sall as President of Senegal in Dakar, Senegal, on April 2:

Daniel W. Yohannes (head of delegation);
Lewis Lukens;
Johnnie Carson; and
Carter F. Ham.

April 2

In the morning, the President had a telephone conversation with President Salva Kiir Mayardit of South Sudan to discuss relations between South Sudan and Sudan, including recent nationality and citizenship agreements and continued violence along their shared border. Then, in the Oval Office, he and Vice President Joe Biden had an intelligence briefing. Later, in the State Dining Room, he hosted a North American Leaders' Summit meeting with Prime Minister Stephen J. Harper of Canada and President Felipe de Jesus Calderon Hinojosa of Mexico.

In the afternoon, in the Green Room, the President, Prime Minister Harper, and President Calderon had a working lunch. Later, in the Oval Office, he and Vice President Biden met with Secretary of State Hillary Rodham Clinton. Then, also in the Oval Office, he had a meeting with his senior advisers.

April 3

In the morning, in the Oval Office, the President had an intelligence briefing. Later, he had a telephone conversation with Prime Minister Nuri al-Maliki of Iraq to congratulate the

Iraqi people on the success of the Summit held in Baghdad, the role of Iraq and the U.S. in regional security efforts, and his support for continued democracy efforts in Iraq.

In the afternoon, in the Oval Office, the President and Vice President Joe Biden met with Secretary of Defense Leon E. Panetta.

During the day, the President had a telephone conversation with Head Coach John Capilari of the University of Kentucky's men's basketball team to congratulate him on his team's victory in the 2012 NCAA championship game.

April 4

In the morning, in the Oval Office, the President and Vice President Joe Biden had an intelligence briefing. Then, also in the Oval Office, he met with his senior advisers.

In the afternoon, in the Vice President's Office, the President dropped by a meeting between Vice President Biden and President Masoud Barzani of the Kurdistan Regional Government in Iraq. Later, in the Dwight D. Eisenhower Executive Office Building, he dropped by a meeting of personal finance and financial news journalists and editors.

During the day, the President had a telephone conversation with Head Coach Kim Mulkey of Baylor University's women's basketball team to congratulate her on her team's historic 40–0 season and their victory in the 2012 NCAA championship game.

The White House announced that the President will attend the White House Forum on Women and the Economy on April 6.

April 5

In the afternoon, in the Oval Office, the President had an intelligence briefing. Then, in the Private Dining Room, he and Vice President Joe Biden had lunch.

In the evening, in the Family Theater, the President hosted a screening of the film "To Kill a Mockingbird."

April 6

In the evening, in the Old Family Dining Room, the President and Mrs. Obama hosted a seder to mark the beginning of Passover.

The White House announced that the President will travel to Boca Raton, FL, on April 10.

April 9

In the morning, in the Oval Office, the President had an intelligence briefing.

In the afternoon, in the Oval Office, the President met with Secretary of State Hillary Rodham Clinton. Later, also in the Oval Office, he met with Secretary of the Treasury Timothy F. Geithner.

April 10

In the morning, the President traveled to Palm Beach Gardens, FL.

In the afternoon, the President traveled to Boca Raton, FL.

In the evening, the President traveled to Hollywood, FL. Then, he traveled to Golden Beach, FL. Later, he returned to Washington, DC.

April 11

In the morning, in the Oval Office, the President had an intelligence briefing.

In the afternoon, in the Oval Office, the President met with Secretary of Defense Leon E. Panetta. Later, at the W Washington DC hotel, he attended a campaign event.

During the day, in the Oval Office, the President met with Prince Salman bin Abd al-Aziz Al Saud, Minister of Defense of Saudi ia. He also had a telephone conversation with Chancellor Angela Merkel of Germany to discuss the situations in Iran and Syria, the upcoming Group of Eight (G–8) summit at Camp David, MD, and Germany-U.S. relations.

The White House announced that the President will travel to Tampa, FL, on April 13.

The White House announced that the President will welcome 2011 NASCAR Sprint Cup Series Champion Tony Stewart and other NASCAR drivers to the White House on April 17.

The President announced his intention to nominate Jay N. Anania to be Ambassador to Suriname.

The President announced his intention to nominate Gene A. Cretz to be Ambassador to Ghana.

The President announced his intention to nominate Susan Marsh Elliott to be Ambassador to Tajikistan.

The President announced his intention to nominate David J. Lane to be U.S. Representative to the United Nations Agencies for Food and Agriculture, with the rank of Ambassador during his tenure of service.

The President announced his intention to nominate Charles P. Rose to be a member of the Board of Trustees of the Morris K. and Stewart L. Udall Foundation.

The President announced his intention to appoint Carol W. Greider to be a member on the President's Committee on the National Medal of Science.

April 12

In the afternoon, in the Diplomatic Room, the President taped separate interviews with Colleen Marshall of WCMH in Columbus, OH, Bruce Aune of KCRG in Cedar Rapids, IA, Larry Connors of KMOV in St. Louis, MO, and Pat Hambright of KOLO in Reno, NV, for later broadcast. Later, in the Oval Office, he met with his senior advisers.

During the day, in the Situation Room, the President had a videoconference with President Nicolas Sarkozy of France to discuss the situations in Iran and Syria and the recent volatility in global oil markets.

April 13

In the morning, the President traveled to Tampa, FL, arriving in the afternoon.

In the afternoon, the President toured the Port of Tampa. Later, he taped in an interview with Jose Diaz-Balart of Telemundo for later broadcast. Then, he traveled to Cartagena, Colombia, where, upon arrival, he traveled to the Hilton Cartagena Hotel.

In the evening, the President traveled to Castillo San Felipe de Barajas, where he attended a Summit of the Americas leaders' dinner. Later, he returned to the Hilton, where he remained overnight.

The White House announced that the President will welcome 2011 BCS National Champion University of Alabama football team to the White House on April 19.

April 14

In the afternoon, the President traveled to the Julio Cesar Turbay Ayala Convention Center, where he participated in an arrival ceremony for Summit of the Americas leaders. Later, also at the Convention Center, he attended the plenary session of the Summit of the Americas. Then, he returned to the Hilton Cartagena Hotel.

In the evening, the President traveled to the Casa de Huespedes Ilustres, where he attended a Summit of the Americas leaders' dinner. Later, he returned to the Hilton Cartagena Hotel, where he remained overnight.

April 15

In the morning, the President traveled to the Julio Cesar Turbay Ayala Convention Center, where he participated in a photographic opportunity and retreat with Summit of the Americas leaders.

In the afternoon, at the Julio Cesar Turbay Ayala Convention Center, the President met with Caribbean leaders. Then, he traveled to the Casa de Huespedes Ilustres, where he had a meeting with President Juan Manuel Santos Calderon of Colombia, followed by a working lunch. Later, he and President Santos toured the Church of San Pedro Claver.

In the evening, the President returned to Washington, DC.

April 16

The White House announced that the President will travel to Elyria, OH, on April 18.

The White House announced that the President will award the Medal of Honor on May 16.

The President announced his intention to nominate Vicki Miles-LaGrange, Ingrid A. Gregg, and James L. Henderson to be members of the Board of Trustees of the Harry S. Truman Scholarship Foundation.

The President announced his intention to appoint James W. Willis as a member of the Cultural Property Advisory Committee.

April 17

In the morning, in the Oval Office, the President and Vice President Joe Biden had an in-telligence briefing. Later, also in the Oval Office, he met with his senior advisers.

In the afternoon, in the Oval Office, the President and Vice President Biden met with Secretary of the Treasury Timothy F. Geithner.

The White House announced that the President will welcome Prime Minister Yoshihiko Noda of Japan to the White House on April 30.

The White House announced that the President will deliver remarks at the U.S. Memorial Holocaust Museum on April 23.

The President announced his intention to nominate Charles Benton, Christie Pearson Brandau, and Norberto J. Castro to be members of the National Museum and Library Services Board.

The President announced his intention to nominate William B. Schultz to be General Counsel at the Department of Health and Human Services.

April 18

In the morning, in the Oval Office, the President had an intelligence briefing. Later, he traveled to Elyria, OH, arriving in the afternoon.

In the afternoon, at Lorain County Community College, the President held a roundtable discussion with David Palmer, Bronson Harwood, Duane Sutton, and Andrea Ashley, unemployed workers enrolled in job training programs. Later, he traveled to Dearborn, MI.

In the evening, the President traveled to Bingham Farms, MI. Later, he returned to Washington, DC.

The President declared a major disaster in Hawaii and ordered Federal aid to supplement State and local recovery efforts in the area struck by severe storms, flooding, and landslides from March 3 through 11.

April 19

In the morning, in the Oval Office, the President had an intelligence briefing.

In the afternoon, in the Oval Office, the President met with his senior advisers. Later, at the W Washington DC hotel, he attended a campaign event.

April 20

In the morning, in the Oval Office, the President had an intelligence briefing, followed by a meeting with his senior advisers.

In the afternoon, in the Oval Office, the President was briefed by U.S. Secret Service Director Mark J. Sullivan on the ongoing investigation into allegations of misconduct by Secret Service personnel in Cartagena, Colombia, on April 11 and 12.

The White House released further details on the President's remarks at the U.S. Memorial Holocaust Museum on April 23.

The White House announced that the President will honor the National Teacher of the Year and finalists on April 24.

The White House announced that the President will travel to Chapel Hill, NC, and Boulder, CO, on April 24, and to Iowa City, IA, on April 25.

April 21

The White House released further details on the President's travel to Iowa City, IA, on April 25.

April 23

In the morning, the President toured exhibits at the U.S. Holocaust Memorial Museum. Later, in the Oval Office, he had an intelligence briefing, followed by a meeting with his senior advisers.

In the afternoon, in the Oval Office, the President met with Secretary of State Hillary Rodham Clinton.

April 24

In the morning, the President traveled to Chapel Hill, NC.

In the afternoon, at the University of North Carolina, the President taped an interview with James T. Fallon, Jr., of NBC's "Late Night With Jimmy Fallon" program for later broadcast. Later, he traveled to Boulder, CO.

In the evening, at the Sink restaurant, the President met with patrons.

The White House announced that the President and Mrs. Obama will travel to Hinesville, GA, on April 27.

April 25

In the morning, the President traveled to Iowa City, IA.

In the afternoon, in the Iowa Memorial Union at the University of Iowa, the President participated in a roundtable discussion with students. Later, he returned to Washington, DC.

In the evening, at the Jefferson hotel, the President attended an Obama Victory Fund 2012 fundraiser.

The President announced that he has nominated Terrence G. Berg to be a judge on the U.S. District Court for the Eastern District of Michigan.

The President announced that he has nominated Jesus G. Bernal to be a judge on the U.S. District Court for the Central District of California.

The President announced that he has nominated Shelly Deckert Dick to be a judge on the U.S. District Court for the Middle District of Louisiana.

The President announced that he has nominated Lorna G. Schofield to be a judge on the U.S. District Court for the Southern District of New York.

The President announced that he has nominated Charles R. Breyer to be a Commissioner on the U.S. Sentencing Commission.

April 26

In the morning, in the Oval Office, the President had an intelligence briefing.

In the afternoon, in the Blue Room and the Situation Room, he taped an interview with Brian Williams of NBC's "Nightly News With Brian Williams" program for later broadcast. Later, in the Oval Office, he met with Vice President Joe Biden.

During the day, in the East Room, the President met with the 2012 spring White House interns.

The President announced his intention to nominate Timothy M. Broas to be Ambassador to the Netherlands.

The President announced his intention to nominate Richard L. Morningstar to be Ambassador to Azerbaijan.

The President announced his intention to nominate Sean Sullivan to be a member of the Defense Nuclear Facilities Safety Board.

The President announced his intention to appoint Nancy Hellman Bechtle to be a member of the Board of Directors of the Presidio Trust.

The President announced his intention to appoint Reginald D. Betts to be a member of the Coordinating Council on Juvenile Justice and Delinquency Prevention.

The President announced his intention to appoint Patricia G. Smith to be a member of the Advisory Board of the National Air and Space Museum.

April 27

In the morning, the President and Mrs. Obama traveled to Hinesville, GA. Later, they toured the Fort Stewart Warriors Walk.

In the afternoon, the President and Mrs. Obama returned to Washington, DC.

The President announced that he has appointed Jodi Archambault Gillette as Senior Policy Adviser for Native American Affairs for the White House Domestic Policy Council.

April 29

In the afternoon, the President traveled to McLean, VA.

In the evening, the President returned to Washington, DC.

April 30

In the morning, in the Oval Office, the President had an intelligence briefing. Later, also in the Oval Office, he met with Prime Minister Yoshihiko Noda of Japan.

In the afternoon, in the Old Family Dining Room, the President and Prime Minister Noda had a working lunch. Later, in the Oval Office, he met with Secretary of the Treasury Timothy F. Geithner.

The President announced the designation of the following individuals as members of a Presidential delegation to attend ceremonies commemorating the 70th anniversary of the Battle of the Coral Sea in Australia from May 3 through 5: Janet A. Napolitano (head of delegation); Jeffrey L. Bleich; and Scott H. Swift.

May 1

In the morning, the President traveled to Bagram Air Base, Afghanistan, arriving in the evening. While en route aboard Air Force One, he had an intelligence briefing.

Later in the evening, the President traveled to Kabul, Afghanistan, where, at the Presidential Palace, he met with President Hamid Karzai of Afghanistan.

The White House announced that the President and Mrs. Obama will travel to Columbus, OH, and Richmond, VA, on May 5.

The White House announced that the President will welcome the 2012 NCAA Champion University of Kentucky men's basketball team to the White House on May 4.

May 2

In the morning, the President traveled to Bagram Air Base, Afghanistan, where he met with U.S. military personnel and presented Purple Hearts to 10 servicemembers. Later, he returned to Washington, DC. While en route aboard Air Force One, he had a telephone conversation with Prime Minister Benjamin Netanyahu of Israel to express his condolences for the death of the Prime Minister's father, Benzion Netanyahu.

In the afternoon, in the Oval Office, the President participated in a credentialing ceremony for newly appointed Ambassadors to the U.S. Later, at the W Washington DC hotel, he attended two campaign events.

The White House announced that the President will travel to Arlington, VA, on May 4.

May 3

In the afternoon, in the Private Dining Room, the President and Vice President Joe Biden had lunch. Later, in the Oval Office, he met with his senior advisers.

The White House announced that the President has invited President Thomas Yayi Boni of Benin, President John Evans Atta Mills of Ghana, President Jakaya Mrisho Kikwete of Tanzania, and Prime Minister Meles Zenawi of Ethiopia to attend a discussion at the Group of Eight (G–8) summit at Camp David, MD, on May 19.

May 4

In the morning, in the Oval Office, the President and Vice President Joe Biden had an intelligence briefing. Then, he traveled to Arlington, VA.

In the afternoon, the President returned to Washington, DC.

The White House announced that the President will travel to Albany, NY, on May 8.

May 5

In the morning, the President and Mrs. Obama traveled to Columbus, OH.

In the afternoon, the President and Mrs. Obama traveled to Richmond, VA.

In the evening, the President and Mrs. Obama returned to Washington, DC.

May 6

In the afternoon, the President had a telephone conversation with President-elect François Hollande of France to congratulate him on his election victory.

May 7

In the morning, in the Oval Office, the President had an intelligence briefing, followed by a meeting with his senior advisers. Later, also in the Oval Office, he met with 2010 Enrico Fermi Award recipients Burton Richter and Mildred S. Dresselhaus and their spouses.

In the afternoon, the President had a telephone conversation with outgoing President Nicolas Sarkozy of France to thank him for his leadership, friendship, and contribution to France-U.S. relations. Later, in the Roosevelt Room, he dropped by a meeting with representatives from organizations concerned about vacancies in Federal courts. Then, in the Oval Office, he participated in a conference call with Governors, mayors, and student government leaders from across the country to discuss student loan interest rates.

The White House announced that the President will welcome Secretary General Anders Fogh Rasmussen of the North Atlantic Treaty Organization to the White House on May 9.

May 8

In the morning, in the Oval Office, the President had an intelligence briefing. Then, he traveled to Albany, NY.

In the afternoon, at the University at Albany, the President toured the NanoTech Complex with Gov. Andrew M. Cuomo of New York and Christopher Borst, associate vice president for G450C technical operations, University at Albany. Later, he returned to Washington, DC.

The President announced his intention to nominate Kristine L. Svinicki to be a Commissioner of the Nuclear Regulatory Commission.

The President announced his intention to nominate Maria Lopez De Leon and Emil J. Kang to be members of the National Council on the Arts.

May 9

In the morning, in the Oval Office, the President and Vice President Joe Biden had an intelligence briefing. Then, also in the Oval Office, he had a telephone conversation with President Vladimir Vladimirovich Putin of Russia to discuss the commemoration of Victory in Europe Day and Russia-U.S. relations.

In the afternoon, in the Oval Office, the President and Vice President Biden met with Secretary General Anders Fogh Rasmussen of the North Atlantic Treaty Organization. Then, also in the Oval Office, they met with Secretary of the Treasury Timothy F. Geithner. Later, in the Oval Office, he met with his senior advisers.

During the day, in the Cabinet Room, the President taped an interview with Robin Roberts of ABC's "Good Morning America" program for later broadcast.

The White House announced that the President will welcome the National Association of Police Organizations TOP COPS awardees to the White House on May 12.

The White House announced that the President will award the Medal of Honor posthumously to Specialist Leslie H. Sabo, Jr., USA, on May 16.

The White House announced that the President will travel to Reno, NV, on May 11.

The President announced his intention to nominate Deborah R. Malac to be Ambassador to Liberia.

The President announced his intention to nominate Thomas S. Sowers II to be Assistant Secretary for Public and Intergovernmental Affairs at the Department of Veterans Affairs.

The President announced his intention to nominate Fernando Torres-Gil to be a member of the National Council on Disability.

The President announced his intention to appoint Lothar von Falkenhausen to be a member of the Cultural Property Advisory Committee.

The President announced his intention to appoint Mark F. Heinrich and Anil Lewis to be members of the Committee for Purchase From People Who Are Blind or Severely Disabled.

May 10

In the morning, the President traveled to Seattle, WA.

In the afternoon, he traveled to Studio City, CA, arriving in the evening.

In the evening, the President traveled to the Beverly Hilton hotel in Beverly Hills, CA.

The White House announced that the President will welcome the Major League Soccer Champion L.A. Galaxy to the White House on May 15.

The White House announced that the President will travel to New York City to deliver the commencement address at Barnard College on May 14.

The President announced his intention to appoint Caitlin Durkovich as Assistant Secretary for Infrastructure Protection at the Department of Homeland Security.

The President announced his intention to appoint Ellen M. Peel and Russell F. Smith III as U.S. Commissioners to the International Commission for the Conservation of Atlantic Tunas.

May 11

In the morning, the President traveled to Reno, NV.

In the afternoon, the President returned to Washington, DC, arriving in the evening.

The President announced his intention to nominate Thomas H. Armbruster to be Ambassador to the Marshall Islands.

The President announced his intention to nominate David B. Wharton to be Ambassador to Zimbabwe.

The President announced his intention to nominate William J. Shaw to be a member of the U.S. Commission on International Religious Freedom.

May 14

In the morning, the President traveled to New York City.

In the afternoon, at the studios of ABC television, the President taped an interview with Barbara Walters, Whoopi Goldberg, Joy Behar, Sherri Shepherd, and Elisabeth Hasselbeck of ABC's "The View" program for later broadcast.

In the evening, the President returned to Washington, DC. Later, he had a telephone conversation with Prime Minister Julia E. Gillard of Australia to discuss the situation in Afghanistan.

The President announced that he has nominated Frank P. Geraci, Jr., to be a judge on the U.S. District Court for the Western District of New York.

The President announced that he has nominated Fernando M. Olguin to be a judge on the U.S. District Court for the Central District of California.

May 15

In the morning, in the Oval Office, the President and Vice President Joe Biden had an intelligence briefing.

In the afternoon, the President had a telephone conversation with Prime Minister Mario Monti of Italy to discuss the security transition in Afghanistan and the economic situation in Europe. Later, in the Oval Office, he and Vice President Biden met with Secretary of the Treasury Timothy F. Geithner. Then, also in the Oval Office, they met with Secretary of Defense Leon E. Panetta. Later, in the Cabinet Room, they met with U.S. military combatant commanders.

In the evening, in the Blue Room, the President and Mrs. Obama hosted a dinner for combatant commanders and their spouses.

May 16

In the afternoon, in the Private Dining Room, the President had a working lunch with Speaker of the House of Representatives John A. Boehner, House Democratic Leader Nancy Pelosi, Senate Majority Leader Harry M. Reid, and Senate Minority Leader A. Mitchell McConnell. Later, in the Oval Office, he met with Secretary of State Hillary Rodham Clinton.

The President made additional disaster assistance available to Vermont by authorizing an increase in the level of Federal funding for public assistance projects undertaken as a result of Tropical Storm Irene from August 27 through September 2, 2011.

May 17

The White House announced that the President and Mrs. Obama will travel to Chicago, IL, on May 19 to host the NATO summit.

The President announced the designation of the following individuals as members of a Presidential delegation to attend the Inauguration of Jose Maria "Taur Matan Ruak" Vasconcelos as President of Timor-Leste in Dili, Timor-Leste, on May 19 and 20: Judith R. Fergin (head of delegation); and Nisha D. Biswal.

The President announced his intention to nominate Derek J. Mitchell to be Ambassador to Burma.

The President announced his intention to appoint Anhlan P. Nguyen and Quyen N. Vuong as members of the Board of Directors of the Vietnam Education Foundation.

The President announced that he has nominated Gary Blankinship to be U.S. marshal for the Southern District of Texas.

The President announced that he has nominated Matthew W. Brann and Malachy E. Mannion to be judges on the U.S. District Court for the Middle District of Pennsylvania.

May 18

In the afternoon, the President traveled to Camp David, MD, to attend the Group of Eight (G–8) summit, arriving in the evening.

In the evening, the President hosted a reception for G–8 leaders, followed by a working dinner.

The White House announced that the President will travel to Joplin, MO, on May 21.

The President announced his intention to nominate Joseph B. Donovan to be a member of the Board of Directors of the National Institute of Building Sciences.

The President announced his intention to nominate Bruce R. Sievers to be a member of the National Council on the Humanities.

The President announced his intention to appoint Miaohong Hsiangju Liu and Barbara Williams-Skinner as members of the President's Advisory Council on Faith-Based and Neighborhood Partnerships.

May 19

In the morning, on the grounds of the Aspen Lodge, the President participated in a photographic opportunity with Group of Eight (G–8) leaders. Then, in the Aspen Lodge, he met with Prime Minister David Cameron of the United Kingdom. Later, on the Laurel Lodge patio, he met with Chancellor Angela Merkel of Germany. Then, in the Laurel Lodge, he attended a working session with G–8 leaders.

In the afternoon, in the Laurel Lodge, the President hosted a working lunch on food safety. Then, he attended three more working sessions.

In the evening, the President again met with Chancellor Merkel of Germany. Later, he traveled to Chicago, IL.

May 20

In the afternoon, at the McCormick Place convention center, the President participated in a welcoming ceremony for North Atlantic Treaty Organization (NATO) leaders, followed by separate photographic opportunities with each of the NATO leaders.

In the evening, at Soldier Field, the President participated in a photographic opportunity with NATO leaders, followed by a working dinner.

May 21

In the morning, at the McCormick Place convention center, the President met with President Asif Ali Zardari of Pakistan.

In the afternoon, at the McCormick Place convention center, the President met with President Zardari and President Hamid Karzai of Afghanistan. Later, he participated in a photographic opportunity with International Security Assistance Force members. Then, he attended a meeting with NATO leaders.

In the evening, the President traveled to Joplin, MO. Later, he returned to Washington, DC.

The White House announced that the President will travel to Colorado Springs, CO, on May 23.

The President announced that he has nominated Thomas M. Durkin to be a judge on the U.S. District Court for the Northern District of Illinois.

May 22

The White House announced that the President will travel to Newton, IA, on May 24.

The White House announced that the President will award the Presidential Medal of Freedom on May 29.

May 23

In the morning, the President traveled to Colorado Springs, CO.

In the afternoon, the President traveled to Denver, CO. Later, he traveled to Atherton, CA, arriving in the evening.

In the evening, the President traveled to Redwood City, CA. Then, he traveled to San Jose, CA.

The President announced his intention to nominate Jonathan Lippman to be a member of the Board of Directors of the State Justice Institute.

The President announced his intention to appoint John F. Sopko as the Special Inspector General for Afghanistan Reconstruction.

May 24

In the morning, at the Fairmont Hotel, the President attended a campaign event. Later, he traveled to Newton, IA.

In the afternoon, the President toured a TPI Composites, Inc., facility. Then, also at TPI Composites, he participated in a question-and-answer session with Twitter users. Later, he traveled to Des Moines, IA, arriving in the evening.

In the evening, the President returned to Washington, DC.

The President declared a major disaster in Kansas and ordered Federal aid to supplement State and local recovery efforts in the area affected by severe storms, tornadoes, straight-line winds, and flooding on April 14 and 15.

The President announced his intention to nominate Greta C. Holtz to be Ambassador to Oman.

The President announced his intention to nominate Alexander M. Laskaris to be Ambassador to Guinea.

The President announced his intention to nominate Allison M. Macfarlane to be a Commissioner of the Nuclear Regulatory Commission, and, upon appointment, to designate her as Chair.

The President announced his intention to nominate Marcie B. Ries to be Ambassador to Bulgaria.

The President announced his intention to nominate Walter M. Shaub, Jr., to be Director of the Office of Government Ethics.

The President announced his intention to appoint Fred P. Hochberg as a member of the Board of Trustees of the Woodrow Wilson International Center for Scholars.

The President announced his intention to appoint Earl W. Stafford as a member of the President's Board of Advisers on Historically Black Colleges and Universities.

May 25

In the morning, in the Oval Office, the President had an intelligence briefing.

The White House announced that the President will welcome President Benigno S. Aquino III of the Philippines to the White House on June 8.

May 28

In the morning, in the Blue Room, the President, Mrs. Obama, Secretary of Defense Leon

E. Panetta, Secretary of the Navy Raymond E. Mabus, Jr., and Vice Chief of Naval Operations Vice Adm. Mark E. Ferguson III, USN, greeted the first contingent of women submariners to be assigned to the Navy's operational submarine force. Then, in the State Dining Room, he and Mrs. Obama hosted a breakfast in honor of Gold Star families. Later, they traveled to Arlington, VA, where they participated in a Memorial Day wreath-laying ceremony at the Tomb of the Unknowns in Arlington National Cemetery.

In the afternoon, the President and Mrs. Obama returned to Washington, DC.

May 29

In the morning, in the Oval Office, the President had an intelligence briefing, followed by a meeting with his senior advisers.

In the afternoon, in the Oval Office, the President met with Secretary of State Hillary Rodham Clinton. Later, in the Blue Room, he met with Presidential Medal of Freedom recipient and author Toni Morrison.

In the evening, in the Oval Office, the President met with Secretary of Defense Leon E. Panetta.

The White House announced that the President will travel to Golden Valley, MN, on June 1.

May 30

In the morning, in the Situation Room, the President participated in a videoconference with President François Hollande of France, Chancellor Angela Merkel of Germany, and Prime Minister Mario Monti of Italy to discuss the economic situation in Europe, the upcoming Group of Twenty (G–20) summit in Mexico, and the situation in Syria. Then, also in the Situation Room, he received the annual hurricane preparedness briefing.

The White House announced that the President and Mrs. Obama will welcome former President George W. Bush and former First Lady Laura Bush to the White House on May 31 for the unveiling of their official portraits.

The President announced the designation of the following individuals as members of a Presidential delegation to attend the 50th anniversary of Samoan independence in Apia, Samoa, on June 1:

David Huebner (head of delegation);
Eni F.H. Faleomavaega;
James L. Loi; and
Cecil D. Haney.

May 31

In the morning, in the Oval Office, the President and Vice President Joe Biden had an intelligence briefing.

In the afternoon, in the Red Room, the President and Mrs. Obama hosted a lunch for former President George W. Bush, former First Lady Laura Bush, former President George H.W. Bush, former First Lady Barbara Bush, and other members of the Bush family. Later, in the Oval Office, he met with Secretary of the Treasury Timothy F. Geithner.

June 1

In the morning, in the Oval Office, the President met with Rep. Steven R. Rothman. Then, he traveled to Golden Valley, MN, where he toured the Honeywell International Inc. manufacturing facility.

In the afternoon, the President traveled to Minneapolis, MN, where, at the Bachelor Farmer restaurant, he attended campaign events. Later, he traveled to Chicago, IL.

June 2

In the afternoon, the President traveled to Camp David, MD.

June 3

In the morning, the President returned to Washington, DC.

In the afternoon, in the Blue Room, the President hosted a reception for Ford's Theatre.

June 4

In the morning, in the Oval Office, the President had an intelligence briefing. Later, also in the Oval Office, he met with Secretary of the Treasury Timothy F. Geithner, Deputy National Security Adviser for International and Economic Affairs Michael B. Froman, and Under Secretary of the Treasury for International Affairs Lael Brainard.

In the afternoon, the President had a telephone conversation with President-elect Danilo Medina Sanchez of the Dominican Republic to congratulate him on his election victory and discuss Dominican Republic-U.S. relations. Later, he traveled to New York City.

In the evening, at the Waldorf-Astoria hotel, the President and former President William J. Clinton met with Francisco Maldonado of Chicago, IL, Rachel Klick of Falls Church, VA, and Joe Ardito of Estes Park, CO, winners of a contest held by his reelection campaign. Later, he returned to Washington, DC.

The White House announced that the President will travel to Las Vegas, NV, on June 7.

June 5

In the morning, the President had a telephone conversation with Prime Minister David Cameron of the United Kingdom to discuss the economic situation in Europe, preparations for the upcoming Group of Twenty (G–20) summit in Los Cabos, Mexico, and the June 1 rescue by British and U.S. special forces of four aid workers held captive in Afghanistan. He also conveyed his congratulations to Queen Elizabeth II of the United Kingdom on the occasion of her Diamond Jubilee.

Later in the morning, in the Oval Office, the President and Vice President Joe Biden had an intelligence briefing. Then, also in the Oval Office, he met with his senior advisers.

The White House announced that the President will welcome the Super Bowl XLVI Champion New York Giants to the White House on June 8.

June 6

In the morning, the President traveled to San Francisco, CA. While en route aboard Air Force One, he had separate telephone conversations with Chancellor Angela Merkel of Germany and Prime Minister Mario Monti of Italy to discuss the economic situation in Europe and preparations for the upcoming Group of Twenty (G–20) summit in Los Cabos, Mexico.

In the afternoon, the President traveled to Los Angeles, CA.

In the evening, the President traveled to Beverly Hills, CA.

The President announced his intention to nominate Mignon L. Clyburn to be a Commissioner of the Federal Communications Commission.

The President announced his intention to nominate Stephen Crawford to be a Governor of the Board of Governors of the U.S. Postal Service.

The President announced his intention to nominate John M. Koenig to be Ambassador to Cyprus.

The President announced his intention to appoint Patrick Gaynor as a member of the Medal of Valor Review Board.

June 7

In the morning, the President traveled to View Park, CA.

In the afternoon, the President traveled to Las Vegas, NV. Later, he returned to Washington, DC, arriving in the evening.

June 8

In the afternoon, in the Private Dining Room, the President and Vice President Joe Biden had lunch. Then, he had a telephone conversation with President François Hollande of France to discuss the economic situation in Europe, preparations for the upcoming Group of Twenty (G–20) summit in Los Cabos, Mexico, and the situation in Syria. Later, at the Jefferson hotel, he attended an Obama Victory Fund 2012 fundraiser.

June 11

In the morning, in the Oval Office, the President and Vice President Joe Biden had an intelligence briefing. Later, in the Cabinet Room, he taped separate television interviews with Don Ward of KKTV in Colorado Springs, CO, Hollani Davis of WDBJ in Roanoke, VA, Kristen Remington of KTVN in Reno, NV, Matthew Breen of KTIV in Sioux City, IA, Matt Smith of WBAY in Green Bay, WI, Michael Cogdill of WYFF in Greenville, SC, Tom Wills of WJXT in Jacksonville, FL, and Warren Armstrong of KFSN in Fresno, CA, for later broadcast.

In the afternoon, in the Oval Office, the President met with representatives of Big Brothers Big Sisters of America. Then, in the Private Dining Room, he and Vice President Biden had lunch. Later, in the Oval Office, they met with Secretary of the Treasury Timothy F. Geithner. Then, also in the Oval Office, they met with Secretary of Defense Leon E. Panetta.

During the day, in the Oval Office, the President met with actor Betty M. White.

The President announced that he has nominated Caitlin J. Halligan and Srikanth Srinivasan to be judges on the U.S. Court of Appeals for the District of Columbia Circuit.

The President announced that he has nominated Kimberly S. Knowles to be a judge on the Superior Court for the District of Columbia.

The President announced that he has nominated Jon S. Tigar and William H. Orrick III to be judges on the U.S. District Court for the Northern District of California.

June 12

In the morning, the President had a telephone conversation with Secretary of Commerce John E. Bryson to discuss Secretary Bryson's health. Later, in the Oval Office, he had an intelligence briefing. Then, he traveled to Owings Mills, MD, arriving in the afternoon.

Later in the afternoon, the President traveled to Baltimore, MD. Later, he had a telephone conversation with Gov. John W. Hickenlooper of Colorado to express his condolences for the loss of life due to the High Park wildfire and discuss Federal assistance for recovery efforts. Then, he traveled to Philadelphia, PA.

In the evening, the President returned to Washington, DC.

The White House announced that the President and Mrs. Obama will travel to New York City on June 14.

June 13

In the afternoon, in the Oval Office, the President and Vice President Joe Biden met with President Shimon Peres of Israel. Later, at the W Washington DC hotel, he attended a campaign event.

During the day, the President had separate telephone conversations with President Herman Van Rompuy of the European Council and President Felipe de Jesus Calderon Hinojosa of Mexico to discuss the economic situation in Europe and preparations for the upcoming Group of Twenty (G–20) summit in Los Cabos, Mexico.

June 14

In the morning, in the Oval Office, the President had an intelligence briefing. Then, also in the Oval Office, he had separate telephone conversations with King Abdallah bin Abd al-Aziz Al Saud of Saudi ia to discuss Saudi ia-U.S. relations and Prime Minister Manmohan Singh of India to discuss the global economy and the upcoming G–20 summit in Los Cabos, Mexico. Later, he traveled to Cleveland, OH, arriving in the afternoon.

In the afternoon, the President visited the Broadway Boys & Girls Club of Cleveland, where he met with children. Then, he and Mrs. Obama traveled to New York City, where they toured the World Trade Center construction site with Gov. Andrew M. Cuomo of New York, Gov. Christopher J. Christie of New Jersey, and Mayor Michael R. Bloomberg of New York City and signed a ceremonial steel beam.

In the evening, the President and Mrs. Obama returned to Washington, DC.

The President announced his intention to nominate Mark D. Gearan to be a member of the Board of Directors of the Corporation for National and Community Service.

The President announced his intention to nominate Michael D. Kirby to be Ambassador to Serbia.

The President announced his intention to appoint David Benton as a member of the Arctic Research Commission.

The President announced his intention to appoint Paula Robinson Collins as a member of the Board of Directors of the Presidio Trust.

The President declared a major disaster in Oklahoma and ordered Federal aid to supplement State and local recovery efforts in the area affected by severe storms, tornadoes, straight-line winds, and flooding from April 28 through May 1.

June 15

In the afternoon, at the Lincoln restaurant, the President had lunch with Janet Jones of Akkokeek, MD, Jim Heath of Aurora, OH, Paula Matyas of Milford, MI, and Wyndi Austin of Gilbert, AZ, winners of a contest held by his reelection campaign.

In the evening, the President, Mrs. Obama, their daughters Sasha and Malia, and his mother-in-law Marian Robinson traveled to Chicago, IL.

The President declared a major disaster in New Hampshire and ordered Federal aid to supplement State and local recovery efforts in the area affected by a severe storm and flooding from May 29 through May 31.

June 17

In the evening, the President traveled to Los Cabos, Mexico, where, upon arrival, he traveled to the Esperanza Resort in Cabo San Lucas.

June 18

In the morning, at the Esperanza Resort in Cabo San Lucas, Mexico, the President met with Chancellor Angela Merkel of Germany.

In the afternoon, the President traveled to the Los Cabos International Convention Center in San Jose del Cabo, where he participated in an official arrival ceremony with President Felipe de Jesus Calderon Hinojosa of Mexico. Then, he attended a Group of Twenty (G–20) plenary session.

In the evening, the President participated in an official photograph with G–20 leaders. Then, he participated in a working dinner with G–20 leaders. Later, he returned to the Esperanza Resort in Cabo San Lucas.

The White House announced that the President will travel to Orlando, FL, on June 22.

June 19

In the morning, the President traveled to the Los Cabos International Convention Center in San Jose del Cabo, where he participated

in two Group of Twenty (G–20) plenary sessions.

In the afternoon, the President participated in a working lunch with G–20 leaders. Later, he attended the closing ceremony of the G–20 summit.

During the day, the President met with Prime Minister Recep Tayyip Erdogan of Turkey to discuss the situations in Syria and Iraq, Turkey-U.S. counterterrorism operations, and the upcoming Framework for Strategic Economic and Commercial Cooperation meeting in Ankara, Turkey.

In the evening, the President returned to Washington, DC.

The President announced the designation of the following individuals as members of a Presidential delegation to offer condolences to King Abdallah bin Abd al-Aziz Al Saud for the death of Crown Prince Nayif bin Abd al-Aziz Al Saud in Riyadh, Saudi ia, on June 20:

Leon E. Panetta (head of delegation);
James B. Smith;
John O. Brennan;
Robert S. Mueller III;
A. Elizabeth Jones;
George J. Tenet; and
Frances Fragos Townsend.

June 20

During the day, the President had a telephone conversation with King Abdallah bin Abd al-Aziz Al Saud of Saudi ia to offer his condolences for the death of Crown Prince Nayif bin Abd al-Aziz Al Saud and congratulate the King on the selection of Prince Salman bin Abd al-Aziz Al Saud as Crown Prince.

The President announced his intention to nominate David Masumoto to be a member of the National Council on the Arts.

The President announced his intention to nominate Polly E. Trottenberg to be Under Secretary for Policy at the Department of Transportation.

June 21

In the morning, in the Oval Office, the President and Vice President Joe Biden had an intelligence briefing. Then, also in the Oval Office, he met with his senior advisers.

In the afternoon, in the Private Dining Room, the President and Vice President Biden had lunch. Later, in the Oval Office, he met with Secretary of Commerce John E. Bryson to discuss his resignation and thank him for his service.

During the day, the President dropped by a meeting between National Security Adviser Thomas E. Donilon and Vice Prime Minister Shaul Mofaz of Israel.

June 22

In the morning, the President traveled to Orlando, FL, arriving in the afternoon.

In the afternoon, the President traveled to Tampa, FL. While en route aboard Air Force One, he had a telephone conversation with Miami Heat Head Coach Erik Spoelstra to congratulate him on his team's victory over the Oklahoma City Thunder in the 2012 NBA Finals.

In the evening, the President returned to Washington, DC.

The President announced the designation of the following individuals as members of a Presidential delegation to attend the opening ceremony of the 2012 Olympic Games in London, England, on June 23:

Michelle Obama (head of delegation);
Louis B. Susman;
Brandi Chastain;
Dominique M. Dawes;
Gabriel Diaz de Leon;
Grant E. Hill; and
Summer Sanders.

The President declared a major disaster in Vermont and ordered Federal aid to supplement State and local recovery efforts in the area affected by a severe storm, tornado, and flooding on May 29.

June 24

In the evening, the President had a telephone conversation with President-elect Muhammad Mursi of Egypt to congratulate him on his election victory and discuss Egypt-U.S. relations. He also had a telephone conversation

with Egyptian Presidential candidate Gen. Ahmed Shafiq to commend him for his campaign efforts and encourage him to continue to play a role in Egyptian politics.

June 25

In the morning, in the Oval Office, the President and Vice President Joe Biden had an intelligence briefing. Then, also in the Oval Office, they met with Secretary of State Hillary Rodham Clinton. Later, he had a telephone conversation with Prime Minister Antonis Samaras of Greece to congratulate him on his election, express his support for Greece, and wish him a speedy recovery following his recent surgery.

In the afternoon, the President traveled to Durham, NH. While en route aboard Air Force One, he had a telephone conversation with Prime Minister Mario Monti of Italy to discuss the recent G–20 meeting and economic stabilization efforts in Europe. Later, at the University of New Hampshire Dairy Bar, he stopped for ice cream and visited with patrons. Then, he traveled to Boston, MA.

Later in the afternoon, at Hamersley's Bistro restaurant, the President attended a campaign event.

In the evening, the President traveled to Weston, MA. Later, he returned to Boston, MA.

The President announced that he has nominated Sheri P. Chappell to be a judge on the U.S. District Court for the Middle District of Florida.

The President announced that he has nominated Katherine P. Failla to be a judge on the U.S. District Court for the Southern District of New York.

The President announced that he has nominated Troy L. Nunley to be a judge on the U.S. District Court for the Eastern District of California.

June 26

In the morning, the President traveled to Atlanta, GA. While en route aboard Air Force Once, he had a telephone conversation with Gov. Richard L. Scott of Florida to express his condolences for the loss of life and damage to property as a result of Tropical Storm Debby and offer Federal assistance.

In the afternoon, the President traveled to the Varsity diner, where he had lunch and greeted students from the Lenora Academy in Snellville, GA. Later, he traveled to Miami Beach, FL.

In the evening, at a private residence, the President attended a campaign fundraiser. Later, he returned to Washington, DC.

June 27

In the morning, the President had a telephone conversation with President François Hollande of France to discuss the economic situation in Europe.

In the afternoon, in the Oval Office, the President had an intelligence briefing. Later, in the Private Dining Room, he had lunch with Crown Prince Mohammed Bin Zayed Al Nahyan of Abu Dhabi, Deputy Supreme Commander of the United Arab Emirates Armed Forces. Then, he traveled to the Jefferson hotel, where he attended a campaign event.

During the day, the President had separate telephone conversations with Gov. John W. Hickenlooper of Colorado and Mayor Steve Bach of Colorado Springs to discuss the wildfires affecting the area and Federal and State assistance efforts.

The White House announced that the President will address the 2012 National Urban League Conference in New Orleans, LA, on July 25.

June 28

In the morning, in the Oval Office, the President and Vice President Joe Biden had an intelligence briefing.

In the afternoon, in the Private Dining Room, the President and Vice President Biden had lunch. Later, he traveled to Bethesda, MD, where, at the Walter Reed National Military Medical Center, he visited with wounded U.S. military personnel and presented a Purple Heart to a servicemember. Then, he returned to Washington, DC.

Later in the afternoon, in the Oval Office, the President and Vice President Biden met with Secretary of Defense Leon E. Panetta.

During the day, the President had a telephone conversation with U.S. Solicitor General Donald B. Verrilli, Jr., to congratulate him on the Supreme Court's ruling on the Patient Protection and Affordable Care Act.

The President announced his intention to nominate Camila A. Alire and Ramon Saldivar to be members of the National Council on the Humanities.

The White House announced that the President will travel to Colorado Springs, CO, on June 29.

June 29

In the morning, in the Oval Office, the President and Vice President Joe Biden had an intelligence briefing. Later, he traveled to Colorado Springs, CO. Upon arrival, he toured damage caused by the wildfires affecting the area. Then, at an American Red Cross evacuation shelter at the Southeast Family Center & Armed Services YMCA, he met with staff members and volunteers.

In the evening, the President returned to Washington, DC.

The President declared a major disaster in Colorado and ordered Federal aid to supplement State and local response efforts in the area struck by wildfires beginning on June 9 and continuing.

June 30

In the afternoon, the President traveled to Camp David, MD.

During the day, the President had separate telephone conversations with Gov. John R. Kasich of Ohio, Gov. Robert F. McDonnell of Virginia, Gov. Martin J. O'Malley of Maryland, Gov. Earl R. Tomblin of West Virginia, and Federal Emergency Management Agency Administrator W. Craig Fugate to discuss damage and recovery efforts related to the severe storms that affected the Midwest and Mid-Atlantic regions on June 29.

The President declared an emergency in West Virginia and ordered Federal aid to supplement State and local response efforts due to the emergency conditions resulting from severe storms beginning on June 29 and continuing.

The President declared an emergency in Ohio and ordered Federal aid to supplement State and local response efforts due to the emergency conditions resulting from severe storms beginning on June 29 and continuing.

Appendix B—Nominations Submitted to the Senate

The following list does not include promotions of members of the Uniformed Services, nominations to the Service Academies, or nominations of Foreign Service officers.

Submitted January 23

Robert E. Bacharach,
of Oklahoma, to be U.S. Circuit Judge for the Tenth Circuit, vice Robert Harlan Henry, resigned.

William J. Kayatta, Jr.,
of Maine, to be U.S. Circuit Judge for the First Circuit, vice Kermit Lipez, retired.

Michael A. Shipp,
of New Jersey, to be U.S. District Judge for the District of New Jersey, vice Mary Little Parell, retired.

Submitted January 24

Anthony T. Clark,
of North Dakota, to be a member of the Federal Energy Regulatory Commission for the term expiring June 30, 2016, vice Marc Spitzer, term expired.

Erin C. Conaton,
of the District of Columbia, to be Under Secretary of Defense for Personnel and Readiness, vice Clifford L. Stanley.

Scott H. DeLisi,
of Minnesota, a career member of the Senior Foreign Service, class of Minister-Counselor, to be Ambassador Extraordinary and Plenipotentiary of the United States of America to the Republic of Uganda.

Deborah S. Delisle,
of South Carolina, to be Assistant Secretary for Elementary and Secondary Education, Department of Education, vice Thelma Melendez de Santa Ana.

Tracey Ann Jacobson,
of the District of Columbia, a career member of the Senior Foreign Service, class of Minister-Counselor, to be Ambassador Extraordinary and Plenipotentiary of the United States of America to the Republic of Kosovo.

James J. Jones,
of the District of Columbia, to be Assistant Administrator for Toxic Substances of the Environmental Protection Agency, vice Stephen Alan Owens, resigned.

Frank Kendall III,
of Virginia, to be Under Secretary of Defense for Acquisition, Technology, and Logistics, vice Ashton B. Carter, resigned.

James N. Miller, Jr.,
of Virginia, to be Under Secretary of Defense for Policy, vice Michele A. Flournoy.

Jerome H. Powell,
of Maryland, to be a member of the Board of Governors of the Federal Reserve System for the unexpired term of 14 years from February 1, 2000, vice Frederic S. Mishkin.

Marietta S. Robinson,
of Michigan, to be a Commissioner of the Consumer Product Safety Commission for a term of 7 years from October 27, 2010, vice Thomas Hill Moore, term expired.

Adam E. Sieminski,
of Pennsylvania, to be Administrator of the Energy Information Administration, vice Richard G. Newell.

Jeremy C. Stein,
of Massachusetts, to be a member of the Board of Governors of the Federal Reserve System for the unexpired term of 14 years from February 1, 2004, vice Kevin M. Warsh, resigned.

John Christopher Stevens,
of California, a career member of the Senior Foreign Service, class of Counselor, to be Ambassador Extraordinary and Plenipotentiary of the United States of America to Libya.

Linda Thomas-Greenfield,
of Louisiana, a career member of the Senior Foreign Service, class of Minister-Counselor, to be Director General of the Foreign Service, vice Nancy J. Powell, resigned.

Constance B. Tobias,
of Maryland, to be Chairman of the Board of Veterans' Appeals for a term of 6 years, vice James Philip Terry, term expired.

Pamela A. White,
of Maine, a career member of the Senior Foreign Service, class of Career Minister, to be Ambassador Extraordinary and Plenipotentiary of the United States of America to the Republic of Haiti.

Jessica Lynn Wright,
of Pennsylvania, to be an Assistant Secretary of Defense, vice Dennis M. McCarthy, resigned.

Withdrawn January 24

Gineen Maria Bresso,
of Florida, to be a Member of the Election Assistance Commission for a term expiring December 12, 2013 (reappointment), which was sent to the Senate on March 17, 2011.

Scott C. Doney,
of Massachusetts, to be Chief Scientist of the National Oceanic and Atmospheric Administration, vice Kathryn D. Sullivan, which was sent to the Senate on January 26, 2011.

Timothy Charles Scheve,
of Pennsylvania, to be a member of the Internal Revenue Service Oversight Board for a term expiring September 14, 2015, vice Nancy Killefer, term expired, which was sent to the Senate on January 26, 2011.

Gloria Wilson Shelton,
of Maryland, to be a Judge of the U.S. Court of Appeals for Veterans Claims for the term of 15 years, vice a new position created by Public Law 110–389, approved October 10, 2008, which was sent to the Senate on June 22, 2011.

Submitted February 1

Michael A. Botticelli,
of Massachusetts, to be Deputy Director of National Drug Control Policy, vice A. Thomas McLellan.

Christy L. Romero,
of Virginia, to be Special Inspector General for the Troubled Asset Relief Program, vice Neil M. Barofsky, resigned.

Withdrawn February 1

Alan D. Bersin,
of California, to be Commissioner of Customs, Department of Homeland Security, vice W. Ralph Basham, which was sent to the Senate on January 26, 2011.

John D. Podesta,
of the District of Columbia, to be a member of the Board of Directors of the Corporation for National and Community Service for a term expiring October 6, 2014, vice Alan D. Solomont, resigned, which was sent to the Senate on January 26, 2011.

Submitted February 2

Jamie A. Hainsworth,
of Rhode Island, to be U.S. Marshal for the District of Rhode Island for the term of 4 years, vice Steven Gerard O'Donnell, resigned.

Louise W. Kelton,
of Tennessee, to be U.S. Marshal for the Middle District of Tennessee for the term of 4 years, vice Denny Wade King, term expired.

Stephanie Marie Rose,
of Iowa, to be U.S. District Judge for the Southern District of Iowa, vice Robert W. Pratt, retiring.

Michael P. Shea,
of Connecticut, to be U.S. District Judge for the District of Connecticut, vice Christopher Droney, elevated.

Submitted February 6

William Joseph Baer,
of Maryland, to be an Assistant Attorney General, vice Christine Anne Varney.

Marcilynn A. Burke,
of North Carolina, to be an Assistant Secretary of the Interior, vice Wilma A. Lewis, resigned.

Joseph G. Jordan,
of Massachusetts, to be Administrator for Federal Procurement Policy, vice Daniel I. Gordon.

John Robert Norris,
of Iowa, to be a member of the Federal Energy Regulatory Commission for the term expiring June 30, 2017 (reappointment).

Jeremiah O'Hear Norton,
of Virginia, to be a member of the Board of Directors of the Federal Deposit Insurance Corporation for the remainder of the term expiring July 15, 2013, vice Sheila C. Bair, resigned.

Heidi Shyu,
of California, to be an Assistant Secretary of the Army, vice Malcolm Ross O'Neill, resigned.

Submitted February 13

Sharon Block,
of the District of Columbia, to be a member of the National Labor Relations Board for the term of 5 years expiring December 16, 2014, vice Craig Becker, to which position she was appointed during last recess of the Senate.

William P. Doyle,
of Pennsylvania, to be a Federal Maritime Commissioner for the term expiring June 30, 2013, vice Joseph E. Brennan, term expired.

Terence Francis Flynn,
of Maryland, to be a member of the National Labor Relations Board for the term of 5 years expiring August 27, 2015, vice Peter Schaumber, term expired, to which position he was appointed during the last recess of the Senate.

Richard F. Griffin, Jr.,
of the District of Columbia, to be a member of the National Labor Relations Board for the term of 5 years expiring August 27, 2016, vice Wilma B. Liebman, term expired, to which position he was appointed during the last recess of the Senate.

Richard A. Lidinsky, Jr.,
of Maryland, to be a Federal Maritime Commissioner for the term expiring June 30, 2017 (reappointment).

Katharina G. McFarland,
of Virginia, to be an Assistant Secretary of Defense (new position).

Kenneth Merten,
of Virginia, a career member of the Senior Foreign Service, class of Minister-Counselor, to be Ambassador Extraordinary and Plenipotentiary of the United States of America to the Republic of Croatia.

Submitted February 14

James M. Demers,
of New Hampshire, to be a member of the Board of Directors of the Overseas Private Investment Corporation for a term expiring December 17, 2014, vice Kevin Glenn Nealer, term expired.

Naomi A. Walker,
of the District of Columbia, to be a member of the Board of Directors of the Overseas Private Investment Corporation for a term expiring

December 17, 2012, vice Christopher J. Hanley, term expired.

Submitted February 16

Elissa F. Cadish,
of Nevada, to be U.S. District Judge for the District of Nevada, vice Philip M. Pro, retired.

Paul William Grimm,
of Maryland, to be U.S. District Judge for the District of Maryland, vice Benson Everett Legg, retiring.

Jill A. Pryor,
of Georgia, to be U.S. Circuit Judge for the Eleventh Circuit, vice Stanley F. Birch, Jr., retired.

Mark E. Walker,
of Florida, to be U.S. District Judge for the Northern District of Florida, vice Stephan P. Mickle, retired.

Submitted February 17

Erica Lynn Groshen,
of New York, to be Commissioner of Labor Statistics, Department of Labor, for a term of 4 years, vice Keith Hall, term expired.

Makila James,
of the District of Columbia, a career member of the Senior Foreign Service, class of Counselor, to be Ambassador Extraordinary and Plenipotentiary of the United States of America to the Kingdom of Swaziland.

Jeffrey D. Levine,
of California, a career member of the Senior Foreign Service, class of Minister-Counselor, to be Ambassador Extraordinary and Plenipotentiary of the United States of America to the Republic of Estonia.

C. Peter Mahurin,
of Kentucky, to be a member of the Board of Directors of the Tennessee Valley Authority for a term expiring May 18, 2016, vice Robert M. Duncan, term expired.

Richard B. Norland,
of Iowa, a career member of the Senior Foreign Service, class of Minister-Counselor, to be Ambassador Extraordinary and Plenipotentiary of the United States of America to Georgia.

Carlos Pascual,
of the District of Columbia, to be an Assistant Secretary of State (Energy Resources), vice John Stern Wolf.

Major General John Peabody,
United States Army, to be a member and President of the Mississippi River Commission.

Mark A. Pekala,
of Maryland, a career member of the Senior Foreign Service, class of Minister-Counselor, to be Ambassador Extraordinary and Plenipotentiary of the United States of America to the Republic of Latvia.

Submitted February 29

Brian J. Davis,
of Florida, to be U.S. District Judge for the Middle District of Florida, vice Richard A. Lazzara, retired.

John E. Dowdell,
of Oklahoma, to be U.S. District Judge for the Northern District of Oklahoma, vice Terry C. Kern, retired.

Submitted March 5

Edward M. Alford,
of Virginia, a career member of the Senior Foreign Service, class of Minister-Counselor, to be Ambassador Extraordinary and Plenipotentiary of the United States of America to the Republic of The Gambia.

Peter William Bodde,
of Maryland, a career member of the Senior Foreign Service, class of Minister-Counselor, to be Ambassador Extraordinary and Plenipotentiary of the United States of America to the Federal Democratic Republic of Nepal.

Piper Anne Wind Campbell,
of the District of Columbia, a career member of the Senior Foreign Service, class of Counselor, to be Ambassador Extraordinary and Plenipotentiary of the United States of America to Mongolia.

Submitted March 12

Arthur Bienenstock,
of California, to be a member of the National Science Board, National Science Foundation for a term expiring May 10, 2016, vice Louis J. Lanzerotti, term expired.

Suravi Gangopadhyay,
of Michigan, to be a member of the National Museum and Library Services Board for a term expiring December 6, 2016, vice Jeffrey Patchen, term expired.

Luis Herrera,
of California, to be a member of the National Museum and Library Services Board for a term expiring December 6, 2014, vice Katina P. Strauch, term expired.

Dorothea-Maria Rosen,
of California, a career member of the Senior Foreign Service, class of Counselor, to be Ambassador Extraordinary and Plenipotentiary of the United States of America to the Federated States of Micronesia.

Suzanne E. Thorin,
of New York, to be a member of the National Museum and Library Services Board for a term expiring December 6, 2015, vice Sandra Pickett, term expired.

Katherine C. Tobin,
of New York, to be a Governor of the U.S. Postal Service for a term expiring December 8, 2016, vice Carolyn L. Gallagher, term expired.

Withdrawn March 12

Carla M. Leon-Decker,
of Virginia, to be a member of the National Credit Union Administration Board for a term expiring

August 2, 2017, vice Gigi Hyland, term expired, which was sent to the Senate on October 20, 2011.

Submitted March 19

Mark L. Asquino,
of the District of Columbia, a career member of the Senior Foreign Service, class of Minister-Counselor, to be Ambassador Extraordinary and Plenipotentiary of the United States of America to the Republic of Equatorial Guinea.

Edward W. Brehm,
of Minnesota, to be a member of the Board of Directors of the African Development Foundation for a term expiring September 22, 2017 (reappointment).

Derek H. Chollet,
of Nebraska, to be an Assistant Secretary of Defense, vice Alexander Vershbow.

Kathleen H. Hicks,
of Virginia, to be a Principal Deputy Under Secretary of Defense, vice James N. Miller, Jr.

Susanna Loeb,
of California, to be a member of the Board of Directors of the National Board for Education Sciences for a term expiring March 15, 2016, vice Craig T. Ramey, term expired.

Submitted March 21

Rainey Ransom Brandt,
of the District of Columbia, to be an Associate Judge of the Superior Court of the District of Columbia for the term of 15 years, vice Joan Z. McAvoy, retired.

John S. Leonardo,
of Arizona, to be U.S. Attorney for the District of Arizona for the term of 4 years, vice Dennis K. Burke, resigned.

Submitted March 27

Michael Peter Huerta,
of the District of Columbia, to be Administrator of the Federal Aviation Administration for the term of 5 years, vice J. Randolph Babbitt.

Brett H. McGurk,
of Connecticut, to be Ambassador Extraordinary and Plenipotentiary of the United States of America to the Republic of Iraq.

James C. Miller, III,
of Virginia, to be a Governor of the United States Postal Service for the term expiring December 8, 2017 (reappointment).

Michele Jeanne Sison,
of Maryland, a career member of the Senior Foreign Service, class of Minister-Counselor, to be Ambassador Extraordinary and Plenipotentiary of the United States of America to the Democratic Socialist Republic of Sri Lanka, and to serve concurrently and without additional compensation as Ambassador Extraordinary and Plenipotentiary of the United States of America to the Republic of Maldives.

Submitted March 28

Robert James Grey, Jr.,
of Virginia, to be a member of the Board of Directors of the Legal Services Corporation for a term expiring July 13, 2014 (reappointment).

John Gerson Levi,
of Illinois, to be a member of the Board of Directors of the Legal Services Corporation for a term expiring July 13, 2014 (reappointment).

Laurie I. Mikva,
of Illinois, to be a member of the Board of Directors of the Legal Services Corporation for a term expiring July 13, 2013 (reappointment).

Martha L. Minow,
of Massachusetts, to be a member of the Board of Directors of the Legal Services Corporation for a term expiring July 13, 2014 (reappointment).

Gloria Valencia-Weber,
of New Mexico, to be a member of the Board of Directors of the Legal Services Corporation for a term expiring July 13, 2014 (reappointment).

Submitted March 29

Yvonne Brathwaite Burke,
of California, to be a Director of the Amtrak Board of Directors for a term of 5 years (new position).

Patricia K. Falcone,
of California, to be an Associate Director of the Office of Science and Technology Policy, vice Philip E. Coyle, III.

Douglas M. Griffiths,
of Texas, a career member of the Senior Foreign Service, Class of Minister-Counselor, to be Ambassador Extraordinary and Plenipotentiary of the United States of America to the Republic of Mozambique.

Maria Rosario Jackson,
of the District of Columbia, to be a member of the National Council on the Arts for a term expiring September 3, 2016, vice Terence Alan Teachout, term expired.

Patrick A. Miles, Jr.,
of Michigan, to be U.S. Attorney for the Western District of Michigan for the term of 4 years, vice Margaret M. Chiara, resigned.

Patrick J. Wilkerson,
of Oklahoma, to be U.S. Marshal for the Eastern District of Oklahoma for the term of 4 years, vice John William Loyd, term expired.

Danny Chappelle Williams, Sr.,
of Oklahoma, to be U.S. Attorney for the Northern District of Oklahoma for the term of 4 years, vice David E. O'Meilia, term expired.

Submitted April 16

Jay Nicholas Anania,
of Maryland, a career member of the Senior Foreign Service, class of Minister-Counselor, to be Ambassador Extraordinary and Plenipotentiary of the United States of America to the Republic of Suriname.

Gene Allan Cretz,
of New York, a career member of the Senior Foreign Service, class of Minister-Counselor, to be Ambassador Extraordinary and Plenipotentiary of the United States of America to the Republic of Ghana.

Susan Marsh Elliott,
of Florida, a career member of the Senior Foreign Service, class of Counselor, to be Ambassador Extraordinary and Plenipotentiary of the United States of America to the Republic of Tajikistan.

Ingrid A. Gregg,
of Michigan, to be a member of the Board of Trustees of the Harry S Truman Scholarship Foundation for a term expiring December 10, 2017, vice John E. Kidde, term expired.

James L. Henderson,
of Kentucky, to be a member of the Board of Trustees of the Harry S Truman Scholarship Foundation for a term expiring December 10, 2017, vice John Peyton, term expired.

David J. Lane,
of Florida, for the rank of Ambassador during his tenure of service as U.S. Representative to the United Nations Agencies for Food and Agriculture.

Vicki Miles-LaGrange,
of Oklahoma, to be a member of the Board of Trustees of the Harry S Truman Scholarship Foundation for a term expiring December 10, 2015, vice Roger L. Hunt, term expired.

Charles P. Rose,
of Illinois, to be a member of the Board of Trustees of the Morris K. Udall and Stewart L. Udall Foundation for a term expiring April 16, 2017, vice Stephen M. Prescott, term expired.

Patricia M. Wald,
of the District of Columbia, to be a member of the Privacy and Civil Liberties Oversight Board for a term expiring January 29, 2019 (reappointment).

Submitted April 18

Charles Benton,
of Illinois, to be a member of the National Museum and Library Services Board for a term expiring December 6, 2013, vice Harry Robinson, Jr., term expired.

Christie Pearson Brandau,
of Iowa, to be a member of the National Museum and Library Services Board for a term expiring December 6, 2016, vice Lotsee Patterson, term expired.

Norberto Jesus Castro,
of Arizona, to be a member of the National Museum and Library Services Board for a term expiring December 6, 2016, vice Douglas G. Myers, term expired.

William B. Schultz,
of the District of Columbia, to be General Counsel of the Department of Health and Human Services, vice Daniel Meron.

Submitted April 25

Terrence G. Berg,
of Michigan, to be U.S. District Judge for the Eastern District of Michigan, vice Arthur J. Tarnow, retired.

Jesus G. Bernal,
of California, to be U.S. District Judge for the Central District of California, vice Stephen G. Larson, resigned.

Charles R. Breyer,
of California, to be a member of the U.S. Sentencing Commission for a term expiring October 31, 2015, vice Ruben Castillo, term expired.

Shelly Deckert Dick,
of Louisiana, to be U.S. District Judge for the Middle District of Louisiana, vice Ralph E. Tyson, deceased.

Lorna G. Schofield,
of New York, to be U.S. District Judge for the Southern District of New York, vice Shira A. Scheindlin, retired.

Submitted April 26

Timothy M. Broas,
of Maryland, to be Ambassador Extraordinary and Plenipotentiary of the United States of America to the Kingdom of the Netherlands.

Richard L. Morningstar,
of Massachusetts, to be Ambassador Extraordinary and Plenipotentiary of the United States of America to the Republic of Azerbaijan.

Sean Sullivan,
of Connecticut, to be a member of the Defense Nuclear Facilities Safety Board for a term expiring October 18, 2015, vice Larry W. Brown, resigned.

Withdrawn April 26

Thomas M. Beck,
of Virginia, to be a member of the National Mediation Board for a term expiring July 1, 2013, vice Elizabeth Dougherty, term expired, which was sent to the Senate on January 5, 2011.

Matthew J. Bryza,
of Illinois, a career member of the Senior Foreign Service, class of Counselor, to be Ambassador Extraordinary and Plenipotentiary of the United States of America to the Republic of Azerbaijan, to which position he was appointed during the recess of the Senate from December 22, 2010, to January 5, 2011, which was sent to the Senate on January 26, 2011.

Submitted May 8

Maria Lopez De Leon,
of Texas, to be a member of the National Council on the Arts for a term expiring September 3, 2016, vice James Ballinger, term expired.

Emil J. Kang,
of North Carolina, to be a member of the National Council on the Arts for a term expiring September 3, 2018, vice Benjamin Donenberg, term expiring.

Kristine L. Svinicki,
of Virginia, to be a member of the Nuclear Regulatory Commission for the term of 5 years expiring June 30, 2017 (reappointment).

Submitted May 10

Deborah Ruth Malac,
of Virginia, a career member of the Senior Foreign Service, class of Counselor, to be Ambassador Extraordinary and Plenipotentiary of the United States of America to the Republic of Liberia.

Thomas Skerik Sowers II,
of Missouri, to be an Assistant Secretary of Veterans Affairs (Public and Intergovernmental Affairs), vice Ladda Tammy Duckworth.

Fernando Torres-Gil,
of California, to be a member of the National Council on Disability for a term expiring September 17, 2014 (reappointment).

Submitted May 21

Joseph Byrne Donovan,
of Virginia, to be a member of the Board of Directors of the National Institute of Building Sciences for a term expiring September 7, 2013, vice Lane Carson, resigned.

Bruce R. Sievers,
of California, to be a member of the National Council on the Humanities for a term expiring January 26, 2018, vice Kenneth R. Weinstein, term expired.

Thomas M. Durkin,
of Illinois, to be U.S. District Judge for the Northern District of Illinois, vice Wayne R. Andersen, retired.

Submitted May 24

Greta Christine Holtz,
of Maryland, a career member of the Senior Foreign Service, class of Minister-Counselor, to be Ambassador Extraordinary and Plenipotentiary of the United States of America to the Sultanate of Oman.

Alexander Mark Laskaris,
of Maryland, a career member of the Senior Foreign Service, class of Counselor, to be Ambassador Extraordinary and Plenipotentiary of the United States of America to the Republic of Guinea.

Jonathan Lippman,
of New York, to be a member of the Board of Directors of the State Justice Institute for a term expiring September 17, 2012, vice Robert A. Miller, term expired.

Jonathan Lippman,
of New York, to be a member of the Board of Directors of the State Justice Institute for a term expiring September 17, 2015 (reappointment).

Allison M. Macfarlane,
of Maryland, to be a member of the Nuclear Regulatory Commission for the remainder of the term expiring June 30, 2013, vice Gregory B. Jaczko, resigned.

Marcie B. Ries,
of the District of Columbia, a career member of the Senior Foreign Service, class of Career-Minister, to be Ambassador Extraordinary and Plenipotentiary of the United States of America to the Republic of Bulgaria.

Walter M. Shaub, Jr.,
of Virginia, to be Director of the Office of Government Ethics for a term of 5 years, vice Robert Irwin Cusick, Jr., term expired.

Submitted June 7

Mignon L. Clyburn,
of South Carolina, to be a member of the Federal Communications Commission for a term of 5 years from July 1, 2012 (reappointment).

Stephen Crawford,
of Maryland, to be a Governor of the U.S. Postal Service for the remainder of the term expiring December 8, 2015, vice Alan C. Kessler, resigned.

John M. Koenig,
of Washington, a career member of the Senior Foreign Service, class of Minister-Counselor, to be Ambassador Extraordinary and Plenipotentiary of the United States of America to the Republic of Cyprus.

Withdrawn June 7

Terence Francis Flynn,
of Maryland, to be a member of the National Labor Relations Board for the term of 5 years expiring August 27, 2015, vice Peter Schaumber, term expired, which was sent to the Senate on January 5, 2011.

Terence Francis Flynn,
of Maryland, to be a member of the National Labor Relations Board for the term of 5 years expiring August 27, 2015, vice Peter Schaumber, term expired, to which position he was appointed during the last recess of the Senate, which was sent to the Senate on February 13, 2012.

Roslyn Ann Mazer,
of Maryland, to be Inspector General, Department of Homeland Security, vice Richard L. Skinner, resigned, which was sent to the Senate on July 21, 2011.

Submitted June 11

Caitlin Joan Halligan,
of New York, to be U.S. Circuit Judge for the District of Columbia Circuit, vice John G. Roberts, Jr., elevated.

Kimberley Sherri Knowles,
of the District of Columbia, to be an Associate Judge of the Superior Court of the District of Columbia for the term of 15 years, vice Zinora M. Mitchell, retired.

William H. Orrick III,
of the District of Columbia, to be U.S. District Judge for the Northern District of California, vice Charles R. Breyer, retired.

Srikanth Srinivasan,
of Virginia, to be U.S. Circuit Judge for the District of Columbia Circuit, vice A. Raymond Randolph, retired.

Jon S. Tigar,
of California, to be U.S. District Judge for the Northern District of California, vice Saundra Brown Armstrong, retired.

Submitted June 14

Mark D. Gearan,
of New York, to be a member of the Board of Directors of the Corporation for National and Community Service for a term expiring December 1, 2015 (reappointment).

Michael David Kirby,
of Virginia, a career member of the Senior Foreign Service, class of Minister-Counselor, to be Ambassador Extraordinary and Plenipotentiary of the United States of America to the Republic of Serbia.

Withdrawn June 19

Brett H. McGurk,
of Connecticut, to be Ambassador Extraordinary and Plenipotentiary of the United States of America to the Republic of Iraq, which was sent to the Senate on March 27, 2012.

Submitted June 20

David Masumoto,
of California, to be a member of the National Council on the Arts for a term expiring September 3, 2018, vice Stephen W. Porter, term expiring.

Polly Ellen Trottenberg,
of Maryland, to be Under Secretary of Transportation for Policy, vice Roy W. Kienitz.

Withdrawn June 20

Patricia M. Wald,
of the District of Columbia, to be member of the Privacy and Civil Liberties Oversight Board for a term expiring January 29, 2019 (reappointment), which was sent to the Senate on April 16, 2012.

Submitted June 25

Sheri Polster Chappell,
of Florida, to be U.S. District Judge for the Middle District of Florida, vice Gregory A. Presnell, retired.

Katherine Polk Failla,
of New York, to be U.S. District Judge for the Southern District of New York, vice Denise Cote, retired.

Troy L. Nunley,
of California, to be U.S. District Judge for the Eastern District of California, vice Garland E. Burrell, Jr., retiring.

Submitted June 27

William R. Brownfield,
of Texas, a career member of the Senior Foreign Service, class of Career Minister, for the personal rank of Career Ambassador in recognition of especially distinguished service over a sustained period.

Kristie Anne Kenny,
of the District of Columbia, a career member of the Senior Foreign Service, class of Career Minister, for the personal rank of Career Ambassador in recognition of especially distinguished service over a sustained period.

Thomas Alfred Shannon, Jr.,
of Virginia, a career member of the Senior Foreign Service, class of Career Minister, for the personal rank of Career Ambassador in recognition of especially distinguished service over a sustained period.

Submitted June 28

Camila Ann Alire,
of Colorado, to be a member of the National Council on the Humanities for a term expiring January 26, 2018, vice Allen C. Guelzo, term expired.

Ramon Saldivar,
of California, to be a member of the National Council on the Humanities for a term expiring January 26, 2018, vice Wilfred M. McClay, term expired.

Withdrawn June 28

Timothy M. Broas,
of Maryland, to be Ambassador Extraordinary and Plenipotentiary of the United States of America to the Kingdom of the Netherlands, which was sent to the Senate on April 26, 2012.

Appendix C—Checklist of White House Press Releases

The following list contains releases of the Office of the Press Secretary that are neither printed items nor covered by entries in the Digest of Other White House Announcements.

Released January 3

Transcript of a press briefing by Press Secretary James F. "Jay" Carney

Statement by the Press Secretary announcing that the President signed H.R. 515, H.R. 789, H.R. 1059, H.R. 1264, H.R. 1801, H.R. 1892, H.R. 2056, H.R. 2422, and H.R. 2845

Released January 4

Transcript of a press gaggle by Press Secretary James F. "Jay" Carney

Statement by the Press Secretary: We Can't Wait: The White House Announces Federal and Private Sector Commitments To Provide Employment Opportunities for Nearly 180,000 Youth (released January 4; embargoed until January 5)

Advance text of the President's remarks at Shaker Heights High School in Shaker Heights, OH

Released January 5

Transcript of a press briefing by Press Secretary James F. "Jay" Carney

Advance text of the President's remarks in Arlington, VA

Released January 6

Text: Statement by Council of Economic Advisers Chairman Alan B. Krueger on the employment situation in December 2011

Released January 9

Transcript of a press briefing by Press Secretary James F. "Jay" Carney

Released January 10

Transcript of a press briefing by Press Secretary James F. "Jay" Carney

Released January 11

Transcript of a press gaggle by Principal Deputy Press Secretary Joshua R. Earnest

Statement by the Press Secretary: President Obama Issues Call to Action To Invest in America at White House "Insourcing American Jobs" Forum

Advance text of the President's remarks at the White House Insourcing American Jobs Forum

Released January 12

Transcript of a press briefing by Press Secretary James F. "Jay" Carney

Released January 13

Transcript of a press gaggle by Press Secretary James F. "Jay" Carney and Office of Management and Budget Deputy Director for Management Jeffrey D. Zients

Statement by the Press Secretary: President Obama Announces Proposal To Reform, Reorganize and Consolidate Government

Advance text of the President's remarks on Government reform

Released January 14

Statement by the Press Secretary: White House Outlines Approach To Protect the Internet While Combatting Online Piracy

Released January 17

Transcript of a press briefing by Press Secretary James F. "Jay" Carney

Text: Statement by National Security Council Spokesman ThomasF. Vietor on violence in South Sudan

Released January 18

Transcript of a press briefing by Press Secretary James F. "Jay" Carney

Statement by the Press Secretary: New Report: States Moving Forward To Implement Health Reform's Affordable Insurance Exchanges

Text: 2012 Progress Report: States Are Implementing Health Reform

Released January 19

Transcript of a press gaggle by Press Secretary James F. "Jay" Carney

Statement by the Press Secretary: We Can't Wait: President Obama Takes Actions To Increase Travel and Tourism in the Untied States

Released January 20

Transcript of a press briefing by Press Secretary James F. "Jay" Carney

Statement by the Press Secretary on the death of Cuban activist Wilmar Villar

Released January 23

Transcript of a press briefing by Press Secretary James F. "Jay" Carney

Released January 24

Statement by the Press Secretary on Egypt's transition to democracy

Text: Blueprint for an America Built To Last

Text: Guest list for the First Lady's Box at the State of the Union Address

Excerpts of the President's State of the Union Address

Advance text of the President's State of the Union Address

Released January 25

Transcript of a press gaggle by Press Secretary James F. "Jay" Carney

Text: National Strategy for Global Supply Chain Security

Text: Statements on the President's State of the Union Address

Fact sheet: President Obama's Blueprint To Make the Most of America's Energy Sources (embargoed until January 26)

Fact sheet: President Obama's Blueprint To Support U.S. Manufacturing Jobs, Discourage Outsourcing, and Encourage Insourcing

Fact sheet: National Strategy for Global Supply Chain Security

Released January 26

Transcript of a press gaggle by Press Secretary James F. "Jay" Carney

Statement by the Press Secretary on legislation to ban insider trading by Members of Congress (dated January 25)

Released January 27

Transcript of a press gaggle by Press Secretary James F. "Jay" Carney

Text: Statement by Council of Economic Advisers Chairman Alan B. Krueger on the advance estimate of GDP for the fourth quarter of 2011 (dated January 25)

Fact sheet: President Obama's Blueprint for Keeping College Affordable and Within Reach for All Americans

Released January 28

Excerpts of the President's remarks at the Alfalfa Club dinner

Released January 30

Transcript of a press briefing by Press Secretary James F. "Jay" Carney

Statement by the Press Secretary on legislation to ban insider trading by Members of Congress

Released January 31

Transcript of a press briefing by Press Secretary James F. "Jay" Carney

Statement by the Press Secretary: On One-Year Anniversary of Startup America Initiative President Obama Sends Startup America Legislative Agenda to Congress

Statement by the Press Secretary announcing that the President signed H.R. 3800

Released February 1

Transcript of a press briefing by Press Secretary James F. "Jay" Carney and Secretary of

Housing and Urban Development Shaun L.S. Donovan

Statement by the Press Secretary announcing that the President signed H.R. 3237

Fact sheet: President Obama's Plan To Help Responsible Homeowners and Heal the Housing Market

Advance text of the President's remarks at the James Lee Community Center in Falls Church, VA

Released February 2

Transcript of a press briefing by Press Secretary James F. "Jay" Carney

Statement by the Press Secretary on the Sudanese Armed Forces' bombardment of civilian populations in Southern Kordofan and Blue Nile States in Sudan

Fact sheet: President Obama's Plan To Put Veterans Back to Work (embargoed until February 3)

Released February 3

Text: Statement by Council of Economic Advisers Chairman Alan B. Krueger on the employment situation in January

Released February 6

Transcript of a press briefing by Press Secretary James F. "Jay" Carney

Released February 7

Transcript of a press briefing by Press Secretary James F. "Jay" Carney

Fact sheet: President Obama To Host White House Science Fair

Released February 8

Transcript of a press briefing by Press Secretary James F. "Jay" Carney

Fact sheet: Harnessing Innovation for Global Development

Released February 9

Statement by the Press Secretary: President Obama: Our Children Can't Wait for Congress To Fix No Child Left Behind, Announces

Flexibility in Exchange for Reform for Ten States

Fact sheet: The President's Global Development Council

Released February 10

Transcript of a press briefing by Deputy National Security Adviser Benjamin J. Rhodes, National Security Adviser to the Vice President Antony J. Blinken, Deputy National Security Adviser for International Economic Affairs Michael B. Froman, and Senior Director for Asian Affairs Daniel R. Russel on the visit of Vice President Xi Jinping of China

Statement by the Press Secretary announcing that the President signed H.R. 3801

Fact sheet: Women's Preventive Services and Religious Institutions

Released February 13

Transcript of a press briefing by Press Secretary James F. "Jay" Carney

Fact sheet: A Blueprint To Train Two Million Workers for High-Demand Industries Through a Community College to Career Fund

Released February 14

Transcript of a press briefing by Press Secretary James F. "Jay" Carney

Statement by the Press Secretary announcing that the President signed H.R. 588 and H.R. 658

Text: Joint Fact Sheet on Strengthening U.S.-China Economic Relations

Released February 15

Transcript of a press gaggle by Press Secretary James F. "Jay" Carney

Advance text of the President's remarks at Master Locks Co. in Milwaukee, WI

Released February 16

Transcript of a press gaggle by Press Secretary James F. "Jay" Carney

Fact sheet: President Obama's Budget Expands, Simplifies Small Business Health Care Tax Credits

Released March 4

Text: Statement by National Security Council Spokesman Thomas F. Vietor on the train accident outside Szczekociny, Poland

Advance text of the President's remarks at the American Israel Public Affairs Committee policy conference

Released March 5

Statement by the Press Secretary on the upcoming Group of Eight (G–8) and NATO summits

Released March 6

Fact sheet: President Obama Announces New Steps To Provide Housing Relief to Veterans and Servicemembers and Help More Responsible Homeowners Refinance

Released March 7

Transcript of a press gaggle by Press Secretary James F. "Jay" Carney

Statement by the Press Secretary: President's Council on Jobs and Competitiveness Launches STAY WITH IT With a Facebook Live Event

Fact sheet: Latest Steps To Implement the President's Export Control Reform Initiative

Fact sheet: All-of-the-Above Approach to American Energy

Released March 8

Transcript of a press briefing by Press Secretary James F. "Jay" Carney

Statement by the Press Secretary announcing that the President signed H.R. 347

Fact sheet: We Can't Wait: White House Launches Ethics.gov To Promote Government Accountability and Transparency

Fact sheet: U.S.-Ghana Development and Economic Relationship

Released March 9

Transcript of a press gaggle by Principal Deputy Press Secretary Joshua R. Earnest

Statement by the Press Secretary: President Obama To Announce New Efforts To Support Manufacturing Innovation, Encourage Insourcing

Text: Statement by Council of Economic Advisers Chairman Alan B. Krueger on the employment situation in February

Released March 12

Transcript of a press briefing by Press Secretary James F. "Jay" Carney, Secretary of the Interior Kenneth L. Salazar, and Deputy Assistant to the President Heather R. Zichal

Statement by the Press Secretary: White House Announces Details on President's Plan To Provide Americans With Job Training and Employment Services

Statement by the Press Secretary: The Blueprint for a Secure Energy Future: One-Year Progress Report

Text: The Blueprint for a Secure Energy Future: Progress Report

Released March 13

Transcript of a press briefing by Press Secretary James F. "Jay" Carney

Statement by the Press Secretary announcing that the President signed H.R. 4105

Text: Joint op-ed by President Obama and Prime Minister David Cameron of the United Kingdom for the Washington Post: An Alliance the World Can Count On

Released March 14

Statement by the Press Secretary on Senate passage of transportation improvement legislation

Statement by the Press Secretary announcing that the President signed S. 1134 and S. 1710

Text: Statement by National Security Council Spokesman Thomas F. Vietor on the bus accident outside Sierre, Switzerland

Text: Statement by National Security Council Spokesman Thomas F. Vietor on the International Criminal Court conviction of Congolese warlord Thomas Lubanga Dyilo in the child soldiers case

Joint fact sheet: U.S.-UK Progress Towards a Freer and More Secure Cyberspace

Joint fact sheet: U.S.-UK Higher Education, Science, and Innovation Collaboration

Joint fact sheet: U.S. and UK Defense Cooperation

Joint fact sheet: U.S.-UK Task Force To Support Our Armed Forces Personnel, Veterans and Their Families

Joint fact sheet: The U.S.-UK Partnership for Global Development

Joint fact sheet: Peace Corps and VSO Partnership on Volunteerism To Promote Global Development

Joint fact sheet: U.S. and UK Counterterrorism Cooperation

Released March 15

Transcript of a press briefing by Press Secretary James F. "Jay" Carney

Statement by the Press Secretary: Obama Administration Establishes White House Council on Strong Cities, Strong Communities

Advance text of the President's remarks at Prince George's Community College

Released March 16

Transcript of a press gaggle by Press Secretary James F. "Jay" Carney

Released March 19

Transcript of a press briefing by James F. "Jay" Carney

Text: Statement by National Security Council Spokesman Thomas F. Vietor on the detention of *las Damas de Blanco* members in Cuba

Text: Statement by National Security Council Spokesman Thomas F. Vietor on the terrorist attack in Toulouse, France

Released March 20

Transcript of a press briefing by Press Secretary James F. "Jay" Carney

Transcript of a press briefing by Deputy National Security Adviser for Strategic Communications Benjamin J. Rhodes, National Security

Council Senior Director for Asia Daniel R. Russel, and White House Coordinator for Arms Control and Weapons of Mass Destruction, Proliferation, and Terrorism Gary Samore on the President's upcoming visit to South Korea

Text: Statement by White House Communications Director H. Daniel Pfeiffer on the House budget proposal

Released March 21

Transcript of a press gaggle by Press Secretary James F. "Jay" Carney

Text: Statement by Office of Management and Budget Acting Director Jeffrey D. Zients: The Ryan Republican Budget: The Consequences of Imbalance

Fact sheet: Obama Administration's All-of-the-Above Approach to American Energy

Fact sheet: Obama Administration Commitment to American Made Energy

Released March 22

Transcript of a press gaggle by Press Secretary James F. "Jay" Carney

Statement by the Press Secretary on the situation in Mali

Statement by the Press Secretary on Senate action on legislation promoting small-business growth

Text: Statement by National Security Council Spokesman Thomas F. Vietor on the U.N. Human Rights Council's resolution on Sri Lanka

Released March 23

Transcript of a press briefing by Press Secretary James F. "Jay" Carney

Statement by the Press Secretary: New Report: Affordable Care Act Gives Americans More Security, Better Benefits

Text: Affordable Care Act: The New Health Care Law at Two Years

Text: Early Reactions to the Nomination of Jim Yong Kim as President of the World Bank

Released March 25

Statement by the Press Secretary on Assistant to the President for Homeland Security Adviser and Counterterrorism John O. Brennan's telephone conversation with President Abd al-Rabuh Mansur Hadi of Yemen

Released March 26

Transcript of a press readout by Deputy National Security Adviser for Strategic Communications Benjamin J. Rhodes on President Obama's bilateral meeting with President Dmitry Anatolyevich Medvedev of Russia

Statement by the Press Secretary: Trilateral Announcement Between Mexico, the United States, and Canada on Nuclear Security

Text: Joint Statement by the United States, Chile, Poland, Nigeria, Morocco, Thailand, and the Republic of Korea on the Nuclear Security Summit Outreach Efforts

Text: Belgium-France-Netherlands-United States Joint Statement—Minimization of HEU and the Reliable Supply of Medical Radioisotopes

Fact sheet: Italy Fact Sheet: Nuclear Security Summit 2012

Advance text of the President's remarks at Hankuk University of Foreign Studies in Seoul, South Korea

Released March 27

Transcript of a press briefing by Press Secretary James F. "Jay" Carney, Deputy National Security Adviser for Strategic Communications Benjamin J. Rhodes, and National Security Council Director for Nuclear Threat Reduction Shawn Gallagher

Transcript of a teleconference press briefing by Deputy National Security Adviser for Strategic Communications Benjamin J. Rhodes on President Obama's bilateral meeting with Prime Minister Syed Yousuf Raza Gilani of Pakistan

Statement by the Press Secretary on clashes along the border of Sudan and South Sudan

Text: Joint Statement of the Presidents of the Republic of Kazakhstan, the Russian Federa-

tion and the United States of America Regarding the Trilateral Cooperation at the Former Semipalatinsk Test Site

Text: Joint Statement on Quadrilateral Cooperation on High-density Low-enriched Uranium Fuel Production

Text: Statement of Activity and Cooperation To Counter Nuclear Smuggling

Text: Joint Statement on Transport Security

Text: Joint Statement on Nuclear Security Training and Support Centers

Text: Joint Statement on Nuclear Terrorism

Text: Joint Statement on National Legislation Implementation Kit on Nuclear Security

Text: Nuclear Security Summit, Seoul, March 2012: Multinational Statement on Nuclear Information Security

Text: 2012 Nuclear Security Summit Deliverable: Global Partnership Against the Spread of Weapons and Materials of Mass Destruction

Fact sheet: Plutonium Removal From Sweden

Fact sheet: History of Trilateral Threat Reduction Cooperation at the Former Semipalatinsk Test Site

Fact sheet: United States-Japan Nuclear Security Working Group Fact Sheet

Fact sheet: Belgium Nuclear Security Summit

Fact sheet: Ukraine Highly Enriched Uranium Removal

Released March 28

Transcript of a press briefing by Principal Deputy Press Secretary Joshua R. Earnest

Released March 29

Transcript of a press briefing by Press Secretary James F. "Jay" Carney

Statement by the Press Secretary on House passage of 90-day surface transportation extension legislation

Statement by the Press Secretary on the Ryan Republican budget

Statement by the Press Secretary on Senate action on the Buffett rule

Advance text of the President's remarks on energy

Released March 30

Transcript of a press gaggle by Principal Deputy Press Secretary Joshua R. Earnest

Transcript of a teleconference background briefing by senior administration officials on the Presidential determination pursuant to section 1245 of the National Defense Authorization Act for Fiscal Year 2012

Statement by the Press Secretary on the Presidential determination pursuant to section 1245(d)(4)(B) and (C) of the National Defense Authorization Act for Fiscal Year 2012

Statement by the Press Secretary announcing that the President signed H.R. 4281

Released April 2

Statement by the Press Secretary on the elections in Burma

Statement by the Press Secretary announcing that the President signed H.R. 473 and H.R. 886

Released April 3

Text: Statement by White House Communications Director H. Daniel Pfeiffer: Three Charts Illustrating Two Different Visions for Our Nation

Text: Statement by National Security Council Spokesman Thomas F. Vietor on Sudan

Released April 4

Transcript of a press briefing by Press Secretary James F. "Jay" Carney

Statement by the Press Secretary on the attack on the National Theater in Mogadishu, Somalia

Statement by the Press Secretary announcing that the President signed S. 2038

Fact sheet: The STOCK Act: Bans Members of Congress From Insider Trading

Released April 5

Transcript of a press briefing by Press Secretary James F. "Jay" Carney

Statement by the Press Secretary announcing that the President signed H.R. 3606

Fact sheet: President Obama To Sign Jumpstart Our Business Startups (JOBS) Act

Released April 6

Statement by the Press Secretary: White House Releases Report on Women and the Economy

Statement on the employment situation in March

Statement by the Press Secretary: White House Announces 2012 Easter Egg Roll Program and Talent Line-Up

Fact sheet: 2012 White House Easter Egg Roll

Released April 10

Transcript of a press gaggle by Press Secretary James F. "Jay" Carney

Excerpts of the President's remarks at Florida Atlantic University in Boca Raton, FL

Released April 11

Transcript of a press briefing by Press Secretary James F. "Jay" Carney

Transcript of a press briefing by Deputy National Security Adviser for Strategic Communications Benjamin J. Rhodes and Senior Director for the Western Hemisphere Daniel A. Restrepo on the President's participation in the Summit of the Americas in Cartagena, Colombia

Statement by the Press Secretary on the situation in Bahrain

Fact sheet: All of the Above: Obama Administration Announces Additional Steps To Increase Energy Security

Released April 12

Transcript of a press briefing by Press Secretary James F. "Jay" Carney

Statement by the Press Secretary: We Can't Wait: Protecting Taxpayer Dollars From Wasteful Payment Errors and Fraud

Statement by the Press Secretary on North Korea's missile launch

Released April 13

Transcript of a press gaggle by Press Secretary James F. "Jay" Carney and Deputy National Security Adviser for Strategic Communications Benjamin J. Rhodes

Statement by the Press Secretary: White House Releases President Obama and Vice President Biden's 2011 Tax Returns

Statement by the Press Secretary on the situation in Guinea Bissau

Text: Statement by Deputy Assistant to the President for Energy and Climate Change Heather R. Zichal: Facilitating Safe and Responsible Expansion of Natural Gas Production

Text: Statements on the President's Executive Order Supporting Safe and Responsible Development of Unconventional Domestic Natural Gas Resources

Fact sheet: Small Business Network of the Americas

Fact sheet: The U.S. Economic Relationship With the Western Hemisphere

Released April 14

Transcript of a press briefing by Press Secretary James F. "Jay" Carney and Deputy National Security Adviser for Strategic Communications Benjamin J. Rhodes

Fact sheet: Summit of the Americas: Connecting the Americas

Advance text of the President's remarks at the opening session of the Summit of the Americas in Cartagena, Colombia

Released April 16

Statement by the Press Secretary: White House Launches 2012 Citizens Medal Nomination Process

Released April 17

Transcript of a press briefing by Press Secretary James F. "Jay" Carney and National Economic Council Deputy Director Brian C. Deese

Text: Report: Equal Pay Task Force Accomplishments: Fighting for Fair Pay in the Workplace

Fact sheet: Increasing Oversight and Cracking Down on Manipulation in Oil Markets

Fact sheet: Fighting for Equal Pay

Released April 18

Transcript of a press gaggle by Press Secretary James F. "Jay" Carney

Statement by the Press Secretary: President Obama's Visit to Lorain County Community College

Fact sheet: Release of National Security Report on Revising U.S. Export Controls on Satellites

Released April 19

Transcript of a press briefing by Press Secretary James F. "Jay" Carney

Statement by the Press Secretary: President Obama Announces Patricia Summit as a Recipient of the Presidential Medal of Freedom

Released April 20

Transcript of a press briefing by Press Secretary James F. "Jay" Carney and Secretary of Education Arne Duncan

Statement by the Press Secretary: President Obama To Sign Proclamation Designating Fort Ord National Monument

Released April 23

Transcript of a press briefing by Press Secretary James F. "Jay" Carney

Statement by the Press Secretary: President Obama Announces Jan Karski as a Recipient of the Presidential Medal of Freedom

Fact sheet: A Comprehensive Strategy and New Tools To Prevent and Respond to Atrocities

Fact sheet: Mitigating and Eliminating the Threat to Civilians Posed by the Lord's Resistance Army

Fact sheet: Sanctions Against Those Complicit in Grave Human Rights Abuses Via Information Technology in Syria and Iran

Fact sheet: Educating Our Way to an Economy Built To Last: Stopping the Student Loan Interest Rate Hike

Released April 24

Transcript of a press gaggle by Press Secretary James F. "Jay" Carney

Statement by the Press Secretary on the humanitarian crisis in the Horn of Africa

Released April 25

Transcript of a press gaggle by Press Secretary James F. "Jay" Carney

Released April 26

Transcript of a press briefing by Press Secretary James F. "Jay" Carney

Statement by the Press Secretary: Obama Administration Urges Reauthorization of the Violence Against Women Act

Statement by the Press Secretary: President Obama Names Presidential Medal of Freedom Recipients

Statement by the Press Secretary: We Can't Wait: President Obama Takes Action To Stop Deceptive and Misleading Practices by Educational Institutions that Target Veterans, Service Members and their Families

Statement by the Press Secretary on the verdict in the trial of Charles Taylor at the Special Court for Sierra Leone

Released April 27

Transcript of a press gaggle by Principal Deputy Press Secretary Joshua R. Earnest

Transcript of a background briefing by a senior administration official on the upcoming visit of Prime Minister Yoshihiko Noda of Japan

Text: Statement by Council of Economic Advisers Chairman Alan B. Krueger on the advance estimate of GDP for the first quarter of 2012

Released April 30

Fact sheet: United States-Japan Cooperative Initiatives

Advance text of the President's remarks at the National Legislative Conference of the Building and Construction Trades Department of the AFL–CIO

Advance text of remarks by Assistant to the President for Homeland Security and Counterterrorism John O. Brennan at the Woodrow Wilson International Center for Scholars

Released May 1

Transcript of a background briefing by senior administration officials

Text: Statement by Domestic Policy Council Director Cecilia Munoz: New Report: Health Care Law Makes Community Health Centers Stronger

Fact sheet: The U.S.-Afghanistan Strategic Partnership Agreement

Excerpts of the President's address to the Nation from Bagram Air Base, Afghanistan

Advance text of the President's address to the Nation from Bagram Air Base, Afghanistan

Released May 2

Transcript of a press briefing by senior administration officials on the strategic partnership agreement between the U.S. and Afghanistan

Statement by the Press Secretary: We Can't Wait: White House Announces Nearly 300,000 Summer Jobs and Other Employment Opportunities for Youth and New Online Tool To Help Youth Access Opportunities

Released May 3

Transcript of a press briefing by Press Secretary James F. "Jay" Carney

Released May 4

Text: Statement by Council of Economic Advisers Chairman Alan B. Krueger on the employment situation in April

Released May 7

Transcript of a press briefing by Press Secretary James F. "Jay" Carney

Released May 8

Transcript of a press gaggle by Press Secretary James F. "Jay" Carney

Statement by the Press Secretary: President Obama Calls on Congress To Act on "To Do List" To Create Jobs

Statement by the Press Secretary on Senate Republicans' blocking of legislation to prevent student loan interest rates from doubling

Fact sheet: An Update on Bringing Jobs Back to the United States

Released May 10

Transcript of a press gaggle by Press Secretary James F. "Jay" Carney

Statement by the Press Secretary: Administration Officials Announce National Strategy To Increase Travel and Tourism in the United States to 100 Million Visitors Annually by 2021

Fact sheet: Obama Administration Continues Efforts To Increase Travel and Tourism in the United States

Fact sheet: White House Announces New Steps To Cut Red Tape, Eliminate Unnecessary Regulations

Fact sheet: White House Announces New Private and Public Sector Commitments To Promote Financial Empowerment Across the Country

Released May 11

Fact sheet: President Obama Announces Impact of October Refinancing Actions, Calls on Congress To Act on "To Do List"

Released May 19

Transcript of a press briefing by Press Secretary James F. "Jay" Carney, Deputy National Security Adviser for International Economic Affairs Michael B. Froman, and Deputy National Security Adviser for Strategic Communications Benjamin B. Rhodes

Transcript of a press gaggle by Deputy National Security Adviser for Strategic Communications Benjamin B. Rhodes

Text: Camp David Declaration

Fact sheet: G–8 Action on Energy and Climate Change

Fact sheet: G–8 Action on the Deauville Partnership with Arab Countries in Transition

Released May 20

Transcript of a press briefing by Deputy National Security Adviser for Strategic Communications Ben Rhodes, Gen. John R. Allen, USMC, commander, NATO International Security Assistance Forces, Afghanistan, and Special Assistant to the President for Afghanistan and Pakistan Douglas E. Lute

Transcript of a press briefing by U.S. Ambassador to NATO Ivo H. Daalder and Deputy National Security Adviser for Strategic Communications Benjamin J. Rhodes

Fact sheet: Chicago Summit—NATO Capabilities

Released May 21

Fact sheet: Chicago Summit—Strengthening NATO's Partnerships

Fact sheet: Chicago Summit—NATO's Enduring Presence after 2014

Fact sheet: Chicago Summit—Afghanistan Transition Interim Milestone

Fact sheet: Chicago Summit—Sufficient and Sustainable ANSF

Advance text of the President's commencement address at Joplin High School in Joplin, MO

Released May 22

Transcript of a press briefing by Press Secretary James F. "Jay" Carney, Deputy Assistant to the President for Energy and Climate Change Heather R. Zichal, and Winergy Drive Systems Corporation Chief Executive Officer Terry R. Royer

Statement by the Press Secretary: President Obama Calls on Congress To Act on Clean Energy Tax Credits in "To Do List"

Released May 23

Transcript of a press gaggle by Press Secretary James F. "Jay" Carney

Statement by the Press Secretary: Obama Administration Launches Sweeping Shift to Mobile

Advance text of the President's commencement address at the U.S. Air Force Academy in Colorado Springs, CO

Released May 24

Transcript of a press gaggle by Press Secretary James F. "Jay" Carney

Statement by the Press Secretary on Senate action on legislation regarding student loan interest rates

Advance text of the President's remarks at TPI Composites, Inc., in Newton, IA

Released May 25

Statement by the Press Secretary announcing that the President signed H.R. 4045 and H.R. 4967

Fact sheet: Memorial Day and Commemoration of the 50th Anniversary of the Vietnam War

Released May 28

Text: Op-ed by President Obama for Military.com, Military Times, and Stars and Stripes: Keeping Faith With Vietnam Veterans

Released May 29

Transcript of a press briefing by Press Secretary James F. "Jay" Carney

Released May 30

Transcript of a press briefing by Press Secretary James F. "Jay" Carney

Statement by the Press Secretary announcing that the President signed H.R. 2072

Fact sheet: President Obama To Sign the Export-Import Bank Reauthorization Act of 2012

Released May 31

Transcript of a press briefing by Press Secretary James F. "Jay" Carney

Statement by the Press Secretary: President Obama Calls on Congress To Act on Veterans

Jobs Corps in "To Do List" and Launches New Military Credentialing Initiative To Fill Workforce Needs

Statement by the Press Secretary announcing that the President signed H.R. 5740

Released June 1

Transcript of a press gaggle by Principal Deputy Press Secretary Joshua R. Earnest

Text: Statement by Council of Economic Advisers Chairman Alan B. Krueger on the employment situation in May

Released June 4

Transcript of a press briefing by Press Secretary James F. "Jay" Carney

Fact sheet: Fighting for Equal Pay and the Paycheck Fairness Act

Released June 5

Transcript of a press briefing by Press Secretary James F. "Jay" Carney, Secretary of Education Arne Duncan, and Consumer Financial Protection Bureau Director Richard A. Cordray

Statement by the Press Secretary on the 2012 National-Level Exercise

Statement by the Press Secretary announcing that the President signed the Border Tunnel Prevention Act of 2012

Statement by the Press Secretary announcing that the President signed H.R. 2415, H.R. 3220, H.R. 3413, H.R. 4119, and H.R. 4849

Released June 6

Transcript of a press gaggle by Press Secretary James F. "Jay" Carney

Fact sheet: Helping Americans Manage Student Loan Debt With Improvements To Repayment Options

Released June 7

Transcript of a press gaggle by Press Secretary James F. "Jay" Carney

Statement by the Press Secretary on the situation in Syria

Fact sheet: Encouraging Reliable Supplies of Molybdenum-99 Produced Without Highly Enriched Uranium

Released June 8

Statement by the Press Secretary on Philippines-U.S. relations

Statement by the Press Secretary announcing that the President signed H.R. 2947, H.R. 3992, and H.R. 4097

Released June 11

Transcript of a press briefing by Press Secretary James F. "Jay" Carney

Transcript of a background briefing by a senior administration official on the Presidential determination regarding the availability of non-Iranian oil in the market

Statement by the Press Secretary: President Obama Honors Outstanding Math and Science Teachers

Statement by the Press Secretary: Obama Administration Releases Report on America's Agricultural Economy and Announces Commitment To Invest over $2 Billion in Rural Small Businesses

Statement by the Press Secretary on the Presidential determination pursuant to section 1245(d)(4)(B) and (C) of the National Defense Authorization Act for Fiscal Year 2012

Released June 12

Transcript of a press gaggle by Principal Deputy Press Secretary Joshua R. Earnest

Released June 13

Transcript of a press briefing by Press Secretary James F. "Jay" Carney

Statement by the Press Secretary: We Can't Wait: President Obama Signs Executive Order To Make Broadband Construction Faster and Cheaper

Statement by the Press Secretary on the President's signing of legislation concerning contract awards for large air tankers

Statement by the Press Secretary announcing that the President signed S. 3261

Excerpts of the President's remarks on presenting the Presidential Medal of Freedom to President Shimon Peres of Israel

Released June 14

Transcript of a press gaggle by Press Secretary James F. "Jay" Carney

Text: Report: U.S. Strategy Toward Sub-Saharan Africa

Fact sheet: Obama Administration Efforts in Sub-Saharan Africa

Fact sheet: The New Strategy Toward Sub-Saharan Africa

Released June 15

Transcript of a press briefing by Under Secretary of the Treasury for International Affairs Lael Brainard, Deputy National Security Adviser for International Economic Affairs Michael B. Froman, and Deputy National Security Adviser for Strategic Communications Benjamin J. Rhodes on the G–20 summit

Statement by the Press Secretary announcing that the President signed S. 292 and S. 363

Text: Statement by Counsel to the President Kathryn H. Ruemmler on the availability of executive branch personnel public financial disclosure reports

Released June 17

Statement by the Press Secretary on the parliamentary elections in Greece

Released June 18

Transcript of a press briefing by Press Secretary James F. "Jay" Carney, Deputy National Security Adviser for Strategic Communications Benjamin J. Rhodes, Under Secretary of the Treasury for International Affairs Lael Brainard, and U.S. Ambassador to Russia Michael A. McFaul

Released June 19

Transcript of remarks by Secretary of the Treasury Timothy F. Geithner in Los Cabos, Mexico

Text: Joint Statement by the United States and Canada

Text: Joint U.S.-EU Statement on the High Level Working Group on Jobs and Growth

Text: G–20 Leaders Declaration

Text: The Los Cabos Growth and Jobs Action Plan

Released June 20

Statement by the Press Secretary: Obama Administration Commemorates 40 Years of Increasing Equality and Opportunity for Women in Education and Athletics

Released June 21

Transcript of a press briefing by Press Secretary James F. "Jay" Carney

Statement by the Press Secretary announcing that the President signed H.R. 5883 and H.R. 5890

Released June 22

Transcript of a press gaggle by Principal Deputy Press Secretary Joshua R. Earnest

Statement by the Press Secretary: On Anniversary of *Olmstead*, Obama Administration Reaffirms Commitment To Assist Americans With Disabilities

Released June 23

Text: Op-ed by President Obama for Newsweek: President Obama Reflects on the Impact of Title IX

Released June 24

Statement by the Press Secretary on Egypt

Released June 25

Transcript of a press gaggle by Press Secretary James F. "Jay" Carney

Statement by the Press Secretary: Obama Administration Awards "Vets to Cops" Hiring Grants

Released June 26

Transcript of a press gaggle by Press Secretary James F. "Jay" Carney

Statement by the Press Secretary on the International Day in Support of Victims of Torture

Statement by the Press Secretary on student loan interest rates

Released June 27

Transcript of a press briefing by Press Secretary James F. "Jay" Carney

Statement by the Press Secretary announcing that the President signed S. 404, S. 684, and S. 997

Released June 28

Transcript of a background press briefing by senior administrations officials on sanctions against Iran

Statement by White House Communications Director H. Daniel Pfeiffer on the House of Representatives vote to hold Attorney General Eric H. Holder, Jr., in contempt of Congress

Fact sheet: The Affordable Care Act: Secure Health Coverage for the Middle Class

Released June 29

Transcript of a press gaggle by Press Secretary James F. "Jay" Carney

Statement by the Press Secretary on student loan interest rate legislation

Statement by the Press Secretary announcing that the President signed H.R. 6064

Released June 30

Statement by the Press Secretary on the death of former Prime Minister Yitzhak Shamir of Israel

Appendix D—Presidential Documents Published in the *Federal Register*

This appendix lists Presidential documents released by the Office of the Press Secretary and published in the Federal Register. The texts of the documents are printed in the Federal Register
(F.R.) at the citations listed below. The documents are also printed in title 3 of the Code of Federal Regulations and in the Compilation of Presidential Documents.

PROCLAMATIONS

PROCLAMATIONS (Continued)

PROCLAMATIONS (Continued)

EXECUTIVE ORDERS

EXECUTIVE ORDERS (Continued)

OTHER PRESIDENTIAL DOCUMENTS

OTHER PRESIDENTIAL DOCUMENTS (Continued)

OTHER PRESIDENTIAL DOCUMENTS (Continued)

OTHER PRESIDENTIAL DOCUMENTS (Continued)

OTHER PRESIDENTIAL DOCUMENTS (Continued)

Subject Index

ABC
  "Good Morning America" program—894
  "The View" program—895
  "World News With Diane Sawyer" program—877
Adoption—66
Aeronautics and Space Administration, National—128, 176
Afghanistan
  Abductions, foreign nationals—899
  Afghan military and security forces—9, 53, 76, 122, 207, 264–265, 288, 293, 296–297, 349, 352, 378, 383, 388, 446, 523, 552, 555–556, 560–562, 573, 609–610, 637, 644–649, 654, 660, 667, 804, 812
  Bagram Air Base—561
  Civilian deaths—287–288, 293
  Democracy efforts—553–554, 559
  Detention facilities, transfer of responsibility to Afghan forces—552, 804
  Economic growth and development—557–558, 562, 645
  Former regime—68, 220, 297, 552, 561–563, 572, 648, 654, 804, 813
  Governmental accountability and transparency, strengthening efforts—558, 562
  Insurgency and terrorist attacks—552, 562
  International diplomatic efforts—880, 882
  International Security Assistance Force—287–288, 573, 644, 647–650, 653–654, 804–805, 882, 895, 897
  NATO, role—207, 264–265, 288, 556, 562, 610, 637, 641, 644–645, 647–650, 653, 661–662, 667
  President—265, 288, 297, 552, 609, 644, 647–648, 882, 884–886, 893, 897
  President Obama's visit—552, 560–561, 893
  Reconciliation efforts—297, 372, 555, 562, 644, 812, 882
  Reconstruction efforts—557, 637, 641
  Relations with Pakistan—563, 650
  Relations with U.S.—265, 287–288, 552–554, 558–560, 573, 610, 644–645, 648, 879, 882, 884
  Security cooperation with U.S.—297, 553, 555–556, 560–562, 573, 886
  Shootings in Panjwai—885
  U.S. Ambassador—288, 560
  U.S. assistance—558–559
  U.S. military forces
    Casualties—298, 553, 561, 563, 660, 674, 882
    Deployment—8–10, 53, 56, 58, 68, 76, 112–113, 122, 159, 179, 234, 264–265, 288, 293, 296–299, 302, 323, 372, 376, 378, 383, 388, 404,

Afghanistan—Continued
  U.S. military forces—Continued
    Casualties—Continued
      419, 446, 450, 483, 522, 529–530, 537, 555–556, 560–563, 572–573, 577, 582, 599, 609, 616, 644, 647–649, 653–654, 660, 667, 670, 672, 674, 685, 689, 692, 705, 709, 715–716, 719, 733, 738, 771, 778, 796, 804, 810, 834, 841, 849, 853, 856
  U.S. Special Inspector General for Afghanistan Reconstruction—897
Africa
  See also Developing countries; *specific country*
  Agricultural production, improvement efforts—634–636
  Democracy efforts—434
  East Africa, famine and humanitarian crisis—294, 634–635
  Economic growth and development—633–634, 636
  Food security, strengthening efforts—633, 644
  Poverty—634
  U.S. assistance—635
African Development Foundation—886
Agriculture
  Food markets and prices—634–635
  Global Agriculture and Food Security, Symposium on—633
Agriculture, Department of—885
  Forest Service, U.S.—872
  Secretary—245, 677, 682
AIDS. *See* HIV/AIDS; *specific country or region*
Air Force, Department of the
  Air Force Academy, U.S.—498–499, 659–660
  Chief of Staff—659
  Secretary—91, 659
Alabama
  Disaster assistance—878
  Governor—488
  Tornadoes, damage and recovery efforts—488–489
Alaska, disaster assistance—878
Alfalfa Club—878
Al Qaida. *See* Terrorism
American. *See other part of subject*
American Indians and Alaska Natives
  Health care system, improvement efforts—106
  Indian Health Care Improvement Act—106
  Job creation and growth—106
  School improvement and renovation—106
  Tribal nations, relations with Federal Government—105–106
  Unemployment—105

Name Index

Document Categories List